AMERICA PAST AND PRESENT

Robert A. Divine

University of Texas

T. H. Breen

Northwestern University

George M. Fredrickson

Stanford University

R. Hal Williams

Southern Methodist University

HarperCollinsCollegePublishers

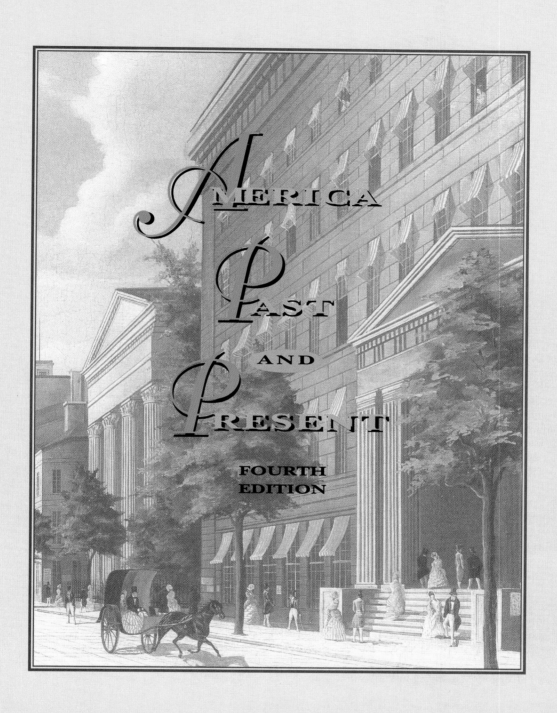

AMERICA PAST AND PRESENT

FOURTH EDITION

Executive Editor: *Bruce Borland*
Director of Development: *Betty Slack*
Project Editors: *Steven Pisano and Shuli Traub*
Design Manager: *Jill Little*
Cover Designer: *Kay Petronio*
Art Studio: *Mapping Specialists Limited*
Photo Researchers: *Leslie Coopersmith and Mary Goljenboom*
Electronic Production Manager: *Mike Kemper*
Electronic Desktop Manager: *Heather A. Peres*
Manufacturing Manager: *Joseph Campanella*
Electronic Page Makeup: *R R Donnelly Barbados*
Printer and Binder: *R. R. Donnelly & Sons Company*
Cover Printer: *Coral Graphic Services, Inc.*

America Past and Present, Fourth Edition

Library of Congress Cataloging-in-Publication Data

America past and present/Robert A. Divine . . . [et. al].—4th ed.
  p. cm.
 Includes bibliographical references and index.
 ISBN 0-673-99192-X
 1. United States—History.I. Divine, Robert A.
E178. 1. A4894 1995   94–39705
973—dc20   CIP

95 96 97 9 8 7 6 5 4 3 2

Brief Contents

Detailed Contents

CHAPTER 33

America in Flux, 1970–1993   1009

Maps

Charts, Tables, and Graphs

Preface

The fourth edition of *America Past and Present* is a major revision that strives to achieve the shared goal of the previous editions: to present a clear, relevant, and balanced history of the United States as an unfolding story of national development, from the days of the earliest inhabitants to the present. We emphasize the *story* because we strongly believe in the value of historical narrative in providing a vivid sense of the past. In each chapter, we sought to blend the excitement and drama of the American experience with insights about the social, economic, and cultural issues that underlie it.

REVISIONS FOR THE FOURTH EDITION

In this edition, we have reviewed each chapter carefully to take account of recent scholarly work, to offer new perspectives, and to sharpen the analysis and the prose. In many cases we have adopted the suggestions offered by those who used the previous editions in their classrooms.

Throughout this revised edition, we devote increased attention to discussion of the ethnic diversity of the United States. New material has been added on Native Americans, African Americans, Hispanic Americans, and Asian Americans. They appear throughout the text, not as witnesses to the historical narrative, but as principals in its development. The opening vignette in Chapter 1 deals with the encounter between Columbus and the Taínos Indians of Hispaniola; Chapter 4 has increased material on settlement in the Spanish borderlands of the eighteenth century as well as on the encounters between Native Americans and European settlers in the "Middle Ground" between the Appalachian Mountains and the Mississippi River. The opening vignette in Chapter 16 discusses the career of Robert Smalls, one of the most famous southern black leaders of the Civil War and Reconstruction era. Material on immigration from China and Japan during the early twentieth century has been added in Chapter 23, and Chapter 33 includes extensive discussion of the ethnic diversity of the United States in the period from the late 1970s to the 1990s.

Another focus of this revision is expanded discussion of the "frontier" in American history. For example, in Chapter 4, material has been added on settlement in the backcountry during the eighteenth century. Chapter 17 now includes discussion of the thesis of the new western historians on the continuing migration to and development and exploitation of the American West.

The final three chapters have been completely rewritten. Chapter 31 discusses politics and diplomacy from the mid-1960s to 1980, the social upheavals of the 1960s, and the energy crisis and inflation of the 1970s. Chapter 32 covers the major political and economic developments of the Reagan-Bush era, the presidential campaign of 1992 and the return of the Democrats to the White House with the election of Bill Clinton, and the momentous political changes of the late 1980s and early 1990s with the collapse of communism in eastern Europe, the dismantling of the Soviet Union, and the end of the Cold War. Chapter 33 is an entirely new chapter covering the social, demographic, ethnic, cultural, and economic changes in American life from the 1970s to the present.

APPROACH AND THEMES

As the title suggests, our book is a blend of the traditional and the new. The strong narrative emphasis and chronological organization are traditional; the incorporation of the many fresh insights that historians have gained from social sciences in the past quarter century is new. We have used significant incidents and episodes to reflect the dilemmas, the choices, and the decisions made by the people as well as by their leaders. After discussion of the colonial period, most of the chapters examine shorter time periods, usually about a decade, permitting us to view these major political and public events as points of reference and orientation around which social themes are integrated. This approach gives unity and direction to the text.

In recounting the story of the American past, we see a nation in flux. The early Africans and Europeans developed complex agrarian folkways that blended Old World customs and New World experiences; as cultural identities evolved, the idea of political independence became more acceptable. People who had been subjects of the British Crown created a system of government that challenged later Americans to work out the full implications of theories of social and economic equality.

The growing sectional rift between the North and South, revolving around divergent models of economic growth and conflicting social values, culminated in civil war. In the post–Civil War period, the development of a more industrialized economy severely tested the values of an agrarian society, engendering a Populist reform movement. In the early twentieth century, Progressive reformers sought to infuse the industrial order with social justice. World War I demonstrated the extent of American power in the world. The resiliency of the maturing American nation was tested by the Great Depression and World War II. The Cold War ushered in an era of crises, foreign and domestic, that revealed both the strengths and the weaknesses of modern America.

The impact of change on human lives adds a vital dimension to our understanding of history. We need to comprehend the way the Revolution affected the lives of ordinary citizens; what it was like for both blacks and whites to live in a plantation society; how men and women fared in the shift from an agrarian to an industrial economy; and what impact technology, in the form of the automobile and the computer, has had on patterns of life in the twentieth century.

Our commitment is not to any particular ideology or point of view; rather, we hope to challenge our readers to rediscover the fascination of the American past and reach their own conclusions about its significance in their lives. At the same time, we have not avoided controversial issues; instead, we have tried to offer reasoned judgments on such morally charged subjects as the nature of slavery and the advent of nuclear weapons. We believe that while history rarely repeats itself, the story of the American past is relevant to the problems and dilemmas facing the nation today, and we have therefore sought to stress themes and ideas that continue to shape our national culture.

STRUCTURE AND FEATURES

The structure and features of the book are intended to stimulate student interest and to reinforce learning. Chapters begin with **vignettes** or incidents, many of them new, that establish direction for chapter themes stated in the introductory sections (which also serve as overviews to the topics covered) and with **expanded summaries**. Each chapter has a **chronology, recommended readings, bibliography** (revised and updated for this revision), and two-page **special feature essay** on a topic that combines high interest and instructional value. Three of the special feature essays are new in this edition: Chapter 4, on etiquette and manners in the eighteenth century; Chapter 13, on the life and experiences of women—black and white, slave and free—on the plantations of the Old South; and Chapter 33, on political, economic, and cultural relations between the United States and Mexico.

New in this edition are the four **four-page essays on "Law and Society."** Each of the essays covers a significant legal case in American history and includes a discussion of the background of the case, excerpts from the trial transcript, and coverage of the case in the news media of the period. Questions at the end of each essay invite students to explore the legal contest from the perspective of social/cultural historians. The cases featured in the essays are the Salem witch trials, the Beecher-Tilton adultery trial of 1875, *Muller* v. *Oregon*, and *Bakke* v. *Regents of the University of California*.

The extensive **full-color map program** has been expanded to provide more information on the ethnic diversity of the United States and more integration of information and action. **New charts, graphs, and tables**—many with a capsulized format for convenient review of factual information—relate to social and economic change. See, for example, the new table in Chapter 26, "Major

New Deal Legislation and Agencies," which lists the principal agencies of the New Deal and summarizes the purposes of each. The rich **full-color illustration program**, bearing directly on the narrative, advances and expands the themes, provides elaboration and contrast, tells more of the story, and generally adds another dimension of learning. The illustrations also present a mini survey of American painting styles. The **"Growth of the United States" series** at the front of the book combines maps, narrative, and a time line of parallel events. The augmented **Appendix** includes the Articles of Confederation (in addition to the Declaration of Independence and the Constitution of the United States and its Amendments). Charts, tables, and graphs present a demographic profile of the American people.

Although this book is a joint effort, each author took primary responsibility for writing one section. T. H. Breen contributed the first eight chapters from the earliest Native American period to the second decade of the nineteenth century. George M. Fredrickson wrote Chapters 9 through 16, carrying the narrative through the Reconstruction era. R. Hal Williams is responsible for Chapters 17 through 24, focusing on the industrial transformation and urbanization, and the events culminating in World War I. Robert A. Divine wrote Chapters 25 through 33, bringing the story through the Great Depression, World War II, and the Cold War from its beginning to its end. Each contributor reviewed and revised the work of his colleagues and helped shape the material into its final form.

SUPPLEMENTS

For Instructors

Instructor's Resource Manual
Prepared by James P. Walsh of Central Connecticut State University, each chapter of this important resource manual contains interpretative essays, anecdotes and references to biographical or primary sources, and a comprehensive summary of the text.

America Through the Eyes of Its People: A Collection of Primary Sources
Prepared by Carol Brown of Houston Community College, this one-volume collection of primary documents portraying the rich and varied tapestry of American life contains documents of women, Native Americans, African Americans, Hispanics, and others who helped to shape the course of U.S. history. Designed to be duplicated by instructors for student use, the documents also have accompanying student exercises.

Discovering American History Through Maps and Views
Created by Gerald Danzer, University of Illinois at Chicago, the recipient of the AHA's 1990 James Harvey Robinson Prize for his work in the development of map transparencies, this set of 140 four-color acetates is a unique instructional tool. It contains an introduction on teaching history through maps and a detailed commentary on each transparency. The collection includes cartographic and pictorial maps, views and photos, urban plans, building diagrams, and works of art.

A Guide to Teaching American History Through Film
Created by Randy Roberts of Purdue University, this guide provides instructors with a creative and practical tool for stimulating classroom discussion. The sections include "American Films: A Historian's Perspective," a listing of "Films for Specific Periods of American History," "Practical Suggestions," and "Bibliography." The film listing is presented in a narrative form, developing the connection between each film and the topics being studied.

Visual Archives of American History, 2/e
This two-sided video laserdisc explores history from a meeting of three cultures to the present and is an encyclopedic chronology of U.S. history offering hundreds of photographs and illustrations, a variety of source and reference maps—several of which are animated—plus approximately 50 minutes of video clips. For ease in planning lectures, a manual listing barcodes for scanning and frame numbers for all the content will be provided.

American Impressions: A CD-ROM for U.S History
This unique, ground-breaking product for the Introduction to U.S. History course is organized in a topical/thematic framework which allows an

in-depth coverage for each topic with a media-centered focus. Hundreds of photos, maps, pieces of art, graphics, and historical film clips are organized into narrated vignettes and interactive activities to create a tool for both professors and students. This first volume of a series includes: When Three Cultures Meet, The Constitution, Labor and Reform, and Democracy and Diversity: The History of Civil Rights. Each topic is explored through three major themes: Politics, Culture and Society, and Science and Health. Available for Macintosh and Windows formats.

Video Lecture Launchers

Prepared by Mark Newman, University of Illinois at Chicago, these video lecture launchers (each 2 to 5 minutes in duration) cover key issues in American history from 1877 to the present. The launchers are accompanied by an Instructor's Manual.

Test Bank

Prepared by Carol Brown and Michael McCormick, Houston Community College, and James S. Olson, Sam Houston State University, this test bank contains over 1,200 multiple-choice, true/false, matching, and completion questions.

TestMaster Computerized Testing System

This flexible, easy-to-master computer test bank includes all the test items in the printed test bank. The TestMaster software allows you to edit existing questions and add your own items. Tests can be printed in several different formats and can include figures such as graphs and tables. Available for IBM and Macintosh computers.

QuizMaster

The new program enables you to design TestMaster generated tests that your students can take on a computer rather than in printed form. QuizMaster is available separate from TestMaster and can be obtained free through your sales representative.

Grades

A grade-keeping and classroom management software program that maintains data for up to 200 students.

For Students

Study Guide and Practice Tests

This two-volume study guide was created by Donald L. Smith, Houston Community College; Richard Bailey, San Jacinto College; Charles M. Cook, Texas Higher Education Coordinating Board, Community and Technical Colleges; and Jon V. Garrett, Houston Community College. Each volume begins with an introductory essay "Skills for Studying and Learning History." Each chapter contains a summary, learning objectives, identification list, map exercises, glossary, and multiple-choice, completion, and essay questions.

Learning to Think Critically: Films and Myths about American History

Randy Roberts and Robert May of Purdue University use well-known films such as *Gone with the Wind* and *Casablanca* to explore some common myths about America and its past. Many widely held assumptions about our country's past come from or are perpetuated by popular films. Which are true? Which are patently not true? And how does a student of history approach documents, sources, and textbooks with a critical and discerning eye? This short handbook subjects some popular beliefs to historical scrutiny to help students develop a method of inquiry for approaching the subject of history in general.

SuperShell II Computerized Tutorial

Prepared by Ron Petrin, Oklahoma State University, this interactive program for IBM computers helps students learn the major facts and concepts through drill and practice exercises and diagnostic feedback. SuperShell II, which provides immediate correct answers and the text page number on which the material is discussed, maintains a running score of the student's performance on the screen throughout the session. This free student supplement is available to instructors through their sales representatives.

Mapping American History: Student Activities

Written by Gerald Danzer of the University of Illinois, Chicago, this free map workbook for students features exercises designed to teach students to interpret and analyze cartographic materials as historical documents. The instructor is entitled to a free copy of the workbook for each copy of the text that is purchased from HarperCollins.

TimeLink Computer Atlas of American History
This atlas, compiled by William Hamblin of Brigham Young University, is an introductory software tutorial and textbook companion. This Macintosh program presents the historical geography of the continental United States from colonial times to the settling of the West and the admission of the last continental state in 1912. The program covers territories in different time periods, provides quizzes, and includes a special Civil War module.

ACKNOWLEDGMENTS

We are most grateful to our consultants and critiquers whose thoughtful and constructive work contributed greatly to this edition. Their many helpful suggestions led to significant improvements in the final product.

Joseph L. Adams
Meramec Community College

Frank Alduino
Anne Arundel Community College

James D. Border
Berkshire Community College

James E. Fell, Jr.
University of Colorado, Denver

Don R. Gerlach
University of Akron

August W. Giebelhaus
Georgia Institute of Technology

Anne Hickling
San Jose City College

I. E. Kirkpatrick
Tyler Junior College

Fred Koestler
Tarleton State University

Robert C. McMath, Jr.
Georgia Institute of Technology

T. Ronald Melton
Brewton-Parker College

Elliot Pasternack
Middlesex County College

J'Nell L. Pate
Tarrant County Junior College

Douglas W. Richmond
University of Texas, Arlington

George G. Suggs, Jr.
Southeast Missouri State University

Clyde D. Tyson
Niagara County Community College

Nancy C. Unger
San Francisco State University

Daniel C. Vogt
Jackson State University

James M. Woods
Georgia Southern University

A large number of instructors, too many to name individually, who used the previous editions were most helpful in reporting on the success of the text in the classroom. We heartily thank them all.

The staff at HarperCollins continued its generous support and assistance for our efforts. We appreciate the thoughtful guidance of Bruce Borland, who was instrumental in initiating the project; developmental editor Betty Slack who helped us augment and enhance the appeal of the text. Project editors Steve Pisano and Shuli Traub and design supervisor Jill Little deftly guided the new edition through the many phases of production. Others of the HarperCollins staff who gave valuable assistance include photo researchers Leslie Coopersmith and Mary Goljenboom.

Finally, each author received aid and encouragement from many colleagues, friends, and family members.

The Authors

About the Authors

ROBERT A. DIVINE

Robert A. Divine, George W. Littlefield Professor in American History at the University of Texas at Austin, received his Ph.D. from Yale University in 1954. A specialist in American diplomatic history, he has taught at the University of Texas since 1954, where he has been honored by the Student Association for teaching excellence. His extensive published work includes *The Illusion of Neutrality* (1962), *Second Chance: The Triumphs of Internationalism in America During World War II* (1967), and *Blowing on the Wind* (1978). He is also the author of *Eisenhower and the Cold War* (1981), and editor of *Exploring the Johnson Years* (1981) and *The Johnson Years,* Vol. II (1987). He has been a fellow at the Center for Advanced Study in the Behavioral Sciences and has given the Albert Shaw Lectures in Diplomatic History at Johns Hopkins University.

T. H. BREEN

T.H. Breen, William Smith Mason Professor of American History at Northwestern University, received his Ph.D. from Yale University in 1968. He has taught at Northwestern since 1970. Breen's major books include *The Character of the Good Rule: A Study of Puritan Political Ideas in New England* (1974), *Puritans and Adventurers: Change and Persistence in Early America* (1980), *Tobacco Culture: The Mentality of the Great Tidewater Planters on the Eve of Revolution* (1985), and with S. Innes of the University of Virginia, *"Myne Owne Ground": Race and Freedom on Virginia's Eastern Shore* (1980). His *Imagining the Past* won the 1990 Historic Preservation Book Award. In addition to receiving an award for outstanding teaching at Northwestern, Breen has been the recipient of research grants from the American Council of Learned Societies, the Guggenheim Foundation, the Insti-

tute for Advanced Study (Princeton), and the National Humanities Center. In 1994 he received the Douglas Adair Award from William and Mary Quarterly for his contribution to colonial American scholarship. He has served as the Fowler Hamilton Fellow at Christ Church, Oxford University (1987–1988), and the Pitt Professor of American History and Institutions, Cambridge University (1990–1991).

GEORGE M. FREDRICKSON

George M. Fredrickson is Edgar E. Robinson Professor of United States History at Stanford University. He is the author or editor of several books, including the *Inner Civil War* (1965), *The Black Image in the White Mind* (1971), and *White Supremacy: A Comparative Study in American and South African History* (1981), which won both the Ralph Waldo Emerson Award from Phi Beta Kappa and the Merle Curti Award from the Organization of American Historians. His most recent work is *The Arrogance of Race: Historical Perspectives on Slavery, Racism, and Social Inequality* (1988). He received both the A.B. and Ph.D. degrees from Harvard and has been the recipient of a Guggenheim Fellowship, two National Endowment for the Humanities Senior Fellowships, and a Fellowship from the Center for Advanced Studies in the Behavioral Sciences. Before coming to Stanford in 1984, he taught at Northwestern. He has also served as Fulbright lecturer in American History at Moscow University and as Harmsworth Professor of American History at Oxford.

R. HAL WILLIAMS

R. Hal Williams is Professor of History at Southern Methodist University. He received his A.B. degree from Princeton University (1963) and his Ph.D. degree from Yale University (1968). His books include *The Democratic Party and*

California Politics, 1880–1896 (1973), *Years of Decision: American Politics in the 1890s* (1978), and *The Manhattan Project: A Documentary Introduction to the Atomic Age* (1990). A specialist in American political history, he taught at Yale University from 1968 to 1975 and came to SMU in 1975 as chair of the Department of History. From 1980 to 1988, he served as dean of Dedman College, the school of humanities and sciences, at SMU. In 1980, he was a visiting professor at University College, Oxford University. Williams has received grants from the American Philosophical Society and the National Endowment for the Humanities, and he has served on the Texas Committee for the Humanities. He is currently at work on a biography of James G. Blaine, the late-nineteenth-century Speaker of the House, secretary of state, and Republican presidential candidate.

Routes of the First Americans

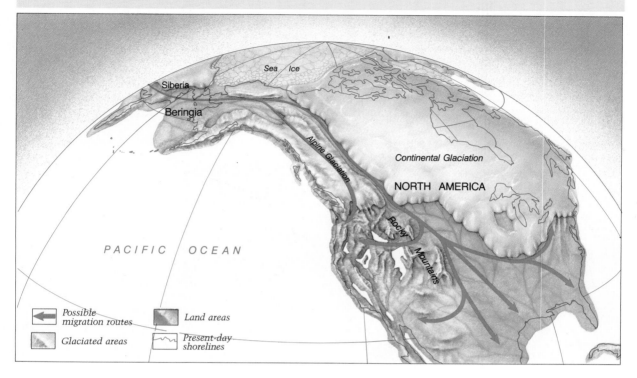

Siberia
Beringia
Sea Ice
Alpine Glaciation
Continental Glaciation
NORTH AMERICA
Rocky Mountains
PACIFIC OCEAN

→ Possible migration routes
Glaciated areas
Land areas
Present-day shorelines

The peopling of North America began about 30,000 years ago, during the Ice Age, and continued for many millennia. Land bridges created by lower sea levels during glaciation formed a tundra coastal plain over what is now the Bering Strait, between Asia and North America. In the postglacial era, the warmer climate supported the domestication and, later, the cultivation of plants. By the first century A.D., intensive farming was established from the southwest to the east coast of what is now the United States. (Ch. 1)

Except for an abortive attempt by Norsemen in the tenth century to settle the New World, contact between North America and Europe was not established until the Age of Exploration at the end of the 1400s. Settlements were founded in Mexico and Florida by Spain in the 1500s, and along the Atlantic littoral by France, England, Sweden, and Holland in the early 1600s.

From the founding of the first colonies along the Atlantic coast to the current involvement of the United States in global affairs, the dominant theme in American life has been growth. The pages that follow chronicle the growth of the United States from its colonial origins to the present in fifty-year intervals, using maps, narrative, and a chronology of major and parallel events.

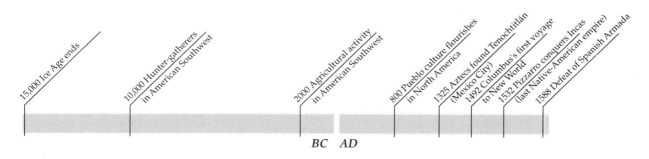

15,000 Ice Age ends

10,000 Hunter-gatherers in American Southwest

2000 Agricultural activity in American Southwest

800 Pueblo culture flourishes in North America

1325 Aztecs found Tenochtitlán (Mexico City)

1492 Columbus's first voyage to New World

1532 Pizzarro conquers Incas (last Native-American empire)

1588 Defeat of Spanish Armada

BC   AD

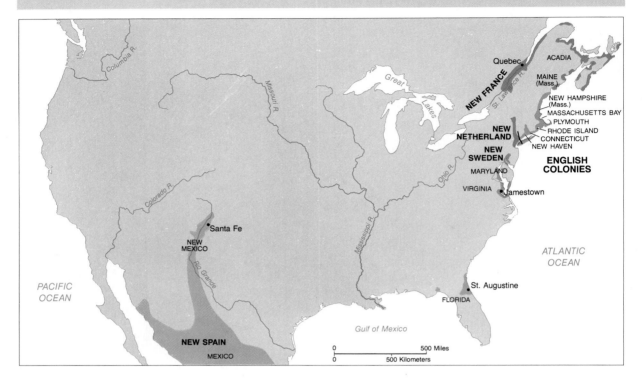

Following up on Columbus's New World discoveries, the Spanish set sail for America and conquered the Native American Aztecs and Incas in the sixteenth century, establishing a vast colonial empire stretching from Mexico to Peru. The search for gold and silver brought Spanish explorers into the present-day American Southwest, where they established outposts in New Mexico in the early 1600s. Even earlier, Spain had begun the settlement of Florida with the founding of St. Augustine in 1565. Far to the north the French, attracted by the profits of the fur trade with the Indians, began settling the St. Lawrence valley in the early part of the seventeenth century.

Between the Spanish to the south and the French to the north, English colonists founded a series of scattered settlements along the Atlantic coast. Driven by the desire for economic gain, religious freedom, or both, colonists in Virginia and Massachusetts Bay endured severe weather and periods of starvation to establish small but permanent colonies. By mid-century, settlements had sprung up in New Hampshire, Connecticut, and Rhode Island. Along Chesapeake Bay, Maryland was founded as a place of refuge for persecuted Catholics. In the midst of these English colonies, the Dutch established New Netherland and took over a small Swedish settlement. By the middle of the century, the seeds had been planted for a future United States.

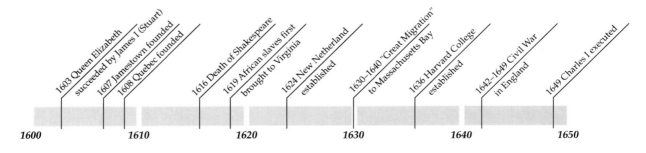

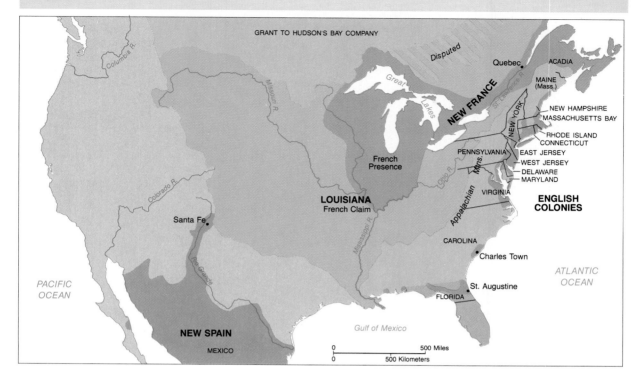

Having established a precarious foothold, the English settlements slowly began to grow and prosper. The later New England colonies received royal charters, separate from the original Massachusetts Bay charter. William Penn established Pennsylvania as a place of refuge for Quakers, welcoming French, Dutch, German, and Swedish settlers, as well as English and Scotch-Irish. Nearby New Jersey became the home for an equally diverse population. Under English rule, New Netherland became New York. In the south, English aristocrats founded Carolina as a plantation society populated in great part by settlers from the Caribbean island of Barbados. What was most remarkable about these English colonies was not their similarities but the differences between them. Bound together only by ties to the mother country, each developed its own character and culture.

Meanwhile, intrepid French explorers based in Quebec penetrated deep into the interior of the continent, driven on by the imperatives of the fur trade. Père Jacques Marquette navigated the Mississippi River and Sieur de La Salle journeyed to the Gulf of Mexico, laying claim for the King of France to a vast territory—all the lands drained by the Mississippi and its tributaries. This French initiative alarmed colonists along the Atlantic coast, many of whom believed that France planned to block English settlement on the lands beyond the Appalachian Mountains. About the same time, Spain established missions in Texas as a token presence. (Ch. 1, 2)

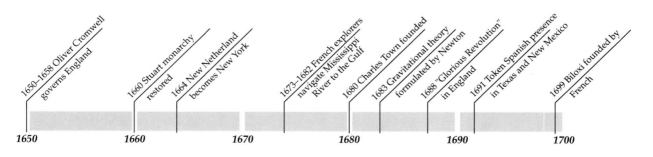

1650

1650–1658 Oliver Cromwell governs England

1660

1660 Stuart monarchy restored

1664 New Netherland becomes New York

1670

1673–1682 French explorers navigate Mississippi River to the Gulf

1680

1680 Charles Town founded

1683 Gravitational theory formulated by Newton

1688 "Glorious Revolution" in England

1690

1691 Token Spanish presence in Texas and New Mexico

1699 Biloxi founded by French

1700

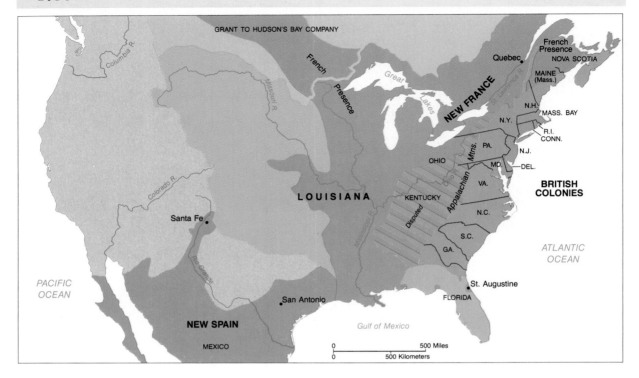

A century-long European struggle for empire between the French and the British led to military confrontation on this side of the Atlantic. Britain's victory in Queen Anne's War changed the map of North America. It gave the British control of the land bordering on Hudson Bay, as well as Newfoundland and Nova Scotia. The French redoubled their efforts to develop Louisiana as a buffer against the westward expansion of the seaboard colonies. Concerned with the Spanish presence in Florida, the British founded the colony of Georgia in 1732 to guard the Carolinas, which had been divided in 1729 into the separate royal colonies of North and South Carolina.

By the middle of the eighteenth century, the American colonists were rapidly moving onto the lands between the Atlantic coast and the foothills of the Appalachian Mountains. Descendents of the original settlers, along with newcomers from England, Northern Ireland, and Germany, filtered into the Shenandoah Valley to settle the backcountry of Virginia and the Carolinas. Other Americans contemplated crossing the mountains to occupy the fertile lands of Kentucky and Ohio. The French, fearful of a floodtide of American settlers, made important alliances with Indian tribes of the Ohio country to strengthen their position, and built a chain of forts to defend the area. Imperial rivalry for control of North America was approaching its climax. (Ch. 4)

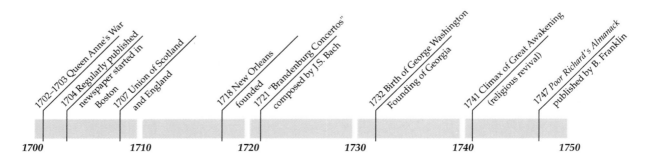

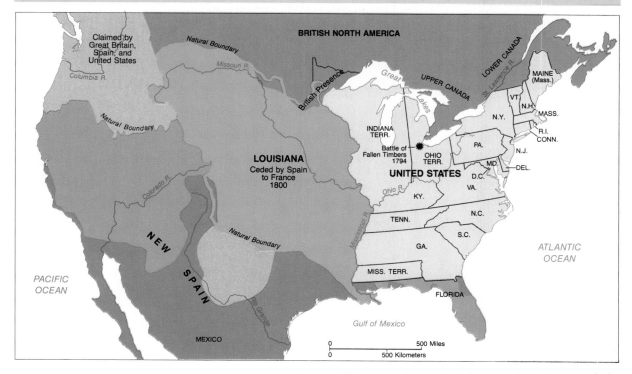

In the half century between 1750 and 1800, the map of North America underwent extensive political change. First, the British defeated the French and drove them from the mainland of the continent. The Peace of Paris in 1763 called for the French to surrender Canada to Great Britain and transfer Louisiana to Spain. The subsequent British Proclamation Line of 1763, designed to preserve a fur trade with the Indians by blocking settlement west of the mountains, angered the colonists and contributed to the unrest that culminated in the Revolutionary War.

Independence stimulated the westward expansion of the American people. Even while the fighting was in progress, pioneers like Daniel Boone began opening up Kentucky and Tennessee to frontier settlement. In the 1783 treaty that ended the war, Britain granted the United States generous boundaries, stretching from the Great Lakes and the St. Lawrence River on the north to Florida on the south, and the Mississippi on the west. But the young nation found it difficult to make good its claims to this new territory. Indians tried to hold on to their land, with British and Spanish encouragement. In the mid-1790s, however, diplomatic agreements with both nations and a crushing defeat of the Indians at Fallen Timbers opened the way to American settlement of the land beyond the mountains. Kentucky and Tennessee became states in the union before the end of the century, and Ohio would follow just a few years later. (Ch. 4, 5, 6, 7)

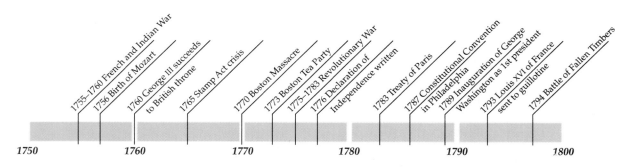

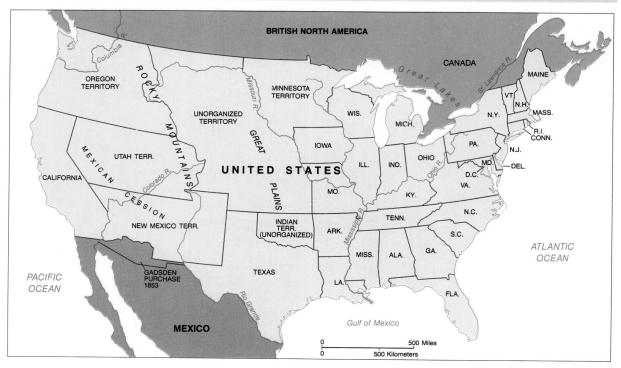

Over the next fifty years, the territory of the United States more than doubled. The purchase of Louisiana from France brought in the vast trans-Mississippi West, stretching across the Great Plains to the Rocky Mountains. From 1804 to 1806, William Lewis and Meriwether Clark and their expedition crossed the continent. Distance, fierce Indian resistance, and an arid climate delayed the settlement of the trans-Mississippi West, but American settlers poured into the area east of the Mississippi. The eastern Indians, their power broken in the War of 1812, were no longer able to resist the tide of settlement; they agreed to evacuate their ancestral homelands and in 1835 the last holdouts, the Cherokees, were forcibly removed to Oklahoma.

The climax of western expansionism came in the 1840s, when the United States extended its boundaries to the Pacific. Proclaiming the nation's "manifest destiny" to occupy the continent, American settlers leapfrogged over the inhospitable Great Plains and rugged Rockies to settle in California and Oregon. Diplomacy with Great Britain secured Oregon to the 49th parallel. Americans moved into Texas in the 1820s, broke away from Mexico in 1836, and joined the union in 1845—a move that led to war with Mexico in 1846. The American victory two years later gave the United States California and the New Mexico territory. The purchase in 1853 of a small strip of southern Arizona from Mexico rounded out the nation's present-day continental boundaries. (Ch. 8, 9, 10, 12)

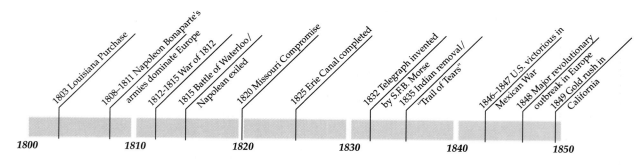

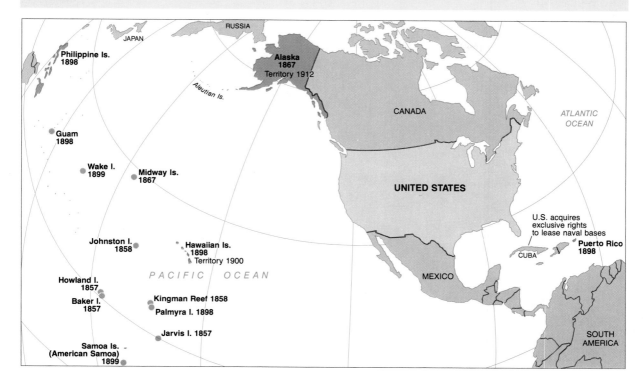

Newly acquired territories brought great opportunities and bitter sectional quarrels. The discovery of gold in California at mid-century was followed by a rush to the Pacific, but the question of extending slavery into the new areas set North against South. That controversy contributed to the outbreak of civil war and the end of slavery. In the three decades following the Civil War, Americans finally settled the last frontier: the Rockies and the Great Plains.

Railroads linked widely separated regions when the first transcontinental line was completed in Utah in 1869. Prospectors flocked to the Rockies, drawn by the bonanza of mineral wealth; ranchers drove cattle through the grasslands of the great open range from the Texas Panhandle to Montana; farmers, using new technology and methods to meet the semiarid conditions, increased the fertility of the soil of the Great Plains. In 1893 historian Frederick Jackson Turner proclaimed the American frontier was disappearing, signaling the end of an era.

With the continent settled, expansionists looked overseas. William Seward added Alaska to the nation's territory in 1867. Three decades later, victory in the Spanish-American War led to an outburst of enthusiasm for empire. The United States acquired Puerto Rico and the Philippines from Spain, and annexed the Hawaiian Islands. (Ch. 14, 15, 17, 21)

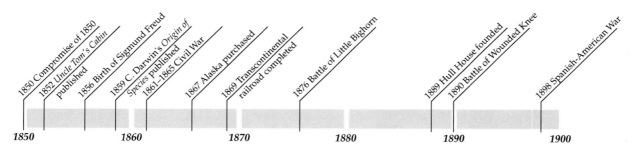

Map Series: The Growth of the United States **xxxix**

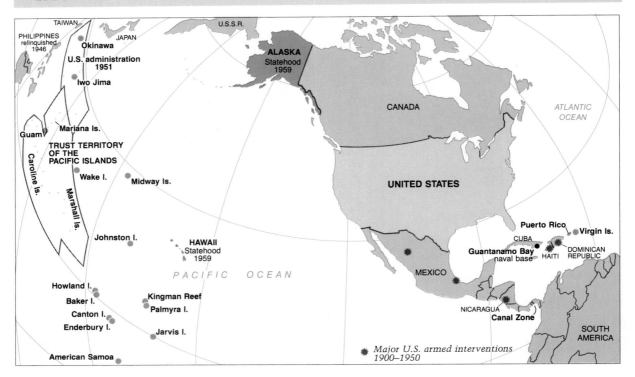

Taking an active role in world affairs led to recurring armed interventions by the United States in distant lands. In 1900, American troops took part in the international effort to put down the antiforeign Boxer Rebellion in China. Over the next decade and a half, the United States intervened in several Latin American countries with armed force, most notably in Panama, where the United States acquired the Canal Zone in 1903, and in Mexico, with the six-month occupation of Vera Cruz in 1914.

America remained neutral for the first three years of World War I in Europe but finally entered the war against the Central Powers (Germany, Austria-Hungary, and Turkey) in 1917, eventually sending more than two million men to fight in France. At the war's end, President Wilson played an active role in negotiating the Treaty of Versailles, even though the United States did not join the League of Nations created by the treaty.

Despite attempts in the 1920s and 1930s to limit American involvement in the world, the 1940s found Americans fighting Germany and Japan around the globe. American forces waged World War II in North Africa, on many Pacific islands, and in Europe. Although the United States took the lead in forming the United Nations, the end of the war did not usher in an era of lasting peace. To the contrary, the United States and the Soviet Union faced off in a Cold War that led to the permanent stationing of American troops from West Germany to the Pacific Trust Territory. The Philippines gained their independence in 1946. (Ch. 21, 24, 27, 28)

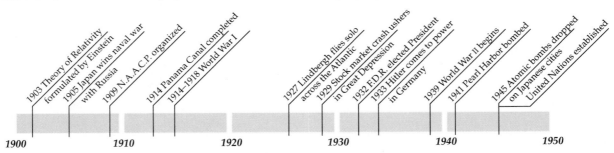

1950 to the Present

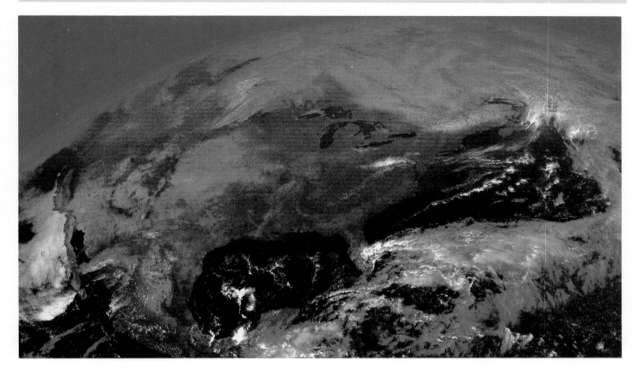

The United States took part in two Asian wars after 1950: a stalemate in Korea and a long, frustrating, losing struggle in Vietnam in the 1960s and 1970s. Closer to home, Russian ties to Fidel Castro led to a dangerous showdown during the Cuban missile crisis in 1962. In the Middle East, European dependence on Persian Gulf oil and American support for Israel made and continue to make this region an area of vital concern for U.S. foreign policy.

There have been changes in the status of America's territorial possessions: Hawaii and Alaska became the forty-ninth and fiftieth states in the late 1950s; and Puerto Rico was granted commonwealth status in 1952. A new frontier—outer space—was opened up with the Soviet launch of *Sputnik* in 1957. In 1969 came the world's most spectacular space achievement

to date when American astronauts landed on the moon. Rockets now launch unmanned probes into the farthest reaches of the solar system, gathering invaluable scientific data. America's space shuttle program—despite setbacks—continues the investigation of space. American horizons, once limited to the confines of thirteen struggling colonies, have expanded over four centuries to embrace the entire world and the nearer reaches of outer space. (Ch. 28, 29, 30, 31; 32, 33)

The greatest changes have come in Europe. The wave of liberation that swept across central and eastern Europe in the summer and fall of 1989 was fittingly exemplified by the crumbling of the Berlin Wall. Germany was reunited, and Communist regimes throughout eastern Europe collapsed. The disintegration of the Soviet Union in 1991 marked the end of the Cold War.

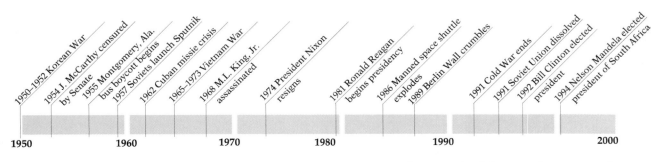

1950–1952 Korean War
1954 J. McCarthy censured by Senate
1955 Montgomery, Ala. bus boycott begins
1957 Soviets launch Sputnik
1962 Cuban missile crisis
1965–1973 Vietnam War
1968 M.L. King, Jr. assassinated
1974 President Nixon resigns
1981 Ronald Reagan begins presidency
1986 Manned space shuttle explodes
1989 Berlin Wall crumbles
1991 Cold War ends
1991 Soviet Union dissolved
1992 Bill Clinton elected president
1994 Nelson Mandela elected president of South Africa

1950   1960   1970   1980   1990   2000

Map Series: The Growth of the United States   xli

AMERICA PAST AND PRESENT

Fourth Edition

Robert A. Divine
University of Texas

T. H. Breen
Northwestern University

George M. Fredrickson
Stanford University

R. Hal Williams
Southern Methodist University

ISBN 0-673-99192-X

This best-selling text for the survey course in U.S. history presents a strong narrative approach and a broad view of the American past that involves traditional themes yet considers social, gender, and ethnic contributions. Reflecting the most recent historical scholarship and working within a cohesive political framework, the authors, all distinguished scholars, allow students to see the chronological unfolding of the American experience. At the same time, students are shown how social and economic factors influence national development. *Volume One: To 1877* chronicles the period of the earliest Native Americans and charts the country's growth up to the Reconstruction. *Volume Two: From 1865* covers the Reconstruction to the present day.

ered a staff of thousands of engineers and technicians, "the largest bureaucracy ever assembled in irrigation history."

Dams and canals channeled water into places like California's Imperial Valley, and as the water streamed in, cotton, cantaloupes, oranges, tomatoes, lettuce, and a host of other crops streamed out to national markets. By 1920, Idaho, Montana, Utah, Wyoming, Colorado, and Oregon had extensive irrigation systems, all drawing on scarce water supplies; California, the foremost importer of water, had 4.2 million acres under irrigation, many of them picked by migrant workers from Mexico, China, and Japan. The work was backbreaking—and poorly paid. A worker from India called picking asparagus a "ghastly" job, paid at the rate of ten cents a box.

> They gave us miles and miles of asparagus rows. As soon as I had knelt down with my knife and cut out one head and put it in the box, there would be another one sprouting before me. Then I would have to stoop again, and it was continuous picking and stooping that made it a terrible form of exercise. It is walk and bend, bend and walk, from half past four [in the morning] or thereabouts, until seven in the evening.

Women at Work

Women worked in larger and larger numbers. In 1900, more than five million worked—one-fifth of all adult women—and among those aged fourteen to twenty-four, the employment rate was almost one-third. Of those employed, single women outnumbered married women by seven to one, yet more than one-third of married women worked. Most women held service jobs. Only a small number held higher paying jobs as professionals

Irrigation and Conservation in the West to 1917
To make the arid lands of the Western states productive, the state and federal governments regulated the water supply through irrigation projects and the creation of water reservoirs. The federal government also created land reserves.

College in New York, became engaged and refused to resign; the dean told her icily that Barnard expected a married woman to "dignify her home-making into a profession, and not assume that she can carry on two full professions at a time."

More women than men graduated from high school, and with professions like medicine and science largely closed

INSIGHTS ON WESTERN HISTORY

New discussions of irrigation, ethnic rivalries, and the impact of settlement on the environment are highlighted. New information is featured on Asian-Americans, migrant labor, and landholding in the West.

Southeast led Spain to colonize St. Augustine (Florida) in 1565. Although this enterprise never flourished, it claims attention as the first permanent European settlement established in what would become the United States, predating the founding of Jamestown and Plymouth by several decades. Pedro Menéndez de Avilés brought some fifteen hundred soldiers and settlers to St. Augustine, where they constructed an impressive fort, but the colony failed to attract additional Spanish migrants. "It is hard to get anyone to go to St. Augustine because of the horror with which Florida is painted," the governor of Cuba complained in 1673. "Only hoodlums and the mischievous go there from Cuba."

California never figured prominently in Spain's plans for the New World. Early explorers reported finding only impoverished Indians living along the Pacific coast. Adventurers saw no natural resources worth mentioning, and since the area proved extremely difficult to reach from Mexico City—the overland trip could take months—California received little attention. Fear that the Russians might seize the entire region belatedly sparked Spanish activity, however, and after 1769, two indomitable servants of empire, Fra Junípero Serra and Don Gaspar de Portolá, organized permanent missions and *presidios* (forts) at San Diego, Monterey, San Francisco, and Santa Barbara.

Land for the Taking

As railroads pushed west in the 1870s and 1880s, locomotive trains replaced wagon trains, but the shift was gradual, and until the end of the century emigrants often combined both modes of travel. Into the 1890s, travelers could be seen making their way across the West by any available means. Early railroad transportation was expensive, and the average farm family could not afford to buy tickets and ship supplies. Many Europeans traveled by rail to designated outfitting places, and then proceeded West with wagons and oxen.

Traffic flowed in all directions, belying the image of a simple "westward" movement. Many people did go west, of course, but others, like migrants from Mexico, became westerners by moving north, and Asian Americans moved eastward from the Pacific coast. Whatever their route, they all ended up in the meeting ground of cultures that formed the modern West.

Why did they come? "The motive that induced us to part with the pleasant associations and the dear friends of our childhood days," explained Phoebe Judson, an early emigrant, "was to obtain from the government of the United States a grant of land that 'Uncle Sam' had promised to give to the head of each family who settled in this new country." A popular camp song reflected the same motive:

Come along, come along—don't be alarmed,
Uncle Sam is rich enough to give us all a farm.

Uncle Sam owned about 1 billion acres of land in the 1860s, much of it mountain and desert land unsuited for agriculture. By 1900, the various land laws had distributed half of it. Between 1862 and 1890, the government gave away 48 million acres under the Homestead Act of 1862, sold about 100 million acres to private citizens and corporations, granted 128 million acres to railroad companies to tempt them to build across the unsettled West, and sold huge tracts to the states over 75 by the 1990s. The Census Bureau projected a slower rate of increase to 2010, when the elderly will make up 13.2 percent of the population, and then a big jump as the baby boomers reach 65. By the year

Of the many dangers faced by those traveling on the overland trails, among the most severe were prairie blizzards. As temperatures fell, cattle would inhale particles of snow and sleet and die of suffocation.

The West: Exploiting an Empire

2030, one out of every five Americans will be over 65.

Six of every ten older Americans were women, and they tended to have a higher rate of chronic disease and to be worse off economically. Many of the oldest old, those over 85, lived in nursing homes and accounted for one-third of all Medicaid payments. Yet only 12.4 percent of the elderly lived below the poverty line; the annual cost of living increases in Social Security payments spared them from the worst ravages of inflation. The average family income of those over 65 was just under $20,000 a year in 1985 and three-fourths owned their own homes. Most impressive of all was their political power: 65 percent of those over 65 voted regularly, compared to just 46 percent of the entire population. The American Association of Retired People (AARP), with more than 30 million members, proved very effective in protecting the interests of the elderly in Washington.

The Revival of Immigration

A change in immigration policy in the 1960s led to a rising flow of immigrants into the United States that reached record proportions by the early 1990s. The Immigration and Nationality Act adopted in 1965 abolished the old national origins quota system, which limited immigration from Europe and Asia to just over 150,000 a year, with no restriction on the Western Hemisphere. The new system place limits of 170,000 visas for persons from Europe, Asia, and Africa and 120,000 for those coming from other Western Hemisphere nations. Instead of national quotas, preferences were allocated on the basis of family relationships and job skills needed in the United States. Immediate family members—spouses, minor children, and parents of U.S. citizens—were exempted from the numerical limits, as were refugees seeking political asylum in the United States.

In the 1970s, immigration rose rapidly, reaching the level of 700,000 a year by the end of the decade. The numbers continued to increase in the 1980s, with over 7 million immigrants entering the United States. Despite some minor changes in the law in 1990, designed mainly to place numerical limits on family-sponsored preferences (226,000) and those based on employment skills (140,000), 704,000 immigrants entered the United States in 1991 and 810,635 in 1992. When the estimated 200,000 illegal immigrants, mainly from Mexico, are added, immigration runs at about 1 million a year, the level of the previous peak years from 1900 to 1910.

The new wave of immigrants came mainly from Latin American and Asia, compared to the earlier overwhelming European majority. In the 1980s, Mexico supplied the largest number of immigrants, 1.6 million, followed by the Philippines with over half a million; in contrast, all of Europe supplied only 761,550 immigrants, just over 10 percent, with the largest number, 159,173, coming from the United Kingdom.

This influx from developing nations created a sharp increase in the number of foreign-born in the United States. By 1990, there were 20 million residents born abroad, 7.9 percent of the population, compared to 4.7 percent in 1970, but much lower than the 13.5 percent in 1910. The new immigrants tended to settle in urban areas in six states—California, Texas, New York, Florida, Illinois, and New Jersey. In California, the influx of immigrants from Asia and Mexico created growing pressure on public services, especially during the recession of the early 1990s. The result was growing resentment of immigrants and demands for a more restrictive policy. A *Newsweek* poll in 1993 found that 60 percent of the American people felt immigration was "a bad thing for this country today." A similar New York Times/CBS survey reported that 61 percent favored a decrease in immigration, up from 49 percent in 1986.

One consequence of the increasing immigration from Latin America and Asia, along with higher birthrates among people from these areas, was a change in the racial and ethnic composition of the United States. In 1990, minority groups, primarily black, Hispanic, and Asian, made up about 25 percent of the total population. By 2050, according to Census Bureau projections, the country would be almost evenly divided between non-Hispanic whites and minorities. Social harmony in the next century would depend on whether the melting pot continued to melt, blending ethnic groups into mainstream America, the American people felt immigration was "a bad thing for this country today." A similar New York Times/CBS survey reported that 61 percent

The Changing American Population

EXPANDED COVERAGE OF IMMIGRATION

Perspectives on immigration trends of the 1980s and early 1990s provide an insightful reference point for a study of current social, ethnic, gender, and economic issues.

CHAPTER CHRONOLOGIES

These helpful chronologies highlight key events that occurred during the time span covered in each chapter.

CHRONOLOGY

1954 Fall of Dien Bien Phu to Vietminh ends French control of Indochina

1955 Eisenhower meets Khrushchev at Geneva summit

1956 England and France touch off Suez crisis

1957 Russia launches *Sputnik* satellite

1959 Fidel Castro takes power in Cuba

1960 America U-2 spy plane shot down over Russia

1961 JFK establishes Peace Corps (March) • U.S.-backed Bay of Pigs invasion crushed by Cubans (April)

1962 Cuban missile crisis takes world to brink of nuclear war

1963 United States, Great Britain, and USSR sign Limited Nuclear Test Ban Treaty (August) • JFK assassinated; Lyndon B. Johnson sworn in as president (November)

1964 Congress overwhelmingly passes Gulf of Tonkin Resolution

1965 LBJ commits 50,000 American troops to combat in Vietnam

1967 Israel wins Six Day War in Middle East

1968 Vietcong launch Tet offensive (January) • Johnson announces he will not seek reelection (March)

Desmond Ball, *Politics and Force Levels* (1981); Harland B. Moulton, *Nuclear Superiority and Parity* (1972); and two broader studies of the arms race since 1945, McGeorge Bundy, *Danger and Survival* (1989), and Ronald Powaski, *March to Armageddon* (1987).

On Latin America, Theodore Draper, *Castro's Revolution* (1962); Richard E. Welch, *Response to Revolution* (1985); Trumbull Higgins, *The Perfect Failure* (1987); and Peter Wyden, *The Bay of Pigs* (1979), all deal with Castro's Cuba. For the Cuban Missile crisis, see Elie Abel, *The Missile Crisis* (1966); Robert F. Kennedy, *Thirteen Days* (1968); Graham Allison, *The Essence of Decision* (1971); Raymond Garthoff, *Reflections on the Cuban Missile Crisis* (1987); James G. Blight and David A. Welch, *On the Brink* (1989); Herbert Dinerstein, *The Making of the Missile Crisis* (1976); Dino Brugioni, *Eyeball to Eyeball* (1990); Robert Smith Thompson, *The Missiles*

of October (1992); and James G. Blight, *The Shattered Crystal Ball* (1990). Books on Johnson's intervention in the Dominican Republic include John B. Martin, *Overtaken by Events* (1966); Jerome Slater, *Intervention and Negotiation* (1970); Abraham Lowenthal, *The Dominican Intervention* (1972); Piero Gleijeses, *The Dominican Crisis* (1976); and Bruce Palmer, *Intervention in the Caribbean* (1989).

Kennedy's handling of a key European problem is traced in Norman Gelb, *The Berlin Wall* (1986), and Honore Catudel, *Kennedy and the Berlin Wall Crisis* (1980). For other regions, see Richard D. Mahoney, *JFK: Ordeal in Africa* (1983); Thomas J. Noer, *Cold War and Black Liberation* (1985); and Timothy P. Maga, *John F. Kennedy and the New Pacific Community, 1961–1963* (1990).

Stanley Karnow offers a broad view of the Vietnam War in *Vietnam: A History* (1983). Other general accounts of the war in Vietnam include Guenther Lewy, *American in Vietnam* (1978); Gabriel Kolko, *Anatomy of a War* (1986); Chester Cooper, *The Lost Crusade* (1970); Leslie H. Gelb and Richard K. Betts, *The Irony of Vietnam* (1979); and David Halberstam, *The Best and the Brightest* (1972). For Kennedy's role, see William J. Rust, *Kennedy in Vietnam* (1985); Ellen J. Hammer, *A Death in November* (1987); and John M. Newman, *JFK and Vietnam* (1992). Neil Sheehan, ed., *The Pentagon Papers* (1971), contains important documents on the war.

Lyndon Johnson's Vietnam decisions and their consequences are traced in two books by Larry Berman, *Planning a Tragedy* (1982) and *Lyndon Johnson's War* (1989); two books on the Gulf of Tonkin incident, Joseph C. Goulden, *Truth Is the First Casualty* (1969), and Anthony Austin, *The President's War* (1971); David Barrett, *Uncertain Warriors: Lyndon Johnson and His Vietnam Advisers* (1993); Kathleen Turner, *Lyndon Johnson's Dual War* (1985), on LBJ and the media; Townsend Hoopes, *The Limits of Intervention* (1969); and Herbert Y. Schandler, *The Unmaking of a President* (1977), on Johnson's change of heart in 1968.

Analyses of the military issues involved in the Vietnam War include Bruce Palmer, Jr., *The 25-Year War* (1984); Harry G. Summers, Jr., *On Strategy* (1982); Timothy Lomperis, *The War Nobody Lost—and Won* (1984); Mark Clodfelter, *The Limits of Air Power: The American Bombing of North Vietnam* (1989); James W. Gipson, *The Perfect War* (1986); Don Oberdorfer, *Tet!* (1971); James J. Wirtz, *The Tet Offensive* (1991); and Larry Cable, *Unholy Grail: The U.S. and the War in Vietnam, 1965–1968* (1992). Neil Sheehan, *A Bright Shining Lie* (1988), explores the war through the eyes of John Paul Vann.

Biographies and memoirs relating to foreign policy include Warren Cohen, *Dean Rusk* (1980); Thomas J.

Additional Bibliography

---

ered a staff of thousands of engineers and technicians, "the largest bureaucracy ever assembled in irrigation history."

Dams and canals channeled water into places like California's Imperial Valley, and as the water streamed in, cotton, cantaloupes, oranges, tomatoes, lettuce, and a host of other crops streamed out to national markets. By 1920, Idaho, Montana, Utah, Wyoming, Colorado, and Oregon had extensive irrigation systems, all drawing on scarce water supplies; California, the foremost importer of water, had 4.2 million acres under irrigation, many of them picked by migrant workers from Mexico, China, and Japan. The work was backbreaking—and poorly paid. A worker from India called picking asparagus a "ghastly" job, paid at the rate of ten cents a box.

> They gave us miles and miles of asparagus rows. As soon as I had knelt down with my knife and cut out one head and put it in the box, there would be another one sprouting before me. Then I would have to stoop again, and it was continuous picking and stooping that made it a terrible form of exercise. It is walk and bend, bend and walk, from half past four [in the morning] or thereabouts, until seven in the evening.

Women at Work

Women worked in larger and larger numbers. In 1900, more than five million worked—one-fifth of all adult women—and among those aged fourteen to twenty-four, the employment rate was almost one-third. Of those employed, single women outnumbered married women seven to one, yet more than one-third of married women worked. Most women held service jobs. Only a small number held higher paying jobs as professionals or managers.

In the 1890s, women made up over one-quarter of medical school graduates. Using a variety of techniques, men gradually squeezed them out, and by the 1920s, only about 5 percent of the graduates were women. Few women taught in colleges and universities, and those who did were expected to resign if they married. In 1906, Harriet Brooks, a promising physicist at Barnard

Irrigation and Conservation in the West to 1917
To make the arid lands of the Western states productive, the state and federal governments regulated the water supply through irrigation projects and the creation of water reservoirs. The federal government also created land reserves.

- Irrigation projects
- Reservoirs and lakes used as reservoirs
- Federal land reserves

0   200   400 Miles
0   200   400 Kilometers

STRONG MAPPING PROGRAM

This sophisticated program teaches students to interpret and analyze history through maps, underscoring their significance in gaining a full appreciation of historical events.

College in New York, became engaged and refused to resign; the dean told her icily that Barnard expected a married woman to "dignify her home-making into a profession, and not assume that she can carry on two full professions at a time."

More women than men graduated from high school, and with professions like medicine and science largely closed to them, they often turned to the new "business schools" that offered training in stenography, typing, and bookkeeping. In 1920, over one-quarter of all employed women held clerical jobs. Many others taught school.

In 1907 and 1908, investigators studied 22,000 women workers in Pittsburgh; 60 percent of them earned less than $7 a week, a minimum for "decent living." Fewer than 1 percent held

L<small>AW</small> & S<small>OCIETY</small> II

The Beecher-Tilton Adultery Trial

Public Image Versus Private Conduct

"LAW AND SOCIETY" ESSAYS

This new feature covers four significant legal cases in American history. Each essay includes a discussion of the background of the case, excerpts from the trial manuscript, and coverage of the case in the media of the period. The concluding paragraph of each essay invites students to explore the legal contest from the perspective of social/cultural historians and to examine its relevance to today's society.

There were no tickets left for the trial. City policemen guarded the door to the Brooklyn city courthouse. Citizens of Brooklyn and New York thronged against the cordon, clamoring to be allowed in. Every now and then someone would wend his or her way to the front of the crowd, show a harried policeman a ticket, and the officers would part just enough to let the ticket holder through.

Inside the courtroom, the judge was preparing to allow the opening arguments to commence. He sternly warned the still settling audience that he would not tolerate outbursts or demonstrations of sentiment from the audience. Nevertheless, the trial, which lasted from January through June of 1875, was repeatedly interrupted, especially by applause when the defendant, the Reverend Mr. Henry Ward Beecher, ridiculed the charges brought against him—charges of adultery. Theodore Tilton, one of Beecher's old friends and a member of his congregation, was suing the minister for having an illicit affair with his wife, Mrs. Elizabeth Tilton.

Beecher, of the famous Beecher family, was then the most prominent minister in the country. The father of the family, Lyman Beecher, had been an influential minister during the early part of the nineteenth century, leading a wing of the revivalist movement to bring religion to the mass of Americans. Henry's sister Catharine wrote tremendously popular tracts advocating expanded roles for women. Another sister Harriet, who wrote under her married name of Stowe, was, in President Lincoln's words, "the little lady who started this big war," with her antislavery novel *Uncle Tom's Cabin*. Henry Ward Beecher was himself something of an antislavery activist, popular for having held auctions at which benevolent Northerners could buy slaves into freedom. His published sermons sold by the thousands. But he was most famous for simply playing his role as the outspoken, charismatic, and ever-popular preacher and public personality, Henry Ward Beecher. Following in his father's footsteps (in method if not in doctrine), Beecher tried to adapt religion to the changing times.

At the time of the trial, only ten years had passed since the end of the Civil War. Middle-class white Northerners—the members of Beecher's congregation and readership—had difficulty reconciling themselves to the drastic changes that were afoot. There were new amendments to the Constitution, reshaping the language of the rights of citizens of the United States. Some people argued that those rights ought to apply not only to the newly freed class of black Americans, but also to the much larger class of free white women, who as yet could not vote or own property as easily as men. In addition to those problems, on the eve of the war Charles Darwin's book *On the Origin of Species* had made its first appearance, sending shock waves through the literate circles of Britain and America, and undermining religious authority on both sides of the Atlantic.

Beecher addressed these issues within the familiar and comfortable language of liberal Protestant Christianity. He presented Darwinian evolution as a benevolent metaphor for the advance of Christian civilization. Evolution thus became progress. He advocated women's rights in a relatively conservative way: like his sister Catharine, he believed women's virtues should be strengthened in order to make the home and the family stronger, not so women could become independent of men and the family.

In the middle of the nineteenth century, Brooklyn was still a separate city from New York. No bridge yet spanned the East River. When Beecher came to Brooklyn, he dedicated himself to reaching as wide an audience as possible. He wanted to bring all the community into his church. He believed he could do that by making himself into a public personality, making the congregation feel they knew him and could trust him. Consequently Beecher always phrased his sermons in colloquial language, and he had Plymouth Church constructed so the audience could sit all around the pulpit. This made the church "perfect," as Beecher said, "because it was built on a principle,—the principle of social and personal magnetism, which emanates reciprocally from a speaker and a close throng of hearers." To achieve his effect, he needed to be near his audience, and his audience needed to be near him, so they could see his whole body, and feel his "magnetic influence."

Beecher made himself into a public figure, a kind of modern celebrity. He acted as the moral and intellectual voice of a large urban community. It was Beecher's prominence and importance that made the trial such a public event. Furthermore, the trial occurred during the last years of the Grant administration, in which the president's personal secretary and some members of his cabinet had already been implicated in scandalous dealings. The war hero president stood accused of surrounding himself with scoundrels and of being unable to govern effectively. Would Beecher become another great man laid low?

Theodore Tilton edited a leading religious newspaper and was a liberal activist, working in the women's rights and abolition movements. He was an old friend and ally of Beecher's; the minister had presided at the marriage of Tilton and his wife Elizabeth. During the Civil War, Beecher and Tilton worked together to join antislavery forces and women's rights advocates into a single organization, the American Equal Rights Association. At a speech in 1866 Beecher linked the two groups, saying "suffrage is the inherent right of mankind" (which, in his mind, included women as well). As Reconstruction wore on, however, some reformers began to argue that those who stood for equal rights ought to focus first on the newly freed slaves, because this was, after all, "the Negro's hour."

This argument occasioned a split in the women's movement. Some women's activists believed they ought to put off their hopes for female suffrage until black suffrage had been secured. Others believed women should not wait, but must push forward with their own agenda. The split became permanent when Congress passed the Fifteenth Amendment, which read "The right of citizens of the United States to vote shall not be denied or abridged by the United States or by any State on account of race, color, or previous condition of servitude." The criterion of sex was conspicuously absent. Elizabeth Cady Stanton and a large group of her supporters opposed the amendment. Soon after, Stanton and Susan B. Anthony withdrew from the Equal Rights Association to form the National Woman Suffrage Association (NWSA). Women who supported the Fifteenth Amendment (including Julia Ward Howe, author of the "Battle Hymn of the Republic") formed the American Woman Suffrage Association (AWSA). The fissure in the feminist movement led to the split between Tilton and Beecher; by 1870, Tilton had become president of the NWSA and Beecher of the rival AWSA.

Tilton's association with the NWSA brought him into contact with the more radical activists of the women's movement. Chief among these was Victoria C. Woodhull, who in 1870 became the first woman to address Congress when she presented the national legislature with a petition on behalf of woman suffrage. Woodhull and her sister, Tennie C. (sometimes "Tennessee") Claflin, founded the first all-female brokerage on Wall Street. They also started the publication *Woodhull and Claflin's Weekly*, in which they advocated the philosophy of free love. Free love, Woodhull said, meant she came into the world "with an inalienable, constitutional, and natural right to love whom I may, to love as long or as short a period as I can, to change that love everyday if I please!" In the postwar period, free love, like socialism, was widely regarded as a threat to American institutions. Woodhull was doubly notorious because she was also a radical socialist; she served a term as leader of the New York division of the Marxist Second International and also published the first English translation of Marx and Engel's *Communist Manifesto*.

Tilton apparently chose Woodhull as a confidant for his troubles. He was having difficulties with his marriage. His wife found him difficult to live with. Elizabeth Tilton had sought out her minister—Beecher—as a sympathetic ear for her unhappiness. Beecher may have advised her to separate from her husband. But Tilton was suspicious of their intimacy for other reasons as well. When he confronted his wife, she confessed—in writing—to having entertained "improper proposals" from Beecher. Tilton took the confession to a conference with Beecher and Frank Moulton, a mutual friend, who could be trusted to act as a neutral party. Beecher and Moulton persuaded Tilton that what had happened was unclear and it was in nobody's best interest to pursue the matter. Tilton tore up the confession.

Beecher visited Elizabeth Tilton, who was in her sickbed. (She had suffered a miscarriage, but she seems not to have told anyone this at the time.) Distraught at the trouble her confession seemed to have caused, she agreed to write out a retraction to quell any possible rumors. "Wearied by importunity and weakened by sickness," she wrote,

> I gave a letter inculpating my friend Henry Ward Beecher, under assurances that would remove all difficulties between me and my husband. That letter I now revoke. I was persuaded—almost forced—when I was in a weakened state of mind. I regret it and recall all of its statements. . . . I desire to say explicitly, Mr. Beecher has never offered any improper solicitations, but has always treated me in a manner becoming a Christian gentleman.

When Tilton learned his wife had given such a letter to Beecher, he immediately worried it might be used against him. So he persuaded his wife to write yet another letter expressing this concern to Beecher. Beecher was now upset. There seemed no way to reassure Tilton. Moulton suggested that Beecher write out an apology. The minister agreed, but was too shaken to write the document himself. Moulton composed the letter, addressed to himself, which Beecher then signed:

My Dear Friend Moulton:

I ask through you Theodore Tilton's forgiveness, and I humble myself before him as I do before my God. He would have been a better man in my circumstances than I have been. I can ask nothing except that he will remember all the other hearts that will ache. I will not plead for myself. I even wish I were dead, but others must live and suffer.

I will die before any one but myself shall be implicated. All my thoughts are running toward my friends, toward the poor child lying there and praying with her folded hands. She is guiltless, sinned against, bearing the transgression of another. Her forgiveness I have. I humbly pray to God that he may put it into the heart of her husband to forgive me. I have trusted this to *Moulton* in confidence.

Things seemed to quiet down after that, but then Victoria Woodhull published a lurid account of the affair in her *Weekly*. She hoped that by exposing Beecher, the spokesman for decent traditional institutions, especially marriage, as an adulterer and thus a hypocrite, she could advance the credibility of her cause. In this, if in nothing else, she was mistaken; she and her sister were soon arrested under the Comstock Laws, which prohibited distributing obscene materials through the mails, and held in jail until Woodhull's health broke down and she had to be released.

The two letters—Mrs. Tilton's retraction and Beecher's apology—constituted the bulk of the real evidence in the trial. Given that Mrs. Tilton had written first a confession and then a retraction and then a conditional statement regarding the retraction—and all under some coercion—and that Beecher hadn't even written his apology himself, the flimsy evidence hardly seem to prove

The members of the examining committee from the Plymouth Church congregation listen intently as Reverend Henry Ward Beecher reads his statement concerning his affair with Elizabeth Tilton. The committee, appointed by Beecher and composed mainly of his close friends and staunch supporters, completely exonerated Beecher.

anything. Nevertheless, as prosecuting attorney Samuel B. Morris noted in his opening remarks, "Adultery is peculiarly a crime of darkness and secrecy. Parties are rarely surprised in it, and so it not only may, but ordinarily must, be established by circumstantial evidence." If Beecher were innocent, then what exactly was he apologizing so abjectly for? What did the note mean to say when it suggested that Mrs. Tilton (the "poor child") had borne the sin of another?

The affair would never have become public knowledge had Victoria Woodhull not chosen to publish it, believing she could implicate Beecher as a free lover and thus advance her own beliefs. Even after she printed her account of the scandal, the case might never have gone to trial. But Woodhull cited Tilton as her source, and Tilton fanned the flames of scandal even as they began to die by publishing a suggestive letter in the newspapers. The leaders of Plymouth Church had had enough and called a meeting to drop Tilton from the roll of the congregation. They had a ready pretext; Tilton had not attended church in four years. Tilton, outraged, carried on an argument in print with various members of the church, all the while hinting that Beecher was guilty of illicit behavior. Finally, Beecher called an examining committee from the congregation to clear his name. Tilton appeared before the committee to accuse Beecher of "criminal intimacy" with his wife. Beecher testified to deny the charges. When Mrs. Tilton came to the stand, the committee asked her just what was the sin of which she and Beecher were so apologetic? "I do not think," she said, "that I felt that it was anything more than giving to another what was due my husband." The committee pressed her further: "When you speak of what was due to him, what do you refer to?" Mrs. Tilton replied, "Why, the all of my nature; I do not think I feel any great sin about it now. . . . I harmed [Theodore] in his pride by allowing any one else into my life at all; I think that was [the] sin."

After hearing all the testimony, the investigating committee reported that "It is proper . . . to state that the offence as alleged by Mr. Tilton during some four years and until recently to numerous persons, in writing and otherwise, was an improper suggestion or solicitation by Mr. Beecher to Mrs. Tilton. But as time passed and purposes matured, this charge passed and matured into another form and substance. . . . The charge, in effect, is that Mr. Beecher . . . committed adultery with Elizabeth R. Tilton."

Did the gradual escalation of the charge from impropriety to adultery reflect Tilton's increasingly outraged imagination, or did it reflect his initial unwillingness to level so monstrous an

"LAW AND SOCIETY" ESSAYS

During the Reconstruction period immediately following the Civil War, African Americans struggled to become equal citizens of a democratic republic. They produced a number of remarkable leaders who showed blacks were as capable as other Americans of voting, holding office, and legislating for a complex and rapidly changing society. Among these leaders was Robert Smalls of South Carolina. Although virtually forgotten by the time of his death in 1915, Smalls was perhaps the most famous and widely respected southern black leader of the Civil War and Reconstruction era. His career reveals some of the main features of the African American experience during that crucial period.

Born a slave in 1839, Smalls had a white father whose identity has never been clearly established. But his white ancestry apparently gained him some advantages, and as a young man he was allowed to live and work independently, hiring his own time from a master who may have been his half-brother. Smalls worked as a sailor and trained himself to be a pilot in Charleston harbor. When the Union Navy blockaded Charleston in 1862, Smalls, who was then working in a Confederate steamship called the *Planter*, saw a chance to win his freedom in a particularly dramatic way. At three o'clock in the morning on May 13, 1862, when the white officers of the *Planter* were ashore, he took command of the vessel and its slave crew, sailed it out of the heavily fortified harbor, and surrendered it to the Union Navy. Smalls immediately became a hero to those antislavery Northerners who were seeking evidence that the slaves were willing and able to serve the Union. The *Planter* was turned into a Union transport and Smalls was made its captain after being commissioned as an officer in the armed forces of the United States. During the remainder of the war, he rendered conspicuous and gallant service as captain and pilot of Union vessels off the coast of South Carolina.

Like a number of other African Americans who had fought valiantly for the Union, Smalls went on to a distinguished political career during Reconstruction, serving in the South Carolina

constitutional convention, the state legislature, and for several terms in the U.S. Congress. He was also a shrewd businessman and became the owner of extensive properties in Beaufort, South Carolina, and its vicinity. (His first purchase was the house of his former master where he had spent his early years as a slave.) As the leading citizen of Beaufort during Reconstruction and for some years thereafter, he acted like many successful white Americans, combining the acquisition of wealth with the exercise of political power. The electoral organization he established resembled in some ways the well-oiled "machines" being established in northern towns and cities. It was so effective that Smalls was able to control local government and get himself elected to Congress even after the election of 1876 had placed the state under the control of white conservatives bent on depriving blacks of political power. Organized mob violence defeated him in 1878, but he bounced back to win by decision of Congress a contested congressional election in 1880. He did not leave the House of Representatives for good until 1886, when he lost another contested election that had to be decided by Congress. It revealed the changing mood of the country that his white challenger was seated despite evidence of violence and intimidation against black voters.

In their efforts to defeat him, Smalls's white opponents frequently charged that he had a hand in the corruption that was allegedly rampant in South Carolina during Reconstruction. But careful historical investigation shows that he was, by the standards of the time, an honest and responsible public servant. In the South Carolina convention of 1868 and later in the state legislature, he was a conspicuous champion of free and compulsory public education. In Congress, he fought for the enactment and enforcement of federal civil rights laws. Not especially radical on social questions, he sometimes bent over backward to accommodate what he regarded as the legitimate interests and sensibilities of South Carolina whites. Like other middle-class black political leaders in Reconstruction-era South Carolina, he can perhaps be faulted in hindsight for not doing more to help poor blacks gain access to land of

e Agony of Reconstruction

Robert Smalls (1839–1915) in an engraving from an 1862 newspaper. Smalls, who commandeered the frigate Planter and delivered it to the Union, served as the highest-ranking African-American officer in the Union navy.

their own. But in 1875 he sponsored congressional legislation that opened for purchase at low prices the land in his own district that had been confiscated by the federal government during the war. As a result, blacks were able to buy most of it, and they soon owned three-fourths of the land in Beaufort and its vicinity.

Smalls spent the later years of his life as U.S. collector of customs for the port of Beaufort, a beneficiary of the patronage that the Republican party continued to provide for a few loyal southern blacks. But the loss of real political clout for Smalls and men like him was one of the tragic consequences of the fall of Reconstruction.

THE PRESIDENT VERSUS CONGRESS

The problem of how to reconstruct the Union in the wake of the South's military defeat was one of the most difficult and perplexing challenges

ever faced by American policymakers. The Constitution provided no firm guidelines, for the framers had not anticipated a division of the country into warring sections. Once emancipation became a northern war aim, the problem was compounded by a new issue: how far should the federal government go to secure freedom and civil rights for four million former slaves?

The debate that evolved led to a major political crisis. Advocates of a minimal Reconstruction policy favored quick restoration of the Union with no protection for the freed slaves beyond the prohibition of slavery. Proponents of a more radical policy wanted readmission of the southern states to be dependent on guarantees that "loyal" men would displace the Confederate elite in positions of power, and that blacks would acquire basic rights of American citizenship. The White House favored the minimal approach, whereas Congress came to endorse the more radical and thoroughgoing form of Reconstruction. The resulting struggle between Congress and the chief executive was the most serious clash between two branches of government in the nation's history.

Wartime Reconstruction

Tension between the president and Congress over how to reconstruct the Union began during the war. Occupied mainly with achieving victory, Lincoln never set forth a final and comprehensive plan for bringing rebellious states back into the fold. But he did take initiatives that indicated he favored a lenient and conciliatory policy toward Southerners who would give up the struggle and repudiate slavery. In December 1863 he issued a Proclamation of Amnesty and Reconstruction; it offered a full pardon to all Southerners (with the exception of certain classes of Confederate leaders) who would take an oath of allegiance to the Union and acknowledge the legality of emancipation. Once 10 percent or more of the voting population of any occupied state had taken the oath, they were authorized to set up a loyal government. Efforts to establish such regimes were quickly undertaken in states that were wholly or partially occupied by Union troops; by 1864

*G*ood Manners and the Creation of an American Middle Class:

The Eighteenth Century

Manners generate anxiety. A wrong dessert spoon, an ill-chosen wine glass, an inappropriate outfit—such errors of judgment can expose a man or woman to the ridicule of polite society. George Washington dreaded the possibility of appearing an "awkward country fellow," and as a young ambitious Virginian, he did what socially insecure persons have done for centuries: he obtained a reliable book of etiquette, the functional equivalent of "Miss Manners" for eighteenth-century Americans.

A teenage Washington busily copied over a hundred points of good manners in a little volume entitled *Rules of Civility & Decent Behaviour in Company and Conversation*. Some entries strike modern readers as uncontroversial: "Associate yourself with Men of good Quality if you Esteem your own Reputation; for 'tis better to be alone than in bad Company" or "When another speaks be attentive yourself and disturb not the audience . . . interrupt him not."

Some of Washington's rules, however, seem bizarre. They suggest that relaxed modern standards of etiquette in this country are still a great deal more demanding than those of the eighteenth century. One wonders, for example, why Washington had to remind himself "When in company, put not your hands to any part of the body, not usually discovered." Another rule counseled polite colonial Americans to "Kill no vermin as fleas, lice, ticks, &c. in the sight of others; if you see any filth or thick spittle, put your foot dexteriously [sic] upon it; if it be upon the clothes of your companions, put it off privately; and if it be upon your own clothes, return thanks to him who puts it off." Even stranger, Washington copied in his little book, "Do not Puff up the Cheeks, Loll not out the tongue . . . thrust out the lips, or bite them or keep the Lips too open or too Close."

The image of Washington puffing up his cheeks or lolling his tongue during a polite conversation is amusing. For the ambitious young planter, however, the fear of exposure was very

Among Washington's Rules of Civility and Decent Behaviour in Company and Conversation *were admonitions to "Let your recreations be manful not sinful" and "Labour to keep alive in your breast that little celestial fire called conscience."*

real. Obsession with gentility swept through the Anglo-American world of the mid-eighteenth century. Everyone thought it important to be polite—or, if not polite in fact, then at least to appear polite. And in their quest for advice, people like Washington turned to surprising sources. The rules he reproduced had a long history stretching back to the Italian Renaissance. Much of this literature had been intended originally for courtiers, for the creatures who flattered Europe's kings and queens, and whatever else he may have been, Washington was no courtier. In eighteenth-century society, manners—the nervous concern over polite behavior—had spread to a fast-growing Anglo-American middle class.

Few Americans of Washington's background questioned the need to maintain visible class distinctions. No one advocated social equality. Indeed, colonists agreed a gentleman should stand apart from ordinary farmers and small merchants. The problem in a largely rural and agrarian society, one that claimed no genuine aristocrats, was discovering who was the authentic gentleman. Any literate person could read the etiquette books and learn the rules of gentility. Moreover, in a relatively open commercial society, almost everyone had opportunities to purchase manufactured goods, such as bright cloth for garments and pretty buckles and buttons. Such widespread access to imported finery and print culture meant a stranger might be a proper gentleman or someone who had managed to dress like a gentleman, in other words, a counterfeit.

A curious exchange between two travelers highlights the difficulty of establishing one's social rank at mid-century. A Scottish physician, Dr. Alexander Hamilton (no relation to the secretary of the treasury), never doubted his own gentility. He refused, however, to accept a Pennsylvania land speculator as his social peer. According to Hamilton, the other man appeared a "very rough spun, forward, clownish blade, much addicted to swearing, [and] at the same time desirous to pass for a gentleman." The Pennsylvanian felt insulted. Although he wore only "a greasy jacket and breeches and a dirty worsted cap," he believed himself as good a gentleman as the physician. In his own defense, the land speculator protested that "though he seemed to be but a plain, homely fellow, yet . . . he was able to afford better [clothes] than many that went finer." In fact, his "little woman at home drank tea twice a day."

The land speculator and his tea-drinking "little woman" were not about to be bullied by the likes of a Hamilton. Such middle-class Americans—white freeholders and artisans—strove to master the trappings of the new gentility. The tea service presented the most demanding test, for during such complex social rituals the chance of making a major faux pas was very great. At such tense moments a young man like Washington may have had to remind himself: "Clense not your teeth with the Table Cloth, Napkin, Fork, or Knife, but if Others do it, let it be done with a Pick Tooth."

The spread of print and the sudden availability of so many consumer goods at mid-century fueled the obsession with "civility and decent behaviour." As middle-class Americans soon discovered, however, there was a heavy price to be paid. The rush to gentility generated new social anxieties. Americans—even those who purchased fancy imports and devoured the etiquette books—worried that manners might represent no more than a polite shell, an external set of appearances that indicated perhaps the absence of sincere principle. The acquisition of a tea set could signal an addiction, leading not to the attainment of true gentility, but rather to the emulation of the moral standards of sniveling European courtiers. The deep tension between private manners and public morality, raised so forcefully for the first time during the mid-eighteenth century, perplexes Americans to this day.

Rigid rules of etiquette prescribed the social ritual of the tea service. In this eighteenth-century overmantle (oil on wood), the family slave attends John Potter and his family of Matunuck, Rhode Island, as they take their tea.

New World Encounters

single dramatic moment altered the course of history for peoples living on three continents. On October 12, 1492, the Taínos, American Indians living in the Bahamas, encountered Europeans and perhaps a few Africans for the first time. How the Taínos regarded the Spanish invaders will never be known. They left no written records. Only the impressions of Admiral Christopher Columbus and his lieutenants have survived. Columbus's journals describe how a group of Europeans rowed to the beach, unfurled a royal standard, raised colorful banners, and, as the natives watched, took possession of territory that generations of Taínos had always called their own.

For contemporary Europeans, Columbus provided a compelling interpretation of the event's historic significance. The discovery of unknown lands and peoples across the seas brought glory to Christianity, to the Spanish monarchs, and not least, to Columbus himself. In a letter circulated throughout Europe upon his return to Spain, Columbus announced, "As I know that you will be pleased at the great victory with which Our Lord has crowned my voyage, I write this to you, from which you will learn how in thirty-three days, I passed from the Canary Islands to the Indies. . . . And there I found very many islands filled with people innumerable, and of them all I have taken possession for their highnesses [King Ferdinand and Queen Isabella]."

Columbus and the adventurers who sailed in his wake wove a narrative of discovery that survived long after the Taínos had become extinct—a fate that befell them in the mid-sixteenth century. The story recounted first in Europe and then in the United States depicted heroic captains, missionaries, and settlers carrying civilization to the peoples of the New World and opening a vast virgin land to economic development. This familiar tale celebrated progress, the inevitable spread of European values, the pushing back of frontiers. It was a history crafted by the victors—usually males—and by the children of the victors to explain how they had come to control the modern world.

This story no longer seems an adequate explanation for European conquest and colonization. It is not so much wrong as incomplete. History from Columbus's perspective inevitably silences the voices of the victims, the peoples who, in this view, resisted economic and technological progress. Heroic tales of the advance of Western civilization fail to acknowledge the millions of Indians who died following conquest or the huge numbers of Africans brought to America as slaves.

By placing these complex, often unsettling events within a framework of *encounters,* we recapture the full human dimensions of conquest and resistance. The New World demanded extraordinary creative energies from the men and women of different cultures who found themselves dealing with one another in unprecedented situations. While the New World was often the scene of tragic violence and systematic exploitation, it allowed ordinary people opportunities to shape their own lives; neither the Indians nor the Africans were passive victims of European colonization. Within their own families and communities they made choices, sometimes rebelling, sometimes accommodating, but always trying to make sense in their own terms out of what was happening to them. Although they occasionally failed to preserve dignity and independence, their efforts poignantly reveal that the history of the New World—be it from the perspective of the Indian, the African American, or the European—is above all else an intensely human drama.

NATIVE AMERICAN CULTURES

As the Taínos well knew, the peopling of America did not begin in 1492. In fact, although the Spanish invaders proclaimed the discovery of a "New World," they really brought into contact three worlds that in the fifteenth century were already old. The first migrants entered North America approximately thirty thousand years ago.

Some archaeologists maintain that human settlement actually occurred much earlier, but the evidence in support of this thesis remains highly controversial. All agree, however, that at the time of the initial migration, the earth's climate was considerably colder than it is today, and that huge glaciers, often more than a mile thick, pushed as far south as the present states of Illinois and Ohio. Much of the world's moisture was transformed into ice, and the oceans dropped

Published in Barcelona in 1493, the first edition of the Carta a Santángel, in which this illustration appeared, announced the news of Columbus's arrival in the New World.

hundreds of feet below their current level. The receding waters created a land bridge between Asia and America, an area now submerged beneath the Bering Sea.

This northern region was largely free from glacial ice, and small bands of spear-throwing Siberian hunters chased giant mammals—woolly mammoths and mastadons, all now extinct—across the open tundra that covered the land bridge. These hunters were the first human beings to set foot on a vast, uninhabited continent. The migrations continued for thousands of years, interrupted only by changing water levels that occasionally flooded the land bridge.

Because these movements took place over such a long period of time and involved small, independent bands of nomadic people, the migrants never developed a sense of themselves as representatives of a single group. Each band pursued its own interests, adjusting to the opportunities presented by various microenvironments. Some groups, presumably those who had first crossed the land bridge, migrated the greatest distances, settling South and Central America. Newer arrivals probably remained in North America.

Whatever their histories, no two groups had precisely the same experience, which helps explain the strikingly different cultures that developed in the New World. Over the centuries, relatively isolated lineage groups—people claiming a common ancestry—developed distinct languages. Anthropologists estimate that, at the time of European conquest, the Native Americans who settled north of Mexico spoke between 300 and 350 separate languages.

Native hunter-gatherer cultures changed substantially during the long period prior to the European colonization. The early Indians developed many of the same technologies that appeared in other parts of the world. Take, for example, the introduction of agriculture in Native American societies. No one knows precisely when people first cultivated plants for food in North America, but archaeologists working in the Southwest have uncovered evidence suggesting that some groups were farming as early as 2000 B.C. These early cultivators depended on maize (corn), beans, and squash. Knowledge of the domestication of these crops spread slowly north and east, and by 800 B.C., cultivation of squash had reached present-day Michigan.

The Agricultural Revolution helps explain obvious differences among the North American Indian communities. Groups living in the Northeast who knew little about the domestication of plants or who learned of it comparatively late relied more heavily on hunting and gathering than did the cultivators of Mexico or the Southwest.

Wherever agriculture developed, it transformed Indian societies. The availability of a more reliable food source helped liberate women and men from some insecurities of a nomadic existence based on hunting and gathering. The vegetable harvest made it possible to establish permanent villages, and as the supply of food increased, the Native American population expanded. It is estimated that approximately four million Indians lived north of Mexico at the time of first contact with Europeans.

Greater population densities in some areas led to the development of a more urban style of life. Mississippian groups who dominated the Southeast around A.D. 1200 constructed large moundlike ceremonial centers and lived in populous towns, at least one of which, Cahokia, near the site of the modern city of St. Louis, contained as many people as did medieval London.

Aztec Society

The stability resulting from the Agricultural Revolution allowed the Indians of Mexico and Central America to structure their societies in different ways. Like the Incas who lived in what is now known as Peru, the Mayan and Toltec peoples of the Valley of Mexico built vast cities, formed complex government bureaucracies that dominated large tributary populations, and developed hieroglyphic writing as well as an accurate solar calendar. Their cities, which housed several thousand people, greatly impressed the Spanish conquerors. Bernal Diaz del Castillo reported, "When we saw all those [Aztec] towns and villages built in the water, and other great towns on dry land, and that straight and level causeway leading to Mexico, we were astounded. . . . Indeed, some of our soldiers asked whether it was not all a dream."

The rise and fall of some Native American civilizations predated the European conquest. Not long before Columbus began his first voyage across the Atlantic, the Aztecs, an aggressive, warlike people, swept through the Valley of Mexico, conquering the great cities that their enemies had constructed. Aztec warriors ruled by force, reducing defeated rivals to tributary status. In 1519, the Aztec's main ceremonial center, Tenochtitlán, contained as many as 250,000 people as compared with only 50,000 in Seville, the port from which the early Spaniards had sailed. Elaborate human sacrifice associated with Huitzilopochtli, the Aztec sun god, horrified Europeans, who apparently did not find the savagery of their own civilization so objectionable. These Aztec ritual killings were connected to the agricultural cycle, and the Indians believed the blood of their victims possessed extraordinary fertility powers. A fragment of an Aztec song-poem captures the indomitable spirit that once pervaded this militant culture.

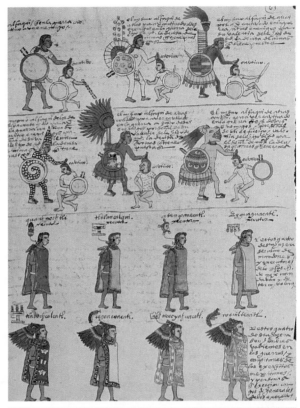

Aztec warriors were organized into regiments and groups distinguished by their distinctive dress. Warriors gained rank—and the right to wear more elaborate attire—by taking captives.

Proud of itself
is the city of Mexico-Tenochtitlán.
Here no one fears to die in war.
This is our glory. . . .

Who could conquer Tenochtitlán?
Who could shake the foundation of heaven?

Eastern Woodland Cultures

In the region along the Atlantic coast claimed by England, the Indians did not practice intensive agriculture. These peoples, numbering less than a million at the time of conquest, generally supplemented mixed farming with seasonal hunting and gathering. Most belonged to what ethnographers term the Eastern Woodland Cultures. Small bands formed villages during the warm summer months. The women cultivated maize and other crops while the men hunted and fished. During

Location of Major Indian Groups and Culture Areas in the 1600s

Native Americans had complex social structures and religious systems and a well-developed agricultural technology when they came into initial contact with Europeans.

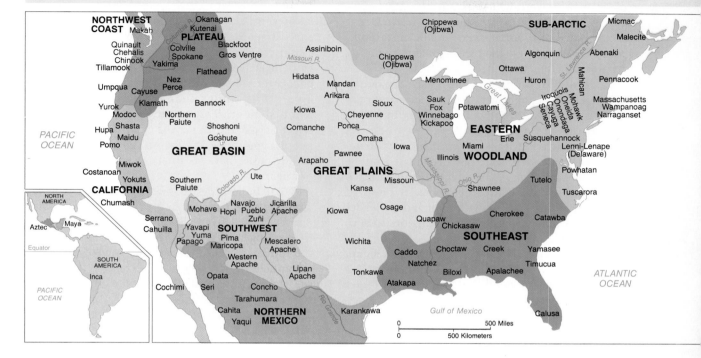

the winter, difficulties associated with feeding so many people forced these communities to disperse. Each family lived off the land as best it could.

Seventeenth-century English settlers were most likely to have encountered the Algonquian-speaking peoples who occupied much of the territory along the Atlantic coast from North Carolina to Maine. Included in this large linguistic family were the Powhatans of Tidewater Virginia, the Narragansetts of Rhode Island, and the Abenakis of northern New England.

Despite common linguistic roots, however, these scattered Algonquian communities would have found communication extremely difficult. In their separate, often isolated environments, they had developed very different dialects. A sixteenth-century Narragansett, for example, would have found it hard to comprehend a Powhatan. The major groups of the Southeast, such as the Creeks, belonged to a separate language group (Muskogean); the Indians of the eastern Great Lakes region and upper St. Lawrence Valley generally spoke Iroquoian dialects.

Linguistic ties had little effect on Indian politics. Algonquian groups who lived in different regions, exploited different resources, and spoke different dialects did not develop strong ties of mutual identity, and when their own interests were involved, they were more than willing to ally themselves with Europeans or "foreign" Indians against other Algonquian speakers. Divisions among Indian groups would in time facilitate European conquest. Local Native American peoples greatly outnumbered the first settlers, and had the Europeans not forged alliances with the Indians, they could not so easily have gained a foothold on the continent.

However divided the Indians of eastern North America may have been, they shared many cultural values and assumptions. Most Native Americans, for example, defined their place in society through kinship. These personal bonds determined the character of economic and political relations. As historian James Axtell explains, "The basic unit of social membership in all tribes was the exogamous clan, a lineal descent group determined through one parent." The farming bands living in areas eventually claimed by England were often matrilineal, which meant in effect that the women owned the planting fields and houses, maintained tribal customs, and had a role in tribal government. Among the native communities of Canada and the northern Great Lakes, patrilineal forms were much more common. In these groups, the men owned the hunting grounds that the family needed to survive.

Eastern Woodland communities organized diplomacy, trade, and war around reciprocal relationships that impressed Europeans as being extraordinarily egalitarian, even democratic. Chains of native authority were loosely structured. Native leaders were such renowned public speakers because persuasive rhetoric was often their only effective source of power. It required considerable oratorial skills for an Indian leader to persuade independent-minded warriors to support a certain policy.

Before the arrival of the white settlers, Indian wars were seldom very lethal. Young warriors attacked neighboring bands largely to exact revenge for a previous insult or the death of a relative, or to secure captives. Fatalities, when they did occur, sparked cycles of revenge. Some captives were tortured to death; others were adopted into the community as replacements for fallen relatives.

THE INDIANS' NEW WORLD

Arrival of large numbers of white men and women on the North American continent profoundly altered Native American cultures. Change did not occur at the same rates of speed in all places. Indian villages located on the Atlantic Coast came under severe pressure almost immediately; inland groups had more time to adjust. Wherever they lived, however, Indians discovered that conquest strained traditional ways of life, and as daily patterns of experience changed almost beyond recognition, native peoples had to devise new answers, new responses, new ways to survive in physical and social environments that mocked tradition. Historian James Merrell reminds us the Indians found themselves living in a world that from their perspective was just as "new" as that which greeted the European invaders.

Native Americans were not passive victims of geopolitical forces beyond their control. So long as they remained healthy, they held their own in the early exchanges, and although they eagerly accepted certain trade goods, they generally resisted other aspects of European cultures. The earliest recorded contacts between Indians and explorers suggest curiosity and surprise rather than hostility. A Southeastern Indian who encountered Hernando de Soto in 1540 expressed awe: "The things that seldom happen bring astonishment. Think, then, what must be the effect on me and mine, the sight of you and your people, whom we have at no time seen . . . things so altogether new, as to strike awe and terror to our hearts."

What Indians desired most was peaceful trade. The earliest French explorers reported that natives waved from shore, urging the Europeans to exchange metal items for beaver skins. In fact, the Indians did not perceive themselves at a disadvantage in these dealings. They could readily see the technological advantage of guns over bows and arrows. Knives made daily tasks a lot easier. And to acquire these goods they gave up pelts, which to them seemed in abundant supply. "The English have no sense," one Indian informed a French priest. "They give us twenty knives like this for one Beaver skin." Another native announced that "the Beaver does everything perfectly well: it makes kettles, hatchets, swords, knives, bread . . . in short, it makes everything." The man who recorded these observations reminded French readers—in case they had missed the point—that the Indian was "making sport of us Europeans."

Trading sessions along the eastern frontier were really cultural seminars. The Europeans tried to make sense out of Indian customs, and although they may have called the natives "savages," they quickly discovered that the Indians drove hard bargains. They demanded gifts; they set the time and place of trade.

The Indians used these occasions to study the newcomers. They formed opinions about the Europeans, some flattering, some less so, but they never concluded from these observations that Indian culture was inferior to that of the colonizers. They regarded the beards worn by European men as particularly revolting. As an eighteenth-century Englishman said of the Iroquois, "They seem always to have Looked upon themselves as far Superior to the rest of Mankind and accordingly Call themselves *Ongwehoenwe,* i.e. Men Surpassing all other men."

For Europeans, communicating with the Indians was always an ordeal. The invaders reported having gained deep insight into Native American cultures through sign languages. How much accurate information explorers and traders took from these crude improvised exchanges is a matter of conjecture. In a letter written in 1493 Columbus expressed frustration: "I did not understand those people nor they me, except for what common sense dictated, although they were saddened and I much more so, because I wanted to have good information concerning everything."

In the absence of meaningful conversation, Europeans often concluded that the Indians held them in high regard, perhaps seeing the newcomers as gods. Such one-sided encounters involved a good deal of projection, a mental process of translating alien sounds and gestures into messages that Europeans wanted to hear. Sometimes the adventurers did not even try to communicate, assuming from superficial observation—as did the sixteenth-century explorer Giovanni da Verrazzano—"that they have no religion, and that they live in absolute freedom, and that everything they do proceeds from Ignorance."

Ethnocentric Europeans tried repeatedly to "civilize" the Indians. In practice that meant persuading natives to dress like the colonists, attend

On the walls of the Canyon del Muerto in present-day Arizona, an Indian artist carved this petroglyph of Spanish conquistadores, whose arrival in the New World so profoundly changed Native American life.

white schools, live in permanent structures, and, most important, accept Christianity. The Indians listened more or less patiently, but in the end, they usually rejected European values. One South Carolina trader explained that when Indians were asked to become more English, they said no, "for they thought it hard, that we should desire them to change their manners and customs, since they did not desire us to turn Indians."

To be sure, some Indians were strongly attracted to Christianity, but most paid it lip service or found it irrelevant to their needs. As one Huron told a French priest, "It would be useless for me to repent having sinned, seeing that I never have sinned." Another Huron announced that he did not fear punishment after death since "we cannot tell whether everything that appears faulty to Men, is so in the Eyes of God."

Among some Indian groups, gender figured significantly in a person's willingness to convert to Christianity. Native men who traded animal skins for European goods had more frequent contact with the whites, and they proved more receptive to the arguments of missionaries. But native women jealously guarded traditional culture, a system that often sanctioned polygamy—a husband having several wives—and gave women substantial authority over the distribution of food within the village. French Jesuits seemed especially eager to undermine the independence of Native American women. Among other demands, missionaries insisted on monogamous marriages, an institution based on Christian values but that made little sense in Indian societies where constant warfare killed off large numbers of young males and increasingly left native women without sufficient marriage partners.

The white settlers' educational system proved no more successful than their religion was in winning cultural converts. Young Indian scholars deserted stuffy classrooms at the first chance. In 1744, Virginia offered several Iroquois boys a free education at the College of William and Mary. The Iroquois leaders rejected the invitation because they found that boys who had gone to college "were absolutely good for nothing being neither acquainted with the true methods of killing deer, catching Beaver, or surprising an enemy."

Even matrimony seldom eroded the Indians' attachment to their own customs. When Native

Americans and whites married—unions the English found less desirable than did the French or Spanish—the European partner usually elected to live among the Indians. Impatient settlers who regarded the Indians simply as an obstruction to progress sometimes developed more coercive methods, such as enslavement, to achieve cultural conversion. Again, from the white perspective, the results were disappointing. Indian slaves ran away or died. In either case, they did not become Europeans.

Disease and Dependency

Over time, cooperative encounters between the two peoples became less frequent. The Europeans found it almost impossible to understand the Indians' relation to the land and other natural resources. English planters cleared the forests and fenced the fields and, in the process, radically altered the ecological systems on which the Indians depended. The European system of land use inevitably reduced the supply of deer and other animals essential to traditional native cultures.

Dependency also came in more subtle forms. The Indians welcomed European commerce, but like so many consumers throughout recorded history, they discovered that the things they most coveted inevitably brought them into debt. To pay for the trade goods, the Indians hunted more aggressively and even further reduced the population of fur-bearing mammals.

Commerce eroded Indian independence in other ways. After several disastrous wars—the Yamasee War in South Carolina (1715), for example—the natives learned that demonstrations of force usually resulted in the suspension of normal trade, on which the Indians had grown quite dependent for guns and ammunition, among other things. A hardened English businessman made the point quite bluntly. When asked if the Catawbas would harm his traders, he responded that "the danger would be . . . little from them, because they are too fond of our trade to lose it for the pleasure of shedding a little English blood."

It was disease, however, that ultimately destroyed the cultural integrity of many North American tribes. European adventurers exposed the Indians to germs and viruses against which they possessed no natural immunity. Smallpox, measles, and influenza decimated the Native American population. Other diseases such as alcoholism took a terrible toll.

Within a generation of initial contact with Europeans, the Caribs, who gave the Caribbean its name, were virtually extinct. The Algonquian communities of New England experienced appalling rates of death. One Massachusetts colonist reported in 1630 that the Indian peoples of his region "above twelve yeares since were swept away by a great & grievous Plague . . . so that there are verie few left to inhabite the Country." Settlers who possessed no knowledge of germ theory—which was not formulated until the mid-nineteenth century—speculated that a Christian God had providentially cleared the wilderness of heathens.

Historical demographers now estimate that some tribes suffered a 90 to 95 percent population loss within the first century of European contact. The death of so many Indians decreased the supply of indigenous laborers needed by the Europeans to work the mines and to grow staple crops such as sugar and tobacco. The decimation of native populations may have persuaded colonists throughout the New World to seek a substitute labor force in Africa. Indeed, the enslavement of blacks has been described as an effort by Europeans to "repopulate" the New World.

Indians who survived the epidemics often found that the fabric of traditional culture had come unraveled. The enormity of the death toll and the agony that accompanied it called traditional religious beliefs and practices into question. These survivors lost not only members of their families, but also elders who might have told them how properly to bury the dead and give spiritual comfort to the living.

Some native peoples, such as the Iroquois, who lived some distance away from the coast and thus had more time to adjust to the challenge, withstood the crisis better than did those who immediately confronted the Europeans and Africans. Refugee Indians from the hardest hit eastern communities were absorbed into healthier western groups. Nonetheless, the cultural and physical shock that the dwindling Native American population experienced is beyond the historian's power ever fully to comprehend.

WEST AFRICA: PEOPLES AND HISTORY

During the era of the European slave trade, a number of enduring myths about sub-Saharan West Africa were propagated. Even today, commentators claim that the people who inhabited this region four hundred years ago were isolated from the rest of the world and had a simple, self-sufficient economy. Indeed, some scholars still depict this vast region stretching from the Senegal River south to modern Angola as a single cultural unit, as if at one time all the men and women living there must have shared a common set of political, religious, and social values.

Sub-Saharan West Africa defies such easy generalizations. The first Portuguese who explored the African coast during the fifteenth century encountered a great variety of political and religious cultures. Many hundreds of years earlier, Africans living in this region had come into contact with Islam, the religion founded by the Prophet Muhammad during the seventh century. Islam spread slowly from Arabia into black Africa. Not until A.D. 1030 did a kingdom located in the Senegal Valley accept the Muslim religion. Many other West Africans, such as those in ancient Ghana, resisted Islam and continued to observe traditional religions.

Muslim traders from North Africa and the Middle East brought a new religion to parts of West Africa, while they expanded sophisticated trade networks that linked the villagers of Senegambia with urban centers in northwest Africa, Morocco, Tunisia, and Cyrenaica. Great camel caravans regularly crossed the Sahara Desert carrying trade goods that were exchanged for gold and slaves. Sub-Saharan Africa's well-developed links with Islam surprised a French priest who in 1686 observed African pilgrims going "to visit Mecca to visit Mahomet's tomb, although they are eleven or twelve hundred leagues distance from it."

West Africans spoke many different languages and organized themselves into diverse political systems. Several populous states, sometimes termed "empires," exercised loose control over large areas. Ancient African empires such as Ghana were vulnerable to external attack as well as internal rebellion, and the oral and written histories of this region record the rise and fall of sev-

Trade Routes in Africa
African trade routes were well established by the late 1600s. Trade restrictions—and a deadly disease environment—confined European settlements primarily to coastal regions.

EUROPE
FRANCE
PORTUGAL SPAIN
Madeira (Port.)
Canary Islands (Spain)
MOROCCO
ALGIERS
TRIPOLI
SAHARA
ATLANTIC OCEAN
Cape Verde Is. (Port.)
Senegal R.
JOLOFF
SENEGAMBIAN STATES
Senegal Valley
GHANA
MALI
AFRICA
Slave Coast
Gold Coast
Ivory Coast
BENIN
BIAFRA
KONGO
Equator

EUROPEAN SETTLEMENTS

□ Portuguese   ■ French
■ Dutch   ■ British

— Major overland trade routes

0   500   1000 Miles
0   500   1000 Kilometers

eral large kingdoms. When European traders first arrived, the list of major states would have included Mali, Benin, and Kongo. Many other Africans lived in what are known as stateless societies, really largely autonomous communities organized around lineage structures. In these respects, African and Native American cultures had much in common.

Whatever the form of government, men and women found their primary social identity within well-defined lineage groups, which consisted of persons claiming descent from a common ancestor. Disputes among members of lineage groups

Ecological Revolution

Sudden and sweeping disruptions of the environment are now almost commonplace, but an even greater ecological revolution than that witnessed following the end of World War II occurred in the century after Columbus's voyages. European explorers, African slaves, and Native Americans brought together three remarkably different worlds, physically separated for millennia. The exchange of plants, animals, and diseases transformed the social history of the Old World as well as the New.

Differences in the forms of life in the two hemispheres astonished the first explorers. They had expected America to be an extension of Europe, a place inhabited by familiar plants and animals. They were surprised. The exotic flora of the New World, sketched here from sixteenth-century drawings, included the food staple maize and the succulent pineapple. Equally strange to European eyes were buffalo, rattlesnakes, catfish, and the peculiar absence of horses and cattle. No domestic animal was common to both sides of the Atlantic except the dog. And perhaps the most striking difference was between the people themselves. Both Native Americans and Europeans found each other to be the most exotic people they had ever encountered.

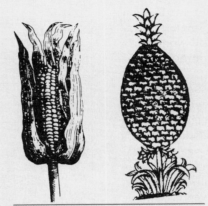

New World plants, including maize and the pineapple, expanded and enriched the European diet.

The most immediate biological consequence of contact between the people of these three startlingly dissimilar continents was the transfer of disease. Within a year of Columbus's return from the Caribbean, syphilis appeared in Europe for the first time and became known as the "American" disease. By 1505, it had spread all the way to China.

The effect of Old World diseases in the Americas was catastrophic. Native Americans had little natural immunity to common African and European diseases because America remained biologically isolated after the reimmersion of the Bering Land Bridge. When they were exposed to influenza, typhus, measles, and especially to smallpox, they died by the millions. Indeed,

European exploration of America set off the worst demographic disaster in world history. Within fifty years of the first contact, epidemics had virtually exterminated the native population of Santo Domingo/Haiti and devastated the densely populated Valley of Mexico.

Also unsettling but by no means as destructive was the transfer of plants and animals from the Old World to the New. Spanish colonizers carried sugar and bananas across the Atlantic, and in time these crops transformed the economies of Latin America. Even more spectacular was the success of European animals in America. During the sixteenth century, pigs, sheep, and cattle arrived as passengers on European ships, and in the fertile New World environment, they multiplied more rapidly than they had in Europe. Some animals survived shipwrecks. On Sable Island, a small, desolate island off the coast of Nova Scotia, one can still see the small, long-haired cattle, the successors of the earliest cattle transported to America. Other animals escaped from the ranches of New Spain, generating new wild breeds, like the fabled Texas longhorn.

No European animal more profoundly affected Native American life than the horse. Once common in North

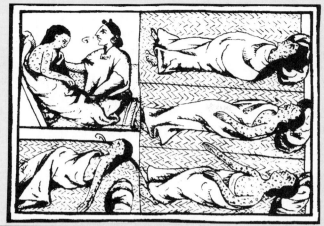

As Native Americans were exposed to common Old World diseases, particularly smallpox, they died by the millions.

European settlers brought plants and animals such as the long-haired steer to the New World, adding to the large variety of flora and fauna that had so amazed the first explorers.

European and African societies. From his first trip to the New World, Columbus brought back a plant that revolutionized the diets of both humans and animals—maize. During the next century, American beans, squash, and sweet potatoes appeared on European tables. The pepper and tomato, other New World discoveries, added a distinctive flavor to Mediterranean cooking. Despite strong prohibitions on the use of tobacco (in Russia, a user might have his nose amputated), European demand for tobacco grew astronomically during the seventeenth century. The potato caught on more slowly in Europe because of a widespread fear that root crops caused disease. The most rapid acceptance of the white potato came in Ireland, where it became a diet staple in the 1600s. Irish immigrants—unaware of the geneology of this native American crop—reintroduced the potato into Massachusetts Bay in 1718. And in West Africa, corn gradually replaced traditional animal feeds of low yield.

These sweeping changes in agriculture and diet helped reshape the Old World economies. Partly because of the rich new sources of nutrition from America, the population of Europe, which had long been relatively stable, nearly doubled in the eighteenth century. Even as cities swelled and industries flourished, European farmers were able to feed the growing population. In many ways, the seeds and plants of the New World were far more valuable in Western economic development than all the silver of Mexico and Peru.

America, the horse mysteriously disappeared from the continent sometime during the last Ice Age. The early Spanish explorers reintroduced the horse to North America, and the sight of this large, powerful animal at first terrified the Indians. Mounted conquistadores discovered that if they could not frighten Indian foes into submission, they could simply outmaneuver them on horseback. The Native Americans of the Southwest quickly adapted the horse to their own use. Sedentary farmers acquired new hunting skills, and soon the Indians were riding across the Great Plains in pursuit of buffalo. The Comanche, Apache Sioux, and Blackfoot tribes—just to name a few—became dependent on the horse. Mounted Indian warriors galloped into battle, unaware that it was their white adversaries who had brought the horse to America.

Equally dramatic was the effect of American crops on

were generally settled by clan elders. These senior leaders allocated economic and human resources. They determined who received land and who might take a wife—critical decisions because within the villages of West Africa, women and children cultivated the fields. These communities were economically self-sufficient. Not only were they able to produce enough food to feed themselves, they also produced trade goods, such as iron, kola, and gum.

The first Europeans to reach the West African coast by sail were the Portuguese. Strong winds and currents along the Atlantic coast moved southward, which meant a ship could sail with the wind from Portugal to West Africa without difficulty. The problem was returning. Advances in maritime technology allowed the Portuguese to overcome these difficulties. By constructing a new type of ship, one uniting European hull design with lateen (triangular) sails from the Middle East, Portuguese caravels were able to navigate successfully against African winds and currents. During the fifteenth century, Portuguese sailors discovered that by sailing far to the west, often as far as the Azores, they could, on their return trips to Europe, catch a reliable westerly wind. Columbus was evidently familiar with this technique. Before attempting to cross the Atlantic Ocean, he sailed to the Gold Coast, and on the way, he undoubtedly studied the wind patterns that would carry his famed caravels to the New World and back again.

The Portuguese journeyed to Africa in search of gold and slaves. Mali and Joloff officials were willing partners in this commerce, but insisted that Europeans respect trade regulations established by Africans. They required the Europeans to pay tolls and other fees and restricted the foreign traders to conducting their business in small forts or castles located at the mouths of the major rivers. Local merchants acquired some slaves and gold in the interior and transported them to the coast where they were exchanged for European manufactures. Transactions were calculated in terms of local African currencies: a slave would be offered to a European trader for so many bars of iron or ounces of gold.

The slave traders accepted these terms largely because they had no other choice. The African states fielded formidable armies, and the Europeans soon discovered they could not impose their will on this region simply by shows of force. Moreover, local diseases proved so lethal for Europeans—six out of ten of whom would die within a single year's stay in Africa—that they were happy to avoid dangerous trips to the interior. The slaves were usually men and women taken captive during wars; others were victims of judicial practices designed specifically to supply the growing American market. By 1650, most West-African slaves were destined for the New World rather than the Middle East.

Even before Europeans colonized the New World, the Portuguese were purchasing almost a thousand slaves a year on the West African coast. The slaves were frequently forced to work on the sugar plantations of Madeira (Portuguese) and the Canaries (Spanish), Atlantic islands on which Europeans experimented with forms of unfree labor that would later be more fully and more ruthlessly established in the American colonies. It is currently estimated that approximately 10.7 million Africans were taken to the New World as slaves. The figure for the eighteenth century alone is about 5.5 million, of which more than one-third came from West-Central Africa. The Bight of Benin, the Bight of Biafra, and the Gold Coast supplied most of the others.

The peopling of the New World is usually seen as a story of European migrations. But in fact, during every year between 1650 and 1831, more Africans than Europeans came to the Americas. As historian Davis Eltis writes, "In terms of immigration alone . . . America was an extension of Africa rather than Europe until late in the nineteenth century."

EUROPE ON THE EVE OF CONQUEST

In ancient times, the West possessed a mythical appeal to people living along the shores of the Mediterranean Sea. Classical writers speculated about the fate of Atlantis, a fabled Western civilization that was said to have sunk beneath the ocean. Fallen Greek heroes allegedly spent eternity in an uncharted western paradise. But because the ships of Greece and Rome were ill designed to sail the open ocean, the lands to the west remained the stuff of legend and fantasy. In the fifth century, an intrepid Irish monk, Saint Brendan, reported finding enchanted islands far out in the

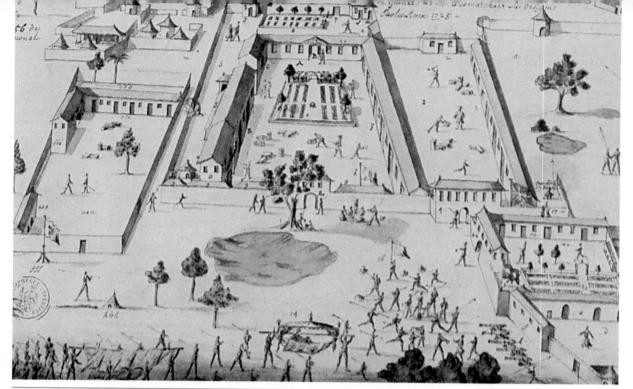

European traders built compounds along the African coast for the sole purpose of expediting the slave trade. Each compound within these "slave factories" served a different European country.

Atlantic. He even claimed to have met a talking whale named Jasconius, who allowed the famished voyager to cook a meal on his back.

In the tenth century, Scandinavian seafarers known as Norsemen or Vikings actually established settlements in the New World, but almost one thousand years passed before they received credit for their accomplishment. In the year 984, a band of Vikings led by Eric the Red sailed west from Iceland to a large island in the North Atlantic. Eric, who possessed a fine sense of public relations, named the island Greenland, reasoning that others would more willingly colonize this icebound region "if the country had a good name." A few years later, Eric's son Leif founded a small settlement he named Vinland at a location in northern Newfoundland now called L'Anse aux Meadows. At the time, the Norse voyages went unnoticed by other Europeans. Soon the hostility of Native Americans, poor lines of communication, and political upheavals in Scandinavia made maintenance of these distant outposts impossible. At the time of his first voyage in 1492, Columbus seemed to have been unaware of these earlier exploits.

European Nation-States

At the time of the Viking settlement, other Europeans were unprepared to sponsor transatlantic exploration. Nor would they be in a position to do so for several more centuries. Medieval kingdoms were loosely organized, and until the early fifteenth century, fierce provincial loyalties, widespread ignorance of classical learning, and dreadful plagues such as the Black Death discouraged people from thinking expansively about the world beyond their own immediate communities.

In the fifteenth century, however, these conditions began to change. Europe became more prosperous, political authority was more centralized, and the Renaissance fostered a more expansive outlook among literate people. A central element in this shift was the slow but steady growth of population after 1450. Historians are uncertain about the cause of this increase—after all, neither the quality of medicine nor sanitation improved much—but the result was a substantial rise in the price of land, since there were more mouths to feed. Landlords profited from these trends, and as their income expanded, they demanded more of the luxury items, such as spices, silks, and jewels, that came from distant ports. Economic prosperity created powerful new incentives for exploration and trade.

This period also witnessed the centralization of political authority under a group of rulers whom historians refer to collectively as the "New Monarchs." Before the mid-fifteenth century, feudal nobles dominated small districts throughout Europe. Conceding only nominal allegiance to larger territorial leaders, these local barons taxed the peasants and waged war pretty much as they pleased. They also dispensed what passed for justice. The New Monarchs challenged the nobles' autonomy. The changes that accompanied these challenges came slowly, and in many areas violently, but the results altered traditional political relationships between the nobility and the Crown, and between the citizen and the state. The New Monarchs of Europe recruited armies and supported these expensive organizations with revenues from national taxes. They created effective national courts. While these monarchs were often despotic, they personified the emergent nation-states of Europe and brought a measure of peace to local communities weary of chronic feudal war.

The story was the same throughout most of western Europe. The Tudors of England, represented by Henry VII (1485–1509), ended a long civil war known as the Wars of the Roses. Louis XI, the French monarch (1461–1483), strengthened royal authority by reorganizing state finances. The political unification of Spain began in 1469 with the marriage of Ferdinand of Aragon and Isabella of Castile. These strong-willed monarchs forged nations out of groups of independent kingdoms. If political centralization had not occurred, the major European countries could not possibly have generated the financial and military resources necessary for worldwide exploration.

A final prerequisite to exploration was solid technical knowledge. Ptolemy (A.D. second century) and other ancient geographers had mapped the known world and had even demonstrated that the world was round. During the Middle Ages, however, Europeans lost effective contact with classical tradition. Within Arab societies, the old learning had survived, indeed flourished, and when Europeans eventually rediscovered the classical texts, in a period known as the Renaissance, they

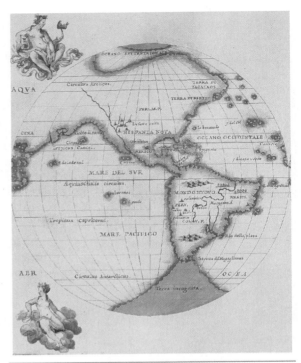

Early sixteenth-century mapmakers thought the New World was really an extension of Asia. Note that on this map of the Western Hemisphere, China appears to be connected to North America.

drew heavily on the work of Arab scholars. This "new" learning generated great intellectual curiosity about the globe and about the possibility of the world that existed beyond the Mediterranean.

The invention of printing from movable type by Johann Gutenberg in the 1440s greatly facilitated the spread of this technical knowledge. Sea captains published their findings as quickly as they could engage a printer, and by the beginning of the sixteenth century, a small, though growing, body of educated readers throughout Europe were well informed about the exploration of the New World. The printing press opened the European mind to exciting prospects that had been hardly perceived when the Vikings sailed the North Atlantic.

EUROPEANS' NEW WORLD

By 1500, centralization of authority and advances in geographic knowledge brought Spain to the first rank as a world power. In the early fifteenth century, though, Spain consisted of several autonomous kingdoms. It lacked rich natural

Improved printing methods in the 1440s allowed navigators to share their geographical findings more easily, spawning a new wave of exploration in the early 1500s.

fact, there was little about this land to suggest its people would take the lead in conquering and colonizing the New World.

By the end of the century, however, Spain suddenly came alive with creative energy. The union of Ferdinand and Isabella sparked a drive for political consolidation that, because of the monarchs' fervid Catholicism, took on the characteristics of a religious crusade. Spurred by the militant faith of its monarchs, the armies of Castile and Aragon waged holy war—known as the *Reconquista*—against the independent states in southern Spain that earlier had been captured by Muslims. In 1492, the Moorish (Islamic) kingdom of Granada fell, and, for the first time in centuries, the entire Iberian peninsula was united under Christian rulers. Spanish authorities showed no tolerance for people who rejected the Catholic faith.

During the Reconquista, thousands of Jews and Moors were driven from the country. Indeed, Columbus undoubtedly encountered such refugees as he was preparing for his famous voyage. From this volatile social and political environment came the *conquistadores,* men eager for personal glory and material gain, uncompromising in matters of religion, and unswerving in their loyalty to the Crown. They were prepared to employ fire and sword in any cause sanctioned by God and king, and these adventurers carried European culture to the most populous regions of the New World.

Long before Spaniards ever reached the West Indies, they conquered the indigenous peoples of the Canary Islands, a strategically located archipelago in the eastern Atlantic. These expeditions, leading eventually to colonization, provided a kind of rehearsal for the invasion of the New World. The harsh lessons the Spanish learned on the Canaries served as models of subjugation in America. Indeed, the Spanish experience paralleled that of the English in Ireland (see "English Colonization in Ireland," pp. 25–26). An early fifteenth-century Spanish chronicle described the Canary natives as "miscreants . . . [who] do not acknowledge their creator and live in part like beasts." Many islanders quickly died of disease; others were killed in battle or enslaved. The new Spanish landholders introduced sugar to the islands, an intensive plantation crop requiring a large labor force. The workers came from Africa, slaves in a place that may truly have been the first American frontier.

Admiral of the Ocean Sea

If it had not been for Christopher Columbus (Cristoforo Colombo), of course, Spain might never have gained an American empire. Little is known about his early life. Born in Genoa in 1451 of humble parentage, Columbus soon devoured the classical learning that had so recently been rediscovered and made available in printed form. He mastered geography and—perhaps while sailing the coast of West Africa—he became obsessed with the idea of voyaging west across the Atlantic Ocean to reach Cathay, as China was then known.

In 1484, Columbus presented his plan to the king of Portugal. However, while the Portuguese were just as interested as Columbus in reaching Cathay, they elected to voyage around the continent of Africa instead of following the route

Indian Slaves Working at a Spanish Sugar Plantation on the Island of Hispaniola *(1595) by Theodore de Bry. Spanish treatment of the Native Americans was often brutal.*

indomitable admiral set sail for Cathay in August 1492, the year of Spain's unification.

Educated Europeans of the fifteenth century knew the world was round. No one seriously believed Columbus and his crew would tumble off the edge of the earth. The concern was with size, not shape. Columbus estimated the distance to the mainland of Asia to be about 3,000 nautical miles, a voyage his small ships would have no difficulty completing. The actual distance is 10,600 nautical miles, however, and had the New World not been in his way, he and his crew would have run out of food and water long before they reached China, as the Portuguese had predicted.

After stopping in the Canary Islands to refit the ships, Columbus continued his westward voyage in early September. When the tiny Spanish fleet sighted an island in the Bahamas after only thirty-three days at sea, the admiral concluded he had reached Asia. Since his mathematical calculations had obviously been correct, he assumed he would soon encounter the Chinese. It never occurred to Columbus he had stumbled upon a new world. He assured his men, his patrons, and perhaps himself that these islands were indeed part of the fabled "Indies." Or if not the Indies themselves, then they were surely an extension of the great Asian landmass. He searched for the splendid cities Marco Polo had described, but instead of meeting wealthy Chinese, Columbus encountered Native Americans, whom he appropriately, if mistakenly, called "Indians."

After his first voyage of discovery, Columbus returned to the New World three more times. But despite his considerable courage and ingenuity, he could never find the wealth his financial supporters in Spain angrily demanded. Columbus died in 1506 a frustrated but wealthy dreamer, unaware he had reached a previously unknown continent separating Asia from Europe. The final disgrace came in December 1500 when an ambitious falsifier, Amerigo Vespucci, published a sensational account of his travels across the Atlantic that convinced German mapmakers he had proven America was distinct from Asia. Before the misconception could be corrected, the name "America" gained general acceptance throughout Europe.

Only two years after Columbus's first voyage, Spain and Portugal almost went to war over the

suggested by Columbus. They suspected Columbus had substantially underestimated the circumference of the earth and that for all his enthusiasm, he would almost certainly starve before reaching Asia. The Portuguese decision eventually paid off quite handsomely. In 1498, one of their captains, Vasco da Gama, returned from the coast of India carrying a fortune in spices and other luxury goods.

Undaunted by rejection, Columbus petitioned Isabella and Ferdinand for financial backing. They were initially no more interested in his grand design than the Portuguese had been. But time was on Columbus's side. Spain's aggressive New Monarchs envied the success of their neighbor, Portugal. Columbus boldly played on the rivalry between these countries, talking of wealth and empire. Indeed, for a person with little success or apparent support, he was supremely confident. One contemporary reported that when Columbus "made up his mind, he was as sure he would discover what he did discover, and find what he did find, as if he held it in a chamber under lock and key."

Columbus's stubborn lobbying on behalf of the "Enterprise of the Indies" gradually wore down opposition in the Spanish court, and the two sovereigns provided him with a small fleet that contained two of the most famous caravels ever constructed, the *Niña* and *Pinta*, as well as the square-rigged *nao Santa Maria*. The

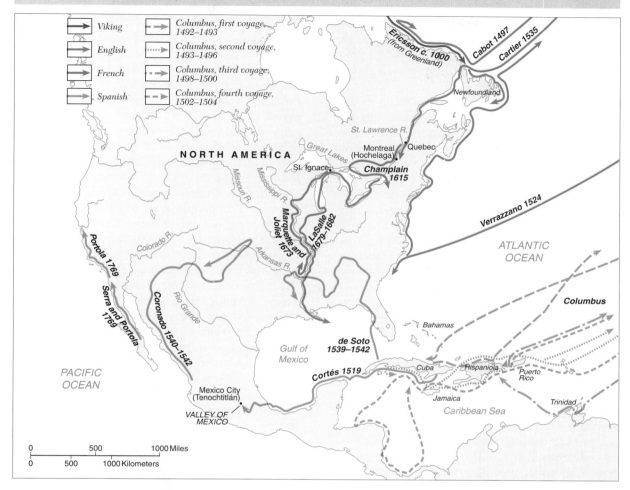

anticipated treasure of Asia. Pope Alexander VI negotiated a settlement that pleased both kingdoms. Portugal wanted to exclude the Spanish from the west coast of Africa and, what was more important, from Columbus's new route to "India." Spain insisted on maintaining complete control over lands discovered by Columbus, then still regarded as an extension of China. The Treaty of Tordesillas (1494) divided the entire world along a line located 270 leagues west of the Azores. Any new lands discovered west of the line belonged to Spain. At the time, no European had ever seen Brazil, which turned out to be on Portugal's side of the line. (To this day Brazilians speak Portuguese.) The treaty failed to discourage future English, Dutch, and French adventurers from trying their luck in the New World.

The Conquistadores

Spain's new discoveries unleashed a horde of conquistadores on the Caribbean. These independent adventurers carved out small settlements on Cuba, Hispaniola, Jamaica, and Puerto Rico in the 1490s and early 1500s. They were not interested in creating a permanent society in the New World. Rather, they came for instant wealth, preferably in gold, and were not squeamish about the means they used to obtain it. Bernal Díaz, one of the first Spaniards to migrate to this region, explained he had traveled to America "to serve God and His Majesty, to give light to those who were in darkness, and to grow rich, as all men desire to do." In less than two decades, the Indians who had inhabited the Caribbean islands had been virtually exterminated, victims of exploitation and disease.

For a quarter century, the conquistadores concentrated their energies on the major islands that Columbus had discovered. Rumors of fabulous wealth in Mexico, however, aroused the interest of many Spaniards, including Hernán Cortés, a minor government functionary in Cuba. Like so many members of his class, he dreamed of glory, military adventure, and riches that would transform him from an ambitious court clerk into an honored *hildago*. On November 18, 1518, Cortés and a small army left Cuba to verify the stories of Mexico's treasure. Events soon demonstrated that Cortés was a leader of extraordinary ability.

His adversary was the legendary Aztec emperor, Montezuma. The confrontation between these two powerful personalities is one of the more exciting of early American history. A fear of competition from rival conquistadores coupled with a burning desire to conquer a vast new empire drove Cortés forward. He was determined to push his men through any obstacle, preventing them from retreating by scuttling the ships that had carried them to Mexico. Cortés led his band of six hundred followers across rugged mountains, and on the way gathered allies from among the Tlaxcalans, a tributary people eager to free themselves from Aztec domination.

In matters of war, Cortés possessed obvious technological superiority over the Aztecs. The sound of gunfire frightened the Indians. Moreover, Aztec troops had never seen horses, much less armored horses carrying sword-wielding Spaniards. But these elements would have counted for little had Cortés not also gained a psychological advantage over his opponents. At first Montezuma thought that the Spaniards were gods, representatives of the fearful plumed serpent, Quetzalcoatl. Instead of resisting immediately, the emperor hesitated. When Montezuma's resolve hardened, it was too late. Cortés's victory in Mexico, coupled with other conquests in South America, transformed Spain into the wealthiest state in Europe.

Managing an Empire

Following the conquest of Mexico, renamed New Spain, the Spanish Crown confronted a difficult problem. Ambitious conquistadores, interested chiefly in their own wealth and glory, had to be brought effectively under royal authority, a task easier said than done. Adventurers like Cortés were stubbornly independent, quick to take offense, and thousands of miles away from the seat of government. The Crown found a partial solution in the *encomienda* system. The monarch rewarded the leaders of the conquest with Indian villages. The people who lived in these settlements provided the *encomenderos* with labor tribute in exchange for legal protection and religious guidance. The system, of course, cruelly exploited Indian laborers. One historian concluded, "The first encomenderos, without known exception, understood Spanish authority as provision for unlimited personal opportunism." Cortés alone was granted the services of over twenty-three thousand Indian workers. The encomíenda system made the colonizers more dependent on the king, for it was he who legitimized their title. In the words of one scholar, the new economic structure helped to transform "a frontier of plunder into a frontier of settlement."

Spain's rulers attempted to maintain tight personal control over their American possessions. The volume of correspondence between the two continents, much of it concerning mundane matters, was staggering. (All documents were duplicated several times by hand.) Because the trip to Madrid took many months, a year often passed before receipt of an answer to a simple request. But somehow the cumbersome system worked. In Mexico, officials appointed in Spain established a rigid hierarchical order, directing the affairs of the countryside from urban centers. Persons born in the New World, even those of Spanish parentage *(criollos)*, were regarded as socially inferior to natives of the mother country *(peninsulares)*.

The Spanish also brought Catholicism to the New World. The Dominicans and Franciscans, the two largest religious orders, established Indian missions throughout New Spain. Some barefoot friars

Spanish priests sought to convert Native Americans to Catholicism. Although the priests and friars could not stop the economic exploitation of the Indians, they frequently condemned the conquistadores' excessive cruelty. In this seventeenth-century work by an anonymous artist, a Spanish friar baptizes a Mexican Indian.

tried to protect the Native Americans from the worst forms of exploitation. One courageous Dominican, Fra Bartolomé de la Casas, published an eloquent defense of Indian rights, *Historia de las Indias,* which among other things questioned the legitimacy of European conquest of the New World. Las Casas's work provoked heated debate in Spain, and while the king had no intention of repudiating his vast American empire, he did initiate certain reforms designed to bring greater "love and moderation" to Spanish-Indian relations. It is impossible to ascertain how many converts these friars made. In 1531, however, a newly converted Christian reported a vision of the Virgin, a dark-skinned woman of obvious Indian ancestry, who became known throughout the region as the Virgin of Guadalupe. This figure—the result of a creative blending of Indian and European cultures—served as a powerful symbol of Mexican nationalism in the wars for independence fought against Spain almost three centuries later.

About 250,000 Spaniards migrated to the New World during the sixteenth century. Another 200,000 made the journey between 1600 and 1650. Most of the colonists were impoverished, single males in their late twenties seeking economic opportunities. They generally came from the poorest agricultural regions of southern Spain—almost 40 percent migrating from Andalusia. Since so few Spanish women migrated, especially in the sixteenth century, the men often married Indians and blacks, unions which produced *mestizos* and *mulattos.* The frequency of interracial marriage indicated that, among other things, the people of New Spain were more tolerant of racial differences than were the English who settled in North America. For the people of New Spain social standing was affected as much, or more, by economic worth, as it was by color.

Spain claimed far more of the New World than it could possibly manage. After the era of the conquistadores, Spain's rulers regarded the American colonies primarily as a source of precious metal, and between 1500 and 1650, an estimated 200 tons of gold and 16,000 tons of silver were shipped back to the Spanish treasury in

Madrid. This great wealth, however, proved a mixed blessing. The sudden acquisition of so much money stimulated a horrendous inflation that hurt ordinary Spaniards. They were hurt further by long, debilitating wars funded by American gold and silver. Moreover, instead of developing its own industry, Spain became dependent on the annual shipment of bullion from America, and, in 1603, one insightful Spaniard declared, "The New World conquered by you, has conquered you in its turn."

FRENCH EXPLORATION AND SETTLEMENT

French interest in the New World developed more slowly. More than three decades after Columbus's discovery, King Francis I sponsored the unsuccessful efforts of Giovanni da Verrazzano to find a short water route to China, via a northwest passage around or through North America. In 1534, the king sent Jacques Cartier on a similar quest. The rocky, barren coast of Labrador depressed the explorer. He grumbled, "I am rather inclined to believe that this is the land God gave to Cain."

Discovery of a large promising waterway the following year raised Cartier's spirits. He reconnoitered the Gulf of Saint Lawrence, traveling up the magnificent river as far as modern Montreal. Despite his high expectations, however, Cartier got no closer to China, and discouraged by the harsh winters, he headed home in 1542. Not until sixty-five years later did Samuel de Champlain resettle this region for France. He founded Quebec in 1608.

As was the case with other colonial powers, the French declared they had migrated to the New World in search of wealth as well as in hopes of converting the Indians to Christianity. As it turned out, these economic and spiritual goals required full cooperation between the French and the Native Americans. In contrast to English settlers who established independent farms and who regarded the Indians at best as obstacles in the path of civilization, the French viewed the natives as necessary economic partners. Furs were Canada's most valuable export, and to obtain the pelts of beaver and other animals, the French were absolutely dependent on Indian hunters and trappers. French traders lived among the Indians, often taking native wives and studying local cultures.

Frenchmen known as *coureurs de bois* (forest runners), following Canada's great river networks, paddled deep into the heart of the continent in search of fresh sources of furs. Some intrepid traders penetrated beyond the Great Lakes into the Mississippi Valley. In 1673, Père Jacques Marquette journeyed down the Mississippi River, and nine years later, Sieur de La Salle traveled all the way to the Gulf of Mexico. In the early eighteenth century, the French established small settlements in Louisiana, the most important being New Orleans. The spreading French influence worried English colonists living along the Atlantic coast, for it appeared the French were about to cut them off from the trans-Appalachian west.

Catholic missionaries also depended on Indian cooperation. Canadian priests were drawn from two orders, the Jesuits and the Recollects, and although measuring their success in the New World is difficult, it seems they converted more Indians to Christianity than did their English counterparts to the south. Like the fur traders, the missionaries lived among the Indians and learned to speak their languages.

The French dream of a vast American empire suffered from serious flaws. The Crown remained largely indifferent to Canadian affairs. Royal officials stationed in New France received limited and sporadic support from the mother country. An even greater problem was the decision to settle what seemed to many rural peasants and urban artisans a cold, inhospitable land. Throughout the colonial period, Canada's European population remained small. A census of 1663 recorded a mere 3,035 French residents. By 1700, the figure had reached only fifteen thousand. Moreover, because of the colony's geography, all exports and imports had to go through Quebec. It was relatively easy, therefore, for crown officials to control that traffic, usually by awarding fur-trading monopolies to court favorites. Such practices created political tensions and hindered economic growth.

THE ENGLISH NEW WORLD

The first English visit to North America remains shrouded in mystery. Fishermen working out of

In the dead of winter, the streams of New France turned to ice. French voyageurs built sledges, placed their canoes and supplies on them, and proceeded down the frozen course into the heart of the continent.

Bristol and other western English ports may have landed in Nova Scotia and Newfoundland as early as the 1480s. The codfish of the Grand Banks undoubtedly drew vessels of all nations, and during the summer months some sailors probably dried and salted their catches on Canada's convenient shores. John Cabot (Giovanni Caboto), a Venetian sea captain, completed the first recorded transatlantic voyage by an English vessel in 1497, while attempting to find a northwest passage to Asia.

Cabot died during a second attempt to find a direct route to Cathay in 1498. Although Sebastian Cabot continued his father's explorations in the Hudson Bay region in 1508–1509, England's interest in the New World waned. For the next three-quarters of a century, the English people were preoccupied with more pressing domestic and religious concerns. When curiosity about the New World revived, however, Cabot's voyages established England's belated claim to American territory.

Religious Turmoil

At the time of Cabot's death, England was not prepared to compete with Spain and Portugal for the riches of the Orient. Although Henry VII, the first Tudor monarch, brought peace to England after a bitter civil war, the country still contained too many "over-mighty subjects," powerful local magnates who maintained armed retainers and who often paid little attention to royal authority. Henry possessed no standing army; his small navy intimidated no one. To be sure, the Tudors gave nominal allegiance to the pope in Rome, but unlike the rulers of Spain, they were not crusaders for Catholicism. Religion did not provide England's impetus for exploration.

A complex web of international diplomacy also worked against England's early entry into New World colonization. In 1509, to cement an alliance between Spain and England, the future Henry VIII married Catherine of Aragon. As a result of this marital arrangement, English merchants enjoyed limited rights to trade in Spain's

American colonies, but any attempt by England at independent colonization would have threatened those rights and would have jeopardized the alliance.

By the end of the sixteenth century, however, conditions within England had changed dramatically, in part as a result of the Protestant Reformation. As they did, the English began to consider their former ally, Spain, as the greatest threat to English aspirations. Tudor monarchs, especially Henry VIII (r. 1509–1547) and his daughter Elizabeth I (r. 1558–1603), developed a strong central administration, while England became more and more a Protestant society. This merger of English Protestantism and English nationalism affected all aspects of public life. It helped propel England into a central role in European affairs and was crucial in creating a powerful sense of an English identity among all classes of people.

Popular anticlericalism helped spark religious reformation in England. The English people had long resented paying monies to a distant pope. Early in the sixteenth century, opposition to and criticism of the clergy grew increasingly vocal. Cardinal Thomas Wolsey, the most powerful prelate in England, flaunted his immense wealth and unwittingly became a symbol of spiritual cor-

ruption. Parish priests were objects of ridicule. Poorly educated men for the most part, they seemed theologically ignorant and perpetually grasping. Anticlericalism did not run as deep in England as it had in Germany, but by the late 1520s, the Catholic church had lost the allegiance of the great mass of the population. The people's pent-up anger is central to an understanding of the English Reformation. Put simply, if common men and women throughout the kingdom had not supported separation from Rome, then Henry VIII could not have forced them to leave the church.

The catalyst for Reformation in England was the king's desire to rid himself of his wife, Catherine of Aragon, who happened to be the daughter of the former king of Spain. Their marriage had produced a daughter, Mary, but, as the years passed, no son. The need for a male heir obsessed Henry. He and his counselors assumed a female ruler could not maintain domestic peace and England would fall once again into civil war. The answer seemed to be remarriage. Henry petitioned Pope Clement VII for a divorce (technically, an annulment), but the Spanish had other ideas. Unwilling to tolerate the public humiliation of Catherine, they forced the pope to procrastinate. In 1527, time ran out. The passionate Henry fell in love with Anne Boleyn, who later bore him a daughter, Elizabeth. The king decided to divorce Catherine with or without papal consent.

The final break with Rome came swiftly. Between 1529 and 1536, the king, acting through Parliament, severed all ties with the pope, seized church lands, and dissolved many of the monasteries. In March 1534, the Act of Supremacy boldly announced, "The King's Majesty justly and rightfully is supreme head of the Church of England." The entire process, which one historian termed a "state reformation," was conducted with impressive unanimity. Land formerly owned by the Catholic church passed quickly into private hands, and within a short period, property holders throughout England had acquired a vested interest in Protestantism. Beyond breaking with the papacy, Henry showed little enthusiasm for theological change. Many Catholic ceremonies survived.

The split with Rome, however, could not be contained. The year 1539 saw the publication of an English Bible. Before then the Scripture had

The Tudor Monarchs

Henry VII
(d. 1509)

m.
Elizabeth of York

Arthur (d.1502) — **Henry VIII** (r. 1509–1547) — Margaret — Mary

m.

Catherine of Aragon — Anne Boleyn — Jane Seymour

Mary I (r. 1553–1558) — **Elizabeth I** (r. 1558–1603) — **Edward VI** (r. 1547–1553)

been available only in Latin, the language of an educated elite. For the first time in English history, ordinary people could read the word of God in the vernacular. It was a liberating experience that persuaded some men and women that Henry had not yet fully reformed the English church.

With Henry's death in 1547, England entered a period of acute political instability. Edward VI, Henry's young son by his third wife, Jane Seymour, came to the throne, but he was still a child and sickly besides. Militant Protestants took advantage of the political uncertainty, insisting the Church of England remove every trace of its Catholic origins. With the death of young Edward in 1553, these ambitious efforts came to a sudden halt. Henry's eldest daughter, Mary, next ascended the throne. Fiercely loyal to the Catholic faith of her mother, Catherine of Aragon, Mary I vowed to return England to the pope.

However misguided were the queen's plans, she possessed her father's iron will. Hundreds of Protestants were executed; others scurried off to the safety of Geneva and Frankfurt where they absorbed the most radical Calvinist doctrines of the day. When Mary died in 1558 and was succeeded by Elizabeth, these "Marian exiles" flocked back to England, more eager than ever to rid the Tudor church of Catholicism. Mary had inadvertently advanced the cause of Calvinism by creating so many Protestant martyrs, reformers burned for their faith and now celebrated in the woodcuts of the most popular book of the period, John Foxe's *Acts and Monuments,* commonly known as the *Book of Martyrs* (1563). The Marian exiles served as the leaders of the Elizabethan church, an institution that remained fundamentally Calvinist until the end of the sixteenth century.

Reformation in Europe

By the time Mary Tudor had come to the throne, the vast popular movement known as the Reformation swept across northern and central Europe, and as much as any of the later great political revolutions, it had begun to transform the character of the modern world. The Reformation started in Germany when, in 1517, a relatively obscure German monk, Martin Luther, publicly challenged the central tenets of

Roman Catholicism. Within a few years, the religious unity of Europe was permanently shattered. The Reformation divided kingdoms, sparked bloody wars, and unleashed an extraordinary flood of religious publication.

Luther's message was straightforward, one ordinary people could easily comprehend. God spoke through the Bible, Luther maintained, not through the pope or priests. Scripture taught that women and men were saved by faith alone. Pilgrimages, fasts, alms, indulgences, none of these traditional ritual activities could assure salvation. Luther's radical ideas challenged the institutional structure of Catholicism, as they spread rapidly across northern Germany and Scandinavia.

Other Protestant theologians—religious thinkers who would determine the course of reform in England, Scotland, and the early American colonies—mounted an even more strident attack on Catholicism. The most influential of these was John Calvin, a lawyer turned theologian, who lived most of his adult life in the Swiss city of Geneva. Calvin stressed God's omnipotence over human affairs. The Lord, he maintained, chose some persons for "election," the gift of salvation, while condemning others to eternal damnation. There was nothing that a man or woman could do to alter this decision.

Common sense suggests that such a bleak doctrine might lead to fatalism or hedonism. After all, why not enjoy the world's pleasures to the fullest if such actions have no effect on God's judgment? But many sixteenth-century Europeans did not share modern notions of what constitutes common sense. Indeed, Calvinists were constantly up and doing, searching for signs that they had received God's gift of grace. The uncertainty of their eternal state proved a powerful psychological spur, for as long as people did not know whether they were scheduled for heaven or hell, they worked diligently to demonstrate that they possessed at least the seeds of grace. The doctrine of *predestination* became the distinguishing mark of this form of Protestantism.

John Calvin's *Institutes of the Christian Religion* (1536) contained a powerful statement of the new faith, and his teachings spawned religious movements in most northern European countries. In France, the Reformed Protestants were known as Huguenots. In Scotland, people of Calvinistic persuasion founded the Presbyterian church. And in

Foxe's Book of Martyrs (1563), depicting the sufferings of those executed under Mary, provided powerful propaganda for the advance of the Protestant religion in England.

seventeenth-century England and America, most of those who put Calvin's teachings into practice were called Puritans.

The Protestant Queen

Elizabeth demonstrated that Henry and his advisers had been mistaken about the capabilities of female rulers. She was a woman of such talent that modern biographers find little to criticize in her decisions. She governed the English people from 1558 to 1603, an intellectually exciting period during which some of her subjects took the first halting steps toward colonizing the New World.

Elizabeth recognized her most urgent duty as queen was to end the religious turmoil that had divided the country for a generation. She had no desire to restore Catholicism. After all, the pope openly referred to her as a woman of illegitimate birth. Nor did she want to recreate the church exactly as it had been in the final years of her father's reign. Rather, Elizabeth established a unique and heterogeneous institution, Catholic in much of its ceremony and government but clearly Protestant in doctrine. Under her so-called Elizabethan settlement, the queen assumed the title "Supreme Head of the Church." Some churchmen who had studied with Calvin in Geneva urged her to drop immediately all Catholic rituals, but she ignored these strident reformers. The young queen understood she could not rule effectively without the full support of her people, and as the examples of Edward and Mary before her demonstrated, neither radical change nor widespread persecution gained a monarch lasting popularity.

The state of England's religion was not simply a domestic concern. One scholar aptly termed this period of European history "the Age of Religious Wars." Catholicism and Protestantism influenced the way ordinary men and women across the continent interpreted the experiences of everyday life. Religion shaped political and economic activities. Protestant leaders, for example, purged the English calendar of the many saints' days that had punctuated the agricultural year in Catholic countries. The Reformation certainly had a profound impact on the economic development of Calvinist countries. Max Weber, a brilliant German sociologist of the early twentieth century, argued in his *Protestant Ethic and Spirit of Capitalism* that a gnawing sense of self-doubt created by the doctrine of "predestination" drove Calvinists to extraordinary diligence. They generated large profits not because they wanted to become rich, but because they wanted to be doing the Lord's work, to show they might be among God's "elect."

Indeed, it is helpful to view Protestantism and Catholicism as warring ideologies, bundles of deeply held beliefs that divided countries and families much as communism and capitalism did during the late twentieth century. The confrontations between these two faiths affected Elizabeth's entire reign. Soon after she became queen, Pope Pius V excommunicated her, and in his papal bull *Regnans in Exelsis* (1570), he stripped Elizabeth of her "pretended title to the kingdom." Spain, the most fervently Catholic state in Europe, vowed to restore England to the "true" faith, and Catholic militants constantly plotted to overthrow the Tudor monarchy.

Religion, War, and Nationalism

Slowly, but steadily, English Protestantism and English nationalism merged. A loyal English subject in the late sixteenth century loved the queen, supported the Church of England, and hated Catholics, especially those who happened to live in Spain. Elizabeth herself came to symbolize this militant new chauvinism. Her subjects adored the Virgin Queen, and they applauded when her famed "Sea Dogs"—dashing figures such as Sir Francis Drake and Sir John Hawkins—seized Spanish treasure ships in American waters. The English sailors' raids were little more than piracy, but in this undeclared state of war, such instances of harassment passed for national victories. There seemed to be no reason that patriotic Elizabethans should not share in the wealth of the New World. With each engagement, each threat, each plot, English nationalism took deeper root. By the 1570s, it had become obvious the English people were driven by powerful ideological forces similar to those that had moved the subjects of Isabella and Ferdinand almost a century earlier.

In the mid-1580s, Philip II, who had united the empire of Spain and Portugal in 1580, decided that England's arrogantly Protestant queen could be tolerated no longer. He ordered the construction of a mighty fleet, hundreds of transport vessels designed to carry Spain's finest infantry across the English channel. When one of Philip's lieutenants viewed the Armada at Lisbon in May 1588, he described it as *la felicissima armada,* the invincible fleet. The king believed that with the support of England's oppressed Catholics, Spanish troops would sweep Elizabeth from power.

It was a grand scheme; it was an even grander failure. In 1588, a smaller, more maneuverable English navy dispersed Philip's Armada, and severe storms finished it off. Spanish hopes for Catholic England lay wrecked along the rocky coasts of Scotland and Ireland. English Protestants interpreted victory in providential terms: "God breathed and they were scattered."

REHEARSAL IN IRELAND FOR AMERICAN COLONIZATION

After the defeat of the Armada, it seemed as if England had fulfilled the prerequisites for American colonization. Before they crossed the Atlantic, however, English settlers moved to Ireland. Their experiences there powerfully shaped how later migrants would view the New World. It was on this island that enterprising Englishmen first learned to subdue a foreign population and to seize its lands. When Elizabeth assumed the throne, Ireland's one million inhabitants were scattered across the countryside. There were few villages, most of which were located along the coast. To the English eye, the Irish people seemed wild and barbaric. They were also fiercely independent and difficult to control. The English dominated a small region around Dublin by force of arms, but much of Ireland's territory remained in the hands of Gaelic-speaking Catholics who presumably lived beyond the reach of civilization.

English Colonization in Ireland

During the 1560s and 1570s, various enterprising English people decided that considerable fortunes could be made in Ireland. There were substantial risks, of course, not the least of which was the hostility of the Irish. Nevertheless, private "projectors" sponsored English settlements, and, in turn, these colonists forced the Irish either into tenancy or off the land altogether. It was during this period that semimilitary colonies were planted in Ulster and Munster.

As one might expect, colonization produced severe cultural strains. The English settlers, however humble their origins, felt superior to the Irish. After all, the English people had championed the Protestant religion. They had constructed a complex market economy and created a powerful nation-state. To the English settlers, the Irish appeared to be lazy, licentious, superstitious, even stupid. English settlers ridiculed unfamiliar local customs, and it is not surprising that even educated representatives of the two cultures found communication almost impossible. English colonists, for example, criticized the pastoral farming methods prevalent in sixteenth-century Ireland. It seemed perversely wasteful for the Irish to be forever moving about, since as any English person could see, such practices retarded the development of towns. Sir John Davies, a leading English colonizer, declared that if the Irish were left to themselves, they would "never (to the end of the world) build houses, make townships or villages or manure or improve the land *as it ought to be*." Such stubborn inefficiency—surely (the English reasoned) the Irish must have known better—became the standard English justification for the seizure of large tracts of land.

English Brutality

English ethnocentrism was relatively benign so long as the Irish accepted the subservient roles the colonizers assigned them. But when they rebelled against the invaders, something they did with great frequency, English condescension turned to violence. Resistance smacked of disrespect and, moreover, to ensure the safety of the English, it had to be crushed. The brutality of Sir Humphrey Gilbert in Ireland would have made even the most insensitive conquistadore uneasy. Gilbert was a talented man who wrote treatises on geography, explored the coast of North America, and entertained Queen Elizabeth with witty conversation. But as a colonizer in a strange land—in what some historians now call England's "permissive frontier"—he tolerated no opposition.

In 1569, he was appointed military governor of Munster, and when the Irish in his district rose up, he executed everyone he could catch, "mane, woman and childe." Gilbert's excesses would never have been permitted in England no matter how serious the rebellion. He cut off the heads of many enemy soldiers killed in battle, and in the words of one contemporary, Gilbert laid his macabre trophies "on the ground by each side of the way leading to his tent, so that none should come into his tent for any cause but commonly he must pass through a lane of heads." Such behavior was not only unprecedented, it was also calamitous. Instead of bringing peace and securi-ty, it helped generate a hatred so deep that Ireland remains divided to this day.

The Irish experiments served as models for later English colonies in the New World. Indeed, one modern Irish scholar argues that "English colonization in Virginia was a logical continuation of the Elizabethan conquest of Ireland." English adventurers in the New World commonly compared Native Americans with the "wild" Irish, a kind of ethnocentric shorthand that equated all alien races. This mental process was a central element in the transfer of English culture to America. The English, like the Spanish and the French, did not perceive America in objective terms. Instead, they saw an America they had already constructed in their imaginations, and the people and objects that greeted them on the other side of the Atlantic were forced into Old World categories, one of which was "Irish."

ENGLAND TURNS TO AMERICA

By the 1570s, English interest in the New World had revived. An increasing number of gentlefolk were in an expansive mood, ready to challenge Spain and reap the profits of Asia and America. Yet the adventurers who directed Elizabethan expeditions were only dimly aware of Cabot's voyages, and their sole experience in settling distant outposts was in Ireland. Over the last three decades of the sixteenth century, English adventurers made almost every mistake one could possibly imagine. They did, however, acquire valuable information about winds and currents, supplies, and finance.

Roanoke Tragedy

In 1584, Sir Walter Ralegh dispatched two captains to the coast of present-day North Carolina to claim land granted to him by Elizabeth. The men returned with glowing reports, no doubt aimed in part at potential financial backers. "The soile," declared Captain Arthur Barlow, "is the most plentifull, sweete, fruitfull, and wholesome of all the world."

Ralegh diplomatically renamed this marvelous region Virginia, in honor of his patron, the Virgin Queen. Elizabeth encouraged her favorite in private conversation but rejected his persistent requests for money. With rumors of war in the air, she did not want to alienate Philip II unnecessarily by sponsoring a colony on land long ago claimed by Spain.

Ralegh finally raised the funds for his adventure, but his enterprise seemed ill fated from the start. Despite careful planning, everything went wrong. The settlement was poorly situated. Located inside the Outer Banks—perhaps to avoid detection by the Spanish—the Roanoke colony proved extremely difficult to reach. Even experienced navigators feared the treacherous currents and storms off Cape Hatteras. Sir Richard Grenville, the leader of the expedition, added to the colonists' troubles by destroying an entire Indian village in retaliation for the suspected theft of a silver cup.

Grenville hurried back to England in the autumn of 1585, leaving the colonists to fend for themselves. Although they coped quite well, a peculiar series of accidents transformed Ralegh's settlement into a ghost town. In the spring of 1586, Sir Francis Drake was returning from a Caribbean voyage and for reasons known only to himself, decided to visit Roanoke. Since an anticipated shipment of supplies was overdue, the colonists climbed aboard Drake's ships and went home.

In 1587, Ralegh launched a second colony. This time he placed in charge John White, a veteran administrator and talented artist, who a few years earlier had produced a magnificent sketchbook of the Algonquian Indians who lived near Roanoke. The new settlement contained women, children, and even two infants who were born within weeks after the colonists crossed the Atlantic. The settlers feasted on Roanoke's fish and game and bountiful harvests of corn and pumpkin.

Once again, Ralegh's luck turned sour. The Spanish Armada severed communication between England and America. Every available English vessel was pressed into military service, and between 1587 and 1590, no ship visited the Roanoke colonists. When rescuers eventually reached the island, they found the village deserted. The fate of the "lost" colonists remains a mystery. The best guess is that they were absorbed by neighboring groups of natives, some

The wife and daughter of an Algonquian chief, drawn by John White, a leader of the 1587 Roanoke settlement. The child is holding an English doll.

from as far as the southern shore of the James River.

Propaganda for Empire

Had it not been for Richard Hakluyt, the Younger, who publicized explorers' accounts of the New World, the dream of American colonization might have died in England. Hakluyt, a supremely industrious man, never saw America. Nevertheless, his vision of the New World powerfully shaped English public opinion. He interviewed captains and sailors upon their return from distant voyages and carefully collected their stories in a massive book entitled *The Principall Navigations, Voyages, and Discoveries of the English Nation* (1589). The work appeared to be

CHRONOLOGY

30,000–20,000 B.C. Indians cross the Bering Strait into North America

2000–1500 B.C. Agricultural revolution trans forms Native American life

1001 A.D. Norsemen establish a small settlement in Vinland (Newfoundland)

1030 Death of War Jaabi (King of Takrur), first Muslim ruler in West Africa

1450 Gutenberg perfects movable type

1469 Marriage of Isabella and Ferdinand leads to the unification of Spain

1481 Portuguese build castle at Elmina on the Gold Coast of Africa

1492 Columbus lands at San Salvador

1497 Cabot leads first English exploration of North America

1498 Vasco da Gama of Portugal reaches India by sailing around Africa

1502 Montezuma becomes emperor of the Aztecs

1506 Columbus dies in Spain after four voyages to America

1517 Martin Luther's protest sparks Reformation in Germany

1521 Cortés defeats the Aztecs at Tenochtitlán

1529–1536 Henry VIII provokes English Reformation

1534 Cartier claims Canada for France

1536 Calvin's *Institutes* published

1540 Coronado explores the Southwest for Spain

1558 Elizabeth I becomes queen of England

1585 First Roanoke settlement established on coast of North Carolina

1588 Spanish Armada defeated by the English

1608 Champlain founds Quebec

a straightforward description of what these sailors had seen across the sea. That was its strength. In reality, Hakluyt edited each piece so it would drive home the book's central point: England needed American colonies. Indeed, they were essential to the nation's prosperity and independence. In Hakluyt's America, there were no losers. "The earth bringeth fourth all things in aboundance, as in the first creations without toil or labour," he wrote of Virginia. His blend of piety, patriotism, and self-interest proved immensely popular, and his *Voyages* went through many editions.

As a salesperson for the New World, Hakluyt was as misleading as he was successful. He failed to appreciate, or purposely ignored, the rich cultural diversity of the Native Americans and the varied backgrounds of the Europeans. He said not a word about the sufferings of Africans in America. Instead, he and many other polemicists for colonization led the ordinary English men and women who traveled to America to expect nothing less than a paradise on earth.

Recommended Reading

The history of first contact has generated provocative, splendidly interdisciplinary scholarship, works that should be read not only to learn something about the conquest of America, but also about the current state of the discipline of history. Two excellent studies of encounters between Native Americans and Europeans—works that attempt to reconstruct the Indians' side of the story—are Inga Clendinnen, *Aztecs: An Interpretation* (1991) and James Axtell, *The Invasion Within: The Contest of Cultures in Colonial North America* (1986). Other innovative books explore how early European invaders imagined the New World, and how they translated what they saw into a familiar and unthreatening language: Stephen Greenblatt, *Marvelous Possessions: The Wonder of the New World* (1991) and Anthony Pagden, *European Encounters with the New World: From Renaissance to Romanticism* (1992). For a readable introduction to the heated controversy over Columbus, consider Kirkpatrick Sale, *The Conquest of Paradise: Christopher Columbus and the Columbian Legacy* (1990). For an excellent investigation of Indian culture in New Spain after the conquest see James Lockhart, *The Nahuas After the Conquest: A Social and Cultural History of the Indians of Central Mexico, Sixteenth Through Eighteenth Centuries* (1992).

Additional Bibliography

A. W. Crosby provides a fascinating study of the ecological impact of exploration on the New World as well as on the Old in *The Columbian Voyages, the Columbian Exchange, and Their Historians* (1987). William Cronon's provocative book, *Changes in the Land* (1983), investigates within early New England a cultural conflict over the meaning and use of land.

A list of the most original investigations of Native American cultures and the Indians' accommodation to radical social and environmental change would include James H. Merrell, *The Indians' New World: Catawbas and Their Neighbors from European Contact Through the Era of Removal* (1989); Neal Salisbury, *Manitou and Providence: Indians, Europeans, and the Making of New England* (1982); Bruce G. Trigger, *Natives and Newcomers: Canada's "Heroic Age" Reconsidered* (1987); Richard White, *The Roots of Dependency: Subsistence, Environment, and Social Change Among the Choctaws, Pawnees, and Navajos* (1983); and James Axtell, *The European and the Indian: Essays in the Ethnohistory of Colonial North America* (1981).

The literature of early West African history often focuses on the American slave trade. But as Philip Curtin and others remind us, the Africans had developed complex economies long before the arrival of the Europeans. An important study is Curtin's *Economic Change in Precolonial Africa: Senegambia in the Era of the Slave Trade* (1975). Other valuable works include Ray A. Kea, *Settlements, Trade, and Politics in the Seventeenth-Century Gold Coast* (1982); Joseph C. Miller, *Way of Death: Merchant Capitalism and the Angolan Slave Trade 1730–1830* (1988); Paul H. Lovejoy, *Transformations in Slavery: A History of Slavery in Africa* (1983).

The complicated and tragic story of the struggle to control Mexico is the subject of several strikingly original studies. See especially Tzvetan Todorov, *The Conquest of America: The Question of the Other* (1984) and Inga Clendinnen, *Ambivalent Conquests: Maya and Spaniard in the Yucatan, 1517–1570* (1987). Also helpful are James Lockhart and Stuart B. Schwartz, *Early Latin America: A History of Colonial Spanish America and Brazil* (1983); and Charles Gibson, *Spain in America* (1966).

The transformation of early modern Europe, especially economic shifts, is discussed in Ralph Davis's brilliant synthesis, *The Rise of Atlantic Economies* (1973). A valuable study that explores the European response to the discovery of the New World is J. H. Elliott, *The Old World and the New, 1492–1650* (1970). On the conquest of the Canary Islands, see Felipe Fernández-Armesto, *Before Columbus* (1987). Anyone curious about the religious background of early English settlement should look at William J. Bouwsma, *John Calvin: A Sixteenth-Century Portrait* (1988); Patrick Collinson, *The Religion of the Protestants: The Church in English Society 1559–1625* (1982); R. W. Scribner, *Popular Culture and Popular Movements in Reformation Germany* (1987).

One can easily obtain many excellent political and social histories of the major European powers on the eve of New World colonization. For Spain, the recommended start remains J. H. Elliott, *Imperial Spain 1469–1716* (1963). For England, G. R. Elton, *England Under the Tudors* (1974); Keith Wrightson, *English Society 1580–1641* (1979); and Lawrence Stone, *The Crisis of the Aristocracy 1558–1641* (1965) provide valuable insights. And for Ireland, the two most readable studies of this period are David B. Quinn, *The Elizabethans and the Irish* (1966) and Nicholas P. Canny, *Kingdom and Colony: Ireland in the Atlantic World, 1560–1800* (1988). Thorough accounts of the development of New France can be found in W. J. Eccles, *France in America* (rev. ed. 1990) and *The Canadian Frontier, 1534–1760* (rev. ed. 1983).

Competing Visions
English Colonization in the Seventeenth Century

*I*n the spring of 1644, John Winthrop, governor of Massachusetts Bay, learned that Indians had overrun the scattered tobacco plantations of Virginia, killing as many as five hundred colonists. Winthrop never thought much of the Chesapeake settlements. He regarded the people who had migrated to that part of America as grossly materialistic, and because Virginia had recently expelled several Puritan ministers, Winthrop decided the Indian hostilities were God's way of punishing the planters for their worldliness. "It was observable," he related, "that this massacre came upon them soon after they had driven out the godly ministers we had sent to them." When Virginians appealed to Massachusetts for military supplies, they received a cool reception. "We were weakly provided ourselves," Winthrop explained, "and so could not afford them any help of that kind."

In 1675, the tables turned. Indian forces declared all-out war against the New Englanders, and soon reports of the destruction of Puritan communities were circulating in Virginia. "The Indians in New England have burned Considerable Villages," wrote one leading tobacco planter, "and have made them [the New Englanders] desert more than one hundred and fifty miles of those places they had formerly seated."

Sir William Berkeley, Virginia's royal governor, was not displeased by news of New England's adversity. He and his friends held the Puritans in contempt. Indeed, the New Englanders reminded them of the religious fanatics who had provoked civil war in England and who in 1649 had executed Charles I. During this particular crisis, Berkeley noted that he might have shown more pity for the beleaguered New Englanders "had they deserved it of the King." The governor, sounding like a Puritan himself, described the warring Indians as the "Instruments" with which God intended "to destroy the King's Enemies." For good measure, Virginia outlawed the export of foodstuffs to their embattled northern neighbors.

Such extraordinary disunity—not to mention lack of compassion—comes as a surprise to anyone searching for the roots of American nationalism in this early period. But the world of Winthrop and Berkeley was most emphatically not that of Washington and Jefferson. English colonization in the seventeenth century did not spring from a desire to build a centralized empire in the New World similar to that of Spain or France. Instead, the English Crown awarded colonial charters to a wide variety of merchants, religious idealists, and aristocratic adventurers who established separate and profoundly different colonies. Not only did New Englanders have little in common with the earliest Virginians and Carolinians, but they were often divided among themselves.

Migration itself helps to explain this striking social diversity. At different times different colonies appealed to different sorts of people. Men and women moved to the New World for various reasons, and as economic, political, and religious conditions changed on both sides of the Atlantic during the course of the seventeenth century, so too did patterns of English migration.

DECISION TO EMIGRATE

English people in the early decades of the seventeenth century observed an accelerating pace of social change. What was most evident was the rapid growth of population. Between 1580 and 1650, a period during which many men and women elected to journey to the New World, the population of England expanded from about 3.5 million to over 5 million. Among other things, this expansion strained the nation's agrarian economy. Competition for food and land drove up prices, and people who needed work increasingly took to the roads. These migrants, many of them drawn into the orbit of London by tales of opportunity, frightened the propertied leaders of English society. To the propertied class, the wandering poor represented a threat to the traditional order, and, particularly during the early decades of the seventeenth century, they urged local magistrates throughout the kingdom to enforce the laws against vagrancy.

Even by modern standards, the English population of this period was quite mobile. To be sure, most men and women lived out their days rooted in the tiny country villages of their birth. A growing number of English people, however, were migrant laborers who took seasonal work. Many others relocated from the countryside to London, already a city of several hundred thousand inhabitants by the early seventeenth century. Because health conditions in London were poor, a large number of these new arrivals quickly died, and had their places not been taken by other migrants from the rural villages, the population of London would almost certainly have decreased.

Other, more exotic destinations also beckoned. A large number of English settlers migrated to Ireland, while lucrative employment and religious freedom attracted people to Holland. The Pilgrims, for example, initially hoped to make a new life in Leyden. These migrations within Europe serve as reminders that ordinary people had choices. A person who was upset about the state of the Church of England or who had lost a livelihood did not have to move to America. That some men and women consciously selected this much more dangerous and expensive journey clearly set them apart from their contemporaries.

English colonists crossed the Atlantic for many different reasons. Some wanted to institute a purer form of worship, more closely based on their reading of Scripture. Others dreamed of owning land and of bettering their social position. A few came to the New World to escape bad marriages, jail terms, and the dreary prospect of lifelong poverty. Since most seventeenth-century migrants, especially those who transferred to the Chesapeake colonies, left almost no records of their previous lives in England, it is futile to try to isolate a single cause or explanation for their decision to leave home.

In the absence of detailed personal information, historians have usually assumed that poverty, or the fear of soon falling into poverty, drove people across the Atlantic. No doubt such considerations figured heavily in the final decision. But so too did religion, and it was not uncommon for the poor of early modern England to be among those demanding the most radical ecclesiastical reform. As a recent historian of seventeenth-century migration concluded, "Individuals left for a variety of motives, some idealistic, others practical, some simple, others complex, many perhaps contradictory and imperfectly understood by the migrants themselves."

Whatever their reasons for crossing the ocean, English migrants to America in this period left a nation wracked by recurrent, often violent political and religious controversy. During the 1620s,

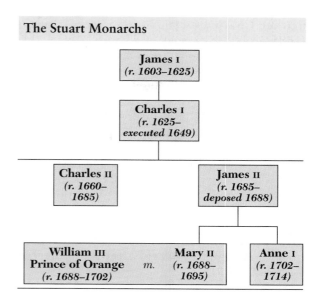

The Stuart Monarchs

the Stuart monarchs—James I (r. 1603–1625) and his son Charles I (r. 1625–1649)—who succeeded Queen Elizabeth on the English throne, fought constantly with the elected members of Parliament.

Many royal policies—the granting of lucrative commercial monopolies to court favorites, for example—fueled popular discontent, but the Crown's hostility to far-reaching religious reform sparked the most vocal protest. Throughout the kingdom, Puritans became adamant in their demand for radical change.

Tensions grew so severe that in 1629, Charles attempted to rule the country without Parliament's assistance. The strategy backfired. When Charles was finally forced to recall Parliament in 1640 because he was running out of money, Parliament demanded major constitutional reforms. Militant Puritans, supported by many members of Parliament, insisted on restructuring the church—abolishing the office of bishop was high on their list. In this angry political atmosphere, Charles took up arms against the supporters of Parliament. The confrontation between Royalists and Parliamentarians set off a long and bloody civil war. In 1649, the victorious Parliamentarians beheaded Charles, and for almost a decade Oliver Cromwell, a skilled general and committed Puritan, governed England.

In 1660, following Cromwell's death from natural causes, the Stuarts returned to the English throne. During a period known as the Restoration, neither Charles II (1660–1685) nor James II (1685–1688)—both sons of Charles I—were able to establish genuine political stability. When the authoritarian James openly patronized his fellow Catholics, the nation rose up in what the English people called the "Glorious Revolution" (1688) and sent James into permanent exile.

The Glorious Revolution altered the course of English political history and, therefore, that of the American colonies as well. The monarchs who followed James II surrendered some of the powers of government that had destabilized English politics for almost a century. The Crown was still a potent force in the political life of the nation, but never again would an English king or queen attempt to govern without an elected assembly.

Such political events, coupled with periodic economic recession and religious repression, determined, in large measure, the direction and flow of migration to America. During times of political turmoil, religious persecution, and economic insecurity, men and women thought more seriously about living in the New World than they did during periods of peace and prosperity. Obviously, people who moved to America at different times came from different social and political environments. A person who emigrated to Pennsylvania in the 1680s, for example, left a homeland unlike the one that a Virginian in 1607 or a Bay Colonist in 1630 might have known. Moreover, the young men and women who migrated to London in search of work and who then, in their frustration and poverty, decided to move to the Chesapeake, carried a very different set of memories than those people who moved directly to New England from the small rural villages of their homeland.

Regardless of the exact timing of departure, English settlers took with them a bundle of ideas and assumptions that helped them make sense of their everyday experiences in an unfamiliar environment. Their values were tested and sometimes transformed in the New World, but they were seldom destroyed. Settlement involved a complex process of adjustment. The colonists developed different subcultures in America, and in each of these, one can trace the interaction between the settlers' values and the physical elements, such as the climate, crops, and soil, of their new surroundings. The Chesapeake, the New England

colonies, the Middle Colonies, and the Southern Colonies formed distinct regional identities that persisted long after the first settlers had passed from the scene.

THE CHESAPEAKE: DREAMS OF WEALTH

After the Roanoke debacle in 1590 (see Chapter 1), interest in American settlement declined, and only a few aging visionaries such as Richard Hakluyt kept alive the dream of English colonies in the New World. These advocates argued that the North American mainland contained resources of incalculable value. An innovative group, they insisted, might reap great profits and at the same time supply the mother country with items that it would otherwise be forced to purchase from European rivals: Holland, France, and Spain.

Moreover, any enterprise that annoyed Catholic Spain or revealed its weakness in America seemed a desirable end in itself to patriotic English citizens. Anti-Catholicism and hatred of Spain became an integral part of English nationalism during this period, and unless one appreciates just how deeply these sentiments ran in the popular mind, one cannot fully understand why ordinary people who had no direct stake in the New World supported English efforts to colonize America. Soon after James I ascended to the throne, adventurers were given an opportunity to put their theories into practice in the colonies of Virginia and Maryland, an area known as the Chesapeake.

Jamestown Disaster

During Elizabeth's reign, the major obstacle to successful colonization of the New World had been money. No single person, no matter how rich or well connected, could underwrite the vast expenses a New World settlement required. The solution to this financial problem was the "joint-stock company," a business organization in which scores of people could invest without fear of bankruptcy. A merchant or landowner could purchase a share of stock at a stated price, and at the end of several years could anticipate recovering the initial investment plus a portion of whatever profits the company had made. Joint-stock

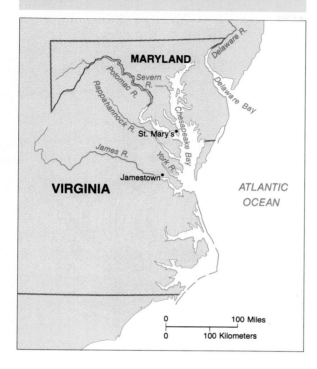

Chesapeake Colonies, 1640

The four regional maps in this chapter depict the full spectrum of English settlement on mainland North America.

MARYLAND

Delaware R.

Potomac R.

Severn R.

Rappahannock R.

Delaware Bay

St. Mary's

Chesapeake Bay

James R.

York R.

Jamestown

VIRGINIA

ATLANTIC OCEAN

0   100 Miles

0   100 Kilometers

ventures sprang up like mushrooms. English citizens of means, and even some of more modest fortunes, rushed to invest in these companies, and as a result, some enterprises were able to amass large amounts of capital, enough certainly to finance a new colony in Virginia.

On April 10, 1606, James issued the first Virginia charter. This document authorized the London Company to establish plantations in Virginia. The London Company was a dynamic business venture. Its leader, Sir Thomas Smith, was reputedly London's wealthiest merchant. Smith and his partners gained possession of the territory lying between Cape Fear and the Hudson River. These were generous but vague boundaries, to be sure, but the Virginia Company—as the London Company soon called itself—set out immediately to find the treasure Hakluyt had promised.

In December 1606, the *Susan Constant,* the *Godspeed,* and the *Discovery* sailed for America. The ships carried 104 men and boys who had been instructed to establish a fortified outpost some hundred miles up a large navigable river. The natural beauty and economic potential of the region was apparent to everyone. A voyager on this expedition reported seeing "faire meaddowes and goodly tall trees, with such fresh waters running through the woods, as almost ravished [us] at first sight."

The leaders of the colony selected—without consulting the local Native Americans—what the Europeans considered a promising location more than 30 miles from the mouth of the James River. A marshy peninsula jutting out into the river became the site for one of America's most ill-fated villages, Jamestown. Modern historians have criticized this choice, for the low-lying ground proved to be a disease-ridden death trap; even the drinking water was contaminated with salt. But the first Virginians were neither stupid nor suicidal. Jamestown seemed the ideal place to build a fort, since surprise attack rather than sickness appeared the more serious threat in the early months of settlement.

Almost immediately the colonists began quarreling. The adventurers were not prepared for the challenges that confronted them in America. Part of the problem was cultural. Most of these people had grown up in a depressed agricultural economy that could not provide full-time employment for all who wanted it. In England laborers shared what little work was available. One man, for example, might perform a certain chore while others simply watched. Later the men who had been idle were given an opportunity to work for an hour or two. This labor system may have been appropriate for England, but in Virginia it nearly destroyed the colony. Adventurers sat around Jamestown while other men performed crucial agricultural tasks. It made little sense, of course, to share work in an environment in which people were starving because too little labor was expended on the planting and harvesting of crops. Not surprisingly, some modern historians—those who assumed all workers should put in an eight-hour day—branded the early Virginians as lazy, irresponsible beings who preferred to play while others labored in the fields. In point of fact, however, these first settlers were merely attempting to replicate a traditional work experience.

Greed exacerbated these problems. The adventurers had traveled to the New World in search of the sort of instant wealth they imagined the

Spaniards to have found in Mexico and Peru. Tales of rubies and diamonds lying on the beach may have inflamed their expectations. Even when it must have been apparent these expectations were unfounded, the first settlers often behaved in Virginia as if they fully expected to become rich. Instead of cooperating for the common good—guarding or farming, for example—each individual pursued personal interests. They searched for gold when they might have helped plant corn. No one was willing to take orders, and those who were supposed to govern the colony looked after their private welfare, while disease, war, and starvation ravaged the settlement.

The Indomitable Captain John Smith

Virginia might have gone the way of Roanoke had it not been for Captain John Smith. By any standard, he was a resourceful man. Before coming to Jamestown, he had traveled throughout Europe, fought with the Hungarian army against the Turks, and if Smith is to be believed, was saved from certain death by various beautiful women. Because of his reputation for boasting, historians have discounted Smith's account of life in early Virginia. Recent scholarship, however,

The title page of a 1609 brochure promoting the colony of Virginia. Pamphlets such as these promised the settlers instant wealth.

Much of our knowledge of early Virginia comes from the accounts and maps of Captain John Smith. Twentieth-century archaeological investigation has confirmed the map's overall accuracy. The vignette in the upper left corner of the map depicts the Indian Powhatan in a longhouse addressing his people.

has reaffirmed the truthfulness of his story. In Virginia, Smith brought order out of anarchy. While members of the council in Jamestown debated petty topics, he traded with the local Indians for food, mapped the Chesapeake Bay, and may even have been rescued from execution by a young Indian girl, Pocahontas. In the fall of 1608, he seized control of the ruling council and instituted a tough military discipline. Under Smith, no one enjoyed special privilege. Individuals whom he forced to work came to hate him. But he managed to keep them alive, no small achievement in such a deadly environment.

Leaders of the Virginia Company in London recognized the need to reform the entire enterprise. After all, they had spent considerable sums and had received nothing in return. In 1609, the company directors obtained a new charter from the king, which completely reorganized the Virginia government. Henceforth all commercial and political decisions affecting the colonists rested with the company, a fact that had not been made sufficiently clear in the 1606 charter. Moreover, in an effort to obtain scarce capital, the original partners opened the "joint-stock" to the general public. For a little more than £12—approximately one year's wages for an unskilled English laborer—a person or group of persons could purchase a stake in Virginia. It was anticipated that in 1616, the profits from the colony would be distributed among the shareholders. The company sponsored a publicity campaign; pamphlets and sermons extolled the colony's potential and exhorted patriotic English citizens to invest in the enterprise.

This burst of energy came to nothing. Bad luck and poor planning plagued the Virginia Company. A vessel carrying settlers and supplies went aground in Bermuda, and while this misadventure did little to help the people at Jamestown, it provided Shakespeare with the idea for *The Tempest*. The governor, Lord De La Warr, added to the confusion by postponing his departure for America. Even the indomitable Captain Smith suffered a gunpowder accident and was forced to return to England.

Between 1609 and 1611, the remaining Virginia settlers lacked capable leadership, and perhaps as a result, they lacked food. The terrible winter of 1609–1610 was termed the "starving time." A few desperate colonists were driven to cannibalism. In England, Smith heard that one colonist had killed his wife, powdered [salted] her, and "had eaten part of her before it was known; for which he was executed." The captain, who possessed a curious sense of humor, observed, "Now, whether she was better roasted, broiled, or carbonadoed, I know not, but such a dish as powdered wife I never heard of." Other people lost the will to live.

The presence of so many Indians complicated the situation. The first colonists found themselves living—or attempting to live—in territory controlled by what was probably the most powerful Native American confederation east of the Mississippi River. Under the leadership of their *werowance*, Powhatan, these Indians had by 1608 created a loose association of some thirty tribes, and when Captain John Smith arrived to lead several hundred adventurers, the Powhatans (named for their king) numbered some 14,000 people, of whom 3,200 were warriors. These natives hoped initially to enlist the Europeans as allies against native enemies. When it became clear that the two peoples, holding such different notions about labor and property and about the exploitation of the natural environment, could not coexist in peace, the Powhatans tried to drive the invaders out of Virginia, once in 1622 and again in 1644. The failure of the second campaign ended in the complete destruction of the Powhatan empire.

In June 1610, the settlers who had survived despite starvation and conflicts with the natives actually abandoned Virginia. Through a stroke of

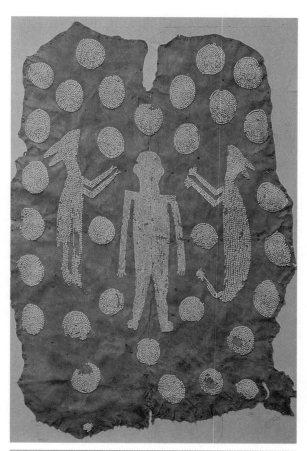

In 1608, Chief Powhatan, the father of Pocahontas, gave this shell-decorated ceremonial cloak to Captain Christopher Newport. Such gestures of friendship were short-lived, however, as coexistence became more and more difficult.

luck, however, they encountered De La Warr just as they commenced their voyage down the James River. The governor and the deputy governors who succeeded him, Sir Thomas Gates and Sir Thomas Dale, ruled by martial law. The new colonists, many of them male and female servants employed by the company, were marched to work by the beat of the drum. Such methods saved the colony but could not make it flourish. In 1616, company shareholders received no profits. Their only reward was the right to a piece of unsurveyed land located 3,000 miles from London.

A "Stinking Weed"

The solution to Virginia's problems grew in the vacant lots of Jamestown. Only Indians bothered to cultivate tobacco until John Rolfe, a settler who achieved notoriety by marrying Pocahontas, realized this local weed might be a valuable export. Rolfe experimented with the crop, eventually growing in Virginia a milder variety that had been developed in the West Indies and was more appealing to European smokers.

Virginians suddenly possessed a means to make money. Tobacco proved relatively easy to grow, and settlers who had avoided work now threw themselves into its production with single-minded diligence. In 1617, one observer found that Jamestown's "streets and all other spare places [are] planted with tobacco . . . the Colony dispersed all about planting tobacco." Although King James I originally considered smoking immoral and unhealthy, he changed his mind when the duties he collected on tobacco imports began to mount. He was neither the first nor the last ruler who decided a vice that generates revenue is not really a vice.

The company launched one last effort to transform Virginia into a profitable enterprise. In 1618, Sir Edwin Sandys (pronounced Sands) led a faction of stockholders that began to pump life into the dying organization by instituting a series of sweeping reforms and eventually ousting Sir Thomas Smith and his friends. Sandys wanted private investors to develop their own estates in Virginia. Before 1618, there had been little incentive to do so, but by relaxing Dale's martial law and promising a representative assembly called

Pocahontas married John Rolfe, a settler who pioneered the cultivation of tobacco as a cash crop. She converted to Christianity, taking the name Rebeka. This portrait, painted during a 1615 visit to London, shows her in court dress.

the House of Burgesses, Sandys thought the colony might be more attractive to wealthy speculators. Even more important was his method for distributing land. Colonists who covered their own transportation cost to America were guaranteed a "headright," a 50-acre lot for which they paid only a small annual rent. Adventurers were granted additional headrights for each servant they brought to the colony. This procedure allowed prosperous planters to build up huge estates at the same time they acquired dependent laborers. This land system persisted long after the company's collapse.

Sandys had only just begun. He also urged the settlers to diversify their economy. Tobacco alone, he argued, was not a sufficient base. He envisioned colonists busily producing iron and tar, silk and glass, sugar and cotton. There was no end to his suggestions. He scoured Europe for skilled artisans and exotic plant cuttings. To finance such a huge project, Sandys relied on a lottery, a game of chance that promised a contin-

The praises sung of tobacco and Virginia on this English tobacco label express the change in King James's attitude toward the "stinking weed" once he recognized the profit to be gained from it.

uous flow of capital into the company's treasury. The final element in the grand scheme was people. Sandys sent new settlers by the thousand to Jamestown, men and women swept up by the same hopes that had carried the colonists of 1607 to the New World.

Mortality in Virginia

Between 1619 and 1622, colonists arrived in Virginia in record number. Company records reveal that during this short period, 3,570 individuals were sent to the colony. These people seldom moved to Virginia in families. Although the first women arrived in Jamestown in 1608, most emigrants were single males in their teens or early twenties who came to the New World as indentured servants. In exchange for transportation across the Atlantic, they agreed to serve a master for a stated number of years. The length of service depended in part on the age of the servant. The younger the servant, the longer he or she served. In return, the master promised to give the laborers proper care and, at the conclusion of their contracts, to provide them with tools and clothes according to "the custom of the country."

Whenever possible, planters in Virginia purchased able-bodied workers, in other words, persons (preferably male) capable of performing hard agricultural labor. This preference dramatically skewed the colony's sex ratio. In the early decades, men outnumbered women by as much as six to one. As one historian, Edmund S. Morgan, explained, "Women were scarcer than corn or liquor in Virginia and fetched a higher price." Such gender imbalance meant that even if a male servant lived to the end of his indenture, he could not realistically expect to start a family of his own. Moreover, despite apparent legal safeguards, masters could treat dependent workers as they pleased; after all, these people were legally considered property. Servants were sold, traded, even gambled away in a hand of cards. It does not require much imagination to see that a society that tolerated such an exploitative labor system might later embrace slavery.

Most Virginians did not live long enough to worry about marriage. Death was omnipresent in this society. Indeed, extraordinarily high mortality was a major reason the Chesapeake colonies developed so differently from those of New England. On the eve of the 1618 reforms, Virginia's population stood at approximately 700. The company sent at least 3,000 more people, but by 1622 only 1,240 were still alive. "It Consequentilie followes," declared one angry shareholder, "that we had then lost 3,000 persons within those 3 yeares." The major killers were contagious diseases. Salt in the water supply also took a toll. And on Good Friday, March 22, 1622, the Powhatans slew 347 Europeans in a well-coordinated surprise attack.

No one knows for certain what effect such a horrendous mortality rate had on the men and women who survived. At the very least, it must have created a sense of impermanence, a desire to escape Virginia with a little money before sickness or Indians tragically ended the adventure. The settlers who drank to excess aboard the tavern ships anchored in the James River described the colony "not as a place of Habitacion but only of a short sojourninge."

Scandal and Reform

On both sides of the Atlantic people wondered who should be blamed. Why had so many colonists died in a land so rich in potential? The burden of responsibility lay in large measure with the Virginia Company. Sandys and his supporters were in too great a hurry to make a profit. Settlers were shipped to America, but neither housing nor food awaited them in Jamestown. Weakened by the long sea voyage, they quickly succumbed to contagious disease.

Company officials in Virginia also bore a share of guilt. They were so eager to line their own pockets that they consistently failed to provide for the common good. Various governors and their councillors grabbed up the indentured servants, sent them to their own private plantations to cultivate tobacco, and, as the 1622 tragedy demonstrated, ignored the colony's crumbling defenses. Jamestown took on the characteristics of a boomtown. There was no shared sense of purpose, no common ideology, except perhaps unrestrained self-advancement, to keep the society from splintering into highly individualistic, competitive fragments.

The company's scandalous mismanagement embarrassed the king, and in 1624 he dissolved the bankrupt enterprise and transformed Virginia into a royal colony. The Crown appointed a governor and a council. No provision was made, however, for continuing the local representative assembly, an institution the Stuarts heartily opposed. The House of Burgesses had first convened in 1619. While elections to the Burgesses were hardly democratic, the assembly did provide wealthy planters with a voice in government. Even without the king's authorization, the representatives gathered annually after 1629, and in 1639, Charles recognized the body's existence.

He had no choice. The colonists who served on the council or in the assembly were strong-willed, ambitious men. They had no intention of surrendering their control over local affairs. Since Charles was having political troubles of his own and lived 3,000 miles from Jamestown, he usually allowed the Virginians to have their own way. In 1634, the assembly divided the colony into eight counties. In each one, a group of appointed justices of the peace—the wealthy planters of the area—sat as a court of law as well as a governing body. The "county court" was the most important institution of local government in Virginia, and long after the American Revolution, it served as a center for social, political, and commercial activities.

Changes in government had little impact on the character of daily life in Virginia. The planters continued to grow tobacco, and as the Indians were killed, made into tributaries, or pushed north and south, Virginians took up large tracts of land along the colony's many navigable rivers. The focus of their lives was the isolated plantation, a small cluster of buildings housing the planter's family and dependent workers. These were modest wooden structures. Not until the eighteenth century did the Virginia gentry build the great Georgian mansions that still attract tourists. The dispersed pattern of settlement retarded the development of institutions such as schools and churches. Besides Jamestown there were no population centers, and as late as 1705, Robert Beverley, a leading planter, reported that Virginia did not have a single place "that may reasonably bear the Name of a Town."

Maryland: A Troubled Sanctuary

By the end of the seventeenth century, Maryland society looked remarkably like that of its Chesapeake neighbor, Virginia. At the time of first settlement in 1634, however, no one would have predicted that Maryland, a colony wholly owned by a Catholic nobleman, would have survived, much less become a flourishing tobacco colony.

The driving force behind the founding of Maryland was Sir George Calvert, later Lord Baltimore. Calvert, a talented and well-educated man, enjoyed the patronage of James I. He was awarded lucrative positions in the government, the most important being the king's secretary of state. In 1625, Calvert shocked almost everyone by publicly declaring his Catholicism; in this fiercely anti-Catholic society, persons who openly supported the Church of Rome were immediately stripped of civil office. Although forced to resign as secretary of state, Calvert retained the Crown's favor.

Before resigning, Calvert sponsored a settlement on the coast of Newfoundland, but after visiting the place, the proprietor concluded that no English person, whatever his or her religion, would transfer to a place where the "ayre [is] so intolerably cold." He turned his attention to the Chesapeake, and on June 30, 1632, Charles I

Cecilius Calvert, the second Lord Baltimore, is shown with his grandson.

granted George Calvert's son, Cecilius, a charter for a colony to be located north of Virginia. The boundaries of the settlement, named Maryland in honor of Charles's queen, were so vaguely defined that they generated legal controversies not fully resolved until the mid-eighteenth century when Charles Mason and Jeremiah Dixon surveyed their famous line between Pennsylvania and Maryland.

Cecilius, the second Lord Baltimore, wanted to create a sanctuary for England's persecuted Catholics. He also intended to make money. Without Protestant settlers, it seemed unlikely Maryland would prosper, and Cecilius instructed his brother Leonard, the colony's governor, to do nothing that might frighten off hypersensitive Protestants. The governor was ordered to "cause all Acts of the Roman Catholic Religion to be done as privately as may be and . . . [to] instruct all Roman Catholics to be silent upon all occa-

sions of discourse concerning matters of Religion." On March 25, 1634, the *Ark* and *Dove,* carrying about one hundred fifty settlers, landed safely, and within days, the governor purchased from the Yaocomico Indians a village that became St. Mary's City, the capital of Maryland.

The colony's charter was an odd document, a throwback to an earlier age. It transformed Baltimore into a "palatine lord," a proprietor with almost royal powers. Settlers swore an oath of allegiance not to the king of England but to Lord Baltimore. In the mother country, such practices had long ago passed into obsolescence, but for reasons not entirely clear, the Calverts obtained the right to create a vast feudal estate in America. As the proprietor, Lord Baltimore owned outright almost 6 million acres; he possessed absolute authority over anyone living in his domain.

On paper at least, everyone in Maryland was assigned a place in an elaborate social hierarchy. Members of a colonial ruling class, persons who purchased 6,000 acres from Baltimore, were called lords of the manor. These landed aristocrats were permitted to establish local courts of law. People holding less acreage enjoyed fewer privileges, particularly in government. Baltimore figured that land sales and rents would adequately finance the entire venture.

Baltimore's feudal system never took root in Chesapeake soil. People simply refused to play the social roles the lord proprietor had assigned. These tensions affected the operation of Maryland's government. Baltimore assumed his brother, acting as his deputy in America, and a small appointed council of local aristocrats would pass necessary laws and carry out routine administration. When an elected assembly first convened in 1635, Baltimore allowed the delegates to discuss only those acts he had prepared. The members of the assembly bridled at such restrictions, insisting on exercising traditional parliamentary privileges. Neither side gained a clear victory in the assembly, and for almost twenty-five years, legislative squabbling contributed to the widespread political instability that almost destroyed Maryland.

The colony drew both Protestants and Catholics, and the two groups might have lived in harmony had civil war not broken out in

England. When Cromwell and the Puritan faction came to power in the mother country, it seemed Baltimore might lose his colony. To head off such an event and to placate Maryland's restless Protestants, in 1649, the proprietor drafted the famous "Act concerning Religion," which extended toleration to all individuals who accepted the divinity of Christ. At a time when European rulers regularly persecuted people for their religious beliefs, Baltimore championed liberty of conscience.

However laudable the act may have been, it did not heal religious divisions in Maryland, and when local Puritans seized the colony's government, they promptly repealed the "Act." For almost two decades, vigilantes roamed the countryside, and during the "Plundering Time" (1644–1646), one armed group temporarily drove Leonard Calvert out of Maryland. In 1655, civil war flared again. No other mainland colony, with the possible exception of Rhode Island, experienced such extreme political disorder.

In this troubled sanctuary, ordinary planters and their workers cultivated tobacco on plantations dispersed along the riverfront. In 1678, Baltimore complained that he could not find fifty houses in a space of 30 miles. Tobacco affected almost every aspect of local culture. "In Virginia and Maryland," one Calvert explained, "Tobacco, as our Staple, is our all, and indeed leaves no room for anything Else." A steady stream of indentured servants supplied the plantations with dependent laborers, that is, until they were replaced by slaves at the end of the seventeenth century. The Europeans sacrificed much by coming to the Chesapeake. For most of the century, their standard of living was primitive when compared with that of people of the same social class who had remained in England. Two-thirds of the planters, for example, lived in houses of only two rooms and of a type associated with the poorest classes in contemporary English society.

CONQUEST OF NEW ENGLAND

The Pilgrims enjoy almost mythic status in American history. These brave refugees crossed the cold Atlantic in search of religious liberty, signed a democratic compact aboard the *Mayflower,* landed at Plymouth Rock, and gave us our Thanksgiving Day. As with most legends, this one contains only a core of truth.

The Pilgrims were not crusaders who set out to change the world. Rather, they were humble English farmers. Their story began in the early 1600s in Scrooby Manor, a small community located approximately 150 miles north of London. Many people living in this area believed the Church of England retained too many traces of its Catholic origin. To support such a corrupt institution was like winking at the devil. Its very rituals compromised God's true believers, and so, in the early years of the reign of James I, the Scrooby congregation formally left the state church. Like others who followed this logic, they were called "Separatists." Since English statute required citizens to attend Anglican services, the Scrooby Separatists moved to Holland in 1608–1609 rather than compromise their souls.

The Netherlands provided the Separatists with a good home—too good. The members of the little church feared they were losing their distinct identity; their children were becoming Dutch. In 1617, therefore, a portion of the original Scrooby congregation vowed to sail to America. Included in this group was William Bradford, a wonderfully literate man who wrote *Of Plymouth Plantation,* one of the first and certainly most moving accounts of an early American settlement. Poverty presented the major obstacle to their plans. They petitioned for a land patent from the Virginia Company of London. At the same time, they looked for someone willing to underwrite the staggering costs of colonization. These negotiations went well, or so it seemed. After stopping in England to take on supplies and laborers, the Pilgrims set off for America in 1620 aboard the *Mayflower,* armed with a patent to settle in Virginia and indebted to a group of English investors who were only marginally interested in separatism.

Because of an error in navigation, the Pilgrims landed not in Virginia, but in New England. The patent for which they had worked so diligently had no validity in this region. In fact, the Crown had granted New England to another company. Without a patent, the colonists possessed no authorization to form a civil government, a serious matter since some sailors who were not Pilgrims threatened mutiny. To preserve the struggling community from anarchy forty-one men agreed on November 11 to "covenant and combine our selves together into a civil body politick."

The Mayflower Compact could not ward off disease and hunger. During the first months in Plymouth, death claimed approximately half of the 102 people who had initially set out from England. Moreover, debts contracted in the mother country severely burdened the new colony. To their credit, the Pilgrims honored their financial obligations, but it took almost twenty years to satisfy the English investors. Without Bradford, whom they elected as governor, the settlers might have allowed adversity to overwhelm them. Through strength of will and self-sacrifice, however, Bradford persuaded frightened men and women that they could survive in America.

In time, the Pilgrims replicated the humble little farm communities they had once known in England. They formed Separatist congregations to their liking; the population slowly increased. The settlers experimented with commercial fishing and the fur trade, but these efforts never generated substantial income. Most families relied on mixed husbandry, grain, and livestock. Because Plymouth offered relatively few economic opportunities, it attracted only a trickle of new settlers. In 1691, the colony was absorbed into its larger and more prosperous neighbor, Massachusetts Bay.

Puritan Commonwealth

In the early decades of the seventeenth century, an extraordinary spirit of religious reform burst forth in England, and before it had burned itself out, Puritanism had transformed the face of England and America. Modern historians have difficulty comprehending this powerful force. Some consider the Puritans rather neurotic individuals who condemned liquor and sex, dressed in drab clothes, and minded their neighbors' business. This crude caricature is based on a fundamental misunderstanding of the actual nature of this broad popular movement. The seventeenth-century Puritans were more like today's radical political reformers, men and women committed to far-reaching institutional change, than like Victorian do-gooders. To their enemies, of course, the Puritans were a bother, always pointing out civil and ecclesiastical imperfections. A

The oldest timepiece in New England was this sundial, owned by John Endecott, first governor of the Massachusetts Bay Colony. The timepiece was made in 1630, the year the colony was established.

great many people, however, shared their vision, and not only did they found several American colonies, but they also sparked the English Civil War, an event that generated bold new thinking about republican government and popular sovereignty.

The Puritans were products of the Protestant Reformation. They accepted the notion that an omnipotent God predestined some people to salvation and damned others throughout eternity (see Chapter 1). But instead of waiting passively for Judgment Day, the Puritans examined themselves for signs of grace, for hints that God had in fact placed them among his "elect." A member of this select group, they argued, would try to live according to Scripture, to battle sin and eradicate corruption.

For the Puritans the logic of everyday life was clear. If the Church of England contained unscriptural elements—clerical vestments, for example—then they must be eliminated. If the pope in Rome was in league with the Antichrist, then Protestant kings had better not form alliances with Catholic states. If God condemned licentiousness and intoxication, then local officials should punish whores and drunks. There was nothing improper about an occasional beer or physical love within marriage, but when sex and drink became ends in themselves, the Puritans thought England's ministers and magistrates should speak out. Persons of this temperament were more combative than the Pilgrims had been. They wanted to purify the Church of England from within, and before the 1630s at least, separatism held little appeal for them.

From the Puritan perspective, the early Stuarts, James I and Charles I, seemed unconcerned about the spiritual state of the nation. James tolerated corruption within his own court; he condoned gross public extravagance. His foreign policy appeased European Catholic powers. At one time, he even tried to marry his son to a Catholic princess. Neither king showed interest in purifying the Anglican church. In fact, Charles assisted the rapid advance of William Laud, a cleric who represented everything the Puritans detested. Laud defended church ceremonies that they found obnoxious. He persecuted Puritan ministers, forcing them either to conform to his theology or lose their licenses to preach. As long as Parliament met, Puritan voters in the various boroughs and countries throughout the nation elected men sympathetic to their point of view. These outspoken representatives criticized royal policies and hounded Laud. Because of their defiance, Charles decided in 1629 to rule England without Parliament and four years later named Laud archbishop of Canterbury. The last doors of reform slammed shut. The corruption remained.

John Winthrop, the future governor of Massachusetts Bay, was caught up in these events. Little about his background suggested such an auspicious future. He owned a small manor in Suffolk, one that never produced sufficient income to support his growing family. He dabbled in law. But the core of Winthrop's life was his faith in God, a faith so intense his contemporaries immediately identified him as a Puritan. The Lord, he concluded, was displeased with England. Time for reform was running out. In May 1629 he wrote to his wife, "I am verily perswaded God will bringe some heavye Affliction upon this lande, and that speedylye." He was, however, confident that the Lord would "provide a shelter and a hidinge place for us."

John Winthrop served many terms as governor of Massachusetts and held the colony together during several major political crises.

Other Puritans, some of them wealthier and politically better connected than Winthrop, reached similar conclusions about England's future. They turned their attention to the possibility of establishing a colony in America, and on March 4, 1629, their Massachusetts Bay Company obtained a charter directly from the king. Charles and his advisers apparently thought the Massachusetts Bay Company was a commercial venture no different from the dozens of other joint-stock companies that had recently sprung into existence.

Winthrop and his associates knew better. On August 26, 1629, twelve of them met secretly and signed the Cambridge Agreement. They pledged to be "ready in our persons and with such of our severall familyes as are to go with us . . . to embark for the said plantation by the first of March next." There was one loophole. The charters of most joint-stock companies designated a specific place where business meetings were to be held. For reasons not entirely clear—a timely bribe is a good guess—the charter of the Massachusetts Bay Company did not contain this standard clause. It could hold meetings anywhere the stockholders, called "freemen," desired, even America, and if they were in America, the king could not easily interfere in their affairs.

"A City on a Hill"

The Winthrop fleet departed England in March 1630. By the end of the first year, almost 2,000 people had arrived in Massachusetts Bay, and before the "Great Migration" concluded in the early 1640s, over 16,000 men and women had arrived in the new Puritan colony.

A great deal is known about the background of these particular settlers. A large percentage of them originated in an area northeast of London called East Anglia, a region in which Puritan ideas had taken deep root. London, Kent, and the West Country also contributed to the stream of emigrants. In some instances, entire villages were reestablished across the Atlantic. Many Bay Colonists had worked as farmers in the mother country, but a surprisingly large number came from English industrial centers, like Norwich, where cloth was manufactured for the export trade.

Whatever their backgrounds, they moved to Massachusetts as nuclear families, fathers, mothers, and their dependent children, a form of migration strikingly different from the one that peopled Virginia and Maryland. Moreover, because the settlers had already formed families in England, the colony's sex ratio was more balanced than that found in the Chesapeake colonies. Finally, and perhaps more significantly, once they had arrived in Massachusetts, these men and women survived. Indeed, their life expectancy compares favorably to that of modern Americans. Many factors help explain this phenomenon—clean drinking water and a healthy climate, for example. While the Puritans could not have planned to live longer than did colonists in other parts of the New World, this remarkable accident reduced the emotional shock of long-distance migration.

The first settlers possessed another source of strength and stability. They were bound together by a common sense of purpose. God, they insisted, had formed a special covenant with the people of Massachusetts Bay. On his part, the Lord expected them to live according to Scripture, to reform the church, in other words, to create a

"city on a hill" that would stand as a beacon of righteousness for the rest of the Christian world. If they fulfilled their side of the bargain, the settlers could anticipate peace and prosperity. No one, not even the lowliest servant, was excused from this divine covenant, for as Winthrop stated, "Wee must be knitt together in this worke as one man." Even as the first ships were leaving England, John Cotton, a popular Puritan minister, urged the emigrants to go forth "with a publicke spirit, looking not on your owne things only, but also on the things of others." Many people throughout the ages have espoused such communal rhetoric, but these particular men and women went about the business of forming a new colony as if they truly intended to transform a religious vision into social reality.

In ecclesiastical affairs, the colonists proceeded by what one founder called "experimental footsteps." They arrived in Massachusetts Bay without a precise plan for their church. Although the rituals and ceremonies enforced by Laud had no place in Massachusetts, the American Puritans refused to separate formally from the Church of England. In this matter, they thought the Pilgrims had made a serious mistake. After all, what was the point of reforming an institution if the reformers were no longer part of it?

The Bay Colonists gradually came to accept a highly innovative form of church government known as Congregationalism. Under this system, each village church was independent of outside interference. The American Puritans, of course, wanted nothing of bishops. The people (the "saints") *were* the church, and as a body, they pledged to uphold God's law. In the Salem Church, for example, the members covenanted "with the Lord and with one another and do bind ourselves in the presence of God to walk together in all his ways."

Simply because a person happened to live in a certain community did not mean he or she automatically belonged to the local church. The churches of Massachusetts were voluntary institutions, and in order to join one a man or woman had to provide testimony—a confession of faith—before neighbors who had already been admitted as full members. It was a demanding process. Whatever the personal strains, however, most men and women in early Massachusetts aspired to full membership, which entitled them to the

Rituals of Public Execution: A Kind of Theater?

Public executions, however ghoulish they might appear to modern Americans, were not unusual events in colonial society. Indeed, they represented what one historian has described as a kind of theater or ritual performance.

Esther Rodgers, aged twenty-one, was hanged in Ipswich, Massachusetts, in July 1701. A local court had convicted her of murdering her own infant, a child fathered out of wedlock. According to a minister who witnessed the woman's last moments, "the manner of her Entertaining DEATH" astonished the crowd of four or five thousand spectators who crowded around the gallows. Rodgers's "Composure of Spirit, Cheerfulness of Countenance, pleasantness of Speech, and a sort of Complaisantness in Carriage towards the Ministers . . . melted the hearts of all that were within seeing or hearing, into Tears of affection."

Various members of a community, including the condemned criminals, played socially sanctioned roles in these public spectacles. It was important that the order of events be correct. Usually the felon—a person allegedly hardened by a life of sin—maintained his or her innocence during the trial. Following conviction, however, such persons often confessed. A

Mr. Richard Mather.

This primitive woodcut depicts Richard Mather, one of early New England's influential Puritan ministers.

minister recorded the full story, and on the day of the execution, he delivered a formal sermon attended by colonists who had sometimes traveled more than 50 miles just to see the hanging. Before they died, the criminals spoke to the spectators, and within a very short time, these last words along with the minister's execution sermon were published as pamphlets.

Clergymen played a central role in these public dramas. They engaged in what today we might call criminal sociology. Why, they asked, had the condemned man or woman come to such a tragic end? What lessons could be drawn from a close study of their lives? Not surprisingly the

answer to these questions involved sin. Long before the condemned person had contemplated murder or some equally heinous act, he or she had engaged in seemingly petty vices—disobedience to parents, pride, lying, profanity, irreligion, drunkenness—a range of ungodly behavior that inevitably led the unwary sinner to more serious transgressions. Seen from this perspective, of course, the average colonists became potential murderers or rapists, and only by resisting small temptations could they ever hope to avoid the fate of poor Esther Rodgers.

The ministers paid special attention to the young people in the audience; in other words, to those persons who seemed most likely to experiment with vice. Standing next to the condemned criminals, clergymen of New England thundered out their warnings. In 1674, for example, the famous Puritan divine Increase Mather observed that when "Children shall rebel against their Parents, their wickedness is excessively great. And such Children do usually die *before their Time.*" Lest the boys and girls missed his point, Mather added, "[it] is greatly to be observed that most of those that die upon the Gallows do confess that they have been guilty of disobedience to Parents."

46

In 1713, Cotton Mather, Increase's son, delivered an execution sermon specifically designed to strike terror in the hearts of the young. Look, he said pointing to a felon about to die, "[Here] is a poor Young man before you, that is just *going to the Dead.* God this day is holding up a *Young man* in Chains, that all the *Young People* of New England, may . . . be withheld from Sinning."

The execution ritual reaffirmed the traditional moral order; rebellion against elders was rebellion against God. The ministers knew the adolescents before them would probably not end their days as murderers or rapists. But by making a spectacle of an extreme case, by transforming the execution into a public drama, they hoped to discourage lesser vices.

Without the cooperation of the condemned, the execution lost much of its social meaning. Most men and women—people about to be hanged and without hope of clemency—not only voluntarily confessed to a host of moral failings, but also admonished the crowds to avoid a life of sin. Esther Rodgers ended her life with these words: "I beg of all to have Care. Be Obedient to your Parents and Masters; Run not at Nights, especially on Sabbath Nights, Refrain bad Company for the Lord's Sake. . . ." Her moving performance made for a "good" execution. James Morgan, a convicted murderer, also fulfilled everyone's expectations. "Have a care of that Sin of Drunkenness," he warned the citizens of Boston in 1686, "for that is a sin that leads to all manner of sins and wickedness." And

The Wages of Sin; OR, Robbery juftly Rewarded: A **POEM;** Occafioned by the untimely Death of **Richard Wilfon,** Who was Executed on *Bofton* Neck, for Burglary, On *Thurfday* the 19th of *October,* 1732.

His Day from Goal muft *Wilfon* be conveyed in a Cart, By Guards unto the Gallows-Tree, to die as his Defert.

Here we may fee what Men for Stealth and Robbing muft endure; And what the Gain of ill got Wealth will in the End procure.

just before he died, Morgan cried out, "I am going out of this World; O take warning by me, and beg God to keep you from this Sin which hath been my ruine."

Though the ministers may have encouraged these public displays of penance—they may have even suggested the actual wording—there is no reason to doubt the criminals' sincerity. They too shared the religious values of the seventeenth-century, and however far from the accepted norms they may have strayed, they desired in some small way to win favor in the sight of the Lord. As the Reverend William Cooper observed in 1733, "It may be [that] there is no Place in the World, where such Pains are taken with condemned Criminals to prepare them for their Death; that *in the Destruction of the Flesh, the Spirit may be saved in the Day of the Lord Jesus.*" Standing on the gallows, men and women rarely expressed even a hint of bitterness. In fact, they frequently praised their judges, noting that the magis-

trates had merely carried out God's will.

Soon after the execution colonial printers issued pamphlets containing the execution sermon, the criminal's dying confession, and in some cases, a lurid woodcut depicting an individual about to hang. These works sold quite well. The account of James Morgan's execution went through several editions. Others bore provocative titles such as *The Wicked Man's Portion* and *Death The Certain Wages of Sin.* The most ambitious production was Cotton Mather's *Pillars of Salt. An HISTORY OF SOME CRIMINALS Executed in this Land; for Capital Crimes. With some of their Dying Speeches; Collected and Published, For the WARNING of such as Live in Destructive Courses of Ungodliness (1699).* What effect the execution rituals had upon colonial Americans—spectators as well as readers—is impossible to judge. Some may have reformed their evil ways; for others the theater of punishment may have involved no more than an "Entertaining DEATH."

sacraments, and gave some of them responsibility for choosing ministers, disciplining backsliders, and determining difficult questions of theology. Although women and blacks could not vote for ministers, they did become members of the Congregational churches. Over the course of the seventeenth century, women made up an increasingly large share of the membership.

There were limits on Congregational autonomy, to be sure, and colonial magistrates sometimes ferreted out heretical beliefs. Those who did not become church members were compelled to attend regular religious services. Perhaps because of the homogeneity of the colony's population, however, the loose polity of the Congregational churches held together for the entire colonial period.

In creating a civil government, the Bay Colonists faced a particularly difficult challenge. Their charter allowed the investors in a joint-stock company to set up a business organization. When the settlers arrived in America, however, company leaders—men like Winthrop—moved quickly to transform the commercial structure into a colonial government. An early step in this direction took place on May 18, 1631, when the category of "freeman" was extended to all adult males who had become members of a Congregational church. This decision greatly expanded the franchise of Massachusetts Bay, and historians estimate that during the 1630s at least 40 percent of the colony's adult males could vote in elections. While this percentage may seem low by modern or even Jacksonian standards, it was higher than anything the emigrants would have known in the mother country. The freemen voted annually for a governor, a group of magistrates called the Court of Assistants, and after 1634, deputies who represented the interests of the individual towns. Even military officers were elected in Massachusetts Bay.

Two popular misconceptions about this government should be dispelled. It was neither a democracy nor a theocracy. The magistrates elected in Massachusetts did not believe they represented the voters, much less the whole populace. They ruled in the name of the electorate; but their responsibility as rulers was to God. In 1638, Winthrop warned against overly democratic forms, since "the best part is always the least, and

of that best part the wiser is always the lesser." And second, the Congregational ministers possessed no formal political authority in Massachusetts Bay. They could not even hold civil office, and it was not unusual for the voters to ignore the recommendations of a respected minister such as John Cotton.

In this colony, the town, rather than the country, became the center of public life. Groups of men and women voluntarily covenanted together to live by certain rules. The community constructed a meetinghouse where church services and town meetings were held, formed a village government, passed bylaws regulating agricultural practices, and "warned out" those individuals who refused to accept local ordinances. Each townsman received land sufficient to build a house and to support a family. The house lots were clustered around the meetinghouse; the fields were located on the village perimeter. The land was given free. No one was expected to pay quitrents or other feudal dues. Villagers were obliged, however, to contribute to the minister's salary, pay local and colony taxes, and serve in the town militia.

Different Voices

The European settlers of Massachusetts Bay managed to live in peace—at least with each other. This was a remarkable achievement considering the chronic instability that plagued other colonies at this time. The Bay Colonists disagreed over many issues, sometimes vociferously; whole towns disputed with neighboring villages over common boundaries. But the people inevitably relied on the courts to mediate differences. They believed in a rule of law, and in 1648 the colonial legislature, called the General Court, drew up the *Lawes and Liberties,* the first alphabetized code of law printed in English. This is a document of fundamental importance in American constitutional history. In clear prose, it explained to the colonists their rights and responsibilities as citizens of the commonwealth. The code engendered public trust in government and discouraged magistrates from the arbitrary exercise of authority.

The most serious challenges to Puritan orthodoxy in Massachusetts Bay came from two remarkable individuals. The first, Roger

Williams, arrived in 1631 and immediately attracted a body of loyal followers. Indeed, everyone seems to have liked Williams as a person.

Williams's *ideas*, however, created controversy. He preached extreme separatism. The Bay Colonists, he exclaimed, were impure in the sight of the Lord so long as they remained even nominal members of the Church of England. Moreover, he questioned the validity of the colony's charter, since the king had not first purchased the land from the Indians, a view that threatened the integrity of the entire colonial experiment. Williams also insisted the civil rulers of Massachusetts had no business punishing settlers for their religious beliefs. It was God's responsibility, not men's, to monitor people's consciences. The Bay magistrates were prepared neither to tolerate heresy nor to accede to Williams's other demands, and in 1636, after attempts to reach a compromise had failed, they banished him from the colony. Williams worked out the logic of his ideas in Providence, a village he founded in what would become Rhode Island.

The magistrates of Massachusetts Bay believed Anne Hutchinson posed an even graver threat to the peace of the commonwealth. This extremely intelligent woman, her husband William, and her children followed John Cotton to the New World in 1634. Even contemporaries found her religious ideas, usually termed Antinomianism, somewhat confusing. Whatever her thoughts, Hutchinson shared them with other Bostonians, many of them women. Her outspoken views scandalized orthodox leaders of church and state. She suggested that all but two ministers in the colony had lost touch with the "Holy Spirit" and were preaching a doctrine in the Congregational churches that was little better than that of Archbishop Laud. When authorities demanded she explain her unusual opinions, she announced she experienced divine inspiration independently of either the Bible or the clergy. In other words, Hutchinson's teachings could not be tested by Scripture, a position that seemed dangerously subjective. Indeed, Hutchinson's theology called the very foundation of Massachusetts Bay into question. Without clear, external standards, one person's truth was as valid as that of anyone else, and from Winthrop's perspective, Hutchinson's teachings invited civil and religious anarchy.

When this woman described Congregational ministers—some of them the leading divines of Boston—as unconverted men, the General Court intervened. For two very tense days in 1637, the ministers and magistrates of Massachusetts Bay cross-examined Hutchinson; in this intense theological debate, she more than held her own. She knew as much about the Bible as did her inquisitors, and no doubt her brilliance at that moment provoked the Court's misogyny.

Hutchinson defied the ministers and magistrates to demonstrate exactly where she had gone wrong. Just when it appeared Hutchinson had outmaneuvered—indeed, thoroughly embarrassed—her opponents, she let down her guard, declaring forcefully that what she knew of God came "by an immediate revelation. . . . By the voice of his own spirit to my soul." Here was what her accusers had suspected all along but could not prove. She had confessed in open court that the Spirit can live without the Moral Law. This Antinomian statement challenged the authority of the Bay rulers, and they were relieved to exile Hutchinson and her followers to Rhode Island.

Breaking Away

Massachusetts Bay spawned four new colonies, three of which survived to the American Revolution. New Hampshire became a separate colony in 1677. Its population grew very slowly, and for much of the colonial period, New Hampshire remained economically dependent on Massachusetts, its neighbor to the south.

Far more people were drawn to the fertile lands of the Connecticut River Valley. In 1636, settlers founded the villages of Hartford, Windsor, and Wethersfield. No one forced these men and women to leave Massachusetts, and in their new surroundings, they created a society that looked much like the one they had known in the Bay Colony. Through his writings, Thomas Hooker, Connecticut's most prominent minister, helped all New Englanders define Congregational church polity. Puritans on both sides of the Atlantic read Hooker's beautifully crafted works. In 1639, representatives from the Connecticut towns passed the Fundamental Orders, a blueprint

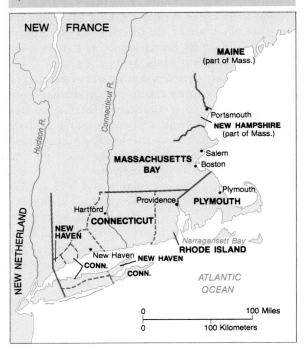

New England Colonies, 1650
The early settlers quickly carved up New England. New Haven briefly flourished as a separate colony before being absorbed into Connecticut in 1662. Long Island later became part of New York; Plymouth later joined Massachusetts.

for civil government, and in 1662, Charles II awarded the colony a charter of its own.

In 1638, another group, led by Theophilus Eaton and the Reverend John Davenport, settled New Haven and several adjoining towns along Long Island Sound. These emigrants, many of whom had come from London, lived briefly in Massachusetts Bay, but then insisted on forming a Puritan commonwealth of their own, one that established a closer relationship between church and state than the Bay colonists had allowed. The New Haven colony never prospered, and in 1662, it was absorbed into Connecticut.

Rhode Island experienced a wholly different history. From the beginning, it was populated by exiles and troublemakers, and according to one Dutch visitor, Rhode Island was "the receptacle of all sorts of riff-raff people. . . . All the cranks of New-England retire thither." This description, of course, was an exaggeration. Roger Williams founded Providence in 1636; two years later Anne

Hutchinson took her followers to Portsmouth. Other groups settled around Narragansett Bay. Not surprisingly, these men and women appreciated the need for toleration. No one was persecuted in Rhode Island for his or her religious beliefs.

One might have thought these separate Rhode Island communities would cooperate for the common good. They did not. Villagers fought over land and schemed with outside speculators to divide the tiny colony into even smaller pieces. In 1644, Parliament issued a patent for the "Providence Plantations," and in 1663, the Rhode Islanders obtained a royal charter. These successes did not calm political turmoil. For most of the seventeenth century, colonywide government existed in name only. Despite their constant bickering, however, the settlers of Rhode Island built up a profitable commerce in agricultural goods.

DIVERSITY IN THE MIDDLE COLONIES

New York, New Jersey, Pennsylvania, and Delaware were settled for quite different reasons. William Penn, for example, envisioned a Quaker sanctuary; the Duke of York worried chiefly about his own income. Despite the founders' intentions, however, some common characteristics emerged. Each colony developed a strikingly heterogeneous population, men and women of different ethnic and religious backgrounds. This cultural diversity became a major influence on the economic, political, and ecclesiastical institutions of the Middle Colonies. The raucous, partisan public life of the Middle Colonies foreshadowed later American society.

Anglo-Dutch Rivalry on the Hudson

By the early decades of the seventeenth century, the Dutch had established themselves as Europe's most aggressive traders. Holland—a small, loosely federated nation—possessed the world's largest merchant fleet. Its ships vied for the commerce of Asia, Africa, and America. Dutch rivalry with Spain, a fading though still formidable power,

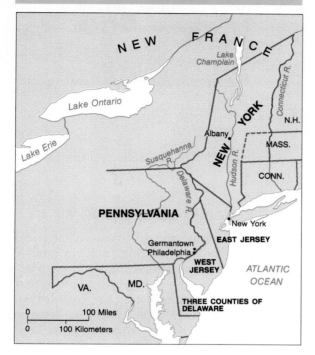

was in large measure responsible for the settlement of New Netherland. While searching for the elusive Northwest Passage in 1609, Henry Hudson, an English explorer employed by a Dutch company, sailed up the river that now bears his name. Further voyages led to the establishment of trading posts in New Netherland, although permanent settlement did not occur until 1624. The area also seemed an excellent base from which to attack Spain's colonies in the New World.

The directors of the Dutch West India Company sponsored two small outposts, Fort Orange (Albany) located well up the Hudson River and New Amsterdam (New York City) on Manhattan Island. The first Dutch settlers were not actually colonists. Rather, they were salaried employees, and their superiors in Holland expected them to spend most of their time gathering animal furs. They did not receive land for their troubles. Needless to say, this arrangement attracted relatively few Dutch immigrants.

The colony's population may have been small, only 270 in 1628, but it contained an extraordinary ethnic mix. One visitor to New Amsterdam in 1644 maintained he had heard "eighteen different languages" spoken in the city. Even if this report was exaggerated, there is no doubt the Dutch colony drew English, Finns, Germans, and Swedes. By the 1640s, a sizable community of free blacks (probably former slaves who had gained their freedom through self-purchase) had developed in New Amsterdam, adding African tongues to the hodgepodge of languages. The colony's culture was further fragmented by New England Puritans who left Massachusetts and Connecticut to stake out farms on eastern Long Island.

New Netherland lacked capable leadership. The company sent a number of director-generals to oversee judicial and political affairs. Without exception, these men were temperamentally unsuited to govern an American colony. They adopted autocratic procedures, lined their own pockets, and in one case, blundered into a war that needlessly killed scores of Indians and settlers. The company made no provision for an elected assembly. As much as they were able, the scattered inhabitants living along the Hudson River ignored company directives. They felt no loyalty to the trading company that had treated them so shabbily. Long Island Puritans complained bitterly about the absence of representative institutions. The Dutch system has aptly been described as "unstable pluralism."

In August 1664, the Dutch lost their tenuous hold on New Netherland. The English Crown, eager to score an easy victory over a commercial rival, dispatched a fleet of warships to New Amsterdam. The commander of this force, Colonel Richard Nicolls, ordered the colonists to surrender. The last director-general, a colorful character named Peter Stuyvesant (1647–1664), rushed wildly about the city urging the settlers to resist the English. But no one obeyed. Even the Dutch remained deaf to Stuyvesant's appeals. They accepted the Articles of Capitulation, a generous agreement that allowed Dutch nationals to remain in the province and to retain their property.

Charles II had already granted his brother, James, the Duke of York, a charter for the newly captured territory and much else besides. The

Het Fort B. de Kerck C. de Wintmolen D. dese Vlagge wert op gehaelt als daer Schepen in de Haven komen. E. t'gevangen huys F. de H. Generaels huys G. t'Gerecht H. de Kaeck I. Compagnies Pachuys

New Amsterdam as it appeared about 1640. This city, which was founded as a trading out-post by the Dutch West Indies Company, was characterized by a diverse ethnic mix and a suc-cession of inept governors.

duke became absolute proprietor over Maine, Martha's Vineyard, Nantucket, Long Island, and the rest of New York all the way to Delaware Bay. The king perhaps wanted to encircle New England's potentially disloyal Puritan population, but whatever his aims may have been, he created a bureaucratic nightmare.

During the English Civil War, the duke acquired a thorough aversion to representative assemblies. After all, Parliament had executed the duke's father, Charles I, and raised up Oliver Cromwell. The new proprietor had no intention of letting participatory government take root in New York. "I cannot *but* suspect," the duke announced, that an assembly "would be of dangerous consequence." The Long Islanders felt betrayed. In part to appease these outspoken critics, Governor Nicolls—one of the few competent administrators to serve in the Middle Colonies—drew up in March 1665 a legal code known as the Duke's Laws. It guaranteed religious toleration and created local governments.

There was no provision, however, for an elected assembly, nor, for that matter, for democratic town meetings. The legal code disappointed the Puritan migrants on Long Island, and when the duke's officers attempted to collect taxes these people protested that "they are inslav'd under an Arbitrary Power."

The Dutch kept silent. For several decades they remained a large unassimilated ethnic group. They continued to speak their own language, worship in their own churches (Dutch Reformed Calvinist), and eye their English neighbors with suspicion. In fact, the colony seemed little different from what it had been under the Dutch West India Company, a loose collection of independent communities ruled by an ineffectual central government.

Confusion in New Jersey

Only three months after receiving a charter for New York, the Duke of York made a terrible blunder—something this stubborn, humorless man was prone to do. As a gift to two courtiers who had served Charles during the English Civil War, the duke awarded the land lying between the Hudson and Delaware rivers to John, Lord Berkeley, and Sir George Carteret. This colony was named New Jersey in honor of Carteret's birthplace, the Isle of Jersey in the English Channel. When Nicolls heard what the duke had done, he exploded. In his estimation this fertile region contained the "most improveable" land in all New York, and to give it away so casually seemed the height of folly.

The duke's impulsive act bred confusion. Soon it was not clear who owned what in New Jersey. Before Nicolls had learned of James's decision, the governor allowed migrants from New England to take up farms west of the Hudson River. He promised these settlers an opportunity to establish an elected assembly, a headright system, and liberty of conscience. In exchange for these privileges, Nicolls asked only that they pay a small annual quitrent to the duke. The proprietors, Berkeley and Carteret, recruited colonists on similar terms. They assumed, of course, that they would receive the rent money.

The result was chaos. Some colonists insisted Nicolls had authorized their assembly. Others, equally insistent, claimed Berkeley and Carteret had done so. Both sides were wrong. Neither the proprietors nor Nicolls possessed any legal right whatsoever to set up a colonial government. James could transfer land to favorite courtiers, but no matter how many times the land changed hands, the government remained his personal responsibility. Knowledge of the law failed to quiet the controversy. Through it all, the duke showed not the slightest interest in the peace and welfare of the people of New Jersey.

Berkeley grew tired of the venture. It generated headaches rather than quitrents, and in 1674, he sold his proprietary rights to a group of surprisingly quarrelsome Quakers. The sale necessitated the division of the colony into two separate governments known as East and West Jersey. Neither half prospered. Carteret and his heirs tried unsuccessfully to turn a profit in East Jersey. In 1677, the Quaker proprietors of West Jersey issued a remarkable democratic plan of government, the Laws, Concessions, and Agreements. But they fought among themselves with such intensity that not even William Penn could bring tranquillity to their affairs. Penn wisely turned his attention to the unclaimed territory across the Delaware River. The West Jersey proprietors went bankrupt, and in 1702, the Crown reunited the two Jerseys into a single royal colony.

In 1700, the population of New Jersey stood at approximately fourteen thousand. Largely because it lacked a good deep-water harbor, the colony never developed a commercial center to rival New York City or Philadelphia. Its residents lived on scattered, often isolated farms; villages of more than a few hundred people were rare. Visitors commented on the diversity of the settlers. There were colonists from almost every European nation. Congregationalists, Presbyterians, Quakers, Baptists, Anabaptists, and Anglicans somehow managed to live together peacefully in New Jersey.

QUAKERS IN AMERICA

The founding of Pennsylvania cannot be separated from the history of the Quaker movement. Believers in an extreme form of Antinomianism, the Quakers saw no need for a learned ministry, since one person's interpretation of Scripture was as valid as anyone else's. This radical religious sect, a product of the social upheaval in England

In this satirical drawing, The Quakers Unmasked (1691), the artist ridicules the mysterious nature of the sect and its leaders, including William Penn. Quakers, who believed that the "Inner Light" of Christ was present in everyone and thus all men and women were equal before the Lord, were harassed for their differences from the traditional social order. In their religious services, or meetings, members sat in silence until the spirit prompted an individual to speak.

during the Civil War, gained its name from the derogatory term that English authorities sometimes used to describe those who "tremble at the word of the Lord." The name persisted even though the Quakers preferred being called Professors of the Light or, more commonly, Friends.

By the time the Stuarts regained the throne in 1660, the Quakers had developed strong support throughout England. One person responsible for their remarkable success was George Fox (1624–1691), a poor shoemaker whose own spiritual anxieties sparked a powerful new religious message that pushed beyond traditional reformed Protestantism. According to Fox, he experienced despair "so that I had nothing outwardly to help me . . . [but] then, I heard a voice which said, 'There is one, even Christ Jesus, that can speak to thy condition.'" Throughout his life, Fox and his growing number of followers gave testimony to the working of the Holy Spirit. Indeed, they informed ordinary men and women that if only they would look, they too would discover they possessed an "Inner Light." This was a wonderfully liberating invitation, especially for persons of lower-class origin. With the Lord's personal assistance, they could attain greater spiritual perfection on earth. Gone was the stigma of original sin; discarded was the notion of eternal predestination. Everyone could be saved.

Quakers practiced humility in their daily lives. They wore simple clothes and employed old-fashioned forms of address that set them apart from their neighbors. Friends refused to honor worldly position and accomplishment or to swear oaths in courts of law. They were also pacifists. According to Fox, all persons were equal in the sight of the Lord, a belief that generally annoyed people of rank and achievement.

Moreover, the Quakers never kept their thoughts to themselves. They preached conversion constantly, spreading the "Truth" throughout England, Ireland, and America. The Friends played important roles in the early history of New Jersey, Rhode Island, and North Carolina, as well as Pennsylvania. In some places, the "publishers of Truth" wore out their welcome. English authorities harassed the Quakers. Thousands, including Fox himself, were jailed, and in Massachusetts Bay between 1659 and 1661, Puritan magistrates ordered several Friends put to death. Such measures proved counterproductive, for persecution only inspired the martyred Quakers to redouble their efforts.

Penn's "Holy Experiment"

William Penn lived according to the Inner Light, a commitment that led eventually to the founding of Pennsylvania. Penn possessed a curiously complex personality. He was an athletic person who threw himself into intellectual pursuits. He was a bold visionary capable of making pragmatic decisions. He came from an aristocratic family and yet spent his entire adult life involved with a reli-

gious movement associated with the lower class.

Penn's father had served with some distinction in the English navy. Through luck and skill, he acquired a considerable estate in Ireland, and as a wealthy landowner, he naturally hoped his son would be a favorite at the Stuart court. He befriended the king, the Duke of York, and several other powerful Restoration figures. But William disappointed his father. He was expelled from Oxford University for holding unorthodox religious views. Not even a grand tour through Europe could dissuade the young man from joining the Society of Friends. His political connections and driving intellect quickly propelled him to a position of prominence within the struggling sect. Penn wrote at least forty-two books testifying to his deep attachment to Quaker principles. Even two years in an English jail could not weaken his faith.

Precisely when Penn's thoughts turned to America is not known. He was briefly involved with the West Jersey proprietorship. This venture may have suggested the possibility of an even larger enterprise. In any case, Penn negotiated in 1681 one of the more impressive land deals in the history of American real estate. Charles II awarded Penn a charter making him the sole proprietor of a vast area called Pennsylvania (literally, Penn's woods). The name embarrassed the modest Penn, but he knew better than to look the royal gift horse in the mouth.

Why the king bestowed such generosity on a leading Quaker who had recently been released from prison remains a mystery. Perhaps Charles wanted to repay an old debt to Penn's father. The monarch may have regarded the colony as a means of ridding England of its troublesome Quaker population, or quite simply, he may have liked Penn. In 1682, the new proprietor purchased from the Duke of York the so-called Three Lower Counties that eventually became Delaware. This astute move guaranteed that Pennsylvania would have access to the Atlantic and determined even before Philadelphia had been established that it would become a commercial center.

Penn lost no time in launching his "Holy Experiment." In 1682, he set forth his ideas in an unusual document known as the Frame of Government. The charter gave Penn the right to create any form of government he desired, and his imagination ran wild. His plan blended traditional notions about the privileges of a landed aristocracy with quite daring concepts of personal liberty. Penn guaranteed that settlers would enjoy among other things liberty of conscience, freedom from persecution, no taxation without representation, and due process of law.

In designing his government, Penn drew heavily on the writings of James Harrington (1611–1677). This English political philosopher argued that no government could ever be stable unless it reflected the actual distribution of landed property within society. Both the rich and poor had to have a voice in political affairs; neither should be able to overrule the legitimate interests of the other class. The Frame of Government envisioned a governor appointed by the proprietor, a 72-member Provincial Council responsible for initiating legislation, and a 200-person Assembly that could accept or reject the bills presented to it. Penn apparently thought the Council would be filled by the colony's richest landholders, or in the words of the Frame, "persons of most note for their wisdom, virtue and ability." The governor and Council were charged with the routine administration of justice. Smaller landowners spoke through the Assembly. It was a clumsy structure, and in America the entire edifice crumbled under its own weight.

Penn promoted his colony aggressively throughout England, Ireland, and Germany. He had no choice. His only source of revenue was the sale of land and the collection of quitrents. Penn commissioned pamphlets in several languages extolling the quality of Pennsylvania's rich farmland. The response was overwhelming. People poured into Philadelphia and the surrounding area. In 1685 alone, eight thousand emigrants arrived. Most of these settlers were Irish, Welsh, and English Quakers, and they generally moved to America as families. But Penn opened the door to men and women of all nations. He asserted that the people of Pennsylvania "are a collection of divers nations in Europe, as French, Dutch, Germans, Swedes, Danes, Finns, Scotch, Irish, and English."

The settlers were by no means all Quakers. The founder of Germantown, Francis Daniel Pastorius, called the vessel that brought him to the New World a "Noah's Ark" of religions, and within his own household, there were servants who subscribed "to the Roman [Catholic], to the Lutheran, to the Calvinistic, to the Anabaptist, and to the Anglican church, and only one Quaker." Ethnic and religious diversity were crucial in the development of Pennsylvania's public institutions, and its politics took on a quarrelsome quality absent in more homogeneous colonies such as Virginia and Massachusetts.

Penn himself emigrated to America in 1682. His stay, however, was unexpectedly short and unhappy. The Council and Assembly—reduced now to more manageable size—fought over the right to initiate legislation. Wealthy Quaker merchants, most of them residents of Philadelphia, dominated the Council. By contrast, the Assembly included men from rural settlements and the Three Lower Counties who showed no concern for the "Holy Experiment."

Penn did not see his colony again until 1699. During his enforced absence much had changed. The settlement had prospered. Its agricultural products, especially its excellent wheat, were in demand throughout the Atlantic world. Despite this economic success, however, the population remained deeply divided. Even the Quakers had briefly split into hostile factions. Penn's handpicked governors had failed to win general support for the proprietor's policies, and one of them exclaimed in anger that each Quaker "*prays* for his neighbor on First Days and then *preys* on him the other six." As the seventeenth century closed, few colonists still shared the founder's desire to create a godly, paternalistic society.

In 1701, legal challenges in England again forced Penn to depart for the mother country. Just before he sailed, Penn signed the Charter of Liberties, a new frame of government that established a unicameral or one-house legislature (the only one in colonial America) and gave the representatives the right to initiate bills. Penn also allowed the Assembly to conduct its business without proprietary interference. The charter provided for the political separation of the Three Lower Counties (Delaware) from Pennsylvania, something people living in this area had demanded for years. This hastily drafted document served as Pennsylvania's constitution until the American Revolution.

His experience in America must have depressed Penn, now both old and sick. In England, Penn was imprisoned for debts incurred by dishonest colonial agents, and in 1718, Pennsylvania's founder died a broken man.

PLANTING THE CAROLINAS

In some ways, Carolina society looked much like the one that had developed in Virginia and Maryland. In both areas, white planters forced African slaves to produce staple crops for a world market. But such superficial similarities masked substantial regional differences. In fact, "the South"—certainly the fabled solid South of the early nineteenth century—did not exist during the colonial period. The Carolinas, joined much later by Georgia, stood apart from their northern neighbors. As a historian of colonial Carolina explained, "the southern colonies were never a cohesive section in the same way that New England was. The great diversity of population groups . . . discouraged southern sectionalism."

Proprietors of the Carolinas

Carolina was a product of the Restoration of the Stuarts to the English throne. Court favorites who had followed the Stuarts into exile during the civil war demanded tangible rewards for their loyalty. New York and New Jersey were obvious plums. So too was Carolina. Sir John Colleton, a successful English planter returned from Barbados, organized a group of eight powerful courtiers who styled themselves the True and Absolute Lords Proprietors of Carolina. On March 24, 1663, the king granted these proprietors a charter to the vast territory between Virginia and Florida and running west as far as the "South Seas."

The failure of similar ventures in the New World taught the Carolina proprietors valuable lessons. Unlike the first Virginians, for example, this group did not expect instant wealth. Rather, the proprietors reasoned that they would obtain a steady source of income from rents. What they needed, of course, were settlers. Recruitment turned out to be no easy task. Economic and social conditions in the mother country improved considerably after the Civil War, and English

A Brief **DESCRIPTION**
OF
The Province
OF
CAROLINA
On the COASTS *of* FLOREDA.
AND
More perticularly of a *New-Plantation* begun by the *ENGLISH* at *Cape-Feare*, on that River now by them called *Charles-River*, the 29th. of *May*. 1664.

Wherein is set forth
The *Healthfulness* of the *Air*; the *Fertility* of the *Earth*, and *Waters*; and the great *Pleasure* and *Profit* will accrue to those that shall go thither to enjoy the same.

Also,
Directions and advice to such as shall go thither whether on their own accompts, or to serve under another.

Together with
A most accurate MAP of the whole *PROVINCE*.

———————————

London, Printed for *Robert Horne* in the first Court of *Gresham-Colledge* neer *Bishopsgate street*. 1666.

This brochure attempted to lure settlers to the province of Carolina by promising pleasure and profit to all who would come to partake of the healthfulness of the air and the fertility of the land and waters.

people were no longer so willing to transfer to the New World. Even if they had shown interest, the cost of transporting settlers across the Atlantic seemed prohibitively expensive. The proprietors concluded, therefore, that with the proper incentives—a generous land policy, for example—they could attract men and women from established American colonies and thereby save themselves a great deal of money. Unfortunately for the men who owned Carolina, such people were not easily persuaded. They had begun to take for granted certain rights and privileges, and as the price of settlement, they demanded a representative assembly, liberty of conscience, and a liberal headright system.

The Carolina proprietors divided their grant into three distinct jurisdictions, anticipating no

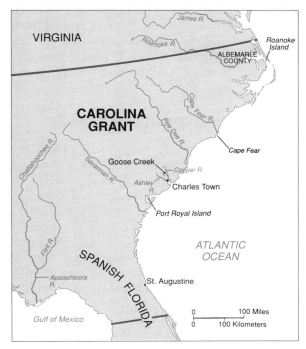

Carolina Proprietorship, 1685
Caribbean sugar planters migrated to the Goose Creek area where, with African American assistance, they eventually mastered rice cultivation. Poor harbors in North Carolina retarded European settlement in that region.

doubt that these areas would become the centers of settlement. The first region, called Albemarle, abutted Virginia. As the earlier ill-fated Roanoke colonists had discovered, the region lacked a good deep-water port. Nevertheless, it attracted a number of dissatisfied Virginians who drifted south in search of fresh land. Further south, the mouth of the Cape Fear River seemed a second likely site for development. And third, within the present state of South Carolina, the Port Royal region contained a maze of fertile islands and meandering tidal streams.

Colleton and his associates waited for the money to roll in, but to their dismay, no one seemed particularly interested in moving to the Carolina frontier. A tiny settlement at Port Royal failed. One group of New Englanders briefly considered taking up land in the Cape Fear area, but these people were so disappointed by what they saw that they departed, leaving behind only a sign that "tended not only to the disparagement of the Land . . . but also to the great discourage-

ment of all those that should hereafter come into these parts to settle." By this time, a majority of surviving proprietors had given up on Carolina.

The Barbadian Connection

Anthony Ashley Cooper, later Earl of Shaftesbury, was the exception. In 1669, he persuaded the remaining Carolinian proprietors to invest their own capital in the colony. Without such financial support, Ashley recognized, the project would surely fail. Once he received sufficient funds, this energetic organizer dispatched three hundred English colonists to Port Royal under the command of Joseph West. The fleet put in briefly at Barbados to pick up additional recruits, and in March 1670, after being punished by Atlantic gales that destroyed one ship, the expedition arrived at its destination. Only one hundred people were still alive. The unhappy settlers did not remain long at Port Royal, an unappealing, low-lying place badly exposed to Spanish attack. They moved northward, locating eventually along the more secure Ashley River. Later the colony's administrative center, Charles Town (it did not become Charleston until 1783) was established at the junction of the Ashley and Cooper rivers.

Ashley also wanted to bring order to the new society. With assistance from John Locke, the famous English philosopher (1632–1704), Ashley devised the Fundamental Constitutions of Carolina. Like Penn, Ashley had been influenced by the writings of Harrington. The constitutions created a local aristocracy consisting of proprietors and lesser nobles called *landgraves* and *cassiques,* terms as inappropriate to the realities of the New World as was the idea of creating an hereditary landed elite. Persons who purchased vast tracts of land automatically received a title and the right to sit in the Council of Nobles, a body designed to administer justice, oversee civil affairs, and initiate legislation. A parliament in which smaller landowners had a voice could accept or reject bills drafted by the council. The very poor were excluded from political life altogether. Ashley thought his scheme maintained the proper "Balance of Government" between aristocracy and democracy, a concept central to Harrington's philosophy. Not surprisingly, the constitutions had little impact on the actual structure of government. It reaffirmed religious toleration, but since so few men bought manors, the Council of Nobles remained a paper dream.

Before 1680, almost half the men and women who settled in the Port Royal area came from Barbados. This small Caribbean island, which produced an annual fortune in sugar, depended upon slave labor. By the third quarter of the seventeenth century, Barbados had become overpopulated. Wealthy families could not provide their sons and daughters with sufficient land to maintain social status, and as the crisis intensified, Barbadians looked to Carolina for relief.

These migrants, many of whom were quite rich, traveled to Carolina both as individuals and family groups. Some even brought gangs of slaves with them to the American mainland. The Barbadians carved out plantations on the tributaries of the Cooper River and established themselves immediately as the colony's most powerful political faction. "So it was," writes historian Richard Dunn, "that these Caribbean pioneers helped to create on the North American coast a slave-based plantation society closer in temper to the islands they fled from than to any other mainland English settlement."

Much of the planters' time was taken up with the search for a profitable crop. The early settlers experimented with a number of plants: tobacco, cotton, silk, and grapes. The most successful items turned out to be beef, skins, and naval stores (especially tar used to maintain ocean vessels). By the 1680s, some Carolinians had built up great herds of cattle—seven or eight hundred head in some cases. Traders who dealt with Indians brought back thousands of deerskins from the interior, and they often returned with Indian slaves as well. These items together with tar and turpentine enjoyed a good market. It was not until the 1690s that the planters came to appreciate fully the value of rice, but once they had done so, it quickly became the colony's main staple.

Proprietary Carolina was in a constant political uproar. Factions vied for special privilege. The Barbadian settlers, known locally as the "Goose Creek Men," resisted the proprietors' policies at every turn. A large community of French Huguenots located in Craven County distrusted the Barbadians. The proprietors—an ineffectual group following the death of Shaftesbury—appointed a series of utterly incompetent governors who only made things worse. One visitor observed that "the Inhabitants of Carolina should be as free from Oppression as any [people] in the Universe . . . if their own Differences amongst themselves do not occasion the contrary." By the end of the century, the Commons House of Assembly had assumed the right to initiate legislation. In 1719, the colonists overthrew the last proprietary governor, and in 1729, the king created separate royal governments for North and South Carolina.

THE FOUNDING OF GEORGIA

The early history of Georgia was strikingly different from that of Britain's other mainland colonies. Its settlement was really an act of aggression against Spain, a country that had as good a claim to this area as did the English. During the eighteenth century, the two nations were often at war (see Chapter 4), and South Carolinians worried that the Spaniards moving up from bases in Florida would occupy the disputed territory between Florida and the Carolina grant.

The colony owed its existence primarily to James Oglethorpe, a British general and member of Parliament who believed that he could thwart Spanish designs on the area south of Charleston while at the same time providing a fresh start for London's worthy poor, saving them from debtors' prison. Although Oglethorpe envisioned Georgia as an asylum as well as a garrison, the military aspects of his proposal were especially appealing to the leaders of the British government. In 1732, the king granted Oglethorpe and a board of trustees a charter for a new colony to be located between the Savannah and Altamaha rivers and from "sea to sea." The trustees living in the mother country were given complete control over Georgia politics, a condition the settlers soon found intolerable.

During the first years of colonization, Georgia fared no better than had earlier utopian experiments. The poor people of England showed little desire to move to an inclement frontier, and the trustees, in their turn, provided little incentive for emigration. Each colonist received only 50 acres. Fifty additional acres could be added for each servant transported to Georgia, but in no case could

England's Principal Mainland Colonies

Name	Original Purpose	Date of Founding	Principal Founder	Major Export	Estimated Population c. 1700
Virginia	Commercial venture	1607	Captain John Smith	Tobacco	64,560
New York (New Amsterdam)	Commercial venture	1613 (Made English colony, 1664)	Peter Stuyvesant, Duke of York	Furs, grain	19,107
Plymouth	Refuge for English Separatists	1620 (Absorbed by Massachusetts 1691)	William Bradford	Grain	Included with Massachusetts
New Hampshire	Commercial venture	1623	John Mason	Wood, naval stores	4,958
Massachusetts	Refuge for English Puritans	1628	John Winthrop	Grain, wood	55,941
Maryland	Refuge for English Catholics	1634	Lord Baltimore (George Calvert)	Tobacco	34,100
Connecticut	Expansion of Massachusetts	1635	Thomas Hooker	Grain	25,970
Rhode Island	Refuge for dissenters from Massachusetts	1636	Roger Williams	Grain	5,894
Delaware (New Sweden)	Commercial venture	1638 (Included in Penn grant, 1681; given separate assembly, 1703)	Peter Minuit William Penn	Grain	2,470
North Carolina	Commercial venture	1663	Anthony Ashley Cooper	Wood, naval stores, tobacco	10,720
South Carolina	Commercial venture	1663	Anthony Ashley Cooper	Naval stores, rice	5,720
New Jersey	Consolidation of new English territory, Quaker settlement	1664	Sir George Cartaret	Grain	14,010
Pennsylvania	Refuge for English Quakers	1681	William Penn	Grain	18,950
Georgia	Discourage Spanish expansion; charity	1733	James Oglethorpe	Silk, rice, wood, naval stores	5,200 (in 1750)

Sources: U.S. Bureau of Census, *Historical Statistics of the United States: Colonial Times to 1970,* Washington, D.C., 1975; John J. McCusker and Russell R. Menard, *The Economy of British America, 1607–1789,* Chapel Hill, 1985.

a settler amass more than 500 acres. Moreover, land could be passed only to an eldest son, and if a planter had no sons at the time of his death, the holding reverted to the trustees. Slavery was prohibited. So too was rum.

Almost as soon as they arrived in Georgia, the settlers complained. The colonists demanded slaves, pointing out to the trustees that unless the new planters possessed an unfree labor force, they could not compete economically with their South Carolina neighbors. The settlers also wanted a voice in local government. In 1738, 121 people living in Savannah petitioned for fundamental reforms in the colony's constitution. Oglethorpe responded angrily, "The idle ones are indeed for Negroes. If the petition is countenanced, the province is ruined." The settlers did not give up. In 1741, they again petitioned Oglethorpe, this time addressing him as "our Perpetual Dictator."

While the colonists grumbled about various restrictions, Oglethorpe tried and failed to capture the Spanish fortress at Saint Augustine (1740). This personal disappointment coupled with the growing popular unrest destroyed his interest in Georgia. The trustees were forced to compromise their principles. In 1738, they eliminated all restrictions on the amount of land a man could own; they allowed women to inherit land. In 1750, they permitted the settlers to import slaves. Soon Georgians could drink rum. In 1751, the trustees returned Georgia to the king, undoubtedly relieved to be free of what had become a hard-drinking, slave-owning plantation society much like that in South Carolina. The king authorized an assembly in 1751, but even with these social and political changes, Georgia attracted very few new settlers.

RUGGED AND LABORIOUS BEGINNINGS

Long after he had returned from his adventures in Virginia, Captain John Smith reflected on the difficulty of establishing colonies in the New World. It was a task for which most people were not temperamentally suited. "It requires," Smith counseled, "all the best parts of art, judgement, courage, honesty, constancy, diligence, and industry, [even] to do neere well." On another occasion, Charles I warned Lord Baltimore that new

CHRONOLOGY

1607	First English settlers arrive at Jamestown
1608–1609	Scrooby Congregation (Pilgrims) leaves England for Holland
1609–1611	"Starving time" in Virginia threatens survival of the colonists
1616–1618	Plague destroys Native American populations of coastal New England
1619	Virginia assembly, called House of Burgesses, meets for the first time • First slaves sold at Jamestown
1620	Pilgrims sign the Mayflower Compact
1622	Surprise Indian attack devastates Virginia
1624	Dutch investors create permanent settlements along Hudson River • James I, king of England, dissolves Virginia Company
1625	Charles I ascends English throne
1630	John Winthrop transfers Massachusetts Bay charter to New England
1634	Colony of Maryland is founded
1636	Harvard College established • Puritan settlers found Hartford and other Connecticut Valley towns
1638	Anne Hutchinson exiled to Rhode Island • Theophilus Eaton and John Davenport lead settlers to New Haven Colony
1639	Connecticut towns accept Fundamental Orders
1644	Second major Indian attack in Virginia
1649	Charles I executed during English Civil War
1660	Stuarts restored to the English throne
1663	Rhode Island obtains royal charter • Proprietors receive charter for Carolina
1664	English soldiers conquer New Netherland
1677	New Hampshire becomes a royal colony
1681	William Penn granted patent for his "Holy Experiment"
1702	East and West Jersey unite to form single colony
1732	James Oglethorpe receives charter for Georgia

settlements "commonly have rugged and laborious beginnings."

Over the course of the seventeenth century, women and men had followed leaders like Baltimore, Smith, Winthrop, Bradford, Penn, and Berkeley to the New World in anticipation of creating a successful new society. Some people were religious visionaries; others were hardheaded businessmen. The results of their efforts, their struggles to survive in an often hostile environment, and their interactions with various Native American groups, yielded a spectrum of settlements along the Atlantic coast, ranging from the quasi feudalism of South Carolina to the Puritan commonwealth of Massachusetts Bay.

The diversity of early English colonization must be emphasized precisely because it is so easy to overlook. Even though the colonists eventually banded together and fought for independence, persistent differences separated New Englanders from Virginians, Pennsylvanians from Carolinians. The interpretive challenge, of course, is to comprehend how European colonists managed over the course of the eighteenth century to overcome fragmentation and to develop the capacity to imagine themselves a nation.

Recommended Reading

The fullest discussion of the separate histories of England's thirteen mainland colonies can be found in Milton Klein and Jacob Cooke, eds., *A History of the American Colonies in Thirteen Volumes* (1973–1986). Each volume in this series has been written by a distinguished specialist. An older but still reliable account of the founding of the various settlements is Charles M. Andrews, *The Colonial Period of American History*, 4 vols. (1934–1938). A provocative guide to this rich historiography is Jack P. Greene and J. R. Pole, eds., *Colonial British America: Essays in the New History of the Early Modern Era* (1984).

Additional Bibliography

Some books that contribute to an understanding of the background of English colonization are Keith Wrightson, *English Society, 1580–1680* (1982); and Virginia D. Anderson, *New England's Generation: The Great Migration and the Formation of Society and Culture in the Seventeenth Century* (1991). T. H. Breen, *Puritans and Adventurers: Change and Persistence in Early America* (1980), specifically explores the problem of cultural transfer. Also helpful is David Grayson Allen, *In English Ways: The Movement of Societies and the Transferal of English Local Law and Custom* (1981).

On the execution ritual, see Lawrence W. Towner, "True Confessions and Dying Warnings in Colonial New England," in *Sibley's Heirs: A Volume in Memory of Clifford Kenyon Shipton*, Publications, Colonial Society of Massachusetts, Vol. 59: 523–539.

The best analysis of the early settlement of Virginia is Edmund S. Morgan, *American Slavery, American Freedom* (1975). For a masterful analysis of the current research on Chesapeake society, see Thad W. Tate and David L. Ammerman, eds., *The Chesapeake in the Seventeenth Century* (1979). New insights are offered in David B. Quinn, ed., *Early Maryland in a Wider World* (1982); Gloria L. Main, *Tobacco Colony: Life in Early Maryland, 1650–1720* (1982); and Lois G. Carr et al., *Robert Cole's World: Agriculture and Society in Early Maryland* (1991).

Two of Colonial New England's most capable historians were William Bradford and John Winthrop. See especially Bradford's *Of Plymouth Plantation*, edited by Samuel E. Morison (1952) and Winthrop's *History of New England*, edited by James K. Hosmer (2 vols., 1908). The most brilliant exploration of Puritan theology remains Perry Miller, *New England Mind: From Colony to Province* (1956). Also, see Stephen Foster, *The Long Argument: English Puritanism and the Shaping of New England Culture, 1570–1700* (1991); George D. Langdon, Jr., *Pilgrim Colony* (1966); T. H. Breen, *Character of the Good Ruler* (1970); David T. Konig, *Law and Society in Puritan Massachusetts* (1979); David D. Hall, *Worlds of Wonder, Days of Judgment: Popular Religious Belief in Early New England* (1989); and Charles E. Hambrick-Stowe, *The Practice of Piety* (1982). The better New England town studies—and there are many—are Kenneth A. Lockridge, *A New England Town: The First Hundred Years* (1970); Philip Greven, Jr., *Four Generations: Population, Land, and Family in Colonial Andover* (1970); and Stephen Innes, *Labor in a New Land* (1983).

Good accounts of early New York history are Oliver A. Rink, *Holland on the Hudson: An Economic and Social History of Dutch New York* (1986) and Robert C. Ritchie, *The Duke's Province* (1977). William Penn's life and political thought are the subject of Mary M. Dunn, *William Penn: Politics and Conscience* (1967). For newer interpretations see Richard and Mary Dunn, eds., *The World of William Penn* (1986).

Anyone curious about the founding of Carolina and Georgia should examine M. Eugene Sirmans, *Colonial South Carolina: A Political History, 1663–1763* (1966); and Harold E. Davis, *The Fledgling Province: Social and Cultural Life in Colonial Georgia, 1733–1776* (1976).

Putting Down Roots

Colonists in an Empire

 he Witherspoon family moved from Great Britain to the South Carolina backcountry early in the eighteenth century. Though otherwise indistinguishable from the thousands of other ordinary families that put down roots in English America, the Witherspoons were made historical figures by the candid account of pioneer life produced by their son, Robert, who was only a small child at the time of their arrival. The Witherspoon's initial reaction to the New World—at least, that of the mother and children—was utter despondence. "My mother and us children were still in expectation that we were coming to an agreeable place," Robert confessed, "but when we arrived and saw nothing but a wilderness and instead of a fine timbered house, nothing but a very mean dirt house, our spirits quite sunk." For many years, the Witherspoons feared they would be killed by Indians, become lost in the woods, or be bitten by snakes.

The Witherspoons managed to survive these early difficult years on the Black River. To be sure, the Carolina backcountry did not look very much like the world they had left behind. The discrepancy, however, apparently did not greatly discourage Robert's father. He had a vision of what the Black River settlement might become. "My father," Robert recounted, "gave us all the comfort he [could] by telling us we would get all these trees cut down and in a short time [there] would be plenty of inhabitants, [and] that we could see from house to house."

Robert Witherspoon's story reminds us just how much the early history of colonial America was in fact a history created by families. Neither the peopling of the Atlantic frontier, the cutting down of the forests, nor the creation of new communities where one could see from "house to house" was a process that involved what we would today recognize as state policy. Men and women made significant decisions about the character of their lives within families. It was within this primary social unit that most colonists earned their livelihoods, educated their children, defined gender, sustained religious tradition, and nursed each other in sickness. In short, the family was the source of their societal and cultural identities.

Early colonial families did not exist in isolation but were part of larger societies. As we have already discovered, the characters of the first English settlements in the New World varied substantially (see Chapter 2). During much of the seventeenth century, these initial differences grew stronger as each region acquired its own history and developed its own traditions. The various local societies in which families like the Witherspoons put down roots reflected several critical elements: supply of labor, abundance of land, unusual demographic patterns, and commercial ties with European markets. In the Chesapeake, for example, an economy based almost entirely on a single commodity—tobacco—created an insatiable demand for indentured servants and black slaves. Moreover, in Massachusetts Bay, the extraordinary longevity of the founders generated a level of social and political stability that Virginians and Marylanders did not attain until the end of the seventeenth century.

By 1660, it seemed these regional differences had undermined the very idea of a unified English empire in America. During the reign of Charles II, however, a trend toward cultural convergence began. Although subcultures had evolved in strikingly different directions, countervailing forces such as common language and religion gradually pulled English American settlers together. Parliament took advantage of this trend and began to establish a uniform set of rules for the expanding American empire. The process was slow and uneven, often sparking violent colonial resistance, but by the end of the seventeenth century, England had made significant progress toward its goal.

TRADITIONAL SOCIETIES: THE NEW ENGLAND COLONIES OF THE SEVENTEENTH CENTURY

Seventeenth-century New Englanders successfully replicated in America a traditional social order they had known in England. The transfer of a familiar way of life to the New World seemed less difficult for these Puritan migrants than it did for the many English men and women who settled in the Chesapeake colonies. Their contrasting experiences, fundamental to an understanding of the development of both cultures, can be explained, at least in part, by the Puritan family tradition.

Immigrant Families and New Social Order

Early New Englanders believed God ordained the family for human benefit. It was essential to the maintenance of social order, since outside the family, men and women succumbed to carnal temptation. Such people had no one to sustain them or remind them of Scripture. "Without *Family care*," declared the Reverend Benjamin Wadsworth, "the labour of Magistrates and Ministers for Reformation and Propagating Religion, is likely to be in great measure unsuccessful."

The godly family, at least in theory, was ruled by a patriarch, father to his children, husband to his wife, the source of authority and object of unquestioned obedience. The wife shared responsibility for the raising of children, but in decisions of importance, especially those related to property, she was expected to defer to her spouse.

The New Englanders' concern about the character of the godly family is not surprising. This institution played a central role in shaping their society. In contrast to those who migrated to the colonies of Virginia and Maryland, New Englanders crossed the Atlantic within *nuclear* families. That is, they moved within established units consisting of a father, mother, and their dependent children, rather than as single youths and adults. People who migrated to America within families preserved local English customs more fully than did the youths who traveled to other parts of the continent as single men and women. The comforting presence of immediate family members reduced the shock of adjusting to a strange environment 3,000 miles from home. Even in the 1630s, the ratio of men to women in New England was fairly well balanced, about three males for every two females. Persons who had not already married in England before coming to the New World could expect to form nuclear families of their own.

The great migration of the 1630s and 1640s brought approximately twenty thousand persons to New England. After 1642, the English Civil War reduced the flood of people moving to Massachusetts Bay to a trickle. Nevertheless, by the end of the century, the population of New

Isaac Royal and Family *(1741) by Robert Feke, known for his portraits of the leading citizens of his day. His portraits are distinguished primarily by an emphasis on elaborate dress.*

England had reached almost 120,000, an amazing increase considering the small number of original immigrants. Historians have been hard pressed to explain this striking rate of growth. Some have suggested that New Englanders married very young, thus giving couples extra years in which to produce large families. Other scholars have maintained that New England women must have been more fertile than their Old World counterparts.

Neither theory adequately explains how so few migrants produced such a large population. Early New England marriage patterns, for example, did not differ substantially from those recorded in seventeenth-century England. The average age for men at first marriage was the mid-twenties. Wives were slightly younger than their husbands, the average age being about twenty-two. There is no evidence that New Englanders favored child brides. Nor, for that matter, were Puritan families unusually large by the standards of the period.

The explanation for the region's extraordinary growth turned out to be survival, rather than fertility. Put simply, people who, under normal conditions, would have died in contemporary Europe, lived in New England. Indeed, the life expectancy of seventeenth-century settlers was not very different from our own. Males who survived infancy might have expected to see their seventieth birthday. Twenty percent of the men of the first generation reached the age of eighty. The figures for women were only slightly lower. Why the early settlers lived so long is not entirely clear.

No doubt, pure drinking water, a cool climate that retarded the spread of fatal contagious disease, and a dispersed population promoted general good health.

Longer life altered family relations. New England males lived not only to see their own children reach adulthood, but also to witness the birth of grandchildren. One historian, John Murrin, has argued that New Englanders "invented" grandparents. In other words, this society produced *real* patriarchs. This may have been one of the first societies in recorded history in which a person could reasonably anticipate knowing his or her grandchildren, a demographic surprise that contributed to social stability. The traditions of particular families and communities literally remained alive in the memories of the colony's oldest citizens.

A Society of Families

The life cycle of the seventeenth-century New England family began with marriage. Young men and women generally initiated courtships. If parents exercised a voice in such matters, it was to discourage union with a person of unsound moral character. Puritan ministers advised single people to choose godly partners, warning:

The Wretch that is alone to Mannon Wed,
May chance to find a Satan in the bed.

In this highly religious society, there was not much chance that young people would stray far from traditional community values. The overwhelming majority of the region's population married, for in New England, the single life was not only morally suspect, but also physically difficult.

A couple without land could not support an independent and growing family in these agrarian communities. While men brought farmland, prospective brides were expected to possess a dowry worth approximately one-half what the bridegroom brought to the union. Women often contributed money or household goods.

The household was primarily a place of work—very demanding work. One historical geographer estimates that a Pennsylvania family of five needed 75 acres of cleared land just to feed itself. Additional cultivation allowed the farmer to produce a surplus that could then be sold or bartered, and since agrarian families required items that could not be manufactured at home—metal tools, for example—they usually grew more than they consumed. Early American farmers were not economically self-sufficient; the belief that they were is a popular misconception.

During the seventeenth century, men and women generally lived in the communities of their parents and grandparents. New Englanders usually managed to fall in love with a neighbor, and most marriages took place between men and women living less than 13 miles apart. Moving to a more fertile region might have increased their earnings, but such thoughts seldom occurred to early New Englanders. Religious values, a sense of common purpose, and the importance of family reinforced traditional communal ties.

Towns, in fact, were collections of families, not individuals. Over time, these families intermarried, so the community became an elaborate kinship network. Social historians have discovered that in many New England towns the original founders dominated local politics and economic affairs for several generations. Not surprisingly, newcomers who were not absorbed into the family system tended to move away from the village with greater frequency than did the sons and daughters of the established lineage groups.

Congregational churches were also built on a family foundation. During the earliest years of settlement, the churches accepted persons who could demonstrate they were among God's "elect." Members were drawn from a broad social spectrum. Once the excitement of establishing a new society had passed, however, New Englanders began to focus more attention on the spiritual welfare of their own families. This quite normal parental concern precipitated a major ecclesiastical crisis. The problem was the status of the children within a gathered church. Sons and daughters of full church members regularly received baptism, usually as infants, but as these people grew to adulthood, they often failed to provide testimony of their own "election." Moreover, they wanted their own children to be baptized. A church synod—a gathering of Congregational ministers—responded to this generational crisis by adopting the so-called Half-Way Covenant (1662). This compromise allowed the grandchildren of persons in full communion

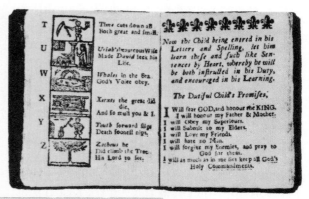

New England parents took seriously their responsibility for the spiritual welfare of their children. To seek the word of God, young people had to learn to read. The New England Primer, *shown here, was their primary vehicle.*

to be baptized even though *their* parents could not demonstrate conversion. Congregational ministers assumed "God cast the line of election in the loins of godly parents." Because of the New Englanders' growing obsession with family—termed *tribalism* by some historians—the Congregational churches by the end of the seventeenth century were increasingly turning inward, addressing the spiritual needs of particular lineage groups rather than reaching out to the larger Christian community.

Colonists regarded education as primarily a family responsibility. Parents were supposed to instruct children in the principles of Christianity; and so it was necessary to teach boys and girls how to read. In 1642, the Massachusetts General Court reminded the Bay Colonists of their obligation to catechize their families. Five years later, the legislature ordered towns containing at least fifteen families to open an elementary school supported by local taxes. Villages of a hundred or more families had to maintain more advanced grammar schools, which taught a basic Latin curriculum. At least eleven schools were operating in 1647, and despite their expense, new schools were established throughout the century.

This family-based education system worked. A large majority of the region's adult males could read and write, an accomplishment not achieved in the Chesapeake colonies for another century. The literacy rate for women was somewhat lower, but by the standards of the period, it was still impressive. A printing press operated in Cambridge as early as 1639. *The New-England Primer,* first published in 1690 in Boston by Benjamin Harris, taught children the alphabet as well as the Lord's Prayer. This primer announced:

He who ne'er learns his ABC,
forever will a blockhead be.
But he who to his book's inclined,
will soon a golden treasure find.

But the best-seller of seventeenth-century New England was Michael Wigglesworth's *The Day of Doom* (1662), a poem of 224 stanzas describing in terrifying detail the fate of sinners on Judgment Day. In words that even young readers could comprehend, Wigglesworth wrote of these unfortunate souls:

They cry, no, no: Alas! and wo!
Our Courage all is gone:
Our hardiness (fool hardiness)
Hath us undone, undone.

Many New Englanders memorized the entire poem.

After 1638, young men could attend Harvard College, the first institution of higher learning founded in England's mainland colonies. The school was originally intended to train ministers, and of the 465 students who graduated during the seventeenth century, over half became Congregational divines. Harvard had a demanding curriculum. The boys read logic, rhetoric, divinity, and several ancient languages, including Hebrew. Yale College followed Harvard's lead, admitting its first students in 1702.

Women in Puritan New England

The role of women in the agrarian societies north of the Chesapeake is a controversial subject among colonial historians. Some scholars point out that common law as well as English custom treated women as inferior to men. Other historians, however, depict the colonial period as a "golden age" for women. According to this interpretation, wives worked alongside their husbands. They were not divorced from meaningful, productive labor. They certainly were not transformed into the frail, dependent beings much admired by middle-class males of the nineteenth century. Both views provide insights into the lives of early American women, but neither fully recaptures their community experiences.

To be sure, women worked on family farms. They did not, however, necessarily do the same jobs that men performed. Women usually handled separate tasks, including cooking, washing, clothes making, dairying, and gardening. Their production of food was absolutely essential to the survival of most households. Sometimes wives—and the overwhelming majority of adult seventeenth-century women were married—raised poultry, and by selling surplus birds achieved some economic independence. When people in one New England community chided a man for allowing his wife to peddle her fowl, he responded, "I meddle not with the geese nor turkeys for they are hers." In fact, during this period women were often described as "deputy husbands," a label that drew attention to their dependence on

family patriarchs as well as to their roles as decision makers.

Women also joined churches in greater number than men. Within a few years of founding, many New England congregations contained two female members for every male, a process historians describe as the "feminization of colonial religion." Contemporaries offered different explanations for this gender shift. Cotton Mather, the leading Congregational minister of Massachusetts Bay, argued that God had created "far more *godly Women*" than men. Others thought the life-threatening experience of childbirth gave women a deeper appreciation of religion. The Quakers gave women an even larger role in religious affairs, which may help to explain the popularity of this sect among ordinary women.

In political and legal matters, society sharply curtailed the rights of colonial women. According to English common law, a wife exercised no control over property. She could not, for example, sell land, although if her husband decided to dispose of their holdings, he was free to do so without her permission. Divorce was extremely difficult to obtain in any colony before the American Revolution. Indeed, a person married to a cruel or irresponsible spouse had little recourse but to run away or accept the unhappy situation.

Yet most women were neither prosperous entrepreneurs nor abject slaves. Surviving letters indicate that men and women generally accommodated themselves to the gender roles they thought God had ordained. One of early America's most creative poets, Anne Bradstreet, wrote movingly of the fulfillment she had found with her husband. In a piece entitled "To my Dear and loving Husband," Bradstreet declared:

If ever two were one, then surely we.
If ever man were lov'd by wife, then thee;
If ever wife was happy in a man,
Compare with me the women if you can.

Although Puritan couples worried that the affection they felt for a husband or a wife might turn their thoughts away from God's perfect love, this was a danger they were willing to risk.

Rank and Status in New England Society

During the seventeenth century, the New England colonies attracted neither noblemen nor paupers. The absence of these social groups meant the American social structure seemed incomplete by contemporary European standards. The settlers were not displeased that the poor remained in the Old World. The lack of very rich persons—and in this period great wealth frequently accompanied noble title—was quite another matter. According to the prevailing hierarchical view of the structure of society, well-placed individuals were *natural rulers,* people intended by God to exercise political authority over the rank and file. Migration forced the colonists, however, to choose their rulers from men of more modest status. One minister told a Plymouth congregation that since its members were "not furnished with any persons of *special eminency above the rest,* to be chosen by you into office of government," they would have to make due with neighbors, "not beholding in them the *ordinariness of their persons.*"

The colonists gradually sorted themselves out into distinct social groupings. Persons who would never have been "natural rulers" in England became provincial gentry in the various northern colonies. It helped, of course, if an individual possessed wealth and education, but these attributes alone could not guarantee a newcomer would be accepted into the local ruling elite, at least not during the early decades of settlement. In Massachusetts and Connecticut, Puritan voters expected their leaders to join Congregational churches and defend orthodox religion.

The Winthrops, Dudleys, and Pynchons—just to cite a few of the more prominent families—fulfilled these expectations, and in public affairs they assumed dominant roles. They took their responsibilities quite seriously and certainly did not look kindly on anyone who spoke of their "ordinariness." A colonist who jokingly called a Puritan magistrate a "just ass" found himself in deep trouble with civil authorities.

The problem was that while most New Englanders accepted a hierarchical view of society, they disagreed over their assigned places. Both Massachusetts Bay and Connecticut passed sumptuary laws—statutes that limited the wearing of fine apparel to the wealthy and prominent—to curb the pretensions of those of lower status. Yet such restraints could not prevent some people from rising and others from falling within the social order.

Governor John Winthrop provided a marvelous description of the unplanned social mobility that occurred in early New England. During the 1640s, he recorded in his diary the story of a master who could not afford to pay a servant's wages. To meet this obligation, the master sold a pair of oxen, but the transaction barely covered the cost of keeping the servant. In desperation, the master asked the employee, a man of lower social status, "how shall I do . . . when all my cattle are gone?" The servant replied, "you shall then serve me, so you may have your cattle again." In the margin of his diary next to this account, Winthrop scribbled "insolent."

Most northern colonists were yeomen (independent farmers) who worked their own land. While few became rich in America, even fewer fell hopelessly into debt. Their daily lives, especially for those who settled New England, centered on scattered little communities where they participated in village meetings, church-related matters, and militia training. Possession of land gave agrarian families a sense of independence from external authority. As one man bragged to those who had stayed behind in England, "Here are no hard landlords to rack us with high rents or extorting fines. . . . Here every man may be master of his own labour and land . . . and if he have nothing but his hands he may set up his trade, and by industry grow rich."

During the seventeenth century, this independence was balanced by an equally strong feeling of local identity. Not until the late eighteenth century, when many New Englanders left their familial villages in search of new land, did many northern yeomen place personal material ambition above traditional community bonds.

It was not unusual for northern colonists to work as servants at some point in their lives. This system of labor differed greatly from the pattern of servitude that developed in seventeenth-century Virginia and Maryland. New Englanders seldom recruited servants from the Old World. The forms of agriculture practiced in this region, mixed cereal and dairy farming, made employment of large gangs of dependent workers uneconomic. Rather, New England families placed their adolescent children in nearby homes. These young persons contracted for four or five years and seemed more like apprentices than servants. Servitude was not simply a means by which one group exploited another. It was a form of vocational training program in which the children of the rich as well as the poor participated.

By the end of the seventeenth century, the New England Puritans had developed a compelling story about their own history in the New World. The founders had been extraordinarily godly men and women, and in an heroic effort to establish a purer form of religion, pious families had passed "over the vast ocean into this vast and howling wilderness." Although the children and grandchildren of the first generation sometimes questioned their ability to please the Lord, they recognized the mission to the New World had been a success: they were "as Prosperous as ever, there is Peace & Plenty, & the Country flourisheth."

THE PLANTERS' WORLD

An entirely different regional society developed in England's Chesapeake colonies. This contrast with New England seems puzzling. After all, the two areas were founded at roughly the same time by men and women from the same mother country. In both regions, settlers spoke English, accepted Protestantism, and gave allegiance to one crown. And yet, to cite an obvious example, seventeenth-century Virginia looked nothing like Massachusetts Bay. In an effort to explain the difference, colonial historians have studied environmental conditions, labor systems, and agrarian economies. The most important reason for the distinctiveness of these early southern plantation societies, however, turned out to be the Chesapeake's death rate, a frighteningly high mortality that tore at the very fabric of traditional family life.

Family Life in a Perilous Environment

Unlike New England's settlers, the men and women who emigrated to the Chesapeake region did not move in family units. They traveled to the New World as young unmarried servants, youths cut off from the security of traditional kin relations. Although these immigrants came from a cross section of English society, most had been poor to middling farmers in the mother country. It is now estimated that 70 to 85 percent of the white colonists who went to Virginia and Maryland during the seventeenth century were not free; that is, they owed four or five years' labor in exchange for the cost of passage to America. If the servant was under fifteen, he or she had to serve a full seven years. The overwhelming majority of these laborers were males between the ages of eighteen and twenty-two. In fact, before 1640, the ratio of males to females stood at 6 to 1. This figure dropped to about $2\frac{1}{2}$ to 1 by the end of the century, but the sexual balance in the Chesapeake was never as favorable as it had been in early Massachusetts.

Most immigrants to the Chesapeake region died soon after arriving. It is difficult to ascertain the exact cause of death in most cases, but malaria and other diseases took a frightful toll. Recent studies also indicate that drinking water contaminated with salt killed many colonists living in low-lying areas. Throughout the entire seventeenth century, high mortality rates had a profound effect on this society. Life expectancy for Chesapeake males was about forty-three, some ten to twenty years less than for men born in New England! For women, life was even shorter. A full 25 percent of all children died in infancy; another 25 percent did not see their twentieth birthdays. The survivors were often weak or ill, unable to perform hard physical labor.

These demographic conditions retarded normal population increase. Young women who might have become wives and mothers could not do so until they had completed their terms of servitude. They thus lost several reproductive years, and in a society in which so many children died in infancy, late marriage greatly restricted family size. Moreover, because of the unbalanced sex ratio, many adult males simply could not find wives. Migration not only cut them off from their English families, but also deprived them of an opportunity to form new ones. Without a constant flow of immigrants, the population of Virginia and Maryland would have actually declined.

High mortality compressed the family life cycle into a few short years. One partner in a marriage usually died within seven years. Only one in three

Seventeenth-century Puritan carvers transformed the production of gravestones into high art.

Chesapeake marriages survived as long as a decade. Not only did children not meet grandparents, they often did not even know their own parents. Widows and widowers quickly remarried, bringing children by former unions into their new homes, and it was not uncommon for a child to grow up with persons to whom he or she bore no blood relation. The psychological effects of such experiences on Chesapeake settlers cannot be measured. People probably learned to cope with a high degree of personal insecurity. However they adjusted, it is clear family life in this region was vastly more impermanent than it was in the New England colonies during the same period.

Women were obviously in great demand in the early southern colonies. Some historians have argued that scarcity heightened the woman's bargaining power in the marriage market. If she was an immigrant, she did not have to worry about obtaining parental consent. She was on her own in the New World and free to select whomever she pleased. If a woman lacked beauty or strength, if she were a person of low moral standards, she could still be confident of finding an American husband. Such negotiations may have provided Chesapeake women with a means of improving their social status. Nevertheless, liberation from some traditional restraints on seventeenth-century women must not be exaggerated. As servants, women were vulnerable to sexual exploitation by their masters. Moreover, in this unhealthy environment, childbearing was extremely dangerous, and women in the Chesapeake usually died twenty years earlier than their New England counterparts.

Rank and Status in Plantation Society

Colonists who managed somehow to survive grew tobacco—as much tobacco as they possibly could. This crop became the Chesapeake staple, and since it was relatively easy to cultivate, anyone with a few acres of cleared land could produce leaves for export. Cultivation of tobacco did not, however, produce a society roughly equal in wealth and status. To the contrary, tobacco generated inequality. Some planters amassed large fortunes; others barely subsisted. Labor made the difference, for to succeed in this staple economy, one had to control the labor of other men and women. More workers in the fields meant larger harvests, and, of course, larger profits. Since free persons showed no interest in growing another man's tobacco, not even for wages, wealthy planters relied on white laborers who were not free, as well as on slaves. The social structure that developed in the seventeenth-century Chesapeake reflected a wild, often unscrupulous scramble to bring men and women of three races—black, white, and Indian—into various degrees of dependence.

Great planters dominated Chesapeake society. The group was small, only a trifling portion of the population of Virginia and Maryland. During the early decades of the seventeenth century, the composition of Chesapeake gentry was continually in flux. Some gentlemen died before they could establish a secure claim to high social status; others returned to England, thankful to have survived. Not until the 1650s did the family names of those who would become famous eighteenth-century gentry appear in the records. The first gentlemen were not—as genealogists sometimes discover to their dismay—dashing Cavaliers who had fought in the English civil war for King Charles I. Rather, such Chesapeake gentry as the Burwells, Byrds, Carters, and Masons consisted originally of the younger sons of English merchants and artisans.

These ambitious men arrived in America with capital. They invested immediately in laborers, and one way or another, they obtained huge tracts of the best tobacco-growing land. The members of this gentry were not technically aristocrats, for they did not possess titles that could be passed from generation to generation. They gave themselves military titles, sat as justices of the peace on the county courts, and directed local (Anglican) church affairs as members of the vestry. Over time, these gentry families intermarried so frequently that they created a vast network of cousins. During the eighteenth century, it was not uncommon to find a half dozen men with the same surname sitting simultaneously in the Virginia House of Burgesses.

Freemen formed the largest class in this society. Their origins were strikingly different from those of the gentry, or for that matter, from those of New England's yeomen farmers. Chesapeake freemen traveled to the New World as indentured servants and, by sheer good fortune, managed to remain alive to the end of their contracts. If they had dreamed of becoming great planters, they were gravely disappointed. Most seventeenth-century freemen lived on the edge of poverty. Some freemen, of course, did better in America than they would have in contemporary England, but in both Virginia and Maryland, historians have found a sharp economic division separating the gentry from the rest of white society.

Below the freemen came indentured servants. Membership in this group was not demeaning; after all, servitude was a temporary status. But servitude in the Chesapeake colonies was not the benign institution it was in New England. Great planters purchased servants to grow tobacco. No one worried whether these laborers received decent food and clothes, much less whether they acquired trade skills. These young people, thousands of them, cut off from family ties, sick often to the point of death, unable to obtain normal sexual release, regarded their servitude as a form of "slavery." Not surprisingly, the gentry worried

that unhappy servants and impoverished freemen, what the planters called the "giddy multitude," would rebel at the slightest provocation, a fear that turned out to be fully justified.

The character of social mobility—and this observation applies only to the whites—changed considerably during the seventeenth century. Until the 1680s, it was relatively easy for a newcomer who possessed capital to become a member of the planter elite. No one paid much attention to the reputation or social standing of one's English family.

Sometime after the 1680s, however—the precise date is impossible to establish—a dramatic demographic shift occurred. Although infant mortality remained high, life expectancy rates for those who survived childhood in the Chesapeake improved significantly, and for the first time in the history of Virginia and Maryland, important leadership positions went to men who had actually been born in America. This transition has been described by one political historian as the "emergence of a creole majority," in other words, as the rise of an indigenous ruling elite. Before this time, immigrant leaders had died without heirs or had returned as quickly as possible to England. The members of the new creole class took a greater interest in local government. Their activities helped give the Tobacco Colonies the kind of political and cultural stability that had eluded earlier generations of planter adventurers. Not surprisingly, it was during this period of demographic transition that creole leaders founded the College of William and Mary (1693) and authorized the construction of an impressive new capital called Williamsburg. These were changes that, in the words of one creole Virginian, provided the colony "with a sense of permanence and legitimacy . . . it had never before possessed."

The key to success in this creole society was ownership of slaves. Those planters who held more blacks could grow more tobacco, and thus could acquire fresh capital needed to purchase additional laborers. Over time, the rich not only became richer, they also formed a distinct ruling elite that newcomers found increasingly difficult to enter.

Opportunities for advancement also decreased for the region's freemen. Studies of mid-seventeenth-century Maryland reveal that some servants managed to become moderately prosperous farmers and small officeholders. But as the gentry consolidated its hold on political and economic institutions, ordinary people discovered it was much harder to rise in Chesapeake society. Those men and women with more ambitious dreams headed for Pennsylvania, North Carolina, or western Virginia.

Social institutions that figured importantly in the daily experience of New Englanders were either weak or nonexistent in the Chesapeake colonies. In part, this sluggish development resulted from the continuation of high infant mortality rates. There was little incentive to build elementary schools, for example, if half the children would die before reaching adulthood. The great planters sent their sons to England or Scotland for their education, and even after the founding of the College of William and Mary in Virginia in 1693, the gentry continued to patronize English schools. As a result of this practice, higher education in the South languished for much of the colonial period.

Tobacco influenced the spread of other institutions in this region. Planters were scattered along the rivers, often separated from their nearest neighbors by miles of poor roads. Since the major tobacco growers traded directly with English merchants, they had no need for towns. Whatever items they required were either made on the plantation or imported from Europe. Other than the centers of colonial government, Jamestown (and later Williamsburg) and St. Mary's (and later Annapolis), there were no villages capable of sustaining a rich community life before the late eighteenth century. Seventeenth-century Virginia did not even possess a printing press. In fact, Governor Sir William Berkeley bragged in 1671, "there are no free schools, nor printing in Virginia, for learning has brought disobedience, and heresy . . . into the world, and printing had divulged them . . . God keep us from both!"

THE AFRICAN AMERICAN EXPERIENCE

Many people who landed in the colonies had no desire to come to the New World. They were Africans taken as slaves to cultivate rice, sugar, and tobacco. As the Native Americans were exterminated and the supply of white indentured servants dried up, European planters demanded even more African laborers.

Roots of Slavery

A great deal is known about the transfer of African peoples across the Atlantic. During the entire history of this human commerce, between the sixteenth and nineteenth centuries, slave traders carried almost eleven million blacks to the Americas. Most of these men and women were sold in Brazil or in the Caribbean. Only a small number of Africans ever reached British North America, and of this group, the majority arrived after 1700. Because slaves performed hard physical labor, planters preferred purchasing young males. In many early slave communities, men outnumbered women by a ratio of two to one.

English colonists did not hesitate to enslave black people, or for that matter, Native Americans. While the institution of slavery had long before died out in the mother country, New World settlers quickly discovered how well this particular labor system operated in the Spanish and Portuguese colonies. The decision to bring African slaves to the colonies, therefore, was based primarily on economic considerations.

English masters, however, seldom justified the practice purely in terms of planter profits. Indeed, they adopted a quite different pattern of rhetoric. English writers associated blacks in Africa with heathen religion, barbarous behavior, sexual promiscuity—in fact, with evil itself. From such a racist perspective, the enslavement of Africans seemed unobjectionable. The planters maintained that if black slaves converted to Christianity, shedding their supposedly savage ways, they would benefit from their loss of freedom.

Africans first landed in Virginia in 1619. For the next fifty years, the status of the colony's black people remained unclear. English settlers classified some black laborers as slaves for life, as chattel to be bought and sold at the master's will. But other Africans became servants, presumably for stated periods of time, and it was even possible for a few blacks to purchase their freedom. Several seventeenth-century Africans became successful Virginia planters (see pp. 76–77).

One reason Virginia lawmakers tolerated such confusion was that the black population remained very small. By 1660, less than 1,500

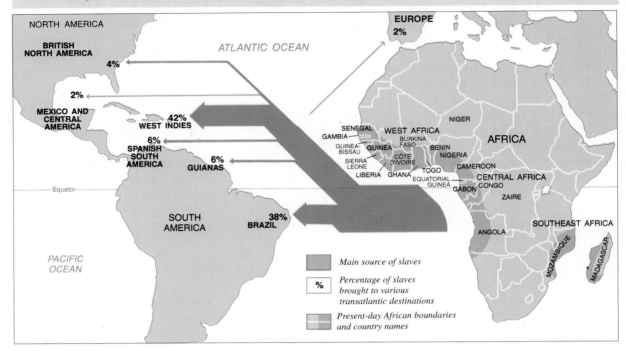

The African Slave Trade

Between 1619 and 1760, about half a million African captives were brought to the thirteen mainland English colonies, far fewer than were taken to other parts of the Americas.

people of African origin lived in the entire colony (compared to a white population of approximately 26,000), and it hardly seemed necessary for the legislature to draw up an elaborate slave code to control so few men and women. If the planters could have obtained more black laborers, they certainly would have done so. There is no evidence that the great planters preferred white indentured servants to black slaves. The problem was supply. During this period, slave traders sold their cargoes on Barbados or the other sugar islands of the West Indies, where they fetched higher prices than Virginians could afford. In fact, before 1680, most blacks who reached England's colonies on the North American mainland came from Barbados or through New Netherland rather than directly from Africa.

By the end of the seventeenth century, the legal status of Virginia's black people was no longer in doubt. They were slaves for life, and so were their children after them. This transformation reflected changes in the supply of Africans to British North America. After 1672, the Royal African Company was chartered to meet the colonial

planters' demands for black laborers. Historian K.G. Davies terms this organization "the strongest and most effective of all European companies formed exclusively for the African trade." Between 1695 and 1709, over eleven thousand Africans were sold in Virginia alone; many others went to Maryland and the Carolinas. Although American merchants—most of them based in Rhode Island—entered the trade during the eighteenth century, the British continued to supply the bulk of the slaves to the mainland market for the entire colonial period.

The expanding black population apparently frightened white colonists, for as the number of Africans increased, lawmakers drew up ever stricter slave codes. It was during this period that racism, always a latent element in New World societies, was fully revealed. By 1700, slavery was unequivocally based on the color of a person's skin. Blacks fell into this status simply because they were black. A vicious pattern of discrimination had been set in motion. Even conversion to Christianity did not free the African from bondage. The white planter could deal with his

This watercolor, Slave Deck of the Albanoz (1846), by naval officer Lieutenant Godfrey Meynell, shows slaves packed with cargo in the hold of a ship after being taken captive in West Africa. Because it was expected that many slaves would die en route, ship captains sometimes attempted to increase their profits by crowding even more slaves into the hold than regulations allowed.

black property as he alone saw fit, and one revolting Virginia statute excused a master who had killed a slave, on the grounds that no rational person would purposely "destroy his own estate." Children born to a slave woman became slaves regardless of the father's race. Unlike the Spanish colonies, where persons of lighter color enjoyed greater privileges in society, the English colonies tolerated no mixing of the races. Mulattoes and pure Africans received the same treatment.

African American Cultures in English America

The slave experience varied substantially from colony to colony. The daily life of a black person in South Carolina, for example, was quite different from that of an African American who happened to live in Pennsylvania or Massachusetts Bay. The size and density of the slave population determined in large measure how successfully blacks could maintain a separate cultural identity.

In the lowlands of South Carolina during the eighteenth century, 60 percent of the population was black. These men and women were placed on large, isolated rice plantations, and their contact with whites was limited. In these areas blacks developed creole languages, which mixed the basic vocabulary of English with words borrowed from various African tongues. Until the end of the nineteenth century, one creole language, Gullah, was spoken on some of the Sea Islands along the Georgia-South Carolina coast. Slaves on these large rice plantations were also able to establish elaborate and enduring kinship networks that may have helped reduce the more dehumanizing aspects of bondage.

In the New England and Middle Colonies, and even in Virginia, African Americans made up a smaller percentage of the population: 40 percent in Virginia, 8 percent in Pennsylvania, and 3 percent in Massachusetts. In such environments, contact between blacks and whites was more frequent than in South Carolina and Georgia. These population patterns had a profound effect on

Anthony Johnson: Black Patriarch of Pungoteague Creek

During the first decades of settlement, a larger proportion of Virginia's black population achieved freedom than at any time until the Civil War ended slavery. Despite considerable obstacles, these free black men and women—their number in these early years was quite small—formed families, acquired property, earned community respect, and helped establish a distinctive African American culture. One member of this group was Anthony Johnson, an immigrant who rose from slavery to prominence on Virginia's Eastern Shore.

Johnson came to Virginia aboard the English vessel *James* in 1621, just two years after the first blacks had arrived in the colony. As a slave known simply as "Antonio a Negro," Johnson found life a constant struggle for survival. Working in the tobacco fields of the Bennett plantation located on the south side of the James River, he endured long hours, poor rations, fearful epidemics, and haunting loneliness, which, more often than not, brought an early death to slaves as well as indentured servants. Johnson, however, was a tough, intelligent, and lucky man.

Exactly how Johnson achieved freedom is not known. Early records reveal that while still living at the Bennett plantation, he took a wife "Mary a

Africans were sometimes given the opportunity to buy their freedom through labor. This arrangement, called self-purchase, may have been the means by which Anthony and Mary Johnson escaped bondage and became property owners.

Negro woman." Anthony was fortunate to find her. Because of an exceedingly unequal sex ratio in early Virginia, few males—regardless of color—had an opportunity to form families. Anthony and Mary reared at least four children. Even more remarkable, in a society in which most unions were broken by death within a decade, their marriage lasted over forty years.

Sometime during the 1630s, Anthony and Mary gained their freedom, perhaps with the help of someone named Johnson. Their bondage probably ended through self-purchase, an arrangement that allowed enterprising slaves to buy their liberty through labor. Later, again

under unknown circumstances, the Johnsons migrated to Northampton County on the Eastern Shore of Virginia. During the 1640s, they acquired an estate of 250 acres on Pungoteague Creek, where they raised cattle, horses, and hogs and cultivated tobacco. To work these holdings, Anthony Johnson apparently relied on the labor of indentured servants and at least one black slave named Casor.

As the "patriarch of Pungoteague Creek," Johnson participated as fully as most whites in Northampton society. He traded with wealthy white landowners and apparently shared their assumptions about the sanctity of property and the

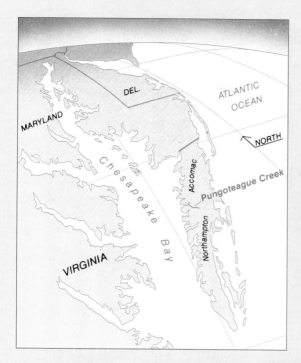

legitimacy of slavery. When two white neighbors attempted to steal Casor, Johnson hauled them into court and forced them to return his laborer. On another occasion, Johnson appealed to the court for tax relief after an "unfortunate fire" destroyed much of his plantation.

The Johnsons also maintained close ties with other free blacks, such as Anthony Payne and Emmanuel Driggus who had similarly attained freedom and prosperity through their own efforts. Johnson's strongest links were with his family. Although his children lived in separate homes after reaching adulthood, his two sons laid out holdings in the 1650s adjacent to their father's plantation, and in times of crisis, parents and children participated in family conferences. These close bonds persisted even after the Johnson clan moved to Somerset County, Maryland, in the 1660s, and Anthony Johnson's subsequent

death. When he purchased land in Somerset in 1677, Johnson's grandson, a third-generation free black colonist, named his plantation "Angola," perhaps in memory of his grandfather's African homeland.

Interpreting Johnson's remarkable life has proved surprisingly difficult. An earlier generation of historians considered Johnson a curiosity, a sort of black Englishman who did not fit neatly into familiar racial categories. Even some recent writers, concerned about tracing the roots of slavery and prejudice in the United States, have paid scant attention to Johnson and the other free blacks on the Eastern Shore.

Most historians would now agree that Johnson's life illustrated the complexity of race relations in early Virginia. His surprising progression from slave to slaveholder and his easy participation in the world of the white gentry and in a network of black

friendships and family ties demonstrated that relations among blacks and whites conformed to no single pattern in the fluid society of mid-seventeenth-century Virginia. Rather, they took a variety of forms—conflict, cooperation, exploitation, accommodation—depending on the goals, status, experience, and environment of the participants. Race was only one—and by no means the decisive—factor shaping relations among colonists.

The opportunities that had been available to Anthony Johnson and other Virginia blacks, however, disappeared during the last quarter of the seventeenth century. A growing reliance on slave labor rather than white indentured servitude brought about a rapid increase in the black population of Virginia and an accompanying curtailment of civil liberties on racial grounds. The rise of a group of great planters who dominated the colonial economy soon drove free black farmers into poverty. No longer did they enjoy the security, as had one black farmer in the 1640s, of having "myne owne ground and I will work when I please and play when I please." It is not surprising that after 1706, a time when Virginia's experiment in a genuinely multiracial free society was all but over, the Johnson family disappeared from the colonial records. When modern Americans discuss the history of race relations in the United States, they might consider the factors that allowed some of the first blacks that settled in America to achieve economic and social success.

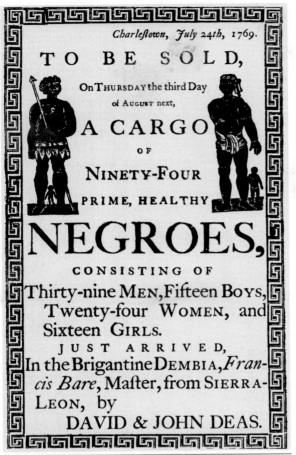

This notice publicizes a slave auction to be held at the Charles Town wharf (1769).

now exceedingly miserable, and thought myself worse off than any . . . of my companions; for they could talk to each other [in English], but I had no person to speak to that I could understand. In this state I was constantly grieving and pining, and wishing for death."

Newly arrived men and women from Africa were far more likely to run away, assault their masters, and organize rebellion than were the creole slaves. The people described in colonial newspaper advertisements as "New Negroes" desperately tried to regain control over their lives. In 1770—just to cite one moving example—two young Africans, both recently sold in Virginia, "went off with several others, being persuaded that they could find their way back to their own Country."

Despite such wrenching experiences, black slaves creatively preserved elements of an African heritage. The process of establishing African American traditions involved an imaginative reshaping of African and European customs into something that was neither African nor European. It was African American. The slaves accepted Christianity, but they did so on their own terms—terms their masters seldom fully understood. Blacks transformed Christianity into an expression of religious feeling in which an African element remained vibrant. In music and folk art, they gave voice to a cultural identity that even the most degrading conditions could not eradicate.

A major turning point in the history of African American people occurred during the early decades of the eighteenth century. At this time, blacks living in England's mainland colonies began to reproduce successfully. The number of live births exceeded deaths, and from that date, the expansion of the African American population owed more to natural increase than to the importation of new slaves. Even though thousands of new Africans arrived each year, the creole population was always much larger than that of the immigrant blacks. This demographic shift did not take place in the Caribbean or South American colonies until a much later date. Historians believe North American blacks enjoyed a healthier climate and better diet than other New World slaves.

Although mainland blacks lived longer than the blacks of Jamaica or Barbados, they were,

northern and Chesapeake blacks, for while they escaped the physical drudgery of rice cultivation, they found the preservation of an independent African identity difficult. In northern cities, slaves working as domestics and living in the houses of their masters saw other blacks, but had little opportunity to develop creole languages or reaffirm a common African past.

In eighteenth-century Virginia, native-born or creole blacks, people who had learned to cope with whites on a daily basis, looked with contempt on slaves who had just arrived from Africa. These "outlandish" Negroes, as they were called, were forced by blacks as well as whites to accept elements of English culture. It was especially important for newcomers to speak English. Consider, for example, the pain of young Olaudah Equiano, an African sold in Virginia in 1757. This twelve-year-old slave declared, "I was

Old Plantation, *a watercolor by an unknown artist (about 1800), shows that some African identity and customs survived plantation life. The man and women in the center dance (possibly to celebrate a wedding) to the music of drum and banjo. Instruments, turbans, and scarves have African elements.*

after all, still slaves. They protested their debasement in many ways, some in individual acts of violence, others in organized revolt. The most serious slave rebellion of the colonial period was the Stono Uprising, which took place in September 1739. One hundred and fifty South Carolina blacks rose up, and seizing guns and ammunition, murdered several white planters. "With Colours displayed, and two Drums beating," they marched toward Spanish Florida where they had been promised freedom. The local militia soon overtook the rebellious slaves and killed most of them. Although the uprising was short-lived, such incidents helped persuade whites everywhere that their own blacks might secretly be planning bloody revolt. Fear bred paranoia. When an unstable white servant woman in New York City announced in 1741 that blacks intended to burn the town, frightened authorities executed 32 suspected arsonists and dispatched 175 others to the West Indies. While the level of inter-racial violence in colonial society was quite low, everyone recognized that the blacks—in the words of one Virginia governor—longed "to Shake off the fetters of Slavery."

BLUEPRINT FOR EMPIRE

In 1661, John Norton, a respected Congregational minister, delivered a remarkable sermon before the assembled legislators of Massachusetts Bay. "It is not a Gospel-spirit to be against Kings," Norton lectured, "'tis neither Gospel nor English Spirit for any of us to be against the Government by Kings, Lords and Commons." It was as if after some thirty years of virtual freedom, the American Puritans had to be reminded of the political ties that bound them to England. As Norton sensed, however, the times were changing. The newly restored Stuart monarchy was beginning to establish rules for the entire empire, and the planters of the Chesapeake as well as the Puritans of New England would soon discover they were not as independent as they had imagined.

Until the middle of the seventeenth century, English political leaders largely ignored the American colonists. Private companies and aristocratic proprietors had created these societies, some for profit, others for religious sanctuary, but in no case did the Crown provide financial or military assistance. After the Restoration of Charles II in 1660, intervention replaced indifference. Englishmen of various sorts—courtiers, merchants, parliamentarians—concluded that the colonists should be brought more tightly under the control of the mother country. The regulatory policies that evolved during this period formed a framework for an empire that survived with only minor adjustment until 1765.

A New Commercial System

The famous eighteenth-century Scottish economist, Adam Smith, coined the term *mercantilist system* to describe Great Britain's commercial regulations, and ever since, his phrase has appeared in history books. Smith's term, however, is misleading. It suggests that English policymakers during the reign of Charles II had developed a well-integrated set of ideas about the nature of international commerce and a carefully planned set of mercantilist government policies to implement them.

They did nothing of the sort. Administrators responded to particular problems, usually on an individual basis. In 1668, Charles informed his sister, "The thing which is nearest the heart of the nation is trade and all that belongs to it." National interest alone, however, did not shape public policy. Instead, the needs of several powerful interest groups led to the rise of English commercial regulation.

Each group looked to colonial commerce to solve a different problem. For his part, the king wanted money. For their part, English merchants were eager to exclude Dutch rivals from lucrative American markets and needed government assistance to compete successfully with the Dutch, even in Virginia or Massachusetts Bay. From the perspective of the landed gentry who sat in

Parliament, England needed a stronger navy and that in turn meant expansion of the domestic shipbuilding industry. And almost everyone agreed England should establish a more favorable balance of trade; that is, increase exports, decrease imports, and grow richer at the expense of other European states. None of these ideas was particularly innovative, but taken together they provided a blueprint for England's first empire.

Navigation Acts Transform Colonial Society

After some legislation in that direction during the Commonwealth, Parliament passed a Navigation Act in 1660. This statute was the most important piece of imperial legislation drafted before the American Revolution. Colonists from New

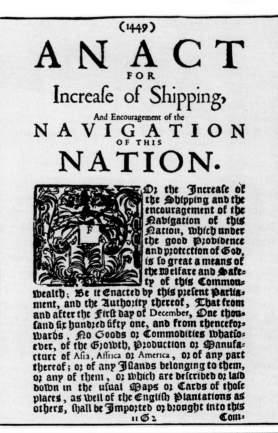

(1449)

AN ACT
FOR
Increafe of Shipping,
And Encouragement of the
NAVIGATION
OF THIS
NATION.

In the 1650s and 1660s Parliament enacted a series of measures known collectively as the Navigation Acts, which were designed to protect English shipping, enrich the treasury, and exploit colonial economies. Shown here is the title page of the Navigation Act of 1651.

Hampshire to Georgia paid close attention to the details of this statute, which stated (1) that no ship could trade in the colonies unless it had been constructed in either England or America and carried a crew that was at least 75 percent English (for these purposes colonists counted as Englishmen), and (2) that certain *enumerated* goods of great value that were not produced in England—tobacco, sugar, cotton, indigo, dye-woods, ginger—could be transported from the colonies *only* to an English or another colonial port. In 1704, Parliament added rice and molasses to the enumerated list; in 1705, rosins, tars, and turpentines needed for shipbuilding were included.

The act of 1660 was masterfully conceived. It encouraged the development of domestic shipbuilding and prohibited European rivals from obtaining enumerated goods anywhere except in England. Since the Americans had to pay import duties in England (for this purpose colonists did *not* count as Englishmen) on such items as sugar and tobacco, the legislation also provided the Crown with another source of income.

In 1663, Parliament supplemented this legislation with a second Navigation Act known as the *Staple Act,* which stated that, with a few noted exceptions, nothing could be imported into America unless it had first been transshipped through the mother country, a process that greatly added to the price ultimately paid by colonial consumers.

The Navigation Acts attempted to eliminate the Dutch, against whom the English fought three wars in this period (1652–1654, 1664–1667, and 1672–1674), as the middlemen of American commerce. Just as English merchants were celebrating their victory, however, an unanticipated rival appeared on the scene. New England merchantmen sailed out of Boston, Salem, and Newport to become formidable world competitors in maritime commerce.

During the 1660s, the colonists showed little enthusiasm for the new imperial system. Reaction to these regulations varied from region to region. Virginians bitterly protested the Navigation Acts. The collection of English customs on tobacco greatly reduced the colonial planters' profits. Moreover, the exclusion of the Dutch from the trade meant that growers often had to sell their crops at artificially low prices. The Navigation Acts hit the small planters especially hard, for

they were least able to absorb increased production costs. Even though the governor of Virginia lobbied on the planters' behalf, the Crown turned a deaf ear. By 1670, import duties on tobacco accounted for almost £100,000, a sum the king could scarcely do without.

At first, New Englanders simply ignored the commercial regulations. Indeed, one Massachusetts merchant reported in 1664 that Boston entertained "near one hundred sail of ships, this year, of ours and strangers." The strangers, of course, were the Dutch, who had no intention of obeying the Navigation Acts so long as they could reach colonial ports. Some New England merchants found clever ways to circumvent the Navigation Acts. These crafty traders picked up cargoes of enumerated goods such as sugar or tobacco, sailed to another colonial port (thereby technically fulfilling the letter of the law), and then made directly for Holland or France. Along the way they paid no customs.

To plug this loophole, Parliament passed the Navigation Act of 1673. This statute established a *plantation duty,* a sum of money equal to normal English customs duties to be collected on enumerated products at the various colonial ports. New Englanders could now sail wherever they pleased within the empire, but they could not escape paying customs. Parliament also extended the jurisdiction of the London Customs Commissioners to America. And in 1675, as part of this new imperial firmness, the Privy Council formed a powerful subcommittee, the Lords of Trade, whose members monitored colonial affairs.

Despite these legal reforms, serious obstacles impeded the execution of imperial policy. The customs service did not have enough effective agents in American ports to enforce the Navigation Acts fully, and some men sent from the mother country did more harm than good. Edward Randolph, head of the imperial customs service in New England, was such a person. He was dispatched to Boston in 1676 to gather information about the conduct of colonial trade. New England Puritans did not look kindly on intervention in their affairs, but even considering their irritability, Randolph seems to have been extraordinarily inept. His behavior was so obnoxious, his reports about New Englanders so condescending, that he became the most hated man in late seventeenth-century Massachusetts.

Parliament passed the last major piece of imperial legislation in 1696. Among other things, the statute tightened enforcement procedures, putting pressure specifically on the colonial governors to keep England's competitors out of American ports. The act of 1696 also expanded the American customs service, and for the first time set up vice-admiralty courts in the colonies. This decision eventually rankled the colonists. Established to settle disputes that occured at sea, vice-admiralty courts required neither juries nor oral cross-examination, both traditional elements of the common law. But they were effective and sometimes even popular for resolving maritime questions quickly enough to send the ships to sea again with little delay. The year 1696 witnessed one other significant change in the imperial system. William III replaced the ineffective Lords of Trade with a body of policy advisers that came to be known as the Board of Trade. This group was expected to monitor colonial affairs closely and to provide government officials with the best available advice on commercial and other problems. For several decades at least, it energetically carried out its responsibilities.

The members of Parliament believed these reforms would belatedly compel the colonists to accept the Navigation Acts, and in large measure they were correct. By 1700, American goods transshipped through the mother country accounted for a quarter of *all* English exports, an indication the colonists found it profitable to obey the commercial regulations. In fact, during the eighteenth century, smuggling from Europe to America dried up almost completely.

The Navigation Acts of the seventeenth century also shaped the colonists' material culture. Over time, Americans grew increasingly accustomed to purchasing English goods; they established close ties with specific merchant houses in London, Bristol, or Glasgow. It is not surprising, therefore, that by the mid-eighteenth century the colonists preferred the manufactures of the mother country over those of England's commercial rivals. In other words, the Navigation Acts influenced the development of consumer habits throughout the empire, and it is not an exaggeration to suggest that this regulatory system was in large part responsible for the anglicization of eighteenth-century American culture (see Chapter 4).

POLITICAL UNREST, 1676–1691: COLONIAL GENTRY IN REVOLT

The Navigation Acts created an illusion of unity. English administrators superimposed a system of commercial regulation on a number of different, often unstable American colonies and called it an empire. But these statutes did not remove longstanding differences. Within each society, men and women struggled to bring order out of disorder, to establish stable ruling elites, to diffuse ethnic and racial tensions, and to cope with population pressures that imperial planners only dimly understood. During the final decades of the seventeenth century, these efforts sometimes sparked revolt.

First, the Virginians rebelled, and then a few years later, political violence swept through Maryland, New York, and Massachusetts Bay, England's most populous mainland colonies. Historians once interpreted these events as rehearsals for the American Revolution, or even for Jacksonian Democracy. They perceived these rebels as frontier democrats, rising in protest against an entrenched aristocracy.

Recent research suggests, however, that this view seriously misconstrued the character of these late seventeenth-century rebellions. These uprisings certainly did not involve confrontations between ordinary people and their rulers. Indeed, these events were not in any modern sense of the word ideological. In each colony, the local gentry split into factions, usually the "outs" versus the "ins," and each side proclaimed its political legitimacy.

Civil War in Virginia: Bacon's Rebellion

After 1660, the Virginia economy steadily declined. Returns from tobacco had not been good for some time, and the Navigation Acts reduced profits even further. Into this unhappy environment came thousands of indentured servants, people drawn to Virginia, as the governor explained, "in hope of bettering their condition in a Growing Country."

The reality bore little relation to their dreams. A hurricane destroyed one entire tobacco crop, and in 1667, Dutch warships captured the tobacco fleet just as it was about to sail for England. Indentured servants complained about lack of food and clothing. No wonder that Virginia's governor, Sir William Berkeley, despaired of ever ruling "a People where six parts of seven at least are Poor, Endebted, Discontented and Armed." In 1670, he and the House of Burgesses disfranchised all landless freemen, persons they regarded as troublemakers, but the threat of social violence remained.

Enter Nathaniel Bacon. This ambitious young man arrived in Virginia in 1674. He came from a respectable English family and set himself up immediately as a substantial planter. But he wanted more. Bacon envied the government patronage monopolized by Berkeley's cronies, a group known locally as the "Green Spring" faction. When Bacon attempted to obtain a license to engage in the fur trade, he was rebuffed. This lucrative commerce was reserved for the governor's friends. If Bacon had been willing to wait, he probably would have been accepted into the ruling clique, but as subsequent events would demonstrate, Bacon was not a man of patience.

Events beyond Bacon's control thrust him suddenly into the center of Virginia politics. In 1675, Indians reacting to white encroachment attacked several outlying plantations, killing a few colonists, and Virginians expected the governor to send an army to retaliate. Instead, early in 1676 Berkeley called for the construction of a line of defensive forts, a plan that seemed to the settlers both expensive and ineffective. Indeed, this strategy raised embarrassing questions. Was Berkeley protecting his own fur monopoly? Was he planning to reward his friends with contracts to build useless forts?

While people speculated about such matters, Bacon stepped forward. He boldly offered to lead a volunteer army against the Indians at no cost to the hard-pressed Virginia taxpayers. All he demanded was an official commission from Berkeley giving him military command, and the right to attack other Indians, not just the hostile Susquehannocks. The governor steadfastly refused. With some justification, Berkeley regarded his upstart rival as a fanatic on the subject of Indians. The governor saw no reason to exterminate peaceful tribes simply to avenge the death of a few white settlers.

What followed would have been comic had not so many people died. Bacon thundered against the governor's treachery; Berkeley labeled Bacon a traitor. Both men appealed to the populace for support. On several occasions, Bacon marched his followers to the frontier, but they either failed to find the enemy, or worse, massacred friendly Indians. At one point, Bacon burned Jamestown to the ground, forcing the governor to flee to the colony's Eastern Shore. Bacon's bumbling lieutenants chased Berkeley across Chesapeake Bay only to be captured themselves. Thereupon, the governor mounted a new campaign.

As the civil war dragged on, it became increasingly apparent that Bacon and his gentry supporters had only the vaguest notion of what they were trying to achieve. The members of the planter elite never seemed fully to appreciate that the rank-and-file soldiers, often black slaves and poor white servants, had serious, legitimate grievances against Berkeley's corrupt government, and they were demanding substantial reforms, not just a share in the governor's fur monopoly.

Although women had not been allowed to vote in colony elections, they made their political views clear enough during the rebellion. Some were apparently more violent than others. Sarah Glendon, for example, agitated so aggressively in support of Bacon that Berkeley later refused to grant her a pardon. Another outspoken rebel, Lydia Chiesman, defended her husband before Governor Berkeley, noting that the man would not have joined Bacon's forces had she not persuaded him to do so. "Therefore," Lydia Chiesman concluded, ". . . since what her husband had done, was by her meanes, and so, by consequence, she most guilty, that she might be hanged and he pardoned."

When Charles II learned of the fighting in Virginia, he dispatched a thousand regular soldiers to Jamestown. By the time they arrived, Berkeley had regained full control over the colony's government. In October 1676, Bacon died after a brief illness, and within a few months, his band of rebel followers had dispersed.

Berkeley, now an old and embittered man, was recalled to England in 1677. His successors, especially Lord Culpeper (1680–1683) and Lord Howard of Effingham (1683–1689), seemed interested primarily in enriching themselves at the expense of the Virginia planters. Their self-serving policies, coupled with the memory of near anarchy, helped heal divisions within the Virginia ruling class. For almost a century, in fact, the local gentry formed a united front against greedy royal appointees.

The Glorious Revolution in the Bay Colony

During John Winthrop's lifetime, Massachusetts settlers developed an inflated sense of their independence from the mother country. After 1660, however, it became difficult even to pretend that the Puritan colony was a separate state. Royal officials like Edward Randolph demanded full compliance with the Navigation Acts. Moreover, the growth of commerce attracted new merchants to the Bay Colony, men who were Anglicans rather than Congregationalists and who maintained close business contacts in London. These persons complained loudly of Puritan intolerance. The Anglican faction was never large, but its presence, coupled with Randolph's unceasing demands, divided Bay leaders. A few Puritan ministers and magistrates regarded compromise with England as treason, a breaking of the Lord's covenant. Other spokesmen, recognizing the changing political realities within the empire, urged a more moderate course.

In 1675, in the midst of this ongoing political crisis, the Indians dealt the New Englanders a terrible setback. Metacomet, a Wampanoag chief the whites called King Philip, declared war against the colonists. The powerful Narragansetts, whose lands the settlers had long coveted, joined Metacomet, and in little more than a year of fighting, the Indians destroyed scores of frontier villages, killed hundreds of colonists, and disrupted the entire regional economy. More than one thousand Indians and New Englanders died in the conflict. The war left the people of Massachusetts deeply in debt and more than ever uncertain of their future. As in other parts of colonial America, the defeated Indians were forced off their lands, compelled by events to become either refugees or economically marginal figures in white society.

In 1684, the debate over the Bay Colony's relation to the mother country ended abruptly. The Court of Chancery, sitting in London and acting on a petition from the king, annulled the charter of the Massachusetts Bay Company. In one stroke of a pen, the patent that Winthrop had so lovingly carried to America in 1630, the founda-

Metacomet, the Wampanoag chief, also known as King Philip, led Native Americans in a major war designed to remove the Europeans from New England.

tion for a "city on a hill," was gone. The decision forced the most stubborn Puritans to recognize they were part of an empire run by people who did not share their particular religious vision.

James II, a monarch who disliked representative institutions—after all, Parliament, a representative assembly, had executed his father, Charles I— decided to restructure the government of the entire region in the Dominion of New England. In various stages from 1686 to 1689, the Dominion incorporated Massachusetts, Connecticut, Rhode Island, Plymouth, New York, New Jersey, and New Hampshire under a single appointed royal governor. For this demanding position, James selected Sir Edmund Andros (pronounced Andrews), a military veteran of tyrannical temperament. Andros arrived in Boston in 1686, and within a matter of months he had alienated every-

William II and Mary II, joint monarchs of England after the Glorious Revolution of 1688. Mary ascended the throne when her father, James II, was deposed. Her husband William ruled Holland before ascending the English throne.

one: Puritans, moderates, and even Anglican merchants. Not only did Andros abolish elective assemblies, but he also enforced the Navigation Acts with such rigor that he brought about commercial depression. Andros declared normal town meetings illegal, collected taxes the people never approved, and packed the courts with strangers who detested the local population. Eighteenth-century historian and governor Thomas Hutchinson compared Andros unfavorably with the Roman tyrant Nero.

Early in 1689, news of the Glorious Revolution reached Boston. The previous fall, the ruling class of England had deposed James II, an admitted Catholic, and placed his daughter Mary and her husband, William of Orange, on the throne as joint monarchs (see the chart of the Stuart monarchs on p. 33). As part of the settlement, William and Mary accepted a Bill of Rights, a document stipulating the constitutional rights of all Englishmen. Almost immediately the Bay Colonists overthrew the hated Andros regime. The New England version of the Glorious Revolution

(April 18, 1689) was so popular that no one came to the governor's defense. Andros was jailed without a single shot having been fired. According to Cotton Mather, a leading Congregational minister, the colonists were united by the "most *Unanimous Resolution* perhaps that was ever known to have Inspir'd any people."

However united as they may have been, the Bay Colonists could not take the Crown's support for granted. William III could have declared the New Englanders rebels and summarily reinstated Andros. But thanks largely to the tireless efforts of Increase Mather, Cotton's father, who pleaded the colonists' case in London, William abandoned the Dominion of New England, and in 1691, Massachusetts received a new royal charter. This document differed substantially from the company patent of 1629. The freemen no longer selected their governor. The choice now belonged to the king. Membership in the General Court was determined by annual election, and these representatives in turn chose the men who sat in the council or upper house, subject always to the governor's veto. Moreover, the franchise, restricted here as in other colonies to adult males, was determined on the basis of personal property rather than church membership, a change that brought Massachusetts into conformity with general English practice. On the local level, town government remained much as it had been in Winthrop's time.

Contagion of Witchcraft

The instability of the Massachusetts government following Andros's arrest—what Reverend Samuel Willard described as "the short *Anarchy* accompanying our late Revolution"—allowed what under normal political conditions would have been an isolated, though ugly, local incident to expand into a major colonial crisis. Hysterical men and women living in Salem Village, a small unprosperous farming community, nearly overwhelmed the new rulers of Massachusetts Bay. Accusations of witchcraft were not uncommon in seventeenth-century New England. Puritans believed an individual might make a compact with the devil, but during the first decades of settlement, authorities executed only about fifteen alleged witches. Sometimes villagers simply left suspected witches alone. Never before had fears of witchcraft plunged an entire community into panic.

The terror in Salem Village began in late 1691, when several adolescent girls began to behave in strange ways. They cried out for no apparent reason; they twitched on the ground. When concerned neighbors asked what caused their suffering, the girls announced they were victims of witches, seemingly innocent persons who lived in the community. The arrest of several alleged witches did not relieve the girls' "fits," nor did prayer solve the problem. Additional accusations were made, and at least one person confessed, providing a frightening description of the devil as "a thing all over hairy, all the face hairy, and a long nose." In June 1692, a special court convened and began to send men and women to the gallows. By the end of the summer, the court had hanged nineteen people; another was pressed to death. Many more suspects awaited trial.

Then suddenly, the storm was over. Led by Increase Mather, a group of prominent Congregational ministers belatedly urged leniency and restraint. Especially troubling to the clergymen was the court's decision to accept "spectral evidence," that is, reports of dreams and visions in which the accused appeared as the devil's agent. Worried about convicting people on such dubious testimony, Mather declared, "It were better that ten suspected witches should escape, than that one innocent person should be condemned." The colonial government accepted the ministers' advice and convened a new court, which promptly acquitted, pardoned, or released the remaining suspects. After the Salem nightmare, witchcraft ceased to be a capital offense.

No one knows exactly what sparked the terror in Salem Village. The community had a history of religious discord, and during the 1680s, the people split into angry factions over the choice of a minister. Economic tensions played a part as well. Poorer, more traditional farmers accused members of prosperous, commercially oriented families of being witches. The underlying misogyny of the entire culture meant the victims were more often women than men. Whatever the ultimate social and psychological sources of this event may have been, jealousy and bitterness apparently festered to the point that adolescent girls who normally would have been disciplined were allowed to incite judicial murder. As so often happens in incidents like this one—the McCarthy hearings of the 1950s, for example—the accusers later came to their senses and apologized to the survivors for the needless suffering they had inflicted on the community. (For further discussion of the Salem witchcraft trials, see the essay "Witches and the Law," pp. 90–95.)

The Glorious Revolution in New York and Maryland

The Glorious Revolution in New York was more violent than it had been in Massachusetts Bay. Divisions within New York's ruling class ran deep and involved ethnic as well as religious differences. English newcomers and powerful Anglo-Dutch families who had recently risen to commercial prominence in New York City opposed the older Dutch elite.

Much like Nathaniel Bacon, Jacob Leisler was a man entangled in events beyond his control. Leisler, the son of a German minister, emigrated to New York in 1660, and through marriage

aligned himself with the Dutch elite. While he achieved moderate prosperity as a merchant, Leisler resented the success of the Anglo-Dutch.

When news of the Glorious Revolution reached New York City in May 1689, Leisler raised a group of militiamen and seized the local fort in the name of William and Mary. He apparently expected an outpouring of popular support, but it was not forthcoming. His rivals waited, watching while Leisler desperately attempted to legitimize his actions. Through bluff and badgering, Leisler managed to hold the colony together, especially after French forces burned Schenectady (February 1690), but he never established a secure political base.

In March 1691, a new royal governor, Henry Sloughter, reached New York. He ordered Leisler to surrender his authority, but when Sloughter refused to prove he had been sent by William rather than by the deposed James, Leisler hesitated. The pause cost Leisler his life. Sloughter declared Leisler a rebel, and in a hasty trial, a court sentenced him and his chief lieutenant, Jacob Milbourne, to be hanged "by the Neck and being Alive their bodyes be Cutt downe to Earth and Their Bowells to be taken out and they being Alive, burnt before their faces. . . ." In 1695, Parliament officially pardoned Leisler, but he not being "Alive," the decision arrived a bit late. Long after his death, political factions calling themselves Leislerians and Anti-Leislerians struggled to dominate New York government. Indeed, in no other eighteenth-century colony was the level of bitter political rivalry so high.

During the last third of the seventeenth century, the colony of Maryland stumbled from one political crisis to another. Protestants in the colony's lower house resisted Lord Baltimore's Catholic friends in the upper house or council. When news of James's overthrow reached Maryland early in 1689, pent-up antiproprietary and anti-Catholic sentiment exploded. John

Coode, a member of the assembly and an outspoken Protestant, formed a group called the Protestant Association, which in August forced Baltimore's governor, William Joseph, to resign.

Coode avoided Leisler's fatal mistakes. The Protestant Association, citing many wrongs suffered at the hands of local Catholics, petitioned the Crown to transform Maryland into a royal colony. After reviewing the case, William accepted Coode's explanation, and in 1691, the king dispatched a royal governor to Maryland. A new assembly dominated by Protestants declared Anglicanism the established religion. Catholics were excluded from public office on the grounds they might be in league with French Catholics in Canada. Lord Baltimore lost control of the colony's government, but he and his family did retain title to Maryland's undistributed lands. In 1715, the Crown restored to full proprietorship the fourth Lord Baltimore, who had been raised a member of the Church of England, and Maryland remained in the hands of the Calvert family until 1776.

COMMON EXPERIENCES, SEPARATE CULTURES

"It is no little Blessing of God," Cotton Mather announced proudly in 1700, "that we are part of the *English* nation." A half century earlier, John Winthrop would not have spoken these words, at least not with such enthusiasm. The two men were, of course, products of different political cultures. It was not so much that the character of Massachusetts society had changed. In fact, the Puritan families of 1700 were much like those of the founding generation. Rather, the difference was in England's attitude toward the colonies. Rulers living more than 3,000 miles away now made political and economic demands that Mather's contemporaries could not ignore.

The creation of a new imperial system did not, however, erase profound sectional differences. By 1700, for example, the Chesapeake colonies were more, not less, committed to the cultivation of tobacco and slave labor. Although the separate regions were being pulled slowly into England's commercial orbit, they did not have much to do with each other. The elements that sparked a powerful sense of nationalism among colonists dispersed over a huge territory would not be evident for a very long time. It would be a mistake, therefore, to anticipate the coming of the American Revolution.

Recommended Reading

The best account of the way seventeenth-century New Englanders thought about the family remains Edmund S. Morgan, *The Puritan Family* (1956). One should complement this book with one of the fine demography studies of a New England town. Philip J. Greven's *Four Generations* (1970) provides an excellent introduction to the field. Morgan has also produced a masterful analysis of development of early Chesapeake society.

His *American Slavery, American Freedom: The Ordeal of Colonial Virginia* (1975) examines the impact of an extraordinarily high death rate upon an evolving triracial plantation society. Anyone interested in the history of slavery in early America would do well to start with Winthrop D. Jordan, *White over Black: American Attitudes Toward the Negro, 1550–1812* (1968) and David B. Davis, *The Problem of Slavery in Western Culture* (1966). A complete discussion of the drafting of the Navigation Acts and England's efforts to enforce them can be found in C. M. Andrews, *The Colonial Period of American History,* vol. 4 (1938). David S. Lovejoy provides a comprehensive survey of the various late seventeenth-century colonial rebellions in *The Glorious Revolution in America* (1972). Perhaps the most readable biography of a leading figure from this period is Kenneth Silverman, *The Life and Times of Cotton Mather* (1984).

Additional Bibliography

The historical literature dealing with early New England is vast. The religious culture is explored in C. Hambrick-Stowe, *Practice of Piety* (1982), D. D. Hall, *Worlds of Wonder; Days of Judgment* (1989); and Patricia U. Bonomi, *Under the Cope of Heaven: Religion, Society, and Politics in Colonial America* (1986). There is no completely satisfactory examination of daily life in the other northern colonies, but James T. Lemon's *Best Poor Man's Country* (1972) is a valuable investigation of the rural economy of early Pennsylvania. Also see Barry Levy, *Quakers and the American Family: British Settlement in the Delaware Valley* (1988) and Joan Jensen, *Loosening the Bonds: Mid-Atlantic Farm Women, 1750–1850* (1986).

The dynamics of gender definition in colonial society is imaginatively explored in Laurel T. Ulrich, *Good Wives: Image and Reality in the Lives of Women in Northern New England 1650–1750* (1982). The best single discussion of colonial women in the Chesapeake is Lois G. Carr and Lorena S. Walsh, "The Planter's Wife: The Experience of White Women in Seventeenth-Century Maryland," *William and Mary Quarterly,* 3rd ser., 34 (1977): 542–571. Julia C. Spruill's *Women's Life and Work in the Southern Colonies* (1938) remains a valuable study.

Education and literacy are examined from different perspectives in James Axtell, *The School upon A Hill* (1974); and Kenneth Lockridge, *Literacy in Colonial New England* (1974).

Various aspects of the development of colonial society in the South are explored in three splendid essay collections: T. Tate and D. L. Ammerman, eds., *The Chesapeake in the Seventeenth Century* (1979); A. C. Land et al., eds., *Law, Society, and Politics in Early Maryland* (1977); and Lois Carr et al., eds., *Colonial Chesapeake Society* (1988). Anyone interested in the sociopolitical history of Virginia should read Bernard Bailyn, "Politics and Social Structure in Virginia," in J. M. Smith, ed., *Seventeenth-Century America* (1959). In *Colonists in Bondage* (1947), A. E. Smith discusses indentured servitude; one should also see David W. Galenson, *White Servitude in Colonial America: An Economic Analysis* (1981). In *Puritans and Adventurers* (1980), T. H. Breen speculates on the cultural values of early Virginians and compares them with those of the New Englanders. A quite different treatment of the same general theme can be found in Jack P. Greene, *Pursuits of Happiness* (1988). A pioneering study of a Virginia community is Darrett B. Rutman and Anita H. Rutman, *A Place in Time: Middlesex County, Virginia, 1650–1750* (1984).

The African American experience has been the topic of several recent interdisciplinary studies of very high quality: Philip D. Curtin, *The Atlantic Slave Trade: A Census* (1969); Patrick Manning, *Slavery and African Life* (1990); Peter Wood, *Black Majority* (1974); Allan Kulikoff, *Tobacco and Slaves: The Development of Southern Cultures in the Chesapeake, 1680–1800* (1986); Mechal Sobel, *The World They Made Together: Black and White Values in Eighteenth-Century Virginia* (1987). The creation of a free black community in early Virginia is the focus of T. H. Breen and Stephen Innes, *"Myne Owne Ground," Race and Freedom on Virginia's Eastern Shore* (1980).

Several good studies of the rebellions in specific colonies are available: W. Washburn, *The Governor and the Rebel* (1957) on Bacon's Rebellion; Thomas J. Archdeacon, *New York City, 1664–1710* (1976) on Leisler's Rebellion; and Lois Carr and D. W. Jordan, *Maryland's Revolution of Government* (1974) on Coode's Uprising. On King Philip's War, the fullest account is Douglas Leach, *Flintlock and Tomahawk* (1958). Of the many studies of witchcraft in seventeenth-century New England, some of the more imaginative are Paul Boyer and Stephen Nissenbaum, *Salem Possessed* (1974); John Demos, *Entertaining Satan: Witchcraft and the Culture of Early New England* (1982); Carol F. Karlsen, *The Devil in the Shape of a Woman: Witchcraft in Colonial New England* (1987); Richard Godbeer, *The Devil's Dominion* (1992); and Richard P. Gildrie, *The Profane, the Civil, and the Godly* (1994).

LAW & SOCIETY I

Witches and the Law

A Problem of Evidence in 1692

The events that occurred at Salem Village in 1692 still haunt modern memory. In popular American culture the incident has come to represent our worst nightmare—a community-sanctioned witch hunt that ferrets out deviants in the name of law. What seems most unsettling about the incident is the failure of allegedly good men and women to bear witness against judicial terror. The ordeal of Salem Village links a distant colonial past with the infamous McCarthy hearings of the 1950s as well as other, more recent witch hunts. The story of this deeply troubled town challenges us to confront the possibility that we, too, might allow law and authority to become instruments of injustice.

Our challenge is how best to interpret the Salem trials. It would be easy to insist that Puritan magistrates were gross hypocrites, figures who consciously manipulated the law for their own hateful purposes. But such conclusions are simplistic; they fail to place the Salem nightmare in proper historical context. The participants in this intense social drama acted on a complex set of seventeenth-century assumptions—legal, religious, and scientific—and if judges and jurors wronged innocent people, they did so by the standards of a society very different from our own.

Few New Englanders doubted the existence of witches. For centuries European communities had identified certain persons as agents of the Devil, and when the Puritans migrated to America, they carried these beliefs with them. They recognized no conflict between rational religion and the possible existence of a satanic world populated by witches. Ordinary farmers regarded unusual events—the strange death of a farm animal, for example—as evidence of witchcraft. New England's intellectual leaders sustained popular superstition in impressive scientific publications. In his *Memorable Providences, Relating to*

Witchcrafts and Possessions (1689), the Reverend Cotton Mather declared, "I am resolv'd . . . never to use . . . one grain of patience with any man that shall . . . impose upon me a Denial of Devils, or of Witches. I shall . . . count him down-right Impudent if he Assert the Non-Existence of things which we have had such palpable Convictions of."

Colonial New Englanders did more than talk and write about witches; as early as 1647 they executed several. Before the Salem outbreak, ninety-one people had been tried for witchcraft in Massachusetts and Connecticut, and eighteen of them were hanged (not burned as some historians have claimed). In addition, hundreds of people had accused neighbors of witchcraft but for many reasons—usually lack of convincing evidence—they stopped short of taking such disputes before the court. These were isolated incidents. Before 1692 fear of witches had not sparked mass hysteria.

Salem Village was different. In this instance charges of witchcraft shattered a community already deeply divided against itself. The predominantly agricultural Salem Village lay a few miles up the Ipswich Road from the bustling commercial port of Salem Town. The farmers of the Village envied their neighbors' prosperity. Even more, they resented the control that Town authorities exerted over the Village church and government. This tension found expression in numerous personal and family rivalries. In 1689, the congregation at Salem Village ordained the Reverend Samuel Parris, a troubled figure who provoked "disquietness" and "restlessness" and who fanned the factionalism that had long plagued the community.

The witchcraft crisis began suddenly in mid-January of 1692 when two girls in the Parris household experienced violent convulsions and frightening visions. A local physician examined the afflicted children but found no "natural" cause for their condition. Soon anxious families raised the possibility of witchcraft, a move which set off a storm of accusations that did not abate until October. By that time, 19 people had died and over 150 prisoners still awaited trial.

Although the witch hysteria affected everyone—men and women, rich and poor, farmers and merchants—the accusers and their targets were not evenly distributed among the population of Salem Village. Twenty of the thirty-four persons who claimed to have been bewitched were girls between the ages of eleven and twenty. Women a full generation older than the accusers were most likely to be identified as witches; over 40 percent of the accused fell into this category. Although men and women from many different backgrounds were accused, one widely shared characteristic was a history of socially unacceptable behavior. Sarah Good, for example, smoked a pipe and was known for cursing her enemies. John Aldin's accusers described him as "a bold fellow . . . who lies with Indian squaws . . . [and stands] with his hat on before the judges." Bridget Bishop ran a scandalous tavern and dressed in a particularly flashy, immodest manner. Those who testified against the supposed witches came from all classes, both genders, and every age group. Indeed, virtually the entire community was drawn into the ugly business of charge and countercharge, fear and betrayal.

No contemporary illustrations of the Salem witchcraft trials exist, but this recreation depicts the wife of Giles Corey standing in the dock as her accuser brings the charge of witchcraft against her.

New England's intellectual leaders—most of them Harvard-educated clergymen—tried to make sense out of reports coming out of Salem. Since the colonies did not yet have a newspaper, the reflections of these prominent figures significantly shaped how the entire society interpreted the frightening events of 1692. During the spring of that year, accusations of witchcraft mounted while magistrates interrogated everyone touched by the contagion.

Arriving from England in mid-May at the height of the witch hunt, the new royal governor of Massachusetts Bay, William Phips, appointed a special court of law (a court of "oyer and terminer") to try the cases at Salem Village. The seven judges he appointed all had previous experience in the colony's law courts. Phips wanted the trials to be as fair as possible and procedurally correct. A proper jury was impaneled. Despite precautions, however, the court itself soon succumbed to the frenzy. Chief judge and deputy governor William Stoughton, for example, staunchly believed the girls had been bewitched, and he had little doubt that "real" witches were responsible for the trouble at Salem Village. By contrast, Nathaniel Saltonstall was highly skeptical of the witchcraft charges. After witnessing the first round of executions, Saltonstall resigned from the court and turned to alcohol to persuade himself the court had not made a terrible mistake. Although the judges and jury may have felt ambivalent about what was happening, the law stated that persons convicted as witches must die.

Everything turned on evidence. Confession offered the most reliable proof of witchcraft, and it occurred surprisingly often. We will never know what compelled people to confess. Some may have actually believed they had cast spells on their neighbors or had foretold the future. Many women, though believing themselves innocent, may have confessed because of guilt for impure thoughts that they had privately entertained. Perhaps the psychological strain of imprisonment, coupled with intense social scrutiny, convinced them they might have unwittingly entered into a contract with the Devil. Regardless, the stories they told undoubtedly mortified those who heard them and fueled the growing frenzy. Imagine the reaction to Ann Foster's July 18 confession:

> Ann Foster . . . confessed that the devil in the shape of a black man appeared to

Increase Mather.

*her with [Martha] Carrier about six yeare
since when they made her a witch and
that she promised to serve the devill two
years: upon which the Devill promised
her prosperity and many things but never
performed it, that she and Martha
Carrier did both ride on a stick or pole
when they went to the witch meeting at
Salem Village and that the stick broak: as
they were carried in the air above the
tops of the trees and they fell but she did
hang fast about the neck of [Martha]
Carrier and were presently at the village,
. . . she further saith that she heard some
of the witches say that there was three
hundred and five in the whole Country
and that they would ruin that place the
Village . . .*

Most of the accused did not confess, however,
forcing the judges to produce tangible evidence of
witchcraft. The charge was difficult because the
crime of bewitchment was, by nature, an invisible
act. Earthly laws and magistrates had difficulty
dealing with crimes that occurred in the spiritual
world. In this situation, the beleaguered judges
used a few customary tests. All witches supposed-

ly had a "witch's teat," usually a flap of skin
located anywhere on the body, from which they
gave suck to the Devil. The judges subjected
almost every defendant to a humiliating physical
examination in order to find such biological
abnormalities. Witches could also be discovered
by having them touch a girl in the midst of her
torments. If the girl's fits ceased, then the person
who touched her was assumed responsible for her
agony. Since this form of evidence was immediately observable, judges relied on it heavily,
oftentimes parading accused witches before the
possessed girls waiting to see whose touch would
calm them.

Had the terrible ordeal turned solely on
unsightly warts, the trials might have ended without further note. But that did not happen. The
judges allowed the jury to entertain a different
sort of evidence, *spectral evidence,* and it was this
material that hanged people at Salem Village.
New Englanders believed that witches worked by
dispatching a specter, a phantom spirit, to torment their victims. This meant that witches had
power over great distances; they were invisible.
They entered people's dreams, and dozens of
good New Englanders complained of having been
bitten, pinched, or even choked by specters that
looked a lot like their neighbors. The judges regularly accepted spectral testimony of the sort
offered by the eighteen-year-old John Cook.

*. . . one morning about sun rising as I
was in bed . . . I saw [Bridget] Bishop . . .
Standing in the chamber by the window
and she looked on me & . . . presently
struck me on the Side of the head w'ch
did very much hurt me & then I Saw her
goe Out under the End window at a little
Creviss about So bigg as I Could thrust
my hand into. I Saw her again the Same
day . . . walke & Cross the roome &
having at the time an apple in my hand it
flew Out of my hand into my mothers
lapp who stood Six or Eight foot distance from me & then She disappeared
& though my mother & Severall others
were in the Same room yet they affirmed
they Saw her not.*

As far as the witch hunters were concerned,
Bridget Bishop had been caught in the act. To the

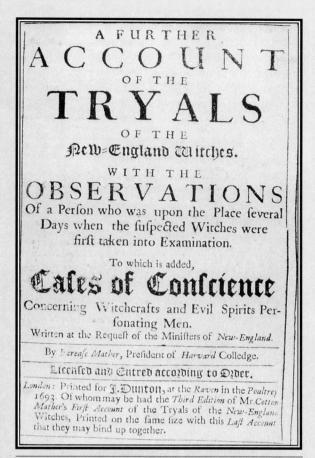

A FURTHER
ACCOUNT
OF THE
TRYALS
OF THE
New-England Witches.
WITH THE
OBSERVATIONS
Of a Person who was upon the Place several
Days when the suspected Witches were
first taken into Examination.

To which is added,

Cases of Conscience
Concerning Witchcrafts and Evil Spirits Per-
sonating Men.
Written at the Request of the Ministers of New-England.

By Increase Mather, President of Harvard Colledge.

Licensed and Entred according to Order.

London: Printed for J. Dunton, at the Raven in the Poultrey
1693. Of whom may be had the Third Edition of Mr. Cotton
Mather's First Account of the Tryals of the New-England
Witches, Printed on the same size with this Last Account
that they may bind up together.

Title page of A Further Account of the Tryals of the New England Witches *(1693), Increase Mather's reflection on the incidents at Salem Village. Mather's* Cases of Conscience Concerning Witchcrafts and Evil Spirits *is credited with helping end the witchcraft executions in Salem.*

modern observer, however, the problems with this kind of evidence seem obvious. First, how could one tell if Cook was lying? The power of his story lay in its inability to be corroborated, for one could never check the authenticity of an intensely private dream or vision. The second problem was that persons accused of being witches had no defense against spectral testimony. When Captain John Aldin stood before his accusers, for example, they immediately fell to the ground, writhing in pain. When asked why he tormented the girls Aldin firmly denied any wrongdoing, inquiring why the judges "suppose[d he had] no better things to do than to come to Salem to afflict these persons that I never knew or saw before?" Aldin's defense did not

carry much weight when set against the testimony of the suffering girls, and rather than conclude the accusers manifested a "lying spirit," the judges admitted all spectral evidence as incontestable proof of witchcraft.

Very early in the trials, a few people expressed doubts about the reliability of this particular form of evidence. Cotton Mather and other ministers, for example, issued a statement urging the judges to use spectral evidence with "a very critical and exquisite caution." Some feared the Devil could assume the shape of innocent people. If this was the case, then the visions of the afflicted proved nothing but the Devil's ability to deceive humans. In the absence of spectral evidence, the cases against most of the witches boiled down to little more than long-standing complaints against obnoxious neighbors. The fury of prosecution silenced these skeptical voices, however, and when the trials resumed in late June, chief judge William Stoughton continued to accept dreams and visions as proof of witchcraft.

Fantastic testimony about flying witches and pinching specters lent an almost circuslike air to the proceedings at Salem. Before the judges and the members of the jury, the afflicted girls would fall to the ground, convulsing and screaming, claiming to see witches that remained invisible to the court. Hundreds of spectators sat horrified as Satan caused suffering before their own eyes. For seventeenth-century New Englanders who felt the presence of the spiritual world in their everyday lives, the courtroom at Salem offered the opportunity to witness the struggle between the forces of darkness and light. Because of the gravity of the situation, no one expected the judges to deal lightly with those who had sworn allegiance to the Devil. Indeed, in the interest of obtaining a confession, the judges conducted harsh interrogations, usually assuming the guilt of the defendant. The intense psychological pressure inflicted on the defendants is revealed in the questioning of Sarah Good, a woman subsequently hanged as a witch.

JUDGE. *Sarah Good, what evil spirit have you familiarity with?*

GOOD. *None.*

JUDGE. *Why do you hurt these children?*

GOOD. *I do not hurt them. I scorn it.*

JUDGE. *Who do you employ then to do it?*

GOOD. *I employ nobody.*

JUDGE. *Have you made a contract with the devil?*

GOOD. *No.*

JUDGE. *Sarah Good . . . why do you not tell us the truth? Why do you thus torment these poor children?*

GOOD. *I do not torment them.*

Even the ministers who advised caution applauded the judges' "assiduous endeavors" and encouraged the "vigorous prosecution" of the witches. As the witch hysteria gained momentum, few people dared to defend the witches for fear of being accused themselves. The humble pleas of those who genuinely thought themselves innocent fell on the deaf ears of a community convinced of its own righteousness.

By late September, with nineteen people already executed, the emotional intensity that had sustained the witch hunt in its early stages began to ebb. For one thing, the accusations spun wildly out of control as the afflicted girls began naming unlikely candidates as witches: prominent ministers, a judge's mother-in-law, and even the governor's wife! Such accusations discredited the entire procedure by which the witches had been discovered. Also, although the jails could barely hold the 150 people still awaiting trial, the accusations kept coming. The terror was feeding on itself.

In mid-October, Governor Phips dismissed the original court and appointed a new one, this time barring spectral evidence. All remaining defendants were quickly acquitted although, curiously enough, three women still confessed to having practiced witchcraft. Phips explained his decision to end the trials in a letter to the king, claiming "the people" had become "dissatisfied and disturbed." Men and women who had been so eager to purify the community of evil, to murder neighbors in the name of a higher good, now spoke of their fear of divine retribution. Perhaps the dying words of Sarah Good, uttered in response to the assistant minister of Salem Town, echoed in their ears: "I am no more a witch than you are a wizard, and if you take away my life, God will give you blood to drink."

Soon after the trials ended, the witch hunters quickly turned confessors. In 1706, Ann Putnam, one of the most prolific accusers, publicly asked for forgiveness: "I desire to be humbled before

God. . . . It was a great delusion of Satan that deceived me in that time." Nine years earlier, the Salem jurors had issued a similar statement, asking the community to understand the particular pressures that compelled them to convict so many people:

> *We confess that we . . . were not capable to understand, nor able to withstand the mysterious delusions of the Powers of Darkness. . . ; but were for want of Knowledge in our selves, and better Information from others, prevailed with to take up with such Evidence against the Accused, as on further consideration, and better Information, we justly fear was insufficient for the touching the Lives of any . . . whereby we fear we have been instrumental with others, tho Ignorantly and unwittingly, to bring upon our selves, and this People of the Lord, the Guilt of Innocent Blood.*

The state never again executed citizens for witchcraft. The experience at Salem had taught New Englanders that, although witches may have existed, no human court could identify a witch beyond a reasonable doubt. The Reverend Increase Mather summed up the attitude of a post-Salem New England: "It were better that ten suspected witches should escape than that one innocent person should be condemned."

What triggered the tragic events of 1692 remains a mystery. Some historians view the witch hunt as a manifestation of Salem Village's socioeconomic troubles. This interpretation helps explain why the primary accusers came from the agrarian village while the alleged witches either resided in or were somehow connected to the market-oriented town. Perhaps the charge of witchcraft masked a deep resentment for their neighbors' monetary success and the new set of values that accompanied the market economy. Other historians believe the witch hunt reflected a deep ambivalence about gender roles in New England society. Young girls lashed out at older nonconforming women because they symbolized a freedom that was achievable within New England society, yet vehemently criticized. Facing the choice between becoming their husbands' servants or being free, the accusers may have expressed this cultural frustration in lethal ways. These and many other factors contributed to the witch phenomenon.

Regardless of which interpretation one favors, however, one must acknowledge that Salem Village had indeed been possessed. The blame rests on the community as a whole, not just on a few vindictive judges. In 1697, another repentant witch hunter, the Reverend John Hale, tried to explain how well-meaning people had caused such harm:

> *I am abundantly satisfyed that those who were most concerned to act and judge in those matters, did not willingly depart from the rules of righteousness. But such was the darkness of that day, . . . that we walked in the clouds, and could not see our way.*

Hale's words ring hollow. They came a little too late to do much good. As other communities have learned, it is easier to apologize after the fact than to stand up courageously against the first injustice.

Frontiers of Empire

Eighteenth-Century America

illiam Byrd II (1674–1744) was a type of English-American that one would not have encountered during the earliest years of settlement. This successful Tidewater planter was a product of a new, more cosmopolitan environment, and as an adult, Byrd seemed as much at home in London as in his native Virginia. In 1728, at the height of his political influence in Williamsburg, the capital of colonial Virginia, Byrd accepted a commission to help survey a disputed boundary between North Carolina and Virginia. During his long journey into the distant backcountry, Byrd kept a detailed journal, a satiric, often bawdy chronicle of daily events that is now regarded as a classic of early American literature.

On his trip into the wilderness, Byrd met many different people. No sooner had he departed a familiar world of tobacco plantations than he came across a self-styled "Hermit," an Englishman who apparently preferred the freedom of the woods to the constraints of society. "He has no other Habitation but a green Bower or Harbour," Byrd reported, "with a Female Domestick as wild & as dirty as himself."

As the boundary commissioners pushed further into the backcountry, they encountered highly independent men and women of European descent, small frontier families that Byrd regarded as living no better than savages. He attributed their uncivilized behavior to a diet of too much pork. "The Truth of it is, these People live so much upon Swine's flesh . . . [that it] makes them . . . extremely hoggish in their Temper, & many of them seem to Grunt rather than Speak in their ordinary conversation." The wilderness journey also brought Byrd's party of surveyors into regular contact with Native Americans, whom he properly distinguished as Catawabas, Tuscaroras, Usherees, and Sapponis.

Byrd's journal invites us to view the eighteenth-century backcountry from a fresh perspective. It was not a vast empty territory awaiting the arrival of European settlers. Maps often sustain this erroneous impression. They depict cities and towns, farms and plantations clustered along the Atlantic Coast; they suggest a "line of settlement" steadily pushing outward into a huge blank area with no mark of civilization. The people Byrd met on his journey into the backcountry would not have understood such maps. After all, the empty space on the maps was their home. They experienced the frontier as a populous multicultural zone stretching from the English and French settlements in the north all the way to the Spanish borderlands in the far southwest.

The point is not to discount the significance of the older Atlantic settlements. During the eighteenth century, Britain's thirteen colonies underwent a profound transformation. The population in the colonies grew at unprecedented rates. German and Scotch-Irish immigrants arrived in huge numbers. So too did African slaves.

Wherever they lived, colonial Americans of this period found they were not as isolated from each other as they had been during most of the seventeenth century. Indeed, after 1690, men and women expanded their cultural horizons, becoming part of a larger Anglo-American world. The change was striking. Colonists whose parents or grandparents had come to the New World to confront a "howling wilderness" now purchased imported European manufactures, read English

William Byrd II. Byrd's History of the Dividing Line Run in the Year 1728 *contains a marvelously satirical account of a survey of the Virginia–North Carolina boundary.*

journals, participated in imperial wars, and sought favors from a growing number of resident royal officials. No one—not even the inhabitants of the distant frontiers—could escape the influence of Britain. The cultural, economic, and political links connecting the colonists to the imperial center in London grew stronger with time.

This surprising development raises a difficult question for the modern historian. If the eighteenth-century colonists were so powerfully attracted to Great Britain, then why did they ever declare independence? The answer may well be that as the colonists became more British, they inevitably became more American as well. This was a development of major significance, for it helps to explain the appearance after mid-century of genuine nationalist sentiment. Political, commercial, and military links that brought the colonists into more frequent contact with Great Britain also made them more aware of other colonists. It was within an expanding, prosperous empire that they first began seriously to consider what it meant to be American.

EXPANDING EMPIRE

The phenomenal growth of British America during the eighteenth century amazed Benjamin Franklin, one of the first persons to bring scientific rigor to the study of demography. The population of the English colonies doubled approximately every twenty-five years, and according to calculations Franklin made in 1751, if the expansion continued at such an extraordinary rate for another century or so, "the greatest Number of Englishmen will be on this Side [of] the water." Not only was the total population increasing at a very rapid rate, it also was becoming more dispersed and heterogeneous. Each year witnessed the arrival of thousands of non-English Europeans, most of whom soon moved to the backcountry of Pennsylvania and the Southern Colonies.

Accurate population data from the colonial period are extremely difficult to find. The first national census did not occur until 1790. Still, various sources surviving from prerevolutionary times indicate quite clearly that the total white population of Britain's thirteen mainland colonies

Estimated Population, 1720–1760			New England Colonies	Middle Colonies	Southern Colonies
1720	White		166,937	92,259	138,110
	Black		3,956	10,825	54,098
1730	White		211,233	135,298	191,893
	Black		6,118	11,683	73,220
1740	White		281,163	204,093	270,283
	Black		8,541	16,452	125,031
1750	White		349,029	275,723	309,588
	Black		10,982	20,736	204,702
1760	White		436,917	398,855	432,047
	Black		12,717	29,049	284,040

New England Colonies New Hampshire, Massachusetts, Rhode Island, and Connecticut

Middle Colonies New York, New Jersey, Pennsylvania, and Delaware

Southern Colonies Maryland, Virginia, North Carolina, South Carolina, and (after 1740) Georgia

Source: From *The American Colonies* by R. C. Simmons. Copyright © 1976 by R. C. Simmons. Reprinted by permission of Harold Matson Company, Inc.

rose from about 250,000 in 1700 to 2,150,000 in 1770, an annual growth rate of 3 percent.

Few societies in recorded history have expanded so rapidly, and if the growth rate had not dropped substantially during the nineteenth and twentieth centuries, the current population of the United States would stand at well over one billion people. Natural reproduction was responsible for most of the growth. More families bore children who in turn lived long enough to have children of their own. Because of this sudden expansion, the population of the late colonial period was strikingly young; approximately one-half of the populace at any given time was under the age of sixteen.

Convicts for America

The African slaves were not the only large group of people coerced into moving to the New World. In 1718, Parliament passed the Transportation Act, allowing judges in England, Scotland, and Ireland to send convicted felons to the American

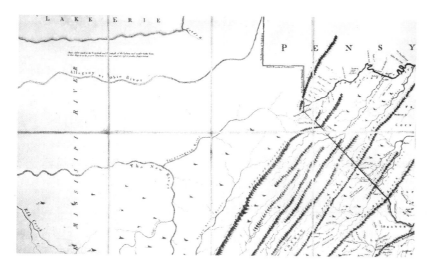

Detail from the 1751 "Map of the Inhabited Part of Virginia" by Joshua Fry and Peter Jefferson showing the northwest quadrant. The map depicts plentiful rivers and mountains but little settlement.

colonies. Between 1718 and 1775, the courts shipped approximately fifty thousand convicts across the Atlantic. Some of these men and women may actually have been dangerous criminals, but the majority seem to have committed minor crimes against property. Although transported convicts—almost 75 percent of whom were young males—escaped the hangman, they found life difficult in the colonies. Eighty percent of them were sold in the Chesapeake colonies as indentured servants. At best they faced an uncertain future, and it is probably not surprising that few former convicts prospered in America.

British authorities lavished praise on this system. According to one writer, transportation drained "the Nation of its offensive Rubbish, without taking away their Lives." Although Americans purchased the convict servants, they expressed fear that these men and women would create a dangerous criminal class. In one irate essay, Benjamin Franklin asked his readers to consider just how the colonists might repay the leaders of Great Britain for shipping so many felons to America. He suggested that rattlesnakes might be the appropriate gift. "I would propose to have them carefully distributed...," Franklin wrote, "in the Gardens of all the Nobility and Gentry throughout the Nation; but particularly in the Gardens of the *Prime Ministers,* the *Lords of Trade* and *Members of Parliament.*" The Revolution forced the British courts to redirect the flow of convicts to another part of the world; an indirect result of American independence was the founding of Australia by transported felons.

CULTURES OF THE BACKCOUNTRY

The eighteenth century also witnessed fresh waves of voluntary European migration. Unlike those seventeenth-century English settlers who had moved to the New World in search of religious sanctuary (see Chapter 2), the newcomers generally transferred in hope of obtaining their own land and setting up as independent farmers. These people often traveled to the backcountry, a region stretching approximately 800 miles from western Pennsylvania to Georgia. Although they planned to follow customs they had known in Europe, they found the challenge of surviving on the British frontier far more demanding than they anticipated. They plunged into a complex, fluid, often violent society that included large numbers of Native Americans and African Americans as well as other Europeans.

Scotch-Irish and Germans

Non-English colonists poured into American ports throughout the eighteenth century, creating rich ethnic diversity in areas originally settled by Anglo-Saxons. The largest group of newcomers consisted of Scotch-Irish. The experiences of these people in Great Britain influenced not only their decision to move to the New World but also their behavior once they arrived.

During the seventeenth century, English rulers thought they could thoroughly dominate Catholic Ireland by transporting thousands of lowland Scottish Presbyterians to the northern region of that war-torn country. The plan failed. English officials who were members of the Anglican church discriminated against the Presbyterians. They passed laws that placed the Scotch-Irish at a severe disadvantage when they traded in England; they taxed them at exorbitant rates. After several poor harvests, many of the Scotch-Irish elected to emigrate to America where they hoped to find the freedom and prosperity that had been denied in Ireland. "I have seen some of their letters to their friends here [Ireland]," one British agent reported in 1729, ". . . in which after they set forth and recommend the fruitfulness and commodities of the country [America], they tell them, that if they will but carry over a little money with them, they may for a small sum purchase considerable tracts of land." It is estimated that about 150,000 Scotch-Irish migrated to the colonies before the Revolution.

Most Scotch-Irish immigrants landed initially in Philadelphia, but instead of remaining in that city, they carved out farms on Pennsylvania's western frontier. The colony's proprietors welcomed the influx of new settlers, for it seemed they would form an ideal barrier between the Indians and the older, coastal communities. The Penn family soon had second thoughts, however. The Scotch-Irish squatted on whatever land looked best, and when colony officials pointed out that large tracts had already been reserved, the immigrants retorted "it was against the laws of God and nature that so much land should be idle when so many Christians wanted it to labour on and to raise their bread." Wherever they located, the Scotch-Irish challenged established authority.

A second large body of non-English settlers, more than 100,000 people, came from the upper Rhine Valley, the German Palatinate. Some of the migrants, especially those who relocated to America around the turn of the century, belonged to small pietistic Protestant sects whose religious views were somewhat similar to those of the Quakers. These Germans moved to the New World primarily in hope of finding religious toleration. Under the guidance of Francis Daniel Pastorius (1651–1720), a group of Mennonites established a prosperous community in Pennsylvania known as Germantown.

By mid-century, however, the characteristics of the German migration had begun to change.

Large numbers of Lutherans transferred to the Middle Colonies. Unlike members of the pietistic sects, these men and women were not in search of religious freedom. Rather, they traveled to the New World looking to better their material lives. The Lutheran church in Germany initially tried to maintain control over the distant congregations, but even though the migrants themselves fiercely preserved many aspects of traditional German culture, they were eventually forced to accommodate to new social conditions. Henry Melchior Muhlenberg (1711–1787), a tireless leader, helped German Lutherans through a difficult cultural adjustment, and in 1748, Muhlenberg organized a meeting of local pastors and lay delegates that ordained ministers of their own choosing, an act of spiritual independence that has been called "the most important single event in American Lutheran history."

The German migrants—mistakenly called Pennsylvania Dutch because the English confused *deutsch* (meaning German) with *Dutch* (a person from Holland)—began reaching Philadelphia in large numbers after 1717, and by 1766, persons of German stock accounted for more than one-third of Pennsylvania's total population. Even their most vocal detractors admitted the Germans were the best farmers in the colony.

Ethnic differences in Pennsylvania bred disputes. The Scotch-Irish as well as the Germans preferred to live with people of their own background, and they sometimes fought to keep members of the other nationality out of their neighborhoods. The English were suspicious of both groups. They could not comprehend why the Germans insisted on speaking German in America. In 1753, for example, Franklin described these settlers as "the most stupid of their nation." He warned that "unless the stream of [German] importation could be turned from this to other colonies . . . they will soon outnumber us, . . . [and] all the advantages we have, will in my opinion, be not able to preserve our language, and even our government will become precarious."

Such prejudice may have persuaded members of both groups to search for new homes. After 1730, Germans and Scotch-Irish pushed south from western Pennsylvania into the Shenandoah Valley, thousands of them settling in the backcountry of Virginia and the Carolinas. The

Elizabeth Canning, convicted of perjury, stands at the bar to receive her sentence from the London court. For her crime, she was sentenced to one month's imprisonment and transport for seven years to the American colonies.

Germans usually remained wherever they found unclaimed fertile land. By contrast, the Scotch-Irish often moved two or three times, acquiring a reputation as a rootless people.

Wherever the newcomers settled, they often found themselves living beyond the effective authority of the various colonial governments. To be sure, backcountry residents petitioned for assistance during wars against the Indians, but most of the time they preferred to be left alone. These conditions heightened the importance of religious institutions within the small ethnic communities. Although the original stimulus for coming to America may have been a desire for economic independence and prosperity, backcountry families—especially the Scotch-Irish—flocked to evangelical Protestant preachers, to Presbyterian, Baptist, and later, Methodist ministers who not only fulfilled the settlers' spiritual needs, but also gave these scattered backcountry communities a pronounced moral character that survived long after the colonial period.

"Middle Ground"

In some histories of the colonial period, Native Americans make only a brief appearance, usually during the earliest years of conquest and settlement. After initial contact with the first European invaders, the Indians seem mysteriously to disappear from the central narrative of colonization, and it is not until the nineteenth century that they turn up again, this time to wage a last desperate battle against the encroachment of white society.

This obviously inadequate account slights one of the richer chapters of Native American history. To be sure, during much of the seventeenth century various Indian groups who contested the English settlers for control of coastal lands suffered terribly, sometimes from war, but more often from the spread of contagious diseases such as smallpox. The two races found it very difficult to live in close proximity. As one Indian informed the members of the Maryland assembly in 1666, "Your hogs & Cattle injure Us, You come too near Us to live & drive Us from place to place.

This folk art painting, from the cover of a clothes box, shows a typical eighteenth-century German farmer.

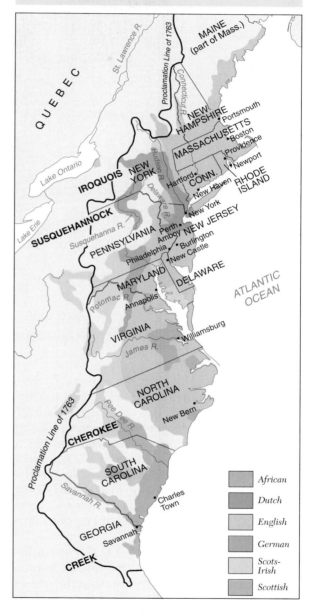

Distribution of European and African Immigrants in the Thirteen Colonies

A flood of non-English immigrants came to the British colonies between 1700 and 1775.

African
Dutch
English
German
Scots-Irish
Scottish

We can fly no farther; let us know where to live & how to be secured for the future from the Hogs & Cattle."

Against such odds the Indians managed to survive. By the eighteenth century, the site of the most intense and creative contact between the races had shifted to the Cis-Mississippian west; that is, to the huge territory between the Appalachian Mountains and the Mississippi River, where several hundred thousand Native Americans made their homes.

Many Indians had only recently migrated to this area. The Delawares, for example, retreated to far western Pennsylvania and the Ohio Valley to escape almost continuous confrontation with advancing European invaders. Other Indians drifted west in less happy circumstances. They were refugees, the remnants of Native American groups who had lost so many people they could no longer sustain an independent cultural identity. These survivors joined with other Indians to establish new multiethnic communities. In this respect the Native American villages may not have seemed all that different from the mixed European settlements of the backcountry.

Stronger groups of Indians such as the Creeks, Choctaws, Chickasaws, Cherokees, and Shawnees generally welcomed the refugees. Strangers were

By the Honorable Sir William Johnson Bart His Majesty's sole Agent and Super-Intendant of Indian Affairs for the Northern Department of North America. Colonel of the Six United Nations their Allies and Dependants &c. &c.

To

Whereas I have received repeated proofs of your Attachment to his Britanic Majesty's Interests, and Zeal for his Service upon Sundry occasions, more particularly

I do therefore give you this public Testimonial thereof as a Proof of his Majesty's Esteem & Approbation, Declaring you the said   to be a   of Your   and recommending it to all his Majesty's Subjects and faithfull Indian Allies to Treat and Consider you upon all occasions agreable to your Character, Station, and Service _____

Given under my Hand and Seal at Arms at Johnson hall the   day of   17

By Command of Sir W. Johnson

This certificate of William Johnson, superintendent of Indian affairs, signifies an alliance between the English settlers and the Native Americans in the "middle ground." Calumets (ceremonial pipes), wampum belts, and medals were other tokens used to mark alliances.

formally adopted to take the places of family members killed in battle or overcome by sickness, and we should appreciate that many seemingly traditional Indian villages of the eighteenth century actually represented innovative responses to rapidly shifting external conditions. As historian Peter Wood explains, "Physically and linguistically diverse groups moved to form loosely organized confederacies, unions of mutual convenience, that effectively restrained interethnic hostilities."

The concept of a *middle ground*—a term that has only recently entered the interpretive vocabulary—helps us more fully to comprehend how eighteenth-century Indians held their own in the backcountry beyond the Appalachian Mountains. The Native Americans never intended to isolate themselves completely from European contact. They relied on white traders, French as well as English, to provide essential metal goods and weapons. The goal of the Indian confederacies was rather to maintain a strong independent voice in these commercial exchanges, and so long

as they had sufficient military strength—that is, large numbers of healthy armed warriors—they compelled everyone who came to negotiate in the "middle ground" to give them proper respect. It would be incorrect, therefore, to characterize their relations with the Europeans as a stark choice between resistance or accommodation, between total war or abject surrender. Native Americans took advantage of rivals when possible; they compromised when necessary. It is best to imagine the Indians' middle ground as an open, dynamic process of creative interaction.

The Susquehannas understood the rules of the middle ground. Indeed, they mastered the eighteenth-century language of commercial negotiation. When backcountry traders charged the Indians seemingly exorbitant prices for European goods, the angry Susquehannas took their complaint to James Hamilton, the lieutenant governor of Pennsylvania. In fact, they forced Hamilton to give them a short lecture on international economics, an event that shows the Indians were fully capable of grasping the essential elements of modern capitalism. "You know we dont make the Goods ourselves," Hamilton whined, "they are made in England, and the Transporting them over the Seas is dangerous in time of War and very expensive, so that . . . their prices change, as the risque and demand for them is greater or less."

The survival of the middle ground depended ultimately on factors over which the Native Americans had little control. Imperial competition between France and Great Britain enhanced the Indians' bargaining position, but after the British defeated the French in 1763, the Indians no longer received the same solicitous attention as they had in earlier times. Keeping old allies happy seemed to the British a needless expense. Moreover, contagious disease continued to take a fearful toll. In the southern backcountry between 1685 and 1790 the Indian population dropped an astounding 72 percent. In the Ohio Valley the numbers suggest similar rates of decline. By the time the United States took control of this region, the middle ground itself had become a casualty of history.

SPANISH BORDERLANDS OF THE EIGHTEENTH CENTURY

Until 1821 when Mexico declared independence from Madrid, Spanish authorities struggled to control a vast northern frontier. During the eighteenth century the Spanish Empire in North America included widely dispersed settlements such as San Francisco, San Diego, Santa Fe, San Antonio, and St. Augustine. In these borderland communities European colonists mixed with peoples of other races and backgrounds, forming multicultural societies. According to historian Ramón A. Gutiérrez, the Spanish provinces present a story of "the complex web of interactions between men and women, young and old, rich and poor, slave and free, Spaniard and Indian, all of whom fundamentally depended on the other for their own self-definition."

Conquering the Northern Frontier

Tales of gold and silver attracted the attention of the earliest Spaniards. Eager to duplicate Cortés's feat (see Chapter 1), several lesser known con-

quistadores explored the lands to the north of Mexico. Between 1539 and 1541, Hernando de Soto trekked across the Southeast in search of treasure. At roughly the same time, Francisco Vázquez de Coronado departed New Spain looking for the fabled "Seven Cities of Cibola," centers of wealth that on closer inspection turned out to be Zuni pueblos. Coronado's quixotic journey took him to the present states of Texas, Kansas, New Mexico, and Arizona.

Not until late in the sixteenth century did Spanish settlers, led by Juan de Oñate, establish European communities north of the Rio Grande. The Pueblos resisted the invasion of colonists, soldiers, and missionaries, and in a major rebellion in 1680 led by El Popé, the native peoples drove the whites completely out of New Mexico. "The heathen have conceived a mortal hatred for our holy faith and enmity for the Spanish nation," concluded one imperial bureaucrat. Not until 1692 were the Spanish able to reconquer this fiercely contested area. By then, Native American hostility coupled with the settlers' failure to find precious metal had cooled Spain's enthusiasm for the northern frontier.

Concern over French encroachment in the Southeast led Spain to colonize St. Augustine (Florida) in 1565. Although this enterprise never flourished, it claims attention as the first permanent European settlement established in what would become the United States, predating the founding of Jamestown and Plymouth by several decades. Pedro Menéndez de Avilés brought some fifteen hundred soldiers and settlers to St. Augustine, where they constructed an impressive fort, but the colony failed to attract additional Spanish migrants. "It is hard to get anyone to go to St. Augustine because of the horror with which Florida is painted," the governor of Cuba complained in 1673. "Only hoodlums and the mischievous go there from Cuba."

California never figured prominently in Spain's plans for the New World. Early explorers reported finding only impoverished Indians living along the Pacific Coast. Adventurers saw no natural resources worth mentioning, and since the area proved extremely difficult to reach from Mexico City—the overland trip could take months—California received little attention. Fear that the Russians might seize the entire region belatedly sparked Spanish activity, however, and after

Spanish America, 1600

The first permanent inland Spanish settlements were established in the early seventeenth century in what is now the state of New Mexico, but they were little more than isolated outposts.

1769 two indomitable servants of empire, Fra Junípero Serra and Don Gaspar de Portolá, organized permanent missions and *presidios* (forts) at San Diego, Monterey, San Francisco, and Santa Barbara.

Peoples of the Spanish Borderlands

In sharp contrast to the English frontier settlements of the eighteenth century, the Spanish outposts in North America grew very slowly. A few Catholic priests and imperial administrators traveled to the northern provinces, but the danger of Indian attack as well as a harsh physical environment discouraged ordinary colonists. The European migrants were overwhelmingly male, most of them soldiers in the pay of the empire. Although some colonists came directly from Spain, most had been born in other Spanish colonies such as Minorca, the Canaries, or New

Spain, and because European women rarely appeared on the frontier, Spanish males formed relationships with Indian women, fathering large numbers of *mestizos,* children of mixed race.

As in other European frontiers of the eighteenth century, encounters with Spanish soldiers, priests, and traders altered Native American cultures. The experience here was quite different from that of the whites and Indians in the British backcountry. The Spanish exploited Native American labor, reducing entire Indian villages to servitude. Many Indians moved to the Spanish towns, and although they lived in close proximity to the Europeans—something rare in British America—they were consigned to the lowest social class, objects of European contempt. However much their material conditions changed, the Indians of the Southwest resisted strenuous efforts to convert them to Catholicism. The Pueblos maintained their own religious forms—often at great personal risk—and they sometimes murdered priests who became too intrusive. Angry Pueblos at Taos reportedly fed the hated Spanish friars corn tortillas containing urine and mice meat.

The Spanish empire never had the resources necessary to secure the northern frontier fully. The small military posts were intended primarily to discourage other European powers such as France, Great Britain, and Russia from taking possession of territory claimed by Spain. It would be misleading, however, to stress the fragility of Spanish colonization. The urban design and public architecture of many southwestern cities still reflect the vision of the early Spanish settlers, and to a large extent, the old borderlands remain Spanish speaking to this day.

BRITISH COLONIES IN AN ATLANTIC WORLD

The character of the older, more established Atlantic colonies changed almost as rapidly as that of the backcountry. The rapid growth of an urban cosmopolitan culture impressed eighteenth-century commentators, and even though most Americans still lived on scattered farms, they had begun to participate aggressively in a exciting consumer marketplace that expanded their imaginative horizons.

Acoma Pueblo near present-day Albuquerque, New Mexico. In 1540, a party sent by the explorer Coronado reached the site, which is situated atop a rock mesa more than 300 feet high with steep sides and approached along a difficult trail. Captured in 1599 by Juan de Oñate, Acoma joined in the revolt against the Spanish led by El Popé in 1680.

Provincial Cities

Considering the rate of population growth, it is surprising to discover how few eighteenth-century Americans lived in cities. Boston, Newport, New York, Philadelphia, and Charleston—the five largest cities—contained only about 5 percent of the colonial population. In 1775, none had more than forty thousand persons. The explanation for the relatively slow development of colonial American cities lies in their highly specialized commercial character. Colonial port towns served as entrepôts, intermediary trade and shipping centers where bulk cargoes were broken up for inland distribution and where agricultural products were gathered for export. They did not support large-scale manufacturing. Indeed, the pool of free urban laborers was quite small, since the type of person who was forced to work for wages in Europe usually became a farmer in America.

Yet despite the limited urban population, cities profoundly influenced colonial culture. It was in the cities that Americans were exposed to and welcomed the latest English ideas. Wealthy colonists—merchants and lawyers—tried to emulate the culture of the mother country. They sponsored concerts and plays; they learned to dance. Women as well as men picked up the new fashions quickly, and even though most of them had never been outside the colony of their birth, they sometimes appeared to be the products of London's best families.

It was in the cities, also, that wealthy merchants transformed commercial profits into architectural splendor, for in their desire to outdo one another, they built grand homes of enduring beauty. Most of these buildings are described as Georgian because they were constructed during the reign of Britain's early Hanoverian kings, who all happened to be named George. Actually these homes were provincial copies of grand country houses of Great Britain. They drew their inspiration from the great Italian Renaissance architect Andrea Palladio (1508–1580), who had incorporated classical themes into a rigidly symmetrical form. Palladio's ideas were popularized in the colonies by James Gibbs, an Englishman whose *Book of Architecture* (1728) provided blueprints for the most spectacular homes of mid-eighteenth-century America.

Their owners filled these houses with fine furniture. Each city patronized certain skilled craftsmen, but the artisans of Philadelphia were known for producing magnificent copies of the works of Thomas Chippendale, Great Britain's most famous furniture designer. These developments gave American cities an elegance they had not possessed in the previous century. One foreign visitor noted of Philadelphia in 1748, ". . . its natural advantages, trade, riches and power, are by no means inferior to any, even of the most ancient towns of Europe." As this traveler understood, the cultural impact of the cities went far beyond the number of people who actually lived there.

Estimated Population of Colonial Cities, 1720–1770, showing decennial percentage increases

	Boston	%	Newport	%	New York	%	Philadelphia	%	Charleston	%
1720	12,000	—	3,800	—	7,000	—	10,000	—	3,500	—
1730	13,000	8	4,640	22	8,622	23	11,500	15	4,500	29
1740	15,601	20	5,840	26	10,451	21	12,654	10	6,269	39
1750	—	—	6,670	14	14,225	36	18,202	44	7,134	14
1760	15,631	—	7,500	12	18,000	27	23,750	30	8,000	12
1770	15,877	2	9,833	31	22,667	26	34,583	46	10,667	33

Source: From *The American Colonies* by R. C. Simmons. Copyright © 1976 by R. C. Simmons. Reprinted by permission of Harold Matson Company, Inc.

Westover, the huge Virginia estate of William Byrd II (see p. 98) shows the influence of the architectural style of Andrea Palladio on eighteenth-century Georgian buildings.

Benjamin Franklin

Benjamin Franklin (1706–1790) absorbed the new cosmopolitan culture. European thinkers regarded him as a genuine *philosophe,* a person of reason and science, a role that he self-consciously cultivated when he visited England and France in later life. Franklin had little formal education, but as a young man working in his brother's print shop, he managed to keep up with the latest intellectual currents. In his *Autobiography,* Franklin described the excitement of discovering a new British journal. It was like a breath of fresh air to a boy growing up in Puritan New England. "I met with an odd volume of *The Spectator,*" Franklin recounted, ". . . I had never before seen any of them. I bought it, read it over and over, and was much delighted with it. I thought the writing excellent, and wished if possible to imitate it."

Franklin's opportunity came in August 1721 when he and his brother founded *The New England Courant,* a weekly newspaper that satirized Boston's political and religious leaders in the manner of the contemporary British press. Writing under the name "Silence Dogood," young Franklin asked his readers "Whether a Commonwealth suffers more by hypocritical Pretenders to Religion, or by the openly Profane?" Proper Bostonians were not prepared for a journal that one minister described as "full freighted with Nonesense, Unmannerliness, Railery, Prophaneness, Immorality, Arrogance,

Benjamin Franklin (left) exemplified the scientific curiosity and search for practical knowledge characteristic of thinkers of the eighteenth century. Franklin's experiments on electricity became world famous and inspired many others to study the effects of this strange force. The ordinary citizens shown above (right), eager to try out a new phenomenon, are rubbing metal rods together to produce static electricity.

Calumnies, Lyes, Contradictions, and what not, all tending to Quarrels and Divisions and to Debauch and Corrupt the Minds and Manners of New England." Franklin got the point; he left Massachusetts in 1723 in search of a less hostile intellectual environment.

After he had moved to Philadelphia, leaving behind an irritable brother as well as New England Puritanism, Franklin devoted himself to the pursuit of useful knowledge, ideas that would increase the happiness of his fellow Americans. Franklin never denied the existence of God. Rather, he pushed the Lord aside, making room for the free exercise of human reason. Franklin tinkered, experimented, and reformed. Almost everything he encountered in his daily life aroused his curiosity. His investigation of electricity brought him world fame, but Franklin was never satisfied with his work in this field until it yielded practical application. In 1756, he invented the lightning rod. He also designed a marvelously

efficient stove that is still used today. In modern America, Franklin has become exactly what he would have wanted to be, a symbol of material progress through human ingenuity.

Franklin energetically promoted the spread of reason. In Philadelphia, he organized groups that discussed the latest European literature, philosophy, and science. In 1727, for example, he "form'd most of my ingenious Acquaintances into a Club for mutual Improvement, which we call'd the Junto." Four years later Franklin took a leading part in the formation of the Library Company, a voluntary association that for the first time allowed people like himself to pursue "useful knowledge." The members of these societies communicated with Americans living in other colonies, providing them not only with new information but also with models for their own clubs and associations. Such efforts broadened the intellectual horizons of many colonists, especially those who lived in cities.

Economic Transformation

The colonial economy kept pace with the stunning growth in population. During the first three-quarters of the eighteenth century, the population increased at least tenfold, and yet even with so many additional people to feed and clothe, the per capita income did not decline. Indeed, with the exception of poor urban dwellers, such as sailors whose employment varied with the season, white Americans did quite well. An abundance of land and the extensive growth of agriculture accounted for their economic success. New farmers were not only able to provide for their families' well-being but also to sell their crops in European and West Indian markets as well. Each year, more Americans produced more tobacco, wheat, or rice—just to cite the major export crops—and by this means, they maintained a high level of individual prosperity without developing an industrial base.

At mid-century, colonial exports flowed along well-established routes. Over half of American goods produced for export went to Great Britain. The Navigation Acts (see Chapter 3) were still in effect and "enumerated" items such as tobacco had to be landed first at a British port. Furs were added to the restricted list in 1722. The White Pines Acts passed in 1711, 1722, and 1729 forbade Americans from cutting white pine trees without a license. The purpose of this legislation was to reserve the best trees for the use of the Royal Navy. The Sugar Act of 1733—also called the Molasses Act—placed a heavy duty on molasses imported from foreign ports; the Hat and Felt Act of 1732 and the Iron Act of 1750 attempted to limit the production of colonial goods that competed with British exports.

These statutes might have created tensions between the colonists and the mother country had they been rigorously enforced. Crown officials, however, generally ignored the new laws. New England merchants imported molasses from French Caribbean islands without paying the full customs; ironmasters in the Middle Colonies continued to produce iron. Even without the Navigation Acts, however, a majority of colonial exports would have been sold on the English market. The emerging consumer society in Great Britain was beginning to create a new generation of buyers who possessed enough income to purchase American goods, especially sugar and tobacco. This rising demand was the major market force shaping the colonial economy.

Colonial merchants operating out of Boston, Newport, and Philadelphia also carried substantial tonnage to the West Indies. In 1768, this market accounted for 27 percent of all American exports. If there was a triangular trade that included the west coast of Africa, it does not seem to have been economically significant. Colonial ships carrying food sailed for the Caribbean and returned immediately to the Middle Colonies or New England with cargoes of molasses, sugar, and rum. In fact, recent research indicates that during the eighteenth century, trade with Africa involved less than 1 percent of all American exports. Slaves were transported directly to colonial ports where they were sold for cash or credit.

The West Indies played a vital role in preserving American credit in Europe. Without this source of income, colonists would not have been able to pay for the manufactured items they purchased in the mother country. To be sure, they exported American products in great quantity to Great Britain, but the value of these exports seldom equaled the cost of British goods shipped back to the colonists. To cover this small but recurrent deficit, colonial merchants relied on profits made in the West Indies.

Birth of a Consumer Society

After mid-century, however, the balance of trade turned dramatically against the colonists. The reasons for this change were complex, but in simplest terms, Americans began buying more English goods than their parents or grandparents had done. Between 1740 and 1770, English exports to the American colonies increased by an astounding 360 percent.

In part, this shift reflected a fundamental transformation in the British economy. Although the Industrial Revolution was still far in the future, the pace of the British economy picked up dramatically after 1690. Small factories produced certain goods more efficiently and more cheaply than the colonists could. The availability of these products altered the lives of most Americans, even those with modest incomes. Staffordshire china replaced crude earthenware; imported cloth replaced homespun. Franklin noted in his *Autobiography* how changing consumer habits affected his life. For years, he had eaten his breakfast in an earthenware bowl with a pewter spoon, but on one morning it was served "in a china bowl, with a spoon of silver." Franklin observed that "this was the first appearance of plate and china in our house which afterwards in the course of years, as our wealth increased, augmented gradually to several hundred pounds in value." In this manner, British industrialization undercut American handicraft and folk art.

To help Americans purchase manufactured goods, British merchants offered generous credit. Colonists deferred settlement by agreeing to pay interest on their debts. The temptation to acquire English finery blinded many people to hard economic realities. They gambled on the future, hoping bumper farm crops would reduce their dependence on the large merchant houses of London and Glasgow. Obviously, some persons lived within their means, but the aggregate American debt continued to grow. By 1760, total indebtedness had reached £2 million. Colonial leaders tried various expedients to remain solvent—issuing paper money, for example—and while these efforts delayed a crisis, the balance of payments problem was clearly very serious.

The eighteenth century also saw a substantial increase in intercoastal trade. Southern planters sent tobacco and rice to New England and the Middle Colonies where these staples were exchanged for meat and wheat as well as goods imported from Great Britain. By 1760, approximately 30 percent of the colonists' total tonnage capacity was involved in this extensive "coastwise" commerce. In addition, backcountry farmers in western Pennsylvania and the Shenandoah Valley carried their grain to market along an old Iroquois trail that became known as the "Great Wagon Road," a rough, hilly highway that by the time of the Revolution stretched 735 miles along the Blue Ridge Mountains to Camden, South Carolina. Most of their produce was carried in long, gracefully designed Conestoga wagons. These vehicles—sometimes called the "wagons of empire"—had been invented by German immigrants living in the Conestoga River Valley in Lancaster County, Pennsylvania.

The shifting patterns of trade had immense effects on the development of an American culture. First, the flood of British imports eroded local and regional identities. Commerce helped to "anglicize" American culture by exposing colo-

The Great Wagon Road
By the mid-eighteenth century, this road had become the major avenue for the settlers in the Virginia and Carolina backcountry.

nial consumers to a common range of British manufactured goods. Deep sectional differences remained, of course, but Americans from New Hampshire to Georgia were increasingly drawn into a sophisticated economic network centered in London. Second, the expanding coastal and overland trade brought colonists of different backgrounds into more frequent contact. Ships that sailed between New England and South Carolina, and between Virginia and Pennsylvania, provided dispersed Americans with a means to exchange ideas and experiences on a more regular basis. Mid-eighteenth-century printers, for example, established several dozen new journals; these were weekly newspapers that carried information not only about the mother country and world commerce but also about events in other colonies.

RELIGIOUS REVIVALS IN PROVINCIAL SOCIETIES

The Great Awakening had a profound impact on the lives of ordinary people. This unprecedented evangelical outpouring altered the course of

Good Manners and the Creation of an American Middle Class

The Eighteenth Century

Manners generate anxiety. A wrong dessert spoon, an ill-chosen wine glass, an inappropriate outfit—such errors of judgment can expose a man or woman to the ridicule of polite society. George Washington dreaded the possibility of appearing an "awkward country fellow," and as a young ambitious Virginian, he did what socially insecure persons have done for centuries: he obtained a reliable book of etiquette, the functional equivalent of "Miss Manners" for eighteenth-century Americans.

A teenage Washington busily copied over a hundred points of good manners in a little volume entitled *Rules of Civility & Decent Behaviour in Company and Conversation*. Some entries strike modern readers as uncontroversial: "Associate yourself with Men of good Quality if you Esteem your own Reputation; for 'tis better to be alone than in bad Company" or "When another speaks be attentive yourself and disturb not the audience . . . interrupt him not."

Some of Washington's rules, however, seem bizarre. They suggest that relaxed modern standards of etiquette in this country are still a great deal more demanding than those of the eighteenth century. One wonders, for example, why Washington had to remind himself "When in company, put not your hands to any part of the body, not usually discovered." Another rule counseled polite colonial Americans to "Kill no vermin as fleas, lice, ticks, &c. in the sight of others; if you see any filth or thick spittle, put your foot dexteriously [sic] upon it; if it be upon the clothes of your companions, put it off privately; and if it be upon your own clothes, return thanks to him who puts it off." Even stranger, Washington copied in his little book, "Do not Puff up the Cheeks, Loll not out the tongue . . . thrust out the lips, or bite them or keep the Lips too open or too Close."

The image of Washington puffing up his cheeks or lolling his tongue during a polite conversation is amusing. For the

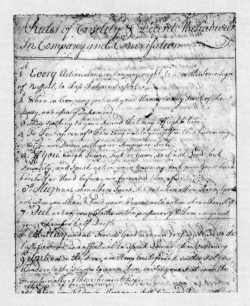

Among Washington's Rules of Civility and Decent Behaviour in Company and Conversation *were admonitions to "Let your recreations be manful not sinful" and "Labour to keep alive in your breast that little celestial fire called conscience."*

ambitious young planter, however, the fear of exposure was very real. Obsession with gentility swept through the Anglo-American world of the mid-eighteenth century. Everyone thought it important to be polite—or, if not polite in fact, then at least to appear polite. And in their quest for advice, people like Washington turned to surprising sources. The rules he reproduced had a long history stretching back to the Italian Renaissance. Much of this literature had been intended originally for courtiers, for the creatures who flattered Europe's kings and queens, and whatever else he may have been, Washington was no courtier. In eighteenth-century society, manners—the nervous concern over polite behavior—had spread to a fast-growing Anglo-American middle class.

Few Americans of Washington's background questioned the need to maintain visible class distinctions. Indeed, colonists agreed a gentleman should stand apart from ordinary farmers and small merchants. The problem in a largely rural and agrarian society, one that claimed no genuine aristocrats, was discovering who was the authentic gentleman. Any literate person could read the etiquette books and learn the rules of gentility. Moreover, in a relatively open commercial society, almost everyone had opportunities to purchase manufactured goods, such as bright cloth for

garments and pretty buckles and buttons. Such widespread access to imported finery and print culture meant a stranger might be a proper gentleman or someone who had managed to dress like a gentleman, in other words, a counterfeit.

A curious exchange between two travelers highlights the difficulty of establishing one's social rank at mid-century. A Scottish physician, Dr. Alexander Hamilton (no relation to the secretary of the treasury), never doubted his own gentility. He refused, however, to accept a Pennsylvania land speculator as his social peer. According to Hamilton, the other man appeared a "very rough spun, forward, clownish blade, much addicted to swearing, [and] at the same time desirous to pass for a gentleman." The Pennsylvanian felt insulted. Although he wore only "a greasy jacket and breeches and a dirty worsted cap," he believed himself as good a gentleman as the physician. In his own defense, the land speculator protested that "though he seemed to be but a plain, homely fellow, yet . . . he was able to afford better [clothes] than many that went finer." In fact, his "little woman at home drank tea twice a day."

The land speculator and his tea-drinking "little woman" were not about to be bullied by the likes of a Hamilton. Such middle-class Americans—white freeholders and artisans—strove

to master the trappings of the new gentility. The tea service presented the most demanding test, for during such complex social rituals the chance of making a major faux pas was very great. At such tense moments a young man like Washington may have had to remind himself: "Clense not your teeth with the Table Cloth, Napkin, Fork, or Knife, but if Others do it, let it be done with a Pick Tooth."

The spread of print and the sudden availability of so many consumer goods at mid-century fueled the obsession with "civility and decent behaviour." As middle-class Americans soon discovered, however, there was a heavy price to be paid. The rush to gentility generated new social anxieties. Americans—even those who purchased fancy imports and devoured the etiquette books—worried that manners might represent no more than a polite shell, an external set of appearances that indicated perhaps the absence of sincere principle. The acquisition of a tea set could signal an addiction, leading not to the attainment of true gentility, but rather to the emulation of the moral standards of sniveling European courtiers. The deep tension between private manners and public morality, raised so forcefully for the first time during the mid-eighteenth century, perplexes Americans to this day.

Rigid rules of etiquette prescribed the social ritual of the tea service. In this eighteenth-century overmantle (oil on wood), the family slave attends John Potter and his family of Matunuck, Rhode Island, as they take their tea.

American history. In our own time, of course, we have witnessed the force of religious revival in different regions throughout the world. It is no exaggeration to claim that a similar populist movement took place in mid-eighteenth-century America, for it caused men and women of all backgrounds to rethink basic assumptions about church and state, institutions and society.

Only with hindsight does the Great Awakening seem a unified religious movement. Revivals occurred in different places at different times; the intensity of the events varied from region to region. The first signs of a spiritual awakening appeared in New England during the 1730s, but within a decade the revivals in this area had burned themselves out. It was not until the 1750s and 1760s that the Awakening made more than a superficial impact on the people of Virginia. The revivals were most important in Massachusetts, Connecticut, Rhode Island, Pennsylvania, New Jersey, and Virginia. Their effect on religion in New York, Delaware, and the Carolinas was marginal. No single religious denomination or sect monopolized the Awakening. In New England, revivals shattered Congregational churches, and in the South, especially in Virginia, they had an impact on Presbyterians, Methodists, and Baptists. Moreover, there was nothing peculiarly American about the Great Awakening. Mid-eighteenth-century Europe experienced a similar burst of religious emotionalism.

Whatever their origins, the seeds of revival were generally sown on fertile ground. In the early decades of the century, many Americans— but especially New Englanders—complained that organized religion had lost vitality. They looked back at Winthrop's generation with nostalgia, assuming that common people at that time must have possessed greater piety than did later, more worldly colonists. Congregational ministers seemed obsessed with dull, scholastic matters; they no longer touched the heart. And in the southern colonies, there were simply not enough ordained ministers to tend to the religious needs of the population.

The Great Awakening arrived unexpectedly in Northampton, a small farm community in western Massachusetts, sparked by Jonathan Edwards, the local Congregational minister. Edwards accepted the traditional teachings of Calvinism (see Chapter 1), reminding his parish-ioners that their eternal fate had been determined by an omnipotent God, there was nothing they could do to save themselves, and they were totally dependent on the Lord's will. He thought his fellow ministers had grown soft. They left men and women with the mistaken impression that sinners might somehow avoid eternal damnation simply by performing good works. "How dismal will it be," Edwards told his complacent congregation, "when you are under these racking torments, to know assuredly that you never, never shall be delivered from them." Edwards was not exaggerating his message in an attempt to be dramatic. He spoke of God's omnipotence with such calm self-assurance that even people who had not thought deeply about religious matters were shaken by his words.

Why this uncompromising message set off several religious revivals during the mid-1730s is not known. Whatever the explanation for the popular response to Edwards's preaching, young people began flocking to the church. They experienced a searing conversion, a sense of "new birth" and utter dependence on God. "Surely," Edwards pronounced, "this is the Lord's doing, and it is marvelous in our eyes." The excitement spread, and evangelical ministers concluded that God must be preparing Americans, his chosen people, for the millennium. "What is now seen in America and especially in New England," Edwards explained, "may prove the dawn of that glorious day."

Religion of the People

Edwards was a brilliant theologian, but he did not possess the dynamic personality required to sustain the revival. That responsibility fell to George Whitefield, a young, inspiring preacher from England who toured the colonies from New Hampshire to Georgia. While Whitefield was not an original thinker, he was an extraordinarily effective public speaker. According to Edwards's wife, Sarah, it was wonderful to witness what a spell Whitefield ". . . casts over an audience . . . I have seen upwards of a thousand people hang on his words with breathless silence, broken only by an occasional half-suppressed sob."

Whitefield's audiences came from all groups of American society: rich and poor, young and old, rural and urban. One obscure Connecticut farmer,

The fervor of the Great Awakening was intensified by the eloquence of itinerant preachers such as George Whitefield, the most popular evangelical of the mid-eighteenth century.

Nathan Cole, left a moving account of a sermon Whitefield delivered in Middletown in 1741. Rushing with his wife Anne along the dirt roads, Cole encountered "a stedy streem of horses & their riders scarcely a horse more than his length behind another all of a lather and fome with swet ther breath rooling out of their noistrels in the cloud of dust every jump every hors seemed to go with all his might to carry his rider to hear the news from heaven for the saving of their Souls." When Cole heard the great preacher, the farmer experienced what he called "a heart wound." While Whitefield described himself as a Calvinist, he welcomed all Protestants. He spoke from any pulpit that was available. "Don't tell me you are a Baptist, an Independent, a Presbyterian, a dissenter," he thundered, "tell me you are a Christian, that is all I want."

Whitefield was a brilliant entrepreneur. Like Franklin, with whom he published many popular volumes, the itinerant minister possessed an almost intuitive sense of how this burgeoning consumer society could be turned to his own advantage, and he embraced the latest merchandising techniques. He appreciated, for example, the power of the press in selling the revival, and he regularly promoted his own work in advertisements placed in British and American newspapers. The crowds flocked to hear Whitefield, while his critics grumbled about the commercialization of religion. One anonymous writer in Massachusetts noted there is "a very wholesome law of the province to discourage Pedlars in Trade" and it seems high time "to enact something for the discouragement of Pedlars in Divinity also."

Other, American-born itinerant preachers followed Whitefield's example. The most famous was Gilbert Tennent, a Presbyterian of Scotch-Irish background who had been educated in the Middle Colonies. His sermon, "On the Danger of an Unconverted Ministry," printed in 1741 set off a storm of protest from established ministers who were understandably insulted. Lesser known revivalists traveled from town to town, colony to colony, challenging local clergymen who seemed hostile to evangelical religion. Men and women who thronged to hear the itinerants were called "New Lights," and during the 1740s and 1750s, many congregations split between defenders of the new emotional preaching and those who regarded the entire movement as dangerous nonsense.

Despite Whitefield's successes, many ministers remained suspicious of the itinerants and their methods. Some complaints may have amounted to little more than sour grapes. One "Old Light" spokesman labeled Tennent "a monster! impudent and noisy." He claimed Tennent told anxious Christians that "they were *damned! damned! damned!* This charmed them; and, in the most dreadful winter I ever saw, people wallowed in snow, night and day, for the benefit of his beastly brayings; and many ended their days under these fatigues." Charles Chauncy, minister of the prestigious First Church of Boston, raised much more troubling issues. How could the revivalists be certain God had sparked the Great Awakening? Perhaps the itinerants had relied too much on emotion? "Let us esteem those as friends of religion," Chauncy warned, ". . . who warn us of the danger of enthusiasm, and would put us on our guard, that we may not be led aside by it."

While Tennent did not condone the excesses of the Great Awakening, his attacks on formal learning invited the crude anti-intellectualism of such fanatics as James Davenport. This deranged revivalist traveled along the Connecticut coast in 1742 playing upon popular emotion. At night, under the light of smoky torches, he danced and stripped, shrieked and laughed. He also urged people to burn books written by authors who had not experienced the new light as defined by Davenport. Like so many fanatics throughout history who have claimed a special knowledge of the "truth," Davenport later recanted and begged pardon for his disruptive behavior.

To concentrate on the bizarre activities of Davenport—as many critics of the Great Awakening have done—is to obscure the positive ways in which this vast revival changed American society. First, despite occasional anti-intellectual outbursts, the New Lights founded several important centers of higher learning. They wanted to train young men who would carry on the good works of Edwards, Whitefield, and Tennent. In 1746, New Light Presbyterians established the College of New Jersey, which later became Princeton University. Just before his death, Edwards was appointed its president. The evangelical minister, Eleazar Wheelock, launched Dartmouth (1769); other revivalists founded Brown (1764) and Rutgers (1766).

The Great Awakening also encouraged men and women who had been taught to remain silent before traditional figures of authority to speak up, to take an active role in their salvation. They could no longer rely on ministers or institutions. The individual alone stood before God. Knowing this, New Lights made religious choices that shattered the old harmony among Protestant sects, and in its place, they introduced a noisy, often bitterly fought competition. As one New Jersey Presbyterian explained, "There are so many particular *sects* and *Parties* among professed Christians . . . that we know not . . . in which of these different *paths,* to steer our course for *Heaven.*"

Expressive evangelicalism struck a particularly responsive chord among African Americans. Itinerant ministers frequently preached to large sympathetic audiences of slaves. Richard Allen (1760–1831), the founder of the African Methodist

Episcopal Church (AME), reported he owed his freedom in part to a traveling Methodist minister who persuaded Allen's master of the sinfulness of slavery. Allen himself was converted, as were thousands of other black colonists. According to one historian, evangelical preaching "shared enough with traditional African styles and beliefs such as spirit possession and ecstatic expression . . . to allow for an interpenetration of African and Christian religious beliefs."

With religious contention came an awareness of a larger community, a union of fellow believers that extended beyond the boundaries of town and colony. In fact, evangelical religion was one of several forces at work during the mid-eighteenth century that brought scattered colonists into contact with one another for the first time. In this sense, the Great Awakening was a "national" event long before a nation actually existed.

People who had been touched by the Great Awakening shared an optimism about the future of America. With God's help, social and political progress was possible, and from this perspective, of course, the New Lights did not sound much different than the mildly rationalist American spokesmen of the Enlightenment. Both groups prepared the way for the development of a revolutionary mentality in colonial America.

CLASH OF POLITICAL CULTURES

The political history of this period illuminates a growing tension within the empire. Americans of all regions repeatedly stated their desire to replicate British political institutions. Parliament, they claimed, provided a model for the American assemblies. They revered the English constitution. However, the more the colonists studied British political theory and practice—in other words, the more they attempted to become British—the more aware they became of major differences. By trying to copy Great Britain, they unwittingly discovered something about being American.

The English Constitution

During the eighteenth century, political discussion began with the British constitution. It was the object of universal admiration. Unlike the

U.S. Constitution, the British constitution was not a formal written document. It was something much more elusive. The English constitution was a growing body of law, court decisions, and statutes, a sense of traditional political arrangements that people of all classes believed had evolved out of the distant past, preserving life, liberty, and property. Eighteenth-century political commentators admitted with great reluctance that the constitution had in fact changed. Historic confrontations between king and parliament had generated new understandings about what the constitution did or did not allow. Nevertheless, almost everyone regarded change as dangerous and destabilizing, a threat to the political tradition that seemed to explain Britain's greatness.

In theory, the English constitution contained three distinct parts. The monarch was at the top, advised by handpicked court favorites. Next came the House of Lords, a body of 180 aristocrats who served with 26 Anglican bishops as the upper house of Parliament. And third was the House of Commons, composed of 558 members elected by various constituencies scattered throughout the realm.

Political theorists waxed eloquent on workings of the British constitution. Each of the three parts of government, it seemed, represented a separate socioeconomic interest: king, nobility, and common people. Acting alone each body would run to excess, even tyranny, but operating within a mixed system, they automatically checked each other's ambitions for the common good. "Herein consists the excellence of the English government," explained the famed eighteenth-century jurist Sir William Blackstone, "that all parts of it form a mutual check upon each other." Unlike the delegates who wrote the Constitution of the United States, eighteenth-century Englishmen did not perceive the constitution as a balance of executive, legislative, and judicial branches.

The Reality of British Politics

The reality of daily political life in Great Britain, however, bore little relation to theory. The three elements of the constitution did not, in fact, represent distinct socioeconomic groups. Men elected to the House of Commons often came from the same social background as those who served in the House of Lords. All represented the inter-

ests of Britain's landed elite. Moreover, there was no attempt to maintain strict constitutional separation. The king, for example, organized parliamentary associations, loose groups of political followers who sat in the House of Commons and who openly supported the monarch's policies in exchange for patronage or pension.

The claim that the members of the House of Commons represented all the people of England also seemed farfetched. As of 1715, roughly no more than 20 percent of Britain's adult males had the right to vote. Property qualifications or other restrictions often greatly reduced the number of eligible voters. In addition, the size of the electoral districts varied throughout the kingdom. In some boroughs, representatives to Parliament were chosen by several thousand voters. In many districts, however, a handful of electors controlled the result. These tiny, or "rotten" boroughs were an embarrassment. The Methodist leader, John Wesley, complained that Old Sarum, an almost uninhabited borough, "in spite of common sense, without house or inhabitant, still sends two members to the parliament." Since these districts were so small, a wealthy lord or ambitious politician could easily bribe or otherwise "influence" the entire constituency, something they did regularly throughout the century.

Before 1760, few people spoke out against these constitutional abuses. The main exception was a group of radical publicists whom historians have labeled the "Commonwealthmen." These writers decried the corruption of political life, noting that a nation that compromised civic virtue, that failed to stand vigilant against fawning courtiers and would-be despots, deserved to lose its liberty and property. The most famous Commonwealthmen were John Trenchard and Thomas Gordon, who penned a series of essays entitled *Cato's Letters* between 1720 and 1723. If England's rulers were corrupt, they warned, then the people could not expect the balanced constitution to save them from tyranny. In one typical article, Trenchard and Gordon observed "The Appitites . . . of Men, especially of Great Men, are carefully to be observed and stayed, or else they will never stay themselves. The Experience of every Age convinces us, that we must not judge of Men by what they ought to do, but by what they will do."

But however shrilly these writers protested, they won little support for political reforms.

The Election by William Hogarth illustrates just one aspect of electoral corruption in England—voters were openly willing to sell their votes to either (or both) sides in an election.

Most eighteenth-century Englishmen admitted there was more than a grain of truth in the commonwealth critique, but they were not willing to tamper with a system of government that had so recently survived a civil war and a Glorious Revolution. Americans, however, took Trenchard and Gordon to heart.

Governing the Colonies: The American Experience

The colonists assumed—perhaps naively—that their own governments were modeled on the balanced constitution of Great Britain. They argued that within their political systems, the governor corresponded to the king, and the governor's council to the House of Lords. The colonial assemblies were perceived as American reproductions of the House of Commons and were expected to preserve the interests of the people against those of the monarch and aristocracy. As the colonists discovered, however, general theories about a mixed constitution were even less relevant in America than they were in Britain.

By mid-century a majority of the mainland colonies had royal governors appointed by the Crown. Many were career army officers who through luck, charm, or family connection had gained the ear of someone close to the king. These patronage posts did not generate income sufficient to interest the most powerful or talented personalities of the period, but they did draw middle-level bureaucrats who were ambitious, desperate, or both. It is perhaps not surprising that most governors decided simply not to "consider any Thing further than how to sit easy."

George Clinton, who served as New York's governor from 1743 to 1753, was probably typical of the men who hoped to "sit easy." Before coming to the colonies, Clinton had compiled an extraordinary record of ineptitude as a naval officer. He gained the governorship more as a means to get him out of England than as a sign of respect. When he arrived in New York City, Clinton ignored the colonists. "In a province given to hospitality," wrote one critic, "he [Clinton] erred by immuring himself in the fort, or retiring to a grotto in the country, where his time was spent with his bottle and a little trifling circle."

Whatever their demerits, royal governors in America possessed enormous powers. In fact, royal governors could do certain things in America that a king could not do in eighteenth-century Britain. Among these were the right to veto legislation and dismiss judges. The governors also served as military commanders in each province.

Political practice in America differed from the British model in another crucial respect. Royal governors were advised by a council, usually a body of about twelve wealthy colonists selected by the Board of Trade in London upon the recommendation of the govenor. During the seventeenth century, the council had played an important role in colonial government, but its ability to exercise independent authority declined steadily over the course of the eighteenth century. Its members certainly did not represent a distinct aristocracy within American society.

If royal governors did not look like kings, nor American councils like the House of Lords, colonial assemblies bore but a faint resemblance to the eighteenth-century House of Commons. The major difference was the size of the American franchise. In most colonies, adult white males who owned a small amount of land could vote in colonywide elections. One historian estimates that 95 percent of this group in Massachusetts were eligible to participate in elections. The number in Virginia was about 85 percent. These high figures—much larger than those of contemporary England—have led some scholars to view the colonies as "middle-class democracies," societies run by moderately prosperous yeomen farmers who—in politics at least—exercised independent judgment. There were too many of them to bribe, no "rotten" boroughs, and when these people moved west, colonial assemblies usually created new electoral districts.

Colonial governments were not democracies in the modern sense of that term. Possessing the right to vote was one thing, exercising it quite another. Americans participated in elections when major issues were at stake—the formation of banks in mid-eighteenth-century Massachusetts, for example—but most of the time they were content to let members of the rural and urban gentry represent them in the assemblies. To be sure, unlike modern democracies, these colonial politics excluded women and nonwhites from voting. The point to remember, however, is that the power to expel legislative rascals was always present in

America, and it was this political reality that kept autocratic gentlemen from straying too far from the will of the people.

Colonial Assemblies

Elected members of the colonial assemblies believed that they had a special obligation to preserve colonial liberties. They perceived any attack on the legislature as an assault on the rights of Americans. The elected representatives brooked no criticism, and several colonial printers landed in jail because they criticized actions taken by a lower house.

So aggressive were these bodies in seizing privileges, determining procedures, and controlling money bills that some historians have described the political development of eighteenth-century America as "the rise of the assemblies." No doubt this is exaggerated, but the long series of imperial wars against the French, demanding large public expenditures, transformed the small, amateurish assemblies of the seventeenth century into the more professional, vigilant legislatures of the eighteenth.

This political system seemed designed to generate hostility. There was simply no reason for the colonial legislators to cooperate with appointed royal governors. Alexander Spotswood, Virginia's governor from 1710 to 1722, for example, attempted to institute a bold new land program backed by the Crown. He tried persuasion and gifts, and when these failed, chicanery. But the members of the House of Burgesses refused to support a plan that did not suit their own interests. Before leaving office, Spotswood gave up trying to carry out royal policy in America. Instead, he allied himself with the local Virginia gentry who controlled the House as well as the Council, and because they awarded their new friend with large tracts of land, he became a wealthy man.

A few governors managed briefly to recreate in America the political culture of patronage, the system that eighteenth-century Englishmen took for granted. Most successful in this endeavor was William Shirley, who held office in Massachusetts from 1741 to 1757. The secret to his political successes in America was connection to people who held high office in Great Britain. But Shirley's practices—and those of men like him—clashed with the colonists' perception of politics. They *really* believed in the purity of the balanced constitution. They insisted on complete separation of executive and legislative authority. Therefore, when Americans suspected a governor, or even some of their own representatives, of employing patronage to influence government decisions, their protests seem to have been lifted directly from the pages of *Cato's Letters.*

A major source of shared political information was the weekly journal, a new and vigorous institution in American life. In New York and Massachusetts especially, weekly newspapers urged readers to preserve civic virtue, to exercise extreme vigilance against the spread of privileged power. In the first issue of the *Independent Reflector* published in New York (November 30, 1752), the editor announced defiantly that no discouragement shall ". . . deter me from vindicating the *civil* and *religious RIGHTS* of my Fellow-Creatures: From exposing the peculiar Deformity of publick *Vice,* and *Corruption;* and displaying the amiable Charms of *Liberty,* with the detestable Nature of *Slavery* and *Oppression.*" Through such journals, a pattern of political rhetoric that in Britain had gained only marginal respectability, became after 1765 America's normal form of political discourse.

The rise of the assemblies shaped American culture in other, subtler ways. Over the course of the century, the language of the law became increasingly anglicized. The Board of Trade, the Privy Council, and Parliament scrutinized court decisions and legislative actions from all thirteen mainland colonies. As a result, varying local legal practices that had been widespread during the seventeenth century became standardized. Indeed, according to one historian, the colonial legal system by 1750 "was substantially that of the mother country." Not surprisingly, many men who served in colonial assemblies were either lawyers or persons who had received legal training. When Americans from different regions met—as they frequently did in the years before the Revolution—they discovered they shared a commitment to the preservation of the English common law.

As eighteenth-century political developments drew the colonists closer to the mother country, they also brought Americans a greater awareness of each other. As their horizons widened, they learned they operated within the same general

North America, 1750

By 1750, the French had established a chain of settlements southward through the heart of the continent from Quebec to New Orleans. The English saw this as a menace to their seaboard colonies, which were expanding westward.

imperial system, and the problems confronting the Massachusetts House of Representatives were not too different from those facing Virginia's House of Burgesses or South Carolina's Commons House. Like the revivalists and merchants—people who crossed old boundaries—colonial legislators laid the foundation for a larger cultural identity.

CENTURY OF IMPERIAL WAR

The scope and character of warfare in the colonies changed radically during the eighteenth century. The founders of England's mainland colonies had engaged in intense local conflicts with the Indians, such as King Philip's War (1675–1676) in New England. But after 1690, the colonists were increasingly involved in hostilities that originated on the other side of the Atlantic, in rivalries between Great Britain and France over political and commercial ambitions. The external threat to security forced people in different colonies to devise unprecedented measures of military and political cooperation.

On paper at least, the British settlements enjoyed military superiority over the settlements of New France. Louis XIV (1643–1715) possessed an impressive army of 100,000 well-armed troops, but he dispatched few of them to the New World. He left the defense of Canada and the Mississippi Valley to the companies engaged in the fur trade. Meeting this challenge seemed almost impossible for the French outposts strung out along the Saint Lawrence River and the Great Lakes. In 1754, New France contained only 75,000 inhabitants as compared to 1.2 million people living in Britain's mainland colonies.

For most of the century, the theoretical advantages enjoyed by the English colonists did them little good. While the British settlements possessed a larger and more prosperous population, they were divided into separate governments that sometimes seemed more suspicious of each other than of the French. When war came, French officers and Indian allies exploited these jealousies with considerable skill. Moreover, although the population of New France was comparatively small, it was concentrated along the Saint Lawrence, so that while the French found it difficult to mount effective offensive operations against the English, they could easily mass the forces needed to defend Montreal and Quebec.

King William's and Queen Anne's Wars

Colonial involvement in imperial war began in 1689, when England's new king, William III, declared war on Louis XIV. Europeans called this struggle the War of the League of Augsburg, but to the Americans, it was simply King William's War. Canadians commanded by the Comte de Frontenac raided the northern frontiers of New York and New England, and while they made no territorial gains, they caused considerable suffering among the civilian populations of Massachusetts and New York.

Native Americans often depended on trade goods supplied by the British and sometimes adopted British dress as shown in this engraving of a Mohawk chief, "Old Hendrick," published in London in 1740.

The war ended with the Treaty of Ryswick (1697), but the colonists were drawn almost immediately into a new conflict. Queen Anne's War, known in Europe as the War of Spanish Succession (1702–1713), was fought across a large geographic area. The bloody combat along the American frontier ended in 1713 when Great Britain and France signed the Treaty of Utrecht. European negotiators showed little interest in the military situation in the New World. Their major concern was preserving a balance of power among the European states. More than two decades of intense fighting had taken a heavy toll in North America, but neither French nor English colonists had much to show for their sacrifice.

After George I replaced Anne on the throne in 1714, parliamentary leaders were determined to preserve peace—mainly because of the rising cost of war. Yet on the American frontier, the hostilities continued with raids and reprisals. As people on both sides of this conflict now realized, the

A Century of Conflict: Major Wars, 1689–1763

Dates	European Name	American Name	Major Allies	Issues
1689–1697	War of the League of Augsburg	King William's War	Britain, Holland, Spain, their colonies, and Native American allies against France, its colonies, and Native American allies	Opposition to French bid for control of Europe
1702–1713	War of the Spanish Succession	Queen Anne's War	Britain, Holland, their colonies, and Native American allies against France, Spain, their colonies, and Native American allies	Austria and France hold rival claims to Spanish throne
1739–1748	War of the Austrian Succession (War of Jenkin's Ear)	King George's War	Britain, its colonies and Native American allies, and Austria against France, Spain, their Native American allies, and Prussia	Struggle among Britain, Spain, and France for control of New World territory; among France, Prussia, and Austria for control of central Europe.
1756–1763	Seven Years' War	French and Indian War	Britain, its colonies, and Native American allies against France, its colonies, and Native American allies.	Struggle among Britain, Spain, and France for worldwide control of colonial markets and raw materials

stakes of war were very high; they were fighting for control over the entire West, including the Mississippi Valley.

Both sides viewed this great contest in conspiratorial terms. From South Carolina to Massachusetts Bay, colonists believed the French planned to "encircle" the English settlements, to confine the English to a narrow strip of land along the Atlantic Coast. The English noted that in 1682, La Salle had claimed for the king of France, a territory—Louisiana—that included all the people and resources located on "streams and Rivers" flowing into the Mississippi River. To make good on their claim, the French constructed forts on the Chicago and Illinois rivers. In 1717, they established a military post 200 miles up the Alabama River, well within striking distance of the Carolina frontier, and in 1718, they settled New Orleans. One New Yorker declared in 1715 that ". . . it is impossible that we and the French can

both inhabit this Continent in peace but that one nation must at last give way to the other."

On their part, the French suspected their rivals intended to seize all of North America. Land speculators and frontier traders pushed aggressively into territory claimed by the French and owned by the Native Americans. In 1716, one Frenchman urged his government to hasten the development of Louisiana, since "it is not difficult to guess that their [the British] purpose is to drive us entirely out . . . of North America."

To their great sorrow and eventual destruction, the original inhabitants of the frontier, the Native Americans, were swept up in this undeclared war. The Indians maneuvered to hold their own in the "middle ground." The Iroquois favored the British; the Algonquian peoples generally supported the French. But regardless of the groups to which they belonged, Indian warriors—acting independently and for their own strategic

Major American Battle	Treaty
New England troops assault Quebec under Sir William Phips (1690)	Treaty of Ryswick (1697)
Deerfield Massacre (1704)	Treaty of Utrecht (1713)
New England forces capture Louisbourg under William Pepperrell (1745)	Treaty of Aix-la-Chappelle (1748)
British and Continental forces capture Quebec under Major General James Wolfe (1759)	Peace of Paris (1763)

reasons—found themselves enmeshed in imperial policies set by distant European kings.

King George's War and Its Aftermath

In 1743, the Americans were dragged once again into the imperial conflict. During King George's War (1743–1748), known in Europe as the War of Austrian Succession, the colonists scored a magnificent victory over the French. Louisbourg, a gigantic fortress on Cape Breton Island, the easternmost promontory of Canada, guarded the approaches to the Gulf of Saint Lawrence and Quebec. It was described as the "Gibraltar of the New World." An army of New England troops under the command of William Pepperrell captured Louisbourg in June 1745, a feat that demonstrated the British colonists were able to fight and to mount effective joint operations.

The Americans, however, were in for a shock. When the war ended with the signing of the Treaty of Aix-la-Chapelle in 1748, the British government handed Louisbourg back to the French in exchange for concessions elsewhere. Such decisions exposed the deep and continuing ambivalence the colonists felt about participation in imperial wars. They were proud to support Great Britain, of course, but the Americans seldom fully understood why the wars were being fought, why certain tactics had been adopted, and why the British accepted treaty terms that so blatantly ignored colonial interests.

The French were not prepared to surrender an inch. But as they recognized, time was running against them. Not only were the English colonies growing more populous, they also possessed a seemingly inexhaustible supply of manufactured goods to trade with the Indians. The French decided in the early 1750s, therefore, to seize the Ohio Valley before the Virginians could do so. They established forts throughout the region, the most formidable being Fort Duquesne, located at the strategic fork in the Ohio River, later renamed Pittsburgh.

Although France and England had not officially declared war, British officials advised the governor of Virginia to "repell force by force." The Virginians needed little encouragement. They were eager to make good their claim to the Ohio Valley, and in 1754, militia companies under the command of a promising young officer, George Washington, constructed Fort Necessity not far from Fort Duquesne. The plan failed. French and Indian troops overran the badly exposed outpost (July 3, 1754). Among other things, this humiliating setback revealed that a single colony could not defeat the French.

Albany Congress and Braddock's Defeat

Benjamin Franklin, for one, appreciated the need for intercolonial cooperation. When British officials invited representatives from the northern colonies to Albany (June 1754) to discuss relations with the Iroquois, Franklin used the occasion to present a bold blueprint for colonial union. His so-called Albany Plan envisioned the formation of a Grand Council, made up of elected delegates from the various colonies, to oversee matters of common defense, western expansion, and Indian affairs. A President General appointed by the king would preside. Franklin's most daring suggestion involved taxation. He insisted the

This mid-eighteenth-century lithograph portrays colonial assault troops, under the command of William Pepperrell, establishing a beachhead at Freshwater Cove near Louisbourg. Pepperrell's troops went on to capture Louisbourg.

council be authorized to collect taxes to cover military expenditures.

First reaction to the Albany Plan was enthusiastic. To take effect, however, it required the support of the separate colonial assemblies as well as Parliament. It received neither. The assemblies were jealous of their fiscal authority, and the English thought the scheme undermined the Crown's power over American affairs.

In 1755, the Ohio Valley again became the scene of fierce fighting. Even though there was still no formal declaration of war, the British resolved to destroy Fort Duquesne, and to that end, they dispatched units of the regular army to America. In command was Major General Edward Braddock, an obese, humorless veteran who inspired neither fear nor respect. One colonist described Braddock as ". . . very indolent, Slave to his passions, women & wine, as great an Epicure as could be in his eating, tho a brave man."

On July 9, Braddock led a joint force of twenty-five hundred British redcoats and colonists to humiliating defeat. The French and Indians opened fire as Braddock's army waded across the Monongahela River, about 8 miles from Fort Duquesne. Along a narrow road already congested with heavy wagons and confused men, Braddock ordered a counterattack, described by one of his officers as "without any form or order but that of a parcell of school boys coming out of s[c]hool." Nearly 70 percent of Braddock's troops were killed or wounded in western Pennsylvania. The general himself died in battle. The French, who suffered only light casualties, remained in firm control of the Ohio Valley.

The entire affair profoundly angered Washington, who fumed, "We have been most scandalously beaten by a trifling body of men." The British thought their allies the Iroquois might desert them after this embarrassing defeat. The Indians, however, took the news in stride, observing that "they were not at all surprised to hear it, as they [Braddock's redcoats] were men who had crossed the Great Water and were unacquainted with the arts of war among the Americans."

Seven Years' War

Britain's imperial war effort had hit bottom. No one in England or America seemed to possess the leadership necessary to drive the French from the Mississippi Valley. The cabinet of George II (1727–1760) lacked the will to organize and finance a sustained military campaign in the New World, and colonial assemblies balked every time Britain asked them to raise men and money. On May 18, 1756, the British officially declared war on the French, a conflict called the French and Indian War in America and the Seven Years' War in Europe.

Had it not been for William Pitt, the most powerful minister in George's cabinet, the military stalemate might have continued. This supremely self-confident Englishman believed he was the only person capable of saving the British empire, an opinion he publicly expressed. When he became effective head of the Ministry in December 1756, Pitt had an opportunity to demonstrate his talents.

In the past, warfare on the European continent had worked mainly to France's advantage. Pitt saw no point in continuing to concentrate on Europe, and in 1757 he advanced a bold new imperial policy, one based on commercial assumptions. In Pitt's judgment, the critical confrontation would take place in North America, where Britain and France were struggling to control colonial markets and raw materials. Indeed, according to Pitt, America was "where England and Europe are to be fought for." He was determined, therefore, to expel the French from the continent, however great the cost.

To effect this ambitious scheme, Pitt took personal command of the army and navy. He mapped strategy. He even promoted young promising officers over the heads of their superiors. He also recognized that the success of the war effort could not depend on the generosity of the colonial assemblies. Great Britain would have to foot most of the bill. Pitt's military expenditures, of course, created an enormous national debt that would soon haunt both Britain and its colonies, but at the time, no one foresaw the fiscal consequences of victory in America.

To direct the grand campaign, Pitt selected two relatively obscure officers, Jeffrey Amherst and James Wolfe. It was a masterful choice, one that

The first political cartoon to appear in an American newspaper was created by Benjamin Franklin in 1754 to emphasize the importance of the Albany Plan.

a less self-assured man than Pitt would never have risked. Both officers were young, talented, and ambitious, and on July 26, 1758, forces under their direction captured Louisbourg, the same fortress the colonists had taken a decade earlier!

This victory cut the Canadians' main supply line with France. The small population of New France could no longer meet the military demands placed on it. As the situation became increasingly desperate, the French forts of the Ohio Valley and the Great Lakes began to fall. Duquesne was simply abandoned late in 1758 as French and Indian troops under the Marquis de Montcalm retreated toward Quebec and Montreal. During the summer of 1759, the French surrendered key forts at Ticonderoga, Crown Point, and Niagara.

The climax to a century of war came dramatically in September 1759. Wolfe, now a major general, assaulted Quebec with nine thousand men. But it was not simply force of arms that brought victory. Wolfe proceeded as if he were preparing to attack the city directly, but under cover of darkness, his troops scaled a cliff to dominate a less well-defended position. At dawn on September 13, 1759, they took the French from the rear by surprise. The decisive action occurred on the Plains of Abraham, a bluff high above the Saint Lawrence River. Both Wolfe and Montcalm were mortally wounded. When an aide informed Wolfe the French had been routed, he

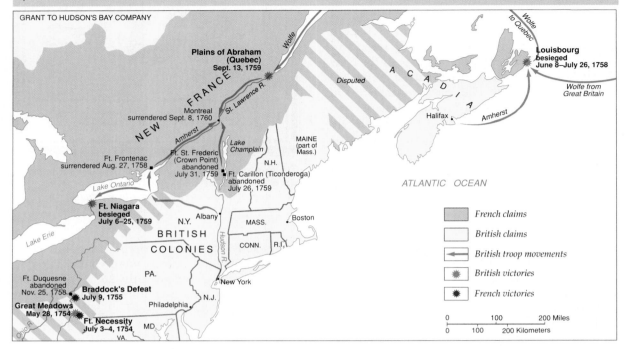

The Seven Years' War, 1756–1763
Major battle sites. The conflict ended with Great Britain driving the French from mainland North America.

sighed, "Now, God be praised, I will die in peace." On September 8, 1760, Amherst accepted the final surrender of the French army at Montreal.

The Peace of Paris signed on February 10, 1763, almost fulfilled Pitt's grandiose dreams. Great Britain took possession of an empire that stretched around the globe. Only Guadeloupe and Martinique, the Caribbean sugar islands, were given back to the French. After a century-long struggle, the French had been driven from the mainland of North America. Even Louisiana passed out of France's control into Spanish hands. The treaty gave Britain title to Canada, Florida, and all the land east of the Mississippi River. Moreover, with the stroke of a diplomat's pen, eighty thousand French-speaking Canadians, most of them Catholics, became the subjects of George III.

The Americans were overjoyed. It was a time of good feelings and national pride. Together, the English and their colonial allies had thwarted the "Gallic peril." Samuel Davies, a Presbyterian who had brought the Great Awakening to Virginia, announced confidently that the long-awaited victory would inaugurate "*a new heaven and a new earth.*"

Perceptions of War

The Seven Years' War made a deep impression on American society. Even though Franklin's Albany Plan had failed, the military struggle had forced the colonists to cooperate on an unprecedented scale. It also drew them into closer contact with Britain. They became aware of being part of a great empire, but in the very process of waging war, they acquired a more intimate sense of an America that lay beyond the plantation and the village. Conflict had carried thousands of young men across colonial boundaries, exposing them to a vast territory full of opportunities for a booming population. Moreover, the war trained a corps of American officers, people like George Washington, who learned from firsthand experience that the British were not invincible.

British officials later accused the Americans of ingratitude. England, they claimed, had sent troops and provided funds to liberate the colonists from the threat of French attack. The Americans, appreciative of the aid from England, cheered on the British but dragged their feet at every stage, refusing to pay the bills. These charges were later incorporated into a general argument justifying parliamentary taxation in America.

The British had a point. The colonists were, in fact, slow in providing the men and materials needed to fight the French. Nevertheless, they did make a significant contribution to the war effort, and it was perfectly reasonable for Americans to regard themselves at the very least as junior partners in the empire. After all, they had supplied almost twenty thousand soldiers and spent well over £2 million. In a single year, in fact, Massachusetts enlisted five thousand men out of an adult male population of about fifty thousand, a commitment that, in the words of one military historian, meant "the war was being waged on a scale comparable to the great wars of modern times." After making such a sacrifice—indeed, after demonstrating their loyalty to the mother country—the colonists would surely have been disturbed to learn that General James Wolfe, the hero of Quebec, had stated, "The Americans are in general the dirtiest, the most contemptible, cowardly dogs that you can conceive. There is no depending upon them in action. They fall down in their own dirt and desert in battalions, officers and all."

RULE BRITANNIA?

James Thomson, an Englishman, understood the hold of empire on the popular imagination of the eighteenth century. In 1740, he composed words that British patriots have proudly sung for more than two centuries:

Rule Britannia, rule the waves
Britons never will be slaves

Colonial Americans—at least, those of British background—joined the chorus. By mid-century they took their political and cultural cues from

North America After 1763
The Peace of Paris (1763) redrew the map of North America. Great Britain received all the French holdings except a few islands in the Caribbean.

Great Britain. They fought its wars, purchased its consumer goods, flocked to hear its evangelical preachers, and read its many publications. Without question, the empire provided the colonists with a compelling source of identity.

An editor justified the establishment of New Hampshire's first newspaper in precisely these terms. "By this Means," the publisher observed, "the spirited *Englishman*, the mountainous *Welshman*, the brave *Scotchman*, and *Irishman*, and the loyal *American*, may be firmly united and mutually RESOLVED to guard the glorious Throne of BRITANNIA. . . . as *British Brothers*, in defending the Common Cause." Even new immigrants, the Germans, Scotch-Irish, and

CHRONOLOGY

1680	Popé leads Pueblo revolt against the Spanish in New Mexico
1689	William and Mary accede to the English throne
1706	Birth of Benjamin Franklin
1714	George I of Hanover becomes monarch of Great Britain
1732	Colony of Georgia is established • Birth of George Washington
1734–1736	First expression of the Great Awakening at Northampton, Massachusetts
1740	George Whitefield electrifies listeners at Boston
1745	Colonial troops capture Louisbourg • First American Lutheran ministers ordained in Philadelphia
1754	Albany Congress meets
1755	Braddock is defeated by the French and Indians in western Pennsylvania
1756	Seven Years' War is formally declared
1759	British are victorious at Quebec. Wolfe and Montcalm are killed in battle
1760	George III becomes king of Great Britain
1763	Peace of Paris ending French and Indian War is signed
1769	Junípero Serra begins to build missions in California
1821	Mexico declares independence from Spain

ent perception. For them, "American" was a way of saying "not quite English."

Recommended Reading

A comprehensive examination of Anglo-American relations in the late colonial period is Lawrence H. Gipson, *British Empire Before the American Revolution*, 8 vols. (1936-1949). A much shorter, and in many ways more useful, introduction to eighteenth-century colonial society is Richard Hofstadter, *America at 1750: A Social Portrait* (1971). A stimulating survey of English culture and politics can be found in Roy Porter, *English Society in the Eighteenth Century* (1982). For the wars of empire, see Howard H. Peckham, *The Colonial Wars, 1689–1762* (1964), and Fred Anderson's splendid social history of colonial soldiering, *A People's Army: Massachusetts Soldiers and Society in the Seven Years' War* (1984). Sydney E. Ahlstrom provides an encyclopedic review of eighteenth-century religion in *Religious History of the American People* (1972). Also valuable is Patricia Bonomi, *Under the Cope of Heaven: Religion, Society, and Politics in Colonial America* (1986). The most imaginative analysis of colonial politics remains Bernard Bailyn, *The Origin of American Politics* (1968). And recently, Bailyn has produced a masterful study of European migration entitled *Voyagers to the West* (1986).

Additional Bibliography

The significance of American population growth in this period is thoughtfully examined in John J. McCusker and Russell R. Menard, *The Economy of British America, 1607–1789* (1985). The transfer of various British subcultures is the topic of David H. Fischer's provocative *Albion's Seed: Four British Folkways in America* (1989). A useful review of the recent literature can be found in Bernard Bailyn and Philip D. Morgan, eds., *Strangers Within the Realm: Cultural Margins of the First British Empire* (1991). A. G. Roeber provides an impressively original interpretation of the transfer of German culture in *Palatines, Liberty, and Property: German Lutherans in Colonial British America* (1993). For the Scots, see Ned Landsman, *Scotland and Its First American Colony* (1985). Roger A. Ekirch offers a thorough analysis of the convict servant trade in *Bound for America* (1987).

The most exciting recent historical literature deals with the formation of a multicultural backcountry. These studies are especially good on the development of Native American societies: Daniel H. Unser, Jr., *Indians, Settlers, and Slaves in a Frontier Exchange Economy* (1992); Michael N. McConnell, *A Country Between: The Upper Ohio Valley and Its Peoples,*

Africans, who felt no political loyalty to Great Britain and no affinity to English culture, had to assimilate to some degree to the dominant English culture of the colonies.

Americans hailed Britannia. In 1763, they were the victors, the conquerors of the backcountry. In their moment of glory the colonists assumed that Britain's rulers saw the Americans as "Brothers," as equal partners in the business of empire. Only slowly would they learn the British had a differ-

1724–1774 (1992); Richard White, *The Middle Ground: Indians, Empires, and Republics in the Great Lakes Region* (1991); Daniel K. Richter, *The Ordeal of the Longhouse: The Peoples of the Iroquois League in the Era of European Colonization* (1992); Peter H. Wood et al., eds., *Powhatan's Mantle: Indians in the Colonial Southeast* (1989); and Peter C. Mancall, *Valley of Opportunity: Economic Culture Along the Upper Susquehanna* (1991).

The complex story of Spanish colonization is told masterfully in David J. Weber, *The Spanish Frontier in North America* (1992). Weber also edited a book of valuable essays entitled *New Spain's Far Northern Frontier* (1979). One of the most original works in this field, one that explores the meaning of gender, is Ramón A. Gutiérrez, *When Jesus Came, the Corn Mothers Went Away: Marriage, Sexuality, and Power in New Mexico, 1500–1846* (1991).

Eighteenth-century English politics, theory and practice, is the subject of an increasingly sophisticated literature. Read Linda Colley, *Britons: Forging the Nation, 1707–1837* (1992); Gerald Newman, *The Rise of English Nationalism: A Cultural History* (1987); and Lawrence Stones, ed., *An Imperial State at War* (1994).

The way Americans living in different colonies interpreted contemporary British political culture is discussed in Bernard Bailyn, *The Origins of American Politics* (1968); Jack P. Greene, *Peripheries and Center* (1986); Richard Bushman, *King and People in Provincial Massachusetts* (1985); and T. H. Breen, *Tobacco Culture: The Great Tidewater Planters on the Eve of Revolution* (1986). Also see J. Greene, *Quest for Power* (1983); Patricia Bonomi, *A Factious People: Politics and Society in Colonial New York* (1977); Robert Weir, *"The Last American Freemen," Studies in the Political Culture of the Colonial and Revolutionary South* (1986).

On the Great Awakening, see George Whitefield's *Journals* (1969) as well as *The Great Awakening* (1967), edited by Alan Heimert and Perry Miller. Also useful are Alan Heimert, *Religion and the American Mind* (1966); Harry S. Stout, *The New England Soul* (1988); John Butler, *Awash in a Sea of Faith* (1990); and Frank Lambert, *"Pedlar in Divinity": George Whitefield and the Transatlantic Revivals* (1994). For an explanation of the eighteenth-century concern for good manners, see Richard L. Bushman, *The Refinement of America: Persons, Houses, Cities* (1992).

The American Revolution

From Gentry Protest to Popular Revolt, 1763–1783

During the revolutionary war, a captured British officer spent some time at the plantation of Colonel Thomas Mann Randolph, a leader of Virginia's gentry. The Englishman described the arrival of three farmers who were members of the local militia. He characterized the militiamen as "peasants," for without asking their host's permission, the Americans drew chairs up to the fire, pulled off their muddy boots, and began spitting. The British officer was appalled; after the farmers departed, he observed they had not shown Randolph proper deference. The colonel responded that such behavior had come to be expected, for "the spirit of independency" had been transformed into "equality." Indeed, every American who "bore arms" during the Revolution considered himself as good as his neighbors. "No doubt," Randolph remarked to the officer, "each of these men conceives himself, in every respect, my equal."

This chance encounter illuminates the character of the American Revolution. The initial stimulus for rebellion came from the gentry, from the rich and wellborn, who resented Parliament's efforts to curtail their rights within the British empire. They voiced their unhappiness in carefully reasoned statements and in speeches before elected assemblies. Passionate rhetoric made them uneasy.

But as these influential planters, wealthy merchants, and prominent clergymen discovered, the revolutionary movement generated a momentum that they could not control. As relations with Britain deteriorated, particularly after 1765, the traditional leaders of colonial society invited the ordinary folk to join the protest—as rioters, as petitioners, and finally, as soldiers. Newspapers, sermons, and pamphlets helped transform what had begun as a squabble among the gentry into a mass movement, and as Randolph learned, once the people had become involved in shaping the nation's destiny, they could never again be excluded.

A second, often overlooked, aspect of the American Revolution involved a massive military commitment. If common American soldiers had not been willing to stand up to seasoned British troops, to face the terror of the bayonet charge, independence would have remained a dream of intellectuals. Proportionate to the population, a greater percentage of Americans died in military service during the Revolution than in any war in American history, with the exception of the Civil War. The concept of liberty so magnificently expressed in revolutionary pamphlets was not, therefore, simply an abstraction, an exclusive concern of political theorists like Thomas Jefferson and John Adams. It also motivated ordinary folk—mud-covered Virginia militiamen, for example—to take up weapons and risk death. Those who survived the ordeal were never quite the same, for the very experience of fighting, of assuming responsibility in battle and perhaps even of taking the lives of British officers, gave dramatic new meaning to social equality.

AN EXPECTANT SOCIETY

Colonists who were alive during the 1760s did not anticipate the coming of independence. It is only from our modern perspective that we see how the events of this period would lead to the formation of a new nation. The colonists, of course, did not know what the future would bring. They would probably have characterized these years as "postwar," as a time of heightened economic and political expectation following the successful conclusion of the Seven Years' War (see Chapter 4).

For many Americans, it was a period of optimism. The population continued to grow. Indeed, in 1776, approximately 2.5 million people, black and white, were living in Great Britain's thirteen mainland colonies. The population was extremely young. Nearly 60 percent of the American people were under twenty-one. This is a fact of considerable significance. At any given time, most people in this society were small children, and many of the young men who fought the British during the Revolution either had not been alive during the Stamp Act crisis or, if they were alive, had been infants. Any explanation for the coming of independence, therefore, must take into account the continuing political mobilization of so many young people.

Postwar Americans also experienced a high level of prosperity. To be sure, some major port cities went through a difficult period as colonists who had been employed during the fighting were thrown out of work. Sailors and ship workers, for example, were especially vulnerable to layoffs of this sort. In general, however, white Americans did very well. In fact, the quality of their material lives was not substantially lower than that of the English. In 1774, the per capita wealth of the Americans—this figure includes blacks as well as whites—was £37.4. This sum exceeds the per capita wealth of most developing countries today. On the eve of revolution, £37.4 would have purchased about 310 bushels of wheat, 1,600 pounds of rice, 11 cows, or 6 horses. A typical white family of five—a father, mother, and three dependent children—would have been able to afford not only decent food, clothing, and housing, but would also have had money left over with which to purchase consumer goods. Even the poorest colonists seem to have benefited from a rising standard of living, and although they may not have done as well as their wealthier neighbors, they too wanted to preserve gains they had made.

Wealth, however, was not evenly distributed in this society. Regional variations were striking. The southern colonies enjoyed the highest levels of personal wealth in America, which can be explained in part by the ownership of slaves. Over 90 percent of America's unfree workers lived in the South, and they represented a huge capital investment. Even without including the slaves in these wealth estimates, the South did quite well. In terms of aggregate wealth, the Middle Colonies also scored impressively. In fact, only New England lagged noticeably behind, a reflection of its relative inability to produce large amounts of exports for a growing world market.

Roots of Imperial Crisis

Ultimate responsibility for preserving the empire fell to George III. When he became king of England in 1760, he was a young man, only twenty-two years of age. In public, contemporaries praised the new monarch. In private, however, they expressed grave reservations. The youth had led a sheltered, loveless life; his father, an irresponsible playboy, died in 1751 before ascending the throne. Young George had not received a good education, and even though he

Despite his insecurity over an inadequate education, George III was determined to take an active role in reigning over Parliament and the colonies.

demonstrated considerable mechanical ability, his grandfather, George II, thought his grandson dull-witted, an opinion widely shared. As one might expect, George grew up hating not only his grandfather, but almost everyone associated with the reign of George II.

To hide his intellectual inadequacies, the new king adopted a pedantic habit of correcting people for small faults, a characteristic made all the more annoying by his obvious inability to grasp the larger implications of government policy. During a difficult period that demanded imagination, generosity, and wisdom, George muddled along as best he could.

The new monarch was determined to play an aggressive role in government. This decision caused considerable dismay among England's political leaders. For decades a powerful, though loosely associated, group of men who called themselves "Whigs" had set policy and controlled patronage. George II had accepted this situation, and so long as the Whigs in Parliament did not meddle with his beloved army, the king had let them rule the nation.

In one stroke, George III destroyed this cozy relationship. He selected as his chief minister the Earl of Bute, a Scot whose only qualification for office appeared to be his friendship with the young king. The Whigs who dominated Parliament were outraged. Bute had no ties with the members of the House of Commons; he owed them no favors. It seemed to the Whigs that with the appointment of Bute, George was trying to turn back the clock, to reestablish a personal Stuart monarchy free from traditional constitutional restraints. The Whigs blamed Bute for every wrong, real or imagined. George did not, in fact, harbor such arbitrary ambitions, but his actions threw customary political practices into doubt.

By 1763, Bute had despaired of public life and left office. His departure, however, neither restored the Whigs to preeminence nor dampened the king's enthusiasm for domestic politics. Everyone agreed George had the right to select whomever he desired for cabinet posts, but until 1770, no one seemed able to please the monarch. Ministers came and went, often for no other reason than George's personal distaste. Because of this chronic instability, subministers (minor bureaucrats who directed routine colonial affairs) did not know what was expected of them. In the absence of long-range policy, some ministers made narrowly based decisions; others did nothing. Most devoted their energies to finding a political patron capable of satisfying the fickle king. Talent played little part in the scramble for office, and incompetent hacks were advanced as frequently as were men of vision. With such turbulence surrounding him, the king showed little interest in the American colonies.

The king, however, does not bear the sole blame for England's loss of empire. The members of Parliament who actually drafted the statutes that gradually drove a wedge between the colonists and Britain must share the blame, for they failed to provide innovative answers to the explosive constitutional issues of the day. The

problem was not stupidity, or even obstinancy, qualities that are found in equal measure among all peoples.

In part, the impasse resulted from sheer ignorance. Few Englishmen active in government had ever visited America. For those who attempted to follow colonial affairs, accurate information proved extremely difficult to obtain. Packet boats carrying passengers and mail sailed regularly between London and the various colonial ports, but the voyage across the Atlantic required at least four weeks. Furthermore, all correspondence was laboriously copied in longhand by overworked clerks serving in understaffed offices. One could not expect to receive from America an answer to a specific question in less than three months. As a result of the lag in communication between England and America, rumors sometimes passed for true accounts, and misunderstanding influenced the formulation of colonial policy.

But failure of communication alone was not to blame for the widening gap between the colonists and England. Even when complete information was available, the two sides were often unable to understand each other's positions. The central element in this Anglo-American debate was a concept known as *parliamentary sovereignty*. The English ruling classes viewed the role of Parliament from a historical perspective that most colonists never shared. They insisted that Parliament was the dominant element within the constitution. Indeed, this elective body protected rights and property from an arbitrary monarch. During the reign of the Stuarts, especially under Charles I (1625–1649), the authority of Parliament had been challenged, and it was not until the Glorious Revolution of 1688 that the English Crown formally recognized Parliament's supreme authority in matters such as taxation. Almost no one, including George III, would have dissented from a speech made in 1766 before the House of Commons in which a representative declared, "The parliament hath, and must have, from the nature and essence of the constitution, has had, and ever will have a sovereign supreme power and jurisdiction over every part of the dominions of the state, *to make laws in all cases whatsoever.*"

Such a constitutional position did not leave much room for compromise. Most members of

Parliament took a hard line on this issue. The notion of dividing or sharing sovereignty simply made no sense to the English ruling class. As Thomas Hutchinson, royal governor of Massachusetts, explained, no middle ground existed "between the supreme authority of Parliament and the total dependence of the colonies: it is impossible there should be two independent legislatures in one and the same state."

The logic of this argument seemed self-evident to the British. In fact, Parliamentary leaders could never quite understand why the colonists were so difficult to persuade. In frustration, Lord Hillsborough, the British Secretary of State, admonished the colonial agent for Connecticut, "It is essential to the constitution to preserve the supremacy of Parliament inviolate; and tell your friends in America . . . that it is as much their interest to support the constitution and preserve the supremacy of Parliament as it is ours."

No Taxation Without Representation: The American Perspective

Americans most emphatically did not see it in their "interest" to maintain the "supremacy of Parliament." The crisis in imperial relations forced the colonists first to define and then to defend principles deeply rooted in their own political culture. For more than a century, their ideas about the colonies' role within the British empire had remained a vague, untested bundle of assumptions about personal liberties, property rights, and representative institutions.

By 1763, however, certain fundamental American beliefs had become clear. From Massachusetts to Georgia, colonists aggressively defended the powers of the provincial assemblies. They drew on a rich legislative history of their own. Over the course of the century, the American assemblies had steadily expanded their authority over taxation and expenditure. Since no one in Britain bothered to clip their legislative wings, these provincial bodies assumed a major role in policy making and routine administration. In other words, by mid-century the assemblies looked like American copies of Parliament. It seemed unreasonable, therefore, for the British suddenly to insist on the supremacy of Parliament, for as the legislators of Massachusetts observed in 1770, "This house has the same inherent rights in this province as the house of commons in Great Britain."

The constitutional debate turned ultimately on the meaning of representation itself. In 1764, a British official informed the colonists that even though they had not elected members to Parliament—indeed, even though they had had no direct contact with the current members—they were nevertheless "virtually" represented by that august body. The members of parliament, he declared, represented the political interests of everyone who lived in the British empire. It did not really matter whether they had cast a vote.

The colonists ridiculed this argument. The only representatives the Americans recognized as legitimate were those actually chosen by the people for whom they spoke. On this crucial point they would not compromise. As John Adams insisted, a representative assembly should actually mirror its constituents: "It should think, feel, reason, and act like them." Since the members of Parliament could not possibly "think" like Americans, it followed logically they could not represent them. And if they were not genuine representatives, the members of Parliament—pretensions to sovereignty not withstanding—had no business taxing the American people. Thus, in 1764 the Connecticut Assembly declared in bold letters, "NO LAW CAN BE MADE OR ABROGATED WITHOUT THE CONSENT OF THE PEOPLE BY THEIR REPRESENTATIVES."

Politics of Virtue

The political ideology that had the greatest popular appeal among the colonists contained a strong moral component, one that British rulers and American loyalists (people who sided with the king and Parliament during the Revolution) never fully understood. The origins of this highly religious perspective on civil government are difficult to locate with precision, but certainly, the Great Awakening created a general awareness of an obligation to conduct public as well as private affairs according to Scripture (see Chapter 4).

Americans expressed their political beliefs in a language they had borrowed from English writers. The person most frequently cited was John Locke, the great seventeenth-century philosopher whose *Two Treatises of Government* (first published in 1690) seemed to colonial readers at least a brilliant description of what was in fact American political practice. Locke claimed that all people possessed natural and inalienable rights. In order to preserve these God-given rights—the rights of life, liberty, and property, for example—free men (the status of women in Locke's work was less clear) formed contracts. These agreements were the foundation of human society as well as civil government, and they required the consent of the people who were actually governed. There could be no coercion. Locke justified rebellion against arbitrary forms of government that were by their very nature unreasonable. Americans delighted in Locke's ability to unite traditional religious values with a spirited defense of popular government, and even when they did not fully understand his technical writings, they seldom missed a chance to quote from the works of "the Great Mr. Locke."

Colonial Americans also enthusiastically subscribed to the so-called Commonwealthman tradition, a body of political assumptions generally identified with two eighteenth-century English publicists, John Trenchard and Thomas Gordon (see Chapter 4). The writings of such figures—most of whom spent their lives in political opposition—helped persuade the colonists that *power* was extremely dangerous, a force that would surely destroy liberty unless it was countered by *virtue*. Persons who shared this highly charged moral outlook regarded bad policy as not simply the result of human error. Rather, it was an indication of sin and corruption.

Insistence on public virtue—sacrifice of self-interest to the public good—became the dominant theme of revolutionary political writing. American pamphleteers seldom took a dispassionate, legalistic approach to their analysis of power and liberty. More commonly, they exposed plots hatched by corrupt courtiers, such as the Earl of Bute. None of them—nor their readers—had any doubt that Americans were more virtuous than were the people of England.

During the 1760s, however, popular writers were not certain how long the colonists could hold out against arbitrary taxation, standing armies, Anglican bishops—in other words, against a host of external threats designed to crush American liberty. In 1774, for example, the people of Farmington, Connecticut, declared that "the present ministry, being instigated by the devil and led by their wicked and corrupt hearts, have a design to take away our liberties and properties, and to enslave us forever." Indeed, these Connecticut farmers described Britain's leaders as "pimps and parasites." This highly emotional, conspiratorial rhetoric sometimes shocks modern readers who assume America's revolutionary leaders were products of the Enlightenment, persons who relied solely on reason to solve social and political problems. Whatever the origins of their ideas may have been, the colonial pamphleteers successfully roused ordinary men and women to resist Britain with force of arms.

Colonial newspapers spread these ideas through a large dispersed population. A majority of adult white males—especially in the Northern Colonies—were literate, and it is not surprising that the number of journals published in this country increased dramatically during the revolutionary period. For the first time in American his-

Samuel Adams, seen here in a portrait by John Singleton Copley, was a fervid republican ideologue who urged the American colonists to defend their political virtue against British corruption.

tory, persons living in various parts of the continent could closely follow events that occurred in distant American cities. Because of the availability of newspapers, the details of Bostonians' confrontations with British authorities were known throughout the colonies, and these shared political experiences drew Americans more closely together, making it possible—in the words of John Adams—for "Thirteen clocks . . . to strike together—a perfection of mechanism which no artist had ever before effected."

ERODING THE BONDS OF EMPIRE: CHALLENGE AND RESISTANCE

The Seven Years' War saddled Great Britain with a national debt so huge that over half of the annual national budget went to pay the interest on it. Almost everyone in government assumed that with the cessation of hostilities, the troops would be disbanded, thus saving a lot of money. George III had other plans. He insisted on keeping the largest peacetime army in British history on active duty, supposedly to protect Indians from predatory frontiersmen and to preserve order in the newly conquered territories of Florida and Quebec.

Maintaining such a force so far distant from the mother country fueled the budgetary crisis. The growing financial burden weighed heavily on restive English taxpayers and sent government leaders scurrying in search of new sources of revenue.

For their part, colonists doubted the value of this very expensive army. First, Britain did not leave enough troops in America to maintain peace effectively. The weakness of the army was dramatically demonstrated during the spring of 1763. The native peoples of the backcountry—the Senecas, Ottawas, Miamis, Creeks, and Cherokees—had begun discussing how they might turn back the tide of white settlement. The powerful spiritual leader Neolin, known as the Delaware Prophet, helped these Indians articulate their fear and anger. He urged them to restore their cultures to the "original state that they were in before the white people found out their country." If moral regeneration required violence, so be it. Neolin converted Pontiac, an Ottawa warrior, to the cause, and he, in turn, coordinated an uprising among the western Indians who had formerly been French allies and who hated all British people—even those sent to protect them from land-grabbing colonists. In May, Pontiac attacked Detroit; other Indians harassed the Pennsylvania and Virginia frontiers. At the end of the year, after his followers began deserting, Pontiac sued for peace. During even this brief outbreak, the British army proved unable to defend exposed colonial settlements, and several thousand Americans lost their lives.

Second, the colonists fully intended to settle the fertile region west of the Appalachian Mountains. After the British government issued the Proclamation of 1763, which prohibited governors from granting land beyond the headwaters of rivers flowing into the Atlantic, disappointed Americans viewed the army as an obstruction to legitimate economic development, a domestic police force that cost too much money.

The task of reducing England's debt fell to George Grenville, the rigid, somewhat unimaginative chancellor of the exchequer who replaced Bute in 1763 as the king's first minister. After carefully reviewing the state of Britain's finances, Grenville concluded that the colonists would have to contribute to the maintenance of the army. The first bill he steered through Parliament was the Revenue Act of 1764, known as the Sugar Act.

This legislation placed a new burden on the Navigation Acts that had governed the flow of colonial commerce for almost a century (see Chapter 3). Those acts had forced Americans to trade almost exclusively with Britain. The statutes were not, however, primarily intended as a means to raise money for the British government. The Sugar Act—and the acts that soon followed—redefined the relationship between America and Great Britain. Parliament now expected the colonies to generate revenue. The preamble of the Sugar Act proclaimed explicitly: "It is just and necessary that a revenue be raised . . . in America for defraying the expenses of defending, protecting, and securing the same." The purpose of the Sugar Act was to discourage smuggling, bribery, and other illegalities that prevented the Navigation Acts from being profitable. Parliament reduced the duty on molasses (set originally by the Molasses Act of 1733) from six to three pence per gallon. At so low a rate, Grenville reasoned, colonial mer-

Colonial Products and Trade

The American colonies produced many goods that were valuable to Britain,
but they were also dependent on British manufactures such as cloth, metal goods, and ceramics.

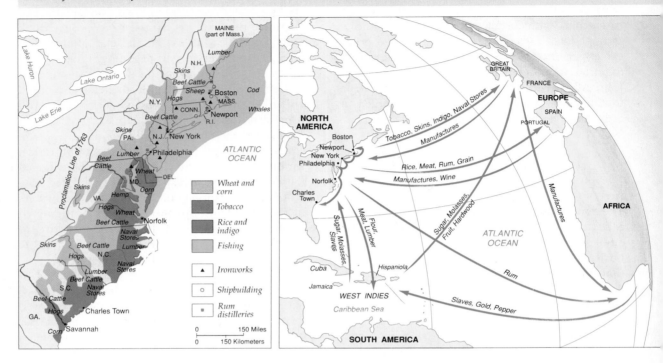

chants would have little incentive to bribe customs collectors. Much needed revenue would be diverted from the pockets of corrupt officials into the Treasury so that it might be used to maintain the army.

Grenville had been too clever by half. The Americans immediately saw through his unconstitutional scheme. According to the members of the Rhode Island Assembly, the Sugar Act taxed the colonists in a manner "inconsistent with their rights and privileges as British subjects." James Otis, a fiery orator from Massachusetts, exclaimed the legislation deprived Americans of "the right of assessing their own taxes."

The Act generated no violence. In fact, ordinary men and women were only marginally involved in the drafting of formal petitions. The protest was still confined to the members of the colonial assemblies, to the merchants, and to the well-to-do Americans who had personal interests in commerce.

Birth of Popular Politics

Passage of the Stamp Act in 1765 transformed conversation among gentlemen into a mass political movement. The crisis might have been avoided. Colonial agents had presented Grenville with alternative schemes for raising money in America. But Grenville was a stubborn man, and he had little fear of parliamentary opposition. The majority of the House of Commons assumed that Parliament possessed the right to tax the colonists, and when the chancellor of the exchequer announced a plan to squeeze £60,000 annually out of the Americans by requiring them to purchase special seals or stamps to validate legal documents, the members responded with enthusiasm. The Stamp Act was scheduled to go into effect on November 1, 1765, and in anticipation of brisk sales, Grenville appointed stamp distributors for every colony.

During discussion of the act in Parliament, several members warned the act would raise a storm of protest in the colonies. Colonel Isaac Barré, a veteran of the Seven Years' War, reminded his colleagues that the Americans were "sons of liberty" and would not surrender their rights without a fight. But Barré's appeal fell on deaf ears.

Word of the Stamp Act reached America in May, and it was soon clear that Barré had gauged the colonists' response correctly. The most dramatic incident occurred in Virginia's House of Burgesses. Patrick Henry, young and eloquent, whom contemporaries compared in fervor to evangelical preachers, introduced five resolutions protesting the Stamp Act on the floor of the assembly. He timed his move carefully. It was late in the session; many of the more conservative burgesses had already departed for their plantations. Even then, Henry's resolves declaring that Virginians had the right to tax themselves as they alone saw fit passed by narrow margins. The fifth resolution, stricken almost immediately from the legislative records, announced that any attempt to collect stamp revenues in America was "illegal, unconstitutional, and unjust, and has a manifest tendency to destroy British as well as American liberty." Henry was carried away by the force of his own rhetoric. He reminded his fellow Virginians that Caesar had had his Brutus, Charles I his Cromwell, and he hoped that "some good American would stand up for his country…" An astonished speaker of the house cut Henry off in mid-sentence, accusing him of treason.

The Virginia Resolves might have remained a local matter had it not been for the colonial press. Newspapers throughout America printed Henry's resolutions, but perhaps because editors did not really know what had happened in Williamsburg, they reported that all five resolutions had received the burgesses' full support. Several journals even carried two resolves that Henry had not dared to introduce. The result of this misunderstanding, of course, was that the Virginians appeared to have taken an extremely radical position on the issue of the supremacy of Parliament, one that other Americans now trumpeted before their own assemblies. No wonder Francis Bernard, royal governor of Massachusetts, called the Virginia Resolves an "alarm bell."

Not to be outdone by Virginia, Massachusetts called a general meeting to protest Grenville's policy. Nine colonies sent representatives to the Stamp Act Congress that convened in New York City in October 1765. It was the first intercolonial gathering held since the abortive Albany Congress of 1754; if nothing else, the new congress provided leaders from different regions with an opportunity to discuss common problems. The delegates drafted petitions to the king and Parliament that restated the colonists' belief "that no taxes should be imposed on them, but with their own consent, given personally, or by their representatives." The tone of the meeting was restrained, even conciliatory. The congress studiously avoided any mention of independence or disloyalty to the Crown.

Resistance to the Stamp Act soon spread from the assemblies to the streets. By taxing deeds, marriage licenses, and playing cards, the Stamp Act touched the lives of ordinary women and men. Anonymous artisans and seamen, angered by Parliament's apparent insensitivity and fearful the statute would increase unemployment and poverty, organized mass protests in the major colonial ports.

In Boston, the "Sons of Liberty" burned in effigy the local stamp distributor, Andrew Oliver, and when that action failed to bring about his resignation, they tore down one of his office buildings. Even after he resigned, the mob nearly demolished the elegant home of Oliver's close associate, Lieutenant Governor Thomas Hutchinson. The violence frightened colonial leaders, yet evidence suggests they encouraged the lower classes to intimidate royal officials. Popular participation in these protests was an exciting experience for people who had traditionally deferred to their social betters. After 1765, it was impossible for either royal governors or patriot leaders to take the ordinary folk for granted.

By November 1, 1765, stamp distributors in almost every American port had publicly resigned, and without distributors, the hated revenue stamps could not be sold. The courts soon reopened; most newspapers were published. Daily life in the colonies was undisturbed with one exception: the Sons of Liberty persuaded—some said coerced—colonial merchants to boycott British goods until Parliament repealed the Stamp Act. The merchants showed little enthusiasm for such tactics, but the threat of tar and feathers stimulated cooperation.

Because the Stamp Act touched the lives of ordinary men and women, they were vocal and demonstrative in their protests against the measure. Here a crowd in New Hampshire displays the hanged effigy of the stamp master.

The boycott movement was in itself a masterful political innovation. The colonists depended on British imports—cloth, metal goods, and ceramics—and each year they imported more consumer goods than they could possibly afford. In this highly charged moral atmosphere, one in which ordinary people talked constantly of conspiracy and corruption, it is not surprising that Americans of different classes and backgrounds advocated a radical change in buying habits. Private acts suddenly became part of the public sphere. Personal excess threatened to contaminate the entire political community. This logic explains the power of an appeal made in a Boston newspaper: "Save your money and you can save your country."

The boycotts mobilized colonial women. They were excluded from voting and civil office, but such legal discrimination did not mean women were not part of the broader political culture. Since wives and mothers spent their days involved with household chores, they assumed special responsibility to reform consumption, to root out luxury, and to promote frugality. Indeed, in this realm they possessed real power; they monitored the ideological commitment of the entire family. Throughout the colonies women altered styles of dress, made homespun cloth, and shunned imported items on which Parliament had placed a tax.

British Reaction

What most Americans did not yet know—after all, communication with Britain required months—was that in July, Grenville had fallen from power. This unexpected shift came about not because the king thought Grenville's policies inept, but rather because George did not like the man. His replacement as first lord of the treasury, Lord Rockingham, was young, inexperienced, and terrified of public speaking, a serious handicap to launching a brilliant parliamentary career. The Rockinghamites—as his followers were called—envisioned a prosperous empire founded on an expanding commerce and local government under the gentle guidance of Parliament. In this unified structure, it seemed improbable that Parliament would ever be obliged to exercise control in a manner likely to offend the Americans. Rockingham wanted to repeal the Stamp Act, but because of the shakiness of his own political coalition, he could not announce such a decision until it enjoyed broad national support. He, therefore, urged merchants and manufacturers throughout England to petition Parliament for repeal of the act, claiming the American boycott would soon drive them into bankruptcy.

Grenville, now simply a member of Parliament, would tolerate no retreat on the issue of supremacy. He urged his colleagues in the House of

Commons to be tough, to condemn "the outrageous tumults and insurrections which have been excited and carried on in North America." But William Pitt, the architect of victory in the Seven Years' War and a hero throughout America, eloquently defended the colonists' position, and after the Rockingham ministry gathered additional support from prominent figures such as Benjamin Franklin, who happened to be visiting England, Parliament felt strong enough to recommend repeal. On March 18, 1766, the House of Commons voted 275 to 167 to rescind the Stamp Act.

Lest its retreat on the Stamp Act be interpreted as weakness, the House of Commons passed the Declaratory Act (March 1766), a shrill defense of parliamentary supremacy over the Americans "in all cases whatsoever." The colonists' insistence on no taxation without representation failed to impress British rulers. England's merchants, supposedly America's allies, claimed sole responsibility for the Stamp Act repeal. The colonists had only complicated the task, the merchants lectured, and if the Americans knew what was good for them, they would keep quiet. To George Mason, a leading political figure in Virginia, such advice sounded patronizing. The British merchants seemed to be saying, "We have with infinite difficulty and fatigue got you excused this one time; pray be a good boy for the future, do what your papa and mama bid you, and hasten to return them your most grateful acknowledgements for condescending to let you keep what is your own." To this, Mason snapped "ridiculous!"

The Stamp Act crisis also eroded the colonists' respect for imperial officeholders in America. Suddenly, these men—royal governors, customs collectors, military personnel—appeared alien, as if their interests were not those of the people over whom they exercised authority. One person who had been forced to resign the post of stamp distributor for South Carolina noted several years later that "The Stamp Act had introduc'd so much Party Rage, Faction, and Debate that the ancient Harmony, Generosity, and Urbanity for which these People were celebrated is destroyed, and at an End." Similar reports came from other colonies, and it is testimony to the Americans' lingering loyalty to the British Crown and constitution that rebellion did not occur in 1765.

Townshend's Boast: Tea and Sovereignty

Rockingham's ministry soon gave way to a government headed once again by William Pitt, who was now the Earl of Chatham. The aging Pitt suffered horribly from gout, and during his long absences from London, Charles Townshend, his chancellor of the exchequer, made important policy decisions. Townshend was an impetuous man whose mouth often outran his mind. During a parliamentary debate in January 1767, he surprised everyone by blithely announcing he knew a way to obtain revenue from the Americans. The members of the House of Commons were so pleased with the news, they promptly voted to lower English land taxes, an action that threatened fiscal chaos.

A budgetary crisis forced Townshend to make good on his extraordinary boast. His scheme turned out to be a grab bag of duties on American imports of paper, glass, paint, lead, and tea, which collectively were known as the Townshend Revenue Acts (June–July 1767). He hoped to generate sufficient funds to pay the salaries of royal governors and other imperial officers, thus freeing them from dependence on the colonial assemblies.

The chancellor recognized that without tough instruments of enforcement, his duties would not produce the promised revenues. Therefore, he created an American Board of Customs Commissioners, a body based in Boston and supported by reorganized vice-admiralty courts located in Boston, Philadelphia, and Charles Town. And for good measure, Townshend induced Parliament to order the governor of New York to veto all bills passed by that colony's assembly until it supplied resident British troops in accordance with the Quartering Act (May 1765) that required the colonies to house soldiers in barracks, taverns, and vacant buildings, and to provide the army with firewood, candles, and beer, among other items. Many Americans regarded this as more taxation without representation, and in New York at least, colonists refused to pay.

Colonists showed no more willingness to pay Townshend's duties than they had to buy Grenville's stamps. No congress was called; none was necessary. Recent events had taught people how to coordinate protest, and they moved to resist the unconstitutional revenue acts. In major ports, the Sons of Liberty organized boycotts of British goods. Protest often involved what one historian has termed "rituals of nonconsumption." In some large towns, these were moments of public moral reaffirmation. Men and women took oaths before neighbors promising not to purchase certain goods until Parliament repealed unconstitutional taxation. In Boston, ordinary people were encouraged to sign "Subscription Rolls." "The Selectmen strongly recommend this Measure to Persons of *all ranks*," announced the *Boston Gazette*," as the most honorable and effectual way of giving *public* Testimony of their Love to their Country, and of endeavouring to save it from ruin."

On February 11, 1768, the Massachusetts House of Representatives drafted a circular letter, which it then sent to other colonial assemblies. The letter requested suggestions on how best to thwart the Townshend Acts; not surprisingly, legislators in other parts of America, busy with local matters, simply ignored this general appeal. But not Lord Hillsborough, England's secretary for American affairs. This rather mild action struck him as gross treason, and he ordered the Massachusetts representatives to rescind their "seditious paper." After considering Hillsborough's demand, the legislators voted 92 to 17 to defy him.

Suddenly, the circular letter became a cause célèbre. The royal governor of Massachusetts hastily dissolved the House of Representatives. That decision compelled the other colonies to demonstrate their support for Massachusetts. Assembly after assembly now felt obligated to take up the circular letter, an action Hillsborough had specifically forbidden. Assemblies in other colonies were dissolved, creating a much broader crisis of representative government. Throughout America, the number 92 (the number of legislators who voted against Hillsborough) immediately became a symbol of patriotism. In fact, Parliament's challenge had brought about the very results it most wanted to avoid: a foundation for intercolonial communication and a strengthening of conviction among the colonists of the righteousness of their position.

The Boston Massacre Heightens Tensions

In October 1768, British rulers made another mistake, one that raised tensions almost to the pitch they had reached during the Stamp Act

riots. The issue at the heart of the trouble was the army. In part to save money and in part to intimidate colonial troublemakers, the ministry transferred four thousand regular troops from Nova Scotia and Ireland to Boston. Most of the army had already been withdrawn from the frontier to the seacoast to save revenue, thereby raising more acutely than ever the issue of why troops were in America at all. The armed strangers camped on Boston Commons, and when citizens passed the site, redcoats shouted obscenities. Sometimes in accordance with martial law, an errant soldier was whipped within an inch of his life, a bloody sight that sickened Boston civilians. To make relations worse, redcoats—men who were ill treated and underpaid—competed in their spare time for jobs with local dockworkers and artisans. Work was already in short supply, and the streets crackled with tension.

When colonists questioned why the army had been sent to a peaceful city, pamphleteers responded that it was there to further a conspiracy originally conceived by Bute to oppress Americans, to take away their liberties, to collect illegal revenues. Grenville, Hillsborough, Townshend: they were all, supposedly, part of the plot. Such rhetoric sounds excessive, but to Americans who had absorbed the political theories of the Commonwealthmen, a pattern of tyranny seemed obvious.

Colonists had no difficulty interpreting the violence that erupted in Boston on March 5, 1770. In the gathering dusk of that afternoon, young boys and street toughs bombarded a small isolated patrol outside the offices of the hated customs commissioners in King Street with rocks and snowballs. The details of this incident are obscure, but it appears that as the mob grew and became more threatening, the soldiers panicked. In the confusion, the troops fired, leaving five Americans dead.

Pamphleteers promptly labeled the incident a "massacre." The victims were seen as martyrs and were memorialized in extravagant terms. In one eulogy, Joseph Warren addressed the dead men's widows and children, dramatically recreating the gruesome scene in King Street. "Behold thy murdered husband gasping on the ground," Warren cried, ". . . take heed, ye orphan babes, lest, whilst your streaming eyes are fixed upon the ghastly corpse, your feet slide on the stones

The BLOODY MASSACRE perpetrated in King Street BOSTON on March 5th 1770 by a party of the 29th REGt

Unhappy BOSTON! see thy Sons deplore,
Thy hallowed Walks besmear'd with guiltless Gore.
While faithless P——n and his savage Bands,
With murdrous Rancour stretch their bloody Hands;
Like fierce Barbarians grinning o'er their Prey,
Approve the Carnage and enjoy the Day.

If scalding drops from Rage from Anguish Wrung
If speechless Sorrows lab'ring for a Tongue
Or if a weeping World can ought appease
The plaintive Ghosts of Victims such as these;
The Patriot's copious Tears for each are shed,
A glorious Tribute which embalms the Dead.

But know, FATE summons to that awful Goal,
Where JUSTICE strips the Murd'rer of his Soul:
Should venal C——ts the scandal of the Land,
Snatch the relentless Villain from her Hand,
Keen Execrations on this Plate inscrib'd,
Shall reach a JUDGE who never can be brib'd.

Outrage over the Boston Massacre was fanned by propaganda, such as this etching by Paul Revere, which showed British red-coats firing on well-dressed men and women. In subsequent editions, the blood spurting from the dying Americans became more conspicuous.

bespattered with your father's brains." Apparently to propagandists like Warren, it mattered little that the five civilians had been bachelors! Paul Revere's engraving of the massacre, appropriately splattered with blood, became an instant best-seller. Confronted with such intense reaction and with the possibility of massive armed resistance, crown officials wisely moved the army to an island in Boston harbor.

At this critical moment, the king's new first minister restored a measure of tranquillity. Lord North, congenial, well meaning, but not very talented, became chancellor of the exchequer following Townshend's death in 1767. North became the first minister in 1770, and for the next twelve years—indeed, throughout most of the American crisis—he managed to retain his office. His secret formula seems to have been an ability to get along with George III and to build an effective majority in Parliament.

One of North's first recommendations to Parliament was the repeal of the Townshend duties. Not only had these ill-conceived duties unnecessarily angered the colonists, they also hurt English manufacturers, a cardinal sin in the mer-

cantilist system. By taxing British exports such as glass and paint, Parliament had only encouraged the Americans to develop their own industries; thus without much prodding, the House of Commons dropped all the Townshend duties—with the notable exception of tea. The tax on tea was retained not for revenue purposes, North insisted, but as a reminder that England's rulers still subscribed to the principles of the Declaratory Act. They would not compromise the supremacy of Parliament. In mid-1770, however, the matter of tea seemed trivial to most Americans. The colonists had drawn back from the precipice, a little frightened by the events of the past two years, and desperately hoped to head off future confrontation with the British.

An Interlude of Order, 1770–1773

For a short while, American colonists and British officials put aside their recent animosities. Like England's rulers, some colonial gentry were beginning to pull back from protest, especially violent confrontation with estab-

Popular Culture and Revolutionary Ferment

No one knows exactly why men and women rebel against governments. Economic deprivation and political frustration contribute to unrest, but the spark that ignites popular passions, that causes common people to risk their lives in battle, often arises from a society's most basic traditions and beliefs.

The American Revolution illustrates this complex process of revolt. The educated elite in the colonies may have found their inspiration in reading classical history or political pamphlets, but the common people, those who protested British taxation in the streets, seem to have gained resolution from a deep Protestant tradition, a set of religious values recently reinforced during the Great Awakening (see Chapter 4). For ordinary men and women, the American Revolution may have seemed a kind of morality play, a drama that transformed complicated issues of representation and sovereignty into a stark conflict between American good and British evil.

Even before colonial protests against British taxation led to bloodshed, religious passions helped draw thousands of people into the streets of Boston on Pope's Day, a traditional anti-Catholic holiday celebrated on November 5. (In England, the holiday was known as Guy Fawkes Day and commemorated exposure of the Gunpowder Plot of 1605, a conspiracy organized by English Catholics to blow up Parliament that was thwarted at the last minute.) For the holiday, Bostonians arranged elaborate processions, complete with effigies of the pope and the devil, which they burned at the climax of the festivities. Sometimes the annual celebration turned ugly, as rival gangs from the north and south ends of the city tried to disrupt each other's parade. During the Seven Years' War, the crowds grew increasingly unruly, as the pageantry triggered an outpouring of emotions that sprang from the New Englanders' fervent commitment to the Reformation and their desire to rid Canada of Catholic domination.

The Pope's Day celebrations provided a model for demonstrations against the Stamp Act. The first public protest against the British law in Boston, on August 14, 1765, began with a rally under a large elm, the original colonial "Liberty Tree." Hanging from its branches were effigies of Andrew Oliver, Boston's first stamp collector, and the devil, whose pitchforks men-

Pope's Day celebrations—complete with burning effigies and more than a touch of rowdyism—provided colonists with a model that they could use for later anti-British political demonstrations.

Description of the POPE, 1769.

Toasts on the Front of the large Lanthorn.
Love and Unity.---The American Whig.---Confusion to the Torries, and a total Banishment to Bribery and Corruption.
On the Right Side of the same.—An Acrostick.

I nsulting Wretch, we'll him expose,
O 'er the whole World his Deeds disclose,
H ell now gaups wide to take him in,
N ow he is ripe, Oh Lump of Sin.
M ean is the Man, M--n is his Name,
E nough he's spread his hellish Fame,
I nfernal Furies hurl his Soul,
N ine Million Times from Pole to Pole.

aced Oliver. A label attached to the effigy of Oliver read:

> *Fair Freedom's glorious cause I've meanly quitted For the sake of self; But ah! the Devil had me outwitted, And instead of stamping others, I've hang'd myself*

As night fell, a diverse crowd of gentlemen, workers, and even a few women carried the effigies through the streets of Boston. After destroying a building owned by Oliver, they marched to Fort Hill where "they made a burnt offering of the effigies for these sins of the people which had caused such heavy judgments as the Stamp Act, etc. to be laid upon them." This symbolic protest ended with a sort of conversion; in much the same way that anxious sinners renounced evil at evangelical meetings, Oliver announced publicly that he would resign as stamp collector.

The devil was a familiar feature in American political cartoons. In one famous illustration, published in 1774, the devil held a list of crimes committed by Governor Thomas Hutchinson of Massachusetts, as the viper of death prepared to punish the royal official for his sins. This gruesome imagery revealed that patriots thought of Hutchinson not only as a political opponent but also as a moral traitor. No one who saw these macabre figures could fail to appreciate the accompanying warning: "Let the destroyers of mankind behold and tremble!"

A similar message was at the heart of the patriot practice of tarring and feathering. Crowds in Boston usually reserved this humiliating punishment for informers who reported violations to the hated customs officers. The victim

became the main actor in a public morality play, in which he was wheeled in a cart before jeering crowds and forced to repent. This spectacle recalled a verse often repeated on Pope's Day:

> *See the informer how he stands If anyone now takes his part An enemy to all the Land He'll go to Hell without a cart.*

Patriots regarded military traitors as the worst of sinners. When General Benedict Arnold, who had been a hero during the early stages of the war, went over to the British in 1780, Americans accused him of selling out to the devil. A huge parade held in Philadelphia included a two-faced Arnold riding in front of Satan. The devil held a bag of gold—presumably the source of Arnold's fall—and a pitchfork that he used to prod the traitor along the path to Hell.

Revolutionary leaders also tapped long-standing Puritan hostility to the theater. Puritans and other strict Protestants indicted the theater for encouraging idleness, hypocrisy, deceit, and even effeminacy, since men usually played women's roles. But their greatest objection was that the stage appealed to those emotions and lusts that God-fearing men and women tried to restrain through knowledge of Scripture. Theaters, they believed, were nothing less than enemies of the church. "Those therefore who serve the Devill in Playes and Playhouses; it's impossible for them to serve the Lord in prayers and Churches," asserted one Puritan thinker.

Patriot leaders also considered the stage a rival for popular loyalties. In 1766, the Sons of Liberty in New York City demolished a theater. And in 1774, the First Continental Congress resolved to

"discontenance and discourage every species of extravagance and dissipation especially . . . shews, plays and other expensive diversions and entertainments." Such proclamations helped to channel Protestant moral fervor into a commitment to the patriot cause.

During the war itself—when soldiers were actually fighting and dying—religion helped sustain patriotism. In 1775, for example, a company of Massachusetts soldiers on their way to Quebec camped briefly at Newburyport, where George Whitefield had been buried. Before the troops resumed their long march to Canada, some of them opened the minister's tomb and cut off small pieces of Whitefield's collar and wristband, an act that seems ghoulish only to those who do not fully comprehend the importance of religion in the lives of the common soldiers.

Religious symbol and ritual thus galvanized common men and women by expressing in moral terms the issues that divided the colonies from England. The Great Awakening had prepared the colonists to view the contest in terms of American virtue and English vice, of God and the devil. By appealing to the strong Protestant tradition in the colonies, patriots mobilized the American people for revolution.

145

lished authority, in fear that the lower orders were becoming too assertive. It was probably in this period that Loyalist Americans emerged as an identifiable group. Colonial merchants returned to familiar patterns of trade, pleased no doubt to end the local boycotts that had depressed the American economy. British goods flooded into colonial ports; the level of American indebtedness soared to new highs. In this period of apparent reconciliation, the people of Massachusetts—even of Boston—decided they could accept their new governor, Thomas Hutchinson. After all, he was one of their own, an American.

But appearances were deceiving. The bonds of imperial loyalty remained fragile, and even as Lord North attempted to win the colonists' trust, crown officials in America created new strains. Customs commissioners whom Townshend had appointed to collect his duties remained in the colonies long after his Revenue Acts had been repealed. If they had been honest, unobtrusive administrators, perhaps no one would have taken notice of their behavior. But the customs commissioners regularly abused their powers of search and seizure and in the process lined their own pockets. In Massachusetts, Rhode Island, and South Carolina—to cite the most notorious cases—these officials drove local citizens to distraction by enforcing the Navigation Acts with such rigor that a skiff could not cross Narragansett Bay with a load of firewood without first obtaining a sheaf of legal documents. One slip, no matter how minor, could bring confiscation of ship and cargo.

The commissioners were not only corrupt, they were also short-sighted. If they had restricted their extortion to the common folk, they might have avoided becoming a major American grievance. But they could not control their greed. Some customs officers harassed the wealthiest, most powerful men around, men like John Hancock of Boston and Henry Laurens of Charles Town. The commissioners' actions drove some members of the colonial ruling class into opposition to the king's government. When in the summer of 1772 a group of disguised Rhode Islanders burned a customs vessel, the *Gaspee*, Americans cheered. A special royal commission sent to arrest the culprits discovered that not a single Rhode Islander had the slightest idea how the ship could have come to such an end.

Samuel Adams (1722–1803) refused to accept the notion that the repeal of the Townshend duties had secured American liberty. During the early 1770s, while colonial leaders turned to other matters, Adams kept the cause alive with a drumfire of publicity. He reminded the people of Boston that the tax on tea remained in force. He organized public anniversaries commemorating the repeal of the Stamp Act and the Boston Massacre. Adams was a genuine revolutionary, an ideologue filled with a burning sense of indignation at the real and alleged wrongs suffered by his countrymen. To his contemporaries, this man resembled a figure out of New England's Puritan past. He seemed obsessed with the preservation of public virtue. The American goal, he declared, was the creation of a "Christian Sparta," an ideal commonwealth in which vigilant citizens would constantly guard against the spread of corruption, degeneracy, and luxury.

With each new attempt by Parliament to assert its supremacy over the colonists, more and more Bostonians listened to what Adams had to say. He observed ominously that the British intended to use the tea revenue to pay judicial salaries, thus freeing the judges from dependence on the assembly. When in November 1772 Adams suggested the formation of a committee of correspondence to communicate grievances to villagers throughout Massachusetts, he received broad support. Americans living in other colonies soon copied his idea. It was a brilliant stroke. Adams developed a structure of political cooperation completely independent of royal government.

The Final Provocation: The Boston Tea Party

In May 1773, Parliament passed the Tea Act, legislation the Americans might have welcomed. After all, it lowered the price for their favorite beverage. Parliament wanted to save one of Britain's largest businesses, the East India Company, from possible bankruptcy. This commercial giant imported Asian tea into England, where it was resold to wholesalers. The tea was also subject to heavy duties. The Company tried to pass these charges on to the consumers, but American tea drinkers preferred the cheaper leaves that were smuggled in from Holland.

The Tea Act changed the rules. Parliament not only allowed the Company to sell directly to American retailers, thus cutting out middlemen, but also eliminated the duties paid in England. If all had gone according to plan, the agents of the East India Company in America would have undersold their competitors, including the Dutch smugglers, and with the new profits would have saved the business.

But Parliament's logic was flawed. First, since the tax on tea, collected in American ports, remained in effect, this new act seemed a devious scheme to win popular support for Parliament's right to tax the colonists without representation. Second, the act threatened to undercut powerful colonial merchants who did a good business trading in smuggled Dutch tea. Considering the American reaction, the British government might have been well advised to devise another plan to rescue the ailing company. In Philadelphia, and then at New York City, colonists turned back the tea ships before they could unload.

In Boston, however, the issue was not so easily resolved. Governor Hutchinson, a strong-willed man, would not permit the vessels to return to England. Local patriots would not let them unload. And so, crammed with the East India Company's tea, the ships sat in Boston Harbor waiting for the colonists to make up their minds. On the night of December 16, 1773, they did so in dramatic style. A group of men disguised as Mohawks boarded the ships and pitched 340 chests of tea worth £10,000 over the side. Whether Samuel Adams organized the famed "Tea Party" is not known. No doubt he and his allies were not taken by surprise. Even at the time, John Adams, Samuel's distant cousin, sensed the event would have far-reaching significance. "This Destruction of the Tea," he scribbled in his diary, "is so bold, so daring, so firm, intrepid, and inflexible, and it must have so important consequences, and so lasting, that I can't but consider it as an epocha in history."

When news of the Tea Party reached London in January 1774, the North ministry was stunned. The people of Boston had treated parliamentary supremacy with utter contempt, and British rulers saw no humor whatsoever in the destruction of private property by subjects of the Crown dressed in costume. To quell such rebelliousness, Parliament passed a series of laws called the Coercive Acts. (In America, they were referred to as the Intolerable Acts.) This legislation (1) closed the port of Boston until the city fully compensated the East India Company for the lost tea, (2) restructured the Massachusetts government by transforming the upper house from an elective to an appointed body and restricting the number of legal town meetings to one a year, (3) allowed the royal governor to transfer British officials arrested for offenses committed in the line of duty to England where there was little likelihood they would be convicted, and (4) authorized the army to quarter troops wherever they were needed, even if this required the compulsory requisition of uninhabited private buildings. George III enthusiastically supported this tough policy; he appointed General Thomas Gage to serve as the colony's new royal governor. Gage apparently won the king's favor by announcing that in America "Nothing can be done but by forcible means."

This sweeping denial of constitutional liberties confirmed the colonists' worst fears. To men like Samuel Adams, it seemed as if Britain really intended to enslave the American people. Colonial moderates found their position shaken by the vindictiveness of the Coercive Acts. Edmund Burke, one of America's last friends in Parliament, noted sadly on the floor of Commons, "this is the day, then, that you wish to go to war with all America, in order to conciliate that country to this . . . "

In the midst of this constitutional crisis, Parliament announced plans to establish a new civil government for the Canadian province of Quebec (Quebec Act, June 22, 1774). This territory had been ruled by military authority following the Seven Years' War. The Quebec Act not only failed to create an elective assembly—an institution the Americans regarded as essential for the protection of liberty—but also awarded French Roman Catholics a large voice in local political affairs. Moreover, since Quebec extended all the way south to the Ohio River and west to the Mississippi River, Americans concluded that Parliament wanted to deny the American settlers and traders in this fast-developing region their constitutional rights, a threat that affected all colonists, not just those of Massachusetts Bay.

If in 1774 the House of Commons thought it could isolate Boston from the rest of America, it was in for a rude surprise. Colonists living in

This drawing of the Boston Tea Party appeared in W. D. Cooper's History of North America, *published in London in 1789. The British lion on the prow of the ship seems to look on disapprovingly as the colonists, disguised as Indians, dump the tea in the harbor.*

other parts of the continent recognized immediately that the principles at stake in Boston affected all Americans. As one Virginian explained, ". . . there were no Heats and Troubles in Virginia till the Blockade of Boston." Few persons advocated independence, but they could not remain passive while Boston was destroyed. They sent food and money and, during the fall of 1774, reflected more deeply than ever on what it meant to be a colonist in the British empire.

The sticking point remained—as it had been in 1765—the sovereignty of Parliament. No one in Britain could think of a way around this constitutional impasse. In 1773, Benjamin Franklin had offered a suggestion. "The Parliament," he observed, "has no right to make any law whatever, binding on the colonies . . . the king, and not the king, lords, and commons collectively, is their sovereign." But so long as it still seemed possible to coerce the Americans into obedience, to punish these errant children, Britain's rulers had little incentive to accept such a humiliating compromise.

DECISION FOR INDEPENDENCE

During the summer of 1774, committees of correspondence analyzed the perilous situation in which the colonists found themselves. Something, of course, had to be done. But what? Would the Southern Colonies support resistance in New England? Would Pennsylvanians stand up to Parliament? Not surprisingly, the committees endorsed a call for a Continental Congress, a gathering of fifty-five elected delegates from twelve colonies (Georgia sent none but agreed to support the action taken). This momentous gathering convened in Philadelphia on September 5. It included some of America's most articulate, respected leaders; among them were John and Samuel Adams, Patrick Henry, Richard Henry Lee, Christopher Gadsden, and George Washington.

The delegates were strangers to one another. They knew little about the customs and values, the geography and economy of Britain's other provinces. As John Adams explained on September 18, "It has taken Us much Time to get acquainted with the Tempers, Views, Characters, and Designs of Persons and to let them into the Circumstances of our Province." During the early sessions of the Congress, the delegates eyed each other closely, trying to gain a sense of the strength and integrity of the men with whom they might commit treason.

Differences of opinion soon surfaced. Delegates from the Middle Colonies—Joseph Galloway of Pennsylvania, for example—wanted to proceed with caution, but Samuel Adams and other more radical members pushed the moderates toward confrontation. Boston's master politician engineered congressional commendation of the Suffolk Resolves, a bold statement drawn up in Suffolk County, Massachusetts, that encouraged forcible resistance of the Coercive Acts.

After this decision, the tone of the meeting was established. Moderate spokesmen introduced conciliatory measures, which received polite discussion but failed to win a majority vote. Just

Legislation	Date	Provisions	Colonial Reaction
Sugar Act	April 5, 1764	Revised duties on sugar, coffee, tea, wine, other imports; expanded juris diction of vice-admiralty-courts	Several assemblies protest taxation for revenue
Stamp Act	March 22, 1765; repealed March 18, 1766	Printed documents (deeds, newspapers, marriage licenses, etc.) issued only on special stamped paper purchased from stamp distributors	Riots in cities; collectors forced to resign; Stamp Act Congress (October 1765)
Quartering Act	May 1765	Colonists must supply British troops with housing other items (candles, firewood, etc.)	Protest in assemblies; New York Assembly punished for failure to comply 1767
Declaratory Act	March 18, 1766	Parliament declares its sovereignty over the colonies "in all cases whatsoever"	Ignored in celebration over repeal of the Stamp Act
Townshend Revenue Acts	June 26, 29, July 2, 1767; all repealed—except duty on tea, March 1770	New duties on glass, lead, paper, paints, tea; customs collections tightened in America	Nonimportation of British goods; assemblies protest; newspapers attack British policy
Tea Act	May 10, 1773	Parliament gives East India Company right to sell tea directly to Americans; some duties on tea reduced	Protests against favoritism shown to monopolistic company; tea destroyed in Boston (December 16, 1773)
Coercive Acts (Intolerable Acts)	March–June 1774	Closes port of Boston; restructures, Massachusetts government; restricts town meetings; troops quartered in Boston; British officials accused of crimes sent to England or Canada for trial	Boycott of British goods; First Continental Congress convenes (September 1774)
Prohibitory Act	December 22, 1775	Declares British intention to coerce Americans into submission; embargo on American goods; American ships seized	Drives Continental Congress closer to decision for independence

before returning to their homes (September 1774), the delegates created the "Association," an intercolonial agreement to halt all commerce with Britain until Parliament repealed the Intolerable Acts. This was a totally revolutionary decision. The Association authorized a vast network of local committees to enforce nonimportation. In many of the communities, they *were* the government, distinguishing in the words of James Madison, "Friends from Foes." George III sneered at these activities. "I am not sorry," he confided, "that the line of conduct seems now chalked out ... the New England Governments are in a state of Rebellion, blows must decide whether they are to be subject to this country or independent."

Shots Heard Around the World

The king was correct. Before Congress reconvened, "blows" fell at Lexington and Concord, two small farm villages in eastern Massachusetts. On the evening of April 18, 1775, General Gage dispatched troops from Boston to seize rebel supplies. Paul Revere, a renowned silversmith and active patriot, warned the colonists the redcoats were coming. The militia of Lexington, a collection of ill-trained farmers, boys as well as old men, decided to stand on the village green on the following morning, April 19, as the British soldiers passed on the road to Concord. No one planned to fight, but in a moment of confusion someone (probably a colonist) fired; the redcoats discharged a volley, and eight Americans lay dead.

Word of the incident spread rapidly, and by the time the British force reached its destination, the countryside swarmed with "minutemen," special companies of Massachusetts militia prepared to respond instantly to military emergencies. The redcoats found nothing of significance in Concord, and so returned. The long march back to Boston turned into a rout. Lord Percy, a British officer who brought up reinforcements, remarked more in surprise than bitterness, "whoever looks upon them [the American soldiers] as an irregular mob, will find himself much mistaken." On June 17, colonial militiamen again held their own against seasoned troops at the battle of Bunker Hill (actually Breed's Hill). The British finally took the hill, but after this costly "victory" in which he suffered 40 percent casualties, Gage complained that the Americans had displayed "a conduct and spirit against us, they never showed against the French."

The Second Continental Congress Directs the War Effort

Members of the Second Continental Congress gathered in Philadelphia in May 1775. They faced an awesome responsibility. British government in the mainland colonies had almost ceased to function, and with Americans fighting redcoats, the country desperately needed strong central leadership. Slowly, often reluctantly, Congress took control of the war. The delegates formed a Continental army and appointed George Washington its commander, in part because he seemed to have greater military experience than anyone else available and in part because he looked like he should be commander in chief. The delegates were also eager to select someone who did not come from Massachusetts, a colony that seemed already to possess too much power in national councils. The members of Congress purchased military supplies and, to pay for them, issued paper money. But while they were assuming the powers of a sovereign government, the congressmen refused to declare independence. They debated and fretted, listened to the appeals of moderates who played on the colonists' remaining loyalty to Britain, and then did nothing.

Indecision drove men like John Adams nearly mad. In one tirade against his timid colleagues, he exclaimed that they possessed "the vanity of the ape, the tameness of the ox, or the stupid servility of the ass." Haste, however, would have been a terrible mistake. While Adams and Richard Henry Lee of Virginia were willing to sever ties with Britain, many Americans were not convinced that such a step was either desireable or necessary. If Congress had moved too quickly, it might have become vulnerable to charges of extremism, in which case the rebellion would have seemed—and indeed, might have been—more like an overthrow by a faction or clique than an expression of popular will.

The British government appeared intent on transforming colonial moderates into angry rebels. In December 1775, Parliament passed the Prohibitory Act, declaring war on American commerce. Until the colonists begged for pardon, they could not trade with the rest of the world. The

This 1775 engraving by Amos Doolittle, an eyewitness, shows the attack on the British regulars as they marched from Concord back to Boston. The minutemen fired from cover. It is not certain who fired the first shot at Lexington.

British navy blockaded their ports and seized American ships on the high seas. Lord North also hired German mercenaries (the Russians drove too hard a bargain) to put down the rebellion. And in America, royal governors like Lord Dunmore further undermined the possibility of reconciliation by urging Virginia's slaves to take up arms against their masters. Few did so, but the effort to stir up black rebellion infuriated the Virginia gentry.

Thomas Paine (1737–1809) pushed the colonists even closer to independence. Nothing in this man's background suggested he would write the most important pamphlet in American history. In England, Paine had tried and failed in a number of jobs, and exactly why he elected to move to America in 1774 is not clear. While still in England, Paine had the good fortune to meet Benjamin Franklin, who presented him with letters of introduction to the leading patriots of Pennsylvania. At the urging of his new American

friends, Paine produced *Common Sense,* an essay that became an instant best-seller. In only three months it sold over 120,000 copies. Paine confirmed in forceful prose what the colonists had been thinking but had been unable to state in coherent form. "My motive and object in all my political works," he declared, ". . . have been to rescue man from tyranny and false systems of government, and enable him to be free."

Common Sense systematically stripped kingship of historical and theological justification. For centuries, the English had maintained the fiction that the monarch could do no wrong. When the government oppressed the people, the royal counselors received the blame. The Crown was above suspicion. To this, Paine cried nonsense. Monarchs ruled by force. George III was simply a "royal brute," who by his arbitrary behavior had surrendered his claim to the colonists' obedience. The pamphlet also attacked the whole idea of a mixed and balanced constitution. Indeed,

Common Sense was a powerful democratic manifesto.

Paine's greatest contribution to the revolutionary cause was persuading common folk to sever their ties with Great Britain. It was not reasonable, he argued, to regard England as the mother country. "Europe, and not England," he explained, "is the parent country of America. This new world hath been the asylum for the persecuted lovers of civil and religious liberty from *every part* of Europe." No doubt that message made a deep impression on Pennsylvania's German population. The time had come for the colonists to form an independent republic. "We have it in our power," Paine wrote in one of his most moving statements, "to begin the world over again . . . the birthday of a new world is at hand."

On July 2, 1776, after a long and tedious debate, Congress finally voted for independence. The motion passed; twelve states for, none against. Thomas Jefferson, a young Virginia lawyer and planter who enjoyed a reputation as a graceful writer, drafted a formal declaration that was accepted with alterations two days later. Much of the Declaration of Independence consisted of a list of specific grievances against George III and his government. Like the skilled lawyer he was, Jefferson presented the evidence for independence. But the document did not become famous for those passages. Long after the establishment of the new Republic, the declaration challenged Americans to make good on the principle that "all men are created equal." John Adams nicely expressed the patriots' fervor when he wrote on July 3: "Yesterday the greatest question was decided, which ever was debated in America, and a greater perhaps, never was or will be decided among men."

WAR FOR INDEPENDENCE

Only fools and visionaries were optimistic about America's prospects of winning independence in 1776. The Americans had taken on a formidable military power. The population of Britain was perhaps four times that of its former colonies. England also possessed a strong manufacturing base, a well-trained regular army supplemented

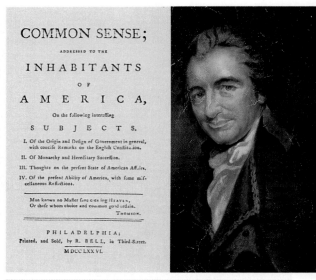

The message of Thomas Paine's pamphlet Common Sense *(title page shown) was clear and direct. Paine's stark phrases calling for "The Free and Independent States of America" reverberated throughout America.*

by thousands of hired German troops (Hessians), and a navy that dominated the world's oceans. Many British officers had battlefield experience. They already knew what the Americans would slowly learn: waging war requires great discipline, money, and sacrifice.

The British government entered the conflict fully confident it could beat the Americans. In 1776, Lord North and his colleagues regarded the war as a police action. They anticipated a mere show of armed force would intimidate the upstart colonists. As soon as the rebels in Boston had been humbled, the British argued, people living in other colonies would desert the cause for independence. General Gage, for example, told the king that the colonists "will be Lions, whilst we are Lambs, . . . if we take a resolute part they will undoubtedly prove very weak." Since this advice confirmed George's views, he called Gage "an honest determined man."

As later events demonstrated, of course, Britain had become involved in an impossible military situation, in some ways analogous to that in which the United States found itself in Vietnam. Three separate elements neutralized advantages held by the larger power over its adversary. First, the British had to transport men and supplies across the Atlantic, a logistic chal-

Congress Voting Independence, *oil painting by Robert Edge Pine and Edward Savage, 1785. The committee appointed by Congress to draft a declaration of independence included (center, standing) John Adams, Roger Sherman, Robert Livingston, Thomas Jefferson, and (center foreground, seated) Benjamin Franklin. The committee members are shown submitting Jefferson's draft to the Speaker.*

lenge of unprecedented complexity. Unreliable lines of communication broke down under the strain of war.

Second, America was too vast to be conquered by conventional military methods. Redcoats might gain control over the major port cities, but as long as the Continental army remained intact, the rebellion continued. As Washington explained, ". . . the possession of our Towns, while we have an Army in the field, will avail them little. . . . It is our Arms, not defenceless Towns, they have to subdue." Even if England had recruited enough soldiers to occupy the entire country, it would still have lost the war. As one Loyalist instructed the king, "if all America becomes a garrison, she is not worth your attention." Britain could only win by crushing the American will to resist.

And third, British strategists never appreciated the depth of the Americans' commitment to a political ideology. In the wars of eighteenth-century Europe, such beliefs had seldom mattered. European troops before the French Revolution served because they were paid or because the military was a vocation, but most certainly not because they hoped to advance a set of constitutional principles. Americans were different. To be sure, some young men were drawn to the military by bounty money or by the desire to escape unhappy families. A few were drafted. But taking

such people into account, one still encounters among the American troops a remarkable commitment to republican ideals. As one French officer reported from the United States, "It is incredible that soldiers composed of men of every age, even of children of fifteen, of whites and blacks, almost naked, unpaid, and rather poorly fed, can march so well and withstand fire so steadfastly."

During the earliest months of rebellion, American soldiers—especially those of New England—suffered no lack of confidence. Indeed, they interpreted their courageous stands at Concord and Bunker Hill as evidence that brave yeomen farmers could lick British regulars on any battlefield. George Washington spent the first years of the war disabusing the colonists of this foolishness, for as he had learned during the French and Indian War, military success depended on endless drill, careful planning, and tough discipline—rigorous preparation that did not characterize the minutemen's methods.

Washington insisted on organizing a regular well-trained field army. Some advisers urged the commander in chief to wage a guerrilla war, one in which small partisan bands would sap Britain's will to rule Americans. But Washington rejected that course. He recognized the Continental army served not only as a fighting force but also as a symbol of the republican cause. Its very existence would sustain American hopes, and so long as the

Overview of the Revolutionary War

Maps that follow on pages 156, 157 and 160 are enlargements of the insets on this map.

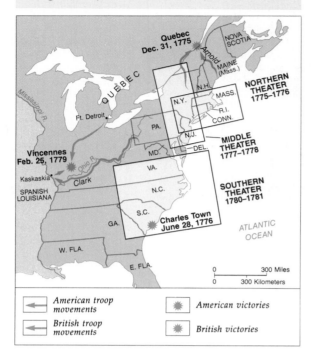

American troop movements

British troop movements

American victories

British victories

Britain . . . [but] They appeared to be penitent of their former conduct, [and] professed themselves convinced . . . that there was no such thing as remaining neuters." Without local political coercion, Washington's task would have been considerably more difficult.

For the half million African American colonists, most of them slaves, the fight for independence took on special poignance. After all, they wanted to achieve personal as well as political freedom, and many African Americans supported those who seemed most likely to deliver them from bondage. As one historian explained, "the black soldier was likely to join the side that made him the quickest and best offer in terms of those 'unalienable rights' of which Mr. Jefferson had spoken." It is estimated that some five thousand African Americans took up arms to fight against the British. The Continental army included two all-black units, one from Massachusetts and the other from Rhode Island. In 1778, the legislature of Rhode Island voted to free any slave who volunteered to serve, since according to the lawmakers, history taught that "the wisest, the

army survived, American agents could plausibly solicit foreign aid. This thinking shaped Washington's wartime strategy; he studiously avoided "general actions" in which the Continental army might be destroyed. Critics complained about Washington's caution, but as they soon discovered, he understood better than they what independence required.

If the commander in chief was correct about the army, however, he failed to comprehend the importance of the militia. These scattered, almost amateur, military units seldom altered the outcome of battle, but they did maintain control over large areas of the country not directly affected by the British army. Throughout the war, they compelled men and women who would rather have remained neutral to support actively the American effort. In 1777, for example, the militia of Farmington, Connecticut, visited a group of suspected Tories, as Loyalists were called, and after "educating" these people in the fundamentals of republican ideology, a militia spokesman announced, "They were indeed grossly ignorant of the true grounds of the present war with Great

In this 1774 woodcut, a Daughter of Liberty stands ready to take up arms in support of colonial militia.

freest, and bravest nations . . . liberated their slaves, and enlisted them as soldiers to fight in defence of their country." In the South, especially in Georgia and South Carolina, more than ten thousand African Americans supported the British, and after the patriots had won the war, these men and women left the United States, relocating to Nova Scotia, Florida, and Jamaica, with some eventually resettling in Africa.

Early Disasters Test the American Will

After the embarrassing defeats in Massachusetts, the king appointed General Sir William Howe to replace the ill-fated Gage. British rulers now understood that a simple police action would not be sufficient to crush the American rebellion. Parliament authorized sending over fifty thousand troops to the mainland colonies, and after evacuating Boston—an untenable strategic position—the British forces stormed ashore at Staten Island in New York harbor on July 3, 1776. From this more central location, Howe believed he could cut the New Englanders off from the rest of America. He enjoyed the powerful support of the British navy under the command of his brother, Admiral Lord Richard Howe.

When Washington learned the British were planning to occupy New York City, he transferred many of his inexperienced soldiers to Long Island, where they suffered a major defeat (August 27, 1776). In a series of disastrous engagements for the Americans, Howe drove the Continental army across the Hudson River into New Jersey. Because of his failure to take full advantage of the situation, however, General Howe lost what seemed in retrospect an excellent opportunity to annihilate Washington's entire army. Nevertheless, the Americans were on the run, and in the fall of 1776, contemporaries predicted the rebels would soon capitulate.

"Times That Try Men's Souls"

Swift victories in New York and New Jersey persuaded General Howe that few Americans enthusiastically supported independence. He issued a general pardon, therefore, to anyone who would swear allegiance to George III. The results were encouraging. Over three thousand men and women who lived in areas occupied by the British army took the oath. This group included one signer of the Declaration of Independence. Howe perceived that a lasting peace in America would require his troops to treat "our enemies as if they might one day become our friends." A member of Lord North's cabinet grumbled that this was "a sentimental manner of making war," a shortsighted view considering England's experience in attempting to pacify the Irish. The pardon plan eventually failed not because Howe lacked toughness but because his soldiers and officers regarded loyal Americans as inferior provincials, an attitude that did little to promote good relations. In any case, as soon as the redcoats left a pardoned region, the rebel militia retaliated against those who had deserted the patriot cause.

In December 1776, Washington's bedraggled army retreated across the Delaware River into Pennsylvania. American prospects appeared bleaker than at any other time during the war. The Continental army lacked basic supplies, and many men who had signed up for short-term enlistments prepared to go home. "These are the times that try men's souls," Paine wrote in a pamphlet entitled *American Crisis*. "The summer soldier and the sunshine patriot will, in this crisis, shrink from the service of their country, but he that stands it *now* deserves . . . love and thanks. . . " Before winter, Washington determined to attempt one last desperate stroke.

Howe played into Washington's hands. The British forces were dispersed in small garrisons across the state of New Jersey, and while the Americans could not possibly have defeated the combined British army, they did possess the capacity—with luck—to capture an exposed post. On the night of December 25, Continental soldiers slipped over the ice-filled Delaware River and at Trenton took nine hundred sleeping Hessian mercenaries by complete surprise.

Cheered by success, Washington returned a second time to Trenton, but on this occasion the Continental army was not so fortunate. A large British force under Lord Cornwallis trapped the Americans. Instead of standing and fighting—really an impossible challenge—Washington secretly, by night, marched his little army around Cornwallis's left flank. On January 3, 1777, the Americans surprised a British garrison at Princeton. Washington then went into winter quarters. The British, fearful of losing more out-

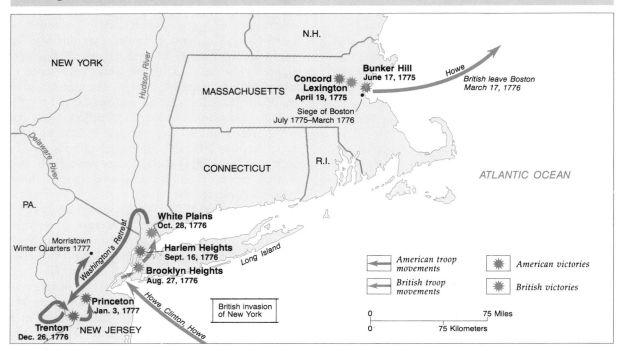

Northern Theater of War, 1775–1776

The major battles of the first years of the war, from the spontaneous rising at Concord in 1775 to Washington's well-coordinated attack on Trenton in December 1776, occurred in the northern colonies.

NEW YORK

N.H.

Hudson River

MASSACHUSETTS

Bunker Hill
June 17, 1775

Howe

British leave Boston
March 17, 1776

**Concord
Lexington**
April 19, 1775

Siege of Boston
July 1775–March 1776

Delaware River

CONNECTICUT

R.I.

ATLANTIC OCEAN

PA.

White Plains
Oct. 28, 1776

Morristown
Winter Quarters 1777

Washington's Retreat

Harlem Heights
Sept. 16, 1776

Brooklyn Heights
Aug. 27, 1776

Long Island

Princeton
Jan. 3, 1777

Howe, Clinton, Howe

Trenton
Dec. 26, 1776

NEW JERSEY

British invasion
of New York

American troop movements

British troop movements

American victories

British victories

0   75 Miles
0'   75 Kilometers

Defeat of the British at the Battle of Princeton, *oil painting by William Mercer, ca. 1786–1790. The painting shows George Washington (left, on horseback) directing cannon fire with his sword. Shouting "It's a fine fox chase, my boys!" he led the rout of the British rear guard. The artist's father was mortally wounded in the battle.*

posts, consolidated their troops, thus leaving much of the state in the hands of the patriot militia.

Victory in a Year of Defeat

In 1777, England's chief military strategist, Lord George Germain, still perceived the war in conventional European terms. A large field army would somehow maneuver Washington's Continental troops into a decisive battle in which the British would enjoy a clear advantage. Complete victory over the Americans certainly seemed within England's grasp. Unfortunately for the men who advocated this plan, the Continental forces proved extremely elusive, and while one British army vainly tried to corner Washington in Pennsylvania, another was forced to surrender in the forests of upstate New York.

In the summer of 1777, General John Burgoyne, a dashing though overbearing officer, descended from Canada with a force of over seven thousand troops. They intended to clear the Hudson Valley of rebel resistance, join Howe's army, which was to come up to Albany, and thereby cut New England off from the other states. Burgoyne fought in a grand style. Accompanied by a German band, thirty carts filled with the general's liquor and belongings, and two thousand dependents and camp followers, the British set out to thrash the Americans. The campaign was a disaster. Military units, mostly from New England, cut the enemy force apart in the deep woods north of Albany. At the battle of Bennington (August 16), the New Hampshire militia under Brigadier General John Stark overwhelmed a thousand German mercenaries. After this setback, Burgoyne's forces struggled forward, desperately hoping Howe would rush to their rescue, but when it became clear their situation at Saratoga was hopeless, the haughty Burgoyne was forced to surrender fifty-eight hundred men to the American General Horatio Gates (October 17).

Soon after Burgoyne left Canada, General Howe quite unexpectedly decided to move his main army from New York City to Philadelphia. Exactly what he hoped to achieve was not clear, even to Britain's rulers, and of course, when Burgoyne called for assistance, Howe was sitting in the new nation's capital still trying to devise a way to destroy the Continental army. Howe's campaign began in late July. The British forces sailed to the head of the Chesapeake Bay and

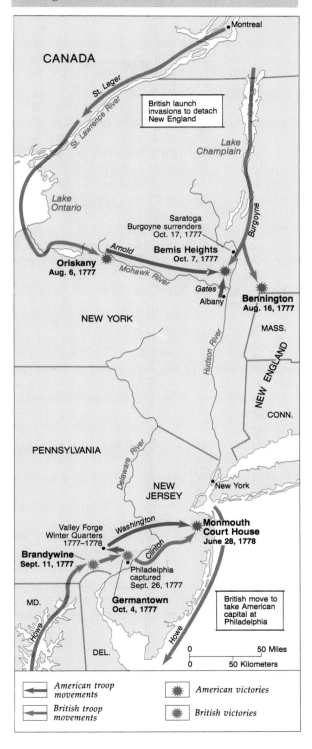

The Middle Years of the War

Burgoyne's attempt to cut New England off from the rest of the states failed when his army was defeated at Saratoga.

then marched north to Philadelphia. Washington's troops obstructed the enemy's progress, first at Brandywine Creek (September 11) and then at Paoli (September 20), but the outnumbered Americans could not stop the British from entering Philadelphia.

Anxious lest these defeats discourage Congress and the American people, Washington attempted one last battle before the onset of winter. In an engagement at Germantown (October 4), the Americans launched a major counterattack on a fog-covered battlefield, but just at the moment when success seemed assured, the Americans broke off the fight. "When every thing gave the most flattering hopes of victory," Washington complained, "the troops began suddenly to retreat." Bad luck, confusion, and incompetence contributed to the failure. A discouraged Continental army dug in at Valley Forge, 20 miles outside of Philadelphia, where camp diseases took twenty-five hundred American lives. In their misery, few American soldiers realized their situation was not nearly as desperate as it had been in 1776.

The French Alliance

Even before the Americans declared their independence, agents of the government of Louis XVI began to explore ways to aid the colonists, not so much because the French monarchy favored the republican cause, but because it hoped to embarrass the English. The French deeply resented the defeat they had sustained during the Seven Years' War. During the early months of the Revolution, the French covertly sent tons of essential military supplies to the Americans. The negotiations for these arms involved secret agents and fictitious trading companies, the type of clandestine operation more typical of modern times than of the eighteenth century. But when American representatives, Benjamin Franklin for one, pleaded for official recognition of American independence or for outright military alliance, the French advised patience. The international stakes were too great for the king openly to back a cause that had little chance of success.

The American victory at Saratoga convinced the French that the rebels had formidable forces and were serious in their resolve. Indeed, Lord North drew the same conclusion. When news of Saratoga reached London, North muttered, "this damned war." In private conversation he expressed doubts about England's ability to win the contest, knowing the French would soon enter the fray.

In April 1778, North tried to avert a greatly expanded war by sending a peace commission to America. He instructed this group, headed by the Earl of Carlisle, to bargain with the Continental Congress "as if it were a legal body." If the colonists would agree to drop their demand for independence, they could turn the imperial calendar back to 1763. Parliament belatedly conceded the right of Americans to tax themselves, even to elect their own governors. It also promised to remove all British troops in times of peace. The proposal might have gained substantial support back in 1776. The war, however, had hardened American resolve; the Congress refused to deal with Carlisle.

In Paris, Franklin performed brilliantly. In meetings with French officials, he hinted that the Americans might accept a British peace initiative. If the French wanted the war to continue, if they really wanted to embarrass their old rival, then they had to do what the English refused: formally recognize the independence of the United States.

The stratagem paid off handsomely. On February 6, 1778, the French presented American representatives with two separate treaties. The first, called the Treaty of Amity and Commerce, established commercial relations between France and the United States. It tacitly accepted the existence of a new, independent republic. The Treaty of Alliance was even more generous, considering America's obvious military and economic weaknesses. In the event that France and England went to war (they did so on June 14 as everyone expected), the French agreed to reject "either Truce or Peace with Great Britain . . . until the independence of the United States shall have been formally or tacitly assured by the Treaty or Treaties that shall terminate the War." Even more amazing, France surrendered its claim to all territories formerly owned by Great Britain east of the Mississippi River. The Americans pledged they would not sign a separate peace with Britain without first informing their new ally. And in return, France made no claim to Canada, asking only for the right to take possession of certain British islands in the Caribbean. Never had

Franklin worked his magic to greater effect.

French intervention instantly transformed British military strategy. What had been a colonial rebellion suddenly became a world conflict, a continuation of the great wars for empire of the late seventeenth century (see Chapter 4). Scarce military resources, especially newer fighting ships, had to be diverted from the American theater to guard the English Channel. In fact, there was talk in London of a possible French invasion. While the threat of such an assault was not very great until 1779, the British did not have cause for concern. The French navy posed a serious challenge to the overextended British fleet. By concentrating their warships in a specific area, the French could hold off or even defeat British squadrons, an advantage that would figure significantly in the American victory at Yorktown.

The Final Campaign

British General Henry Clinton replaced Howe, who resigned after the battle of Saratoga. Clinton was a strangely complex individual. As a subordinate officer, he had impressed his superiors as imaginative but easily provoked to anger. When he took command of the British army, his resolute self-confidence suddenly dissolved. Perhaps he feared failure. Whatever the explanation for his vacillation, Clinton's record in America was little better than Howe's or Gage's.

Military strategists calculated that Britain's last chance of winning the war lay in the Southern Colonies, a region largely untouched in the early years of fighting. Intelligence reports reaching London indicated that Georgia and South Carolina contained a sizable body of Loyalists, men who would take up arms for the Crown if only they received support and encouragement from the regular army. The southern strategy devised by Germain and Clinton in 1779 turned the war into a bitter guerrilla conflict, and during the last months of battle, British officers worried that their search for an easy victory had inadvertently opened a Pandora's box of uncontrollable partisan furies.

The southern campaign opened in the spring of 1780. Savannah had already fallen, and Clinton reckoned that if the British could take Charles Town, they would be able to control the entire South. A large fleet carrying nearly eight thousand redcoats reached South Carolina in February. Complacent Americans had allowed the city's fortifications to decay, and in a desperate, last-minute effort to preserve Charles Town, General Benjamin Lincoln's forces dug trenches and reinforced walls, but to no avail. Clinton and his second in command, General Cornwallis, gradually encircled the city, and on May 12, Lincoln surrendered an American army of almost six thousand men.

The defeat took Congress by surprise, and without making proper preparations, it dispatched a second army to South Carolina under Horatio Gates, the hero of Saratoga. He too failed. At Camden, Cornwallis outmaneuvered the raw American recruits, capturing or killing 750 during the course of battle (August 16). Poor Gates galloped from the scene and did not stop until he reached Hillsboro, North Carolina, 200 miles away.

Even at this early stage of the southern campaign, the dangers of partisan warfare had become evident. Tory raiders showed little interest in serving as regular soldiers in Cornwallis's army. They preferred night riding, indiscriminate plundering or murdering of neighbors against whom they harbored ancient grudges. The British had unleashed a horde of banditti across South Carolina. Men who genuinely supported independence or who had merely fallen victim to the Loyalist guerrillas bided their time. They retreated westward waiting for their enemies to make a mistake. Their chance came on October 7 at King's Mountain, North Carolina. The backwoodsmen decimated a force of British regulars and Tory raiders who had strayed too far from base. This was the most vicious fighting of the Revolution. One witness reported that when a British officer tried to surrender, he was summarily shot down by at least seven American soldiers.

Cornwallis, badly confused and poorly supplied, proceeded to squander his strength chasing American forces across the Carolinas. Whatever military strategy had compelled him to leave Charles Town had long since been abandoned, and in early 1781, Cornwallis informed Clinton that "Events alone can decide the future Steps." Events, however, did not run in the British favor. Congress sent General Nathanael Greene to the South with a new army. This young Rhode Islander was the most capable general on Washington's staff. Greene joined Daniel

Southern Theater of War, 1780–1781
Major battles from the fall of Savannah to the final victory at Yorktown.

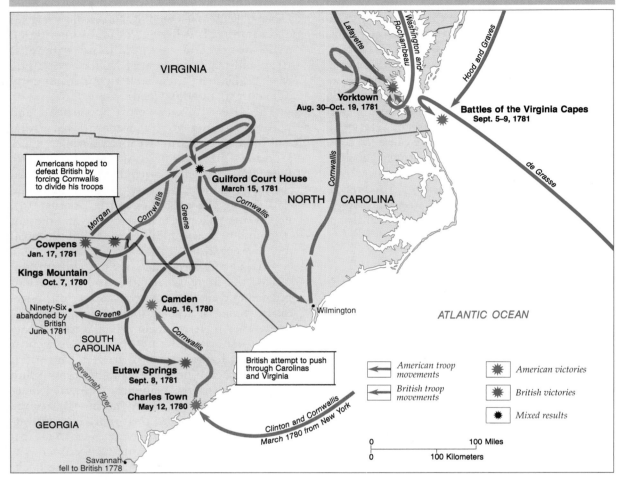

Morgan, leader of the famed Virginia Riflemen, and in a series of tactically brilliant engagements, they sapped the strength of Cornwallis's army, first at Cowpens, South Carolina (January 17, 1781), and later at Guilford Courthouse, North Carolina (March 15). Clinton fumed in New York City. In his estimation, the inept Cornwallis had left "two valuable colonies behind him to be overrun and conquered by the very army which he boasts to have completely routed but a week or two before."

Cornwallis pushed north into Virginia, planning apparently to establish a base of operations on the coast. He selected Yorktown, a sleepy tobacco market town located on a peninsula bounded by the York and James rivers. Washington watched these maneuvers closely.

The canny Virginia planter knew this territory intimately, and he sensed that Cornwallis had made a serious blunder. When Washington learned the French fleet could gain temporary dominance in the Chesapeake Bay, he rushed south from New Jersey. With him marched thousands of well-trained French troops under Comte de Rochambeau. All the pieces fell into place. The French admiral, Comte de Grasse, cut Cornwallis off from the sea, while Washington and his lieutenants encircled the British on land. On October 19, 1781, Cornwallis surrendered his entire army of six thousand men. When Lord North heard of the defeat at Yorktown, he moaned, "Oh God! It is all over." The British still controlled New York City and Charles Town, but except for a few skirmishes, the fighting ended. The task of securing the independence of the United States was now in the hands of the diplomats.

THE LOYALIST DILEMMA

The war lasted longer than anyone had predicted in 1776. While the nation won its independence, many Americans paid a terrible price. Indeed, a large number of men and women decided that however much they loved living in America, they could not accept the new government.

No one knows for certain how many Americans actually supported the Crown during the Revolution. Some Loyalists undoubtedly kept silent and avoided making a public commitment that might have led to banishment or loss of property. But for many persons, neutrality proved impossible. Almost one hundred thousand men and women permanently left America. While a number of these exiles had served as imperial officeholders—Thomas Hutchinson, for example—in the main, they came from all ranks and backgrounds. A large number of humble farmers, more than thirty thousand, resettled in Canada. Others relocated to England, the West Indies, or Africa.

The political ideology of the Loyalists was not substantially different from that of their opponents. Like other Americans, they believed men and women were entitled to life, liberty, and the pursuit of happiness. The Loyalists were also convinced that independence would destroy those values by promoting disorder. By turning their backs on Britain, a source of tradition and stability, the rebels seemed to have encouraged licentiousness, even anarchy in the streets. The Loyalists suspected that Patriot demands for freedom were self-serving, even hypocritical, for as Perserved Smith, a Loyalist from Ashfield, Massachusetts, observed, "Sons of liberty . . . did not deserve the name, for it was evident all they wanted was liberty from oppression that they might have liberty to oppress!"

The Loyalists were caught in a difficult squeeze. The British never quite trusted them. After all, they were Americans. During the early stages of the war, Loyalists organized militia companies and hoped to pacify large areas of the countryside with the support of the regular army.

The British generals were unreliable partners, however, for no sooner had they called on loyal Americans to come forward, than the redcoats marched away, leaving the Tories exposed to rebel retaliation. And in England, the exiles found themselves treated as second-class citizens. While many of them received monetary compensation for their sacrifice, they were never regarded as the equals of native-born English citizens. Not surprisingly, the Loyalist community in London was gradually transformed into a collection of bitter men and women who felt unwelcome on both sides of the Atlantic.

Americans who actively supported independence saw these people as traitors who deserved their fate of constant, often violent, harassment. In many states—but especially in New York—revolutionary governments confiscated Loyalist property. Other friends of the king received beatings, or as the rebels called them, "grand Toory [sic] rides." A few were even executed. According to one patriot, "A Tory is a thing whose head is in England, and its body in America, and its neck ought to be stretched."

Long after the victorious Americans turned their attentions to the business of building a new republic, Loyalists remembered a receding colonial past, a comfortable, ordered world that had been lost forever at Yorktown. Although many Loyalists eventually returned to their homes, a sizable number could not do so. For them, the sense of loss remained a heavy emotional burden. Perhaps the most poignant testimony came from a young mother living in exile in Nova Scotia. "I climbed to the top of Chipman's Hill and watched the sails disappear in the distance," she recounted, "and such a feeling of loneliness came over me that though I had not shed a tear through all the war I sat down on the damp moss with my baby on my lap and cried bitterly."

WINNING THE PEACE

Congress appointed a splendid delegation to negotiate a peace treaty: Benjamin Franklin, John Adams, and John Jay. According to their official instructions, they were to insist only on the recognition of the independence of the United States. On other issues, Congress ordered

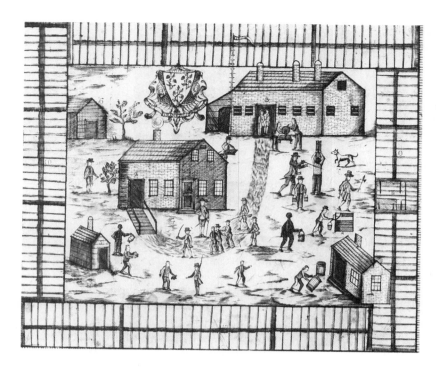

Between 1776 and 1783, the revolutionary state governments passed "Test Acts" requiring repudiation of the British Crown and setting various punishments for those who remained loyal to Britain. The Connecticut assembly, for example, passed a law threatening imprisonment for anyone who criticized the state assembly or the Continental Congress. This engraving, "A Prospective View of Old Newgate Connecticut's State Prison" is attributed to Richard Brunton and was probably done ca. 1800–1801 while Brunton was imprisoned for counterfeiting.

its delegates to defer to the counsel of the French government.

But the political environment in Paris was much different than the diplomats had been led to expect. The French had formed a military alliance with Spain, and French officials announced that they could not consider the details of an American settlement until after the Spanish had recaptured Gibraltar from the British. The prospects for a Spanish victory were not good, and in any case, it was well known that Spain coveted the lands lying between the Appalachian Mountains and the Mississippi River. Indeed, there were even rumors afloat in Paris that the great European powers might intrigue to deny the United States its independence.

While the three American delegates publicly paid their respects to French officials, they secretly entered into negotiations with an English agent. The peacemakers drove a remarkable bargain, a much better one than Congress could have expected. The prelimi-

nary agreement signed on September 3, 1783, not only guaranteed the independence of the United States, it also transferred all the territory east of the Mississippi River, except Spanish Florida, to the new Republic. The treaty established generous boundaries on the north and south and gave the Americans important fishing rights in the North Atlantic. In exchange, Congress promised to help British merchants collect debts contracted before the Revolution and compensate Loyalists whose lands had been confiscated by the various state governments. Even though the Americans negotiated separately with the British, they did not sign a separate peace. The preliminary treaty did not become effective until France reached its own agreement with Great Britain. Thus did the Americans honor the French alliance. It is difficult to imagine how Franklin, Adams, and Jay could have negotiated a more favorable conclusion to the war. In the fall of 1783, the last redcoats sailed from New York City, ending 176 years of colonial rule.

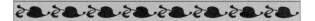

CHRONOLOGY

1763	Peace of Paris ends the Seven Years' War
1764	Parliament passes Sugar Act to collect American revenue
1765	Stamp Act receives support of House of Commons (March) • Stamp Act Congress meets in New York City (October)
1766	Stamp Act repealed the same day that Declaratory Act becomes law (March 18)
1767	Townshend Revenue Acts stir American anger (June–July)
1768	Massachusetts assembly refuses to rescind circular letter (February)
1770	Parliament repeals all Townshend duties except one on tea (March) • British troops "massacre" Boston civilians (March)
1772	Samuel Adams forms committee of correspondence
1773	Lord North's government passes Tea Act (May) • Bostonians hold Tea Party (December)
1774	Parliament punishes Boston with Coercive Acts (March–June) • First Continental Congress convenes (September)
1775	Patriots take stand at Lexington and Concord (April) • Second Continental Congress gathers (May) • Americans hold their own at Bunker Hill (June)
1776	Congress votes for independence; Declaration of Independence is signed • British defeat Washington at Long Island (August) • Americans score victory at Trenton (December)
1777	General Burgoyne surrenders at Saratoga (October)
1778	French treaties recognize independence of the United States (February)
1780	British take Charles Town (May)
1781	Washington forces Cornwallis to surrender at Yorktown (October)
1783	Peace treaty signed (September) • British evacuate New York City (November)

REPUBLICAN CHALLENGE

The American people had waged war against the most powerful nation in Europe and emerged victorious. The treaty marked the conclusion of a colonial rebellion, but it remained for the men and women who had resisted taxation without representation to work out the full implications of republicanism. What would be the shape of the new government? What powers would be delegated to the people, the states, the federal authorities? How far would the wealthy, well-born leaders of the rebellion be willing to extend political, social, and economic rights? No wonder that Dr. Benjamin Rush explained, "There is nothing more common than to confound the terms of American Revolution with those of the late American war. The American war is over, but this is far from being the case with the American Revolution. On the contrary, nothing but the first act of the great drama is closed."

Recommended Reading

The Revolution has generated a rich historiography. No sooner had the fighting ceased than the participants, Loyalists as well as Patriots, began to interpret the events leading to the creation of an independent republic. The most enjoyable book is David Ramsay's *The History of the American Revolution*, originally published in 1789, but recently reprinted in volumes edited by Lester H. Cohen (1990). A general guide to the period is provided by Jack Greene and J. R. Pole, eds., *Blackwell Encyclopedia of the American Revolution* (1991). Two reliable surveys are Merrill Jensen, *The Founding of a Nation* (1968), and Edmund S. Morgan, *Birth of the Republic* (rev. ed. 1992). Two books that transformed how an entire generation interpreted the revolution are Edmund S. Morgan and Helen M. Morgan, *The Stamp Act Crisis* (1953), and Bernard Bailyn, *The Ideological Origins of the American Revolution* (1967).

Additional Bibliography

The literature dealing with British politics on the eve of the American Revolution is impressive. One important study is John Brooke, *King George III* (1974). The most useful recent investigation of parliamentary politics is John Brewer, *Party Ideology and Popular Politics at the Accession of George III* (1976). Also helpful are J. C. D. Clark, *The Language of Liberty 1660–1832: Political Discourse and Social Dynamics in the Anglo-American World* (1994) and P. D. G.

Thomas's *The Townshend Duties Crisis* (1987) and *Tea Party to Independence* (1991).

The American interpretation of changing British politics can be explored in Pauline Maier, *From Resistance to Revolution: Colonial Radicals and the Development of American Opposition to Britain* (1972), and John Phillip Reid, *Constitutional History of the American Revolution* (1986). Other more specialized studies include John Shy, *Toward Lexington* (1965); Richard D. Brown, *Revolutionary Politics in Massachusetts: The Boston Committee of Correspondence and the Towns* (1970); and David Hackett Fischer, *Paul Revere's Ride* (1994). For an innovative interpretation of the cultural tensions in revolutionary society, see Jay Fliegelman's *Declaring Independence: Jefferson, Natural Language, and the Culture of Performance* (1993) as well as his *Prodigals and Pilgrims: The American Revolution Against Patriarchal Authority* (1982).

Several studies show how local communities tried to make sense out of political and social change: Rhys Isaac, *Transformation of Virginia, 1740–1790* (1983); Robert A. Gross, *The Minutemen and Their World* (1976); Edward Countryman, *A People in Revolution: The American Revolution and Political Society in New York* (1982); and T. H. Breen, *Tobacco Culture: The Mentality of the Great Tidewater Planters on the Eve of Revolution* (1985). For a balanced biography of the author of *Common Sense*, see Eric Foner, *Tom Paine and Revolutionary America* (1976). An excellent essay collection remains Alfred F. Young, ed., *The American Revolution: Explorations in American Radicalism* (1976).

Alice H. Jones provides a full analysis of the economic structure of colonial America in *Wealth of a Nation to Be* (1980). The experiences of the merchants are discussed in Thomas Doerflinger, *A Vigorous Spirit of Enterprise* (1986) and John W. Tyler, *Smugglers and Patriots* (1986). A splendid reconstruction of city life, especially the growth of class tensions, can be found in Gary Nash, *Urban Crucible: Social Change, Political Consequences, and the Origins of the American Revolution*

(1979). Also see Billy G. Smith, *The "Lower Sort": Philadelphia's Laboring People, 1750–1800* (1990).

Anyone interested in the experiences of American women during this period should start with Linda Kerber, *Women of the Republic* (1980). Also helpful are Mary Beth Norton, *Liberty's Daughters: The Revolutionary Experience of American Women, 1750–1800* (1980) and Marylynn Salmon, *Women and the Law of Property in Early America* (1986). The rituals of rebellion are interpreted in T. H. Breen, "Narrative of Commercial Life: Consumption, Ideology, and Community on the Eve of the American Revolution," *William & Mary Quarterly*, 3rd ser., 50 (1993), 471–501. A good account of the Iroquois remains Barbara Graymont, *The Iroquois in the American Revolution* (1972).

Two valuable studies of the war are Don Higginbotham, *The War of Independence: Military Attitudes, Policies, and Practices* (1983), and Howard H. Peckham, *The War for Independence: A Military History* (1958). The British side of the story is well told in Piers Mackesy, *The War for America, 1775–1783* (1964). For an innovative interpretation of the political role of the militia see John Shy, *A People Numerous and Armed* (rev. ed. 1990). The Americans' changing attitudes toward the Continental army are traced in Charles Royster, *A Revolutionary People at War* (1979). Also see a classic study of African American soldiers, Benjamin Quarles, *The Negro in the American Revolution* (1961) as well as Sidney Kaplan, *The Black Presence in the Era of the American Revolution 1770–1800* (1973).

The Loyalists are examined in Wallace Brown, *The King's Friends: The Composition and Motives of the American Loyalist Claimants* (1965); Robert M. Calhoon, *The Loyalists in Revolutionary America, 1760–1781* (1973); and Janice Potter, *Liberty We Seek: Loyalist Ideology in Colonial New York and Massachusetts* (1983). A good study of American relations with foreign powers is Jonathan Dull, *The Diplomatic History of the American Revolution* (1985).

The Republican Experiment

A curious controversy shattered the harmony of Boston in 1785. The dispute broke out soon after a group of young adults, sons and daughters of the city's wealthiest families, announced the formation of a tea assembly or "Sans Souci Club." The members of this select group gathered once a week for the pleasure of good conversation, a game of cards, some dancing, and perhaps a glass of Madeira wine.

These meetings outraged other Bostonians, many of them old patriots. Samuel Adams, who dreamed of creating a "Christian Sparta," a virtuous society committed to republican purity, sounded the alarm. "Say, my country," he thundered, "why do you suffer all the intemperances of Great Britain to be fostered in our bosom, in all their vile luxuriance?" The club's very existence threatened the "republican principles" for which Americans had so recently fought a revolution.

FROM MONARCHY TO REPUBLIC

Today, the term *republican* no longer possesses the evocative powers it did for Americans of the late eighteenth century. Adams and his contemporaries—some of whom probably visited the Sans Souci Club—believed creating a new nation-state involved more than simply winning independence from Great Britain. The American people had taken on a responsibility to establish an elective system of government. It was a bold experiment, and the precedents were not very encouraging. Indeed, the history books of that period offered disturbing examples of failure, of young republics that after a promising beginning had succumbed to political instability and military impotence.

More than did any other form of government, a republic demanded an exceptionally high degree of public morality. If American citizens substituted "luxury, prodigality, and profligacy" for "prudence, virtue, and economy," then their revolution surely would have been in vain. Maintaining popular virtue was crucial to success. An innocent tea party, therefore, set off alarm bells. Such "foolish gratifications" in Boston seemed to compromise republican goals. It is not surprising that

in this situation Adams thundered, "Rome, Athens, and all the cities of renown, whence came your fall?"

White Americans were optimistic about their country's chances. They came out of the Revolution with an almost euphoric sense of America's special destiny. This expansive outlook, encountered among so many ordinary men and women, owed much to the spread of Protestant evangelicalism. However skeptical Jefferson and Franklin may have been about revealed religion, the great mass of American people subscribed to a millennial vision of the country's future. To this republic, God had promised progress and prosperity. The signs were there for everyone to see. "There is not upon the face of the earth a body of people more happy or rising into consequence with more rapid stride," one man announced in 1786, "than the Inhabitants of the United States of America. Population is increasing, new houses building, new lands clearing, new settlements forming, and new manufactures establishing with a rapidity beyond conception."

Such optimism did not translate easily or smoothly into the creation of a strong central government. Modern Americans tend to take for granted the acceptance of the Constitution. Its merits seem self-evident largely because it has survived for two centuries. But in the early 1780s, no one could have predicted the Constitution as we know it would have been written, much less ratified. It was equally possible the Americans would have supported a weak confederation, or perhaps, allowed the various states and regions to go their separate ways.

In this uncertain political atmosphere, Americans divided sharply over the relative importance of *liberty* and *order*. The revolutionary experience had called into question the legitimacy of any form of special privilege. As one republican informed an aristocratic colleague in the South Carolina assembly, "the day is Arrived when *goodness,* and not *Wealth,* are the only *Criterions of greatness.*" A legislative leader in Pennsylvania put the point even more bluntly: "no man has a greater claim of special privilege for his $100,000 than I have for my $5." The man who passionately defended social equality for those of varying economic status, however, may still have resisted the extension of civil rights to women or blacks. Nevertheless, liberty was contagious, and Americans of all backgrounds began to make new demands on society and government. For them, the Revolution had suggested radical alternatives, and in many forums throughout the nation—especially in the elected state assemblies—they insisted on being heard.

In certain quarters, the celebration of liberty met with mixed response. Some Americans—often the very men who had resisted British tyranny—worried the citizens of the new nation were caught up in a wild, destructive scramble for material wealth. Democratic excesses seemed to threaten order, to endanger the rights of property. Surely a republic could not long survive unless its citizens showed greater self-control. For people concerned about the loss of order, the state assemblies appeared the greatest source of instability. Popularly elected representatives lacked what men of property defined as real civic virtue.

Working out the tensions between order and liberty, between property and equality, generated an outpouring of political genius. At other times in American history, persons of extraordinary talent have been drawn to theology, commerce, or science, but during the 1780s, the country's intellectual leaders—Thomas Jefferson, James Madison, Alexander Hamilton, and John Adams among others—focused their creative energies on the problem of how republicans ought to govern themselves.

REPUBLICAN SOCIETY

Revolution changed American society, often in ways no one had planned. This phenomenon is not surprising. The great revolutions of modern times produced radical transformations in French, Russian, and Chinese societies. By comparison, the immediate results of the American Revolution appear much tamer, less wrenching. Nevertheless, national independence compelled people to reevaluate hierarchical social relations that they had taken for granted during the colonial period. The faltering first steps of independence raised fundamental questions about the meaning of equality in American society, many that still have not been answered satisfactorily.

Social and Political Reform

Following the war, Americans aggressively ferreted out and, with republican fervor, denounced any traces of aristocratic presence. As colonists, they had long resented the claims that certain Englishmen made to special privilege simply because of noble birth. Even so committed a republican as George Washington had to be reminded that artificial status was contrary to republican principles. In 1783, he and the officers who had served during the Revolution formed the Society of the Cincinnati, a hereditary organization in which membership passed from father to eldest son. The soldiers meant no harm; they simply wanted to maintain old friendships. But anxious republicans throughout America let out a howl of protest and one South Carolina legislator, Aedanus Burke, warned that the Society intended to create "an hereditary peerage . . . [which would] undermine the Constitution and destroy civil liberty." After an embarrassed Washington called for appropriate reforms of the Society's bylaws, the Cincinnati crisis receded. The fear of privilege remained, however, and wealthy Americans dropped honorific titles such as "esquire." Lawyers of republican persuasion chided judges who had adopted the English custom of wearing great flowing wigs to court.

The appearance of equality was as important as its actual achievement. In fact, the distribution of wealth in postwar America was more uneven than it had been in the mid-eighteenth century. The sudden accumulation of large fortunes by new families made other Americans particularly sensitive to aristocratic display, for it seemed intolerable that a revolution waged against a monarchy should produce a class of persons legally, or even visibly, distinguished from their fellow citizens.

In an effort to root out the notion of a privileged class, states abolished laws of primogeniture and entail. In colonial times, these laws allowed a landholder either to pass his entire estate to his eldest son or to declare that his property could never be divided, sold, or given away. Jefferson claimed that the repeal of these practices would eradicate "antient [sic] and future aristocracy; a foundation [has been] laid for a government truly republican." Jefferson exaggerated the social impact of this reform. In neither Virginia nor North Carolina did the abolition of

Questions of equality in the new Republic extended to the rights of women. In this illustration, which appeared as the frontispiece in the 1792 issue of The Lady's Magazine and Repository of Entertaining Knowledge, *the "Genius of the Ladies Magazine" and the "Genius of Emulation" (holding in her hand a laurel crown) present to Liberty a petition for the rights of woman.*

no man can be "free & independent" unless he possesses "a voice . . . in the choice of the most important Officers in the Legislature." Pennsylvania and Georgia allowed all white male taxpayers to participate in elections. Other states were less democratic, but with the exception of Massachusetts, they reduced property qualifications. These reforms, however, did not significantly expand the American electorate. Long before the Revolution, an overwhelming percentage of free white males had owned enough land to vote. In any case, during the 1780s republican lawmakers were not prepared to experiment with universal manhood suffrage, for as John Adams observed, if the states pushed these reforms too far, "New claims will arise, women will demand a vote . . . and every man who has not a farthing, will demand an equal vote with any other."

The most important changes in voting patterns were the result of western migration. As Americans moved to the frontier, they received full political representation in their state legislatures, and because new districts tended to be poorer than established coastal settlements, their representatives seemed less cultured, less well trained than those sent by eastern voters. Moreover, western delegates resented traveling so far to attend legislative meetings, and they lobbied successfully to transfer state capitals to more convenient locations. During this period, Georgia moved the seat of its government from Savannah to Augusta, South Carolina from Charles Town to Columbia, North Carolina from New Bern to Raleigh, Virginia from Williamsburg to Richmond, New York from New York City to Albany, and New Hampshire from Portsmouth to Concord.

After gaining independence, Americans also reexamined the relation between church and state. Republican spokespersons like Thomas Jefferson insisted that rulers had no right to interfere with the free expression of an individual's religious beliefs. As governor of Virginia, he strenuously advocated the disestablishment of the Anglican church, an institution that had received tax monies and other benefits during the colonial period. Jefferson and his allies regarded such special privilege not only as a denial of religious freedom—after all, rival denominations did not receive tax money—but also as a vestige of aristocratic society.

primogeniture greatly affect local custom. The great tobacco planters had seldom encumbered their estates with entail, and they generally provided all their children—daughters as well as sons—with land. Nonetheless, republican legislators wanted to cleanse traces of the former feudal order from the statute books.

Republican ferment also encouraged many states to lower property requirements for voting. After the break with Great Britain, such a step seemed logical. As one group of farmers declared,

In 1786, Virginia cut the last ties between church and state. Other southern states disestablished the Anglican church, but in Massachusetts and New Hampshire, Congregational churches continued to enjoy special status. Moreover, while Americans championed toleration, they seldom favored philosophies that radically challenged Christian values.

African Americans in the New Republic

Revolutionary fervor forced Americans to confront the most appalling contradiction to republican principles—slavery. The Quaker leader, John Woolman (1720–1772), probably did more than any other white person of the era to remind people of the evils of this institution. A trip he took through the Southern Colonies as a young man forever impressed upon Woolman "the dark gloominess" of slavery. In a sermon, this outspoken humanitarian declared "that Men having Power too often misapplied it; that though we made Slaves of the Negroes, and the Turks made Slaves of the Christians, I believed that Liberty was the natural Right of all Men equally."

During the revolutionary period, abolitionist sentiment spread. Both in private and in public, people began to criticize slavery in other than religious language. No doubt, the double standard of their own political rhetoric embarrassed many white Americans. They hotly demanded liberation from parliamentary enslavement at the same time that they held several hundred thousand blacks in permanent bondage.

By keeping the issue of slavery before the public by writing and petitioning, African Americans powerfully undermined arguments advanced in favor of human bondage. They demanded freedom, reminding white lawmakers that African American men and women had the same right to liberty as did other Americans. In 1779, for example, a group of African Americans living in Connecticut pointedly asked the members of the state assembly "whether it is consistent with the present Claims, of the United States, to hold so many Thousands, of the Race of Adam, our Common Father, in perpetual Slavery." In New Hampshire, nineteen persons who called themselves "natives of Africa" reminded local legislators that "private or public tyranny and slavery are alike detestable to minds conscious of the equal dignity of human nature."

The scientific accomplishments of Benjamin Banneker (1731–1806), Maryland's African American astronomer and mathematician, and the international fame of Phillis Wheatley (1753–1784), Boston's celebrated "African muse," made it increasingly difficult for white Americans to maintain credibly that African Americans could not hold their own in a free society. Wheatley's poems went through many editions, and after reading her work, the great French philosopher, Voltaire, rebuked a friend who had claimed "there never would be Negro poets." As Voltaire discovered, Wheatley "writes excellent verse in English." Banneker, like Wheatley, enjoyed a well-deserved reputation for his contributions as a scientist. After receiving a copy of an almanac that Banneker had published in Philadelphia, Thomas Jefferson concluded "that nature has given to our black brethren, talents equal to those of the other colors of men."

In the northern states, there was no real economic justification for slavery, and white laborers, often recent European immigrants, resented having to compete in the workplace against slaves. This economic situation, combined with the acknowledgment of the double standard represented by slavery, contributed to the establishment of antislavery societies. In 1775, Franklin helped organize a group in Philadelphia called The Society for the Relief of Free Negroes, Unlawfully Held. John Jay, Alexander Hamilton, and other prominent New Yorkers founded a Manumission Society in 1785. By 1792, antislavery societies were meeting from Virginia to Massachusetts, and in the northern states at least, these groups working for the same ends as various Christian evangelicals put slaveholders on the intellectual defensive for the first time in American history.

In several states north of Virginia, the abolition of slavery took a number of different forms. Even before achieving statehood, Vermont drafted a constitution (1777) that specifically prohibited slavery. In 1780, the Pennsylvania legislature passed a law effecting the gradual emancipation of slaves. Although the Massachusetts assembly refused to address the issue directly, the state courts took up the challenge and liberated the African Americans. A judge ruled slavery unconstitutional in Massachusetts because it conflicted with a clause in the state bill of rights declaring "all men . . . free and equal." According to one enthusiast, this decision freed "a Grate [sic] number of Blacks . . . who . . . are held in a state of slavery within the bowels of a free and christian Country." By 1800, slavery was well on the road to extinction in the northern states.

These positive developments did not mean white people accepted blacks as equals. In fact, in the very states that outlawed slavery, African Americans faced systematic discrimination. Free blacks were generally excluded from voting, juries, and militia duty—they were denied rights and responsibilities usually associated with full citizenship. They rarely enjoyed access to education, and in cities like Philadelphia and New York, where African Americans went to look for work, they wound up living in segregated wards or neighborhoods. Even in the churches—institutions that had often spoken out against slavery—

Born to slaves, Richard Allen became a zealous minister and converted his master, who allowed him to buy his freedom. Allen was ordained a bishop in 1799.

This engraving of Phillis Wheatley appeared in her volume of verse, Poems on Various Subjects, Religious and Moral *(1773), the first book published by an African American.*

free African Americans were denied equal standing with white worshippers. Humiliations of this sort persuaded African Americans to form their own churches. In Philadelphia, Richard Allen, a former slave, founded the Bethel Church for Negro Methodists (1793). This man later organized the African Methodist Episcopal Church (1814), an institution of great cultural as well as religious significance for nineteenth-century American blacks.

Even in the South, where African Americans made up a large percentage of the population, slavery disturbed thoughtful white republicans. Some planters simply freed their slaves, and by 1790, the number of free blacks living in Virginia numbered 12,766. By 1800, the figure had reached 30,750. There is no question that this trend reflected the uneasiness among white masters. Richard Randolph, one of Virginia's wealthier planters, explained that he freed his slaves "to make retribution, as far as I am able, to an unfortunate race of bond-men, over whom my ancestors have usurped and exercised the most lawless and monstrous tyranny." George Washington also manumitted his slaves. To be sure, most southern slaveholders, especially those living in South Carolina and Georgia, rejected this course of action. Their economic well-being depended on slave labor. Perhaps more significant, however, is the fact that no southern leader during the era of republican experimentation defended slavery as a positive good. Such overtly racist rhetoric did not become part of the public discourse until the nineteenth century.

Despite promising starts in that direction, the southern states did not abolish slavery. The economic incentives to maintain a servile labor force, especially after the invention of the cotton gin in 1793, and the opening up of the Alabama and Mississippi frontier, overwhelmed the initial abolitionist impulse. An opportunity to translate the principles of the American Revolution into social practice had been lost, at least temporarily. Jefferson reported sadly in 1805, "I have long since given up the expectation of any early provision for the extinction of slavery among us." Unlike some contemporary Virginians, the man who wrote the Declaration of Independence could not bring himself to free his own slaves.

Rethinking Gender

The revolutionary experience accelerated changes in the way ordinary people viewed the family. At the beginning of the eighteenth century, fathers claimed authority over other members of their families simply on the grounds that they were fathers. As patriarchs, they merited obedience. If they behaved like brutal despots, so be it; fathers could treat wives and children however they pleased. The English philosopher John Locke (1632–1704) helped to expose the fallacy of this view, and at the time of the American Revolution few seriously accepted the notion that fathers—be they tyrannical kings or heads of ordinary families—enjoyed unlimited powers over women and children. Indeed, people in England as well as America increasingly described the family in terms of love and companionship. Instead of duties, they spoke of affection. This transformation in the way men and women viewed relations of power within the family was most evident in the popular novels of the period. Americans devoured *Pamela* and *Clarissa,* stories by the English writer Samuel Richardson about women

who were the innocent victims of unreformed males, usually deceitful lovers and unforgiving fathers.

It was in this changing intellectual environment that American women began making new demands not only on their husbands, but also on republican institutions. Abigail Adams, one of the generation's most articulate women, instructed her husband, John, as he set off for the opening of the Continental Congress: "I desire you would Remember the Ladies, and be more generous and favourable to them than your ancestors. Do not put such unlimited power into the hands of the Husbands." John responded in a condescending manner. The "Ladies" would have to wait until the country achieved independence. In 1777, Lucy Knox took an even stronger line with her husband, General Henry Knox. When he was about to return home from the army, she warned him, "I hope you will not consider yourself as commander in chief in your own house—but be convinced . . . that there is such a thing as equal command."

If Knox accepted Lucy's argument, he did so because she was a good republican wife and mother. In fact, women justified their assertiveness largely on the basis of political ideology. If survival of republics really depended on the virtue of its citizens, they argued, then it was the special responsibility of women as mothers to nurture the right values in their children and as wives to instruct their husbands in proper behavior. Contemporaries claimed that the woman who possessed "virtue and prudence" could easily "mold the taste, the manners, and the conduct of her admirers, according to her pleasure." In fact, "nothing short of a general reformation of manners would take place, were the ladies to use their power in discouraging our licentious manners."

Ill-educated women could not possibly fulfill these high expectations. Women required education that was at least comparable to what men received. Scores of female academies were established during this period to meet what many Americans, men as well as women, now regarded as a pressing social need. These schools may have received widespread encouragement precisely because they did not radically alter traditional gender roles. After all, the educated republican woman of the late eighteenth century did not pursue a career; she returned to the home where she

Abigail Adams, wife of patriot John Adams, was a brilliant woman whose plea to limit the power of husbands gained little sympathetic attention.

and she sued successfully for divorce. Studies of divorce patterns in Connecticut and Pennsylvania show that after 1773, women divorced on about the same terms as men.

The war itself presented some women with fresh opportunities. In 1780, Ester DeBerdt Reed founded a large volunteer women's organization in Philadelphia—the first of its kind in the United States—that raised over $300,000 for Washington's army. Other women ran family farms and businesses while their husbands fought the British. And in 1790, the New Jersey legislature explicitly allowed women who owned property to vote.

Despite these scattered gains, republican society still defined women's roles exclusively in terms of mother, wife, and homemaker. Other pursuits seemed unnatural, even threatening, and it is perhaps not surprising, therefore, that in 1807, New Jersey lawmakers—apparently angry over a close election in which women voters apparently determined the result—repealed female suffrage in the interests of "safety, quiet, and good order and dignity of the state."

The Promise of Liberty

The Revolution did not bring about a massive restructuring of American society, at least not in the short term. Nevertheless, republicans like Samuel Adams and Thomas Jefferson raised issues of immense significance for the later history of the United States. They insisted that equality, however narrowly defined, was an essential element of republican government. Even though they failed to abolish slavery, institute universal manhood suffrage, or apply equality to women, they vigorously articulated a set of assumptions about people's rights and liberties that challenged future generations of Americans to make good on the promise of the Revolution.

THE STATES: THE LESSONS OF REPUBLICANISM

In May 1776, the Second Continental Congress invited the states to adopt constitutions. The old colonial charters filled with references to king and Parliament were clearly no longer adequate, and within a few years, most states had taken action. Rhode Island and Connecticut already enjoyed republican government by virtue of their

followed a familiar routine as wife and mother. The frustration of not being allowed to develop her talents may explain the bitterness of a graduation oration delivered by an otherwise obscure woman in 1793: "Our high and mighty Lords . . . have denied us the means of knowledge, and then reproached us for want of it. . . . They doom'd the sex to servile or frivolous employments, on purpose to degrade their minds, that they themselves might hold unrivall'd, the power and preeminence they had usurped."

During this period, women began to petition for divorce on new grounds. One case is particularly instructive concerning changing attitudes toward women and the family. In 1784, John Backus, an undistinguished Massachusetts silversmith, was hauled before a local court and asked why he beat his wife. He responded that "it was Partly owing to his Education for his father treated his mother in the same manner." The difference between Backus's case and his father's was that Backus's wife refused to tolerate such abuse,

Westtown Boarding School in Pennsylvania was established by the Society of Friends to expand educational opportunities for women in the mid-Atlantic states. Instituted in 1794, the school opened in 1799.

unique seventeenth-century charters that allowed the voters to select both governors and legislators. Eleven other states plus Vermont created new political structures, and their deliberations reveal how Americans living in different regions and reacting to different social pressures defined fundamental republican principles.

Several constitutions were boldly experimental, and some states later rewrote documents that had been drafted in the first flush of independence. These early constitutions were provisional, but they nevertheless provided the framers of the federal Constitution of 1787 with invaluable insights into the strengths and weaknesses of government based on the will of the people.

Blueprints for State Government

Despite disagreements over details, Americans who wrote the various state constitutions shared certain political assumptions. First, they insisted on preparing *written* documents. For many of them, of course, this seemed a natural step. As colonists, they had lived under royal charters, documents that described the workings of local government in detail. The Massachusetts Bay Charter of 1629, for example (see Chapter 2), guaranteed that the Puritans would enjoy the rights of Englishmen even after they had moved to the New World. And in New England, Congregationalists drew up church covenants stating in clear contractual language the rights and responsibilities of the entire congregation.

However logical the decision to produce written documents may have seemed to the Americans, it represented a major break with English practice. Political philosophers in the mother country had long boasted of Britain's unwritten constitution, a collection of judicial reports and parliamentary statutes. But this highly vaunted system had not protected the colonists from oppression; hence, after declaring independence, Americans demanded that their state constitutions explicitly define the rights of the people as well as the power of their rulers.

Natural Rights and the State Constitutions

The authors of the state constitutions believed men and women possessed certain natural rights over which government exercised no control whatsoever. So that future rulers—potential tyrants—would know the exact limits of authority, these fundamental rights were carefully spelled out. Indeed, the people of Massachusetts rejected the proposed state constitution of 1778 largely because it lacked a full statement of their basic rights. They demanded a guarantee of "rights of conscience, and . . . security of persons and property, which every member in the State hath a right to expect from the supreme power."

Eight state constitutions contained specific "Declarations of Rights." The length and character of these lists varied, but in general, they affirmed three fundamental freedoms: religion, speech, and press. They protected citizens from unlawful searches and seizures; they upheld trial by jury. George Mason, a shrewd political thinker who had written important revolutionary pamphlets, penned the most influential Declaration of Rights. It was appended to the Virginia Constitution of 1776, and the words were incorporated into other state constitutions as well as the famed Bill of Rights of the federal Constitution.

In almost every state, delegates to constitutional conventions drastically reduced the power of the governor. The constitutions of Pennsylvania and Georgia abolished the governor's office. In four other states, terms like *president* were substituted for *governor*. Even when those who designed the new state governments provided for a governor, they severely circumscribed his authority. He was allowed to make almost no political appointments, and while the state legislators closely monitored his activities, he possessed no veto over their decisions (Massachusetts being the lone exception). Most early constitutions lodged nearly all effective power in the legislature. This decision made good sense to men who had actually served under powerful royal governors during the late colonial period. These ambitious crown appointees had used executive patronage to influence members of the colonial assemblies, and as the Americans drafted their new republican constitutions, they were determined to bring their governors under tight control. In fact, the writers of the state constitutions were so fearful of the concentration of power in the hands of a single person, they failed to appreciate that elected governors—like the representatives themselves—were now the servants of a free people.

The legislature dominated early state government. The constitutions of Pennsylvania and Georgia provided for a unicameral, or one-house system, and since any male taxpayer could cast a ballot in these states, their legislatures became the nation's most democratic. Other states authorized the creation of two houses, but even as they did so, some of the more demanding republicans wondered why America needed a senate or upper house at all. What social and economic interests, they asked, did that body represent that could not be more fully and directly voiced in the lower house? After all, America had just freed itself of an aristocracy. The two-house form survived the Revolution largely because it was familiar and because some persons had already begun to suspect that certain checks on the popular will, however arbitrary they might appear, were necessary to preserve minority rights.

Power to the People

Massachusetts did not adopt a constitution until 1780, several years after the other states had done so. The experience of the people of Massachusetts is particularly significant because in their efforts to establish a workable system of republican government they hit on a remarkable political innovation. After the rejection of two constitutions drafted by the state legislature, the responsibility fell to a specially elected convention of delegates whose sole purpose was the "formation of a new Constitution."

John Adams took a position of leadership at this convention and served as the chief architect of the governmental framework of Massachusetts. This framework included a house and senate, a popularly elected governor—who, unlike the chief executives of other states, possessed a veto over legislative bills—and property qualifications for officeholders as well as voters. The most striking aspect of the 1780 constitution, however, was its opening sentence: "We . . . the people of Massachusetts . . . agree upon, ordain, and establish." This powerful vocabulary would be echoed in the federal Constitution. The Massachusetts experiment reminded Americans that ordinary officeholders could not be trusted to define fundamental rights. That important task required a convention of delegates who could legitimately claim to speak for the people.

In 1780, no one knew whether the state experiments would succeed. There was no question a different type of person had begun to appear in public office, one that seemed, to the local gentry at least, a little poorer and less polished than they would have liked. When one Virginian surveyed the newly elected House of Burgesses in 1776, he discovered it was "composed of men not quite so well dressed, nor so politely educated, nor so highly born as some Assemblies I have formerly seen." This particular Virginian approved of such change, for he believed that "the People's men," however plain they might appear, possessed honesty and sincerity. They were, in fact, representative republicans, people who insisted they were anyone's equal in this burgeoning society.

Other Americans were less optimistic about the nation's immediate prospects. The health of a small republic depended entirely on the virtue of its people. If they or their elected officials succumbed to material temptation, if they failed to comprehend the moral dimensions of political power, or if personal liberty threatened the rights of property, then the state constitutions were no more than worthless pieces of paper. The risk of excess seemed great. In 1778, a group of New Englanders, fearful unbridled freedom would create political anarchy, observed, "The idea of liberty has been held up in so dazzling colours that some of us may not be willing to submit to that subordination necessary in the freest states."

CREATING A NEW NATIONAL GOVERNMENT

When the Second Continental Congress convened in 1775, the delegates found themselves waging war in the name of a country that did not yet exist. As the military crisis deepened, Congress gradually—often reluctantly—assumed greater authority over national affairs, but everyone agreed such narrowly conceived measures were a poor substitute for a legally constituted government. The separate states could not possibly deal with the range of issues that now confronted the American people. Indeed, if independence meant anything in a world of sovereign nations, it implied the creation of a central authority capable of conducting war, borrowing money, regulating trade, and negotiating treaties.

Articles of Confederacy

The challenge of creating a viable central government proved more difficult than anyone anticipated. Congress appointed a committee to draw up a plan for confederation. John Dickinson, the lawyer who had written an important revolutionary pamphlet entitled *Letters from a Farmer in Pennsylvania,* headed the committee. Dickinson envisioned the creation of a strong central government, and the report his committee presented on July 12, 1776, shocked delegates who assumed the constitution would authorize a loose confederation of states. Dickinson's plan placed the western territories, land claimed by the separate states, under congressional control. In addition,

John Dickinson, a highly respected lawyer, conceived a bold plan in 1776 for a strong central government, but the members of Congress saw it as a dangerous threat to the sovereignty of the states.

Dickinson's committee called for equal state representation in Congress.

Since some states, such as Virginia and Massachusetts, were more populous than others, the plan fueled tensions between large and small states. Also unsettling was Dickinson's recommendation that taxes be paid to Congress on the basis of a state's total population, black as well as white, a formula that angered Southerners who did not think slaves should be counted. Indeed, even before the British evacuated Boston, Dickinson's committee raised many difficult political questions that would divide Americans for several decades.

Not surprisingly, the draft of the plan—the Articles of Confederation—that Congress finally approved in November 1777 bore little resemblance to Dickinson's original plan. The Articles jealously guarded the sovereignty of the states. The delegates who drafted this framework shared a general republican conviction that power—especially power so far removed from the people—was inherently dangerous and that the only way to preserve liberty was to place as many constraints as possible on federal authority.

The result was a government that many people regarded as powerless. The Articles provided for a single legislative body consisting of representatives selected annually by the state legislatures. Each state possessed a single vote in Congress. It could send as many as seven delegates, as few as two, but if they divided evenly on a certain issue, the state lost its vote. There was no independent executive and no veto over legislative decisions. The Articles also denied Congress the power of taxation, a serious oversight in time of war. The national government could obtain funds only by asking the states for contributions, called requisitions, but if a state failed to cooperate—and many did—Congress limped along without financial support. Amendments to this constitution required assent by *all* thirteen states. The authors of the new system expected the weak national government to handle foreign relations, military matters, Indian affairs, and interstate disputes. They most emphatically did not award Congress ownership of the lands west of the Appalachian Mountains.

The new constitution sent to the states for ratification encountered apathy and hostility. Most Americans were far more interested in local affairs than in the actions of Congress. When a British army marched through a state, creating a need for immediate military aid, people spoke positively about central government, but as soon as the threat had passed, they sang a different tune. During this period, even the slightest encroachment on state sovereignty rankled the republicans who feared centralization would inevitably promote corruption.

Meeting a Crisis

The major bone of contention with the Articles, however, was the disposition of the vast, unsurveyed territory west of the Appalachians that everyone hoped the British would soon surrender. Some states, such as Virginia and Georgia, ¹aimed land all the way from the Atlantic Ocean the elusive "South Sea," in effect extending their boundaries to the Pacific Coast by virtue of royal charters. State legislators—their appetites whetted by aggressive land speculators—anticipated generating large revenues through land sales. Connecticut, New York, Pennsylvania, and North Carolina also announced intentions to seize blocks of western land.

Other states were not blessed with vague or ambiguous royal charters. The boundaries of Maryland, Delaware, and New Jersey had been established many years earlier, and it seemed as if people living in these states would be permanently cut off from the anticipated bounty. In protest, these "landless" states stubbornly refused to ratify the Articles of Confederation. Marylanders were particularly vociferous. All the states had made sacrifices for the common good during the Revolution, they complained, and it appeared only fair that all states should profit from the fruits of victory, in this case, from the sale of western lands. Maryland's spokesmen feared that if Congress did not void Virginia's excessive claims to all of the Northwest Territory (the land west of Pennsylvania and north of the Ohio River) as well as to a large area south of the Ohio, beyond the Cumberland Gap, known as Kentucky, then Marylanders would desert their home state in search of cheap Virginia farms, leaving Maryland an underpopulated wasteland.

Virginians scoffed at these pleas for equity. They knew that behind the Marylanders' statements of high purpose lay the greed of speculators. Private land companies had sprung up before the Revolution and purchased large tracts from the Indians in areas claimed by Virginia. Their agents petitioned Parliament to legitimize these questionable transactions. Their efforts failed. After the Declaration of Independence, however, the companies shifted the focus of their lobbying to Congress, particularly to the representatives of landless states like Maryland. By liberally distributing shares of stock, officials of the Indiana, Illinois, and Wabash companies gained powerful supporters such as Benjamin Franklin, Robert Morris, and Thomas Johnson, governor of Maryland. These activities encouraged Delaware and New Jersey to modify their demands and join the Confederation, while Maryland held out for five years. The leaders of Virginia, though, remained firm. Why, they asked, should Virginia surrender its historic claims to western lands to enrich a handful of selfish speculators?

The states resolved this bitter controversy in 1781 as much by accident as by design. Virginia agreed to cede its holdings north of the Ohio River to the Confederation on condition that Congress nullify the land companies' earlier purchases from the Indians. A practical consideration had softened Virginia's resolve. Republicans such as Jefferson worried about expanding their state beyond the mountains; with poor transportation links, it seemed impossible to govern such a large territory effectively from Richmond. The western settlers might even come to regard Virginia as a colonial power insensitive to their needs. Marylanders who dreamed of making fortunes on the land market grumbled, but when a British army appeared on their border, they prudently accepted the Articles (March 1, 1781). Congress required another three years to work out the details of the Virginia cession. Other landed states followed Virginia's example. These transfers established an important principle, for after 1781, it was agreed the West belonged not to the separate states, but to the United States. In this matter at least, the national government now exercised full sovereignty.

No one greeted ratification of the Articles with much enthusiasm. When they thought about national politics at all, Americans concerned themselves primarily with winning independence. The new government gradually developed an administrative bureaucracy, and in 1781, it formally created the Departments of War, Foreign Affairs, and Finance. By far the most influential figure in the Confederation was Robert Morris (1734–1806), a freewheeling Philadelphia merchant who was appointed the first superintendent of finance. Although he was a brilliant manager, Morris's decisions as superintendent provoked controversy, indeed, deep suspicion. He hardly seemed a model republican. Morris mixed public funds under his control with personal accounts, and he never lost an opportunity to make a profit. While such practices were not illegal, his apparent improprieties undermined his own political agenda. He desperately wanted to strengthen the central government, but highly vocal critics resisted, labeling Morris a "pecuniary dictator."

The Confederation's Major Achievement

Whatever the weaknesses of Congress may have been, it did score one impressive triumph. Congressional action brought order to western settlement, especially in the Northwest Territory, and incorporated frontier Americans into an expanding federal system. In 1781, the prospects for success did not seem promising. For years, colonial authorities had ignored people who migrated far inland, sending neither money nor soldiers to protect them from Indian attack. Tensions between the seaboard colonies and the frontier regions had sometimes flared into violence. In 1763, a group of Scotch-Irish frontiersmen calling themselves the "Paxton Boys" had protested Pennsylvania's inadequate defenses by killing innocent Indians and marching on the colonial capital. Similar disorders occurred in South Carolina in 1767, in North Carolina in 1769, and in Vermont in 1777. With thousands of men and women, most of them squatters, pouring across the Appalachian Mountains, Congress had to act quickly to avoid the past errors of royal and colonial authorities.

The initial attempt to deal with this explosive problem came in 1784. Jefferson, then serving as a member of Congress, drafted an ordinance that became the basis for later, more enduring legislation. Jefferson recommended carving ten new states out of the western lands located north of the Ohio River and recently ceded to the United States by Virginia. He specified that each new state establish a republican form of government. When the population of a territory equaled that of the smallest state already in the Confederation, the region could apply for full statehood. In the meantime, free white males could participate in local government, a democratic guarantee that frightened some of Jefferson's more conservative colleagues.

The impoverished Congress was eager to sell off the western territory as quickly as possible. After all, the frontier represented a source of income that did not depend on the unreliable generosity of the states. A second ordinance, passed in 1785 and called the Land Ordinance, established an orderly process for laying out new townships and marketing public lands.

The 1785 scheme possessed geometric elegance. Surveyors marked off townships, each running directly from east to west. These units, 6

Western Land Claims Ceded by the States

After winning the war, the major issue facing the Continental Congress under the Articles of Confederation was mediating conflicting states' claims to rich western land. By 1802, the states had ceded all rights to the federal government.

miles square, were subdivided into 36 separate sections of 640 acres (1 square mile) each. (Roads and property boundaries established according to this grid pattern survived long after the Confederation had passed into history.) The government planned to auction off its holdings at prices of not less than $1 an acre. Congress set the minimum purchase at 640 acres, and near-worthless paper money was not accepted as payment. Section 16 was set aside for public education; the federal government reserved four other sections for its own use.

Public response disappointed Congress. Surveying the lands took far longer than antici-

Land Ordinance of 1785

Grid pattern of a township
36 sections of 640 acres (1 square mile each)

36	30	24	18	12	6
35	29	23	17	11	5
34	28	22	16	10	4
33	27	21	15	9	3
32	26	20	14	8	2
31	25	19	13	7	1

6 miles (vertical) — 6 miles (horizontal)

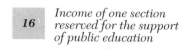

16 *Income of one section reserved for the support of public education*

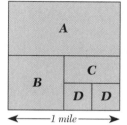

← 1 mile →

A Half-section   320 acres
B Quarter-section   160 acres
C Half-quarter section   80 acres
D Quarter-quarter section   40 acres

pated, and few persons possessed enough hard currency to make even the minimum purchase. Finally, a solution to the problem came from Manasseh Cutler, a New England minister turned land speculator and congressional lobbyist, and his associates, who included several former officers of the Continental army.

Cutler and his associates, representing the Ohio and Scioto companies, offered to purchase more than 6 million unsurveyed acres of land located in present-day southeastern Ohio by persuading Congress to accept, at full face value, government loan certificates that had been issued to soldiers during the Revolution. On the open market, the Ohio company could pick up these certificates for as little as 10 percent of their face value; thus, the company stood to make a fortune. Like so many other get-rich-quick schemes, however, this one failed to produce the anticipated millions. Unfortunately for Cutler and his friends, small homesteaders settled wherever they pleased, refusing to pay either government or speculators for the land.

Congress worried about the excess liberty on the frontier. In the 1780s, the West seemed to be filling up with people who by eastern standards were uncultured. Timothy Pickering, a New Englander, declared that "the emigrants to the frontier lands are the least worthy subjects in the United States. They are little less savage than the Indians; and when possessed of the most fertile spots, for want of industry, live miserably." The charge was as old as the frontier itself. Indeed,

seventeenth-century Englishmen had said the same things of the earliest Virginians. The lawless image stuck, however, and even a sober observer like Washington insisted the West crawled with "banditti." The Ordinance of 1784 placed the government of the territories in the hands of people about whom congressmen and speculators had second thoughts.

These various currents shaped the Ordinance of 1787, one of the final acts passed under the Confederation. This bill, also called the Northwest Ordinance, provided a new structure for government of the Northwest Territory. The plan authorized the creation of between three and five territories, each to be ruled by a governor, a secretary, and three judges appointed by Congress. When the population reached five thousand, voters who owned property could elect an assembly, but its decisions were subject to the governor's absolute veto. Once sixty thousand persons resided in a territory, they could write a constitution and petition for full statehood. While these procedures represented a retreat from Jefferson's original proposal, the Ordinance of 1787 contained several significant features. A bill of rights guaranteed the settlers the right to trial by jury, freedom of religion, and due process of law. In addition, this act outlawed slavery, a prohibition that freed the future states of Ohio, Indiana, Illinois, Michigan, and Wisconsin from the curse of human bondage.

By contrast, settlement south of the Ohio River received far less attention from Congress. Long before the end of the war, thousands of Americans streamed through the Cumberland Gap into a part of Virginia known as Kentucky. The most famous of these settlers was Daniel Boone. In 1775, the population of Kentucky was approximately one hundred; by 1784, it had jumped to thirty thousand. Speculators purchased large tracts from the Indians, planning to resell this acreage to settlers at handsome profits. In 1776, one land company asked Congress to reorganize the company's holdings into a new state called Transylvania. While nothing came of this self-serving request, another, even more aggressive group of speculators in 1784 carved the state of Franklin out of a section of present-day Tennessee, then claimed by North Carolina. Rival speculators prevented formal recognition of Franklin's government. By 1790, the entire region south of the Ohio River had been transformed into a crazy quilt of claims and counterclaims that generated lawsuits for many years to come.

SEARCH FOR ORDER

Despite its success in bringing order to the Northwest Territory, the Confederation increasingly came under heavy fire from critics who wanted a stronger central government. Complaints varied from region to region, from person to person, but most disappointment reflected economic frustration. Americans had assumed that peace would restore economic growth, but recovery following the Revolution was slow.

The Nationalist Critique

Even before England signed a treaty with America, its merchants flooded American ports with consumer items and offered easy credit. Families that had postponed purchases of imported goods—either because of British blockade or personal hardship—now rushed to buy European finery.

This sudden renewal of trade with Great Britain on such a large scale strained the American economy. Gold and silver flowed back across the Atlantic, leaving the United States desperately short of hard currency, and when large merchant houses called in their debts, ordinary American consumers often found themselves on the brink of bankruptcy. "The disagreeable state of our commerce," observed James Wilson, an advocate of strong national government, has been the result "of extravagant and injudicious importation. . . . [w]e seemed to have forgot that to pay was as necessary in trade as to purchase."

To blame the Confederation alone for the economic depression would be unfair. Nevertheless, during the 1780s, many people agreed a stronger central government could somehow have brought greater stability to the struggling economy. In their rush to acquire imported luxuries, Americans seemed to have deserted republican

The widespread land speculation in the territory south of the Ohio River did not go unnoticed by European political cartoonists of the day. The French caption to the original cartoon explained that "Citizen Mignard signs today for some English companions who are selling imaginary lands in the United States. The better to ensnare dupes, they draw geological maps, converting rocky deserts into fertile plains, show roads cutting through impassable cliffs, and offer shares in lands that do not belong to them."

principles, and a weak Congress was helpless to restore national virtue.

Critics pointed to the government's inability to regulate trade. Whenever a northern congressman suggested restricting British access to American markets, southern representatives, who feared any controls on the export of tobacco or rice, bellowed in protest. Southerners anticipated that navigation acts written by the Confederation would put planters under the yoke of northern shipping interests.

The country's chronic fiscal instability increased public anxiety. While the war was still in progress, Congress printed well over $200 million in paper money, but because of extraordinarily high inflation, the rate of exchange for Continental bills soon declined to a fraction of their face value. In 1781, Congress, facing insolvency, turned to the states for help. They were asked to retire the depreciated currency. The situation was spinning out of control. Several states—pressed to pay their own war-related debts—not only recirculated the Continental bills, but also issued nearly worthless money of their own.

A heavy burden of state and national debt compounded the general sense of economic crisis. Revolutionary soldiers had yet to be paid. Women and men who had loaned money and goods to the government clamored for reimbursement. Foreign creditors demanded interest on funds advanced during the Revolution. These pressures grew, but Congress was unable to respond. The Articles specifically prohibited Congress from taxing the American people. It required little imagination to see the Confederation would soon default on its legal obligations unless something was done quickly.

In response, an aggressive group of men announced they knew how to save the Confederation. The "nationalists"—persons like Alexander Hamilton, James Madison, and Robert Morris—called for major constitutional reforms, the chief of which was an amendment allowing Congress to collect a 5 percent tax on imported goods sold in the states. Revenues generated by the proposed Impost of 1781 would be used by the Confederation to reduce the national debt. On this point they were adamant. The nationalists recognized that whoever paid the public debt would gain the public trust. If the states assumed

"Not worth a Continental!" became a common oath when inflation eroded the value of Continental currency. Most currency issued by the states was equally valueless.

the responsibility, then the country could easily fragment into separate republics. "A national debt," Hamilton explained in 1781, "if it is not excessive, will be to us a national blessing. It will be a powerful cement to our union." Twelve states accepted the Impost amendment, but Rhode Island—where local interests argued the tax would make Congress "independent of their constituents"—resolutely refused to cooperate. One negative vote on this proposed constitutional change and the taxing scheme was dead. Subsequent attempts to put the country's finances on a firm footing were also narrowly defeated on the state level.

State leaders frankly thought the nationalists were up to no good. The "localists" were especially apprehensive of fiscal plans advanced by Robert Morris. His profiteering as superintendent of finance appeared a threat to the moral fiber of the young republic. Richard Henry Lee and Samuel Adams, men of impeccable patriotic credentials, decried Morris's efforts to create a national bank. Such an institution would bring forth a flock of social parasites, the kind of persons that Americans associated with corrupt monarchical government. One person declared that if an impost ever passed, Morris "will have all [the money] in his Pocket."

The nationalists regarded their opponents as economically naive. A country with the potential of the United States required a complex, centralized fiscal system. But for all their pretensions to realism, the nationalists of the early 1780s were politically inept. They underestimated the depth of republican fears, and in their rush to strengthen the Articles, they overplayed their hand.

A group of extreme nationalists even appealed to the army for support. To this day, no one knows the full story of the Newburgh Conspiracy of 1783. Officers of the Continental army stationed at Newburgh, New York, worried Congress would disband them without funding their pensions, began to lobby intensively for relief. In March, they scheduled general meetings to protest the weakness and duplicity of Congress. The officers' initial efforts were harmless enough, but frustrated nationalists such as Morris and Hamilton hoped that if the army exerted sufficient pressure on the government, perhaps even threatened a military takeover, then stubborn Americans might be compelled to amend the Articles.

The conspirators failed to take George Washington's integrity into account. No matter how much he wanted a strong central government, he would not tolerate insubordination by the military. Washington confronted the officers directly at Newburgh, intending to read a prepared statement. Fumbling with his glasses before his men, he commented, "Gentlemen, you must pardon me. I have grown gray in your service and now find myself growing blind." The unexpected vulnerability of this great soldier reduced the troops to tears, and in an instant, the rebellion was broken. Washington deserves credit for preserving civilian rule in this country.

In April 1783, Congress proposed a second impost, but it too failed to win unanimous ratification. Even a personal appeal by Washington could not save the amendment. As one opponent explained, if "permanent Funds are given to Congress, the aristocratic Influence, which predominates in more than a major part of the

United States, will fully establish an arbitrary Government." With this defeat, nationalists gave up on the Confederation. Morris retired from government, and Madison returned to Virginia utterly depressed by what he had witnessed.

Diplomatic Humiliation

In foreign affairs, Congress endured further embarrassment. It could not even enforce the provisions of its own peace treaty. American negotiators had promised Great Britain that its citizens could collect debts contracted before the Revolution. The states, however, dragged their heels, and several even passed laws obstructing the settlement of legitimate prewar claims. Congress was powerless to force compliance. The British responded to this apparent provocation by refusing to evacuate troops from posts located in the Northwest Territory. A strong national government would have driven the redcoats out, but without adequate funds, the weak Congress could not provide soldiers for such a mission.

Congress's postrevolutionary dealings with Spain were equally humiliating. That nation refused to accept the southern boundary of the United States established by the Treaty of Paris. Spain claimed sovereignty over much of the land located between Georgia and the Mississippi River, and its agents schemed with Indian tribes in this region to resist American expansion. On July 21, 1784, Spain fueled the controversy by closing the lower Mississippi River to citizens of the United States.

This unexpected decision devastated western farmers. Free use of the Mississippi was essential to the economic development of the entire Ohio Valley. Because of the prohibitively high cost of transporting freight for long distances over land, western settlers—and southern planters eyeing future opportunities in this area—demanded a secure water link with the world's markets. Their spokesmen in Congress denounced anyone who claimed that navigation of the Mississippi was a negotiable issue.

In 1786, a Spanish official, Don Diego de Gardoqui, opened talks with John Jay, a New Yorker appointed by Congress to obtain rights to navigation of the Mississippi. Jay soon discovered that Gardoqui would not compromise. After making little progress, Jay seized the initiative. If

Gardoqui would allow American merchants to trade directly with Spain, thus opening up an important new market to ships from New England and the middle states, then the United States might forgo navigation of the Mississippi for twenty-five years. When southern delegates heard of Jay's concessions, they were outraged. It appeared to them as if representatives of northern commerce were ready to abandon the southern frontier. Angry congressmen accused New Englanders of attempting to divide the United States into separate confederations, for as one Virginian exclaimed, the proposed Spanish treaty "would weaken if not destroy the union by disaffecting the Southern States . . . to obtain a trivial commercial advantage." Congress wisely terminated the negotiations with Spain.

By the mid-1780s, the Confederation could claim several notable achievements. It designed an administrative system that lasted far longer than did the Articles. It also brought order out of the chaos of conflicting western land claims. Still, as anyone could see, the government was struggling. Congress met irregularly. Some states did not even bother to send delegates, and pressing issues often had to be postponed for lack of a quorum. The nation even lacked a permanent capital, and Congress drifted from Philadelphia to Princeton, to Annapolis to New York City, prompting one humorist to suggest the government purchase an air balloon. This newly invented device, he explained, would allow the members of Congress to "float along from one end of the continent to the other" and "suddenly pop down into any of the states they please."

RESTRUCTURING THE REPUBLIC

Many Americans, especially those who had provided leadership during the Revolution, agreed something had to be done. By 1785, the country seemed to have lost direction. The buoyant optimism that sustained revolutionary patriots had dissolved into pessimism and doubt. In 1786, Washington bitterly observed, "What astonishing changes a few years are capable of producing. Have we fought for this? Was it with these expectations that we launched into a sea of trouble, and have bravely struggled through the most threatening dangers?"

A Crisis Mentality

The conviction of people such as Washington that the nation was indeed in a state of crisis reflected tensions within republican thought. To be sure, they supported open elections and the right of individuals to advance their own economic well-being, but when these elements seemed to undermine social and political order, they expressed the fear that perhaps liberty had been carried too far. The situation had changed quite rapidly. As recently as the 1770s, men of republican persuasion had insisted the greatest threat to the American people was concentration of power in the hands of unscrupulous rulers. With this principle in mind, they transformed state governors into mere figureheads and emasculated the Confederation in the name of popular liberties.

By the mid-1780s, persons of property and standing saw the problem in a different light. Recent experience suggested to them that ordinary citizens did not in fact possess sufficient virtue to sustain a republic. The states had been plagued not by executive tyranny but by an excess of democracy, by a failure of the majority to preserve the property rights of the minority, by an unrestrained individualism that promoted anarchy rather than good order.

Many state leaders did not seem particularly concerned about the fiscal health of the national government. Local presses churned out worthless currency, and in some states, assemblies passed laws impeding the collection of debt. In Rhode Island, the situation became absurd. State legislators made it illegal for merchants to reject Rhode Island money even though everyone knew it had no value. No wonder Governor William Livingston of New Jersey declared in 1787, "We do not exhibit the virtue that is necessary to support a republican government."

As Americans tried to interpret these experiences within a republican framework, they were checked by the most widely accepted political wisdom of the age. Baron de Montesquieu (1689–1755), a French political philosopher of immense international reputation, declared flatly that a republican government could not flourish in a large territory. The reasons were clear. If the people lost direct control over their representatives, they would fall prey to tyrants. Large distances allowed rulers to hide their corruption; physical separation presented aristocrats with opportunities to seize power.

In the United States, most learned men treated Montesquieu's theories as self-evident truths. His writings seemed to demonstrate the importance of preserving the sovereignty of the states, for however much these small republics abused the rights of property and ignored minority interests, it was plainly unscientific to maintain that a republic consisting of thirteen states, several million people, and thousands of acres of territory could long survive.

James Madison rejected Montesquieu's argument, and in so doing, helped Americans to think of republican government in radical new ways. This soft-spoken, rather unprepossessing Virginian was the most brilliant American political thinker of his generation. One French official described Madison as "a man one must study a long time in order to make a fair appraisal." Those who listened carefully to what Madison had to say, however, soon recognized his genius for translating theory into practice.

Madison delved into the writings of a group of Scottish philosophers, the most prominent being David Hume (1711–1776), and from their works he concluded that Americans need not fear a greatly expanded republic. Madison perceived that "inconveniences of popular States contrary to prevailing Theory, are in proportion not to the extent, but to the narrowness of their limits." Indeed, it was in small states like Rhode Island that legislative majorities tyrannized the propertied minority. In a large territory, Madison explained, "the Society becomes broken into a greater variety of interest, of pursuits, of passions, which check each other, whilst those who may feel a common sentiment have less opportunity of communication and contact."

Madison did not, however, advocate a modern "interest-group" model of political behavior. The contending parties were incapable of working for the common good. They were too mired in their own local, selfish concerns. Rather, Madison thought competing factions would neutralize each other, leaving the business of running the central government to the ablest, most virtuous persons the nation could produce. In other words, Madison's federal system was not a small state writ large; it was something entirely different, a government based on the will of the people and yet detached from their narrowly based demands. This thinking formed the foundation of Madison's most famous political essay, *The Federalist* No. 10.

Movement Toward Constitutional Reform

A concerted movement to overhaul the Articles of Confederation began in 1786 when Madison and his friends persuaded the Virginia assembly to recommend a convention to explore the creation of a unified system of "commercial regulations." Congress supported the idea. In September, delegates from five states arrived in Annapolis, Maryland, to discuss issues that extended far beyond commerce. The small turnout was disappointing, but the occasion provided strong nationalists with an opportunity to hatch an even bolder plan. The Annapolis delegates advised Congress to hold a second meeting in Philadelphia "to take into consideration the situation of the United States, to devise such further provisions as shall appear to them necessary to render the constitution of the Federal Government adequate to the exigencies of the Union." Whether staunch states' rights advocates in Congress knew what was afoot is not clear. In any case, Congress authorized a grand convention to gather in May 1787.

Events played into Madison's hands. Soon after the Annapolis meeting, an uprising known as Shays's Rebellion, involving several thousand impoverished farmers, shattered the peace of western Massachusetts. No matter how hard these men worked the soil, they always found themselves in debt to eastern creditors. They complained of high taxes, of high interest rates, and, most of all, of a state government insensitive to their problems. In 1786, Daniel Shays, a veteran of the battle of Bunker Hill, and his armed neighbors closed a county courthouse where creditors were suing to foreclose farm mortgages. At one point, the rural insurgents threatened to seize the federal arsenal located at Springfield. Congress did not have funds sufficient to support an army, and the arsenal might have fallen had not a group of wealthy Bostonians raised an army of four thousand troops to put down the insurrection. The victors were in for a surprise. At the next general election, the voters of Massachusetts

This 1787 woodcut portrays Daniel Shays with one of his chief officers, Jacob Shattucks. Shays led a band of fellow farmers in revolt against a state government that was insensitive to rural needs. Their rebellion strengthened the demand for a strong new federal government.

selected representatives sympathetic to Shays's demands, and a new liberal assembly reformed debtor law.

Nationalists throughout the United States were not so forgiving. From their perspective, Shays' Rebellion symbolized the breakdown of law and order that they had long predicted. "Great commotions are prevailing in Massachusetts," Madison wrote. "An appeal to the sword is exceedingly dreaded." The time had come for sensible people to speak up for a strong national government. The unrest in Massachusetts persuaded persons who might otherwise have ignored the Philadelphia meeting to participate in drafting a new constitution.

The Philadelphia Convention

In the spring of 1787, fifty-five men representing twelve states traveled to Philadelphia. Rhode Island refused to take part in the proceedings, a decision that Madison attributed to its "wickedness and folly." Thomas Jefferson described the convention as an "assembly of demi-Gods," but this flattering depiction is misleading. However much modern Americans revere the Constitution, they should remember that the individuals who wrote it did not possess divine insight into the nature of government. They were practical people—lawyers, merchants, and planters—many of

whom had fought in the Revolution and served in the Congress of the Confederation. The majority were in their thirties or forties. The gathering included George Washington, James Madison, George Mason, Robert Morris, James Wilson, John Dickinson, Benjamin Franklin, and Alexander Hamilton, just to name some of the more prominent participants. Absent were John Adams and Thomas Jefferson, who were conducting diplomacy in Europe; Patrick Henry, a localist suspicious of strong central government, remained in Virginia, announcing he "smelled a rat."

As soon as the convention opened on May 25, the delegates made several procedural decisions of the utmost importance. First, they voted "that nothing spoken in the House be printed, or communicated without leave." The rule was stringently enforced. Sentries guarded the doorways to keep out uninvited visitors, windows stayed shut in the sweltering heat to prevent sound from either entering or leaving the chamber, and members were forbidden to copy the daily journal without official permission. As Madison explained, the secrecy rule saved "both the convention and the community from a thousand erroneous and perhaps mischievous reports." It also has made it extremely difficult for modern lawyers and judges to determine exactly what the delegates had in mind when they wrote the

Constitution (see pages 188–189, "The Elusive Constitution: Search for Original Intent").

In a second procedural move, the delegates decided to vote by state, but to avoid the kinds of problems that had plagued the Confederation, they ruled that key proposals needed the support of only a majority instead of the nine states required under the Articles.

Inventing a Federal Republic

Madison understood that whoever sets the agenda, controls the meeting. Even before all the delegates had arrived, he drew up a framework for a new federal system known as the "Virginia Plan." Madison wisely persuaded Edmund Randolph, Virginia's popular governor, to present this scheme to the convention on May 29. Randolph claimed the Virginia Plan merely revised sections of the Articles, but everyone, including Madison, knew better. "My ideas," Madison confessed, "strike . . . deeply at the old Confederation." He was determined to restrain the state assemblies, and in the original Virginia Plan, Madison gave the federal government power to veto state laws.

The Virginia Plan envisioned a national legislature consisting of two houses, one elected *directly* by the people, the other chosen by the first house from nominations made by the state assemblies. Representation in both houses was proportional to the state's population. The Virginia Plan also provided for an executive elected by Congress. Since most delegates at the Philadelphia convention sympathized with the nationalist position, Madison's blueprint for a strong federal government initially received broad support, and the Virginia Plan was referred to further study and debate. A group of men who allegedly had come together to reform the Confederation found themselves discussing the details of "a *national* Government . . . consisting of a *supreme* Legislature, Executive, and Judiciary."

The Virginia Plan had been pushed through the convention so fast that opponents hardly had an opportunity to present their objections. On June 15, they spoke up. William Paterson, a New Jersey lawyer, advanced the so-called New Jersey Plan, a scheme that retained the unicameral legislature in which each state possessed one vote, and at the same time gave Congress extensive new powers to tax and regulate trade. Paterson argued that these revisions, while more modest than Madison's plan, would have greater appeal for the American people. "I believe," he said, "that a little practical virtue is to be preferred to the finest theoretical principles, which cannot be carried into effect." The delegates listened politely and then soundly rejected the New Jersey Plan on June 19. Indeed, only New Jersey, New York, and Delaware voted in favor of Paterson's scheme.

Rejection of this framework did not resolve the most controversial issue before the convention. Paterson and others feared that under the Virginia Plan, small states would lose their separate identities. These delegates maintained that unless each state possessed an equal vote in Congress, the small states would find themselves at the mercy of their larger neighbors.

This argument outraged the delegates who favored a strong federal government. It awarded too much power to the states. "For whom [are we] forming a Government?" Wilson cried. "Is it for men, or for the imaginary beings called States?" It seemed absurd to claim that Rhode Island with only 68,000 people should have the same voice in Congress as Virginia's 747,000 inhabitants.

Compromise Saves the Convention

The mood of the convention was tense. Hard work and frustration, coupled with Philadelphia's sweltering summer heat, frayed nerves, prompted some members to predict that this meeting would accomplish nothing of significance. But despite the growing pessimism, the gathering did not break up. The delegates desperately wanted to produce a constitution, and they refused to give up until they had explored every avenue of reconciliation. Perhaps cooler heads agreed with Washington: "To please all is impossible, and to attempt it would be vain. The only way, therefore, is . . . to form such a government as will bear the scrutinizing eye of criticism, and trust it to the good sense and patriotism of the people."

Mediation clearly offered the only way to overcome what Roger Sherman, a Connecticut delegate, called "a full stop." On July 2, a "grand committee" of one person from each state was elected by the convention to resolve persistent differences between the large and small states. Franklin, at eighty-one the oldest delegate, served as chair. The two fiercest supporters of proportional representation based on population, Madison and Wilson, were left off the "grand committee," a sure sign the small states would salvage something from the compromise.

The committee recommended the states be equally represented in the upper house of Congress, while representation was to be proportionate in the lower house. Only the lower house could initiate money bills. Franklin's committee also decided one member of the lower house should be selected for every forty thousand inhabitants of a state. Southern delegates insisted this number include slaves. In the so-called three-fifths rule, the committee agreed that for the purpose of determining representation in the lower house slaves would be counted, but not as much as free persons. For every five slaves, a congressional district received credit for three free voters, a deal that gave the South much greater power in the new government than it would have otherwise received. As with most compromise solutions, the one negotiated by Franklin's committee fully satisfied no one. It did, however, overcome a major impasse, and after the small states gained an assured voice in the upper house, the Senate, they cooperated enthusiastically in creating a strong central government.

A Republic with Slaves

During the final days of August, a deeply disturbing issue came before the convention. It was a harbinger of the great sectional crisis of the nineteenth century. Many northern representatives detested the slave trade and wanted it to end immediately. They despised the three-fifths ruling that seemed to award slaveholders extra power in government simply because they owned slaves. "It seemed now to be pretty well understood," Madison jotted in his private notes, "that the real difference of interest lay, not between the large and small but between the N. and Southn. States. The institution of slavery and its consequences formed a line of discrimination."

Whenever northern delegates—and on this point they were by no means united—pushed too aggressively, Southerners threatened to bolt the convention, thereby destroying any hope of establishing a strong national government. Curiously, even recalcitrant Southerners avoided using the word *slavery*. They seemed embarrassed to call an institution by its true name, and in the Constitution itself, slaves were described as "other persons," "such persons," "persons held to Service or Labour," in other words, as everything but slaves.

A few northern delegates such as Roger Sherman of Connecticut sought at every turn to mollify the Southerners, especially the South Carolinians who spoke so passionately about preserving slavery. Gouverneur Morris, a Pennsylvania representative, would have none of it. He regularly reminded the Convention that, "the inhabitant of Georgia and S.C. who goes to the Coast of Africa, and in defiance of the most sacred laws of humanity tears away his fellow creatures from their dearest connections and damns them to the most cruel bondage, shall have more votes in a Government instituted for the protection of the rights of mankind, than the Citizen of Pa. or N. Jersey."

Largely ignoring Morris's stinging attacks, the delegates reached an uneasy understanding on the continuation of the slave trade. Southerners feared the new Congress would pass commercial regulations adversely affecting the planters—taxes on the export of rice and tobacco, for example. They demanded, therefore, that no trade laws be passed without a two-thirds majority of the federal legislature. They backed down on this point, however, in exchange for guarantees that Congress would not interfere with the slave trade until 1808 (see Chapter 8). The South even came away with a clause assuring the return of fugitive slaves. "We have obtained," Charles Cotesworth Pinckney told the planters of South Carolina, "a right to recover our slaves in whatever part of America they may take refuge, which is a right we had not before."

Although these deals revolted many Northerners, they conceded that establishing a strong national government was of greater immediate importance than ending the slave trade. "Great as the evil is," Madison wrote, "a dismemberment of the union would be worse."

The Elusive Constitution
Search for Original Intent

Many prominent national leaders, alarmed at a perceived "judicial imperialism" in recent activist courts, have urged that judges interpret the Constitution strictly according to the "intent of the Framers." Arguing that a "jurisprudence of original intent" is the "only legitimate basis for constitutional decision making," *intentionalists* demand that judges measure decisions against a "demonstrable consensus among the Framers and ratifiers as to principles stated or implied in the Constitution."

Yet when one considers circumstances surrounding the Constitution's framing, demonstration of the Founders' intent proves elusive indeed. Delegates to Philadelphia in 1787 deliberately veiled the purpose of the Convention in secrecy to avoid pressure by local constituencies who harbored deep suspicions concerning strong central government. Newspapers, barred from access to the Convention, printed only occasional rumors. Delegates refused to speak or correspond with outsiders concerning the proceedings.

The strictness with which delegates observed the rule of secrecy not only restricted contemporary knowledge of what transpired, but has also limited the number of sources in which subsequent generations may search for original intent. Only three members preserved complete accounts of Convention debates. These records remained unpublished for more than thirty years, forcing the first generation of lawyers and federal judges to rely on the words of the Constitution alone for clues to the Framers' intent.

The publication of the three accounts did not necessarily make the delegates' intent more accessible. The *Journal, Acts and Proceedings of the Convention Assemblies in Philadelphia,* recorded by the Convention Secretary, William Jackson, provided only a chronological listing of motions, resolutions, and vote tallies. His unpublished manuscript of convention debates, which could have fleshed out the published *Journal's* "mere skeleton" of the proceedings, was lost.

The notes of New York delegate Robert Yates appeared in 1821 as *Secret Proceedings and Debates of the Convention Assembled at Philadelphia,* but the circumstances of their publication rendered them thoroughly unreliable. Their editor, the for-

---

Though complete sets of notes were penned by both the convention secretary, William Jackson (center, left) and James Madison (opposite page), neither set provides indisputable evidence to support a particular theory of original intent. Jackson's published notes provide only listings to parliamentary procedures; Madison's notes, though accurate, must be considered incomplete.

mer French minister Citizen Edmond Genêt, attained notoriety in the 1790s when he violated American neutrality in the Anglo-French war by commissioning American privateers against British shipping. Genêt supported states' rights and popular government and manipulated Yates's notes to support his views. A comparison of *Secret Proceedings* with the two surviving pages of Yates's manuscript reveals that Genêt altered or deleted more than half the original text.

If the intent of the delegates survives anywhere, Madison's *Notes of Debates in the Federal Convention of 1787* provides its likeliest repository. The "father of the Constitution" as contemporaries called him, carefully preserved notes on Convention proceedings and took every measure to ensure their accuracy. Recognizing his own limitations as a stenographer, Madison did not try to record everything said, but sought manuscript copies of delegates' speeches that he incorporated into his notes at the end of each day. Madison also waited until the end of each day to record his own speeches, every one of which was extemporaneous, from memory. At the convention's end, he obtained a manuscript copy of Secretary Jackson's notes, which he used to supplement and correct his own. Though Madison tinkered at times with his notes over the next thirty years, recent analysis has demonstrated that none of these minor corrections impaired the faithfulness of the text.

Yet in spite of the meticulous care that Madison lavished on his notes, they remain, at best, incomplete repositories of the

Framers' original intent. Each day's notes contain only a few minutes of oral discourse, whereas actual delivery occupied between five and seven hours. Furthermore, written manuscripts of speeches may have approximated only roughly what the debaters actually said. Madison's speech on the benefits of a large republic, for example, occupies two closely reasoned pages in his notes. Yet others who took notes seem to have recorded a much shorter and far less impressive oral version. Such discrepancies raise important questions. How did Framers understand the actual speeches on the Convention floor? How did understanding shape their intentions? How much of their intent is lost in the vast omissions?

These questions take on even greater significance when one considers that the Constitution was forged through a series of compromises among representatives whose interests and intentions differed widely. No delegate was completely satisfied, and the finished document permitted some functions none had intended. Madison himself complained, for example, that the principle of judicial review "was never intended and can never be proper."

Moreover, he thought it would be a mistake to search for the original intent of Convention delegates. The delegates' intent could never possibly determine Constitutional interpretation, he argued, for "the only authoritative intentions were those of the people of the States, as expressed thro' the Conventions which ratified the Constitution."

Yet the works most common-

James Madison

ly cited from the time of state ratification raise problems with the application of this principle as well. Stenographers who recorded the *Debates of the Several State Conventions on the Adoption of the Federal Constitution* did not possess skills adequate to their task, and Federalist partisans edited the speeches with abandon in order to promote their own views. Evidence also suggests that Jonathan Eliot, the journalist who published the debates in 1836, altered them further.

Given the limitations of sources most often cited by modern judges and lawyers, the original intent of most Framers remains as elusive today as it was for the first generation who had no access to those documents. The Constitution's often ambiguous wording, which furnished the sole guide to the Framers' intent in their day, remains the best recourse in our own.

The Last Details

On July 26, the convention formed a Committee of Detail, a group that prepared a rough draft of the Constitution. After it completed its work—writing a document that still, after so many hours of debate, preserved the fundamental points of the Virginia Plan—the delegates reconsidered each article. The task required the better part of a month.

During these sessions, the members of the convention concluded that the president, as they now called the executive, should be selected by an electoral college, a body of prominent men in each state chosen by local voters. The number of "electoral" votes held by each state equaled its number of representatives and senators. This awkward device guaranteed the president would not be indebted to the Congress for his office. Whoever received the second largest number of votes in the electoral college automatically became vice president. In the event that no person received a majority of the votes, the election would be decided by the lower house—the House of Representatives—with each state casting a single vote. Delegates also armed the chief executive with veto power over legislation as well as the right to nominate judges. Both privileges, of course, would have been unthinkable a decade earlier, but the state experiments revealed the importance of having an independent executive to maintain a balanced system of republican government.

As the meeting was concluding, some delegates expressed concern about the absence in the Constitution of a bill of rights. Such declarations had been included in most state constitutions, and Virginians like George Mason insisted that the states and their citizens needed explicit protection from possible excesses by the federal government. While many delegates sympathized with Mason's appeal, they noted that the hour was late and, in any case, that the proposed Constitution provided sufficient security for individual rights. During the hard battles over ratification, the delegates to the convention may have regretted passing over the issue so lightly.

We, the People

The delegates adopted an ingenious procedure for ratification. Instead of submitting the Constitution to the various state legislatures, all of which had a vested interest in maintaining the status quo and most of which had two houses, either of which could block approval, they called for the election of thirteen state conventions especially chosen to review the new federal government. The delegates may have picked up this idea from the Massachusetts experiment of 1780. Moreover, the Constitution would take effect after the assent of only nine states. There was no danger, therefore, that the proposed system would fail simply because a single state like Rhode Island withheld approval.

The convention asked Gouverneur Morris, a delegate from Pennsylvania noted for his urbanity, to make final stylistic changes in the wording of the Constitution. When Morris examined the working draft, he discovered it spoke of the collection of states forming a new government. This wording presented problems. Ratification required only nine states. No one knew whether all the states would accept the Constitution, and if not, which nine would. A strong possibility existed that several New England states would reject the document. Morris's brilliant phrase, "We, the People of the United States," eliminated this difficulty. The new nation was a republic of the people, not of the states.

On September 17, thirty-nine men signed the Constitution. A few members of the convention, like Mason, could not support the document. Others had already gone home. For over three months, Madison had served as the convention's driving intellectual force. He now generously summarized the experience: "There never was an assembly of men, charged with a great and arduous trust, who were more pure in their motives, or more exclusively or anxiously devoted to the object committed to them."

WHOSE CONSTITUTION? THE STRUGGLE FOR RATIFICATION

Supporters of the Constitution recognized ratification would not be easy. After all, the convention had been authorized only to revise the Articles, but instead it produced a new plan that fundamentally altered relations between the states and the central government. The delegates dutifully dispatched copies of the Constitution to the Congress of Confederation, then meeting in New

Revolution or Reform? The Articles of Confederation and the Constitution Compared

	Articles of Confederation	Constitution
Mode of ratification or amendment	Require confirmation by every state legislature	Requires confirmation by $3/4$ of state conventions or legislatures
Number of houses in legislature	One	Two
Mode of representation	1–7 Delegates represent each state, each state holding only one vote in Congress	Two senators represent each state in upper house; each senator holds one vote. One representative to lower house represents every 30,000 people (in 1788) in a state; each representative holds one vote
Mode of election and term of office	Delegates appointed annually by state legislatures	Senators chosen by state legislatures for six-year term (direct election after 1913); representatives chosen by vote of citizens for two-year term
Executive	No separate executive: delegates annually elect one of their number as president, who possesses no veto, no power to appoint officers or to conduct policy. Administrative functions of government theoretically carried out by Committee of States; practically by various single-headed departments	Separate executive branch: president elected by electoral college to four-year term, granted veto, power to conduct policy, to appoint ambassadors, judges, and officers of executive departments established by legislation
Judiciary	Most adjudication left to state and local courts, Congress final court of appeal in disputes between states	Separate branch consisting of Supreme Court and inferior courts established by Congress to enforce federal law
Taxation	States alone can levy taxes, Congress funds the Common Treasury by making requisitions for state contributions	Federal government granted powers of taxation
Regulation of commerce	Congress regulates foreign commerce by treaty, but holds no check on conflicting state regulations	Congress regulates foreign commerce by treaty; all state regulations must obtain congressional consent

York City, and that powerless body referred the document to the separate states without any specific recommendation. The fight for ratification had begun.

Federalists and Antifederalists

Proponents of the Constitution enjoyed great advantages over the unorganized opposition. In the contest for ratification, they took no chances.

Their most astute move was the adoption of the label *Federalist*. This term cleverly suggested that they stood for a confederation of states rather than for the creation of a supreme national authority. Critics of the Constitution, who tended to be somewhat poorer, less urban, and less well educated than their opponents, cried foul, but there was little they could do. They were stuck with the name *Antifederalist*, a misleading term that made their cause seem far more obstructionist than it actually was.

The Federalists recruited the most prominent public figures of the day. In every state convention, speakers favoring the Constitution were more polished and more fully prepared than were their opponents. In New York, the campaign to win ratification sparked publication of *The Federalist,* a brilliant series of essays written by Madison, Hamilton, and Jay during the fall and winter of 1787 and 1788. The nation's newspapers threw themselves overwhelmingly behind the new government. In fact, few journals even bothered to carry Antifederalist writings. In some states, the Federalists adopted tactics of questionable propriety in order to gain ratification. In Pennsylvania, for example, they achieved a legal quorum for a crucial vote by dragging several opposition delegates into the meeting from the streets. In New York, Hamilton intimidated upstate Antifederalists with threats that New York City would secede from the state unless the state ratified the Constitution.

In these battles, the Antifederalists articulated a political philosophy that had broad popular appeal. They spoke the language of the Commonwealthmen (see Chapter 4). Like the extreme republicans who drafted the first state constitutions, the Antifederalists were deeply suspicious of political power. During the debates over ratification, they warned that public officials, however selected, would be constantly scheming to expand their authority.

The preservation of individual liberty required constant vigilance. It seemed obvious that the larger the republic, the greater the opportunity for political corruption. Local voters could not possibly know what their representatives in a distant national capital were doing. The government outlined in the Constitution invited precisely the kinds of problems that Montesquieu had described in his famous essay. "In so extensive a republic," one Antifederalist declared, "the great officers of government would soon become above the control of the people, and abuse their power."

Antifederalists demanded direct, personal contact with their representatives. They argued that elected officials should reflect the character of their constituents as closely as possible. It seemed unlikely that in large congressional districts, the people would be able to preserve such close ties with their representatives. According to the Antifederalists, the Constitution favored persons wealthy enough to have forged a reputation that extended beyond a single community. Samuel Chase told the members of the Maryland ratifying convention that under the new system "the distance between the people and their representatives will be so great that there is no probability of a farmer or planter being chosen . . . only the *gentry,* the *rich,* and the well-born will be elected."

Federalist speakers mocked their opponents' localist perspective. The Constitution deserved general support precisely because it ensured future Americans would be represented by "natural aristocrats," individuals possessing greater insights, skills, and training than did the ordinary citizen. These talented leaders, the Federalists insisted, could discern the interests of the entire population. They were not tied to the selfish needs of local communities. "The little demagogue of a petty parish or country will find his importance annihilated [under the Constitution] and his intrigues useless," predicted Charles Cotesworth Pinckney, a South Carolina Federalist.

Historians have generally accepted the Federalist critique. It would be a mistake, however, to see the Antifederalists as "losers" or as persons who could not comprehend social and economic change. Although their rhetoric echoed an older moral view of political culture, they accepted more easily than did many Federalists a liberal marketplace in which ordinary citizens competed as equals with the rich and well-born. They believed the public good was best served by allowing individuals like themselves to pursue their own private interests. That is what they had been doing on the local level during the 1780s, and they resented the imposition of elite controls over their affairs. Although the Antifederalists lost the battle over ratification, their ideas about political economy later found many champions in the "Age of Andrew Jackson."

The Constitution drew support from many different types of people. In fact, historians have been unable to discover sharp correlations between wealth and occupation on the one hand

and attitudes toward the proposed system of central government on the other. In general, Federalists lived in more commercialized areas than did their opponents. In the cities, artisans as well as merchants called for ratification, while those farmers who were only marginally involved in commercial agriculture frequently voted Antifederalist.

Despite passionate pleas from Patrick Henry and other Antifederalists, most state conventions quickly adopted the Constitution. Delaware acted first (December 7, 1787), and a number of other states soon followed. Within eight months of the Philadelphia meeting, eight of the nine states required to launch the government had ratified

the document. The contests in New York and Virginia (June 1788) generated bitter debate, but they too joined the union, leaving only North Carolina and Rhode Island outside the United States. Eventually (November 21, 1789 and May 29, 1790), even these states ratified the Constitution. Still, the vote had been very close. The Constitution was ratified in New York by a tally of 30 to 27, in Massachusetts by 187 to 168, and in Virginia by 89 to 79. A swing of a few votes in several key states could have defeated the new government.

While the state conventions sparked angry rhetoric, Americans soon closed ranks behind the Constitution. An Antifederalist who represented

Ratification of the Constitution
Advocates of the new Constitution called themselves Federalists and those who opposed its ratification were known as Antifederalists.

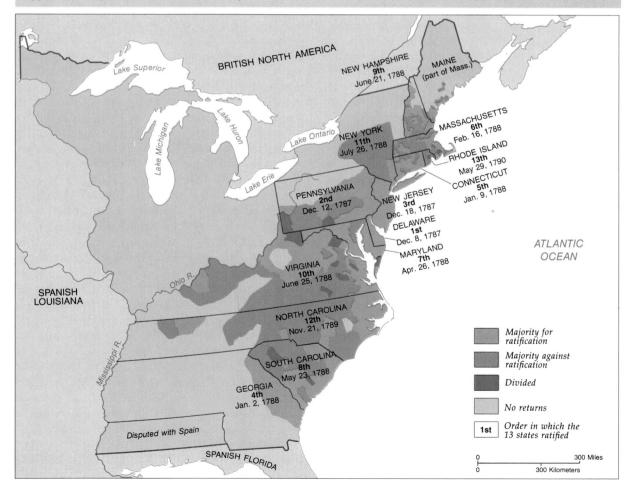

one Massachusetts village explained that "he had opposed the adoption of this Constitution; but that he had been overruled . . . by a majority of wise and understanding men [and that now] he should endeavor to sow the seeds of union and peace among the people he represented."

Adding the Bill of Rights

The first ten amendments to the Constitution are the major legacy of the Antifederalist argument. In almost every state convention, opponents of the Constitution pointed to the need for greater protection of individual liberties, rights that people presumably had possessed in a state of nature. "It is necessary," wrote one Antifederalist, "that the sober and industrious part of the community should be defended from the rapacity and violence of the vicious and idle. A bill of rights, therefore, ought to set forth the purposes for which the compact is made, and serves to secure the minority against the usurpation and tyranny of the majority." The list of fundamental rights varied from state to state, but most Antifederalists demanded specific guarantees for jury trial and freedom of religion. They wanted prohibitions against cruel and unusual punishments. There was also considerable, though not universal, support for freedom of speech and freedom of the press.

Madison and others regarded these proposals with little enthusiasm. In *The Federalist* No. 84, Hamilton bluntly reminded the American people that "the constitution is itself . . . a BILL OF RIGHTS." But after the adoption of the Constitution had been assured, Madison moderated his stand. If nothing else, passage of a bill of rights would appease able men such as George Mason and Edmund Randolph, who might otherwise remain alienated from the new federal system. "We have in this way something to gain," Madison concluded, "and if we proceed with caution, nothing to lose."

The crucial consideration was caution. A number of people throughout the nation advocated calling a second constitutional convention, one that would take Antifederalist criticism into account. Madison wanted to avoid such a meeting, and he feared some members of the first Congress might use a bill of rights as an excuse to revise the entire Constitution or to promote a second convention.

Madison carefully reviewed these recommendations as well as the various declarations of rights that had appeared in the early state constitutions, and on June 8, 1789, he placed before the House of Representatives a set of amendments designed to protect individual rights from government interference. Madison told the members of Congress that the greatest dangers to popular liberties came from "the majority [operating] against the minority." A committee compressed and revised his original ideas into ten amendments that were ratified and became known collectively as the Bill of Rights. For many modern Americans these amendments are the most important section of the Constitution. Madison had hoped that additions would be inserted into the text of the Constitution at the appropriate places, not tacked onto the end, but he was overruled.

The Bill of Rights protected the freedoms of assembly, speech, religion, and the press; guaranteed speedy trial by an impartial jury; preserved the people's right to bear arms; and prohibited unreasonable searches. Other amendments dealt with legal procedure. Some opponents of the Constitution urged Congress to provide greater safeguards for states' rights, but Madison had no intention of backing away from a strong central government. Only the Tenth Amendment addressed the states' relation to the federal system. This crucial article, designed to calm Antifederalist fears, specified that those "powers not delegated to the United States by the Constitution, nor prohibited by it to the States, are reserved to the States respectively, or to the people."

On September 25, 1789, the Bill of Rights passed both houses of Congress, and by December 15, 1791, these amendments had been ratified by three-fourths of the states. Madison was justly proud of his achievement. He had effectively secured individual rights without undermining the Constitution. When he asked his friend Jefferson for his opinion of the Bill of Rights, Jefferson responded with typical republican candor: "I like [it] . . . as far as it goes; but I should have been for going further."

The Signing of the Constitution (*1875*) by Thomas Rossiter. *Paintings like this, in which Washington appears enthroned in a radiant aura, contributed to the mythic reputations of the men who framed the Constitution at the 1787 convention in Independence Hall, Philadelphia.*

A NEW BEGINNING

By 1789, one phase of American political experimentation had come to an end. During these years, the people gradually, often haltingly, learned that in a republican society they themselves were sovereign. They could no longer blame the failure of government on inept monarchs or greedy aristocrats. They bore a great responsibility. Americans had demanded a government of the people only to discover during the 1780s that in some situations the people could not be trusted with power, majorities could tyrannize minorities, and the best of governments could abuse individual rights.

Contemporaries had difficulty deciding just what had been accomplished. A writer in the *Pennsylvania Packet* thought the American people had preserved *order*. "The year 1776 is cele-brated," the newspaper observed, "for a revolution in favor of liberty. The year 1787 . . . will be celebrated with equal joy, for a revolution in favor of Government." But some aging patriots grumbled that perhaps order had been achieved at too high a price. In 1788, Richard Henry Lee remarked, "Tis really astonishing that the same people, who have just emerged from a long and cruel war in defense of liberty, should now agree to fix an elective despotism upon themselves and their posterity."

But most Americans probably would have accepted Franklin's optimistic assessment. As he watched the delegates to the Philadelphia convention come forward to sign the Constitution, he noted that there was a sun carved on the back of George Washington's chair. "I have," the aged philosopher noted, ". . . often in the course of the session . . . looked at [the sun] behind the

CHRONOLOGY

1776 Second Continental Congress authorizes colonies to create republican government (May) • Eight states draft new constitutions; two others already enjoy republican government by virtue of former colonial charters

1777 Congress accepts Articles of Confederation after long debate (November)

1780 Massachusetts finally ratifies state constitution

1781 States ratify Articles of Confederation following settlement of Virginia's western land claims • British army surrenders at Yorktown (October)

1782 States fail to ratify proposed Impost tax

1783 Newburgh Conspiracy thwarted (March) • Society of the Cincinnati raises a storm of criticism • Treaty of peace signed with Great Britain (September)

1785 Land Ordinance for Northwest Territory passed by Congress

1786 Jay-Gardoqui negotiations over Mississippi navigation anger southern states • Annapolis Convention suggests second meeting to revise the Articles of Confederation (September) • Shays's Rebellion frightens American leaders

1787–1788 The federal Constitution is ratified by all states except North Carolina and Rhode Island

1791 Bill of Rights (first ten amendments of the Constitution) ratified by states

---

President without being able to tell whether it was rising or setting; but now at length I have the happiness to know that it is a rising and not a setting sun."

Recommended Reading

The best general accounts of this period have been written by Merrill Jensen and Jackson Turner Main. Of

enduring value are Jensen's *Articles of Confederation* (1959) and *The New Nation: A History of the United States During the Confederation, 1781–1789* (1950) as well as Main's *The Sovereign States, 1775–1783* (1973) and *The Antifederalists, Critics of the Constitution, 1781–1788* (1961). Gordon S. Wood brilliantly reinterpreted this entire period in *The Creation of the American Republic, 1776–1787* (1969), a work now supplemented by his provocative *Radicalism of the American Revolution* (1992). The failure of Congress during the 1780s is the subject of Jack N. Rakove's *The Beginning of National Politics: An Interpretive History of the Continental Congress* (1979). Peter S. Onuf provides a penetrating analysis of one major piece of legislation in *Statehood and Union: A History of the Northwest Ordinance* (1987). A splendid collection of contempory writings can be found in Bernard Bailyn, ed., *The Debate on the Constitution* (1993).

Additional Bibliography

In a masterful essay, *The American Revolution Considered as a Social Movement* (1926), Franklin Jameson challenged American historians not only to explore social effects of the Revolution, but also to compare the patriots' achievement with the actions of other revolutionaries throughout the world. Although no one responded fully to this ambitious challenge, some scholars provide a provocative comparative framework. See, for example, Patrice Higonnet, *Sister Republics: The Origins of French and American Republicanism* (1988). Good general discussions of some of these issues can be found in Joyce Appleby, *Liberalism and Republicanism in the Historic Imagination* (1992) and Peter Onuf, ed., *Jeffersonian Legacies* (1993).

Many able studies focus on specific reforms. The extension of political participation is discussed in J. R. Pole, *Political Representation in England and the Origins of the American Republic* (1966). On African Americans, see Winthrop Jordan, *White Over Black: American Attitudes Toward the Negro, 1550–1812* (1968); Benjamin Quarles, *The Negro in the American Revolution* (1961); Arthur Zilversmit, *The First Emancipation* (1961); Gary Nash, *Race and Revolution* (1990); Ira Berlin and Ronald Hoffman, eds., *Slavery and Freedom in the Age of the American Revolution* (1983); and Sylvia R. Frey, *Water from the Rock: Black Resistance in a Revolutionary Age* (1991).

Recent historians have transformed our understanding of women in postrevolutionary society. One might start an investigation of this field with Linda Kerber, *Women of the Republic* (1980); Mary Beth Norton, *Liberty's Daughters* (1980); and Ronald Hoffman and Peter J. Albert, eds., *Women in the Age of the*

American Revolution (1990). Important articles are Jan Lewis, "The Republican Wife," *William and Mary Quarterly,* 3rd ser., 44(1987): 689–721; and Ruth H. Bloch, "The Gendered Meaning of Virtue in Revolutionary America," *Signs: Journal of Women in Culture and Society,* 8(1987): 37–58. Bernard Bailyn writes about immigrants and speculators in his *Voyagers to the West: A Passage in the Peopling of America on the Eve of the Revolution* (1986).

The early state constitutions are discussed in Wood's *Creation of the American Republic* (1969); and Willi Paul Adams, *The First American Constitutions: Republican Ideology and the Making of the State Constitutions* (1980). A classic exploration of political and economic history at the state level is Oscar and Mary Handlin, *Commonwealth: A Study of the Role of Government in the American Economy, Massachusetts, 1774–1861,* rev. ed. (1969). The Newburgh Conspiracy is covered in Richard H. Kohn, *Eagle and Sword: The Federalists and the Creation of the Military Establishment in America, 1783–1802* (1975). On Shays's Rebellion, see Robert A. Gross, ed., *In Debt to Shays: The Bicentennial of an Agrarian Rebellion* (1993).

The best source on the Constitution remains Max Farrand, ed., *Records of the Federal Convention of 1787,* 4 vols. (1911–1937). Charles A. Beard's *Economic Interpretation of the Constitution of the United States* (1913) caused a generation of historians to examine the financial accounts of convention delegates, but as Forrest McDonald demonstrates in *We The People* (1958), Beard's thesis simply does not hold up. The intellectual background of the Founders is examined in Forrest McDonald, *Novus Ordo Seclorum: The Intellectual Origins of the Constitution* (1985); Douglass Adair, *Fame and the Founding Fathers,* edited by Trevor Colbourn (1974); Garrett W. Sheldon, *Political Philosophy of Thomas Jefferson* (1991); and J. G. A. Pocock, *The Machiavellian Moment: Florentine Political Thought and the Atlantic Republican Tradition* (1975). The practical implications of republican ideas on state government are explored in Rosemarie Zagarri, *The Politics of Size: Representation in the United States, 1776–1850* (1987).

In *Visionary Republic: Millennial Themes in American Thought, 1756–1800* (1985), Ruth H. Bloch argues persuasively that historians of this period have not fully appreciated evangelical Protestantism in shaping political ideas. For a thoughtful investigation of the many different meanings of republicanism, see Richard Beeman, et al., eds., *Beyond Confederation: Origins of the Constitution and American National Identity* (1987). The best introduction to Antifederalist thought is Herbert J. Storing, ed., *The Complete Antifederalist,* 7 vols. (1981).

Setting the Agenda
Federalists and Republicans, 1788–1800

hile presiding over the first meeting of the U.S. Senate in 1789, Vice President John Adams called the senators' attention to a pressing procedural question.

How would they address George Washington, the newly elected president? Adams insisted that Washington deserved an impressive title, a designation lending dignity and weight to his office. The vice president warned the senators that if they called Washington simply "president of the United States," the "common people of foreign countries [as well as] the sailors and soldiers [would] despise him to all eternity." Adams recommended "His Highness, the President of the United States, and Protector of their Liberties," but some senators favored "His Elective Majesty" or "His Excellency."

Adams's initiative caught many persons, including Washington, completely by surprise. They regarded the entire debate as ridiculous. James Madison, a member of the House of Representatives, announced that pretentious European titles were ill suited to the "genius of the people" and "the nature of our Government." Thomas Jefferson, who was then residing in Paris, could not comprehend what motivated the vice president, and in private correspondence, he repeated Benjamin Franklin's judgment that Adams "means well for his Country, is always an honest Man, often a wise one, but sometimes, and in some things, absolutely out of his senses." When the senators learned their efforts embarrassed Washington, they dropped the topic. The leader of the new republic would be called president of the United States. One wag, however, dubbed the portly Adams, "His Rotundity."

FORCE OF PUBLIC OPINION

The comic-opera quality of this debate should not obscure the participants' serious concern about setting government policy. The members of the first Congress could not take the survival of republican government for granted. All of them, of course, wanted to secure the Revolution. The recently ratified Constitution transferred sovereignty from the states to the people, a bold and unprecedented decision that many Americans feared would generate chronic instability.

Translating constitutional abstractions into practical legislation would under the most favorable conditions have been difficult. But these were especially trying times. Great Britain and France, rivals in a century of war, put nearly unbearable pressures on the leaders of the new republic and, in the process, made foreign policy a bitterly divisive issue.

Although no one welcomed them, political parties gradually took shape during this period. Neither the Jeffersonians nor the Federalists—as the two major groups were called—doubted that the United States would one day become a great commercial power. They differed, however, on how best to manage the transition from an agrarian household economy to an international system of trade and industry. The Federalists encouraged rapid integration of the United States into a world economy, but however enthusiastic they were about capitalism, they did not trust the people or local government to do the job effectively. A modern economy, they insisted, required strong national institutions that would be directed by a social elite who understood the financial challenge and who would work in the best interests of the people.

Such claims frightened persons who called themselves Jeffersonians. Strong financial institutions, they thought, had corrupted the government of Great Britain from which they had just dissociated themselves. They searched for alternative ways to accommodate to the needs of commerce and industry. Unlike the Federalists, the Jeffersonians put their political faith in the people. The Jeffersonians felt that if ordinary entrepreneurs could be freed from too many government regulations, they could be trusted to resist greed and crass materialism and to sustain the virtue of the republic.

During the 1790s, former friends were surprised to discover themselves at odds over such basic political issues. One person—Hamilton, for example—would stake out a position. Another, such as Jefferson or Madison, would respond, perhaps speaking a little more extravagantly than a specific issue demanded, goaded by the rhetorical nature of public debate. The first in turn would rebut passionately the new position. By the middle of the decade, this dialectic had almost spun out of control, taking the young republic to the brink of political violence.

Leaders of every persuasion had to learn to live with "public opinion." The revolutionary gentry had invited the people to participate in government, but the gentlemen assumed ordinary voters would automatically defer to their social betters. Instead, the founders discovered they had created a rough-and-tumble political culture. The "public" followed the great debates of the period through articles they read in hundreds of highly partisan newspapers and magazines. Just as television has done in our own century, print journalism opened politics to a large audience that previously might have been indifferent to the activities of elected officials. By the time John Adams left the presidency in 1800, he had learned this lesson well. The ordinary workers and farmers of the United States, feisty individuals who thought they were as good as anyone else and who were not afraid to let their political opinions be known, were not likely to let their president become an "Elective Majesty."

ESTABLISHING GOVERNMENT

In 1788, George Washington enjoyed great popularity throughout the nation. The people remembered him as the selfless leader of the Continental army, and even before the states had ratified the Constitution, everyone assumed he would be chosen president of the United States. He received the unanimous support of the electoral college, an achievement that no subsequent president has duplicated. Adams, a quick-tempered New Englander who championed national independence in 1776, was selected vice president. As Washington left his beloved Virginia plantation, Mount Vernon, for New York City, he recognized that the people—now so vocal in their support—could be fickle. "I fear," he explained with mature insight, "if the issue of public measures should not correspond with their sanguine expectations, they will turn the extravagant . . . praise . . . into equally extravagant . . . censures."

Washington bore great responsibility. The political stability of the young republic depended in large measure on how he handled himself in office. In the eyes of his compatriots, he had been transformed into a living symbol of the new government (see "The Man Who Could Not Tell a Lie," pp. 202–203), and during his presidency (1789–1797), he carried himself with studied dignity and reserve—never ostentatious, the embodiment of classical republican values. Contemporaries sensed that although Washington put himself forward for elective office, he somehow stood above the hurly-burly of routine politics. A French diplomat who witnessed Washington's first inauguration in New York City reported in awe: "He has the soul, look and figure of a hero united in him." But the adulation of Washington—however well meant—seriously affected the conduct of public affairs, for criticism of his administration was regarded as an attack on the president and by extension, on the republic itself. During the early years of Washington's presidency, therefore, American public opinion discouraged partisan politics.

Washington created a strong, independent presidency. While he discussed pressing issues with the members of his cabinet—indeed, solicited their opinions—he left no doubt that he alone made policy. Moreover, the first president resisted congressional efforts to restrict executive authority, especially in foreign affairs.

The first Congress quickly established executive departments. Some congressmen wanted to prohibit presidents from dismissing cabinet-level appointees without Senate approval, but James Madison—still a voice for a strong, independent executive—led a successful fight against this restriction on presidential authority. Madison recognized that the chief executive could not function unless he had personal confidence in the people with whom he worked. In 1789, Congress created the Departments of War, State, and the Treasury, and as secretaries, Washington nominated Henry Knox, Thomas Jefferson, and Alexander Hamilton, respectively. Edmund Randolph served as part-time attorney general, a position that ranked slightly lower in prestige than the head of a department. Since the secretary of the treasury oversaw the collection of customs and other future federal taxes, Hamilton could anticipate having several thousand jobs to dispense, an obvious source of political patronage.

To modern Americans accustomed to a large federal bureaucracy, the size of Washington's government seems amazingly small. When Jefferson arrived in New York to take over the State Department, for example, he found two chief clerks, two assistants, and a part-time trans-

The Man Who Could Not Tell a Lie

The American Star, *painted by Frederick Kemmelmeyer, commemorates Washington's first inauguration.*

Every schoolchild can recite the more memorable incidents of George Washington's life: how as a small boy, the future father of his country chopped down a cherry tree or how he threw a stone across the broad Rappahannock River, a feat no contemporary had the strength to duplicate. Yet these stories are false, wholly without historical foundation. That such tall tales came to provide the most enduring images of Washington is attributable to the scribblings of one man, Mason Locke Weems, better known as "Parson" Weems.

Credited with inventing many Washington myths, Weems grew up in colonial Maryland, the youngest of nineteen children. He studied abroad during the Revolutionary War, first for the medical profession and then for the ministry. Ordained in England in 1784, he returned to become the rector of a Maryland parish. Apparently, he soon tired of being a parson and took up a more lucrative calling—selling books, mainly Bibles. Weems traveled widely with his literary offerings, dabbling at times in writing and publishing. Although he wrote several advice pamphlets, like *Hymen's Recruiting Sergeant,* a tract recommending premarital chastity, and the *Bad Wife's Looking Glass,* Weems's greatest success as an author came with his first biography, *The Life of Washington,* a book that went through eighty editions.

Several months before Washington's death in December 1799, Weems began to gather anecdotes about the first president. Always on the lookout for a quick profit, Weems wrote to his publisher friend Matthew Carey that a pamphlet on Washington "could make [Carey] a world of pence and popularity." Shortly after Washington's fatal illness plunged the nation into mourning, Weems wrote again to Carey, "Millions are gaping to read something about him. I am very nearly primed and cocked for 'em." Weems wanted to print a morally uplifting history that would "show that [Washington's] unparalleled rise & elevation were due to his Great Virtues."

When Carey ignored Weems's scheme, the persistent parson turned to another publisher, this time with more satisfactory results. At least three editions of his eighty-page pamphlet appeared in 1800. *The Life of Washington* proved extremely popular, outselling everything else in Weems's mobile bookstore. In the sixth edition and in all future editions, Weems described himself as the former rector of Mount Vernon parish, although no such parish existed. By 1808, he had lengthened the pamphlet to two hundred pages filled with exciting new anecdotes "Equally Honourable to [Washington] and Exemplary To His Young Countrymen."

Among the stories Weems invented to pad the original pamphlet was the unforgettable fable of the cherry tree. Supposedly, a distant relative who frequently visited Washington's family during her girlhood recounted the inci-

The image of the first president, captured in tapestry.

Cincinnatus seemed plausible to nineteenth-century Americans, since much of Washington's behavior had in fact corresponded to that of the mythic hero. After crushing the enemy, Cincinnatus had returned without hesitation to his farm, unmoved by the civic honors that others attempted to thrust on him. Like that virtuous Roman, Washington had neglected his plantation while in the service of his countrymen. At the conclusion of the Revolution, he enthusiastically threw himself into farming. And after two terms as a reluctant though popular president, America's agrarian warrior retired to his beloved Mount Vernon, content to exchange political authority for the joys of country life.

However outlandish Weems's images of Washington as Cincinnatus or as a child hero now appear, they reveal something important about the way Americans perceive national character. Washington embodied humility, quiet dignity, and a selfless devotion to country. A comparison with his famed contemporary Napoleon is instructive. The French celebrated Napoleon's martial triumphs; he was depicted in extravagant splendor as the god of war or as Zeus, the king of the gods. Washington remained, even in Weems's account, a somewhat plain figure, a republican soldier, a reluctant politician, a farmer rather than a warrior. Yet if Washington seems somewhat dull to modern Americans, his reserve in office and virtue in private life may have set a tone that discouraged later would-be presidents from attempting to become military adventurers.

dent for Weems. Calling the anecdote "too valuable to be lost, and too true to be doubted," Weems explained how the six-year-old George had received a hatchet as a gift. He chopped down everything in sight, including his father's favorite cherry tree. When the elder Washington discovered the mischief, he questioned his son, who in Weems's rich imagination at least, admitted to the crime, crying "I can't tell a lie, Pa." This extraordinary show of honesty earned young George his father's praise rather than his punishment. "Run to my arms, you dearest boy," exclaimed his father. "Such an act of heroism in my son is worth more than a thousand trees."

Also new to the 1808 *Life* was a prophetic dream that Washington's mother, Mary Ball Washington, had allegedly had

long before the Revolution. She dreamed that the family home was on fire and no adult seemed capable of extinguishing the blaze. Five-year-old George, playing with a plow in the fields, rushed to the scene and inspired the confused servants to attack the flames just as he would later inspire American soldiers to fight the British. With this dream, Weems symbolically linked Washington to Cincinnatus, the patriot who set aside his plow to defend Rome. As Weems explained, Cincinnatus "unyoked his oxen [and] . . . hastened to the army—who at his appearance, felt as did our troubled fathers in 1774 [sic] when the godlike figure of Washington stood before them on the plains of Boston to fight the battles of liberty."

Portraying Washington as a

The First Cabinet, *engraving from a painting by Alonzo Chappell (1866). The first meeting of the cabinet took place at Washington's Mount Vernon home.*

created a Supreme Court staffed by a chief justice and five associate justices. In addition, the statute set up thirteen district courts authorized to review the decisions of the state courts. John Jay, a leading figure in New York politics, agreed to serve as chief justice, but since federal judges in the 1790s were expected to travel hundreds of miles over terrible roads to attend sessions of the inferior courts, few persons of outstanding talent and training joined Jay on the federal bench. One who did, Judge James Iredell, complained that service on the Supreme Court had transformed him into a "travelling postboy."

Remembering the financial insecurity of the old Confederation government, the newly elected congressmen passed the tariff of 1789, a tax of approximately 5 percent on imports. Even before it went into effect, however, the act sparked controversy. Southern planters, who relied heavily on European imports and the northern shippers who could control the flow of imports into the South, claimed the tariff discriminated against southern interests in favor of those of northern merchants. The new levy generated considerable revenue for the young republic.

JEFFERSON AND HAMILTON

Washington's first cabinet included two extraordinary personalities, Alexander Hamilton and Thomas Jefferson. Both had served the country with distinction during the Revolution, were recognized by contemporaries as men of special genius as well as high ambition, and brought to public office a powerful vision of how the American people could achieve greatness. The story of their opposing views during the decade of the 1790s provides insight into the birth and development of political parties. It also reveals how a common political ideology, republicanism, could be interpreted in such vastly different ways that decisions about government policy turned friends into adversaries. Indeed, the falling out of Hamilton and Jefferson reflected deep, potentially explosive political divisions within American society.

Hamilton was a brilliant, dynamic young lawyer who had distinguished himself as Washington's aide-de-camp during the Revolution. Born in the West Indies, the child of an adulterous relationship, Hamilton employed

lator. With this tiny staff, he not only maintained contacts with the representatives of foreign governments, collected information about world affairs, and communicated with U.S. officials living overseas, but also organized the entire federal census! Jefferson immediately recognized that his new job would allow him little leisure for personal interests. The situation in other departments was similar. Overworked clerks scribbled madly just to keep up with the press of correspondence. John Adams, reviewing a bundle of letters and memos, grumbled "often the handwriting is almost illegible." Considering these working conditions, it is not surprising that the president had difficulty persuading able people to accept positions in the new government. It is even more astonishing that Hamilton and Jefferson were able to accomplish as much as they did with so little assistance.

Congress also provided for a federal court system. The Judiciary Act of 1789, the work primarily of Connecticut Congressman Oliver Ellsworth,

charm, courage, and intellect to fulfill his inexhaustible ambition. He strove not for wealth but reputation. Men and women who fell under his spell found him almost irresistible, but to enemies, Hamilton appeared a dark, calculating, even evil, genius. He advocated a strong central government and refused to be bound by the strict wording of the Constitution, a document Hamilton once called "a shilly shally thing." While he had fought for American independence, he admired British culture, and during the 1790s, he advocated closer commercial and diplomatic ties with the former mother country with whom "we have a similarity of tastes, language, and general manners."

Jefferson possessed a profoundly different temperament. This tall Virginian was more reflective and shone less brightly in society than Hamilton. Contemporaries sometimes interpreted his retiring manner as lack of ambition. They misread Jefferson. He thirsted not for power or wealth but for an opportunity to advance the democratic principles that he had stated so eloquently in the Declaration of Independence. When Jefferson became secretary of state in January 1790, he had just returned from Paris where he witnessed the first exhilarating moments of the French Revolution. These earthshaking events, he believed, marked the beginning of a worldwide republican assault on absolute monarchy and aristocratic privilege. His European experiences biased Jefferson in favor of France over Great Britain when the two nations clashed.

The contrast between these two powerful figures during the early years of Washington's administration should not be exaggerated. They shared many fundamental beliefs. Indeed, both Hamilton and Jefferson insisted they were working for the creation of a strong, prosperous republic, one in which commerce would play an important role. Hamilton was publicly accused of being a secret monarchist, but he never repudiated the ideals of the American Revolution. Rather than being spokespersons for competing ideologies, Hamilton and Jefferson were different kinds of republicans who, during the 1790s, attempted as best they could to cope with unprecedented political challenges.

However much these two men had in common, serious differences emerged. Washington's secretaries disagreed on precisely how the United States should fulfill its destiny. As head of the treasury department, Hamilton urged his fellow citizens to think in terms of bold commercial development, of farms and factories embedded within a complex financial network that would reduce the nation's reliance on foreign trade. Because Great Britain had already established an elaborate system of banking and credit, the secretary looked to that country for economic models that might be reproduced on this side of the Atlantic.

Hamilton also voiced concerns about the role of the people in shaping public policy. His view of human nature caused him to fear total democracy. He assumed that in a republican society, the gravest threat to political stability was anarchy rather than monarchy. "The truth," he claimed, "unquestionably is, that the only path to a subversion of the republican system of the Country is, by flattering the prejudices of the people, and exciting their jealousies and apprehensions, to throw affairs into confusion and bring on civil commotion." The best hope for the survival of the republic, Hamilton believed, lay with the country's monied classes. If the wealthiest people could be persuaded their economic self-interest could be advanced—or at least made less insecure—by the central government, then they would work to strengthen it, and by so doing, bring a greater measure of prosperity to the common people. From Hamilton's perspective, there was no conflict between private greed and public good; one was the source of the other.

On almost every detail, Jefferson challenged Hamilton's analysis. The secretary of state assumed the strength of the American economy lay not in its industrial potential, but in its agricultural productivity. The "immensity of land" represented the country's major economic resource. Contrary to the claims of some critics, Jefferson did not advocate agrarian self-sufficiency or look back nostalgically to a golden age dominated by simple yeomen. He recognized the necessity of change, and while he thought that persons who worked the soil were more responsible citizens than were those who labored in factories for wages, he encouraged the nation's farmers to participate in an expanding international market. Americans could exchange raw materials "for finer manufactures than they are able to execute themselves."

Unlike Hamilton, Jefferson expressed faith in the ability of the American people to shape policy. Throughout this troubled decade, even when the very survival of constitutional government seemed in doubt, Jefferson maintained a boundless optimism in the judgment of the common folk. He instinctively trusted the people, feared that uncontrolled government power might destroy their liberties, and insisted public officials follow the letter of the Constitution, a frame of government he described as "the wisest ever presented to men." The greatest threat to the young republic, he argued, came from the corrupt activities of pseudo aristocrats, persons who placed the protection of "property" and "civil order" above the preservation of "liberty." To tie the nation's future to the selfish interests of a privileged class—bankers, manufacturers, speculators— seemed cynical as well as dangerous. He despised speculators who encouraged "the rage of getting rich in a day," since such "gaming" activities inevitably promoted the kinds of public vice that threatened republican government. To mortgage the future of the common people by creating a large national debt struck Jefferson as particularly insane. But the responsibility for shaping the economy of the new nation fell mainly to Alexander Hamilton as the first secretary of the treasury.

HAMILTON'S GRAND DESIGN

The unsettled state of the nation's finances presented the new government with a staggering challenge. In August 1789, the House of Representatives announced that "adequate provision for the support of public credit [is] a matter of high importance to the national honor and prosperity." However pressing the problem appeared, no one was prepared to advance a solution, and the House asked the secretary of the treasury to make suggestions.

Congress may have received more than it bargained for. Hamilton threw himself into the task. He read deeply in abstruse economic literature. He even developed a questionnaire designed to find out how the U.S. economy really worked and sent it to scores of commercial and political leaders throughout the country. But when Hamilton's three major reports—on public credit, on banking, and on manufacturers—were complete, they bore the unmistakable stamp of his own creative genius. The secretary synthesized a vast amount of information into an economic blueprint so complex, so innovative that even his allies were slightly baffled. Theodore Sedgwick, a congressman who supported Hamilton's program, explained weakly that the secretary's ideas were "difficult to understand . . . while we are in our infancy in the knowledge of Finance." Certainly, Washington never fully grasped the subtleties of Hamilton's plan.

The secretary presented his *Report on the Public Credit* to Congress on January 14, 1790. His research revealed that the nation's outstanding debt stood at approximately $54 million. This sum represented various obligations that the U.S. government had incurred during the Revolutionary War. In addition to foreign loans, the figure included loan certificates the government had issued to its own citizens and soldiers. But that was not all. The states still owed creditors approximately $25 million. During the 1780s, Americans desperate for cash had been forced to sell government certificates to speculators at greatly discounted prices, and it was estimated that approximately $40 million of the nation's debt was owed to twenty thousand people, only 20 percent of whom were the original creditors.

Funding and Assumption

Hamilton's *Report on the Public Credit* contained two major recommendations covering the areas of funding and assumption. First, under his plan the United States promised to fund its foreign and domestic obligations at full face value. Current holders of loan certificates, whoever they were and no matter how they obtained them, could exchange the old certificates for new government bonds bearing a moderate rate of interest. Second, the secretary urged the federal government to assume responsibility for paying the remaining state debts.

Hamilton reasoned that his credit system would accomplish several desirable goals. It would significantly reduce the power of the individual states in shaping national economic policy, something Hamilton regarded as essential in maintaining a strong federal government. Moreover, the creation of a fully funded national debt signaled to investors throughout the world that the United States was now solvent, that its bonds represented a good risk. Hamilton argued that investment capital, which might otherwise flow to Europe, would remain in this country, providing a source of money for commercial and industrial investment. In short, Hamilton invited the country's wealthiest citizens to invest in the future of the United States. Critics claimed that

the only people who stood to profit from the scheme were Hamilton's friends—some of whom sat in Congress and who had purchased great numbers of public securities at very low prices.

To Hamilton's great surprise, Madison—his friend and collaborator in writing *The Federalist*—attacked the funding scheme in the House of Representatives. The Virginia congressman agreed that the United States should honor its debts. He worried, however, about the citizens and soldiers who, because of personal financial hardship, had been compelled to sell their certificates at prices far below face value. Why should wealthy speculators now profit from their hardship? If the government treated the current holders of certificates less generously, Madison declared, then there might be sufficient funds to provide equitable treatment for the distressed patriots. Whatever the moral justification for Madison's plan may have been, it proved unworkable on the national level. Far too many records had been lost since the Revolution for the Treasury Department to be able to identify all the original holders. In February 1790, Congress soundly defeated Madison's proposal.

Assumption unleashed even greater criticism. Some states had already paid their revolutionary debts, and Hamilton's program seemed designed to reward certain states—Massachusetts and South Carolina, for example—simply because they had failed to put their finances in order. In addition, the secretary's opponents in Congress became suspicious that assumption was merely a ploy to increase the power and wealth of Hamilton's immediate friends. "The Secretary's people scarce disguise their design," observed William Maclay, a crusty Scotch-Irish senator from Pennsylvania, "which is to create a mass of debts which will justify them in seizing all the sources of government."

No doubt, Maclay and others expressed genuine fears. Some of those who protested, however, were simply looking after their own speculative schemes. These men had contracted to purchase huge tracts of vacant western lands from the state and federal governments. They anticipated that when settlers finally arrived in these areas, the price of land would skyrocket. In the meantime, the speculators had paid for the land with revolutionary certificates, often purchased on the open market at fifteen cents on the dollar. This meant that one could obtain 1,000 acres for only $150. Hamilton's assumption proposal threatened to destroy these lucrative transactions by cutting off the supply of cut-rate securities. On April 12, a rebellious House led by Madison defeated assumption.

The victory was short-lived. Hamilton and congressional supporters resorted to legislative horse trading to revive his foundering program. In exchange for locating the new federal capital on the Potomac River, a move that would stimulate the depressed economy of northern Virginia, several key congressmen who shared Madison's political philosophy changed their votes on assumption. Hamilton may also have offered to give the state of Virginia more federal money than it actually deserved. Whatever the details of these negotiations may have been, in August, Washington signed assumption and funding into law. The first element of Hamilton's design was now securely in place.

The Controversial Bank of the United States

The persistent Hamilton submitted his second report to Congress in January 1791. He proposed that the U.S. government charter a national bank, much like the Bank of England. This privately owned institution would be funded in part by the federal government. Indeed, since the bank would own millions of dollars of new U.S. bonds, its financial stability was tied directly to the strength of the federal government and, of course, to the success of the Hamiltonian program. The secretary of the treasury argued that a growing financial community required a central bank to facilitate increasingly complex commercial transactions. The institution not only would serve as the main depository of the U.S. government but also would issue currency acceptable in payment of federal taxes. Because of that guarantee, the money would maintain its value while in circulation.

Madison and others in Congress immediately raised a howl of protest. While they were not oblivious to the many important services a national bank might provide for a growing country, they suspected that banks—especially those modeled on British institutions—might "perpetuate a larged monied interest" in this country. And what about the Constitution? That document said nothing specifically about chartering financial corporations, and they warned that if Hamilton and his supporters were allowed to stretch fundamental law on this occasion, they could not be held back in the future. Popular liberties would be at the mercy of whoever happened to be in office. "To take a single step," Jefferson warned, "beyond the boundaries thus specifically drawn around the powers of Congress is to take possession of a boundless field of power, no longer susceptible to definition." On this issue, Hamilton stubbornly refused to compromise, announcing angrily, "This is the first symptom of a spirit which must either be killed or will kill the constitution of the United States."

This intense controversy involving his closest advisers worried the president. Even though the bank bill passed Congress (February 8), Washington seriously considered vetoing the legislation on constitutional grounds. Before doing so, however, he requested written opinions from the members of his cabinet. Jefferson's rambling, wholly predictable attack on the bank was not one of his more persuasive performances. By contrast, in only a few days, Hamilton prepared a masterful essay entitled "Defense of the Constitutionality of the Bank." He assured the president that Article I, Section 8 of the Constitution—"The Congress shall have Power. . . . To make all Laws which shall be necessary and proper for carrying into Execution the foregoing Powers"—justified issuing charters to national banks. The "foregoing Powers" on which Hamilton placed so much weight were taxation, regulation of commerce, and making war. He boldly articulated a doctrine of *implied powers,* an interpretation of the Constitution that neither Madison nor Jefferson had anticipated. Hamilton's "loose construction" carried the day, and on February 25, 1791, Washington signed the bank act into law.

Hamilton triumphed in Congress, but the general public looked on his actions with growing fear and hostility. Many persons associated huge national debts and privileged banks with the decay of public virtue. Men of Jefferson's temperament believed Great Britain—a country Hamilton held in high regard—had compromised the purity of its ancient constitution by allowing speculators to worm their way into positions of political power.

Hamilton seemed intent on reproducing this corrupt system in the United States. When news of his proposal to fund the national debt at full face value leaked out, for example, urban speculators rushed to rural areas, where they purchased loan certificates from unsuspecting citizens at bargain prices. To backcountry farmers, making money without actually engaging in physical labor appeared immoral, unrepublican, and certainly, un-American. When the greed of a former treasury department official led to several serious bankruptcies in 1792, ordinary citizens began to listen more closely to what Madison, Jefferson, and their associates were saying about growing corruption in high places.

Setback for Hamilton

In his third major report, *Report on Manufactures,* submitted to Congress in December 1791, Hamilton revealed the final details of his grand design for the economic future of the United States. This lengthy document suggested ways by which the federal government might stimulate manufacturing. If the country wanted to free itself from dependence on European imports, Hamilton observed, then it had to develop its own industry, textile mills for example. Without direct government intervention, however, the process would take decades. Americans would continue to invest in agriculture. But, according to the secretary of the treasury, protective tariffs and special industrial bounties would greatly accelerate the growth of a balanced economy, and with proper planning, the United States would soon hold its own with England and France.

In Congress, the battle lines were clearly drawn. Hamilton's opponents—not yet a disciplined party but a loose coalition of men who shared Madison's and Jefferson's misgivings about the secretary's program—ignored his economic arguments. Instead, they engaged him on moral and political grounds. Madison railed against the dangers of "consolidation," a process that threatened to concentrate all power in the federal government, leaving the states defenseless. Under the Confederation, of course, Madison had stood with the nationalists against the advocates of extreme states' rights (see Chapter 6). His disagreements with Hamilton over economic policy, coupled with the necessity of pleasing the voters of his Virginia congressional district every two years, transformed Madison into a spokesman for the states.

Jefferson attacked the *Report on Manufactures* from a different angle. He assumed—largely because he had been horrified by Europe's urban poverty—that cities breed vice. The government, Jefferson argued, should do nothing to promote their development. He believed Hamilton's proposal guaranteed that American workers would leave the countryside and crowd into urban centers. "I think our government will remain virtuous for many centuries," Jefferson explained, "as long as they [the people] are chiefly agricultural. . . . When they get piled upon one another in large cities, as in Europe, they will become corrupt as in Europe." And southern congressmen saw tariffs and bounties as vehicles for enriching Hamilton's northern friends at the planters' expense. The recommendations in the *Report on Manufactures* were soundly defeated in the House of Representatives.

Washington detested political squabbling. The president, of course, could see the members of his cabinet disagreed on many issues, but in 1792, he still believed that Hamilton and Jefferson—and the people who looked to them for advice—could be reconciled. In August, he begged them personally to rise above the "internal dissensions [which are] . . . harrowing and tearing at our vitals." The appeal came too late. By the conclusion of Washington's first term, neither secretary trusted the other's judgment. Their sparring had produced congressional factions, but as yet no real political parties with permanent organizations that engaged in campaigning had come into existence. At this point, Hamilton and Jefferson only dimly appreciated the force of public opinion in shaping federal policy.

FOREIGN AFFAIRS: A CATALYST TO THE BIRTH OF POLITICAL PARTIES

During Washington's second term (1793–1797), war in Europe dramatically thrust foreign affairs into the forefront of American life. The impact of this development on the conduct of domestic politics was devastating. Officials who had formerly disagreed on economic policy now began to identify their interests with either Britain or France, the world's most powerful nations. Differences of political opinion, however trivial, were suddenly cited as evidence that one group or the other had entered into treasonous correspondence with external enemies eager to compromise the independence and prosperity of the United States. As Jefferson observed in the troubled summer of 1793, European conflict "kindled and brought forward the two parties with an ardour which our own interests merely, could never excite."

Formal political organizations—the Federalists and Republicans—were born in this poisonous atmosphere. The clash between these groups developed over how best to preserve the new republic. The Republicans (Jeffersonians) advocated states' rights, strict interpretation of the Constitution, friendship with France, and vigilance against "the avaricious, monopolizing Spirit of Commerce and Commercial Men." The Federalists urged a strong national government, central economic planning, closer ties with Great Britain, and maintenance of public order, even if that meant calling out federal troops.

Threats to U.S. Neutrality

Great Britain treated the United States with arrogance. The colonists had defeated the redcoats on land, but on the high seas, the Americans were no match for the British navy, the strongest in the world. Indeed, the young republic could not even compel its old adversary to comply with the Treaty of 1783, in which the British had agreed to vacate military posts in the Northwest Territory. In 1794, approximately a thousand British soldiers still occupied American land, an obstruction that Governor George Clinton of New York claimed had excluded U.S. citizens "from a very valuable trade to which their situation would naturally have invited them." Moreover, even though 75 percent of American imports came from Great Britain, that country refused to grant the United States full commercial reciprocity. Among other provocations, it barred American shipping from the lucrative West Indian trade.

France presented a very different challenge. In May 1789, Louis XVI, desperate for revenue, authorized a meeting of a representative assembly known as the Estates General. By so doing, the king unleashed explosive revolutionary forces that toppled the monarchy and cost him his life (January 1793). The men who seized power—and they came and went rapidly—were militant republicans, ideologues eager to liberate all Europe from feudal institutions. In the early years of the Revolution, France drew on the American experience, and Thomas Paine and the Marquis de Lafayette enjoyed great popularity. But the French found they could not stop the Revolution. Constitutional reform turned into bloody purges, and one radical group, the Jacobins, guillotined thousands of people—many wrongfully—who were suspected of monarchist sympathies during the so-called Reign of Terror (October 1793–July 1794). These events left Americans confused. While those who shared Jefferson's views cheered the spread of republicanism, those others who sided with Hamilton condemned French expansionism and political violence.

In the face of growing international tension, neutrality seemed the most prudent course for the United States. But that policy was easier for a weak country to proclaim than to defend. In February 1793, France declared war on Great Britain—what the leaders of revolutionary France called the "war of all peoples against all kings"—and these powerful European rivals immediately challenged the official American position on shipping: "free ships make free goods," meaning that belligerents should not interfere with the shipping of neutral carriers. To make matters worse, no one was certain whether the Franco-American Treaties of 1778 (see Chapter 5) legally bound the United States to support its old ally against Great Britain.

Both Hamilton and Jefferson wanted to avoid war. The secretary of state believed nations desiring American goods should be forced to honor American neutrality. If Britain treated the United States as a colonial possession, if the Royal Navy stopped American ships on the high seas and forced seamen to serve the king—in other words, if it impressed American sailors—then the United States should award France special commercial advantages. Hamilton thought Jefferson's scheme insane. He pointed out that Britain possessed the largest navy in the world and was not likely to be coerced by American threats. The United States, he counseled, should appease the former mother country even if that meant swallowing national pride.

A newly appointed French minister to the United States, Edmond Genêt, precipitated the first major diplomatic crisis. This unstable young

The execution of Louis XVI by French revolutionaries served to deepen the growing political division in America. Republicans, although they deplored the excesses of the Reign of Terror, continued to support the French people. Federalists feared that the violence and lawlessness would spread to the United States.

man arrived in Charleston, South Carolina, in April 1793. He found considerable popular enthusiasm for the French Revolution and, buoyed by this reception, he authorized privately owned American vessels to seize British ships in the name of France. Such actions clearly violated U.S. neutrality and invited British retaliation. When government officials warned Genêt to desist, he threatened to take his appeal directly to the American people, who presumably loved France more than members of the Washington administration.

This confrontation particularly embarrassed Jefferson, the most outspoken pro-French member of the cabinet. He described Genêt as "hot headed, all imagination, no judgment, passionate, disrespectful and even indecent towards the President." Washington did not wait to discover if the treaties of 1778 were still in force. Before he had formally received the impudent French minister, the president issued a Proclamation of Neutrality (April 22). Ironically, when Genêt

learned the Jacobins intended to cut off his head if he returned to France, he requested asylum, married into an extremely wealthy family, and spent the remainder of his life residing in New York.

Jay's Treaty Divides the Nation

Great Britain failed to take advantage of Genêt's insolence. Instead, it pushed the United States to the brink of war. British forts in the Northwest Territory remained a constant source of tension. In June 1793, a new element was added. The London government blockaded French ports to neutral shipping, and in November, its navy captured several hundred American vessels trading in the French West Indies. The British had not even bothered to give the United States advance warning of a change in policy. Outraged members of Congress, especially those who identified with Jefferson and Madison, demanded retaliation, an embargo, a stoppage of debt payment, even war.

Before this rhetoric produced armed struggle, Washington made one final effort to preserve peace. In May 1794, he sent Chief Justice John Jay to London to negotiate a formidable list of grievances. Jay's main objectives were removal of the British forts, payment for ships taken in the West Indies, improved commercial relations, and acceptance of the American definition of neutral rights.

Jefferson's supporters—by now openly called the "Republican interest"—anticipated a treaty favorable to the United States. After all, they explained, the war with France had not gone well for Great Britain, and the British people were surely desperate for American foodstuffs. Even before Jay departed, however, his mission stood little chance of success. Hamilton, anxious as ever to placate the British, had already secretly informed British officials that the United States would compromise on most issues.

Not surprisingly, when Jay reached London, he encountered polite but firm resistance. The chief justice did persuade the British to abandon their frontier posts and to allow small American ships to trade in the British West Indies, but they rejected out of hand the U.S. position on neutral rights. The Royal Navy would continue to search American vessels on the high seas for contraband and to impress sailors suspected of being British citizens. Moreover, there would be no compensation for the ships seized in 1793 until the Americans paid British merchants for debts contracted before the Revolution. And to the particular annoyance of Southerners, not a word was said about the slaves the British army had carried off at the conclusion of the war. While Jay salvaged the peace, he appeared to have betrayed the national interest.

News of Jay's Treaty—perhaps more correctly called Hamilton's Treaty—produced an angry outcry in the nation's capital. Even Washington was apprehensive. He submitted the document to the Senate without recommending ratification, a sign the president was not entirely happy with the results of Jay's mission. After an extremely bitter debate, the upper house, controlled by Federalists, accepted a revised version of the treaty (June 1795). The vote was 20 to 10, a bare two-thirds majority.

The details of the Jay agreement soon leaked to the press. This was an important moment in American political history. The popular journals

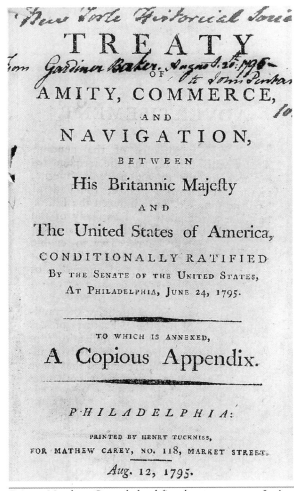

Printer Matthew Carey helped fire the protest over Jay's Treaty by printing the terms of the agreement and adding a series of comments to the appendix.

sparked a firestorm of protest. Throughout the country, people who had generally been apathetic about national politics were swept up in a wave of protest. Urban mobs condemned Jay's alleged sellout; rural settlers burned him in effigy. Jay jokingly told friends he could find his way across the country simply by following the light of these fires. Southerners announced they would not pay prerevolutionary debts to British merchants. The Virginia legislature proposed a constitutional amendment reducing the Senate's role in the treaty-making process. As Fisher Ames, a Federalist congressman, noted darkly, "These little whirlwinds of dry leaves and dirt portend a hurricane."

His prediction proved accurate. The storm broke in the House of Representatives. Republican congressmen, led by Madison, thought they could stop Jay's Treaty by refusing to appropriate funds for its implementation. As part of their plan, they demanded that Washington show the House state papers relating to Jay's mission. The challenge raised complex issues of constitutional law. The House, for example, was claiming a voice in treaty ratification, a power explicitly reserved to the Senate. Second, there was the question of executive secrecy in the interest of national security. Could the president withhold information from the public? According to Washington—as well as all subsequent presidents—the answer was yes. He took the occasion to lecture the rebellious representatives that "the nature of foreign negotiations requires caution; and their success must often depend on secrecy."

The president still had a trump card to play. He raised the possibility that the House was really contemplating his impeachment. Such an action was, of course, unthinkable. Even criticizing Washington in public was politically dangerous, and as soon as he redefined the issue before Congress, petitions supporting the president flooded into the nation's capital. The Maryland legislature, for example, declared its "unabated reliance on the integrity, judgment, and patriotism of the President of the United States," a statement that clearly called into question the patriotism of certain Republican congressmen. The Federalists won a stunning tactical victory over the opposition. Had a less popular man than Washington occupied the presidency, however, they would not have fared so well. The division between the two parties was beyond repair. The Republicans labeled the Federalists "the British party"; the Federalists believed the Republicans were in league with the French.

By the time Jay's Treaty became law (June 14, 1795), the two giants of Washington's first cabinet had retired. Late in 1793, Jefferson returned to his Virginia plantation, Monticello, where despite his separation from day-to-day political affairs, he remained the chief spokesman for the Republican party. His rival, Hamilton, left the Treasury in January 1795 to practice law in New York City. He maintained close ties with important Federalist officials, and even more

than Jefferson, Hamilton concerned himself with the details of party organization.

Diplomacy in the West

Before Great Britain finally withdrew its troops from the Great Lakes and Northwest Territory, its military officers encouraged local Indian groups—the Shawnee, Chippewa, and Miami—to attack settlers and traders from the United States. The Indians, who even without British encouragement fully appreciated the newcomers intended to seize their land, won several impressive victories over federal troops in the area that would become western Ohio and Indiana. In 1790, General Josiah Harmar led his soldiers into an ambush. The following year, an army under General Arthur St. Clair suffered more than nine hundred casualties near the Wabash River. But the Indians were militarily more vulnerable than they realized, for when confronted with a major U.S. army under the command of General Anthony Wayne, they received no support from their former British allies. At the battle of Fallen Timbers (August 20, 1794), Wayne's forces crushed Indian resistance in the Northwest Territory, and the native peoples were compelled to sign the Treaty of Greenville, formally ceding to the U.S. government the land that became Ohio. In 1796, the last British soldiers departed for Canada.

Shrewd negotiations mixed with pure luck helped secure the nation's southwestern frontier. For complex reasons having to do with the state of European diplomacy, Spanish officials in 1795 encouraged the U.S. representative in Madrid to discuss the navigation of the Mississippi River. Before this initiative, the Spanish government not only had closed the river to American commerce but also had incited the Indians of the region to harass settlers from the United States (see Chapter 6). Relations between the two countries would probably have deteriorated further had the United States not signed Jay's Treaty. The Spanish assumed—quite erroneously—that Great Britain and the United States had formed an alliance to strip Spain of its North American possessions.

To avoid this imagined disaster, officials in Madrid offered the American envoy, Thomas Pinckney, extraordinary concessions: the opening

Conquest of the West

Withdrawal of the British, defeat of Native Americans, and negotiations with Spain secured the nation's frontiers.

British Military Posts

■ British-held forts

Great Lakes

LOWER CANADA
St. Lawrence R.

MAINE (part of Mass.)

Pointe-au-Fer
Oswegatchie
Dutchman's Point
VT.
N.H.

Ft. Michilimackinac

UPPER CANADA

Ft. Oswego
N.Y.
MASS.

Ft. Niagara

R.I.
CONN.

Ft. Detroit

Ft. Miami (built 1794)

NORTHWEST TERRITORY

PA.

N.J.

MD.
DEL.

ATLANTIC OCEAN

VA.

Mississippi R.

Ohio R.

SPANISH LOUISIANA

0   150 Miles
0   150 Kilometers

Major Indian Battles

✳ Major Indian battles

UPPER CANADA

N.Y.

Ft. Detroit

Lake Erie

Fallen Timbers
Aug. 20, 1794

Ft. Miami (Br.)

Harmer's Defeat
Oct. 22, 1790

Maumee R.

PA.

Treaty of Greenville Line, 1795

Pittsburgh

St. Clair's Defeat
Nov. 4, 1791

NORTHWEST TERRITORY

Wabash R.

Cincinnati

Ohio R.

VA.

KY.

0   100 Miles
0   100 Kilometers

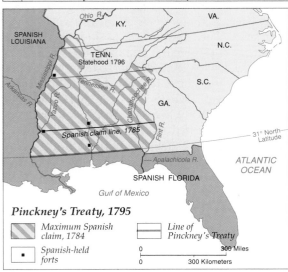

Ohio R.

KY.

VA.

SPANISH LOUISIANA

TENN.
Statehood 1796

N.C.

Mississippi R.

Tennessee R.

S.C.

Arkansas R.

Yazoo R.

Chattahoochee R.

GA.

Spanish claim line, 1785

Flint R.

31° North Latitude

Apalachicola R.

ATLANTIC OCEAN

SPANISH FLORIDA

Gulf of Mexico

Pinckney's Treaty, 1795

▨ Maximum Spanish claim, 1784

▢ Line of Pinckney's Treaty

■ Spanish-held forts

0   300 Miles
0   300 Kilometers

GEORGE WASHINGTON PRESIDENT. 1792.

This engraved medallion is typical of the commemorative medals the United States presented to the chief of the Native American groups with whom it signed treaties.

of the Mississippi, the right to deposit goods in New Orleans without paying duties, a secure southern boundary on the thirty-first parallel (a line roughly parallel to the northern boundary of Florida and running west to the Mississippi), and a promise to stay out of Indian affairs. An amazed Pinckney signed the Treaty of San Lorenzo (also called Pinckney's Treaty) on October 27, 1795, and in March the Senate ratified the document without a single dissenting vote. Pinckney, who came from a prominent South Carolina family, instantly became the hero of the Federalist party.

POPULAR POLITICAL CULTURE

More than any other event during Washington's administration, ratification of Jay's Treaty generated intense political strife. Even as members of Congress voted as Republicans or Federalists, they condemned the rising partisan spirit as a grave threat to the stability of the United States. Popular writers equated "party" with "faction," and "faction" with "conspiracy to overthrow legitimate authority." Party conflict also suggested that Americans had lost the sense of common purpose that had united them during the Revolution. Contemporaries did not appreciate the beneficial role that parties could play by presenting alternative solutions to foreign and domestic problems. Organized opposition smacked of disloyalty and therefore had to be eliminated by any means—fair or foul. These intellectual currents coupled with the existence of two parties created an atmosphere that bred suspicion. In the name of national unity, Federalists as well as Republicans advocated the destruction of political adversaries.

The Partisan Role of Newspapers and Political Clubs

More than any other single element, newspapers transformed the political culture of the United States. Americans were voracious readers. In 1789, a foreign visitor observed, "The common people [here] are on a footing, in point of literature, with the middle ranks of Europe. They all read and write, and understand arithmetic; almost every little town now furnishes a circulating library."

A rapidly expanding number of newspapers appealed to this large literate audience. John Fenno established the *Gazette of the United States* (1789), a journal that supported Hamilton's political philosophy. The Republicans responded in October 1790 with Philip Freneau's influential *National Gazette*. While the format of these publications was similar to that of the colonial papers, their tone was quite different. These fiercely partisan journals presented rumor and opinion as fact. Public officials were regularly dragged through the rhetorical mud. Jefferson, for example, was accused of cowardice; Hamilton, vilified as an adulterer. As party competition became more bitter, editors showed less restraint. One Republican paper even suggested George Washington had been a British agent during the Revolution. No wonder Fisher Ames announced in 1801, "The newspapers are an overmatch for any government."

Even poets and essayists were caught up in the political fray. The better writers—and this was not a period of outstanding artistic achievement in the United States—often produced party propaganda. However much Freneau aspired to fame as a poet, he is remembered today chiefly as a champion of the Republican cause. Noah Webster, who later published *An American Dictionary of the English Language* (1828), spent the 1790s editing a strident Federalist journal, *American Minerva*, in New York City. And Joel Barlow, a Connecticut poet of modest talent, celebrated the French Revolution in verse, thus clearly identifying himself with the party of Jefferson. American writers sometimes complained that the culture of the young republic was too materialistic, too unappreciative of the subtler forms of art then popular in Europe. But it was clear that poets who ignored patriotism and politics simply did not sell well in the United States.

This decade also witnessed the birth of political clubs. These "Democratic" or "Republican" associations, as they were called, first appeared in 1793 and were modeled on the political debating societies that sprang up in France during the early years of the French Revolution. Perhaps because of the French connection, Federalists assumed the American clubs represented the interests of the Republican party. Their purpose was clearly political indoctrination. The Philadelphia Society announced it would "cultivate a just knowledge of rational liberty." A "Democratic" club in New York City asked each member to declare himself a "firm and steadfast friend of the EQUAL RIGHTS OF MAN."

By 1794, at least twenty-four clubs were holding regular meetings. How many Americans actually attended their debates is not known, but regardless of the number, the clubs obviously complemented the newspapers in providing the common people with highly partisan political information.

Whiskey Rebellion Linked to Republican Incendiaries

Political tensions became explosive in 1794. The Federalists convinced themselves the Republicans were actually prepared to employ violence against the U.S. government. Though the charge was without foundation, it took on plausibility in the context of growing party strife.

The crisis developed when a group of farmers living in western Pennsylvania protested a federal excise tax on distilled whiskey that Congress had originally passed in 1791. These men did not relish paying any taxes, but this tax struck them as particularly unfair. They made a good deal of money distilling their grain into whiskey, and the excise threatened to put them out of business.

Largely because the Republican governor of Pennsylvania refused to suppress the angry farmers, Washington and other leading Federalists assumed the insurrection represented a direct political challenge. The president called out fifteen thousand militiamen, and accompanied by Hamilton, he marched against the rebels. The expedition was an embarrassing fiasco. The distillers disappeared, and predictably enough, no one living in the Pittsburgh region seemed to know where the troublemakers had gone. Two supposed rebels were convicted of high crimes against the United States, one reportedly a "simpleton" and the other insane. Washington eventually pardoned both men. As peace returned to the frontier, Republicans gained much electoral support from voters the Federalists had alienated.

In the national political forum, however, the Whiskey Rebellion had just begun. Spokesmen for both parties offered sinister explanations for this seemingly innocuous affair. Washington blamed the "Republican" clubs for promoting civil unrest. He apparently believed the opposition party had dispatched French agents to western Pennsylvania to undermine the authority of the federal government. In November 1794, Washington informed Congress that these "self-created societies"—in other words, the Republican political clubs—had inspired "a spirit inimical to all order." Indeed, the Whiskey Rebellion had been "fomented by combinations of men who . . . have disseminated, from an ignorance or perversion of facts, suspicions, jealousies, and accusations of the whole Government."

The president's interpretation of this rural tax revolt was no less charitable than the conspiratorial explanation offered by the Republicans. Jefferson labeled the entire episode a Hamiltonian device to create an army for the purpose of intimidating Republicans. How else could one explain the administration's gross overreaction to a few disgruntled farmers? "An insurrection was announced and proclaimed and armed against," Jefferson noted, "but could never be found." The response of both parties reveals a pervasive fear of some secret evil design to destroy the republic. The clubs and newspapers—as yet unfamiliar tools for mobilizing public opinion—fanned these anxieties, convincing many government officials

Tarring and feathering federal officials was one way in which western Pennsylvanians protested the tax on whiskey in 1794. Washington's call for troops to put down the insurrection drew more volunteers than he had been able to raise during most of the Revolution.

that the First Amendment should not be interpreted as protecting political dissent.

Washington's Farewell

In September 1796, Washington published his famed "Farewell Address," formally declaring his intention to retire from the presidency. In the address, which was printed in newspapers throughout the country, Washington warned against all political factions. Written in large part by Hamilton, who drew on a draft prepared several years earlier by Madison, the address served narrowly partisan ends. The product of growing political strife, it sought to advance the Federalist cause in the forthcoming election. By waiting until September to announce his retirement, Washington denied the Republicans valuable time to organize an effective campaign. There was an element of irony in this initiative. Washington had always maintained he stood above party. While he may have done so in the early years of his presidency, events such as the signing of Jay's Treaty and the suppression of the Whiskey Rebellion transformed him in the eyes of many Americans into a spokesman solely for Hamilton's Federalist party.

Washington also spoke to foreign policy matters in the address. He counseled the United States to avoid making any permanent alliances with distant nations that had no real interest in promoting American security. This statement guided foreign relations for many years and became the credo of later American isolationists, who argued the United States should steer clear of foreign entanglements.

THE ADAMS PRESIDENCY

The election of 1796 took place in an atmosphere of mutual distrust. Jefferson, soon to be the vice president, informed a friend that "an Anglican and aristocratic party has sprung up, whose avowed object is to draw over us the substance, as they have already done the forms, of British government." On their part, the Federalists were convinced their Republican opponents wanted to hand the government over to French radicals. By modern standards, the structures of both political parties were still primitive. Leaders of national stature such as Madison and Hamilton wrote let-

Candidate	Party	Electoral Vote
J. Adams	Federalist	71
Jefferson	Republican	68
T. Pinckney	Federalist	59
Burr	Republican	30

The Election of 1796

ters encouraging local gentlemen around the country to support a certain candidate, but no one attempted to canvass the voters in advance of the election.

During the campaign the Federalists sowed the seeds of their eventual destruction. Party stalwarts agreed John Adams should stand against the Republican candidate, Thomas Jefferson. Hamilton, however, could not leave well enough alone. From his law office in New York City, he schemed to deprive Adams of the presidency. His motives were obscure. He apparently feared an independent-minded Adams would be difficult to manipulate. He was correct.

Hamilton exploited an awkward feature of the electoral college. In accordance with the Constitution, each elector cast two ballots, and the person who gained the most votes became president. The runner-up, regardless of party affiliation, served as vice president. Ordinarily the Federalist electors would have cast one vote for Adams and one for Thomas Pinckney, the hero of the negotiations with Spain and the party's choice for vice president. Everyone hoped, of course, there would be no tie. Hamilton secretly urged southern Federalists to support only Pinckney even if that meant throwing away an elector's second vote. If everything had gone according to plan, Pinckney would have received more votes than Adams, but when New Englanders loyal to Adams heard of Hamilton's maneuvering, they dropped Pinckney. When the votes were counted, Adams had 71, Jefferson 68, and Pinckney 59. Hamilton's treachery not only angered the new president but also heightened tensions within the Federalist party.

Adams assumed the presidency under intolerable conditions. He found himself saddled with the members of Washington's old cabinet, a group of second-raters who regularly consulted with

Hamilton behind Adams's back. The two most offensive were Timothy Pickering, secretary of state, and James McHenry, secretary of war. But to have dismissed them summarily would have called Washington's judgment into question, and Adams was not prepared to take that risk publicly.

Adams also had to work with a Republican vice president. Adams hoped he and Jefferson could cooperate as they had during the Revolution—they had served together on the committee that prepared the Declaration of Independence—but partisan pressures soon overwhelmed the president's good intentions. Jefferson recorded their final attempt at reconciliation. Strolling home one night after dinner, Jefferson and Adams reached a place "where our road separated, his being down Market Street, mine along Fifth, and we took leave; and he [Adams] never after that . . . consulted me as to any measure of the government."

The XYZ Affair and Domestic Politics

Foreign affairs immediately occupied Adams's full attention. The French government regarded Jay's Treaty as an affront. By allowing Great Britain to define the conditions for neutrality, the United States had in effect sided with that nation against the interests of France.

Relations between the two countries had steadily deteriorated. The French refused to receive Charles Cotesworth Pinckney, the U.S. representative in Paris. Pierre Adet, the French minister in Philadelphia, openly tried to influence the 1796 election in favor of the Republicans. His meddling in domestic politics not only embarrassed Jefferson, it also offended the American people. The situation then took a violent turn. In 1797, French privateers began seizing American ships. Since neither the United States nor France officially declared war, the hostilities came to be known as the Quasi-War.

Hamilton and his friends welcomed a popular outpouring of anti-French sentiment. The "High Federalists"—as Hamilton's wing of the party was called—counseled the president to prepare for all-out war, hoping war would purge the United States of French influence. Adams was not persuaded to escalate the conflict. He dispatched a special commission in a final attempt to remove the sources of antagonism. This famous negotiat-ing team consisted of Charles Pinckney, John Marshall, and Elbridge Gerry. They were instructed to obtain compensation for the ships seized by French privateers as well as release from the treaties of 1778. Federalists still worried that this old agreement might oblige the United States to defend French colonies in the Caribbean against British attack, which they were extremely reluctant to do. In exchange, the commission offered France the same commercial privileges granted to Great Britain in Jay's Treaty. While the diplomats negotiated for peace, Adams talked of strengthening American defenses, rhetoric that pleased the militant members of his own party.

The commission was shocked by the outrageous treatment it received in France. Instead of dealing directly with Talleyrand, the minister of foreign relations, they met with obscure intermediaries who demanded a huge bribe. The commission reported that Talleyrand would not open negotiations unless he was given $250,000. In addition, the French government expected a "loan" of millions of dollars. The Americans refused to play this insulting game. Pinckney angrily sputtered, "No, no, not a sixpence," and with Marshall he returned to the United States. When they arrived home, Marshall offered his much-quoted toast: "Millions for defense, but not one cent for tribute."

Diplomatic humiliation set off a domestic political explosion. When Adams presented the commission's official correspondence before Congress—the names of Talleyrand's lackeys were labeled X, Y, and Z—the Federalists burst out with a war cry. At last, they would be able to even old scores with the Republicans. In April 1798, a Federalist newspaper in New York City announced ominously that any American who refused to censure France" . . . must have a soul black enough to be *fit* for *treasons, strategems,* and *spoils.*" Rumors of conspiracy spread throughout the country. Personal friendships between Republicans and Federalists were shattered. Jefferson described the tense political atmosphere in a letter to an old colleague: "You and I have formerly seen warm debates and high political passions. But gentlemen of different politics would then speak to each other, and separate the business of the Senate from that of society. It is not so now. Men who have been intimate all their lives, cross the streets to avoid meeting, and

This cartoon, Property Protected, a la Francoise (1798), *captures the anti-French sentiment many Americans felt after President Adams disclosed the papers of the XYZ affair. America—depicted as a young maiden—is being plundered by five Frenchmen, who represent the five directors of the French government.*

turn their heads another way, lest they should be obliged to touch their hats."

Crushing Political Dissent

In the spring of 1798, High Federalists assumed that it was just a matter of time until Adams asked Congress for a formal declaration of war. In the meantime, they pushed for a general rearmament, new fighting ships, additional harbor fortifications, and most important, a greatly expanded U.S. Army. About the need for land forces, Adams remained understandably skeptical. He saw no likelihood of French invasion.

The president missed the political point. The army the Federalists wanted was intended not to thwart French aggression but to stifle internal opposition. Indeed, militant Federalists used the XYZ affair as the occasion to institute what Jefferson termed the "reign of witches." The threat to the Republicans was not simply a figment of the vice president's overwrought imagination. When Theodore Sedgwick, now a Federalist senator from Massachusetts, first learned of the commission's failure, he observed in words that capture the High Federalists' vindictiveness, "It will afford a glorious opportunity to destroy faction. Improve it."

During the summer of 1798, a provisional army gradually came into existence. George Washington agreed to lead the troops, but he would do so only on condition that Adams appoint Hamilton as second-in-command. This demand placed the president in a terrible dilemma. Several revolutionary veterans—Henry Knox, for example—outranked Hamilton. Moreover, the former secretary of the treasury had consistently undermined Adams's authority, and to give Hamilton a position of real power in the government seemed awkward at best. When Washington insisted, however, Adams was forced to support Hamilton.

The chief of the High Federalists threw himself into the task of recruiting and supplying the troops. No detail escaped his attention. He and Secretary of War McHenry made certain that in this political army only loyal Federalists received commissions. They even denied Adams's son-in-law a post. The entire enterprise took on an air of unreality. Hamilton longed for military glory, and he may have contemplated attacking Spain's Latin American colonies. His driving obsession, however, was the restoration of political order. No doubt, he agreed with a Federalist senator from Connecticut who predicted the Republicans "never will yield till violence is introduced; we must have a partial civil war . . . and the bayonet must convince some, who are beyond the reach of other arguments."

Hamilton should not have treated Adams with such open contempt. After all, the Massachusetts statesman was still the president, and without presidential cooperation, Hamilton could not fulfill his grand military ambitions. Yet whenever pressing questions concerning the army arose, Adams was nowhere to be found. He let commissions lie on his desk unsigned; he took overlong vacations to New England. He made it quite clear his first love was the navy. In May 1798, the president persuaded Congress to establish the Navy Department. For this new cabinet position, he selected Benjamin Stoddert, a person who did not take orders from Hamilton. Moreover, Adams further infuriated the High Federalists by refusing to ask Congress for a formal declaration of war. When they pressed him, Adams threatened to resign, making Jefferson president. As the weeks passed, the American people increasingly regarded the idle army as an expensive extravagance.

Silencing Political Opposition: The Alien and Sedition Acts

The Federalists did not rely solely on the army to crush political dissent. During the summer of 1798, the party's majority in Congress passed a group of bills known collectively as the Alien and Sedition Acts. This legislation authorized the use of federal courts and the powers of the presidency to silence the Republicans. The acts were born of fear and vindictiveness, and in their efforts to punish the followers of Jefferson, the Federalists created the nation's first major crisis over civil liberties.

Congress drew up three separate Alien Acts. The first, the Alien Enemies Law, vested the president with extraordinary wartime powers. On his own authority, he could detain or deport citizens of nations with which the United States was at war and who behaved in a manner he thought suspicious. Since Adams refused to ask for a declaration of war, this legislation never went into effect. A second act, the Alien Law, empowered the president to expel any foreigner from the United States simply by executive decree. Congress limited the acts to two years, and while Adams did not attempt to enforce them, the mere threat of arrest caused some Frenchmen to flee the country. The

third act, the Naturalization Law, was the most flagrantly political of the group. The act established a fourteen-year probationary period before foreigners could apply for full U.S. citizenship. Federalists recognized that recent immigrants, especially the Irish, tended to vote Republican. The Naturalization Law, therefore, was designed to keep "hordes of wild Irishmen" away from the polls for as long as possible.

The Sedition Law struck at the heart of free political exchange. It defined criticism of the U.S. government as criminal libel; citizens found guilty by a jury were subject to fines and imprisonment. Congress entrusted enforcement of the act to the federal courts. Republicans were justly worried that the Sedition Law undermined rights guaranteed by the First Amendment. When they protested, however, the High Federalists dismissed their complaints. The Constitution, they declared, did not condone "the most groundless and malignant lies, striking at the safety and existence of the nation." They were determined to shut down the opposition press and were willing to give the government what seemed almost dictatorial powers to achieve that end. The Jeffersonians also expressed concern over the federal judiciary's expanded role in punishing sedition. They believed such matters were best left to state officials.

Americans living in widely scattered regions of the country soon witnessed political repression firsthand. District courts staffed by Federalist appointees indicted seventeen people for criticizing the government. Several cases were absurd. In Newark, New Jersey, for example, a drunkard staggered out of a tavern to watch a sixteen-gun salute fired in honor of President Adams. When the man expressed the hope a cannonball might lodge in Adams's ample posterior, he was arrested. No wonder a New York City journal declared, "joking may be very dangerous even to a free country."

The most celebrated trial occurred in Vermont. A Republican congressman, Matthew Lyon, who was running for reelection, publicly accused the Adams administration of mishandling the Quasi-War. This was not the first time this Irish immigrant had angered the Federalists. On the floor of the House of Representatives, Lyon once spit in the eye of a Federalist congressman from Connecticut. Lyon was immediately labeled the "Spitting Lyon," and one Bostonian declared, "I

In the early years of the republic, political dissent sometimes escalated to physical violence. This fistfight took place on the floor of Congress, February 15, 1798. The combatants are Republican Matthew Lyon and Federalist Roger Griswold.

feel grieved that the saliva of an Irishman should be felt upon the face of an American & he, a New Englandman." A Federalist court was pleased to have the opportunity to convict him of libel. But Lyon enjoyed the last laugh. While he sat in jail, his constituents reelected him to Congress.

As this and other cases demonstrated, the federal courts had become political tools. While the fumbling efforts at enforcement of the Sedition Law did not silence opposition—indeed, they sparked even greater criticism and created martyrs—the actions of the administration persuaded Republicans the survival of free government was at stake. Time was running out. "There is no event," Jefferson warned, " . . . however atrocious, which may not be expected."

The Republicans Appeal to the States

By the fall of 1798, Jefferson and Madison were convinced the Federalists envisioned the creation of a police state. According to Madison, the Sedition Law "ought to produce universal alarm." It threatened the free communication of ideas which he "deemed the only effectual guardian of every other right." Some extreme Republicans such as John Taylor of Virginia recommended secession from the Union; others advocated armed resistance. But Jefferson wisely counseled against such extreme strategies. "This is not the kind of opposition the American people

will permit," he reminded his desperate supporters. The last best hope for American freedom lay in the state legislatures.

As the crisis deepened, Jefferson and Madison drafted separate protests known as the Virginia and Kentucky Resolutions. Both statements vigorously defended the right of individual state assemblies to interpret the constitutionality of federal law. Jefferson wrote the Kentucky Resolutions in November 1798, and in an outburst of partisan anger, he flirted with a doctrine of nullification as dangerous to the survival of the United States as anything advanced by Hamilton and his High Federalist friends.

In the Kentucky Resolutions, Jefferson described the federal union as a compact. The states transferred certain explicit powers to the national government, but in his opinion, they retained full authority over all matters not specifically mentioned in the Constitution. Jefferson rejected Hamilton's broad interpretation of the "general welfare" clause. "Every state," Jefferson argued, "has a natural right in cases not within the compact . . . to *nullify* of their own authority all assumptions of power by others within their limits." Carried to an extreme, this logic could have led to the breakup of the federal government, and in 1798, Kentucky legislators were not prepared to take such a radical stance. While they diluted Jefferson's prose, they fully accepted his belief that the Alien and Sedition Acts were unconstitutional and ought to be repealed.

When Madison drafted the Virginia Resolutions in December, he took a stand more temperate than Jefferson's. Madison urged the states to defend the rights of the American people, but he resisted the notion that a single state legislature could or should have the authority to overthrow federal law.

The Virginia and Kentucky Resolutions must be viewed in proper historical context. They were not intended as statements of abstract principles and most certainly not as a justification for southern secession. They were pure political party propaganda. Jefferson and Madison dramatically reminded American voters during a period of severe domestic tension that the Republicans offered a clear alternative to Federalist rule. No other state legislatures passed the Resolutions, and even in Virginia where the Republicans enjoyed broad support, several important figures such as John Marshall and George Washington censured the states' rights argument.

Adams's Finest Hour

In February 1799, President Adams belatedly declared his independence from the Hamiltonian wing of the Federalist party. Throughout the confrontation with France, Adams had shown little enthusiasm for war. Following the XYZ debacle, he began to receive informal reports that Talleyrand had changed his tune. The French foreign minister told Elbridge Gerry and other Americans that the bribery episode had been an unfortunate misunderstanding and that if the United States sent new representatives, he was prepared to negotiate in good faith. The High Federalists ridiculed this report. But Adams, still brooding over Hamilton's appointment to the army, decided to throw his own waning prestige behind peace. In February, he suddenly asked the Senate to confirm William Vans Murray as U. S. representative to France.

The move caught the High Federalists totally by surprise. They sputtered with outrage. "It is solely the President's act," Pickering cried, "and we were all thunderstruck when we heard of it." Adams was just warming to the task. In May, he fired Pickering and McHenry, an action he should have taken months earlier. With peace in the offing, American taxpayers complained more and more about the cost of maintaining an unnecessary army. The president was only too happy to dismantle Hamilton's dream.

When the new negotiators—Oliver Ellsworth and William Davie joined Murray—finally arrived in France in November 1799, they discovered that yet another group had come to power there. This government, headed by Napoleon Bonaparte, cooperated in drawing up an agreement known as the Convention of Mortefontaine. The French refused to compensate the Americans for vessels taken during the Quasi-War, but they did declare the treaties of 1778 null and void. Moreover, the convention removed annoying French restrictions on U.S. commerce. Not only had Adams avoided war, he had also created an atmosphere of mutual trust that paved the way for the purchase of the Louisiana Territory. The president declared with considerable justification that the second French mission was "the most disinterested, the most determined and the most

John Adams in the suit and sword he wore for his 1797 inauguration. The portrait is by English artist William Winstanley, 1798. Throughout his presidency, Adams was plagued by political extremists, Federalist as well as Republican.

successful [act] of my whole life." It also cost him reelection.

THE PEACEFUL REVOLUTION: THE ELECTION OF 1800

On the eve of the election of 1800, the Federalists were fatally divided. Adams enjoyed wide popularity among the Federalist rank and file, especially in New England, but articulate party spokesleaders such as Hamilton vowed to punish the president for his betrayal of their militant policies. Hamilton even composed a scathing pamphlet entitled *Letter Concerning the Public Conduct and Character of John Adams,* an essay that questioned Adams's ability to hold high office.

Once again the former secretary of the treasury attempted to rig the voting in the electoral college so that the party's vice presidential candidate, Charles Cotesworth Pinckney, would receive more ballots than Adams, and America would be saved from "the fangs of Jefferson." As in 1796, the conspiracy backfired. The Republicans gained 73 votes, while the Federalists trailed with 65.

But to everyone's surprise, the election was not resolved in the electoral college. When the ballots were counted, Jefferson and his running mate, Aaron Burr, had tied. This accident—a Republican elector should have thrown away his second vote—sent the selection of the next president to the House of Representatives, a "lame duck" body still controlled by members of the Federalist party.

As the House began its work on February 27, 1801, excitement ran high. Each state delegation cast a single vote, with nine votes needed for election. On the first ballot, Jefferson received the support of eight states, Burr six, and two states divided evenly. People predicted a quick victory for Jefferson, but after dozens of ballots, the House had still not selected a president. "The scene was now ludicrous," observed one witness. "Many had sent home for night-caps and pillows, and wrapped in shawls and great-coats, lay about the floor of the committee-rooms, or sat sleeping in their seats." The drama dragged on for days. To add to the confusion, Burr unaccountably refused to withdraw. Contemporaries thought his ambition had overcome his good sense.

The Election of 1800		
Candidate	Party	Electoral Vote
Jefferson	Republican	73
Burr	Republican	73
J. Adams	Federalist	65
C. Pinckney	Federalist	64

The logjam finally broke when leading Federalists decided that Jefferson, whatever his faults, would make a more responsible president than would the shifty Burr. Even Hamilton labeled Burr "the most dangerous man of the community." On the thirty-sixth ballot, Representative James A. Bayard of Delaware announced he no longer supported Burr. This decision, coupled with Burr's inaction, gave Jefferson the presidency, ten states to four.

The Twelfth Amendment, ratified in 1804, saved the American people from repeating this potentially dangerous turn of events. Henceforth, the electoral college cast separate ballots for president and vice president.

During the final days of his presidency, Adams appointed as many Federalists as possible to the federal bench. Jefferson protested the hasty manner in which these "midnight judges" were selected. One of them, John Marshall, became chief justice of the United States, a post he held with distinction for thirty-four years. But behind the last-minute flurry of activity lay bitterness and disappointment. Adams never forgave Hamilton. "No party," the Federalist president wrote, "that ever existed knew itself so little or so vainly overrated its own influence and popularity as ours. None ever understood so ill the causes of its own power, or so wantonly destroyed them." On the morning of Jefferson's inauguration, Adams slipped away from the capital—now located in Washington, D.C.—unnoticed and unappreciated.

Peaceful Transition

In the address that Adams missed, Jefferson attempted to quiet partisan fears. "We are all republicans; we are all federalists," the new president declared. By this statement he did not mean to suggest party differences were no longer important. Jefferson reminded his audience that whatever the politicians might say, the people shared a deep commitment to a federal Union based on republican ideals set forth during the American Revolution. Indeed, the president interpreted the election of 1800 as a revolutionary episode, a fulfillment of the principles of 1776.

Recent battles, of course, colored Jefferson's judgment. The contests of the 1790s had been hard fought; the outcome often in doubt. Jefferson looked back at this period as a confrontation between the "advocates of republican and those of kingly government," and he believed only the vigilance of his own party had saved the country from Federalist "liberticide."

The Federalists were thoroughly dispirited by the entire experience. In the end, it had not been Hamilton's foolish electoral schemes that destroyed the party's chances in 1800. Rather, the Federalists had lost touch with a majority of the American people. In office, Adams and Hamilton—whatever their own differences may have been—betrayed their doubts about popular sovereignty too often, and when it came time to marshal broad support, to mobilize public opinion in favor of the party of wealth and privilege, few responded. As Secretary of War Oliver Wolcott observed on hearing of Jefferson's victory, "Have our party shown that they possess the necessary skill and courage to deserve . . . to govern? What have they done? . . . They write *private* letters. To whom? To each other, but they do nothing to give a proper direction to the public mind."

From a broader historical perspective, the election of 1800 seems noteworthy for what did not occur. There were no riots in the streets, no attempted coup by military officers, no secession from the Union, nothing except the peaceful transfer of government from the leaders of one political party to those of the opposition. Americans had weathered the Alien and Sedition Acts, the meddling by predatory foreign powers in domestic affairs, the shrilly partisan rhetoric of hack journalists, and now at the start of a new century, they were impressed with their own achievement. As one woman who attended Jefferson's inauguration noted, "The changes of administration which in every government and in every age have most generally been epochs of

CHRONOLOGY

1787   Constitution of the United States signed (September)

1789   George Washington inaugurated (April) • Louis XVI of France calls meeting of the Estates General (May)

1790   Congress approves Hamilton's plan for funding and assumption (July)

1791   Bank of the United States is chartered (February) • Hamilton's *Report on Manufactures* rejected by Congress (December)

1793   France's revolutionary government announces a "war of all people against all kings" (February) • Genêt affair strains relations with France (April) • Washington issues Proclamation of Neutrality (April) • Spread of "Democratic" Clubs alarms Federalists • Jefferson resigns as secretary of state (December)

1794   Whiskey Rebellion put down by U.S. Army (July–November) • General Anthony Wayne defeats Indians at Battle of Fallen Timbers (August)

1795   Hamilton resigns as secretary of the treasury (January) • Jay's Treaty divides the nation (June) • Pinckney's Treaty with Spain is a welcome surprise (October)

1796   Washington publishes "Farewell Address" (September) • John Adams elected president (December)

1797   XYZ Affair poisons U.S. relations with France (October)

1798–1800   Quasi-War with France

1798   Congress passes the Alien and Sedition Acts (June and July) • Provisional army is formed • Virginia and Kentucky Resolutions protest the Alien and Sedition Acts (November and December)

1799   George Washington dies (December)

1800   Convention of Mortefontaine is signed with France, ending Quasi-War (September)

1801   House of Representatives elects Thomas Jefferson president (February)

confusion, villainy and bloodshed, in this our happy country take place without any species of distraction, or disorder."

Recommended Reading

The best general survey of political events is Stanley Elkins and Eric McKitrick, *The Age of Federalism: The Early American Republic* (1993). Forrest McDonald has produced two highly original portraits of major figures of this period: *The Presidency of George Washington* (1974) and *Alexander Hamilton* (1979). Merrill D. Peterson provides an encyclopedic account of Jefferson's political career in *Thomas Jefferson and the New Nation: A Biography* (1970). For a thoughtful reinterpretation of the ideological issues separating Hamilton from Jefferson, see Drew McCoy, *The Elusive Republic: The Political Economy in Jeffersonian America* (1980). Richard Hofstadter offers a valuable discussion of the development of political parties in this period in *The Idea of a Party System, 1780–1840* (1969).

Additional Bibliography

Some of the better biographies of Hamilton, Madison, and Jefferson include Dumas Malone's classic *Jefferson and the Rights of Man* (1951) and *Jefferson and the Ordeal of Liberty* (1962); Gerald Stourzh, *Alexander Hamilton and the Idea of Republican Government* (1970); Jacob Ernest Cooke, *Alexander Hamilton* (1982); and Jack N. Rakove, *James Madison and the Creation of the American Republic* (1990). For students doing research in this period or for people just curious about the powerful personalities that shaped the politics of the new nation, the published papers of George Washington, John Adams, Thomas Jefferson, Alexander Hamilton, John Jay, and James Madison provide invaluable insights.

Political ideologies of the 1790s are discussed in Lance Banning, *The Jeffersonian Persuasion: Evolution of Party Ideology* (1978); Richard Buel, Jr., *Securing the Revolution: Ideology in American Politics, 1789–1815* (1972); Joyce Appleby, *Capitalism and a New Social Order* (1984); and Robert E. Shalhope, *The Roots of Democracy: American Thought and Culture* (1990). Two good regional studies are Andrew Cayton, *Frontier Republic: Ideology and Politics in the Ohio Country, 1780–1825* (1986) and Alan Taylor, *Liberty Men and Great Proprietors* (1990).

Several books take a more cultural perspective on the period: Steven Watts, *The Republic Reborn: War and the Making of Liberal America, 1790–1820* (1987); and David Shi, *The Simple Life: Plain Living and High Thinking in American Culture* (1985).

For a discussion of Parson Weems as well as the changing public image of Washington throughout American history, see Mason Locke Weems, *The Life of Washington,* edited by Marcus Cunliffe (1962); Gary Wills, *Cincinnatus: George Washington and the Enlightenment* (1984); and Paul K. Longmore, *Invention of George Washington* (1989).

The problems associated with the development of political parties are examined in William N. Chambers, *Political Parties in a New Nation: The American Experience, 1776–1809* (1963); Noble E. Cunningham, Jr., *The Jeffersonian Republicans: The Formation of Party Organization, 1789–1801* (1957); and Alfred F. Young, *The Democratic Republicans of New York: The Origins 1763–1797* (1963). The relation between literature and society is the topic of three challenging books: Michael Warner, *Letters of the Republic: Publication and the Public Sphere* (1990); Emory Elliott, *Revolutionary Writers: Literature and Authority in the New Republic, 1725–1810* (1982); and Cathy N. Davidson, *Revolution and the Word: The Rise of the Novel in America* (1986).

Detailed treatments of the complex negotiations and treaty fights include Alexander De Conde, *Entangling Alliance: Politics and Diplomacy Under George Washington* (1958) and *The Quasi-War: Politics and Diplomacy of the Undeclared War with France 1797–1801* (1966); Gerald A. Combs, *The Jay Treaty: Political Battleground of the Founding Fathers* (1970); Albert H. Bowman, *The Struggle for Neutrality: Franco-American Diplomacy During the Federalist Era* (1974); and William Stinchcombe, *The XYZ Affair* (1960).

The attempts by the Federalists to restrict constitutional rights is masterfully explored in James Morton Smith, *Freedom's Fetters: The Alien and Sedition Laws and American Civil Liberties* (1956). Richard H. Kohn's *Eagle and Sword: The Federalists and the Creation of the Military Establishments in America, 1783–1803* (1975) describes the plans to form a Federalist army. The implications of using armed force against citizens are analyzed in Thomas P. Slaughter, *The Whiskey Rebellion: Frontier Epilogue to the American Revolution* (1986).

Jeffersonian Ascendancy

Theory and Practice of Government

*B*ritish visitors often expressed contempt for Jeffersonian society. Wherever they traveled in the young republic, they met ill-mannered people inspired with a ruling passion for liberty and equality. Charles William Janson, an Englishman who lived in the United States for thirteen years, recounted an exchange he found particularly unsettling that had occurred at the home of an American acquaintance. "On knocking at the door," he reported, "it was opened by a servant maid, whom I had never before seen." The woman's behavior astonished Janson. "The following is the dialogue, word for word, which took place on this occasion:—'Is your master at home?'—'I have no master.'—'Don't you live here?'—'I *stay* here.'—'And who are you then?'—'Why, I am Mr. ——— 's *help*. I'd have you know, *man,* that I am no *sarvant* [sic]; none but *negers* [sic] are *sarvants.*'"

Standing on his friend's doorstep, Janson encountered the authentic voice of Jeffersonian republicanism—self-confident, assertive, blatantly racist, and having no intention of being relegated to low social status. The maid who answered the door believed she was her employer's equal, perhaps not in wealth but surely in character. She may have even dreamed of someday owning a house staffed with "*help*." American society fostered such ambition. In the early nineteenth century, thousands of settlers poured across the Appalachian Mountains or moved to cities in search of opportunity. Thomas Jefferson and individuals who stood for public office under the banner of the Republican party spoke for these people.

The limits of the Jeffersonian vision were obvious even to contemporaries. The people who spoke most eloquently about equal opportunity often owned slaves. As early as the 1770s, the famed English essayist Samuel Johnson had chided Americans for their hypocrisy. "How is it," he asked the indignant rebels, "that we hear the loudest yelps for liberty from the drivers of Negroes?" Little had changed since the Revolution. African Americans, who represented one-fifth of the population of the United States, were totally excluded from the new opportunities opening up in the cities and the West. Indeed, the maid in the incident just described insisted—with

no apparent sense of inconsistency—that her position was superior to that of blacks, who were brought to lifelong servitude involuntarily.

It is not surprising that leaders of the Federalist party accused the Republicans, especially those who lived in the South, of disingenuousness, and in 1804, one Massachusetts Federalist sarcastically defined "Jeffersonian" as "an Indian word, signifying '*a great tobacco planter, who had herds of black slaves.*'" The race issue simply would not go away. Beneath the political maneuvering over the acquisition of the Louisiana Territory and the War of 1812 lay fundamental disagreement about the spread of slavery to the western territories.

In other areas, the Jeffersonians did not fulfill even their own high expectations. As members of an opposition party during the presidency of John Adams, they insisted on a strict interpretation of the Constitution, peaceful foreign relations, and a reduction of the role of the federal government in the lives of the average citizens. But following the election of 1800, Jefferson and his supporters discovered that unanticipated pressures, foreign and domestic, forced them to moderate these goals. Before he retired from public office, Jefferson interpreted the Constitution in a way that permitted the government to purchase the Louisiana Territory when the opportunity arose; he regulated the national economy with a rigor that would have made Alexander Hamilton blush, and he led the country to the brink of war. Some Americans praised the president's pragmatism; others felt betrayed. For a man who had played a leading role in the revolt against George III, it must have been shocking in 1807 to find himself labeled a "despot" in a popular New England newspaper. "Give ear no longer to the siren voice of democracy and Jeffersonian liberty," the editor shrieked. "It is a cursed delusion, adopted by traitors, and recommended by sycophants."

DEVELOPING REGIONAL IDENTITIES

During the early decades of the nineteenth century, the population of the United States experienced substantial growth. The 1810 census counted 7,240,000 Americans, a jump of almost two million in just ten years. Of this total, approximately 20 percent were blacks, the majority of whom lived in the South. The large population increase in the nation was the result primarily of natural reproduction, since during Jefferson's presidency few immigrants moved to the New World. The largest single group in this society was children, boys and girls who were born after Washington's administration and who came of age at a time when the nation's boundaries were rapidly expanding.

Even as Americans defended the rights of individual states, they were forming strong regional identifications. In commerce and politics, they perceived themselves as representatives of distinct subcultures—as Southerners, New Englanders, or Westerners. No doubt, the broadening geographic horizons reflected improved transportation links that enabled people to travel more easily within the various sections. But the growing regional mentality was also the product of defensiveness. While local writers celebrated New England's cultural distinctiveness, for example, they were clearly uneasy about the region's rejection of the democratic values that were sweeping the rest of the nation. Moreover, during this period people living south of the Potomac River began describing themselves as Southerners, not as citizens of the Chesapeake or the Carolinas as they had done in colonial times.

This shifting focus of attention resulted not only from an awareness of shared economic interests but also from a sensitivity to outside attacks on slavery. Several times during the first fifteen years of the nineteenth century, conspirators actually advocated secession, and while these harebrained schemes failed, they revealed the powerful sectional loyalties that undermined national unity.

Western Conquest

The most striking changes occurred in the West. Before the end of the American Revolution, only Indian traders and a few hardy settlers had ventured across the Appalachians. After 1790, however, a flood of people rushed west to stake out farms on the rich soil. Many settlers followed the so-called northern route across Pennsylvania or New York into the old Northwest Territory. Pittsburgh and Cincinnati, both strategically located on the Ohio River, became important commercial ports. In 1803, Ohio joined the Union, and territorial governments were formed

in Indiana (1800), Louisiana (1805), Michigan (1805), Illinois (1809), and Missouri (1812). Southerners poured into the new states of Kentucky (1792) and Tennessee (1796). Wherever they located, Westerners depended on water transportation. Because of the extraordinarily high cost of hauling goods over land, riverboats represented the only economical means of carrying agricultural products to distant markets. The Mississippi River was the crucial commercial link for the entire region, and Westerners did not feel secure so long as New Orleans, the southern gate to the Mississippi, remained under Spanish control.

Families who moved west attempted to transplant familiar eastern customs to the frontier. In some areas such as the Western Reserve, a narrow strip of land along Lake Erie in northern Ohio, the influence of New England remained strong. In general, however, a creative mixing of peoples of different backgrounds in a strange environment generated distinctive folkways. Westerners developed their own heroes like Mike Fink, the legendary keelboatman of the Mississippi River; Daniel Boone, the famed trapper and Indian fighter; and the eye-gouging "alligatormen" of Kentucky and Tennessee. Americans who crossed the mountains were ambitious and self-confident, excited by the challenge of almost unlimited geographic mobility. A French traveler observed in 1802 that throughout the region he visited there was not a single farm "where one cannot with confidence ask the owner from whence he had emigrated, or, according to the light manners of the Americans, 'What part of the world do you come from?'" These rootless people, he explained, "incline perpetually toward the most distant fringes of American settlement."

At the beginning of the nineteenth century, a substantial number of Native Americans lived in the region; the land belonged to them. The tragedy was that the Indians, many dependent on trade with the white people and ravaged by disease, lacked unity. Small groups of Native Americans, allegedly representing the interests of an entire tribe, sold off huge pieces of land, often for whiskey and trinkets.

Such fraudulent transactions disgusted the two Shawnee leaders, Tecumseh and his brother Tenskwatawa (known as the Prophet). Tecumseh rejected classification as a Shawnee and may have been the first native leader to identify himself self-

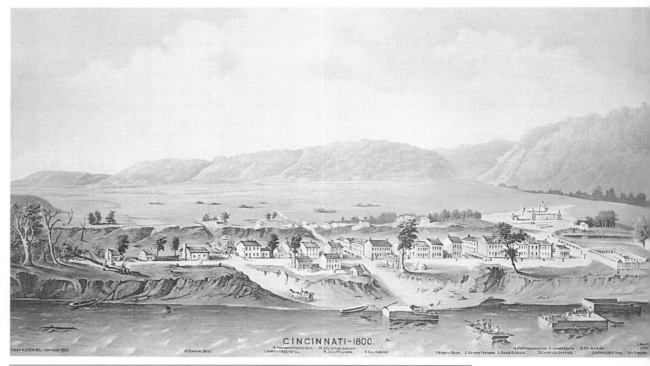

By 1800, Cincinnati—one of the new western cities—had become a busy trading center on the Ohio River with a post office, a Presbyterian church, and the Green Tree Hotel.

consciously as "Indian." These men desperately attempted to revitalize native cultures, and against overwhelming odds, they briefly persuaded Native Americans living in the Indiana Territory to avoid contact with whites, to resist alcohol, and most important, to hold on to their land. White intruders saw Tecumseh as a threat to progress, and during the War of 1812, they shattered the Indians' dream of cultural renaissance (see discussion on p. 252). The populous Creek nation, located in the modern states of Alabama and Mississippi, also resisted the settlers' advance, but its warriors were crushed by Andrew Jackson's Tennessee militia at the battle of Horseshoe Bend (March 1814).

Well-meaning Jeffersonians disclaimed any intention to destroy the Indians. The president talked of creating a vast reservation beyond the Mississippi River, just as the British had talked before the Revolution of a sanctuary beyond the Appalachian Mountains. He sent federal agents to "civilize" the Indians, to transform them into yeoman farmers. But even the most enlightened white thinkers of the day did not believe the Indians possessed cultures worth preserving. In

fact, in 1835 the Democratic national convention selected a vice presidential candidate whose major qualification for high office seemed to be that he killed Tecumseh.

Commercial Capitalism

Before 1820, the prosperity of the United States depended primarily on its agriculture and trade. Jeffersonian America was by no stretch of the imagination an industrial economy. The overwhelming majority of the population—84 percent in 1810—was directly involved in agriculture. Southerners concentrated on staple crops, tobacco, rice, and cotton, which they sold on the European market. In the North, people generally produced livestock and cereal crops. Regardless of location, however, the nation's farmers followed a back-breaking work routine that did not differ substantially from that of their parents and grandparents. Except for the cotton gin, important chemical and mechanical inventions did not appear in the fields for another generation. Probably the major innovation of this period was the agricultural fair, an idea first advanced in

1809 by a Massachusetts farmer, Elkanah Watson. In hopes of improving animal breeding, he offered prizes for the best livestock in the country. The experiment was a great success, for as Watson reported, "Many farmers, and even women, were excited by curiosity to attend this first novel, and humble exhibition."

The merchant marine represented an equally important element in America's preindustrial economy. At the turn of the century, ships flying the Stars and Stripes transported a large share of the world's trade. Merchants in Boston, New York, and Philadelphia received handsome profits from this commerce. Their ships provided essential links between European countries and their Caribbean colonies. France, for example, relied heavily on American vessels for its sugar. These lucrative transactions, coupled with the export of domestic staples, especially cotton, generated great fortunes. Between 1793 and 1807, the year that Jefferson imposed the embargo against Britain and France, American commerce enjoyed a more than 300 percent increase in the value of exports and in net earnings. Unfortunately, the boom did not last. The success of the "carrying trade" depended in large measure on friendly relations between the United States and the major European powers. When England and France began seizing American ships—as they both did after 1805—national prosperity suffered.

The cities of Jeffersonian America functioned chiefly as depots for international trade. Only about 7 percent of the nation's population lived in urban centers, and most of these people owed their livelihoods either directly or indirectly to the "carrying trade." Artisans maintained the fleet; skilled workers produced new ships; laborers loaded cargoes. And as some merchant families became wealthy, they demanded luxury items such as fine furniture. This specialized market drew a small, but highly visible, group of master craftspeople, and their extraordinarily beautiful and intricate pieces—New England tall clocks, for example—were perhaps the highest artistic achievement of the period.

Despite these accomplishments, American cities exercised only a marginal influence on the nation's vast hinterland. Because of the high cost of land transportation, urban merchants seldom purchased goods for export—flour, for example—from a distance of more than 150 miles. The

Tenskwatawa, known as the Prophet, provided spiritual leadership for the union of the native peoples he and his brother Tecumseh organized to resist white encroachment on Native American lands.

separation between rural and urban Americans was far more pronounced during Jefferson's presidency than it was after the development of canals and railroads a few decades later.

The booming carrying trade may actually have retarded the industrialization of the United States. The lure of large profits drew investment capital—a scarce resource in a developing society—into commerce. By contrast, manufacturing seemed too risky. One contemporary complained, "The brilliant prospects held out by commerce, caused our citizens to neglect the mechanical and manufacturing branches of industry."

He may have exaggerated slightly to make his point. Samuel Slater, an English-born designer of textile machinery, did establish several cotton spinning mills in New England, but before the 1820s these plants employed only a small number of workers. In fact, during this period far more cloth was produced in individual households than in factories. Another farsighted inventor, Robert Fulton, sailed the first American steamship up the Hudson River in 1807. In time, this marvelous innovation opened new markets for domestic

Although cotton was an important trade item in the early nineteenth century, technological advances in textile production were slow in taking hold. Some spinning mills such as the one pictured here were built in New England.

manufacturers, especially in the West. At the conclusion of the War of 1812, however, few people anticipated how greatly power generated by fossil fuel would eventually transform the character of the American economy.

Ordinary workers often felt threatened by the new machines. Skilled artisans who had spent years mastering trade and who took pride in producing an object that expressed their own personalities found the industrial workplace alienating (see "Machines Ingeniously Constructed," pp. 234–235). Moreover, they rightly feared that innovative technology designed to achieve greater efficiency might throw traditional craftspeople out of work or, if not that, transform independent entrepreneurs into dependent wage laborers. One New Yorker, for example, writing in the *Gazette and General Advertiser* in 1801 warned the tradespeople to be on guard against those who "will screw down the wages to the last thread . . . [and destroy] the independent spirit, so distinguished at present in our mechanics, and so useful in republics."

REPUBLICAN ASCENDANCY

The District of Columbia seemed an appropriate capital for a Republican president. At the time of Jefferson's first inauguration, Washington was still an isolated rural village, a far cry from the cosmopolitan centers of Philadelphia and New York. Jefferson fit comfortably into Washington society. He despised formal ceremony and sometimes shocked foreign dignitaries by meeting them in his slippers or a threadbare jacket. He spent as much time as his official duties allowed in reading and reflection. Isaac, one of Jefferson's slaves, recounted, "Old master had abundance of books: sometimes would have twenty of 'em down on the floor at once; read fust one then tother."

The president was a poor public speaker. He wisely refused to deliver annual addresses before Congress. In personal conversation, however, Jefferson exuded considerable charm. His dinner parties were major intellectual as well as social events, and in this forum, the president regaled politicians with his knowledge of literature, philosophy, and science. According to Margaret Bayard Smith, the wife of a congressman, the president "has more ease than grace—all the winning softness of politeness, without the artificial polish of courts."

Notwithstanding his commitment to the life of the mind, Jefferson was a politician to the core. He ran for the presidency in order to achieve specific goals: the reduction of the size and cost of federal government, the repeal of obnoxious Federalist legislation such as the Alien Acts, and the maintenance of international peace. To

The busy carrying trade conducted in the harbor surrounding lower Manhattan in New York is pictured in Cannon House and Wharf *(1792) by Jonathan Budington.*

accomplish his program, Jefferson realized he needed the full cooperation of congressional Republicans, some of whom were fiercely independent men. Over such figures Jefferson exercised political mastery. He established close ties with the leaders of both houses of Congress, and while he seldom announced his plans in public, he made certain his legislative lieutenants knew exactly what he desired. Contemporaries who described Jefferson as a weak president—and some Federalists did just that—did not read the scores of memoranda he sent to political friends or witness the informal meetings he held at the executive mansion with important Republicans. In two terms as president, Jefferson never had to veto a single act of Congress.

Jefferson carefully selected the members of his cabinet. During Washington's administration, he had witnessed—even provoked—severe infighting; as president, he nominated only those who enthusiastically supported his programs. James Madison, the leading figure at the Constitutional Convention, became secretary of state. For the Treasury, Jefferson chose Albert Gallatin, a Swiss-born financier who understood the complexities of the federal budget. "If I had the universe to choose from," the president announced,

"I could not change one of my associates to my better satisfaction."

Jeffersonian Reforms

A top priority of the new government was cutting the national debt. Throughout American history, presidents have advocated such reductions, but in the twentieth century, few have achieved them. Jefferson succeeded. He and Gallatin regarded a large federal deficit as dangerous to the health of republican institutions. In fact, both men associated debt with Alexander Hamilton's Federalist financial programs (see Chapter 7), measures they considered harmful to republicanism. Jefferson claimed that legislators elected by the current generation did not have the right to mortgage the future of unborn Americans.

Jefferson also wanted to diminish the activities of the federal government. He urged Congress to repeal all direct taxes, including the hated Whiskey Tax that had sparked an insurrection in 1794. Secretary Gallatin linked federal income to the carrying trade. He calculated that the entire cost of national government could be borne by customs receipts. As long as commerce flourished, revenues provided sufficient sums. When

"Machines Ingeniously Constructed"
Tensions of Technology in the Early Republic

On July 4, 1788, a parade sponsored by the Pennsylvania Society for the Encouragement of Manufactures and the Useful Arts sparked a mild workers' protest as its members marched in Philadelphia's Federal Procession. A 30-foot carriage at the head of the parade carried several operators who demonstrated the latest devices for making cloth: a carding machine that prepared cotton for spinning, a spinning jenny that produced eighty spindles of yarn at once, a large handloom, and a cloth-printing machine. Independent weavers and Society wage earners marched proudly behind the carriage. Handspinners, however, refused to parade with the jenny that threatened their livelihoods by replacing their wheels.

Eli Whitney's inventions (such as the cotton gin shown here in a cutaway) had a tremendous impact on the growth of manufacturing at the turn of the nineteenth century.

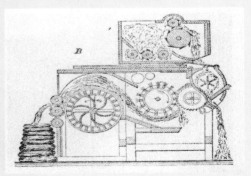

From the earliest days of independence, a tension between mechanization and craftsmanship marked the American quest for technological advance. Manufacturing enthusiasts such as Alexander Hamilton joined Enlightenment figures like Benjamin Rush to celebrate the advent of "machines ingeniously constructed." George Washington urged the First Congress to pass a patent law for the "effectual encouragement" of new inventions that could improve American productivity, reduce reliance on foreign manufactures, and thereby promote genuine independence.

Yet other Americans expressed grave misgivings about the new technology. Thomas Jefferson urged citizens of the new republic to preserve individual independence by letting "our work-shops remain in Europe." While few craftspeople followed his advice, most resisted mechanization and clung to the methods their fathers had taught them.

To be sure, the U. S. Patent Office recognized several important technological achievements among the 1,179 patents it issued between 1790 and 1810. Eli Whitney secured fame by modifying the design of earlier cotton gins so that his model could separate fibers from seeds and husks of the short staple cotton grown in the South. Samuel Slater made great strides in importing and improving English textile technology for northeastern merchant investors. The New York patrician Robert Livingston's financing enabled Robert Fulton's *Claremont* to succeed in 1807 where steamboats of the 1790s had failed, and the Hudson River provided the enterprising inventor a profitable route.

Despite such achievements, traditional methods of transportation and production comprised the bulk of the early republic's economic activity. Even textile manufacturers, the first to mechanize extensively, were still relying as late as the mid-nineteenth century on weavers using hand looms to make the finer grades of cloth. Managers sought to increase productivity by moving weaving from the household to the factory where they could impose stricter work discipline, hoping thus to gain as much from "the labor of thirty men" as they could from "one hundred loom weavers in families."

Such attempts met with resistance from weavers who, like other craftspeople, had traditionally enjoyed the freedom to set their own hours, work at their own pace, and interrupt their professional duties to tend to small farms or simply to socialize. Most master weavers refused to make cloth on factory-owned looms, and many less skilled journeymen worked in textile factories only long enough to acquire the means and experience needed to set up independent shops.

Despite the risk of antagonizing craftspeople, other fledgling American industries increased productivity by combining small technological advances with an imposition of industrial discipline and a reorganization of the manufacturing process through the division of labor. Connecticut clockmakers, for example, increased output by applying water power to conventional drills and lathes and by introducing templates, gauges, and pattern pieces for measuring parts. Craftspeople lacking such tools had built the entire works of every clock, custom shaping each piece to ensure proper operation. Now each worker could use the pattern piece to shape a single interchangeable part for later assembly. By 1820, the new division of labor was enabling the workers of a small factory to turn out more clocks in a month than a traditional clockmaker could produce in a lifetime.

Where imposition of labor discipline had undermined the craftsperson's traditional independence, specialization threatened to reduce his or her competence to a small portion of a manufacturing process that the worker had earlier performed in its entirety. The decrease in requisite skills often undermined wages by enabling employers to hire unskilled workers for simple tasks formerly carried out by craftspeople.

Gunsmiths at the federal armory in Harpers Ferry, Virginia, were keenly aware of this and carried on a running battle with the federal Ordinance Department to prevent mechanization of their trade. The secretary of war and his chief of ordinance, however, were anxious on their part to increase efficiency and to develop guns with interchangeable parts that could be repaired quickly on the field. True interchangeability eluded arms manufacturers until 1830, but the drive for uniformity and efficiency fostered technological advances that enabled Harpers Ferry manager James Stubblefield to employ extensive specialization. Where the armory had begun operations in the 1790s with a threefold division of labor, by 1816 Stubblefield

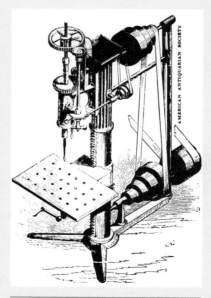

Drill presses like the one shown here were used in musket factories to make identical, interchangeable parts.

doubled the productivity of his work force by increasing to fifty-five the number of specialized tasks involved in manufacturing each gun.

While Stubblefield's gunsmiths acquiesced in the division of labor, they clung to many of their traditional craft prerogatives. Armorers resisted changes in labor discipline, retaining control of their own hours, working at their own pace, taking frequent holidays and drinking on the job. They welcomed machines such as a new barrel lathe, which improved work conditions by replacing a dangerous method. Yet older craftspeople, refusing to become "slaves of machines," continued practicing much that they had learned in Pennsylvania workshops. Metalworkers still hand-welded barrels long after other arms manufacturers were welding by machine. Woodworkers, scorning stock-turning lathes, meticulously hand-carved and custom-fitted each stock to its barrel until the 1830s. Yankee technicians sent to introduce machine-assisted processes at Harpers Ferry complained of poor treatment and sabotaged equipment.

Such behavior slowed but did not halt mechanization and the division of labor. By 1825, even Thomas Jefferson was boasting of "manufactures . . . now very nearly on a footing with those of England." Yet his early admonition—that Americans not sacrifice personal independence merely to achieve independence from foreign manufactured goods—voiced a deep-rooted ambivalence toward the new methods of production that has persisted into the modern age.

Georgetown and Federal City (which would later be renamed Washington, D.C.) are visible in this 1801 view of the Potomac. The Capitol moved here from Philadelphia in 1800, during John Adams's presidency.

international war closed foreign markets, however, the flow of funds dried up.

To help pay the debt inherited from the Adams administration, Jefferson ordered substantial cuts in the national budget. The president closed several American embassies in Europe. He also slashed military spending. In his first term, Jefferson reduced the size of the U.S. Army by 50 percent. This decision left only three thousand soldiers to guard the entire frontier. In addition, he retired a majority of the navy's warships. When New Englanders claimed these cuts left the country defenseless, Jefferson countered with a disarming argument. As ships of the U.S. Navy sailed the world's oceans, he claimed, they were liable to provoke hostilities, perhaps even war; hence by reducing the size of the fleet, he promoted peace.

More than budgetary considerations prompted Jefferson's military reductions. He was deeply suspicious of standing armies. In the event of foreign attack, he reasoned, the militia would rise in defense of the republic. No doubt, his experiences during the Revolution influenced his thinking on military affairs, for in 1776, an aroused populace had taken up arms against the British. To ensure that the citizen soldiers would receive professional leadership in battle, Jefferson created the Army Corps of Engineers and the military academy at West Point in 1802.

Political patronage was a great burden to the new president. Loyal Republicans throughout the United States had worked hard for Jefferson's victory, and as soon as he took office, they stormed the executive mansion seeking federal employment. While the president controlled several hundred jobs, he refused to dismiss all the Federalists. To be sure, he acted quickly to remove the so-called midnight appointees, highly partisan selections that Adams had made after learning of Jefferson's election. But to transform federal hiring into an undisciplined spoils system, especially at the highest levels of the federal bureaucracy, seemed to Jefferson to be shortsighted. Moderate Federalists might be converted to the Republican party, and in any case, there was a good chance they possessed the expertise needed to run the government. At the end of his first term, one-half of the people holding office were appointees of Washington and Adams.

Jefferson's political moderation helped hasten the demise of the Federalist party. This loose organization had nearly destroyed itself during the election of 1800 (see Chapter 7), and following Adams's defeat, prominent Federalist spokesmen such as Fisher Ames and John Jay withdrew from national affairs. They refused to adopt the popular forms of campaigning that the Republicans had developed so successfully during the late 1790s. The mere prospect of flattering the common people was odious enough to drive some Federalists into political retirement.

Many of them also sensed that national expansion worked against their interests. The creation of new states and congressional reapportionment inevitably seemed to increase the number of Republican representatives in Washington. By 1805, the Federalists retained only a few seats in New England and Delaware. "The power of the [Jefferson] Administration," confessed John Quincy Adams in 1802, "rests upon the support of a much stronger majority of the people throughout the Union than the former administrations ever possessed since the first establishment of the Constitution."

After 1804, a group of younger Federalists belatedly attempted to pump life into the dying party. They experimented with popular election techniques. In some states they tightened party organization, held nominating conventions, and campaigned energetically for office. These were essential reforms, but with the exception of a brief Federalist revival in the Northeast between 1807 and 1814, the results of these activities were disappointing. Even the younger Federalists felt it was demeaning to appeal for votes. The diehards like Timothy Pickering promoted wild secessionist schemes in New England, while the most promising moderates—John Quincy Adams, for example—joined the Republicans.

The Louisiana Purchase

When Jefferson first took office, he was confident that Louisiana as well as Florida would eventually become part of the United States. After all, Spain owned the territory, and Jefferson assumed he could persuade the rulers of that notoriously weak nation to sell their colonies. If that peaceful strategy failed, the president was prepared to threaten forceable occupation.

In May 1801, however, prospects for the easy or inevitable acquisition of Louisiana suddenly darkened. Jefferson learned that Spain had secretly transferred title to the entire region to France, its powerful northern neighbor. To make matters worse, the French leader Napoleon seemed intent on reestablishing an empire in North America. Even as Jefferson sought additional information concerning the details of the transfer, Napoleon was dispatching a large army to put down a rebellion in France's sugar-rich Caribbean colony, Haiti. From that island stronghold in the West Indies, French troops could occupy New Orleans and close the Mississippi River to American trade.

A sense of crisis enveloped Washington. Some congressmen urged Jefferson to prepare for war

President Jefferson recognized the strategic location of New Orleans and determined to buy it from the French. By 1803, when this view was painted, New Orleans was already a thriving port and an important outlet for products from the growing frontier.

UNDER MY WINGS EVERY THING PROSPERS

The Louisiana Purchase and the Route of Lewis and Clark

Not until Lewis and Clark had explored the far West did citizens of the United States realize just how much territory Jefferson had acquired through the Louisiana Purchase.

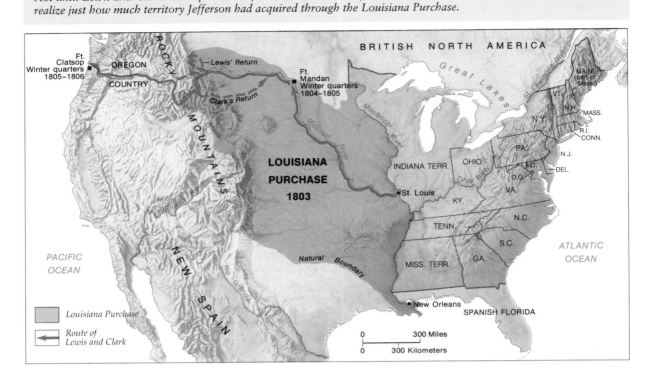

against France. Tensions increased when the Spanish officials who still governed New Orleans announced the closing of that port to American commerce (October 1802). Jefferson and his advisers assumed the Spanish had acted on orders from France, but despite this serious provocation, the president preferred negotiations to war. In January 1803, he asked James Monroe, a loyal Republican from Virginia, to join the American minister, Robert Livingston, in Paris. The president instructed the two men to explore the possibility of purchasing the city of New Orleans. Lest they underestimate the importance of their diplomatic mission, Jefferson reminded them, "There is on the globe one single spot, the possessor of which is our natural and habitual enemy. It is New Orleans." If Livingston and Monroe failed, Jefferson realized he would be forced to turn to Great Britain for military assistance. Dependence on that country seemed repellent, but he recognized that as soon as French troops moved into Louisiana, "we must marry ourselves to the British fleet and nation."

By the time Monroe joined Livingston in France, Napoleon had lost interest in establishing an American empire. The army he sent to Haiti succumbed to tropical diseases. By the end of 1802, over thirty thousand veteran troops had died. In a fit of disgust, Napoleon announced, "Damn sugar, damn coffee, damn colonies . . . I renounce Louisiana." The diplomats from the United States knew nothing of these developments. They were taken by complete surprise, therefore, when they learned that Talleyrand, the French minister for foreign relations, had offered to sell the entire Louisiana Territory in April 1803. For only $15 million, the Americans doubled the size of the United States. In fact, Livingston and Monroe were not certain how much land they had actually purchased. When they asked Talleyrand whether the deal included Florida, he responded ambiguously, "You have made a noble bargain for yourselves, and I suppose you will make the most of it." Even at that moment, Livingston realized the transaction would alter the course of American history.

"From this day," he wrote, "the United States take their place among the powers of first rank."

The American people responded enthusiastically to news of the Louisiana Purchase. The only criticism came from a few disgruntled Federalists in New England who thought the United States was already too large. Jefferson, of course, was immensely relieved. The nation had avoided war with France. Nevertheless, he worried that the treaty might be unconstitutional. The president pointed out that the Constitution did not specifically authorize the acquisition of vast new territories and the incorporation of thousands of foreign citizens. To escape this apparent legal dilemma, Jefferson proposed an amendment to the Constitution. Few persons, even his closest advisers, shared the president's scruples. Events in France soon forced Jefferson to adopt a more pragmatic course. When he heard that Napoleon had become impatient for his money, Jefferson rushed the treaty to a Senate eager to ratify the agreement, and nothing more was said about amending the Constitution.

Jefferson's fears about the incorporation of this new territory were not unwarranted. The area that eventually became the state of Louisiana (1812) contained many people of French and Spanish background who possessed no familiarity with representative institutions. Their laws had been autocratic; their local government corrupt. To allow such persons to elect a representative assembly struck the president as dangerous. He did not even know whether the population of Louisiana would remain loyal to the United States. Jefferson, therefore, recommended to Congress a transitional government consisting entirely of appointed officials. In March 1804, the Louisiana Government Bill narrowly passed the House of Representatives. Members of the president's own party attacked the plan. After all, it imposed taxes on the citizens of Louisiana without their consent. According to one outspoken Tennessee congressman, the bill "establishes a complete despotism." Most troubling perhaps was the fact that the legislation ran counter to Jefferson's well-known republican principles.

The Lewis and Clark Expedition

In the midst of the Louisiana controversy, Jefferson dispatched a secret message to Congress requesting $2,500 for the exploration of the Far West (January 1803). How closely this decision was connected to the Paris negotiations is not clear. Whatever the case may have been, the president asked his talented private secretary, Meriwether Lewis, to discover whether the Missouri River "may offer the most direct & practicable water communication across this continent for the purposes of commerce." The president also regarded the expedition as a wonderful opportunity to collect precise data about flora and fauna. He personally instructed Lewis in the latest techniques of scientific observation. While preparing for this great adventure, Lewis's second-in-command, William Clark, assumed such a prominent role that the effort became known as the Lewis and Clark Expedition. The exploring party set out from St. Louis in May 1804, and after barely surviving crossing the snow-covered Rocky Mountains, with their food supply running dangerously low, the Americans reached the Pacific Ocean in November 1805. The group returned safely the following September. The results of this expedition not only fulfilled Jefferson's scientific expectations, but also reaffirmed his faith in the future economic prosperity of the United States.

Conflict with the Barbary States

During this period, Jefferson dealt with another problem. For several decades, Morocco, Algiers, Tripoli, and Tunis—the Barbary States—had preyed on commercial shipping. Most European nations paid these pirates tribute, hoping thereby to protect merchants trading in the Mediterranean. In 1801, Jefferson, responding to Tripoli's increased demand for tribute, decided this extortion had become intolerable, and dispatched a small fleet to the Barbary Coast, where according to one commander, the Americans intended to negotiate "through the mouth of a cannon." Tripoli put up stiff resistance, however, and in one mismanaged engagement it captured the U. S. frigate *Philadelphia*. Ransoming the crew cost Jefferson's government another $60,000. An American land assault across the Libyan desert provided inspiration for the words of the Marine hymn—"to the shores of Tripoli"—but no smashing victory.

Despite a generally unimpressive American military record, a vigorous naval blockade

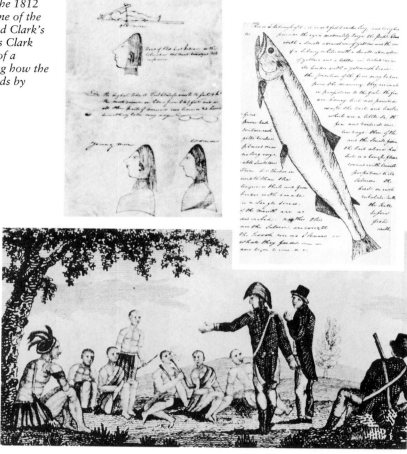

The large drawing at right is from the 1812 edition of Patrick Gass's Journal, *one of the first authentic accounts of Lewis and Clark's expedition. Samples of the drawings Clark made in his field diary include one of a salmon trout and a diagram showing how the Chinook flattened their infants' heads by binding them between two boards.*

brought hostilities to a conclusion. In 1805, the president signed a treaty formally ending the Barbary War. One diplomat crowed, "It must be mortifying to some of the neighboring European powers to see that the Barbary States have been taught their first lessons of humiliation from the Western World."

Jefferson concluded his first term on a wave of popularity. He had maintained the peace, reduced taxes, and expanded the boundaries of the United States. Not surprisingly, he overwhelmed his Federalist opponent in the presidential election of 1804. In the electoral college, Jefferson received 162 votes to Charles Cotesworth Pinckney's 14. Republicans controlled Congress. John Randolph, the most articulate member of the House of Representatives, exclaimed, "Never was there an administration more brilliant than that of Mr.

Jefferson up to this period. We were indeed in 'the full tide of successful experiment!'"

SOURCES OF POLITICAL DISSENSION

At the moment of Jefferson's greatest electoral victory, a perceptive person might have seen signs of serious division within the Republican party and within the country. The president's heavy-handed attempts to reform the federal courts stirred deep animosities. Republicans had begun sniping at other Republicans, and one leading member of the party, Aaron Burr, became involved in a bizarre plot to separate the West from the rest of the nation. Congressional debates over the future of the slave trade revealed the

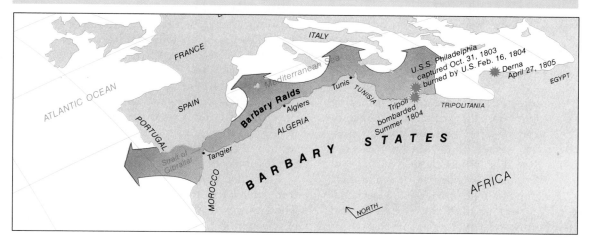

The Barbary States

In 1801, President Jefferson refused to continue paying the tribute that pirates of the Barbary States had received for decades.

existence of powerful sectional loyalties and profound disagreement on the issue.

Attack on the Judges

Jefferson's controversy with the federal bench commenced the moment he first became president. The Federalists, realizing they would soon lose control over the executive branch, had passed the Judiciary Act of 1801. This bill created several circuit courts and sixteen new judgeships. Through his "midnight" appointments, Adams had quickly filled these positions with stalwarts of the Federalist party. Such blatantly partisan behavior angered Jefferson. In the courts, he explained, the Federalists hoped to preserve their political influence, and "from that battery all the works of Republicanism are to be beaten down and erased." Even more infuriating was Adams's appointment of John Marshall as the new chief justice. This shrewd, largely self-educated Virginian of Federalist background, whose training in the law consisted of a series of lectures he attended at William and Mary College in 1780, was clearly a man who could hold his own against the new president.

In January 1802, Jefferson's congressional allies called for repeal of the Judiciary Act. In public debate they studiously avoided the obvious political issue. The new circuit courts should be closed not only because they were staffed by

Federalists but also, as they argued, because they were needlessly expensive. The judges did not hear enough cases to warrant continuance. The Federalists mounted an able defense. The Constitution, they observed, provided for the removal of federal judges only when they were found guilty of high crimes and misdemeanors. By repealing the Judiciary Act, the legislative branch would in effect be dismissing judges without a trial, a clear violation of their constitutional rights. This argument made little impression on the Republican party. In March, the House, following the Senate, voted for repeal.

While Congress debated the Judiciary Act, another battle erupted. One of Adams's "midnight" appointees, William Marbury, complained that the new administration would not give him his commission for the office of justice of the peace for the District of Columbia. He sought redress before the Supreme Court, demanding that the federal justices compel James Madison, the secretary of state, to deliver the necessary papers. When they learned that Marshall had agreed to hear this case, the Republicans were furious. Apparently the chief justice wanted to provoke a confrontation with the executive branch.

Marshall was too clever to jeopardize the independence of the Supreme Court over this relatively minor issue. In his celebrated *Marbury* v. *Madison* decision (February 1803), Marshall

The Election of 1804

Candidate	Party	Electoral Vote
Jefferson	Republican	162
Pinckney	Federalist	14

berated the secretary of state for withholding Marbury's commission. Nevertheless, he concluded that the Supreme Court did not possess jurisdiction over such matters. Poor Marbury was out of luck. The Republicans proclaimed victory. In fact, they were so pleased with the outcome, they failed to examine the logic of Marshall's decision. He had ruled that part of the earlier act of Congress, the one on which Marbury based his appeal, was unconstitutional. This was the first time the Supreme Court asserted its right to judge the constitutionality of congressional acts, and while contemporaries did not fully appreciate the significance of Marshall's doctrine, *Marbury* v. *Madison* later served as an important precedent for judicial review of federal statutes.

Neither Marbury's defeat nor repeal of the Judiciary Act placated extreme Republicans. They insisted that federal judges should be made more responsive to the will of the people. One solution, short of electing federal judges, was impeachment. This clumsy device provided the legislature with a way of removing particularly offensive individuals. Early in 1803, John Pickering, an incompetent judge from New Hampshire, presented the Republicans with a curious test case. This Federalist appointee suffered from alcoholism as well as insanity. While his outrageous behavior on the bench embarrassed everyone, Pickering had not committed any high crimes against the U. S. government. Ignoring such legal niceties, Jefferson's congressional allies pushed for impeachment. Although the Senate convicted Pickering (March 1804), many senators refused to compromise the letter of the Constitution and were conspicuously absent on the day of the final vote.

Jefferson was apparently so eager to purge the courts of Federalists that he failed to heed these warnings. By the spring of 1803, he had set his sights on a target far more important than John Pickering. In a Baltimore newspaper, the presi-

dent stumbled on the transcript of a speech allegedly delivered before a federal grand jury. The words seemed almost treasonous. The person responsible was Samuel Chase, a justice of the Supreme Court, who had frequently attacked Republican policies. Jefferson leapt at the chance to remove Chase from office. Indeed, the moment he learned of Chase's actions, the president wrote to a leading Republican congressman, asking, "Ought the seditious and official attack on the principles of our Constitution . . . go unpunished?" The congressman took the hint. In a matter of weeks, the Republican-controlled House of Representatives indicted Chase.

Even at this early stage of the impeachment, some members of Congress expressed uneasiness. The charges drawn up against the judge were purely political. There was no doubt the judge's speech had been indiscreet. He had told the Baltimore jurors that "our late reformers"—in other words, the Republicans—threatened "peace and order, freedom and property." But while Chase lacked good judgment, his attack on the Jefferson administration hardly seemed criminal. Nathaniel Macon, a powerful Republican congressman from North Carolina, wondered aloud, "Is error of opinion to be dreaded where enquiry is free?" This was the sort of question that Jefferson himself had asked the Federalists following passage of the Alien and Sedition Acts, but in 1804, Macon went unanswered. It was clear that if the Senate convicted Chase, every member of the Supreme Court, including Marshall, might also be dismissed.

Chase's trial before the U. S. Senate was one of the most dramatic events in American legal history. Aaron Burr, the vice president, organized the proceedings. For reasons known only to himself, Burr redecorated the Senate chamber so that it looked more like the British House of Lords than the meeting place of a republican legislature. In this luxurious setting, Chase and his lawyers conducted a masterful defense. By contrast, John Randolph, the congressman who served as chief prosecutor, behaved in an erratic manner, betraying repeatedly his ignorance of relevant points of law. While most Republican senators personally disliked the arrogant Chase, they refused to expand the constitutional definition of impeachable offenses to suit Randolph's argument, and on March 1, 1805, the Senate acquitted the jus-

REPORT

OF THE

T R I A L

OF THE

HON. SAMUEL CHASE,

ONE OF THE ASSOCIATE JUSTICES

OF THE

SUPREME COURT OF THE UNITED STATES,

BEFORE THE

HIGH COURT OF IMPEACHMENT,

COMPOSED OF THE

Senate of the United States,

FOR CHARGES EXHIBITED AGAINST HIM BY THE

HOUSE OF REPRESENTATIVES,

In the name of themselves, and of all the People of the United States,

FOR

HIGH CRIMES & MISDEMEANORS,

SUPPOSED TO HAVE BEEN BY HIM COMMITTED;

WITH THE NECESSARY

DOCUMENTS AND OFFICIAL PAPERS,

From his Impeachment to final Acquital.

TAKEN IN SHORT HAND,

BY CHARLES EVANS,

AND THE ARGUMENTS OF COUNSEL REVISED BY THEM

FROM HIS MANUSCRIPT.

BALTIMORE:

PRINTED FOR SAMUEL BUTLER AND GEORGE KEATINGE.

1805.

Presiding officer Aaron Burr ordered extra seating installed in the Senate chamber to accommodate the spectators who attended Justice Chase's impeachment trial.

tice of all charges. The experience apparently convinced Chase of the need for greater moderation. After returning to the federal bench, he refrained from attacking Republican policies. His Jeffersonian opponents also learned something important. American politicians did not like tampering with the Constitution in order to get rid of specific judges, even an imprudent one like Chase.

Politics of Desperation

The collapse of the Federalists on the national level encouraged dissension within the Republican party. Extremists in Congress insisted on monopolizing the president's ear, and when he listened to political moderates, they rebelled. The members of the most vociferous faction called themselves "the *good old* republicans"; the newspapers labeled them the "Tertium Quids," loosely translated as "nothings" or "No Accounts." During Jefferson's second term, the Quids argued that the president's policies, foreign and domestic, sacrificed virtue for pragmatism. Their chief spokesmen were two members from Virginia, John Randolph and John Taylor of Caroline (the name of his plantation), both of whom were convinced that Jefferson had betrayed the republican purity of the Founding Fathers. They both despised commercial capitalism. Taylor urged Americans to return to a simple agrarian way of life. Randolph's attacks were particularly shrill. He saved his sharpest barbs for Gallatin and Madison, Republican moderates who failed to appreciate the congressman's self-righteous posturing.

The Yazoo controversy raised the Quids from political obscurity. This complex legal battle began in 1795 when a thoroughly corrupt Georgia assembly sold 35 million acres of western land, known as the Yazoo claims, to private companies at bargain prices. It soon became apparent that every member of the legislature had been bribed, and in 1796, state lawmakers rescinded the entire agreement. Unfortunately, some land had already changed hands. When Jefferson became president, a specially appointed federal commission attempted to clean up the mess. It recommended that Congress set aside 5 million acres for buyers who had unwittingly purchased land from the discredited companies.

Randolph immediately cried foul. Such a compromise, however well meaning, condoned fraud. Republican virtue hung in the balance. For months the Quids harangued Congress about the Yazoo business, but in the end their impassioned oratory accomplished nothing. The Marshall Supreme Court upheld the rights of the original purchasers in *Fletcher* v. *Peck* (1810). The justices unanimously declared that legislative fraud did not impair private contracts and that the Georgia assembly of 1796 did not have authority to take away lands already sold to innocent buyers. This important case upheld the Supreme Court's authority to rule on the constitutionality of state laws.

The Burr Conspiracy

Vice President Aaron Burr created far more serious difficulties for the president. The two men had never been close. Burr's strange behavior during the election of 1800 (see Chapter 7) raised suspicions that he had conspired to deprive Jefferson of the presidency. Whatever the truth may have been, the vice president entered the new administration under a cloud. He played only a marginal role in shaping policy, a situation extremely frustrating for a person as ambitious as Burr.

In the spring of 1804, Burr decided to run for the governorship of New York. Although he was a Republican, he entered into political negotiations with High Federalists who were plotting the secession of New England and New York from the Union. In a particularly scurrilous contest—and New York politics were always abusive—Alexander Hamilton described Burr as ". . . a dangerous man . . . who ought not to be trusted with the reins of government" and urged Federalists in the state to vote for another candidate.

Whether Hamilton's appeals influenced the voters is not clear. Burr, however, blamed Hamilton for his subsequent defeat and challenged his tormentor to a duel. Even though Hamilton condemned this form of violence—his own son had recently been killed in a duel—he accepted Burr's "invitation." On July 11, 1804, at Weehawken, New Jersey, the vice president shot and killed the former secretary of the treasury. Both New York and New Jersey indicted Burr for murder. If he returned to either state, he would immediately be arrested. His political career lay in shambles.

In his final weeks as vice president, Burr hatched a scheme so audacious that the people with whom he dealt could not decide whether he was a genius or a madman. On a trip down the Ohio River in April 1805 after his term as vice president was over, he hinted broadly that he was planning a private military adventure against a Spanish colony, perhaps Mexico. Burr also suggested that he envisioned separating the western states and territories from the Union. The region certainly seemed ripe for secession. The citizens of New Orleans acted as if they wanted no part of the United States. Burr covered his tracks well.

Frustrated in his attempt to win national political power, Aaron Burr initiated a series of maneuvers that led eventually to his downfall.

No two contacts ever heard the same story. Wherever Burr traveled, he recruited adventurers; he mingled with the leading politicians of Kentucky, Ohio, and Tennessee. James Wilkinson, commander of the U. S. Army in the Mississippi Valley, accepted an important role in this vaguely defined conspiracy. The general was a thoroughly corrupt opportunist. Randolph described him as "the only man that I ever saw who was from bark to the very core a villain."

In the late summer of 1806, Burr put his ill-defined plan into action. A small group of volunteers constructed riverboats on a small island in the Ohio River owned by Harman Blennerhassett, an Irish immigrant who found Burr's charm irresistible. By the time this armed band set out to join Wilkinson's forces, however, the general had experienced a change of heart. He frantically dispatched letters to Jefferson denouncing Burr.

Wilkinson's betrayal destroyed any chance of success, and conspirators throughout the West rushed pell-mell to save their own skins. Facing certain defeat, Burr tried to escape to Spanish Florida. It was already too late. Federal authorities arrested Burr in February 1807 and took him to Richmond to stand trial for treason. The prospect of humiliating his old rival was hardly displeasing to the president. Even before a jury had been called, Jefferson announced publicly that Burr's guilt "is placed beyond all question."

Jefferson spoke prematurely. John Adams wisely observed, if Burr's "guilt is as clear as the Noon day Sun, the first Magistrate ought not to have pronounced it so before a Jury had tryed him." The trial judge was John Marshall, a strong Federalist not likely to do the Republican administration any favors. During the entire proceedings, Marshall insisted on a narrow constitutional definition of treason. He refused to hear testimony regarding Burr's supposed intentions. "Troops must be embodied," Marshall thundered, "men must be actually assembled." He demanded two witnesses to each overt act of treason.

Burr, of course, had been too clever to leave this sort of evidence. While Jefferson complained bitterly about the miscarriage of justice, the jurors declared on September 1, 1807, that the defendant was "not proved guilty by any evidence submitted to us." The public was outraged, and Burr prudently went into exile in Europe. The president threatened to introduce an amendment to the Constitution calling for the election of federal judges. Nothing came of his proposal. And Marshall, who behaved in an undeniably partisan manner, inadvertently helped protect the civil rights of all Americans. If the chief justice had allowed circumstantial evidence into the Richmond courtroom, if he had listened to rumor and hearsay, he would have made it much easier for later presidents to use trumped-up conspiracy charges to silence legitimate political opposition.

The Slave Trade

Slavery sparked angry debate at the Constitutional Convention of 1787 (see Chapter 6). If delegates from the northern states had refused to compromise on this issue, Southerners would not have supported the new government. The slave states demanded a great deal in return for cooperation. According to an agreement that determined the size of a state's congressional delegation, a slave counted as three-fifths of a free white male. This political formula meant that while blacks did not vote, they helped increase the number of southern representatives. The South in turn gave up very little, agreeing only that after 1808 Congress *might consider* banning the importation of slaves into the United States. Slaves even influenced the outcome of national elections. Had the three-fifths rule not been in effect in 1800, for example, Adams would surely have had the votes to defeat Jefferson in the electoral college.

In an annual message sent to Congress in December 1806, Jefferson urged the representatives to prepare legislation outlawing the slave trade. During the early months of 1807, congressmen debated various ways of ending this embarrassing commerce. It was clear that the issue cut across party lines. Northern representatives generally favored a strong bill; some even wanted to make smuggling slaves into the country a capital offense. But there was a serious problem. The northern congressmen could not figure out what to do with black people captured by the customs agents who would enforce the legislation. To sell these Africans would involve the federal government in slavery, which many Northerners found morally repugnant. Nor was there much sympathy for freeing them. Ignorant of the English language and lacking personal possessions, it seemed unlikely that these blacks could long survive free in the American South.

Southern congressmen responded with threats and ridicule. They explained to their northern colleagues that no one in the South regarded slavery as evil. It appeared naive, therefore, to expect local planters to enforce a ban on the slave trade or to inform federal agents when they spotted a smuggler. The notion that these culprits deserved capital punishment seemed viciously inappropriate. At one point in the debate, Peter Early, a congressman from Georgia, announced that the South wanted "no civil wars, no rebellions, no insurrections, no resistance to the authority of government." All he demanded, in fact, was to let the *states* regulate slavery. To this, a Republican congressman from western Pennsylvania retorted that Americans who hated slavery would not be "terrified by the threat of civil war."

The bill that Jefferson finally signed in March 1807 probably pleased no one. The law prohibited the importation of slaves into the United States after the new year. Whenever customs officials captured a smuggler, the slaves were turned over to state authorities and disposed of according to local custom. Southerners did not cooperate, and for many years African slaves continued to pour into southern ports. Even more blacks would have been imported had Great Britain not outlawed the slave trade in 1807. As part of their ban of the slave trade, ships of the Royal Navy captured American slave smugglers off the coast of Africa, and when anyone complained, the British explained that they were merely enforcing the laws of the United States.

FAILURE OF FOREIGN POLICY

During Jefferson's second term (1805–1809), the United States found itself in the midst of a world at war. A brief peace in Europe ended abruptly in 1803, and the two military giants of the age, France and Great Britain, fought for supremacy on land and sea. This was a kind of total war unknown in the eighteenth century. Napoleon's armies carried the ideology of the French Revolution across the Continent. The emperor—as Napoleon Bonaparte called himself after December 1804—transformed conquered nations into French satellites. Only Britain offered effective resistance. On October 21, 1805, Admiral Horatio Nelson destroyed the main French fleet at the battle of Trafalgar, demonstrating decisively the absolute supremacy of the Royal Navy. But only a few weeks later (December 2, 1805), Napoleon crushed Britain's allies, Austria and Russia, at the battle of Austerlitz and confirmed his clear superiority on land.

During the early stages of the war, the United States profited from European adversity. As "neutral carriers," American ships transported goods to any port in the world where they could find a buyer, and American merchants grew wealthy serving Britain and France. Since the Royal Navy did not allow direct trade between France and its colonies, American captains conducted "broken voyages." American vessels sailing out of French ports in the Caribbean would put in briefly in the United States, pay nominal

customs, and then leave for France. For several years, the British did little to halt this obvious subterfuge.

Napoleon's successes on the battlefield, however, quickly strained Britain's economic resources. In July 1805, a British admiralty court announced in the *Essex* decision that henceforth "broken voyages" were illegal. The Royal Navy began seizing American ships in record number. Moreover, as the war continued, the British stepped up the impressment of sailors on ships flying the U. S. flag. Estimates of the number of men impressed ranged as high as nine thousand.

Beginning in 1806, the British government issued a series of trade regulations known as "Orders in Council." These proclamations forbade neutral commerce with the Continent and threatened any ship that violated these orders with seizure. The declarations created what were in effect "paper blockades," for even the powerful British navy could not monitor the activities of every Continental port.

Napoleon responded to Britain's commercial regulations with his own "paper blockade," called the Continental System. In the Berlin Decree of November 1806 and the Milan Decree of December 1807, he announced the closing of all Continental ports to British trade. Since French armies occupied most of the territory between Spain and Germany, the decrees obviously cut the British out of a large market. The French emperor also declared that neutral vessels carrying British goods were liable to seizure. For the Americans there was no escape. They were caught between two conflicting systems. The British ordered American ships to stop off to pay duties and secure clearances in England on the way to the Continent; Napoleon was determined to seize any vessel that obeyed the British.

This unhappy turn of international events baffled Jefferson. He had assumed that civilized countries would respect neutral rights; justice obliged them to do so. Appeals to reason, however, made little impression on states at war. "As for France and England," the president growled, ". . . the one is a den of robbers, the other of pirates." In a desperate attempt to avoid hostilities for which the United States was ill prepared, Jefferson ordered James Monroe and William Pinckney to negotiate a commercial treaty with Great Britain. The document they signed on

December 31, 1806, said nothing about impressment, and an angry president refused to submit the treaty to the Senate for ratification.

The United States soon suffered an even greater humiliation. A ship of the Royal Navy, the *Leopard*, sailing off the coast of Virginia, commanded an American warship to submit to a search for deserters (June 22, 1807). When the captain of the *Chesapeake* refused to cooperate, the *Leopard* opened fire, killing three men and wounding eighteen. The attack clearly violated the sovereignty of the United States. Official protests received only a perfunctory apology from the British government, and the American people demanded revenge.

Despite the pressure of public opinion, however, Jefferson played for time. He recognized that the United States was unprepared for war against a powerful nation like Great Britain. The president worried that an expensive conflict with Great Britain would quickly undo the fiscal reforms of his first term. As Gallatin explained, in the event of war the United States "will be poorer, both as a nation and as a government, our debt and taxes will increase, and our progress in every respect be interrupted."

Embargo Divides the Nation

Jefferson found what he regarded as a satisfactory way to deal with European predators with a policy he called "peaceable coercion." If Britain and France refused to respect the rights of neutral carriers, then the United States would keep its ships at home. Not only would this action protect them from seizure, it would also deprive the European powers of much needed American goods, especially food. The president predicted that a total embargo of American commerce would soon force Britain and France to negotiate with the United States in good faith. "Our commerce is so valuable to them," he declared, "that they will be glad to purchase it when the only price we ask is to do us justice." Congress passed the Embargo Act by large majorities, and it became law on December 22, 1807.

"Peaceable coercion" turned into a Jeffersonian nightmare. The president apparently believed the American people would enthusiastically support the embargo. That was a naive assumption. Compliance required a series of enforcement acts that over fourteen months became increasingly harsh.

By the middle of 1808, Jefferson and Gallatin were involved in the regulation of the smallest details of American economic life. Indeed, in the words of one of Jefferson's biographers, the president assumed the role of "commissar of the nation's economy." The federal government supervised the coastal trade, lest a ship sailing between two states slip away to Europe or the West Indies. Overland trade with Canada was proscribed. When violations still occurred, Congress gave customs collectors the right to seize a vessel merely on suspicion of wrongdoing. A final desperate act, passed in January 1809, prohibited the loading of any U. S. vessel, regardless of size, without authorization from a customs officer who was supported by the army, navy, and local militia. Jefferson's eagerness to pursue a reasonable foreign policy blinded him to the fact that he and a Republican Congress would have had to establish a police state to make it work.

Northerners hated the embargo. Persons living near Lake Champlain in upper New York state simply ignored the regulations, and they roughed up collectors who interfered with the Canadian trade. The administration was determined to stop the smugglers. Jefferson urged the governor of

The Ograb me (embargo spelled backwards) snapping turtle, created by cartoonist Alexander Anderson, is shown here grabbing at an American tobacco smuggler who is breaking the embargo.

New York to call out the militia. "I think it so important," the president explained in August 1808, ". . . to crush these audacious proceedings, and to make the offenders feel the consequences of individuals daring to oppose a law by force, that no effort should be spared to compass the object." In a decision that Hamilton might have applauded, Jefferson dispatched federal troops—led by the conspiratorial General Wilkinson—to overawe the citizens of New York.

New Englanders regarded the embargo as lunacy. Merchants of the region were willing to take their chances on the high seas, but for reasons that few people understood, the president insisted that it was better to preserve ships from possible seizure than to make profits. Sailors and artisans were thrown out of work. The popular press maintained a constant howl of protest. One writer observed that embargo in reverse spelled "O grab me!" A poem published in July 1808 captured the growing frustration:

Our ships, all in motion,
Once whitened the ocean,
    They sail'd and returned with a cargo;
Now doom'd to decay
They have fallen a prey
    To Jefferson, worms, and Embargo.

Dolly Madison, in a portrait by Gilbert Stuart, 1804, hosted popular informal entertainments at the White House.

Not surprisingly, the Federalist party experienced a brief revival in New England, and a few extremists suggested the possibility of state assemblies nullifying federal law.

By 1809, the bankruptcy of Jefferson's foreign policy was obvious. The embargo never seriously damaged the British economy. In fact, British merchants rushed to take over the lucrative markets that the Americans had been forced to abandon. Napoleon liked the embargo, since it seemed to harm Great Britain more than it did France. Faced with growing popular opposition, the Republicans in Congress panicked. One newly elected representative declared that "peaceful coercion" was a "miserable and mischievous failure" and joined his colleagues in repealing the embargo a few days before James Madison's inauguration. Relations between the United States and the great European powers were much worse in 1809 than they had been in 1805. During his second term, the pressures of office weighed heavily on Jefferson, and after so many years of public service, he welcomed retirement to Monticello.

A New Administration Goes to War

As president, James Madison suffered from several personal and political handicaps. Although his intellectual abilities were great, he lacked the qualities necessary for effective leadership. In public gatherings, he impressed people as being "exceedingly modest," and one foreign visitor claimed that the new president ". . . always seems to grant that the one with whom he talks is his superior in mind and training." Critics argued that Madison's humility revealed a weak, vacillating character.

During the election of 1808, Randolph and the Quids tried unsuccessfully to persuade James

The Election of 1808		
Candidate	Party	Electoral Vote
Madison	Republican	122
Pinckney	Federalist	47

Monroe to challenge Madison's candidacy. Jefferson favored his old friend Madison. In the end, a caucus of Republican congressmen gave the official nod to Madison, the first time in American history that such a congressional group controlled a presidential nomination. The former secretary of state defeated his Federalist rival, Charles Cotesworth Pinckney, in the electoral college by a vote of 122 to 47, with New Yorker George Clinton receiving six ballots. The margin of victory was substantially lower than Jefferson's had been in 1804, a warning of political troubles ahead. The Federalists also made impressive gains in the House of Representatives, raising their delegation from 24 to 48.

The new president confronted the same foreign policy problems that had occupied his predecessor. Neither Britain nor France showed the slightest interest in respecting American neutral rights. Threats against either nation rang hollow so long as the United States failed to develop its military strength. Out of weakness, therefore, Madison was compelled to put the Non-Intercourse Act into effect. Congress passed this clumsy piece of legislation at the same time it repealed the embargo (March 1, 1809). The new bill authorized the resumption of trade between the United States and all nations of the world *except* Britain and France. Either of these countries could restore full commercial relations simply by promising to observe the rights of neutral carriers.

The British immediately took advantage of this offer. Their minister to the United States, David M. Erskine, informed Madison that the British government had modified its position on a number of sensitive commercial issues. The president was so encouraged by these talks that he publicly announced that trade with Great Britain could resume in June 1809. Unfortunately, Erskine had not conferred with his superiors on the details of these negotiations. George Canning, the British foreign secretary, rejected the agreement out of hand, and while an embarrassed Madison fumed in Washington, the Royal Navy seized the American ships that had already put to sea.

Canning's apparent betrayal led the artless Madison straight into a French trap. In May 1810, Congress passed Macon's Bill Number Two, an act sponsored by Nathanial Macon of North Carolina. In a complete reversal of strategy, this poorly drafted legislation reestablished trade with *both* England and France. It also contained a curious carrot-and-stick provision. As soon as either of these European states repealed restrictions upon neutral shipping, the U. S. government promised to halt all commerce with the other.

Napoleon spotted a rare opportunity. He informed the U. S. minister in Paris that France would no longer enforce the hated Berlin and Milan decrees. Again, Madison acted impulsively. Without waiting for further information from Paris, he announced that unless Britain repealed the Orders in Council by November, the United States would cut off commercial relations. Only later did the president learn that Napoleon had no intention of living up to his side of the bargain; his agents continued to seize American ships. Madison, who had been humiliated by the Erskine experience, decided to ignore the French provocations, to pretend the emperor was behaving in an honest manner. The British could not explain why the United States tolerated such obvious deception. No one in London would have suspected that the president really had no other options left.

Events unrelated to international commerce fueled anti-British sentiment in the newly conquered parts of the United States. Westerners believed—incorrectly as it turned out—that British agents operating out of Canada had persuaded Tecumseh's warriors to resist the spread of American settlement. According to the rumors that ran through the region, the British dreamed of monopolizing the fur trade. In any case, General William Henry Harrison, governor of the Indiana Territory, marched an army to the edge of a large Shawnee Village at the mouth of Tippecanoe Creek near the banks of the Wabash River. On the morning of November 7, 1811, the American troops routed the Indians at the battle of Tippecanoe. Harrison immediately became a

This colored lithograph from 1889 commemorates the Battle of Tippecanoe. While Tecumseh was away, Shawnee warriors engaged U. S. troops led by General William Henry Harrison. Although his troops lost more men than did the Shawnee, Harrison claimed the victory.

national hero, and several decades later the American people rewarded "Tippecanoe" by electing him president. This incident forced Tecumseh—a brilliant leader who was trying to restore the confidence and revitalize tribal cultures of the Indians of the Indiana Territory—to seek British military assistance in battling the Americans, something he probably would not have done had Harrison left him alone.

Fumbling Toward Conflict

In 1811, the anti-British mood of Congress intensified. A group of militant representatives, some of them elected to Congress for the first time in the election of 1810, announced they would no longer tolerate national humiliation. They called for action, for resistance to Great Britain, for any course that promised to achieve respect for the United States and security for its republican institutions. These aggressive nationalists, many of them elected in the South and West, have sometimes been labeled the "War Hawks." The group included Henry Clay, an earthy Kentucky congressman who served as Speaker of the House, and John C. Calhoun, a brilliant South Carolinian. These fiery orators spoke of honor and pride, as if foreign relations were a sort of duel between gentlemen. While the War Hawks were Republicans, they repudiated Jefferson's policy of peaceful coercion.

Madison surrendered to the "War Hawks." On June 1, 1812, he sent Congress a declaration of war against Great Britain. The timing of his action was peculiar. Over the preceding months, tensions between the two nations had relaxed. No new attacks had occurred. Indeed, at the very moment Madison called for war, the British government was suspending the Orders in Council, a conciliatory gesture that in all likelihood would have preserved the peace.

However inadequately Madison communicated his goals, he did seem to have had a plan. His major aim was to force the British to respect American maritime rights, especially in Caribbean waters. The president's problem was to figure out how a small, militarily weak nation like the United States could bring effective pressure on Great Britain. Madison's answer seemed to be Canada. This colony supplied Britain's Caribbean possessions with much needed foodstuffs. The president reasoned, therefore, that by threatening to seize Canada, the Americans might compel the British to make concessions on maritime issues. It was this logic that Secretary of State James Monroe had in mind when he explained in June 1812 that "it might be necessary to invade Canada, not as an object of the war but as a means to bring it to a satisfactory conclusion."

Congressional War Hawks, of course, may have had other goals in mind. Some expansionists were probably more concerned about conquering Canada than they were about the impressment of American seamen. For others, the whole affair may have truly been a matter of national pride. Andrew Jackson wrote, "*For what are we going to fight? . . . we are going to fight for the reestablishment of our national character, misunderstood and vilified at home and abroad.*" New

Englanders in whose commercial interests the war would supposedly be waged ridiculed such chauvinism. The vote in Congress was close, 79 to 49 in the House, 19 to 13 in the Senate. With this doubtful mandate, the country marched to war against the most powerful maritime nation in Europe. Division over the war question was reflected in the election of 1812. A faction of antiwar Republicans nominated De Witt Clinton of New York, who was endorsed by the Federalists. Nevertheless Madison, the Republican, won narrowly, gaining 128 electoral votes to Clinton's 89.

THE STRANGE WAR
OF 1812

Optimism ran high. The War Hawks apparently believed that even though the United States possessed only a small army and navy, it could easily sweep the British out of Canada. Such predictions flew in the face of political and military realities. Not only did the Republicans fail to appreciate how unprepared the country was for war, they also refused to mobilize needed resources. The House rejected proposals for direct taxes and authorized naval appropriations only with the greatest reluctance. Indeed, even as they planned for battle, the Republican members of Congress were haunted by the consequences of their political and economic convictions. They did not seem to understand that a weak, highly decentralized government—the one that Jeffersonians championed—was incapable of waging an expensive war against the world's greatest sea power.

New Englanders refused to cooperate with the war effort. In July 1812, one clergyman in Massachusetts urged the people of the region to "proclaim an honourable neutrality." Many persons did just that. New Englanders carried on a lucrative, though illegal, commerce with the enemy. When the U. S. Treasury appealed for loans to finance the war, wealthy northern merchants failed to respond. The British government apparently believed the New England states might negotiate a separate peace, and during the first year of war, the Royal Navy did not bother to blockade the major northern ports.

American military operations focused initially on the western forts. The results were discourag-

The Election of 1812

Candidate	Party	Electoral Vote
Madison	Republican	128
Clinton	Republican* (antiwar faction)	89

*Clinton was nominated by a convention of antiwar Republicans and endorsed by the Federalists.

ing. On August 16, 1812, Major General William Hull surrendered an entire army to a smaller British force at Detroit. Michilimackinac was lost. Poorly coordinated marches against the enemy at Niagara and Montreal achieved nothing. These experiences demonstrated that the militia, led by aging officers with little military aptitude, no matter how enthusiastic, was no match for well-trained European veterans. On the sea, the United States did much better. In August, Captain Isaac Hull's *Constitution* defeated the H. M. S. *Guerriere* in a fierce battle, and American privateers destroyed or captured a number of British merchantmen. These successes were somewhat deceptive, however. So long as Napoleon threatened the Continent, Great Britain could spare few warships for service in America. As soon as peace returned to Europe in the spring of 1814, Britain redeployed its fleet and easily blockaded the tiny U. S. Navy.

The campaigns of 1813 revealed that conquering Canada would be more difficult than the War Hawks ever imagined. Both sides in this war recognized that whoever controlled the Great Lakes controlled the West. On Lake Erie, the Americans won the race for naval superiority. On September 10, 1813, Oliver Hazard Perry destroyed a British fleet at Put-in-Bay, and in a much quoted letter written immediately after the battle, Perry exclaimed, "We have met the enemy; and they are ours." On October 5, General Harrison overran an army of British troops and Indian warriors at the battle of Thames River. During this engagement Tecumseh was killed. On the other fronts, however, the war went badly for the Americans. General Wilkinson suffered an embarrassing defeat near Montreal (battle of Chrysler's Farm,

The War of 1812
Major battles of the War of 1812 brought few lasting gains to either the British or the Americans.

November 11), and the British Navy held its own on Lake Ontario.

In 1814, the British took the offensive. Following their victory over Napoleon, British strategists planned to increase pressure on three separate American fronts: the Canadian frontier,

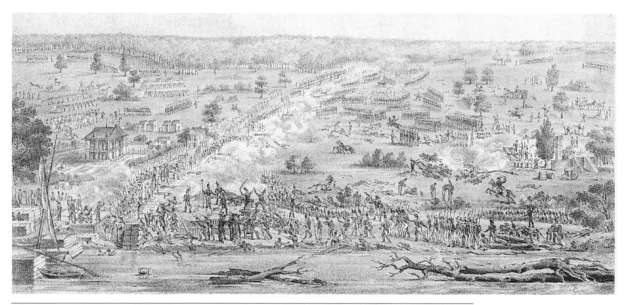

This scene of the battle of New Orleans, painted from sketches drawn during the engagement, shows the Americans standing their ground against the British frontal assault. The Americans suffered only light casualties in the battle, but more than two thousand British soldiers were killed or wounded.

Chesapeake coastal settlements, and New Orleans. Sir George Prevost, commander of the British forces in Canada, marched his army south into upper New York State. A hastily assembled American fleet led by Captain Thomas Macdonough turned back a British flotilla off Plattsburg on Lake Champlain (September 11, 1814). When Prevost learned of this setback, he retreated quickly into Canada. Although the Americans did not realize the full significance of this battle, the triumph accelerated peace negotiations, for after news of Plattsburg reached London, the British government concluded that major land operations along the Canadian border were futile.

Throughout the year, British warships harassed the Chesapeake coast. To their surprise, the British found the region almost totally undefended, and on August 24, 1814, in retaliation for the Americans' destruction of the capital of Upper Canada (York, Ontario), a small force of British marines burned the American capital, a victory more symbolic than strategic. Encouraged by their easy success and contemptuous of America's ragtag soldiers, the

British launched a full-scale attack on Baltimore (September 14). To everyone's surprise, the fort guarding the harbor held out against a heavy naval bombardment, and the British gave up the operation. The survival of Fort McHenry inspired Francis Scott Key to write "The Star-Spangled Banner."

The battle of New Orleans should never have occurred. The British landed a large assault force under General Edward Pakenham at precisely the same time that diplomats in Europe were preparing the final drafts of a peace treaty. The combatants, of course, knew nothing of these distant developments, and on January 8, 1815, Pakenham foolishly ordered a frontal attack against General Andrew Jackson's well-defended positions. In a short time, the entire British force had been destroyed. The Americans suffered only light casualties. The victory not only transformed Jackson into a national folk hero, it also provided the people of the United States with a much needed source of pride. Even in military terms, the battle was significant, for if the British had managed to occupy New Orleans, they would have been difficult to dislodge regardless of the specific provisions of the peace treaty.

Hartford Convention: The Demise of the Federalists

In the fall of 1814, a group of leading New England politicians, most of them moderate Federalists, gathered in Hartford to discuss relations between the people of their region and the federal government. The delegates were angry and hurt by the Madison administration's seeming insensitivity to the economic interests of the New England states. The embargo had soured New Englanders on Republican foreign policy, but the events of the War of 1812 added insult to injury. When British troops occupied the coastal villages of Maine, then part of Massachusetts, the president did nothing to drive out the enemy. Of course, the self-righteous complaints of convention organizers overlooked New England's tepid support for the war effort.

The men who met at Hartford on December 15 did not advocate secession from the Union. Although people living in other sections of the country cried treason, the convention delegates only recommended changes in the Constitution. They drafted a number of amendments that reflected the New Englanders' growing frustration. One proposal suggested that congressional representation be calculated on the basis of the number of white males living in a state. New England congressmen were tired of the three-fifths rule that gave southern slaveholders a disproportionally large voice in the House. The convention also wanted to limit each president to a single term in office, a reform that New Englanders hoped might end Virginia's monopoly of the executive mansion. And finally, the delegates insisted that a two-thirds majority was necessary before Congress could declare war, pass commercial regulations, or admit new states to the Union. The moderate Federalists of New England were confident these changes would protect their region from the tyranny of southern Republicans.

The convention dispatched its resolutions to Washington, but soon after an official delegation reached the federal capital, the situation became extremely awkward. Everyone was celebrating the victory of New Orleans and the announcement of peace. Republican leaders in Congress accused the hapless New Englanders of disloyalty, and people throughout the country were persuaded that a group of wild secessionists had attempted to destroy the Union. The Hartford Convention accelerated the final demise of the Federalist party.

Treaty of Ghent Ends the War

In August 1814, the United States dispatched a distinguished negotiating team to Ghent, a Belgian city where the Americans opened talks with their British counterparts. During the early weeks of discussion, the British made impossible demands. They insisted on territorial concessions from the United States, the right to navigate the Mississippi River, and the creation of a large Indian buffer state in the Northwest Territory. The Americans listened to this presentation, more or less politely, and then rejected the entire package. In turn, they lectured their British counterparts about maritime rights and impressment.

Fatigue finally broke the diplomatic deadlock. The British government realized no amount of military force could significantly alter the outcome of hostilities in the United States. When one important minister asked the Duke of Wellington, the hero of the Napoleonic Wars, for his assessment of British prospects following the battle of Plattsburg, the general replied, "I do not know where you could carry on . . . an operation which would be so injurious to the Americans as to force them to sue for peace."

Weary negotiators signed the Treaty of Ghent on Christmas Eve 1814. The document dealt with virtually none of the topics contained in Madison's original war message. Neither side surrendered territory; Great Britain refused even to discuss the topic of impressment. In fact, after more than two years of hostilities, the adversaries merely agreed to end the fighting, postponing the vexing issues of neutral rights until a later date. The Senate apparently concluded that stalemate was preferable to continued conflict and ratified the treaty 35 to 0.

Most Americans—except perhaps the diehard Federalists of New England—viewed the War of 1812 as an important success. Even though the country's military accomplishments had been unimpressive, the people of the United States had been swept up in a contagion of nationalism. The Hartford debacle served to discredit secessionist fantasies for several decades. Americans had waged a "second war of independence" and in the process transformed the Union into a symbol of national destiny. "The war," reflected Gallatin, had made Americans "feel and act more as a nation; and I hope that the permanency of the Union is thereby better secured." That nationalism had flourished in times of war was an irony that Gallatin's contemporaries did not fully appreciate. After the Treaty of Ghent, however, Americans came gradually to realize they had nothing further to fear from Europe, and in an era of peace, the process of sectional divergence began to quicken, threatening to destroy the republic that Jefferson and Madison had worked so hard to preserve.

REPUBLICAN LEGACY

During the 1820s, it became fashionable to visit retired presidents. These were not, of course, ordinary leaders. Jefferson, Adams, and Madison linked a generation of younger men and women to the heroic moments of the early republic. When they spoke about the Declaration of Independence or the Constitution of the United States, their opinions carried symbolic weight for a burgeoning society anxious about its political future.

A remarkable coincidence occurred on July 4, 1826, the fiftieth anniversary of the Declaration of Independence. On that day, Thomas Jefferson died at Monticello. His last words were "Is it the Fourth?" On the same day several hundred miles to the north, John Adams also passed his last day on earth. His mind was on his old friend and sometimes adversary, and during his final moments, Adams found comfort in the assurance that "Thomas Jefferson still survives."

James Madison lived on at his Virginia plantation, the last of the "founding fathers." Throughout a long and productive career, he had fought for republican values. He championed a Jeffersonian vision of a prosperous nation in which virtuous, independent citizens pursued their own economic interests. He tolerated no aristocratic pretensions. Leaders of a Jeffersonian persuasion—and during his last years that probably

included John Adams—brought forth a democratic, egalitarian society. Although they sometimes worried that the obsessive grubbing for wealth might destroy public virtue, they were justly proud of the republic they had helped to create.

But many visitors who journeyed to Madison's home at Montpelier before he died in 1836 were worried about another legacy of the founding generation. Why, they asked the aging president, had the early leaders of this nation allowed slavery to endure? How did African Americans fit into the republican scheme? Try as they would, neither Madison nor the politicians who claimed the Jeffersonian mantle could provide satisfactory answers. In an open, egalitarian society, there seemed no place for slaves, and a few months before Madison died, a visitor reported sadly, "With regard to slavery, he owned himself almost to be in despair."

Recommended Reading

The best written and in many ways the fullest account of the first two decades of the nineteenth century remains Henry Adams's classic *History of the United States During the Administration of Jefferson and Madison,* 9 vols. (1889–1891). A solid account of the period is Marshall Smelser, *The Democratic Republic, 1801–1815* (1968). Anyone interested in the problems that Jefferson faced as president should start with Merrill D. Peterson, *Thomas Jefferson and the New Nation: A Biography* (1970) and Forrest McDonald, *The Presidency of Thomas Jefferson* (1976). A brilliant exploration of the evolution of republican ideas after the retirement of Madison is Drew R. McCoy, *The Last of the Founding Fathers: James Madison and the Republican Legacy* (1989). Nathan O. Hatch provides an excellent account of popular religion in his *The Democratization of American Christianity* (1989). Laurel Ulrich has written a splendid study of a remarkable woman in the age of Jefferson: *A Midwife's Tale* (1990).

Additional Bibliography

The economic developments of this period are the subject of several valuable studies. The most provocative is Thomas C. Cochran, *Frontiers of Change: Early Industrialization of America* (1981). Also see Stuart Bruchey, *The Roots of American Economic Growth, 1607–1861* (1965); Douglass C. North, *The Economic Growth of the United States, 1790–1860* (1961); Winifred B. Rothenberg, *From Market-Places to a*

CHRONOLOGY

1800   Thomas Jefferson elected president

1801   Adams makes "midnight" appointments of federal judges

1802   Judiciary Act is repealed (March)

1803   Chief Justice John Marshall rules on *Marbury* v. *Madison* (February); sets precedent for judicial review • Louisiana Purchase concluded with France (May)

1803–1806   Lewis and Clark explore the Northwest

1804   Aaron Burr kills Alexander Hamilton in a duel (July) •Jefferson elected to second term

1805   Justice Samuel Chase acquitted by   Senate (March)

1807   Burr is tried for conspiracy (August-September) • Embargo Act passed (December)

1808   Slave trade is ended (January) • Madison elected president

1809   Embargo is repealed; Non-Intercourse Act passed (March)

1811   Harrison defeats Indians at Tippecanoe (November)

1812   Declaration of war against Great Britain (June) • Madison elected to second term, defeating De Witt Clinton of New York

1813   Perry destroys British fleet at battle of Put-in-Bay (September)

1814   Jackson crushes Creek Indians at Horseshoe Bend (March) • British marines burn Washington, D.C. (August) • Hartford Convention meets to recommend constitutional changes (December) • Treaty of Ghent ends War of 1812 (December)

1815   Jackson routs British at battle of New Orleans (January)

Merritt Roe Smith, *Harper's Ferry Armory and the New Technology: The Challenge of Change* (1977) and Brooke Hindle and Steven Lubar, *Engines of Change: The American Industrial Revolution, 1790–1860* (1986).

A thoughtful study of working class culture is Howard B. Rock, *Artisans of the New Republic: The Tradesmen of New York City in the Age of Jefferson* (1979). Charles W. Jansen's account of American society along with other contemporary documents can be found in Gordon S. Wood, ed., *The Rising Glory of America, 1760–1820* (1971).

A good introduction to the history of the western settlements is Reginald Horsman, *The Frontier in the Formative Years, 1783–1815* (1970). Also see John M. Faragher, *Daniel Boone, the Life and Legend of an American Pioneer* (1992); Andrew R. L. Cayton, *The Midwest and the Nation* (1990); Anthony F. C. Wallace, *Death and Rebirth of the Seneca* (1970); William McLoughlin, *Cherokees and Missionaries, 1789–1839* (1984); and B. Gilbert, *God Gave Us This Country: Takamthi and the First American Civil War* (1989).

The challenges confronting Jefferson as president are discussed in Dumas Malone, *Jefferson and His Time,* vols. 4 and 5 (1970, 1974). Several works focus more narrowly on political problems: Noble E. Cunningham, Jr., *The Process of Government Under Jefferson* (1978); and James Sterling Young, *The Washington Community, 1800–1828* (1966). See also Richard E. Ellis's masterful *The Jeffersonian Crisis: Courts and Politics in the Young Republic* (1971); Leonard W. Levy, *Emergence of a Free Press* (1985); and Morton J. Horowitz, *The Transformation of American Law, 1780–1860* (1977).

The Louisiana Purchase is the subject of Alexander DeConde, *The Affair of Louisiana* (1976). On the Lewis and Clark expedition, see James P. Ronda, *Lewis and Clark Among the Indians* (1984); and Donald Jackson, *Thomas Jefferson and the Stony Mountains: Exploring the West from Monticello* (1981).

Two Republicans who gave Jefferson so much trouble are discussed in Robert E. Shalhope, *John Taylor of Caroline: Pastoral Republican* (1980); and Robert Dawidoff, *The Education of John Randolph* (1979). For Burr's strange career, see Milton Lomask, *Aaron Burr,* vols. 1 and 2 (1979, 1982). Thoughtful explorations of the relation of slavery to politics are Donald L. Robinson, *Slavery in the Structure of American Politics, 1765–1820* (1971); and John C. Miller, *Wolf by the Ears: Thomas Jefferson and Slavery* (1991).

The country's foreign policy is analyzed in Bradford Perkins, *Prologue to War: England and the United States, 1805–1812* (1961); and Burton Spivak, *Jefferson's English Crisis: Commerce, Embargo, and*

Market Economy: The Transformation of Rural Massachusetts, 1750–1850 (1992).The problems of adjusting to new industrial technologies is addressed in

the Republican Revolution (1974). For Madison's presidency, see Irving Brant, *James Madison*, vols. 4–6 (1953–1961) as well as Ralph Ketcham, *James Madison: A Biography* (1971). A good account of the War of 1812 can be found in J. C. A. Stagg, *Mr. Madison's War: Politics, Diplomacy, and Warfare in the Early American Republic* (1983).

The problems facing the Federalist party are the subject of David Hackett Fischer, *The Revolution of American Conservatism* (1965); Linda Kerber, *Federalists in Dissent: Imagery and Ideology in Jeffersonian America* (1970); and James M. Banner, Jr., *To the Hartford Convention* (1970).

Nationalism and Nation-Building

When the Marquis de Lafayette revisited the United States in 1824, he marveled at how the country had changed in the more than forty years since he had served with George Washington. During his thirteen-month grand tour, the great French hero of the American Revolution traveled to all parts of the country. He was greeted by adoring crowds in places that had been unsettled or beyond the nation's borders four decades earlier. Besides covering the eastern seaboard, Lafayette went west to New Orleans, then up the Mississippi and the Ohio by steamboat. He thus sampled a new mode of transportation that was helping to bring the far-flung outposts and settlements of a much enlarged nation into regular contact with each other. Such travel was still hazardous. Lafayette had to be rescued from a sinking steamboat on the Ohio before he could complete his journey to Cincinnati, hub city of the newly settled trans-Appalachian West.

Everywhere Lafayette was greeted with patriotic oratory celebrating the liberty, prosperity, and progress of the new nation. Speaking before a joint session of both houses of Congress, the old hero responded in kind, telling his hosts exactly what they wanted to hear. He hailed "the immense improvements" and "admirable communications" that he had witnessed and declared himself deeply moved by "all the grandeur and prosperity of these happy United States, which . . . reflect on every part of the world the light of a far superior political civilization."

Americans had good reasons to make Lafayette's return the occasion for patriotic celebration and reaffirmation. Since the War of 1812, the nation had been free from serious foreign threats to its independence and way of life. It was growing rapidly in population, size, and wealth. Its republican form of government, which many had considered a risky experiment at the time of its origin, was apparently working well. James Monroe, the current president, had proclaimed in his first inaugural address that "the United States have flourished beyond example. Their citizens individually have been happy and the nation prosperous." Expansion "to the Great Lakes and beyond the sources of the great rivers which communicate through our whole interior," meant that "no country was ever happier with respect to

its domain." As for the government, it was so near to perfection that "in respect to it we have no essential improvement to make."

Beneath the optimism and self-confidence, however, lay undercurrents of doubt and anxiety about the future. The visit of the aged Lafayette signified the passing of the Founding Fathers. Less than a year after his departure, Jefferson and Adams, the last of the great Founders, would die within hours of each other on the fiftieth anniversary of the Declaration of Independence. Could their example of republican virtue and self-sacrifice be maintained in an increasingly prosperous and materialistic society? Many in fact believed public virtue had declined since the heroic age of the Revolution. And what about the place of black slavery in a "perfect" democratic republic? Lafayette himself noted with disappointment that the United States had not yet extended freedom to southern slaves.

But the peace following the War of 1812 did open the way for a great surge of nation-building. As new lands were acquired or opened up for settlement, hordes of pioneers often rushed in. Improvements in transportation soon gave many of them access to distant markets, and advances in the processing of raw materials led to the first stirrings of industrialization. Politicians looked for ways to encourage this process of growth and expansion, and an active judiciary handed down decisions that served to promote economic development and assert the priority of national over state and local interests. To guarantee the peace and security essential for internal progress, statesmen proclaimed a foreign policy designed to insulate America from external involvements. A new nation of great potential wealth and power was emerging.

EXPANSION AND MIGRATION

The peace concluded with Great Britain in 1815 allowed Americans to shift their attention from Europe and the Atlantic to the vast lands of North America. Although the British had withdrawn from the region north of the Ohio, they continued to lay claim to the Pacific Northwest. Spain still possessed Florida and much of the present-day American West. Between the Appalachians and the Mississippi, settlement had already begun in earnest, especially in the new states of Ohio, Kentucky, and Tennessee. In the lower Mississippi Valley, the former French colony of Louisiana had been admitted as a state in 1812, and a thriving settlement existed around Natchez in the Mississippi Territory. Elsewhere, however, the trans-Appalachian West was only sparsely settled by whites, and much good land remained in Indian hands. Diplomacy, military action (or at least the threat of it), and the westward movement of vast numbers of settlers were all needed before the continent would yield up its wealth.

Extending the Boundaries

The first goal of postwar expansionists was to obtain Florida from Spain. In the eyes of the Spanish, their possession extended along the Gulf Coast to the Mississippi. Between 1810 and 1812, however, the United States had annexed the area between the Mississippi and the Perdido rivers in what became Alabama, claiming it was part of the Louisiana Purchase. The remainder, known as East Florida, became a prime object of territorial ambition for President James Monroe and his energetic secretary of state, John Quincy Adams. Adams had a grand design for continental expansion that required nullifying or reducing Spanish claims west of the Mississippi as well as east of it; he eagerly awaited an opportunity to apply pressure for that purpose.

General Andrew Jackson provided such an opportunity. In 1816, U. S. troops first crossed into East Florida in pursuit of hostile Seminole Indians. This raid touched off a wider conflict, and after taking command in late 1817, Jackson went beyond his official orders and occupied East Florida in April and May of 1818. Except for Adams, all the members of Monroe's cabinet privately condemned this aggressive action; so did a report of the House of Representatives. But no disciplinary action was taken, mainly because public opinion rallied behind the hero of New Orleans.

In November 1818, Secretary Adams informed the Spanish government the United States had acted in self-defense and that further conflict would be avoided only if East Florida was ceded to the United States. The Madrid government, weakened by Latin American revolutions and the

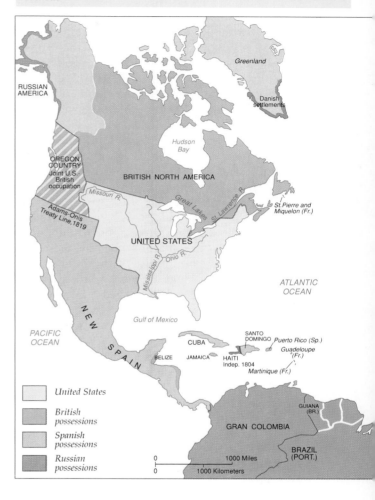

North America, 1819
Historian Henry Adams described the North American continent as "an uncovered ore bed." But it would take diplomacy, military action, and massive settlement before its riches could be mined.

breaking up of its empire, was in no position to resist American bullying. As part of the Adams-Onís Treaty, signed on February 22, 1819, Spain relinquished Florida to the United States. In return, the United States assumed $5 million of the financial claims of American citizens against Spain.

A strong believer that the United States had a continental destiny, Adams also used the confrontation over Florida to make Spain give up its claim to the Pacific Coast north of California, thus opening a path for future American expansion. Taking advantage of Spain's desire to keep its title to Texas—a portion of which the United States had previously claimed as part of the Louisiana Purchase—Adams induced the Spanish minister Luis de Onís to agree to the creation of a new boundary between American and Spanish territory that ran north of Texas but extended all the way to the Pacific. Great Britain and Russia still had competing claims to the Pacific Northwest, but the United States was now in a better position to acquire some frontage on a second ocean.

Interest in exploitation of the Far West continued to grow during the second and third decades of the nineteenth century. In 1811, a New York merchant, John Jacob Astor, founded the fur trading post of Astoria at the mouth of the Columbia River in the Oregon country. Astor's American Fur Company, which later sold its interests to a British firm, operated out of St. Louis in the 1820s and 1830s, with fur traders working their way up the Missouri to the northern Rockies and beyond. First they limited themselves to trading for furs with the Indians, but later, businesses such as the Rocky Mountain Fur Company, founded in 1822, relied on trappers or "mountain men" who went after game on their own and sold the furs to agents of the company at an annual "rendezvous."

These colorful characters, who included such legendary figures as Jedediah Smith, Jim Bridger, Kit Carson, and Jim Beckwourth (one of the many African Americans who contributed to the opening of the West as fur traders, scouts, or settlers), accomplished prodigious feats of survival under harsh natural conditions. Following Indian trails, they explored many parts of the Rockies and the Great Basin. They often married Indian women and assimilated much of the culture and technology of the Native Americans. Although they actually depleted the animal resources on which the Indians depended, these mountain men were portrayed in American literature and popular mythology as exemplars of a romantic ideal of lonely self-reliance in harmony with unspoiled nature.

Reports of military expeditions provided better documented information about the Far West than the tales of illiterate mountain men. The most notable of the postwar expeditions was mounted by Major Stephen S. Long in 1819–1820. Long surveyed parts of the Great Plains and Rocky Mountains, but his reports encouraged the mis-leading view that the plains beyond the Missouri were a "great American desert" unfit for cultivation or settlement. For the time being, the Far West remained beyond American dreams of agrarian expansion. The real focus of attention between 1815 and the 1840s was the nearer West, the rich agricultural lands between the Appalachians and the Mississippi that were being opened up for settlement.

Settlement to the Mississippi

To completely occupy and exploit the trans-Appalachian interior, white Americans generally believed they had to displace the Indian communities still inhabiting that region in 1815. In the Ohio Valley and the Northwest Territory, military defeat had already made Native Americans only a minor obstacle to the ambitions of white settlers and land speculators. When the British withdrew from the Old Northwest in 1815, they left their former Indian allies virtually defenseless before the tide of whites who rushed into the region. Consigned by treaty to reservations outside the main lines of white advance, most of the tribes were eventually forced west of the Mississippi. The last stand of the Indians in this region occurred in 1831–1832, when a faction of the confederated Sac and Fox Indians under Chief Black Hawk refused to abandon their lands east of the Mississippi. Federal troops and Illinois state militia pursued Black Hawk's band and drove it back to the river, where it was almost exterminated while attempting to cross to the western bank.

Uprooting once populous Indian communities of the Old Northwest was part of a national program for removing Indians of the eastern part of the country to an area beyond the Mississippi. Whites of the time viewed Indian society and culture as radically inferior to their own and doomed by the march of "progress." Furthermore, the fact that Indians based property rights to land on use rather than absolute ownership was regarded as an insuperable obstacle to economic development. As originally conceived by Thomas Jefferson, removal would have allowed those Indians who became "civilized" to remain behind on individually owned farms and qualify for American citizenship. This policy

Mountain men like Jim Beckwourth (far left) and Native Americans met at a rendezvous to trade their furs to company agents in exchange for food, ammunition, and other goods. Feasting, drinking, gambling, and sharing exploits were also part of the annual event. Moccasins (left) trimmed with trade beads and worn by both Native Americans and trappers, show how trade influenced both cultures. The painting Rendezvous (ca. 1837) is by Alfred Jacob Miller.

would reduce Indian holdings without appearing to violate American standards of justice. But during the Monroe era it became clear that white settlers wanted nothing less than the removal of all Indians, civilized or not. The issue was particularly pressing in the South. Greed combined with racism as land-grabbing state governments pressed for the total extinction of Indian land titles within their borders.

In the South, as in the Old Northwest, a series of treaties negotiated between 1815 and 1830 reduced tribal holdings and provided for the eventual removal of most Indians to the trans-Mississippi West. But some southern tribes held on tenaciously to their homelands. Many members of the five so-called civilized tribes—the Cherokees, Creeks, Seminoles, Choctaws, and Chickasaws—had become settled agriculturalists. It was no easy task to induce the civilized tribes to give up the substantial and relatively prosperous enclaves in Georgia, Florida, Alabama, and Mississippi that they still held in the 1820s. But the pressure continued to mount. The federal government used a combination of deception, bribery, and threats to induce land cessions. When federal action did not yield results fast enough to suit southern whites who coveted Indian land for mining, speculation, and cotton production, state governments began to act on their own, proclaiming state jurisdiction over lands still allotted by federal treaty to Indians within the state's borders. The stage was thus set for the forced removal of the five civilized tribes to Oklahoma during the administration of

View of the Great Treaty Held at Prairie du Chien (1825). *Representatives of eight Native American tribes met with government agents at Prairie du Chien, Wisconsin, in 1825 to define the boundaries of their respective land claims. The United States claimed the right to make "an amicable and final adjustment" of the claims. Within twenty-five years most of the tribes present at Prairie du Chien had ceded their land to the government.*

Andrew Jackson. (See Chapter 10 for a more complete discussion.)

While Indians were being hustled or driven beyond the Mississippi, settlers poured across the Appalachians and filled the agricultural heartland of the United States. In 1810, only about one-seventh of the American population lived beyond the Appalachians; by 1840, more than one-third did. During that period, Illinois grew from a territory with 12,282 inhabitants to a state with 476,183; Mississippi's population of about 40,000 increased tenfold; and Michigan grew from a remote frontier area with less than 5,000 people into a state with more than 200,000. Eight new western states were added to the Union during this period. Because of the government's removal policies, few settlers actually had to fight Indians. But they did have to obtain possession of land and derive a livelihood from it. For many, this was no easy task.

Much of the vast acreage opened up by the westward movement passed through the hands of land speculators before it reached farmers and planters. Government lands in the western territories were first surveyed and then sold at auction. After a financial panic in 1819 brought ruin to many who had purchased tracts on credit, the minimum price was lowered from $2.00 to $1.25 an acre, but full payment was required in cash.

Since few settlers could afford the necessary outlays, wealthy speculators continued to acquire most good land. In the prosperous period following the War of 1812, and again during the boom of the early to mid-1830s, speculation in public lands proceeded at a massive and feverish rate.

Eventually most of the land did find its way into the hands of actual cultivators. In some areas, squatters arrived before the official survey and formed claims associations that policed land auctions to prevent "outsiders" from bidding up the price and buying their farms out from under them. Squatters also agitated for formal "preemption" rights from the government. Between 1799 and 1830, Congress passed a number of special acts that granted squatters in specific areas the right to buy the land that they had already improved at the minimum price. In 1841, the right to farm on public lands with the assurance of a *future* preemption right was formally acknowledged by Congress.

Settlers who arrived after speculators had secured title had to deal with land barons. Fortunately for the settlers, most speculators operated on credit and needed a quick return on their investment. They did this by selling land at a profit to settlers who had some capital, renting out farms until tenants had earned enough to buy them, or loaning money to squatters until they

Indian Removal

Because so many Native Americans, uprooted from their lands in the East, died on the forced march to Oklahoma, the route they followed became known as the "Trail of Tears."

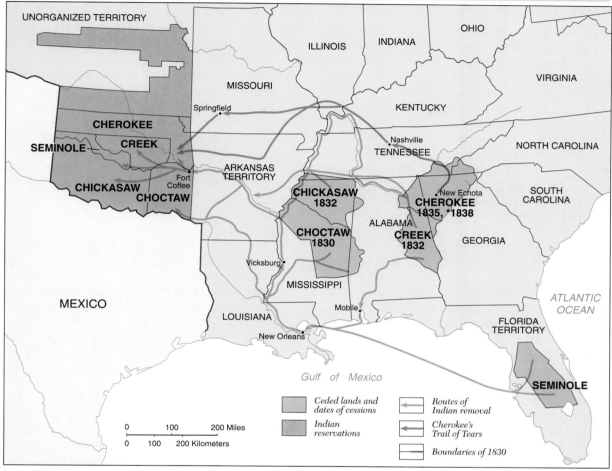

* Treaty signed in 1835 by minority factions forced removal in 1838.

were in a position to pay for the land in installments. As a result, the family farm or owner-operated plantation became the characteristic unit of western agriculture.

Since the pioneer family was likely to be saddled with debt of one kind or another, it was often forced from the beginning to do more than simply raise enough food to subsist. Farmers also had to produce something for market. Not surprisingly, most of the earliest settlement was along rivers that provided a natural means of transportation for flatboats loaded with corn, wheat, cotton, or cured meat. From more remote areas, farmers drove livestock over primitive trails and roads to eastern markets. To turn bulky

grain, especially corn, into a more easily transportable commodity, farmers in these remote regions often distilled it into whiskey. To meet the needs of farmers, local marketing centers quickly sprung up, usually at river junctions. Some of these grew into small cities virtually overnight. In the Midwest especially, the rapid rise of towns and cities serving surrounding farming areas greatly accelerated regional development.

Most frontier people welcomed the opportunity to sell some of their crops in order to acquire the consumer goods they could not produce for themselves, but many of them also valued self-sufficiency and tried to produce enough of the necessities of life to survive when cash crops failed or prices were low.

The People and Culture of the Frontier

Most of the settlers who populated the West were farmers from the seaboard states. Rising land prices and declining fertility of the soil in the older regions often motivated their migration. Few sought to escape or repudiate the "civilized" and settled way of life they had known in the East. Most moved in family units and tried to recreate their former ways of life as soon as possible. Women were often reluctant to migrate in the first place, and when they arrived in new areas, they strove valiantly to recapture the comfort and stability they had left behind.

New Englanders moving to western New York or northern Ohio, Indiana, and Illinois brought with them their churches, schools, notions of community uplift, Puritan ideals of hard work and self-denial, and respect for law and government. The Southerners who emigrated from Virginia, the Carolinas, and Georgia to Kentucky, Tennessee, Alabama, and Mississippi, as well as the lower part of the Midwest, were more devoted to the defense of personal or family honor and independence. They therefore tended to be less committed to the development of public authority and institutions.

In general, pioneers sought out the kind of terrain and soil with which they were already familiar. People from eastern uplands favored western hill country. Piedmont and tidewater farmers or planters usually made for the lower and flatter areas. The fertile prairies of the Midwest were avoided by early settlers, who preferred river bottoms or wooded sections because they were more like home and could be farmed by tried-and-true methods. Rather than being the bold and deliberate innovators pictured in American mythology, typical agricultural pioneers were deeply averse to changing their habits.

Yet adjustments were necessary simply to survive under frontier conditions. Initially, at least, a high degree of self-sufficiency was required on isolated homesteads. Men usually cut down trees, built cabins, broke the soil, and put in crops; besides cooking, keeping house, and caring for children, women made clothes, manufactured soap and other household necessities, churned butter, preserved food for the winter, and worked in the fields at busy times; at one time or another, women performed virtually all the tasks required by frontier farming. Crops had to be planted, harvested, and readied for home consumption with simple tools brought in wagons from the East—often little more than an axe, a plow, and a spinning wheel.

But this picture of frontier self-reliance is not the whole story. Most settlers in fact found it extremely difficult to accomplish all these tasks using only family labor. A more common practice was the sharing of work by a number of pioneer families. Except in parts of the South, where frontier planters had taken slaves with them, the normal way to get heavy labor done in newly settled regions was through mutual aid. Assembling the neighbors to raise a house, burn the woods, roll logs, harvest wheat, husk corn, pull flax, or make quilts helped turn collective work into a festive social occasion. Passing the jug was a normal feature of these "bees," and an uproarious good time often resulted from the various contests or competitions that speeded the work along. These communal events represented a creative response to the shortage of labor and at the same time provided a source for community solidarity. They probably tell us more about the "spirit of the frontier" than the conventional image of the pioneer as a lonely individualist.

While some settlers remained in one place and "grew up with the country," many others moved on after a relatively short time. The wandering of young Abraham Lincoln's family from Kentucky to Indiana and finally to Illinois between 1816 and 1830 was fairly typical. The physical mobility characteristic of nineteenth-century Americans in general was particularly pronounced in frontier regions. Improved land could be sold at a profit and the proceeds used to buy new acreage beyond the horizon where the soil was reportedly richer. The temptations of small-scale land speculation and the lure of new land further west induced a large proportion of new settlers to pull up stakes and move on after only a few years. Few early nineteenth-century American farmers developed the kind of attachment to the land that often characterized rural populations in other parts of the world.

Americans who remained in the East often ignored the frontier farmers and imagined the West as an untamed American wilderness inhabited by Indians and solitary white "pathfinders"

American Log House (1822), *a watercolor by John Hackett. The log cabin and split rail fence of the typical frontier farmstead were cut from trees on the land. Other trees were burnt to clear the land for farming.*

who turned their backs on civilization and learned to live in harmony with nature. James Fenimore Cooper, the first great American novelist, fostered this mythic view of the West in his stories of the frontier. He began in 1823 to publish a series of novels featuring Natty Bumppo, or "Leatherstocking"—a character who became the prototype for the western hero of popular fiction. Natty Bumppo was a hunter and scout who preferred the freedom of living in the forest to the constraints of civilization. Through Natty Bumppo, Cooper engendered a main theme of American romanticism—the superiority of a solitary life in the wilderness to the kind of settled existence among families, schools, and churches to which most real pioneers aspired.

TRANSPORTATION AND THE MARKET ECONOMY

It took more than the spread of settlements to bring prosperity to new areas and ensure that they would identify with older regions or with the country as a whole. Along the eastern seaboard, land transportation was so primitive that in 1813 it took seventy-five days for one wagon of goods drawn by four horses to make a trip of about 1,000 miles from Worcester, Massachusetts, to Charleston, South Carolina. Coastal shipping eased the problem to some extent in the East and stimulated the growth of port cities. Traveling west over the mountains, however, meant months on the trail.

After the War of 1812, political leaders realized that national security, economic progress, and political unity were all more or less dependent on a greatly improved transportation network. Accordingly, President Madison called for a federally supported program of "internal improvements" in 1815. Recommending such a program in Congress, Congressman John C. Calhoun described it as a great nationalizing enterprise: "Let us, then, bind the nation together with a perfect system of roads and canals. Let us conquer space." In ensuing decades, Calhoun's vision of a transportation revolution was realized to a considerable extent, although the direct role of the federal government proved to be less important than anticipated.

A Revolution in Transportation: Roads and Steamboats

Americans who wished to get from place to place rapidly and cheaply needed, as a bare minimum, new and improved roads. The first great federal transportation project was the building of the National Road between Cumberland, Maryland, on the Potomac, and Wheeling, Virginia, on the Ohio (1811–1818). This impressive toll road had a crushed stone surface and immense stone bridges. It was subsequently extended to reach Vandalia, Illinois, in 1838. Another thoroughfare to the west completed during this period was the Lancaster Turnpike connecting Philadelphia and Pittsburgh. Other major cities were also linked by

On the frontier, women were responsible for preparing all the food, even for sometimes butchering the animals (top). The sketch, by artist Lewis Miller, is from the early 1800s. Quilting bees (bottom), depicted in Quilting Bee, *a ca. 1855 work by an anonymous artist, offered men and women a rare opportunity to socialize.*

"turnpikes"—privately owned toll roads chartered by the states. By about 1825, southern New England, upstate New York, much of Pennsylvania, and northern New Jersey were crisscrossed by thousands of miles of turnpikes.

By themselves, however, the toll roads failed to meet the demand for low-cost transportation over long distances. For the most part, travelers benefited more than transporters of bulky freight. The latter usually found that total expenses—toll plus the cost and maintenance of heavy wagons and great teams of horses—were too high to guarantee a satisfactory profit from haulage. Hence traffic was less than anticipated, and the tolls collect-

ed were often insufficient to provide an adequate return to investors.

Even the National Road itself had severe limitations. Although it was able to carry a substantial east-west traffic of settler parties and wagonloads of manufactured goods, as well as a reverse flow of livestock being driven to market, it could not offer the low freight costs required for the long-distance hauling of wheat, flour, and the other bulky agricultural products of the Ohio valley. For these commodities, water transportation of some sort was required.

The United States's natural system of river transportation was one of the most significant reasons for its rapid economic development. The Ohio-Mississippi system in particular provided ready access to the rich agricultural areas of the interior and a natural outlet for their products. By 1815, large numbers of flatboats loaded with wheat, flour, and salt pork were making the 2,000-mile trip from Pittsburgh to New Orleans. On the lower Mississippi and its main tributaries, cotton could be loaded from plantation or town wharfs onto river craft or small seagoing vessels and carried to the same destination. Even after the coming of the steamboat, flatboats continued to carry a major share of the downriver trade.

The flatboat trade, however, was necessarily one way. A farmer from Ohio or Illinois, or someone hired to do the job, could float down to New Orleans easily enough, but there was generally no way to get back except by walking overland through rough country. Until the problem of upriver navigation was solved, the Ohio-Mississippi could not carry the manufactured goods that farmers desired in exchange for their crops.

Fortunately, a solution was readily at hand—the use of steam power. Late in the eighteenth century, a number of American inventors had experimented with steam-driven riverboats. John Fitch even exhibited an early model to delegates at the Constitutional Convention. But making a commercially successful craft required further refinement. In 1807, inventor Robert Fulton, backed by Robert R. Livingston—a New Yorker of great wealth and political prominence—demonstrated the full potential of the steamboat by successfully propelling the *Clermont* 150 miles up the Hudson River. The first steamboat launched in the West was the *New Orleans*, which made the long trip from Pittsburgh to New

Fairview Inn or Three Mile House, Frederick Road, Baltimore *(1889), a watercolor by*
Thomas Ruckle. On their way west to the Alleghenies, a party of settlers leads their Conestoga
wagons, loaded with freight, past the Fairview Inn on the National Road near Baltimore.
Heading east is a herd of cattle being driven to market.

Orleans in 1811–1812. Besides becoming a principal means of passenger travel on the inland waterways of the East, the river steamboat revolutionized western commerce. In 1815, the *Enterprise* made the first return trip from New Orleans to Pittsburgh. Within five years, sixty-nine steamboats with a total capacity of 13,890 tons were plying western waters.

Steam transport was a great boon for farmers and merchants. It reduced costs, increased the speed of moving goods and people, and allowed a two-way commerce on the Mississippi and Ohio. Eastern manufacturers and merchants now had a better way to reach interior markets than the old method of hauling everything over the Appalachians by road.

The steamboat quickly captured the American imagination. Great paddle wheelers became luxurious floating hotels, the natural habitats of gamblers, confidence men, and mysterious women. For the pleasure of passengers and onlookers, steamboats sometimes raced against each other, and their more skillful pilots became folk heroes. But the boats also had a lamentable safety record, frequently running aground, colliding, or blowing up. The most publicized disasters of antebellum

America were spectacular boiler explosions that claimed the lives of hundreds of passengers. As a result of such accidents, the federal government began in 1838 to attempt to regulate steamboats and monitor their construction and operation. This legislation, which failed to create an agency capable of enforcing minimum safety standards, stands as virtually the only federal effort in the pre–Civil War period to regulate domestic transportation.

The Canal Boom

A transportation system based solely on rivers and roads had one enormous gap—it did not provide an economical way to ship western farm produce directly east to ports engaged in transatlantic trade or to the growing urban market of the seaboard states. The solution offered by the politicians and merchants of the Middle Atlantic and midwestern states was to build a system of canals that linked seaboard cities directly to the Great Lakes, the Ohio, and ultimately the Mississippi.

The best natural location for a canal connect-

The Clermont on the Hudson *(probably 1830–1835) by Charles Pensee. Although some called his Clermont "Fulton's Folly," Robert Fulton immediately turned a profit from his fleet of steamboats, which reduced the cost and increased the speed of river transport.*

ing a river flowing into the Atlantic with one of the Great Lakes was between Albany and Buffalo, a relatively flat stretch of 364 miles. The potential value of such a project had long been recognized, but when it was actually approved by the New York legislature in 1817, it was justly hailed as an enterprise of breathtaking boldness. At that time, no more than about 100 miles of canal existed in the entire United States, and the longest single canal extended only 26 miles. Credit for the project belongs mainly to New York's vigorous and farsighted governor, De Witt Clinton. He persuaded the New York state legislature to underwrite the project by issuing bonds, and construction began in 1818. In less than two years, 75 miles were already finished, and the first tolls were being collected. In 1825, the entire canal was opened with great public acclaim and celebration.

At 364 miles long, 40 feet wide, 4 feet deep, and containing 84 locks, the Erie Canal was the most spectacular engineering achievement of the young republic. Furthermore, it was a great economic success. It reduced the cost of moving goods from Buffalo to Albany to one-twelfth the previous rate. It not only lowered the cost of western products in the East but caused an even sharper decline in the price of goods imported

from the East by Westerners. It also helped to make New York City the commercial capital of the nation.

The great success of the Erie Canal inspired other states to extend public credit for canal building. Between 1826 and 1834, Pennsylvania constructed an even longer and more elaborate canal, covering the 395 miles from Philadelphia to Pittsburgh and requiring twice as many locks as its New York competitor. But the Pennsylvania Main Line Canal did not do as well as the Erie, partly because of a bottleneck at the crest of the Alleghenies where an inclined-plane railroad had to haul canal boats over a high ridge. Ohio also embarked on an ambitious program of canal construction, completing an artificial waterway from the Ohio River to Cleveland on Lake Erie in 1833. Shorter canals were built in many other states connecting navigable rivers with sea or lake ports. The last of these was the Illinois and Michigan Canal, completed in 1848. It linked Chicago and the Great Lakes with the Illinois River and the Mississippi.

The canal boom ended when it became apparent in the 1830s and 1840s that most of these waterways were unprofitable. State credit had been overextended, and the panic and depression of the late 1830s and early 1840s forced retrenchment. Moreover, by this time railroads were beginning to compete successfully for the same traffic, and a new phase in the transportation revolution was beginning.

But canals should not be written off as economic failures that contributed little to the improvement of transportation. Some of them continued to be important arteries up to the time of the Civil War and well beyond. Furthermore, the "failure" of many of the canals was due solely to their inability to yield an adequate return on the money invested in them. Concerning one failing canal, a contemporary argued it "has been more useful to the public, than to the owners." Had the canals been thought of as providing a service rather than yielding a profit—in the manner, for example, of modern interstate highways—their vital contribution to the nation's economic development would have been better appreciated.

Emergence of a Market Economy

The desire to reduce the costs and increase the speed of shipping heavy freight over great distances laid the groundwork for a new economic system. Canals made it less expensive and more profitable for western farmers to ship wheat and flour to New York and Philadelphia and also gave manufacturers in the East ready access to an interior market. Steamboats reduced shipping costs on the Ohio and Mississippi, and put farmers in the enviable position of receiving more for their crops and paying less for the goods they needed to import. Hence improved transport increased farm income and stimulated commercial agriculture.

At the beginning of the nineteenth century, the typical farming household consumed most of what it produced and sold only a small surplus in nearby markets. Most manufactured articles were produced at home. Easier and cheaper access to distant markets caused a decisive change in this pattern. Between 1800 and 1840, agricultural output increased at an annual rate of approximately 3 percent a year, and a rapidly growing portion of this production consisted of commodities grown for sale rather than consumed at home. This rise in productivity was partly due to technological advances. Iron or steel plows proved better than wooden ones, the grain cradle displaced the scythe for harvesting, and better varieties or strains of crops, grasses, and livestock were introduced. But the availability of good land and the revolution in marketing were the most important spurs to profitable commercial farming. Good land made for high yields, at least for a time; and when excessive planting wore out the soil, a farmer could migrate to more fertile lands farther west. The existence or extension of transportation facilities made distant markets available and plugged farmers into a commercial network that provided credit and relieved them of the need to do their own selling.

Erie Canal Scene *(1884) by William R. Miller. Shallow-draft canal barges were used to transport goods on the four-foot deep Erie Canal. These barges were often towed by horses or mules from footpaths on the shore.*

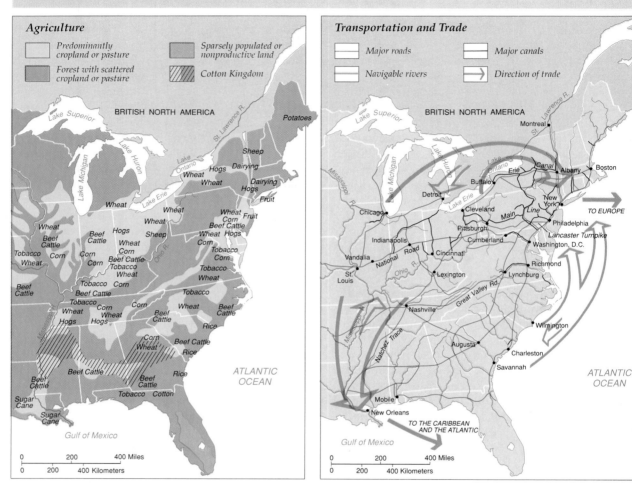

Agriculture, Transportation, and Trade

Connecting the new crop-producing regions of the frontier with eastern markets depended on improved transportation networks. Although the new toll roads helped in some of the inland areas, most trade was still carried out along the major waterways—the Mississippi River, the Great Lakes, and the Atlantic seaboard.

This emerging exchange network encouraged movement away from diversified farming and toward regional concentration on staple crops. Wheat was the main cash crop of the North, and the center of its cultivation moved westward as soil depletion, pests, and plant diseases lowered yields in older regions. In 1815, the heart of the wheat belt was New York and Pennsylvania. By 1839, Ohio was the leading producer and Indiana and Illinois were beginning to come into their own. On the rocky hillsides of New England, sheep raising was displacing the mixed farming of an earlier era. But the prime examples of successful staple production in this era were in the South. Tobacco continued to be a major cash crop of the upper South (despite declining fertility and a shift to wheat in some areas), rice was important in coastal South Carolina, and sugar was a staple of southern Louisiana. Cotton, however, was the "king" crop in the lower South as a whole. In the course of becoming the nation's principal export commodity, it brought wealth and prosperity to a belt of states running from South Carolina to Louisiana.

A number of factors made the Deep South the world's greatest producer of cotton. First was the great demand generated by the rise of textile manufacturing in England and, to a lesser extent, in New England. Second was the effect of the cotton gin on processing. Invented by Eli Whitney in

1793, this simple device cut the labor costs involved in cleaning short-staple cotton, thus making it an easily marketable commodity.

A third reason for the rise of cotton was the availability of good land in the Southwest. As yields fell in original areas of cultivation—mainly South Carolina and Georgia—the opening of the rich and fertile plantation areas or "black belts" of Alabama, Mississippi, and Louisiana shifted the Cotton Kingdom westward and resulted in a vast increase in total production. In 1816, New Orleans, the great marketing center for western crops, received 37,000 bales; in 1830, 428,000 arrived; and in 1840, the annual number had reached 923,000. Between 1817 and 1840, the amount of cotton produced in the South tripled from 461,000 bales to 1,350,000.

A fourth factor—the existence of slavery, which provided a flexible system of forced labor—permitted operations on a scale impossible for the family labor system of the agricultural North. Finally, the cotton economy benefited from the South's splendid natural transportation system—its great network of navigable rivers extending deep into the interior from the cotton ports of Charleston, Savannah, Mobile, and, of course, New Orleans. The South had less need than other agricultural regions for artificial internal improvements such as canals and good roads. Planters could simply establish themselves on or near a river and ship their crops to market via natural waterways.

Commerce and Banking

As regions specialized in growing commercial crops, a new system of marketing emerged. During the early stages in many areas, farmers did their marketing personally, even when it required long journeys overland or by flatboat. With the growth of country towns, local merchants took charge of the crops near their sources, bartering clothing and other manufactured goods for produce. These intermediaries shipped the farmers' crops to larger local markets like Pittsburgh, Cincinnati, and St. Louis. From there the commodities could be sent on to Philadelphia, New York, or New Orleans. Cotton growers in the South were more likely to deal directly with factors or agents in the port cities from which their crop was exported. But even in the South, commission merchants in such inland

towns as Macon, Atlanta, Montgomery, Shreveport, and Nashville became increasingly important as intermediaries.

Credit was a crucial element in the whole system. Farmers borrowed from local merchants, who received an advance of their own when they consigned crops to a commission house or factor. The commission agents relied on credit from merchants or manufacturers at the ultimate destination, which might be Liverpool or New York City. The intermediaries all charged fees and interest, but the net cost to the farmers was less than when they had handled their own marketing. The need for credit encouraged the growth of money and banking.

Before the revolutions in transportation and marketing, small-scale local economies could survive to a considerable extent on barter. Farmers could give grain to blacksmiths who could in turn exchange grain for iron from a local forge. But long-distance transactions involving credit and deferred payment required money and lots of it. Under the Constitution, the U. S. government is the only agency authorized to coin money and regulate its value. But in the early to mid-nineteenth century, the government printed no paper money and produced gold and silver coins in such small quantities that it utterly failed to meet the expanding economy's need for a circulating currency.

Private or state banking institutions filled the void by issuing bank notes, promises to redeem their paper in *specie*—gold or silver—on the bearer's demand. After Congress failed to recharter the Bank of the United States in 1811, existing state-chartered banks took up the slack. Many of them, however, lacked adequate reserves and were forced to suspend specie payments during the War of 1812. The demand for money and credit during the immediate postwar boom led to a vast increase in the number of state banks—from 88 to 208 within two years. The resulting flood of state bank notes caused this form of currency to depreciate well below its face value and threatened a runaway inflation. In an effort to stabilize the currency, Congress established a second Bank of the United States in 1816. The Bank was expected to serve as a check on the state banks by forcing them to resume specie payments.

But it did not perform this task well in its early years. In fact, its own free lending policies contributed to the overextension of credit that led to financial panic and depression in 1819. When the economy collapsed, as it would do again in 1837, many Americans questioned whether the new system of banking and credit was as desirable as it had seemed to be in times of prosperity. As a result, hostility to banks became a prominent feature of American politics.

Early Industrialism

The growth of a market economy also created new opportunities for industrialists. In 1815, most manufacturing in the United States was carried on in households, in the workshops of skilled artisans, or in small mills, which used waterpower to turn wheat into flour or timber into boards. The factory form of production, in which supervised workers tended or operated machines under one roof, was rare. It was found mainly in southern New England where a number of small spinning mills, relying heavily on the labor of women and children, accomplished one step in the manufacture of cotton textiles. But most spinning of thread, as well as the weaving, cutting, and sewing of cloth, was still done by women working at home.

As late as 1820, about two-thirds of the clothing worn by Americans was made entirely in households by female family members—wives and daughters. A growing proportion, however, was produced for market rather than direct home consumption. Under the "putting-out system" of manufacturing, merchant capitalists provided raw material to people in their own homes, picked up finished or semifinished products, paid the workers, and took charge of distribution. Items such as simple shoes and hats were also made under the putting-out system. Home manufacturing of this type was centered in the Northeast and often involved farm families making profitable use of their slack seasons. It did not usually present a direct challenge to the economic preeminence of agriculture, nor did it seriously disrupt the rural pattern of life.

The making of articles that required greater skill—such as high-quality shoes and boots, carriages or wagons, mill wheels, and barrels or kegs—was mostly carried on by artisans working in small shops in towns. But in the decades after 1815, shops expanded in size, masters tended to become entrepreneurs rather than working artisans, and journeymen often became wage earners rather than aspiring masters. At the same time, the growing market for low-priced goods led to a stress on speed, quantity, and standardization in the methods of production. Even where no substantial mechanization was involved, shops dealing in handmade goods for a local clientele tended to become small factories turning out cheaper items for a wider public.

A fully developed factory system emerged first in textile manufacturing. The establishment of the first cotton mills utilizing the power loom as well as spinning machinery—thus making it possible to turn fiber into cloth in a single factory—resulted from the efforts of a trio of Boston merchants: Francis Cabot Lowell, Nathan Appleton, and Patrick Tracy Jackson. On a visit to England in 1810 and 1811, Lowell succeeded in memorizing the closely guarded industrial secret of how a power loom was constructed. Returning to Boston, he joined with Appleton and Jackson to acquire a water site at Waltham and to obtain a corporate charter for textile manufacturing on a new and expanded scale.

Under the name of the Boston Manufacturing Company, the associates began their Waltham operation in 1813. Its phenomenal success led to the erection of a larger and even more profitable mill at Lowell in 1822 and another at Chicopee in 1823. Lowell became the great showplace for early American industrialization. Its large and seemingly contented work force of unmarried young women residing in supervised dormitories, its unprecedented scale of operation, its successful mechanization of almost every stage of the production process—all captured the American middle-class imagination in the 1820s and 1830s. (See "The Evolution of a 'Mill Girl,'" pp. 276–277.) Other mills using similar methods sprang up throughout New England, and the region became the first important manufacturing area in the United States.

The shift in textile manufacture from domestic to factory production shifted the locus of female economic activity. As the New England textile industry grew, the putting-out system rapidly declined. Between 1824 and 1832, household production of textiles dropped from 90 to 50 percent in most parts of New England. The shift to factory production changed the course of capitalistic activity in the region. Before the 1820s, New England merchants concentrated mainly on international trade, and Boston mercantile houses made great profits. A major source of capital was the lucrative China trade carried on by fast, well-built New England vessels. When the success of Waltham and Lowell became clear, many merchants shifted their capital away from oceanic trade and into manufacturing. This change had important political consequences, as leading politicians such as Daniel Webster no longer advocated a low tariff that favored importers over exporters. They now became leading proponents of a high duty rate designed to protect manufacturers from foreign competition.

The development of other "infant industries" of the postwar period was less dramatic and would not come to fruition until the 1840s and 1850s. Technology to improve the rolling and refining of iron was imported from England; it gradually encouraged a domestic iron industry centered in Pennsylvania. The use of interchangeable parts in the manufacture of small arms, pioneered by Eli Whitney and Simeon North, not only helped to modernize the weapons industry but also contributed more generally to the growth of new forms of mass production.

Although most manufacturing was centered in the Northeast, the West also experienced modest industrial progress. Increasing rapidly in number and size were facilities for processing farm products, such as grist mills, slaughterhouses, and tanneries. Distilleries in Kentucky and Ohio began during the 1820s to produce vast quantities of corn whiskey for a seemingly insatiable public.

One should not assume, however, that America had already experienced an industrial revolution by 1840. In that year, 63.4 percent of the nation's labor force was still employed in agriculture. Only 8.8 percent were directly involved in factory production (others were employed in trade, transportation, and the professions). Although this represented a significant shift since 1810 when the figures were 83.7 and 3.2 percent, the numbers would have to change a good deal more before it could be said that industrialization had really arrived. The revolution that did occur during these years was essentially one of distribution rather than production. The growth of a market economy of national scope—still based mainly on agriculture but involving a rapid flow of capital, commodities, and services from region to region—was the major economic development of this period. And it was one that had vast repercussions for all aspects of American life.

For those who benefited from it most directly, the market economy provided firm evidence of progress and improvement. But many of those who suffered from its periodic panics and depressions regretted the loss of the individual independence and security that had existed in a localized economy of small producers. These victims of boom and bust were receptive to politicians and reformers who attacked corporations and "the money power."

THE POLITICS OF NATION-BUILDING AFTER THE WAR OF 1812

Geographic expansion, economic growth, and the changes in American life that accompanied them were bound in the long run to generate political controversy. Farmers, merchants, manufacturers, and laborers were affected by the changes in different ways. So were Northerners, Southerners, and Westerners. Federal and state policies meant to encourage or control growth and expansion did not benefit all these groups or sections equally, and unavoidable conflicts of interest and ideology occurred.

But for a time these conflicts were not prominently reflected in the national political arena. During the period following the War of 1812, a single party dominated politics. Without a party system in place, politicians did not have to band together to offer the voters a choice of programs and ideologies. A myth of national harmony prevailed, culminating in the "Era of Good Feeling" during James Monroe's two terms as president. Behind this facade, individuals and groups fought for advantage, as always, but without the public accountability and need for broad popular approval that a party system would have required. As a result, popular interest in national politics fell.

The absence of party discipline and programs did not completely immobilize the federal government. Congress did manage to legislate on some matters of national concern. Although the president had little control over congressional action, he could still take important initiatives in foreign policy. The third branch of government—the Supreme Court—was in a position to make far-reaching decisions affecting the relationship between the federal government and the states. The common theme of the public policies that

The Evolution of a "Mill Girl"

Sarah Bagley became a "mill girl" when she left home in 1837 to work in a textile factory in Lowell, Massachusetts. In their own quiet way, Bagley and her fellow workers at the cotton mills, nearly all of them young women from rural families, initiated a struggle for women's rights that still continues.

The struggle was not planned. The mills of the 1820s and 1830s utilized amazing new machines for transforming raw cotton into textiles, but initially lacked people to run them. Cheap land and entrepreneurial opportunities had drained away the pool of potential male laborers; the early part of the nineteenth century was still a time when men would work under no boss unless absolutely necessary.

Women, with few other opportunities for earning a living, were perceived as a willing and docile labor alternative. As the *Lowell Offering* (a magazine published by the mills and written by the women operatives) said, women were to be "submissive, cheerful and contented" and to "remain entirely neutral in political and economic matters." Operating within that dominant ideology, the owners of the mills, understandably, considered women the perfect solution to the labor shortage.

Initially the mill owners were

right. Visitors and new operatives alike marvelled at the early mills' corporate paternalism. The assigned boardinghouses where most women operatives lived were clean and "morally pure," which is to say the supervisors prohibited any behavior that deviated from a church-defined norm. At night, until their 10 P.M. curfew, operatives read books, magazines, and newspapers made available by the mills and attended lyceum lectures and evening classes. Sunday church attendance was required.

Such paternalism inspired Sarah Bagley in her early mill-working days to write about

such topics as "The Pleasures of Factory Life," in which she spoke of her male bosses as kindly patriarchs: "We are placed in the care of overseers who feel under moral obligation to look after our interests."

Soon, however, she began with other operatives to write about an increasingly oppressive working environment: conditions had begun to contradict the image of benign paternalism. Her new ideas carried her into labor organization. In 1844, she helped found the Lowell Female Labor Reform Association (FLRA), making the New England Workingmen's Association the first labor organization in America to include both men and women. Quasi-spontaneous strikes in 1834 and 1836, called "turn-outs," had generally failed because they lacked an organizational backing, a clearly focused complaint, and the sympathetic intervention of outsiders. Women strikers had stressed their hereditary ties to the American Revolution and its yeomanry by calling themselves "daughters of freemen," but in most cases mill owners ("Tories in disguise") had simply fired all strikers. In the 1840s, owners slashed wages and instituted harsher work rules to maintain factory profits in the face of increased competition and a depressed economy.

Lowell, Massachusetts, ca. 1849.

The economic burden fell largely on the operatives. "It is *very* hard indeed," a two-year veteran of the mills wrote about her work, "and sometimes I think I shall not be able to endure it." Her pay, "about two dollars a week," must have been enough to keep her on the job, but it was less than one-third of the average weekly pay for a farmhand. "Perhaps you would like [to know] something about our regulations about going in and coming out of the mill," wrote a seventeen-year-old operative to her widowed father in 1845. "At half past 4 in the morning the bell rings for us to get up and at five for us to go into the mill. At seven we are called out to breakfast, are allowed half an hour between bells and the same at noon. . . . We have dinner at half past 12 and supper at seven."

Operatives worked a daily average of thirteen and a half hours: monotonous, noisy, and stifling labor. The mills were poorly ventilated, with fumes from whale-oil lamps permeating stale, lint-filled air that could not circulate because, in order to maintain the high humidity nec-essary to keep threads from breaking, overseers nailed all windows shut. Operatives often became ill, reportedly "going home to die" after working at the mills for a few years.

The FLRA responded by orga-nizing the Ten-Hour-Day move-ment—gathering petitions and lobbying for legislation limiting factory workers to ten-hour days. The FLRA objected not only to the length of working days but also to the absolute power of employers to set inhu-man work assignments for the operatives. In particular, the FLRA attempted to introduce legislation to regulate three employer innovations: the speedup, the stretch-out, and the bonus system. Speeding up referred simply to making each machine turn faster; stretching-out was the practice of gradually forcing operatives to control more machines at once; and the bonus system rewarded some overseers for getting more pro-duction from their operatives than other overseers could. Efforts at regulating those prac-tices through political channels failed. (Not until 1874 did Massa-chusetts pass a ten-hour-day law.)

Under its "Try again!" motto the FLRA then turned to a strat-egy of direct agitation against such innovations. In May 1846, when one mill tried to get its mill girls to operate four instead of three looms simultaneously, the *Voices of Industry* threatened to print the name of any woman who refused to sign a pledge against "stretching-out" to four looms. All the women in the plant signed the pledge, and management yielded.

Such victories on behalf of the women operatives were rare. By the end of the 1840s, immi-grants, many coming from con-ditions worse than those at the mills, replaced most native-born mill girls. Sarah Bagley dropped out of the labor movement in 1847 to live in a utopian com-munity, but would soon reap-pear as the nation's first female telegraph operator. (See discus-sion of utopian societies in Chapter 10.) Her refusal to stay "submissive, cheerful and con-tented" typified the reactions of many nineteenth-century women whose reality differed from the contemporary ideal of "true womanhood."

emerged between the War of 1812 and the Age of Jackson, which began in the late 1820s, was an awakening nationalism—a sense of American pride and purpose that reflected the expansionism and material progress of the period.

The Republicans in Power

By the end of the War of 1812, the Federalist party was no longer capable of winning a national election. The party of Jefferson, now known simply as the Republicans, was so completely dominant that it no longer had to distinguish itself from its opponents. Retreating from their original philosophy of states' rights and limited government, party leaders now openly embraced some of the programs of their former Federalist rivals—policies that seemed dictated by postwar conditions. In December 1815, President Madison proposed to Congress that it consider such measures as the reestablishment of a national bank, a mildly protective tariff for industry, and a program of federally financed internal improvements to bind "more closely together the various parts of our extended confederacy." Thus did Jefferson's successor endorse parts of a program enunciated by Alexander Hamilton.

In Congress, Henry Clay of Kentucky took the lead in advocating that the government take action to promote economic development. The keystone of what Clay called the "American system" was a high protective tariff to stimulate industrial growth and provide a "home market" for the farmers of the West, making the nation economically self-sufficient and free from a dangerous dependence on Europe.

In 1816, Congress took the first step toward establishing a neo-Federalist "American System." It enacted a tariff raising import duties an average of 25 percent. This legislation was deemed necessary because a flood of British manufactured goods was beginning to threaten the infant industries that had sprung up during the period when imports had been shut off by the embargo and the war. The tariff had substantial support in all parts of the country, both from a large majority of congressmen from New England and the Middle Atlantic states, and from a respectable minority of the southern delegation. In 1816, manufacturing was not so much a powerful interest as a patriotic concern. Many Americans

believed the preservation of political independence and victory in future wars required industrial independence for the nation. Furthermore, important sectors of the agricultural economy also felt the need of protection—especially hemp growers of Kentucky, sugar planters of Louisiana, and wool producers of New England.

Later the same year, Congress voted to establish the second Bank of the United States. The new national Bank had a twenty-year charter, an authorized capital of $35 million, and the right to establish branches throughout the country as needed. Organized much like the first bank, it was a mixed public-private institution, with the federal government owning one-fifth of its stock and appointing five of its twenty-five directors. The Bank served the government by providing a depository for its funds, an outlet for marketing its securities, and a source of redeemable bank notes that could be used to pay taxes or purchase public lands. The bank bill was opposed by state banking interests and strict constructionists, but the majority of Congress found it a necessary and proper means for promoting financial stability and meeting the constitutional responsibility of the federal government to raise money from taxation and loans.

Legislation dealing with internal improvements made less headway in Congress because it aroused stronger constitutional objections and invited disagreements among sectional groups over who would benefit from specific projects. Except for the National Road, the federal government undertook no major transportation projects during the Madison and Monroe administrations. Both presidents believed that internal improvements were desirable but that a constitutional amendment was required before federal monies could legally be used for the building of roads and canals within individual states. In 1817, just before leaving office, Madison vetoed a bill that would have distributed $1.5 million among the states for local transportation projects.

The following year, the House of Representatives held a lengthy debate on the question of whether Congress had the authority to make appropriations for internal improvements. Although a preliminary vote approved the principle, further discussion led to its rejection. In 1822, Monroe vetoed legislation for the repair and administration of the National Road, arguing

The Election of 1816

Candidate	Party	Electoral Vote
Monroe	Republican	183
King	Federalist	34

that even this modest activity was beyond the constitutional powers of Congress. Consequently, public aid for the building of roads and canals continued to come mainly from state and local governments.

Monroe as President

As did Jefferson before him, President Madison chose his own successor in 1816. James Monroe thus became the third successive Virginian to occupy the White House. He served two full terms and was virtually uncontested in his election to each. Monroe was well qualified in terms of experience, having been an officer in the Revolution, governor of Virginia, a special emissary to France, and secretary of state. He was reliable, dignified, and high principled, as well as stolid and unimaginative, lacking the intellectual depth and agility of his predecessors. He projected an image of a disinterested statesman in the tradition of the Founders. (He even dressed in the outmoded fashions of the revolutionary era.) Nominated, as was the custom of the time, by a caucus of Republicans in the House of Representatives, Monroe faced only nominal Federalist opposition in the general election.

Monroe avoided controversy in his effort to maintain the national harmony that was the keynote of his presidency. His first inaugural address expressed the complacency and optimism of the time, and he followed it up with a goodwill tour of the country, the first made by a president since Washington. A local newspaper was so impressed with Monroe's warm reception in Federalist Boston that it announced that party strife was a thing of the past and that an "era of good feelings" had begun.

A principal aim of Monroe's administrations was to encourage these good feelings. He hoped to accommodate or conciliate all the sectional or economic interests of the country and devote his main attention to the task of asserting American power and influence on the world stage.

The first challenge to Monroe's hopes for domestic peace and prosperity was the panic of 1819, which brought an abrupt end to the postwar boom. After a period of rampant inflation, easy credit, and massive land speculation, the Bank of the United States pricked the bubble by calling in loans and demanding the immediate redemption in specie of the state bank notes in its possession. This retrenchment brought a drastic downturn in the economy, as prices fell sharply, businesses failed, and land bought on credit was foreclosed upon.

In 1821, Congress responded weakly to the resulting depression by passing a relief act that eased the terms for paying debts owed on public land. Monroe himself had no program to relieve the economic crisis because he did not feel called on to exert this kind of leadership, and the voters did not seem to have expected it of him. The one-party system then prevailing left the president without the ability to work through an organized majority party in Congress; one-party rule had in fact degenerated into a chaotic "no-party" system. More easily than later presidents, Monroe could retain his popularity during a depression.

Monroe prized national harmony even more than economic prosperity. But during his first administration, a bitter controversy developed between the North and the South over the admission of Missouri to the Union. Once again Monroe remained above the battle and suffered little damage to his own prestige. It was left entirely to the legislative branch of the government to deal with the nation's most serious domestic political crisis between the War of 1812 and the late 1840s.

The Election of 1820

Candidate	Party	Electoral Vote
Monroe	Republican	231
J. Q. Adams -	No party designation	1

The Missouri Compromise

In 1817, the Missouri territorial assembly applied for statehood. Since there were two to three thousand slaves already in the territory and the petition made no provision for their emancipation or for curbing further introduction of slaves, it was clear that Missouri would enter the Union as a slave state unless Congress took special action. Missouri was slated to be the first state, other than Louisiana, to be carved out of the Louisiana Purchase, and resolution of the status of slavery there would have implications for the rest of the trans-Mississippi West.

When the question came before Congress in early 1819, sectional fears and anxieties bubbled to the surface. Many Northerners resented southern control of the presidency and the fact that the three-fifths clause of the Constitution, by which every five slaves were counted as three persons in figuring the state's population, gave the South's free population added weight in the House of Representatives and the electoral college. The South, on the other hand, feared for the future of what it regarded as a necessary balance of power between the sections. Up until 1819, a strict equality had been maintained by alternately admitting slave and free states; in that year, there were eleven of each. But northern population was growing more rapidly than southern, and the North had built up a decisive majority in the House of Representatives. Hence the South saw its equal vote in the Senate as essential for preservation of the balance.

In February 1819, Congressman James Tallmadge of New York introduced an amendment to the statehood bill banning further introduction of slaves into Missouri and requiring steps toward the gradual elimination of slavery within the state. After a heated debate, the House approved the Tallmadge amendment by a narrow margin. The Senate, however, voted it down. The issue remained unresolved until a new Congress convened in December 1819. In the great debate that ensued in the Senate, the Federalist leader Rufus King of New York argued that Congress was within its rights to require restriction of slavery before Missouri could become a state. Southern senators protested that denying Missouri's freedom in this matter was an attack on the principle of equality among the states and showed that Northerners were conspiring to upset the balance of power between the sections.

A separate statehood petition from the people of Maine, who were seeking to be separated from Massachusetts, suggested a way out of the impasse. In February 1820, the Senate voted to couple the admission of Missouri as a slave state with the admission of Maine as a free state. A further amendment was also passed prohibiting slavery in the rest of the Louisiana Purchase north of the southern border of Missouri, or above the latitude of 36°30', and allowing it below that line. The Senate's compromise then went to the House, where it was initially rejected. Through the adroit maneuvering of Henry Clay—who broke the proposal into three separate bills—it eventually won House approval. The measure authorizing Missouri to frame a constitution and apply for admission as a slave state passed by a razor-thin margin of 90 to 87 with most northern representatives remaining opposed.

A major sectional crisis had been resolved. But the Missouri affair had ominous overtones for the future of North-South relations. Thomas Jefferson described the controversy as "a fire bell in the night," threatening the peace of the Union. In 1821, he wrote prophetically of future dangers: "All, I fear, do not see the speck on our horizon which is to burst on us as a tornado, sooner or later. The line of division lately marked out between the different portions of our confederacy is such as will never, I fear, be obliterated." The congressional furor had shown that when the issue of slavery or its extension came directly before the people's representatives, regional loyalties took precedence over party or other considerations. An emotional rhetoric of morality and fundamental rights issued from both sides, and votes followed sectional lines much more closely than on any other issue. If the United States were to acquire any new territories in which the status of slavery had to be determined by Congress, renewed sectional strife would be unavoidable.

Postwar Nationalism and the Supreme Court

While the Monroe administration was proclaiming national harmony and congressional leaders were struggling to reconcile sectional differences, the third branch of government—the Supreme Court—was making a more substantial and enduring contribution to the growth of national-

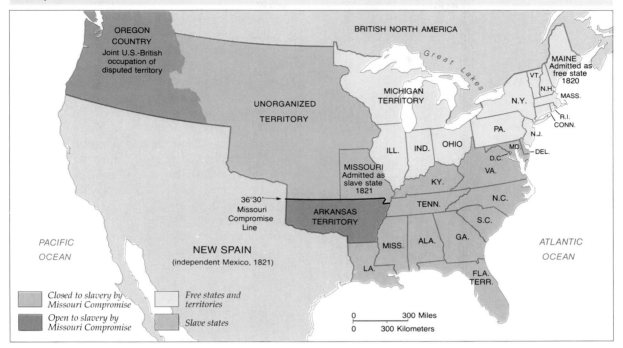

The Missouri Compromise, 1820–1821

The Missouri Compromise kept the balance of power in the Senate by admitting Missouri as a slave state and Maine as a free state. The agreement temporarily settled the argument over slavery in the territories.

ism and a strong federal government. Much of this achievement was due to the firm leadership and fine legal mind of the chief justice of the United States, John Marshall.

A Virginian, a Federalist, and the devoted disciple and biographer of George Washington, Marshall served as chief justice from 1801 to 1835, and during that entire period dominated the Court as no other chief justice has ever done. Discouraging dissent and seeking to hammer out a single opinion on almost every case that came before the Court, he played a role that has been compared to that of a symphony conductor who is also composer of the music and principal soloist.

As the author of most of the major opinions issued by the Supreme Court during its formative period, Marshall gave shape to the Constitution and clarified the crucial role of the Court in the American system of government. He placed the protection of individual liberty, especially the right to acquire property, above the attainment of political, social, or economic equality. Ultimately he was a nationalist, believing the strength, secu-

rity, and happiness of the American people depended mainly on economic growth and the creation of new wealth.

The role of the Supreme Court, in Marshall's view, was to interpret and enforce the Constitution in a way that encouraged economic development, especially against efforts of state legislatures to interfere with the constitutionally protected rights of individuals or combinations of individuals to acquire property through productive activity. To limit state action, he cited the contract clause of the Constitution that prohibited a state from passing a law "impairing the obligation of contracts." As the legal watchdog of an enterprising, capitalistic society, the Court could also approve a liberal grant of power for the federal government so the latter could fulfill its constitutional responsibility to promote the general welfare by encouraging economic growth and prosperity.

In a series of major decisions between 1819 and 1824, the Marshall Court enhanced judicial power and used the contract clause of the Constitution to limit the power of state legislatures.

Chief Justice John Marshall affirmed the Supreme Court's authority to overrule state laws and congressional legislation that it held to be in conflict with the Constitution. The portrait is by Chester Harding, ca. 1829.

It also strengthened the federal government by sanctioning a broad or loose construction of its constitutional powers and by clearly affirming its supremacy over the states.

In *Dartmouth College* v. *Woodward* (1819), the Court was asked to rule on whether the legislature of New Hampshire had the right to convert Dartmouth from a private college into a state university. Daniel Webster, arguing for the college and against the state, contended Dartmouth's original charter of 1769 was a valid and irrevocable contract. The Court accepted his argument. Speaking for all the justices, Marshall made the far-reaching determination that any charter granted by a state to a private corporation was fully protected by the contract clause.

In practical terms, the Court's ruling in the Dartmouth case meant that the kind of business enterprises then being incorporated by state governments—such as turnpike or canal companies and textile manufacturing firms—could hold on indefinitely to any privileges or favors that had been granted in their original charters. The deci-

sion therefore increased the power and independence of business corporations by weakening the ability of the states to regulate them or withdraw their privileges. This ruling helped foster the growth of the modern corporation as a profit-making enterprise with only limited public responsibilities.

About a month after the Dartmouth ruling, in March 1819, the Marshall Court handed down its most important decision. The case of *McCulloch* v. *Maryland* arose because the state of Maryland had levied a tax on the Baltimore branch of the Bank of the United States. The unanimous opinion of the Court, delivered by Marshall, was that the Maryland tax was unconstitutional. The two main issues were whether Congress had the right to establish a national bank and whether a state had the power to tax or regulate an agency or institution created by Congress.

In response to the first question, Marshall set forth his doctrine of "implied powers." Conceding that no specific authorization to charter a bank could be found in the Constitution, the chief justice argued that such a right could be deduced from more general powers and from an understanding of the "great objects" for which the federal government had been founded. Marshall thus struck a blow for "loose construction" of the Constitution and a broad grant of power to the federal government to encourage economic growth and stability.

In answer to the second question—the right of a state to tax or regulate a federal agency—Marshall held that the Bank was indeed such an agency and that giving a state the power to tax it would also give the state the power to destroy it. In an important assertion of the supremacy of the national government, Marshall argued that the American people "did not design to make their government dependent on the states." This opinion ran counter to the view of many Americans, particularly in the South, that the Constitution did not take away sovereignty from the states. This debate over federal-state relations was not finally resolved until the northern victory in the Civil War decisively affirmed the dominance of federal authority. But Marshall's decision gave great new weight to a nationalist constitutional philosophy.

The case of *Gibbons* v. *Ogden* in 1824 led to a decision that bolstered the power of Congress to regulate interstate commerce. A steamboat monopoly granted by the state of New York was challenged by a competing ferry service operating between New York and New Jersey. The Court declared the New York grant unconstitutional because it amounted to state interference with Congress's exclusive right to regulate interstate commerce. Until this time, it had not been clearly established that "commerce" included navigation, and the Court's ruling went a long way toward freeing private interests engaged in furthering the transportation revolution from state interference.

This case clearly showed the dual effect of Marshall's decision making. It broadened the power of the federal government at the expense of the states while at the same time encouraging the growth of a national market economy. The actions of the Supreme Court provide the clearest and most consistent example of the main nationalistic trends of the postwar period—the acknowledgment of the federal government's major role in promoting the growth of a powerful and prosperous America and the rise of a nationwide capitalist economy.

Nationalism in Foreign Policy: The Monroe Doctrine

The new spirit of nationalism was also reflected in foreign affairs. The main diplomatic challenge facing Monroe after his reelection in 1820 was how to respond to the successful revolt of most of Spain's Latin American colonies after the Napoleonic wars. In Congress, Henry Clay called for immediate recognition of the new republics. In doing so, he expressed the belief of many Americans that their neighbors to the south were simply following the example of the United States in its own struggle for independence.

Before 1822, the administration stuck to a policy of neutrality. Monroe and Secretary of State Adams feared that recognizing the revolutionary governments would antagonize Spain and impede negotiations to acquire Florida. But pressure for recognition grew in Congress; in 1821, the House of Representatives, responding to Clay's impassioned oratory, passed a resolution of sympathy for Latin American revolutionaries and made it clear to the president that he would have the support of Congress if and when he decided to accord recognition. After the Florida treaty had

been formally ratified in 1821, Monroe agreed to recognition and the establishment of diplomatic ties with the Latin American republics. Mexico and Colombia were recognized in 1822, Chile and Argentina in 1823, Brazil (which had separated from Portugal) and the Federation of Central American States in 1824, and Peru in 1826.

Recognizing the republics put the United States on a possible collision course with the major European powers. Austria, Russia, and Prussia were committed to rolling back the tides of liberalism, self-government, and national self-determination that had arisen during the French Revolution and its Napoleonic aftermath. After Napoleon's first defeat in 1814, the monarchs of Europe had joined in a "Grand Alliance" to protect "legitimate" authoritarian governments from democratic challenges. Originally Great Britain was a member of this concert of nations but withdrew when it found its own interests conflicted with those of the other members. In 1822, the remaining alliance members, joined now by the restored French monarchy, gave France the green light to invade Spain and restore a Bourbon regime that might be disposed to reconquer the empire. Both Great Britain and the United States were alarmed by this prospect.

Particularly troubling to American policymakers was the role of Tsar Alexander I of Russia in these maneuverings. Not only was the tsar an outspoken and active opponent of Latin American independence, but he was attempting to extend Russian claims on the Pacific Coast of North America south to the fifty-first parallel—into the Oregon country the United States wanted for itself.

The threat from the Grand Alliance pointed to a need for American cooperation with Great Britain, which had its own reasons for wanting to prevent a restoration of Spanish or French power in the New World. Independent nations offered better and more open markets for British manufactured goods than the colonies of other nations, and the spokesmen for burgeoning British industrial capitalism anticipated a profitable economic dominance over Latin America. In early 1823, the British foreign secretary, George Canning, tried to exact from the French a pledge that they would make no attempt to acquire territories in Spanish America. When that venture failed, he sought to involve the United States in a joint policy to prevent the Grand Alliance from intervening in Latin America.

In August 1823, Canning broached the possibility of joint Anglo-American action against the designs of the Alliance to Richard Rush, U. S. minister to Great Britain, and Rush referred the suggestion to the president. Monroe welcomed the British initiative because he believed the United States should take an active role in trans-Atlantic affairs by playing one European power against another. When Monroe presented the question to his cabinet, however, he encountered the opposition of Secretary of State Adams, who favored a different approach. Adams distrusted the British and differed from the president in his general view of proper relations between the United States and Europe. Adams believed the national interest would best be served by avoiding all entanglements in European politics while at the same time discouraging European intervention in the Americas.

Political ambition also predisposed Adams against joint action with Great Britain; he hoped to be the next president and did not wish to give his rivals the chance to label him as pro-British. He therefore advocated unilateral action by the United States rather than some kind of joint declaration with the British. As he told the cabinet in November, "It would be more candid, as well as more dignified, to avow our principles explicitly to Russia and France, than to come in as a cockboat of the British man-of-war."

In the end, Adams managed to swing Monroe and the cabinet around to his viewpoint. In his annual message to Congress on December 2, 1823, Monroe included a far-reaching statement on foreign policy that was actually written mainly by Adams. What came to be known as the Monroe Doctrine solemnly declared the United States opposed any further colonization in the Americas or any effort by European nations to extend their political systems outside of their own hemisphere. In return, the United States pledged not to involve itself in the internal affairs of Europe or to take part in European wars. The statement envisioned a North and South America composed entirely of independent republics—with the United States preeminent among them.

Although the Monroe Doctrine made little impression on the great powers of Europe at the time it was proclaimed, it signified the rise of a new sense of independence and self-confidence in American attitudes toward the Old World. The United States would now go its own way free of involvement in European conflicts and would energetically protect its own sphere from European interference.

Adams and the End of the Era of Good Feelings

Monroe endorsed John Quincy Adams to succeed him as president. An intelligent and high-minded New Englander and the son of the second president, Adams seemed remarkably well qualified for the highest office in the land. More than anyone, except perhaps Monroe himself, he seemed to stand for a nonpartisan nationalism that put the public good above special interests. Early in

John Quincy Adams, in an 1828 portrait by Gilbert Stuart, the outstanding American portrait painter. As secretary of state under James Monroe, Adams advocated a policy of national self-interest and freedom from entanglement in European affairs.

his career, he had lost a seat in the Senate for supporting the foreign policies of Thomas Jefferson in defiance of the Federalist majority of his home state of Massachusets. After becoming a National Republican, he served mainly in diplomatic posts, culminating in his tenure as secretary of state. In this office, he did more than negotiate treaties. Believing the rising greatness of America should be reflected not only in economic development and territorial expansion but also in scientific and intellectual achievement, he single-handedly produced a monumental report prescribing a uniform system of weights and measures for the United States. For three years, he rose early every morning in order to put in several hours of research on this project before doing a full day's work conducting the nation's foreign policy. Uniformity of weights and measures, he argued, was essential to scientific and technological progress. Showing that his nationalism was not of a narrow and selfish kind, he called for an agreement with Great Britain and France to promote a single universal system.

Adams represented a type of leadership that could not survive the growth of the sectional and economic divisions foreshadowed by the Missouri controversy and the fallout from the panic of 1819. Adams did become president, but only after a hotly contested election that led to the revival of partisan political conflict (see Chapter 10). As the nation's chief executive, he tried to gain support for government-sponsored scientific research and higher education, only to find the nation was in no mood for public expenditures that offered nothing immediate and tangible to most voters. As a highly educated "gentleman," he projected an image that was out of harmony with a rising spirit of democracy and veneration of "the common man."

The consensus on national goals and leadership that Monroe had represented could not sustain itself. The "era of good feelings" turned out to be a passing phase and something of an illusion. Although the pursuit of national greatness would continue, there would be sharp divisions over how it should be achieved. A general commitment to settlement of the West and the development of agriculture, commerce, and industry would endure despite serious differences over what role government should play in the process; but the idea that an elite of nonpartisan states-

men could define common purposes and harmonize competing elements—the concept of leadership that Monroe and Adams had advanced—would no longer be viable in the more contentious and democratic America of the Jacksonian era.

CHRONOLOGY

1813	Boston Manufacturing Company founds cotton mill at Waltham, Massachusetts
1815	War of 1812 ends
1816	James Monroe elected president
1818	Andrew Jackson invades Florida
1819	Supreme Court hands down far-reaching decision in Dartmouth College case and in *McCulloch* v. *Maryland* • Adams-Onís treaty cedes Spanish territory to the United States • Financial panic is followed by a depression lasting until 1823
1820	Missouri Compromise resolves nation's first sectional crisis • Monroe reelected president unanimously
1823	Monroe Doctrine proclaimed
1824	Lafayette revisits the United States • Supreme Court decides *Gibbons* v. *Ogden*
1825	Erie Canal completed; Canal Era begins

Recommended Reading

The standard surveys of the period between the War of 1812 and the Age of Jackson are two works by George Dangerfield: *The Era of Good Feelings* (1952) and *Awakening of American Nationalism, 1815–1828* (1965); but see also the early chapters of Charles Sellers, *The Market Revolution: Jacksonian America, 1815–1846* (1991). A lively narrative of westward expansion is Dale Van Every, *The Final Challenge: The American Frontier, 1804–1845* (1964); but Malcolm J. Rohrbough, *The Trans-Appalachian Frontier* (1978), is more comprehensive and authoritative. Outstanding studies of economic transformation and the rise of a market economy are George R. Taylor, *The Transportation Revolution, 1815–1860* (1951); Paul

W. Gates, *The Farmer's Age: Agriculture, 1815–1860* (1960); Stuart Bruchey, *Growth of the Modern American Economy* (1975); and Douglas C. North, *The Economic Growth of the United States, 1790–1860* (1961). An incisive study of the Marshall Court's decisions is Robert K. Faulkner, *The Jurisprudence of John Marshall* (1968). Samuel F. Bemis, *John Quincy Adams and the Foundations of American Policy* (1949), provides the classic account of the statesmanship that led to the Monroe Doctrine. But see also Ernest May, *The Making of the Monroe Doctrine* (1976), for a persuasive newer interpretation of how the doctrine originated.

Additional Bibliography

Good accounts of Lafayette's visit and what Americans made of it can be found in Fred Somkin, *Unquiet Eagle: Memory and Desire in the Idea of American Freedom, 1815–1860* (1967) and Anne C. Loveland, *Emblem of Liberty: The Image of Lafayette in the American Mind* (1971). For general accounts of the westward movement, see Frederick Jackson Turner, *The Frontier in American History* (1920), Ray A. Billington, *Westward Expansion* (1974), and Richard White, *It's Your Misfortune and None of My Own* (1992). On the removal of Native Americans, see A. H. DeRosier, *The Removal of the Choctaw Indians* (1970); Francis P. Prucha, *American Indian Policy in the Formative Years* (1962); Dale Van Every, *Disinherited: The Lost Birthright of the American Indian* (1966); and William G. McLoughlin, *Cherokee Renascence in the New Republic* (1986). Insights into life in the frontier areas can be derived from Frank Owsley, *Plain Folk of the Old South* (1948); Allen G. Bogue, *From Prairie to Corn Belt* (1963); Richard L. Power, *Planting Corn Belt Culture* (1953); and R. C. Buley, *The Old Northwest: Pioneer Period*, 2 vols. (1950). On exploration and fur trading in the trans-Mississippi West, see William H. Goetzmann, *Exploration and Empire* (1966) and David J. Wishart, *The Fur Trade of the American West, 1817–1840* (1979). On popular and literary images of the West and the frontier, see Henry Nash Smith, *Virgin Land: The American West as Symbol and Myth* (1950), and Richard Slotkin, *The Fatal Environment: The Myth of the Frontier in the Age of Industrialization* (1985).

Major works on the development of internal waterways are Carter Goodrich, *Government Promotion of American Canals and Railroads* (1960); Harry N. Schieber, *Ohio Canal Era* (1969); Ronald E. Shaw, *Erie Water West* (1966); and Erik E. Haites et al., *Western River Transportation* (1975). On agricultural development, see Percy W. Bidwell and John I. Falconer, *History of Agriculture in the Northern United States* (1925) and Lewis C. Gary, *History of Agriculture in the Southern United States to 1860*, 2 vols. (1933). The early growth of manufacturing is treated in Caroline F. Ware *The Early New England Cotton Manufacture* (1931); Arthur H. Cole, *The American Wool Manufacture*, 2 vols. (1926); Peter Temin, *Iron and Steel in Nineteenth Century America* (1964); H. J. Habakkuk, *American and British Technology in the Nineteenth Century* (1962); David J. Jeremy, *Transatlantic Industrial Revolution* (1981); and Robert F. Dalzell, *The Boston Associates and the World They Made* (1987). On early mill workers, see Bernice Selden, *The Mill Girls* (1983), and Thomas Dublin, *Women at Work: The Transformation of Work and Community in Lowell, Massachusetts, 1826–1860* (1979).

The politics of postwar nationalism are examined in Shaw Livermore, Jr., *The Twilight of Federalism* (1962); Harry Ammon, *James Monroe* (1971); James S. Young, *The Washington Community, 1800–1828* (1966); and Robert V. Remini, *Henry Clay: Statesman for the Union* (1991). The Marshall Court is covered in Leonard Baker, *John Marshall* (1974); Albert J. Beveridge, *John Marshall*, 4 vols. (1916–1919); and R. Kent Newmyer, *The Supreme Court Under Marshall and Taney* (1968). Morton J. Horwitz, *The Transformation of American Law, 1780–1860* (1977), deals with broader aspects of legal change.

On diplomacy and the Monroe Doctrine, see Philip C. Brooks, *Diplomacy and the Borderlands* (1939); Walter LaFeber, ed., *John Quincy Adams and American Continental Empire* (1965); and Dexter Perkins, *The Monroe Doctrine, 1823–1826* (1927) and *Hands Off: A History of the Monroe Doctrine* (1941).

The Triumph of
White Men's Democracy

So many Americans were moving about in the 1820s and 1830s that new industries sprung up just to meet their needs. To service the rising tide of travelers, transients, and new arrivals, entrepreneurs erected large hotels in the center of major cities. There they provided lodging, food, and drink on an unprecedented scale. These establishments were as different from the inns of the eighteenth century as the steamboat was from the flatboat. A prototype of the new hotel was the Boston Exchange Hotel with its 8 stories and 300 rooms. Opened in 1809, the Exchange burned down nine years later; and the depression that followed the financial panic of 1819 put a damper on hotel building. After the return of prosperity in 1825, the "first-class hotel" soon became a prominent feature of the American scene. The splendor and comforts of the Baltimore City Hotel, Gadsby's National Hotel in Washington, and the Tremont House of Boston—all of which opened in the late 1820s—dazzled travelers and local residents alike. By the 1830s, imposing hotels were springing up in commercial centers all over the country. The grandest of these was New York's Astor House, completed in 1836.

According to the historian Doris Elizabeth King, "the new hotels were so obviously 'public' and 'democratic' in their character that foreigners were often to describe them as a true reflection of American society." Their very existence showed that many people, white males in particular, were on the move geographically and socially. Among the hotels' patrons were traveling salesmen, ambitious young men seeking to establish themselves in a new city, and restless pursuers of "the main chance" (unexpected economic opportunities) not yet ready to put down roots.

Hotel managers shocked European visitors by failing to enforce traditional social distinctions among their clientele. Under the "American plan," guests were required to pay for their meals, and to eat at a common "table d'hôte" with anyone who happened to be there, including servants traveling with their employers. Ability to pay was the only requirement for admission (unless one happened to be an unescorted female or dark-skinned), and every white patron, regardless of social background and occupation, enjoyed the kind of personal service previously available only to a privileged class. Many patrons experienced such amenities as gaslight, indoor plumbing, and steam heat for the first time in their lives. Because a large proportion of the American population stayed in hotels at one time or another—a privilege that was, in Europe, reserved for the elite—foreigners inferred that there was widespread prosperity and a much greater "equality of condition" than existed in Europe.

The hotel culture also revealed some of the limitations of the new era of democratic ideals and aspirations. African Americans, Native Americans, and women were excluded or discriminated against, just as they were denied suffrage at a time when it was being extended to all white males. The genuinely poor—of whom there were more than met the eye of most European visitors—simply could not afford to patronize the hotels and were consigned to squalid rooming houses. If the social equality *within* the hotel reflected a decline in traditional rigid class lines, the broad gulf between potential patrons and those who could not pay the rates signaled the growth of inequality based squarely on wealth rather than inherited status.

The hotel life also reflected the emergence of democratic politics. Professional politicians of a new breed, pursuing the votes of a mass electorate, spent much of their time in hotels as they traveled about. Those elected to Congress or a state legislature often stayed in hotels during the session, and the political deals and bargains required for effective party organization or legislative success were sometimes concluded in these establishments.

When Andrew Jackson arrived in Washington to prepare for his administration in 1829, he took residence at the new National Hotel. After a horde of well-wishers had made a shambles of the White House during his inaugural reception, Jackson retreated to the National for peace and quiet. The hotel was more than a public and "democratic" gathering place; it could also serve as a haven where the rising men of politics and business could find rest and privacy. In its lobbies, salons, and private rooms the spirit of an age was expressing itself.

DEMOCRACY IN THEORY AND PRACTICE

During the 1820s and 1830s, the term *democracy* first became a generally accepted term to describe how American institutions were supposed to work. The Founders had defined democracy as direct rule by the masses; most of them rejected this concept of a democratic approach to government because it was at odds with their conception of a well-balanced republic led by a "natural aristocracy." For champions of popular government in the Jacksonian period, however, the "people" were truly sovereign and could do no wrong. "The voice of the people is the voice of God" was their clearest expression of this principle. Conservatives were less certain of the wisdom of the common folk. But even they were coming to recognize that public opinion had to be won over before major policy decisions could be made.

Besides evoking a heightened sense of "popular sovereignty," the democratic impulse seemed to stimulate a process of social leveling. Earlier Americans had usually assumed the rich and well-born should be treated with special respect and recognized as natural leaders of the community and guardians of its culture and values. By the 1830s, the disappearance of inherited social ranks and clearly defined aristocracies or privileged groups struck European visitors like Alexis de Tocqueville as the most radical feature of democracy in America. Historians have described this development as a decline of the spirit of "deference."

The decline of deference meant that "self-made men" of lowly origins could now rise more readily to positions of power and influence and that exclusiveness and aristocratic pretensions were likely to provoke popular hostility or scorn. But economic equality, in the sense of an equitable

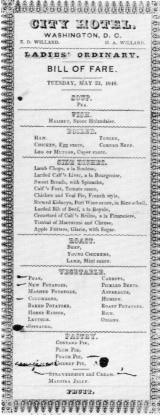

The democratic mingling of social classes was especially apparent in the dining rooms of major hotels that sprang up during the early nineteenth century. Under the "American plan," guests paid for each meal and chose their food from hearty menus like the ladies' ordinary menu from the City Hotel in Washington, D.C. in 1848 (left). Of course, dining at long tables with strangers of uncertain breeding and table manners did have its hazards, as illustrated by the contemporary cartoon, "Pass the Mustard."

sharing of wealth, was not part of the mainstream agenda of the Jacksonian period. This was, after all, a competitive capitalistic society. The watchword was equality of *opportunity* not equality of *reward*. Life was a race, and so long as white males appeared to have an equal start, there could be no reason for complaint if some were winners and some were losers. Historians now generally agree that economic inequality—the gap between rich and poor Americans—was actually increasing during this period of political and social democratization.

The Democratic Ferment

The supremacy of democracy was most obvious in the new politics of universal white manhood suffrage and mass political parties. By the 1820s, most states had removed the last remaining barriers to voting participation by all white males. This change was not as radical or controversial as it would be later in nineteenth-century Europe; ownership of land was so common in the United States that a general suffrage did not mean men without property became a voting majority.

Accompanying this broadening of the electorate was a rise in the proportion of public officials who were elected rather than appointed. More and more judges, as well as legislative and executive officeholders, were chosen by "the people." A new style of politicking developed. Politicians had to get out and campaign, demonstrating in their speeches on the stump that they could mirror the fears and concerns of the voters. Electoral politics began to assume a more festive and dramatic quality.

Skillful and farsighted politicians—like Martin Van Buren in New York—began in the 1820s to build stable statewide political organizations out of what had been loosely organized factions. Before the rise of effective national parties, politicians created true party organizations on the state level by dispensing government jobs to friends and supporters, and by attacking rivals as enemies of popular aspirations. Earlier politicians had regarded parties as a threat to republican virtue and had embraced them only as a temporary expedient, but Van Buren regarded a permanent two-party system as essential to democratic government. In his opinion, parties were an effective check on the temptation to abuse power, a tendency deeply planted in the human heart. The major break-through in American political thought during the 1820s and 1830s was the idea of a "loyal opposition," ready to capitalize politically on the mistakes or excesses of the "ins," without denying the right of the "ins" to act in the same way when they became the "outs."

Changes in the method of nominating and electing a president fostered the growth of a two-party system on the national level. By 1828, presidential electors were chosen by popular vote rather than by state legislatures in all but two of the twenty-four states. The new need to mobilize grass-roots voters behind particular candidates required national organization. Coalitions of state parties that could agree on a single standard-bearer gradually evolved into the great national parties of the Jacksonian era—the Democrats and the Whigs. When national nominating conventions made their appearance in 1831, candidate selection became a matter to be taken up by representative party assemblies, not congressional caucuses or ad hoc political alliances.

New political institutions and practices encouraged a great upsurge of popular interest and participation. In the presidential election of 1824, the proportion of adult white males voting was less than 27 percent. In 1828, it rose sharply to 55 percent, held at about the same level for the elections of 1832 and 1836, and then shot up to 78 percent in 1840—the first election in which two fully organized national parties each nominated a single candidate and campaigned for their choices in every state in the Union.

Economic questions dominated the political controversies of the 1820s and 1830s. The panic of 1819 and the subsequent depression heightened popular interest in government economic policy, first on the state and then on the national level. No one really knew how to solve the problems of a market economy that went through cycles of boom and bust, but many people thought they had the answer. Some, especially small farmers, favored a return to a simpler and more "honest" economy without banks, paper money, and the easy credit that encouraged speculation. Others, particularly emerging entrepreneurs, saw salvation in government aid and protection for venture capital. Entrepreneurs appealed to state governments for charters that granted special privileges to banks, transportation enterprises, and manufacturing corporations. Politicians attempted to respond to these conflicting views about the best way to restore and maintain prosperity. Out of the economic distress of the early 1820s came rapid growth of state-level political activity and organization that foreshadowed the rise of national parties, which would be organized around economic programs.

The party disputes that arose over corporations, tariffs, banks, and internal improvements involved more than the direct economic concerns of particular interest groups. The republican ideology of the revolutionary period survived in the form of widespread fears of conspiracy against American liberty and equality. Whenever any group appeared to be exerting decisive influence over public policy, people who did not identify with that group's aspirations were quick to charge them with corruption and the unscrupulous pursuit of power.

The notion that the American experiment was a fragile one, constantly threatened by power-hungry conspirators, eventually took two principal forms. Jacksonians believed "the money power" endangered the survival of republicanism; their opponents feared that populist politicians like Jackson himself—alleged "rabble-rousers"— would gull the electorate into ratifying high-handed and tyrannical actions contrary to the true interests of the nation.

An object of increasing concern for both sides was the role of the federal government. Should it take positive steps to foster economic growth, as the National Republicans and later the Whigs contended, or should it simply attempt to destroy what Jacksonians decried as "special privilege" or "corporate monopoly"? Almost everyone favored equality of opportunity, but there was serious disagreement over whether this goal could best be achieved by active governmental support of commerce and industry or by divorcing the government from the economy in the name of laissez-faire and free competition.

For one group of dissenters, democracy took on a more radical meaning. Workingmen's parties and trade unions emerged in eastern cities during the late 1820s and early 1830s. Their leaders condemned the growing gap between the rich and the poor resulting from early industrialization and the growth of a market economy. They argued that an expansion of low-paying labor was putting working people under the dominance of their employers to such an extent that the American tradition of "equal rights" was in grave

danger. Society, in their view, was divided between "producers"—laborers, artisans, farmers, and small business owners who ran their own enterprises—and nonproducing "parasites"— bankers, speculators, and merchant capitalists. Their aim was to give the producers greater control over the fruits of their labor.

These radicals called for a number of reforms to achieve their goal of equal rights. Thomas Skidmore, a founder of the New York Working Men's party, advocated the abolition of inheritance and a redistribution of property. Champions of the rights of labor also demanded greatly extended and improved systems of public education. But educational reform, however radical or extensive, could only provide equal opportunities to future generations. To relieve the plight of adult artisans and craftspeople at a time when their economic and social status was deteriorating, labor reformers and trade unionists experimented with cooperative production and called for a ten-hour workday, abolition of imprisonment for debt, and a currency system based exclusively on hard money so workers could no longer be paid in depreciated bank notes.

Philadelphia was an especially active center of labor politics and trade union activity. In 1827, the city's skilled artisans formed the Mechanics Union of Trade Associations, the nation's first metropolitan labor movement, and shortly thereafter launched the Working Men's party to compete in local elections. In 1834, fifty craft associations incorporated into the General Trades' Union of the City and County of Philadelphia, and within a year took the leading role in the first general strike in American history. The strike was successful in getting the ten-hour day accepted in most Philadelphia industries, but the depression that began in 1837 destroyed the General Trades' Union and nullified most of its gains. The same pattern of temporary success and ultimate defeat was repeated in other major cities. Nevertheless, American labor had set a precedent for the use of mass action aimed at the achievement of better working conditions.

In the 1830s and 1840s, northern abolitionists and early proponents of women's rights made other efforts to extend the meaning and scope of democracy. Radical abolitionists sought an immediate end to southern slavery and supported extension of the franchise and other civil rights to free blacks. A women's rights movement also

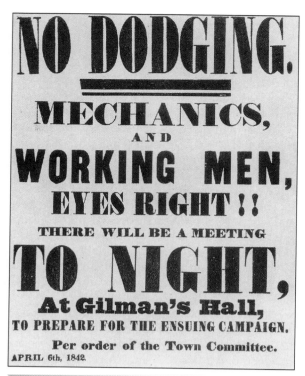

Working Men's parties of the late 1820s and 1830s sought to close the widening gap between the rich and the poor and acted to improve working conditions.

developed, partially out of women's involvement in the abolitionist crusade and the enlarged conception of equal rights that their experiences had fostered. But Jacksonian America was too permeated with racism and male chauvinism to give much heed to claims that the equal rights prescribed by the Declaration of Independence should be extended to blacks and women. Most of those who advocated democratization explicitly limited its application to white males, and in some ways the civil and political status of blacks and women actually deteriorated during "the age of the common *man.*" (See Chapter 11 for a more detailed discussion of these movements.)

Democracy and Society

Although some types of inequality persisted or even grew during the age of democracy, they did so in the face of a growing belief that equality was the governing principle of American society. What this meant in practice was that no one could expect special privileges because of family connections. The plain folk, who in an earlier period would have known their place and deferred to their betters, were now likely to greet claims for special treatment with indifference or scorn. High-status Europeans who traveled in America were constantly affronted by democratic attitudes and manners. One aristocrat was rudely rebuffed when he tried to hire an entire stagecoach for himself and his valet. On other occasions these blue-blooded tourists were forced to eat at the same table as teamsters and stagecoach drivers or share rooms in country inns with rough characters of all kinds. Another irritation to European visitors was the absence of special first-class accommodations on steamboats and railroads.

With the exception of slaveholders, wealthy Americans could not depend on a distinctive social class for domestic service. Instead of keeping "servants," they hired "help"—household workers who refused to wear livery, agreed to work for only short periods of time, and sometimes insisted on eating at the same table as their employers. As noted in the maid's comments quoted in Chapter 8, no true American was willing to be considered as a member of a servant class, and those who engaged in domestic work regarded it as a temporary stopgap. Except as a euphemistic substitute for the word *slave,* the term *servant* virtually disappeared from the American vocabulary.

The decline of distinctive modes of dress for upper and lower classes conveyed the principle of equality in yet another way. The elaborate periwigs and knee breeches worn by eighteenth-century gentlemen gave way to short hair and pantaloons, a style that was adopted by men of all social classes. Fashionable dress among women also ceased to be a sure index of gentility; serving girls on their day off wore the same kind of finery as the wives and daughters of the wealthy. Those with a good eye for detail might detect subtle differences in taste or in quality of materials, but the casual observer of crowds in a large city could easily conclude that all Americans belonged to a single social class.

Of course Americans were not all of one social class. In fact, inequality based on control of productive resources was increasing during the Jacksonian period. A growing percentage of the population, especially in urban areas, possessed no real estate and little other property. The rise of industrialization was creating a permanent class of low-paid, unorganized wage earners. In rural areas, there was a significant division between successful commercial farmers and smallholders or tenants who subsisted on marginal land, as well as enormous inequality of status between southern planters and their black slaves. But most foreign observers overlooked the widening gap between the propertied middle class and the laboring population; their attention was riveted on the fact that all white males were equal before the law and at the polls, a situation that was genuinely radical by European standards.

Traditional forms of privilege and elitism were also under strong attack, as evidenced by changes in the organization and status of the learned professions. Under Jacksonian pressure, state legislatures abolished the licensing requirements for physicians previously administered by local medical societies. As a result, practitioners of unorthodox modes of healing were permitted to compete freely with established medical doctors. One popular therapy was Thomsonianism, a form of treatment based entirely on the use of common herbs and roots. Thomsonians argued that their own form of medicine would make every man his own physician. The democratic tide also struck the legal profession. Local bar associations continued to set the qualifications for practicing attorneys, but in many places they lowered standards and admitted persons with little or no formal training and only the most rudimentary knowledge of the law.

For the clergy, "popular sovereignty" meant they were increasingly under the thumb of the laity. The growing dependence of ministers on the support and approval of their congregations forced them to develop a more popular and emotional style of preaching. Ministers had ceased to command respect merely because of their office. To succeed in their calling, they had to please the public, in much the same way a politician had to satisfy the electorate.

Democratic Culture

The democratic spirit also found expression in the rise of new forms of literature and art directed at a mass audience. The intentions of individual artists and writers varied considerably. Some sought success by pandering to popular taste in defiance of traditional standards of high culture. Others tried to capture the spirit of the age by portraying the everyday life of ordinary Americans rather than the traditional subjects of "aristocratic" art. A notable few hoped to use literature and art as a way of improving popular taste and instilling deeper moral and spiritual values. But all of them were aware their audience was the broad citizenry of a democratic nation rather than a refined elite.

The romantic movement in literature, which came to the fore in the early nineteenth century in both Europe and America, valued strong feeling and mystical intuition over the calm rationality and appeal to common experience that had prevailed in the writing of the eighteenth century. Romanticism was not necessarily connected with democracy; in Europe it sometimes went along with a reaffirmation of feudalism and the right of a superior few to rule over the masses. In the American setting, however, romanticism often appealed to the feelings and intuitions of ordinary people: the innate love of goodness, truth, and beauty that all people were thought to possess. Writers in search of popularity and economic success, however, often deserted the high plane of romantic art for crass sentimentalism—a willingness to pull out all emotional stops to thrill readers or bring tears to their eyes.

A mass market for popular literature was made possible by a rise in literacy and a revolution in the technology of printing. An increase in potential readers and a decrease in publishing costs led to a flood of lurid and sentimental novels, some of which became the first American best-sellers. By the 1840s and 1850s, writers like George Lippard, Mrs. Southworth, and Augusta Jane Evans had perfected the formulas that led to commercial success. Gothic horror and the perils of virtuous heroines threatened by dastardly villains were among the ingredients that readers came to expect from popular fiction. Many of the new sentimental novels were written by and for women. Some women writers implicitly protested against their situation by portraying men in general as tyrannical, unreliable, or vicious, and the women they abandoned or failed to support as resourceful individualists capable of making their own way in a man's world. But the standard happy endings sustained the convention that a woman's place was in the home, for a virtuous and protec-

James Fenimore Cooper's descriptions of the frontier shoreline of Lake Ontario in The Pathfinder *are examples of the romantic style in literature.*

tive man usually turned up and saved the heroine from independence.

In the theater, melodrama became the dominant genre. Despite religious objections, theatergoing was a popular recreation in the cities during the Jacksonian era. The standard fare involved the inevitable trio of beleaguered heroine, mustachioed villain, and a hero who asserted himself in the nick of time. Patriotic comedies extolling the common sense of the rustic Yankee who foiled the foppish European aristocrat were also popular and served to arouse the democratic sympathies of the audience. Men and women of all classes went to the theater, and those in the cheap seats often behaved raucously and even violently when they did not like what they saw. Unpopular actors or plays could even provoke serious riots. In an 1849 incident in New York,

134 people were killed in disorders stemming from hostility toward an English actor who was the rival of Edwin Forrest, the most popular American thespian of the time.

The spirit of "popular sovereignty" expressed itself less dramatically in the visual arts, but its influence was felt nonetheless. Beginning in the 1830s, painters turned from portraying great events and famous people to the depiction of scenes from everyday life. Democratic genre painters like William S. Mount and George Caleb Bingham captured the lives of plain folk with great skill and understanding. Mount, who painted lively rural scenes, expressed the credo of the democratic artist: "Paint pictures that will take with the public—never paint for the few but the many." Bingham was noted for his graphic images of Americans voting, carrying goods on riverboats, and engaging in other everyday activities.

Architecture and sculpture reflected the democratic spirit in a different way; they were viewed as civic art forms meant to glorify the achievements of the republic. In the 1820s and 1830s, the Greek style with its columned facades not only predominated in the architecture of public buildings but was also favored for banks, hotels, and private dwellings. Besides symbolizing an identification of the United States with the democracy of ancient Greece, it achieved monumental impressiveness at a fairly low cost. Even in newly settled frontier communities, it was relatively easy and inexpensive to put up a functional square building and then add a classical facade. Not everyone could live in structures that looked like Greek temples, but almost everyone could admire them from the outside or conduct business within their walls.

Sculpture was intended strictly for public admiration or inspiration, and its principal subjects were the heroes of the republic. The sculptors who accepted public commissions had to make sure their work met the expectations of politicians and taxpayers, who favored stately, idealized images. Horatio Greenough, the greatest sculptor of the pre–Civil War era, got into trouble when he unveiled a seated George Washington, dressed in classical garb and nude from the waist up. Much more acceptable was the equestrian figure of Andrew Jackson executed for the federal government by Clark Mills and unveiled in 1853.

William Sidney Mount, Rustic Dance After a Sleigh Ride, *1830. Mount's portrayals of country folk dancing, gambling, playing music, or horse-trading were pieces that appealed strongly to contemporaries, but art historians have found much to praise in his use of architecture, particularly that of the common barn, to achieve striking compositional effects.*

What most impressed the public was that Mills had succeeded in balancing the horse on two legs.

Serious exponents of a higher culture and a more refined sensibility sought to reach the new public in the hope of enlightening or uplifting it. The "Brahmin poets" of New England—Henry Wadsworth Longfellow, James Russell Lowell, and Oliver Wendell Holmes—offered lofty sentiments and moral messages to a receptive middle class; Ralph Waldo Emerson carried his philosophy of spiritual self-reliance to lyceums and lecture halls across the country, and great novelists like Nathaniel Hawthorne and Herman Melville experimented with the popular romantic genres. But Hawthorne and Melville failed to gain a large readership. The ironic and pessimistic view of life that pervaded their work clashed with the optimism of the age. For later generations of American critics, however, the works of Melville and Hawthorne became centerpieces of the American literary "renaissance" of the mid-nineteenth century. Hawthorne's *The Scarlet Letter* (1850) and Melville's *Moby-Dick* (1851) are now commonly regarded as masterworks of American fiction.

The great landscape painters of the period— Thomas Cole, Asher Durand, and Frederic Edwin Church—believed their representations of untamed nature would elevate popular taste and convey moral truths. The modern ideal of art for art's sake was utterly alien to the instructional spirit of mid-nineteenth-century American culture. The responsibility of the artist in a democratic society, it was generally assumed, was to contribute to the general welfare by encouraging virtue and proper sentiments. Only Edgar Allan Poe seemed to fit the European image of romantic genius, rebelling against middle-class pieties. But in his own way, Poe exploited the popular fascination with death in his verse and used the conventions of Gothic horror in his tales. The most original of the antebellum poets, Walt Whitman, sought to be a direct mouthpiece for the rising democratic spirit, but his abandonment of traditional verse forms and his freedom in dealing with the sexual side of human nature left him isolated and unappreciated during his most creative years.

JACKSON AND THE POLITICS OF DEMOCRACY

The public figure who came to symbolize the triumph of democracy was Andrew Jackson, who came out a loser in the presidential election of 1824. His victory four years later, his actions as

Asher Durand's paintings, such as In the Catskills (1859), *helped establish an image of a young and optimistic republic, as noble as its wilderness.*

president, and the great political party that formed around him refashioned national politics in a more democratic mold.

The Election of 1824 and J. Q. Adams's Administration

As Monroe's second term ended, the ruling Republican party was in disarray and could not agree on who should succeed to the presidency. The party's congressional caucus chose William Crawford of Georgia, an old-line Jeffersonian. But a majority of congressmen showed their disapproval of this outmoded method of nominating candidates by refusing to attend the caucus. Monroe himself favored John Quincy Adams of Massachusetts. This gave the New England statesman an important boost but did not discourage others from entering the contest. Supporters of Henry Clay and John C. Calhoun mounted campaigns for their favorites, and a group of local leaders in his home state of Tennessee tossed Jackson's hat into the ring.

Initially, Jackson was not given much of a chance. Unlike other aspirants, he had not played

a conspicuous role in national politics; his sole claim to fame was as a military hero, and not even his original supporters believed this would be sufficient to catapult him into the White House. But after testing the waters, Calhoun withdrew and chose instead to run for vice president. Then Crawford suffered a debilitating stroke that weakened his chances. With one Southerner out of the race and another disabled, Jackson began to pick up support in slaveholding states. He also found favor among those in the North and West who were disenchanted with the economic nationalism of Clay and Adams.

In the election, Jackson won a plurality of the electoral votes, but lacked the necessary majority. The contest was thrown into the House of Representatives, where the legislators were to choose from among the three top candidates. Here Adams emerged victorious over Jackson and Crawford. Clay, who had just missed making the final three, provided the winning margin by persuading his supporters to vote for Adams. When Adams proceeded to appoint Clay as his secretary of state, the Jacksonians charged that a "corrupt bargain" had deprived their favorite of the presidency. Although there was no evidence Clay had bartered votes for the promise of a high office, the corrupt bargain charge was widely believed. As a result, Adams assumed office under a cloud of suspicion.

Adams had a difficult and frustrating presidency. The political winds were blowing against nationalistic programs, partly because the country was just recovering from a depression that many thought had been caused or worsened by federal banking and tariff policies. Adams refused to bow to public opinion and called for an expansion of federal activity. Advocates of states' rights and a strict construction of the Constitution were aghast, and the opposition that developed in Congress turned the administration's domestic program into a pipe dream.

The new Congress elected in 1826 was clearly under the control of men hostile to the administration and favorable to the presidential aspirations of Andrew Jackson. The tariff issue was the main business on their agenda. Pressure for greater protection came not only from manufacturers but also from many farmers, especially wool and hemp growers, who would supply critical votes in the upcoming presidential election. The cotton-growing South—the only section

The Election of 1824

Candidate	Party	Popular Vote	Electoral Vote*
J. Q. Adams	No party	113,122	84
Jackson	designations	151,271	99
Clay		47,531	37
Crawford		40,856	41

No candidate received a majority of the electoral votes. Adams was elected by the House of Representatives.

where tariffs of all kinds were unpopular—was assumed to be safely in the general's camp regardless of his stand on the tariff. Therefore, promoters of Jackson's candidacy felt safe in supporting a high tariff to swing critical votes in Jackson's direction. Jackson himself had never categorically opposed protective tariffs so long as they were "judicious."

As it turned out, the resulting tariff law was anything but judicious. Congress had operated on a give-and-take principle, trying to provide something for everybody. Those favoring protection for farmers agreed to protection for manufacturers and vice versa. The substantial across-the-board increase in duties that resulted, however, angered southern free traders and became known as the "tariff of abominations." Historians long erred in explaining the 1828 tariff as a complex Jacksonian plot that backfired; it was in fact an early example of how special interest groups can achieve their goals in democratic politics through the process of legislative bargaining known as logrolling.

Jackson Comes to Power

The campaign of 1828 actually began with Adams's election in 1824. Rallying around the charge of a corrupt bargain between Adams and Clay, Jackson's supporters began to organize on the state and local level with an eye to reversing the outcome of the election. By late 1827, a Jackson committee was functioning in virtually every county and important town or city in the nation. Influential state or regional leaders who had supported other candidates in 1824 now rallied behind the Tennessean to create a formidable coalition.

The most significant of these were Vice President Calhoun, who now spoke for the militant states' rights sentiment of the South; Senator Martin Van Buren, who dominated New York politics through the political machine known as the Albany Regency; and two Kentucky editors, Francis P. Blair and Amos Kendall, who worked in the West to mobilize opposition to Henry Clay and his "American system" (a plan for government-sponsored economic development emphasizing protective tariffs and internal improvements). As they prepared themselves for the canvass of 1828, these leaders and their many local followers laid the foundations for the first modern American political party—the Democrats. The fact that the Democratic party was founded to promote the cause of a particular presidential candidate revealed a central characteristic of the emerging two-party system. From this time on, according to historian Richard P. McCormick, national parties existed primarily "to engage in a contest for the presidency." Without this great prize, there would have been little incentive to create national organizations out of the parties and factions developing in the several states.

The election of 1828 saw the birth of a new era of mass democracy. The mighty effort on behalf of Jackson featured the widespread use of such electioneering techniques as huge public rallies, torchlight parades, and lavish barbecues or picnics paid for by the candidate's supporters. Personalities and mudslinging dominated the campaign. The Democratic party press and a legion of pamphleteers bombarded the public with vicious personal attacks on Adams and praise of "Old Hickory" as Jackson was called. The supporters of Adams responded in kind; they even sunk to the level of accusing Jackson's wife Rachel of bigamy and adultery because she had unwittingly married Jackson before being officially divorced from her first husband. The Democrats then came up with the utterly false charge that Adams's wife was born out of wedlock!

What gave Jacksonians the edge was their success in portraying their candidate as an authentic man of the people, despite his substantial fortune in land and slaves. His backwoods upbringing, his record as a popular military hero and Indian fighter, and even his lack of education were touted as evidence that he was a true representative of the common people, especially the plain folk of the South and the West. In the words of one of

When it was clear that he would not win the presidency in 1824, Henry Clay, shown here in an 1822 portrait by Charles Bird King, threw his support to John Quincy Adams.

An 1835 painting of Andrew Jackson in the heroic style by Thomas Sully. The painting shows Jackson as the common people saw him.

his supporters, Jackson had "a judgment unclouded by the visionary speculations of the academician." Adams, according to Democratic propagandists, was the exact opposite—an over-educated aristocrat, more at home in the salon and the study than among plain people. Nature's nobleman was pitted against the aloof New England intellectual, and Adams never really had a chance.

Jackson won by a popular vote margin of 150,000 and by more than 2 to 1 in the electoral college. Clearly Jackson's organization had been more effective and his popular appeal substantially greater. He had piled up massive majorities in the Deep South, but the voters elsewhere divided fairly evenly. Adams, in fact, won a majority of the electoral vote in the northern states. Furthermore, it was not clear what kind of a mandate Jackson had won. Most of the politicians in his camp favored states' rights and limited government as against the nationalism of Adams and Clay, but the general himself had never taken a clear public stand on such issues as banks, tariffs, and internal improvements. He did, however, stand for the removal of Indians from the Gulf states, and this was the key to his immense popularity in that region.

Jackson turned out to be one of the most forceful and domineering of American presidents. His most striking character traits were an indomitable will, an intolerance of opposition, and a prickly pride that would not permit him to forgive or forget an insult or supposed act of betrayal. It is sometimes hard to determine whether his political actions were motivated by principle or personal spite. As a young man on his own in a frontier environment, he had learned to fight his own battles. Somewhat violent in temper and action, he fought a number of duels and served in wars against the British, the Spanish, and the Indians with a zeal his critics found excessive. His experiences had made him tough and resourceful but had also deprived him of the

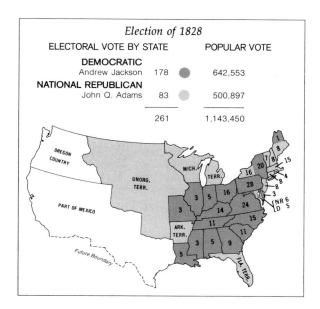

Election of 1828

ELECTORAL VOTE BY STATE   POPULAR VOTE

DEMOCRATIC
Andrew Jackson   178   642,553
NATIONAL REPUBLICAN
John Q. Adams   83   500,897

261   1,143,450

Jackson's resigning cabinet members were, according to this cartoon, rats deserting a crumbling house.

flexibility normally associated with successful politicians. Yet he generally got what he wanted.

Jackson's presidency commenced with his open endorsement of rotation of officeholders or what his critics called "the spoils system." Although he did not actually depart radically from his predecessors in the extent to which he removed federal officeholders and replaced them with his supporters, he was the first president to defend this practice as a legitimate application of democratic doctrine. He proclaimed in his first annual message that "the duties of all public officers are . . . so plain and simple that men of intelligence may readily qualify themselves for their performance" and that "no man has any more intrinsic claim to office than another."

Midway through his first administration Jackson completely reorganized his cabinet, replacing almost all of his original appointees. At the root of this upheaval was a growing feud between Jackson and Vice President Calhoun, but the incident that brought it to a head was the Peggy Eaton affair. Peggy O'Neale Eaton was the daughter of a Washington tavern owner who married Secretary of War John Eaton in 1829. Because of gossip about her moral character, the wives of other cabinet members refused to receive her socially. Jackson became her fervent champion, partly because he found the charges against her reminiscent of the slanders against his late wife Rachel. When he raised the issue of Mrs. Eaton's social status at a cabinet meeting, only

Secretary of State Van Buren, a widower, supported his stand. This seemingly trivial incident led to the resignation of all but one of the cabinet members, and the president was able to begin again with a fresh slate. Although Van Buren resigned with the rest to promote a thorough reorganization, his loyalty was rewarded by his appointment as minister to England and strong prospects of future favor.

Indian Removal

The first major policy question facing the Jackson administration concerned the fate of Native Americans. Jackson had long favored removing eastern Indians to lands beyond the Mississippi. In his military service on the southern frontier, he had been directly involved in persuading and coercing tribal groups to emigrate. Jackson's support of removal was no different from the policy of previous administrations. The only real issues to be determined were how rapidly and thoroughly the process should be carried out and by what means. At the time of Jackson's election, the states of Georgia, Alabama, and Mississippi, distressed by the federal government's failure to eliminate the substantial Indian enclaves remaining within their boundaries, were clamoring for quick action. Since Adams seemed to have dragged his feet on the issue, voters in these states turned overwhelmingly to Jackson, who promised to expel the Indians without delay.

The greatest obstacle to voluntary relocation was the Cherokee nation, which held lands in Georgia, Alabama, North Carolina, and Tennessee. The Cherokees refused to move. They had instituted a republican form of government for themselves, achieved literacy in their own language, and made considerable progress toward adopting a settled agrarian way of life similar to that of southern whites. The professed aim of the government's Indian policy was the "civilization" of the Indians, and the official reason given for removal was that this aim could not be accomplished in areas surrounded by white settlements, subject to demoralizing frontier influences. Missionaries and northeastern philanthropists argued the Cherokees were a major exception and should be allowed to remain where they were.

The southern states disagreed. Immediately after Jackson's election, Georgia extended its state laws over the Cherokees. Before his inauguration, Alabama and Mississippi took similar action by asserting state authority over the tribes in their own states. This legislation defied provisions of the Constitution giving the federal government exclusive jurisdiction over Indian affairs and also violated specific treaties. As anticipated, Jackson quickly gave his endorsement to the state actions. His own attitude toward Indians was that they were children when they did the white man's bidding and savage beasts when they resisted. He was also keenly aware of his political debt to the land-hungry states of the South. Consequently, in his December 1829 message to Congress, he advocated a new and more coercive removal policy. He denied Cherokee autonomy, asserted the primacy of states' rights over Indian rights, and called for the speedy and thorough

Sequoyah's invention of the Cherokee alphabet enabled thousands of Cherokees to read and write primers and newspapers published in their own language.

removal of all eastern Indians to designated areas beyond the Mississippi.

Early in 1830, the president's congressional supporters introduced a bill to implement this policy. The ensuing debate was vigorous and heated. Opponents took up the cause of the Cherokees in particular and charged that the president had defied the Constitution by removing federal protection from the southeastern tribes. But Jackson and his supporters were determined to ride roughshod over humanitarian or constitutional objections to Indian dispossession. With strong support from the South and the western border states, the removal bill passed the Senate by a vote of 28 to 19 and the House by the narrow margin of 102 to 97.

Jackson then moved quickly to conclude the necessary treaties, using the threat of unilateral state action to bludgeon the tribes into submission. In 1832, he condoned Georgia's defiance of a Supreme Court decision (*Worcester* v. *Georgia*) that denied the right of a state to extend its jurisdiction over tribal lands. By 1833, all the southeastern tribes except the Cherokees had agreed to evacuate their ancestral homes. In 1838, a stubbornly resisting majority faction of the Cherokees were rounded up by federal troops and forcibly marched to Oklahoma. This trek—known as the "Trail of Tears"—was made under such harsh conditions that almost 4,000 of approximately 13,000 marchers died on the way. The Cherokee removal exposed the prejudiced and greedy side of Jacksonian democracy.

The Nullification Crisis

During the 1820s, Southerners became increasingly fearful of federal encroachment on the rights of the states. Behind this concern, in South Carolina at least, was a strengthened commitment to the preservation of slavery and a resulting anxiety about possible uses of federal power to strike at the "peculiar institution." Hoping to keep the explosive slavery issue out of the political limelight, South Carolinians seized on another genuine grievance—the protective tariff—as the issue on which to take their stand in favor of a state veto power over federal actions they viewed as contrary to their interests. As a staple-producing and exporting region, the South had sound economic reasons for favoring free trade. Tariffs increased the prices that southern agriculturalists paid for manufactured goods and threatened to undermine their foreign markets by inciting counterprotection. An economic crisis in the South Carolina upcountry during the 1820s made that state particularly receptive to extreme positions on the tariff and states' rights.

Vice President John C. Calhoun emerged as the leader of the states' rights insurgency in South Carolina, abandoning his earlier support of nationalism and the American system. After the passage of the tariff of abominations in 1828, the state legislature declared the new duties unconstitutional and endorsed a lengthy statement—written anonymously by Calhoun—that affirmed the right of an individual state to nullify federal law. Calhoun supported Jackson in 1828 and planned to serve amicably as his vice president, expecting Jackson would support his native region on questions involving the tariff and states' rights. He also entertained hopes of succeeding Jackson as president.

Early in his administration, Jackson appeared well attuned to the southern slave-holding position on state versus federal authority. Besides acquiescing in Georgia's de facto nullification of federal treaties upholding Indian tribal rights, he vetoed a major internal improvements bill in 1830, invoking a strict construction of the Constitution to deny federal funds for the building of the Maysville Road in Kentucky.

In the meantime, however, a bitter personal feud developed between Jackson and Calhoun. The vice president and his wife were viewed by Jackson as prime movers in the ostracism of Peggy Eaton. Furthermore, evidence came to light that Calhoun, as secretary of war in Monroe's cabinet in 1818, had privately advocated punishing Jackson for his incursion into Florida. As Calhoun lost favor with Jackson, it became clear that Van Buren rather than the vice president would be Jackson's designated successor. The personal breach between Jackson and Calhoun colored and intensified their confrontation over nullification and the tariff.

The two men differed on matters of principle as well. Although generally a defender of states' rights and strict construction of the Constitution, Jackson opposed the theory of nullification as a threat to the survival of the Union. In his view, federal power should be held in check, but this did not mean the states were truly sovereign. His nationalism was that of a military man who had fought for the United States against foreign enemies and was not about to permit the nation's disintegration at the hands of domestic dissidents. The differences between Jackson and Calhoun came into the open at the Jefferson Day Dinner in 1830, when Jackson offered the toast "Our Union: It must be preserved"; to which Calhoun responded: "The Union next to Liberty most dear. May we always remember that it can only be preserved by distributing equally the benefits and the burdens of the Union."

In 1830 and 1831, the movement against the tariff gained strength in South Carolina. Calhoun openly took the lead, elaborating further on his view that states had the right to set aside federal laws. In 1832, Congress passed a new tariff that lowered the rates slightly but retained the principle of protection. Supporters of nullification argued that the new law simply demonstrated that no genuine relief could be expected from Washington. They then succeeded in persuading the South Carolina state legislature to call a special convention. When the convention met in

Robert Lindneux, The Trail of Tears *(1942). Cherokees, carrying their few possessions, are prodded along by U. S. soldiers on the "Trail of Tears." Several thousand Native Americans died on the ruthless, forced march from their homelands in the East to the newly established Indian Territory in Oklahoma.*

November 1832, the members voted overwhelmingly to nullify the tariffs of 1828 and 1832 and to forbid the collection of customs duties within the state.

Jackson reacted with characteristic decisiveness. He alerted the secretary of war to prepare for possible military action, issued a proclamation denouncing nullification as a treasonous attack on the Union, and asked Congress to vote him the authority to use the army to enforce the tariff. At the same time, he sought to pacify the nullifiers somewhat by recommending a lower tariff. Congress responded by enacting the Force Bill—which gave the president the military powers he sought—and the compromise tariff of 1833. The latter was primarily the work of Jackson's political enemy Henry Clay, but the president signed it anyway. Faced with Jackson's clear intention to use force if necessary and somewhat appeased by the prospect of a lower tariff, South Carolina suspended the nullification ordinance in late January 1833 and formally rescinded it in March, after the new tariff had been enacted. To demonstrate they had not conceded their constitutional position, the convention delegates concluded their deliberations by nullifying the Force Bill.

The nullification crisis revealed South Carolinians would not tolerate any federal action that seemed contrary to their interests or raised doubts about the institution of slavery. The nullifiers' philosophy implied the right of secession as well as the right to declare laws of Congress null and void. As subsequent events would show, a fear of northern meddling with slavery was the main spur to the growth of a militant doctrine of state sovereignty in the South. At the time of the nullification crisis, the other slave states had not yet developed such strong anxieties about the future of the "peculiar institution" and had not embraced South Carolina's radical conception of state sovereignty. Jackson was himself a Southerner and a slaveholder, a man who detested abolitionists and everything they stood for. In general, he was a proslavery president; later he would use his executive power to stop antislavery literature from being carried by the U. S. mails.

Some far-sighted southern loyalists, however, were alarmed by the Unionist doctrines Jackson propounded in his proclamation against nullification. More strongly than any previous president, he had asserted the federal government was supreme over the states and that the Union was indivisible. What was more, he had justified the

Vice President John C. Calhoun emerged as a champion of states' rights during the nullification crisis, a time when cartoons depicted the emaciated South burdened by tariffs while the North grew fat at southern expense.

use of force against states that denied federal authority.

THE BANK WAR AND THE SECOND PARTY SYSTEM

Jackson's most important and controversial use of executive power was his successful attack on the Bank of the United States. "The Bank War" revealed some of the deepest concerns of Jackson and his supporters and dramatically expressed their concept of democracy. It also aroused intense opposition to the president and his policies, an opposition that crystallized in a new national party—the Whigs. The destruction of the Bank and the economic disruption that followed brought to the forefront the issue of the government's relationship to the nation's financial system. Differences on this question helped to sustain the new two-party system.

Mr. Biddle's Bank

The Bank of the United States had long been embroiled in public controversy. Its role in precipitating the panic of 1819 by first extending credit freely and then suddenly calling in its loans had led many, especially in the South and the West, to blame the Bank for the subsequent depression. But after Nicholas Biddle took over the Bank's presidency in 1823, it regained public confidence. Biddle was an able manager who probably understood the mysteries of banking

and currency better than any other American of his generation. A Philadelphia gentleman of broad culture, extensive education, and some political experience, his major faults were his arrogance and his vanity. He was inclined to rely too much on his own judgment and refused to admit his mistakes until it was too late to correct them. But his record prior to the confrontation with Jackson was a good one. In 1825 and again in 1828, he acted decisively to curb an overextension of credit by state banks and helped avert a recurrence of the boom-and-bust cycle.

The actual performance of the Bank was not the only target of criticism about it. Old-line Jeffersonians had always opposed it on principle, both because they viewed its establishment as unconstitutional and because it placed too much power in the hands of a small, privileged group. The Bank was a chartered monopoly, an essentially private corporation that performed public services in return for exclusive economic rights. "In 1828," according to historian Robert Remini, "the Bank was a financial colossus, entrenched in the nation's economy, possessing the means of draining specie from state banks at will and regulating the currency according to its own estimate of the nation's needs."

Because of the Bank's great influence, it was easy to blame it for anything that went wrong with the economy. For those who had misgivings about the rise of the national market, it epitomized the forces threatening the independence and prosperity of small producers. In an era of rising white men's democracy, an obvious and telling objection to the Bank was simply that it possessed great power and privilege without being under popular control.

The Bank Veto and the Election of 1832

Jackson came into office with strong reservations about banking and paper money in general—in part as a result of his own brushes with bankruptcy after accepting promissory notes that depreciated in value. He also harbored suspicions that branches of the Bank of the United States had illicitly used their influence on behalf of his opponent in the presidential election. In his annual messages in 1829 and 1830, Jackson called on Congress to begin discussing "possible modification of a system which cannot continue to exist in its present form without . . . perpetual apprehensions and discontent on the part of the States and the People."

Biddle began to worry about the fate of the Bank's charter when it came up for renewal in 1836. At the same time, Jackson was listening to the advice of close friends and unofficial advisers—members of his "Kitchen Cabinet"—especially Amos Kendall and Francis P. Blair, who thought an attack on the Bank would provide a good party issue for the election of 1832. Biddle then made a fateful blunder. Panicked by the presidential messages and the anti-Bank oratory of congressional Jacksonians like Senator Thomas Hart Benton of Missouri, he determined to seek recharter by Congress in 1832, four years ahead of schedule. Senator Henry Clay, leader of the antiadministration forces on Capitol Hill, encouraged this move because he was convinced Jackson had chosen the unpopular side of the issue and would be embarrassed or even discredited by a congressional endorsement of the Bank.

The bill to recharter, which was introduced in the House and Senate in early 1832, aroused Jackson and unified his administration and party against renewal. The bill found many supporters in Congress, however. A number of legislators had received loans from the Bank, and the economy seemed to be prospering under the Bank's guidance. As a result, the bill to recharter passed Congress with ease.

The next move was Jackson's, and he made the most of the opportunity. He vetoed the bill and defended his action with ringing statements of principle. After repeating his opinion that the Bank was unconstitutional, notwithstanding the Supreme Court's ruling on the issue, he went on to argue that it violated the fundamental rights of the people in a democratic society: "In the full enjoyment of the gifts of Heaven and the fruits of superior industry, economy, and virtue, every man is equally entitled to protection by law; but when the laws undertake to add to those natural and just advantages artificial distinctions, to grant . . . exclusive privileges, the humble members of society—the farmers, mechanics, and laborers—who have neither the time nor the means of securing like favors to themselves, have a right to complain of the injustice of their government." Government, he added, should "confine itself to equal protection."

Jackson thus called on the common people to join him in fighting the "monster" corporation. His veto message was the first ever to use more than strictly constitutional arguments and to deal directly with social and economic issues. Congressional attempts to override the veto failed, and Jackson resolved to take the entire issue to the people in the upcoming presidential election.

The 1832 election, the first in which candidates were chosen by national nominating conventions, pitted Jackson against Henry Clay, standard-bearer of the National Republicans. Although the Democrats did not adopt a formal platform, the party stood firmly behind Jackson in his opposition to rechartering the Bank. Clay and the National Republicans attempted to marshal the pro-Bank sentiment that was strong in many parts of the country. But Jackson won a great personal triumph, garnering 219 electoral votes to 49 for Clay. His share of the popular vote was not quite as high as it was in 1828, but it was substantial enough to be interpreted as a mandate for continuing the war against the Bank.

Killing the Bank

Not content with preventing the Bank from getting a new charter, the victorious Jackson now resolved to attack it directly by removing federal deposits from Biddle's vaults. Jackson told Van Buren, "The bank . . . is trying to kill me, but I will kill it." The Bank had indeed used all the political influence it could muster in an attempt to prevent Jackson's reelection, in an act of self-defense. Old Hickory regarded Biddle's actions as a personal attack, part of a devious plot to destroy the president's reputation and deny him the popular approval he deserved. Although he presided over the first modern American political party, Jackson did not really share Van Buren's belief in the legitimacy of a competitive party system. In his view, his opponents were not merely wrong, they were evil and deserved to be destroyed. Furthermore, the election results convinced him he was the people's chosen instrument in the struggle against corruption and privilege, the only man who could save the pure republicanism of Jefferson and the Founders from the "monster bank."

In order to remove the deposits from the Bank, Jackson had to overcome strong resistance in his own cabinet. When one secretary of the treasury refused to support the policy, he was shifted to another cabinet post. When a second balked at carrying out removal, he was replaced by Roger B. Taney, a Jackson loyalist and dedicated opponent of the Bank. Beginning in late September

Aided by Van Buren (center), Jackson wields his veto rod against the Bank, whose heads represent the directors of the state branches. Biddle is wearing the top hat.

1833, Taney ceased depositing government money in the Bank of the United States and began to withdraw the funds already there. Although Jackson had earlier suggested the government keep its money in some kind of public bank, he had never worked out the details and made a specific proposal to Congress. The problem of how to dispose of the funds was therefore resolved by an ill-advised decision to place them in selected state banks. By the end of 1833, twenty-three state banks had been chosen as depositories. Opponents charged the banks had been selected for political rather than fiscal reasons and dubbed them Jackson's "pet banks." Since Congress refused to approve administration proposals to regulate the credit policies of these banks, Jackson's effort to shift to a hard-money economy was quickly nullified by the use the state banks made of these new deposits. They extended credit more recklessly than before and increased the amount of paper money in circulation.

The Bank of the United States counterattacked by calling in outstanding loans and instituting a policy of credit contraction that helped bring on an economic recession. Biddle hoped to win support for recharter by demonstrating that weakening the Bank's position would be disastrous for the economy. With some justice, the president's

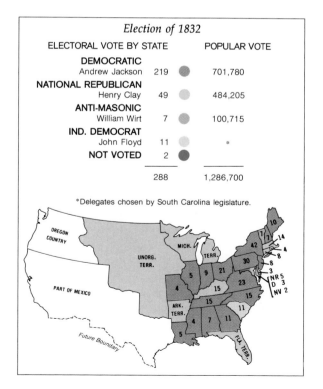

Election of 1832

ELECTORAL VOTE BY STATE		POPULAR VOTE
DEMOCRATIC		
Andrew Jackson	219	701,780
NATIONAL REPUBLICAN		
Henry Clay	49	484,205
ANTI-MASONIC		
William Wirt	7	100,715
IND. DEMOCRAT		
John Floyd	11	*
NOT VOTED	2	
	288	1,286,700

*Delegates chosen by South Carolina legislature.

supporters accused Biddle of deliberately and unnecessarily causing economic distress out of personal resentment and a desire to maintain his unchecked powers and privileges. The Bank never did regain its charter.

Strong opposition to Jackson's fiscal policies developed in Congress. Henry Clay and his supporters contended that the president had violated the Bank's charter and exceeded his constitutional authority when he removed the deposits. They eventually persuaded the Senate to approve a motion of censure. Jacksonians in the House were able to block such action, but the president was further humiliated when the Senate refused to confirm Taney as secretary of the treasury. Not all of this criticism and obstructionism can be attributed to sour grapes on the part of pro-Bank politicians. Some congressmen who originally defended Jackson's veto now became disenchanted with the president because they thought he had gone too far in asserting the powers of his office.

The Emergence of the Whigs

The coalition that passed the censure resolution in the Senate provided the nucleus for a new national party—the Whigs. The leadership of the new party and a majority of its support came from National Republicans associated with Clay and New England ex-Federalists led by Senator Daniel Webster of Massachusetts. The Whigs also picked up critical support from southern proponents of states' rights who had been upset by the political nationalism of Jackson's stand on nullification and now saw an unconstitutional abuse of power in his withdrawal of federal deposits from the Bank of the United States. Even Calhoun and his nullifiers occasionally cooperated with the Whig camp. The initial rallying cry for this diverse anti-Jackson coalition was "executive usurpation." The Whig label was chosen because of its associations with both English and American Revolutionary opposition to royal power and prerogatives. In their propaganda, the Whigs portrayed the tyrannical designs of "King Andrew" and his court.

The Whigs also gradually absorbed the Anti-Masonic party, a surprisingly strong political movement that had arisen in the northeastern states in the late 1820s and early 1830s.

Capitalizing on the hysteria aroused by the 1826 disappearance and apparent murder of a New Yorker who had threatened to reveal the secrets of the Masonic order, the Anti-Masons exploited traditional American fears of secret societies and conspiracies. They also appealed successfully to the moral concerns of the northern middle class under the sway of an emerging evangelical Protestantism. (For more on the evangelical movement, see Chapter 11.) Anti-Masons detested Jacksonianism mainly because it stood for a toleration of diverse lifestyles. Democrats did not think government should be concerned about people who drank, gambled, or found better things to do than go to church on Sundays. Their opponents from the Anti-Masonic tradition believed government should restrict such "sinful" behavior. This desire for moral and religious uniformity contributed an important cultural dimension to northern Whiggery.

As the election of 1836 approached, the government's fiscal policies also provoked a localized rebellion among the urban working-class elements of the Democratic coalition. In New York City, a dissident faction broke with the regular Democratic organization mainly over issues involving banking and currency. These radicals—called "Loco-Focos" after the matches they used for illumination when their opponents turned off the gaslights at a party meeting—favored a strict hard-money policy and condemned Jackson's transfer of federal deposits to the state banks as inflationary. Because they wanted working people to be paid in specie rather than bank notes, the Loco-Focos went beyond opposition to the Bank of the United States and attacked state banks as well. Seeing no basis for cooperation with the Whigs, they established the independent Equal Rights Party and nominated a separate state ticket for 1836.

Jackson himself had hard-money sentiments and regarded the "pet bank" solution as a stopgap measure rather than a final solution to the money problem. Somewhat reluctantly, he surrendered to congressional pressure in early 1836 and signed legislation allocating surplus federal revenues to the deposit banks, increasing their numbers, and weakening federal controls over them. The result was runaway inflation. State banks in the South and West responded to demands from land-speculating interests by issuing a new flood of paper money. Reacting somewhat belatedly to the speculative mania he had inadvertently helped to create, Jackson pricked the bubble on July 11, 1836. He issued his "specie circular," requiring that after August 15 only gold and silver would be accepted in payment for public lands. This action served to curb inflation and land speculation but did so in such a sudden and drastic way that it helped precipitate the financial panic of 1837.

The Rise and Fall of Van Buren

As his successor, Jackson chose Martin Van Buren, who had served him loyally as vice president during his second term. Van Buren was the greatest master of practical politics in the Democratic party, and the Democratic National Convention of 1835 unanimously confirmed Jackson's choice. In accepting the nomination, Van Buren promised to "tread generally in the footsteps of General Jackson."

The newly created Whig party, reflecting the diversity of its constituency, did not try to decide on a single standard-bearer. Instead, each region chose candidates—Daniel Webster in the East, William Henry Harrison of Ohio (also the Anti-Masonic nominee) in the Old Northwest, and Hugh Lawson White of Tennessee (a former Jackson supporter) in the South. Whigs hoped to deprive Van Buren of enough electoral votes to throw the election into the House of Representatives where one of the Whigs might stand a chance.

This stratagem proved unsuccessful. Van Buren carried fifteen of the twenty-six states and won a clear majority in the electoral college. But the election foreshadowed future trouble for the Democrats, particularly in the South. There the Whigs ran virtually even, erasing the enormous majorities that Jackson had run up in 1828 and 1832. The emergence of a two-party system in the previously solid Deep South resulted from two factors—opposition to some of Jackson's policies and the image of Van Buren as an unreliable Yankee politician. The division did not reflect basic disagreement on the slavery issue. Whigs and Democrats shared a commitment to protecting slavery, and each tried to persuade the electorate they could do the job better than the opposition.

An adroit politician and a loyal vice president to Jackson, Martin Van Buren was Jackson's choice and the Democratic party's nominee for president in 1836.

As he took office Van Buren was immediately faced with a catastrophic depression. The price of cotton fell by almost 50 percent, banks all over the nation suspended specie payments, many businesses went bankrupt, and unemployed persons demonstrated in several cities. The sale of public lands fell off so drastically that the federal surplus, earmarked in 1836 for distribution to the states, now became a deficit.

The panic of 1837, economic historians have concluded, was not exclusively, or even primarily, the result of government policies. It was in fact international in scope and reflected some complex changes in the world economy that were beyond the control of American policymakers. But the Whigs were quick to blame the state of the economy on Jacksonian finance, and the administration had to make a politically effective response. Since Van Buren and his party were committed to a policy of laissez-faire on the federal level, there was little or nothing they could do to relieve economic distress through subsidies or relief measures. But Van Buren could at least try to salvage the federal funds deposited in shaky state banks and devise a new system of public finance that would not contribute to future panics by fueling speculation and credit expansion.

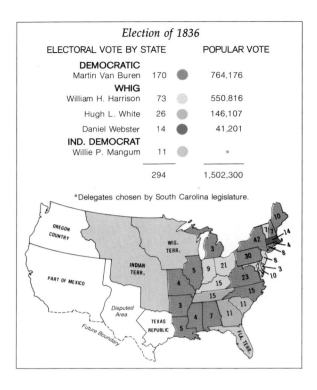

Election of 1836

ELECTORAL VOTE BY STATE			POPULAR VOTE
DEMOCRATIC			
Martin Van Buren	170		764,176
WHIG			
William H. Harrison	73		550,816
Hugh L. White	26		146,107
Daniel Webster	14		41,201
IND. DEMOCRAT			
Willie P. Mangum	11		*
	294		1,502,300

*Delegates chosen by South Carolina legislature.

Van Buren's solution was to establish a public depository for government funds with no connections whatsoever to commercial banking. His proposal for such an "independent subtreasury" aroused intense opposition from the congressional Whigs, who strongly favored the reestablishment of a national bank as the only way to restore economic stability. Whig resistance stalled the subtreasury bill for three years; it was not until 1840 that it was enacted into law. In the meantime, the economy had temporarily revived in 1838 only to sink again into a deeper depression the following year.

Van Buren's chances for reelection in 1840 were undoubtedly hurt by the state of the economy. But the fact that he lacked the popular appeal and personal charisma of Jackson left him vulnerable to a Whig campaign based on personalities and symbolism. In 1836, the Whigs had been disorganized and had not fully mastered the new democratic politics. But in 1840, they settled on a single nominee and outdid the Democrats in grass-roots organization and popular electioneering. The Whigs passed over the true leader of their party, Henry Clay, because he was identified with too many controversial positions. Instead they found their own Jackson in William Henry Harrison, a military hero of advanced age who was associated in the public mind with the battle of Tippecanoe and the winning of the West.

Harrison's views on public issues were little known, and the Whigs ran him without a platform to void distracting the electorate from his personal qualities. They pretended Harrison had been born in a log cabin—actually it was a pillared mansion—and that he preferred hard cider to more effete beverages. To balance the ticket and increase its appeal in the South they chose John Tyler of Virginia, a converted states' rights Democrat, to be Harrison's running mate.

Using the slogan, "Tippecanoe and Tyler, Too," the Whigs pulled out all stops in their bid for the White House. Rallies and parades were organized in every locality, complete with posters, placards, campaign hats and emblems, special songs, and even movable log cabins filled with coonskin caps and barrels of cider for the faithful. Imitating the Jacksonian propaganda against Adams in 1828, they portrayed Van Buren as a luxury-loving aristocrat and compared him with their own homespun candidate. The Democrats countered by using many of the same methods, but they simply could not project an image of Van Buren that rivaled Harrison's grass-roots appeal. There was an enormous turnout on election day—78 percent of those eligible to vote. When it was over, Harrison had parlayed a narrow edge in the popular vote into a landslide in the electoral college. He carried 19 of the 26 states and won 234 electoral votes to 60 for Van Buren. Buoyed by the electorate's belief that their policies might revive the economy, the Whigs also won control of both houses of Congress.

HEYDAY OF THE SECOND PARTY SYSTEM

America's "second party system" came of age in the election of 1840. Unlike the earlier competition between Federalists and Jeffersonian Republicans, the rivalry of Democrats and Whigs made the two-party pattern a normal feature of electoral politics in the United States. During the 1840s, the two national parties competed on fair-

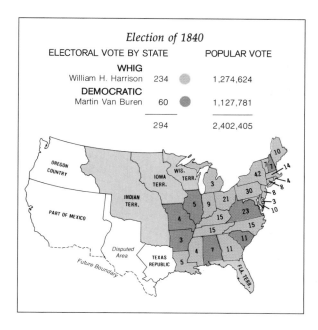

Election of 1840

ELECTORAL VOTE BY STATE		POPULAR VOTE
WHIG		
William H. Harrison	234	1,274,624
DEMOCRATIC		
Martin Van Buren	60	1,127,781
	294	2,402,405

ly equal terms for the support of the electorate. Allegiance to one party or the other became an important source of personal identity for many Americans and increased their interest and participation in politics.

In addition to drama and entertainment, the parties offered the voters a real choice of programs and ideologies. Whigs stood for a "positive liberal state"—which meant government had the right and duty to subsidize or protect enterprises that could contribute to general prosperity and economic growth. Democrats normally advocated a "negative liberal state." According to them, government should keep its hands off the economy; only by doing nothing could it avoid favoring special interests and interfering with free competition. They charged that granting subsidies or special charters to any group would create pockets of privilege or monopoly and put ordinary citizens under the thumb of the rich and powerful.

Conflict over economic issues helped determine each party's base of support. In the Whig camp were most industrialists and merchants, plus a majority of those farmers and planters who had adapted successfully to a market economy. Democrats appealed mainly to smaller farmers,

workers, declining gentry, and emerging entrepreneurs who were excluded from the established commercial groups that stood to benefit most from Whig programs. Democratic rhetoric about monopoly and privilege appealed to those who had mixed or negative feelings about the rise of a national market economy. To some extent, this division pitted richer and more privileged Americans against those who were poorer and less economically or socially secure. But it did not follow class lines in any simple or direct way. Many businessmen were Democrats, and large numbers of wage earners voted Whig. Merchants engaged in the import trade had no use for Whiggish high tariffs, whereas workers in industries clamoring for protection often concluded that their jobs depended on such duties.

Economic interest and ideology was not the only factor behind the choice of parties. Lifestyles and ethnic or religious identities strongly affected party loyalties during this period. In the northern states, one way to tell the typical Whig from the typical Democrat was to see what each did on Sunday. A person who went to one of the evangelical Protestant churches was very likely to be a Whig. On the other hand, the person who attended a ritualized service—Catholic, Lutheran, or Episcopalian—or did not go to church at all was most probably a Democrat.

The Democrats were the favored party of immigrants, Catholics, freethinkers, backwoods farmers, and those of all classes who enjoyed traditional amusements condemned by the new breed of moral reformers. One thing all these groups had in common was a desire to be left alone, free of restrictions on their freedom to think and behave as they liked. The Whigs enjoyed particularly strong support among Protestants of old stock living in smaller cities, towns, and prosperous rural areas devoted to market farming. In general, the Whigs welcomed a market economy but wished to restrain the individualism and disorder it created by enforcing cultural and moral values derived from the Puritan tradition. Most of those who sought to be "their brothers' keepers" were Whigs. Some of the roots of party allegiance can be found in local divisions between old stock Americans and immigrants over such matters as temperance, keeping the Sabbath, and reading the Protestant Bible in public schools.

On the Hustings in Michigan

Political candidates of the Jacksonian era traveled from town to town giving stump speeches. The political gatherings at which they spoke provided entertainment as well as an excellent source of political news. The sketch is by George Caleb Bingham, one of the most prolific of the democratic genre painters.

In 1838, Martin Van Buren's cousin Ephriam, a farmer in western Michigan, marched to the polls in rank with some seventy or eighty other Democrats, each carrying a hickory stick in honor of Andrew Jackson. An enthusiastic supporter of the Whig party fearlessly attempted to break the line. Ephriam Van Buren was called on to restrain him, which

he did. A few days after this event, an old Democrat told the Whig that if he wished to succeed in politics, he must vote with them. "What, I join you?" he exclaimed. "Sooner than vote the Democratic ticket, I would crawl on my hands and knees from Battle Creek to Detroit, and be struck by lightning every other mile." Others told a similar story of the old Democrat who once voted the Whig ticket, and the next day, goaded by his sins, bought half a dozen candles and took them home "to light them and sit up and hate himself by them." Politics was very serious business for the common voter in the age of Jackson, full of important ritual; it was also the best show in town.

As did revivalistic "camp meetings," political gatherings brought crowds and speakers into direct contact with the speakers working to entertain, inform, and convert the crowd. Between the first of July and the autumn election day, wandering political orators and local candidates would go from village to township, speaking to ready audiences on the topics of the day. An old tree stump or "husting" would often be the only stage, leading citizens to call all small-town political orators "stump" speakers. These "hustings" visits would inform the voters of each party's stance on the issues of the day; before the era of the telegraph, stump

speakers were the best source of political news.

Party workers organized parades and barbeques to boost the size and enthusiasm of the crowds. The parades would begin in the morning, at first informally as people arrived in groups from surrounding areas, and then with great pageantry, with brass bands, and wagons full of farmers and artisans joining in. A Michigan college student in 1851 recalled a time eleven years earlier, in "those glorious days of Tippecanoe and Tyler, too," when a nine-year-old from Troy, Michigan, a boy who had earnestly declared himself a Whig, was seen "on the fourth of July of that eventful year, seated upon the reach of a double wagon 45 feet long, in company with some fifty others of his party, on his way to assist in the ceremonies of the day." The informant added that "our youthful politician, in his zeal, inflicted a severe castigation upon a young gentleman of about his age because he had the audacity to mar the solemnity of the occasion, by shouting for 'Young Hickory.'" The youthful Whig, it seems, had become "gloriously fuddled" by a combination of partisan spirit and hard cider.

Such festivities would lead into the speeches. Candidates for office would either speak on their own or debate their opponents. Before and after speaking, the politicians would mix with the crowd. A Michigan schoolteacher described a favorite politician "familiarly mingling among the Democrats at their meetings, taking seat with them before the speaking began, and as one of them, talking freely on the subjects incident to the occasion. I used to think that here was where [he] got his power with the masses." That practice of elbow rubbing closed the distance between audience and speaker, between the leader and the led.

The audiences did their part to fill the gap, typically responding generously during the stump speech and filling the air with political songs between addresses. A conservative observer from Michigan noted in 1845 that prior to a typical political speech the "miserable rabble" would greet the prospective speaker with "unmeaning and bacchana-

lian cries." The hurrahs of the audience (and songs with lyrics such as "Van, Van, he's a used-up man," and "The mustang colt has a killing pace/he's bound to win in the White House race") would inspire the orator. "It is well known that unless heartily cheered the 'stump orator' can do nothing," the sanctimonious onlooker continued. "It has therefore been supposed that in this kind of oratory the elements of eloquence are latently contained in cheers and are then conveyed through some unknown medium, perhaps animal magnetism, to the speaker."

Good stump speakers possessed a dramatic ability to communicate to the audience its own fears and concerns. The nearly mystic communication between speaker and hearer comes through in the following depiction of a Michigan Whig's elo-

quence and sincerity on the stump: "In whatever crowd or assembly he might be his mind would catch with marvelous facility the general tendency of the mind of the audience, and a chemical process, as it were, would take place within his mind. How could he fail then to force attention of those to whom he returned their own thoughts strengthened, broadened, and adorned with superb flights of eloquence."

In retrospect, these spectacular stump-speaking trips to where the voters lived helped to affirm the democratic nature of Jacksonian politics. Politicians in the era were typically far more educated and wealthy than their constituents, but were supposed to represent faithfully the concerns of the common citizens. Mutual participation in the ritual of the hustings celebrated the people's significance in a manner that no faraway convention or latter-day press release could.

In a later era, popular politics would be less critical to a politician's election. The post–Civil War period was an era of stenography and telegraph, of industrialism and class strife. Political speeches would be widely reported, and constituencies were more economically heterogeneous. Those conditions forced politicians to become far more cautious about what they would say, when, and to whom. To a large degree the technology of the industrial age put an end to the stump speeches of Jacksonian America, and to a certain extent that same technology severed— for better or worse—the intimate bond between America's politicians and the rural electorate.

Political gatherings like that shown here in First State Election in Detroit *(1837) by Thomas Mickell Burnham gave candidates and their constituents the opportunity to meet and generated a high voter turnout on election day.*

Nevertheless, party conflict in Congress continued to center on national economic policy. Whigs stood firm for a loose construction of the Constitution and federal support for business and economic development. The Democrats persisted in their defense of strict construction, states' rights, and laissez-faire. Debates over tariffs, banking, and internal improvements remained vital and vigorous during the 1840s.

True believers in both parties saw a deep ideological or moral meaning in the clash over economic issues. Whigs and Democrats had conflicting views of the good society, and their policy positions reflected these differences. The Democrats were the party of white male equality and personal liberty. They perceived the American people as a collection of independent and self-sufficient white males. The role of government was to see to it that the individual was not interfered with—in his economic activity, in his personal habits, and in his religion (or lack of it). Democrats were ambivalent about the rise of the market economy because of the ways it threatened individual independence. The Whigs, on the other hand, were the party of orderly progress under the guidance of an enlightened elite. They believed the propertied, the well-educated, and the pious were responsible for guiding the masses toward the common good. Believing sincerely a market economy would benefit everyone in the long run, they had no qualms about the rise of a commercial and industrial capitalism.

De Tocqueville's Wisdom

The French traveler Alexis de Tocqueville, author of the most influential account ever written of the emergence of American democracy, visited the United States in 1831 and 1832. He departed well before the presidential election and had relatively little to say about national politics and the formation of political parties. For him, the essence of American democracy was local self-government, such as he observed in the town meetings of New England. The participation of ordinary citizens in the affairs of their communities impressed him greatly, and he praised Americans for not conceding their liberties to a centralized state, as he believed the French had done.

CHRONOLOGY

1824	House of Representatives elects John Quincy Adams president
1828	Congress passes "tariff of abominations" • Jackson elected president over J. Q. Adams
1830	Jackson vetoes the Maysville Road bill • Congress passes Indian Removal Act
1831	Jackson reorganizes his cabinet • First national nominating conventions meet
1832	Jackson vetoes the bill rechartering the Bank of the United States • Jackson reelected, defeating Henry Clay (National Republican candidate)
1832–1833	Crisis erupts over South Carolina's attempt to nullify the tariff of 1832
1833	Jackson removes federal deposits from the Bank of the United States
1834	Whig party comes into existence
1836	Jackson issues "specie circular" • Martin Van Buren elected president
1837	Financial panic occurs, followed by depression lasting until 1843
1840	Congress passes the Independent Subtreasury Bill • Harrison (Whig) defeats Van Buren (Democrat) for the presidency

Despite his generally favorable view of the American experiment, Tocqueville was acutely aware of the limitations of American democracy and of the dangers facing the republic. He believed the nullification crisis foreshadowed destruction of the Union and predicted the problem of slavery would lead eventually to civil war and racial conflict. He also noted the power of white supremacy, providing an unforgettable firsthand description of the sufferings of an Indian community in the course of forced migration to the West, as well as a graphic account of the way free blacks were segregated and driven from the polls in northern cities like Philadelphia. White Americans, he believed, were deeply prejudiced against people of color, and he doubted it was possible "for a whole people to rise . . . above itself." Perhaps a despot could force the equality and mingling of the races, but "while American democracy remains at the head of affairs, no one would dare attempt any such thing, and it is possible to forsee [sic] that the freer the whites in America are, the more they will seek to isolate themselves." Tocqueville was equally sure the kind of democracy men were practicing was not meant for women. Observing how women were strictly assigned to a separate domestic sphere, he concluded that Americans had never supposed "that democratic principles should undermine the husband's authority and make it doubtful who is in charge of the family." His observations have value because of their clearsighted insistence that the democracy and equality of the Jacksonian era were meant for only some of the people. The democratic idea could not be so limited; it would soon begin to burst the boundaries of white male supremacy.

Recommended Reading

Arthur M. Schlesinger, Jr., *The Age of Jackson* (1945), sees Jacksonian Democracy as a progressive protest against big business and stresses the participation of urban workers. Marvin Meyers, *The Jacksonian Persuasion: Politics and Belief* (1960), argues that Jacksonians appealed to nostalgia for an older America—"an idealized ancestral way" they believed was threatened by commercialization. Lee Benson, *The Concept of Jacksonian Democracy: New York as a Test Case* (1964), finds an ethnocultural basis for democratic allegiance. A sharply critical view of Jacksonian leadership—one that stresses opportunism, greed, and demagoguery—can be found in Edward Pessen, *Jacksonian America: Society, Personality, and Politics,* rev. ed. (1979). This work also offers a comprehensive survey of the social, economic, and political developments of the period. An excellent recent survey of Jacksonian politics is Harry L. Watson, *Liberty and Power* (1990). It stresses the crisis of "republicanism" at a time of "market revolution." Development of the view that Jacksonianism was a negative reaction to the rise of market capitalism can be found in Charles Sellers, *The Market Revolution* (1991).

The classic study of the new party system is Richard P. McCormick, *The Second Party System: Party Formation in the Jacksonian Era* (1966). On what the anti-Jacksonians stood for, see especially Daniel Walker Howe, *The Political Culture of the American Whigs* (1979). James C. Curtis, *Andrew Jackson and the Search for Vindication* (1976), provides a good introduction to Jackson's career and personality. On Jackson's popular image, see John William Ward, *Andrew Jackson: Symbol for an Age* (1955). On the other towering political figures of the period, see Merrill D. Peterson, *The Great Triumvirate: Webster, Clay, and Calhoun* (1987). The culture of the period is well-surveyed in Russel B. Nye, *Society and Culture in America, 1830–1860* (1960). Alexis de Tocqueville, *Democracy in America*, 2 vols. (1945), is a foreign visitor's wise and insightful analysis of American life in the 1830s.

Additional Bibliography

On the hotel as a symbolic institution, see Doris Elizabeth King, "The First Class Hotel and the Age of the Common Man," *Journal of Southern History* 23 (1957): 173–188. On the new politics, see Chilton Williamson, *American Suffrage from Property to Democracy* (1960), Richard Hofstadter, *The Idea of a Party System* (1970), and Harry D. Watson, *Jacksonian Politics and Community Conflict* (1981). On Jacksonian ideology and political culture, see John Ashworth, *"Aristocrats and Agrarians"* (1982) and Lawrence Kohl, *The Politics of Individualism: Parties and the American Character in the Jacksonian Era* (1989). On radical working-class movements, see Edward Pessen, *Most Uncommon Jacksonians: The Radical Leaders of the Early Labor Movement* (1967); Bruce Laurie, *Working People of Philadelphia, 1800–1850* (1980); and Sean Wilentz, *Chants Democratic: New York City and the Rise of the American Working Class, 1788–1850* (1984). Social manifestations of the democratic character are covered in Douglas T. Miller, *Jacksonian Aristocracy: Class and Democracy in New York, 1830–1860* (1967); Joseph F. Kett, *The Formation of the American Medical Profession* (1968); Daniel H. Calhoun, *Professional Lives in America: Structure and Aspiration, 1750–1850* (1965); and Donald M. Scott, *From Office to Profession: The New England Ministry, 1750–1850* (1978). On democratic culture, see E. Douglas Branch, *The Sentimental Years, 1836–1860* (1934); David Grimstad, *Melodrama Unveiled: American Theater and Culture, 1800–1850* (1968); Oliver W. Larkin, *Art and Life in America* (1960); Neil Harris, *The Artist in American Society: The Formative Years, 1790–1860* (1966); and Henry Nash Smith, *Democracy and the Novel: Popular Resistance to Classic American Writers* (1978).

The emergence of Andrew Jackson and the Democratic party is described in Samuel F. Bemis, *John Quincy Adams and the Union* (1956) and in several works by Robert V. Remini: *Martin Van Buren and the Making of the Democratic Party* (1959); *Andrew*

Jackson and the Course of American Empire, 1767–1821 (1977); Andrew Jackson and the Course of American Freedom, 1822–1832 (1981); and Andrew Jackson and the Course of American Democracy, 1833–1845 (1984). Jackson's presidency is also examined in Richard B. Latner, The Presidency of Andrew Jackson: White House Politics, 1829–1837 (1979). On Jackson's Indian policy, see Bernard W. Sheehan, The Seeds of Extinction: Jeffersonian Philanthropy and the American Indian (1973); Michael Paul Rogin, Fathers and Children: Andrew Jackson and the Subjugation of the American Indian (1975); and Ronald N. Satz, American Indian Policy in the Jacksonian Era (1975). On nullification, see William W. Freehling, Prelude to Civil War: The Nullification Controversy in South Carolina, 1816–1836 (1966), and Richard B. Ellis, The Union at Risk: Jacksonian Democracy, States' Rights, and the Nullification Crisis (1987).

The Bank War is discussed in Bray Hammond, Banks and Politics in America from the Revolution to the Civil War (1957); Thomas P. Govan, Nicholas Biddle (1959); and John M. Paul, The Politics of Jacksonian Finance (1972). On Van Buren, see James C. Curtis, The Fox at Bay: Martin Van Buren and the Presidency (1970); and Donald B. Cole, Martin Van Buren and the American Political System (1984).

For more on the rise of the Whigs, see two biographies of their principal leaders: Robert V. Remini, Henry Clay: Statesman for the Union (1991), and Maurice G. Baxter, One and Inseparable: Daniel Webster and the Union (1984). The growth of a two-party system in the South is described in William J. Cooper, Jr., The South and the Politics of Slavery (1978). The politics of the 1840s is surveyed in William R. Brock, Parties and Political Conscience, 1840–1850 (1979). See also Ronald P. Formisano, The Birth of Mass Political Parties: Michigan, 1827–1861 (1971).

The Pursuit of Perfection

*I*n the winter of 1830 to 1831 a wave of religious revivals swept the northern states. The most dramatic and successful took place in Rochester, New York. Large audiences, composed mostly of respectable and prosperous citizens, heard evangelist Charles G. Finney preach that every man or woman had the power to choose Christ and a godly life. For six months, Finney held prayer meetings almost daily, putting intense pressure on those who had not experienced salvation. Hundreds came forth to declare their faith, and church membership doubled during his stay. The newly awakened Christians of Rochester were urged to convert relatives, neighbors, and employees. If enough people enlisted in the evangelical crusade, Finney proclaimed, the millennium would be achieved within months.

Finney's call for religious and moral renewal fell on fertile ground in Rochester. This bustling boomtown on the Erie Canal was suffering from severe growing pains and tensions arising from rapid economic development. Leading families were divided into quarreling factions, and workers were threatening to break free from the control their employers had previously exerted over their daily lives. Most of the early converts were from the middle class. Businessmen who had been heavy drinkers and irregular churchgoers now abstained from alcohol and went to church at least twice a week. They also pressured the employees in their workshops, mills, and stores to do likewise. More rigorous standards of proper behavior and religious conformity unified Rochester's elite and increased its ability to control the rest of the community. As in other cities swept by the revival, evangelical Protestantism provided the middle class with a stronger sense of identity and purpose.

But the war on sin was not always so unifying. Among those converted in Rochester and elsewhere were some who could not rest easy until the nation as a whole conformed to the pure Christianity of the Sermon on the Mount. Finney expressed such a hope himself, but he concentrated on religious conversion and moral uplift of the individual, trusting that the purification of American society and politics would automatically follow. Other religious and moral reformers were inspired to crusade against those social and political institutions that failed to measure up to the standards of Christian perfection. They proceeded to attack such collective "sins" as the liquor traffic, war, slavery, and even government. Religiously inspired reformism cut two ways. On the one hand, it imposed a new order and cultural unity to previously divided and troubled communities like Rochester. But it also inspired a variety of more radical movements or experiments that threatened to undermine established institutions that failed to live up to the principles of the more idealistic reformers. One of these movements—abolitionism—challenged the central social and economic institution of the southern states and helped trigger political upheaval and civil war.

According to some historians, evangelical revival and the reform movements it inspired reflected the same spirit as the new democratic politics. In a sense this is true: Jacksonian politicians and evangelists both sought popular favor and assumed individuals were free agents capable of self-direction and self-improvement. But leaders of the two types of movements made different kinds of demands on ordinary people. Jacksonians idealized common folk pretty much as they found them and saw no danger to the community if individuals pursued their worldly interests. Evangelical reformers, who tended to support the Whigs or to reject both parties, believed the common people needed to be redeemed and uplifted—committed to a higher goal than self-interest. They did not trust a democracy of unbelievers and sinners. The republic would be safe, they insisted, only if a right-minded minority preached, taught, and agitated until the mass of ordinary citizens was reborn into a higher life.

THE RISE OF EVANGELICALISM

American Protestantism was in a state of constant ferment during the early nineteenth century. The separation of church and state, a process that began during the Revolution, was now complete. Government sponsorship and funding had ended, or would soon end, for the established churches of the colonial era, such as the Congregationalists of New England and the Episcopalians of the South. Dissenting groups, such as Baptists and

Graphic portrayals of good and evil like this 1862 litho-graph, Way of Good and Evil, *reminded people of the message of some evangelists that wicked ways would lead to everlasting punishment.*

The Second Great Awakening: The Frontier Phase

The Second Great Awakening began in earnest on the southern frontier around the turn of the century. In 1801, a crowd estimated at nearly fifty thousand gathered at Cane Ridge, Kentucky. According to a contemporary observer:

> *The noise was like the roar of Niagara. The vast sea of human beings seemed to be agitated as if by a storm. I counted seven ministers all preaching at once. . . . Some of the people were singing, others praying, some crying for mercy . . . while others were shouting most vociferously. . . .At one time I saw at least five hundred swept down in a moment, as if a battery of a thousand guns had been opened upon them, and then followed immediately shrieks and shouts that rent the heavens.*

Methodists, welcomed full religious freedom because it offered a better chance to win new converts. All pious Protestants, however, were concerned about the spread of "infidelity"—their word for secular-humanistic beliefs. Some of the Founders of the nation had set a troubling example by their casual or even unfriendly attitude toward religious orthodoxy. Secular ideas drawn from the Enlightenment (see Chapter 4) had achieved wide acceptance as a basis for the establishment of a democratic republic, and opposition to mixing religion with public life remained strong during the age of Jackson.

Revivalism provided the best way to extend religious values and build up church membership. The Great Awakening of the mid-eighteenth century had shown the wonders that evangelists could accomplish, and new revivalists repeated this success by greatly increasing the proportion of the population that belonged to Protestant churches. They also capitalized on the growing willingness of Americans to form voluntary organizations. Spiritual renewals were often followed by mobilization of the faithful into associations to spread the gospel and reform American morals.

Highly emotional camp meetings, organized usually by Methodists or Baptists but sometimes by Presbyterians, became a regular feature of religious life in the South and the lower Midwest (see the illustration on p. 315). On the frontier, the camp meeting met social as well as religious needs. In the sparsely settled southern backcountry, it was difficult to sustain local churches with regular ministers. Methodists solved part of the problem by sending out circuit riders. Baptists licensed uneducated farmers to preach to their neighbors. But for many people the only way to get baptized, married, or have a communal religious experience was to attend a camp meeting.

Rowdies and scoffers also attended, drinking whiskey, carousing, and fornicating on the fringes of the small city of tents and wagons. Sometimes they were "struck down" by a mighty blast from the pulpit. Evangelists loved to tell stories of such conversions or near conversions. According to Methodist preacher Peter Cartwright, one scoffer was seized by the "jerks"—a set of involuntary bodily movements often observed at camp meetings. Normally such an exercise would lead to conversion, but this particular sinner was so hard-hearted that he refused to surrender to God.

The result was that he kept jerking until his neck was broken.

Camp meetings obviously provided an emotional outlet for rural people whose everyday lives were often lonely and tedious. They could also promote a sense of community and social discipline. Conversion at a camp meeting could be a rite of passage, signifying that a young man or woman had outgrown wild or antisocial behavior and was now ready to become a respectable member of the community.

In the southern states, Baptists and Presbyterians eventually deemphasized camp meetings in favor of "protracted meetings" in local churches, which featured guest preachers holding forth day after day for up to two weeks. Southern evangelical churches, especially Baptist and Methodist, grew rapidly in membership and influence during the first half of the nineteenth century and became the focus of community life in rural areas. Although they fostered societies to improve morals—to encourage temperance and discourage dueling, for example—they generally shied away from social reform. The conservatism of a slave-holding society discouraged radical efforts to change the world.

The Second Great Awakening in the North

Reformist tendencies were more evident in the distinctive kind of revivalism that originated in New England and western New York. Northern evangelists were mostly Congregationalists and Presbyterians, strongly influenced by New England Puritan traditions. Their greatest successes were not in rural or frontier areas but in small- to medium-sized towns and cities. Their revivals could be stirring affairs but were less extravagantly emotional than the camp meetings of the South. The northern brand of evangelism resulted in formation of societies devoted to the redemption of the human race in general and American society in particular.

The reform movement in New England began as an effort to defend Calvinism against the liberal views of religion fostered by the Enlightenment. The Reverend Timothy Dwight, who became president of Yale College in 1795, was alarmed by the younger generation's growing acceptance of the belief that the Deity was the benevolent master architect of a rational universe rather than an all-powerful, mysterious God. Dwight was particularly disturbed by those religious liberals whose rationalism reached the point of denying the doctrine of the Trinity and who proclaimed themselves to be "Unitarians."

To Dwight's horror, Unitarians captured some fashionable and sophisticated New England congregations and even won control of the Harvard Divinity School. He fought back by preaching to Yale undergraduates that they were "dead in sin" and succeeded in provoking a series of campus revivals. But the harshness and pessimism of orthodox Calvinist doctrine, with its stress on original sin and predestination, had limited appeal in a republic committed to human freedom and progress.

A younger generation of Congregational ministers reshaped New England Puritanism to increase its appeal to people who shared the prevailing optimism about human capabilities. The main theologian of early nineteenth-century neo-Calvinism was Nathaniel Taylor, a disciple of Dwight, who also held forth at Yale. Taylor softened the doctrine of predestination almost out of existence by contending that every individual was a free agent who had the ability to overcome a natural inclination to sin.

The first great practitioner of the new evangelical Calvinism was Lyman Beecher, another of Dwight's pupils. In the period just before and after the War of 1812, Beecher helped promote a series of revivals in the Congregational churches of New England. Using his own homespun version of Taylor's doctrine of free agency, Beecher induced thousands—in his home church in Litchfield, Connecticut, and in other churches that offered him their pulpits—to acknowledge their sinfulness and surrender to God.

During the late 1820s, Beecher was forced to confront the new and more radical form of revivalism being practiced in western New York by Charles G. Finney. Upstate New York was a seedbed for religious enthusiasms of various kinds. A majority of its population were transplanted New Englanders who had left behind their close-knit village communities and ancestral churches but not their Puritan consciences. Troubled by rapid economic changes and the social dislocations that went with them, they were ripe for a new faith and a fresh moral direction.

The Beecher family, shown here in a photograph by Matthew Brady, contributed four influential members to the reform movement. Lyman Beecher (seated center) was a successful preacher and a master strategist in the organized campaign against sin and infidelity. His eldest daughter, Catharine (on his right) was a leader in the movement supporting higher education for women. Another daughter, Harriet (seated far right) wrote the novel Uncle Tom's Cabin. *Lyman's son, Henry Ward Beecher (standing far right) was an ardent antislavery advocate and later became one of the most celebrated preachers of the post–Civil War era. He also became involved in a notorious scandal and trial; see the essay* The Beecher–Tilton Adultery Trial: Public Image Versus Private Conduct *on pp. 430–435.*

Although he worked within Congregational and Presbyterian churches (which were then cooperating under a plan of union established in 1804), Finney departed radically from Calvinist doctrines. In his hands, free agency became unqualified free will. One of his sermons was entitled "Sinners Bound to Change Their Own Hearts." Finney was relatively indifferent to theological issues. His appeal was to emotion or to the heart rather than to doctrine or reason. He wanted converts to feel the power of Christ and become new men and women. He eventually adopted the extreme view that redeemed Christians could be totally free of sin—as perfect as their Father in Heaven.

Beginning in 1823, Finney conducted a series of highly successful revivals in towns and cities of western New York, culminating in the aforementioned triumph in Rochester in 1830–1831. Even more controversial than his freewheeling approach to theology were the means he used to win converts. Finney sought instantaneous conversions through a variety of new methods. These included protracted meetings lasting all night or several days in a row, the placing of an "anxious bench" in front of the congregation where those in the process of repentance could receive special atten-

tion, and encouraging women to pray publicly for the souls of male relatives.

The results could be dramatic. Sometimes listeners fell to the floor in fits of excitement. "If I had had a sword in my hand," Finney recalled, "I could not have cut them off as fast as they fell." Although he appealed to emotion, Finney had a practical, almost manipulative, attitude toward the conversion process: It "is not a miracle or dependent on a miracle in any sense. . . . It is purely a philosophical result of the right use of constituted means."

Lyman Beecher and eastern evangelicals were disturbed by Finney's new methods and by the emotionalism that accompanied them. They were also upset because he violated long-standing Christian tradition by allowing women to pray aloud in church. An evangelical summit meeting between Beecher and Finney, held at New Lebanon, New York, in 1827, failed to reach agreement on this and other issues. Beecher even threatened to stand on the state line if Finney attempted to bring his crusade into Connecticut. But it soon became clear that Finney was not merely stirring people to temporary peaks of excitement; he was also leaving strong and active churches behind him, and eastern opposition gradually weakened.

Finney eventually founded a tabernacle in New York City that became a rallying point for evangelical efforts to reach the urban masses.

From Revivalism to Reform

The northern wing of the Second Great Awakening, unlike the southern, inspired a great movement for social reform. Converts were organized into voluntary associations that sought to stamp out sin and social evil and win the world for Christ. An activist and outgoing Christianity was being advanced, not one that called for withdrawal from a sinful world. Most of the converts of northern revivalism were middle-class citizens already active in the lives of their communities. They were seeking to adjust to the bustling world of the market revolution in ways that would not violate their traditional moral and social values. Their generally optimistic and forward-looking attitudes led to hopes that a wave of conversions would save the nation and the world.

In New England, Beecher and his evangelical associates were behind the establishment of a great network of missionary and benevolent societies. In 1810, Presbyterians and Congregationalists founded a Board of Commissioners for Foreign Missions and soon dispatched two missionaries to India. In 1816, the Reverend Samuel John Mills took the leading role in organizing the American Bible Society. By 1821, the society had distributed 140,000 Bibles, mostly in parts of the West where there was a scarcity of churches and clergymen.

Another major effort went into publication and distribution of religious tracts, mainly by the American Tract Society, founded in 1825. Groups beyond the reach of regular churches were the target of special societies, such as missions to seamen, Native Americans, and the urban poor. In 1816 to 1817, middle-class women in New York, Philadelphia, Charleston, and Boston formed societies to spread the gospel in lower-class wards—where, as one of their missionaries put it, there was "a great mass of people beyond the restraints of religion."

Evangelicals founded moral reform societies as well as missions. Some of these aimed at curbing irreligious activity on the Sabbath; others sought to stamp out dueling, gambling, and prostitution. In New York in 1831, a zealous young clergyman published a sensational report claiming there were ten thousand prostitutes in the city laying their snares for innocent young men. As a result of this exposé, an asylum was established for the redemption of "abandoned women." When middle-class women became involved in this crusade, they shifted its focus to the men who patronized prostitutes, and proposed that teams of observers record and publish the names of those seen entering brothels. This plan was abandoned because it offended those who thought the cause of virtue would be better served by suppressing public discussion and investigation of sexual vices.

Beecher was especially influential in the temperance crusade, the most successful of the reform movements; his published sermons against drink were the most important and widely distributed of the early tracts calling for total abstinence from "demon rum." The temperance movement was directed at a real social evil. Since the Revolution, whiskey had become the most popular American beverage. Made from corn by individual farmers or, by the 1820s, in commercial distilleries, it was cheaper than milk or beer and safer than water (which was often contaminated). In some parts of the country, rum and brandy were also popular. Hard liquor was frequently consumed with food as a table beverage, even at breakfast, and children sometimes imbibed along with adults. Per capita annual consumption of distilled beverages in the 1820s was almost triple what it is today, and alcoholism had reached epidemic proportions.

The temperance reformers viewed indulgence in alcohol as a threat to public morality. Drunkenness was seen as a loss of self-control and moral responsibility that spawned crime, vice, and disorder. Above all, it threatened the family. Drinking was mainly a male vice, and the main target of temperance propaganda was the husband and father who abused, neglected, or abandoned his wife and children because he was a slave to the bottle. Women played a vital role in the movement and were instrumental in making it a crusade for the protection of the home. The drinking habits of the poor or laboring classes also aroused great concern. Particularly in urban areas, the "respectable" and propertied elements lived in fear that lower-class mobs, crazed with drink, would attack private property and destroy the social order.

Many evangelical reformers regarded intemperance as the greatest single obstacle to a repub-

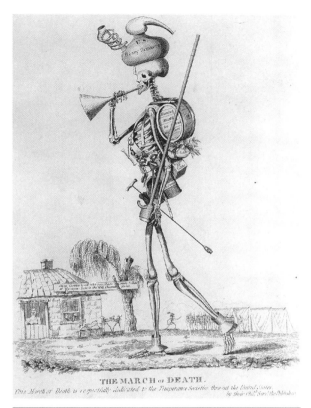

THE MARCH OF DEATH.
This March of Death is respectfully dedicated to the Temperance Societies thro'out the United States, by their obt. Sevt. the Publisher.

Temperance propaganda, like this broadside, warned that "demon rum" would lead the drinker down the direct path to poverty and wretchedness and would bring about the ruin of his entire family.

in altering the drinking habits of middle-class American males by making temperance a mark of respectability. Per capita consumption of hard liquor declined more than 50 percent during the 1830s.

Cooperating missionary and reform societies—collectively known as "the benevolent empire"—were a major force in American culture by the early 1830s. Efforts to modify American attitudes and institutions seemed to be bearing fruit. A new ethic of self-control and self-discipline was being instilled in the middle class, equipping individuals to confront a new world of economic growth and social mobility without losing their cultural and moral bearings.

DOMESTICITY AND CHANGES IN THE AMERICAN FAMILY

The evangelical culture of the 1820s and 1830s influenced the family as an institution and inspired new conceptions of its role in American society. For many parents, child rearing was viewed as essential preparation for self-disciplined Christian life, and they performed their nurturing duties with great seriousness and self-consciousness. Women—regarded as particularly susceptible to religious and moral influences—were increasingly confined to the domestic circle, but assumed a greater importance within it.

Marriage and Sex Roles

The white middle-class American family underwent major changes in the decades between the revolution and the mid-nineteenth century. One was the triumph of marriage for love. Parents now exercised even less control over their children's selection of mates than they had in the colonial period. The desire to protect family property and maintain social status remained strong, but mutual affection was now considered absolutely essential to a proper union. Beginning in the late eighteenth century, romantic novels popularized the idea that marriage should be based exclusively on the promptings of the heart. It became easier for sons to marry while their fathers were still alive and for younger daughters to wed before their oldest sisters—trends that reflected a weakening of the traditional parental role.

lic of God-fearing, self-disciplined citizens. In 1826, a group of clergymen previously active in mission work organized the American Temperance Society to coordinate and extend the work already begun by local churches and moral reform societies. The original aim was to encourage abstinence from "ardent spirits" or hard liquor; there was no agreement on the evils of beer and wine. The society sent out lecturers, issued a flood of literature, and sponsored essay contests. Its agents organized revival meetings and called on those in attendance to sign a pledge promising abstinence from spirits.

The campaign was enormously effective. By 1834, there were five thousand local branches with more than a million members, a large proportion of them women. Although it may be doubted whether huge numbers of confirmed drunkards were cured, the movement did succeed

The Shakers

Ritualized dances were part of the Shakers' spiritual preparation for the Second Coming. The dancers in this nineteenth-century etching exemplify the mixed heritage of the Shaker community.

One of the communitarian religious movements that sprang up in the pre–Civil War period had a special fascination for outsiders. The Shakers—officially known as the Millennial Church or the United Society of Believers—welcomed curious travelers to their settlements, and many of the visitors reported in great detail on the unusual way of life they observed.

The Shakers were descended from a small English sect of the same name that appeared in the early to mid-eighteenth century. The English Shakers were radical millennialists, which meant they expected Christ's Second Coming to occur momentarily. Their name was derived from the fact that they expressed their religious fervor through vigorous bodily movements, which eventually took the form of a ritualized dance. Most of the Shakers were from the working class, and one of their converts was a woman named Ann Lee, who joined the sect in 1758.

After she had been jailed several times for preaching strange and unorthodox doctrines in public places, Lee immigrated to America in 1774. Mother Ann, as she was known to her followers, came to believe she was the one sent by God to save the world. It would not be farfetched to call her the great feminist of Christian millennialism. She preached that God was both masculine and feminine and that Christ had incarnated only the masculine side. It was her vocation to bring on the millennium by embodying the feminine attributes of the Almighty. Hence the American Shakers venerated Ann Lee and expressed belief in a new theology based squarely on the principle of sexual equality.

Mother Ann died in 1784, but not before she had made enough American converts to establish a permanent sect. Taking advantage of the great availability of land in America, the Shakers drew apart from the rest of society and established communities where they could practice their own version of Christian perfectionism free of harassment. The mother colony was at Mount Lebanon, New York, but other Shaker communities were established in the New England states before 1800 and in Ohio and Kentucky thereafter. By the 1830s, twenty settlements in seven states had a combined membership of approximately six thousand.

In the Shaker communities all property was owned in common and political authority was vested in a self-perpetuating group of ministers. Hence the Shakers practiced a form of "theocratic communism." Reflecting their belief in sexual equality, they required that the ministry of each community be composed of an equal number of elders and elderesses. What most attracted the interest of outsiders, however, was the fact that Shakers banned sexual intercourse and marriage, requiring strict celibacy of all members. To enforce this rule they segregated men and women in most social and economic activities. This novel arrangement resulted from a belief that the end of the world was at hand; thus there was no need to reproduce the human race, and those anticipating salvation should begin to live in the pure spiritual state that would arrive with the millennium. The rule of chastity obviously limited the growth of the Shaker communities, but a willingness to adopt orphans and to accept converts allowed some of them to survive well into the twentieth century.

Visitors to the Shaker settlements were, for the most part, impressed with the order, decorum, cleanliness, and quiet prosperity that prevailed. But beginning in 1837 religious services in the communities suddenly became wildly ecstatic. Relatively formalized dancing was replaced by spontaneous and violent "shaking and turning exercizes." Shakers had always believed in spiritualism, or direct communication with departed souls, but now there was an epidemic of spiritual possession. In almost every service, members fell into trances, conveyed messages from the spirit world, and spoke in what were thought to be foreign tongues. Some observers concluded that the Shakers had literally gone mad, and for a time the ministers thought it advisable to close their services to the public.

At a time when religious revivalism had recently swept the country as a whole, the Shakers were simply having their own outburst of enthusiasm, showing perhaps that they were not completely cut off from the outside world. Since Shakers were already intensely religious, their revivals were even more violent and frantic than those taking place elsewhere. Modern psychologists might attribute this frenzy to sexual frustration, but such an interpretation would not explain why the Shaker ecstatic revival ended about 1845. After that time, the calm and sober spirit of earlier years again prevailed.

The Shakers, despite their isolation and singularity, made some important contributions to American culture. They valued simplicity in all things, and this ideal became a basis for creative achievement. The virtue of simplicity was expressed in the words of the hauntingly beautiful Shaker hymn (which later became the theme for Aaron Copland's twentieth-century symphonic work *Appalachian Spring*), "'Tis a gift to be simple." Their aesthetic ideal of simplicity inspired Shaker artisans to design buildings and furnishings that were purely functional and without ornamentation. In the eyes of modern art critics and historians, Shaker handiwork achieved an elegance and purity of form that ranks it among the most beautiful ever produced in America. The Tree of Life emblem (opposite page) is from a Shaker spirit drawing that was received as a vision and recorded by Sister Hannah Cohoon in 1854.

Wives now began to behave more like the companions of their husbands and less like their servants or children. In the main, eighteenth-century correspondence between spouses had been formal and distant in tone. The husband often assumed a patriarchal role, even using such salutations as "my dear child" and rarely confessing that he missed his wife or craved her company. Letters from women to their husbands were highly deferential and did not usually give advice or express disapproval.

By the early nineteenth century first names, pet names, and terms of endearment like "honey" or "darling" were increasingly used by both sexes, and absent husbands frequently confessed they felt lost without their mates. In their replies, wives assumed a more egalitarian tone and offered counsel on a wide range of subjects. One wrote to a husband who had admitted to flirting with pretty women that she was more than "a little jealous." She asked him angrily how he would feel if she made a similar confession—"would it be more immoral in me than in you?"

The change in middle- and upper-class marriage should not be exaggerated or romanticized. In law, and in cases of conflict between spouses, the husband remained the unchallenged head of the household. True independence or equality for women was impossible at a time when men held exclusive legal authority over a couple's property and children. Divorce was difficult for everyone, but the double standard made it easier for husbands than wives to dissolve a marriage on grounds of adultery.

Such power as women exerted within the home came from their ability to affect the decisions of men who had learned to respect their moral qualities and good sense. The evangelical movement encouraged this quiet expression of feminine influence. The revivals not only gave women a role in converting men but made a Christ with stereotypical feminine characteristics the main object of worship. A nurturing, loving, merciful saviour, mediating between a stern father and his erring children, provided the model for woman's new role as spiritual head of the home. Membership in evangelical church-based associations inspired and prepared women for new roles as civilizers of men and guardians of domestic culture and morality. Female reform societies taught them the strict ethical code they were to instill in other family members; organized mothers' groups gave instruction in how to build character and encourage piety in children.

Historians have described the new conception of woman's role as the "Cult of True Womanhood" or the "ideology of domesticity." In the view of most men, a woman's place was in the home and on a pedestal. The ideal wife and mother was "an angel in the house," a model of piety and virtue who exerted a wholesome moral and religious influence over members of the coarser sex. A masculine view of the true woman was well expressed in a poem published in 1846:

> I would have her as pure as the snow on the
>   mount—
>   As true as the smile that to infancy's given—
> As pure as the wave of the crystalline fount,
>   Yet as warm in the heart as the sunlight of
>   heaven.

The sociological reality behind the Cult of True Womanhood was an increasing division between the working lives of men and women. In the eighteenth century and earlier, most economic activity had been centered in and near the home, and husbands and wives often worked together in a common enterprise. By the early to mid-nineteenth century this way of life was declining, especially in the Northeast. In towns and cities, the rise of factories and countinghouses severed the home from the workplace. Men went forth every morning to their places of labor, leaving their wives at home to tend the house and the children. Married women were therefore increasingly deprived of a productive economic role. The cult of domesticity made a virtue of the fact that men were solely responsible for running the affairs of the world and building up the economy.

A new conception of sex roles justified and glorified this pattern. The "doctrine of two spheres"—as set forth in novels, advice literature, and the new ladies' magazines—sentimentalized the woman who kept a spotless house, nurtured her children, and offered her husband a refuge from the heartless world of commerce and industry. From a modern point of view, it is easy to condemn the cult of domesticity as a rationalization for male dominance; to a considerable extent

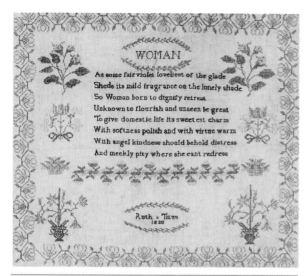

The sentiment on this sampler, stitched in 1820 by Ruth Titus, typifies beliefs about woman's proper role, according to the Cult of True Womanhood.

it was. But many women of the early to mid-nineteenth century do not seem to have felt oppressed or degraded by the new arrangement. The earlier pattern of cooperation had not implied sexual equality—normally men had been very much in charge of farms or home industries and had often treated their wives more like servants than partners. The new norm of confinement to the home did not necessarily imply women were inferior. By the standards of evangelical culture, women in the domestic sphere could be viewed as superior to men, since women were in a good position to cultivate the "feminine" virtues of love and self-sacrifice and thus act as official guardians of religious and moral values.

The domestic ideology had real meaning only for relatively affluent women. Working-class wives were not usually employed outside the home during this period, but they labored long and hard within the household. Besides cleaning, cooking, and taking care of large numbers of children, they often took in washing or piecework to supplement a meager family income. Their endless domestic drudgery made a sham of the notion that women had the time and energy for the "higher things of life."

In urban areas, unmarried working-class women often lived on their own and toiled as household servants, in the sweatshops of the garment indus-

try, and in factories. Barely able to support themselves and at the mercy of male sexual predators, they were in no position to identify with the middle-class ideal of elevated, protected womanhood. For some of them, the relatively well-paid and gregarious life of the prostitute seemed to offer an attractive alternative to a life of loneliness and privation.

For middle-class women whose husbands or fathers earned a good income, freedom from industrial or farm labor offered some tangible benefits. They now had the leisure to read extensively in the new literature directed primarily at housewives, to participate in female-dominated charitable activities, and to cultivate deep and lasting friendships with other women. The result was a distinctively feminine subculture emphasizing "sisterhood" or "sorority." This growing sense of solidarity with other women and of the importance of sexual identity could transcend the private home and even the barriers of social class. Beginning in the 1820s, urban women of the middle and upper classes organized societies for the relief and rehabilitation of poor or "fallen women." The aim of these organizations was not economic and political equality with men but the elevation of all females to true womanhood.

For some women, the domestic ideal even sanctioned efforts to extend their sphere until it conquered the masculine world outside the home. This domestic feminism was reflected in women's involvement in crusades to stamp out such masculine sins as intemperance, gambling, and sexual vice.

In the benevolent societies and reform movements of the Jacksonian era, especially those designated as female organizations, women handled money, organized meetings and public appeals, made contracts, and sometimes even gave orders to male subordinates—activities they could not usually perform in their own households. The desire to extend the feminine sphere was the motivating force behind Catharine Beecher's campaign to make schoolteaching a woman's occupation. A prolific and influential writer on the theory and practice of domesticity, this unmarried daughter of Lyman Beecher saw the spinster-teacher as equivalent to a mother. By instilling in young males the virtues that only women could teach, the schoolmarm could help liberate America from corruption and materialism.

But Beecher and other domestic feminists continued to emphasize the role of married women who stayed home and did their part simply by being wives and mothers. Reforming husbands was difficult: they were away much of the time and tended to be preoccupied with business. But this very fact gave women primary responsibility for the rearing of children—an activity to which nineteenth-century Americans attached almost cosmic significance. Since women were considered particularly well qualified to transmit piety and morality to future citizens of the republic, the cult of domesticity exalted motherhood and encouraged a new concern with childhood as the time of life when "character" was formed.

The Discovery of Childhood

The nineteenth century has been called "the century of the child." More than before, childhood was seen as a distinct stage of life requiring the special and sustained attention of adults. The family now became "child-centered," which meant the care, nurture, and rearing of children was viewed as the family's main function. In earlier times, adults treated children in a more casual way, often sending them away from home for education or apprenticeship at a very early age. Among the well-to-do, children spent more time with servants or tutors than with their parents.

By the early decades of the nineteenth century, however, children were staying at home longer and receiving much more attention from parents, especially mothers. Almost completely abandoned was the colonial custom—nearly inconceivable today—of naming a living child after a sibling who had died in infancy. Each child was now looked on as a unique and irreplaceable individual.

New customs and fashions heralded the "discovery" of childhood. Books aimed specifically at juveniles began to roll off the presses. Parents became more self-conscious about their responsibilities and sought help from a new literature providing expert advice on child rearing. One early nineteenth-century mother wrote, "There is scarcely any subject concerning which I feel more anxiety than the proper education of my children. It is a difficult and delicate subject, the more I feel how much is to be learnt by myself."

The new concern for children resulted in more intimate relations between parents and children.

The ideal family described in the advice manuals and sentimental literature was bound together by affection rather than authority. Firm discipline remained at the core of "family government," but there was a change in the preferred method of enforcing good behavior. Corporal punishment declined, partially displaced by shaming or withholding of affection. Disobedient middle-class children were now more likely to be confined to their rooms to reflect on their sins than to receive a good thrashing. Discipline could no longer be justified as the constant application of physical force over naturally wayward beings. In an age of moral perfectionism, the role of discipline was to induce repentance and change basic attitudes. The intended result was often described as "self-government"; to achieve it parents used guilt, rather than fear, as their main source of leverage. A mother's sorrow or a father's stern and prolonged silence was deemed more effective in forming character than blows or angry words.

Child-centered families also meant smaller families. If nineteenth-century families had remained as large as those of earlier times, it would have been impossible to lavish so much care and attention on individual offspring. For reasons that are still not completely understood, the average number of children born to each woman during her fertile years dropped from 7.04 in 1800 to 5.42 in 1850. As a result, average family size declined about 25 percent, beginning a long-range trend lasting to the present day.

The practice of various forms of birth control undoubtedly contributed to this demographic revolution. Ancestors of the modern condom and diaphragm were openly advertised and sold during the pre–Civil War period, but it was likely most couples controlled family size by practicing the withdrawal method or limiting the frequency of intercourse. Abortion was also surprisingly common and was on the rise. One historian has estimated that by 1850 there was one abortion for every five or six live births.

Parents seemed to understand that having fewer children meant they could provide their offspring with a better start in life. Such attitudes were appropriate to a society that was beginning to shift from agriculture to commerce and industry. For rural households short of labor, large families were an economic asset. For urban couples who hoped to send their children into a competitive world that demanded special talents and training, they were a liability.

INSTITUTIONAL REFORM

The family could not carry the whole burden of socializing and reforming individuals. Children needed schooling as well as parental nurturing, and many lacked the advantage of a real home environment. Some adults, too, seemed to require special kinds of attention and treatment. Seeking to extend the advantages of "family government" beyond the domestic circle, reformers worked to establish or improve public institutions that were designed to shape individual character and instill a capacity for self-discipline.

The Extension of Education

The period from 1820 to 1850 saw an enormous expansion of free public schools. The new resolve to put more children in school for longer periods reflected many of the same values that exalted the child-centered family. Up to a certain age children could be effectively nurtured and educated at home. But after that they needed formal training at a character-molding institution that would prepare them to make a living and bear the burdens of republican citizenship. Purely intellectual training at school was regarded as less important than moral indoctrination.

Sometimes more than just an extension of the family, the school served as a substitute for it. Educational reformers were alarmed at the masses of poor and immigrant children who allegedly lacked a proper home environment. It was up to schools to make up for this disadvantage. Otherwise, the republic would be in danger from masses of people "incapable of self-government."

Before the 1820s, schooling in the United States was a haphazard affair. The wealthy sent their children to private schools, and some of the poor sent their children to charity or "pauper" schools that were usually financed in part by local governments. Public education was most highly developed in New England states, where towns were required by law to support elementary schools. It was weakest in the South where almost all education was private.

The agitation for expanded public education began in the 1820s and early 1830s as a central demand of the workingmen's movements in eastern cities. These hard-pressed artisans viewed free schools open to all as a way of countering the growing gap between rich and poor. Initially, strong opposition came from more affluent tax-payers who did not see why they should pay for the education of other people's children. But middle-class reformers soon seized the initiative, shaped educational reform to their own end of social discipline, and provided the momentum needed for legislative success.

The most influential spokesman for the common school movement was Horace Mann of Massachusetts. As a lawyer and member of the state legislature, Mann worked tirelessly to establish a state board of education and adequate tax support for local schools. In 1837, he persuaded the legislature to enact his proposals, and he subsequently resigned his seat to become the first secretary of the new board, an office he held with great distinction until 1848. He believed children were clay in the hands of teachers and school officials and could be molded to a state of perfection. Like advocates of child rearing through moral influence rather than physical force, he discouraged corporal punishment except as a last resort. His position on this issue led to a bitter controversy with Boston schoolmasters who retained a Calvinist sense of original sin and favored a freer use of the rod.

Against those who argued that school taxes violated property rights, Mann contended private property was actually held in trust for the good of the community. "The property of this commonwealth," he wrote, "is pledged for the education of all its youth up to such a point as will save them from poverty and vice, and prepare them for the adequate performance of their social and civil duties." Mann's conception of public education as a means of social discipline converted the middle and upper classes to the cause. By teaching middle-class morality and respect for order, the schools could turn potential rowdies and revolutionaries into law-abiding citizens. They could also encourage social mobility by opening doors for lower-class children who were determined to do better than their parents.

In practice, new or improved public schools often alienated working-class pupils and their families rather than reforming them. Compulsory attendance laws in Massachusetts and other states deprived poor families of needed wage earners without guaranteeing new occupational opportunities for those with an elementary education. As the laboring class became increasingly immigrant and Catholic in the 1840s and 1850s, dissatisfaction arose over the evangelical Protestant tone of "moral instruction" in the schools. Quite consciously, Mann and his disciples were trying to impose a uniform culture on people who valued differing traditions.

In addition to the "three Rs," reading, writing, and arithmetic, the public schools of the mid-nineteenth century taught the "Protestant ethic"—industry, punctuality, sobriety, and frugality. These were the virtues stressed in the famous McGuffey readers, which first appeared in 1836. Millions of children learned to read by digesting McGuffey's parables about the terrible fate of those who gave in to sloth, drunkenness, or wastefulness. Such moral indoctrination helped produce generations of Americans with personalities and beliefs adapted to the needs of an industrializing society—people who could be depended on to adjust to the precise and regular routines of the factory or the office. But as an education for self-government—in the sense of learning to think for oneself—it left much to be desired.

Fortunately, however, education was not limited to the schools nor devoted solely to children. Every city and almost every town or village had a lyceum, debating society, or mechanics' institute where adults of all social classes could broaden their intellectual horizons. Lyceums featured discourses on such subjects as "self-reliance" or "the conduct of life" by creative thinkers such as Ralph Waldo Emerson, explanations and demonstrations of the latest scientific discoveries, and debates among members on controversial issues.

Young Abraham Lincoln, who had received less than two years of formal schooling as a child in backwoods Indiana, sharpened his intellect in the early 1830s as a member of the New Salem (Illinois) debating society. In 1838, after moving to Springfield, he set forth his political principles when he spoke at the local lyceum on "The Perpetuation of Our Political Institutions." Unlike public schools, the lyceums and debating societies fostered independent thought and encouraged new ideas.

LESSON XXI.

1. IN'DO-LENT; *adj.* lazy; idle.
2. COM-MER'CIAL; *adj.* trading.
3. COM'IC-AL; *adj.* amusing.
3. DRONE; *n.* an idler.
4. NAV'I-GA-BLE; *adj.* in which boats can sail.

THE IDLE SCHOOL-BOY.

PRONOUNCE correctly. Do not say *indorlunt* for in-do-lent; *creepin* for creep-ing; *sylubble* for syl-*la*-ble; *colud* for col-ored; *scarlit* for scar-let; *ignerunt* for ig-no-rant.

1. I WILL tell you about the †laziest boy you ever heard of. He was indolent about every thing. When he played, the boys said he played as if the teacher told him to. When he went to school, he went creep-ing along like a snail. The boy had sense enough; but he was too lazy to learn any thing.

2. When he spelled a word, he †drawled out one syllable after another, as if he were afraid the †syllables would quarrel, if he did not keep them a great way apart.

3. Once when he was †reciting, the teacher asked him, "What is said of †Hartford?" He answered, "Hartford is a †flourishing *comical* town." He meant that it was a "flourishing *commercial* town;" but he was such a drone, that he never knew what he was about.

4. When asked how far the River †Kennebec was navigable, he said, "it was navigable for *boots* as far as †Waterville." The boys all laughed, and the teacher could not help laughing, too. The idle boy †colored like scarlet.

5. "I say it is so in my book," said he. When one of the boys showed him the book, and pointed to the

The lessons and examples in McGuffey's Readers upheld the basic virtues of thrift, honesty, and charity, and taught that evil deeds never went unpunished.

Discovering the Asylum

Some segments of the population were obviously beyond the reach of family government and character training provided in homes and schools. In the 1820s and 1830s, reformers became acutely aware of the danger to society posed by an apparently increasing number of criminals, lunatics, and paupers. Their answer was to establish special institutions to house those deemed incapable of self-discipline. Their goals were humanitarian; they believed reform and rehabilitation were possible in a carefully controlled environment.

In earlier times, the existence of paupers, lawbreakers, and insane persons had been taken for

In this 1876 woodcut, prisoners—in hand-on-shoulder lockstep—march into the dining room at Sing Sing Prison in New York. Rigid discipline and extensive rules restricting the inmates' movements, speech, and actions were thought to reform criminals. In most prisons, a strict silence was enforced at all times to allow the prisoners to reflect on the error of their ways.

granted. Their presence was viewed as the consequence of divine judgment or original sin. For the most part these people were dealt with in ways that did not isolate them from local communities. The insane were allowed to wander about if harmless and were confined at home if they were dangerous; the poor were supported by private charity or the dole provided by towns or counties; convicted criminals were whipped, held for limited periods in local jails, or—in the case of very serious offenses—executed.

By the early nineteenth century these traditional methods had come to seem both inadequate and inhumane. Dealing with deviants in a neighborly way broke down as economic development and urbanization made communities less cohesive. At the same time, reformers were concluding that all defects of mind and character were correctable—the insane could be cured, criminals reformed, and paupers taught to pull themselves out of destitution. The result was what historian David Rothman termed "the discovery of the asylum"—the invention and establishment of special institutions for the confinement and reformation of deviants.

The 1820s and 1830s saw the emergence of state-supported prisons, insane asylums, and poorhouses. New York and Pennsylvania led the way in prison reform. Institutions at Auburn, New York, and Philadelphia attracted international attention as model penitentiaries, mainly because of their experiments in isolating inmates

from one another. Solitary confinement was viewed as a humanitarian and therapeutic policy because it gave inmates a chance to reflect on their sins, free from the corrupting influence of other convicts. In theory, prisons and asylums substituted for the family. Custodians were meant to act as parents, providing moral advice and training.

In practice, these institutions were far different from the affectionate families idealized by the cult of domesticity. Most accommodated only a single sex or maintained a strict segregation of male and female inmates. Their most prominent feature was the imposition of a rigid daily routine. The early superintendents and wardens believed the enforcement of a rigorous set of rules and procedures would encourage self-discipline. The French observers Alexis de Tocqueville and Gustave de Beaumont summed up these practical expectations after a tour of American prisons in 1831 and 1832: "The habits or order to which the prisoner is subjected for several years . . . the obedience of every moment to inflexible rules, the regularity of a uniform life . . . are calculated to produce a deep impression upon his mind. Perhaps, leaving the prison he is not an honest man, but he has contracted honest habits. . . ."

Prisons, asylums, and poorhouses did not achieve the aims of their founders. Public support was inadequate to meet the needs of a growing inmate population and the personnel of these institutions often lacked the training needed to help the incarcerated. The results were overcrowding and the use of brutality to keep order. For the most part, prisons failed to reform hardened criminals, and the primitive psychotherapy known as "moral treatment" failed to cure most asylum patients. Poorhouses rapidly degenerated into sinkholes of despair. A combination of naive theories and poor performance doomed these institutions to a custodial rather than a reformatory role.

Conditions would have been even worse had it not been for Dorothea Dix. Between 1838 and the Civil War, this remarkable woman devoted her energies and skills to publicizing the inhumane treatment prevailing in prisons, almshouses, and insane asylums and lobbying for corrective action. As a direct result of her activities fifteen states opened new hospitals for the insane and others improved their supervision of penitentiaries, asylums, and poorhouses. Dix ranks as one of the most practical and effective of all the reformers of the pre–Civil War era.

REFORM TURNS RADICAL

During the 1830s, internal dissension split the great reform movement spawned by the Second Great Awakening. Efforts to promote evangelical piety, improve personal and public morality, and shape character through familial or institutional discipline continued and even flourished. But bolder spirits went beyond such goals and set their sights on the total liberation and perfection of the individual.

Divisions in the Benevolent Empire

Early nineteenth-century reformers were, for the most part, committed to changing existing attitudes and practices gradually and in ways that would not invite conflict or disrupt the society. But by the mid-1830s a new mood of impatience and perfectionism surfaced within the benevolent societies. In 1836, for example, the Temperance Society split over two issues—whether the abstinence pledge should be extended to include beer and wine and whether pressure should be applied to producers and sellers of alcoholic beverages as well as to consumers. Radicals insisted on a total commitment to "cold water" and were prepared to clash head on with an important economic interest. Moderates held back from such goals and tactics because they wished to avoid hostility from prominent citizens who drank wine or had money invested in the liquor industry.

A similar rift occurred in the American Peace Society, an antiwar organization founded in 1828 by clergymen seeking to promote Christian concern for world peace. Most of the founders admitted the propriety of "defensive wars" and were shocked when some members of the society began to denounce all use of force as a violation of the Sermon on the Mount. Dissidents, who called themselves "nonresistants," withdrew from the organization in 1838. Led by Henry C. Wright, they formed the New England Non-Resistance Society to promote an absolute pacifism, which denied the right of self-defense to nations or individuals and repudiated all forms of governmental coercion.

Dorothea Dix (1802–1887). Her efforts on behalf of the mentally ill led to the building of more than thirty institutions in the United States and the reform and restaffing—with well-trained personnel—of already existing hospitals. She died in Trenton, New Jersey, in 1887, in a hospital that she had founded.

The new perfectionism realized its most dramatic and important success within the antislavery movement. Before the 1830s, most people who expressed religious and moral concern over slavery were affiliated with the American Colonization Society, a benevolent organization founded in 1817. Most colonizationists admitted slavery was an evil, but they also viewed it as a deeply rooted social and economic institution that could only be eliminated very gradually and with the cooperation of slaveholders. Reflecting the power of racial prejudice, they proposed to transport freed blacks to Africa as a way of relieving southern fears that a race war would erupt if slaves were simply released from bondage and allowed to remain in America. In 1821, the society established the colony of Liberia in West Africa, and during the next decade a few thousand African Americans were settled there.

Colonization proved to be grossly inadequate as a step toward the elimination of slavery. Many of the blacks taken to Africa were already free, and those liberated by masters influenced by the movement represented only a tiny percentage of the natural increase of the southern slave population. Northern blacks denounced this enterprise because it denied the prospect of racial equality in America. Black opposition to colonizationism helped persuade William Lloyd Garrison and other white abolitionists to repudiate the Colonization Society and support immediate emancipation without emigration.

Garrison launched a new and more radical antislavery movement in 1831 when he began to publish a journal called the *Liberator* in Boston. Most of the small number of early subscribers to Garrison's *Liberator* were free blacks, and radical abolitionists depended heavily on black support from then on. Black orators, especially escaped slaves like Frederick Douglass, were featured at antislavery meetings, and some African Americans became officers of antislavery societies.

Besides calling for immediate and unconditional emancipation, Garrison denounced colonization as a slaveholder's plot to remove troublesome free blacks and an ignoble surrender to un-Christian prejudices. His rhetoric was as severe as his proposals were radical. As he wrote in the first issue of the *Liberator,* "I will be as harsh as truth and as uncompromising as justice. . . . I am in earnest—I will not equivocate—I will

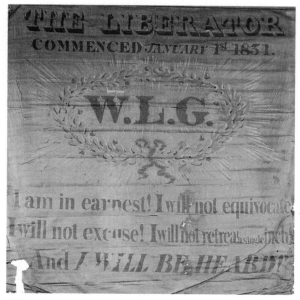

In the inaugural issue of his antislavery weekly the Liberator, *William Lloyd Garrison announced that he was launching a militant battle against the evil and sin of slavery. The stirring words that appeared in that first issue are repeated on the* Liberator's *banner.*

not excuse—I will not retreat a single inch—AND I WILL BE HEARD."

Heard he was. In 1833, Garrison and other abolitionists founded the American Anti-Slavery Society. "We shall send forth agents to lift up the voice of remonstrance, of warning, of entreaty, and of rebuke," its Declaration of Sentiments proclaimed. The colonization movement was placed on the defensive, and during the 1830s many of its most active northern supporters became abolitionists.

The Abolitionist Enterprise

The abolitionist movement, like the temperance crusade, was a direct outgrowth of the Second Great Awakening. Many leading abolitionists had undergone conversion experiences in the 1820s and were already committed to a life of Christian activism before they dedicated themselves to freeing the slaves. Several were ministers or divinity students seeking a mission in life that would fulfill spiritual and professional ambitions.

The career of Theodore Dwight Weld exemplified the connection between revivalism and abolitionism. Weld came from a long line of New England ministers. After dropping out of divinity school because of a combination of physical and spiritual ailments, he migrated to western New York. There he fell under the influence of Charles G. Finney and, after a long struggle, underwent a conversion experience in 1826. He then became an itinerant lecturer for various reform causes. By the early 1830s, he focused his attention on the moral issues raised by the institution of slavery. After a brief flirtation with the colonization movement, Weld was converted to abolitionism in 1832, recognizing that colonizationists did not really accept blacks as equals or "brothers-in-Christ." In 1834, he instigated what amounted to a series of abolitionist revivals at Lane Theological Seminary in Cincinnati. When the trustees of the seminary attempted to suppress further discussion of the case for immediate emancipation, Weld led a mass walkout of most students. "The Lane rebels" subsequently founded Oberlin College as a center for abolitionist activity.

In 1835 and 1836, Weld toured Ohio and western New York preaching abolitionism. He also supervised and trained other agents and orators as part of a campaign to convert the entire region to immediate emancipation. The tried and true methods of the revival—fervent preaching, protracted meetings, and the call for individuals to come forth and announce their redemption—were put at the service of the antislavery movement. Weld and his associates often had to face angry mobs, but they left behind them tens of thousands of new abolitionists and hundreds of local antislavery societies. As a result of their efforts, northern Ohio and western New York became hotbeds of abolitionist sentiment.

Antislavery orators and organizers tended to have their greatest successes in the small- to medium-sized towns of the upper North. The typical convert came from an upwardly mobile family engaged in small business, the skilled trades, or market farming. In larger towns and cities, or when they ventured close to the Mason-Dixon line, abolitionists were more likely to encounter fierce and effective opposition. In 1835, Garrison was mobbed in the streets of Boston and almost lynched. In New York City, the Tappan brothers—Lewis and Arthur—were frequent objects of threats and violence. These two successful merchants were key figures in the movement because they used their substantial wealth to finance antislavery activities. In 1835–1836, they supported a massive effort to print antislavery pamphlets and distribute them through the U. S. mails. But they made relatively few converts in their own city; most New Yorkers regarded them as dangerous radicals.

Abolitionists who thought of taking their message to the fringes of the South had reason to pause, given the fate of the antislavery editor Elijah Lovejoy. In 1837, while attempting to defend himself and his printing press from a mob in Alton, Illinois, just across the Mississippi River from slaveholding Missouri, Lovejoy was shot and killed.

Racism was a major cause of antiabolitionist violence in the North. Rumors that abolitionists advocated or practiced interracial marriage could easily incite an urban crowd. If it could not find white abolitionists, the mob was likely to turn on local blacks. Working-class whites tended to fear that economic and social competition with blacks would increase if abolitionists succeeded in freeing slaves and making them citizens. But a striking feature of many of the mobs was that they were dominated by "gentlemen of property and standing." Solid citizens resorted to violence, it would appear, because abolitionism threatened their conservative notions of social order and hierarchy.

By the end of the 1830s, the abolitionist movement was under great stress. Besides the burden of external repression, there was dissension within the movement. Becoming an abolitionist required an exacting conscience and an unwillingness to compromise on matters of principle. These character traits also made it difficult for abolitionists to work together and maintain a united front. Relations between black and white abolitionists were, for the most part, tense and uneasy. Blacks protested that they did not have a fair share of leadership positions or influence over policy. Not even abolitionists were entirely free of the prejudices rife in the larger white society, and blacks resented the paternalism and condescension that often resulted.

During the late 1830s, Garrison, the most visible spokesman for the cause, began to adopt positions that some other abolitionists found extreme and divisive. He embraced the nonresistant or "no-government" philosophy of Henry C. Wright and urged abolitionists to abstain from voting or otherwise participating in a corrupt political system. He also attacked the clergy and the churches for refusing to take a strong antislavery stand and

African American leaders in the abolitionist movement included Frederick Douglass (right) and William Whipper (left). Douglass, who escaped from slavery in 1838, became one of the most effective voices in the crusade against slavery. In 1837, twelve years before Thoreau's essay "Civil Disobedience," Whipper published an article entitled "An Address on Non-Resistance to Offensive Aggression." Whipper was also one of the founders of the American Moral Reform Society, an African American abolitionist organization.

encouraged his followers to "come out" of the established denominations rather than continuing to work within them.

These positions alienated those members of the Anti-Slavery Society who continued to hope that organized religion and the existing political system could be influenced or even taken over by abolitionists. But it was Garrison's stand on women's rights that led to an open break at the national convention of 1840. Following their leader's principle that women should be equal partners in the crusade, a Garrison-led majority elected a female abolitionist to the executive committee of the Anti-Slavery Society. A minority, led by Lewis Tappan, then withdrew to form a competing organization—the American and Foreign Anti-Slavery Society.

The new organization never amounted to much, but the schism did weaken Garrison's influence within the movement. When he later repudiated the U. S. Constitution as a proslavery document and called for northern secession from the Union, few antislavery people in the mid-Atlantic or midwestern states went along. Outside of New England, most abolitionists worked *within* the churches and avoided controversial side issues like women's rights and nonresistant pacifism. Some antislavery advocates chose the path of political action. The Liberty party, organized in 1840, was their first attempt to enter the electoral arena under their own banner; it signaled a new effort to turn antislavery sentiment into political power.

Historians have debated the question of whether the abolitionist movement of the 1830s and early 1840s was a success or failure. It obviously failed to convert a majority of Americans to its position that slavery was a sinful institution that should be abolished immediately. Since that position implied that blacks should be granted equality as American citizens, it ran up against the powerful conviction of white supremacy prevailing in all parts of the country. In the South, abolitionism caused a strong counterreaction and helped inspire a more militant and uncompromising defense of slavery. The belief that peaceful agitation, or what abolitionists called "moral suasion," would convert slaveholders and their northern sympathizers to abolition was obviously unrealistic.

But in another sense the crusade was successful. It brought the slavery issue to the forefront of public consciousness and convinced a substantial and growing segment of the northern population that the South's peculiar institution was morally wrong and potentially dangerous to the American way of life. The South helped the antislavery cause in the North by responding hysterically and repressively to abolitionist agitation. In 1836, Southerners in Congress forced adoption of a "gag rule" requiring that abolitionist petitions be tabled without being read; at about the same time, the Post Office refused to carry antislavery literature into the slave states. Prominent Northerners who had not been moved to action by abolitionist depictions of slave suffering became more responsive to the movement when it appeared their own civil liberties might be threatened. The politicians who later mobilized the North against the expansion of slavery into the territories drew strength from the antislavery and antisouthern sentiments that abolitionists had already called forth.

From Abolitionism to Women's Rights

Abolitionism also served as a catalyst for the women's rights movement. From the beginning women were active participants in the abolitionist crusade. Between 1835 and 1838, the American Anti-Slavery Society bombarded Congress with petitions, mostly calling for abolition of slavery in the District of Columbia. Over half of the thousands of antislavery petitions sent to Washington had women's signatures on them.

Some antislavery women went further and defied conventional ideas of their proper sphere by becoming public speakers and demanding an equal role in the leadership of antislavery societies. The most famous of these were the Grimké sisters, Sarah and Angelina, who attracted enormous attention because they were the rebellious daughters of a South Carolina slaveholder. When some male abolitionists objected to their speaking in public to mixed audiences of men and women, Garrison came to their defense and helped forge a link between black and female struggles for equality.

The battle to participate equally in the antislavery crusade made a number of female abolitionists acutely aware of male dominance and oppression. For them, the same principles that justified the liberation of the slaves also applied to the emancipation of women from all restrictions on their rights as citizens. In 1840, Garrison's American followers withdrew from the first World's Anti-Slavery Convention in London because the sponsors refused to seat the female members of their delegation. Among the women thus excluded were Lucretia Mott and Elizabeth Cady Stanton.

Wounded by male reluctance to extend the cause of emancipation to include women, Stanton and Mott organized a new and independent movement for women's rights. The high point of their campaign was the famous convention at Seneca Falls, New York, in 1848. The "Declaration of Sentiments" issued by this first national gathering of feminists charged that "the history of mankind is a history of repeated injuries and usurpations on the part of man toward woman, having in direct object the establishment of an absolute

Elizabeth Cady Stanton, a leader of the women's rights movement, reared seven children. In addition to her pioneering work, especially for women's suffrage, she also lectured frequently on family life and child care.

tyranny over her." It went on to demand that all women be given the right to vote and that married women be freed from unjust laws giving husbands control of their property, persons, and children. Rejecting the cult of domesticity with its doctrine of separate spheres, these women and their male supporters launched the modern movement for gender equality.

Radical Ideas and Experiments

Hopes for individual or social perfection were not limited to reformers inspired by evangelicalism. Between the 1820s and 1850s, a great variety of schemes for human redemption came from those who had rejected orthodox Protestantism. Some were secular humanists carrying on the freethinking tradition of the Enlightenment, but most were seeking new paths to spiritual or religious fulfillment. These philosophical and religious radicals attacked established institutions, prescribed new modes of living, and founded utopian communities to put their ideas into practice.

A radical movement of foreign origin that gained a toehold in Jacksonian America was utopian socialism. In 1825–1826, the British manufacturer and reformer Robert Owen visited the United States and founded a community based on common and equal ownership of property at New Harmony, Indiana. About the same time, Owen's associate Frances Wright gathered a group of slaves at Nashoba, Tennessee, and set them to work earning their freedom in an atmosphere of "rational cooperation." The rapid demise of both of these model communities suggested that utopian socialism did not easily take root in American soil.

But the impulse survived. In the 1840s, a number of Americans, including the prominent editor Horace Greeley, became interested in the ideas of the French utopian theorist Charles Fourier. Fourier called for cooperative communities in which everyone did a fair share of the work and tasks were allotted to make use of the natural abilities and instincts of the members. Between 1842 and 1852, about thirty Fourierist "phalanxes" were established in the northeastern and midwestern states, and approximately a hundred thousand people lived for a time in these communities or otherwise supported the movement. The phalanxes were not purely socialistic; in fact they were organized as joint-stock companies. But they did give the members an opportunity to live and work in a communal atmosphere. Like the Owenite communities, they were short-lived, surviving for an average of only two years. The common complaint of the founders was that Americans were too individualistic to cooperate in the ways that Fourier's theories required.

The most successful and long-lived of the pre–Civil War utopias was established in 1848 at Oneida, New York, and was inspired by an unorthodox brand of Christian perfectionism. Its founder, John Humphrey Noyes, believed the Second Coming of Christ had already occurred; hence human beings were totally free from sin and were no longer obliged to follow the moral rules that their previously fallen state had required. At Oneida, traditional marriage was outlawed and a carefully regulated form of "free love" was put into practice.

It was a literary and philosophical movement known as transcendentalism that inspired the era's most memorable experiments in thinking and living on a higher plane. The main idea was that the individual could transcend material reality and ordinary understanding, attaining through a higher form of reason—or intuition—a oneness with the universe as a whole and with the spiritual forces that lay behind it. Transcendentalism was the major American version of the romantic and idealist thought that emerged in the early nineteenth century. Throughout the western world, romanticism was challenging the rationalism and materialism of the Enlightenment in the name of exalted feeling and cosmic spirituality. Most American transcendentalists were Unitarians or ex-Unitarians who were dissatisfied with the sober rationalism of their denomination and sought a more intense kind of spiritual experience. Unable to embrace evangelical Christianity because of intellectual resistance to its doctrines, they sought inspiration from a philosophical and literary idealism of German origin.

Their prophet was Ralph Waldo Emerson, a brilliant essayist and lecturer who preached that each individual could commune directly with a benign spiritual force that animated nature and the universe, which he called the "oversoul." Emerson was a radical individualist committed to "self-culture" and "the sufficiency of the private man." He carefully avoided all involvement in organized movements or associations because they limited the freedom of the individual to develop inner resources and find a personal path to spiritual illumination. In the vicinity of Emerson's home in Concord, Massachusetts, a group of like-minded seekers of truth and spiritual fulfillment gathered during the 1830s and 1840s. Among them for a time was Margaret Fuller, the leading female intellectual of the age. In *Woman in the Nineteenth Century* (1845), she made a strong claim for the spiritual and artistic equality of women.

One group of transcendentalists, led by the Reverend George Ripley, rejected Emerson's radical individualism and founded a cooperative community at Brook Farm, near Roxbury, Massachusetts, in 1841. For the next four years group members worked the land in common, conducted an excellent school on the principle that spontaneity rather than discipline was the key to education, and allowed ample time for conversation, meditation, communion with nature, and artistic activity of all kinds. Visitors and guest lecturers included such luminaries as Emerson, Margaret Fuller, and Theodore Parker, the Unitarian theologian and radical reformer. In 1845, Brook Farm was reconstituted as a Fourieristic phalanx, but some of the original spirit persisted until its dissolution in 1849.

Another experiment in transcendental living adhered more closely to the individualistic spirit of the movement. Between 1845 and 1847, Henry David Thoreau, a young disciple of Emerson, lived by himself in the woods along the shore of Walden Pond and carefully recorded his thoughts and impressions. In a sense, he pushed the ideal of self-culture to its logical outcome—a utopia of one. The result was *Walden* (published in 1854), one of the greatest achievements in American literature.

Fads and Fashions

Not only venturesome intellectuals experimented with new beliefs and lifestyles. Between the 1830s and 1850s, a number of fads, fashions, and medical cure-alls appeared on the scene, indicating that a large segment of the middle class was obsessed with the pursuit of personal health, happiness, and moral perfection. Dietary reformers like Sylvester Graham convinced many people to give up meat, coffee, tea, and pastries in favor of fruit, vegetables, and whole wheat bread. Some women, especially feminists, began to wear loose-fitting pantalettes, or "bloomers," popularized by Amelia Bloomer. These clothes were more convenient and less restricting than the elaborate structure of corsets, petticoats, and hooped skirts currently in fashion. A concern with understanding and improving personal character and abilities was reflected in the craze for phrenology, a popular pseudoscience that studied the shape of the skull to determine natural aptitudes and inclinations.

In an age of perfectionism, even the dead could be enlisted on the side of universal reform. In the 1850s, spiritualists like Andrew Jackson Davis and the Fox sisters—Margaret, Leah, and Catharine—convinced an extraordinary number of people that it was possible to make direct contact with the departed, who were viewed as having "passed on" to a purer state of being and a higher wisdom. Seances were held in parlors all over the

Henry David Thoreau explained that he went to live in solitude in the woods because he wished to "front only the essential facts of life." The sketch at right appeared on the title page of the first edition of Walden, *published in 1854, the remarkable record of his experiment in living.*

nation, and large crowds turned out for demonstrations of "spirit-rapping" and other psychic manifestations. Spiritualist beliefs were a logical outgrowth (some might say to the point of absurdity) of the perfectionist dream pursued so ardently by antebellum Americans.

Counterpoint on Reform

One great American writer observed at close quarters the perfectionist ferment of the age but held himself aloof, suggesting in his novels and tales that pursuit of the ideal led to a distorted sense of human nature and possibilities. Nathaniel Hawthorne lived in Concord, knew Emerson and Margaret Fuller, and even spent time at Brook Farm. But his sense of human frailty and sinfulness made him skeptical about the claims of transcendentalism and Utopianism. He satirized transcendentalism as unworldly and overoptimistic in his allegorical tale "The Celestial Railroad" and gently lampooned the denizens of Brook Farm in his novel *The Blithedale Romance* (1852). His view of the dangers of pursuing perfection too avidly came out in his tale of a father who kills his beautiful daughter trying to remove her one blemish, a birthmark. His greatest novels, *The Scarlet Letter* (1850) and *The House of Seven Gables* (1851), imaginatively probed New England's Puritan past and the shadows it cast on the present. By dwelling on the psychological reality of original sin, Hawthorne told his contemporaries that their efforts to escape from guilt and evil were futile. One simply had to accept the world as an imperfect place. Although he did not engage in polemics against humanitarian reformers and cosmic optimists, Hawthorne wrote parables and allegories that implicitly questioned the fundamental assumptions of pre–Civil War reform.

One does not have to agree with Hawthorne's antiprogressive view of the human condition to acknowledge that the dreams of perfectionist reformers promised more than they could possibly deliver. Revivals could not make all men like Christ; temperance could not solve all social problems; abolitionist agitation could not bring a peaceful end to slavery; and transcendentalism (as Emerson himself sometimes conceded) could not fully emancipate people from the limitations and frustrations of daily life. The consequences of

Known primarily for works expressing his skepticism about reform and the pursuit of perfection, Nathaniel Hawthorne also published lighter pieces of imagination and fancy. His Tanglewood Tales *(1853) was a collection of children's stories. Pictured here is the title page from the 1854 edition.*

perfectionist efforts were often far different from what their proponents expected. In defense of the reformers however, one could argue that Hawthorne's skepticism and fatalism were a prescription for doing nothing in the face of intolerable evils. If the reform impulse was long on inspirational rhetoric but somewhat short on durable, practical achievements, it did at least disturb the complacent and opportunistic surface of American life and open the way to necessary changes. Nothing could possibly change for the better unless people were willing to dream of improvement.

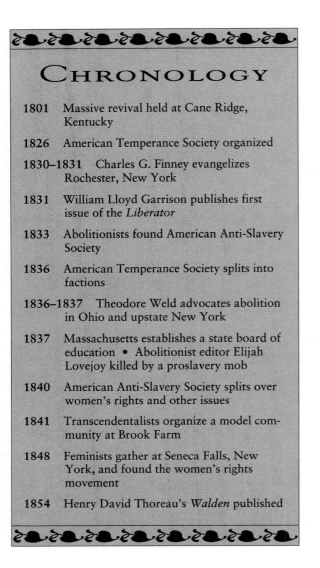

CHRONOLOGY

1801	Massive revival held at Cane Ridge, Kentucky
1826	American Temperance Society organized
1830–1831	Charles G. Finney evangelizes Rochester, New York
1831	William Lloyd Garrison publishes first issue of the *Liberator*
1833	Abolitionists found American Anti-Slavery Society
1836	American Temperance Society splits into factions
1836–1837	Theodore Weld advocates abolition in Ohio and upstate New York
1837	Massachusetts establishes a state board of education • Abolitionist editor Elijah Lovejoy killed by a proslavery mob
1840	American Anti-Slavery Society splits over women's rights and other issues
1841	Transcendentalists organize a model community at Brook Farm
1848	Feminists gather at Seneca Falls, New York, and found the women's rights movement
1854	Henry David Thoreau's *Walden* published

Recommended Reading

Alice Felt Tyler, *Freedom's Ferment: Phases of American Social History from the Colonial Period to the Outbreak of the Civil War* (1944), gives a lively overview of the varieties of pre-Civil War reform activity. Ronald G. Walters, *American Reformers, 1815–1860* (1978), provides a modern interpretation of these movements. A particularly useful selection of articles and essays is David Brion Davis, ed., *Ante-Bellum Reform* (1967). The best general work on the revivalism of the Second Great Awakening is William G. McLoughlin, *Modern Revivalism* (1959). Paul E. Johnson, *A Shopkeeper's Millennium: Society and Revivals in Rochester, New York, 1815–1837* (1978), incisively describes the impact of the revival on a single community. A good introduction to the changing roles

of women and the family in nineteenth-century America is Carl N. Degler, *At Odds: Women and the Family in America from the Revolution to the Present* (1980). On the rise of the domestic ideology see Nancy Cott, *The Bonds of Womanhood: "Woman's Sphere" in New England, 1780–1835* (1977). The condition of working-class women is incisively treated in Christine Stansell, *City of Women: Sex and Class in New York, 1789–1860* (1986).

David J. Rothman, *The Discovery of the Asylum: Social Order and Disorder in the New Republic* (1971), provides a penetrating analysis of the movement for institutional reform. For a good survey of abolitionism, see James Brewer Stewart, *Holy Warriors: The Abolitionists and American Slavery* (1976).

Additional Bibliography

The various dimensions of evangelical religion are covered in William G. McLoughlin, *Revivals, Awakenings, and Reform: An Essay on Religion and Social Change in America, 1607–1977* (1978); John B. Boles, *The Great Revival* (1972); Donald G. Mathews, *Religion in the Old South* (1977); Anne C. Loveland, *Southern Evangelicals and the Social Order, 1800–1860* (1980); Charles A. Johnson, *The Frontier Camp Meeting* (1955); Whitney R. Cross, *The Burned-Over District* (1950); Perry Miller, *The Life of the Mind in America from the Revolution to the Civil War* (1965); and Charles C. Cole, *The Social Ideas of the Northern Evangelists* (1954). The connection between revivalism and organized benevolence is treated in Clifford Griffen, *Their Brothers' Keepers: Moral Stewardship in the United States, 1800–1865* (1960); Charles I. Foster, *An Errand of Mercy: The Evangelical United Front* (1960); John R. Bodo, *The Protestant Clergy and Public Issues, 1812–1848* (1954); and Timothy L. Smith, *Revivalism and Social Reform in Mid-Nineteenth-Century America* (1957). On the temperance movement, see John A. Krout, *The Origins of Prohibition* (1925); Joseph R. Gusfield, *Symbolic Crusade: Status, Politics, and the American Temperance Movement* (1963); W. J. Rorabaugh, *The Alcoholic Republic: An American Tradition* (1979); and Ian R. Tyrrell, *Sobering Up: From Temperance to Prohibition in Antebellum America, 1800–1860* (1979).

The cult of domesticity and the status of women are the subjects of Barbara Welter, "The Cult of True Womanhood," *American Quarterly*, 18 (1966): 217–240; Kathryn Kish Sklar, *Catharine Beecher: A Study in American Domesticity* (1973); Mary Ryan, *The Cradle of the Middle Class: The Family in Oneida County New York, 1790–1865* (1981); and Suzanne Lebsock, *The Free Women of Petersburg* (1984). On women's reform activities, see Lori D. Ginzberg, *Women and the Work of Benevolence* (1990). Bernard Wishy, *The Child and the Republic: The Dawn of Modern American Child Nurture* (1968), treats childhood and child rearing. Light is shed on the limitation of family size in James Reed, *From Private Vice to Public Virtue: The Birth Control Movement and American Society Since 1830* (1978) and James C. Mohr, *Abortion in America: The Origins and Evolution of National Policy, 1800–1900* (1978). On educational reform, see Lawrence Cremin, *American Education: The National Experience, 1783–1876* (1980); Rush Welter, *Popular Education and Democratic Thought* (1962); and Michael B. Katz, *The Irony of Early School Reform: Educational Innovation in Mid-Nineteenth-Century Massachusetts* (1968). The emergence of modern prisons is described in Blake McKelvy, *American Prisons* (1936) and W. David Lewis, *From Newgate to Dannemora: The Rise of the Penitentiary in New York* (1965). On the rise of asylums, see Gerald N. Grob, *Mental Institutions in America: Social Policy to 1875* (1973).

There is a vast literature on the abolitionist movement. Among the most significant works are Gilbert H. Barnes, *The Antislavery Impulse* (1934); John L. Thomas, *The Liberator: William Lloyd Garrison* (1963); Aileen S. Kraditor, *Means and Ends in American Abolitionism: Garrison and His Critics on Strategy and Tactics* (1967); Bertram Wyatt-Brown, *Lewis Tappan and the Evangelical War Against Slavery* (1969); Lewis Perry, *Radical Abolitionism: Anarchy and the Government of God in Antislavery Thought* (1973); Ronald G. Walters, *The Antislavery Appeal: American Abolitionists After 1830* (1976); Robert H. Abzug, *Passionate Liberator: Theodore Dwight Weld and the Dilemma of Reform* (1980); Lawrence J. Friedman, *Gregarious Saints: Self and Community in American Abolitionism* (1982); Louis S. Gerteis, *Morality and Utility in Antislavery Reform* (1987); and William S. McFeely, *Frederick Douglass* (1991). Leonard L. Richards, *"Gentlemen of Property and Standing": Anti-Abolition Mobs in Jacksonian America* (1970), interprets violence against the abolitionists. On the connection between abolition and women's rights, see Gerda Lerner, *The Grimké Sisters from South Carolina: Rebels Against Slavery* (1967); Blanche Glassman Hersh, *The Slavery of Sex: Feminist Abolitionists in America* (1978); and Shirley J. Yee, *Black Women Abolitionists* (1992).

The utopian impulse is the subject of Arthur Bestor, *Backwoods Utopias* (1950); Michael Fellman, *The Unbounded Frame: Freedom and Community in Nineteenth-Century Utopianism* (1973); and Carl Guarneri, *The Utopian Alternative: Fourierism in Nineteenth-Century America* (1991). On the transcendentalists, see Anne C. Rose, *Transcendentalism as a Social Movement, 1830–1850* (1981). R. Laurence Moore, *In Search of White Crows: Spiritualism, Parapsychology, and American Culture* (1977), is the best study of spiritualism.

An Age of Expansionism

In the 1840s and early 1850s politicians, journalists, writers, and entrepreneurs frequently proclaimed themselves champions of "Young America." One of the first to use the phrase was Ralph Waldo Emerson, who told an audience of merchants and manufacturers in 1844 that the nation was entering a new era of commercial development, technological progress (as exemplified in the railroads just beginning to crisscross the landscape), and territorial expansion. Emerson suggested that a progressive new generation—the "Young Americans"—would lead this surge of physical development. More than a slogan and less than an organized movement, Young America stood for a positive attitude toward the market economy and industrial growth, a more aggressive and belligerent foreign policy, and a celebration of America's unique strengths and virtues. The idea of a young country led by young men into new paths of prosperity and greatness was bound to appeal to many. It did, however, have its opponents—cautious, tradition-minded people who had doubts about where "progress" and expansionism might lead. The Young Americans had no patience with such "old fogeys." "The spirit of young America," noted a Boston newspaper in 1844, "will not be satisfied with what has been attained but plumes its wings for more glorious flight. . . . The steam is up, the young overpowering spirit of the country will press onward."

Although the Young America ideal attracted support across party lines, it came to be identified mainly with young Democrats who sought to purge their party of its traditional fear of the expansion of commerce and industry. Unlike old-line Jeffersonians and Jacksonians, Young Americans had no qualms about the market economy and the speculative, materialistic spirit it called forth.

Furthermore, the Young Americans favored enlarging the national market by acquiring new territory. They called in turn for annexation of Texas, assertion of an American claim to all of Oregon, and the appropriation of vast new territories from Mexico. They also celebrated the technological advances that would knit this new empire together, especially the telegraph and the railroad. Telegraphs, according to one writer,

would "flash sensation and volition . . . and to and from towns and provinces as if they were organs and limbs of a single organism"; railroads would provide "a vast system of iron muscles which, as it were, move the limbs of the mighty organism."

Young America was a cultural and intellectual as well as an economic and political movement. In 1845, a Washington journal hailed the election of the relatively young James K. Polk to the presidency as a sign that youth will "dare to take antiquity by the beard, and tear the cloak from hoary-headed hypocrisy. Too young to be corrupt . . . it is Young America, awakened to a sense of her own intellectual greatness by her soaring spirit. It stands in strength, the voice of the majority." During the Polk administration, "Young American" writers and critics—mostly based in New York—called for a new and distinctive national literature, free of subservience to European themes or models and expressive of the democratic spirit. Their organ was the *Literary World*, founded in 1847, and its ideals influenced two of the greatest writers the nation has produced—Walt Whitman and Herman Melville.

Whitman captured much of the exuberance and expansionism of Young America in his "Song of the Open Road"

> *From this hour I ordain myself loos'd of limits and imaginary lines,*
> *Going where I list, my own master total and absolute,*
> . . . .
> *I inhale great draughts of space,*
> *The east and the west are mine, and the north and the south are mine.*
> *I am larger, better than I thought.*

In *Moby-Dick,* Herman Melville produced a novel sufficiently original in form and conception to more than fulfill the demand of Young Americans for "a New Literature to fit the New Man in the New Age." But Melville was too deep a thinker not to see the perils that underlay the soaring ambition and aggressiveness of the new age. The whaling captain, Ahab, who brings destruction on himself and his ship by his relentless pursuit of the white whale symbolized— among other things—the dangers facing a nation that was overreaching itself by indulging its pride and exalted sense of destiny with too little concern for moral and practical consequences.

MOVEMENT TO THE FAR WEST

In the 1830s and 1840s, the westward movement of population left the valley of the Mississippi behind and penetrated the Far West all the way to the Pacific. Pioneers pursued fertile land and economic opportunity beyond the existing boundaries of the United States and thus helped set the stage for the annexations and international crises of the 1840s. Some went for material gain, others for adventure, and a significant minority sought freedom from religious persecution. Whatever their reasons, they brought American attitudes into regions that were already occupied or claimed by Mexico or Great Britain.

Borderlands of the 1830s

U.S. expansionists directed their ambitions to the north, west, and southwest. For a time it seemed that both Canada and Mexico might be frontiers

New York native Herman Melville, shown here in an 1870 portrait by Joseph Oriel Eaton, shaped the knowledge he gained as a merchant sailor into Moby-Dick, *a cautionary saga about the dark side of human ambition.*

Walt Whitman in the "carpenter portrait" that appeared in the first edition of his great work, Leaves of Grass, *in 1855. The poet's rough clothes and slouch hat signify his identification with the common people.*

for expansionism. Conflicts over the border between the United States and British North America led periodically to calls for diplomatic or military action to wrest the northern half of the continent from the British; similar conflicts in Mexican territory led ultimately to the United States's capture and acquisition of much of northern Mexico.

Since the birth of the republic there had been a major dispute over the boundary between Maine and the Canadian province of New Brunswick. In 1839, fighting broke out between Canadian lumberjacks and the Maine militia. This long-festering controversy poisoned Anglo-American relations until 1842, when Secretary of State Daniel Webster concluded an agreement with the British government, represented by Lord Ashburton. The Webster-Ashburton Treaty gave over half of the disputed territory to the United States and established a definite northeastern boundary with Canada.

On the other side of the continent, the United States and Britain both laid claim to Oregon, a vast area that lay between the Rockies and the Pacific from the forty-second parallel (the northern boundary of California) to the latitude of 54°40′ (the southern boundary of Alaska). In 1818, the two nations agreed to joint occupation for ten years, an agreement that was renewed indefinitely in 1827. Meanwhile, the Americans had strengthened their claim by acquiring Spain's rights to the Pacific Northwest in the Adams-Onís Treaty (see Chapter 9), and the British had gained effective control of the northern portion of the Oregon country through the activities of the Hudson's Bay Company, a well-financed fur-trading concern. Blocking an equitable division was the reluctance on both sides to surrender access to the Columbia River basin and the adjacent territory extending north to the forty-ninth parallel (which later became the northern border of the state of Washington).

The Oregon country was scarcely populated before 1840. The same could not be said of the Mexican borderlands that lay directly west of Jacksonian America. Spanish settlements in present-day New Mexico dated from the end of the sixteenth century. By 1820, about forty thousand

people populated this province, engaging mainly in sheep-raising and mining. In 1821, Spain granted independence to Mexico, which then embraced areas that currently make up the states of Texas, New Mexico, Arizona, California, Nevada, Utah, and much of Colorado. Spain's mercantilistic policies had closed the region to outside traders, but the Republic of Mexico opted for a free trade policy. Mexico in 1821 informed its northern neighbors of the changed laws encouraging trade. This action succeeded in stimulating commercial prosperity, but also whetted expansionist appetites on the Anglo side of the border.

California was the other major northward extension of Mexico. Spanish missionaries and soldiers had taken control of the region in the late eighteenth century. In the 1820s and 1830s, this land of huge estates and enormous cattle herds was far less populous than New Mexico—only about four thousand Mexicans of Spanish origin lived in California in 1827. The region's other inhabitants were the thirty thousand Indians,

Territorial Expansion by the Mid-Nineteenth Century

Fervent nationalists identified the growth of America through territorial expansion as the divinely ordained "Manifest Destiny" of a chosen people.

many of whom were forced to work on vast land tracts owned by Spanish missions. At the beginning of the 1830s, a chain of twenty-one mission stations, stretching from San Diego to San Francisco, controlled most of the province's land and wealth. Great as the Indian population may seem, the number represented only a small fraction of the original indigenous population; there had been a dramatic and catastrophic decline in Indian population during the previous sixty years of Spanish rule. The stresses and strains of forced labor and exposure to European diseases had taken an enormous toll.

In 1833, the Mexican Congress's "secularization act" emancipated the Indians from church control and opened the mission lands to settlement. The government awarded immense tracts of the mission land to Mexican citizens and left the Indians landless. A new class of large landowners, or *rancheros*, replaced the *padres* as rulers of Old California and masters of the province's indigenous population. Seven hundred grantees took possession of *ranchos* ranging up to nearly 50,000 acres and proceeded to subject the Indians to a new and even harsher form of servitude. During the fifteen years they held sway, the rancheros created an American legend through their lavish hospitality, extravagant dress, superb horsemanship, and taste for violent and dangerous sports. Their flamboyant lifestyle and devotion to the pursuit of pleasure captured the fancy and aroused the secret envy of many American visitors and traders.

The Americans who saw California in the 1830s were mostly merchants and sailors involved in the oceanic trade between Boston and California ports. New England clipper ships sailed around Cape Horn at the southern tip of South America to barter manufactured goods for cowhides. One Boston firm came away with over 500,000 hides in a twenty-year period. By the mid-1830s, several Yankee merchants had taken up permanent residence in towns like Monterey and San Diego in order to conduct the California end of the business. The reports they sent back about the Golden West sparked interest in eastern business circles.

The Texas Revolution

At the same time some Americans were trading with California, others were taking possession of Texas. In the early 1820s, Mexican officials encouraged settlers from the United States to settle in Texas. Newly independent Mexico granted Stephen F. Austin, son of a one-time Spanish citizen, a huge piece of land in hopes he would help attract and settle new colonists from the United States. Some fifteen other Anglo-American *empresarios* were similarly granted land in the 1820s. In 1823, three hundred families from the United States were settled on the Austin grant, and within a year the colony's population had swelled to 2,021. American immigrants were drawn by the offer of fertile and inexpensive land.

An extravagantly dressed ranchero *directs his Indian overseer in this 1839 lithograph. With their thrilling lifestyles and exotic costumes, these hacienda owners contributed to the vivid images associated with California in the 1830s.*

Friction soon developed between the Mexican government and the Anglo-American colonists over slavery's status and the Catholic church's authority. At its core, the dispute was a misunderstanding about whether the settlers were Anglo-Americans or Mexicans. Under the terms of settlement, all people living in Texas adopted Mexican citizenship and the Roman Catholic faith. Slavery presented a problem, for in 1829 Mexico freed all slaves under its jurisdiction. Slaveholders in Texas were given a special exemption that allowed them to emancipate their slaves and then sign them to lifelong contracts as indentured servants, but many refused to limit their ownership rights in any way. Settlers similarly either converted to Catholicism only superficially or ignored the requirement entirely.

A Mexican government commission reported in 1829 that Americans were the great majority of the Texas population and were flagrantly violating Mexican law—refusing to emancipate their slaves, evading import duties on goods from the United States, and failing to convert to Catholicism. The following year the Mexican Congress prohibited further American immigration and importation of slaves to Texas.

Enforcement of the new law was feeble, and the flow of settlers, slaves, and smuggled goods continued virtually unabated. A long-standing complaint of the Texans was the failure of the Mexican constitution to grant them local self-government. Under the Mexican federal system, Texas was joined to the state of Coahuila, and Texan representatives were outnumbered three to one in the state legislature. In 1832, the colonists showed their displeasure with Mexican rule by rioting in protest against the arrest of several Anglo-Americans by a Mexican commander.

Stephen F. Austin went to Mexico City in 1833 to present the Texans' grievances and seek concessions from the central government. He succeeded in having the ban against American immigration lifted, but got only vague promises about tariff relief, and failed to win agreement to the separation of Texas from Coahuila. As he was about to return to Texas, Austin was arrested and imprisoned for writing a letter recommending that Texans set up a state government without Mexico City's consent.

In 1835, some Texans revolted against Mexico's central government. The insurrection-ists claimed they were fighting for freedom against a long experience of oppression. Actually, Mexican rule had not been harsh; the worst that can be said was that it was inefficient, inconsistent, and sometimes corrupt. Furthermore, the Texans' devotion to "liberty" did not prevent them from defending slavery against Mexico's attempt to abolish it. Texans had done pretty much what they pleased, despite laws to the contrary and angry rumblings from south of the Río Grande.

Developments in 1834 had threatened their status as "tolerated guests." In that year, General Antonio López de Santa Anna made himself dictator of Mexico and abolished the federal system of government. When news of these developments reached Texas late in the year, it was accompanied by rumors of the impending disfranchisement and even expulsion of American immigrants. The rebels, already aroused by earlier restrictive policies, were influenced by these rumors and prepared to resist Santa Anna's effort to enforce tariff regulations by military force.

When he learned that Texans were resisting customs collections, Santa Anna sent reinforcements. On June 30, 1835, before any additional troops could arrive, a band of settlers led by W. B. Travis captured the Mexican garrison at Anahuac without firing a shot. The settlers first engaged Mexican troops at Gonzales in October and forced the retreat of a cavalry detachment. Shortly thereafter, Stephen F. Austin laid siege to San Antonio with a force of five hundred men and after six weeks forced its surrender, thereby capturing most of the Mexican troops then in Texas.

The Republic of Texas

While this early fighting was going on, delegates from the American communities in Texas met in convention and after some hesitation voted overwhelmingly to declare their independence on March 2, 1836. A constitution, based closely on that of the United States, was adopted for the new Republic of Texas, and a temporary government was installed to carry on the military struggle. Although the ensuing conflict was largely one of Americans against Mexicans, some Texas-Mexicans, or *Tejanos*, joined the fray on the side of the Anglo rebels. They too wanted to be free of

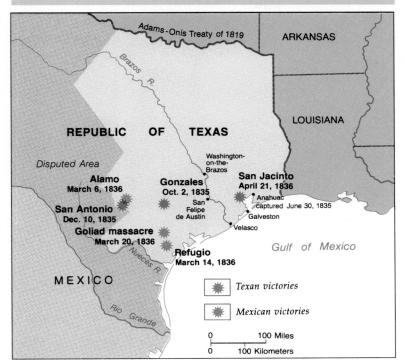

Texas Revolution
Major battles of the Texas Revolution. The Texans suffered severe losses at the Alamo and Goliad, but they scored a stunning victory at San Jacinto.

Santa Anna's heavy-handed rule. (Most of the Tejanos would become victims of the same anti-Mexican prejudice that spurred the revolt. Tejano leader Juan Seguin, who served as captain in the Texas army and became a hero of the independence struggle, was driven off his land by Anglo-Texans in 1841.)

Within days after Texas declared itself a republic, rebels and Mexican troops in San Antonio fought the famous battle of the Alamo. Myths about that battle have magnified the Anglo rebels' valor at the Mexicans' expense. The folklore is based on fact—only 187 rebels fought off a far larger number of Mexican soldiers for more than a week before eventually capitulating—but it is not true that all rebels, including the folk hero Davy Crockett, fought to the death. Crockett and seven other survivors were captured and then executed. Moreover, the rebels fought from inside a strong fortress with superior weapons against march-weary Mexican conscripts. Nevertheless, a tale that combined actual and mythical bravery inside the Alamo gave the

insurrection new inspiration, moral sanction, outside support, and the rallying cry "Remember the Alamo."

The revolt ended with an exchange of slaughters. A few days after the Alamo battle, another Texas detachment was surrounded and captured in an open plain near the San Antonio River and was marched to the town of Goliad, where most of its 350 members were executed. The next month, on April 21, 1836, the main Texas army, under General Sam Houston, assaulted Santa Anna's troops at an encampment near the San Jacinto River during the siesta hour. The final count showed that 630 Mexicans and only a handful of Texans had been killed. Santa Anna was captured and marched to Velasco, the meeting place of the Texas government, where he was forced to sign treaties recognizing the independence of Texas and its claim to territory all the way to the Río Grande. The Mexican Congress immediately repudiated the treaty, but their argument was in vain; although a strip of land between the Nueces and the Río Grande rivers

William H. Huddle, Surrender of Santa Anna at the Battle of San Jacinto, *ca. 1900. After the battle of San Jacinto, its hero Sam Houston, lying wounded under a tree, accepts the surrender of Santa Anna, at left in white breeches. The man cupping his ear at right is Erastus "Deaf" Smith, a famous scout and important man in Houston's army.*

would be disputed during the next decade, Mexico failed to impose its authority on the victorious Texas rebels.

Sam Houston, the hero of San Jacinto, became the first president of Texas. His platform sought annexation to the United States, and one of his first acts in office was to send an emissary to Washington to test the waters. Houston's agent found much sympathy for Texas independence but was told by Andrew Jackson and others that domestic politics and fear of a war with Mexico made immediate annexation impossible. The most that he could win from Congress and the Jackson administration was formal recognition of Texas sovereignty.

In its ten-year career as the "Lone Star Republic," Texas drew settlers from the United States at an accelerating rate. The panic of 1837 impelled many debt-ridden and land-hungry farmers to take advantage of the free grants of 1,280 acres that Texas offered to immigrating heads of white families. In the decade after independence, the population of Texas soared, from 30,000 to 142,000. Most of the newcomers assumed, as did the old settlers, that they would soon be annexed and restored to American citizenship.

Trails of Trade and Settlement

After New Mexico opened its trade to American merchants, a thriving commerce developed along the trail that ran from Missouri to Santa Fe. The first of these merchants to reach the New Mexican capital was William Becknell, who arrived with his train of goods late in 1821. Others followed rapidly. To protect themselves from the hostile Indians whose territory they had to cross, the traders traveled in large caravans, one or two of which would arrive in Santa Fe every summer. The federal government assisted them by providing troops when necessary and by appropriating money to purchase rights of passage from various tribes. Even so, the trip across the Cimarron desert and the southern Rockies was often difficult and hazardous. But profits from the exchange of textiles and other manufactured goods for furs, mules, and precious metals were substantial enough to make the risk worth taking.

Relations between the United States and Mexico soured following the Texas revolution, and this had a devastating effect on the Santa Fe trade. Much of the ill feeling was caused by further Anglo-American aggressions. An expedition of Texas businessmen and soldiers to Santa Fe in 1841 alarmed the Mexican authorities, and they arrested its members. In retaliation, a volunteer force of Texas avengers attacked Mexican troops along the Santa Fe Trail. The Mexican government then moved to curtail the Santa Fe trade. In April 1842, it passed a new tariff banning the importation of many of the goods sold by American merchants and prohibiting the export of gold and silver. Further restrictions in 1843 denied American traders full access to the Santa Fe market.

The famous Oregon Trail was the great overland route that brought the wagon trains of American migrants to the West Coast during the 1840s. Extending for 2,000 miles, across the northern Great Plains and the mountains beyond, it crossed the Rockies at the South Pass and then forked; the main northern route led to the Willamette Valley of Oregon, but various alternative trails were opened during the decade for overlanders heading for California. The journey from Missouri to the West Coast took about six months; most parties departed in May, hoping to arrive in November before the great snows hit the last mountain barriers.

After small groups had made their way to both Oregon and California in 1841 and 1842, a mass migration—mostly to Oregon—began in 1843. Within two years, five thousand Americans, living in the Willamette Valley south of the Columbia River, were demanding the extension of full American sovereignty over the Oregon country.

The Mormon Trek

An important and distinctive group of pioneers followed the Oregon Trail as far as the South Pass and then veered southwestward to establish a thriving colony in the region of the Great Salt Lake. These were Mormons, members of the largest religious denomination founded on American soil—the Church of Jesus Christ of Latter Day Saints.

The background of the Mormon trek was a history of persecution in the eastern states. Joseph Smith, founder of Mormonism, encountered strong opposition from the time he announced in Palmyra, New York, in 1830 that he had received a new divine revelation. According to this new revelation, the lost tribes of Israel had come to the New World in ancient times. One group had founded a Christian civilization, only to be exterminated by the heathen tribes that were the ancestors of the Indian peoples now being encountered by American settlers. Smith and those he converted to his new faith were committed to restoring the pure religion that had once thrived on American soil by founding a western Zion where they could practice their faith unmolested and carry out their special mission to convert the Native Americans.

In the 1830s, the Mormons established communities in Ohio and Missouri, but the former went bankrupt in the panic of 1837 and the latter was the target of angry mobs and vigilante violence. After the Mormons lost the "war" they fought against the Missourians in 1839, Smith led his followers back across the Mississippi to Illinois, where he received a liberal charter from the state legislature to found a town at Nauvoo. Here the Mormons had a temporary measure of security and self-government, but Smith soon reported new revelations that engendered dissension among his followers and hostility from neighboring "gentiles." Most controversial was his authorization of polygamy, or plural marriage. In 1844, Smith was killed by a mob while being held in jail in Carthage, Illinois, on a charge stemming from his quarrels with dissident Mormons who objected to his new policies.

The death of Smith confirmed the growing conviction of the Mormon leadership that they needed to move beyond the borders of the United States to establish their Zion in the wilderness. In late 1845, Smith's successor, Brigham Young, decided to send a party of fifteen hundred men to assess the chances of a colony in the vicinity of the Great Salt Lake (then part of Mexico). Nauvoo was quickly depopulated as twelve thousand Mormons took to the trail in 1846. The following year Young himself arrived in Utah and sent back word to the thousands encamped along the trail that he had found the promised land.

Western Trails

Among the greatest hazards faced by those migrating to the West was the rough and unfamiliar terrain over which their wagon trains traveled.

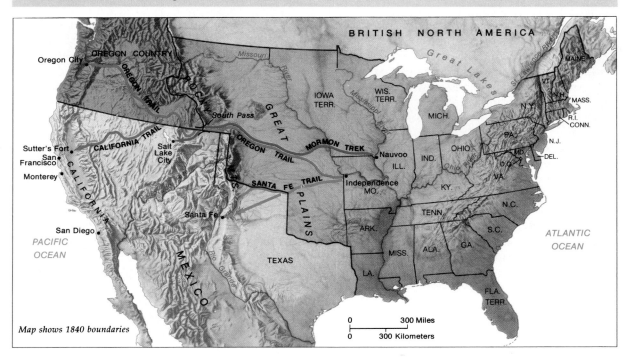

Map shows 1840 boundaries

The Mormon community that Young established in Utah is one of the great success stories of western settlement. In contrast to the rugged individualism and disorder that often characterized mining camps and other new communities, "the state of Deseret" (as Utah was originally called) was a model of discipline and cooperation. Because of its communitarian form of social organization, its centralized government, and the religious dedication of its inhabitants, this frontier society was able to expand settlement in a planned and efficient way and develop a system of irrigation that "made the desert bloom."

Utah's main problem was the determination of its political status. When the Mormons first arrived, they were encroaching illegally into Mexican territory. After Utah came under American sovereignty in 1848, the state of Deseret fought to maintain its autonomy and its custom of polygamy against the efforts of the federal government to extend American law and set up the usual type of territorial administration. In 1857, President Buchanan sent a military force to

bring Utah to heel, and the Mormons prepared to repel this "invasion." But after a heavy snow prevented the army from crossing the Rockies, Buchanan offered an olive branch in the form of a general pardon for Mormons who had violated federal law but agreed to cooperate with U. S. authorities in the future. The Mormons accepted, and in return, Brigham Young called off his plan to resist the army by force and accepted the nominal authority of an appointed territorial governor.

MANIFEST DESTINY AND THE MEXICAN WAR

The rush of settlers beyond the nation's borders in the 1830s and 1840s inspired politicians and propagandists to call for annexation of those areas occupied by migrants. Some went further and proclaimed it was the "Manifest Destiny" of the United States to expand until it had absorbed all of North America, including Canada and

Carl Christian Anton Christensen, Handcart, ca. 1840. Lacking funds to buy sufficient wagons and oxen, the Mormon colonists made their trek to Deseret on foot, hauling their possessions in handcarts and working together as families to move their heavy loads.

Mexico. Such ambitions—and the policies they inspired—led to a major diplomatic confrontation with Great Britain and a war with Mexico.

Tyler and Texas

President John Tyler initiated the politics of Manifest Destiny. He was vice president when William Henry Harrison died in office in 1841 after serving scarcely a month. The first of America's "accidental presidents," Tyler was a states' rights, proslavery Virginian who had been picked as Harrison's running mate to broaden the appeal of the Whig ticket. Profoundly out of sympathy with the mainstream of his own party, he soon broke with the Whigs in Congress, who had united behind Henry Clay's nationalistic economic program. Although he lacked a base in either of the major parties, Tyler hoped to be elected president in his own right in 1844. To accomplish this difficult feat, he needed a new issue around which he could build a following that would cut across established party lines.

In 1843, Tyler decided to put the full weight of his administration behind the annexation of Texas. He anticipated that incorporation of the Lone Star Republic would be a popular move, especially in the South where it would feed the appetite for additional slave states. With the South solidly behind him, Tyler expected to have a good chance in the election of 1844.

To achieve his objective, Tyler enlisted the support of John C. Calhoun, the leading political defender of slavery and southern rights. Calhoun saw the annexation issue as a way of uniting the South and taking the offensive against the abolitionists. Success or failure in this effort would constitute a decisive test of whether the North was willing to give the southern states a fair share of national power and adequate assurances for the future of their way of life. If antislavery sentiment succeeded in blocking the acquisition of Texas, the Southerners would at least know where they stood and could begin to "calculate the value of the union."

To prepare the public mind for an annexation, the Tyler administration launched a propaganda campaign in the summer of 1843 based on reports of British designs on Texas. According to information supplied by Duff Green, an unofficial American agent in England, the British were preparing to guarantee Texas independence and make a loan to the financially troubled republic in return for the abolition of slavery. It is doubtful the British had such intentions, but the stories were believed and used to give urgency to the annexation cause.

Secretary of State Abel Upshur, a proslavery Virginian and protégé of Calhoun, began negotiating an annexation treaty. After Upshur was killed in an accident, Calhoun replaced him and carried the negotiations to a successful conclusion. When the treaty was brought before the Senate in 1844, Calhoun denounced the British for attempting to subvert the South's essential system of labor and racial control by using Texas as a base for abolitionist operations. According to the supporters of Tyler and Calhoun, the South's security and well-being—and by extension that of the nation—required the immediate incorporation of Texas into the Union.

The strategy of linking annexation explicitly to the interests of the South and slavery led northern antislavery Whigs to charge the whole scheme was a proslavery plot meant to advance the interest of one section of the nation against the other. Consequently, the Senate rejected the treaty by a decisive vote of 35 to 16 in June 1844. Tyler then attempted to bring Texas into the Union through an alternative means—a joint resolution of both houses of Congress admitting it as a state—but Congress adjourned before the issue came to a vote, and the whole question hung fire in anticipation of the election of 1844.

The Triumph of Polk and Annexation

Tyler's initiative made the future of Texas the central issue in the 1844 campaign. But party lines held firm, and the president himself was unable to capitalize on the issue because his stand was not in line with the views of either party. Tyler tried to run as an independent, but his failure to gain significant support eventually forced him to withdraw from the race.

If the Democratic party convention had been held in 1843—as originally scheduled—ex-President Martin Van Buren would have won the nomination easily. But postponement of the Democratic conclave until May 1844 weakened his chances. In the meantime the annexation question came to the fore, and Van Buren was

forced to take a stand on it. He persisted in the view he had held as president—that incorporation of Texas would risk war with Mexico, arouse sectional strife, and destroy the unity of the Democratic party. Fears of sectional and party division seemed confirmed in 1844 when the dominant party faction in Van Buren's home state of New York came out against Tyler's Texas policy. In an effort to keep the issue out of the campaign, Van Buren struck a gentleman's agreement with Henry Clay, the overwhelming favorite for the Whig nomination, that both of them would publicly oppose immediate annexation.

Van Buren's letter opposing annexation appeared shortly before the Democratic convention and it cost him the nomination. Angry southern delegates secured a rule requiring approval by a two-thirds vote to block Van Buren's nomination. After several ballots, a dark horse candidate—James K. Polk of Tennessee—emerged triumphant. Polk, a protégé of Andrew Jackson, had been Speaker of the House of Representatives and governor of Tennessee.

Polk was an avowed expansionist, and he ran on a platform calling for the simultaneous annexation of Texas and assertion of American claims to all of Oregon. He identified himself and his party with the popular cause of turning the United States into a continental nation, an aspiration that attracted support from all parts of the country. His was a much more astute political strategy than the overtly prosouthern expansionism advocated by Tyler and Calhoun. The Whig nominee, Henry Clay, was basically antiexpansionist, but his sense of the growing popularity of Texas annexation among southern Whigs caused him to waffle on the issue during the campaign. This in turn cost Clay the support of a small but crucial group of northern antislavery Whigs, who defected to the abolitionist Liberty party.

Polk won the fall election by a relatively narrow popular margin. His triumph in the electoral college—170 votes to 105—was secured by victories in New York and Michigan, where the Liberty party candidate, James G. Birney, had taken away enough votes from Clay to affect the outcome. (See the charts of the election of 1844 on the opposite page.) The closeness of the election meant the Democrats had something less than a clear mandate to implement their expan-

The Liberty Party Swings an Election

Candidate	Party	Actual Vote in New York	National Electoral Vote	If Liberty Voters Had Voted Whig	Projected Electoral Vote
Polk	Democrat	237,588	170	237,588	134
Clay	Whig	232,482	105	248,294	141
Birney	Liberty	15,812	0	—	—

The Election of 1844

Candidate	Party	Popular Vote	Electoral Vote
Polk	Democrat	1,338,464	170
Clay	Whig	1,300,097	105
Birney	Liberty	62,300	—

sionist policies, but this did not prevent them from claiming that the people had backed an aggressive campaign to extend the borders of the United States.

After the election, Congress reconvened to consider the annexation of Texas. The mood had changed as a result of Polk's victory, and some leading senators from both parties who had initially opposed Tyler's scheme for annexation by joint resolution of Congress now changed their position. As a result, annexation was approved a few days before Polk took office.

The Doctrine of Manifest Destiny

The expansionist mood that accompanied Polk's election and the annexation of Texas was given a name and a rationale in the summer of 1845. John L. O'Sullivan, a proponent of the Young America movement and editor of the influential *United States Magazine and Democratic Review* charged that foreign governments were conspiring to block the annexation of Texas in an effort to thwart "the fulfillment of our manifest destiny to overspread the continent allotted by providence for the free development of our yearly multiplying millions."

Besides coining the phrase *Manifest Destiny,* O'Sullivan pointed to the three main ideas that lay behind it. One was that God was on the side of American expansionism. This notion came naturally out of the long tradition, going back to the New England Puritans, that identified the growth of America with the divinely ordained success of a chosen people. A second idea, implied in the phrase *free development,* was that the spread of American rule meant what other propagandists for expansion described as "extending the area of freedom." Democratic institutions and local self-government would follow the flag if areas claimed by autocratic foreign governments were annexed to the United States. O'Sullivan's third premise was that population growth required the outlet that territorial acquisitions would provide. Behind this notion lurked a fear that growing numbers would lead to diminished opportunity and a European-type polarization of social classes if the restless and the ambitious were not given new lands to settle and exploit.

In its most extreme form, Manifest Destiny meant the United States would someday occupy the entire North American continent, that nothing less would appease its land-hungry population. "Make way, I say, for the young American Buffalo," bellowed a Democratic orator in 1844"—he has not yet got land enough. . . . I tell you we will give him Oregon for his summer shade, and the region of Texas as his winter pasture. (Applause) Like all of his race, he wants salt, too. Well, he shall have the use of two oceans—the mighty Pacific and the turbulent

Atlantic. . . . He shall not stop his career until he slakes his thirst in the frozen ocean. (Cheers)"

Polk and the Oregon Question

In 1845 and 1846, the United States came closer to armed conflict with Great Britian than at any time since the War of 1812. The willingness of some Americans to go to war over Oregon was expressed in the rallying cry "fifty-four forty or fight" (referring to the latitude of the northern boundary of the desired territory). This slogan was actually coined by Whigs seeking to ridicule Democratic expansionists, but Democrats later took it over as a vivid expression of their demand for what is now British Columbia. Polk fed this expansionist fever by laying claim in his inaugural address to all of the Oregon country, then jointly occupied by Britain and the United States. Privately, however, he was willing to accept the forty-ninth parallel as a dividing line. What made the situation so tense was that Polk was dedicated to an aggressive diplomacy of bluff and bluster. As historian David M. Pletcher has put it, Polk "set forth on a foreign policy of strong stands, over-stated arguments, and menacing public announcements, not because he wanted war but because he felt that this was the only policy which his foreign adversaries would understand."

In July 1845, Polk authorized Secretary of State James Buchanan to reply to the latest British request for terms by offering a boundary along the forty-ninth parallel. Because this did not meet the British demand for all of Vancouver Island and free navigation of the Columbia River, the British ambassador rejected the proposal out of hand. This rebuff infuriated Polk; in his view the offer was a generous and conciliatory retreat from his public position. He subsequently withdrew it and refused a British request of December 1845 that he renew the offer and submit the dispute to international arbitration. Instead he called on Congress to terminate the agreement for joint occupation of the Pacific Northwest. Congress complied in April 1846, and Polk submitted the required year's notice to the British on May 21.

Since abrogation of the joint agreement implied that the United States would attempt to extend its jurisdiction north to 54°40, the British government decided to take the diplomatic initiative in an effort to avert war, while at the same time dispatching warships to the Western Hemisphere in case conciliation failed. Their new proposal accepted the forty-ninth parallel as the border to a point where the boundary would veer south so that Britain could retain Vancouver Island. It also provided for British navigation rights on the Columbia River. When the draft treaty was received in June, Polk refused either to endorse or reject it and took the unusual step of submitting it directly to the Senate for advice. The Senate recommended the treaty be accepted with the single change that British rights to navigate the Columbia be made temporary. It was ratified in that form on June 15.

Polk was prompted to settle the Oregon question because he now had a war with Mexico on his hands. His reckless and aggressive diplomacy had brought the nation within an eyelash of being involved in two wars at the same time. American policymakers got what they wanted from the Oregon treaty, namely Puget Sound and the strait that led into it south of Vancouver Island. Acquisition of this splendid natural harbor gave the United States its first deep-water port on the Pacific. Polk's initial demand for all of Oregon was made partly for domestic political consumption and partly to bluff the British into making more concessions. It was a dangerous game on both fronts. When Polk finally agreed to the solution, he alienated expansionist advocates in the Old Northwest who had supported his call for "all of Oregon."

For many Northerners, the promise of new acquisitions in the Pacific Northwest was the only thing that made annexation of Texas palatable. They hoped new free states could be created to counterbalance the admission of slave-holding Texas to the Union. As this prospect receded, the charge of antislavery advocates that Texas annexation was a southern plot became more believable; to Northerners Polk began to look more and more like a president concerned mainly with furthering the interests of his native region.

War with Mexico

While the United States was avoiding a war with Great Britain, it was getting into one with Mexico. Although they had recognized Texas independence in 1845, the Mexicans rejected the Lone Star Republic's dubious claim to the unset-

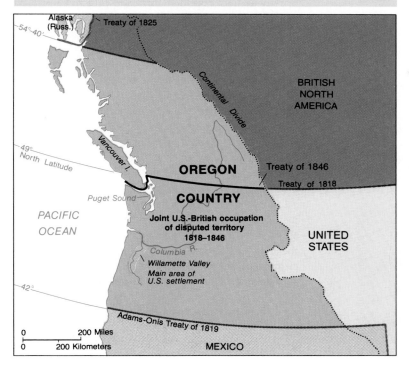

Northwest Boundary Dispute
President Polk's policy of bluff and bluster nearly involved the United States in a war with Great Britain over the disputed boundary in Oregon.

tled territory between the Nueces River and the Río Grande. When the United States annexed Texas and assumed its claim to the disputed area, Mexico broke off diplomatic relations and prepared for armed conflict.

Polk responded by placing troops in Louisiana on the alert and by dispatching John Slidell as an emissary to Mexico City in the hope he could resolve the boundary dispute and also persuade the Mexicans to sell New Mexico and California to the United States. The Mexican government refused to receive Slidell because the nature of his appointment ignored the fact that regular diplomatic relations were suspended. While Slidell was cooling his heels in Mexico City in January 1846, Polk ordered General Zachary Taylor, commander of American forces in the Southwest, to advance well beyond the Nueces and proceed toward the Río Grande, thus invading territory claimed by both sides.

By April, Taylor had taken up a position near Matamoros on the Río Grande. On the opposite bank of the river, Mexican forces had assembled and erected a fort. On April 24, sixteen hundred Mexican soldiers crossed the river and the following day met and attacked a small American detachment, killing eleven and capturing the rest. After learning of the incident, Taylor sent word to the president: "Hostilities," he reported, "may now be considered as commenced."

This news was neither unexpected nor unwelcome. Polk in fact was already preparing his war message to Congress when he learned of the fighting on the Río Grande. A short and decisive war, he had concluded, would force the cession of California and New Mexico to the United States. When Congress declared war on May 13, American agents and an "exploring expedition" under John C. Frémont were already in California stirring up dissension against Mexican rule, and ships of the U.S. Navy lay waiting expectantly off the shore. Two days later, Polk ordered a force under Colonel Stephen Kearny to march to Santa Fe and take possession of New Mexico.

This 1846 cartoon entitled "This Is the House That Polk Built" shows President Polk sitting forlornly in a house of cards, which represents the delicately balanced issues facing him.

The war lasted much longer than expected because the Mexicans refused to make peace despite a succession of military defeats. In the first major campaign of the conflict, Taylor followed up his victory in two battles fought north of the Río Grande by crossing the river, taking Matamoros and marching on Monterrey. In September, his forces assaulted and captured this major city of northern Mexico after overcoming fierce resistance.

Taylor's controversial decision to allow the Mexican garrison to go free and his unwillingness or inability to advance further into Mexico angered Polk and led him to adopt a new strategy for winning the war and a new commander to implement it. General Winfield Scott was ordered to prepare an amphibious attack on Vera Cruz with the aim of placing an American army within striking distance of Mexico City itself. With half his forces detached for the new invasion, Taylor was left to hold his position in northern Mexico.

But this did not deprive him of a final moment of glory. At Buena Vista, in February 1847, he claimed victory over a sizable Mexican army sent northward to dislodge him. Despite his unpopularity with the administration, Taylor was hailed as a national hero and a possible candidate for president

Meanwhile, the Kearny expedition captured Santa Fe, proclaimed the annexation of New Mexico by the United States, and set off for California. There they found that American settlers, in cooperation with John C. Frémont's exploring expedition, had revolted against Mexican authorities and declared their independence as the "Bear Flag Republic." The navy had also captured the port of Monterey. With the addition of Kearny's troops, a relatively small number of Americans were able to take possession of California against scattered and disorganized Mexican opposition, a process that was completed by the beginning of 1847.

The decisive Veracruz campaign was slow to develop because of the massive and careful preparations required. But in March 1847, the main American army under General Scott finally landed near that crucial port city and laid siege to it. Veracruz fell after eighteen days, and then Scott began his advance on Mexico City. In the most important single battle of the war, Scott met forces under General Santa Anna at Cerro Gordo on April 17 and 18. The Mexicans occupied an apparently impregnable position on high ground blocking the way to Mexico City. A daring flanking maneuver that required soldiers to scramble up the mountainsides enabled Scott to win the decisive victory that opened the road to the Mexican capital. By August American troops were drawn up in front of Mexico City. After a temporary armistice, a brief respite that was actually used by the Mexicans to regroup and improve their defenses, Scott ordered the massive assault that captured the city on September 14.

Settlement of the Mexican War

Accompanying Scott's army was a diplomat, Nicholas P. Trist, who was authorized to negotiate a peace treaty whenever the Mexicans decided they had had enough. Despite a sequence of American victories and the imminent fall of Mexico City, Trist made little progress. No

The Mexican War

The Mexican War added half a million square miles of territory to the United States, but the cost was high: $100 million and 13,000 lives.

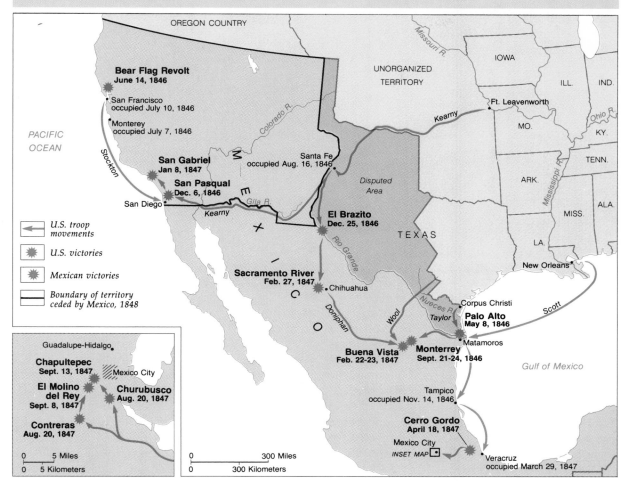

Mexican leader was willing to invite the wrath of an intensely proud and patriotic citizenry by agreeing to the kind of terms that Polk wanted to impose. Even after the United States had achieved an overwhelming military victory, Trist found it difficult to exact an acceptable treaty from the Mexican government. In November, Polk ordered Trist to return to Washington. Radical adherents of Manifest Destiny were now clamoring for the annexation of all Mexico, and Polk himself may have been momentarily tempted by the chance to move from military occupation to outright annexation.

Trist ignored Polk's instructions and lingered in Mexico City. On February 2, 1848, he signed a treaty that gained all the concessions he had been commissioned to obtain. The Treaty of Guadalupe Hidalgo ceded New Mexico and California to the United States for $15 million, established the Río Grande as the border between Texas and Mexico, and promised that the U. S. government would assume the substantial claims of American citizens against Mexico. The treaty also provided that the Mexican residents of the new territories would become U. S. citizens. When the agreement reached Washington, Polk censured Trist for disobeying orders but approved most of his treaty, which he sent to the Senate for ratification. Senate approval by a vote of 38 to 14 came on March 10.

When popular hero Zachary Taylor (left) displeased President Polk with his actions in the capture of Monterrey, he was replaced by Winfield Scott. Scott carried out Polk's plans for the attack on the port city of Veracruz (right), which led to the capture of Mexico City.

As a result of the Mexican War, the United States gained 500,000 square miles of territory. The treaty of 1848 enlarged the size of the nation by about 20 percent, adding to its domain the present states of California, Utah, New Mexico, Nevada, and Arizona, and parts of Colorado and Wyoming. Soon those interested in a southern route for a transcontinental railroad pressed for even more territory along the southern border of the cession. That pressure led in 1853 to the Gadsden Purchase, through which the United States acquired the southernmost parts of present-day Arizona and New Mexico. But one intriguing question remains. Why, given the expansionist spirit of the age, did the campaign to acquire *all* of Mexico fail?

According to the historian Frederick Merk, a major factor was the peculiar combination of racism and anticolonialism that dominated American opinion. It was one thing to acquire thinly populated areas that could be settled by "Anglo-Saxon" pioneers. It was something else again to incorporate a large population that was mainly of mixed Spanish and Indian origin. These "mongrels," charged racist opponents of the "All Mexico" movement, could never be fit citizens of a self-governing republic. They would have to be

ruled in the way the British governed India, and the possession of colonial dependencies was contrary to American ideals and traditions.

Merk's thesis sheds light on why the general public had little appetite for swallowing all of Mexico, but those actually making policy had more mundane and practical reasons for being satisfied with what was obtained at Guadalupe Hidalgo. What they had really wanted all along, historian Norman Graebner contends, were the great California harbors of San Francisco and San Diego. From these ports Americans could trade directly with the Orient and dominate the commerce of the Pacific. Once acquisition of California had been assured, policymakers had little incentive to press for more Mexican territory.

The war with Mexico divided the American public and provoked political dissension. A majority of the Whig party opposed the war in principle, arguing that the United States had no valid claims to the area south of the Nueces. Whig congressmen voted for military appropriations while the conflict was going on, but they constantly criticized the president for starting it. More ominous was the charge of some Northerners from both parties that the real purpose of the war was to spread the institution of slavery and increase the political power of the southern states. While battles were being fought in Mexico, Congress was debating the Wilmot Proviso, a proposal to prohibit slavery in any territories that might be acquired from Mexico. A bitter sectional quarrel over the status of slavery in new areas was a major legacy of the Mexican War (see Chapter 14).

The domestic controversies aroused by the war and the propaganda of Manifest Destiny revealed the limits of mid-nineteenth-century American expansionism and put a damper on additional efforts to extend the nation's boundaries. Concerns about slavery and race impeded acquisition of new territory in Latin America and the Caribbean. Resolution of the Oregon dispute clearly indicated that the United States was not willing to go to war with a powerful adversary to obtain large chunks of British North America, and the old ambition of incorporating Canada faded. From 1848 until the revival of expansionism in the late nineteenth century, American growth usually took the form of populating and developing the vast territory already acquired.

INTERNAL EXPANSIONISM

Young American expansionists saw a clear link between acquisition of new territory and other forms of material growth and development. In 1844, Samuel F. B. Morse perfected and demonstrated his electric telegraph, a device that would make it possible to communicate rapidly over the expanse of a continental nation. Simultaneously, the railroad was becoming increasingly important as a means of moving people and goods over the same great distances. Improvements in manufacturing and agricultural methods led to an upsurge in the volume and range of internal trade, and the beginnings of mass immigration were providing human resources for the exploitation of new areas and economic opportunities.

After gold was discovered in newly acquired California in 1848, a flood of emigrants from the East and several foreign nations arrived by ship or wagon train, their appetites whetted by the thought of striking it rich. The gold they unearthed spurred the national economy, and the rapid growth of population centers on the Pacific Coast inspired projects for transcontinental telegraph lines and railroad tracks.

Despite the best efforts of the Young Americans, the spirit of Manifest Destiny, and the thirst for acquiring new territory waned after the Mexican War, and the expansionist impulse was channeled mainly into internal development. Although the nation ceased to grow in size, the technological advances and population increase of the 1840s continued during the 1850s. The result was an acceleration of economic growth, a substantial increase in industrialization and urbanization, and the emergence of a new American working class.

The Triumph of the Railroad

More than anything else, the rise of the railroad transformed the American economy during the 1840s and 1850s. The technology came from England, where steam locomotives were first used to haul cars along tracks at the beginning of the century. In 1830 and 1831 two American railroads began commercial operation—the Charleston and Hamburg in South Carolina and the Baltimore and Ohio in Maryland. After these pioneer lines had shown that steam locomotion was practical and profitable, several other railroads were built and began to carry passengers and freight during the 1830s.

Canals, however, proved to be strong competitors, especially for the freight business. By 1840, railroads had 2,818 miles of track—a figure almost equal to the combined length of all canals—but the latter still carried a much larger volume of goods. Passengers might prefer the speed of trains, which reached astonishing velocities of 20 to 30 miles an hour, but the lower unit cost of transporting freight on the canal boats prevented most shippers from changing their habits. Furthermore, states like New York and Pennsylvania had invested heavily in canals and resisted chartering a competitive form of transportation. Most of the early railroads reached out from port cities, such as Boston and Baltimore, that did not have good canal routes to the interior. Steam locomotion provided them a chance to cut into the enormous commerce that flowed along the Erie Canal and gave New York an advantage in the scramble for western trade.

During the 1840s, rails extended beyond the northeastern and Middle Atlantic states, and mileage increased more than threefold, reaching a

Railroads, 1850 and 1860

During the 1840s and 1850s, railroad lines moved rapidly westward. By 1860, more than 30,000 miles of track had been laid.

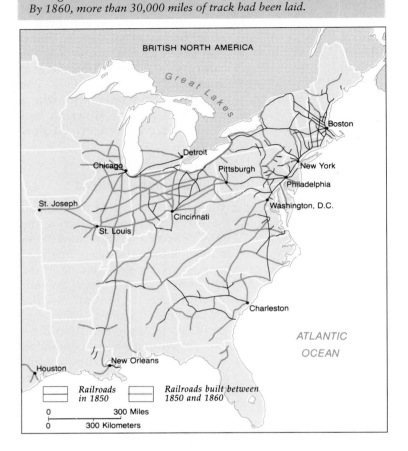

total of more than 9,000 miles by 1850. Expansion, fueled by massive European investment, was even greater in the following decade when about 20,000 miles of additional track were laid. By 1860, all the states east of the Mississippi had rail service, and a traveler could go by train from New York to Chicago and return by way of Memphis. Throughout the 1840s and 1850s, railroads cut deeply into the freight business of the canals and succeeded in driving many of them out of business. The cost of hauling goods by rail decreased dramatically because of improved track construction and the introduction of powerful locomotives that could haul more cars. New York and Pennsylvania were slow to encourage rail transportation because of their early commitment to canals, but by the 1850s both states had accepted the

inevitable and were promoting massive railroad building.

The development of railroads had an enormous effect on the economy as a whole. Although the burgeoning demand for iron rails was initially met mainly by importation from England, it eventually spurred development of the domestic iron industry. Since railroads required an enormous outlay of capital, their promoters pioneered new methods for financing business enterprise. At a time when most manufacturing and mercantile concerns were still owned by families or partnerships, the railroad companies sold stock to the general public and helped to set the pattern for the separation of ownership and control that characterizes the modern corporation. They also developed new types of securities, such as "preferred stock" with no voting rights but the assur-

Railroad Mileage, ca. 1860	
Area	Miles
New England	3,660
Middle Atlantic	6,353
Old Northwest	9,592
Southeast	5,463
Southwest	4,072
Far West	1,495
Total	30,636

Source: Adapted from George R. Taylor and Irene D. Neu, *The American Railroad Network, 1861 to 1890 (1956;* reprint ed., Salem, N.H.: Arno, 1981*).*

ance of a fixed rate of return, and long-term bonds at a set rate of interest.

The gathering and control of private capital did not fully meet the desires of the early railroad barons. State and local governments, convinced that railroads were the key to their future prosperity, loaned the railroads money, bought their stock, and guaranteed their bonds. Despite the dominant philosophy of laissez-faire, the federal government became involved by surveying the routes of projected lines and providing land grants. In 1850, for example, several million acres of public land were granted to the Illinois Central. In all, forty companies received such aid before 1860, and a precedent was set for the massive land grants of the post–Civil War era.

The Industrial Revolution Takes Off

While railroads were initiating a revolution in transportation, American industry was entering a new phase of rapid and sustained growth. The factory mode of production, which had originated before 1840 in the cotton mills of New England, was extended to a variety of other products (see Chapter 9). Woolen manufacturing was concentrated in single production units beginning in the 1830s, and by 1860 some of the largest textile mills in the country were producing wool cloth. In the coal and iron regions of eastern Pennsylvania, iron was being forged and rolled in factories by 1850. Among the other industries that adopted the factory system during this period were those producing firearms, clocks, and sewing machines.

The essential features of the emerging mode of production were the gathering of a supervised work force in a single place, the payment of cash wages to workers, the use of interchangeable parts, and manufacture by "continuous process." Within a factory setting, standardized parts, manufactured separately and in bulk, could be efficiently and rapidly assembled into a final product by an ordered sequence of continuously repeated operations. Mass production, which involved the division of labor into a series of relatively simple and repetitive tasks, contrasted sharply with the traditional craft mode of production, in which a single worker produced the entire product out of raw materials. The bulk of American manufacturing of the 1840s and 1850s, however, was still carried on by traditional methods. Small workshops continued to predominate in most industries and some relatively large factories were not yet mechanized. But mass production was clearly the wave of the future. The transformation of a craft into a modern industry is well illustrated by the evolution of shoemaking. The independent cobbler producing shoes for order was first challenged by a putting-out system involving the assignment of various tasks to physically separated workers, and then was virtually displaced by the great shoe factories that by the 1860s were operating in cities like Lynn, Massachusetts.

New technology often played an important role in the transition to mass production. Just as power looms and spinning machinery had made textile mills possible, the development of new and more reliable machines or industrial techniques revolutionized other industries. Elias Howe's invention of the sewing machine in 1846 laid the basis for the ready-to-wear clothing industry and also contributed to the mechanization of shoemaking. During the 1840s, iron manufacturers adopted the British practice of using coal rather than charcoal for smelting and thus produced a metal better suited to industrial needs. Charles Goodyear's discovery in 1839 of the process for the vulcanization of rubber made a new range of manufactured items available to the American consumer, most notably the overshoe.

The Age of Practical Invention

(Dates refer to patent or first successful use)

Year	Inventor	Contribution	Importance/Description
1787	John Fitch	Steamboat	First successful American steamboat
1793	Eli Whitney	Cotton gin	Simplified process of separating fiber from seeds; helped make cotton a profitable staple of southern agriculture
1798	Eli Whitney	Jig for guiding tools	Facilitated manufacture of interchangeable parts
1802	Oliver Evans	Steam engine	First American steam engine; led to manufacture of high-pressure engines used throughout eastern United States
1813	Richard B. Chenaworth	Cast-iron plow	First iron plow to be made in three separate pieces, thus making possible replacement of parts
1830	Peter Cooper	Railroad locomotive	First steam locomotive built in America
1831	Cyrus McCormick	Reaper	Mechanized harvesting; early model could cut six acres of grain a day
1836	Samuel Colt	Revolver	First successful repeating pistol
1837	John Deere	Steel plow	Steel surface kept soil from sticking; farming thus made easier on rich prairies of Midwest
1839	Charles Goodyear	Vulcanization of rubber	Made rubber much more useful by preventing it from sticking and melting in hot weather
1842	Crawford W. Long	First administered ether in surgery	Reduced pain and risk of shock in surgery during operations
1844	Samuel F. B. Morse	Telegraph	Made long-distance communication almost instantaneous
1846	Elias Howe	Sewing machine	First practical machine for automatic sewing
1846	Norbert Rillieux	Vacuum evaporator	Improved method of removing water from sugar cane; revolutionized sugar industry and was later applied to many other products
1847	Richard M. Hoe	Rotary printing press	Printed an entire sheet in one motion; vastly speeded up printing process
1851	William Kelly	"Air-boiling process"	Improved method of converting iron into steel (usually known as Bessemer process because English inventor Bessemer had more advantageous patent and financial arrangements)
1853	Elisha G. Otis	Passenger elevator	Improved movement in buildings; when later electrified, stimulated development of skyscrapers
1859	Edwin L. Drake	First American oil well	Initiated oil industry in the United States
1859	George M. Pullman	Pullman car	First sleeping car suitable for long-distance travel

Source: From *Freedom and Crisis: An American History,* Third Edition, by Allen Weinstein and Frank Otto Gatell. Copyright © 1974, 1978, 1981 by Random House, Inc. Reprinted by permission of Random House, Inc.

Perhaps the greatest triumph of American technology during the mid-nineteenth century was the development of the world's most sophisticated and reliable machine tools. Such advances as the invention of the extraordinarily accurate measuring device known as the *vernier caliper* in 1851 and the first production of turret lathes in 1854 were signs of a special American aptitude for the kind of precision toolmaking that was essential to efficient industrialization.

Progress in industrial technology and organization did not mean the United States had become an industrial society by 1860. Factory workers remained a small fraction of the work force, and agriculture retained first place both as a source of livelihood for individuals and as a contributor to the gross national product. Nearly 60 percent of the gainfully employed still worked on the land. But farming itself, at least in the North, was undergoing a technological revolution of its own. John Deere's steel plow, invented in 1837 and mass produced by the 1850s, enabled midwestern farmers to cultivate the tough prairie soils that had resisted cast-iron implements. The mechanical reaper, patented by Cyrus McCormick in 1834, offered an enormous saving in the labor required for harvesting grain; by 1851, McCormick was producing more than a thousand reapers a year in his Chicago plant. Other new farm implements that came into widespread use before 1860 included seed drills, cultivators, and threshing machines.

A dynamic interaction between advances in transportation, industry, and agriculture gave great strength and resiliency to the economy of the northern states during the 1850s. Railroads offered western farmers better access to eastern markets. After Chicago and New York were linked by rail in 1853, the flow of most midwestern farm commodities shifted from the north-south direction based on river-borne traffic that had still predominated in the 1830s and 1840s, to an east-west pattern.

The mechanization of agriculture did more than lead to more efficient and profitable commercial farming; it also provided an additional impetus to industrialization, and its labor-saving features released manpower for other economic activities. The growth of industry and the modernization of agriculture can thus be seen as mutually reinforcing aspects of a single process of economic growth.

Mass Immigration Begins

The original incentive to mechanize northern industry and agriculture came in part from a shortage of

A revolution in farming followed the introduction of new farm implements like Cyrus McCormick's reaper, which could do ten times the work of a single person. The lithograph, by an anonymous artist, is entitled The Testing of the First Reaping Machine near Steele's Tavern, Virginia, 1831.

cheap labor. Compared with that of industrializing nations of Europe, the economy of the United States in the early nineteenth century was labor-scarce. Since it was difficult to attract able-bodied men to work for low wages in factories or on farms, women and children were used extensively in the early textile mills, and commercial farmers had to rely heavily on the labor of their family members. In the face of such limited and uncertain labor supplies, producers were greatly tempted to experiment with labor-saving machinery. By the 1840s and 1850s, however, even the newly industrialized operations were ready to absorb a new influx of unskilled workers. Factories required increasing numbers of operatives, and railroad builders needed construction gangs. The growth of industrial work opportunities helped attract a multitude of European immigrants during the two decades before the Civil War.

Between 1820 and 1840, an estimated 700,000 immigrants arrived in the United States, mainly from the British Isles and German-speaking areas of continental Europe. During the 1840s, this substantial flow suddenly became a flood. No less than 4.2 million crossed the Atlantic between 1840 and 1860, and about 3 million of these arrived in the single decade between 1845 and 1855. This was the greatest influx in proportion to total population—then about 20 million—that the nation has ever experienced. The largest single source of the new mass immigration was Ireland, but Germany was not far behind. Smaller contingents came from Switzerland, Norway, Sweden, and the Netherlands.

This massive transatlantic movement had many causes; some people were "pushed" out of their homes, while others were "pulled" toward America. The great push factor that caused 1.5 million Irish to forsake the Emerald Isle between 1845 and 1854 was the great potato famine. Escape to America was made possible by the low fares then prevailing on sailing ships bound from England to North America. Ships involved in the timber trade carried their bulky cargoes from Boston or Halifax to Liverpool; as an alternative to returning to America partly in ballast, they packed Irish immigrants into their holds. The squalor and misery in these steerage accommodations were almost beyond belief.

Because of the ports involved in the lumber trade—Boston, Halifax, Saint John's, and Saint Andrews—the Irish usually arrived in Canada or the northeastern states. Immobilized by poverty and a lack of the skills required for pioneering in

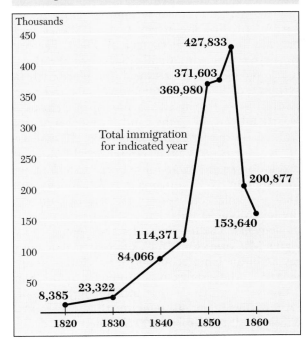

Immigration to the United States, 1820–1860

Thousands

Total immigration for indicated year

427,833
371,603
369,980
200,877
153,640
114,371
84,066
23,322
8,385

1820 1830 1840 1850 1860

the West, most of them remained in the northeast. By the 1850s, they constituted a substantial portion of the total population of Boston, New York, Philadelphia, and many smaller cities of the New England and Middle Atlantic states (see "The Irish in Boston," pp. 370–371). Forced to subsist on low-paid menial labor and crowded into festering urban slums, they were looked down on by most native-born Americans. Their devotion to Catholicism aroused Protestant resentment and mob violence (see Chapter 14 for a discussion of the growth of nativism and anti-Catholicism).

The million or so Germans who also came in the late 1840s and early 1850s were somewhat more fortunate. Most of them were also peasants, but they had fled hard times rather than outright catastrophe. Changes in German landholding patterns and a fluctuating market for grain crops put pressure on small operators. Those whose mortgages were foreclosed—or who could no longer make the regular payments to landlords that were the price of emancipation from feudal obligations—frequently opted for immigration to America. Unlike the Irish, they often escaped with

a small amount of capital with which to make a fresh start in the New World.

Many German immigrants were artisans and sought to ply their trades in cities like New York, St. Louis, Cincinnati, and Milwaukee—all of which became centers of German-American population. But a large portion of those with peasant backgrounds went back to the land. The possession of diversified agricultural skills and small amounts of capital enabled many Germans to become successful midwestern farmers. In general, they encountered less prejudice and discrimination than the Irish. For those who were Protestant, religious affinity with their American neighbors made for relative tolerance. But even Germans who were Catholic normally escaped the virulent scorn heaped on the Irish, perhaps because they were not so poverty stricken and did not carry the added burden of being members of an ethnic group Anglo-Americans had learned to despise from their English ancestors and cousins.

What attracted most of the Irish, German, and other European immigrants to America was the promise of economic opportunity. A minority, like some of the German revolutionaries of 1848, chose the United States because they admired its democratic political system. But most immigrants were more interested in the chance to make a decent living than in voting or running for office. The force of the economic motive can be seen in the fact that peak periods of immigration—1845

to 1854 is a prime example—coincided very closely with times of domestic prosperity and high demand for labor. During depressed periods, such as 1837 to 1842 and the mid-to-late 1850s, immigration dropped off significantly.

The arrival of large numbers of immigrants exacerbated the already serious problems of America's rapidly growing cities. The old "walking city" in which rich and poor lived in close proximity near the center of town was changing to a more segregated environment. The advent of railroads and horse-drawn streetcars enabled the affluent to move to the first American suburbs, while areas nearer commercial and industrial centers became the congested abode of newcomers from Europe. Emerging slums, such as the notorious "Five Points" district in New York City, were characterized by overcrowding, poverty, disease, and crime. Recognizing that these conditions created potential dangers for the entire urban population, middle-class reformers worked for the professionalization of police forces, introduction of sanitary water and sewage disposal systems, and the upgrading of housing standards. They made some progress in these endeavors in the period before the Civil War, but the lot of the urban poor, mainly immigrants, was not dramatically improved. Except to the extent that their own communal activities—especially those sponsored by churches and mutual aid societies—provided a sense of security and solidarity, the exis-

The Irish in Boston, 1845–1865

For the city of Boston, the period between 1845 and 1865 was an era of great change. Events half a world away rudely plucked more than fifty thousand Irish Catholic peasants from their homeland and transplanted them to a city that had hitherto been a homogeneous bastion of old-stock New England Puritanism. Some Bostonians viewed this mass of poor immigrants as an urban calamity. But the "invasion" was also a blessing, reinvigorating Boston with a substantial—and inimitable—Irish-American contribution to its social, economic, and political life.

The Irish came to America because they had no other choice. By the early nineteenth century, large landowners on the "isle of wondrous beauty"—mainly of English descent—were masters over impoverished tenant farmers who had been forced by their wretched circumstances to live on a diet consisting mostly of potatoes. When a blight caused the potato crop to rot in the mid-1840s, Ireland entered a period known as the Great Hunger. During this "state of social decomposition" between 1845 and 1851, the only alternative to starvation was emigration for most Irish peasants. One million people emigrated and another million died of starvation or disease.

The immigrants disembarked at the large northeastern seaboard cities. Although the newcomers were of rural origins, they were too poor and sick to continue westward to America's rich agricultural regions; they settled where they were dropped. Boston's population nearly doubled, growing from 93,000 to 177,000 between 1840 and 1860. In part this increase reflected the movement of a burgeoning native population

The corner saloon was the Irish workingman's version of a men's club. Irishmen gathered regularly, not only to partake of food and drink, but more important, to meet with friends, discuss politics, tell stories, or play cards.

from the country to the cities, but mainly it was the product of Ireland's Great Hunger.

Penniless and unskilled, the immigrants crowded into old buildings and warehouses that Boston's Yankees had abandoned—dark, unheated, unventilated, and unsanitary tenements. But as a social worker observed of the people living in Boston's Irish ghettos, "The Hibernian is first, last, and always a social being." In Ireland, poor tenant farmers had found comfort in lively conversation, sometimes made even more spirited by a convivial round of distilled refreshment, and nothing the immigrants found in Boston altered these customs. Talk came naturally to the Irish. They talked in the streets, in the shops, in the churches, in their homes—and in their saloons.

For men, by far the most popular locus of sociability was the corner saloon—where it was said a working man could not die of thirst. The Irish bar in Boston was devoid of frills. It featured wooden chairs, a long wooden bar with brass railings, card tables, sawdust-covered floors, and a philosophical bartender, who extended beer, whiskey, credit, and advice, in roughly equal doses. Irishmen sang, told stories, talked politics, or reminisced about the green fields and deep blue lakes of the Emerald Isle. In 1846, there were 850 liquor dealers in Boston, but by 1850 fully 1,500 saloons catered to the residents of the changing city.

Fortunately for Boston's capitalists and large-scale entrepreneurs, the most immediate need of the immigrants was employment—of any kind. At first the newcomers, who had been peasants in the "Ould Country," became street or yard laborers, but as it became apparent that the Irish were a potential pool of long-term proletarians—a large supply of workers who would remain in the least desirable jobs for low pay—capitalists responded by accelerating the Industrial Revolution in the Boston area. The number of industrial employees in Boston doubled in the decade of 1845 to 1855, and doubled again in the following decade. Moreover, Irish immigrants replaced much of the labor force from the early industrial era (see Chapter 9), especially in the textile mills of Boston's outlying suburbs. Irish men and unmarried women were willing to work for lower wages than those paid to Yankees and were not so insistent on decent working conditions.

Although reluctant to work outside the home for wages, married Irish-American women—who were usually raising a large family—often found themselves taking in lodgers, sewing at home for piece work rates on men's shirts and women's millinery, and doing other people's laundry. Their lot was frequently made more difficult by the long absences of their "railroading" husbands (Irishmen contracted out for months at a time to build and lay rails).

A large proportion of the Great Hunger immigrants from Ireland were unmarried women who, like their male counterparts, were desperate for employment. Some replaced Yankee "mill girls" but a larger number relieved an acute shortage of domestics in New England. Few native-born American women would do household work for pay, not only because the job carried the stigma of servanthood, but also because New Englanders were not willing to pay good wages for what was sometimes a 24-hour responsibility. Many maids and cooks suffered from "shattered health." But for the single Irish-American woman, the life of a domestic was often the best of a narrow range of alternatives..

Few of the first generation of Boston Irish escaped from the ranks of low-paid manual labor. The discriminatory attitudes of Yankee employers contributed significantly to this relative lack of mobility. (Many good jobs were advertised with the qualification that "no Irish need apply.") But occupational mobility was also inhibited to some extent by the tendency of the Irish immigrants to save up for the purchase of land and houses rather than starting small businesses or investing in the acquisition of education and skills. They also tended to place group security above individual advancement. They used strong communal activities and neighborhood organizations to their advantage in politics and union-building; success in local political clubs and the labor movement meant Irish politicians and labor leaders in Boston channeled several generations of Irish-Americans into secure but dead-end municipal and industrial jobs.

Although they were slow to rise out of the working class, the Irish energized the economy of Boston and soon won for themselves respect and power. They were the first large immigrant group to test the notion of America as a great melting pot. More than 150,000 Irish-Americans served in the Civil War, eager to demonstrate their loyalty to their adopted country. By 1865 the Irish, through their persistent efforts, their skill at local organization, and their willingness to be Boston's reliable working class, had found a permanent place in America's most venerable Puritan stronghold.

(a) Baron Biesele, upon his arrival in America (in German): "Hey, fellow countryman, where can we find a German tavern?" Countryman (in German): "Damme. Do you think I'm a no-good like you? I am an American."

(b) Baron Biesele, first week after arrival (in German): "Well, Marianel, how do you like it in America?" Marianel (in German): "Oh, Baron, the language, the language. I'll never learn it in all my life."

(c) Baron Biesele, two weeks after arrival (in German): "Can you tell us –Hey, beautiful Marianel, isn't that you?" Marianel (in English): "You are mistaken. I don't talk Dutch."

These lithographs from the Fliegende Blatter *(Cincinnati, 1847) feature the antics of Baron Biesele, a cartoon character popular in the German prototype of this short-lived Cincinnati periodical.*

tence of most urban immigrants remained unsafe, unhealthy, and unpleasant.

The New Working Class

A majority of immigrants ended up as wage workers in factories, mines, and construction camps, or as casual day laborers doing the many unskilled tasks required for urban and commercial growth. By providing a vast pool of cheap labor, they fueled and accelerated the Industrial Revolution. During the 1850s, factory production in Boston and other port cities previously devoted to commerce grew—partly because thousands of recent Irish immigrants worked for the kind of low wages that almost guaranteed large profits for entrepreneurs.

In established industries and older mill towns of the Northeast, immigrants gradually displaced the native-born workers who had predominated in the 1830s and 1840s. The changing work force of the textile mills in Lowell, Massachusetts, provided a striking example of this process. In 1836, only 3.7 percent of the workers in one Lowell

mill were foreign born; most members of the labor force at that time were young unmarried women from New England farms. By 1860, immigrants constituted 61.7 percent of the work force. A related development was a great increase in the number of men who tended machines in textile and other factories. Irish males, employers found, were willing to perform tasks that native-born men had generally regarded as women's work.

This trend reveals much about the changing character of the American working class. In the 1830s, most male workers were artisans, and factory work was still largely the province of women and children. Both groups were predominantly of American stock. In the 1840s, the proportion of men engaged in factory work increased, although the work force in the textile industry remained predominantly female. During that decade work conditions in many mills deteriorated. Workdays of twelve to fourteen hours were not new, but the paternalism that had earlier evoked a spirit of cooperation from workers was replaced by a more impersonal and cost-

Five Points, New York City, by an anonymous artist. At the time this work was done (ca. 1829), the area was reputedly the most dangerous neighborhood in the United States. Beggars, pimps, prostitutes, and hoodlums frequented the area, a notorious center of crime, disease, and poverty.

conscious form of management. During the depression that followed the panic of 1837, bosses attempted to reduce expenses and increase productivity by cutting wages, increasing the speed of machinery, and "stretching out"—giving each worker more machinery to operate.

The result was a new upsurge of labor militancy involving female as well as male factory workers. Mill girls in Lowell, for example, formed a union of their own—the Female Labor Reform Association—and agitated for shorter working hours. On a broader front, workers' organizations petitioned state legislatures to pass laws limiting the workday to ten hours. Some such laws were actually passed, but they turned out to be ineffective because employers could still require a prospective worker to sign a special contract agreeing to longer hours.

The employment of immigrants in increasing numbers between the mid-1840s and the late 1850s made it more difficult to organize industrial workers. Impoverished fugitives from the Irish potato famine tended to have lower economic expectations and more conservative social attitudes than native-born workers. Consequently the Irish immigrants were willing to work for less and were not so prone to protest bad working conditions. Most industrial laborers remained unorganized and resisted appeals for solidarity along class lines.

But the new working class of former rural folk did not make the transition to industrial wage labor easily or without protesting in subtle and indirect ways. Tardiness, absenteeism, drunkenness, loafing on the job, and other forms of resistance to factory discipline reflected deep hostility to the unaccustomed and seemingly unnatural routines of industrial production. The adjustment to new styles and rhythms of work was painful and took time. Historians are only now beginning to examine the inner world of the early generations of industrial workers, and they are finding evidence of discontent rather than docility, cultural resistance rather than easy adaptation.

By 1860, industrial expansion and immigration had created a working class of men and women who seemed destined for a life of low-paid wage labor. This reality stood in contrast to America's self-image as a land of opportunity and upward mobility. Wage labor was popularly viewed as a temporary condition from which workers were supposed to extricate themselves by hard work and frugality. According to Abraham Lincoln, speaking in 1850 of the North's "free labor" society, "there is no such thing as a freeman being fatally fixed for life, in the condition of a hired laborer." This ideal still had some validity in rapidly developing regions of the western states, but it was mostly myth when applied to the increasingly foreign born industrial workers of the Northeast.

Both internal and external expansion had come at a heavy cost. Tensions associated with class and ethnic rivalries were only one part of the price of rapid economic development. The acquisition of new territories became politically divisive and would soon lead to a catastrophic sectional controversy. The Young America wing of the Democratic party fought vainly to prevent this from happening. Its leader in the late 1840s and early 1850s was Senator Stephen A. Douglas of Illinois, called "the little giant" because of his small stature and large public presence. More than anyone else of this period, he sought political power for himself and his party by combining an expansionist foreign policy with the encouragement of economic development within the territories already acquired. Furthermore, his youthful dynamism made him seem the very embodiment of the Young America ideal. Recognizing that the slavery question was the main obstacle to his program, he sought to neutralize it through compromise and evasion (see Chapter 14). His failure to win the presidency or even the Democratic nomination before 1860 showed the Young Americans' dream of a patriotic consensus supporting headlong expansion and economic development could not withstand the tensions and divisions that expansionist policies created or brought to light.

CHRONOLOGY

1822	Santa Fe opened to American traders
1823	Earliest American settlers arrive in Texas
1830	Mexico attempts to halt American migration to Texas
1831	American railroads begin commercial operation
1834	Cyrus McCormick patents mechanical reaper
1835	Revolution breaks out in Texas
1836	Texas becomes independent republic
1837	John Deere invents steel plow
1841	President John Tyler inaugurated
1842	Webster-Ashburton Treaty fixes border between Maine and New Brunswick
1843	Mass migration to Oregon begins • Mexico closes Santa Fe trade to Americans
1844	Samuel F. B. Morse demonstrates electric telegraph • James K. Polk elected president on platform of expansionism
1845	Mass immigration from Europe begins • United States annexes Texas • John L. O'Sullivan coins slogan *Manifest Destiny*
1846	War with Mexico breaks out • United States and Great Britain resolve diplomatic crisis over Oregon
1847	American conquest of California completed • Mormons settle Utah • American forces under Zachary Taylor defeat Mexicans at Buena Vista • Winfield Scott's army captures Veracruz and defeats Mexicans at Cerro Gordo • Mexico City falls to American invaders
1848	Treaty of Guadalupe Hidalgo consigns California and New Mexico to United States • Gold discovered in California
1849	"Forty-niners" rush to California to dig for gold
1858	War between Utah Mormons and U. S. forces averted

Recommended Reading

An overview of expansion to the Pacific is Ray A. Billington, *The Far Western Frontier, 1830–1860* (1956). The impulse behind Manifest Destiny has been variously interpreted. Albert K. Weinberg's classic *Manifest Destiny: A Study of National Expansionism in American History* (1935) describes and stresses the ideological rationale. Frederick Merk, *Manifest Destiny and Mission in American History* (1963), analyzes public opinion and shows how divided it was on the question of territorial acquisitions. Norman A. Graebner, *Empire on the Pacific: A Study in American Continental Expansionism* (1956), highlights the desire for Pacific harbors as a motive for adding new territory. The most complete and authoritative account of the diplomatic side of expansionism in this period is David M. Pletcher, *The Diplomacy of Annexation: Texas, Oregon, and the Mexican War* (1973). Charles G. Sellers, *James K. Polk: Continentalist, 1843–1846* (1966) is the definitive work on Polk's election and the expansionist policies of his administration. For a lively narrative of Manifest Destiny at its climax, see Bernard De Voto, *The Year of Decision, 1846* (1943). A very good recent account of the Mexican War is provided by John S. D. Eisenhower, *So Far from God: The U. S. War with Mexico* (1989).

Economic developments of the 1840s and 1850s are well covered in George R. Taylor, *The Transportation Revolution, 1815–1960* (1952) and Albert Fishlow, *American Railroads and the Transformation of the Ante-Bellum Economy* (1965). A good short introduction to immigration is Maldwyn Allen Jones, *American Immigration* (1960). On the Irish, see Kerby A. Miller, *Emigrants and Exiles: Ireland and the Irish Exodus to America* (1985). Oscar Handlin, *Boston Immigrants: A Study in Acculturation*, rev. ed. (1959) is a classic study of immigration to one city. A standard work on the antebellum working class is Sean Wilentz, *Chants Democratic: New York City and the Rise of the American Working Class, 1788–1850* (1984); for the new approach to labor history that emphasizes working-class culture, see Herbert G. Gutman, *Work, Culture, and Society in Industrializing America* (1976). A pathbreaking and insightful study of workers in the textile industry is Thomas Dublin, *Women at Work: The Transformation of Work and Community in Lowell, Massachusetts, 1826–1860* (1979).

Additional Bibliography

Other important works on American penetration and settlement of the Far West include William H. Goetzmann, *Exploration and Empire: The Explorer and the Scientist in the Winning of the American West* (1966); John D. Unruh, Jr., *The Plains Across: The Overland Immigrants and the Trans-Mississippi West, 1840–1860* (1979); Thomas O'Dea, *The Mormons* (1957); Wallace Stegner, *The Gathering of Zion: The Story of the Mormon Trail* (1964); and R. W. Paul, *California Gold* (1947). On the struggle for Texas independence, see W. C. Binkley, *The Texas Revolution* (1952) and Michael A. Lofaro, ed., *Davy Crockett: The Man, the Legend, the Legacy* (1983). The politics and diplomacy of expansionism are treated in two books by Frederick Merk: *Slavery and the Annexation of Texas* (1972) and *The Monroe Doctrine and American Expansion, 1843–1849* (1966). For further insight into the expansionist motives of the Tyler administration, see William J. Cooper, *The South and the Politics of Slavery, 1828–1856* (1978). On the Mexican War, see K. Jack Bauer, *The Mexican War, 1846–1848* (1974), and Otis Singletary, *The Mexican War* (1960). John H. Schroeder, *Mr. Polk's War: American Opposition and Dissent* (1973), and Robert W. Johannsen, *To the Halls of Montezuma: The Mexican War and the American Imagination* (1985), deal with the way the war was viewed on the home front. The Mexican side of the struggle for the Southwest is well presented in Rudolfo Acuña, *Occupied America: A History of Chicanos* (1988), David J. Weber, *The Mexican Frontier, 1821–1846: The American Southwest Under Mexico* (1982), and in the early chapters of David Montejano, *Anglos and Mexicans in the Making of Texas* (1988). The ideas associated with Manifest Destiny and Young America are further explored in Reginald Horsman, *Race and Manifest Destiny* (1981), and Perry Miller, *The Raven and the Whale* (1956).

Economic growth and technological development in the late antebellum period are covered in Douglass C. North, *The Economic Growth of the United States, 1790–1860* (1961); Thomas C. Cochran and William Miller, *The Age of Enterprise: A Social History of Industrial America* (1942); Robert W. Fogel, *Railroads and American Economic Growth* (1964); Stuart Bruchey, *The Roots of American Economic Growth, 1607–1861* (1965); Peter Temin, *Iron and Steel in Nineteenth Century America* (1964); and Merritt Roe Smith, *Harpers Ferry Armory and the New Technology* (1977). For further insight into immigration, see Marcus L. Hansen, *The Atlantic Migration, 1607–1860* (1940); Katherine Neils Conzen, *Immigrant Milwaukee, 1836–1860* (1976); Robert Ernst, *Immigrant Life in New York City, 1825–1863* (1949); Philip Taylor, *The Distant Magnet: European Immigration to the United States of America* (1971); and Dale T. Knobel, *Paddy and the Republic: Ethnicity and Nationality in*

Antebellum America (1986). On urban life in this period, see Edward K. Spann, *The New Metropolis: New York City, 1840–1857* (1981). Important works that deal with the working-class experience include Alan Dawley, *Class and Community: The Industrial Revolution in Lynn* (1976); Bruce Laurie, *Working People of Philadelphia, 1800–1850* (1980); and Christine Stansell, *City of Women: Sex and Class in New York* (1986).

CHAPTER

13

Masters and Slaves

O n August 22, 1831, the worst nightmare of southern slaveholders became reality. A group of slaves in Southampton County, Virginia, rose in open and bloody rebellion. Their leader was Nat Turner, a preacher and prophet who believed God had given him a sign that the time was ripe to strike for freedom; a vision of black and white angels wrestling in the sky had convinced him that divine wrath was about to be visited upon the white oppressor.

Beginning with a few followers and rallying others as he went along, Turner led his band from plantation to plantation and oversaw the killing of nearly sixty whites. The rebellion was short-lived; after only forty-eight hours, white forces dispersed the rampaging slaves. The rebels were then rounded up and executed, along with dozens of other slaves who were vaguely suspected of complicity. Nat Turner was the last to be captured, and he went to the gallows unrepentant, convinced he had acted in accordance with God's will.

After the initial panic and rumors of a wider insurrection had passed, white Southerners went about the grim business of making sure such an incident would never happen again. Their anxiety and determination were strengthened by the fact that 1831 also saw the emergence of a more militant northern abolitionism. Nat Turner and William Lloyd Garrison were viewed as two prongs of a revolutionary attack on the southern way of life. Although no evidence came to light that Turner was directly influenced by abolitionist propaganda, many whites believed he must have been or that future rebels might be. Consequently, they launched a massive campaign to quarantine the slaves from possible exposure to antislavery ideas and attitudes.

A series of new laws severely restricted the rights of slaves to move about, assemble without white supervision, or learn to read and write. The wave of repression did not stop at the color line; laws and the threat of mob action prevented white dissenters from publicly criticizing or even questioning the institution of slavery. For the most part, the South became a closed society with a closed mind. Loyalty to the region was firmly identified with defense of it and proslavery agitators sought to create a mood of crisis and danger requiring absolute unity and single-mindeness among the white population. This embattled attitude lay behind the growth of a more militant sectionalism and inspired threats to secede from the Union unless the South's peculiar institution could be made safe from northern or abolitionist attack.

The campaign for repression apparently achieved its original aim. Between 1831 and the Civil War, there were no further uprisings resulting in the mass killing of whites. This fact has led some historians to conclude that African American slaves were brainwashed into a state of docility. But resistance to slavery simply took less dangerous forms than open revolt. The brute force employed in response to the Turner rebellion and the elaborate precautions taken against its recurrence provided slaves with a more realistic sense of the odds against direct confrontation with white power. As a result they sought and perfected other methods of asserting their humanity and maintaining their self-esteem. This heroic effort to endure slavery without surrendering to it gave rise to an African American culture of lasting value.

SLAVERY AND THE SOUTHERN ECONOMY

Slavery would not have lasted as long as it did—and Southerners would not have reacted so strongly to real or imagined threats to its survival—if an influential class of whites had not had a vital and growing economic interest in this form of human exploitation. Since the early colonial period, forced labor had been considered essential to the South's plantation economy. In the period between the 1790s and the Civil War, plantation agriculture expanded enormously and so did dependence on slave labor; unfree blacks were the only workers readily available to landowners who sought to profit from expanding market opportunities by raising staple crops on a large scale.

By the time of the Civil War, 90 percent of the South's 4 million slaves worked on plantations and farms. In the seven cotton-producing states of the lower South (see the map in Chapter 9, p. 272) slaves constituted close to half the total population and were responsible for producing 90 percent of the cotton and almost all of the rice and sugar. In the upper South whites outnumbered slaves by more than 3 to 1 and were less dependent on their labor. To understand southern thought and behavior, it is necessary to bear in mind these major differences between the cotton kingdom with its entrenched one-crop plantation system and the upper South, which was actually moving away from this pattern during the pre–Civil War period.

Economic Adjustment in the Upper South

Tobacco, the original plantation crop of the colonial period, continued to be the principal slave-cultivated commodity of the upper tier of southern states during the pre–Civil War era. But markets were often depressed, and profitable tobacco cultivation was hard to sustain for very long in one place because it rapidly depleted the soil. As a result, there were continual shifts in the areas of greatest production and much experimentation with new crops and methods of farming in the original tobacco-growing regions of Virginia and Maryland. By 1860 more tobacco was grown in the new western states than in the older eastern ones, and Kentucky had emerged as a major producer.

During the lengthy depression of the tobacco market that lasted from the 1820s to the 1850s, agricultural experimentation was widespread in Virginia and Maryland. Increased use of fertilizer, systematic rotation of tobacco with other crops, and the growth of diversified farming based on a mix of wheat, corn, and livestock contributed to a gradual revival of agricultural prosperity. Such changes increased the need for capital but reduced the demand for labor. Improvements were financed in part by selling surplus slaves from the upper South to regions of the lower South, where staple crop production was more profitable. The interstate slave trade, which sent hundreds of thousands of slaves in a southwesterly direction between 1815 and 1860, was thus a godsend to the slaveowners of the upper South and a key to their survival and returning prosperity.

Some economic historians have concluded that the most important crop produced in the tobacco kingdom was not the "stinking weed" but human beings cultivated for the auction block. Respectable planters did not think of themselves

as raising slaves for market, but few would refuse to sell some of their "people" if they needed money to get out of debt or make expensive improvements. The economic effect was clear: the natural increase of their slaves beyond what the planters needed for their operations provided them with a crucial source of capital in a period of transition and innovation and, as a result, encouraged the export of surplus slaves from the upper South to the Deep South.

Nevertheless, the fact that slave labor was declining in importance in the upper South meant the peculiar institution had a weaker hold on public loyalty there than in the cotton states. Diversification of agriculture was accompanied by a more rapid rate of urban and industrial development than was occurring elsewhere in the South. As a result, Virginians, Marylanders, and Kentuckians were seriously divided on whether their ultimate future lay with the Deep South's plantation economy or with the industrializing free labor system that was flourishing just north of their borders.

The Rise of the Cotton Kingdom

The warmer climate and good soils of the lower tier of southern states made it possible to raise crops more naturally suited than tobacco or cereals to the plantation form of agriculture and the heavy use of slave labor. Since the colonial period, rice and a special variety of fine cotton (known as "long staple") had been grown profitably on vast estates along the coast of South Carolina and Georgia. In lower Louisiana, between New Orleans and Baton Rouge, sugar was the cash crop. As in the West Indies, sugar production required a large investment and a great deal of back-breaking labor: in other words, large, well-financed plantations and small armies of slave laborers. Cultivation of rice, long-staple cotton, and sugar was limited by natural conditions to peripheral, semitropical areas. It was the rise of "short-staple" cotton as the South's major crop that strengthened the hold of slavery and the plantation on the southern economy.

Short-staple cotton differed from the long-staple variety in two important ways: its bolls contained seeds that were much more difficult to extract by hand, and it could be grown almost anywhere south of Virginia and Kentucky—the

Lewis Miller, Slave Sale, Virginia, *probably 1853. Slave auctions, such as the one depicted in this sketch from Lewis Miller's sketchbook, were an abomination and embarrassment to many Americans. To southern plantation owners dependent on slave labor, however, such activities were essential.*

main requirement was a guarantee of two hundred frost-free days. Before the 1790s, the seed extraction problem had prevented short-staple cotton from becoming a major market crop. The invention of the cotton gin in 1793 resolved that difficulty, however, and the subsequent westward expansion opened vast areas for cotton cultivation. Unlike rice and sugar, cotton could be grown on small farms as well as on plantations. But large planters enjoyed certain advantages that made them the main producers. Only relatively large operators could afford their own gins or possessed the capital to acquire the fertile bottomlands that brought the highest yields. They also had lower transportation costs because they were able to monopolize land along rivers and streams that were the South's natural arteries of transportation.

Cotton was well suited to a plantation form of production. Required tasks were relatively simple and could be performed by supervised gangs of unfree workers. Furthermore, there was enough work to be done in all seasons to keep the force occupied throughout the year. Unlike cereals, which had only to be planted, allowed to grow, and then harvested rapidly, cotton required constant weeding or "chopping" during the growing season and then could be picked over an extended period. The relative absence of seasonal variations in work needs made the use of slave laborers advantageous.

The first major cotton-producing regions were inland areas of Georgia and South Carolina that were already thinly settled at the time the cotton gin was introduced. The center of production shifted rapidly westward during the nineteenth century. By the 1830s, Alabama and Mississippi had surpassed Georgia and South Carolina as cotton-growing states. By the 1850s, Arkansas, northwest Louisiana, and east Texas were the most prosperous and rapidly growing plantation regions. The rise in total production that accompanied this geographical expansion was phenomenal. Between 1792 and 1817, the South's output of cotton rose from about 13,000 bales to 461,000; by 1840, it was 1.35 million; nine years later it had risen to 2.85 million; and in 1860 production peaked at the colossal figure of 4.8 million bales. Most of this cotton went to supply the booming textile industry of Great Britain. Lesser proportions went to the manufacturers of continental Europe and the northeastern United States.

"Cotton is king!" proclaimed a southern orator in the 1850s, and he was right. By that time, three-quarters of the world's supply of cotton came from the American South, and this single commodity accounted for over half of the total dollar value of American exports. Cotton growing and the network of commercial and industrial enterprises that marketed and processed this crop constituted the most important economic interest

The Cotton Trade, 1857

Cotton output in the South increased rapidly as production moved westward. By the 1850s, the American South was the supplier of three-quarters of the world's cotton.

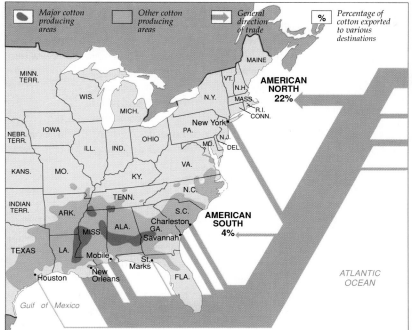

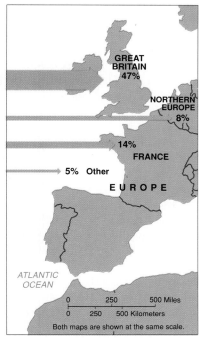

in the United States on the eve of the Civil War. Since slavery and cotton seemed inextricably linked, it appeared obvious to many Southerners that their peculiar institution was the keystone of national wealth and economic progress.

Despite its overall success, however, the rise of the cotton kingdom did not bring a uniform or steady prosperity to the lower South. Many planters worked the land until it was exhausted and then took their slaves westward to richer soils, leaving depressed and ravaged areas in their wake.

Planters were also beset and sometimes ruined by fluctuations in markets and prices. Boom periods and flush times were followed by falling prices and a wave of bankruptcies. The great periods of expansion and bonanza profits were 1815–1819, 1832–1837, and 1849–1860. The first two booms were deflated by a fall in cotton prices resulting from overproduction. During the eleven years of rising output and high prices preceding the Civil War, however, the planters grad-

ually forgot their earlier troubles and began to imagine they were immune to future economic disasters.

Despite the insecurities associated with cotton production, most of the time this crop represented the Old South's best chance for profitable investment. Prudent planters who had not borrowed too heavily during flush times could survive periods of depression by cutting costs and making their plantations self-sufficient by shifting acreage away from cotton and planting subsistence crops. For those with worn-out land, two options existed: they could sell their land and move west or they could sell their slaves to raise capital for fertilization, crop rotation, and other improvements that could help them survive where they were. Hence planters had little incentive to seek alternatives to slavery, the plantation, and dependence on a single cash crop. From a purely economic point of view they had every reason to defend slavery and insist on their right to expand it.

Slavery and Industrialization

As the sectional quarrel with the North intensified, Southerners became increasingly alarmed by their region's lack of economic self-sufficiency. Dependence on the North for capital, marketing facilities, and manufactured goods was seen as evidence of a dangerous subservience to "external" economic interests. Southern nationalists like J. D. B. DeBow, editor of the influential *DeBow's Review,* called during the 1850s for the South to develop its own industries, commerce, and shipping. As a fervent defender of slavery, DeBow did not believe such diversification would require a massive shift to free wage labor. He saw no reason for slaves not to be used as the main work force in an industrial revolution. But his call for a diversified economy went unanswered. Men with capital were doing too well in plantation agriculture to risk their money in other ventures.

It is difficult to determine whether it was some inherent characteristic of slavery as a labor system or simply the strong market demand for cotton and the South's capacity to meet it that kept most slaves working on plantations and farms. A minority—about 5 percent during the 1850s—were, in fact, successfully employed in industrial tasks. Besides providing most of the labor for mining, lumbering, and constructing roads, canals, and railroads, slaves also worked in cotton mills and tobacco factories.

In the 1840s and 1850s, a debate raged among white capitalists over whether the South should use free whites or enslaved blacks as the labor supply for industry. William Gregg of South Carolina, the foremost promoter of cotton mills in the Old South, defended a white labor policy, arguing that factory work would provide new economic opportunities for a degraded class of poor whites. But other advocates of industrialization feared that the growth of a free working class would lead to social conflict among whites and preferred using slaves for all supervised manual labor. In practice, some factories employed slaves, others white workers, and a few even experimented with integrated work forces.

It is clear, however, that the union of slavery and cotton that was central to the South's prosperity impeded industrialization and left the region dependent on a one-crop agriculture and on the North for capital and marketing. Slaves were the only available workers who could be employed on plantations; rural whites refused to work for low wages when they had the alternative of subsistence farming on marginal lands in the southern backcountry. Industry, on the other hand, was concentrated in towns and cities where white labor was more readily available. When agriculture was booming—as it was during the 1850s—urban and industrial slaves tended to be displaced by whites and shifted to farming. So long as plantations yielded substantial profits, there could be no major movement of slaves from agriculture to industry. If anything, the trend was in the opposite direction.

The "Profitability" Issue

Some Southerners were obviously making money, and a great deal of it, using slave labor to raise cotton. The great mansions of the Alabama "black belt" and the lower Mississippi could not have been built if their owners had not been successful. But did slavery yield a good return for the great majority of slaveholders who were not large planters? Did it provide the basis for general prosperity and a relatively high standard of living for the southern population in general, or at least for the two-thirds of it who were white and free? These questions have been hotly debated by economic historians. Some knowledge of the main arguments regarding its "profitability" is helpful to an understanding of the South's attachment to slavery.

For many years historians believed slave-based agriculture was, on the average, not very lucrative. Planters' account books seemed to show at best a modest return on investment. In the 1850s, the price of slaves rose at a faster rate than the price of cotton, allegedly squeezing many operators. Some historians even concluded that slavery was a dying institution by the time of the Civil War. Profitability, they argued, depended on access to new and fertile land suitable for plantation agriculture, and virtually all such land within the limits of the United States had already been taken up by 1860. Hence slavery had allegedly reached its natural limits of expansion and was on the verge of becoming so unprofitable it would fall of its own weight in the near future.

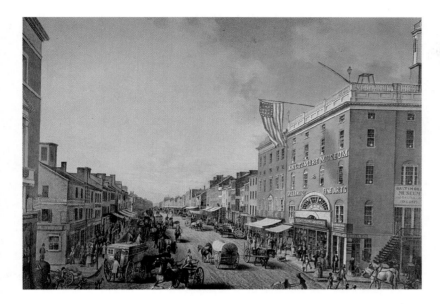

Slaves are evident in this illustration, Baltimore Street Looking West from Calvert Street, Baltimore Maryland, *ca. 1853. Only a small number of slaves worked in industry. Slaves who were not employed in agriculture worked in textile mills, tobacco factories, and ironworks; built roads and railroads; or served as dockworkers and longshoremen.*

A more recent interpretation, based on modern economic theory, holds that slavery was in fact still an economically sound institution in 1860 and showed no signs of imminent decline. A reexamination of planters' records using modern accounting methods shows that during the 1850s planters could normally expect an annual return of 8 to 10 percent on capital invested. This yield was roughly equivalent to the best that could then be obtained from the most lucrative sectors of northern industry and commerce.

Furthermore, it is no longer clear that plantation agriculture had reached its natural limits of expansion by 1860. Production in Texas had not yet peaked, and construction of railroads and levees was opening up new areas for cotton growing elsewhere in the South. With the advantage of hindsight, economic historians have pointed out that improvements in transportation and flood control would enable the post-Civil War South to double its cotton acreage. Those who now argue that slavery was profitable and had an expansive future have made a strong and convincing case.

But the larger question remains: what sort of economic development did a slave plantation system foster? The system may have made slaveholders wealthy, but did the benefits trickle down to the rest of the population—to the majority of whites who owned no slaves and to the slaves themselves? Did it promote efficiency and progressive change? Economists Robert Fogel and

Stanley Engerman have argued that slave plantation agriculture was more efficient than northern family farming. They came to this conclusion using a measure of productivity involving a ratio of "input"—capital, labor, and land—to "output"—the dollar value of the crop when sold. Critics have pointed out, however, that the higher efficiency rate for plantation agriculture may be due entirely to market conditions, or, in other words, to the fact that cotton was in greater demand than such northern commodities as wheat and livestock. Hence Fogel and Engerman's calculations would not prove their assertion that the plantation's success was due to an internally efficient enterprise with good managers and industrious, well-motivated workers.

Other evidence suggests that large plantation owners were the only segment of the population to profit so greatly. Small slaveholders and non-slaveholders shared only to a very limited extent in the bonanza profits of the cotton economy. Because of various insecurities—lack of credit, high transportation costs, and a greater vulnerability to market fluctuations—they had to devote a larger share of their acreage to subsistence crops, especially corn and hogs, than did the planters. They were thus able to survive, but their standard of living was lower than that of most northern farmers. Slaves benefited from planter profits only to the extent that they were better fed, housed, and clothed than they would have been

Slave Concentration, 1820

In 1820, most slaves lived in the eastern seaboard states of Virginia and South Carolina and in Louisiana on the Gulf of Mexico.

had their owners been less prosperous. But it is proslavery propaganda rather than documented fact to suggest they were better off than northern wage laborers.

The South's economic development was skewed in favor of a single route to wealth, open only to the minority possessing both a white skin and access to capital. The concentration of capital and business energies on cotton production foreclosed the kind of diversified industrial and commercial growth that would have provided wider opportunities. Thus, in comparison to the industrializing North, the South was an underdeveloped region in which much of the population had little incentive to work hard. A lack of public education for whites and the denial of even mini-

mal literacy to slaves represented a critical failure to develop human resources. The South's economy was probably condemned to backwardness so long as it was based on slavery.

THE SLAVEHOLDING SOCIETY

If the precise effect of slavery on the South's economic life remains debatable, there is less room for disagreement concerning its impact on social arrangements and attitudes. More than any other factor, the ownership of slaves determined gradations of social prestige and influence among whites. The large planters were the dominant class, and nonslaveholders were of lower social rank. But the fact that all whites were free and

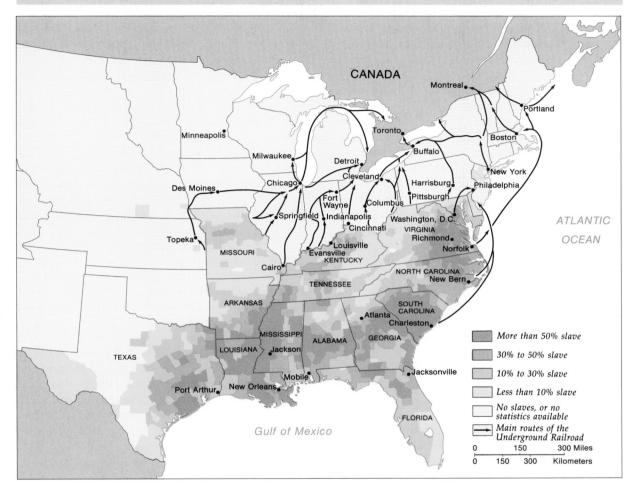

Slave Concentration, 1860

In 1860, slavery had extended throughout the southern states, with the greatest concentrations of slaves in the states of the Deep South. There were also sizable slave populations in the new states of Missouri, Arkansas, Texas, and Florida.

Legend:
- More than 50% slave
- 30% to 50% slave
- 10% to 30% slave
- Less than 10% slave
- No slaves, or no statistics available
- → Main routes of the Underground Railroad

0   150   300 Miles
0   150   300 Kilometers

---

most blacks were slaves created a sharp cleavage between the races that could create the impression (some would say the illusion) of a basic equality within "the master race." In the language of sociologists, inequality in the Old South was determined in two ways: by "class"—differences in status resulting from unequal access to wealth and productive resources—and by "caste"—inherited advantages or disadvantages associated with racial ancestry. Awareness of both systems of social ranking is necessary for an understanding of southern society.

The Planters' World

Those who know the Old South only from modern novels, films, and television programs are likely to envision a land filled with majestic plantations. Pillared mansions behind oak-lined carriageways are portrayed as scenes of aristocratic splendor, where courtly gentlemen and elegant ladies, attended by hordes of uniformed black servants, lived in refined luxury. It is easy to conclude from such images that the typical white Southerner was an aristocrat who belonged to a family that owned large numbers of slaves.

The great houses existed—many of them can still be seen in places like the low country of South Carolina and the lower Mississippi Valley—and some wealthy slaveholders did maintain as aristocratic a lifestyle as was ever seen in the United States. But census returns indicate that this was the world of only a small percentage of slaveowners and a minuscule portion of the total white population.

In 1850, only 30 percent of all white Southerners belonged to families owning slaves; by 1860, the proportion had shrunk to 25 percent. Even in the cotton belt of the Deep South, slaveholders were a minority of whites on the eve of the Civil War—about 40 percent. Planters, defined by the census takers as agriculturalists owning twenty or more slaves, were the minority of a minority. In 1860, planters and their families constituted about 12 percent of all slaveholders and less than 4 percent of the total white population of the South. Even the master of twenty to fifty slaves could rarely live up to the popular image of aristocratic grandeur. To build a great house and entertain lavishly, a planter had to own at least fifty slaves. In 1860, these substantial planters comprised less than 3 percent of all slaveholders and less than 1 percent of all whites.

Although few in numbers, the great planters had a weighty influence on southern life. They set the tone and values for much of the rest of society, especially for the less wealthy slaveowners who sought to imitate the planters' style of living to the extent that resources allowed. Although many of them were too busy tending to their plantations to become openly involved in politics, wealthy planters held more than their share of high offices and often exerted a decisive influence on public policy. Within those regions of the South in which plantation agriculture predominated, they were a ruling class in every sense of the term.

Contrary to legend, a majority of the great planters of the pre-Civil War period were self-made rather than descendants of the old colonial gentry. Some were ambitious young men who married planters' daughters. Others started as lawyers and used their fees and connections to acquire plantations.

As the cotton kingdom spread westward from South Carolina and Georgia to Alabama, Mississippi, and Louisiana, the men who became the largest slaveholders were less and less likely to have come from old and well-established planter families. A large proportion of them began as hard-driving businessmen who built up capital from commerce, land speculation, banking, and even slave-trading. They then used their profits to buy plantations. The highly competitive, boom-or-bust economy of the western Gulf states put a greater premium on sharp dealing and business skills than on genealogy. Stephen Duncan of Mississippi, probably the most prosperous cotton planter in the South during the 1850s (he owned eight plantations and 1,018 slaves), had invested the profits from his banking operations. Among the largest sugar planters of southern Louisiana at this time were Maunsel White and John Burnside, Irish immigrants who had prospered as New Orleans merchants, and Isaac Franklin, former king of the slave traders.

To be successful, a planter had to be a shrewd businessman who kept a careful eye on the market, the prices of slaves and land, and the extent of his indebtedness. Reliable "factors"—the agents who marketed the crop and provided advances against future sales—could assist him in making decisions, but a planter who failed to spend a good deal of time with his account books could end up in serious trouble. Managing the slaves and plantation production was also difficult and time consuming, even when overseers were available to supervise day-to-day activities. Hence few planters could be the men of leisure featured in the popular image of the Old South. Likewise, the responsibility of running an extended household that produced much of its own food and clothing kept plantation mistresses from being the idle ladies of legend.

Some of the richest and most secure plantation families did aspire to live in the manner of a traditional landed aristocracy. A few were so successful that they were accepted as equals by visiting English nobility. Big houses, elegant carriages, fancy-dress balls, and excessive numbers of house servants all reflected aristocratic aspirations. The romantic cult of chivalry, described in the popular novels of Sir Walter Scott, was in vogue in some circles and even led to the nonviolent reenactment of medieval tournaments. Dueling, despite efforts to repress it, remained the standard way to settle "affairs of honor" among gentlemen. Another sign of gentility was the tenden-

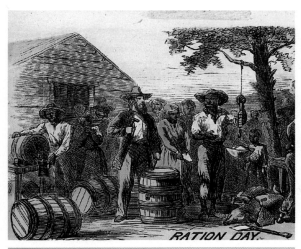

Ration Day on the Plantation, *an illustration by A. R. Waud for* Harper's Weekly, *February 2, 1867. The planter's need to keep track of all expenses was evident on ration day, when field slaves received their weekly food allotment—usually cornmeal and three to four pounds of meat, frequently bacon.*

cy of planters' sons to avoid "trade" as a primary or secondary career in favor of law or the military. Planters' daughters were trained from girlhood to play the piano, speak French, dress in the latest fashions, and sparkle in the drawing room or on the dance floor. The aristocratic style originated among the older gentry of the seaboard slave states, but by the 1840s and 1850s it had spread southwest as a second generation of wealthy planters began to displace the rough-hewn pioneers of the cotton kingdom.

Planters and Slaves

No assessment of the planters' outlook or "worldview" can be made without considering their relations with their slaves. Planters, by the census definition, owned more than half of all the slaves in the South and set standards for treatment and management. Most planters, it is clear from their private letters and journals, as well as from proslavery propaganda, liked to think of themselves as kindly and paternalistic. Often they referred to their slaves as if they were members of an extended patriarchal family—a favorite phrase was "our people." Blacks in general were described as a race of perpetual children requiring constant care and supervision by superior whites. Paternalistic rhetoric increased greatly after aboli-

tionists began to charge that most slaveholders were sadistic monsters. To some extent, the planters' response was part of a defensive effort to redeem the South's reputation and self-respect.

There was, nevertheless, a grain of truth in the planters' claim that their slaves were relatively well provided for. Recent comparative studies have suggested that North American slaves of the pre–Civil War period enjoyed a somewhat higher standard of living than those in other New World slave societies, such as Brazil and the West Indian sugar islands. Their food, clothing, and shelter were normally sufficient to sustain life and labor at slightly above a bare subsistence level and the rapid increase of the slave population in the Old South stands in sharp contrast to the usual failure of slave populations to reproduce themselves.

The concern of many planters for slave health and nutrition does not prove they put ethical considerations ahead of self-interest. The ban on the transatlantic slave trade in 1808 was effective enough to make the domestic reproduction of the slave force an economic necessity if the system was to be perpetuated. Rising slave prices thereafter inhibited extreme physical abuse and deprivation. Slaves were valuable property and the main tools of production for a booming economy, and it was in the interest of masters to see that their property remained in good enough condition to work hard and bear large numbers of children. Furthermore, a good return on their investment enabled southern planters to divert a significant portion of their profits to slave maintenance, a luxury not available to masters in less prosperous plantation economies. But some planters did not behave rationally. They failed to control their tempers or tried to work more slaves than they could afford to maintain. Consequently, there were more cases of physical abuse and undernourishment than a purely economic calculation would lead us to expect.

The testimony of slaves themselves and of some independent white observers suggests that masters of large plantations generally did not have close and intimate relationships with the mass of field slaves. The kind of affection and concern associated with a father figure appears to have been limited mainly to relationships with a few favored house servants or other elite slaves, such as drivers and highly skilled artisans. The field hands on large estates dealt mostly with

Slave cabins, such as these on a prosperous plantation, were small and crude, but still were better than many that had only a doorway leading into a dirt-floored hovel.

overseers who were hired or fired on their ability to meet production quotas.

When they were being most realistic, planters conceded that the ultimate basis of their authority was the slaves' fear of force and intimidation, rather than the natural obedience resulting from a loving parent-child relationship. Scattered among their statements are admissions that they relied on the "principle of fear," "more and more on the power of fear," or—most graphically—that it was necessary "to make them stand in fear." Devices for inspiring fear including whipping—a common practice on most plantations—and the threat of sale away from family and friends. Planters' manuals and instructions to overseers reveal that certain and swift punishment for any infraction of the rules or even for a surly attitude was the preferred method for maintaining order and productivity.

When some masters inevitably yielded to the temptations of power or to their bad tempers and tortured or killed their slaves or raped slave women, the slaves had little recourse. Slaves had little legal protection against such abuse because slave testimony was not accepted in court. Abolitionists were correct in condemning slavery on principle because it gave one human being nearly absolute power over another. Human nature being what it is, such a situation was bound to result in atrocities. Even Harriet Beecher Stowe acknowledged in *Uncle Tom's Cabin,* her celebrated antislavery novel of 1852, that most slaveholders were not as sadistic and brutish as Simon Legree. But—and this was her real point—there was something terribly wrong with an institution that made a Simon Legree possible.

The World of the Plain Folk

As we have seen, 88 percent of all slaveholders in 1860 owned fewer than twenty slaves and thus were not planters in the usual sense of the term. Of these, the great majority had fewer than ten.

Not all slaves and masters had the benevolent relationship often cited in defense of slavery. Whippings that could produce scars like these were common on most plantations.

Some of the small slaveholders were urban merchants or professional men who needed slaves only for domestic service, but more typical were farmers who used one or two slave families to ease the burden of their own labor. Relatively little is known about life on these small slaveholding farms; unlike the planters, the owners left few records behind. We do know that life was relatively spartan. Masters lived in log cabins or small frame cottages and slaves lived in lofts or sheds that were not usually up to plantation housing standards.

For better or worse, relations between owners and their slaves were more intimate than on larger estates. Unlike planters, these farmers often worked in the fields alongside their slaves and sometimes ate at the same table or slept under the same roof. But such closeness did not necessarily result in better treatment. Slave testimony reveals that both the best and the worst of slavery could be found on these farms, depending on the char-

acter and disposition of the master. Given a choice, most slaves preferred to live on plantations because they offered the sociability, culture, and kinship of the quarters, as well as better prospects for adequate food, clothing, and shelter. Marginal slaveholders often sank into poverty and were forced either to sell their slaves or give them short rations.

Just below the small slaveholders on the social scale was a substantial class of yeoman farmers who owned land they worked themselves. Contrary to another myth about the Old South, most of these people did not fit the image of the degraded, shiftless poor white. Such poor whites did exist, mainly as squatters on stretches of barren or sandy soil that no one else wanted. In parts of the South, a significant proportion of those working the land were tenants; some of these were "shiftless poor whites," but others were ambitious young men seeking to accumulate the capital to become landowners. The majority of the nonslaveholding rural population were proud, self-reliant farmers whose way of life did not differ markedly from that of family farmers in the Midwest during the early stages of settlement. If they were disadvantaged in comparison with farmers elsewhere in the United States, it was because the lack of economic development and urban growth perpetuated frontier conditions and denied them the opportunity to produce a substantial surplus for market.

The yeomen were mostly concentrated in the backcountry where slaves and plantations were rarely seen. In every southern state, there were hilly sections unsuitable for plantation agriculture. The foothills or interior valleys of the Appalachians and the Ozarks offered reasonably good soils for mixed farming, and long stretches of piney barrens along the Gulf Coast were suitable for raising livestock. In such regions slaveless farmers concentrated, giving rise to the "white counties" that complicated southern politics. A somewhat distinct group were the genuine mountaineers, who lived too high up to succeed at farming and relied heavily on hunting, lumbering, and distilling whiskey.

The lack of transportation facilities, more than some failure of energy or character, limited the prosperity of the yeomen. A large part of their effort was devoted to growing subsistence crops, mainly corn. They raised a small percentage of

Plantation Women—White and Black

Fanny Cannady, a former slave girl, had mixed recollections of her mistress. Miss Sally was always kind, except when her husband Jordan was around. Her mother, Fanny recalled, had once spilled some coffee, and Jordan had ordered Miss Sally to slap her. Sally did so, but not hard enough to satisfy Master Jordan. "Hit her, Sally, hit the black bitch like she deserves to be hit," he told his wife. Then Miss Sally slapped her again—hard. After Master Jordan left the room, Sally began to cry, and she hugged Fanny's mother. "I loved Miss Sally when Marse Jordan wasn't around," Fanny said.

Fanny's memories illustrate that planters ruled their wives and children as well as their slaves. The planter's wife, in accordance with the conventions of the time, was supposed to exercise a softening influence on her lord and husband. As the lady of the manor, she was to provide a delicate and pure feminine presence within the big family of the plantation. This could lead planters' wives to have sympathy for their fellow subjects. But ultimately, the planter's wife was still a white lady and lived in a world apart from her enslaved counterparts.

Although they supervised the operations of the household and were actually kept very busy making sure everyone on the plantation was fed and clothed, women of the planter's family were supposed to be ladies. They had servants to wait on them, so they could give the impression to visitors they had nothing to do. Ladies could identify each other—and, just as important, townspeople could identify ladies—by their manners, their dress, and the number, behavior, and dress of their personal servants. Unmarried ladies were pure (if sometimes flirtatious), and married ladies demure. Their honor was reinforced by the wealth and weapons of their male relatives. If someone were so unwise as to insult a lady's honor, a duel with her brother, father, or husband would most likely follow.

Plantation women were able to be ladies at social functions. They made social calls on each other, to gossip and to confirm their status, which was defined by their husbands' wealth and honor. They also made charity calls on the less fortunate, thus fulfilling their religious and social obligations to help the poor of their community. Sometimes, they nursed sick slaves and supervised the lying-in of preg-

This satiric illustration, in which a slave woman kneels before and attends to her white mistress, appeared in The Life and Adventure of Jonathan Jefferson Whitlaw, or Scenes in Mississippi, *by Frances Trollope, an English author of novels and travel books and mother of the English novelist Anthony Trollope.*

nant slave women. In the evenings came the balls, which were the underpinning of plantation society and the chief opportunity for ladies to flash their finery among respectable company. The unmarried ladies reigned at the balls, attracting as many suitors as they could handle.

Ladies often expressed themselves privately in writing, or even, in rare cases, in print. One such lady was Mary Boykin Chesnut. In her journal of the Civil War years, she often commented caustically on the customs of southern slave society. She wrote about the evils she believed slavery caused, how it made violence a perpetual presence in society and corrupted the character of the slaveholder. She also equated the institution of slavery with the constraints placed on southern women: "There is no slave, after all, like a wife," she wrote. Still, even though she apparently felt sympathy for mistreated slaves and wives, she could never bring herself to believe either ought to liberate themselves.

Trapped though southern ladies were, theirs was a gilded cage, a prison decked with lace and perfumed with magnolia. Everything they strove to be stood out in stark contrast against the lives of their counterparts on the plantation: women slaves. While white women on plantations tried to uphold the standards of ladyhood, black women had to struggle to maintain some semblance of womanhood. Sojourner Truth escaped slavery to become a prominent spokesperson for abolition and gave voice to the plight of black women by demanding of a northern audience, "Ar'n't I a woman?"

Black women had the worst of two important prejudices: as blacks, they could be owned as slaves, and as owned women, they could be sexually exploited. The guilt caused by sex between masters and slaves helped create polarized stereotypes of black women's sexuality: on the one hand there was the Jezebel, the woman who was all sexuality, and on the other, Mammy, who had none. A mammy took care of the white children and often exercised considerable authority in household matters, especially if a young mistress had earlier been in her charge. But she often lacked the time to pay adequate attention to her own slave family.

Masters' control over the bodies of female slaves extended to their wombs. It was in the master's interest to promote procreation among slaves. As Thomas Jefferson said, "I consider a woman who brings a child every two years as more profitable than the best man of the farm. What she produces is an addition to the capital, while his labors disappear in mere consumption." For a black woman to be owned as a slave meant that her womb was owned and her children were owned.

Black women nevertheless managed to create private lives and communities. Most lived in two-parent slave families in which husbands and wives normally shared responsibilities in a more equitable way than was the case with their owners. But labor gangs were often separated into men and women, and the sort of work women did usually allowed them to be with each other. This was probably the beginning of a sense of female community. The persistence of African traditions of spirituality and healing helped as well. Women acting as midwives, or known to have an understanding of folk medicine, had a certain authority.

Perhaps most important in terms of rebelling against the master, women in the slave quarters sometimes worked together to avoid bringing more children into slavery by the use of contraceptives, abortifacients, and even infanticide. More often, however, they valued their children and sought to teach them how to survive under slavery.

Slave women also resisted in smaller ways, particularly against their mistresses. When the master was not about, they were that much more likely to shirk work, to talk back to the mistress, and to play tricks, for they knew the master would invariably put it down to his wife's weakness as a woman and inability to wield authority effectively.

Black women were subject to special hardships because they were women, but unlike white ladies, they were not entitled to special treatment because of their gender. This was especially graphic when masters punished slaves. White men who would consider it unthinkable to strike a white lady had no qualms about whipping slave women. An extreme and illustrative example is that of the man who shot a slave named Lydia while she was running away from punishment. The Supreme Court of North Carolina held that the master had a right to do so because "The Power of the master must be absolute to render the submission of the slave perfect."

Power was the first and final fact of life under slavery. The southern economy had made slavery indispensable. White Southerners had to ensure their dominion over blacks. This kept plantation ladies and female slaves from finding their potential solidarity as women.

the South's cotton and tobacco, but production was severely limited by the difficulty of marketing. Their main source of cash was livestock, especially hogs. Hogs could be walked to market over long distances, and massive droves from the backcountry to urban markets were commonplace. But southern livestock, which was generally allowed to forage in the woods rather than being fattened on grain, was of poor quality and did not bring high prices or big profits to raisers.

Although they did not benefit directly from the peculiar institution, most yeomen and other nonslaveholders tolerated slavery and were fiercely opposed to abolitionism in any form. A few anti-slavery Southerners, most notably Hinton R. Helper of North Carolina, tried to convince the yeomen they were victimized by planter dominance and should work for its overthrow. These dissenters presented a plausible set of arguments, emphasizing that slavery and the plantation system created a privileged class and severely limited the economic opportunities of the nonslaveholding white majority.

Most yeomen were staunch Jacksonians who resented aristocratic pretensions and feared concentrations of power and wealth in the hands of the few. When asked about the gentry, they commonly voiced their disdain of "cotton snobs" and rich planters generally. In state and local politics, they sometimes expressed these feelings by voting against planter interests on issues involving representation, banking, and internal improvements. Why, then, did they fail to respond to antislavery appeals that called on them to strike at the real source of planter power and privilege?

One reason was that some nonslaveholders hoped to get ahead in the world, and in the South this meant acquiring slaves of their own. Just enough of the more prosperous yeomen broke into the slaveholding classes to make this dream seem believable. Planters, anxious to ensure the loyalty of nonslaveholders, strenuously encouraged the notion that every white man was a potential master.

Even if they did not aspire to own slaves, white farmers often viewed black servitude as providing a guarantee of their own liberty and independence. A society that gave them the right to vote and the chance to be self-sufficient on land of their own encouraged the feeling they were fundamentally equal to the largest slaveholders.

Although they had no natural love of planters and slavery, they believed—or could be induced to believe—that abolition would threaten their liberty and independence. In part their anxieties were economic; freed slaves would compete with them for land or jobs. But an intense racism deepened their fears and made their opposition to black freedom implacable. "Now suppose they was free," a nonslaveholder told a northern traveler, "you see they'd think themselves just as good as we . . . just suppose you had a family of children, how would [you] like to hev a niggar feeling just as good as a white man? how'd you like to hev a niggar steppin' up to your darter?" Emancipation was unthinkable because it would remove the pride and status that automatically went along with a white skin in this acutely race-conscious society. Slavery, despite its drawbacks, served to keep blacks "in their place" and to make all whites, however poor and uneducated they might be, feel they were free and equal members of a master race.

A Closed Mind and a Closed Society

Despite the tacit assent of most nonslaveholders, the dominant planters never lost their fear that lower-class whites would turn against slavery. They felt threatened from two sides: from the slave quarters where a new Nat Turner might be gathering his forces, and from the backcountry where yeomen and poor whites might heed the call of abolitionists and rise up against planter domination. Beginning in the 1830s, the ruling element tightened the screws of slavery and used their control of government and communications to create a mood of impending catastrophe designed to ensure that all southern whites were of a single mind on the slavery issue.

Before the 1830s, open discussion of the rights or wrongs of slavery had been possible in many parts of the South. Apologists commonly described the institution as "a necessary evil." In the upper South, as late as the 1820s, there had been significant support for the American Colonization Society, with its program of gradual voluntary emancipation accompanied by deportation of the freedmen. In 1831 and 1832—in the wake of the Nat Turner uprising—the Virginia state legislature debated a gradual emancipation plan. Major support for ensuring white safety by getting rid of both slavery and blacks came from representatives of the yeoman farmers living west of the Blue Ridge Mountains. But the defeat of the proposal effectively ended the discussion. The argument that slavery was "a positive good"—rather than an evil slated for gradual elimination—won the day.

The positive good defense of slavery was an answer to the abolitionist charge that the institution was inherently sinful. The message was carried in a host of books, pamphlets, and newspaper editorials published between the 1830s and the Civil War. Who, historians have asked, was it meant to persuade? Partly, the argument was aimed at the North, as a way of bolstering the strong current of antiabolitionist sentiment. But Southerners themselves were a prime target; the message was clearly calculated to resolve the kind of doubts and misgivings that had been freely expressed before the 1830s. Much of the message may have been over the heads of nonslaveholders, many of whom were semiliterate, but some of the arguments, in popularized form, were used to arouse racial anxieties that tended to neutralize antislavery sentiment among the lower classes.

The proslavery argument was based on three main propositions. The first and foremost was that enslavement was the natural and proper status for people of African descent. Blacks, it was alleged, were innately inferior to whites and suited only for slavery. Biased scientific and historical evidence was presented to support this claim. Secondly, slavery was held to be sanctioned by the Bible and Christianity—a position made necessary by the abolitionist appeal to Christian ethics. Ancient Hebrew slavery was held up as a divinely sanctioned model, and Saint Paul was quoted endlessly on the duty of servants to obey their masters. Southern churchmen took the lead in reconciling slavery with religion and also made renewed efforts to convert the slaves as a way of showing that enslavement could be a means for spreading the gospel.

Finally, efforts were made to show that slavery was consistent with the humanitarian spirit of the nineteenth century. The premise that blacks were naturally dependent led to the notion they needed some kind of "family government" or special regime equivalent to the asylums that existed for the small numbers of whites who were also inca-

pable of caring for themselves. The plantation allegedly provided such an environment, as benevolent masters guided and ruled this race of "perpetual children."

By the 1850s, the proslavery argument had gone beyond mere apology for the South and its peculiar institution and featured an ingenious attack on the free labor system of the North. According to the Virginian George Fitzhugh, the master-slave relationship was *more* humane than the one prevailing between employers and wage laborers in the North. Slaves had security against unemployment and a guarantee of care in old age, whereas free workers might face destitution and even starvation at any time. Worker insecurity in free societies led inevitably to strikes, bitter class conflicts, and the rise of socialism; slave societies, on the other hand, could more effectively protect property rights and maintain other traditional values because its laboring class was both better treated, and at the same time, more firmly controlled.

In addition to arguing against the abolitionists, proslavery Southerners attempted to seal off their region from antislavery ideas and influences. Whites who were bold enough to criticize slavery publicly were mobbed or persecuted. One of the last and bravest of the southern abolitionists, Cassius M. Clay of Kentucky, armed himself with a brace of pistols when he gave speeches, until the threat of mob violence finally forced him across the Ohio. In 1856, a University of North Carolina professor was fired because he admitted he would vote for the moderately antislavery Republican party if he had a chance. Clergymen who questioned the morality of slavery were driven from their pulpits, and northern travelers suspected of being abolitionist agents were tarred and feathered. When abolitionists tried to send their literature through the mails during the 1830s, it was seized in southern post offices and publicly burned.

Such flagrant denials of free speech and civil liberties were inspired in part by fears that nonslaveholding whites and slaves would get subversive ideas about slavery. Hinton R. Helper's book, *The Impending Crisis of the South,* an 1857 appeal to nonslaveholders to resist the planter regime, was suppressed with particular vigor; those found with copies were beaten up or even lynched. But the deepest fear was that slaves

This proslavery cartoon of 1841 contends that the slave in America had a better life than did the working-class white in England. Supposedly, the grateful slaves were clothed, fed, and cared for in their old age by kindly and sympathetic masters, while starving English workers were mercilessly exploited by factory owners.

would hear the abolitionist talk or read antislavery literature and be inspired to rebel. Such anxieties rose to panic pitch after the Nat Turner rebellion. Consequently, new laws were passed making it a crime to teach slaves to read and write. Other repressive legislation aimed at slaves banned meetings unless a white man was present, severely restricted the activities of black preachers, and suppressed independent black churches. Free blacks, thought to be possible instigators of slave revolt, were denied basic civil liberties and were the object of growing surveillance and harassment.

All these efforts at thought control and internal security did not allay the fears of abolitionist subversion, lower-class white dissent, and, above all, slave revolt. The persistent barrage of proslavery propaganda and the course of national events in the 1850s created a mood of panic and despera-

tion. By this time an increasing number of Southerners had become convinced that safety from abolitionism and its associated terrors required a formal withdrawal from the Union—secession.

THE BLACK EXPERIENCE UNDER SLAVERY

Most African Americans of the early to mid-nineteenth century experienced slavery on plantations; the majority of slaves lived on units owned by planters who had twenty or more slaves. The masters of these agrarian communities sought to ensure their personal safety and the profitability of their enterprises by using all the means—physical and psychological—at their command to make slaves docile and obedient. By word and deed, they tried to convince the slaves that whites were superior and had a right to rule over blacks. Masters also drew constant attention to their awesome power and ability to deal harshly with rebels and malcontents. As increasing numbers of slaves were converted to Christianity and attended white-supervised services, they were forced to hear, over and over again, that God had commanded slaves to serve and obey their masters.

It is a great tribute to the resourcefulness and spirit of African Americans that most of them resisted these pressures and managed to retain an inner sense of their own worth and dignity. When conditions were right, they openly asserted their desire for freedom and equality and showed their disdain for white claims that slavery was a positive good. But the struggle for freedom involved more than the confrontation between master and slave; free blacks, in both the North and the South, did what they could to speed the day when all African Americans would be free.

This woman is believed to be the granddaughter of Marie Therese, a freed slave who married a Frenchman and built Melrose Plantation in Louisiana. Despite its slave heritage, even this planter family owned slaves.

Forms of Slave Resistance

Open rebellion, the bearing of arms against the oppressors by organized groups of slaves, was the most dramatic and clear-cut form of slave resistance. In the period between 1800 and 1831, a number of slaves participated in revolts that showed their willingness to risk their lives in a desperate bid for liberation. In 1800, a Virginia slave named Gabriel Prosser mobilized a large band of his fellows to march on Richmond. But a violent storm dispersed "Gabriel's army" and enabled whites to suppress the uprising without any loss of white life.

In 1811, several hundred Louisiana slaves marched on New Orleans brandishing guns, waving flags, and beating drums. It took three hundred soldiers of the U.S. Army, aided by armed planters and militiamen, to stop the advance and to end the rebellion. In 1822, whites in Charleston, South Carolina, uncovered an extensive and well-planned conspiracy, organized by a free black man named Denmark Vesey, to seize local armories, arm the slave population, and take possession of the city. Although the Vesey conspiracy was nipped in the bud, it convinced South Carolinians that blacks were "the Jacobins of the country [a reference to the militants of the French Revolution] against whom we should always be on guard."

Only a year after the Vesey affair, whites in Norfolk County, Virginia, complained of the activities of a marauding band of runaway slaves that had killed several whites. The militia was sent out and captured the alleged leader—a fugitive of several years' standing named Bob Ferebee. Groups of runaways, who hid for years in places like the Great Dismal Swamp of Virginia, continued to raid plantations throughout the antebellum period and were inclined to fight to the death rather than be recaptured.

As we have already seen, the most bloody and terrifying of all slave revolts was the Nat Turner insurrection of 1831. Although it was the last slave rebellion of this kind during the pre-Civil War period, armed resistance had not ended. Indeed, the most sustained and successful effort of slaves to win their freedom by force of arms took place in Florida between 1835 and 1842 when hundreds of black fugitives fought in the Second Seminole War alongside the Indians who had given them a haven. The Seminoles were resisting removal to Oklahoma, but for the blacks who took part, the war was a struggle for their own freedom, and when it ended most of them were allowed to accompany their Indian allies to the trans-Mississippi West.

Only a tiny fraction of all slaves ever took part in organized acts of violent resistance against white power. Most realized the odds against a successful revolt were very high, and bitter experience had shown them that the usual outcome was death to the rebels. As a consequence, they characteristically devised safer or more ingenious ways to resist white dominance.

One way of protesting against slavery was to run away, and thousands of slaves showed their discontent and desire for freedom in this fashion. Most fugitives never got beyond the neighborhood of the plantation; after "lying out" for a time, they would return, often after negotiating immunity from punishment. But many escapees remained free for years by hiding in swamps or other remote areas, and a fraction made it to freedom in the North or Mexico. Some fugitives stowed away aboard ships heading to northern ports; others traveled overland for hundreds of miles, avoiding patrols and inquisitive whites by staying off the roads and moving only at night. Light-skinned blacks sometimes made it to freedom by passing for whites, and one resourceful slave even had himself packed in a box and shipped to the North.

The typical fugitive was a young, unmarried male from the upper South. For the majority of slaves, however, flight was not a real option. Either they lived too deep in the South to have any chance of reaching free soil, or they were reluctant to leave family and friends behind. Slaves who did not or could not leave the plantation had to register their opposition to the masters' regime while remaining under the yoke of bondage.

The normal way of expressing discontent was engaging in a kind of indirect or passive resistance. Many slaves worked slowly and inefficiently, not because they were naturally lazy (as whites supposed), but as a gesture of protest or alienation as conveyed in the words of a popular slave song, "You may think I'm working/But I ain't." Others withheld labor by feigning illness or

Running away was one way to escape slavery, but for most slaves, flight was impossible. Instead, they sought other means by which to improve their condition as slaves.

injury. Stealing provisions—a very common activity on most plantations—was another way to show contempt for authority. According to the code of ethics prevailing in the slave quarters, theft from the master was no sin; it was simply a way for slaves to get a larger share of the fruits of their own labors.

Substantial numbers of slaves committed acts of sabotage. Tools and agricultural implements were deliberately broken, animals were willfully neglected or mistreated, and barns or other outbuildings were set afire. Often masters could not identify the culprits because slaves did not readily inform on one another. The ultimate act of clandestine resistance was poisoning the master's food. Some slaves, especially the "conjure" men and women who practiced a combination of folk medicine and witchcraft, knew how to mix rare, virtually untraceable poisons; and a suspiciously large number of plantation whites became suddenly and mysteriously ill. Sometimes whole families died from obscure "diseases" that did not infect the slave quarters.

The basic attitude behind such actions was revealed in the folk-tales that slaves passed down from generation to generation. The famous Brer Rabbit stories showed how a small, apparently defenseless animal could overcome a bigger and stronger one through cunning and deceit. Although these tales often had an African origin, they also served as an allegory for the black view of the master-slave relationship. Other stories—which were not told in front of whites—openly portrayed the slave as a clever trickster outwitting the master. In one such tale a slave reports to his master that seven hogs have died of "malitis." Thinking this is a dread disease, the master agrees to let the slaves have all the meat. What really happened, so the story goes, was that "One of the strongest Negroes got up early in the morning" and "skitted to the hog pen with a heavy mallet in his hand. When he tapped Mister Hog 'tween the eyes with that mallet, 'malitis' set in mighty quick."

The Struggles of Free Blacks

In addition to the 4 million blacks in bondage, there were approximately 500,000 free African Americans in 1860, about half of them living in slave states. Whether they were in the North or in the South, "free Negroes" were treated as social outcasts and denied legal and political equality with whites. Public facilities were strictly segregated, and after the 1830s blacks in the United States could vote only in four New England states. Nowhere but in Massachusetts could they testify in court cases involving whites.

Free blacks had difficulty finding decent jobs; most employers preferred immigrants or other whites over blacks, and the latter were usually relegated to menial and poorly paid occupations: casual day labor or domestic service. Many states excluded blacks entirely from public schools, and the federal government barred them from serving in the militia, working for the postal service, and laying claim to public lands. Free blacks were even denied U. S. passports; in effect they were stateless persons even before the 1857 Supreme Court ruling that no Negro could claim American citizenship.

In the South, free blacks were subject to a set of direct controls that tended to make them semi-slaves. They were often forced to register or have white guardians who were responsible for their behavior. Invariably they were required to carry papers proving their free status, and in some states they had to obtain official permission to move from one county to another. Licensing laws were invoked to exclude blacks from several occupations, and attempts by blacks to hold meetings or form organizations were frequently blocked by the authorities. Sometimes vagrancy and apprenticeship laws were used to force free blacks into a state of economic dependency barely distinguishable from outright slavery. Just before the outbreak of the Civil War, a campaign developed in some southern states to carry this pattern of repression and discrimination to its logical conclusion: several state legislatures proposed laws giving free Negroes the choice of emigrating from the state or being enslaved.

Although beset by special problems of their own, most free blacks identified with the suffering of the slaves; when circumstances allowed, they protested against the peculiar institution and worked for its abolition. Many of them had once been slaves themselves or were the children of slaves; often they had close relatives who were still in bondage. Furthermore, they knew the discrimination from which they suffered was rooted in slavery and the racial attitudes that accompanied it. So long as slavery existed, their own rights were likely to be denied and even their freedom was at risk; former slaves who could not prove they had been legally freed were subject to reenslavement. This threat existed even in the North: under federal fugitive slave laws, escaped slaves could be returned to bondage. Even blacks who were born free were not perfectly safe. Kidnapping or fraudulent seizure by slave-catchers was always a possibility.

Because of the elaborate system of control and surveillance, free blacks in the South were in a relatively weak position to work against slavery. The case of Denmark Vesey showed that a prosperous and well-situated free black might make a stand in the struggle for freedom, but it also revealed the dangers of revolutionary activity and the odds against success. The wave of repression against the free black population that followed the Vesey conspiracy heightened the dangers and increased the odds. Consequently, most free blacks found that survival depended on creating the impression of loyalty to the planter regime. In some parts of the lower South, groups of relatively privileged free Negroes, mostly of racially mixed origin, were sometimes persuaded it was to their advantage to preserve the status quo. As skilled craftsmen and small businessmen dependent on white favors and patronage, they had little incentive to risk everything by taking the side of the slaves. In southern Louisiana, there was even a small group of mulatto planters who lived in luxury, supported by the labor of other African Americans.

Free blacks in the North were in a better position to join the struggle for freedom. Despite all the prejudice and discrimination they faced, they still enjoyed some basic civil liberties denied to southern blacks. They could protest publicly against slavery or white supremacy and could form associations for the advancement and liberation of African Americans. Frederick Douglass, the escaped slave who became an abolitionist orator, was their most eloquent spokesman. Among the other leading black male abolitionists were Charles Remond, William Wells Brown, Robert Purvis, and Henry Highland Garnet. Outspoken women like Sojourner Truth, Maria Stewart, and Frances Harper also played a significant role in black antislavery activity. The Negro Convention movement, which sponsored national meetings of black leaders beginning in 1830, provided an important forum for independent black expression. Their most eloquent statement came in 1854, when black leaders met in Cleveland to declare their faith in a separate racial identity, proclaiming, "We pledge our integrity to use all honorable means, to unite us, as one people, on this continent."

Black newspapers, such as *Freedom's Journal*, first published in 1827, and *The North Star*, founded by Douglass in 1847, gave black writers a chance to preach their gospel of liberation to black readers. African American authors also produced a stream of books and pamphlets attacking slavery, refuting racism, and advocating various forms of resistance. One of the most influential publications was David Walker's *Appeal . . . to the Colored Citizens of the World*, which appeared in 1829. Walker denounced slavery in the most vigorous language possible and called for a black revolt against white tyranny.

Free blacks in the North did more than make verbal protests against racial injustice. They were also the main conductors on the fabled underground railroad that opened a path for fugitives from slavery. It has been supposed that benevolent whites were primarily responsible for organized efforts to guide and assist fugitive slaves, but modern research has shown that the underground railroad was largely a black-operated enterprise. Courageous ex-slaves like Harriet Tubman and Josiah Henson made regular forays into the slave states to lead other blacks to freedom, and many of the "stations" along the way were manned by free Negroes. In northern towns and cities, free blacks organized "vigilance committees" to protect fugitives and thwart the slave catchers. Groups of blacks even used force to rescue recaptured fugitives from the authorities. In Boston in 1851, one such group seized a slave named Shadrack from a U. S. marshal who was in the process of returning him to bondage. In deeds as well as words, free blacks showed their unyielding hostility to slavery and racism.

African American Religion

African Americans could not have resisted or even endured slavery if they had been utterly demoralized by its oppressiveness. What made the struggle for freedom possible were inner resources and patterns of thought that gave some dignity to their lives and inspired hopes for a brighter future. From the realm of culture and fundamental beliefs African Americans drew the strength to hold their heads high and look beyond their immediate condition.

Religion was the cornerstone of this emerging African American culture. Black Christianity may have owed its original existence to the efforts of white missionaries, but it was far from a mere imitation of white religious forms and beliefs. This distinctive variant of evangelical Protestantism incorporated elements of African religion and stressed those portions of the Bible that spoke to the aspirations of an enslaved people thirsting for freedom.

Harriet Tubman, on the extreme left, is shown here with some of the slaves she helped escape on the underground railroad. Born a slave in Maryland, she escaped to Philadelphia in 1849. She is said to have helped as many as three hundred African Americans flee slavery. She led many of them all the way to Canada, where they would be beyond the reach of the Fugitive Slave Law.

Free blacks formed the first independent black churches by seceding from white congregations that discriminated against them in seating and church governance. Out of these secessions came a variety of autonomous Baptist groups and the highly successful African Methodist Episcopal (AME) church, organized as a national denomination under the leadership of Reverend Richard Allen of Philadelphia in 1816. But the mass of blacks did not have access to these independent churches. These churches mainly served free blacks and urban slaves with indulgent masters. In the deep South, whites regarded AME churches with suspicion and sometimes suppressed them; a thriving congregation in Charleston was forced to close its doors in 1822 after some of its members had been implicated in the Vesey conspiracy.

Plantation slaves who were exposed to Christianity either attended neighboring white churches or worshiped at home. On large estates masters or white missionaries often conducted Sunday services. But the narratives and recollections of ex-slaves reveal that white-sanctioned religious activity was only a superficial part of the slaves' spiritual life. The true slave religion was practiced at night, often secretly, and was led by black preachers. Historian Albert J. Raboteau has described this underground black Christianity as "the invisible institution."

This covert slave religion was a highly emotional affair that featured singing, shouting, and dancing. In some ways the atmosphere resembled a backwoods revival meeting. But much of what went on was actually an adaptation of African religious beliefs and customs. The chanting mode of preaching—with the congregation responding at regular intervals—and the expression of religious feelings through rhythmical movements, especially the counterclockwise movement known as "the ring shout," were clearly African in origin. The black conversion experience was normally a state of ecstasy more akin to possession by spirits—a major form of African religious expression—than to the agony of those "struck down" at white revivals. The emphasis on sinfulness and fear of damnation that were core themes of white evangelicalism played a lesser role among blacks. For them, religion was more an affirmation of the joy of life than a rejection of worldly pleasures and temptations.

Slave sermons and religious songs spoke directly to the plight of a people in bondage and implicitly asserted their right to be free. The most popular of all biblical subjects was the deliverance of the children of Israel from slavery in Egypt. The book of Exodus provided more than its share of texts for sermons and images for songs. In one moving spiritual, God commands Moses to "tell Old Pharaoh" to "let my people

Go." In another, Mary is told she can stop weeping and begin to rejoice because "Pharaoh's army got drownded" trying to cross the Red Sea. Many sermons and songs referred to the crossing of Jordan and the arrival in the Promised Land. "Oh Canaan, sweet Canaan, I am bound for the land of Canaan" and "Oh brothers, don't get weary . . . . We'll land on Canaan's shore" are typical of lines from spirituals known to have been sung by slaves. Other songs invoked the liberation theme in different ways. One recalled that Jesus had "set poor sinners free," and another prophesied that "We'll soon be free, when the Lord will call us home."

Most of the songs of freedom and deliverance can be interpreted as referring exclusively to religious salvation and the afterlife—and this was undoubtedly how slaves hoped their masters would understand them. But the slaves did not forget that God had once freed a people from slavery in this life and punished their masters. The Bible thus gave African Americans the hope that they, as a people, would repeat the experience of the Israelites and be delivered from bondage. During the Civil War, observers noted that freed slaves seemed to regard their emancipation as something that had been preordained and were inclined to view Lincoln as the reincarnation of Moses.

Besides being the basis for a deep-rooted hope for eventual freedom, religion helped the slaves endure bondage without losing their sense of inner worth. Unless their masters were unusually pious, religious slaves could regard themselves as superior to their owners. Some slaves even believed all whites were damned because of their unjust treatment of blacks, while all slaves would be saved because any sins they committed were the involuntary result of their condition.

More important, "the invisible institution" of the church gave African Americans a chance to create and control a world of their own. Preachers, elders, and other leaders of slave congregations could acquire a sense of status within their own community that had not been conferred by whites; the singers who improvised the spirituals found an outlet for independent artistic expression. Although religion seldom inspired slaves to open rebellion, it must be regarded as a prime source of resistance to the dehumanizing effects of enslavement. It helped create a sense of community, solidarity, and self-esteem among slaves by giving them something of their own that they found infinitely precious.

The Slave Family

The African American family was the other institution that prevented slavery from becoming utterly demoralizing. Contrary to what historians and sociologists used to believe, the majority of slaves lived in two-parent households. Although slave marriages were not legally binding, many masters encouraged stable unions, and the slaves themselves apparently preferred monogamy to more casual or promiscuous relationships. Plantation registers reveal that many slave marriages lasted for as long as twenty or thirty years and were more often broken by death or sale than by voluntary dissolution of the union. The breakup of marriages and families by sale occurred frequently enough to introduce an element of desperation and instability into slave family relationships. Nevertheless, the black family ethic valued marital fidelity and a sense of responsibility for children, attitudes strongly influenced by Christian teachings. Relations between spouses and between parents and children were normally close and affectionate. Slave husbands and fathers did not, of course, have the same power and authority as free heads of families; they could not play the role of breadwinner or even protect their wives and children from harsh punishment or sexual abuse by masters or overseers. But they usually did what they could, and this included supplementing the family diet by hunting, fishing, or pilfering plantation stores. Husbands and wives tried to relieve each other's burdens; together they taught their children how to survive slavery and plantation life.

The terrible anguish that usually accompanied the breakup of families through sale showed the depth of kinship feelings. Masters knew the first place to look for a fugitive was in the neighborhood of a family member who had been sold away. After emancipation, thousands of freed slaves wandered about looking for spouses, children, or parents from whom they had been forcibly separated years before. The famous spiritual, "Sometime I feel like a motherless child," was far more than an expression of religious need; it also reflected the family anxieties and personal tragedies of many slaves.

John Antrobus, Plantation Burial, *ca. 1860. The painting depicts slaves gathering in a forest to bury a fellow slave. Many spirituals sung by the slaves on such occasions portrayed death as a welcome release from bondage and created an image of an afterlife where the trials and cares of this life were unknown.*

Feelings of kinship and mutual obligation extended beyond the nuclear family. Grandparents, uncles, aunts, and even cousins were often known to slaves through direct contact or family lore. A sense of family continuity over three or more generations was revealed in the names that slaves gave to their children or took for themselves. Infants were frequently named after grandparents, and those slaves who assumed surnames often chose that of an ancestor's owner rather than the family name of a current master.

Kinship ties were not limited to blood relations. When families were broken up by sale, individual members who found themselves on plantations far from home were likely to be "adopted" into new kinship networks. Orphans or children without responsible parents were quickly absorbed without prejudice into new families.

What becomes apparent from studies of the slave family is that kinship provided a model for personal relationships and the basis for a sense of community. For some purposes, all the slaves on a plantation were in reality members of a single extended family, as their forms of address clearly reveal. Elderly slaves were addressed by everyone else as "uncle" and "aunty," and younger unre-

Some slave families managed to stay together, as shown by the footnote to this 1835 bill of sale: "I did intend to leave Nancy['s] child but she made such a damned fuss I had to let her take it. . . ."

lated slaves commonly called each other "brother" or "sister." Slave culture was a family culture, and this was one of its greatest sources of strength and cohesion. Strong kinship ties, whether real or fictive, meant slaves could depend on one another in times of trouble. The kinship network also provided a vehicle for the transmission of African American folk traditions from one generation to the next. Together with slave religion, kinship gave African Americans some sense they were members of a community, not just a collection of individuals victimized by oppression.

Some historians have argued that a stress on the strength of slave culture obscures the harshness and cruelty of the system and its damaging effect on the African American personality. Slavery was of course often a demoralizing and even brutalizing experience, and it provided little opportunity for learning about the world outside the plantation, developing mental skills, and exercising individual initiative. Compared with serfs in Russia or even with slaves on some of the large sugar plantations of the Caribbean, bondspeople

on the relatively small southern plantations or farms with their high turnover of personnel had less chance to develop communal ties of the kind associated with peasant villages. Nevertheless, their sense of being part of a distinctive group with its own beliefs and ways of doing things, fragile and precarious though it may have been, made *psychic survival* possible and helped engender an African American ethnicity that would be a source of strength in future struggles. Although slave culture did not normally provoke violent resistance to the slaveholders' regime, the inner world that slaves made for themselves gave them the spiritual strength to thwart the masters' efforts to take over their hearts and minds. After emancipation, this resilient cultural heritage would combine with the tradition of open protest created by rebellious slaves and free black abolitionists to inspire and sustain new struggles for equality.

If slaves lived to some extent in a separate and distinctive world of their own, so did planters, less affluent whites, and even free blacks. The Old South was thus a deeply divided society. The northern traveler Frederick Law Olmsted, who made three journeys through the slave states in the 1850s, gives us a vivid sense of how diverse in outlook and circumstances southern people could be. Visiting a great plantation, he watched the slaves stop working as soon as the overseer turned away; on a small farm he saw a slave and his owner working in the fields together. Treatment of slaves, he found, ranged from humane paternalism to flagrant cruelty. Olmsted heard nonslaveholding whites damn the planters as "cotton snobs" but also talk about blacks as "niggars" and express fear of interracial marriages if slaves were freed. He received hospitality from poor whites living in crowded one-room cabins as well as from fabulously wealthy planters in pillared mansions and found life in the "backcountry" radically different than in the plantation belts. In short, he showed that the South was a kaleidoscope of groups divided by class, race, culture, and geography. What held it together and provided some measure of unity was a booming plantation economy and a web of customary relationships and loyalties that could obscure the underlying cleavages and antagonisms. The fractured and fragile nature of this society would soon become apparent when it was subjected to the pressures of civil war.

Chronology

Recommended Reading

Major works that take a broad view of slavery are Kenneth M. Stampp, *The Peculiar Institution: Slavery in the Antebellum South* (1956), which stresses its coercive features; John W. Blassingame, *The Slave Community: Plantation Life in the Antebellum South* (1972), which focuses on slave culture and psychology; and Eugene D. Genovese, *Roll, Jordan, Roll: The World the Slaves Made* (1974), which probes the paternalistic character of the institution and the way in which slaves made a world for themselves within its bounds.

On the economics of slavery, see Gavin Wright, *The Political Economy of the Cotton South: Households, Markets, and Wealth in the Nineteenth Century* (1978). Clement Eaton, *The Growth of Southern Civilization, 1790–1860* (1961), provides a good introduction to life in the Old South. A more recent and insightful interpretation of antebellum southern society is James Oakes, *Slavery and Freedom* (1990). On the effect of slavery and the plantation on women, see Elizabeth Fox-Genovese, *Within the Plantation Household* (1988), and Deborah Gray White, *Ar'n't I a Woman: Female Slaves in the Plantation South* (1985).

Black resistance to slavery is described in Vincent Harding, *There Is a River: The Black Struggle for Freedom in America* (1981). Slave culture is examined in Albert J. Raboteau, *Slave Religion* (1978); Herbert G. Gutman, *The Black Family in Slavery and Freedom, 1750–1925* (1976); Lawrence W. Levine, *Black Culture and Consciousness: Afro-American Folk Thought from Slavery to Freedom* (1977); and Sterling Stuckey, *Slave Culture: Nationalist Theory and the Foundations of Black America* (1987).

Additional Bibliography

The classic account of southern agriculture is Lewis C. Gray, *History of Agriculture in the Southern United States to 1860*, 2 vols. (1941). On the economics of slavery, see Eugene D. Genovese, *The Political Economy of Slavery: Studies in the Economy and Society of the Slave South* (1965); Robert William Fogel and Stanley L. Engerman, *Time on the Cross: The Economics of American Negro Slavery,* 2 vols. (1974); and Paul A. David et al., *Reckoning with Slavery: A Critical Study of the Quantitative History of American Negro Slavery* (1976). Unsurpassed as a contemporary account of the economic and social aspects of slavery is Frederick L. Olmsted, *The Cotton Kingdom* (1962).

Nonagricultural slavery is examined in Robert S. Starobin, *Industrial Slavery in the Old South* (1970); Richard C. Wade, *Slavery in the Cities* (1964); and Claudia Dale Goldin, *Urban Slavery in the American South, 1820–1860: A Quantitative History* (1976).

On the slave trade, see Michael Tadman, *Speculators and Slaves* (1989). For comparisons with slavery elsewhere, see Frank Tannebaum, *Slave and*

Citizen: The Negro in the Americas (1946), Carl N. Degler, *Neither Black Nor White: Slavery and Race Relations in Brazil and the United States* (1971); George M. Fredrickson, *White Supremacy: A Comparative Study in American and South African History* (1981), Peter Kolchin, *Unfree Labor: American Slavery and Russian Serfdom* (1987); and Shearer Davis Bowman, *Masters and Lords: Mid-19th Century U.S. Planters and Prussian Junkers* (1993).

On the society and culture of the southern white population, see W. J. Cash, *The Mind of the South* (1941); Dickson D. Bruce, Jr., *Violence and Culture in the Antebellum South* (1979); Clement Eaton, *The Mind of the Old South* (1964); Drew Gilpin Faust, *A Sacred Circle: The Dilemma of the Intellectual in the Old South, 1840–1860* (1977); Bertram Wyatt-Brown, *Southern Honor: Ethics and Behavior in the Old South* (1982); John McCardell, *The Idea of a Southern Nation: Southern Nationalists and Southern Nationalism, 1830–1860* (1979); James Oakes, *The Ruling Race: A History of American Slaveholders* (1982); Steven M. Stowe, *Intimacy and Power: Ritual in the Lives of the Planters* (1987), and Kenneth S. Greenberg, *Masters and Statesmen: The Political Culture of American Slavery* (1985). On the relation of white society and culture to political attitudes and behavior, see two excellent studies: J. Mills Thorton, *Politics and Power in a Slave Society: Alabama, 1800–1860* (1978); and Lacy K. Ford, *The Origins of Southern Radicalism: The South Carolina Upcountry, 1800–1860* (1988).

Proslavery consciousness is treated in William Sumner Jenkins, *Pro-Slavery Thought in the Old South* (1935); George M. Fredrickson, *The Black Image in the White Mind: The Debate on Afro-American Character and Destiny, 1817–1914* (1971); Eugene D. Genovese, *The World the Slaveholders Made: Two Essays in Interpretation* (1969); and H. Shelton Smith, *In His Image, But . . . : Racism in Southern Religion, 1780–1910* (1972). Southern dissent and efforts to repress it are well covered in Carl N. Degler, *The Other South: Southern Dissenters in the Nineteenth Century* (1974).

On slave revolts, see Herbert Aptheker, *American Negro Slave Revolts* (1943), and Eugene D. Genovese, *From Rebellion to Revolution: Afro-American Slave Revolts in the Making of the Modern World* (1979). The plight of southern free blacks is covered in Ira Berlin, *Slaves Without Masters: The Free Negro in the Antebellum South* (1974), and Michael P. Johnson and James L. Roark, *Black Masters: A Free Family of Color in the Old South* (1984), while racial discrimination in the North is described in Leon Litwack, *North of Slavery: The Free Negro in the Free States, 1790–1860* (1961). On the antislavery activities of northern blacks, see Benjamin Quarles, *Black Abolitionists* (1969); Jane H. Pease and William H. Pease, *They Who Would Be Free* (1974); William S. McFeely, *Frederick Douglass* (1991), and Shirley Yee, *Black Women Abolitionists* (1992). On life in the slave quarters, see George P. Rawick, *From Sundown to Sunup: The Making of the Black Community* (1972), and Thomas L. Webber, *Deep Like Rivers: Education in the Slave Quarters, 1831–1865* (1978). Further insight into the family life of both races in the Old South can be found in Orville Vernon Burton, *In My Father's House Are Many Mansions: Family and Community in Edgefield, South Carolina* (1983).

CHAPTER
14

The Sectional Crisis

O n May 22, 1856, Representative Preston Brooks of South Carolina erupted onto the floor of the Senate with a cane in his hand. He approached Charles Sumner, the antislavery senator from Massachusetts who had recently given a fiery oration condemning the South for plotting to extend slavery to the Kansas Territory. What was worse, the speech had included insulting references to Senator Andrew Butler of South Carolina, a kinsman of Brooks. When he found Sumner seated at his desk, Brooks proceeded to batter him over the head. Amazed and stunned, Sumner made a desperate effort to rise and ripped his bolted desk from the floor. He then collapsed under a continued torrent of blows.

Sumner was so badly injured by the assault that he did not return to the Senate for three years. But his home state reelected him in 1857 and kept his seat vacant as testimony against southern brutality and "barbarism." In parts of the North that were up in arms against the expansion of slavery, Sumner was hailed as a martyr to the cause of "free soil." Brooks, denounced in the North as a bully, was lionized by his fellow Southerners. When he resigned from the House after a vote of censure had narrowly failed because of solid southern opposition, his constituents reelected him unanimously.

These contrasting reactions show how bitter sectional antagonism had become by 1856. Sumner spoke for the radical wing of the new Republican party, which was making a bid for national power by mobilizing the North against the alleged aggressions of "the slave power." Southerners viewed the very existence of this party as an insult to their section of the country and a threat to its vital interests. Sumner came closer to being an abolitionist than any other member of Congress, and nothing created greater fear and anxiety among Southerners than their belief that antislavery forces were plotting against their way of life. To many Northerners, "bully Brooks" stood for all the arrogant and violent slaveholders who were allegedly conspiring to extend their barbaric labor system. By 1856, therefore, the sectional cleavage that would lead to the Civil War had already undermined the foundations of national unity.

The crisis of the mid-1850s came only a few years after the elaborate compromise of 1850 had seemingly resolved the dispute over the future of slavery in the territories acquired as a result of the Mexican War. The renewed agitation over the extension of slavery that led to Brooks's attack on Sumner was set in motion by the Kansas-Nebraska Act of 1854. This legislation revived the sectional conflict and led to the emergence of the Republican party. From that point on, a dramatic series of events increased sectional confrontation and destroyed the prospects for a new compromise. The caning of Charles Sumner was one of these events, and violence on the Senate floor foreshadowed violence on the battlefield.

THE COMPROMISE OF 1850

The "irrepressible conflict" over slavery in the territories began in the late 1840s. The positions taken on this issue between 1846 and 1850 established the range of options that would reemerge after 1854. But during this earlier phase of the sectional controversy, the leaders of two strong national parties, each with substantial followings in both the North and the South, had a vested interest in resolving the crisis. Efforts to create uncompromising sectional parties failed to disrupt what historians call the second party system—the vigorous competition between Whigs and Democrats that had characterized elections since the 1830s. Furthermore, the less tangible features of sectionalism—emotion and ideology—were not as divisive as they would later become. Hence a fragile compromise was achieved through a kind of give-and-take that would not be possible in the changed environment of the mid-1850s.

The Problem of Slavery in the Mexican Cession

As the price of union between states committed to slavery and those in the process of abolishing it, the Founders had attempted to limit the role of the slavery issue in national politics. The Constitution gave the federal government the right to abolish the international slave trade but no definite authority to regulate or destroy the institution where it existed under state law. Although many of the Founders hoped for the

eventual demise of slavery, they provided no direct means to achieve this end except voluntary state action. These ground rules limited the effect of northern attacks on the South's peculiar institution. It was easy to condemn slavery in principle but very difficult to develop a practical program to eliminate it without defying the Constitution.

Radical abolitionists saw this problem clearly and resolved it by rejecting the law of the land in favor of a "higher law" prohibiting human bondage. In 1844, William Lloyd Garrison publicly burned the Constitution, condemning it as "A Covenant with Death, an Agreement with Hell." But Garrison spoke for a small minority dedicated to freeing the North, at whatever cost, from the sin of condoning slavery.

During the 1840s, the majority of Northerners showed that while they disliked slavery, they also detested abolitionism. They were inclined to view slavery as a backward and unwholesome institution, much inferior to their own free labor system, and could be persuaded that slaveholders were power-hungry aristocrats seeking more than their share of national political influence. But they regarded the Constitution as a binding contract between slave and free states and were likely to be prejudiced against blacks and reluctant to accept large numbers of them as free citizens. Consequently, they saw no legal or desirable way to bring about emancipation within the southern states.

But the Constitution had not predetermined the status of slavery in *future* states. Since Congress had the power to admit new states to the Union under any conditions it wished to impose, a majority could arguably require the abolition of slavery as the price of admission. An effort to use this power had led to the Missouri crisis of 1819–1820 (see Chapter 9). The resulting compromise was designed to decide future cases by drawing a line between slave and free states and extending it westward through the unsettled portions of what was then American soil. When specific territories were settled, organized, and prepared for statehood, slavery would be permitted south of the line and prohibited north of it.

This tradition of providing both the free North and the slave South with opportunities for expansion and the creation of new states broke down when new territories were wrested from Mexico in the 1840s. When Texas was admitted as a slave state, northern expansionists could still look forward to the admission of Oregon as a counterbalancing free state. But the Mexican War raised the prospect that California and New Mexico, both south of the Missouri Compromise line, would also be acquired. Since it was generally assumed in the North that Congress had the power to prohibit slavery in new territories, a movement developed in Congress to do just that.

The Wilmot Proviso Launches the Free-Soil Movement

The "Free-Soil" crusade began in August 1846, only three months after the start of the Mexican

War, when Congressman David Wilmot, a Pennsylvania Democrat, proposed an amendment to the military appropriations bill that would ban slavery in any territory that might be acquired from Mexico.

Wilmot spoke for the large number of northern Democrats who felt neglected and betrayed by the party's choice of Polk over Van Buren in 1844 and by the "pro-southern" policies of the Polk administration. Pennsylvanians like Wilmot were upset because the tariff of 1846 reduced duties to a level unacceptable to the manufacturing interests of their state. Others, especially midwesterners, were annoyed that Polk had vetoed a bill to provide federal funds for the improvement of rivers and harbors. Democratic expansionists also felt betrayed because Polk had gone back on his pledge to obtain "all of Oregon" up to 54°40′ and then had proceeded to wage war to win all of Texas. This twist in the course of Manifest Destiny convinced them that the South and its interests were dominating the party and the administration. David Wilmot spoke for many when he wrote that he was "jealous of the power of the South."

These pioneer Free-Soilers had a genuine interest in the issue actually at hand—the question of who would control and settle the new territories. Combining an appeal to racial prejudice with opposition to slavery as an institution, Wilmot defined his cause as involving the "rights of white freemen" to go to areas where they could live "without the disgrace which association with negro slavery brings on white labor." Wilmot proposed that slavery as well as settlement by free African Americans be prohibited in the territory obtained in the Mexican cession, thus giving the common folk of the North a fair chance by preventing job competition from slaves and free blacks. By linking racism with resistance to the spread of slavery, Wilmot appealed to a broad spectrum of northern opinion.

Northern Whigs backed Wilmot's Proviso because they shared his concern about the outcome of an unregulated competition between slave and free labor in the territories. Furthermore, voting for the measure provided a good outlet for their frustration at being unable to halt the annexation of Texas and the Mexican War. The preferred position of some Whig leaders was no expansion at all, but when expansion could not be avoided the northern wing of the party endorsed the view that acquisition of Mexican territory should not be used to increase the power of the slave states.

In the first House vote on the Wilmot Proviso, party lines crumbled and were replaced by a sharp sectional cleavage. Every northern congressman with the exception of two Democrats voted for the amendment, and every Southerner except two Whigs went on record against it. After passing the House, the Proviso was blocked in the Senate by a combination of southern influence and Democratic loyalty to the administration. When the appropriation bill went back to the House without the Proviso, the administration's arm-twisting succeeded in changing enough northern Democratic votes to pass the bill and thus send the Proviso down to defeat.

Reactions to the Proviso on the state and local level provided further evidence of the polarizing effect of the territorial issue. Northern state legislatures, with one exception, endorsed the Proviso, while southern orators proclaimed that its passage would insult their section and violate the principle of equality among the states by denying slaveholding citizens access to federal territories.

The end of the Mexican War, the formal acquisition of New Mexico and California, and the approaching election of 1848 gave new urgency to a search for politically feasible solutions to the crisis. The extreme alternatives—the Proviso policy of free soil and the radical southern response that slavery could be extended to any territory—threatened to destroy the national parties because there was no bisectional support for either of them.

Squatter Sovereignty and the Election of 1848

After a futile attempt was made to extend the Missouri Compromise line to the Pacific—a proposal that was unacceptable to Northerners because most of the Mexican cession lay south of the line—a new approach was devised that appealed especially to Democrats. Its main proponent was Senator Lewis Cass of Michigan, an aspirant for the party's presidential nomination. Cass, who described his formula as "squatter sovereignty," would leave the determination of the status of slavery in a territory to the actual settlers. From the beginning this proposal contained an ambiguity that allowed it to be interpreted differently in the North and the South. For northern Democrats squatter sovereignty—or "popular sovereignty" as it was later called—meant the settlers could vote slavery up or down at the first meeting of a territorial legislature. For the southern wing of the party, it meant a decision would only be made at the time a convention drew up a constitution and applied for statehood. It was in the interest of national Democratic leaders to leave this ambiguity unresolved for as long as possible.

Congress failed to resolve the future of slavery in the Mexican cession in time for the election of 1848, and the issue entered the arena of presidential politics. The Democrats nominated Cass on a platform of squatter sovereignty. The Whigs evaded the question by running General Zachary Taylor—the hero of the battle of Buena Vista—without a platform. Taylor refused to commit himself on the status of slavery in the territories, but northern Whigs favoring restriction took heart from the general's promise not to veto any territorial legislation passed by Congress. Southern Whigs went along with Taylor mainly because he was a Southerner who owned slaves and would presumably defend the interests of his native region.

Northerners who strongly supported the Wilmot Proviso—and felt betrayed that neither the Whigs nor the Democrats were supporting it—were attracted by a third party movement. In August a tumultuous convention in Buffalo nominated former president Van Buren to carry the banner of the Free-Soil party. Support for the Free-Soilers came from antislavery Whigs dismayed by their party's nomination of a slaveholder and its evasiveness on the territorial issue, disgruntled Democrats who had backed the Proviso and resented southern influence in their party, and some of the former adherents of the abolitionist Liberty party. Van Buren himself was motivated less by antislavery zeal than by bitterness at being denied the Democratic nomination in 1844 because of southern obstructionism. The founding of the Free-Soil party was the first significant effort to create a broadly based sectional party addressing itself to voters' concerns about the extension of slavery.

After a noisy and confusing campaign, Taylor came out on top, winning a majority of the elec-

The Election of 1848			
Candidate	Party	Popular Vote	Electoral Vote
Taylor	Whig	1,360,967	163
Cass	Democratic	1,222,342	127
Van Buren	Free Soil	291,263	—

toral votes in both the North and the South and a total of 1,361,000 popular votes to 1,222,000 for Cass and 291,000 for Van Buren. The Free-Soilers failed to carry a single state but did quite well in the North, coming in second behind Taylor in New York, Massachusetts, and Vermont.

Taylor Takes Charge

Once in office, Taylor devised a bold plan to decide the fate of slavery in the Mexican cession. A brusque military man who disdained political give-and-take, he tried to engineer the immediate admission of California and New Mexico to the Union as states, thus bypassing the territorial stage entirely and avoiding a congressional debate on the status of slavery in the federal domain. Under the administration's urging, California, which was filling up rapidly with settlers drawn by the lust for gold, convened a constitutional convention and applied for admission to the Union as a free state.

Instead of resolving the crisis, President Taylor's initiative only worsened it. Once it was clear that California was going to be a free state, the administration's plan aroused intense opposition in the South. Fearing that New Mexico would also be free because Mexican law had prohibited slavery there, Southerners of both parties accused the president of trying to impose the Wilmot Proviso in a new form. The prospect that only free states would emerge from the entire Mexican cession inspired serious talk of secession.

In Congress, Senator John C. Calhoun of South Carolina saw a chance to achieve his longstanding goal of creating a southern voting bloc that would cut across regular party lines. State legislatures and conventions throughout the South denounced

In this cartoon, Democrats Lewis Cass and John C. Calhoun and antislavery radicals Horace Greeley, William Lloyd Garrison, and Abby Folsom look on as Martin Van Buren, the Free-Soil party candidate in the election of 1848, attempts to bridge the chasm between the Democratic platform and that of the antislavery Whigs. The Free-Soil influence was decisive in the election; it split the New York Democratic vote, thus allowing Whig candidate Zachary Taylor to win New York and the presidency.

"northern aggression" against the rights of the slave states. As signs of southern fury increased, Calhoun rejoiced that the South had never been so "united . . . bold, and decided." In the fall and winter of 1849–1850 several southern states agreed to participate in a convention, to be held in Nashville in June, where grievances could be aired and demands made. For an increasing number of southern political leaders the survival of the Union would depend on the North's response to the demands of the southern rights movement.

Forging a Compromise

When it became clear that the president would not abandon or modify his plan in order to appease the South, independent efforts began in Congress to arrange a compromise. Hoping that he could again play the role of "great pacificator" as he had in the Missouri Compromise of 1820, Senator Henry Clay of Kentucky offered a series of resolutions meant to restore sectional harmony. He hoped to reduce tension by providing mutual concessions on a range of divisive issues. On the critical territorial question, his solution was to admit California as a free state and organize the rest of the Mexican cession with no explicit prohibition of slavery—in other words, without the Wilmot Proviso. Noting that Mexican law had already abolished slavery there, he also pointed to the arid climate of the New Mexico region, which made it unsuitable for cotton culture and slavery. He also sought to resolve

a major boundary dispute between New Mexico and Texas by granting the disputed region to New Mexico while compensating Texas through federal assumption of its state debt. As a concession to the North on another issue—the existence of slavery in the District of Columbia—he recommended prohibiting the buying and selling of slaves at auction and permitting the abolition of slavery itself with the consent of the District's white inhabitants. He also called for a more effective fugitive slave law.

The compromise plan, which was proposed in February 1850, took several months to get through Congress. One obstacle was President Taylor's firm resistance to the proposal; another was the difficulty of getting congressmen to vote for it in the form of a single package or "omnibus bill." Few politicians from either section were willing to go on record as supporting the key concessions to the *other* section. The logjam was broken in July by two crucial developments: President Taylor died and was succeeded by Millard Fillmore, who favored the compromise; and a decision was made to abandon the omnibus strategy in favor of a series of measures that could be voted on separately. After the breakup of the omnibus bill, Democrats replaced the original Whig sponsors as leaders of the compromise movement and some of Clay's proposals were modified to make them more acceptable to the South and the Democrats. Senator Stephen A. Douglas, a Democrat from Illinois, was particularly influential in maneuvering the separate provisions of the plan through Congress.

As the price of Democratic support, the popular sovereignty principle was included in the bills organizing New Mexico and Utah. Territorial legislatures in the Mexican cession were explicitly granted power over "all rightful subjects of legislation," which might include slavery. Half of the compensation to Texas for giving up its claims to New Mexico was paid directly to holders of Texas bonds, a decision that reflected intense lobbying by interested parties.

Abolition of slave auctions and depots in the District of Columbia and a new fugitive slave law were also enacted. The latter was a particularly outrageous piece of legislation. As the result of southern pressures and amendments, suspected fugitives were now denied a jury trial, the right to testify in their own behalf, and other basic constitutional rights. As a result, there were no effective safeguards against false identification by accusers or against the kidnapping of blacks who were legally free.

The compromise passed because its key measures were supported by northern Democrats, southern Whigs, and representatives of both parties from the border states. No single bill was backed by a majority of the congressmen from both sections, and few senators or representatives actually voted for the entire package. Many northern Whigs and southern Democrats thought the end result conceded too much to the other section. Doubts therefore persisted over the value of workability of a "compromise" that was really more like an armistice or a cease-fire.

Yet the Compromise of 1850 did serve for a short time as a basis for sectional peace. In southern state elections during 1850–1851 moderate coalitions won out over the radicals who viewed the compromise as a sellout to the North. But this emerging "unionism" was conditional. Southerners demanded strict northern adherence to the compromise, especially to the Fugitive Slave Law, as the price for suppressing threats of secession. In the North, the compromise was backed by virtually the entire Democratic party and by one faction of the Whigs.

The Fugitive Slave Law was unpopular in areas where abolitionism was particularly strong because it required Northerners to enforce slavery, and there were a few sensational rescues or attempted rescues of escaped slaves. In Boston in 1854, an antislavery mob led by armed abolitionists tried to free fugitive Anthony Burns from the courthouse where his extradition hearing was to take place. One of the men guarding Burns was killed but the fugitive himself could not be reached. After the hearing had declared Burns an escaped slave, he was escorted by units of the U. S. Army through a hissing and groaning crowd of twenty thousand to a waiting ship. Despite such abolitionist resistance, the Fugitive Slave Law was enforced fairly successfully in the early 1850s. Other parts of the compromise were less troublesome. In 1852, when the Democrats endorsed the compromise in their platform and the Whigs failed to condemn it in theirs, it seemed that sharp differences on the slavery issue had once again been banished from national politics.

POLITICAL UPHEAVAL, 1852–1856

The second party system—Democrats versus Whigs—survived the crisis over slavery in the Mexican cession, but in the long run the Compromise of 1850 may have weakened it. Although both national parties had been careful during the 1840s not to take stands on the slavery issue that would alienate their supporters in either section of the country, they had in fact offered voters alternative ways of dealing with the question. Democrats had endorsed headlong territorial expansion with the promise of a fair division of the spoils between slave and free states. Whigs had generally opposed annexations or acquisitions, because they were likely to bring the slavery question to the fore and threaten sectional harmony. With some shifts of emphasis and interpretation, each strategy could be presented to southern voters as a good way to protect slavery and to Northerners as a good way to contain it.

The consensus of 1852 meant the parties had to find other issues on which to base their distinctive appeals. Their failure to do so encouraged voter apathy and a disenchantment with the major parties. When the Democrats sought to revive the Manifest Destiny issue in 1854, they reopened the explosive issue of slavery in the territories. By this time, the Whigs were too weak and divided to respond with a policy of their own, and a purely sectional Free-Soil party—the Republicans—gained prominence. The collapse of the second party system released sectional agitation from the earlier constraints imposed by the competition of strong national parties.

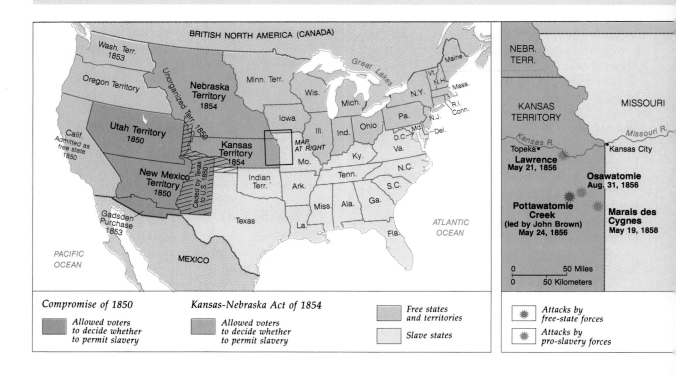

Compromise of 1850
Allowed voters to decide whether to permit slavery

Kansas-Nebraska Act of 1854
Allowed voters to decide whether to permit slavery

Free states and territories

Slave states

Attacks by free-state forces

Attacks by pro-slavery forces

The Party System in Crisis

The presidential campaign of 1852 was singularly devoid of major issues. With the slavery question under wraps, some Whigs tried to revive interest in the nationalistic economic policies that were the traditional hallmarks of their party. But convincing arguments in favor of a protective tariff, a national bank, and internal improvements were hard to make in a period of sustained prosperity. Business was thriving under the Democratic program of virtual laissez-faire.

Another tempting issue was immigration. Many Whigs were upset by the massive influx from Europe, partly because most of the new arrivals were Catholics, and the Whig following was largely evangelical Protestant. For office-seeking Whig politicians a more urgent problem was the fact that immigrants voted overwhelmingly for their Democratic opponents. The Whig leadership was divided on whether to compete with the Democrats for the immigrant vote or

respond to the prejudices of the party rank and file by calling for restrictions on immigrant voting rights.

The Whigs nominated General Winfield Scott of Mexican War fame who supported the faction that resisted nativism and sought to broaden the appeal of the party. The fact that Scott's daughters were being raised as Catholics was publicized to demonstrate his good intentions toward immigrant communities. This strategy backfired and contributed to disaster at the polls. For the most part, Catholic immigrants retained their Democratic allegiance, and some nativist Whigs apparently sat out the election to protest their party's disregard of their cultural prejudices.

But the main cause for Scott's crushing defeat was the support he lost in the South when he allied himself with the dominant northern anti-slavery wing of the party, led by Senator William Seward of New York. The Democratic candidate, Franklin Pierce of New Hampshire, was a color-

CAUTION!!

COLORED PEOPLE
OF BOSTON, ONE & ALL,

You are hereby respectfully CAUTIONED and advised, to avoid conversing with the

Watchmen and Police Officers of Boston,

For since the recent ORDER OF THE MAYOR & ALDERMEN, they are empowered to act as

KIDNAPPERS
AND
Slave Catchers,

And they have already been actually employed in KIDNAPPING, CATCHING, AND KEEPING SLAVES. Therefore, if you value your LIBERTY, and the *Welfare of the Fugitives* among you, *Shun* them in every possible manner, as so many *HOUNDS* on the track of the most unfortunate of your race.

Keep a Sharp Look Out for KIDNAPPERS, and have TOP EYE open.
APRIL 24, 1851.

THEODORE PARKER'S PLACARD

Placard written by Theodore Parker and printed and posted by the Vigilance Committee of Boston after the rendition of Thomas Sims to slavery in April, 1851.

This abolitionist broadside was printed in response to a ruling that fugitive slave Thomas Sims must be returned to his master in Georgia.

less nonentity compared to his rival, but he ran up huge majorities in the Deep South where Whigs stayed home in massive numbers. He also edged out Scott in most of the free states. In the most one-sided election since 1820, Pierce received 254 electoral votes from 27 states while Scott carried only 4 states with 42 electoral votes. This outcome revealed the Whig party was in deep trouble because it lacked a program that would distinguish it from the Democrats and would appeal to voters in both sections of the country.

Despite their overwhelming victory in 1852, the Democrats had reasons for anxiety about the loyalty of their supporters. Because the major parties had ceased to offer clear-cut alternatives to the electorate, voter apathy or alienation was a

The Election of 1852

Candidate	Party	Popular Vote	Electoral Vote
Pierce	Democratic	1,601,117	254
Scott	Whig	1,385,453	42
Hale	Free Soil	155,825	

growing trend in the early 1850s. The Democrats won majorities in both North and South in 1852 primarily because the public viewed them as the most reliable supporters of the Compromise of 1850, not because of long-term party allegiance.

The Kansas-Nebraska Act Raises a Storm

In January 1854, Senator Stephen A. Douglas proposed a bill to organize the territory west of Missouri and Iowa. Since this region fell within the area where slavery had been banned by the Missouri Compromise, Douglas anticipated objections from Southerners concerned about the creation of more free states. To head off this opposition and keep the Democratic party united, Douglas disregarded the compromise line and sought to set up the territorial government in Kansas and Nebraska on the basis of popular sovereignty, relying on the alleged precedent set in the Compromise of 1850.

Douglas wanted to organize the Kansas-Nebraska area quickly because he was a strong supporter of the expansion of settlement and commerce. Along with other midwestern promoters of the economic development of the frontier, he hoped a railroad would soon be built to the Pacific with Chicago (or another midwestern city) as its eastern terminus. A long controversy over the status of slavery there would slow down the process of organization and settlement and might hinder the building of the railroad through the territory in question. As a leader of the Democratic party, Douglas also hoped his Kansas-Nebraska bill would revive the spirit of Manifest Destiny that had given the party cohesion and electoral success in the mid-1840s (see Chapter 12). As the main spokesman for a new expansionism, he expected to win the Democratic nomination and the presidency.

The price of southern support, Douglas soon discovered, was the addition of an amendment explicitly repealing the Missouri Compromise. Although he realized this would "raise a hell of a storm," he reluctantly agreed. In this more provocative form, the bill made its way through Congress, passing the Senate by a large margin and the House by a narrow one. The vote in the House showed that Douglas had split his party rather than uniting it; exactly half of the northern Democrats voted against the legislation.

The Democrats who broke ranks created the storm Douglas had predicted but underestimated. A manifesto of "independent Democrats" denounced the bill as "a gross violation of a sacred pledge." A memorial from three thousand New England ministers described it as a craven and sinful surrender to the slave power. For many Northerners, probably a majority, the Kansas-Nebraska Act was an abomination because it permitted the possibility of slavery in an area where it had previously been prohibited. Except for an aggressive minority, Southerners had not pushed for such legislation or even shown much interest in it, but now they felt obligated to support it. Their support provided deadly ammunition to those who were seeking to convince the northern public that there was a conspiracy to extend slavery.

Douglas's bill had a catastrophic effect on sectional harmony. It repudiated a compromise that many in the North regarded as a binding sectional compact, almost as sacred and necessary to the survival of the Union as the Constitution itself. In defiance of the whole compromise tradition, it made a concession to the South on the issue of slavery extension without providing an equivalent concession to the North. It also shattered the fragile sectional accommodation of 1850 and made future compromises less likely. From now on, northern sectionalists would be fighting to regain what they had lost, while Southerners would battle to maintain rights already conceded.

The act also destroyed what was left of the second party system. The already weakened and tottering Whig party totally disintegrated when its congressional representation split cleanly along sectional lines on the Kansas-Nebraska issue. The Democratic party survived, but its ability to act as a unifying national force was seriously

impaired. Northern desertions and southern gains (resulting from the recruitment of proslavery Whigs) combined to destroy the sectional balance within the party and place it under firm southern control.

The congressional elections of 1854 revealed the political chaos Douglas had created. In the North, "anti-Nebraska" coalitions of Whigs, dissident Democrats, and Free-Soilers swept regular Democrats out of office. Most congressmen who had voted for the act were decisively defeated, and sixty-six of the ninety-one House seats held by northern Democrats were lost to opponents running under various labels. In some states, these anti-Democratic coalitions would evolve directly into a new and stronger Free-Soil party—the Republicans. In the Deep South, however, the Democrats routed the remaining Whigs and came close to ending two-party competition on the state level.

The furor over Kansas-Nebraska also doomed the efforts of the Pierce administration to revive an expansionist foreign policy. Pierce and Secretary of State William Marcy were committed to acquiring Cuba from Spain. In October 1854, the American ministers to England, France, and Spain met in Ostend, Belgium, and drew up a memorandum for the administration urging acquisition of Cuba by any means necessary—including force, if Spain refused to sell the island. The "Ostend Manifesto" became public in the midst of the controversy resulting from the Kansas-Nebraska Act, and those Northerners who were convinced that the administration was trying to extend slavery to the Great Plains were enraged to discover it was also scheming to fulfill the southern expansionist dream of a "Caribbean slave empire." The resulting storm of protest forced Pierce and his cohorts to abandon their scheme.

An Appeal to Nativism: The Know-Nothing Episode

The collapse of the Whigs created the opening for a new political party. The anti-Nebraska coalitions of 1854 suggested that such a party might be organized on the basis of northern opposition to the extension of slavery to the territories. Before such a prospect could be realized, however, an alternative emerged in the form of a major political movement based on hostility to immi-

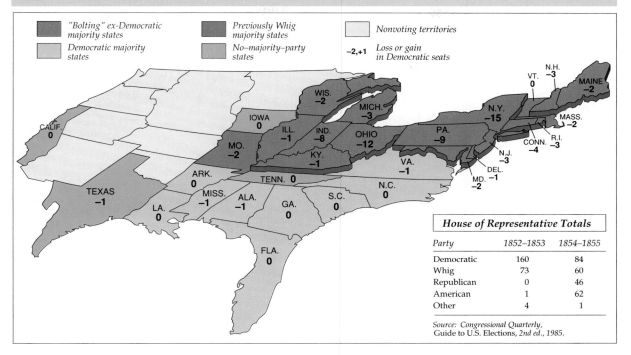

Congressional Election of 1854

The impact of the Kansas–Nebraska Act was immediately felt in the election of 1854. "Anti-Nebraska" coalitions and the fledgling Republican party made gains in the North; the Democrats remained dominant in the South.

Legend:
- "Bolting" ex-Democratic majority states
- Democratic majority states
- Previously Whig majority states
- No–majority–party states
- Nonvoting territories
- −2,+1 Loss or gain in Democratic seats

State values:
N.H. −3, VT. 0, MAINE −2, WIS. −2, MICH. −3, N.Y. −15, MASS. −2, IOWA 0, ILL. −1, IND. −8, OHIO −12, PA. −9, CONN. −4, R.I. −3, CALIF. 0, MO. −2, KY. −1, N.J. −3, DEL., VA. −1, MD. −1, ARK. 0, TENN. 0, N.C. 0, TEXAS −1, MISS. −1, ALA. −1, GA. 0, S.C. 0, LA. 0, FLA. 0

House of Representative Totals

Party	1852–1853	1854–1855
Democratic	160	84
Whig	73	60
Republican	0	46
American	1	62
Other	4	1

Source: Congressional Quarterly, Guide to U.S. Elections, *2nd ed., 1985.*

grants. For a time, it appeared that the Whigs would be replaced by a nativist party rather than an antislavery one.

Massive immigration of Irish and Germans (see Chapter 12), most of whom were Catholic, led to increasing tension between ethnic groups during the 1840s and early 1850s. The fact that most of these new arrivals clustered in their own separate communities or neighborhoods helped arouse the suspicion and distrust of older-stock Americans. Native-born and even immigrant Protestants viewed the newcomers as bearers of an alien culture. Their fears were demonstrated in bloody anti-Catholic riots, church and convent burnings, and in a barrage of propaganda and lurid literature trumpeting the menace of "popery" to the American way of life. Nativist agitators charged that immigrants were agents of a foreign despotism, based in Rome, that was bent on overthrowing the American republic.

Political nativism first emerged during the 1840s in the form of local "American" parties protesting immigrant influence in cities like New York and Philadelphia. In 1849, a secret fraternal organization, the Order of the Star-Spangled Banner, was founded in New York as a vehicle for anti-immigrant attitudes. When members were asked about the organization, they were instructed to reply, "I know nothing." The order grew rapidly in size, and in 1854 it had a membership of somewhere between 800,000 and 1,500,000. The political objective of the Know-Nothings was to extend the period of naturalization in order to undercut immigrant voting strength and to keep aliens in their place.

From 1854 to 1855 the movement surfaced as a major political force, calling itself the American party. Much of its backing came from Whigs looking for a new home, but the party also attracted some ex-Democrats. Know-Nothingism also appealed to native-born workers fearful of competition from low-paid immigrants. Many others supported the American party simply because it was an alternative for those who wanted to vote against the Democrats. In the North, Know-Nothing candidates generally opposed the

Know-Nothings often charged that immigrant voters were stealing American elections. In the cartoon above, German and Irish immigrants, represented by German beer and Irish whiskey, steal a ballot box. An anti-Know-Nothing cartoon (left) portrays the Know-Nothings as gun-wielding ruffians.

Kansas-Nebraska Act, and some of their support came from voters who were more anxious about the expansion of slavery than about the evils of immigration.

The success of the new party was so dramatic that it was compared to a hurricane. In 1854, it won complete control in Massachusetts, capturing the governorship, most of the seats in the legislature, and the entire congressional delegation. In 1855, the Know-Nothings took power in three more New England states, swept Maryland, Kentucky, and Texas, and emerged as the principal opposition to the Democrats everywhere else, except in the Midwest. By late 1855, the Know-Nothings showed every sign of displacing the Whigs as the nation's second party.

Yet, almost as rapidly as it had risen, the Know-Nothing movement collapsed. Its demise in 1856 is one of the great mysteries of American political history. As an intersectional party, its failure is understandable enough. When the Know-Nothings attempted to hold a national convention in 1856, northern and southern delegates split on the question of slavery in the territories, showing that former Whigs were still at

odds over the same issue that had destroyed their old party.

Less clear is why the Know-Nothings failed to become the major opposition party to the Democrats in the North. The most persuasive explanation is that their Free-Soil Republican rivals, who were seeking to build a party committed to the containment of slavery, had an issue with wider appeal. In 1855 and 1856, the rate of immigration declined noticeably, and the conflict in Kansas heightened the concern about slavery. Consequently, voters who opposed both the expansion of slavery and unrestricted immigration were inclined to give priority to the former threat.

But the movement's peculiar "antipolitical" character also contributed to its rapid disintegration. Besides being a manifestation of real ethnic tensions, Know-Nothingism was a grass-roots protest against the professional politicians who had led the Whig and Democratic parties. Concern about the effects of immigration on American culture and society would not have generated a mass political movement with the initial appeal of the Know-Nothings had it not been for the belief that political bosses were recruiting immigrant voters for their own corrupt purposes. As a result of the Know-Nothing party's distrust of conventional politics, most of its spokesmen and elected officials were neither professional politicians nor established community leaders. The very inexperience that was a major source of voter attraction to the party may have made it hard for it to develop organizational discipline. With inexperienced leaders and a lack of cohesion, the Know-Nothings were unable to make effective use of power once they had it. When voters discovered the Know-Nothings also *did* nothing, or at least failed to do anything that a more conventional party could not do better, they looked for more competent and experienced leadership.

Kansas and the Rise of the Republicans

The new Republican party was an outgrowth of the anti-Nebraska coalition of 1854. The Republican name was first used in midwestern states like Wisconsin and Michigan where Know-Nothingism failed to win a mass following. A new political label was required because Free-Soil Democrats—who were an especially important element in the midwestern coalitions—refused to march under the Whig banner or even support any candidate for high office who called himself a Whig.

When the Know-Nothing party split over the Kansas-Nebraska issue in 1856, most of the northern nativists went over to the Republicans. The Republican argument that "the slave power conspiracy" was a greater threat to American liberty and equality than an alleged "popish plot" proved to be persuasive. But nativists did not have to abandon their ethnic and religious prejudices to become Republicans. Although Republican leaders generally avoided taking anti-immigrant positions—some out of strong principle and others with an eye to the votes of the foreign born—the party showed a clear commitment to the values of native-born evangelical Protestants. On the local level Republicans generally supported causes that reflected an anti-immigrant or anti-Catholic bias—such as prohibition of the sale of alcoholic beverages, observance of the Sabbath, defense of Protestant Bible-reading in schools, and opposition to state aid for parochial education.

Unlike the Know-Nothings, the Republican party was led by seasoned professional politicians, men who had earlier been prominent Whigs or Democrats. Adept at organizing the grass roots, building durable coalitions, and employing all the techniques of popular campaigning, they built up an effective party apparatus in an amazingly short time. By late 1855, the party had won the adherence of two-thirds of the anti-Nebraska congressmen elected in 1854. One of these, Nathaniel Banks of Massachusetts, was elected Speaker of the House after a lengthy struggle. By early 1856, the new party was well established throughout the North and was preparing to make a serious bid for the presidency.

Underlying the rapid growth of the Republican party was the strong and growing appeal of its position on slavery in the territories. Republicans viewed the unsettled West as a land of opportunities, a place to which the ambitious and hard-working could migrate in the hope of improving their social and economic position. Free soil would serve as a guarantee of free competition or "the right to rise." But if slavery was permitted to expand, the rights of "free labor" would be denied. Slaveholders would monopolize the best land, use their slaves to compete unfairly with free white workers, and block efforts at commercial and industrial development. They could also use their political control of new western states to dominate the federal government in the interest of the "slave power." Some Republicans also pandered to race prejudice: they presented their policy as a way to keep African Americans out of the territories, thus preserving the new lands for exclusive white occupancy.

Although passage of the Kansas-Nebraska Act raised the territorial issue and gave birth to the Republican party, it was the turmoil associated with attempts to implement popular sovereignty in Kansas that kept the issue alive and enabled the Republicans to increase their following throughout the North. When Kansas was organized in the fall of 1854, a bitter contest began for control of the territorial government. New Englanders founded an Immigrant Aid Society to encourage antislavery settlement in Kansas, but the earliest arrivals came from slaveholding Missouri. In the first territorial elections, proslavery settlers were joined at the polls by thousands

FREE STATE CONVENTION!

All persons who are favorable to a union of effort, and a permanent organization of all the Free State elements of Kansas Territory, and who wish to secure upon the broadest platform the co-operation of all who agree upon that point, are requested to meet at their several places of holding elections, in their respective districts on the 25th of August, instant, at one o'clock, P. M., and appoint five delegates to each representative to which they are entitled in the Legislative Assembly, who shall meet in general Convention at

Big Springs, Wednesday, Sept. 5th '55,

at 10 o'clock A.M., for the purpose of adopting a Platform upon which all may act harmoniously who prefer Freedom to Slavery. The nomination of a Delegate to Congress, will also come up before the General Convention.

Let no sectional or party issue distract or prevent the perfect co-operation of Free State men. Union and harmony are absolutely necessary to success. The pro-slavery party are fully and effectually organized. No pure nor minor issues divide them. And to contend against them successfully, we also must be united.—Without prudence and harmony of action we are certain to fail. Let every man then do his duty and we are certain of victory.

All Free State men, without distinction, are earnestly requested to take immediate and effective steps to insure a full and correct representation for every District in the Territory. "United we stand; divided we fall."

By order of the Executive Committee of the Free State Party of the Territory of Kansas, as per resolution of the Mass Convention in session at Lawrence. Aug 15th and 16th, 1855.

J. K. GOODIN, Sec'y.   C. ROBINSON, Chairman.
                                                    Herald of Freedom, Print.

Free-Soil settlers in Kansas, outraged by the manner in which the proslavery forces had seized control of the territorial legislature, called for a new state convention to draw up a constitution outlawing slavery.

of Missouri residents who crossed the border to vote illegally. The result was a decisive victory for the slave-state forces. The legislature then proceeded to pass laws that not only legalized slavery but made it a crime to speak or act against it.

Settlers favoring free soil, most of whom came from the Midwest, were already a majority of the actual residents of the territory when the fraudulently elected legislature stripped them of their civil liberties. To defend themselves and their convictions, they took up arms and established a rival territorial government under a constitution that outlawed slavery. The Pierce administration and its appointed local agents refused to recognize this "free-state" initiative, but Republicans in Congress defended it.

A small-scale civil war then broke out between the rival regimes, culminating in May 1856 when proslavery adherents raided the free-state capital at Lawrence. Portrayed in Republican propaganda as "the sack of Lawrence," this incursion resulted in substantial property damage but no loss of life. More bloody was the reprisal carried out by the antislavery zealot John Brown. Upon hearing of the attack on Lawrence, Brown and a few followers murdered five proslavery settlers in cold blood. During the next few months—until a truce was arranged by an effective territorial governor in the fall of 1856—a hit-and-run guerrilla war raged between free-state and slave-state factions. (See the map of "Bleeding Kansas" on p. 408.)

The national Republican press had a field day with the events in Kansas, exaggerating the extent of the violence but correctly pointing out that the federal government was favoring rule by a proslavery minority over a Free-Soil majority. Since the "sack of Lawrence" occurred at about the same time that Charles Sumner was assaulted on the Senate floor, the Republicans launched their 1856 campaign under the twin slogans, "Bleeding Kansas and Bleeding Sumner." The image of an evil and aggressive "slave power," using violence to deny constitutional rights to its opponents, was a potent device for arousing northern sympathies and winning votes.

Sectional Division in the Election of 1856

The Republican nominating convention revealed the strictly sectional nature of the new party. Only a handful of the delegates from the slave states attended, and all of these were from the upper South. The platform called for liberation of Kansas from the slave power and congressional prohibition of slavery in all territories. The nominee was John C. Frémont, explorer of the West and participant in the conquest of California during the Mexican War.

The Democratic convention dumped the ineffectual Pierce, passed over Stephen A. Douglas, and nominated James Buchanan of Pennsylvania who had a long career in public service. The Democrats' platform endorsed popular sovereignty in the territories. The American party, a Know-Nothing remnant that survived mainly as the rallying point for anti-Democratic conservatives in the border states and parts of the South, chose ex-President Millard Fillmore as its standard-bearer and received the backing of those northern Whigs who resisted the Republicans and hoped to revive the tradition of sectional compromise.

The election was really two separate races—one in the North, where the main contest was between Frémont and Buchanan, and the other in the South, which pitted Fillmore against Buchanan. The Pennsylvania Democrat emerged victorious because he outpolled Fillmore in all but one of the slave states (Maryland) and edged out Frémont in four crucial northern states—Pennsylvania, New Jersey, Indiana, and Illinois. But the Republicans did remarkably well for a party that was scarcely more than a year old. Frémont won eleven of the sixteen free states,

The Election of 1856

Candidate	Party	Popular Vote	Electoral Vote
Buchanan	Democratic	1,832,955	174
Frémont	Republican	1,339,932	114
Fillmore	American (Know-Nothing)	871,731	8

sweeping the upper North with substantial majorities and winning a larger proportion of the northern popular vote than either of his opponents. Since the free states had a substantial majority in the electoral college, a future Republican candidate could win the presidency simply by overcoming a slim Democratic edge in the lower North.

In the South, where the possibility of a Frémont victory had revived talk of secession, the results of the election brought a momentary sense of relief tinged with deep anxiety about the future. The very existence of a sectional party committed to restricting the expansion of slavery constituted an insult to the Southerners' way of life. That such a party was genuinely popular in the North was profoundly alarming and raised grave doubts about the security of slavery within the Union. The continued success of a unified Democratic party under southern control was widely viewed as the last hope for the maintenance of sectional balance and "southern rights."

THE HOUSE DIVIDED, 1857–1860

The sectional quarrel deepened and became virtually "irreconcilable" in the years between the election of Buchanan in 1856 and Lincoln's victory in 1860. A series of incidents provoked one side or the other, heightened the tension, and ultimately brought the crisis to a head. Behind the panicky reaction to public events lay a growing sense that the North and South were so different in culture and so opposed in basic interests that they could no longer coexist in the same nation.

Cultural Sectionalism

Signs of cultural and intellectual cleavage had appeared well before the triumph of sectional politics. In the mid-1840s, the Methodist and Baptist churches split into northern and southern denominations because of differing attitudes toward slaveholding. Presbyterians remained formally united, but had informal northern and southern factions that went their separate ways on the slavery issue. Instead of unifying Americans around a common Protestant faith, the churches became nurseries of sectional discord. Increasingly, northern preachers and congregations denounced slaveholding as a sin, while most southern church leaders rallied to a biblical defense of the peculiar institution and became influential apologists for the southern way of life. Prominent religious leaders—such as Henry Ward Bseecher, George B. Cheever, and Theodore Parker in the North, and James H. Thornwell, Leonidas Polk, and Bishop Stephen Elliott in the South, were in the forefront of sectional mobilization. As men of God, they helped to turn political questions into moral issues and reduced the prospects for a compromise.

American literature also became sectionalized during the 1840s and 1850s. Southern men of letters, including such notable figures as the novelist William Gilmore Simms and Edgar Allan Poe, wrote proslavery polemics. Popular novelists produced a flood of "plantation romances" that seemed to glorify southern civilization and sneer at that of the North. The notion that planter "cavaliers" were superior to money-grubbing Yankees was the message that most Southerners derived from the homegrown literature they read. In the North, prominent men of letters—Emerson, Thoreau, James Russell Lowell, and Herman Melville—expressed strong antislavery sentiments in prose and poetry, particularly after the outbreak of the Mexican War.

Literary abolitionism reached a climax in 1852 when Harriet Beecher Stowe published *Uncle Tom's Cabin,* an enormously successful novel (it sold more than 300,000 copies in a single year) that fixed in the northern mind the image of the slaveholder as a brutal Simon Legree. Much of its emotional impact came from the book's portrayal of slavery as a threat to the family and the cult of domesticity. When the saintly Uncle Tom was sold away from his adoring wife and children,

The Webb family, pictured here, toured the northern states giving dramatic readings from Uncle Tom's Cabin.

Northerners shuddered with horror and some Southerners felt a painful twinge of conscience.

Southern defensiveness gradually hardened into cultural and economic nationalism. Northern textbooks were banished from southern schools in favor of those with a prosouthern slant; young men of the planter class were induced to stay in the South for higher education rather than going North (as had been the custom); and a movement developed to encourage southern industry and commerce as a way of reducing dependence on the North. Almost without exception, prominent southern educators and intellectuals of the late 1850s rallied behind southern sectionalism, and many even endorsed the idea of a southern nation.

The Dred Scott Case

When James Buchanan was inaugurated on March 4, 1857, the dispute over the legal status of slavery in the territories was an open door through which sectional fears and hatreds could enter the political arena. Buchanan hoped to close that door by encouraging the Supreme Court to resolve the constitutional issue once and for all.

The Court was then about to render its decision in the case of *Dred Scott* v. *Sandford*. The plaintiff in this case was a Missouri slave whose owner had taken him to the Wisconsin Territory for a time during the 1830s. After his master's death, Dred Scott sued for his freedom on the grounds that he had lived for many years in an area where slavery had been outlawed by the Missouri Compromise. The Supreme Court could have decided the issue on the narrow ground that a slave was not a citizen and therefore had no right to sue in federal courts. But President-elect Buchanan, in the days just before the inauguration, encouraged the Court to render a broader decision that would settle the slavery issue.

On March 6, Chief Justice Roger B. Taney announced that the majority had ruled against Scott. One argument on which the Court based its decision was that Scott could not sue because he was not a citizen. Taney, in fact, argued further that *no* African American—slave or free—could be a citizen of the United States. But the real bombshell in the decision was the ruling that Dred Scott would not have won his case even if he had been a legal plaintiff. His residence in the Wisconsin Territory established no right to freedom because Congress had no power to prohibit slavery there. The Missouri Compromise was thus declared unconstitutional and so, implicitly, was the main plank in the Republican platform.

If Buchanan expected the decision to reduce sectional tension, he was quickly proved wrong. In the North, and especially among Republicans, the Court's verdict was viewed as the latest diabolical act of the "slave power conspiracy." The charge that the decision was a political maneuver rather than a disinterested interpretation of the Constitution was supported by strong circumstantial evidence. Five of the six judges who voted in the majority were proslavery Southerners, and their resolution of the territorial issue was close to the extreme southern rights position long advocated by John C. Calhoun.

Republicans denounced the decision as "a wicked and false judgment" and as "the greatest crime in the annals of the republic"; but they stopped short of openly defying the Court's authority. Instead, they argued on narrow technical grounds that the decision as written was not binding on Congress and that a ban on slavery in the territories could still be enacted. The decision actually helped the Republicans build support; it lent credence to their claim that an aggressive slave power was dominating all branches of the federal government and attempting to use the Constitution to achieve its own ends.

The Lecompton Controversy

While the Dred Scott case was being decided, leaders of the proslavery faction in Kansas concluded that the time was ripe to draft a constitution and seek admission to the Union as a slave state. Since settlers with free-state views were now an overwhelming majority in the territory, the success of the plan required a rigged, gerrymandered election for convention delegates. When it became clear the election was fixed, the free-staters boycotted it, and the proslavery forces won complete control. The resulting constitution, drawn up at Lecompton, was certain to be voted down if submitted to the voters in a fair election, and sure to be rejected by Congress if no referendum of any kind was held.

To resolve this dilemma, supporters of the constitution decided to permit a vote on the slavery provision alone, giving the electorate the narrow choice of allowing or forbidding the future importation of slaves. Since there was no way to vote for total abolition, the free-state majority again resorted to a boycott, thus allowing ratification of a constitution that protected existing slave property and placed no restriction on importations. Meanwhile, however, the free-staters had finally gained control of the territorial legislature, and they authorized a second referendum on the constitution as a whole. This time, the proslavery party boycotted the election, and the Lecompton constitution was overwhelmingly rejected.

The Lecompton constitution was such an obvious perversion of popular sovereignty that Stephen A. Douglas spoke out against it. But the Buchanan administration, bowing to southern pressure, tried to push it through Congress in early 1858, despite overwhelming evidence that the people of Kansas did not wish to enter the Union as a slave state. The resulting debate in Congress became so bitter and impassioned that it provoked fistfights between northern and southern members. Buchanan, using all the political muscle he could command, scored a victory in the Senate, which voted to admit Kansas under the Lecompton constitution on March 23. But on April 1, a coalition of Republicans and Douglas Democrats defeated the bill in the House. A face-saving compromise was then devised. It allowed resubmission of the constitution to the Kansas voters on the pretext that a change in the provisions for a federal land grant was required. Finally, in August 1858, the people of Kansas killed the Lecompton constitution when they voted it down by a margin of 6 to 1.

The Lecompton controversy aggravated the sectional quarrel and made it truly "irreconcilable," if it had not been before. For Republicans, the administration's frantic efforts to admit Kansas as a slave state exposed southern dominance of the Democratic party and the lengths to which proslavery conspirators would go to achieve their ends. Among Democrats, the affair opened a deep rift between the followers of Douglas and the backers of the Buchanan administration. Because of his anti-Lecompton stand, Douglas gained popularity in the North, and some Republicans even flirted with the idea of joining forces with him against the "doughfaces"—prosouthern Democrats—who stood with Buchanan.

For Douglas himself, however, the affair was a disaster; it destroyed his hopes of uniting the Democratic party and defusing the slavery issue through the application of popular sovereignty. What had happened in Kansas suggested that popular sovereignty in practice was an invitation to civil war. Furthermore, the Dred Scott decision implied that the voters of a territory could not legally decide the fate of slavery at any time before the constitution-making stage. Hence, the interpretation of popular sovereignty favored in the North was undermined, and Southerners could insist on full protection of their right to own human property in all federal territories. For his stand against Lecompton, Douglas was denounced as a traitor in the South, and his hopes of being elected president were seriously diminished.

Debating the Morality of Slavery

Douglas's more immediate problem was to win reelection to the Senate from Illinois in 1858. Here he faced surprisingly tough opposition from

The Case of Dred and Harriet Scott

Dred Scott and his wife Harriet both wanted to be free; the North and South both wanted to find a way to end the crisis over slavery in the territories. On March 6, 1857, the U. S. Supreme Court handed down a decision that fulfilled neither the Scotts's nor the nation's hopes. The case began when the Scotts brought suit against the widow of Dred's owner, an army doctor who had taken Dred from the slave state of Missouri to Fort Snelling in the Wisconsin Territory, where slavery was prohibited by the Missouri Compromise. It was there that Dred and Harriet Scott met and married. Two daughters were born to the couple. In their suit, filed after they had been brought back to Missouri, the Scotts argued that the doctor, now the master of Harriet as well, had made them permanently free by taking them into free territory. Ten years after it was filed, the case made its way to the Supreme Court.

The first question faced by the Court was whether or not Dred Scott was a citizen. Until 1857, neither the wording of the Constitution nor the legal system of the young nation had addressed the question of black citizenship. It was clear enough that slaves were denied the rights of citizenship, including the right to sue in court, but the status of free blacks had not been estab-

The case of Dred and Harriet Scott resulted in a Supreme Court ruling that has been called the "most overturned decision in history."

lished. Although lower courts considered Dred Scott at least a potential citizen by allowing his case to proceed, the Supreme Court attempted to make such a future eventuality impossible by ruling that all blacks, free or slave, were barred from citizenship.

Chief Justice Roger B. Taney's opinion stated that at the time the Constitution was framed, blacks were "so far inferior" to whites "that they had no rights which the white man was bound to respect; and . . . might justly and lawfully be reduced to slavery for their benefit." Although he did not say so, Taney implied that such racist judgments still

418

prevailed. Astute contemporaries agreed. "Judge Taney's decision, infamous as it is," said Susan B. Anthony, "is but the reflection of the spirit and practice of the American people, North as well as South." One scholar concluded that the Scott decision contained "an argument weak in its law, logic, history, and factual accuracy"; but that in its ruling on black citizenship the Taney Court interpreted the Constitution with its finger on the public pulse. Only when the Civil War had helped them consolidate power did Republicans begin the process of giving blacks the legal basis for full citizenship that culminated in the Fourteenth Amendment to the Constitution.

A second constitutional question rising out of the Dred Scott case was whether Congress had the authority to prohibit slavery in the federal territories. Because Dred Scott had lived in a territory for four years, his suit for freedom rested in part on the contention that residency in a territory where slavery was outlawed by the Missouri Compromise had rendered him legally free. In response, the Court ruled that Congress had *unconstitutionally* restricted slavery when it enacted the Missouri Compromise. Although the Constitution authorized Congress "to dispose of and make all needful rules and regulations respecting the territory or other property belonging to the United States," Chief Justice Taney argued that this passage

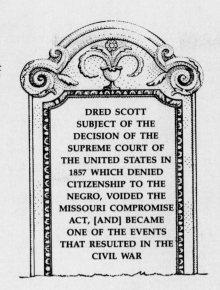

DRED SCOTT SUBJECT OF THE DECISION OF THE SUPREME COURT OF THE UNITED STATES IN 1857 WHICH DENIED CITIZENSHIP TO THE NEGRO, VOIDED THE MISSOURI COMPROMISE ACT, [AND] BECAME ONE OF THE EVENTS THAT RESULTED IN THE CIVIL WAR

allowed Congress to set rules for the disposal of federally owned land, not to determine the rights of those who settled there. Furthermore, Taney maintained, the clause affected only land already owned or claimed when the Constitution was signed in 1789. If the first construction is somewhat flimsy, the second argument verges on the absurd. (Taney found authority elsewhere in the Constitution for Congress to govern the territories—namely in the power to admit new states.) Such was the questionable logic that the Supreme Court used in 1857 to invalidate the Missouri Compromise.

A third major constitutional issue raised by the case pertained to the limits of judicial sovereignty, and, unlike the other issues, it has never been fully resolved. In its famous *Marbury v. Madison* ruling in 1803, the Court under Chief Justice John

Marshall effectively claimed the role of final arbiter of constitutional questions. But in *Dred Scott* the Court went much further. For the first time, it actually invalidated a major piece of legislation. The Court could have voided Scott's suit, resolved the immediate question of Scott's status, and left the territorial issue to the politicians. But tremendous pressure was brought to bear on the justices to convince them that they had the duty and the authority to settle the most stubborn and divisive political problem of the time. It turned out that they did not settle it; the Dred Scott ruling has been called the "most overturned decision in history." Nonetheless, it forced the country to confront great constitutional issues and marked the beginning of a dynamic movement toward judicial activism.

Ironically, Dred and Harriet Scott were freed by a later master soon after the Court handed down its decision. They remained in St. Louis, where Dred worked as a hotel porter and Harriet as a laundress. They both died of natural causes on the eve of the Civil War.

Several of the descendents of their daughter Lizzie, including Dred Scott Madison, a great-grandson of Dred and Harriet, attended a centennial observation in 1957 during which Dred Scott's grave was at long last marked with a headstone. The inscription on the stone, shown above, notes the political and constitutional importance of the case.

Stephen Douglas, the "Little Giant" from Illinois, won election to Congress when he was just thirty years old. Four years later he was elected to the Senate.

dence of a plot to extend and nationalize slavery and called for defensive actions to stop the spread of slavery and place it "where the public mind shall rest in the belief that it is in the course of ultimate extinction." He tried to link Douglas to this proslavery conspiracy by pointing to his rival's unwillingness to take a stand on the morality of slavery, to his professed indifference about whether slavery was voted up or down in the territories. For Lincoln, the only security against the triumph of slavery and the slave power was moral opposition to human bondage. Neutrality on the moral issue would lull the public into accepting the expansion of slavery until it was legal everywhere.

In the subsequent series of debates that focused national attention on the Illinois senatorial contest, Lincoln hammered away at the theme that Douglas was a covert defender of slavery because he was not a principled opponent of it. Douglas responded by accusing Lincoln of endangering the Union by his talk of putting slavery on the path to extinction. Denying that he was an abolitionist, Lincoln made a distinction between tolerating slavery in the South, where it was protected by the Constitution, and allowing it to expand to places where it could legally be prohibited. Restriction of slavery, he argued, had been the policy of the Founders, and it was Douglas and the Democrats who had departed from the great tradition of containing an evil that could not be immediately eliminated.

In the debate at Freeport, Illinois, Lincoln questioned Douglas on how he could reconcile popular sovereignty with the Dred Scott decision. The Little Giant, as Douglas was called by his admirers, responded that slavery could not exist without supportive legislation to sustain it and that territorial legislatures could simply refrain from passing a slave code if they wanted to keep it out. Historians formerly believed that Douglas's "Freeport doctrine" suddenly alienated his southern supporters. In truth, Douglas's anti-Lecompton stand had already undermined his popularity in the slave states. But the Freeport speech undoubtedly hardened southern opposition to his presidential ambitions.

Douglas's most effective debating point was to charge that Lincoln's moral opposition to slavery implied a belief in racial equality. Lincoln, facing an intensely racist electorate, vigorously denied

a Republican candidate who, in defiance of precedent, was nominated by a party convention. (At this time senators were elected by state legislatures.) Douglas's rival, former Whig Congressman Abraham Lincoln, set out to convince the voters that Douglas could not be relied on to oppose the extension of slavery, even though he had opposed the admission of Kansas under a proslavery constitution.

In the famous speech that opened his campaign, Lincoln tried to distance himself from his opponent by taking a more radical position. He argued that the nation had reached the crisis point in the struggle between slavery and freedom: "'A house divided against itself cannot stand.' I believe this government cannot endure, permanently half *slave* and half *free*." He then described the chain of events between the Kansas-Nebraska Act and the Dred Scott decision as evi-

Abraham Lincoln, shown here in his first full-length portrait. Although Lincoln lost the contest for the Senate seat in 1858, the Lincoln–Douglas debates established his reputation as a rising star of the Republican party.

this charge and affirmed his commitment to white supremacy. He would grant blacks the right to the fruits of their own labor while denying them the "privileges" of citizenship. This was an inherently contradictory position, and Douglas made the most of it.

Although Republican candidates for the state legislature won a majority of the popular votes, the Democrats carried more counties and thus were able to send Douglas back to the Senate. Lincoln lost an office, but he won respect in Republican circles throughout the country. By stressing the moral dimension of the slavery question and undercutting any possibility of fusion between Republicans and Douglas Democrats, he had sharpened his party's ideological focus and had stiffened its backbone against any temptation to compromise its Free-Soil position.

The South's Crisis of Fear

After Kansas became a free territory instead of a slave state in August 1858, the issue of slavery in the territories lost some of its immediacy, although it continued to carry great emotional and symbolic meaning. The remaining unorganized areas, which were in the Rockies and northern Great Plains, were unlikely to attract slaveholding settlers. Southern expansionists still dreamed of annexations in the Caribbean and Central America but had little hope of winning congressional approval. Nevertheless, Southerners continued to demand the "right" to take their slaves into the territories, and Republicans persisted in denying it to them. Although the Republicans repeatedly promised they would not interfere with slavery where it already existed, Southerners refused to believe them and interpreted their unyielding stand against the extension of slavery as a threat to southern rights and security.

A chain of events in late 1859 and early 1860 turned southern anxiety about northern attitudes and policies into a "crisis of fear." These events alarmed slaveholders because they appeared to threaten their safety and dominance in a new and direct way.

The first of these incidents was John Brown's raid on Harpers Ferry, Virginia, in October 1859. Brown had shown in Kansas that he was prepared to use violence against the enemies of black freedom. He had the appearance and manner of an Old Testament prophet and thought of himself as God's chosen instrument "to purge this land with blood" and eradicate the sin of slaveholding. On October 16, he led eighteen men from his band of twenty-two (which included five free blacks) across the Potomac River from his base in Maryland and seized the federal arsenal and armory in Harpers Ferry.

Brown's aim was to arm the local slave population to commence a guerrilla war from havens in the Appalachians that would eventually extend to the plantation regions of the lower South. But the neighboring slaves did not rise up to join him, and Brown's raiders were driven out of the armory and arsenal by the local militia and forced to take refuge in a fire-engine house. There they held out until their bastion was stormed by a force of U. S. Marines commanded by Colonel Robert E. Lee. In the course of the fighting, ten of Brown's men were killed or mortally wounded, along with seven of the townspeople and soldiers who opposed them.

The wounded Brown and his remaining followers were put on trial for treason against the state of Virginia. The subsequent investigation produced evidence that several prominent north-ern abolitionists had approved of Brown's plan—to the extent they understood it—and had raised money for his preparations. This seemed to confirm southern fears that abolitionists were actively engaged in fomenting slave insurrection.

After Brown was sentenced to be hanged, Southerners were further stunned by the outpouring of sympathy and admiration that his impending fate aroused in the North. As Ralph Waldo Emerson expressed it, Brown "would make the gallows as glorious as the cross." His actual execution on December 2 completed Brown's elevation to the status of a martyred saint of the antislavery cause. The day of his death was marked in parts of the North by the tolling of bells, the firing of cannons, and the holding of memorial services.

Although Republican politicians were quick to denounce John Brown for his violent methods, Southerners interpreted the wave of northern sympathy as an expression of the majority opinion and the Republicans' "real" attitude. According to historian James McPherson, "They identified Brown with the abolitionists, the abolitionists with Republicans, and Republicans with the whole North." Within the South, the raid and its aftermath touched off a frenzy of fear, repres-

John Brown, shown here barricaded at Harpers Ferry with his followers and hostages, looked on his fight against slavery as a holy campaign ordained by God. In his last speech to the court before his execution for conviction of murder, promoting slave insurrection, and treason, Brown proclaimed, "Now, if it is deemed necessary that I should forfeit my life for the furtherance of the ends of justice and mingle my blood further with the blood of my children and with the blood of millions in this slave country whose rights are disregarded by wicked, cruel, and unjust enactments—I say, let it be done!"

sion, and mobilization. Witch-hunts searched for the agents of a vast imagined conspiracy to stir up slave rebellion; vigilance committees were organized in many localities to resist subversion and ensure control of slaves, and orators pointed increasingly to secession as the only way to protect southern interests.

Brown was scarcely in his grave when another set of events put southern nerves on edge once more. Next to abolitionist-abetted rebellions, the slaveholding South's greatest fear was that the nonslaveholding majority would turn against the master class and the solidarity of southern whites behind the peculiar institution would crumble. When Congress met to elect a Speaker of the House on December 5, the Republican candidate—John Sherman of Ohio—was bitterly denounced by Southerners because he had endorsed as a campaign document Hinton R. Helper's *Impending Crisis of the South.* Helper's book, which called on lower-class whites to resist planter dominance and abolish slavery in their own interest, was regarded by slaveholders as even more seditious than *Uncle Tom's Cabin,* and they feared the spread of "Helperism" among poor whites almost as much as they feared the effect of "John Brownism" on the slaves.

The ensuing contest over the speaker's office lasted almost two months. As the balloting went on, southern congressmen threatened secession if Sherman was elected, and feelings became so heated that some representatives began to carry weapons on the floor of the House. Since the Republicans did not have an absolute majority and needed the votes of a few members of the American party, it eventually became clear that Sherman could not be elected, and his name was withdrawn in favor of a moderate Republican who had refrained from endorsing Helper's book. The impasse over the speakership was thus resolved, but the contest helped persuade Southerners that the Republicans were committed to stirring up class conflict among southern whites.

Republicans' identification with Helper's ideas may have been decisive in convincing many conservative planters that a Republican victory in the presidential election of 1860 would be intolerable. Anxiety about the future allegiance of nonslaveholding whites had been growing during the 1850s because of changes in the pattern of slave ownership. A dramatic rise in the price of slaves was undermining the ambition of slaveless farmers to join the slaveholding ranks. During the decade, the proportion of white heads of families owning slaves had shrunk from 30 to 25 percent in all the slave states and from 50 to 40 percent in the cotton belt of the lower South. Perceiving in this trend the seeds of class conflict, proslavery extremists had called for the reopening of the Atlantic slave trade as a way to reduce the price of slaves and make them more widely available. Although the interest of large owners in preserving the appreciated value of their human property had helped prevent this "proslavery crusade" from gaining broad support, many slaveholders were concerned about the social and political consequences of their status as a shrinking minority. Even those most strongly committed to the Union were terrified by the prospect that a Republican party in control of the federal government would use its power to foster "Helperism" among the South's nonslaveholding majority.

The Election of 1860

The Republicans, sniffing victory and generally insensitive to the depth of southern feeling against them, met in Chicago on May 16 to nominate a presidential candidate. The initial front-runner, Senator William H. Seward of New York, had two strikes against him: he had a reputation for radicalism and a long record of strong opposition to the nativist movement. What a majority of the delegates wanted was a less controversial nominee who could win two or three of the northern states that had been in the Democratic column in 1856. Abraham Lincoln met their specifications: he was from Illinois, a state the Republicans needed to win, he had a more moderate image than Seward, and he had kept his personal distaste for Know-Nothingism to himself. In addition, he was a self-made man, whose rise from frontier poverty to legal and political prominence embodied the Republican ideal of equal opportunity for all. After trailing Seward by a large margin on the first ballot, Lincoln picked up enough strength on the second to pull virtually even and was nominated on the third.

The platform, like the nominee, was meant to broaden the party's appeal in the North. Although a commitment to halt the expansion of

slavery remained, economic matters received more attention than they had in 1856. With an eye on Pennsylvania, the delegates called for a high protective tariff; other planks included endorsement of free homesteads, which was popular in the Midwest and among working men, and federal aid for internal improvements, especially a transcontinental railroad. The platform was cleverly designed to bring most ex-Whigs into the Republican camp while also accommodating enough renegade Democrats to give the party a solid majority in the northern states.

The Democrats failed to present a united front against this formidable challenge. When the party first met in the sweltering heat of Charleston in late April, Douglas commanded a majority of the delegates but was unable to win the two-thirds required for nomination because of unyielding southern opposition. He did succeed in getting the convention to endorse popular sovereignty as its slavery platform, but the price was a walkout by Deep South delegates who favored a federal slave code for the territories.

Unable to agree on a nominee, the convention adjourned to reconvene in Baltimore in June. The next time around, a fight developed over whether to seat newly selected pro-Douglas delegations from some Deep South states in place of the bolters from the first convention. When the Douglas forces won most of the contested seats, another and more massive southern walkout took place. The result was a fracture of the Democratic party. The delegates who remained nominated Douglas and reaffirmed the party's commitment to popular sovereignty, while the bolters convened elsewhere to nominate John Breckinridge of Kentucky on a platform of federal protection for slavery in the territories.

By the time the campaign was underway, four parties were running presidential candidates. In addition to the Republicans, the Douglas Democrats, and the "Southern Rights" Democrats, a remnant of conservative Whigs and Know-Nothings nominated John Bell of Tennessee under the banner of the Constitutional Union party. Taking no explicit stand on the issue of slavery in the territories, the Constitutional Unionists tried to represent the spirit of sectional accommodation that had led to compromise in 1820 and 1850. In effect, the race became a separate two-party contest in each section: in the North the real choice was between Lincoln and Douglas, and in the South the only candidates with a fighting chance were Breckinridge and Bell. Douglas alone tried to carry on a national campaign, gaining some support in every state, but actually winning only in Missouri.

When the results came in, the Republicans had achieved a stunning victory. By gaining the electoral votes of all the free states except a fraction of New Jersey's, Lincoln won a decisive majority—180 to 123 over his combined opponents. In the North, his 54 percent of the popular vote annihilated Douglas. In the South, where Lincoln

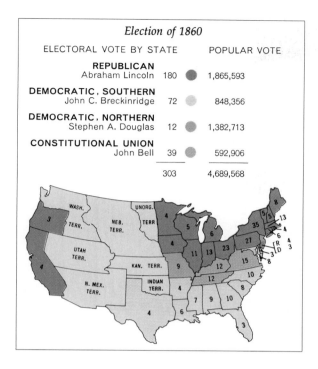

Election of 1860

ELECTORAL VOTE BY STATE		POPULAR VOTE
REPUBLICAN Abraham Lincoln	180	1,865,593
DEMOCRATIC, SOUTHERN John C. Breckinridge	72	848,356
DEMOCRATIC, NORTHERN Stephen A. Douglas	12	1,382,713
CONSTITUTIONAL UNION John Bell	39	592,906
	303	4,689,568

EXPLAINING THE CRISIS

Generations of historians have searched for the underlying causes of the crisis leading to disruption of the Union but have failed to agree on exactly what they were. Some have stressed the clash of economic interests between agrarian and industrializing regions. But this interpretation does not reflect the way people at the time expressed their concerns. The main issues in the sectional debates of the 1850s were whether slavery was right or wrong and whether it should be extended or contained. Disagreements over protective tariffs and other economic measures benefiting one section or the other were clearly secondary. Furthermore, it has never been clear why the interests of northern industry and those of the South's commercial agriculture were irreconcilable. From a purely economic point of view, there was no necessity for producers of raw materials to go to war with those who marketed or processed them.

Another group of historians have blamed the crisis on "irresponsible" politicians and agitators on both sides of the Mason-Dixon line. Public opinion, they argue, was whipped into a frenzy over issues that competent statesmen could have resolved. But this viewpoint has been sharply criticized for failing to acknowledge the depths of feeling that could be aroused by the slavery question and for underestimating the obstacles to a peaceful solution.

The dominant modern view is that the crisis was rooted in profound ideological differences over the morality and utility of slavery as an institution. Most interpreters are now agreed that the roots of the conflict lay in the fact that the South was a slave society and determined to stay that way, while the North was equally committed to a free labor system. In the words of historian David Potter, "slavery really had a polarizing effect, for the North had no slaveholders—at least not of resident slaves—and the South had virtually no abolitionists." No other differences divided the regions in this decisive way, and it is hard to imagine that secessionism would have developed if the South had followed the North's example and abolished slavery in the postrevolutionary period.

Nevertheless, the existence or nonexistence of slavery will not explain why the crisis came when it did and in the way that it did. Why did the con-

was not even on the ballot, Breckinridge triumphed everywhere except in Virginia, Kentucky, and Tennessee, which went for Bell and the Constitutional Unionists. The Republican strategy of seeking power by trying to win decisively in the majority section was brilliantly successful. Although less than 40 percent of those who went to the polls throughout the nation actually voted for Lincoln, his support in the North was so solid that he would have won in the electoral college even if his opponents had been unified behind a single candidate.

Most Southerners saw the result of the election as a catastrophe. A candidate and a party with no support in their own section had won the presidency on a platform viewed as insulting to southern honor and hostile to vital southern interests. Since the birth of the republic, Southerners had either sat in the White House or exerted considerable influence over those who did. Those days might now be gone forever. Rather than accepting permanent minority status in American politics and facing the resulting dangers to black slavery and white "liberty," the political leaders of the lower South launched a movement for immediate secession from the Union.

A "Wide-Awakes" torchlight parade in New York City, 1860. In the presidential campaign of 1860, the Republicans organized their supporters into "Wide-Awake Clubs," whose uniformed members marched in small towns and large cities to drum up support for Lincoln and a Republican victory.

flict become "irreconcilable" in the 1850s and not earlier or later? Why did it take the form of a political struggle over the future of slavery in the territories? Adequate answers to both questions require an understanding of political developments that were not directly caused by tensions over slavery.

By the 1850s, the established Whig and Democratic parties were in trouble partly because they no longer offered the voters clear-cut alternatives on the economic issues that had been the bread and butter of politics during the heyday of the second party system. This situation created an opening for new parties and issues. After the Know-Nothings failed to make attitudes toward immigrants the basis for a political realignment, the Republicans used the issue of slavery in the territories to build the first successful sectional party in American history. They called for "free

soil" rather than freedom for blacks because abolitionism conflicted with the northern majority's commitment to white supremacy and its respect for the original constitutional compromise that established a hands-off policy toward slavery in the southern states. For Southerners, the Republican party now became the main issue, and they fought against it from within the Democratic party until it ceased to function as a national organization in 1860.

If politicians seeking new ways to mobilize an apathetic electorate are seen as the main instigators of sectional crisis, the reasons that certain appeals were more effective than others must still be uncovered. Why did the slavery extension issue arouse such strong feelings in the two sections during the 1850s? The same issue had arisen earlier and had proved adjustable, even in 1820 when the second party system—with its vested interest in compromise—had not yet emerged. If the expansion of slavery had been as vital and emotional a question in 1820 as it was in the 1850s, the declining Federalist party would presumably have revived in the form of a northern sectional party adamantly opposed to the admission of slave states to the Union.

Ultimately, therefore, the crisis of the 1850s must be understood as having a deep social and cultural dimension as well as a purely political one. In *Uncle Tom's Cabin,* Harriet Beecher Stowe personified the cultural conflict in her depiction of two brothers with similar personalities, one of whom settled in Vermont "to rule over rocks and stones" and the other in Louisiana "to rule over men and women." The first became a deacon in the church, a member of the local abolition society, and, despite his natural authoritarianism, the adherent of "a democratic theory." The second became indifferent to religion, openly aristocratic, a staunch defender of slavery, and an extreme racist—"he considered the negro, through all possible gradations of color, as the intermediate link between man and animals." Stowe's comparison may have been biased, but she showed a good understanding of how the contrasting environments of slavery and freedom could lead very similar men to have sharply conflicting views of the world.

This divergence in basic beliefs and values had increased and become less manageable between the 1820s and the 1850s. Both sections continued to profess allegiance to the traditional "republican" ideals of individual liberty and independence, and both were strongly influenced by evangelical religion. But differences in the way each region developed economically and socially transformed a common culture into two conflicting cultures. In the North a rising middle class adapted to the new market economy with the help of an evangelical Christianity that sanctioned self-discipline and social reform (see Chapter 11). The South, on the other hand, embraced slavery as a foundation for the liberty and independence of whites. Its evangelicalism encouraged personal piety but not social reform and gave only limited attention to building the kind of personal character that made for commercial success. The notion that white liberty and equality depended on resistance to social and economic change and—to get to the heart of the

CHRONOLOGY

1846   David Wilmot introduces proviso banning slavery in the Mexican cession

1848   Free-Soil party is founded • Zachary Taylor (Whig) elected president, defeating Lewis Cass (Democrat) and Martin Van Buren (Free-Soil)

1849   California seeks admission to the Union as a free state

1850   Congress debates sectional issues and enacts Compromise of 1850

1852   Harriet Beecher Stowe publishes *Uncle Tom's Cabin* • Franklin Pierce (Democrat) elected president by a large majority over Winfield Scott (Whig)

1854   Congress passes Kansas-Nebraska Act, repealing Missouri Compromise • Republican party founded in several northern states • Anti-Nebraska coalitions score victories in congressional elections in the North

1854–1855   Know-Nothing party achieves stunning successes in state politics

1854–1856   Free-state and slave-state forces struggle for control of Kansas Territory

1856   Preston Brooks assaults Charles Sumner on Senate floor • James Buchanan wins presidency despite strong challenge in the North from John C. Frémont.

1857   Supreme Court decides Dred Scott case and legalizes slavery in all territories

1858   Congress refuses to admit Kansas to Union under the proslavery Lecompton constitution • Lincoln and Douglas debate slavery issue in Illinois

1859   John Brown raids Harpers Ferry, is captured and executed

1859–1860   Fierce struggle takes place over election of a Republican as Speaker of the House (December–February)

1860   Republicans nominate Abraham Lincoln for presidency (May) • Democratic party splits into northern and southern factions with separate candidates and platforms (June) • Lincoln wins the presidency over Douglas, Breckinridge, and Bell.

matter—on continuing to have enslaved blacks to do menial labor became more deeply entrenched.

When politicians appealed to sectionalism during the 1850s, therefore, they could evoke conflicting views of what constituted the good society. The South—with its allegedly idle masters, degraded unfree workers, and shiftless poor whites—seemed to a majority of Northerners to be in flagrant violation of the Protestant work ethic and the ideal of open competition in "the race of life." From the dominant southern point of view, the North was a land of hypocritical money-grubbers who denied the obvious fact that the virtue, independence, and liberty of free citizens was only possible when dependent laboring classes—especially racially inferior ones—were kept under the kind of rigid control that only slavery could provide. According to the ideology of northern Republicans, the freedom of the individual depended on equality of opportunity for everyone; in the minds of southern sectionalists, it required that part of the population be enslaved. Once these contrary views of the world had become the main themes of political discourse, sectional compromise was no longer possible.

Recommended Reading

The best general account of the politics of the sectional crisis is David M. Potter, *The Impending Crisis, 1848–1861* (1976). This well-written and authoritative work combines a vivid and detailed narrative of events with a shrewd and detailed interpretation of them. A provocative analysis of the party system in crisis is Michael F. Holt, *The Political Crisis of the 1850s* (1978). Holt incorporates the social-scientific approaches and methods of the "new political history." The most important studies of northern political sectionalism are Eric Foner, *Free Soil, Free Labor, Free Men: The Ideology of the Republican Party Before the Civil War* (1970), and William E. Gienapp, *The Origins of the Republican Party, 1852–1856* (1987), on the Republican party generally, and Don E. Fehrenbacher, *Prelude to Greatness: Lincoln in the 1850s* (1962), on Lincoln's rise to prominence. On the background of southern separatism, see William W. Freehling, *The Road to Disunion: Secessionists at Bay, 1776–1854* (1990); and William L. Barney, *The Road to Secession: A New Perspective on the Old South* (1972).

Additional Bibliography

The most detailed and thorough discussion of the events leading up to the Civil War is Allan Nevins, *The Ordeal of the Union*, vols. 1–4 (1947–1950). More concise efforts to cover the same ground are Avery Craven, *The Coming of the Civil War*, 2d ed. (1957); John Niven, *The Coming of the Civil War, 1837–1861* (1990); and Bruce Levine, *Half Slave and Half Free: The Roots of the Civil War* (1992). Craven has also produced an extensive study of southern responses to the events of the crisis period in *The Growth of Southern Nationalism, 1848–1861* (1953).

There are good books on most of the specific political events and personalities of the period. On developments between 1846 and 1850, see Chaplain W. Morrison, *Democratic Politics and Sectionalism: The Wilmot Proviso Controversy* (1967), and Holman Hamilton, *Prologue to Conflict: The Crisis and Compromise of 1850* (1964). Enforcement of the fugitive slave law is the subject of Stanley W. Campbell, *The Slave Catchers* (1970). The rise of antislavery politics in the 1840s and 1850s is well described in Richard H. Sewell, *Ballots for Freedom: Antislavery Politics in the United States, 1837–1860* (1976). Eugene H. Berwanger, *The Frontier Against Slavery: Western Anti-Negro Prejudice in the Slavery Extension Controversy* (1967), stresses the role of racial attitudes in the Free-Soil movement. Insights into the origin and nature of the Republican party—specifically its relation to nativism—can be derived from Ronald P. Formisano, *The Birth of Mass Political Parties: Michigan, 1827–1861* (1971); Michael F. Holt, *Forging a New Majority: The Formation of the Republican Party in Pittsburgh, 1848–1860* (1969); and Dale Baum, *The Civil War Party System: The Case of Massachusetts, 1848–1876* (1984). On nativism generally, see Ray Allen Billington, *The Protestant Crusade, 1800–1860* (1938). The best treatment of the Know-Nothing movement is Tyler Anbinder, *Nativism and Slavery: The Northern Know-Nothings and the Politics of the 1850s* (1992). James A. Rawley, *Race and Politics: "Bleeding Kansas" and the Coming of the Civil War* (1969), deals with the struggle over slavery in the Kansas Territory. Stephen A. Douglas, a key participant in the crisis of the 1850s, is the subject of a major biography by Robert W. Johannsen: *Stephen A. Douglas* (1973). David Donald, *Charles Sumner and the Coming of the Civil War* (1960), puts another important political figure into context. Don E. Fehrenbacher, *The Dred Scott Case: Its Significance in American Law and Politics* (1978), is the definitive work on the subject. The best treatment of the Lecompton controversy and its significance can be found in Kenneth M. Stampp, *America in 1857: A*

Nation on the Brink (1990). An incisive analysis of the "great debates" is Harry V. Jaffa, *Crisis of the House Divided: An Interpretation of the Lincoln-Douglas Debates* (1959). A stimulating psychoanalytic interpretation of the Lincoln-Douglas rivalry is George B. Forgie, *Patricide in the House Divided: A Psychological Interpretation of Lincoln and His Age* (1979). Roy Franklin Nichols, *The Disruption of American Democracy* (1948), treats the breakdown of the Democratic party between 1856 and 1860. On John Brown and his raid, see Stephen B. Oates, *To Purge This Land with Blood: A Biography of John Brown* (1970). Stephen A. Channing, *Crisis of Fear: Secession in South Carolina,* (1970), details the hysteria that seized one southern state after Brown's raid. On the controversy over Helper's inflammatory book, see the introduction to Hinton R. Helper, *The Impending Crisis of the South: How to Meet It,* edited by George M. Fredrickson (1968).

Perspectives on the intellectual, social, and cultural aspects of the sectional conflict can be derived from William R. Taylor, *Cavalier and Yankee: The Old South and American National Character* (1961); John McCardell, *The Idea of a Southern Nation: Southern Nationalists and Southern Nationalism, 1830–1860* (1979); Major L. Wilson, *Space and Freedom: The Quest for Nationality and the Irrepressible Conflict* (1974); Paul C. Nagel, *One Nation Indivisible: The Union in American Thought* (1964); Donald G. Mathews, *Slavery and Methodism: A Chapter in American Morality, 1780–1845* (1965); and Ronald T. Takaki, *A Pro-Slavery Crusade: The Agitation to Reopen the African Slave Trade* (1971). See also works cited in the bibliographies of earlier chapters dealing with evangelicalism, abolitionism, and proslavery arguments.

LAW & SOCIETY II

The Beecher-Tilton Adultery Trial

Public Image Versus Private Conduct

There were no tickets left for the trial. City policemen guarded the door to the Brooklyn city courthouse. Citizens of Brooklyn and New York thronged against the cordon, clamoring to be allowed in. Every now and then someone would wend his or her way to the front of the crowd, show a harried policeman a ticket, and the officers would part just enough to let the ticketholder through.

Inside the courtroom, the judge was preparing to allow the opening arguments to commence. He sternly warned the still-settling audience that he would not tolerate outbursts or demonstrations of sentiment from them. Nevertheless, the trial, which lasted from January through June of 1875, was repeatedly interrupted, especially by applause when the defendant, the Reverend Mr. Henry Ward Beecher, ridiculed the charges brought against him—charges of adultery. Theodore Tilton, one of Beecher's old friends and a member of his congregation, was suing the minister for having an illicit affair with his wife, Mrs. Elizabeth Tilton.

Beecher, of the famous Beecher family, was then the most prominent minister in the country. The father of the family, Lyman Beecher, had been an influential minister during the early part of the nineteenth century, leading a wing of the revivalist movement to bring religion to the mass of Americans. Henry's sister Catharine wrote tremendously popular tracts advocating expanded roles for women. Another sister Harriet, who wrote under her married name of Stowe, was, in President Lincoln's words, "the little lady who started this big war," with her antislavery novel *Uncle Tom's Cabin*. Henry Ward Beecher was himself something of an antislavery activist, popular for having held auctions at which benevolent Northerners could buy slaves into freedom. His published sermons sold by the thousands. But he

was most famous for simply playing his role as the outspoken, charismatic, and ever-popular preacher and public personality, Henry Ward Beecher. Following in his father's footsteps (in method if not in doctrine), Beecher tried to adapt religion to the changing times.

At the time of the trial, only ten years had passed since the end of the Civil War. Middle-class white Northerners—the members of Beecher's congregation and readership—had difficulty reconciling themselves to the drastic changes that were afoot. There were new amendments to the Constitution, reshaping the language of the rights of citizens of the United States. Some people argued that those rights ought to apply not only to the newly freed class of black Americans, but also to the much larger class of free white women, who as yet could not vote or own property as easily as men. In addition to those problems, on the eve of the war Charles Darwin's book *On the Origin of Species* had made its first appearance, sending shock waves through the literate circles of Britain and America, and undermining religious authority on both sides of the Atlantic.

Beecher addressed these issues within the familiar and comfortable language of liberal Protestant Christianity. He presented Darwinian evolution as a benevolent metaphor for the advance of Christian civilization. Evolution thus became progress. He advocated women's rights in a relatively conservative way: like his sister Catharine, he believed women's virtues should be strengthened in order to make the home and the family stronger, not so women could become independent of men and the family.

In the middle of the nineteenth century, Brooklyn was still a separate city from New York. No bridge yet spanned the East River. When Beecher came to Brooklyn, he dedicated himself to reaching as wide an audience as possible. He wanted to bring all the community into his church. He believed he could do that by making himself into a public personality, making the congregation feel they knew him and could trust him. Consequently Beecher always phrased his sermons in colloquial language, and he had Plymouth Church constructed so the audience could sit all around the pulpit. This made the church "perfect," as Beecher said, "because it was built on a principle,—the principle of social and personal magnetism, which emanates reciprocally from a speaker and a close throng of hearers." To achieve his effect, he needed to be near his audience, and his audience needed to be near him, so they could see his whole body, and feel his "magnetic influence."

Beecher made himself into a public figure, a kind of modern celebrity. He acted as the moral and intellectual voice of a large urban community. It was Beecher's prominence and importance that made the trial such a public event. Furthermore, the trial occurred during the last years of the Grant administration, in which the president's personal secretary and some members of his cabinet had already been implicated in scandalous dealings. The war hero president stood accused of surrounding himself with scoundrels and of being unable to govern effectively. Would Beecher become another great man laid low?

Theodore Tilton edited a leading religious newspaper and was a liberal activist, working in the women's rights and abolition movements. He was an old friend and ally of Beecher's; the minister had presided at the marriage of Tilton and his wife Elizabeth. During the Civil War, Beecher and Tilton worked together to join antislavery forces and women's rights advocates into a single organization, the American Equal Rights Association. At a speech in 1866 Beecher linked the two groups, saying "suffrage is the inherent right of mankind" (which, in his mind, included women as well). As Reconstruction wore on, however, some reformers began to argue that those who stood for equal rights ought to focus first on the newly freed slaves, because this was, after all, "the Negro's hour."

This argument occasioned a split in the women's movement. Some women's activists believed they ought to put off their hopes for female suffrage until black suffrage had been secured. Others believed women should not wait, but must push forward with their own agenda. The split became permanent when Congress passed the Fifteenth Amendment, which read "The right of citizens of the United States to vote shall not be denied or abridged by the United States or by any State on account of race, color, or previous condition of servitude." The criterion of sex was conspicuously absent. Elizabeth Cady Stanton and a large group of her supporters opposed the amendment. Soon after, Stanton and Susan B. Anthony withdrew from the Equal Rights Association to form the National Woman Suffrage Association (NWSA). Women who supported the Fifteenth Amendment (including Julia Ward Howe, author of the "Battle Hymn of the Republic") formed the American Woman Suffrage Association (AWSA). The fissure in the feminist movement led to the split between Tilton and Beecher; by 1870, Tilton had become president of the NWSA and Beecher of the rival AWSA.

Tilton's association with the NWSA brought him into contact with the more radical activists of the women's movement. Chief among these was Victoria C. Woodhull, who in 1870 became the first woman to address Congress when she presented the national legislature with a petition on behalf of woman suffrage. Woodhull and her sister, Tennie C. (sometimes "Tennessee") Claflin, founded the first all-female brokerage on Wall Street. They also started the publication *Woodhull and Claflin's Weekly,* in which they advocated the philosophy of free love. Free love, Woodhull said, meant she came into the world "with an inalienable, constitutional, and natural right to love whom I may, to love as long or as short a period as I can, to change that love everyday if I please!" In the postwar period, free love, like socialism, was widely regarded as a threat to American institutions. Woodhull was doubly notorious because she was also a radical socialist; she served a term as leader of the New York division of the Marxist Second International and also published the first English translation of Marx and Engel's *Communist Manifesto.*

Tilton apparently chose Woodhull as a confidant for his troubles. He was having difficulties with his marriage. His wife found him difficult to live with. Elizabeth Tilton had sought out her minister—Beecher—as a sympathetic ear for her unhappiness. Beecher may have advised her to separate from her husband. But Tilton was suspicious of their intimacy for other reasons as well. When he confronted his wife, she confessed—in writing—to having entertained "improper proposals" from Beecher. Tilton took the confession to a conference with Beecher and Frank Moulton, a mutual friend, who could be trusted to act as a neutral party. Beecher and Moulton persuaded Tilton that what had happened was unclear and it was in nobody's best interest to pursue the matter. Tilton tore up the confession.

Beecher visited Elizabeth Tilton, who was in her sickbed. (She had suffered a miscarriage, but she seems not to have told anyone this at the time.) Distraught at the trouble her confession seemed to have caused, she agreed to write out a retraction to quell any possible rumors. "Wearied by importunity and weakened by sickness," she wrote,

> I gave a letter inculpating my friend Henry Ward Beecher, under assurances that would remove all difficulties between me and my husband. That letter I now revoke. I was persuaded—almost forced—when I was in a weakened state of mind. I regret it and recall all of its statements. . . . I desire to say explicitly, Mr. Beecher has never offered any improper solicitations, but has always treated me in a manner becoming a Christian gentleman.

When Tilton learned his wife had given such a letter to Beecher, he immediately worried it might be used against him. So he persuaded his wife to write yet another letter expressing this concern to Beecher. Beecher was now upset. There seemed no way to reassure Tilton. Moulton suggested that Beecher write out an apology. The minister agreed, but was too shaken to write the document himself. Moulton composed the letter, addressed to himself, which Beecher then signed:

My Dear Friend Moulton:

> I ask through you Theodore Tilton's forgiveness, and I humble myself before him as I do before my God. He would have been a better man in my circumstances than I have been. I can ask nothing except that he will remember all the other hearts that will ache. I will not

> plead for myself. I even wish I were dead, but others must live and suffer.

> I will die before any one but myself shall be implicated. All my thoughts are running toward my friends, toward the poor child lying there and praying with her folded hands. She is guiltless, sinned against, bearing the transgression of another. Her forgiveness I have. I humbly pray to God that he may put it into the heart of her husband to forgive me. I have trusted this to Moulton in confidence.

Things seemed to quiet down after that, but then Victoria Woodhull published a lurid account of the affair in her *Weekly*. She hoped that by exposing Beecher, the spokesman for decent traditional institutions, especially marriage, as an adulterer and thus a hypocrite, she could advance the credibility of her cause. In this, if in nothing else, she was mistaken; she and her sister were soon arrested under the Comstock Laws, which prohibited distributing obscene materials through the mails, and held in jail until Woodhull's health broke down and she had to be released.

The two letters—Mrs. Tilton's retraction and Beecher's apology—constituted the bulk of the real evidence in the trial. Given that Mrs. Tilton had written first a confession and then a retraction and then a conditional statement regarding the retraction—and all under some coercion—and that Beecher hadn't even written his apology himself, the flimsy evidence hardly seem to prove anything. Nevertheless, as prosecuting attorney Samuel B. Morris noted in his opening remarks, "Adultery is peculiarly a crime of darkness and secrecy. Parties are rarely surprised in it, and so it not only may, but ordinarily must, be established by circumstantial evidence." If Beecher were innocent, then what exactly was he apologizing so abjectly for? What did the note mean to say when it suggested that Mrs. Tilton (the "poor child") had borne the sin of another?

The affair would never have become public knowledge had Victoria Woodhull not chosen to publish it, believing she could implicate Beecher as a free lover and thus advance her own beliefs. Even after she printed her account of the scandal, the case might never have gone to trial. But Woodhull cited Tilton as her source, and Tilton fanned the flames of scandal even as they began to die by publishing a suggestive letter in the newspapers. The leaders of Plymouth Church had had enough and called a meeting to drop Tilton from the roll of the congregation. They had a ready pretext; Tilton had not attended church in four years. Tilton, outraged, carried on an argument in print with various members of the church, all the while hinting that Beecher was guilty of illicit behavior. Finally, Beecher called an examining committee from the congregation to clear his name. Tilton appeared before the committee to accuse Beecher of "criminal intimacy" with his wife. Beecher testified to deny the charges. When Mrs. Tilton came to the stand, the committee asked her just what was the sin of which she and Beecher were so apologetic? "I do not think," she said, "that I felt that it was anything more than giving to another what was due my husband." The committee pressed her further: "When you speak of what was due to him, what do you refer to?" Mrs. Tilton replied, "Why, the all of my nature; I do not think I feel any great sin about it now. . . . I harmed [Theodore] in his pride by allowing any one else into my life at all; I think that was [the] sin."

After hearing all the testimony, the investigating committee reported that "It is proper . . . to state that the offence as alleged by Mr. Tilton during some four years and until recently to numerous persons, in writing and otherwise, was an improper suggestion or solicitation by Mr. Beecher to Mrs. Tilton. But as time passed and purposes matured, this charge passed and matured into another form and substance. . . . The charge, in effect, is that Mr. Beecher . . . committed adultery with Elizabeth R. Tilton."

Did the gradual escalation of the charge from impropriety to adultery reflect Tilton's increasingly outraged imagination, or did it reflect his initial unwillingness to level so monstrous an accusation at such a public figure? Elizabeth Tilton believed her husband was jealous because Beecher had become a closer friend to his wife than he. She never even mentioned adultery. Beecher claimed that the apology, which he had not written himself, referred only to his sorrow at the apparent bad feeling. The committee acquitted him. Tilton, in order to preserve what remained of his dignity, felt he had to sue Beecher for adultery.

The evidence the court would hear was the same as that presented to the church committee—the letters and Mrs. Tilton's and Beecher's respective denials. There was again the confusion over what the charge had actually been—improper suggestions or actual adultery. Public interest in the scandal soared. The court, in order to ensure there would be room for the participants and the jury, limited audience admission by issuing tick-

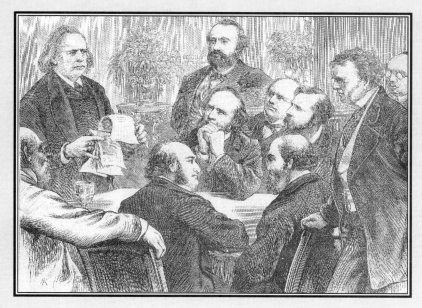

The members of the examining committee from the Plymouth Church congregation listen intently as Reverend Henry Ward Beecher reads his statement concerning his affair with Elizabeth Tilton. The committee, appointed by Beecher and composed mainly of his close friends and staunch supporters, completely exonerated Beecher.

MR. MOULTON ANSWERS AN EASY QUESTION.   MRS. TILTON GAZES AT HER HUSBAND.   MR. TILTON CATCHES A MOMENTARY GLIMPSE OF HIS WIFE.

THE TILTON-BEECHER SCANDAL CASE.—See Page 343.

The popular media of the day carried detailed accounts—complete with illustrations—of the Tilton-Beecher scandal case, as it was called. The sketches shown here of three of the principal figures in the trial, Frank Moulton, Elizabeth Tilton, and Theodore Tilton, are from a pictorial history of the trial.

ets. On the streets of New York and in cities throughout the country, Americans purchased various accounts of the infamous "Brooklyn scandal," each of which included reprints of the correspondence, profiles of the participants, and, after discussing the details of the case for many pages, a comment regretting the whole affair had come before the public. One concluded, "Ten thousand immoral and obscene novels could not have done the harm which this case has done, in teaching the science of wrong to thousands of quick-witted and curious boys and girls." Benjamin F. Butler, who had been a Union general during the Civil War and was an acquaintance of both Beecher and Tilton, summed up this sentiment when he declared, "I don't care who is right and who is wrong. This exposure will work harm. . . . The thing to be advised in the case was to keep it hidden."

Butler believed, as did others, that the country did not need to have its moral authority challenged. It was a time of crisis economically as well as politically; the country had been in a depression for two years. Beecher represented the moral rectitude of the new nation that had emerged from the Civil War. To have his authority challenged could only hurt the whole country.

Beecher apparently thought in such public terms as well. At the trial, he testified grandly that he cared but little for the damage done to him personally and spoke of "the intensity with which I [have] expressed my sorrow to lie in the sorrow of other people." Beecher probably exaggerated his unselfishness a bit, but it is true he was more concerned with the well-being of his public persona than the truth of his own behavior. When the prosecutor asked him why he did not step forth immediately to quell the rumors that surrounded him, Beecher said he was only aware of a few suspicions.

PROSECUTOR. *Well, suspicion of what?*

BEECHER. *Suspicion of moral conduct and character.*

PROSECUTOR. *Well, Sir, did you not want to clear up that suspicion?*

BEECHER. *I wanted to have it [his "moral conduct and character"] unquestioned.*

(Beecher would have preferred the affair to remain private and his public character to remain unstained.)

Butler's and Beecher's instincts appear to have been correct. The trial did nobody any good, and it probably harmed some worthy causes. Beecher was acquitted, but he never again commanded the same moral authority once his character had been questioned. Tilton had lost his job as editor of the religious newspaper and alienated his wife. Elizabeth Tilton had been forced to defend her character in public. Victoria Woodhull nearly died in jail, and free love came no closer to respectability.

The feminist movement suffered by having two of its leading figures quarreling in court over a sex scandal. In a broader sense, the cause of reform overall was hurt: the Beecher case added to the list of scandals that beset the country during the Grant administration and fueled public skepticism regarding the ability of government, institutions, and prominent leaders to act in the public interest.

For a time, the Plymouth Church community took care of Elizabeth Tilton. She earned money by privately tutoring children of the congregation. On April 16, 1878, however, the *New York Times* printed this letter, from Mrs. Tilton to her lawyer, on its front page:

> *A few weeks since, after long months of mental anguish, I told, as you know, a few friends, whom I had bitterly deceived, that the charge brought by my husband, of adultery between myself and the Rev. Henry Ward Beecher, was true, and that the lie I had lived as well the last four years had become intolerable to me . . . . I know full well the explanations that will be sought by many for this acknowledgment; a desire to return to my husband, insanity, malice, everything except the true and only one—my quickened conscience, and the sense of what is due to the cause of truth and justice.*

In the next column the *Times* printed this letter:

> *I confront Mrs. Tilton's confession with complete and absolute denial. The testimony to her own innocence and to mine which, for four years, she has made to hundreds in private and in public, before the court, in writing and orally, I declare to be true. And the allegations now made in contradiction of her uniform, solemn, and unvarying statements hitherto I utterly deny.*
>
> *I declare her to be innocent of the great transgression.*
>
> *Henry Ward Beecher*

The public's taste for the scandal appeared to have long gone, and no great consequence came of this new twist on the case. The story was replaced in the *Times* after two days by the description of Boss Tweed's funeral. Plymouth Church removed Elizabeth Tilton from its rolls four years after it had dropped her husband.

The case raises several intriguing legal questions. Most obviously, was Beecher innocent or guilty of the charges against him? The jury seems to have reached a sensible verdict given the evidence presented to them. But if Elizabeth Tilton's later confession had been before them, they might have come to a different conclusion—or would they? A second question is whether or not a jury could fairly judge a famous public figure about whom they already held strong feelings of approval or disapproval. Would a panel of middle-class Protestant males have believed the testimony of an apparently overwrought woman against a man like Beecher? Finally, what does the affair tell us about American efforts to extend the law into the most private and most intimate areas of life? Adultery was a crime, but—as this case suggests—it was rarely prosecuted successfully. Virtually unenforceable laws concerning private moral conduct are still on the books in many states. The real function of such laws may be to discourage people from violating community norms rather than to punish them for their transgressions.

Secession and the Civil War

he man elected to the White House in 1860 was striking in appearance—he was 6 feet 4 inches in height and seemed even taller because of his disproportionately long legs and his habit of wearing a high silk "stovepipe" hat. But Abraham Lincoln's previous career provided no guarantee he would tower over most of our other presidents in more than physical height. When Lincoln sketched the main events of his life for a campaign biographer in June 1860, he was modest almost to the point of self-deprecation. Especially regretting his "want of education," he assured the biographer that "he does what he can to supply the want."

Born to poor and illiterate parents on the Kentucky frontier in 1809, Lincoln received a few months of formal schooling in Indiana after the family moved there in 1816. But mostly he educated himself, reading and rereading a few treasured books by firelight. In 1831, when the family migrated to Illinois, he left home to make a living for himself in the struggling settlement of New Salem, where he worked as a surveyor, shopkeeper, and local postmaster. His brief career as a merchant was disastrous: he went bankrupt and was saddled with debt for years to come. But he eventually found a path to success in law and politics. While studying law on his own in New Salem, he managed to get elected to the state legislature. In 1837, he moved to Springfield, a growing town that offered bright prospects for a young lawyer-politician. Lincoln combined exceptional political and legal skills with a down-to-earth, humorous way of addressing jurors and voters. Consequently, he became a leader of the Whig party in Illinois and one of the most sought after of the lawyers who rode the central Illinois judicial circuit.

The high point of his political career as a Whig was one term in Congress (1847–1849). Lincoln did not seek reelection, but he would have faced certain defeat had he done so. His strong stand against the Mexican War alienated much of his constituency, and the voters expressed their disaffection in 1848 by electing a Democrat over the Whig who tried to succeed Lincoln. In 1849, President Zachary Taylor, for whom Lincoln had campaigned vigorously and effectively, failed to appoint him to a patronage job he coveted. Having been repudiated by the electorate and ignored by the national leadership of a party he had served loyally and well, Lincoln concentrated on building his law practice.

The Kansas-Nebraska Act of 1854, with its advocacy of popular sovereignty, provided Lincoln with a heaven-sent opportunity to return to politics with a stronger base of support. For the first time, his driving ambition for political success and his personal convictions about what was best for the country were easy to reconcile. Lincoln had long believed slavery was an unjust institution that should be tolerated only to the extent the Constitution and the tradition of sectional compromise required. He attacked Douglas's plan of popular sovereignty because it broke with precedents for federal containment or control of the growth of slavery. After trying in vain to rally free-soilers around the Whig standard, Lincoln threw in his lot with the Republicans, assumed leadership of the new party in Illinois, attracted national attention in his bid for Douglas's Senate seat in 1858, and turned out to have the right qualifications when the Republicans chose a presidential nominee in 1860.

After Lincoln's election provoked southern secession and plunged the nation into the greatest crisis in its history, there was understandable skepticism about him in many quarters: was the former rail-splitter from Illinois up to the responsibilities he faced? Lincoln had less experience relevant to a wartime presidency than any previous chief executive, never having been a governor, senator, cabinet officer, vice president, or high-ranking military officer. But some of his training as a prairie politician would prove extremely useful in the years ahead.

Lincoln had shown himself adept at the art of party leadership; he was able to accommodate various factions and define party issues and principles in a way that would encourage unity and dedication to the cause. Since the Republican party would serve during the war as the main vehicle for mobilizing and maintaining devotion to the Union effort, these political skills assumed crucial importance. When a majority of the party came around to the view that freeing the slaves was necessary to the war effort, Lincoln found a way to comply with their wishes while minimizing the disenchantment of the conservative minority. Lincoln held the party together by persuasion,

This Matthew Brady photograph of Abraham Lincoln was taken when Lincoln arrived in Washington for his inauguration. In his inaugural address, Lincoln appealed for preservation of the Union.

patronage, and flexible policy making; this cohesiveness was essential to Lincoln's success in unifying the nation by force.

Another reason for Lincoln's effectiveness as a war leader was that he identified wholeheartedly with the northern cause and could inspire others to make sacrifices for it. In his view, the issue in the conflict was nothing less than the survival of the kind of political system that gave men like himself a chance for high office. In addressing a special session of Congress in 1861, Lincoln provided a powerful statement of what the war was all about.

> *And this issue embraces more than the fate of these United States. It presents to the whole family of man, the question of whether a constitutional republic, or a democracy—a government of the people*

by the same people—can or cannot, maintain its territorial integrity against its own domestic foes.

The Civil War put on trial the very principle of democracy at a time when most European nations had rejected political liberalism and accepted the conservative view that popular government would inevitably collapse into anarchy. It also showed the shortcomings of a purely white man's democracy and brought the first hesitant steps toward black citizenship. As Lincoln put it in the Gettysburg Address, the only cause great enough to justify the enormous sacrifice of life on the battlefields was the struggle to preserve and extend the democratic ideal, or to ensure that "government of the people, by the people, for the people, shall not perish from the earth."

THE STORM GATHERS

Lincoln's election provoked the secession of seven states of the Deep South but did not lead immediately to armed conflict. Before the sectional quarrel would turn from a cold war into a hot one, two things had to happen: a final effort to defuse the conflict by compromise and conciliation had to fail, and the North needed to develop a firm resolve to maintain the Union by military action. Both of these developments may seem inevitable in retrospect, but for most of those living at the time it was not clear until the guns blazed at Fort Sumter that the sectional crisis would have to be resolved on the battlefield.

The Deep South Secedes

South Carolina, which had long been in the forefront of southern rights and proslavery agitation, was the first state to secede. On December 20, 1860, a convention meeting in Charleston declared unanimously that "the union now subsisting between South Carolina and other states, under the name of the 'United States of America,' is hereby dissolved." The constitutional theory behind secession was that the Union was a "compact" among sovereign states, each of which could withdraw from the Union by the vote of a

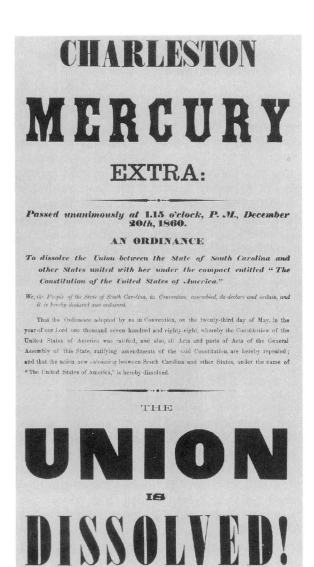

CHARLESTON MERCURY

EXTRA:

Passed unanimously at 1.15 o'clock, P. M., December 20th, 1860.

AN ORDINANCE

To dissolve the Union between the State of South Carolina and other States united with her under the compact entitled "The Constitution of the United States of America."

We, the People of the State of South Carolina, in Convention assembled, do declare and ordain, and it is hereby declared and ordained,

That the Ordinance adopted by us in Convention, on the twenty-third day of May, in the year of our Lord one thousand seven hundred and eighty-eight, whereby the Constitution of the United States of America was ratified, and also, all Acts and parts of Acts of the General Assembly of this State, ratifying amendments of the said Constitution, are hereby repealed; and that the union now subsisting between South Carolina and other States, under the name of "The United States of America," is hereby dissolved.

THE

UNION

IS

DISSOLVED!

A South Carolina newspaper announces the dissolution of the Union. South Carolina's secession was celebrated in the South with bonfires, parades, and fireworks.

convention similar to the one that had ratified the Constitution in the first place. The South Carolinians justified seceding at this time by charging that "a sectional party" had elected a president "whose opinions and purposes are hostile to slavery."

In other states of the cotton kingdom there was similar outrage at Lincoln's election but less certainty about how to respond to it. Those who advocated immediate secession by each state individually were opposed by the "cooperationists," who believed the slave states should act as a unit. If the cooperationists had triumphed, secession would have been delayed until a southern convention had agreed on it. Some of these moderates hoped a delay would provide time to extort major concessions from the North and thus remove the need for dissolving the Union. But South Carolina's unilateral action set a precedent that weakened the cooperationists' cause.

Elections for delegates to secession conventions in six other Deep South states were hotly contested. Cooperationists did especially well in Georgia, Louisiana, and Texas. But nowhere did they stop secessionists from winning a majority. By February 1, seven states had removed themselves from the Union—South Carolina, Alabama, Mississippi, Florida, Georgia, Louisiana, and Texas. In the upper South, however, calls for immediate secession were unsuccessful; majority opinion in Virginia, North Carolina, Tennessee, and Arkansas did not subscribe to the view that Lincoln's election was a sufficient reason for breaking up the Union. In these states, a moderate unionist element, deriving mainly from the old Whig party, had maintained its strength and cohesion despite the sectional crisis. Economic diversification had increased the importance of free labor and ties to the northern economy. Consequently, leaders in the border slave states were more willing than those in the lower South to seek a sectional compromise.

Without waiting for their sister slave states to the north, delegates from the Deep South met in Montgomery, Alabama, on February 4 to establish the Confederate States of America. The convention acted as a provisional government while at the same time drafting a permanent constitution. Relatively moderate leaders, most of whom had not supported secession until *after* Lincoln's election, dominated the proceedings and defeated or modified some of the pet schemes of a radical faction composed of extreme southern nationalists. Voted down were proposals to reopen the Atlantic slave trade, to abolish the three-fifths clause (in favor of counting all slaves in determining congressional representation), and to prohibit the admission of free states to the new Confederacy.

The resulting constitution was surprisingly similar to that of the United States. Most of the differences merely spelled out traditional southern interpretations of the federal charter: the central government was denied the authority to impose protective tariffs, subsidize internal improvements, or interfere with slavery in the states, and was required to pass laws protecting slavery in the territories. As provisional president and vice president, the convention chose Jefferson Davis of Mississippi and Alexander Stephens of Georgia, men who had resisted secessionist agitation. Stephens, in fact, had led the cooperationist forces in his home state. Radical "fire eaters" like William Yancey of Alabama and Robert Barnwell Rhett of South Carolina were denied positions of authority in the new government.

The moderation shown in Montgomery resulted in part from a desire to win support for the cause of secessionism in the reluctant states of the upper South, where such radical measures as reopening the slave trade were unpopular. But it also revealed something important about the nature of the separatist impulse even in the lower South. Proslavery reactionaries, who were totally lacking in reverence for the Union and wished to found an aristocratic nation very different from the democratic United States, had never succeeded in getting a majority behind them. Most Southerners had been opposed to dissolving the Union and repudiating their traditional patriotic loyalties so long as there had been good reasons to believe slavery was safe from northern interference.

Lincoln's election and the panic that ensued gave Southerners cause to fear that Northerners would no longer keep their "hands off" southern slavery; but it was clear from the actions of the Montgomery convention that the goal of the new converts to secessionism was not to establish a slaveholder's reactionary utopia. What they really wanted was to recreate the Union as it had been before the rise of the new Republican party, and they opted for secession only when it seemed clear that separation was the only way to achieve their aim. The decision to allow free states to join the Confederacy reflected a hope that much of the old Union could be reconstituted under southern direction. Some optimists even predicted that all of the North except New England would eventually transfer their loyalty to the new government.

Secession and the formation of the Confederacy thus amounted to a very conservative and defensive kind of "revolution." The only justification for southern independence on which a majority could agree was the need for greater security for the "peculiar institution." Vice President Stephens spoke for all the founders of the Confederacy

when he described the cornerstone of the new government as "the great truth that the negro is not equal to the white man—that slavery—subordination to the superior race—is his natural condition."

The Failure of Compromise

While the Deep South was opting for independence, moderates in the North and border slave states were trying to devise a compromise that would stem the secessionist tide before it could engulf the entire South. When the lame-duck Congress reconvened in December 1860, strong sentiment existed, even among some Republicans, to seek an adjustment of sectional differences. Senator John Crittenden of Kentucky presented a plan that served as the focus for discussion. Crittenden's proposal, which resembled Henry Clay's earlier compromises, advocated extending the Missouri Compromise line to the Pacific to guarantee the protection of slavery in the southwestern territories and in any territories south of the line that might be acquired in the future. It also recommended federal compensation to the owners of escaped slaves and a constitutional amendment that would forever prohibit the federal government from abolishing or regulating slavery in the states.

Initially, congressional Republicans showed some willingness to give ground and take these proposals seriously. At one point William Seward of New York, the leading Republican in the Senate, leaned toward supporting a version of the Crittenden plan. Somewhat confused about how firmly they should support the party position that slavery must be banned in all territories, Republicans in Congress turned for guidance to the president-elect, who had remained in Springfield and was refusing to make public statements on the secession crisis. An emissary brought back word that Lincoln was adamantly opposed to the extension of the compromise line. In the words of one of his fellow Republicans, he stood "firm as an oak."

This resounding "no" to the central provision of the Crittenden plan and other similar compromise proposals stiffened the backbone of congressional Republicans, and they voted against compromise in committee. Also voting against it, and thereby ensuring its defeat, were the remaining senators and congressmen of the seceding states, who had vowed in advance to support no compromise unless the majority of Republicans also endorsed it. Their purpose in taking this stand was to obtain guarantees that the northern sectional party would end its attacks on "southern rights." The Republicans did in the end agree to support Crittenden's "unamendable" amendment guaranteeing that slavery would be immune from future federal action. This action was not really a concession to the South, because Republicans had always acknowledged that the federal government had no constitutional authority to meddle with slavery in the states.

Some historians have blamed Lincoln and the Republicans for causing an unnecessary war by rejecting a compromise that would have appeased southern pride without providing any immediate practical opportunities for the expansion of slavery. But it is questionable whether approval of the compromise would have halted secession of the Deep South. If we take the secessionists at their word, they would have been satisfied with nothing less than federal protection of slavery in *all* territories and the active suppression of antislavery agitation in the North.

Furthermore, Lincoln and those who took his advice had what they considered to be very good reasons for not making territorial concessions. One of these derived from the mistaken northern notion that the secession movement was a conspiracy that reflected the will of only a minority of Southerners. Concessions would allegedly demoralize southern Unionists and moderates by showing that the "rule-or-ruin" attitude of the radical sectionalists paid dividends. It is doubtful, however, that Lincoln and the dedicated free-soilers for whom he spoke would have given ground even if they had realized the secession movement was genuinely popular in the Deep South. In their view, extending the Missouri Compromise line of 36° 30′ to the Pacific would not halt agitation for extending slavery to new areas. South of the line were Cuba and Central America, long the target of southern expansionists who dreamed of a Caribbean slave empire. The only way to resolve the crisis over the future of slavery and to reunite "the house divided" was to remove any chance that slaveholders could enlarge their domain.

Lincoln was also convinced that backing down in the face of secessionist threats would fatally undermine the democratic principle of majority rule. In his inaugural address of March 4, 1861, he recalled that during the winter many "patriotic men" had urged him to accept a compromise that would "shift the ground" on which he had been elected. But to do so would have signified that a victorious presidential candidate "cannot be inaugurated till he betrays those who elected him by breaking his pledges, and surrendering to those who tried and failed to defeat him at the polls." Making such a concession would mean that "this government and all popular government is already at an end."

And the War Came

By the time of Lincoln's inauguration, seven states had seceded, formed an independent confederacy, and seized most federal forts and other installations in the Deep South without firing a shot. Lincoln's predecessor, James Buchanan, had denied the right of secession but had also refused to use "coercion" to maintain federal authority. In January, he sent an unarmed merchant ship, the *Star of the West,* to reinforce the federal garrison in Charleston Harbor, but the vessel turned back after being fired upon. Buchanan's doubts about whether a Union held together by force was worth keeping were, for a time, widely shared in the North. Besides the business community, which was fearful of breaking commercial links with the cotton-producing South, some antislavery Republicans and abolitionists opposed coercive action because they thought the nation might be better off if "the erring sisters" of the Deep South were allowed "to depart in peace."

The collapse of compromise efforts eliminated the option of peaceful maintenance of the Union and narrowed the choices to peaceful separation or war between the sections. By early March, the tide of public opinion was beginning to shift in favor of strong action to preserve the Union. Once the business community realized conciliation would not keep the cotton states in the Union, it put most of its weight behind coercive measures, reasoning that a temporary disruption of commerce was better than the permanent loss of the South as a market and source of raw materials.

In his inaugural address, Lincoln called for a cautious and limited use of force. He would defend federal forts and installations not yet in Confederate hands but would not attempt to recapture the ones already taken. He thus tried to shift the burden for beginning hostilities to the Confederacy, which would have to attack before it would be attacked.

As Lincoln spoke, only four military installations within the seceded states were still held by U. S. forces. Two of these were in the remote Florida Keys and thus attracted little attention. The others were Fort Pickens in northern Florida, which was located in a defensible position on an island outside of the port of Pensacola, and Fort Sumter inside Charleston Harbor. Attention focused on Sumter because the Confederacy, egged on by South Carolina, was demanding the surrender of a garrison that was within easy reach of shore batteries and running low on supplies. Shortly after taking office, Lincoln was informed Sumter could not hold out much longer and that he would have to decide whether to reinforce it or let it fall.

Initially, the majority of Lincoln's cabinet opposed efforts to reinforce or provision Sumter on the grounds that it was indefensible anyway. Secretary of State Seward was so certain this would be the ultimate decision that he so advised representatives of the Confederacy. Lincoln kept his options open in regard to Sumter. On April 4, he ordered that an expedition be prepared to bring food and other provisions to the beleaguered troops in Charleston Harbor. Two days later, he discovered his orders to reinforce Fort Pickens had not been carried out. Later that same day, he sent word to the governor of South Carolina that the relief expedition was being sent.

The expedition sailed on April 8 and 9; but before it arrived, Confederate authorities decided the sending of provisions was a hostile act and proceeded to attack the fort. Early on the morning of April 12, shore batteries opened fire; the bombardment continued for forty hours without loss of life but with heavy damage to the walls of the fort. Finally, on April 13, the Union forces under Major Robert Anderson surrendered, and the Confederate flag was raised over Fort Sumter. The South had won a victory but had also assumed responsibility for firing the first shot. Lincoln had taken pains to ensure that if the South was really determined to fight for its independence, it would have to begin by taking an aggressive action.

On April 15, Lincoln proclaimed that an insurrection against federal authority existed in the Deep South and called on the militia of the loyal states to provide 75,000 troops for short-term service to put it down. Two days later, a sitting Virginia convention, which had earlier rejected secession, reversed itself and voted to join the Confederacy. Within the next five weeks, Arkansas, Tennessee, and North Carolina followed suit. These slave states of the upper South had been unwilling to secede just because Lincoln was elected, but when he called on them to provide troops to "coerce" other southern states, they had to choose sides. Believing secession was a constitutional right, they were quick to cut their ties with a government that opted for the use of force to maintain the Union and called on them to join in the effort.

In the North, the firing on Sumter evoked strong feelings of patriotism and dedication to the Union. "It seems as if we were never alive till now; never had a country till now," wrote a New Yorker; and a Bostonian noted that "I never before knew what a popular excitement can be." Stephen A. Douglas, Lincoln's former political rival, pledged his full support for the crusade against secession and literally worked himself to death rallying midwestern Democrats behind the government. By firing on the flag, the Confederacy united the North. Everyone assumed the war would be short and not very bloody. It remained to be seen whether Unionist fervor could be sustained through a long and costly struggle.

The entire Confederacy, which now moved its capital from Montgomery to Richmond, Virginia, contained only eleven of the fifteen states in which slavery was lawful. In the border slave states of Maryland, Delaware, Kentucky, and Missouri, secession was thwarted by a combination of local Unionism and federal intervention. Kentucky, the most crucial of these states, greeted the outbreak of war by proclaiming its neutrality. Kentucky eventually sided with the Union, mainly because Lincoln, who was careful to respect this tenuous neutrality, provoked the South into violating neutrality first by sending regular troops into the state. Maryland, which surrounded the nation's capital and provided it with access to the free states, was kept in the Union by more ruthless methods, which included the use of martial law to suppress Confederate sympathizers. In Missouri, the presence of regular troops, aided significantly by a staunchly pro-Union German immigrant population, stymied the secession

Secession

The fall of Fort Sumter was a watershed for the secessionist movement. With no room left for compromise, slave states of the upper South chose to join the Confederacy.

Slave states seceding before the fall of Ft. Sumter, April 1861

Slave states seceding after the fall of Ft. Sumter, April 1861

Slave states loyal to the Union

Free states

Free territories

movement. But pro-Union forces failed to establish order in this deeply divided frontier state. Brutal guerrilla fighting made wartime Missouri an unsafe and bloody place.

Hence the Civil War was not, strictly speaking, a struggle between slave and free states. Nor did it simply pit states that could not tolerate Lincoln's election against those that could. More than anything else, conflicting views on the right of secession determined the ultimate division of states and the choices of individuals in areas where sentiment was divided. General Robert E. Lee, for example, was neither a defender of slavery nor a southern nationalist. But he followed Virginia out of the Union because he was the loyal son of a "sovereign state." General George Thomas, another Virginian, chose the Union because he believed it was indissoluble. Although concern about the future of slavery had driven the Deep South to secede in the first place, the actual lineup of states and supporters meant the two sides would define the war less as a struggle over slavery than as a contest to determine whether the Union was indivisible.

ADJUSTING TO TOTAL WAR

The Civil War was a "total war" involving every aspect of society because the North could achieve its aim of restoring the Union only by defeating the South so thoroughly that its separatist government would be overthrown. It was a long war because the Confederacy put up "a hell of a fight" before it would agree to be put to death. Total war is a test of societies, economies, and political systems, as well as a battle of wits between generals and military strategists—and the Civil War was no exception.

Prospects, Plans, and Expectations

If the war was to be decided by sheer physical strength, then the North had an enormous edge in population, industrial capacity, and railroad mileage. Nevertheless, the South had some advantages that went a long way toward counterbalancing the North's demographic and industrial superiority. It could do more with less, because its armies faced an easier task. To achieve its aim

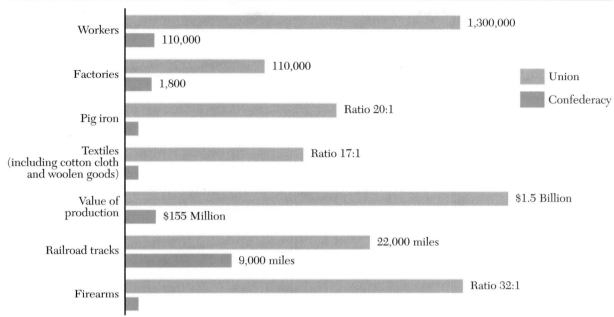

Workers — Union: 1,300,000 | Confederacy: 110,000

Factories — Union: 110,000 | Confederacy: 1,800

Pig iron — Ratio 20:1

Textiles (including cotton cloth and woolen goods) — Ratio 17:1

Value of production — Union: $1.5 Billion | Confederacy: $155 Million

Railroad tracks — Union: 22,000 miles | Confederacy: 9,000 miles

Firearms — Ratio 32:1

Legend: Union | Confederacy

of independence, the Confederacy needed only to defend its own territory successfully. The North, on the other hand, had to invade and conquer the South. Consequently, the Confederacy faced a less serious supply problem, had a greater capacity to choose the time and place of combat, and could take advantage of familiar terrain and a friendly civilian population.

The nature of the war meant southern leaders could define their cause as defense of their homeland against an alien invader and thus appeal to the fervid patriotism of a white population that viewed Yankee domination as a form of slavery. The northern cause, however, was not nearly as clear cut as that of the South. It seemed doubtful in 1861 that Northerners would be willing to give equally fervent support to a war fought for the seemingly abstract principle that the Union was sacred and perpetual.

Confederate optimism on the eve of the war was also fed by other—and more dubious—calculations. It was widely assumed that Southerners would make better fighting men than Yankees. Farm boys used to riding and shooting could allegedly whip several times their number among the clerks and factory workers (many of them immigrants) who, it was anticipated, would make up a large part of the Union Army. (Actually a majority of northern soldiers would also be farm boys.) When most of the large proportion of

Confederate volunteers at the start of the war.

high-ranking officers in the U S. Army who were of southern origin resigned to accept Confederate commands, Southerners confidently expected that their armies would be better led. If external help was needed, such major foreign powers as England and France might come to the aid of the Confederacy because the industrial economies of those European nations depended on southern cotton.

As they thought about strategy in the weeks and months after Fort Sumter, the leaders of both sides tried to find the best way to capitalize on their advantages and compensate for their limitations. The choice before President Davis, who assumed personal direction of the Confederate military effort, was whether to stay on the defensive or seek a sudden and dramatic victory by invading the North. He chose to wage a mainly defensive war in the hope he could make the Union pay so dearly for its incursions into the South that the northern populace would soon tire of the effort. But this plan did not preclude invading the North for psychological or military effect when good opportunities presented themselves. Nor did it inhibit Confederate aggressiveness against exposed northern forces within the South. Although their primary strategic orientation was defensive, it was an "offensive defense" that southern commanders put into effect.

Northern military planners had greater difficulty in working out a basic strategy, and it took a good deal of trial and error (mostly error) before there was a clear sense of what had to be done. Some optimists believed the war could be won quickly and easily by sending an army to capture the Confederate capital of Richmond, scarcely 100 miles from Washington. The "On to Richmond" solution died on the battlefields of Virginia when it soon became clear that difficult terrain and an ably led, hard-fighting Confederate army blocked the way. Aware of the costs of invading the South at points where its forces were concentrated, the aged General Winfield Scott—who commanded the Union Army during the early months of the war—recommended an "anaconda policy." Like a great boa constrictor, the North would squeeze the South into submission by blockading the southern coasts, seizing control of the Mississippi, and cutting off supplies of food and other essential commodities. This plan pointed to the West as the main locus of military operations.

Overview of Civil War Strategy

Confederate military leaders were convinced the South could not be defended unless they took the initiative to determine where critical battles would be fought.

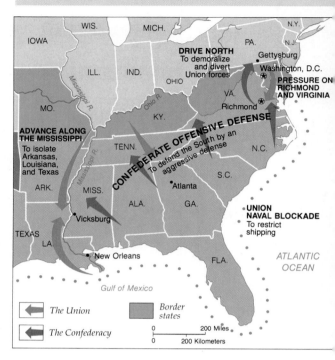

Eventually Lincoln decided on a two-front war. He would keep the pressure on Virginia in the hope a breakthrough would occur there, while at the same time, he would authorize an advance down the Mississippi Valley with the aim of isolating Texas, Arkansas, and Louisiana. Lincoln also attached great importance to the coastal blockade and expected naval operations to seize the ports through which goods entered and left the Confederacy. His basic plan of applying pressure and probing for weaknesses at several points simultaneously was a good one because it took maximum advantage of the North's superiority in manpower and matériel. But it required better military leadership than the North possessed at the beginning of the war and took a painfully long time to put into effect.

Mobilizing the Home Fronts

The North and South faced similar problems in trying to create the vast support systems needed by armies in the field. At the beginning of the conflict, both sides had more volunteers than could be armed and outfitted. The South was forced to reject about 200,000 men in the first year of the war, and the North could commit only a fraction of its forces to battle. Further confusion resulted from the fact that recruiting was done primarily by the states, which were reluctant to surrender control of the forces they had raised. Both Lincoln and Davis had to deal with governors who resisted centralized direction of the military effort.

As it became clear that hopes for a short and easy war were false, the pool of volunteers began to dry up. Many of the early recruits, who had been enrolled for short terms, showed a reluctance to reenlist. To resolve this problem, the Confederacy passed a conscription law in April 1862, and the Union edged toward a draft in July when Congress gave Lincoln the power to assign manpower quotas to each state and resort to conscription if they were not met (see "Soldiering in the Civil War," pp. 448– 449).

To produce the materials of war, both governments relied mainly on private industry. In the North, especially, the system of contracting with private firms and individuals to supply the army resulted in much corruption and inefficiency. The government at times bought shoddy uniforms that disintegrated in a heavy rain, defective rifles, and broken-down horses unfit for service. But the North's economy was strong at the core, and by 1863 its factories and farms were producing more than enough to provision the troops without significantly lowering the living standards of the civilian population.

The southern economy was much less adaptable to the needs of a total war. Because of the weakness of its industrial base, the South of 1861 depended on the outside world for most of its manufactured goods. As the Union blockade became more effective, the Confederacy had to rely increasingly on a government-sponsored crash program to produce war materials. In addition to encouraging and promoting private initiative, the government built its own munitions plants, including a gigantic powder factory at Augusta, Georgia. Astonishingly, the Confederate Ordnance Bureau, under the able direction of General Josiah Gorgas, succeeded in producing or procuring sufficient armaments to keep southern armies well supplied throughout the conflict.

Southern agriculture, however, failed to meet the challenge. Planters were reluctant to shift from staples that could no longer be readily exported to foodstuffs that were urgently needed. But more significant was the inadequacy of the South's internal transportation system. Its limited rail network was designed to link plantation regions to port cities rather than to connect food-producing areas with centers of population, as was the pattern in the North. New railroad construction during the war did not resolve the problem; most of the new lines were aimed to facilitate the movement of troops rather than the distribution of food.

When northern forces penetrated parts of the South, they created new gaps in the system. As a result, much of the corn or livestock that was raised could not reach the people who needed it. Although well armed, Confederate soldiers were increasingly undernourished, and by 1863 civilians in urban areas were rioting to protest shortages of food. To supply the troops, the Confederate commissary resorted to the impressment of available agricultural produce at below the market price, a policy resisted so vigorously by farmers and local politicians that it eventually had to be abandoned.

Another challenge faced by both sides was how to finance an enormously costly struggle. Although special war taxes were imposed, neither side was willing to resort to the heavy taxation that was needed to maintain fiscal integrity. Americans, it seems, were more willing to die for their government than to pay for it. Besides floating loans and selling bonds, both treasuries deliberately inflated the currency by printing large quantities of paper money that could not be redeemed in gold and silver. In August 1861, the Confederacy issued $100 million of such currency, and the Union followed suit by printing $150 million in early 1862. The presses rolled throughout the war, and runaway inflation was the inevitable result. The problem was much less severe in the North because of the overall strength of its economy. War taxes on income were more readily collectable than in the South, and bond issues were more successful.

The Confederacy was hampered from the outset by a severe shortage of readily disposable wealth that could be tapped for public purposes. Land and cotton could not easily be turned into rifles and cannons, and the southern treasury had to accept payments "in kind." As a result, Confederate "assets" eventually consisted mainly

*S*oldiering in the Civil War

Early in the Civil War, William Tecumseh Sherman told an audience of fresh-faced recruits that "There's many a boy here today who looks on war as all glory, but, boys, it is all hell." Letters from Civil War soldiers reveal that Sherman's lesson was painfully learned by young men in both armies over the four years of conflict. At the outset, the firing on Fort Sumter infected both North and South with war fever. What later became a national nightmare began as a glorious defense of home and country. Young men rushed to join up in great numbers, taxing the ability of the authorities to process enlistments.

Initially, the creation and supply of Union and Confederate army units was in the hands of local communities. A leading citizen—or politician—would advertise for men to fill a company or regiment. Once a unit was assembled, it elected its own officers and chose a commander—usually the man who had led the recruiting drive. The entire procedure, with its solicitation of votes and promises of patronage, was much like a peacetime local election.

Early Union defeats and a strategic stalemate not only ended talk on both sides of a "short engagement filled with glory" but also revealed how undisciplined the troops were. Of the more than 3 million Civil War servicemen, two-thirds were younger than twenty-three years of age and came from rural areas. They were not accustomed to the regimentation necessary to military life; as a young recruit from Illinois put it, "It comes rather hard at first to be deprived of liberty." Inadequate leadership, as well as the beginnings of war weariness and the arrival of letters from home pleading for help with the harvest, led to a degree of military anarchy. The early battles were contests between armed mobs that might break and run with little provocation. Moreover, the long casualty lists from these early battles discouraged new waves of enlistments.

Both governments hit on similar methods of recruiting and disciplining troops. Enlistment and reenlistment bounties were instituted, and the nation's first conscription laws were passed. The dual aim was to maintain the ranks of the original volunteers, while at the same time stimulating more enlistments. Terms of service were lengthened, in most cases to three years, and all nonenlisted men of military age were registered and called on either to volunteer or be faced with the disgrace of being drafted. Although some Southerners were exempted to oversee their large numbers of slaves, and Northerners could escape military duty by paying a $300 fee, the laws did spur enlistments. Between 1861 and 1865, more than half of the nation's 5.5 million men of military age were mustered into service.

The solution to the problem of training the troops was the army training camp. With its "50,000 pup tents and wigwams," the camp was the volunteer's way station between home and battlefield. It was the place the raw recruit received his first bitter taste of the tedium, hardship, and deprivation of soldiering. "A soldier is not his own man," a Louisiana recruit wrote, astonished at how markedly camp routines differed from civilian life. "He has given up all claim on himself. . . . I will give you a little information concerning evry day business. consider youreself a private soldier and in camp . . . the drum beats for drill. you fall in and start. you here feel youre inferirority. even the Sargeants is hollering at you close up; Ketch step. dress to the right, and sutch like."

Professional noncommissioned officers from the peacetime army were used, most effectively by the Union, to turn men into soldiers who could fire a rifle and understand simple commands. The liberal use of the court martial and the board of review enabled the professional soldiers to rid the army of its most incompetent officer-politicians and instill discipline in the ranks. Many recruits spent their entire terms of service within these tent cities, forming a reserve on which field commanders could call to replace casualties.

The camps were themselves the sites of hundreds of thousands of Civil War casualties. Fewer men died of battle wounds than of dysentery, typhoid fever, and other water-borne diseases contracted in the camps, which were often located on swampy land without adequate fresh water. The army food was always the butt of soldier humor—one soldier complained

the beef issued to him must have been carved from a bull "too old for the conscript law"—but it was also the source of its own set of diseases, particularly scurvy. Men in the field were condemned to a diet of "hardtack and half-cooked beans," and no soldier could expect to receive fresh fruits or vegetables. But food became steadily more plentiful in the Union camps; and doctors, officers, and agents of the U. S. Sanitary Commission teamed up to improve camp cleanliness. "Johnny Reb," however, had to survive under steadily worsening conditions. The Confederate supply system did not improve significantly during the course of the war and grew worse wherever the North invaded or blockaded. Nevertheless, the battlefield performance of fighting men on the two sides remained roughly on a par throughout the war.

Camp lessons were often forgotten in the heat of battle, particularly by green troops who "saw the elephant" (went into battle for the first time) and ran from it. Like the youth in Stephen Crane's *The Red Badge of Courage*, a Mississippian anxiously admitted after his first fight that "though i did not run i

mite have if i had thought of it in time." The Union's ability to call more new men into service may have guaranteed ultimate victory, but it meant that battle-hardened Confederate veterans faced large numbers of raw northern recruits in every major battle. Since experience often counted for more than basic training and equipment, southern troops could expect to engage the enemy on fairly equal terms.

The Civil War was the most costly and brutal struggle in which American soldiers have ever been engaged. More American servicemen died in that war (618,000) than in the two world wars and Vietnam combined. Contests were decided by deadly charges in which muskets were exploded at such close range as to sear the faces of the contestants. The survivors, in their letters home, attempted to describe the inhuman events but, as a Maine soldier wrote to his parents after the battle of Gettysburg: "You can form no idea of a battlefield. . . . no pen can describe it. No tongue can tell its horror[.] I hope none of my brothers will ever have to go into a fight."

Fresh recruits cannot avoid seeing battle casualties and field amputations as they wait to join the battle of Fredericksburg in this painting The Battle of Fredericksburg *(1862) by John Richards, based on an engraving that appeared in* Harper's *shortly after the battle.*

of bales of cotton that were unexportable because of the blockade. As the Confederate government fell deeper and deeper into debt and printed more and more paper money, its rate of inflation soared out of sight. By August 1863, a Confederate dollar was worth only eight cents in gold. Late in the war, it could be said with little exaggeration that it took a wheelbarrow full of money to buy a purse full of goods.

Political Leadership: Northern Success and Southern Failure

Total war also forced political adjustments, and both the Union and the Confederacy had to face the question of how much democracy and individual freedom could be permitted when military success required an unprecedented exercise of governmental authority. Since both constitutions made the president commander in chief of the army and navy, Lincoln and Davis took actions that would have been regarded as arbitrary or even tyrannical in peacetime. Nevertheless, "politics as usual"—in the form of free elections, public political controversy, and the maneuverings of parties, factions, and interest groups—persisted to a surprising degree.

Lincoln was especially bold in assuming new executive powers. After the fighting started at Fort Sumter, he expanded the regular army and advanced public money to private individuals without authorization by Congress. On April 27, 1861, he declared martial law, which enabled the military to arrest civilians suspected of aiding the enemy, and suspended the writ of habeas corpus in the area between Philadelphia and Washington, an action deemed necessary because of mob attacks on Union troops passing through Baltimore. Suspension of the writ enabled the government to arrest Confederate sympathizers and hold them without trial, and in September 1862 Lincoln extended this authority to all parts of the United States where "disloyal" elements were active. Such willingness to interfere with civil liberties was unprecedented and possibly unconstitutional, but Lincoln argued that "necessity" justified a flexible interpretation of his war powers. For critics of suspension he had a question: "are all the laws, *but one,* to go unexecuted, and the government itself to go to pieces, lest that one be violated?" In fact, however, most of the

thousands of civilians arrested by military authorities were not exercising their right to criticize the government but were suspected deserters and draft dodgers, refugees, smugglers, or people who were simply found wandering in areas under military control.

For the most part, the Lincoln administration showed restraint and tolerated a broad spectrum of political dissent. Although the government closed down a few newspapers for brief periods when they allegedly published false information or military secrets, antiadministration journals were allowed to criticize the president and his party at will. A few politicians, including an Ohio Congressman, were arrested for proconfederate activity, but a large number of "Peace Democrats"— who called for restoration of the Union by negotiation rather than force—ran for office, sat in Congress and in state legislatures, and thus had ample opportunity to present their views to the public. Lincoln's hand was in fact strengthened by the persistence of vigorous two-party competition in the North during the Civil War. Since his war policies were also the platform of his party,

Jefferson Davis, inaugurated as president of the Confederacy on February 18, 1861, was a West Point graduate and had served as secretary of war under President Franklin Pierce.

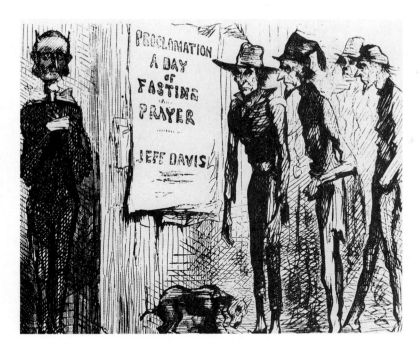

Gaunt southern citizens stare unbelievingly at a poster announcing a day of fasting proclaimed by a horned Jefferson Davis. Davis's insistent demands for his army aroused the hard-pressed Southerners' anger.

he could usually rely on unified partisan backing for the most controversial of his decisions.

Jefferson Davis, most historians agree, was a less effective war leader than Lincoln. He defined his powers as commander in chief narrowly and literally, which meant he assumed personal direction of the armed forces but left policy making for the mobilization and control of the civilian population primarily to the Confederate Congress. Unfortunately, he overestimated his capacities as a strategist and lacked the tact to handle field commanders who were as proud and testy as he was. Two of the South's best generals—Joseph E. Johnston and P. G. T. Beauregard—were denied the commands they deserved because they could not get along with Davis. One of the worst—Braxton E. Bragg—happened to be a personal favorite of the president and was allowed to keep a major command even after he had clearly demonstrated his incompetence.

Davis's greatest failing, however, was his lack of initiative and leadership in dealing with the problems of the home front. He devoted little attention to a deteriorating economic situation that caused great hardship and sapped Confederate morale. Although the South had a much more serious problem of internal division and disloyalty than the North, he refrained from declaring martial law on his own authority. The Confederate Congress grudgingly voted him such power when he asked for it but allowed it to be applied only in limited areas and for short periods.

As the war dragged on, Davis's political and popular support eroded. He was opposed and obstructed by state governors—such as Joseph E. Brown of Georgia and Zebulon Vance of North Carolina—who resisted conscription and other Confederate policies that violated the tradition of states' rights. The Confederate Congress served as a forum for bitter attacks on the administration's conduct of the war, and by 1863 a majority of southern newspapers were taking an anti-Davis stand. Even if he had been a more able and inspiring leader, Davis would have had difficulty maintaining his authority and credibility. Unlike Lincoln, he did not have an organized party behind him, for the Confederacy never developed a two-party system. As a result, it was difficult to mobilize the support required for hard decisions and controversial policies.

Early Campaigns and Battles

The war's first major battle was a disaster for northern arms. Against his better judgment, General Winfield Scott responded to the "On to Richmond" clamor and ordered poorly trained Union troops under General Irvin McDowell to

The battle of the ironclads between the huge Merrimack *and the smaller* Monitor *ended in the* Merrimack *being forced into port. Both ships were later lost; the* Merrimack *was blown up in Norfolk harbor in May 1862 and the* Monitor *went down in a gale in December.*

advance against the Confederate forces gathered at Manassas Junction, Virginia. They attacked the enemy position near Bull Run Creek on July 21, 1861, and seemed on their way to victory until Confederate reinforcements arrived from the Shenandoah Valley. After Confederate General Thomas J. Jackson had earned the nickname "Stonewall" for holding the line against the northern assault, the augmented southern army counterattacked and routed the invading force. As they retreated toward Washington, the raw Union troops gave in to panic and broke ranks in their stampede to safety.

The humiliating defeat at Bull Run led to a shake-up of the northern high command. The man of the hour was George McClellan, who first replaced McDowell as commander of troops in the Washington area and then became general-in-chief when Scott was eased into retirement. A cautious disciplinarian, McClellan spent the fall and winter drilling his troops and whipping them into shape. President Lincoln, who could not understand why McClellan was taking so long to go into the field, became increasingly impatient and finally tried to order the army into action.

Before McClellan made his move, Union forces in the West won some important victories. In February 1862, a joint military-naval operation, commanded by General Ulysses S. Grant, captured Fort Henry on the Tennessee River and Fort Donelson on the Cumberland. Fourteen thousand prisoners were taken at Donelson, and the Confederate Army was forced to withdraw from Kentucky and middle Tennessee. Southern forces in the West then massed at Corinth, Mississippi, just across the border from Tennessee. When a slow-moving Union Army arrived just north of the Mississippi state line, the South launched a surprise attack on April 6. In the battle of Shiloh, one of the bloodiest of the war, only the timely arrival of reinforcements prevented the annihilation of Union troops backed up against the Tennessee River. After a second day of fierce fighting, the Confederates retreated to Corinth, leaving the enemy forces battered and exhausted.

Although the Union's military effort to seize control of the Mississippi Valley was temporarily halted at Shiloh, the Union Navy soon contributed dramatically to the pursuit of that objec-

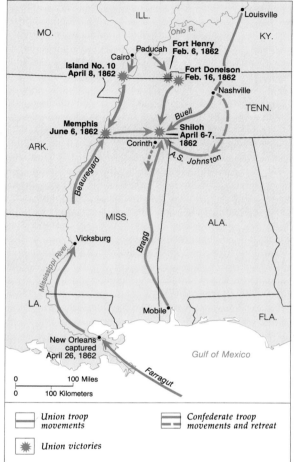

repulsed by the *Monitor,* an armored and turreted Union gunship.

Successes around the edges of the Confederacy did not relieve northern frustration at the inactivity or failure of Union forces on the eastern front. Only after Lincoln had relieved him of supreme command and ordered him to take the offensive at the head of the Army of the Potomac did McClellan start campaigning. Spurning the treacherous overland route to Richmond, he moved his forces by water to the peninsula southeast of the Confederate capital. After landing at Fortress Monroe, which had remained in Union hands, McClellan began moving up the peninsula in early April 1862. For a month he was bogged down before Yorktown, which he chose to besiege rather than assault directly. After Yorktown fell on May 4, he pushed ahead to a point 20 miles from Richmond, where he awaited the additional troops that he expected Lincoln to send.

These reinforcements were not forthcoming. While McClellan was inching his way up the peninsula, a relatively small southern force under Stonewall Jackson was on the rampage in the Shenandoah Valley, where it succeeded in pinning down a much larger Union Army and defeating its detached units in a series of lightning moves. When it appeared by late May that Jackson might be poised to march east and attack the Union capital, Lincoln decided to withhold troops from McClellan so they would be available to defend Washington.

If McClellan had moved more boldly and decisively, he probably could have captured Richmond with the forces he had. But a combination of faulty intelligence reports and his own natural caution led him to falter in the face of what he wrongly believed to be superior numbers. At the end of May, the Confederates under Joseph E. Johnston took the offensive when they discovered McClellan's army was divided into two segments by the Chickahominy River. In the battle of Seven Pines, McClellan was barely able to hold his ground on the side of the river under attack until a corps from the other side crossed over just in time to save the day. During the battle, General Johnston was severely wounded; succeeding him in command of the Confederate Army of Northern Virginia was native Virginian and West Point graduate Robert E. Lee.

tive. On April 26 a fleet under Flag Officer David Farragut, coming up from the Gulf, captured the port of New Orleans after boldly running past the forts below the city. The occupation of New Orleans, besides securing the mouth of the Mississippi, climaxed a series of naval and amphibious operations around the edges of the Confederacy that had already succeeded in capturing South Carolina's Sea Islands and North Carolina's Roanoke Island. Strategically located bases were thus available to enforce a blockade of the southern coast. The last serious challenge to the North's naval supremacy ended on March 9, 1862, when the Confederate ironclad vessel *Virginia* (originally the USS *Merrimack*)—which had demolished wooden-hulled northern ships in the vicinity of Hampton Roads, Virginia—was

After Antietam, Lincoln visited McClellan's headquarters to urge the general to take action. McClellan is on the left facing the President.

Toward the end of June, Lee began an all-out effort to expel McClellan from the outskirts of Richmond. In a series of battles that lasted for seven days, the two armies clawed at each other indecisively. Although McClellan repulsed Lee's final assaults at Malvern Hill, the Union general decided to retreat down the peninsula to a more secure base. This backward step convinced Lincoln that the peninsula campaign was an exercise in futility.

On July 11 Lincoln appointed General Henry W. Halleck, who had been in overall command in the western theater, to be the new general-in-chief and through Halleck ordered McClellan to withdraw his army from the peninsula to join a force under General John Pope that was preparing to move on Richmond by the overland route. As usual, McClellan was slow in responding, and the Confederates got to Pope before he did. At the end of August, in the second battle fought near Bull Run, Lee established his reputation for brilliant generalship; he sent Stonewall Jackson to Pope's rear, provoked the rash Union general to attack Jackson with full force, and then threw the main Confederate Army against the Union's flank. Badly beaten, Pope retreated to the defens-es of Washington, where he was stripped of command. Out of sheer desperation, Lincoln reappointed McClellan to head the Army of the Potomac.

Lee proceeded to lead his exuberant troops on an invasion of Maryland, in the hope of isolating Washington from the rest of the North. McClellan caught up with him near Sharpsburg, and the bloodiest one-day battle of the war ensued. When the smoke cleared at Antietam on September 17, almost five thousand men had been killed on the two sides and more than eighteen thousand were wounded. The result was a draw, but Lee was forced to fall back south of the Potomac to protect his dangerously extended supply lines. McClellan was slow in pursuit, and Lincoln blamed him for letting the enemy escape.

Convinced that McClellan was fatally infected with "the slows," Lincoln once again sought a more aggressive general and put Ambrose E. Burnside in command of the Army of the Potomac. Burnside was aggressive enough, but he was also rather dense. His limitations were disastrously revealed at the battle of Fredericksburg, Virginia, on December 13, 1862, when he launched a direct assault to try to capture an entrenched and elevated position. Throughout the Civil War such uphill charges almost invariably failed because of the range and deadly accuracy of small arms fire when concentrated on exposed troops. The debacle at Fredericksburg, where Union forces suffered more than twice as many casualties as their opponents, ended a year of bitter failure for the North on the eastern front.

The Diplomatic Struggle

The critical period of Civil War diplomacy was 1861 to 1862, when the South was making every effort to induce major foreign powers to recognize its independence and break the Union blockade. The hope that England and France could be persuaded to intervene on the Confederate side stemmed from the fact that these nations depended on the South for three-quarters of their cotton supply. In the case of Britain, the uninterrupted production of cotton textiles appeared essential to economic prosperity; an estimated 20 to 25 percent of its entire population was supported either directly or indirectly by this single industry.

The Confederate commissioners sent to England and France in May 1861 succeeded in gaining recognition of southern "belligerency," which meant the new government could claim some international rights of a nation at war. The North protested vigorously, but by declaring a blockade of southern ports, it had undermined its official position that the rebellion was merely a domestic insurrection. The main advantage of belligerent status was that it permitted the South to purchase and outfit privateers in neutral ports. As a result, Confederate raiders, built and armed in British shipyards, like the *Alabama*—which single-handedly sank sixty-two vessels—devastated northern shipping to such an extent that insurance costs eventually forced most of the American merchant marine off the high seas for the duration of the war.

In the fall of 1861 the Confederate government dispatched James M. Mason and John Slidell to be its permanent envoys to England and France, respectively, and instructed them to push for full recognition of the Confederacy. They took passage on the British steamer *Trent,* which was stopped and boarded in international waters by a U. S. warship. Mason and Slidell were taken into custody by the Union captain, causing a diplo-

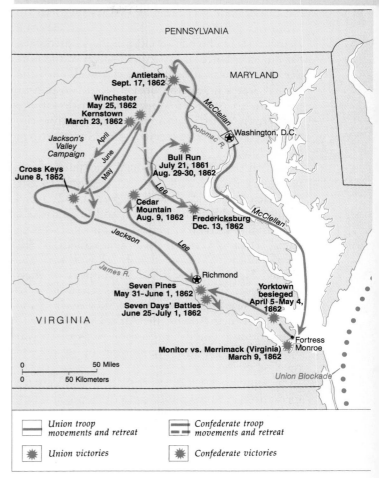

Eastern Theater of War, 1861–1862
Defeats on the battlefield forced a change in the Union's initial military campaign of capturing Richmond, the Confederate capital.

matic crisis that nearly led to war between England and the United States. Refusing to tolerate this flagrant violation of its maritime rights, Britain threatened war if the Confederate emissaries were not released. After a few weeks of ferocious posturing by both sides, Lincoln and Secretary of State Seward made the prudent decision to allow Mason and Slidell to proceed to their destinations.

These envoys may as well have stayed at home; they failed in their mission to obtain full recognition of the Confederacy from either England or France. The anticipated cotton shortage was slow to develop, for the bumper crop of 1860 had created a large surplus in British and French warehouses. Recognition did seem likely for a brief period in the fall of 1862. Napoleon III, the emperor of France, personally favored the southern cause, mainly because he was trying to set up a puppet government in Mexico and saw the chance to trade French support of the Confederacy for an acceptance of his regime south of the border. But he was unwilling to risk war with the United States unless the British would cosponsor his plan to offer European mediation of the American conflict and then recognize the Confederacy if—as expected—the North refused to go along.

British opinion, both official and public, was seriously divided on how to respond to the American conflict. In 1861 and 1862, Lord Palmerston, the prime minister, and Lord Russell, the foreign secretary, played a cautious waiting game. Their government was sympathetic to the South but wary of the danger of war with the United States if they acted in support of their preference. Northern diplomats knew how to play on these fears: Secretary of State Seward and Charles Francis Adams, the American minister to Great Britain, could be relied on to threaten war at any hint of British recognition or support of the Confederacy.

In September 1862, the British cabinet debated mediation and recognition as serious possibilities. Lord Russell pressed for a pro-Confederate policy because he was convinced the South was now strong enough to secure its independence. But when word arrived that Lee had failed to win a clear victory at Antietam and was retreating, Lord Palmerston overruled the foreign secretary and decided to maintain a hands-off policy. The British would intervene, his decision suggested, only if the South won decisively on the battlefield.

The cotton famine finally hit in late 1862, causing massive unemployment in the British textile industry. But, contrary to southern hopes, public opinion did not compel the government to abandon its neutrality and use force to break the Union blockade. Historians used to believe that unselfish pro-Union sympathy among the suffering mill workers was a main cause of restraint, but the British working class still lacked the right to vote and thus had relatively little influence over policy.

Lord Punch: "That was Jeff Davis. . . . Don't you recognize him?" Lord [Palmerston]: "Not exactly—may have to do so one of these days." Britain never recognized the Confederacy.

Influential interest groups, which actually benefited from the famine, provided the crucial support for continuing a policy of nonintervention. Among these groups were owners of large cotton mills who had made bonanza profits on their existing stocks and were happy to see weaker competitors go under while they awaited new sources of supply. By early 1863, cotton from Egypt and India put the industry back on the track toward full production. Other obvious beneficiaries of nonintervention were manufacturers of wool and linen textiles, munition makers who supplied both sides, and shipping interests that profited from the decline of American competition on the world's sea lanes. Since the British economy as a whole gained more than it lost from neutrality, it is not surprising that there was little effective pressure for a change in policy.

By early 1863, when it was clear that "King Cotton Diplomacy" had failed, the Confederacy broke off formal relations with Great Britain. Its hopes for foreign intervention came to nothing because the European powers acted out of self-interest and calculated that the advantages of getting involved were not worth the risk of a long and costly war with the United States. Only a decisive military victory would have gained recognition for southern independence, and if the Confederacy had actually won such a victory, it would not have needed foreign backing.

FIGHT TO THE FINISH

The last two and a half years of the struggle saw the implementation of more radical war measures. The most dramatic and important of these was the North's effort to follow through on Lincoln's decision to free the slaves and bring the black population into the war on the Union side. The tide of battle turned in the summer of 1863, but the South continued to resist valiantly for two more years, until finally overcome by the sheer weight of the North's advantages in manpower and resources.

The Coming of Emancipation

At the beginning of the war, when the North still hoped for a quick and easy victory, only dedicated abolitionists favored turning the struggle for the Union into a crusade against slavery. In the summer of 1861 Congress voted almost unanimously for a resolution affirming that the war was being fought only to preserve the Union and not to change the domestic institutions of any state. But as it became clear how hard it was going to be to subdue the "rebels," sentiment developed for striking a blow at the South's economic and social system by freeing its slaves. In a tentative move toward emancipation, Congress in July 1862 authorized the government to confiscate the slaves of masters who supported the Confederacy. By this time, the actions of the slaves themselves were influencing policy making. They were voting for freedom with their feet by deserting their plantations in areas where the Union forces were close enough to offer a haven. In this way, they put pressure on the government to determine their status and, in effect, offered themselves as a source of manpower to the Union on the condition that they be made free.

Although Lincoln favored freedom for blacks as an ultimate goal, he was reluctant to commit his administration to a policy of immediate emancipation. In the fall of 1861 and again in the spring of 1862, he had disallowed the orders of field commanders who sought to free slaves in areas occupied by their forces, thus angering abolitionists and the strongly antislavery Republicans known as "Radicals." Lincoln's caution stemmed from a fear of alienating Unionist elements in the border slave states and from his own preference for a gradual, compensated form of emancipation. He hoped that such a plan could be put into effect in loyal slaveholding areas and then extended to the rebellious states as the basis for a voluntary restoration of the Union.

Lincoln was also aware that one of the main obstacles to any program leading to emancipation was the strong racial prejudice of most whites in both the North and the South. Although personally more tolerant than most, Lincoln was pessimistic about prospects of equality for blacks in the United States. He therefore coupled moderate proposals with a plea for government subsidies to support the voluntary "colonization" of freed blacks outside of the United States, and he actively sought places that would accept them.

But the slaveholding states that remained loyal to the Union refused to endorse Lincoln's gradual plan, and the failure of Union arms in the spring and summer of 1862 increased the public clamor for striking directly at the South's peculiar institution. The Lincoln administration also realized emancipation would win sympathy for the Union cause in England and France and thus might counter the growing threat that these nations would come to the aid of the Confederacy. In July Lincoln drafted an emancipation proclamation and read it to his cabinet but was persuaded by Secretary of State Seward not to issue it until the North had won a victory and could not be accused of acting out of desperation. Later in the summer Lincoln responded publicly to critics of his cautious policy, indicating that he would take any action in regard to slavery that would further the Union cause.

Finally, on September 22, 1862, Lincoln issued his preliminary Emancipation Proclamation. McClellan's success in stopping Lee at Antietam provided the occasion, but the president was also responding to growing political pressures. Most Republican politicians were now firmly committed to an emancipation policy, and many were on the verge of repudiating the administration for its

The Emancipation Proclamation, here being read to slaves on a Carolina Sea Island plantation, committed the Union to the abolition of slavery as a war aim.

inaction. Had Lincoln failed to act, his party would have been badly split, and he would have been in the minority faction. The proclamation gave the Confederate states one hundred days to give up the struggle without losing their slaves. There was little chance they would do so, but in offering them the chance, Lincoln left the door open for a more conservative and peaceful way of ending slavery than sudden emancipation at the point of a gun. In December Lincoln proposed to Congress that it approve a series of constitutional amendments providing for gradual, compensated emancipation and subsidized colonization.

Since there was no response from the South and little enthusiasm in Congress for Lincoln's gradual plan, the president went ahead on January 1, 1863, and declared that all slaves in those areas under Confederate control "shall be . . . thenceforward, and forever free." He justified the final proclamation as an act of "military necessity" sanctioned by the war powers of the president and authorized the enlistment of freed slaves in the Union Army. The language and tone of the document—one historian has described it as having "all the moral grandeur of a bill of lading"—made it clear that blacks were being freed for reasons of state and not out of humanitarian conviction.

Despite its uninspiring origin and limited appli-cation—it did not extend to slave states loyal to the Union or to occupied areas and thus did not immediately free a single slave—the proclamation did commit the Union to the abolition of slavery as a war aim. It also accelerated the breakdown of slavery as a labor system, a process that was already well under way by early 1863. The blacks who had remained in captured areas or deserted their masters to cross Union lines before 1863 had been kept in a kind of way station between slavery and freedom, in accordance with the theory that they were "contraband of war." As word spread among the slaves that emancipation was now offi-cial policy, larger numbers of them were inspired to run off and seek the protection of approaching northern armies. One slave who crossed the Union lines summed up their motives: "I wants to be free. I came in from the plantation and don't want to go back;. . . I don't want to be a slave again." Approximately one-quarter of the slave popula-tion gained freedom during the war under the terms of the Emancipation Proclamation and thus deprived the South of an important part of its agricultural work force.

African Americans and the War

Almost 200,000 African Americans, most of them newly freed slaves, eventually served in the

Union armed forces and made a vital contribution to the North's victory. Although they were enrolled in segregated units under white officers, were initially paid less than their white counterparts, and were used disproportionately for garrison duty or heavy labor behind the lines, "blacks in blue" fought heroically in several major battles during the last two years of the war. The assistant secretary of war observed them in action at Millikin's Bend on the Mississippi in June 1863 and reported that "the bravery of blacks in the battle . . . completely revolutionized the sentiment of the army with regard to the employment of Negro troops."

Those freed during the war who did not serve in the military were often conscripted to serve as contract wage laborers on cotton plantations owned or leased by "loyal" white planters within the occupied areas of the Deep South. Abolitionists protested that the coercion used by military authorities to get blacks back into the cotton fields amounted to slavery in a new form, but those in power argued that the necessities of war and the northern economy required such "temporary" arrangements. To some extent, regimentation of the freedmen within the South was a way of assuring racially prejudiced Northerners, especially in the Midwest, that emancipation would not result in a massive migration of black refugees to their region of the country.

The heroic performance of African American troops and the easing of northern fears of being swamped by black migrants led to a deepening commitment to emancipation as a permanent and comprehensive policy.

Realizing his proclamation had a shaky constitutional foundation and might apply only to slaves actually freed while the war was going on, Lincoln sought to organize and recognize loyal state governments in southern areas under Union control on condition that they abolish slavery in their constitutions. He also encouraged local

This 1890 lithograph by Kurz and Allison commemorates the 54th Massachusetts Colored Regiment charging Fort Wagner, South Carolina, in July 1863. The 54th was the first African American unit recruited during the war. Charles and Lewis Douglass, sons of Frederick Douglass, served with this regiment.

campaigns to emancipate the slaves in the border states and saw these programs triumph in Maryland and Missouri in 1864.

Finally, Lincoln pressed for an amendment to the federal constitution outlawing involuntary servitude. After supporting its inclusion as a central plank in the Republican platform of 1864, Lincoln used all his influence to win congressional approval for the new Thirteenth Amendment. On January 31, 1865, the House approved the amendment by a narrow margin. There was an explosion of joy on the floor and in the galleries, and then the House voted to adjourn for the rest of the day "in honor of this immortal and sublime event." The cause of freedom for blacks and the cause of the Union had at last become one and the same. Lincoln, despite his earlier hesitations and misgivings, had earned the right to go down in history as "the great emancipator."

The Tide Turns

By early 1863, the Confederate economy was in shambles and its diplomacy had collapsed. The social order of the South was also showing signs of severe strain. Masters were losing control of their slaves, and nonslaveholding whites were becoming disillusioned with the hardships of a war that some of them described as a "rich man's war and a poor man's fight." As slaves fled from the plantations, increasing numbers of lower-class whites deserted the army or refused to be drafted in the first place. Whole counties in the southern backcountry became "deserter havens," which Confederate officials could enter only at the risk of their lives. Appalachian mountaineers, who had remained loyal to the Union, resisted the Confederacy more directly by enlisting in the Union Army or joining guerrilla units operating behind southern lines.

Yet the North was slow to capitalize on the South's internal weaknesses because it had its own serious morale problems. The long series of defeats on the eastern front had engendered war weariness, and the new policies that "military necessity" forced the government to adopt encountered fierce opposition.

Although popular with Republicans, emancipation was viewed by most Democrats as a betrayal of northern war aims. Racism was a main ingredient in their opposition to freeing blacks. According to one Democratic senator, "We mean that the United States . . . shall be the white man's home . . . and the nigger shall never be his equal." Riding a backlash against the preliminary proclamation, Democrats made significant gains in the congressional elections of 1862, especially in the Midwest, where they also captured several state legislatures.

The Enrollment Act of March 1863, which provided for outright conscription of white males, but permitted men of wealth to hire substitutes or pay a fee to avoid military service, provoked a violent response from those unable to buy their way out of service and unwilling to "fight for the niggers." A series of antidraft riots broke out, culminating in one of the bloodiest domestic disorders in American history—the New York riot of July 1863. The New York mob, composed mainly of Irish-American laborers, burned the draft offices, the homes of leading Republicans, and an orphanage for black children. They also lynched more than a dozen defenseless blacks who fell into their hands. At least 120 people died before federal troops restored order. Besides racial prejudice, the draft riots also reflected working-class anger at the wartime privileges and prosperity of the middle and upper classes; they showed how divided the North really was on the administration's conduct of the war.

To fight dissension and "disloyalty," the government used its martial law authority to arrest a few alleged ringleaders, including one prominent Democratic congressman—Clement Vallandigham of Ohio. Private patriotic organizations also issued a barrage of propaganda aimed at what they believed was a vast secret conspiracy to undermine the northern war effort. Historians disagree about the real extent of covert and illegal antiwar activity. No vast conspiracy existed, but militant advocates of "peace at any price"—popularly known as Copperheads—were certainly active in some areas, especially among the immigrant working classes of large cities and in southern Ohio, Indiana, and Illinois. Many Copperheads presented themselves as Jeffersonian believers in limited government who feared a war-induced growth of federal power. But it was opposition to emancipation on racial grounds rather than anxiety about big government that gave the movement most of its emotional force.

The only effective way to overcome the disillu-

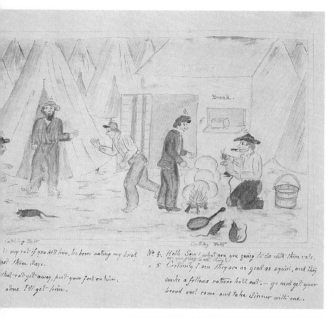

The prison camps of the North (like Point Lookout, Maryland, above) and the South (like Andersonville, Georgia, right) were both deadly, but Andersonville was worse because the South ran out of food. Nearly 50,000 prisoners died in the camps during the war.

sionment that fed the peace movement was to start winning battles and thus convince the northern public that victory was assured. Before this could happen, the North suffered one more humiliating defeat on the eastern front. In early May 1863, Union forces under General Joseph Hooker were routed at Chancellorsville, Virginia, by a Confederate Army less than half its size. Once again, Robert E. Lee demonstrated his superior generalship, this time by dividing his forces and sending Stonewall Jackson to make a devastating surprise attack on the Union right. The Confederacy prevailed, but it did suffer one major loss: Jackson himself died as a result of wounds he received in the battle.

In the West, however, a major Union triumph was taking shape. For over a year, General Ulysses S. Grant had been trying to put his forces in position to capture Vicksburg, Mississippi, the almost inaccessible Confederate bastion that stood between the North and control of the Mississippi River. Finally, in late March 1863, he crossed to the west bank north of the city and moved his forces to a point south of it, where he joined up with naval forces that had run the Confederate batteries mounted on Vicksburg's high bluffs. In one of the boldest campaigns of the war, Grant crossed the river, deliberately cutting himself off from his sources of supply, and marched into the interior of Mississippi. Living off the land and out of communication with an anxious and perplexed Lincoln, his troops won a series of victories over two separate Confederate Armies and advanced on Vicksburg from the east. After unsuccessfully assaulting the city's defenses, Grant settled down for a siege on May 22.

The Confederate government considered and rejected proposals to mount a major offensive

An 1863 draft call in New York first provoked violence against African Americans, viewed by the rioters as the cause of an unnecessary war, and rage against the rich men who had been able to buy exemptions from the draft.

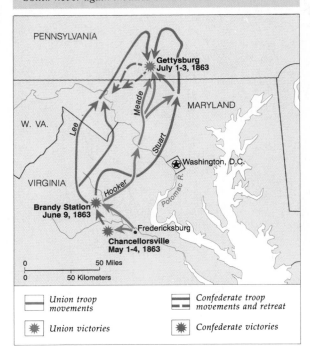

into Tennessee and Kentucky in the hope of drawing Grant away from Vicksburg. Instead, President Davis approved Robert E. Lee's plan for an all-out invasion of the Northeast. Although this option provided no hope for relieving Vicksburg, it might lead to a dramatic victory that would more than compensate for the probable loss of the Mississippi stronghold. Lee's army crossed the Potomac in June and kept going until it reached Gettysburg, Pennsylvania. There Lee confronted a Union Army that had taken up strong defensive positions on Cemetery Ridge and Culp's Hill. This was one of the few occasions in the war when the North could capitalize on the tactical advantage of choosing its ground and then defending it against an enemy whose supply lines were extended.

On July 2 a series of Confederate attacks failed to dislodge General George Meade's troops from the high ground they occupied. The following day, Lee faced the choice of retreating to protect his lines of communication or launching a final, desperate assault. With more boldness than wisdom, he chose to make a direct attack on the strongest part of the Union line. The resulting charge on Cemetery Ridge was disastrous; advancing Confederate soldiers dropped like flies under the barrage of Union artillery and rifle fire. Only a few made it to the top of the ridge, and they were killed or captured.

Retreat was now inevitable, and Lee withdrew his battered troops to the Potomac, only to find that the river was at flood stage and could not be crossed for several days. But Meade failed to follow up his victory with a vigorous pursuit, and Lee was allowed to escape a predicament that could have resulted in his annihilation. Vicksburg fell to Grant on July 4, the same day Lee began his withdrawal, and Northerners rejoiced at the simultaneous Independence Day victories that turned the tide of the war. The Union had secured control of the Mississippi and had at last

Bold and decisive, Confederate General Robert E. Lee (left) often faced an enemy army that greatly outnumbered his own troops. Union General Ulysses S. Grant (right) demonstrated a relentless determination that eventually triumphed.

Western Theater of War, 1863
Grant's victories at Port Gibson, Champion's Hill, and Jackson cleared the way for his siege of Vicksburg.

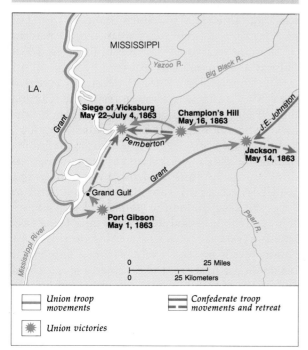

won a major battle in the East. But Lincoln's joy turned to frustration when he learned his generals had missed the chance to capture Lee's army and bring a quick end to the war.

Last Stages of the Conflict

Later in 1863 the North finally gained control of the middle South, an area where indecisive fighting had been going on since the beginning of the conflict. The main Union target was Chattanooga, "the gateway to the Southeast." In September, troops under General William Rosecrans managed to maneuver the Confederates out of the city only to be outfought and driven back at Chickamauga. The Union Army then retreated into Chattanooga, where it was surrounded and besieged by southern forces. After Grant arrived from Vicksburg to take command, the encirclement was broken by daring assaults on the Confederate positions on Lookout Mountain and Missionary Ridge. As a result of its success in the battle of Chattanooga, the North was poised for an invasion of Georgia.

Grant's victories in the West earned him promotion to general-in-chief of all the Union armies. After assuming that position in March 1864, he ordered a multipronged offensive to finish off the Confederacy. The offensive's main movements were a march on Richmond under Grant's personal command and a thrust by the western armies, now led by General William T. Sherman, to Atlanta and the heart of Georgia.

In May and early June, Grant and Lee fought a series of bloody battles in northern Virginia that tended to follow a set pattern. Lee would take up an entrenched position in the path of the invading force, and Grant would attack it, sustaining heavy losses but also inflicting casualties the shrinking Confederate Army could ill afford. When his direct assault had failed, Grant would move to his left, hoping in vain to maneuver Lee into a less defensible position. In the battles of the Wilderness, Spotsylvania, and Cold Harbor, the Union lost about sixty thousand men—more than twice the number of Confederate casualties—without defeating Lee or opening the road to Richmond. After losing twelve thousand men in a single day at Cold Harbor, Grant decided to change his tactics and moved his army to the south of Richmond. There he drew up before Petersburg, a rail center that linked Richmond to the rest of the Confederacy; after failing to take it by assault, he settled down for a siege.

The siege of Petersburg was a long, drawn-out affair, and the resulting stalemate in the East caused northern morale to plummet during the summer of 1864. Lincoln was facing reelection, and his failure to end the war dimmed his prospects. Although nominated with ease in June—with Andrew Johnson, a proadministration Democrat from Tennessee, as his running mate—Lincoln confronted growing opposition within his own party, especially from Radicals who disagreed with his apparently lenient approach to the future restoration of seceded states to the Union. After Lincoln vetoed a Radical-supported congressional reconstruction plan in July, some Radicals began to call for a new convention to nominate another candidate.

The Democrats seemed to be in a good position to capitalize on Republican divisions and make a strong bid for the White House. Their platform appealed to war weariness by calling for a cease-fire followed by negotiations to reestablish the Union. The party's nominee, General George McClellan, announced he would not be bound by the peace plank and would pursue the war. But he promised to end the conflict sooner than Lincoln could because he would not insist on emancipation as a condition for reconstruction. By late summer Lincoln confessed privately that he would probably be defeated.

But northern military successes changed the political outlook. Sherman's invasion of Georgia went well; between May and September he employed a series of skillful flanking movements to force the Confederates to retreat to the outskirts of Atlanta. On September 2, the city fell, and northern forces occupied the hub of the Deep South. The news unified the Republican party behind Lincoln and improved his chances for defeating McClellan in November. The election itself was almost an anticlimax: Lincoln won 212 of a possible 233 electoral votes and 55 percent of the popular vote. The Republican cause of "liberty and Union" was secure.

The concluding military operations revealed the futility of further southern resistance. Cutting himself off from his supply lines and living off the land, Sherman marched unopposed through Georgia to the sea, destroying almost everything of possible military or economic value in a corridor 300 miles long and 60 miles wide. The Confederate Army that had opposed him at Atlanta, now under the command of General John B. Hood, moved northward into Tennessee, where it was defeated and almost destroyed by Union forces under General George Thomas at Nashville in mid-December. Sherman captured Savannah on December 22 and presented the city to Lincoln as a Christmas present. He then turned north and marched through the Carolinas with

The Election of 1864			
Candidate	Party	Popular Vote	Electoral Vote*
Lincoln	Republican	2,218,388	212
McClellan	Democrat	1,812,807	21

*Out of a total of 233 electoral votes. The eleven secessionist states—Alabama, Arkansas, Florida, Georgia, Louisiana, Mississippi, North Carolina, South Carolina, Tennessee, Texas, and Virginia—did not vote.

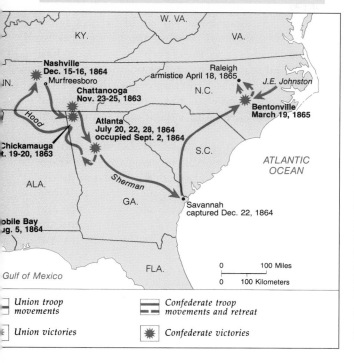

Sherman's March to the Sea
Leaving Atlanta in flames, Sherman marched to the Georgia coast, took Savannah, then moved his troops north through the Carolinas.

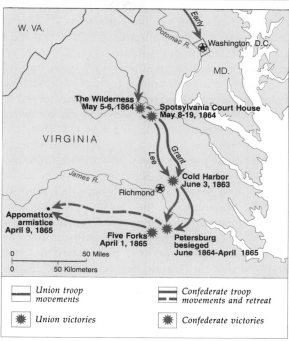

The Road to Appomattox
Grant's terms of surrender were generous, allowing the Confederate soldiers to take home their horses and mules so that they might "put in a crop."

the aim of joining up with Grant at Petersburg near Richmond.

While Sherman was bringing the war to the Carolinas, Grant finally ended the stalemate at Petersburg. When Lee's starving and exhausted army tried to break through the Union lines, Grant renewed his attack and forced the Confederates to abandon Petersburg and Richmond on April 2, 1865. He then pursued them westward for 100 miles, placing his forces in position to cut off their line of retreat to the south. Recognizing the hopelessness of further resistance, Lee surrendered his army at Appomattox Courthouse on April 9.

But the joy of the victorious North turned to sorrow and anger when John Wilkes Booth, a pro-Confederate actor, assassinated Abraham Lincoln as the president watched a play at Ford's Theater in Washington on April 14. Although Booth had a few accomplices—one of whom attempted to murder Secretary of State Seward—popular theories that the assassination was the

result of a vast conspiracy involving Confederate leaders or (according to another version) Radical Republicans have never been substantiated and are extremely implausible.

The man who had spoken of the need to sacrifice for the Union cause at Gettysburg had himself given "the last full measure of devotion" to the cause of "government of the people, by the people, for the people." Four days after Lincoln's death, the only remaining Confederate force of any significance (the troops under Joseph E. Johnston who had been opposing Sherman in North Carolina) laid down its arms. The Union was saved.

Effects of the War

The nation that emerged from four years of total war was not the same America that had split apart in 1861. The 618,000 young men who were in their graves, victims of enemy fire or the diseases that spread rapidly in military encampments in this era before modern medicine and sanitation, would otherwise have married, raised families, and contributed their talents to building up the country. The widows and sweethearts they left behind temporarily increased the proportion of unmarried women in the population, and some members of this generation of involuntary "spinsters" sought new opportunities for making a living or serving the community that went beyond the purely domestic roles previously prescribed for women. The large number who had served as nurses or volunteer workers during the war were especially responsive to calls for broadening "the woman's sphere." Some of the northern women who were prominent in wartime service organizations—like Louise Lee Schuyler, Josephine Shaw Lowell, and Mary Livermore—became leaders of postwar philanthropic and reform movements.

At enormous human and economic cost, the nation had emancipated four million African Americans from slavery, but it had not yet resolved that they would be equal citizens. At the time of Lincoln's assassination, most northern states still denied blacks equality under the law and the right to vote. Whether the North would extend more rights to southern freedmen than it had granted to "free Negroes" was an open question.

The impact of the war on white working people was also unclear. Those in the industrializing parts of the North had suffered and lost ground economically because prices had risen much faster than wages during the conflict. But Republican rhetoric stressing "equal opportunity" and the "dignity of labor" raised hopes that the crusade against slavery could be broadened into a movement to improve the lot of working people in general. Foreign-born workers had additional reason to be optimistic; the fact that so many immigrants had fought and died for the Union cause had—for the moment—weakened nativist sentiment and encouraged ethnic tolerance.

What the war definitely decided was that the federal government was supreme over the states and had a broad grant of constitutional authority to act on matters affecting "the general welfare." The southern principle of state sovereignty and strict construction died at Appomattox, and the United States was on its way to becoming a true nation-state with an effective central government. But it retained a federal structure; although states could no longer claim the right to secede or nullify federal law, they still had primary responsibility for most functions of government. Everyone agreed that the Constitution placed limits on what the national government could do, and questions would continue to arise about where federal authority ended and states' rights began.

A broadened definition of federal powers had

Casualties of War

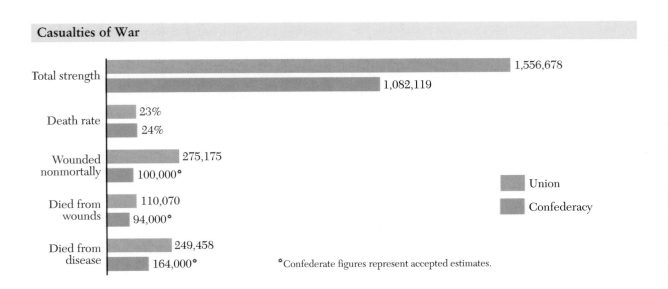

	Union	Confederacy
Total strength	1,556,678	1,082,119
Death rate	23%	24%
Wounded nonmortally	275,175	100,000*
Died from wounds	110,070	94,000*
Died from disease	249,458	164,000*

*Confederate figures represent accepted estimates.

During the war, many women replaced skilled male workers in the manufacturing labor force. These women are filling cartridges in the United States Arsenal at Watertown, New York.

its greatest impact in the realm of economic policy. During the war, Republican-dominated Congresses passed a rash of legislation designed to give encouragement and direction to the nation's economic development. Taking advantage of the absence of southern opposition, Republicans rejected the pre–Civil War tradition of virtual laissez-faire and enacted a Whiggish program of active support for business and agriculture. In 1862, Congress passed a high protective tariff, approved a homestead act intended to encourage settlement of the West by providing free land to settlers, granted huge tracts of public land to railroad companies to support the building of a transcontinental railroad, and gave the states land for the establishment of agricultural colleges. The following year, Congress set up a national banking system that required member banks to keep adequate reserves and invest one-third of their capital in government securities. The notes the national banks issued became the country's first standardized and reliable circulating currency.

These wartime achievements added up to a decisive shift in the relationship between the federal government and private enterprise. The Republicans took a limited government that did little more than seek to protect the marketplace from the threat of monopoly and changed it into an activist state that promoted and subsidized the efforts of the economically industrious.

The most pervasive effect of the war on northern society was to encourage an "organizational revolution." Aided by government policies, venturesome businessmen took advantage of the new national market created by military procurement to build larger firms that could operate across state lines; some of the huge corporate enterprises of the postwar era began to take shape. Philanthropists also developed more effective national associations; the most notable of these were the Sanitary and Christian Commissions that ministered to the physical and spiritual needs of the troops. Efforts to care for the wounded influenced the development of the modern hospital and the rise of nursing as a female profession. Both the men who served in the army and those men and women who supported them on the home front or behind the lines became accustomed to working in large, bureaucratic organizations of a kind that had scarcely existed before the war.

Ralph Waldo Emerson, the era's most prominent man of letters, revealed in his wartime writ-

ment in an inner world of imagination and cosmic intuition. During the conflict, he began to exalt the claims of organization, government, and "civilization" over the endeavors of "the private man" to find fulfillment through "self-culture." He even extolled military discipline and became an official visitor to West Point. In 1837, he had said of young men who aspired to political office: "Wake them up and they shall quit the false good and leap to the true, and leave governments to clerks and desks." Now he affirmed almost the opposite: "Government must not be a parish clerk, a justice of the peace. It has, of necessity, in any crisis of the state, the absolute powers of a dictator." In purging his thoughts of extreme individualism and hailing the need to accept social discipline and participate in organized, cooperative activity, Emerson epitomized the way the war affected American thought and patterns of behavior.

The North won the war mainly because it had shown a greater capacity than the South to organize, innovate, and "modernize." Its victory meant the nation as a whole would now be ready to embrace the conception of progress that the North had affirmed in its war effort—not only advances in science and technology, but also in bringing together and managing large numbers of men and women for economic and social goals. The Civil War was thus a catalyst for the great transformation of American society from an individualistic society of small producers into the more highly organized and "incorporated" America of the late nineteenth century.

Recommended Reading

The best one-volume history of the Civil War is James M. McPherson, *Battle Cry of Freedom: The Civil War Era* (1988). Other valuable surveys of the war and its aftermath are J. G. Randall and David Herbert Donald, *The Civil War and Reconstruction,* 2d ed. (1969); and James M. McPherson, *Ordeal by Fire: The Civil War and Reconstruction* (1981). An excellent shorter account is David Herbert Donald, *Liberty and Union* (1978). The Confederate experience is well covered in Clement Eaton, *A History of the Southern Confederacy* (1954), and Emory M. Thomas, *The Confederate Nation: 1861–1865* (1979). Eaton stresses internal problems and weaknesses; Thomas highlights achievements under adversity. On the North's war effort, see Phillip Paludan, *"A People's Contest: The Union and the Civil War, 1861–1865"* (1988). The best one-vol-

ings that the conflict encouraged a dramatic shift in American thought about the relationship between the individual and society. Before the war, Emerson had generally championed "the transcendent individual," who stood apart from institutions and organizations and sought fulfill-

ume introduction to the military side of the conflict is still Bruce Catton, *This Hallowed Ground* (1956).

Lincoln's career and wartime leadership are treated in two competent biographies: Benjamin P. Thomas, *Abraham Lincoln* (1954), and Stephen B. Oates, *With Malice Toward None: The Life of Abraham Lincoln* (1977). A penetrating analysis of events immediately preceding the fighting is Kenneth M. Stampp, *And the War Came: The North and the Sectional Crisis* (1950). John Hope Franklin, *The Emancipation Proclamation* (1963) is a good short account of the North's decision to free the slaves. An incisive account of the transition from slavery to freedom is Barbara Jeanne Fields, *Slavery and Freedom on the Middle Ground: Maryland in the Nineteenth Century* (1985). Five leading historians offer conflicting interpretations in their attempts to explain the South's defeat in *Why the North Won the Civil War,* edited by David Donald (1960). A brilliant study of the writings of those who experienced the war is Edmund Wilson, *Patriotic Gore: Studies in the Literature of the American Civil War* (1962). On the intellectual impact see George M. Fredrickson, *The Inner Civil War: Northern Intellectuals and the Crisis of the Union,* 2d ed. (1993).

Additional Bibliography

The most thorough modern history of the Civil War is Allan Nevins, *The War for the Union,* 4 vols. (1959–1971). Bruce Catton, *Centennial History of the Civil War,* 3 vols. (1961–1965) is the most detailed account of the military aspects of the conflict. The day-to-day drama of the war is well conveyed in Shelby Foote, *The Civil War: A Narrative,* 3 vols. (1958–1974). Among the many collections of essays that deal with general issues of the period are Allan Nevins, *The Statesmanship of the Civil War* (1962); David Donald, *Lincoln Reconsidered: Essays on the Civil War Era* (1956); Eric Foner, *Politics and Ideology in the Age of the Civil War* (1980); and David M. Potter, *The South and the Sectional Conflict* (1968).

Further insight into the Confederate side of the struggle can be derived from Charles P. Roland, *The Confederacy* (1960); Frank E. Vandiver, *Their Tattered Flags: The Epic of the Confederacy* (1970); Emory M. Thomas, *The Confederacy as a Revolutionary Experience* (1971); and Bell I. Wiley, *The Road to Appomattox* (1956). Jefferson Davis's leadership is assessed in Paul D. Escott, *After Secession: Jefferson Davis and the Failure of Confederate Nationalism* (1978); Hudson Strode, *Jefferson Davis,* 3 vols. (1955–1964); Clement Eaton, *Jefferson Davis* (1977); and Frank E. Vandiver, *Jefferson Davis and the Confederate States* (1964). The most detailed works on Lincoln's stewardship of the Union cause are James G. Randall, *Lincoln the President,* 4 vols. (1945–1955,

vol. 4 completed by Richard N. Current), and Carl Sandburg's less reliable *Abraham Lincoln: The War Years,* 4 vols. (1939). For illuminating essays on Lincoln's leadership, see Don E. Fehrenbacher, *Lincoln in Text and Context* (1987). On Lincoln's most notable speech, see Garry Wills, *Lincoln at Gettysburg* (1992).

Events leading up to the outbreak of hostilities are covered in Dwight L. Dumond, *The Secession Movement* (1931); Ralph Wooster, *The Secession Conventions of the South* (1962); Daniel W. Crofts, *Reluctant Confederates: Upper South Unionists in the Secession Crisis* (1989); Charles R. Lee, *The Confederate Constitutions* (1963); David M. Potter, *Lincoln and His Party in the Secession Crisis,* 2d ed. (1962); and Richard N. Current, *Lincoln and the First Shot* (1963).

The literature on military commanders, campaigns, and battles is enormous, but mention must be made of Douglas Southall Freeman's outstanding works on southern generalship: *R. E. Lee: A Biography,* 4 vols. (1934–1935) and *Lee's Lieutenants,* 3 vols. (1942–1944). Also of exceptional merit is Bruce Catton's trilogy on the Army of the Potomac: *Mr. Lincoln's Army* (1951), *Glory Road* (1952), and *A Stillness at Appomattox* (1953). See also T. Harry Williams, *Lincoln and His Generals* (1952). A provocative interpretation of the ethos of total war is Charles B. Royster, *The Destructive War: William Tecumseh Sherman and the Americans* (1991). On the guerilla war in Missouri see Michael Fellman, *Inside War* (1989). On the common soldier's experience of the war, see two books by Bell I. Wiley: *The Life of Johnny Reb* (1943) and *The Life of Billy Yank* (1952), as well as Reid Mitchell, *The Northern Soldier Leaves Home* (1993).

Major works on northern politics during the war are William B. Hesseltine, *Lincoln and the War Governors* (1948); T. Harry Williams, *Lincoln and the Radicals* (1941); Hans Trefousse, *The Radical Republicans: Lincoln's Vanguard for Racial Justice* (1969); David Donald, *Charles Sumner and the Rights of Man* (1970); Allan G. Bogue, *The Earnest Men: Republicans of the Civil War Senate* (1981); Joel Silbey, *A Respectable Minority: The Democratic Party in the Civil War Era* (1977); Wood Gray, *The Hidden Civil War: The Story of the Copperheads* (1942); Frank L. Klement, *Copperheads in the Middle West* (1960); and Leonard P. Curry, *Blueprint for Modern America: Non-Military Legislation of the First Civil War Congress* (1968). On legal and constitutional issues, see James G. Randall, *Constitutional Problems Under Lincoln,* rev. ed. (1961); Harold M. Hyman, *A More Perfect Union: The Impact of the Civil War and Reconstruction on the Constitution* (1973); Phillip S. Paludan, *A Covenant with Death: The Constitution, the Law, and Equality in the Civil War Era* (1975);

and Mark E. Neely, Jr., *The Fate of Liberty: Abraham Lincoln and Civil Liberties* (1991).

Other aspects of northern life during the war are treated in Paul W. Gates, *Agriculture and the Civil War* (1965); Iver Bernstein, *The New York Draft Riots* (1990); Lori D. Ginzberg, *Women and the Work of Benevolence* (1990); Daniel Aaron, *The Unwritten War: American Writers and the Civil War* (1973); and James H. Morehead, *American Apocalypse: Yankee Protestants and the Civil War* (1978).

For an understanding of the South's internal problems, see Frank Owsley, *States' Rights in the Confederacy* (1925); Curtis A. Amlund, *Federalism in the Southern Confederacy* (1966); Wilfred B. Yearns, *The Confederate Congress* (1960); Richard C. Todd, *Confederate Finance* (1954); Bell I. Wiley, *The Plain People of the Confederacy* (1943); and J. William Harris, *Plain Folk and Gentry in a Slave Society* (1985).

Emancipation and the role of blacks in the war are the subject of a number of excellent studies, including Benjamin Quarles, *The Negro in the Civil War* (1953) and *Lincoln and the Negro* (1962); Bell I. Wiley, *Southern Negroes, 1861–1865* (1938); James M. McPherson, *The Struggle for Equality: Abolitionists and the Negro in the Civil War and Reconstruction* (1964); LaWanda Cox, *Lincoln and Black Freedom* (1981); V. Jacque Voegeli, *Free But Not Equal: The Midwest and the Negro During the Civil War;* Forrest G. Wood, *Black Scare: The Racist Response to the Civil War and Reconstruction* (1968); Louis Gerteis, *From Contraband to Freedman: Federal Policy Toward Southern Blacks 1861–1865* (1973); Willie Lee Rose, *Rehearsal for Reconstruction: The Port Royal Experiment* (1964); Herman Belz, *A New Birth of Freedom: The Republican Party and Freedmen's Rights, 1861–1866* (1976); Robert F. Durden, *The Gray and the Black: The Confederate Debate on Emancipation* (1972).

On wartime diplomacy, see David P. Crook, *The North, the South and the Powers, 1861–1865* (1974); Frank Owsley, *King Cotton Diplomacy,* rev. ed. (1959); Brian Jenkins, *Britain and the War for the Union* (1974); and Mary Ellison, *Support for Secession: Lancashire and the American Civil War* (1972).

CHAPTER

16

The Agony of Reconstruction

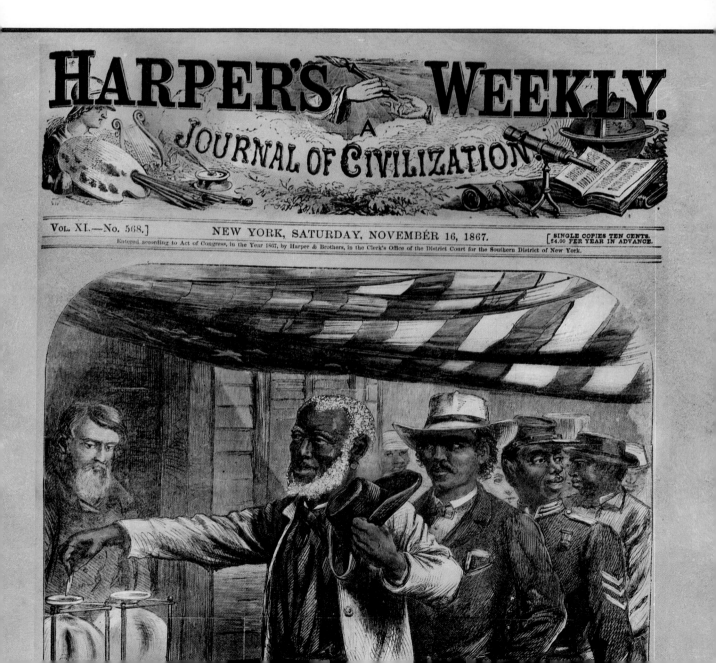

HARPER'S WEEKLY.

A JOURNAL OF CIVILIZATION.

Vol. XI.—No. 568.] NEW YORK, SATURDAY, NOVEMBER 16, 1867. [SINGLE COPIES TEN CENTS. $4.00 PER YEAR IN ADVANCE.

Entered according to Act of Congress, in the Year 1867, by Harper & Brothers, in the Clerk's Office of the District Court for the Southern District of New York.

uring the Reconstruction period immediately following the Civil War, African Americans struggled to become equal citizens of a democratic republic. They produced a number of remarkable leaders who showed that blacks were as capable as other Americans of voting, holding office, and legislating for a complex and rapidly changing society. Among these leaders was Robert Smalls of South Carolina. Although virtually forgotten by the time of his death in 1915, Smalls was perhaps the most famous and widely respected southern black leader of the Civil War and Reconstruction era. His career reveals some of the main features of the African American experience during that crucial period.

Born a slave in 1839, Smalls had a white father whose identity has never been clearly established. But his white ancestry apparently gained him some advantages, and as a young man he was allowed to live and work independently, hiring his own time from a master who may have been his half-brother. Smalls worked as a sailor and trained himself to be a pilot in Charleston Harbor. When the Union Navy blockaded Charleston in 1862, Smalls, who was then working in a Confederate steamship called the *Planter,* saw a chance to win his freedom in a particularly dramatic way. At three o'clock in the morning on May 13, 1862, when the white officers of the *Planter* were ashore, he took command of the vessel and its slave crew, sailed it out of the heavily fortified harbor, and surrendered it to the Union Navy. Smalls immediately became a hero to those antislavery Northerners who were seeking evidence that the slaves were willing and able to serve the Union. The *Planter* was turned into a Union transport and Smalls was made its captain after being commissioned as an officer in the Armed Forces of the United States. During the remainder of the war, he rendered conspicuous and gallant service as captain and pilot of Union vessels off the coast of South Carolina.

Like a number of other African Americans who had fought valiantly for the Union, Smalls went on to a distinguished political career during Reconstruction, serving in the South Carolina constitutional convention, the state legislature, and for several terms in the U.S. Congress. He

was also a shrewd businessman and became the owner of extensive properties in Beaufort, South Carolina, and its vicinity. (His first purchase was the house of his former master where he had spent his early years as a slave.) As the leading citizen of Beaufort during Reconstruction and for some years thereafter, he acted like many successful white Americans, combining the acquisition of wealth with the exercise of political power. The electoral organization he established resembled in some ways the well-oiled "machines" being established in northern towns and cities. It was so effective that Smalls was able to control local government and get himself elected to Congress even after the election of 1876 had placed the state under the control of white conservatives bent on depriving blacks of political power. Organized mob violence defeated him in 1878, but he bounced back to win by decision of Congress a contested congressional election in 1880. He did not leave the House of Representatives for good until 1886, when he lost another contested election that had to be decided by Congress. It revealed the changing mood of the country that his white challenger was seated despite evidence of violence and intimidation against black voters.

In their efforts to defeat him, Smalls's white opponents frequently charged that he had a hand in the corruption that was allegedly rampant in South Carolina during Reconstruction. But careful historical investigation shows that he was, by the standards of the time, an honest and responsible public servant. In the South Carolina convention of 1868 and later in the state legislature, he was a conspicuous champion of free and compulsory public education. In Congress, he fought for the enactment and enforcement of federal civil rights laws. Not especially radical on social questions, he sometimes bent over backward to accommodate what he regarded as the legitimate interests and sensibilities of South Carolina whites. Like other middle-class black political leaders in Reconstruction-era South Carolina, he can perhaps be faulted in hindsight for not doing more to help poor blacks gain access to land of their own. But in 1875 he sponsored congressional legislation that opened for purchase at low prices the land in his own district that had been confiscated by the federal government during the war. As a result, blacks were able to buy most of

Robert Smalls (1839–1915) in an engraving from an 1862 newspaper. Smalls, who commandeered the frigate Planter and delivered it to the Union, later served in congress.

it, and they soon owned three-fourths of the land in Beaufort and its vicinity.

Smalls spent the later years of his life as U. S. collector of customs for the port of Beaufort, a beneficiary of the patronage that the Republican party continued to provide for a few loyal southern blacks. But the loss of real political clout for Smalls and men like him was one of the tragic consequences of the fall of Reconstruction.

THE PRESIDENT VERSUS CONGRESS

The problem of how to reconstruct the Union in the wake of the South's military defeat was one of the most difficult and perplexing challenges ever faced by American policymakers. The Constitution provided no firm guidelines, for the framers had not anticipated a division of the country into warring sections. Once emancipation became a northern war aim, the problem was compounded by a new issue: how far should the federal government go to secure freedom and civil rights for 4 million former slaves?

The debate that evolved led to a major political crisis. Advocates of a minimal Reconstruction policy favored quick restoration of the Union with no protection for the freed slaves beyond the prohibition of slavery. Proponents of a more radical policy wanted readmission of the southern states to be dependent on guarantees that "loyal" men would displace the Confederate elite in positions of power, and that blacks would acquire basic rights of American citizenship. The White House favored the minimal approach, whereas Congress came to endorse the more radical and thoroughgoing form of Reconstruction. The resulting struggle between Congress and the chief executive was the most serious clash between two branches of government in the nation's history.

Wartime Reconstruction

Tension between the president and Congress over how to reconstruct the Union began during the war. Occupied mainly with achieving victory, Lincoln never set forth a final and comprehensive plan for bringing rebellious states back into the fold. But he did take initiatives that indicated he favored a lenient and conciliatory policy toward Southerners who would give up the struggle and repudiate slavery. In December 1863, he issued a Proclamation of Amnesty and Reconstruction; it offered a full pardon to all Southerners (with the exception of certain classes of Confederate leaders) who would take an oath of allegiance to the Union and acknowledge the legality of emancipation. Once 10 percent or more of the voting population of any occupied state had taken the oath, they were authorized to set up a loyal government. Efforts to establish such regimes were quickly undertaken in states that were wholly or partially occupied by Union troops; by 1864 Louisiana and Arkansas had fully functioning Unionist governments.

Lincoln's policy was meant to shorten the war. The president hoped that granting pardons and political recognition to oath-taking minorities would weaken the southern cause by making it easy for disillusioned or lukewarm Confederates to switch sides. He also hoped to further his emancipation policy by insisting the new governments abolish slavery, an action that might prove crucial if—as seemed possible before Lincoln's reelection in 1864 and Congress's subsequent passage of the Thirteenth Amendment—the courts or a future Democratic administration were to disallow or revoke the Emancipation Proclamation. When constitutional conventions operating under the 10 percent plan in Louisiana and Arkansas dutifully abolished slavery in 1864, emancipation came closer to being irreversible.

Congress was unhappy with the president's reconstruction experiments and in 1864 refused to seat the Unionists elected to the House and Senate from Louisiana and Arkansas. A minority of congressional Republicans—the strongly anti-slavery Radicals—favored protection for black rights as a precondition for the readmission of southern states. These Republican militants were upset because Lincoln had not insisted the constitution makers provide for black male suffrage. But a larger group in Congress was not yet prepared to implement civil and political equality for blacks. Many of these moderates also opposed Lincoln's plan, but they did so primarily because they did not trust the repentant Confederates who would play a major role in the new governments. No matter what their position on black rights, most congressional Republicans feared that hypocritical oath taking would allow the old ruling class to return to power and cheat the North of the full fruits of its impending victory.

Congress also felt the president was exceeding his authority by using executive powers to restore the Union. Lincoln operated on the theory that secession, being illegal, did not place the Confederate states outside the Union in a constitutional sense. Since individuals and not states had defied federal authority, the president could use his pardoning power to certify a loyal electorate, which could then function as the legitimate state government.

The dominant view in Congress, on the other hand, was that the southern states had forfeited their place in the Union and that it was up to Congress to decide when and how they would be readmitted. The most popular justification for congressional responsibility was based on the clause of the Constitution providing that "the United States shall guarantee to every State in this Union a Republican Form of Government." By seceding, Radicals argued, the Confederate states had ceased to be republican, and Congress must set the conditions to be met before they could be readmitted.

After refusing to recognize Lincoln's 10 percent governments, Congress passed a Reconstruction bill of its own in July 1864. Known as the Wade-Davis bill, this legislation required that 50 percent of the voters must take an oath of future loyalty before the restoration process could begin. Once this had occurred, those who could swear they had never willingly supported the Confederacy could vote in an election for delegates to a constitutional convention. The bill in its final form did not require black suffrage, but it did give federal courts the power to enforce emancipation. Faced with this attempt to nullify his own program, Lincoln exercised a pocket veto by refusing to sign the bill before Congress adjourned. He justified his action by announcing he did not wish to be committed to any single Reconstruction plan. The sponsors of the bill responded with an angry manifesto, and Lincoln's relations with Congress reached their low.

Congress and the president remained stalemated on the Reconstruction issue for the rest of the war. During his last months in office, however, Lincoln showed some willingness to compromise. He persisted in his efforts to obtain full recognition for the governments he had nurtured in Louisiana and Arkansas but seemed receptive to the setting of other conditions—perhaps including black suffrage—for readmission of those states where wartime conditions had prevented execution of his plan. However, he died without clarifying his intentions, leaving historians to speculate on whether his quarrel with Congress would have worsened or been resolved. Given Lincoln's past record of political flexibility, the best bet is that he would have come to terms with the majority of his party.

Andrew Johnson at the Helm

Andrew Johnson, the man suddenly made president by an assassin's bullet, attempted to put the Union back together on his own authority in 1865. But his policies eventually set him at odds with Congress and the Republican party and provoked the most serious crisis in the history of relations between the executive and legislative branches of the federal government.

Nearly insurmountable problems with a Congress determined to enact its own Reconstruction policy plagued Andrew Johnson through his presidency. Impeached in 1868, he escaped conviction by a single vote.

Johnson's background shaped his approach to Reconstruction. Born in dire poverty in North Carolina, he migrated as a young man to eastern Tennessee, where he made his living as a tailor. Lacking formal schooling, he did not learn to read and write until adult life. Entering politics as a Jacksonian Democrat, he became known as an effective stump speaker. His railing against the planter aristocracy made him the spokesman for Tennessee's nonslaveholding whites and the most successful politician in the state. He advanced from state legislator to congressman to governor and in 1857 was elected to the U. S. Senate.

When Tennessee seceded in 1861, Johnson was the only senator from a Confederate state who remained loyal to the Union and continued to serve in Washington. But his Unionism and defense of the common people did not include antislavery sentiments. Nor was he friendly to blacks. While campaigning in Tennessee, he had objected only to the fact that slaveholding was the privilege of a wealthy minority. He revealed his attitude when he wished that "every head of family in the United States had one slave to take the drudgery and menial service of his family."

During the war, while acting as military governor of Tennessee, Johnson endorsed Lincoln's emancipation policy and carried it into effect. But he viewed it primarily as a means of destroying the power of the hated planter class rather than as a recognition of black humanity. He was chosen as Lincoln's running mate in 1864 because it was thought that a proadministration Democrat, who was a southern Unionist in the bargain, would strengthen the ticket. No one expected Johnson to succeed to the presidency; it is one of the strange accidents of American history that a southern Democrat, a fervent white supremacist, came to preside over a Republican administration immediately after the Civil War.

Some Radical Republicans initially welcomed Johnson's ascent to the nation's highest office. Their hopes make sense in the light of Johnson's record of fierce loyalty to the Union and his apparent agreement with the Radicals that ex-Confederates should be severely treated. More than Lincoln, who had spoken of "malice toward none and charity for all," Johnson seemed likely to punish southern "traitors" and prevent them from regaining political influence. Only gradually did the deep disagreement between the president and the Republican majority in Congress become evident.

The Reconstruction policy that Johnson initiated on May 29, 1865, created some uneasiness among the Radicals, but most Republicans were willing to give it a chance. Johnson placed North Carolina and eventually other states under appointed provisional governors chosen mostly from among prominent southern politicians who had opposed the secession movement and had rendered no conspicuous service to the Confederacy. The governors were responsible for calling constitutional conventions and ensuring that only "loyal" whites were permitted to vote for delegates. Participation required taking the oath of allegiance that Lincoln had prescribed earlier. Once again Confederate leaders and former officeholders who had participated in the rebellion were excluded. To regain their political and property rights, those in the exempted categories had to apply for individual presidential pardons. Johnson made one significant addition to the list of the excluded: all those possessing taxable property exceeding $20,000 in value. In this fashion, he sought to prevent his longtime adversaries—the wealthy planters—from participating in the Reconstruction of southern state governments.

Once the conventions met, Johnson urged them to do three things: declare the ordinances of secession illegal, repudiate the Confederate debt, and ratify the Thirteenth Amendment abolishing slavery. After governments had been reestablished under constitutions meeting these conditions, the president assumed the Reconstruction process would be complete and that the ex-Confederate states could regain their full rights under the Constitution.

The conventions, dominated by prewar Unionists and representatives of backcountry yeoman farmers, did their work in a way satisfactory to the president but troubling to many congressional Republicans. Rather than quickly accepting Johnson's recommendations, delegates in several states approved them begrudgingly or with qualifications. Furthermore, all the resulting constitutions limited suffrage to whites, disappointing the large number of Northerners who hoped, as Lincoln had, that at least some African Americans—perhaps those who were educated or had served in the Union army—would be given the vote. Johnson on the whole seemed eager to give southern white majorities a free hand in determining the civil and political status of the freed slaves.

Republican uneasiness turned to disillusionment and anger when the state legislatures elected under the new constitutions proceeded to pass "Black Codes" subjecting former slaves to a variety of special regulations and restrictions on their freedom. Especially troubling were vagrancy and apprenticeship laws that forced African Americans to work and denied them a free choice of employers. Blacks in some states were also prevented from testifying in court on the same basis as whites and were subject to a separate penal code. To Radicals, the Black Codes looked suspiciously like slavery under a new guise. More upsetting to northern public opinion in general, a number of prominent ex-Confederate leaders were elected to Congress in the fall of 1865.

Johnson himself was partly responsible for this turn of events. Despite his lifelong feud with the planter class, he was generous in granting pardons to members of the old elite who came to him, hat in hand, and asked for them. When for-

mer Confederate Vice President Alexander Stephens and other proscribed ex-rebels were elected to Congress although they had not been pardoned, Johnson granted them special amnesty so they could serve.

The growing rift between the president and Congress came into the open in December when the House and Senate refused to seat the recently elected southern delegation. Instead of endorsing Johnson's work and recognizing the state governments he had called into being, Congress established a joint committee, chaired by Senator William Pitt Fessenden of Maine, to review Reconstruction policy and set further conditions for readmission of the seceded states.

Congress Takes the Initiative

The struggle over how to reconstruct the Union ended with Congress doing the job of setting policy all over again. The clash between Johnson and Congress was a matter of principle and could not be reconciled. Johnson's personality—his prickly pride, sharp tongue, intolerance of opposition, and stubborn refusal to give an inch—did not help his political cause. But the root of the problem was that he disagreed with the majority of Congress on what Reconstruction was supposed to accomplish. An heir of the Democratic states' rights tradition, he wanted to restore the prewar federal system as quickly as possible and without change except that states would no longer have the right to legalize slavery or to secede.

Most Republicans wanted firm guarantees that the old southern ruling class would not regain regional power and national influence by devising new ways to subjugate blacks. Since emancipation had nullified the three-fifths clause of the Constitution by which slaves had been counted as three-fifths of a person, all blacks were now to be counted in determining representation. Consequently, Republicans worried about increased southern strength in Congress and the electoral college. The current Congress favored a Reconstruction policy that would give the federal government authority to limit the political role of ex-Confederates and provide some protection for black citizenship.

Republican leaders—with the exception of a few extreme Radicals like Charles Sumner—

lacked any firm conviction that blacks were inherently equal to whites. They *did* believe, however, that in a modern democratic state, all citizens must have the same basic rights and opportunities, regardless of natural abilities. Principle coincided easily with political expediency; southern blacks, whatever their alleged shortcomings, were likely to be loyal to the Republican party that had emancipated them. They could be used, if necessary, to counteract the influence of resurgent ex-Confederates, thus preventing the Democrats from returning to national dominance through control of the South.

The disagreement between the president and Congress became irreconcilable in early 1866 when Johnson vetoed two bills that had passed with overwhelming Republican support. The first extended the life of the Freedmen's Bureau—a temporary agency set up to aid the former slaves by providing relief, education, legal help, and assistance in obtaining land or employment. The second was a civil rights bill meant to nullify the Black Codes and guarantee to freedmen "full and equal benefit of all laws and proceedings for the security of person and property as is enjoyed by white citizens."

Johnson's vetoes shocked moderate Republicans who had expected the president to accept these relatively modest measures as a way of heading off more radical proposals, such as black suffrage and a prolonged denial of political rights to ex-Confederates. Presidential opposition to policies that represented the bare minimum of Republican demands on the South alienated moderates in the party and ensured a wide opposition to Johnson's plan of Reconstruction. Johnson succeeded in blocking the Freedmen's Bureau bill, although a modified version later passed. But the Civil Rights Act won the two-thirds majority necessary to override his veto, signifying that the president was now hopelessly at odds with most of the congressmen from what was supposed to be his own party. Never before had Congress overridden a presidential veto.

Johnson soon revealed that he intended to abandon the Republicans and place himself at the head of a new conservative party uniting the small minority of Republicans who supported him with a reviving Democratic party that was rallying behind his Reconstruction policy. In

THE RECONSTRUCTION DOSE.

According to this 1867 cartoon from Frank Leslie's Illustrated Newspaper, *Congress's program for Reconstruction was a bitter dose for the South, and President "Naughty Andy" urged Southerners not to accept the plan. Mrs. Columbus insisted, however, that Dr. Congress knew what was best.*

preparation for the elections of 1866, Johnson helped found the National Union movement to promote his plan to readmit the southern states to the Union without further qualifications. A National Union convention meeting in Philadelphia in August 1866 called for the election to Congress of men who endorsed the presidential plan for Reconstruction.

Meanwhile, the Republican majority on Capitol Hill, fearing that Johnson would not enforce civil rights legislation or that the courts would declare such federal laws unconstitutional, passed the Fourteenth Amendment. This, perhaps the most important of all our constitutional amendments, gave the federal government responsibility for guaranteeing equal rights under the law to all Americans. The first section defined national citizenship for the first time as extending to "all persons born or naturalized in the United States." The states were prohibited from abridg-

Amendment	Main Provisions	Congressional Passage (2/3 majority in each house required)	Ratification Process (3/4 of all states including ex-Confederate states required)
13	Slavery prohibited in United States	January 1865	December 1865 (twenty-seven states, including eight southern states)
14	1. National citizenship 2. State representation in Congress reduced proportionally to number of voters disfranchised 3. Former Confederates denied right to hold office 4. Confederate debt repudiated	June 1866	Rejected by twelve southern and border states, February 1867 Radicals make readmission of southern states hinge on ratification Ratified July 1868
15	Denial of franchise because of race, color, or past servitude explicitly prohibited	February 1869	Ratification required for readmission of Virginia, Texas, Mississippi, Georgia Ratified March 1870

ing the rights of American citizens and could not "deprive any person of life, liberty, or property, without due process of law; nor deny to any person . . . equal protection of the laws."

The other sections of the amendment were important in the context of the time but had fewer long-term implications. Section two sought to penalize the South for denying voting rights to black males by reducing the congressional representation of any state that formally deprived a portion of its male citizens of the right to vote. The third section denied federal office to those who had taken an oath of office to support the U. S. Constitution and then had supported the Confederacy, and the fourth repudiated the Confederate debt. The amendment was sent to the states with the understanding that Southerners would have no chance of being readmitted to Congress unless their states ratified it.

The congressional elections of 1866 served as a referendum on the Fourteenth Amendment. Johnson opposed the amendment on the grounds that it created a "centralized" government and denied states the right to manage their own affairs; he also counseled southern state legislatures to reject it, and all except Tennessee followed his advice. But the president's case for state autonomy was weakened by the publicity resulting from bloody race riots in New Orleans and Memphis. These and other reported atrocities against blacks made it clear that the existing southern state governments were failing abysmally to protect the "life, liberty, or property" of the ex-slaves.

Johnson further weakened his cause by taking the stump on behalf of candidates who supported his policies. In his notorious "swing around the circle," he toured the nation, slandering his opponents in crude language and engaging in undignified exchanges with hecklers. Enraged by southern inflexibility and the antics of a president who acted as if he were still campaigning in the backwoods of Tennessee, northern voters repudiated the administration. The Republican majority in Congress increased to a solid two-thirds in both houses, and the Radical wing of the party gained strength at the expense of moderates and conservatives.

Congressional Reconstruction Plan Enacted

Congress was now in a position to implement its own plan of Reconstruction. In 1867 and 1868 it passed a series of acts that nullified the president's initiatives and reorganized the South on a new basis. Generally referred to as "Radical Reconstruction," these measures actually represented a compromise between genuine Radicals and more moderate elements within the party.

Consistent Radicals like Senator Charles Sumner of Massachusetts and Congressmen Thaddeus Stevens of Pennsylvania and George Julian of Indiana wanted to reshape southern society before readmitting ex-Confederates to the Union. Their program of "regeneration before reconstruction" required an extended period of military rule, confiscation and redistribution of large landholdings among the freedmen, and federal aid for schools to educate blacks and whites for citizenship. But the majority of Republican congressmen found such a program unacceptable because it broke too sharply with American traditions of federalism and regard for property rights and might mean that decades would pass before the Union was back in working order.

The First Reconstruction Act, passed over Johnson's veto on March 2, 1867, did place the South under the rule of the army by reorganizing the region into five military districts. But military rule would last for only a short time. Subsequent acts of 1867 and 1868 opened the way for the quick readmission of any state that framed and ratified a new constitution providing for black suffrage. Ex-Confederates disqualified from holding federal office under the Fourteenth Amendment were prohibited from voting for delegates to the constitutional conventions or in the elections to ratify the conventions' work. Since blacks were allowed to participate in this process, Republicans thought they had found a way to ensure that "loyal" men would dominate the new governments. Speed was essential because some Republican leaders anticipated they would need votes from the reconstructed South in order to retain control of Congress and the White House in 1868.

"Radical Reconstruction" was based on the dubious assumption that once blacks had the vote, they would have the power to protect themselves against white supremacists' efforts to deny them their rights. The Reconstruction Acts thus signaled a retreat from the true Radical position that a sustained use of federal authority was needed to complete the transition from slavery to

This cartoon of Columbia (the personification of a united America) and Robert E. Lee, which appeared in the August 5, 1865, issue of Harper's Weekly, depicts the Radical Republicans' demand for signs of "regeneration" before readmitting Confederate states to the Union.

freedom and prevent the resurgence of the South's old ruling class. (Troops were used in the South after 1868 but only in a very limited and sporadic way.) The majority of Republicans were unwilling to embrace centralized government and an extended period of military rule over civilians. Such drastic steps went beyond the popular northern consensus on necessary and proper Reconstruction measures. Thus, despite strong reservations, Radicals like Thaddeus Stevens supported the plan of readmitting the southern states on the basis of black suffrage, recognizing this was as far as the party and the northern public were willing to go.

Even so, congressional Reconstruction did have a radical aspect. Although the program won

Among the most influential of the radicals was Congressman Thaddeus Stevens of Pennsylvania. He advocated seizing land from southern planters and distributing it among the freed slaves.

Republican support partly because it promised practical political advantages, a genuine spirit of democratic idealism gave legitimacy and fervor to the cause of black male suffrage. Enabling people who were so poor and downtrodden to have access to the ballot box was a bold and innovative application of the principle of government by the consent of the governed. The problem was finding a way to enforce equal suffrage under conditions then existing in the postwar South.

The Impeachment Crisis

The first obstacle to enforcement of congressional Reconstruction was resistance from the White House. Johnson thoroughly disapproved of the new policy and sought to thwart the will of Congress by administering the plan in his own obstructive fashion. He immediately began to dismiss officeholders who sympathized with Radical

Reconstruction, and he countermanded the orders of generals in charge of southern military districts who were zealous in their enforcement of the new legislation. Some Radical generals were transferred and replaced by conservative Democrats. Congress responded by passing laws designed to limit presidential authority over Reconstruction matters. One of these measures was the Tenure of Office Act, requiring Senate approval for the removal of cabinet officers and other officials whose appointment had needed the consent of the Senate. Another measure—a rider to an army appropriations bill—sought to limit Johnson's authority to issue orders to military commanders.

Johnson objected vigorously to these restrictions on the grounds, that they violated the constitutional doctrine of the separation of powers. When it became clear that the president was resolute in fighting for his powers and using them to resist the establishment of Radical regimes in the southern states, some congressmen began to call for his impeachment. A preliminary effort foundered in 1867, but when Johnson tried to discharge Secretary of War Edwin Stanton—the only Radical in the cabinet—and persisted in his efforts despite the disapproval of the Senate, the proimpeachment forces gained in strength.

In January 1868, Johnson ordered General Grant, who already commanded the army, to replace Stanton as head of the War Department. But Grant had his eye on the Republican presidential nomination and refused to defy Congress. Johnson subsequently appointed General Lorenzo Thomas, who agreed to serve. Faced with this apparent violation of the Tenure of Office Act, the House voted overwhelmingly to impeach the president on February 24, and he was placed on trial before the Senate.

Because seven Republican senators broke with the party leadership and voted for acquittal, the effort to convict Johnson and remove him from office fell one vote short of the necessary two-thirds. This outcome resulted in part from a skillful defense. Attorneys for the president argued for a narrow interpretation of the constitutional provision that a president could be impeached only for a "high crime and misdemeanor," asserting that this referred only to an indictable crime. Responding to the charge that Johnson had delib-

The record of the Senate vote on Andrew Johnson's impeachment trial. Charles Sumner, one of the leaders of the pro-impeachment forces, spoke of the trial as "one of the last great battles with slavery" and urged that "every sentiment, every conviction, every vow against slavery must now be directed against him [Johnson]." James Grimes, who spoke for Johnson's acquittal, argued that "This government can only be preserved and the liberty of the people maintained by preserved intact the coordinate branches of it—legislative, executive, judicial—alike. I am no convert to any doctrine of the omnipotence of Congress."

erately violated the Tenure of Office Act, the defense contended that the law did not apply to the removal of Stanton because he had been appointed by Lincoln, not Johnson.

The prosecution countered with a different interpretation of the Tenure of Office Act, but the core of their case was that Johnson had abused the powers of his office in an effort to sabotage the congressional Reconstruction policy. Obstructing the will of the legislative branch, they claimed, was sufficient grounds for conviction even if no crime had been committed. The Republicans who broke ranks to vote for acquit-

tal could not endorse such a broad view of the impeachment power. They feared that removal of a president for essentially political reasons would threaten the constitutional balance of powers and open the way to legislative supremacy over the executive. In addition, the man who would have succeeded Johnson—Senator Benjamin Wade of Ohio, the president pro tem of the Senate—was unpopular with conservative Republicans because of his radical position on labor and currency questions.

Although Johnson's acquittal by the narrowest of margins protected the American presidency from congressional domination, the impeachment episode helped create an impression in the public mind that the Radicals were ready to turn the Constitution to their own use to gain their objectives. Conservatives were again alarmed when Congress took action in 1868 to deny the Supreme Court's appellate jurisdiction in cases involving the military arrest and imprisonment of anti-Reconstruction activists in the South. But the evidence of congressional ruthlessness and illegality is not as strong as most historians used to think. Modern legal scholars have found merit in the Radicals' claim that their actions did not violate the Constitution.

Failure to remove Johnson from office was an embarrassment to congressional Republicans, but the episode did ensure that Reconstruction in the South would proceed as the majority in Congress intended. During the trial, Johnson helped influence the verdict by pledging to enforce the Reconstruction Acts, and he held to this promise during his remaining months in office. Unable to depose the president, the Radicals had at least succeeded in neutralizing his opposition to their program.

RECONSTRUCTION IN THE SOUTH

The Civil War left the South devastated, demoralized, and destitute. Slavery was dead, but what this meant for future relationships between whites and blacks was still in doubt. The overwhelming majority of southern whites wanted to keep blacks adrift between slavery and freedom—without rights, in a status resembling that of the "free Negroes" of the Old South. Blacks sought to be independent of their former masters and viewed the acquisition of land, education, and the vote as the best means of achieving this goal. The thousands of Northerners who went south after the war for materialistic or humanitarian reasons hoped to extend Yankee "civilization" to what they viewed as an unenlightened and barbarous region. For most of them this reformation required the aid of the freedmen; not enough southern whites were willing to accept the new order and embrace northern middle-class values.

The struggle of these groups to achieve their conflicting goals bred chaos, violence, and instability. Unsettled conditions created many opportunities for corruption, crime, and terrorism. This was scarcely an ideal setting for an experiment in interracial democracy, but one was attempted nonetheless. Its success depended on massive and sustained support from the federal government. To the extent that this was forthcoming, progressive reform could be achieved. When it faltered, the forces of reaction and white supremacy were unleashed.

Social and Economic Adjustments

The Civil War scarred the southern landscape and wrecked its economy. One devastated area—central South Carolina—looked to an 1865 observer "like a broad black streak of ruin and desolation—the fences are gone; lonesome smokestacks, surrounded by dark heaps of ashes and cinders, marking the spots where human habitations had stood; the fields all along the roads widely overgrown with weeds, with here and there a sickly patch of cotton or corn cultivated by negro squatters." Other areas through which the armies had passed were similarly ravaged. Several major cities—including Atlanta, Columbia, and Richmond—were gutted by fire. Most factories were dismantled or destroyed, and long stretches of railroad were torn up.

Physical ruin would not have been so disastrous if investment capital had been available for rebuilding. But the substantial wealth represented by Confederate currency and bonds had melted away, and emancipation of the slaves had divested the propertied classes of their most valuable and productive assets. According to some estimates, the South's per capita wealth in 1865 was only about half what it had been in 1860.

Recovery could not even begin until a new labor system replaced slavery. It was widely assumed in both the North and the South that southern prosperity would continue to depend on cotton and that the plantation was the most efficient unit for producing the crop. Hindering efforts to rebuild the plantation economy were lack of capital, the deep-rooted belief of southern whites that blacks would work only under compulsion, and the freedmen's resistance to labor conditions that recalled slavery.

Blacks strongly preferred to be small independent farmers rather than plantation laborers, and for a time they had reason to hope the federal government would support their ambitions. General Sherman, hampered by the huge numbers of black fugitives that followed his army on its famous march, issued an order in January 1865 that set aside the islands and coastal areas of Georgia and South Carolina for exclusive black occupancy on 40-acre plots. Furthermore, the Freedmen's Bureau, as one of its many responsibilities, was given control of hundreds of thousands of acres of abandoned or confiscated land and was authorized to make 40-acre grants to black settlers for three-year periods, after which they would have the option to buy at low prices. By June 1865, forty thousand black farmers were at work on 300,000 acres of what they thought would be their own land.

But for most of them the dream of "forty acres and a mule" was not to be realized. President Johnson pardoned the owners of most of the land consigned to the ex-slaves by Sherman and the Freedmen's Bureau, and proposals for an effective program of land confiscation and redistribution failed to get through Congress. Among the considerations prompting most congressmen to oppose land reform were a tenderness for property rights, fears of sapping the freedmen's initiative by giving them something they allegedly had not earned, and the desire to restore cotton production as quickly as possible to increase agricultural exports and stabilize the economy. Consequently, most blacks in physical possession of small farms failed to acquire title, and the mass of freedmen were left with little or no prospect of becoming landowners. Recalling the plight of southern blacks in 1865, an ex-slave later wrote that "they were set free without a dollar, without a foot of land, and without the wherewithal to get the next meal even."

Painting of a sharecropper's cabin, by William Aiken Walker. Too often freed slaves discovered that sharecropping led to a new form of economic servitude.

Despite their poverty and landlessness, ex-slaves were reluctant to settle down and commit themselves to wage labor for their former masters. Many took to the road, hoping to find something better. Some were still expecting grants of land, but others were simply trying to increase their bargaining power. "One ob de rights ob bein' free," one freedman later recalled, "wuz dat we could move around en change bosses." As the end of 1865 approached, many freedmen had still not signed up for the coming season; anxious planters feared they were plotting to seize the land by force. Within a few weeks, however, most holdouts signed for the best terms they could get.

One common form of agricultural employment in 1866 was a contract labor system. Under this system, workers committed themselves for a year in return for fixed wages, a substantial portion of which was withheld until after the harvest. Since many planters were inclined to drive hard bargains, abuse their workers, or cheat them at the end of the year, the Freedmen's Bureau assumed the role of reviewing the contracts and enforcing them. But bureau officials had differing notions of what it meant to protect African Americans from exploitation. Some stood up strongly for the rights of the freedmen; others served as allies of the planters, rounding up available workers, coercing them to sign contracts for low wages, and then helping keep them in line.

The Bureau's influence waned after 1867 (it was phased out completely by 1869), and the experiment with contract wage labor was abandoned. Growing up alongside the contract system and eventually displacing it was an alternative capital-labor relationship—sharecropping. First in small groups known as "squads" and later as individual families, blacks worked a piece of land independently for a fixed share of the crop, usually one-half. The advantage of this arrangement for credit-starved landlords was that it did not require much expenditure in advance of the harvest. The system also forced the tenant to share the risks of crop failure or a fall in cotton prices. These considerations loomed larger after disastrous harvests in 1866 and 1867.

African Americans initially viewed sharecropping as a step up from wage labor in the direction of land-ownership. But during the 1870s this form of tenancy evolved into a new kind of servitude. Croppers had to live on credit until their cotton was sold, and planters or merchants seized the chance to "provision" them at high prices and exorbitant rates of interest. Creditors were entitled to deduct what was owed to them out of the tenant's share of the crop and this left most sharecroppers with no net profit at the end of the year—more often than not with a debt that had to be worked off in subsequent years. Various methods, legal and extralegal, were eventually devised in an effort to bind indebted tenants to a single landlord for extended periods, but considerable movement was still possible.

While landless African Americans in the countryside were being reduced to economic dependence, those in towns and cities found themselves living in an increasingly segregated society. The Black Codes of 1865 attempted to require separation of the races in public places and facilities; when most of the codes were set aside by federal authorities as violations of the Civil Rights Act of 1866, the same end was often achieved through private initiative and community pressure. In some cities, blacks successfully resisted being consigned to separate streetcars by appealing to the military during the brief period when it exercised authority or by organizing boycotts. But they found it almost impossible to gain admittance to most hotels, restaurants, and other privately owned establishments catering to whites. On railroads, separate black, or "Jim Crow," cars were not yet the rule, but African Americans were normally denied first-class accommodations. After 1868, black-supported Republican governments passed civil rights acts requiring equal access to public facilities, but little effort was made to enforce the legislation.

Some forms of racial separation were not openly discriminatory, and blacks accepted or even endorsed them. Freedmen who had belonged to white churches as slaves welcomed the chance to join all-black denominations like the African Methodist Episcopal church, which provided freedom from white dominance and a more congenial style of worship. The first schools for ex-slaves were all-black institutions established by the Freedmen's Bureau and various northern missionary societies. Having been denied all education during the antebellum period, most blacks viewed separate schooling as an opportunity rather than as a form of discrimination. When Radical governments set up public school systems, they condoned de facto educational segregation. Only in city schools of New Orleans and at the University of South Carolina were there

serious attempts during Reconstruction to bring white and black students together in the same classrooms.

The upshot of all forms of racial separatism—whether produced by white prejudice or black independence—was to create a divided society, one in which blacks and whites lived much of the time in separate worlds. There were two exceptions to this pattern: one was at work, where blacks necessarily dealt with white employers; the other was in the political sphere, where blacks sought to exercise their rights as citizens.

Political Reconstruction in the South

The state governments that emerged in 1865 had little or no regard for the rights of the freed slaves. Some of their codes even made black unemployment a crime, which meant blacks had to make long-term contracts with white employers or be arrested for vagrancy. Others limited the rights of African Americans to own property or engage in occupations other than those of servant or laborer. The codes were set aside by the actions of Congress, the military, and the Freedmen's Bureau, but private violence and discrimination against blacks continued on a massive scale unchecked by state authorities. Hundreds, perhaps thousands, of blacks were murdered by whites in 1865–1866, and few of the perpetrators were brought to justice.

The imposition of military rule in 1867 was designed in part to protect former slaves from violence and intimidation, but the task was beyond the capacity of the few thousand troops stationed in the South. When new constitutions were approved and states readmitted to the Union under the congressional plan in 1868, the problem became more severe. White opponents of Radical Reconstruction adopted systematic terrorism and organized mob violence to keep blacks away from the polls. Yet the military presence was progressively reduced, leaving the new Republican regimes to fight a losing battle against armed white supremacists. In the words of historian William Gillette, "there was simply no federal force large enough to give heart to black Republicans or to bridle southern white violence."

Hastily organized in 1867, the southern Republican party dominated the constitution-

At left, an African-American soldier and his sweetheart are wed by a Freedmen's Bureau chaplain. Many black soldiers asked that the unions they made in slave days be legalized so that their families would qualify for survivors' benefits when they died.

Below is a Freedmen's school, one of the more successful endeavors supported by the Freedmen's Bureau. The Bureau, working with teachers from northern abolitionist and missionary societies, founded thousands of schools for freed slaves and poor whites.

making of 1868 and the regimes that came out of it. The party was an attempted coalition of three social groups (which varied in their relative strength from state to state). One was the same class that was becoming the backbone of the Republican party in the North—businessmen with an interest in enlisting government aid for private enterprise. Many Republicans of this stripe were recent arrivals from the North—the so-called carpetbaggers—but some were scalawags, former Whig planters or merchants who were born in the South or had immigrated to the region before the war and now saw a chance to realize their dreams for commercial and industrial development.

Poor white farmers, especially those from upland areas where Unionist sentiment had been strong during the Civil War, were a second element in the original coalition. These owners of small farms expected the party to favor their interests at the expense of the wealthy landowners and to come to their aid with special legislation when—as was often the case in this period of economic upheaval—they faced the loss of their homesteads to creditors. Newly enfranchised blacks were the third group to which the Republicans appealed. Blacks formed the vast majority of the Republican rank and file in most states and were concerned mainly with education, civil rights, and land-ownership.

Under the best of conditions, these coalitions would have been difficult to maintain. Each group had its own distinct goals and did not fully support the aims of the other segments. White yeomen, for example, had a deeply rooted resistance to black equality. And for how long could one expect essentially conservative businessmen to support costly measures for the elevation or relief of the lower classes of either race? In some states, astute Democratic politicians exploited these divisions by appealing to disaffected white Republicans.

But during the relatively brief period when they were in power in the South—varying from one to nine years depending on the state—the Republicans chalked up some notable achievements. They established (on paper at least) the South's first adequate systems of public education, democratized state and local government, and appropriated funds for an enormous expansion of public services and responsibilities.

Important as these social and political reforms were, they took second place to the Republicans' major effort—to foster economic development and restore southern prosperity by subsidizing the construction of railroads and other internal improvements. But the policy of aiding railroads turned out to be disastrous, even though it addressed the region's real economic needs and was initially very popular. Extravagance, corruption, and routes laid out in response to local

political pressure rather than on sound economic considerations made for an increasing burden of public debt and taxation. The policy did not produce the promised payoff of efficient, cheap transportation. Subsidized railroads frequently went bankrupt, leaving the taxpayers holding the bag. When the panic of 1873 brought many southern state governments to the verge of bankruptcy, and railroad building came to an end, it was clear the Republicans' "gospel of prosperity" through state aid to private enterprise had failed miserably. Their political opponents, many of whom had originally favored such policies, now saw an opportunity to take advantage of the situation by charging that Republicans had ruined the southern economy.

In general, the Radical regimes failed to conduct public business honestly and efficiently. Embezzlement of public funds and bribery of state lawmakers or officials were common occurrences. State debts and tax burdens rose enormously, mainly because governments had undertaken heavy new responsibilities, but partly because of waste and graft. The situation varied from state to state; ruling cliques in Louisiana and South Carolina were guilty of much wrongdoing, yet Mississippi had a relatively honest and frugal regime.

Furthermore, southern corruption was not exceptional, nor was it a special result of the extension of suffrage to uneducated African Americans, as critics of Radical Reconstruction have claimed. It was part of a national pattern during an era when private interests considered buying government favors to be a part of the cost of doing business, and many politicians expected to profit by obliging them.

Blacks bore only a limited responsibility for the dishonesty of the Radical governments. Although sixteen African Americans served in Congress—two in the Senate—between 1869 and 1880, only in South Carolina did blacks constitute a majority of even one house of the state legislature. Furthermore, no black governors were elected during Reconstruction (although P. B. S. Pinchback served for a time as acting governor of Louisiana). The biggest grafters were opportunistic whites. Some of the most notorious were carpetbaggers but others were native Southerners. Businessmen offering bribes included members of the prewar gentry who were staunch opponents

Although African Americans represented a majority in many of the former slave states in the Deep South, they constituted a majority only in the South Carolina state legislature (above right). A small number of African Americans were elected to Congress. Among them was Senator Blanche K. Bruce (left) who championed the causes of citizenship for Native Americans and improvement of the Mississippi River.

of Radical programs. Some black legislators went with the tide and accepted "loans" from those railroad lobbyists who would pay most for their votes, but the same men could usually be depended on to vote the will of their constituents on civil rights or educational issues.

If blacks served or supported corrupt and wasteful regimes it was because they had no alternative. Although the Democrats, or "Conservatives" as they called themselves in some states, made sporadic efforts to attract African American voters, it was clear that if they won control they would attempt to strip blacks of their civil and political rights. But opponents of Radical Reconstruction were able to capitalize on racial prejudice and persuade many Americans that "good government" was synonymous with white supremacy.

Contrary to myth, the small number of African Americans elected to state or national office during Reconstruction demonstrated on the average more integrity and competence than their white counterparts. Most were fairly well educated,

having been free Negroes or unusually privileged slaves before the war. Among the most capable were Robert Smalls (whose career was described earlier); Senator Blanche K. Bruce of Mississippi, elected to the Senate in 1874 after rising to deserved prominence in the Republican party of his home state; Congressman Robert Brown Elliott of South Carolina, an adroit politician who was also a consistent champion of civil rights; and Congressman James T. Rapier of Alabama, who stirred Congress and the nation in 1873 with his eloquent appeals for federal aid to southern education and new laws to enforce equal rights for African Americans.

THE AGE OF GRANT

Ulysses S. Grant was the only president between Jackson and Wilson to serve two full and consecutive terms. But unlike other chief executives so favored by the electorate, Grant is commonly regarded as a failure. Historians used to blame him mainly for the corruption that surfaced in his administration. More recently he also has been condemned for the inconsistency and ultimate failure of his southern policy. The charges have some validity, and no one is likely to make the case that he was a great statesman. At times Grant's highest priority seemed to be loyalty to old friends and to politicians who supported him. But the problems he faced were certainly difficult. A president with a clearer sense of duty might have done little better.

Rise of the Money Question

The impeachment crisis of 1868 represented the high point of popular interest in Reconstruction issues. Already competing for public attention was the question of how to manage the nation's currency, and more specifically, what to do about greenbacks—paper money issued during the war. Hugh McCulloch, secretary of the treasury under Johnson, favored a return to "sound" money, and in 1866 he had initiated a policy of withdrawing greenbacks from circulation. Opposition to this hard-money policy and the resulting deflation came from a number of groups. In general, the "greenbackers" were strongest in the credit-hungry West and among expansion-minded manufacturers. Defenders of hard money were mostly the commercial and financial interests in the East; they received crucial support from intellectuals who regarded government-sponsored inflation as immoral or contrary to the natural laws of classical economics.

In 1868, the money question surged briefly to the forefront of national politics. Faced with a business recession blamed on McCulloch's policy of contracting the currency, Congress voted to stop the retirement of greenbacks. The Democratic party, responding to midwestern pressure, included in its platform a plan calling for the redemption of much of the Civil War debt in greenbacks rather than the gold that bondholders had been anticipating. But divisions within the parties prevented the money question from becoming a central issue in the presidential campaign. The Democrats nominated Governor Horatio Seymour of New York, a sound-money supporter, thus nullifying their pro-greenback platform. Republicans based their campaign mainly on a defense of their Reconstruction policy and a celebration of their popular candidate. With the help of votes from the Republican-dominated southern states, Grant won a decisive victory.

In 1869 and 1870, a Republican-controlled Congress passed laws that assured payment in gold to most bondholders but eased the burden of the huge Civil War debt by exchanging bonds soon coming due for those that would not be payable for ten, fifteen, or thirty years. In this way the public credit was protected.

Still unresolved was the problem of what to do about the $356 million in greenbacks that remained in circulation. Hard-money proponents wanted to retire them quickly; inflationists thought more should be issued to stimulate the economy. The Grant administration followed the middle course of allowing the greenbacks to float until economic expansion would bring them to a par with gold, thus permitting a painless return to specie payments. But the panic of 1873, which brought much of the economy to its knees, led to a revival of agitation to inflate the currency. Debt-ridden farmers, who would be the backbone of the greenback movement for years to come, now joined the soft-money clamor for the first time.

Responding to the money and credit crunch, Congress moved in 1874 to authorize a modest issue of new greenbacks. But Grant, influenced by the opinions of hard-money financiers, vetoed the bill. In 1875, Congress, led by Senator John Sherman of Ohio, enacted the Specie Resumption Act, which provided for a limited reduction of greenbacks leading to full resumption of specie payments by January 1, 1879. Its action was widely interpreted as deflation in the midst of depression. Farmers and workers, who were already suffering acutely from deflation, reacted with dismay and anger.

The Democratic party could not capitalize adequately on these sentiments because of the influence of its own hard-money faction, and in 1876 an independent Greenback party entered the national political arena. The party's nominee for president, Peter Cooper, received an insignificant number of votes, but in 1878 the Greenback Labor party polled more than a million votes and

Shown seated at the table are feminist leaders Elizabeth Cady Stanton and Susan B. Anthony. They and their adherents split with Lucy Stone (right) and her followers over the Fifteenth Amendment and its failure to extend the vote to women.

The Election of 1868

Candidate	Party	Popular Vote	Electoral Vote
Grant	Republican	3,013,421	214
Seymour	Democratic	2,706,829	80
Not voted*			23

Unreconstructed states did not participate in the election.

elected fourteen congressmen. The Greenbackers were able to keep the money issue alive into the following decade.

Retreat from Reconstruction

The Republican effort to make equal rights for blacks the law of the land culminated in the Fifteenth Amendment. Passed by Congress in 1869 and ratified by the states in 1870, the amendment prohibited any state from denying a citizen the right to vote because of race, color, or previous condition of servitude. A more radical version, requiring universal manhood suffrage, was rejected partly because it departed too sharply from traditional views of federal-state relations. States therefore could still limit the suffrage by imposing literacy tests, property qualifications, or poll taxes allegedly applying to all racial groups; such devices would eventually be

used to strip southern blacks of the right to vote. But the makers of the amendment did not foresee this result. They believed their action would prevent future Congresses or southern constitutional conventions from repealing or nullifying the provisions for black male suffrage included in the Reconstruction Acts. A secondary aim was to enfranchise African Americans in those northern states that still denied them the vote.

Many feminists were bitterly disappointed that the amendment did not extend the vote to women as well as freedmen. A militant wing of the woman's rights movement led by Elizabeth Cady Stanton and Susan B. Anthony was so angered that the Constitution was being amended to make gender an explicit qualification for voting that they campaigned against ratification of the Fifteenth Amendment. Another group of feminists led by Lucy Stone supported the amendment on the grounds that this was "the Negro's hour" and that women could afford to wait a few years for the vote. This disagreement divided the women's suffrage movement for a generation to come.

The Grant administration was charged with enforcing the amendment and protecting black voting rights in the reconstructed states. Since survival of the Republican regimes depended on African American support, political partisanship dictated federal action, even though the North's emotional and ideological commitment to black citizenship was waning.

Changing Views of Reconstruction

A central issue of Reconstruction was the place of blacks in American life after slavery. Changing attitudes on this question strongly influenced later representations of the Reconstruction era, whether in historical writing or in the popular media. Indeed, what later generations imagined had happened in the South in the years immediately after the Civil War is a fairly reliable index of how they viewed black/white relations in their own time.

In the early twentieth century, when white supremacists were in control in the South and northern public opinion was learning to tolerate southern policies of rigid segregation and disfranchisement of blacks, historians played a major role in rationalizing the new order in southern race relations. According to historians like Professor John W. Burgess of Columbia University, writing in 1902, Reconstruction governments represented an unholy alliance of corrupt northern "carpetbaggers" seeking to profit at the expense of the "prostrate South"; southern white opportunists of mean origins, known as "scalawags"; and black demagogues who sought power by putting false and dangerous aspirations for equality into the heads of newly freed slaves. What made this orgy of misrule possible, said Burgess, was the colossal blunder that Congress made when it extended the vote to "ignorant and vicious" blacks. In the eyes of Burgess and a whole school of historians, Reconstruction was "the most soul-sickening spectacle that Americans have ever been called upon to behold . . . here was government by the most ignorant and vicious part of the population for the vulgar, materialistic, brutal benefit of the governing set."

In 1915 the most ambitious film yet made by the fledgling American movie industry— D. W. Griffith's *Birth of a Nation*—popularized this image of Reconstruction and made its racism more lurid and explicit. To underscore the message of this technically brilliant film, words flashed on the screen describing Reconstruction as a callous attempt to "<u>put the white South under the heel of the black South.</u>" In the film, leering blacks carry signs advocating interracial marriage. Mainly responsible for this state of affairs is a vengeful Congressman meant to represent Thaddeus Stevens, who hatches a devilish plot to oppress and humiliate the white South. One famous scene portrays the South Carolina state legislature as a mob of grinning barefoot blacks, carousing at the taxpayers' expense. The film's melodramatic plot features the suicide of one southern white maiden to escape the embraces of a black pursuer and the Ku Klux Klan's epic res-cue of another damsel from a forced marriage to a mulatto politician.

Birth of a Nation's depiction of the Klan as saving white civilization from bestial blacks inspired vigorous protests from the recently founded National Association for the Advancement of Colored People (NAACP), and censors in a few northern cities deleted some of the more blatantly racist scenes. But President Woodrow Wilson endorsed the film. "My only regret is that it is all so terribly true," he is reported to have said. Most white moviegoers seemed to agree with the president rather than with the NAACP. Millions of Americans saw and applauded this cinematic triumph.

During the period between 1915 and the 1940s, most historians echoed the judgment of

A scene from Birth of a Nation. *Note that the role of the black man at right is played by a white actor in dark makeup.*

Birth of a Nation that efforts to enforce equal rights for blacks after the Civil War had been a grave mistake. One popular work of that era was entitled *The Tragic Era,* and another summed up Reconstruction as "the blackout of honest government." The biases of mainstream historiography served to justify the Jim Crow system of the South by portraying blacks as unqualified for citizenship.

A few black historians of the 1920s and 1930s advanced the contrary view that Reconstruction was a noble effort to achieve a color-blind democracy that failed because of the strength of white racism and conservative economic interests. The most powerful example of this early revisionism was W. E. B. DuBois's *Black Reconstruction in America* (1935).

During the 1950s and 1960s another image of Reconstruction emerged. The majority of historians writing about the era finally rejected the exaggerations, distortions, and racist assumptions of the traditional view. The triumph of "revisionism" was evident in 1965 when Kenneth M. Stampp published his *Era of Reconstruction.* As influential northern opinion shifted from tolerance of segregation to support for the black struggle for equality in the South, a more favorable view of earlier efforts on behalf of civil rights became acceptable. White liberal historians like Stampp concentrated on rehabilitating the Radical Republicans by stressing their idealism, while black scholars like John Hope Franklin highlighted the constructive policies and positive achievements of the much maligned black leaders of the Reconstruction South.

Previous moral judgments thus tended to be reversed; white and black Republicans became the heroes, and the southern whites who resisted and eventually overthrew Reconstruction became the villains. The analogy between these earlier adversaries and the civil rights activists and southern segregationists of the 1960s was clear.

During the 1970s and early 1980s, a "postrevisionism" began to develop. As it became apparent that the dream of equality for blacks was still unrealized, historians responded to the changing perceptions and complex crosscurrents of black/white relations in their own time by taking another look at Reconstruction. They found, among other things, that those in charge of efforts to make blacks equal citizens in the late 1860s had views that were quite moderate by the standards of the post–civil rights era of the 1970s and early 1980s. "Radical Reconstruction" no longer seemed very radical. The reputations of carpetbaggers and upper-class scalawags went down again as historians emphasized their opportunism and probusiness economic policies at the expense of social justice. Black politicians, too, came in for critical reassessment. It was argued that many worked more for their own interests as members of a black middle class than for the kinds of policies—such as land reform—that would have met the vital needs of their impoverished constituents.

The postrevisionists seem to be agreed that Reconstruction failed because it was inadequately motivated, conceived, and enforced. But the causes of this failure remain in doubt. Some recent historians explain it in terms of an underlying racism that prevented white Republicans from identifying fully with the cause of black equality. Others stress the gulf between the class interests of those in charge of implementing and managing Reconstruction and the poor people of the South who were supposed to be its beneficiaries.

The basic issue raised by Reconstruction—how to achieve racial equality in America—has not yet been resolved. So long as this is the case, we will continue to look at our first effort in this direction for whatever guideposts it provides.

491

Between 1868 and 1872, the main threat to southern Republican regimes came from the Ku Klux Klan and other secret societies bent on restoring white supremacy by intimidating blacks who sought to exercise their political rights. First organized in Tennessee in 1866, the Klan spread rapidly to other states, adopting increasingly lawless and brutal tactics. A grass-roots vigilante movement and not a centralized conspiracy, the Klan thrived on local initiative and gained support from whites of all social classes. Its secrecy, decentralization, popular support, and utter ruthlessness made it very difficult to suppress. As soon as blacks had been granted the right to vote, hooded night riders began to visit the cabins of those who were known to be active Republicans; some victims were only threatened, but others were whipped or even murdered. A typical incident was related by a black Georgian: "They broke my door open, took me out of bed, took me to the woods and whipped me three hours or more and left me for dead. They said to me, 'Do you think you will vote for another damned radical ticket?'"

These methods were first used effectively in the presidential election of 1868. Grant lost in Louisiana and Georgia mainly because the Klan—or the Knights of the White Camelia as the Louisiana variant was called—launched a reign of terror to prevent prospective black voters from exercising their right. In Louisiana political violence claimed more than a thousand lives, and in Arkansas, which Grant managed to carry, more than two hundred Republicans, including a congressman, were assassinated.

Thereafter, Klan terrorism was directed mainly at Republican state governments. Virtual insurrections broke out in Arkansas, Tennessee, North Carolina, and parts of South Carolina. Republican governors called out the state militia to fight the Klan, but only the Arkansas militia succeeded in bringing it to heel. In Tennessee, North Carolina, and Georgia, Klan activities helped undermine Republican control, thus allowing the Democrats to come to power in all of these states by 1870.

Faced with the violent overthrow of the southern Republican party, Congress and the Grant administration were forced to act. A series of laws passed in 1870–1871 sought to enforce the Fifteenth Amendment by providing federal protection for black suffrage and authorizing use of the army against the Klan. These "Ku Klux Klan" or "Force" Acts made interference with voting rights a federal crime and established provisions for government supervision of elections. In addition, the legislation empowered the president to call out troops and suspend the writ of habeas corpus to quell insurrection. In 1871–1872, thousands of suspected Klansmen were arrested by the military or U. S. marshals, and the writ was suspended in nine counties of South Carolina that had been virtually taken over by the secret order. Although most of the accused Klansmen were never brought to trial, were acquitted, or received suspended sentences, the enforcement effort was vigorous enough to put a damper on hooded terrorism and ensure relatively fair and peaceful elections in 1872.

In these elections, a heavy black turnout enabled the Republicans to hold on to power in most states of the Deep South, despite efforts of the Democratic-Conservative opposition to cut into the Republican vote by taking moderate positions on racial and economic issues. As a result of this setback, the Democratic-Conservatives made a significant change in their strategy and ideology. No longer did they try to take votes away from the Republicans by proclaiming their support of black suffrage and government aid to business. They began instead to appeal openly to white supremacy and to the traditional Democratic and agrarian hostility to governmental promotion of economic development. Consequently, they were able to bring back to the polls a portion of the white electorate, mostly small farmers, who had not been turning out because they were alienated by the leadership's apparent concessions to Yankee ideas.

This new and more effective electoral strategy dovetailed with a resurgence of violence meant to reduce Republican, especially black Republican, voting. The new reign of terror differed from the previous Klan episode; its agents no longer wore masks but acted quite openly. They were effective because the northern public was increasingly disenchanted with federal intervention on behalf of what were widely viewed as corrupt and tottering Republican regimes. Grant used force in the South for the last time in 1874 when an overt paramilitary organization in Louisiana, known as the White League, tried to overthrow a Republican government accused of stealing an election. When another unofficial militia—in Mississippi—insti-

Members of the Ku Klux Klan, a secret white supremacist organization, in typical regalia. Before elections, hooded Klansmen terrorized AfricanAmericans to discourage them from voting.

By 1876, Republicans held on to only three southern states: South Carolina, Louisiana, and Florida. Partly because of Grant's hesitant and inconsistent use of presidential power but mainly because the northern electorate would no longer tolerate military action to sustain Republican governments and black voting rights, Radical Reconstruction was falling into total eclipse.

Spoilsmen Versus Reformers

One reason Grant found it increasingly difficult to take strong action to protect southern Republicans was the bad odor surrounding his stewardship of the federal government and the Republican party. Reformers charged that a corrupt national administration was propping up bad governments in the South for personal and partisan advantage. An apparent case in point was Grant's intervention in Louisiana in 1872 on behalf of an ill-reputed Republican faction headed by his wife's brother-in-law, who controlled federal patronage as collector of customs in New Orleans.

The Republican party in the Grant era was losing the idealism and high purpose associated with the crusade against slavery. By the beginning of the 1870s, the men who had been the conscience of the party—old-line radicals like Thaddeus Stevens, Charles Sumner, and Benjamin Wade— were either dead, out of office, or at odds with the administration. New leaders of a different stamp, whom historians have dubbed "spoilsmen" or "politicos," were taking their place. When he made common cause with hard-boiled manipulators like senators Roscoe Conkling of New York and James G. Blaine of Maine, Grant lost credibility with reform-minded Republicans.

During Grant's first administration, an aura of scandal surrounded the White House but did not directly implicate the president. In 1869, the financial buccaneer Jay Gould enlisted the aid of a brother-in-law of Grant to further his fantastic scheme to corner the gold market. Gould failed in the attempt, but he did manage to save himself and come away with a huge profit.

Grant's first-term vice president, Schuyler Colfax of Indiana, was directly involved in the notorious Crédit Mobilier scandal. Crédit

gated a series of bloody race riots prior to the state elections of 1875, Grant refused the governor's request for federal troops. As a result, black voters were successfully intimidated—one county registered only seven Republican votes where there had been a black majority of two thousand, and Mississippi fell to the Democratic-Conservatives. According to one account, Grant decided to withhold troops because he had been warned that intervention might cost the Republicans the crucial state of Ohio in the same off-year elections.

Mobilier was a construction company that actually served as a fraudulent device for siphoning off profits that should have gone to the stockholders of the Union Pacific Railroad, which was the beneficiary of massive federal land grants. In order to forestall government inquiry into this arrangement, Crédit Mobilier stock was distributed to influential congressmen, including Colfax (who was Speaker of the House before he was elected vice president). The whole business came to light just before the campaign of 1872.

Republicans who could not tolerate such corruption or had other grievances against the administration broke with Grant in 1872 and formed a third party committed to "honest government" and "reconciliation" between the North and the South. Led initially by high-minded reformers like Senator Carl Schurz of Missouri, the "Liberal Republicans" endorsed reform of the civil service to curb the corruption-breeding patronage system and advocated laissez-faire economic policies—which meant low tariffs, an end to government subsidies for railroads, and hard money. Despite their rhetoric of idealism and reform, the Liberal Republicans were extremely conservative in their notions of what government should do to assure justice for blacks and other underprivileged Americans.

The Liberal Republicans' national convention nominated Horace Greeley, editor of the respected New York *Tribune*. This was a curious and divisive choice, since Greeley was at odds with the founders of the movement on the tariff question and was indifferent to civil service reform. The Democrats also endorsed Greeley, mainly because he promised to end Radical Reconstruction by restoring "self-government" to the South.

But the journalist turned out to be a poor campaigner who failed to inspire enthusiasm from lifelong supporters of either party. Most Republicans stuck with Grant, despite the corruption issue, because they still could not stomach the idea of ex-rebels returning to power in the South. Many Democrats, recalling Greeley's previous record as a staunch Republican, simply stayed away from the polls. The result was a decisive victory for Grant, whose 56 percent of the popular vote was the highest percentage won by any candidate between Andrew Jackson and Theodore Roosevelt.

The Election of 1872			
Candidate	Party	Popular Vote	Electoral Vote*
Grant	Republican	3,598,235	286
Greeley	Democrat and Liberal Republican	2,834,761	Greeley died before the electoral college voted.

Out of a total of 366 electoral votes. Greeley's votes were divided among the four minor candidates.

Grant's second administration seemed to bear out the reformers' worst suspicions about corruption in high places. In 1875, the public learned that federal revenue officials had conspired with distillers to defraud the government of millions of dollars in liquor taxes. Grant's private secretary, Orville E. Babcock, was indicted as a member of the "Whiskey Ring" and was saved from conviction only by the president's personal intercession. The next year, Grant's secretary of war, William E. Belknap, was impeached by the House after an investigation revealed he had taken bribes for the sale of Indian trading posts. He avoided conviction in the Senate only by resigning from office before his trial. Grant fought hard to protect Belknap, to the point of participating in what a later generation might call a "cover-up."

There is no evidence that Grant profited personally from any of the misdeeds of his subordinates. Yet he is not entirely without blame for the corruption in his administration. He failed to take firm action against the malefactors, and even after their guilt had been clearly established, he sometimes tried to shield them from justice.

REUNION AND THE NEW SOUTH

Congressional Reconstruction prolonged the sense of sectional division and conflict for a dozen years after the guns had fallen silent. Its final liquidation in 1877 opened the way to a reconciliation of North and South. But the costs of reunion were high for less privileged groups in the South. The civil and political rights of African

In this Puck cartoon, U. S. Grant clutches the Whiskey and Navy rings and supports an assortment of bosses, profiteers, and scandals associated with the Grant administration.

Americans, left unprotected, were progressively and relentlessly stripped away by white supremacist regimes. Lower-class whites saw their interests sacrificed to those of capitalists and landlords. Despite the rhetoric hailing a prosperous "New South," the region remained poor and open to exploitation by northern business interests.

The Compromise of 1877

The election of 1876 pitted Rutherford B. Hayes of Ohio, a Republican governor untainted by the scandals of the Grant era, against Governor Samuel J. Tilden of New York, a Democratic reformer who had battled against Tammany Hall and the Tweed Ring. Honest government was apparently the electorate's highest priority. When the returns came in, Tilden had clearly won the popular vote and seemed likely to win a narrow victory in the electoral college. But the result was placed in doubt when the returns from the three southern states still controlled by the Republicans—South Carolina, Florida, and Louisiana—were contested. If Hayes were to be awarded these three states, plus one contested electoral vote in Oregon, Republican strategists realized, he would triumph in the electoral college by a single vote.

The outcome of the election remained undecided for months, plunging the nation into a major political crisis. To resolve the impasse, Congress appointed a special electoral commission of fifteen members to determine who would receive the votes of the disputed states. Originally composed of seven Democrats, seven Republicans, and an independent, the commission fell under Republican control when the independent member resigned to run for the Senate and a Republican was appointed to take his place. The commission split along party lines and voted 8 to 7 to award Hayes all of the disputed votes. But this decision still had to be ratified by both houses of Congress. The Republican-dominated Senate readily approved it, but Democrats in the House planned a filibuster to delay the final counting of the electoral votes until after inauguration day. If the filibuster succeeded, neither candidate would have a majority and, as provided in the Constitution, the election would be decided by the House, where the Democrats controlled enough states to elect Tilden.

To ensure Hayes's election, Republican leaders negotiated secretly with conservative southern Democrats, some of whom seemed willing to abandon the filibuster if the last troops were withdrawn and "home rule" was restored to the South. Eventually an informal bargain was struck, which historians have dubbed "the Compromise of 1877." What precisely was agreed to and by whom remains a matter of dispute; but one thing at least was understood by both sides—Hayes would be president and southern blacks would be abandoned to their fate. In a sense, Hayes did not concede anything, because he had already decided to end federal support for the crumbling Radical regimes. But southern negotiators were heartened by firm assurances that this would indeed be the policy. Some were also influenced by vaguer promises involving federal support for southern railroads and internal improvements.

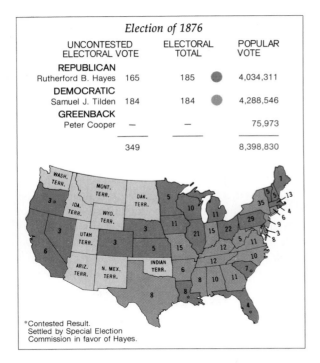

Election of 1876

	UNCONTESTED ELECTORAL VOTE	ELECTORAL TOTAL		POPULAR VOTE
REPUBLICAN				
Rutherford B. Hayes	165	185	●	4,034,311
DEMOCRATIC				
Samuel J. Tilden	184	184	●	4,288,546
GREENBACK				
Peter Cooper	—	—		75,973
		349		8,398,830

*Contested Result.
Settled by Special Election
Commission in favor of Hayes.

With southern Democratic acquiescence, the filibuster was broken and Hayes took the oath of office. He immediately ordered the army not to resist a Democratic takeover of state governments in South Carolina and Louisiana. Thus fell the last of the Radical governments, and the entire South was firmly under the control of white Democrats. The trauma of the war and Reconstruction had destroyed the chances for a renewal of two-party competition among white Southerners.

Northern Republicans soon reverted to denouncing the South for its suppression of black suffrage. But this "waving of the bloody shirt," which also served as a reminder of the war and northern casualties, quickly degenerated into a campaign ritual aimed at northern voters who could still be moved by sectional antagonism.

The New South

The men who came to power after Radical Reconstruction fell in one southern state after another are usually referred to as the "Redeemers." They had differing backgrounds and previous loyalties. Some were members of the Old South's ruling planter class who had warmly supported secession and now sought to reestablish the old order with as few changes as possible. Others, of middle-class origin or outlook, favored commer-

cial and industrial interests over agrarian groups and called for a "New South," committed to diversified economic development. A third group were professional politicians bending with the prevailing winds—like Joseph E. Brown of Georgia who had been a secessionist, a wartime governor, and a leading scalawag Republican, before becoming a Democratic "Redeemer."

Although historians have tried to assign the Redeemers a single coherent ideology or view of the world and have debated whether it was Old South agrarianism or New South industrialism they endorsed, these leaders can perhaps best be understood as power brokers mediating among the dominant interest groups of the South in ways that served their own political advantage. In many ways, the "rings" that they established on the state and county level were analogous to the political machines developing at the same time in northern cities.

They did, however, agree on and endorse two basic principles: laissez-faire and white supremacy. Laissez-faire—the notion that government should be limited and should not intervene openly and directly in the economy—could unite planters, frustrated at seeing direct state support going to businessmen, and capitalist promoters who had come to realize that low taxes and freedom from government regulation were even more advantageous than state subsidies. It soon became clear that the Redeemers responded only to privileged and entrenched interest groups, especially landlords, merchants, and industrialists, and offered little or nothing to tenants, small farmers, and working people. As industrialization began to gather steam in the 1880s, Democratic regimes became increasingly accommodating to manufacturing interests and hospitable to agents of northern capital who were gaining control of the South's transportation system and its extractive industries.

White supremacy was the principal rallying cry that brought the Redeemers to power in the first place. Once in office, they found they could stay there by charging that opponents of ruling Democratic cliques were trying to divide "the white man's party" and open the way for a return to "black domination." Appeals to racism could also deflect attention away from the economic grievances of groups without political clout.

The new governments were more economical than those of Reconstruction, mainly because

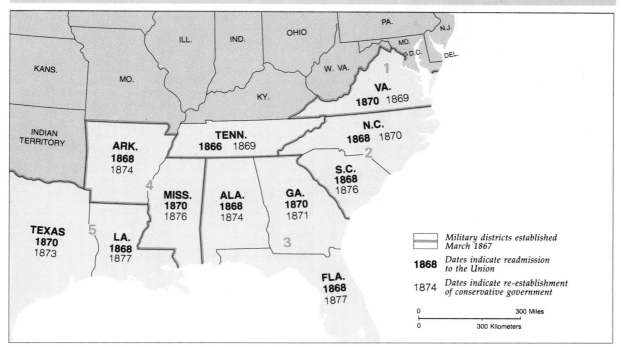

Reconstruction
During the Reconstruction era, the southern state governments passed through three phases: control by white ex-Confederates; domination by Republican legislators, both white and black; and, finally, the regain of control by conservative white Democrats.

□ Military districts established March 1867

1868 Dates indicate readmission to the Union

1874 Dates indicate re-establishment of conservative government

they cut back drastically on appropriations for schools and other needed public services. But they were scarcely more honest—embezzlement of funds and bribery of officials continued to occur to an alarming extent. Louisiana, for example, suffered for decades from the flagrant corruption associated with a state-chartered lottery.

The Redeemer regimes of the late 1870s and 1880s badly neglected the interests of small white farmers. Whites, as well as blacks, were suffering from the notorious "crop lien" system, which gave local merchants who advanced credit at high rates of interest during the growing season the right to take possession of the harvested crop on terms that buried farmers deeper and deeper in debt. As a result, increasing numbers of whites lost title to their homesteads and were reduced to tenancy. When a depression of world cotton prices added to the burden of a ruinous credit system, agrarian protesters began to challenge the ruling elite, first through the Southern Farmers' Alliance of the late 1880s and then by supporting its political descendant—the Populist party of the 1890s (see Chapter 20).

But the greatest hardships imposed by the new order were reserved for African Americans. The Redeemers promised, as part of the understanding that led to the end of federal intervention in 1877, that they would respect the rights of blacks as set forth in the Fourteenth and Fifteenth amendments. Governor Wade Hampton of South Carolina was especially vocal in pledging that African Americans would not be reduced to second-class citizenship by the new regimes. But when blacks tried to vote Republican in the "redeemed" states, they encountered renewed violence and intimidation. "Bulldozing" African American voters remained common practice in state elections during the late 1870s and early 1880s; those blacks who withstood the threat of losing their jobs or being evicted from tenant farms if they voted for the party of Lincoln were visited at night and literally whipped into line. The message was clear: vote Democratic or vote not at all.

Furthermore, white Democrats now controlled the electoral machinery and were able to manipulate the black vote by stuffing ballot boxes, dis-

The first industries of the New South were usually processing plants for the agricultural products of the region. In this 1871 drawing by A. R. Waud for Harper's Weekly, *African American laborers on a sugar plantation in Gretna, Louisiana, across the river from New Orleans, are cutting sugarcane to be processed in the plantation's refinery.*

carding unwanted votes, or reporting fraudulent totals. Some states also imposed complicated new voting requirements to discourage black participation. Full-scale disfranchisement did not occur until literacy tests and other legalized obstacles to voting were imposed in the period from 1890 to 1910, but by that time less formal and comprehensive methods had already made a mockery of the Fifteenth Amendment.

Nevertheless, blacks continued to vote freely in some localities until the 1890s; a few districts, like the one Robert Smalls represented, even elected black Republicans to Congress during the immediate post-Reconstruction period. The last of these, Representative George H. White of North Carolina, served until 1901. His farewell address eloquently conveyed the agony of southern blacks in the era of Jim Crow (strict segregation).

These parting words are in behalf of an outraged, heart-broken, bruised, and bleeding but God-fearing people, faithful, industrious, loyal people—rising people, full of potential force. . . . The only apology that I have to make for the earnestness with which I have spoken is that I am pleading for the life, the liberty, the future happiness, and manhood suffrage of one-eighth of the entire population of the United States.

The dark night of racism that fell on the South after Reconstruction seemed to unleash all the baser impulses of human nature. Between 1889 and 1899, an average of 187 blacks were lynched every year for alleged offenses against white supremacy. Those convicted of petty crimes against property were often little better off; many

Lynching accounted for more than 3,000 deaths between 1899 and 1918, and lynchings were not confined to the South. During that period, only seven states reported no lynchings.

Henry M. Turner, who was born in freedom, became a bishop of the African Methodist Episcopal Church and was elected to the Georgia legislature.

were condemned to be leased out to private contractors whose brutality rivaled that of the most sadistic slaveholders. (Annual death rates in the convict camps ranged as high as 25 percent.) Finally, the dignity of blacks was cruelly affronted by the wave of segregation laws passed around the turn of the century, which served to remind them constantly that they were deemed unfit to associate with whites on any basis that implied equality. To some extent, the segregation laws were a white reaction to the refusal of many blacks to submit to voluntary segregation of railroads, streetcars, and other public facilities.

The North and the federal government did little or nothing to stem the tide of racial oppression in the South. A series of Supreme Court decisions between 1875 and 1896 gutted the Reconstruction amendments and the legislation passed to enforce them, leaving blacks virtually defenseless against political and social discrimination.

The career of Henry McNeal Turner sums up the bitter side of the black experience in the South during and after Reconstruction. Born free in South Carolina in 1834, Turner became a minister of the African Methodist Episcopal church (AME) just before the outbreak of the Civil War.

During the war, he recruited African Americans for the Union Army and later served as chaplain for black troops. After the fighting was over, he went to Georgia to work for the Freedmen's Bureau but encountered racial discrimination from white Bureau officers and left government service for church work and Reconstruction politics. Elected to the 1867 Georgia constitutional convention and to the state legislature in 1868, he was one of a number of black clergymen who assumed leadership roles among the freedmen. But whites won control of the Georgia legislature and expelled all the black members. Turner's reaction was an angry speech in which he proclaimed that white men were never to be trusted. As the inhabitant of a state in which blacks never gained the degree of power that they achieved in some other parts of the South, Turner was one of the first black leaders to see the failure of

Hall v. *DeCuir* (1878)	Struck down Louisiana law prohibiting racial discrimination by "common carriers" (railroads, steamboats, buses). Court declared the law a "burden" on interstate commerce, over which states had no authority.
United States v. *Harris* (1882)	Declared federal laws to punish crimes such as murder and assault unconstitutional. Such crimes declared to be the sole concern of local government. Court ignored the frequent racial motivation behind such crimes in the South.
Civil Rights Cases (1883)	Struck down Civil Rights Act of 1875. Congress may not legislate on civil rights unless a *state* passes a discriminatory law. Court declared the Fourteenth Amendment silent on racial discrimination by private citizens.
Plessy v. *Ferguson* (1896)	Upheld Louisiana statute requiring "separate but equal" accommodations on railroads. Court declared that segregation is *not* necessarily discrimination.
Williams v. *Mississippi* (1898)	Upheld state law requiring a literacy test to qualify for voting. Court refused to find any implication of racial discrimination in the law, although it permitted illiterate whites to vote if they "understood" the Constitution. Using such laws, sou

Reconstruction as the betrayal of African American hopes for citizenship.

Becoming a bishop of the AME church in 1880, Turner emerged as the late nineteenth century's leading proponent of black emigration to Africa. Because he believed white Americans were so deeply prejudiced against blacks that they would never grant them equal rights, Turner became an early advocate of black nationalism and a total separation of the races. Emigration became a popular movement among southern blacks who were especially hard hit by terror and oppression just after the end of Reconstruction, but a majority of blacks in the nation as a whole and even in Turner's own church refused to give up on the hope of eventual equality on American soil. But Bishop Turner's anger and despair were the understandable responses of a proud man to the way that he and his fellow African Americans had been treated in the post–Civil War period.

By the late 1880s, the wounds of the Civil War were healing, and white Americans were seized by the spirit of sectional reconciliation. Union and Confederate veterans were tenting together and celebrating their common Americanism. "Reunion" was becoming a cultural as well as political reality. But whites could come back together only because Northerners had tacitly agreed to give Southerners a free hand in their efforts to reduce blacks to a new form of servitude. The "outraged, heart-broken, bruised, and bleeding" African Americans of the South paid the heaviest price for sectional reunion.

Recommended Reading

The best one-volume account of Reconstruction is Eric Foner, *Reconstruction: America's Unfinished Revolution* (1988). Two excellent short surveys are Kenneth M. Stampp, *The Era of Reconstruction, 1865–1877* (1965), and John Hope Franklin, *Reconstruction: After the Civil War* (1961). Both were early efforts to synthesize modern "revisionist" interpretations. W. E. B. DuBois, *Black Reconstruction in America, 1860–1880* (1935) remains brilliant and provocative. Reconsiderations of Reconstruction issues can be found in J. Morgan Kousser and James M. McPherson, eds., *Region, Race, and Reconstruction: Essays in Honor of C. Vann Woodward* (1982), and Eric Foner, *Nothing But Freedom: Emancipation and Its Legacy* (1983). Morton Keller, *Affairs of State: Public Life in Late Nineteenth Century America* (1977), provides an insightful analysis of American government and politics during Reconstruction and afterward. A perspective on the corruption of the period is provided by Mark Wahlgren Summers in *The Era of Good Stealings* (1993).

Formulation and implementation of northern policies on Reconstruction are covered in Eric L. McKitrick, *Andrew Johnson and Reconstruction, 1865–1867* (1960); W. R. Brock, *An American Crisis: Congress and Reconstruction, 1865–1867* (1963); and

CHRONOLOGY

1863 Lincoln sets forth 10 percent Reconstruction plan

1864 Wade-Davis Bill passes Congress but is pocket vetoed by Lincoln

1865 Johnson moves to reconstruct the South on his own initiative • Congress refuses to seat representatives and senators elected from states reestablished under presidential plan (December)

1866 Johnson vetoes Freedmen's Bureau Bill (February) • Johnson vetoes Civil Rights Act; it passes over his veto (April) • Congress passes Fourteenth Amendment (June) • Republicans increase their congressional majority in the fall elections

1867 First Reconstruction Act is passed over Johnson's veto (March)

1868 Johnson is impeached; he avoids conviction by one vote (February–May) • Southern blacks vote and serve in constitutional conventions • Grant wins presidential election, defeating Horatio Seymour

1869 Congress passes Fifteenth Amendment, granting African Americans the right to vote

1870–1871 Congress passes Ku Klux Klan Acts to protect black voting rights in the South

1872 Grant relected president, defeating Horace Greeley, candidate of Liberal Republicans and Democrats

1873 Financial panic plunges nation into depression

1875 Congress passes Specie Resumption Act • "Whiskey Ring" scandal exposed

1876–1877 Disputed presidential election resolved in favor of Republican Hayes over Democrat Tilden

1877 "Compromise of 1877" results in end to military intervention in the South and fall of the last Radical governments

William Gillette, *Retreat from Reconstruction, 1869–1879* (1979). Leon F. Litwack, *Been in the Storm So Long: The Aftermath of Slavery* (1979), provides a moving portrayal of the black experience of emancipation. On what freedom meant in economic terms, see Gerald David Jaynes, *Branches Without Roots: Genesis of the Black Working Class in the American South, 1862–1882* (1986). The best overview of the postwar southern economy is Gavin Wright, *Old South, New South* (1986). The best introduction to the Grant era is William S. McFeeley, *Grant: A Biography* (1981). On the end of Reconstruction and the character of the post-Reconstruction South, see two classic works by C. Vann Woodward: *Reunion and Reaction*, rev. ed. (1956) and *Origins of the New South, 1877–1913* (1951). A good recent survey of the South after Reconstruction is Edward Ayers, *The Promise of the New South* (1992).

Additional Bibliography

The Reconstruction era is surveyed briefly but well in Michael L. Perman, *Emancipation and Reconstruction, 1862–1879* (1987). The conflict between the president and Congress is examined in David Donald, *The Politics of Reconstruction, 1863–1867* (1965); Michael Les Benedict, *A Compromise of Principle: Congressional Republicans and Reconstruction* (1974) and *The Impeachment and Trial of Andrew Johnson* (1973). On constitutional issues, Stanley I. Kutler, *Judicial Power and Reconstruction Politics* (1968), and Harold M. Hyman, *A More Perfect Union: The Impact of the Civil War and Reconstruction on the Constitution* (1973), are useful.

Presidential Reconstruction in the South is surveyed in Dan T. Carter, *When the War Was Over: Self-Reconstruction in the South* (1985). A major aspect of Radical Reconstruction is covered in Mark W. Summers, *Railroads, Reconstruction, and the Gospel of Prosperity* (1984).

Michael Perman, *Reunion Without Compromise: The South and Reconstruction, 1865–1868* (1973), and *The Road to Redemption: Southern Politics, 1869–1879* (1984), deal authoritatively with southern politics in the postwar years. On the Freedmen's Bureau, see George R. Bentley, *A History of the Freedmen's Bureau* (1965); William McFeeley, *Yankee Stepfather: General O. O. Howard and the Freedmen* (1968); and Donald G. Nieman, *To Set the Law in Motion: The Freedmen's Bureau and Legal Rights for Blacks, 1865–1869* (1979).

On carpetbaggers, see Richard N. Current, *Those Terrible Carpetbaggers: A Reinterpretation* (1989). Among the most valuable of the many state studies of Reconstruction in the South are Joel Williamson, *After Slavery: The Negro in South Carolina, 1861–77* (1965); Elizabeth Studley Nathans, *Losing the Peace: Georgia Republicans and Reconstruction, 1865–1871* (1968); and Thomas Holt, *Black over White: Negro*

Political Leadership in South Carolina During Reconstruction (1977). Essays on black leadership in several southern states can be found in Howard N. Rabinowitz, ed., *Southern Black Leaders of the Reconstruction Era* (1982). See also Okon Edet Uya, *From Slavery to Public Service: Robert Smalls, 1839–1915* (1971); and Peggy Lawson, *The Glorious Failure: Congressmen Robert Brown Elliott and Reconstruction in South Carolina* (1973).

Howard N. Rabinowitz, *Race Relations in the Urban South, 1865–1890* (1977); C. Vann Woodward, *The Strange Career of Jim Crow*, 3d rev. ed. (1974); and Joel Williamson, *The Crucible of Race: Black-White Relations in the American South Since Emancipation* (1984) cover race relations in the postwar South. Economic and social adjustments are analyzed in Lawrence N. Powell, *New Masters: Northern Planters During the Civil War and Reconstruction* (1980); Michael Wayne, *The Reshaping of Plantation Society* (1983); Roger L. Ransom and Richard Sutch, *One Kind of Freedom: The Economic Consequences of Emancipation* (1977); Daniel A. Novak, *The Wheel of Servitude: Black Forced Labor After Emancipation*

(1978); Stephen Hahn, *The Roots of Southern Populism: Yeoman Farmers and the Transformation of the Georgia Upcountry, 1850–1896* (1983); and Charles L. Flynn, Jr., *White Land, Black Labor: Caste and Class in Late Nineteenth-Century Georgia* (1983).

American labor during Reconstruction is the subject of David Montgomery, *Beyond Equality: Labor and the Radical Republicans, 1861–1872* (1967). Liberal republicanism is examined in Ari A. Hoogenboom, *Outlawing the Spoils: A History of Civil Service Reform* (1961), and John G. Sproat, *"The Best Men": Liberal Reformers in the Gilded Age* (1968).

Keith I. Polakoff, *The Politics of Inertia* (1977), challenges C. Vann Woodward's interpretation of the Compromise of 1877. Woodward's conclusions on the Redeemer period have been confirmed or disputed in Paul M. Gaston, *The New South Creed* (1970); William Cooper, *The Conservative Regime: South Carolina, 1877–1890* (1968); Jonathan M. Weiner, *Social Origins of the New South: Alabama, 1860–1885* (1978); and J. Morgan Kousser, *The Shaping of Southern Politics: Suffrage Restriction and the Establishment of the One-Party South* (1974).

The West
Exploiting an Empire

*I*n the last three decades of the nineteenth century, a flood of settlers ventured into the vast lands across the Mississippi River. James H. Kyner, a railroad contractor in Oregon, saw in the 1880s "an almost unbroken stream of emigrants from horizon to horizon. . . . Teams and covered wagons, horsemen, little bunches of cows, more wagons, some drawn by cows, men walking, women and children riding—an endless stream of hardy, optimistic folk, going west to seek their fortunes and to settle an empire."

Prospectors poured into unsettled areas in search of "paydirt," railroads crisscrossed the continent, eastern and foreign capitalists invested in cattle and land bonanzas, and farmers took up the promise of free western lands. In 1867, Horace Greeley, editor of the New York *Tribune,* told New York City's unemployed: "If you strike off into the broad, free West, and make yourself a farm from Uncle Sam's generous domain, you will crowd nobody, starve nobody, and neither you nor your children need evermore beg for something to do."

With the end of the Civil War, white Americans again claimed a special destiny to expand across the continent. In the process, they crushed the culture of the Native Americans and ignored the special contributions of those of other nationalities, such as the Chinese miners and laborers and the Mexican herdsmen. As millions moved west, the states of Colorado, Washington, Montana, the Dakotas, Idaho, Wyoming, and Utah were carved out of the vast lands across the Mississippi. At the turn of the century, only Arizona, New Mexico, and Oklahoma remained as territories.

The West became a great colonial empire, harnessed to eastern capital and tied increasingly to national and international markets. Its raw materials, sent east by wagon, train, and ship, helped fuel eastern factories. Western economies depended to an unusual degree on the federal government, which subsidized their railroads, distributed their land, and spent millions of dollars for the upkeep of soldiers and Indians. Regional variations persisted; and Westerners remained proud of their hardly, individualistic traditions. Yet they imitated the East's social, cultural, and political patterns.

By the 1890s, the West of the lands beyond the Mississippi had undergone substantial change. In place of buffalo and unfenced vistas, there were cities and towns, health resorts, Paris fashions, homesteads, sheep ranches, and in the arid regions, the beginnings of the irrigated agriculture that would reshape the West in the twentieth century. Ghost towns, abandoned farms, and the scars in the earth left by miners and farmers spoke to the less favorable side of settlement. As the new century dawned, the West had become a place of conquest and exploitation, as well as a mythic land of cowboys and quick fortunes.

BEYOND THE FRONTIER

The line of white settlement had reached the edge of the Missouri timber country by 1840. Beyond lay an enormous land of rolling prairies, parched deserts, and rugged, majestic mountains. Emerging from the timber country, travelers first encountered the Great Plains—treeless, nearly flat, an endless "sea of grassy hillocks." The Prairie Plains, the eastern part of the region, enjoyed rich soil and good rainfall; it included parts of present-day Wisconsin, Minnesota, the Dakotas, Nebraska, Kansas, Oklahoma, and Texas. To the west—covering Montana, Wyoming, Colorado, New Mexico, and Arizona—were the High Plains, rough, semiarid, rising gently to the foothills of the Rocky Mountains.

Running from Alaska to central New Mexico, the Rockies presented a formidable barrier. There were valuable beaver in the streams and gold near Pike's Peak. But most travelers hurried through the northern passes, emerging in the desolate basin of present-day southern Idaho and Utah. Native Americans lived there—the Utes, Paiutes, Bannocks, and Shoshoni—surviving in the harsh environment by digging for roots, seeds, and berries. On the west, the lofty Coast ranges—the Cascades and Sierra Nevada—held back rainfall; beyond were the temperate lands of the Pacific Coast.

Early explorers like Zebulon Pike thought the country beyond the Mississippi was uninhabitable, fit only, Pike said, for "wandering and uncivilized aborigines." Mapmakers agreed; between 1825 and 1860, American maps showed

Physiographic Map of the United States

In the Great Plains and Rocky Mountains, the topography, climate, altitudes, crops, and especially the lack of rain led to changes in a mode of settlement that had been essentially uniform from the Atlantic Coast through Kentucky and Ohio and on to Missouri. The rectangular land surveys and quarter-section lots that were traditional in woods and prairie could not accommodate Great Plains conditions.

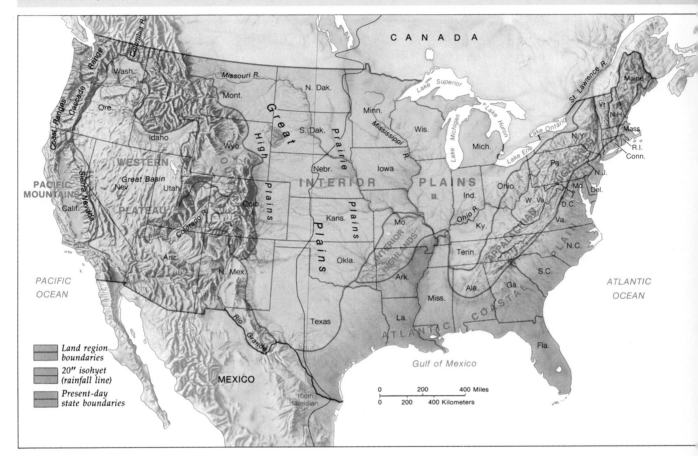

this land as "The Great American Desert." As a result, settlement paused on the edge of the Plains, and most early settlers headed directly for California and Oregon.

The Plains daunted even those hurrying across them. "You look on, on, on, out into space, out almost beyond time itself," John Noble, a painter reared in Kansas, remarked.

You see nothing but the rise and swell of land and grass, and then more grass—the monotonous, endless prairie! A stranger traveling on the prairie would get his hopes up, expecting to see something different on making the next rise. To him the disappointment and monotony were

terrible. "He's got loneliness," we would say of such a man.

Few rivers cut through the Plains; those that did raged in the winter and trickled in the summer. Rainfall usually did not reach 15 inches a year, not enough to support extensive agriculture. There was little lumber for homes and fences, and the tools of eastern settlement—the cast-iron plow, the boat, and the ax—were virtually useless on the tough and treeless Plains soil. "East of the Mississippi," historian Walter Prescott Webb noted, "civilization stood on three legs—land, water, and timber; west of the Mississippi not one but two of these legs were withdrawn—water and timber—and civilization was left on one leg—land."

Hot winds seared the Plains in summer, and northers, blizzards, and hailstorms froze them in winter. Wildlife roamed in profusion. Antelope shared the open prairies with wolves, coyote, and millions of jackrabbits and prairie dogs. The American bison, better known as the buffalo, grazed in enormous herds from Mexico to Canada. In 1865, perhaps fifteen million buffalo lived on the Plains, so many they seemed like "leaves in a forest" to an early observer. A single herd sighted in 1871 had four million head.

CRUSHING THE NATIVE AMERICANS

When Greeley urged New Yorkers to move West and "crowd nobody," he—like almost all his white countrymen—ignored the fact that large numbers of people already lived there. At the close of the Civil War, Native Americans inhabited nearly half the United States. By 1880, they had been driven onto smaller and smaller reservations and were no longer an independent people. A decade later, even their culture had crumbled under the impact of white domination.

In 1865, nearly a quarter of a million Native Americans lived in the western half of the country. Tribes like the Winnebago, Menominee, Cherokee, and Chippewa were resettled there, forced out of their eastern lands by advancing white settlement. Other tribes were native to the region. In the Southwest there were the Pueblo groups, including the Hopi, Zuñi, and Río Grande Pueblos. Peaceful farmers and herders, they had built up complex traditions around a settled way of life.

The Pueblo groups were cultivators of corn. They lived on the subdesert plateau of present-day western New Mexico and eastern Arizona. Harassed by powerful neighboring tribes, they built communal houses of adobe brick on high mesas or in cracks in the cliffs. More nomadic were the Camp Dwellers, the Jicarilla Apache and Navajo who roamed eastern New Mexico and western Texas. Blending elements of the Plains and Plateau environments, they lived in teepees or mud huts, grew some crops to supplement their hunting, and moved readily from place to place. The Navajo herded sheep and produced beautiful ornamental silver, baskets, and blankets. Fierce fighters, Apache horsemen were feared by whites and fellow Indians across the southwestern Plains.

Farther west were the tribes that inhabited present-day California. Divided into many small bands, they eked out a difficult existence living on roots, grubs, berries, and small game. In the Pacific Northwest, where fish and forest animals made life easier, the Klamath, Chinook, Yurok, and Shasta tribes developed a rich civilization. They built plank houses and canoes, worked extensively in wood, and evolved a complex social and political organization. Settled and determined, they resisted the invasion of the whites.

By the 1870s, most of these tribes had been destroyed or beaten into submission. The powerful Ute, crushed in 1855, ceded most of their Utah lands to the United States and settled on a small reservation near Great Salt Lake. The Navajo and Apache fought back fiercely, but between 1865 and 1873 they too were confined to reservations. The Native Americans of California succumbed to the contagious diseases carried by whites during the Gold Rush of 1849. Miners burned their villages and by 1880 there were fewer than twenty thousand Indians in California.

Life of the Plains Indians

Nearly two-thirds of the Native Americans lived on the Great Plains. The Plains tribes included the Sioux of present-day Minnesota and the Dakotas, the Blackfoot of Idaho and Montana, the Cheyenne, Crow, and Arapaho of the central Plains, the Pawnee of western Nebraska, and the Kiowa, Apache, and Comanche of present-day Texas and New Mexico.

Nomadic and warlike, the Plains Indians depended on the buffalo and horse. The modern horse, first brought by Spanish explorers in the 1500s, spread north from Mexico onto the Plains, and by the 1700s had changed the Plains Indians' way of life. They gave up farming almost entirely to hunt the buffalo, ranging widely over the rolling plains. They also became superb warriors and horsemen, among the best light cavalry in the world.

Equipped with stout wooden bows, 3 feet or less in length, Plains Indians were fierce warriors. Hiding their bodies behind their racing ponies, they drove deadly arrows clear through buffalo. Against white troops or settlers, the skillful Comanche rode 300 yards and shot twenty arrows in the time it took a soldier to load his firearm once. The introduction of the new Colt six-shooters during the 1850s gave government troops a rapid-fire weapon but did not entirely offset the Indians' advantage.

Migratory in culture, the Plains Indians formed tribes of several thousand people but lived in smaller "bands" of three to five hundred. The Comanche, who numbered perhaps seven thousand, had thirteen bands with such names as Burnt Meat, Making Bags While Moving, and Those Who Move Often. Each band was governed by a chief and a council of elder men, and Indians of the same tribe transferred freely from band to band. Bands acted independently, making it difficult for the U.S. government to deal with the fragmented tribes.

The bands followed and lived off the buffalo. Buffalo provided food, clothing, and shelter; and the Indians, unlike later white hunters, used every part of the animal. The meat was dried or "jerked" in the hot Plains air. The skins made teepees, blankets, and robes. Buffalo bones became knives; tendons were made into bow strings; horns and hooves were boiled into glue. Buffalo "chips"—dried manure—were burned as fuel. All in all, the buffalo was "a galloping department store."

Warfare between tribes usually took the form of brief raids and skirmishes. Plains Indians fought few prolonged wars and rarely coveted territory. Most conflicts involved only a few warriors intent on stealing horses or "counting coups"—touching an enemy's body with the hand or a special stick. Tribes developed a fierce and trained warrior class, recognized for achievements in battle. Speaking different languages, Native Americans of various tribes were nevertheless able to communicate with one another through a highly developed sign language.

The Plains tribes divided labor tasks according to gender. Men hunted, traded, supervised ceremonial activities, and cleared ground for planting. They usually held the positions of authority, such as chief or medicine man. Women were responsible for child rearing and artistic activity. They also performed the camp work, grew vegetables, prepared buffalo meat and hides, and gathered berries and roots. In most tribes, women played an important role in political, economic, and religious activities. Among the Navajo and Zuñi, kinship descended from the mother's side,

and Navajo women were in charge of most of the family's property. In tribes like the Sioux, there was little difference in status. Men were respected for hunting and war, women for their artistic skills with quill and paint.

"As Long as Waters Run"

Before the Civil War, Americans used the land west of the Mississippi as "one big reservation." The government named the area "Indian Country," moved eastern tribes there with firm treaty guarantees, and in 1834 passed the Indian Intercourse Act, which prohibited any white person from entering Indian country without a license.

The situation changed in the 1850s. Wagon trains wound their way to California and Oregon, miners pushed into western gold fields, and there was talk of a transcontinental railroad. To clear the way for settlement, the federal government in 1851 abandoned "One Big Reservation" in favor of a new policy of "concentration." For the first time, it assigned definite boundaries to each tribe. The Sioux, for example, were given the Dakota country north of the Platte River, the Crows a large area near the Powder River, and the Cheyenne and Arapaho the Colorado foothills between the North Platte and Arkansas rivers for "as long as waters run and the grass shall grow."

The "concentration" policy lasted only a few years. Accustomed to hunting widely for buffalo, many Native Americans refused to stay within their assigned areas. White settlers poured into Indian lands, then called on the government to protect them. Indians were pushed out of Kansas and Nebraska in the 1850s, even as white reformers fought to hold those territories open for free blacks. In 1859, gold miners moved into the Pikes Peak country, touching off warfare with the Cheyenne and Arapaho.

In 1864, tired of the fighting, the two tribes asked for peace. Certain the war was over, Chief Black Kettle led his seven hundred followers to camp on Sand Creek in southeastern Colorado. Early on the morning of November 29, 1864, a group of Colorado militia led by Colonel John M. Chivington attacked the sleeping group. "Kill and scalp all, big and little," Chivington told his men. "Nits make lice." Black Kettle tried to stop the ambush, raising first an American flag and

The Buffalo Hunt *by Charles Russell [below]. At first the Plains Indians hunted the buffalo on foot; then, with the arrival of the horse, on horseback. After the buffalo was killed, women skinned the hide, cut up the meat, and then cured the hide as shown in the painting* Halcyon Days *[right] by George Catlin. Women also decorated the teepees and preserved the meat by drying it in the sun.*

Native Americans in the West: Major Battles and Reservations

"They made us many promises, more than I remember, but they never kept but one; they promised to take our land, and they took it." So said Red Cloud of the Oglala Sioux, summarizing Native American–white relations in the 1870s.

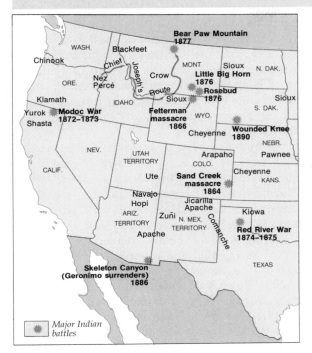

Major Indian battles

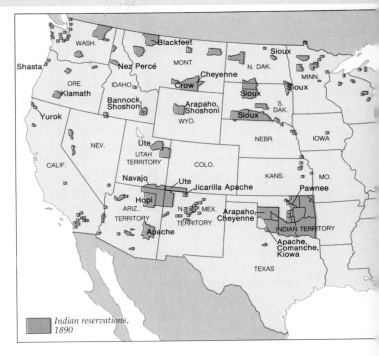

Indian reservations, 1890

then a white flag. Neither worked. The Native American men, women, and children were clubbed, stabbed, and scalped.

The Chivington massacre set off angry protests in Colorado and the East. Congress appointed an investigating committee, and the government concluded a treaty with the Cheyenne and Arapaho condemning "the gross and wanton outrages." Still, the two tribes were forced to surrender their Sand Creek reservation in exchange for lands elsewhere. The Kiowa and Comanche were also ousted from areas they had been granted "forever" only a few years before. As the Sioux chief Spotted Tail said, "Why does not the Great Father put his red children on wheels so that he can move them as he will?"

Before long, the powerful Sioux were on the warpath in the great Sioux War of 1865–1867. Once again an invasion of gold miners touched off the war, which flared even more intensely when the federal government announced plans to connect the various mining towns by building the Bozeman Trail through the heart of the Sioux hunting grounds in Montana. Red Cloud, the

Sioux chief, determined to stop the trail. In December 1866, pursued by an army column under Captain William J. Fetterman, he lured the incautious Fetterman deep into the wilderness, ambushed him, and wiped out all eighty-two soldiers in his command.

The Fetterman massacre, coming so soon after the Chivington massacre, sparked a public debate over the nation's Indian policy. Like the policy itself, the debate reflected differing white views of the Native Americans. In the East, some reform, humanitarian, and church groups wanted a humane peace policy, directed toward educating and "civilizing" the tribes. Many white people, in the East and West, questioned this approach, convinced that Native Americans were savages unfit for civilization. Westerners, of course, had some reason to fear Indian attacks, and the fears often fed on wild rumors of scalped settlers and besieged forts. As a result, Westerners in general favored firm control over the Native Americans, including swift punishment of any who rebelled.

In 1867, the peace advocates won the debate. Halting construction on the Bozeman Trail,

Congress created a Peace Commission of four civilians and three generals to end the Sioux War and eliminate permanently the causes of Indian wars. Setting out for the West, the Peace Commissioners agreed that only one policy offered a permanent solution: a policy of "small reservations" to isolate the Native Americans on distant lands, teach them to farm, and gradually "civilize" them.

The commissioners chose two areas to hold all the Plains Indians. The 54,000 Native Americans on the northern Plains would be moved north of the Black Hills in Dakota Territory, far from prospective white settlement. On the southern Plains, the 86,000 Native Americans would be moved into present-day Oklahoma, a region also considered difficult to farm and unattractive to whites. In both areas, tribes would be assigned specific reservations where government agents could supervise them.

The Kiowa, Comanche, Cheyenne, and Arapaho agreed to the plan in 1867, the Sioux in 1868. Extending the policy beyond the Plains, the Ute, Shoshoni, Bannock, Navajo, and Apache also accepted small reservations. "We have now selected and provided reservations for all, off the great road," an army commander wrote. "All who cling to their old hunting-grounds are hostile and will remain so till killed off."

Final Battles on the Plains

Few Native Americans settled peacefully into life on the new reservations. The reservation system not only changed their age-old customs; it chained them in a situation of poverty and isolation. Soon, young warriors and minor chiefs denounced the treaties and drifted back to the open countryside. In late 1868, warfare broke out again, and it took over a decade of violence to beat the Indians into submission. The Kiowa and Comanche rampaged through the Texas Panhandle, looting and killing, until the U.S. Army crushed them in the Red River War of 1874–1875 and ended warfare in the Southwest.

On the northern Plains fighting resulted from the Black Hills Gold Rush of 1875. As prospectors tramped across Native American hunting grounds, the Sioux gathered to stop them. They were led by Rain-in-the-Face, the great war chief Crazy Horse, and the famous medicine man

Sitting Bull. The army sent several columns of troops after the Indians, but one, under flamboyant Lieutenant Colonel George A. Custer, pushed recklessly ahead, eager to claim the victory. On the morning of June 25, 1876, thinking he had a small band of Native Americans surrounded in their village on the banks of the Little Bighorn River in Montana, Custer divided his column and took 265 men toward it. Instead of finding a small band, he discovered he had stumbled on the main Sioux camp with 2,500 warriors. It was the largest Native American army ever assembled in the United States.

By mid-afternoon it was over; Custer and his men were dead. Custer was largely responsible for the loss, but "Custer's Last Stand," set in blazing headlines across the country, signaled a nationwide demand for revenge. Within a few months, the Sioux were surrounded and beaten, three thousand of them surrendering in October 1876. Sitting Bull and a few followers who had fled to Canada gave up in 1881.

The Sioux War ended the major Indian warfare in the West, but occasional outbreaks occurred for several years thereafter. In 1877, the Nez Percé tribe of Oregon, a people who had warmly welcomed Lewis and Clark in 1805, rebelled against government policy. Hoping to reach Canada, Chief Joseph led the tribe on a courageous flight lasting 75 days and covering 1,321 miles. They defeated the pursuing army at every turn but then ran out of food, horses, and ammunition. Surrendering, they were sent to barren lands in the Indian Country of Oklahoma, and there, most of them died from disease.

In 1890, the Teton Sioux of South Dakota, bitter and starving, became restless. Many of them turned to the "Ghost Dances," a set of dances and rites that grew from a vision of a Paiute messiah named Wovoka. Performance of the dances, Wovoka said, would bring back Native American lands and would cause the whites to disappear. All Native Americans would reunite, the earth would be covered with dust, and a new earth would come upon the old. The vanished buffalo would return in great herds.

The army intervened to stop the dancing, touching off violence that killed Sitting Bull and a number of other warriors. Frightened Native Americans fled southwest to join other Ghost Dancers under the aging chief Big Foot. Moving

This pictogram by Oglala Sioux Amos Bad Heart Bull is a Nastive American version of the Battle of Little Bighorn, also known as "Custer's Last Stand."

quickly, troops of the Seventh Cavalry, Custer's old regiment, caught up with Big Foot's band and took them to the army camp on Wounded Knee Creek in South Dakota. A Native American, it is thought, fired the first shot, returned by the army's new machine guns. Firing a shell a second, they shredded teepees and people. About two hundred men, women, and children were massacred in the snow.

The End of Tribal Life

The final step in Indian policy came in the 1870s and 1880s. Some reformers had long argued against segregating the Native Americans on reservations, urging instead that the nation assimilate them individually into white culture. These "assimilationists" wanted to use education, land policy, and federal law to eradicate tribal society.

Congress began to adopt the policy in 1871 when it ended the practice of treaty-making with Native American tribes. Since tribes were no longer separate nations, they lost many of their political and judicial functions, and the power of

the chiefs was weakened. In 1882, Congress created a Court of Indian Offenses to try Native Americans who broke government rules, and soon thereafter it made them answerable in regular courts for certain crimes.

While Congress worked to break down the tribes, educators trained young Native Americans to adjust to white culture. In 1879, fifty Pawnee, Kiowa, and Cheyenne youths were brought east to the new Carlisle Indian School in Carlisle, Pennsylvania. Other Native American schools soon opened, including the Haskell Institute in Kansas and numerous day schools on the western reservations. The schools taught students to fix machines and farm; they forced them to trim their long hair, made them speak English, banned the wearing of tribal paint or clothes, and forbade tribal ceremonies and dances. "Kill the Indian and save the man," said Richard H. Pratt, the army officer who founded the Carlisle School.

Land ownership was the final and most important link in the new policy. Native Americans who owned land, it was thought, would become responsible, self-reliant citizens. Deciding to give

Tom Torlino, a Navajo Indian, photographed before and after his "assimilation." Torlino attended the Carlisle Indian School in Pennsylvania.

each Native American a farm, Congress in 1887 passed the Dawes Severalty Act, the most important legal development in Indian-white relations in over three centuries.

Aiming to end tribal life, the Dawes Act divided tribal lands into small plots for distribution among members of the tribe. Each family head received 160 acres, single adults 80 acres, and children 40 acres. Once the land was distributed, any surplus was sold to white settlers, with the profits going to Native American schools. To keep the Indians' land from falling into the hands of speculators, the federal government held it in trust for twenty-five years. Finally, American citizenship was granted to Native Americans who accepted their land, lived apart from the tribe, and "adopted the habits of civilized life."

Through the Dawes Act, 47 million acres of land were distributed to Native Americans and their families. There were another 90 million acres in the reservations, and these lands, often the most fertile, were sold to white settlers. Speculators evaded the twenty-five-year rule, leasing rather than purchasing the land from the Native Americans. Many Native Americans knew little about farming. Their tools were rudimentary, and in the culture of the Plains Indians men had not ordinarily participated in farming. In 1934, the government returned to the idea of tribal land ownership, but by then 138 million acres of Indian land had shrunk to 48 million acres, half of which was barren.

The final blow to tribal life came not in the Dawes Act but in the virtual extermination of the buffalo, the Plains Indians' chief resource and the basis for their unique way of life. The killing began in the 1860s as the transcontinental railroads pushed west, and it stepped up as settlers found they could harm the Indians by harming the buffalo. "Kill every buffalo you can," an army officer said. "Every buffalo dead is an Indian gone." Then, in 1871, a Pennsylvania tannery discovered that buffalo hides made valuable leather. Professional hunters like William F. "Buffalo Bill" Cody swarmed across the Plains, killing millions of the beasts.

Between 1872 and 1874, professional hunters slaughtered three million buffalo a year. In a frontier form of a factory system, riflemen, skinners, and transport wagons pushed through the vast herds, which shrank steadily behind them. A good hunter killed a hundred buffalo a day; skinners took off the hides, removed the tongue, hump, and tallow, and left the rest. "I have seen their bodies so thick after being skinned," a hunter said, "that they would look like logs where a hurricane had passed through a forest."

By 1883, the buffalo were almost gone. When the government set out to produce the famous "buffalo nickel," the designer had to go to the Bronx Zoo in New York City to find a buffalo.

By 1900, there were only 250,000 Native Americans in the country. (There were 600,000 within the limits of the present-day United States

Huge buffalo herds grazing along railroads in the West frequently blocked the path of passing trains. Passengers often killed for sport, shooting at the beasts with no intention of using or removing the animal carcasses, glad to know that they were harming the Native Americans by destroying their most important reserve.

in 1800, and more than 5 million in 1492, when Columbus first set foot in the New World.) Most of the Indians lived on reservations. Many lived in poverty. Alcoholism and unemployment were growing problems, and Native Americans, no longer able to live off the buffalo, became wards of the state. They lost their special distinctiveness as a culture. Once possessors of the entire continent, they had been crowded into smaller and smaller areas, overwhelmed by the demand to become settled, literate, and English-speaking. "Except for the internment of the West Coast Japanese during World War II," said historian Roger L. Nichols, "Indian removal is the only example of large-scale government-enforced migration in American history. For the Japanese, the move was temporary; for the Indians it was not."

Even as the Native Americans lost their identity, they entered the romantic folklore of the West. Dime novels, snapped up by readers young and old, told tales of Indian fighting on the Plains. Buffalo Bill Cody turned it all into a profitable business. Beginning in 1883, his Wild West Show ran for over three decades, playing to millions of viewers in the United States, Canada, and Europe. It featured Plains Indians chasing buffalo, performing a war dance, and attacking a settler's cabin. In 1885, Sitting Bull himself, victor

over Custer at the battle of Little Bighorn, performed in the show.

SETTLEMENT OF THE WEST

Between 1870 and 1900, white—and some African, Hispanic, and Asian—Americans settled the enormous total of 430 million acres west of the Mississippi; they occupied more land than had been occupied by Americans in all the years before 1870.

People moved West for many reasons. Some sought adventure; others wanted to escape the drab routine of factory or city life. Many moved to California for their health. The Mormons settled Utah to escape religious persecution. Others followed the mining camps, the advancing railroads, and the farming and cattle frontier. "Most of the time we were solitary adventurers in a great land as fresh and new as a spring morning, and we were free and full of the zest of darers," said Charles Goodnight, a Texas cattleman and founder of the famous Goodnight Trail.

Whatever the specific reason, most people moved West to better their lot. On the whole, their timing was good, for as the nation's population grew, so did demand for the livestock and the agricultural, mineral, and lumber products of the expanding West. Contrary to older historical views, the West did not act as a major "safety valve," an outlet for social and economic tensions. The poor and unemployed did not have the means to move there and establish farms. "Moreover," as Douglass C. North, an economic historian, said, "most people moved West in good times . . . in periods of rising prices, of expanding demand, when the prospects for making money from this new land looked brightest; and this aspect characterized the whole pattern of settlement."

Men and Women on the Overland Trail

The first movement west aimed not for the nearby Plains but for California and Oregon on the continent's far shore. It started in the 1849 Gold Rush to California, and in the next three decades perhaps as many as half a million individuals made the long journey. Some walked; others rode horses alone or in small groups. About half joined great caravans, numbering 150 wagons or more, that inched across the 2,000 miles between the Missouri River and the Pacific Coast.

More often than not, men made the decision to make the crossing, but except for the stampedes to the mines, migration usually turned out to be a family affair. Wives were consulted, though in some cases they had little real choice. They could either go along or live alone at home. While many women regretted leaving family and friends, they agreed to the trip, sometimes as eagerly as the men. "With good courage and not one sigh of regret I mounted my pony," Lydia Rudd said. "I would not be left behind," said Luzena Wilson, whose husband ached to join the Gold Rush to California. "I thought where he could go I could, and where I went I could take my two little toddling babies." Like the Wilsons, the majority of people traveled in family groups, including in-laws, grandchildren, aunts, and uncles. As one historian said, "The quest for something new would take place in the context of the very familiar."

Individuals and wagon trains set out from various points along the Missouri River. Leaving in the spring and traveling through the summer, they hoped to reach their destination before the first snowfall. During April, travelers gradually assembled in spring camp just across the Missouri River, waiting for the new grass to ripen into for-

age. They packed and repacked the wagons and elected the train's leaders, who would set the line of march, look for water and campsites, and impose discipline. Some trains adopted detailed rules, fearing a lapse into savagery in the wild lands across the Missouri. "Every man to carry with him a Bible and other religious books, as we hope not to degenerate into a state of barbarism," one agreement said.

Setting out in early May, travelers divided the enormous route into manageable portions. The first leg of the journey followed the Platte River west to Fort Kearney in central Nebraska Territory, a distance of about 300 miles. The land was even, with good supplies of wood, grass, and water. From a distance the white-topped wagons seemed driven by a common force, but in fact, internal discipline broke down almost immediately. Arguments erupted over the pace of the march, the choice of campsites, the number of guards to post, whether to rest or push on. Elected leaders quit; new ones were chosen. Every train was filled with individualists, and as the son of one train captain said, "If you think it's any snap to run a wagon train of 66 wagons with every man in the train having a different idea of what is the best thing to do, all I can say is that some day you ought to try it."

Men, women, and children had different tasks on the trail. Men concerned themselves almost entirely with hunting, guard duty, and transportation. They rose at 4 A.M. to hitch the wagons, and after breakfast began the day's march. At noon, they stopped and set the teams to graze while the women prepared the midday meal. The march continued until sunset. Then, while the men relaxed, the women fixed dinner and the next day's lunch, and the children kindled the fire, brought water to camp, and searched for wood or other fuel. Walking 15 miles a day, in searing heat and mountain cold, travelers were exhausted by late afternoon. "We can all, as soon as we stop, lie down on the grass or anywhere and be asleep in less than no time almost," Rebecca Ketcham, an Oregon-bound emigrant, reported.

For women, the trail was lonely, and they worked to exhaustion. Before long, some adjusted their clothing to the harsh conditions, adopting the new bloomer pants, shortening their skirts, or wearing regular "wash dresses"—so called because they had shorter hemlines that did not drag on the wet ground on washday. Other women continued to wear their long dresses, thinking bloomers "indecent." Men hunted buffalo and antelope for fresh meat. Both men and women carried firearms in case of Indian attacks, but most emigrants saw few Indians en route.

What they often did see was trash, miles of it, for the wagon trains were an early example of the impact of migration and settlement on the western environment. On the Oregon and other trails, travelers sidestepped mounds of garbage, tin cans, furniture, cooking stoves, kegs, tools, and clothing, all discarded by people who had passed through before. Along a 40-mile trail in the Nevada desert, a migrant tallied two thousand abandoned wagons. On some trails, animals and people stirred up so much dust that drivers wore goggles to see.

The first stage of the journey was deceptively easy, and travelers usually reached Fort Kearney by late May. The second leg led another 300 miles up the Platte River to Fort Laramie on the eastern edge of Wyoming Territory. The heat of June had burned the grass, and there was no wood. Anxious to beat the early snowfalls, travelers rested a day or two at the fort, then hurried on to South Pass, 280 miles to the west, the best route through the forbidding Rockies. The land was barren. It was now mid-July, but the mountain nights were so cold that ice formed in the water buckets.

Beyond South Pass, some emigrants turned south to the Mormon settlements on Great Salt Lake, but most headed 340 miles north to Fort Hall on the Snake River in Idaho. It took another three months to cover the remaining 800 miles. California-bound travelers followed the Humboldt River through the summer heat of Nevada. Well into September, they began the final arduous push: first, a 55-mile stretch of desert; then 70 difficult miles up the eastern slopes of the Sierra Nevada, hoisting wagons laboriously over massive outcrops of rock; and finally the last 100 miles down the western slopes to the welcome October greenness of the Sacramento Valley.

Under the best of conditions the trip took six months, sixteen hours a day, dawn to dusk, of hard, grueling labor. Walking halfway across the continent was no easy task, and it provided a never-to-be-forgotten experience for those who did it. The wagon trains, carrying the dreams of thousands of individuals, reproduced society in small focus: individualistic, hopeful, mobile, divided by age and gender roles, apprehensive, yet willing to strike out for the distant and new.

Of the many dangers faced by those traveling on the overland trails, among the most severe were prairie blizzards. As temperatures fell to −40°, cattle would inhale particles of snow and sleet and die of suffocation.

Blacks in Blue
The Buffalo Soldiers in the West

On Saturday afternoons, youngsters used to sit in darkened movie theaters and cheer the victories of the U.S. Cavalry over the Indians. Typically, the Indians were about to capture a wagon train, when army bugles suddenly sounded. Then the blue-coated cavalry charged over the hill. Few in the theaters cheered for the Indians; fewer still noticed the absence of black faces among the on-charging cavalry. But in fact, more than two thousand African American cavalrymen served on the western frontier between 1867 and 1890. Known as the "buffalo soldiers," they made up one-fifth of the U.S. Cavalry.

Black troops were first used on a large scale during the Civil War (see Chapter 15). Organized in segregated units, with white officers, they fought with distinction. Nearly 180,000 blacks served in the Union Army; 34,000 of them died. When the war ended in 1865, Congress for the first time authorized black troops to serve in the regular peacetime army. In addition to infantry, it created two cavalry regiments—the Ninth and Tenth, which became known as the famous buffalo soldiers.

Like other black regiments, the Ninth and Tenth Cavalry had white officers who took special examinations before they could serve. The chaplains were assigned not only to preach but to teach reading, writing, and arithmetic. The food was poor; racism was wide-spread. The army stocked the first black units with worn-out horses, a serious matter to men whose lives depended on the speed and stamina of their mounts. "Since our first mount in 1867 this regiment has received nothing but broken down horses and repaired equipment," an officer said in 1870.

Many white officers refused to serve with black troops. George A. Custer, the handsome "boy general," turned down a position in the Ninth and joined the new Seventh Cavalry, headed for disaster at Little Bighorn. The *Army and Navy Journal* carried ads that told a similar story:

**A FIRST LIEUTENANT
OF INFANTRY**
(white)
Stationed at a
very desirable post
*in the Department of the
South
desires a transfer with
an officer of the same grade*
on equal terms
*if in a white regiment
but if in a colored regiment*
a reasonable bonus
would be expected.

Although they were not, in fact, treated as well as the white soldiers in their regiments, many African American cavalrymen such as those pictured here were probably drawn into service by hard-sell recruitment posters like the one shown on the facing page.

There was no shortage of black troops for the officers to lead. Blacks enlisted because the army offered some advancement in a closed society. It also paid $13 a month, plus room and board.

In 1867, the Ninth and Tenth Cavalry were posted to the West, where they remained for two decades. Under Colonel Benjamin H. Grierson, a Civil War hero, the Tenth went to Fort Riley, Kansas; the regiment arrived in the midst of a great Indian war. Kiowas, Comanches, Cheyennes, Arapahoes, and Sioux were on the warpath. Troopers of the Tenth defended farms, stages, trains, and work crews building railroad tracks to the west. Cornered by a band of Cheyennes, they beat back the attack and won a new name. Earlier known as the "brunettes" or "Africans," the Cheyenne now called them the buffalo soldiers, a name that soon applied to all African American soldiers in the West. (Some of the "buffalo soldiers" are shown in the photo opposite).

From 1868 to 1874, the Tenth served on the Kansas frontier. The dull winter days were filled with drills and scouting parties outside the post. In spring and summer the good weather brought forth new forays. Indian bands raided farms and ranches and stampeded cattle herds on the way north from Texas. They struck and then melted back into the reservations.

The Ninth Cavalry also had a difficult job. Commanded by Colonel Edward Hatch, who had served with Grierson in the Civil War, it was stationed in West Texas and along the Rio Grande. The summers were so hot that men collapsed with sunstroke, the winters so cold that water froze in the canteens. Native Americans from outside the area

ATTENTION! INDIAN FIGHTERS

Having been authorized by the Governor to raise a Company of 100 day

U. S. VOL CAVALRY!

For immediate service against hostile Indians. I call upon all who wish to engage in such service to call at my office and enroll their names immediately.

Pay and Rations the same as other U. S. Volunteer Cavalry.

Parties furnishing their own horses will receive 40c per day, and rations for the same while in the service.
The Company will also be entitled to all horses and other plunder taken from the Indians.

Office first door East of Recorder's Office.
HAL. SAYR.

Central City, Aug. 13, '64.

frequently raided it. From the north Kiowa and Comanche warriors rode down the Great Comanche War Trail; Kickapoos crossed the Rio Grande from Mexico. Gangs of Mexican bandits and restless Civil War veterans roamed and plundered at will.

From 1874 to 1875, the Ninth fought in the great Red River War, in which the Kiowas and Comanches, fed up with conditions on the reservations, revolted against Grant's peace policy. Marching, fighting, then marching again, the soldiers harried and wore out the Indians, who finally surrendered in the spring of 1875. Herded into a new and desolate reservation, the Mescalero Apaches of New Mexico took to the warpath in 1877 and again in 1879. Each time it took a year of grueling warfare to effect their surrender. In 1886, black cavalrymen surrounded and captured the famous Apache chief Geronimo. In that and other campaigns, several buffalo soldiers won the

Congressional Medal of Honor.

Black troops hunted Big Foot and his band before the slaughter at Wounded Knee in 1890 (see p. 512), and they served in many of the West's most famous Indian battles. While one-third of all army recruits deserted between 1865 and 1890, the Ninth and Tenth Cavalry had few desertions. In 1880, the Tenth had the fewest desertions of any regiment in the country.

It was ironic that in the West, black men fought red men to benefit white men. Once the Indian wars ended, the buffalo soldiers worked to keep illegal settlers out of Indian or government land; much of this land was later opened to settlement. Both regiments saw action in the Spanish-American War, the Ninth at San Juan Hill, the Tenth in the fighting around Santiago. The old buffalo soldiers were forgotten in retirement, although some of them had the satisfaction of settling on the western lands they had done so much to pacify.

Land for the Taking

As railroads pushed west in the 1870s and 1880s, locomotive trains replaced wagon trains, but the shift was gradual, and until the end of the century emigrants often combined both modes of travel. Into the 1890s, travelers could be seen making their way across the West by any available means. Early railroad transportation was expensive, and the average farm family could not afford to buy tickets and ship supplies. Many Europeans traveled by rail to designated outfitting places, and then proceeded West with wagons and oxen.

Traffic flowed in all directions, belying the image of a simple "westward" movement. Many people did go west, of course, but others, like migrants from Mexico, became westerners by moving north, and Asian Americans moved eastward from the Pacific coast. Whatever their route, they all ended up in the meeting ground of cultures that formed the modern West.

Why did they come? "The motive that induced us to part with the pleasant associations and the dear friends of our childhood days," explained Phoebe Judson, an early emigrant, "was to obtain from the government of the United States a grant of land that 'Uncle Sam' had promised to give to the head of each family who settled in this new country." A popular camp song reflected the same motive:

Come along, come along—don't be alarmed,
Uncle Sam is rich enough to give us all a farm.

Uncle Sam owned about 1 billion acres of land in the 1860s, much of it mountain and desert land unsuited for agriculture. By 1900, the various land laws had distributed half of it. Between 1862 and 1890, the government gave away 48 million acres under the Homestead Act of 1862, sold about 100 million acres to private citizens and corporations, granted 128 million acres to railroad companies to tempt them to build across the unsettled West, and sold huge tracts to the states.

The Homestead Act of 1862, a law of great significance, gave 160 acres of land to anyone who would pay a $10 registration and pledge to live on it and cultivate it for five years. The offer set off a mass migration of land-hungry Europeans, dazzled by a country that gave its land away. Americans also seized on the act's provisions, and between 1862 and 1900, nearly 600,000 families claimed free homesteads under it.

Yet the Homestead Act did not work as Congress had hoped. Few farmers and laborers had the cash to move to the frontier, buy farm equipment, and wait out the year or two before the farm became self-supporting. Tailored to the timber and water conditions of the East, the act did not work as well in the semiarid West. In the fertile valleys of the Mississippi, 160 acres provided a generous farm. A farmer on the Great Plains needed either a larger farm for dry farming or a smaller one for irrigation.

The Timber Culture Act of 1873 attempted to adjust the Homestead Act to western conditions. It allowed homesteaders to claim an additional 160 acres if they planted trees on a quarter of it within four years. A successful act, it distributed 10 million acres of land, encouraged needed forestation, and enabled homesteaders to expand their farms to a workable size. Cattle ranchers lobbied for another law, the Desert Land Act of 1877, which allowed individuals to obtain 640 acres in the arid states for $1.25 an acre, provided they irrigated part of it within three years. This act invited fraud. Irrigation sometimes meant a bucket of water dumped on the ground, and ranchers used their hired hands to claim large tracts. More than 2.6 million acres were distributed, much of it fraudulently.

The Timber and Stone Act of 1878 applied only to lands "unfit for cultivation" and valuable chiefly for timber or stone. It permitted anyone in California, Nevada, Oregon, and Washington to buy up to 160 acres of forestland for $2.50 an acre. Like ranchers, lumber companies used employees to file false claims. Company agents rounded up seamen on the waterfront, marched them to the land office to file their claims, took them to a notary public to sign over the claims to the company, and then marched them back to the waterfront for payment in beer or cash. By 1900, 3.6 million acres of rich forest land had been claimed under the measure.

Speculators made ingenious use of the land laws. Sending agents in advance of settlement, they moved along choice river bottoms or irrigable areas, accumulating large holdings to be held for high prices. In the arid West, where control of water meant control of the surrounding land, shrewd ranchers plotted their holdings accordingly. In Colorado, one cattleman, John F. Iliff, owned only 105 small parcels of land, but by placing them around the few waterholes, he effectively dominated an empire stretching over 6,000 square miles.

Water, in fact, became a dominant western issue, since aside from the Pacific Northwest, northern California, parts of the Rocky Mountain West, and the eastern half of the Great Plains, much of the trans-Mississippi West was arid, receiving less than twenty inches of rainfall annually. People speculated in water as if it were gold and planned great irrigation systems in Utah, eastern Colorado, and California's central valleys to "make the desert bloom." A sign in Modesto, California, read, "Water, Wealth, Contentment, Health."

Irrigators received a major boost in 1902 when the National Reclamation Act (the Newlands Act) set aside most of the proceeds from the sale of public lands in sixteen western states to finance irrigation projects in the arid states. Over the next decades, dams, canals, and irrigation systems channeled water into dry areas, creating a "hydraulic" society that was rich in crops and cities (like Los Angeles and Phoenix), but ever thirstier and in danger of outrunning the precious water on which it all depended.

As beneficiaries of the government's policy of land grants for railway construction, the railroad companies were the West's largest landowners. Eager to have immigrants settle on the land they owned near the railroad right-of-way, and eager to boost their freight and passenger business, the companies sent agents to the East and Europe. Attractive brochures touted life in the West. The Union Pacific called the rocky Platte Valley in Nebraska "a flowery meadow of great fertility, clothed in nutritious grasses."

Railroad lines set up Land Departments and Bureaus of Immigration. The Land Departments priced the land, arranged credit terms, and even gave free farming courses to immigrants. The Bureau of Immigration employed agents in Europe, met immigrants at eastern seaports, and ran special cars for land seekers heading West.

Half a billion acres of western land were given or sold to speculators and corporations. At the same time, only 600,000 homestead patents were issued, covering 80 million acres. Thus, only one acre in every nine initially went to individual pioneers, the intended beneficiaries of the nation's largesse. Two-thirds of all homestead claimants before 1890 failed in their efforts to farm their new land.

Territorial Government

As new areas of the West opened, they were organized as territories under the control of Congress and the president. The territorial system started with the famous Northwest Ordinance of 1787 (see Chapter 6), which established the rules by which territories became states. Washington ran the territories like "a passive group of colonial mandates." The president appointed the governor and judges in each territory; Congress detailed their duties, set their budgets, and over-saw their

Railroad companies distributed elaborately illustrated brochures and broadsides to lure people to the West, where they could settle on land owned by the railroad.

activities. Territorial officials had almost absolute power over the territories.

Until they obtained statehood, then, the territories depended on the federal government for their existence. They became an important part of the patronage system, as sources of jobs for deserving politicians.

The national political parties, especially the Republicans, funneled government funds into the territorial economies, and in areas like Wyoming and the Dakotas, where resources were scarce, economic growth depended on them. Many early settlers held patronage jobs or hoped for them, traded with government-supported Native Americans, sold supplies to army troops, and speculated in government lands.

In a large portion of the trans-Mississippi West, a generation grew up under territorial rule. Inevitably, they developed distinct ideas about politics, government, and the economy.

The Spanish-Speaking Southwest

In the nineteenth century almost all Spanish-speaking people in the United States lived in California, Arizona, New Mexico, Texas, and Colorado. Their numbers were small—California had only 8,086 Mexican residents in 1900—but the influence of their culture and institutions was large. In some respects the southwestern frontier was more Spanish-American than Anglo-American.

Pushing northward from Mexico, the Spanish gradually established the present-day economic structure of the Southwest. They brought with them techniques of mining, stock raising, and irrigated farming. After winning independence in the 1820s, the Mexicans brought new laws, ranching methods, chaps, and the burro. Both Spanish and Mexicans created the legal framework for distributing land and water, a precious resource in the Southwest. They gave large grants of land to communities for grazing, to individuals as rewards for service, and to the various Native American pueblos.

In Southern California the Californios, descendants of the original colonizers, began after the 1860s to lose their once vast landholdings to drought and mortgages. Some turned to crime and became feared bandidos; others, like José María Amador, lived in poverty and remembered better days:

E. P. Caldwell, a small-town attorney in Huron, Dakota Territory, ran this newspaper advertisement to attract investors from the East.

When I was but a little boy I drained the chocolate pot,
But now I am a poor man and am condemned to slop.

In 1875, Romualdo Pacheco, an aristocratic native son, served as governor of California and then went on to Congress. But as the Californios died out, Mexican Americans continued the Spanish-Mexican influence. In 1880, one-fourth of the residents of Los Angeles County were Spanish speaking.

In New Mexico, Spanish-speaking citizens remained the majority ethnic group until the 1940s, and the Spanish-Mexican culture dominated the territory. Contests over land grants became New Mexico's largest industry; lawyers who dealt in them amassed huge holdings. After 1888, *Las Gorras Blancas*, The White Caps, a secret organization of Spanish Americans, attacked the movement of Anglo ranchers into the Las Vegas community land grant. Armed and hooded, they cut down fences and scattered the stock of those they viewed as intruders.

Throughout the Southwest, the Spanish-Mexican heritage gave a distinctive shape to society. Men headed the families and dominated economic life. Women had substantial economic rights (though few political ones), and they enjoyed a status their English-American counterparts did not have. Wives kept full control of property acquired before their marriage; they also held half title to all property in a marriage, which later caused many southwestern states to pass community property laws.

In addition, the Spanish-Mexican heritage fostered a modified economic caste system, a strong Roman Catholic influence, and the primary use of the Spanish language. Continuous immigration from Mexico kept language and cultural ties strong. Spanish names and customs spread, even among Anglos. David Starr Jordan, arriving from Indiana to become the first president of Stanford University in California, bestowed Spanish names on streets, houses, and a Standford dormitory. Spanish was the region's first or second language. Confronted by Sheriff Pat Garrett in a darkened room, New Mexico's famous outlaw, Billy the Kid, died asking *"Quién es? Quién es?"* ("Who is it? Who is it?").

THE BONANZA WEST

Between 1850 and 1900, wave after wave of newcomers swept across the trans-Mississippi West. There were riches for the taking, hidden in gold-washed streams, spread lushly over grass-covered prairies, or available in the gullible minds of greedy newcomers. The nineteenth-century West took shape in the search for mining, cattle, and land bonanzas that drew eager settlers from the East and around the world.

As with all bonanzas, its consequences in the West were uneven growth, boom-and-bust economic cycles, and wasted resources. Society seemed constantly in the making. People moved here and there, following river bottoms, gold strikes, railroad tracks, and other opportunities. "Instant cities" arose. San Francisco, Salt Lake City, and Denver were the most spectacular examples, but every cow town and mining camp witnessed similar phenomena of growth. Boston needed more than two centuries to attract one-third of a million people; San Francisco did the same in a little more than twenty years.

Many Westerners had left home to get rich quickly, and they adopted institutions that reflected that goal. As a contemporary poem said,

Love to see the stir an' bustle
In the busy town,
Everybody on the hustle
Saltin' profits down.

Everybody got a wad a'
Ready cash laid by;
Ain't no flies on Colorado—
Not a cussed fly.

In their lives, the West was an idea as well as a region, and the idea molded them as much as they molded it.

The Mining Bonanza

Mining was the first important magnet to attract people to the West. Many hoped to "strike it rich" in gold and silver, but at least half the newcomers had no intention of working in the mines. Instead, they provided food, clothing, and services to the thousands of miners. Leland Stanford and Collis P. Huntington, who later built the Central Pacific Railroad, set up a general store in Sacramento where they sold shovels and supplies. Stephen J. Field, later a prominent justice of the U.S. Supreme Court, followed the Gold Rush to California to practice law.

The California Gold Rush of 1849 began the mining boom and set the pattern for subsequent strikes in other regions. Individual prospectors made the first strikes, discovering pockets of gold along streams flowing westward from the Sierra Nevada. To get the gold, they used a simple process called placer mining, which required little skill, technology, or capital. A placer miner needed only a shovel, washing pan, and a good claim. As the placers gave out, a great deal of gold remained, but it was locked in quartz or buried deep in the earth. Mining became an expensive business, far beyond the reach of the average miner.

Large corporations moved in to dig the deep shafts and finance costly equipment. Quartz mining required heavy rock crushers, mercury vats to dissolve the gold, and large retorts to recapture it. Eastern and European financiers assumed control, labor became unionized, and mining towns took on some of the characteristics of the industrial city. Individual prospectors meanwhile dashed on to the next find. Unlike other frontiers, the mining frontier moved from west to east, as the original California miners—the "yonder-siders," they were called—hurried eastward in search of the big strike.

Before the California Gold Rush of 1849, San Francisco was a sleepy little Spanish-Mexican village called Yerba Buena. Gold seekers turned it into a boom town with an international population. Here, Spanish-Mexican rancheros, white prospectors, Chinese laborers, and a top-hatted professional gambler mingle in a San Francisco saloon.

In 1859, fresh strikes were made near Pikes Peak in Colorado and in the Carson River Valley of Nevada. News of both discoveries set off wild migrations—100,000 miners were in Pikes Peak country by June 1859. The gold there quickly played out, but the Nevada find uncovered a thick bluish black ore that was almost pure silver and gold. A quick-witted drifter named Henry T. P. Comstock talked his way into partnership in the claim, and word of the Comstock Lode—with ore worth $3,876 a ton—flashed over the mountains.

Thousands of miners climbed the Sierra Nevada that summer. On the rough slopes of Davidson Mountain, they created Virginia City, the prototype of the tumultuous western mining town. Mark Twain was there and described the scene in *Roughing It* (1872): "The sidewalks swarmed with people. . . . Joy sat on every countenance, and there was a glad, almost fierce, intensity in every eye, that told of the money-getting schemes that were seething in every brain and the high hope that held sway in every heart."

The biggest strike was yet to come. In 1873, John W. Mackay and three partners formed a company to dig deep into the mountain, and at 1,167 feet they hit the Big Bonanza, a seam of

gold and silver more than 54 feet wide. It was the richest discovery in the history of mining. Between 1859 and 1879, the Comstock Lode produced gold and silver worth $306 million. Most of it went to financiers and corporations. Mackay himself became the richest person in the world, earning (according to a European newspaper) $25 a minute, $5 a minute more than Czar Alexander II of Russia.

In the 1860s and 1870s, important strikes were made in Washington, Idaho, Nevada, Colorado, Montana, Arizona, and Dakota. Extremely mobile, miners flocked from strike to strike, and new camps and mining towns sprang up overnight. "The miners of Idaho were like quicksilver," said Hubert Howe Bancroft, an early historian. "A mass of them dropped in any locality, broke up into individual globules, and ran off after any atom of gold in their vicinity. They stayed nowhere longer than the gold attracted them."

The final fling came in the Black Hills rush of 1874 to 1876. The army had tried to keep miners out of the area, the heart of the Sioux hunting grounds, and even sent a scientific party under Colonel George A. Custer to disprove the rumors of gold and stop the miners' invasion. Instead,

Custer found gold all over the hills, and the rush was on. Miners, gamblers, desperadoes, and prostitutes flocked to Deadwood, the most lawless of all the mining camps. There, Martha Jane Canary—a crack shot who, as Calamity Jane, won fame as a scout and teamster—fell in love with Wild Bill Hickok; and Hickok himself—a western legend who had tamed Kansas cow towns, killed an unknown number of men, and toured in Buffalo Bill's Wild West Show—died, shot in the back of the head. Hickok was thirty-nine.

Towns such as Deadwood, in the Dakota Territory; Virginia City, Nevada; Leadville, Colorado; and Tombstone, Arizona, demonstrated a new development process in the frontier experience. The farming frontier had developed naturally in a rural setting. On the mining frontier, the germ of a city—the camp—appeared almost simultaneously with the first "strike." Periodicals, the latest fashions, theaters, schools, literary clubs, and lending libraries came quickly to the camps, providing civilized refinements not

Martha Jane Canary—Calamity Jane—in the uniform of a U.S. Army scout. She boasted of her marksmanship and her exploits as a Pony Express rider and a scout.

Mining Camps
Gold and silver mines dotted the West, drawing settlers and encouraging political organization in many areas.

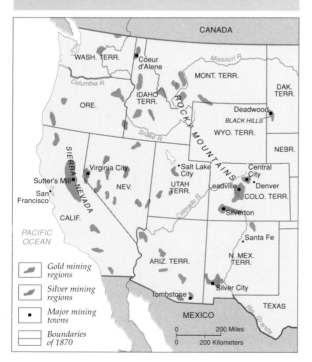

available on other frontiers. Urbanization also created the need for municipal government, sanitation, and law enforcement.

Mining camps were governed by a simple democracy. Soon after a strike, the miners in the area met to organize a mining "district" and adopted rules governing behavior in it. Rules regulated the size and boundaries of claims, established procedures for settling disputes, and set penalties for crimes. Petty criminals were banished from the district; serious offenders were hanged. In the case of a major dispute, the whole camp gathered, chose legal counsel for both sides, and heard the evidence. If all else failed, miners formed secret vigilance committees to hang a few offenders as a lesson to the rest. Early visitors to the mining country were struck by the way miners, solitary and competitive, joined together, founded a camp, and created a society.

The camps were mostly male, made up of "men who can rough it" and a few "ladies of spirit and energy." In 1870, men outnumbered women in the mining districts by more than two to one; there were few children. Prostitutes followed the camps around the West, and "respectable" women were an object of curiosity. Four arrived in Nevada City in 1853, and as one observed, "The men stand and gaze at us with mouth and eyes wide open, every time we go out." Some women worked claims, but more often they took jobs as cooks, housekeepers, and seamstresses—for wages considerably higher than in the East.

In most camps, between one-quarter and one-half of the population was foreign born. The lure of gold drew large numbers of Chinese, Chileans, Peruvians, Mexicans, French, Germans, and English. Experienced miners, the Latin Americans brought valuable mining techniques. At least 6,000 Mexicans joined the California rush of 1849, and by 1852, there were 25,000 Chinese in California. Painstaking, the Chinese profitably worked claims others had abandoned. In the 1860s, almost one-third of the miners in the West were Chinese.

Hostility often surfaced against foreign miners, particularly the French, Latin Americans, and Chinese. In 1850, California passed a Foreign Miners' Tax that charged foreign miners a $20 monthly licensing fee. As intended, it drove out Mexican and other miners. Riots against Chinese laborers occurred in the 1870s and 1880s in Los Angeles, San Francisco, Seattle, Reno, and Denver. Responding to pressure, Congress passed the Chinese Exclusion Act of 1882, which suspended immigration of Chinese laborers for ten years. The number of Chinese in the United States fell drastically.

By the 1890s, the early mining bonanza was over. All told, the western mines contributed billions of dollars to the economy. They helped finance the Civil War and provided needed capital for industrialization. The vast boost in silver production from the Comstock Lode changed the relative value of gold and silver, the base of American currency. Bitter disputes over the currency affected politics and led to the famous "battle of the standards," the presidential election of 1896 (see Chapter 20).

The mining frontier populated portions of the West and sped its process of political organization. Nevada, Idaho, and Montana were granted early statehood because of mining. Merchants,

editors, lawyers, and ministers moved with the advancing frontier, establishing permanent settlements. Women in the mining camps helped to foster family life and raised the moral tone by campaigning against drinking, gambling, and prostitution. But not all the effects of the mining boom were positive. The industry also left behind painful scars in the form of invaded Indian reservations, pitted hills, and lonely ghost towns.

Gold from the Roots Up

"There's gold from the grass roots down," said California Joe, a guide in the gold districts of Dakota in the 1870s, "but there's more gold from the grass roots up." Ranchers began to recognize the potential of the vast grasslands of the West. The Plains were covered with buffalo or grama grass, a wiry variety with short hard stems. Cattle thrived on it.

For twenty years after 1865, cattle ranching dominated the "open range," a vast fenceless area extending from the Texas Panhandle north into Canada. The techniques of the business came

Cattle Trails
Cattle raised in Texas were driven along the cattle trails to the northern railheads that carried them to market.

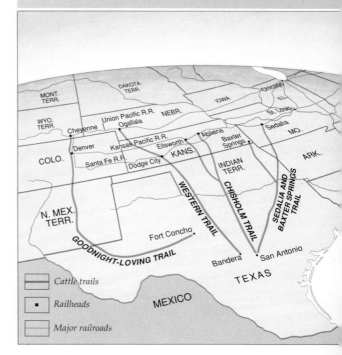

from Mexico, where long before American cowboys moved herds north, their Mexican counterparts, the *vaqueros,* developed the essential techniques of branding, roundups, and roping. The cattle themselves, the famous Texas longhorns, also came from Mexico. Spreading over the grasslands of southern Texas, the longhorns multiplied rapidly. Although their meat was coarse and stringy, they fed a nation hungry for beef at the end of the Civil War.

The problem was getting the beef to eastern markets, and Joseph G. McCoy, a livestock shipper from Illinois, solved it. Looking for a way to market Texas beef, McCoy conceived the idea of taking the cattle to railheads in Kansas. He talked first with the president of the Missouri Pacific, who ordered him out of his office, and then with the head of the Kansas Pacific, who laughed at the idea. The persistent McCoy finally signed a contract in 1867 with the Hannibal and St. Joseph Railroad. Searching for an appropriate rail junction, he settled on the sleepy Kansas town of Abilene, "a very small, dead place," he remembered, with about a dozen log huts and one near-bankrupt saloon.

In September 1867, McCoy shipped the first train of twenty cars of longhorn cattle. By the end of the year, a thousand carloads had followed, all headed for Chicago markets. In 1870, 300,000 head of Texas cattle reached Abilene, followed the next year—the peak year—by 700,000 head. The Alamo Saloon, crowded with tired cowboys at the end of the drive, now employed seventy-five bartenders, working three eight-hour shifts.

The profits were enormous. Drivers bought cheap Texas steers for $4 a head and sold them for $30 or $40 a head at the northern railhead. The most famous trail was the Chisholm, running from southern Texas through Oklahoma Territory to Ellsworth and Abilene, Kansas, on the Kansas Pacific Railroad. Dodge City, Kansas, became the prime shipping center between 1875 and 1879.

Cowboys pushed steers northward in herds of two to three thousand. Novels and films have portrayed them as white, but at least a quarter were black and possibly another quarter were Mexicans. A typical crew on the trail north might have eight men, half of them black or Mexican. Most of the trail bosses were white; they earned about $125 a month. As James "Jim" Perry, a

renowned black cowboy who worked for more than twenty years as a rider, roper, and cook for the XIT ranch, said, "If it weren't for my damned old black face, I'd have been a boss long ago."

Like miners, cattlemen lived beyond the formal reach of the law and so established their own. Before each drive, Charles Goodnight drew up rules governing behavior on the trail. A cowboy who shot another was hanged on the spot. Ranchers adopted rules for cattle ownership, branding, roundups, and drives; and they formed associations to enforce them. The Wyoming Stock Growers' Association, the largest and most formidable, had 400 members owning 2 million cattle; its reach extended well beyond Wyoming into Colorado, Nebraska, Montana, and the Dakotas. Throughout this vast territory, the "laws" of the association were often the law of the land.

Hollywood images to the contrary, there was little violence in the booming cow towns. The number of homicides in a year never topped five in any town, and in many years no one was killed. Doc Holliday and William B. (Bat) Masterson never killed anyone. John Wesley Hardin, a legendary teenaged gunman, shot only one man, firing blindly through a hotel room wall to stop him from snoring. Famous western sheriffs had everyday duties. Wild Bill Hickok served as Abilene's street commissioner, and the Wichita city council made its lawmen, including Wyatt Earp, repair streets and sidewalks before each cattle season.

By 1880, more than six million cattle had been driven to northern markets. But the era of the great cattle drive was ending. Farmers were planting wheat on the old buffalo ranges; barbed wire, a recent invention, cut across the trails and divided up the big ranches. Mechanical improvements in slaughtering, refrigerated transportation, and cold storage modernized the industry. Ranchers bred the Texas longhorns with heavier Hereford and Angus bulls, and as the new breeds proved profitable, more and more ranches opened on the northern ranges.

By the mid-1880s, some 4.5 million cattle grazed the High Plains, reminding people of the once great herds of buffalo. Stories of vast profits circulated, attracting outside capital. Large investments transformed ranching into big business, often controlled by absentee owners and subject to new problems.

By 1885, experienced cattlemen were growing alarmed. A presidential order that year forced stockmen out of the Indian Territory in Oklahoma, adding 200,000 cattle to the over-crowded northern ranges. The winter of 1885 to 1886 was cold, and the following summer was one of the hottest on record. Waterholes dried up; the grass turned brown. Beef prices fell.

The winter of 1886 to 1887 was one of the worst in western history. Temperatures dropped to 45 degrees below zero, and cattle that once would have saved themselves by drifting ahead of the storms came up against the new barbed wire fences. Herds jammed together, pawing the frozen ground or stripping bark from trees in search of food. Cattle died by the tens of thousands. In the spring of 1887, when the snows thawed, ranchers found stacks of carcasses piled up against the fences.

The melting snows did, however, produce a lush crop of grass for the survivors. The cattle business recovered, but it took different directions. Outside capital, so plentiful in the boom years, dried up. Ranchers began fencing their lands, reducing their herds, and growing hay for winter food. To the dismay of cowboys, mowing machines and hay rakes became as important as chuck wagons and branding irons. "I tell you times have changed," one cowboy said sadly.

The last roundup on the northern ranges took place in 1905. Ranches grew smaller, and some ranchers, at first in the scrub country of the Southwest, then on the Plains themselves, switched to raising sheep. By 1900, there were nearly 38 million sheep west of the Missouri River, far more than there were cattle. In Montana, there were six or seven sheep for each cow, and even Wyoming, the great center of the northern ranches, had more sheep than cows.

Ranchers and sheepherders fought bitterly to control the grazing lands, but they had one problem in common: there were troubles ahead. Homesteaders, armed with barbed wire and new strains of wheat, were pushing onto the Plains, and the day of the open range was over.

FARMING ON THE FRONTIER

Like miners and cattlemen, millions of farmers moved into the West in the decades after 1870 to seek crop bonanzas and new ways of life. Some

Nat Love, born a slave in Tennessee in 1854, claimed to be the original "Deadwood Dick," having won the title in a cowboy contest in Deadwood, South Dakota, in 1876.

realized their dreams; many fought just to survive.

Said a folksong from Greer County, Oklahoma,

> Hurrah for Greer County! The land of the free,
> The land of the bedbug, grasshopper, and flea;
> I'll sing of its praises, I'll tell of its fame,
> While starving to death on my government claim.

Between 1870 and 1900, farmers cultivated more land than ever before in American history. They peopled the Plains from Dakota to Texas, pushed the Indians out of their last sanctuary in Oklahoma, and poured into the basins and foothills of the Rockies. By 1900, the western half of the nation contained almost 30 percent of the population, compared to less than 1 percent just a half century earlier.

Sodbusters on the Plains

Unlike mining, farm settlement often followed predictable patterns, taking population from states east of the settlement line and moving gradually westward. Crossing the Mississippi, farmers settled first in South Dakota, Minnesota, western Iowa, Nebraska, Kansas, and Texas. The movement slumped during the depression of the 1870s, but then a new wave of optimism carried thousands more west. Several years of above-average rainfall convinced farmers that the Dakotas, western Nebraska and Kansas, and eastern Colorado were the "rain belt of the Plains." Between 1870 and 1900, the population on the Plains tripled.

In some areas the newcomers were blacks who had fled the South, fed up with beatings and murders, crop liens, and the "Black Codes" (see Chapter 16) that institutionalized their subordinate status. In 1879, about six thousand African Americans, known as the Exodusters, left their homes in Louisiana, Mississippi, and Texas to establish new and freer lives in Kansas, the home of John Brown and the free-soil campaigns of the 1850s. Once there, they farmed or worked as laborers; women worked in the fields alongside the men or cleaned houses and took in washing to make ends meet. All told, the Exodusters homesteaded 20,000 acres of land, and though they met prejudice, it was not as extreme as they had known at home. "I asked my wife did she know the ground she stands on," said John Solomon Lewis, a Louisianan, soon after arriving. "She said, 'No!' I said it is free ground; and she cried like a child for joy."

Other African Americans moved to Oklahoma, thinking they might establish the first African American state. Whether headed for Oklahoma or Kansas, they picked up and moved in sizable groups that were based on family units; they took with them the customs they had known, and in their new homes they were able, for the first time, to have some measure of self-government.

For blacks and whites alike, farming on the Plains presented new problems. There was little surface water, and wells ranged between 50 and 500 feet deep. Well drillers charged up to $2 a foot. Taking advantage of the steady Plains winds, windmills brought the water to the surface, but they too were expensive, and until 1900, many farmers could not afford them. Lumber for homes and fences was also scarce. Some settlers imported it from distant Wisconsin, but a single homestead of 160 acres cost $1,000 to fence, an amount few could pay.

Unable to afford wood, farmers often started out in dreary sod houses. Cut into 3-foot sections, the thick prairie sod was laid like brick, with space left for two windows and a door. Since glass was scarce, cloth hung over the windows; a blanket was hung from the ceiling to make two rooms. Sod houses were small, provided little light and air, and were impossible to keep clean. When it rained, water seeped through the roof. Yet a sod house cost only $2.78 to build.

Outside, the Plains environment sorely tested the men and women who moved there. Neighbors were distant; the land stretched on as far as the eye could see. Always the wind blew. "As long as I live I'll never see such a lonely country," a woman said of the Texas Plains; a Nebraska woman said, "These unbounded prairies have such an air of desolation—and the stillness is very oppressive."

In the winters, savage storms swept the open grasslands. Ice caked on the cattle until their heads were too heavy to hold up. Summertime temperatures stayed near 110 degrees for weeks at a time. Fearsome rainstorms, building in the summer's heat, beat down the young corn and wheat. The summers also brought grasshoppers, arriving without warning, flying in clouds so huge they shut out the sun. The grasshoppers ate everything in sight: crops, clothing, mosquito netting, tree bark, even plow handles. In the summer of 1874, they devastated the whole Plains from Texas to the Dakotas, eating everything "but the mortgage," as one farmer said.

New Farming Methods

Farmers adopted new techniques to meet these conditions. For one thing, they needed cheap and effective fencing material, and in 1874, Joseph F. Glidden, a farmer from De Kalb, Illinois, provided it with the invention of barbed wire. By 1883, his factory was turning out 600 miles of barbed

Long Drive to Kansas *by Clara McDonald Williamson is the artist's recollection of the cattle she watched being driven north out of Texas to Abilene, Kansas, along the Chisholm Trail.*

wire every day, and farmers were buying it faster than it could be produced.

Dry farming, a new technique, helped compensate for the lack of rainfall. By plowing furrows 12 to 14 inches deep, and creating a dust mulch to fill the furrow, farmers loosened the soil and slowed evaporation. Wheat farmers imported European varieties of plants that could withstand the harsh Plains winters. Hard-kerneled varieties like "Turkey Red" wheat from Russia required new milling methods, developed during the 1870s. By 1881, Minneapolis, St. Louis, and Kansas City had become milling centers for the rich "new process" flour.

Farm technology changed long before the Civil War, but later developments improved it. In 1877, James Oliver of Indiana patented a chilled-iron plow with a smooth-surface mold board that did not clog in the thick prairie soils. The spring-tooth harrow (1869) sped soil preparation; the grain drill (1874) opened furrows and scientifically fed seed into the ground. The lister (1880) dug

a deep furrow, planted corn at the bottom, and covered the seed—all in one operation.

The first baling press was built in 1866, and the hay loader was patented in 1876. The first successful harvester, the cord binder (1878), cut and tied bundles of grain, enabling two men and a team of horses to harvest 20 acres of wheat a day. Invented earlier, threshers grew larger; employing as many as nine men and ten horses, they threshed 300 bushels of grain a day.

In 1890, over nine hundred corporations manufactured farm machinery. Scientific agriculture flourished under new discoveries linking soil minerals and plant growth. Samuel Johnson of Yale University wrote books on *How Crops Grow* (1868) and *How Crops Feed* (1870), and one of his students pioneered work on nitrogen, the base of many modern fertilizers. The Hatch Act, passed in 1887, supported agricultural experiment stations that spread the discoveries among farmers. Four years later, these stations employed over 450 persons and distributed more than 300

A work crew on the Dalrymple farm in the Red River Valley gathers grain wired into bundles by self-binding harvesters. In 1877 Dalrymple used 100 workers to harvest his 4000 acres of wheat; by 1884 the number of harvesters employed on the farm had increased to 1000.

published reports annually to some 350,000 readers.

In the late 1870s, huge bonanza farms rose, run by the new machinery and financed with outside capital. Oliver Dalrymple, the most famous of the bonanza farmers, headed an experiment in North Dakota's Red River Valley in 1875, then moved on to manage the Grandin Bonanza of 61,000 acres, five times the size of Manhattan Island. Dalrymple hired armies of workers, bought machinery by the carload, and planted on a scale that dazzled the West.

The bonanza farms—thanks to their size and machinery—captured the country's imagination. Using 200 pairs of harrows, 155 binders, and 16 threshers, Dalrymple produced 600,000 bushels of wheat in 1881. He and other bonanza managers profited from the economies of scale, buying materials at wholesale prices and receiving rebates from the railroads. Then a period of drought began. Rainfall dropped between 1885 and 1890, and the large-scale growers found it hard to compete with smaller farmers who diversified their crops and cultivated more intensively.

Many of the large bonanzas slowly disintegrated, and Dalrymple himself went bankrupt in 1896.

Discontent on the Farm

Touring the South in the 1860s, Oliver H. Kelley, a clerk in the Department of Agriculture, was struck by the drabness of rural life. In 1867, he founded the National Grange of the Patrons of Husbandry, known simply as the Grange. The Grange provided social, cultural, and educational activities for its members. Its constitution banned involvement in politics, but Grangers often ignored the rules and supported railroad regulation and other measures.

The Grange grew rapidly during the depression of the 1870s, and by 1875, it had over 800,000 members in 20,000 local Granges. Most were in the Midwest and South. The Granges set up cooperative stores, grain elevators, warehouses, insurance companies, and farm machinery factories. Many failed, but in the meantime the organization made its mark. Farm-oriented groups like the Farmers' Alliance, with branches in both

South and West, began to attract followers. (See Chapter 20 for a more detailed discussion of the Alliance.)

Like the cattle boom, the farming boom ended sharply after 1887. A severe drought that year cut harvests, and other droughts followed in 1889 and 1894. Thousands of new farmers were wiped out on the western Plains. Between 1888 and 1892, more than half the population of western Kansas left. Farmers grew angry and restless. They complained about declining crop prices, rising railroad rates, and heavy mortgages.

Though many farmers were unhappy, the peopling of the West in these years transformed American agriculture. The states beyond the Mississippi became the garden land of the nation. California sent fruit, wine, and wheat to eastern markets. Under the Mormons, Utah flourished with irrigation. Texas beef stocked the country's tables, and vast wheat fields, stretching to the horizon, covered Minnesota, the Dakotas, Montana, and eastern Colorado. All produced more than Americans could consume. By 1890, American farmers were exporting large amounts of wheat and other crops.

Farmers became more commercial and scientific. They needed to know more and work harder. Mail-order houses and rural free delivery diminished their isolation and tied them ever closer to the national future. "This is a new age to the farmer," said a statistician in the Department of Agriculture in 1889. "He is now, more than ever before, a citizen of the world."

The Final Fling

As the West filled in with people, pressure mounted on the president and Congress to open the last Indian territory, Oklahoma, to settlers. In March 1889, Congress acted and forced the Creeks and Seminoles, two tribes who had been moved into Oklahoma in the 1820s, to surrender their rights. With arrangements complete, President Benjamin Harrison announced the opening of the Oklahoma District as of noon, April 22, 1889.

Preparations were feverish all along the frontier. "From all the West," historian Ray Allen Billington noted, "the homeless, the speculators, the adventurers, flocked to the still forbidden land." On the morning of April 22, nearly 100,000 people lined the Oklahoma borders; "for miles on end horsemen, wagons, hacks, carriages, bicycles, and a host of vehicles beggaring description stood wheel to wheel awaiting the signal." Fifteen Santa Fe trains were jammed with people from platform to roof.

At noon the starting flag dropped. Bugles and cannon signaled the opening of the "last" territory. Horsemen lunged forward, overloaded wagons collided and overturned. The trains steamed slowly forward, forced by army troops to keep a pace that would not give their passengers an undue advantage.

By sunset that day, settlers claimed 12,000 homesteads, and the 1.92 million acres of the Oklahoma District were officially settled. Homesteaders threw up shelters for the night. By evening, Oklahoma City, that morning merely a spot on the prairie with cottonwoods and grass, had 10,000 people; Guthrie to the north had 15,000. Speculators swiftly erected pay toilets, and drinking water cost as much as a beer.

The "Boomers" and "Sooners"—those who had jumped the gun—reflected the speed of western settlement. "Creation!" a character in Edna Ferber's novel *Cimarron* declared. "Hell! That took six days. This was done in one. It was History made in an hour—and I helped make it."

Between the Civil War and 1900, the West witnessed one of the greatest migrations in history. With the Native Americans driven into smaller and smaller areas, farms, ranches, mines, and cities took over the vast lands from the Mississippi to the Pacific. The 1890 census noted that for the first time in the country's history, "there can hardly be said to be a frontier line." Picking up the theme, Frederick Jackson Turner, a young history instructor at the University of Wisconsin, examined its importance in an influential 1893 paper, "The Significance of the Frontier in American History."

"The existence of an area of free land," Turner wrote, "its continuous recession, and the advance of American settlement westward, explain American development." It shaped customs and character; gave rise to independence, self-confidence, and individualism; and fostered invention and adaptation. Historians have substantially modified Turner's thesis by pointing to frontier conservatism and imitativeness, the influence of

Agricultural Land Use in the 1880s

New farming technology and crops enabled more and more land to be distributed for productive use.

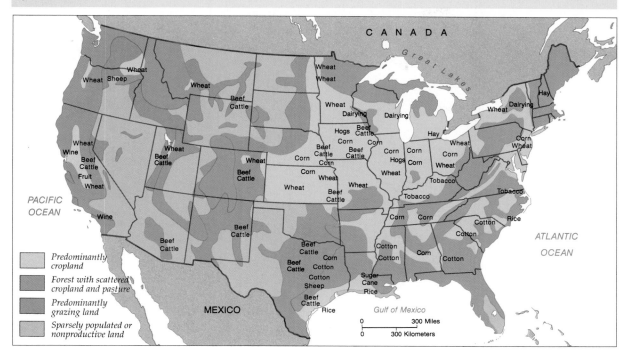

varying racial groups, and the persistence of European ideas and institutions. Most recently, they have shown that family and community loomed as large as individualism on the frontier; men, women, and children played very much the same roles as they had back home.

Rejecting Turner almost completely, a group of "new Western historians" has advanced a different and complex view of the West, and one with few heroes and heroines. Emphasizing the region's racial and ethnic diversity, these historians stress the role of women as well as men, trace struggles between economic interests instead of fights between gunslingers, and question the impact of development on the environment. White English-speaking Americans, they suggest, could be said to have conquered the West rather than settled it.

The West, in this view, was not settled by a wave of white migrants moving west across the continent (Turner's "frontier"), but by a set of waves—Anglo, Mexican American, African American, Asian American, and others—moving

in many directions and interacting with each other and with Native American cultures to produce the modern West. Nor did Western history end in 1890 as Turner would have it. Instead, migration, development, and economic exploitation continued into the twentieth century, illustrated in the fact that the number of people who moved to the West after 1900 far exceeded those who had moved there before.

In both the nineteenth and twentieth centuries, there can be no doubt that the image of the frontier and the West influenced American development. Western lands attracted European, Latin American, and Asian immigrants, adding to the society's talent and diversity. The mines, forests, and farms of the West fueled the economy, sent raw materials to eastern factories, and fed the growing cities. Though defeated in warfare, Indian and Spanish influence persisted in art, architecture, law, and western folklore. The West was the first American empire, and it had a profound impact on the American mind and imagination.

The Receding Frontier

Population patterns closely followed the development of mining and agriculture, as well as the physiography of the land. By 1890, population density in the West was high enough that the frontier was no longer clearly defined.

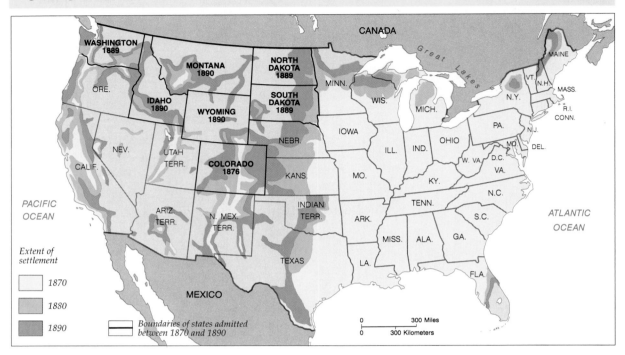

Recommended Reading

The best traditional account of the movement west is Ray Allen Billington, *Westward Expansion* (1967), which also has a first-rate bibliography. See also Frederick Merk, *History of the Westward Movement* (1978). Frederick Jackson Turner's influential interpretation of frontier development, "The Significance of the Frontier in American History," is in his *Frontier in American History* (1920). Walter Prescott Webb, *The Great Plains* (1931), offers a fascinating analysis of development on the Plains.

For examples of the work of "new Western historians," see Donald Worster, *Rivers of Empire: Water, Aridity, and the Growth of the American West* (1985), a powerful study of the "hydraulic" society; the same author's *Under Western Skies: Nature and History in the American West* (1992); William Cronon, *Nature's Metropolis: Chicago and the Great West* (1991), a provocative analysis of the relationship of Chicago and the West; Patricia Nelson Limerick, *The Legacy of Conquest: The Unbroken Past of the American West* (1987); Richard White, *"It's Your Misfortune and None of My Own": A History of the American West* (1991); and William Cronon, George Miles, and Jay

Gitlin, eds., *Under an Open Sky: Rethinking American's Western Past* (1992).

Howard R. Lamar, *The Far Southwest, 1846–1912* (1966), and Rodman W. Paul, *The Far West and the Great Plains in Transition, 1859–1900* (1988), are excellent surveys of the era. Paul gives a thorough survey of the mining bonanza in *Mining Frontiers of the Far West* (1963); Fred A. Shannon provides similar coverage for agriculture in *The Farmer's Last Frontier* (1945). Lewis Atherton, *The Cattle Kings* (1961), and E. S. Osgood, *The Day of the Cattleman* (1929), cover the cattle industry. Louis B. Wright, *Culture on the Moving Frontier* (1955), argues that settlers did not give up books and other cultural assets as they moved West; Henry Nash Smith, *Virgin Land: The American West as Symbol and Myth* (1950), is superb on the literary images of the West in the nineteenth century.

More recent authors have taken fresh and stimulating looks at older or ignored questions. Robert R. Dykstra, *The Cattle Towns* (1968), examines five Kansas cattle towns, with interesting results. Gunther Barth traces the rapid rise of San Francisco and Denver in *Instant Cities* (1975), and Earl Pomeroy, *The Pacific Slope* (1965), looks at urban and other developments in the Far West. Elliott West discusses childhood in *Growing Up with the Country: Childhood on the Far Western Frontier* (1989). Julie Roy Jeffrey, *Frontier Women: The Trans-Mississippi West* (1979); Sandra L. Myres, *Westering Women and the Frontier Experience, 1880–1915* (1982); Paula Petrik, *No Step Backward: Women and Family on the Rocky Mountain Mining Frontier, Helena, Montana, 1865–1900* (1987); and Joanna L. Stratton, *Pioneer Women: Voices from the Kansas Frontier* (1981), are perceptive works on a neglected topic. John Mack Faragher, *Women and Men on the Overland Trail* (1979), and John Phillip Reid, *Law for the Elephant* (1980), examine relationships on the trails west. Faragher's *Sugar Creek: Life on the Illinois Prairie* (1986) brilliantly explores the influence of community in western life.

Additional Bibliography

On the Native Americans, there are a number of valuable works, including R. Douglas Hurt's excellent *Indian Agriculture in America: Prehistory to the Present* (1987); Janet A. McDonnell, *The Dispossession of the American Indian, 1887–1934* (1991); Robert A. Trennert, Jr., *The Phoenix Indian School* (1988); William T. Hagan, *American Indians* (1961); Wilcomb E. Washburn, *The Indian in America* (1975); Russell Thornton, *American Indian Holocaust and Survival* (1987); Frederick E. Hoxie, *A Final Promise: The Campaign to Assimilate the Indians* (1984); Robert Wooster, *The Military and United States Indian Policy, 1865–1903* (1988); Robert M. Utley, *The Last Days of the Sioux Nation* (1963), *Frontier Regulars: The United States Army and the Indian* (1973), and *The Indian Frontier of the American West, 1846–1890* (1984); Francis Paul Prucha, *American Indian Policy in Crisis* (1976); Robert A. Keller, Jr., *American Protestantism and United States Indian Policy, 1869–1882* (1983); and R. K. Andrist, *The Long Death: The Last Days of the Plains Indians* (1964). See also, Margaret Coel, *Chief Left Hand: Southern Arapaho* (1981); Robert S. McPherson, *The Northern Navaho Frontier, 1860–1900: Expansion Through Adversity* (1988); Robert M. Utley, *The Lance and the Shield: The Life and Times of Sitting Bull* (1993); Loretta Fowler, *Arapahoe Politics, 1851–1978* (1982), and Albert L. Hurtado, *Indian Survival on the California Frontier* (1988). Helen Hunt Jackson, *A Century of Dishonor* (1881) is a stinging contemporary account.

Dwight W. Hoover, *The Red and the Black* (1976), contrasts Indian policy with the treatment of other minorities. Leonard Pitt looks at *The Decline of the Californios: A Social History of the Spanish-Speaking Californians* (1966); Mario T. Garcia at the Mexican immigrants to El Paso in *Desert Immigrants* (1981);

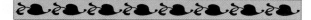

and Gunther Barth at the treatment of the Chinese in *Bitter Strength* (1964). Also, Sucheng Chan, *This Bittersweet Soil: The Chinese in California Agriculture, 1860–1910* (1986); Roger Daniels, *Asian America: Chinese and Japanese in the United States Since 1850* (1988); Sarah Deutsch, *No Separate Refuge: Culture, Class, and Gender on an Anglo-Hispanic Frontier in the American Southwest, 1880–1940* (1987); Richard Griswold del Castillo, *The Los Angeles Barrio, 1850–1890: A Social History* (1979); Albert Camarillo, *Chicanos in a Changing Society* (1979); and two studies by Arnoldo DeLeon, *The Tejano Community, 1836–1900* (1982), and *They Called Them Greasers: Anglo Attitudes Toward Mexicans in Texas* (1983).

George R. Stewart, *The California Trail* (1962) and John D. Unruh, Jr., *The Plains Across* (1979) are good, but read some of the extraordinary diaries, including David M. Potter, ed., *The Trail to California* (1962); Dale Morgan, ed., *Overland in 1846* (1963); Lillian Schlissel, *Women's Diaries of the Westward Journey* (1982); and the letters and diaries in Lillian Schlissel, Byrd Gibbens, and Elizabeth Hampsten, *Far from Home: Families of the Westward Journey* (1989).

Books on the mining bonanza include Rodman W. Paul, *California Gold* (1948); William T. Jackson, *Treasure Hill: Portrait of a Silver Mining Camp* (1963); Odie B. Faulk, *Tombstone* (1972); D. A. Smith, *Rocky Mountain Mining Camps: The Urban Frontier* (1967); Dan DeQuille, *History of the Big Bonanza* (1876); Eliot Lord, *Comstock Mining and Miners* (1883); Joseph R. Conlin, *Bacon, Beans, and Galantines: Food and Foodways on the Western Mining Frontier* (1986); and Mark Twain, *Roughing It* (1872).

The best works on the cowboy are E. E. Dale, *Cow Country* (1942); Andy Adams, *The Log of a Cowboy* (1902); and J. B. Frantz and J. E. Choate, *The American Cowboy: The Myth and Reality* (1955). Also see C. Robert Haywood, *Victorian West: Class and Culture in Kansas Cattle Towns* (1991). Gene M. Gressley, *Bankers and Cattlemen* (1966), details outside investment in cattle. Roger D. McGrath, *Gunfighters, Highwaymen, and Vigilantes: Violence on the Frontier* (1984), and Robert N. Utley, *High Noon in Lincoln: Violence on the Western Frontier* (1987), are recent studies.

Nell Irvin Painter, *Exodusters: Black Migration to Kansas After Reconstruction* (1976), tells the story of the Exodusters, as Monroe Lee Billington does for *New Mexico's Buffalo Soldiers, 1866–1900* (1991). Federal land policy is surveyed in Roy M. Robbins, *Our Landed Heritage* (1942), and Paul Wallace Gates, *Fifty Million Acres* (1954). Valuable studies of farming include Gilbert C. Fite, *The Farmer's Frontier* (1966); Allan G. Bogue, *From Prairie to Corn Belt* (1963); Everett Dick, *The Sod-House Frontier* (1937); and on water and irrigation, Norris Hundley, *The Great Thirst* (1992); Donald J. Pisani, *From the Family Farm to Agribusiness: The Irrigation Crusade in California, 1850–1930* (1984); and William Kahrl, *Water and Power* (1982). Solon J. Buck, *The Granger Movement* (1913); Thomas A. Woods, *Knights of the Plow: Oliver H. Kelley and the Origins of the Grange in Republican Ideology* (1991); and Donald B. Marti, *Women of the Grange: Mutuality and Sisterhood in Rural America, 1866–1920* (1991), study early farm discontent and the Grange.

Jules David Prown et al., *Discovered Lands, Invented Pasts* (1992), studies western American art of the past three centuries. Patricia Nelson Limerick, *Desert Passages: Encounters with the American Deserts* (1985), examines how Americans have responded to the Great Plains. Ruth Moynihan, *Rebel for Rights: Abigail Scott Duniway* (1983); Glenda Riley, *The Female Frontier: A Comparative View of Women on the Prairie and the Plains* (1988), and *Women and Indians on the Frontier* (1984); Lillian Schlissel, Vicki Ruiz, and Janice Monk, eds., *Western Women: Their Land, Their Lives* (1988); Peggy Pascoe, *Relations of Rescue: The Search for Female Moral Authority in the American West, 1874–1939* (1990); H. Elaine Lindgren, *Land in Her Own Name: Women as Homesteaders in North Dakota* (1991); and Polly Welts Kaufman, *Women Teachers on the Frontier* (1984), examine the role of women in the West; the impact of the West itself is treated in Vera Norwood and Janice Monk, eds., *The Desert Is No Lady: Southwestern Landscapes in Women's Writing and Art* (1987). Richard Hogan, *Class and Community in Frontier Colorado* (1990), stresses economic and class relations; Kathleen Underwood, *Town Building on the Colorado Frontier* (1987), is an informative study of the growth of one town.

The Industrial Society

*I*n 1876, Americans celebrated their first century of independence. Survivors of a recent civil war, they observed the centenary proudly and rather self-consciously, in song and speech, and above all in a grand Centennial Exposition held in Philadelphia, Pennsylvania.

Spread over 13 acres, the exposition focused more on the present than the past. Fairgoers strolled through exhibits of life in colonial times, then hurried off to see the main attractions: machines, inventions, and products of the new industrial era. They saw linoleum, a new, easy-to-clean floor covering. For the first time they tasted root beer, supplied by a young druggist named Charles Hires, and the exotic banana, wrapped in foil and selling for a dime. They saw their first bicycle, an awkward high-wheeled contraption with solid tires.

A Japanese pavilion generated widespread interest in the culture of Japan. There was also a women's building, the first ever in a major exposition. Inside were displayed paintings and sculpture by women artists, along with rows of textile machinery staffed by female operators.

In the entire exposition, machinery was the focus, and Machinery Hall was the most popular building. Here were the products of an ever-improving civilization. Long lines of the curious waited to see the telephone, Alexander Graham Bell's new device. ("My God, it talks!" the emperor of Brazil exclaimed.) Thomas A. Edison displayed several recent inventions, while nearby, whirring machines turned out bricks, chewing tobacco, and other products. Fairgoers saw the first public display of the typewriter, Elisha Otis's new elevator, and the Westinghouse railroad air brake.

But above all, they crowded around the mighty Corliss engine, the focal point of the exposition. A giant steam engine, it dwarfed everything in Machinery Hall, its twin vertical cylinders towering almost four stories in the air. Alone, it supplied power for the eight thousand other machines, large and small, on the exposition grounds. Poorly designed, the Corliss was soon obsolete, but for the moment it captured the nation's imagination. It symbolized swift movement toward an industrial and urban society. John Greenleaf Whittier, the aging rural poet,

likened it to the snake in the Garden of Eden and refused to see it.

As Whittier feared, the United States was fast becoming an industrial society. Developments earlier in the century laid the basis, but the most spectacular advances in industrialization came during the three decades after the Civil War. At the start of the war, the country lagged well behind industrializing nations such as Great Britain, France, and Germany. By 1900, it had vaulted far into the lead, with a manufacturing output that exceeded the *combined* output of its three European rivals. Over the same years, cities grew, technology advanced, and farm production rose. Developments in manufacturing, mining, agriculture, transportation, and communication changed society.

Many Americans eagerly sought the change. William Dean Howells, a leading novelist, visited the Centennial Exposition and stood in awe before the Corliss. Comparing it to the paintings and sculpture on display, Howells preferred the machine: "It is in these things of iron and steel," he said, "that the national genius most freely speaks."

INDUSTRIAL DEVELOPMENT

American industry owed its remarkable growth to several considerations. It fed on an abundance of natural resources: coal, iron, timber, petroleum, waterpower. An iron manufacturer likened the nation to "a gigantic bowl filled with treasure." Labor was also abundant, drawn from American farm families and the hosts of European immigrants who flocked to American mines, cities, and factories. Nearly 8 million immigrants arrived in the 1870s and 1880s; another 15 million came between 1890 and 1914—large figures for a nation whose total population in 1900 was about 76 million people.

The burgeoning population led to expanded markets, which new devices like the telegraph and telephone helped to exploit. The swiftly growing urban populations devoured goods, and the railroads, spreading pell-mell across the land, linked the cities together and opened a national market. Within its boundaries, the United States had the largest free-trade market in the world,

The Corliss engine, a "mechanical marvel" at the Centennial Exposition, was a prime example of the giantism so admired by the public.

while tariff barriers partially protected its producers from outside competition.

Expansive market and labor conditions buoyed the confidence of investors, European and American, who provided large amounts of capital. Technological progress, so remarkable in these years, doomed some older industries (tallow, for example) but increased productivity in others, such as the kerosene industry, and created entirely new industries as well. Through inventions like the harvester and the combine, it also helped foster a firm agricultural base, on which industrialization depended.

Eager to promote economic growth, government at all levels—federal, state, and local—gave manufacturers money, land, and other resources. Other benefits, too, flowed from the American system of government: stability, commitment to the concept of private property, and initially at

least, a reluctance to regulate industrial activity. Unlike their European counterparts, American manufacturers faced few legal or social barriers, and their main domestic rivals, the southern planters, had lost political power in the Civil War.

In this atmosphere, entrepreneurs flourished. Taking steps crucial for industrialization, they organized, managed, and assumed the financial risks of the new enterprises. Admirers called them "captains of industry"; foes labeled them "robber barons." To some degree, they were both—creative *and* acquisitive. If sometimes they seemed larger than life, it was because they dealt in concepts, distances, and quantities often unknown to earlier generations.

Industrial growth, it must be remembered, was neither a simple nor steady nor inevitable process. It involved human decisions and brought with it large social benefits and costs. Growth varied from industry to industry and from year to year. It was concentrated in the Northeast, where in 1890, more than 85 percent of America's manufactured goods originated. The more sparsely settled West provided raw materials, while the South, although making major gains in iron, textiles, and tobacco, had to rebuild after wartime devastation. In 1890, the industrial production of the entire South amounted in value to about half that of the state of New York.

Still, industrial development proceeded at an extraordinary pace. Between 1865 and 1914, the real gross national product (GNP)—the total monetary value of all goods and services produced in a year, with prices held stable—grew at a rate of more than 4 percent a year, increasing about eightfold overall. As Robert Higgs, an economic historian, noted, "Never before had such rapid growth continued for so long."

AN EMPIRE ON RAILS

Genuine revolutions happen rarely, but a major one occurred in the nineteenth century: a revolution in transportation and communications. When the nineteenth century began, people traveled and communicated much as they had for centuries before; when it ended, the railroad, the telegraph, the telephone, and the ocean-going steamship had wrought enormous changes.

The steamship sliced in half the time of the Atlantic crossing and, not dependent on wind and tide, introduced new regularity in the movement of goods and passengers. The telegraph, flashing messages almost instantaneously along miles of wire (400,000 miles of it in the early 1880s), transformed communications, as did the telephone a little later. But the railroad worked the largest changes of all. Along with Bessemer steel, it was the most significant technical innovation of the century.

"Emblem of Motion and Power"

The railroad dramatically affected economic and social life. Economic growth would have occurred without it, of course; canals, inland steamboats, and the country's superb system of interior waterways already provided the outlines of an effective transportation network. But the railroad added significantly to the network and contributed advantages all its own.

Those advantages included more direct routes, greater speed, greater safety and comfort than other modes of land travel, more dependable schedules, a larger volume of traffic, and year-round service. A day's land travel on stagecoach or horseback might cover 50 miles. The railroad covered 50 miles in about an hour, 700 miles in a day. It went where canals and rivers did not go—directly to the loading platforms of great factories or across the arid West. As construction crews pushed tracks onward, vast areas of the continent opened for settlement.

Consequently, American railroads differed from European ones. In Europe, railroads were usually built between cities and towns that already existed; they carried mostly the same goods that earlier forms of transportation had. In the United States, they did that and more: they often created the very towns they then served, and they wound up carrying cattle from Texas, fruit from Florida, and other goods that had never been carried before.

Linking widely separated cities and villages, the railroad ended the relative isolation and self-sufficiency of the country's "island communities." It tied people together, brought in outside products, fostered greater interdependence, and encouraged economic specialization. Under its stimulus, Chicago supplied meat to the nation; Minneapolis supplied grain, and Saint Louis,

beer. For these and other communities, the railroad made possible a national market and in so doing pointed the way toward mass production and mass consumption, two of the hallmarks of twentieth-century society.

It also pointed the way toward later business development. The railroad, as Alfred D. Chandler, the historian of business, has written, was "the nation's first big business"; it worked out "the modern ways of finance, management, labor relations, competition, and government regulation."

A railroad corporation, far-flung and complex, was a new kind of business. It stretched over thousands of miles, employed thousands of people, dealt with countless customers, and required a scale of organization and decision making unknown in earlier business. Railroad managers never met most customers or even many employees; thus arose new problems in marketing and labor relations. Year by year, railroad companies consumed large quantities of iron, steel, coal, lumber, and glass, stimulating growth and employment in numerous industries.

No wonder, then, that the railroad captured so completely the country's imagination. Walt Whitman, the poet who celebrated American achievement, chanted the locomotive's praises:

Thy black cylindric body, golden brass and silvery steel . . .
Thy great protruding head-light fix'd in front,
Thy long, pale, floating vapor-pennants, tinged with delicate purple . . .
Thy knitted frame, thy springs and valves, the tremulous twinkle of thy wheels,
Thy train of cars behind, obedient, merrily following . . .
Type of the modern—emblem of motion and power—pulse of the continent . . . Fierce-throated beauty!

For nearly a hundred years—the railroad era lasted through the 1940s—children gathered at depots, paused in the fields to wave as the fast express flashed by, listened at night to far-off whistles, and wondered what lay down the tracks. They lived in a world grown smaller.

Building the Empire

When Lee surrendered at Appomattox in 1865, the country already had 35,000 miles of track, and much of the railroad system east of the Mississippi River was in place (see Chapter 12). Farther west, the rail network stood poised on the edge of settlement. Although southern railroads were in shambles from the war, the United States had nearly as much railroad track as the rest of the world.

After the Civil War, rail construction increased by leaps and bounds. From 35,000 miles in 1865, the network expanded to 93,000 miles in 1880; 166,000 in 1890; and 193,000 in 1900—more than in all Europe including Russia. Mileage peaked at 254,037 miles in 1916, just before the industry began its long decline into the mid-twentieth century.

To build such an empire took vast amounts of capital—over $4.5 billion by 1880, before even half of it was complete. American and European investors provided some of the money; government supplied the rest. In all, local governments gave railroad companies about $300 million, and state governments added $228 million more. The federal government loaned nearly $65 million to a half dozen western railroads and donated mil-lions of acres of the public domain. Between 1850 and 1871, some 80 railroads received more than 170 million acres of land.

Almost 90 percent of the federal land grants lay in twenty states west of the Mississippi River. Federal land grants helped build 18,738 miles of track, less than 8 percent of the system. The land was frequently distant and difficult to market. Railroad companies sometimes sold it to raise cash, but more often used it as security for bonds or loans.

Beyond doubt, the grants of cash and land promoted waste and corruption. The companies built fast and wastefully, eager to collect the subsidies that went with each mile of track. Wanting quick profits, some owners formed separate construction companies to which they awarded lavish contracts. In this way the notorious Crédit Mobilier, a construction company controlled by an inner ring on the Union Pacific, enriched its owners in the 1860s, while the Contract and Finance Company did the same on the Central Pacific. The Crédit Mobilier bribed congressmen and state legislators in order to avoid congressional investigation of its activities (see Chapter 16). The grants also enabled railroads to build into territories that were pledged to the Indians,

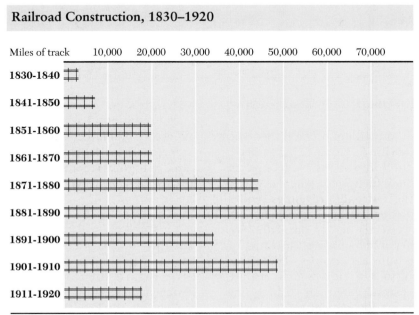

Railroad Construction, 1830–1920

Source: U.S. Bureau of the Census. Historical Statistics of the United States, Colonial Times to 1970, *Bicentennial Edition, Washington, D.C., 1975.*

Federal Land Grants to Railroads as of 1871

Besides land, the government provided loans of $16,000 for each mile built on level land, $32,000 for each mile built on hilly terrain, and $48,000 for each mile in high mountain country.

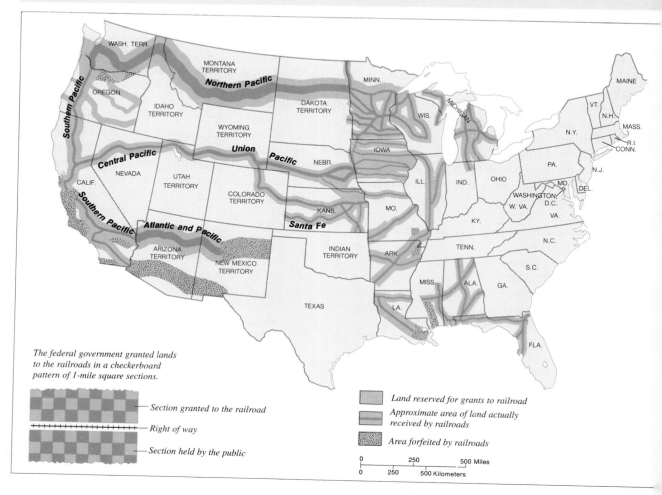

The federal government granted lands to the railroads in a checkerboard pattern of 1-mile square sections.

—— Section granted to the railroad
+++++ Right of way
—— Section held by the public

Land reserved for grants to railroad

Approximate area of land actually received by railroads

Area forfeited by railroads

thus contributing to the wanton destruction of Indian life.

Yet, on balance, the grants probably worked more benefits than evils. As Congress had hoped, the grants were the lure for railroad building across the rugged, unsettled West, where it would be years before the railroads' revenues would repay their construction. Farmers, ranchers, and merchants poured into the newly opened areas, settling the country and boosting the value of government and private land nearby. The grants seemed necessary in a nation which, unlike Europe, expected private enterprise to build the railroads. In return for government aid, Congress required the railroads to carry government freight, troops, and mail at substantially reduced rates—resulting in savings to the government of almost $1 billion between 1850 and 1945. In no other cases of federal subsidies to carriers— canals, highways, and airlines—did Congress exact specific benefits in return.

Linking the Nation via Trunk Lines

The early railroads may seem to have linked different regions, but in fact they did not. Built with little regard for through traffic, they were designed more to protect local interests than to tap outside markets. Many extended fewer than 50 miles. To avoid cooperating with other lines, they adopted conflicting schedules, built separate depots, and above all, used different gauges. Gauges, the distance between the rails, ranged from 4 feet 8½ inches, which became the standard gauge, to 6 feet. Without special equipment, trains of one gauge could not run on tracks of another.

The Civil War showed the value of fast long-distance transportation, and after 1865, railroad managers worked to provide it. In a burst of consolidation, the large companies swallowed the small; integrated rail networks became a reality. Railroads also adopted standard schedules, signals, equipment, and finally in 1886, the standard gauge. In 1866, in a dramatic innovation to speed traffic, railroad companies introduced fast freight lines that pooled cars for service between cities.

In the Northeast, four great trunk lines took shape, all intended to link eastern seaports with the rich traffic of the Great Lakes and western rivers. Like a massive river system, trunk lines drew traffic from dozens of tributaries (feeder lines) and carried it to major markets. The Baltimore and Ohio (B & O), which reached Chicago in 1874, was one; the Erie Railroad, which ran from New York to Chicago, was another. The Erie competed bitterly with the New York Central Railroad, the third trunk line, and its owner, Cornelius Vanderbilt—the "Commodore"—a crusty old multimillionaire from the shipping business.

Nearly seventy years old when he first entered railroading, Vanderbilt wasted no time. In 1867, he took over the New York Central and merged it with other lines to provide a track from New York City to Buffalo and Chicago. When he died in 1877, his Central operated over 4,500 miles of track.

J. Edgar Thomson and Thomas A. Scott built the fourth trunk line, the Pennsylvania Railroad, which initially ran from Philadelphia to Pittsburgh. Restless and energetic, they dreamed of a rail empire stretching through the South and West. An aggressive business leader, Scott expanded the Pennsylvania system to Cincinnati, Indianapolis, Saint Louis, and Chicago in 1869, New York City in 1871, and Baltimore and Washington soon thereafter.

In the war-damaged South, consolidation took longer. As Reconstruction waned, northern and European capital rebuilt and integrated the south-ern lines, especially during the 1880s, when rail construction in the South led the nation. By 1900, the South had five large systems linking its major cities and farming and industrial regions. Four decades after the secession crisis, these systems tied the South into a national transportation network.

Over that rail system, passengers and freight moved in relative speed, comfort, and safety. Automatic couplers (1867), air brakes (1869), refrigerator cars (1867), dining cars, heated cars, electric switches, and stronger locomotives transformed railroad service. George Pullman's lavish sleeping cars became popular. Handsome depots, like New York's Grand Central and Washington's Union Station, were erected at major terminals. Passenger miles per year increased from 5 billion in 1870 to 16 billion in 1900.

In November 1883, the railroads even changed time. Ending the crazy quilt jumble of local times that caused scheduling difficulties, the American Railway Association divided the country into four time zones and adopted the modern system of standard time. Congress took thirty-five years longer; it adopted standard time in 1918, in the midst of World War I.

Rails Across the Continent

The dream of a transcontinental railroad, linking the Atlantic and Pacific oceans, stretched back many years but had always been lost to sectional quarrels over the route. In 1862 and 1864, with the South out of the picture, Congress moved to build the first transcontinental. It chartered the Union Pacific Railroad Company to build westward from Nebraska and the Central Pacific Railroad Company to build eastward from the Pacific Coast. For each mile built, the two companies received from Congress 20 square miles of land in alternate sections along the track. For each mile, they also received a thirty-year loan of $16,000, $32,000, or $48,000, depending on the difficulty of the terrain over which they built.

Construction began simultaneously at Omaha and Sacramento in 1863, lagged during the war, and moved vigorously ahead after 1865. It became a race, each company vying for land, loans, and potential markets. General Grenville M. Dodge, a tough Union army veteran, served as

Railroads, 1870 and 1890

In the last quarter of the nineteenth century, railroads expanded into Texas, the far Southwest, and the Northwest, carrying settlers, businesses, and government to these far-flung areas.

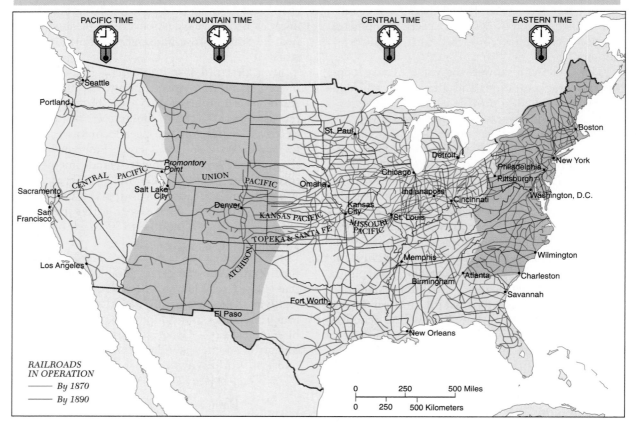

construction chief for the Union Pacific, while Charles Crocker, a former Sacramento dry goods merchant, led the Central Pacific crews. Dodge organized an army of ten thousand workers, many of them ex-soldiers and Irish immigrants. Pushing rapidly westward, he encountered frequent attacks from Native Americans defending their lands, but had the advantage of building over flat prairie.

Crocker faced more trying conditions in the high Sierra Nevada along California's eastern border. After several experiments he decided that Chinese laborers worked best, and he hired six thousand of them, most brought directly from China. "I built the Central Pacific," Crocker enjoyed boasting, but the Chinese crews in fact did the awesome work. Under the most difficult conditions they dug, blasted, and pushed their way slowly east.

On May 10, 1869, the two lines met at Promontory, Utah, near the northern tip of the Great Salt Lake. Dodge's crews had built 1,086 miles of track, Crocker's 689. The Union Pacific and Central Pacific presidents hammered in a golden spike (both missed it on the first try), and the dreamed-of connection was made. The telegraph flashed the news east and west, setting off wild celebrations. A photograph was taken, but it included none of the Chinese who had worked so hard to build the road; they were all asked to step aside.

The transcontinental railroad symbolized American unity and progress. Along with the Suez Canal, completed the same year, it helped

After the last spike was hammered in at Promontory, Utah, the pilots of the two locomotives exchanged champagne toasts. The chief engineers of the two lines are seen shaking hands.

knit the world together. Bret Harte, the exuberant poet of the West, wrote of Promontory:

> *What was it the Engines said,*
> *Pilots touching,—head to head*
> *Facing on the single track,*
> *Half a world behind each back?*

In the next twenty-five years, four more railroads reached the coast: the Northern Pacific (completed in 1883), running from Minnesota to Oregon; the Atchison, Topeka, and Santa Fe (1883), connecting Kansas City and Los Angeles; the powerful Southern Pacific (1883), running from San Francisco and Los Angeles to New Orleans; and James J. Hill's superbly built Great Northern Railway (1893), running from Minneapolis-Saint Paul to Seattle, Washington.

By the 1890s, business leaders talked comfortably of railroad systems stretching deep into South America and across the Bering Strait to Asia, Europe, and Africa. In an age of progress, anything seemed possible. "The American," said the *Chicago Tribune,* "intelligent and self-reliant, has banished forever the impossible from his philosophy."

Problems of Growth

Overbuilding during the 1870s and 1880s caused serious problems for the railroads. Lines paralleled each other, and where they did not, speculators such as Jay Gould often laid one down to force a rival line to buy it at inflated prices. While many managers worked to improve service, Gould and others bought and sold railroads like toys, watered their stock, and milked their assets. By 1885, almost one-third of railroad stock rep-

Cornelius, the "Commodore," Vanderbilt, in this cartoon of the "Modern Colossus of (Rail) Roads," is shown towering over his rail empire and pulling the strings to control its operations. In addition to the New York Central, Vanderbilt gained control of the Hudson River Railroad, the Lake Shore and Michigan Southern Railway, and the Canadian Southern Railway.

resented "water," that is, stock distributed in excess of the real value of the assets.

Competition was severe, and managers fought desperately for traffic. They offered special rates and favors: free passes for large shippers; low rates on bulk freight, carload lots, and long hauls; and above all, rebates—secret privately negotiated reductions below published rates. Fierce rate wars broke out frequently, convincing managers that ruthless competition helped no one. Rebates made more enemies than friends.

Managers like Albert Fink, the brilliant vice president of the Louisville & Nashville, tried first to arrange pooling agreements, a way to control competition by sharing traffic. Fink directed the

Eastern Trunk Line Association (1877), which divided westbound traffic among the four trunk lines. Similar associations pooled traffic in the South and West, but none survived the intense pressures of competition. Legally unenforceable, pools were handshake agreements among individuals who did not always keep their word. Customers grew adept at bargaining for rebates and other privileges, and railroads rarely felt able to refuse them. In the first six months of 1880, the New York Central alone granted six thousand special rates.

Failing to cooperate, railroad owners next tried to consolidate. Through purchase, lease, and merger, they gobbled up competitors and built "self-sustaining systems" that dominated entire regions. But many of these systems, expensive and unwieldy, collapsed in the panic of 1893. By mid-1894, a quarter of the railroads were bankrupt. The victims of the panic included such legendary names as the Erie, B & O, Santa Fe, Northern Pacific, and Union Pacific.

Needing money, railroads turned naturally to bankers, who finally imposed order on the industry. J. Pierpont Morgan, head of the New York investment house of J.P. Morgan and Company, took the lead. Massively built, with eyes so piercing they seemed like the headlights of an onrushing train, Morgan was the most powerful figure in American finance. He liked efficiency, combination, and order. He disliked "wasteful" competition. In 1885, during a bruising rate war between the New York Central and the Pennsylvania, Morgan invited the combatants to a conference aboard his palatial steam yacht, *Corsair*. Cruising on Long Island Sound, he arranged a traffic-sharing agreement and collected a million-dollar fee. Bringing peace to an industry could be profitable. It also satisfied Morgan's passion for stability.

After 1893, Morgan and a few other bankers refinanced ailing railroads, and in the process they took control of the industry. Their methods were direct: fixed costs and debt were ruthlessly cut; new stock was issued to provide capital; rates were stabilized; rebates and competition were eliminated; and control was vested in a "voting trust" of hand-picked trustees. Between 1894 and 1898, Morgan reorganized—critics said "Morganized"—the Southern Railway, the Erie, the Northern Pacific, and the B & O. In addition, he took over a half dozen other important railroads. By 1900, he was a dominant figure in American railroading.

As the new century began, the railroads had pioneered the patterns followed by most other industries. Seven giant systems controlled nearly two-thirds of the mileage, and they in turn answered to a few investment banking firms like the house of Morgan. For good and ill, a national transportation network, centralized and relatively efficient, was now in place.

AN INDUSTRIAL EMPIRE

The new industrial empire was based on steel as well as on railroads. Harder and more durable than other kinds of iron, steel wrought changes in manufacturing, agriculture, transportation, and architecture. It permitted longer bridges, taller buildings, stronger railroad track, newer weapons, better plows, heavier machinery, and faster ships. Made in great furnaces by strong men, it symbolized the tough, often brutal nature of industrial society. From the 1870s onward, steel output became the worldwide accepted measure of industrial progress, and nations around the globe vied for leadership.

The Bessemer process, developed in the late 1850s by Henry Bessemer in England and independently by William Kelly in the United States, made greater steel production possible. Both Bessemer and Kelly discovered that a blast of air forced through molten iron burned off carbon and other impurities, resulting in steel of a more uniform and durable quality. The discovery transformed the industry. While earlier methods produced amounts a person could lift, a Bessemer converter handled 5 tons of molten metal at a time. The mass production of steel was now possible.

Carnegie and Steel

Bessemer plants demanded extensive capital investment, abundant raw materials, and sophisticated production techniques. Using chemical and other processes, they required research departments, which became critical components of later American industries. Costly to build, they limited entry into the industry to the handful who could afford them.

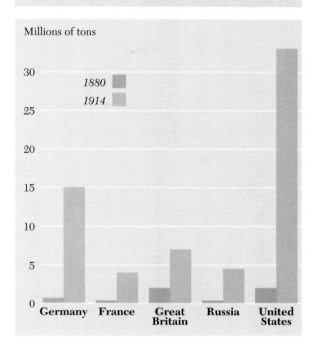

International Steel Production, 1880–1914

Millions of tons

1880
1914

Great steel districts arose in Pennsylvania, Ohio, and Alabama—in each case around large coal deposits that fueled the huge furnaces. Pittsburgh became the center of the industry, its giant mills employing thousands of workers. Output shot up. In 1874, the United States produced less than half the pig iron produced in Great Britain. By 1890, it took the lead, and in 1900, it produced four times as much as Britain.

Iron ore abounded in the fabulous deposits near Lake Superior, the greatest deposits in the world. In the mines of the Mesabi Range in Minnesota, giant steam shovels loaded ore onto railroad cars for transport to ships on the Great Lakes. Powered lifts, self-loading devices, and other innovations sped the process. "By the turn of the century," historian Peter Temin noted, "the transport of Lake ores had become an intricate ballet of large and complex machines."

Like the railroads, steel companies grew larger and larger. In 1880, only nine companies could produce more than 100,000 tons a year. By the early 1890s, several companies exceeded 250,000 tons, and two—including the great Carnegie Steel Company—produced over 1 million tons a year. As operations expanded, managers needed greater skills. Product development, marketing,

The machinery dwarfs the workers in this engraving of the Bessemer converters in one of Andrew Carnegie's Pittsburgh steel mills. The illustration is from an 1886 issue of Harper's Weekly.

and consumer preferences became important. Competition was fierce, and steel companies, like the railroads, tried secret agreements, pools, and consolidation. During the 1880s and 1890s, they moved toward vertical integration, a type of organization in which a single company owns and controls the entire process from the unearthing of the raw materials to the manufacture and sale of the finished product. Such companies combined coal and iron mines, transportation companies, blast furnaces, and rolling mills into integrated networks.

Andrew Carnegie emerged as the undisputed master of the industry. Born in Scotland, he came to the United States in 1848 at the age of twelve. Settling near Pittsburgh, he went to work as a bobbin boy in a cotton mill, earning $1.20 a week. He soon took a job in a telegraph office, where in 1852 his hard work and skill caught the eye of Thomas A. Scott of the Pennsylvania Railroad. Starting as Scott's personal telegrapher, Carnegie spent a total of twelve years on the Pennsylvania, a training ground for company managers. By 1859, he had become a divisional superintendent. He was twenty-four.

Soon rich from shrewd investments, Carnegie plunged into the steel industry in 1872. On the Monongahela River south of Pittsburgh he built the giant J. Edgar Thomson Steel Works, named after the president of the Pennsylvania Railroad, his biggest customer. With his warmth and salesmanship, he attracted able partners and subordinates such as Henry Clay Frick and Charles M. Schwab, whom he drove hard and paid well. Although he had written magazine articles defending the rights of workers, Carnegie kept the wages of the laborers in his mills low, disliked unions, and, with the help of Frick, crushed a violent strike at his Homestead works in 1892 (see p. 560).

In 1878, he won the steel contract for the Brooklyn Bridge. During the next decade, as city building boomed, he converted the huge Homestead works near Pittsburgh to the manufacture of structural beams and angles, which went into the New York City elevated railway, the first skyscrapers, and the Washington Monument. Carnegie profits mounted: from $2 million in 1888 to $40 million in 1900. That year, Carnegie Steel alone produced more steel than Great Britain. Employing twenty thousand people, it was the largest industrial company in the world.

In 1901, Carnegie sold it. Believing that wealth brought social obligations, he wanted to devote his full time to philanthropy. He found a buyer in J. Pierpont Morgan, who in the late 1890s had put together several steel companies, including Federal Steel, Carnegie's chief rival. Carnegie Steel had blocked Morgan's well-known desire for control, and in mid-1900, when a war loomed between the two interests, Morgan decided to buy Carnegie out. In early January 1901, Morgan told Charles M. Schwab: "Go and find his price." Schwab cornered Carnegie on the golf course, Carnegie listened, and the next day handed Schwab a note, scribbled in blunt pencil, asking almost a half-billion dollars. Morgan glanced at it and said, "I accept this price."

Drawing other companies into the combination, Morgan on March 3, 1901, announced the creation of the United States Steel Corporation. The new firm was capitalized at $1.4 billion, the first billion-dollar company. It absorbed over 200 other companies, employed 168,000 people, and produced 9 million tons of iron and steel a year. It controlled three-fifths of the country's steel business. Soon there were other giants, including Bethlehem Steel, Republic Steel, and National Steel. As the nineteenth century ended, steel products—rare just thirty years before—had altered the landscape. Huge firms, investment bankers, and professional managers dominated the industry.

Rockefeller and Oil

Petroleum worked comparable changes in the economic and social landscape, although mostly after 1900. Distilled into oil, it lubricated the machinery of the industrial age. There seemed little use for gasoline (the internal combustion engine had only just been developed), but kerosene, another major distillate, brought inexpensive illumination into almost every home. Whale oil, cottonseed oil, and even tallow candles were expensive to burn; consequently, many people went to bed at nightfall. Kerosene lamps opened the evenings to activity, which altered the patterns of life.

Like other changes in these years, the oil boom happened with surprising speed. In the mid-1850s, petroleum was a bothersome, smelly fluid that occasionally rose to the surface of springs and streams. Clever entrepreneurs bottled it in patent medicines; a few scooped up enough to burn. Other entrepreneurs soon found that drilling reached pockets of oil beneath the earth. In 1859, Edwin L. Drake drilled the first oil well near Titusville in northwest Pennsylvania, and the "black gold" fever struck. Chemists soon discovered ways to transform petroleum into lubricating oil, grease, paint, wax, varnish, naphtha, and paraffin. Within a few years, there was a world market in oil.

At first, growth of the oil industry was chaotic. Early drillers and refiners produced for local markets, and since drilling wells and even erecting refineries cost little, competition flourished. Output fluctuated dramatically; prices rose and fell with devastating effect. Refineries—usually a collection of wooden shacks and tanks—were centered in Cleveland and Pittsburgh, near the original oil-producing regions.

A young merchant from Cleveland named John D. Rockefeller imposed order on the industry. "I had an ambition to build," he later recalled, and beginning in 1863, at the age of twenty-four, he built the Standard Oil Company, soon to become one of the titans of corporate business. Like Morgan, Rockefeller considered competition wasteful, small-scale enterprise inefficient, and consolidation the path of the future. Consolidation "revolutionized the way of doing business all over the world," he said. "The time was ripe for it. It had to come, though all we saw at the moment was the need to save ourselves from wasteful conditions."

Methodically, Rockefeller absorbed or destroyed competitors in Cleveland and elsewhere. As ruthless in his methods as Carnegie, he lacked the steel master's spontaneous charm. He was distant and taciturn, a man of deep religious beliefs who taught Bible classes at Cleveland's Erie Street Baptist Church. Like Carnegie, he demanded efficiency, relentless cost cutting, and the latest technology. He attracted exceptional lieutenants—although, as one said, he could see further ahead than any of them, "and then see around the corner."

"Nothing in haste, nothing ill-done," Rockefeller often said to himself. "Your future hangs on every day that passes." Paying careful attention to detail, he counted the stoppers in barrels, shortened barrel hoops to save metal, and in one famous incident, reduced the number of drops of solder on kerosene cans from forty to thirty-nine. In large-scale production, Rockefeller realized, even small reductions meant huge savings. Research uncovered other ways of lowering costs and improving products, and Herman Frasch, a brilliant Standard chemist, solved problem after problem in the refining of oil.

In the end, Rockefeller triumphed over his competitors by marketing products of high quality at the lowest unit cost. But he employed other, less savory methods as well. He threatened rivals and bribed politicians. He employed spies to harass the customers of competing refiners. Above all, he extorted railroad rebates that lowered his transportation costs and undercut com-

John D. Rockefeller, satirized in a 1901 Puck *cartoon, is enthroned on oil, the base of his empire; his crown is girded by other holdings.*

petitors. By 1879, he controlled 90 percent of the country's entire oil-refining capacity.

Vertically integrated, Standard Oil owned wells, timberlands, barrel and chemical plants, refineries, warehouses, pipelines, and fleets of tankers and oil cars. Its marketing organization served as the model for the industry. Standard exported oil to Asia, Africa, and South America; and its 5-gallon kerosene tin, like Coca-Cola bottles and cans during a later era, was a familiar sight in the most distant parts of the world.

To manage it all, the company developed a new plan of business organization, the trust, which had profound significance for American business. In 1881, Samuel T. C. Dodd, Standard's attorney, set up the Standard Oil Trust, with a board of nine trustees empowered "to hold, control, and manage" all Standard's properties. Stockholders exchanged their stock for trust certificates, on which dividends were paid. On January 2, 1882, the first of the modern trusts was born. As Dodd intended, it immediately centralized control of Standard's far-flung empire.

Competition almost disappeared; profits soared. A trust movement swept the country, as industries with similar problems—whiskey, lead, and sugar, among others—followed Standard's example. The word *trust* became synonymous with monopoly, amid vehement protests from the public. *Antitrust* became a watchword for a generation of reformers from the 1880s through the era of Woodrow Wilson. But Rockefeller's purpose had been *management* of a monopoly, not monopoly itself, which he had already achieved.

During the 1890s, Rockefeller helped pioneer another form of industrial consolidation, the holding company. Taking advantage of an 1889 New Jersey law that allowed companies to purchase other companies, he moved Standard Oil to New Jersey and brought up his own subsidiaries to form a holding company. The trust, he had learned, was somewhat cumbersome, and it was under attack in Congress and the courts. Holding companies offered the next step in industrial management. They were simply large-scale mergers, in which a central corporate organization purchased the stock of the member companies and established direct formal control.

Other companies followed suit, including American Sugar Refining, the Northern Securities Company, and the National Biscuit Company. (See Chapter 23 for further discussion of Northern Securities.) Merger followed merger. By 1900, 1 percent of the nation's companies controlled more than one-third of its industrial production. A decade later, a congressional investigation showed that two individuals, Rockefeller and Morgan, between them controlled businesses worth more than $22 billion.

In 1897, Rockefeller retired with a fortune of nearly $900 million, but for Standard Oil and petroleum in general, the most expansive period was yet to come. The great oil pools of Texas and Oklahoma had not yet been discovered. Plastics and other oil-based synthetics were several decades in the future. There were only four usable automobiles in the country, and the day of the gasoline engine, automobile, and airplane lay just ahead.

The Business of Invention

"America has become known the world around as the home of invention," boasted the Commissioner of Patents in 1892. It had not always been so; until the last third of the nineteenth century, the country had imported most of its technology. Then an extraordinary group of inventors and tinkerers—"specialists in invention," Thomas A. Edison called them—began to study the world around them. Some of their inventions gave rise to new industries; a few actually changed the quality of life.

The number of patents issued to inventors reflected the trend. During the 1850s, fewer than 2,000 patents were issued each year. By the 1880s and 1890s, the figure reached more than 20,000 a year. Between 1790 and 1860, the Patent Office issued just 36,000 patents; in the decade of the 1890s alone, it issued more than 200,000.

Some of the inventions transformed communications. In 1866, Cyrus W. Field improved the

transatlantic cable linking the telegraph networks of Europe and the United States. By the early 1870s, land and submarine cables ran to Brazil, Japan, and the China coast; in the next two decades, they reached Africa and spread across South America. Diplomats and business leaders could now "talk" to their counterparts in Berlin or Hong Kong. Even before the telephone, the cables quickened the pace of foreign affairs, revolutionized journalism, and allowed businesses to expand and centralize.

The typewriter (1867), stock ticker (1867), cash register (1879), calculating machine (1887), and adding machine (1888) helped business transactions. High-speed spindles, automatic looms, and electric sewing machines transformed the clothing industry, which for the first time in history turned out ready-made clothes for the masses. In 1890, the Census Bureau first used machines to sort and tabulate data on punched cards, a portent of a new era of information storage and treatment.

In 1879, George Eastman patented a process for coating gelatine on photographic dry plates, which led to celluloid film and motion pictures. By 1888, he was marketing the Kodak camera, which weighed 35 ounces, took 100 exposures, and cost $25. Even though early Kodaks had to

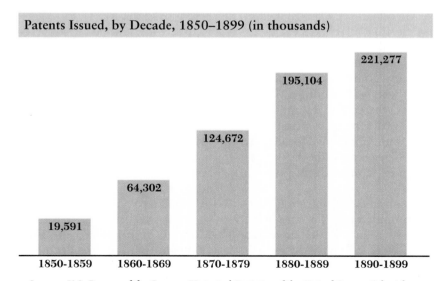

Patents Issued, by Decade, 1850–1899 (in thousands)

Decade	Patents
1850-1859	19,591
1860-1869	64,302
1870-1879	124,672
1880-1889	195,104
1890-1899	221,277

Source: U.S. Bureau of the Census. Historical Statistics of the United States, Colonial Times to 1970, *Bicentennial Edition, Washington, D.C., 1975.*

be returned to the factory, camera and all, for film developing, they revolutionized photography. Now almost anyone could snap a picture.

Other innovations changed the diet. There were new processes for flour, canned meat, vegetables, condensed milk, and even beer (from an offshoot of Louis Pasteur's discoveries about bacteria). Packaged cereals appeared on breakfast tables. Refrigerated railroad cars, ice-cooled, brought fresh fruit from Florida and California to all parts of the country. In the 1870s, Gustavus F. Swift, a Chicago meatpacker, hit on the idea of using the cars to distribute meat nationwide. Setting up "dissembly" factories to butcher meat (Henry Ford later copied them for his famous "assembly" lines), he started an "era of cheap beef," as a newspaper said.

No innovation, however, rivaled the importance of the telephone and the use of electricity for light and power. The telephone was the work of Alexander Graham Bell, a shrewd and genial Scotsman who settled in Boston in 1871. Interested in the problems of the deaf, Bell experimented with ways to transmit speech electrically, and after several years developed electrified metal disks that, much like the human ear, converted sound waves to electrical impulses and back again. On March 10, 1876, he transmitted the first sentence over a telephone: "Mr. Watson, come here; I want you." Later that year, he exhibited the new device to excited crowds at the Centennial Exposition in Philadelphia.

In 1878—the year a telephone was installed in the White House—the first telephone exchange opened in New Haven, Connecticut. Fighting off competitors who challenged the patent, the young Bell Telephone Company dominated the growing industry. By 1895, there were about 310,000 phones; a decade later, there were 10 million— one for almost every ten people. American Telephone and Telegraph Company, formed by the Bell interests in 1885, became another of the vast holding companies, consolidating over a hundred local systems.

If the telephone dissolved communications barriers as old as the human race, Thomas Alva Edison, the "Wizard of Menlo Park," invented processes and products of comparable significance. Born in 1847, Edison had little formal education, although he was an avid reader. Like Carnegie, he went into the new field of telegraphy. Tinkering in his spare time, he made several important improvements, including a telegraph capable of sending four messages over a single wire. Gathering teams of specialists to work on specific problems, Edison built the first modern research laboratory at Menlo Park, New Jersey. It may have been his most important invention.

The laboratory, Edison promised, would turn out "a minor invention every ten days and a big thing every six months or so." In 1877, it turned out a big thing. Worried about a telephone's high cost, Edison set out to invent a "telephone repeater," which became the phonograph. Those unable to afford a phone, he thought, could record their voices for replay from a central telephone station. Using tin foil wrapped around a grooved rotating cylinder, he shouted the verses of "Mary had a little lamb" and then listened in awe as the machine played them back. "I was never so taken aback in all my life," he later said. "Everybody was astonished. I was always afraid of things that worked the first time."

In 1896, records made of hard rubber and shellac appeared on the market; the following year, a phonograph sold for $20. In 1904, someone had the idea of recording on both sides of the disc, and the phonograph record in its modern form was born. For the first time in history, people could listen again and again to a favorite symphony or piano solo. The phonograph made human experience repeatable in a way never before possible.

In 1879 came an even larger triumph, the incandescent lamp. Sir Joseph William Swan, an English inventor, had already experimented with the carbon filament, but Edison's task involved more than finding a durable filament. He set out to do nothing less than change light. A trial-and-error inventor, Edison tested sixteen hundred materials before producing, late in 1879, the carbon filament he wanted. Then he had to devise a complex system of conductors, meters, and generators, by which electricity could be divided and distributed to homes and businesses.

With the financial backing of J. Pierpont Morgan, he organized the Edison Illuminating Company and built the Pearl Street power station in New York City, the testing ground of the new apparatus. On September 4,1882, as Morgan and

In 1891, Thomas Edison patented his kinetoscopic camera, which took moving pictures on a strip of film. The film images, called a peepshow, could be viewed by one person looking into a lighted box and turning a crank. Later, Edison came up with the Vitascope, in which the images were projected onto a screen so that many people could see them simultaneously.

others watched, Edison threw a switch and lit the house of Morgan, the stock exchange, the *New York Times,* and a number of other buildings. Amazed, a *Times* reporter marveled that writing stories in the office at night "seemed almost like writing in daylight." Power stations soon opened in Boston, Philadelphia, and Chicago. By 1900, there were 2,774 stations, lighting some 2 million electric lights around the country. In a nation alive with light, the habits of centuries changed. A flick of the switch lit homes and factories at any hour of the day or night.

In a rare blunder, Edison based his system on low-voltage direct current, which could be transmitted only about 2 miles. George Westinghouse, the inventor of the railroad air brake, demonstrated the advantages of high-voltage alternating current for transmission over great distances. In 1886, he formed the Westinghouse Electric Company and with the inventor Nikola Tesla, a

Hungarian immigrant, developed an alternating-current motor that could convert electricity into mechanical power. Electricity could light a lamp or illuminate a skyscraper; pull a streetcar or drive an entire railroad; run a sewing machine or power a mammoth assembly line. Transmitted easily over long distances, it freed factories and cities from location near water or coal. Electricity, in short, brought a revolution.

Taking advantage of the new devices, Frank J. Sprague, a young engineer, electrified the Richmond, Virginia, streetcar system in 1887. Other cities quickly followed. Electric-powered subway systems opened in Boston in 1897 and New York City in 1904. Overhead wires and third rails made urban transportation quieter, faster, and cleaner. Buried under pavement or strung from pole to pole, wires of every description—trolley, telephone, and power—marked the birth of the modern city.

THE SELLERS

The increased output of the industrial age alone was not enough to ensure huge profits. The products still had to be sold, and that gave rise to a new "science" of marketing. Some business leaders—like Swift in meatpacking, James B. Duke in tobacco, and Rockefeller in oil—built extensive marketing organizations of their own. Others relied on retailers, merchandising techniques, and advertising, developing a host of methods to convince consumers to buy.

In 1867, businesses spent about $50 million on advertising; in 1900, they spent over $500 million, and the figure was increasing rapidly. The first advertising agency, N. W. Ayer and Son, of Philadelphia, began to service businesses in the mid-1870s, and it was followed by numerous imitators. The rotary press (1875) churned out newspapers and introduced a new era in newspaper advertising. Woodcuts, halftones, and photoengraving added illustrations to catch the consumer's eye. Brand names became popular, and already Kellogg was promising cornflake eaters "Genuine Joy, Genuine Appetite, Genuine Health and therefore Genuine Complexion."

Bringing producer and consumer together, nationwide advertising was the final link in the national market. From roadside signs to newspaper ads, it pervaded American life. "Do you know why we publish the *Ladies' Home Journal?*" the magazine's owner asked an audience of manufacturers. "The editor thinks it is for the benefit of American women. That is an illusion, but a very proper one for him to have. But I will tell you; the real reason, the publisher's reason, is to give you people who manufacture things that American women want and buy a chance to tell them about your products."

R. H. Macy in New York, John Wanamaker in Philadelphia, and Marshall Field in Chicago turned the department store into a national institution. There people could browse (a relatively new concept) and buy. Innovations in pricing, display, and advertising helped customers develop wants they did not know they had. In 1870, Wanamaker took out the first full-page newspaper ad, and Macy, an aggressive advertiser, touted "goods suitable for the millionaire at prices in reach of the millions."

The "chain store"—an American term—spread across the country. The A & P grocery stores, begun in 1859, numbered 67 by 1876, all marked by a familiar red-and-gold facade. By 1915, there were a thousand of them. In 1880, F. W. Woolworth, bored with the family farm, opened the first "Five and Ten Cent Store" in Utica, New York. He had fifty-nine stores in 1900, the year he adopted the bright red storefront and heaping counters to lure customers in and persuade them to buy.

In similar fashion, Sears, Roebuck and Montgomery Ward sold to rural customers through mail-order catalogs—a means of selling that depended on effective transportation and a high level of customer literacy. As a traveler for a dry goods firm, Aaron Montgomery Ward had seen an unfulfilled need of people in the rural West. He started the mail-order trend in 1872, with a one-sheet price list offered from a Chicago loft. By 1884, he offered almost ten thousand items in a catalog of 240 pages.

Richard W. Sears also saw the possibilities in the mail-order business. Starting with watches and jewelry, he gradually expanded his list. In the early 1880s, he moved to Chicago, and with Alvah C. Roebuck, founded Sears, Roebuck and Company. Sears sold anything and everything, prospering in a business that relied on mutual faith between unseen customers and distant distributors. Sears catalogs, soon over five hundred pages long, exploited four-color illustrations and other new techniques. By the early 1900s, Sears distributed six million catalogs annually.

Advertising, brand names, chain stores, and mail-order houses brought Americans of all varieties into a national market. Even as the country grew, a certain homogeneity of goods bound it together, touching cities and farms, East and West, rich and poor. There was a common language of consumption. The market, some contemporaries thought, also bridged ethnic and other differences. A prominent English economist wrote in 1919, "Widely as the Scandinavians are separated from the Italians, and the native Americans from the Poles, in sentiment, in modes of living, and even in occupations, they are yet purchasers of nearly the same goods. . . . [T]hey buy similar clothes, furniture, and implements."

Shoppers crowd the aisles to hunt for bargains in New York City's Siegel Cooper department store in 1897.

The theory had severe limits; ethnic and racial differences remained entrenched in the society. But Americans *had* become a community of consumers, surrounded by goods unavailable just a few decades before, and able to purchase them. They had learned to make, want, and buy. "Because you see the main thing today is—shopping," Arthur Miller, a twentieth-century playwright, said in *The Price*.

> *Years ago a person, he was unhappy, didn't know what to do with himself—he'd go to church, start a revolution—something. Today you're unhappy? Can't figure it out? What is the salvation? Go shopping.*

THE WAGE EARNERS

Although entrepreneurs were important, it was the labor of millions of men and women that built the new industrial society. In their individual stories, nearly all unrecorded, lay much of the achievement, drama, and pain of these years.

In a number of respects, their lot improved during the last quarter of the nineteenth century.

Real wages rose, working conditions got better, and the workers' influence in national affairs increased. Between 1880 and 1914, wages of the average worker rose about $7 a year. Like others, workers also benefited from expanding health and educational services.

But life was not easy. Before 1900, most wage earners worked at least ten hours a day, six days a week. If skilled, they earned about 20¢ an hour; if unskilled, just half that. On average they earned between $400 and $500 a year. It took about $600 for a family of four to live decently. Construction workers, machinists, government employees, printers, clerical workers, and western miners made more than the average. Eastern coal miners, agricultural workers, garment workers, and unskilled factory hands made considerably less.

There were few holidays or vacations and there was little respite from the grueling routine. Skilled workers could turn the system to their own ends—New York City cigar makers, for example, paid someone to read to them while they worked—but the unskilled seldom had such luxury. They were too easily replaced. "A bit of advice to you," said a guidebook for immigrant Jews in the 1890s: "do not take a moment's rest.

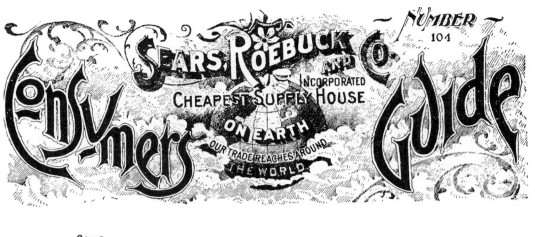

Saws.
Patent Gullet-Tooth Circular Saws.
Henry Disston & Sons'.

Patent ground and tempered solid teeth, of extra quality, superior workmanship.

Among the items offered for sale in the 1897 Sears, Roebuck catalog were tools such as the circular saw, chairs—a "great bargain for 85 cents"—and the celebrated Acme power windmill, available from the agricultural implement department of the company.

Run, do, work, and keep your own good in mind."

Work was not only grueling; it was very dangerous. Safety standards were low, and accidents were common, more common in fact than in any industrial nation in the world at that time. On the railroads, 1 in every 26 workers was injured, 1 in every 399 killed each year. Thousands suffered from chronic illness, unknowing victims of dust, chemicals, and other pollutants. In the early 1900s, Dr. Alice Hamilton established a link between jobs and disease, but meanwhile, illness weakened or struck down many a breadwinner.

The breadwinner might be a woman or child; both worked in increasing numbers. In 1870,

about 15 percent of women over the age of sixteen were employed for wages; in 1900, 20 percent (5.3 million women) were. Of 303 occupations listed in the 1900 census, women were represented in 296. The textile industry was their largest single employer. Between 1870 and 1900, the number of working children rose nearly 130 percent to 1.8 million. In 1900, one out of every ten girls and one out of every five boys between the ages of ten and fifteen held jobs. In Paterson, New Jersey, an important industrial city, about half of all boys and girls aged eleven to fourteen had jobs.

There were so many children in the labor force that when people spoke of "child labor," they often meant boys and girls *under* the age of fourteen. Boys were paid little enough, but girls made even less. Girls, it was argued, were headed for marriage; those who worked were just doing so in order to help out their families. "We try to employ girls who are members of families," a box manufacturer said, "for we don't pay the girls a living wage in this trade."

Most working women were young and single. Many began working at sixteen or seventeen, worked a half-dozen years or so, married, and quit. In 1900, only 5 percent of all married women were employed outside the home, although black women were an important exception. Among them, 25 percent of married women worked in 1900, usually on southern farms or as low-paid laundresses and domestic servants. As clerical work expanded, women learned new skills like typing and stenography. Moving into formerly male occupations, they became secretaries, bookkeepers, typists, telephone operators, and clerks in the new department stores.

A few women—very few—became ministers, lawyers, and doctors. Arabella Mansfield, admitted to the Iowa bar in 1869, was the first woman lawyer in the country. But change was slow, and in the 1880s, some law schools were still refusing to admit women because they "had not the mentality to study law." Among women entering the professions, the overwhelming majority became nurses, schoolteachers, and librarians. In such professions a process of *feminization* occurred, in which women became a majority of the workers, a small number of men took the management roles, and most men left for other jobs, lowering the profession's status.

In most jobs, status and pay were divided unequally between men and women. Many of both sexes thought a woman's place was in the home, "queen of a little house—no matter how humble—where there are children rolling on the floor." When employed in factories, women tended to occupy jobs that were viewed as natural extensions of household activity. They made clothes and textiles, processed food, and made cigars, tobacco, and shoes. In the ladies' garment industry, which employed large numbers of women, they were the sewers and finishers, jobs that paid less; men were the higher paid cutters and pressers.

In *The Long Day: The Story of a New York Working Girl as Told by Herself* (1906), the girl,

It was not unusual for children in some cities to grow up along with their peers in the factory instead of on the playground, like these girls working in the garment industry.

a young schoolteacher, earned $2.50 a week, paid $1.00 for her room, and had $1.50 for food, clothes, carfare, and any social life. For breakfast, she had bread, butter, and coffee; for lunch, bread and butter; for dinner, potato soup, bread, and butter. In Pittsburgh, a worker in a pickle factory said of her day: "I have stood ten hours; I have fitted 1,300 corks; I have hauled and loaded 4,000 jars of pickles. My pay is seventy cents." Exhausted, such workers fell into bed at night and crawled out again at dawn to begin another "long day."

In general, adults earned more than children, the skilled more than the unskilled, native born more than foreign born, Protestants more than Catholics or Jews, and whites more than blacks and Asians. On average, women made a little more than half as much as men, according to contemporary estimates. In some cases, employers defended the differences—the foreign born, for example, might not speak English—but most simply reflected bias against race, creed, or gender. In the industrial society white, native-born

A typing pool in the Audit Division of the Metropolitan Life Insurance Company, 1897. As demand for clerical workers grew, women took over many of the secretarial duties formerly performed by men. Despite their prominence in the workplace, however, the women were usually overseen by male supervisors.

Protestants—the bulk of the population—reaped the greatest rewards.

Black labored on the fringes, usually in menial occupations. The last hired and first fired, they earned less than other workers at almost every level of skill. On the Pacific Coast, the Chinese— and later the Japanese—lived in enclaves and suffered periodic attacks of discrimination. In 1879, the Workingmen's party of California got a provision in the state constitution forbidding corporations to employ Chinese, and in 1882, Congress prohibited the immigration of Chinese workers for ten years (see Chapter 17).

Culture of Work

Among almost all groups, industrialization shattered age-old patterns, including work habits and the culture of work, as Herbert G. Gutman, a social historian, noted. It made people adapt "older work routines to new necessities and strained those wedded to premodern patterns of labor." Adaptation was difficult and often demeaning. Virtually everyone went through it, and newcomers repeated the experiences of those who came before.

Men and women fresh from farms were not accustomed to the factory's disciplines. Now they worked indoors rather than out, paced themselves to the clock rather than the movements of the sun, and followed the needs of the market rather than the natural rhythms of the seasons. They had foremen and hierarchies and strict rules. Piece work determined wages, and always—as Morris Rosenfeld, a clothing presser, wrote—there was the relentless clock:

The Clock in the workshop,—it rests not a moment;
It points on, and ticks on: eternity-time;
Once someone told me the clock had a meaning,

In pointing and ticking had reason and rhyme.
At times, when I listen, I hear the clock plainly;
The reason of old—the old meaning—is gone!
The maddening pendulum urges me forward
To labor and still labor on.
The tick of the clock is the boss in his anger.
The face of the clock has the eyes of the foe.
The clock—I shudder—Dost hear how it draws me?
It calls me "Machine" and it cries [to] me "Sew"!

As industries grew larger, work became more impersonal. Machines displaced skilled artisans, and the unskilled tended them for employers they never saw. Workers picked up and left their jobs with startling frequency, and factories drew on a churning, highly mobile labor supply. Historian Stephan Thernstrom, who has carefully studied the census records, found that only about half the people recorded in any census still lived in the same community ten years later. "The country had an enormous reservoir of restless and foot-loose men, who could be lured to new destinations when opportunity beckoned."

Thernstrom and others have also found substantial economic and social mobility. The Horatio Alger stories, of course, had always said so, and careers like Andrew Carnegie's—the impoverished immigrant boy who made good—seemed to confirm it. The actual record was considerably more limited. Most business leaders in the period came from well-to-do or middle-class families of old American stock. Of 360 iron and steel barons in Pittsburgh, Carnegie's own city, only 5 fit the Carnegie characteristics, and one of those was Carnegie himself. Still, if few workers became steel magnates, many workers made major progress during their lifetimes. Thernstrom discovered that a quarter of the manual laborers rose to middle-class positions, and working-class children were even more likely to move up the ladder. In Boston, about half the Jewish immigrants rose from manual to middle-class jobs, and English, Irish, and Italian immigrants were not far behind.

The chance for advancement played a vital role in American industrial development. It gave workers hope, wedded them to the system, and tempered their response to the appeal of labor unions and working-class agitation. Very few workers rose from rags to riches, but a great many rose to better jobs and higher status.

Labor Unions

Weak throughout the nineteenth century, labor unions never included more than 2 percent of the total labor force nor more than 10 percent of industrial workers. To many workers, unions seemed "foreign," radical, and out of step with the American tradition of individual advancement. Craft, ethnic, and other differences fragmented the labor force, and its extraordinary mobility made organization difficult. Employers opposed unions. "I have always had one rule," said an executive of U.S. Steel. "If a worker sticks up his head, hit it."

Although immigrants comprised a good portion of the industrial work force, prejudice existed against certain groups. This 1877 cartoon from a San Francisco paper, the San Francisco Illustrated WASP, *shows the working-men's prejudice against Asians in that city.*

As the national economy emerged, however, national labor unions gradually took shape. The early unions often represented skilled workers in local areas, but in 1866, William H. Sylvis, a Pennsylvania iron molder, united several unions into a single national organization, the National Labor Union. Like many of the era's labor leaders, Sylvis sought long-range humanitarian reforms, such as the establishment of workers' cooperatives, rather than specific bread-and-butter goals. A talented propagandist, he attracted many members—some 640,000 by 1868—but he died in 1869, and the organization did not long survive him.

The year Sylvis died, Uriah S. Stephens and a group of Philadelphia garment workers founded a far more successful organization, the Noble and Holy Order of the Knights of Labor. A secret fraternal order, it grew slowly through the 1870s, until Terence V. Powderly, the new Grand Master Workman elected in 1879, ended the secrecy and embarked on an aggressive recruitment program. Wanting to unite all labor, the Knights welcomed everyone who "toiled," regardless of skill, creed, sex, or color. Unlike most unions it organized female workers, and at its peak had sixty thousand black members.

Harking back to the Jacksonians, the Knights set the "producers" against monopoly and special privilege. As members they excluded only "nonproducers"—bankers, lawyers, liquor dealers, and gamblers. Since employers were "producers," they could join; and since workers and employers had common interests, the Knights maintained that workers should not strike. The order's platform included the eight-hour day and the abolition of child and prisoner labor, but more often it focused on uplifting utopian reform. Powderly, the eloquent and idealistic leader, spun dreams of a new era of harmony and cooperation. He wanted to sweep away trusts and end drunkenness. Workers should pool their resources, establish worker-run factories, railroads, and mines, and escape from the wage system. "The aim of the Knights of Labor—properly understood—is to make each man his own employer," Powderly said.

Membership grew steadily—from 42,000 in 1882 to 110,000 in 1885. In March 1885, ignoring Powderly's dislike of strikes, local Knights in Saint Louis, Kansas City, and other cities won a victory against Jay Gould's Missouri Pacific Railroad, and membership soared. It soon reached almost 730,000, but neither Powderly nor the union's loose structure could handle the growth. In 1886, the wily Gould struck back, crushing the Knights on the Texas and Pacific Railroad. The defeat punctured the union's growth and revealed the ineffectiveness of its national leaders. Tens of thousands of unskilled laborers, who had recently rushed to join, deserted the ranks. The Haymarket riot (see p. 560) turned public sympathy against unions like the Knights. By 1890, the order had shrunk to 100,000 members, and a few years later it was virtually defunct.

Even as the Knights waxed and waned, another organization emerged that was to endure. Founded in 1886, the American Federation of Labor (AFL) was a loose alliance of national craft unions. Unlike the Knights, the AFL rejected industrial unions in favor of trade unions. It organized only skilled workers along craft lines, avoided politics, and worked for specific practical objectives. "I have my own philosophy and my own dreams," Samuel Gompers, the founder and longtime president, said, "but first and foremost I want to increase the workingman's welfare year by year."

Born in a London tenement in 1850, Gompers was a child of the union movement. Settling in New York, he worked as a cigar maker, took an active hand in union activities, and experimented for a time with socialism and working-class politics. As leader of the AFL, he adopted a pragmatic approach to labor's needs. Gompers accepted capitalism and did not argue for fundamental changes in it. For labor he wanted simply a recognized place within the system and a greater share of the rewards.

Unlike Powderly, Gompers and the AFL assumed that most workers would remain workers throughout their lives. The task, then, lay in improving lives in "practical" ways: higher wages, shorter hours, and better working conditions. They offered some attractive assurances to employers. As trade unionists, they would use the strike and boycott, but only to achieve limited gains, and if treated fairly, they would provide a stable labor force. They would not oppose monopolies and trusts, as Gompers said, "so long as we obtain fair wages."

By the 1890s, the AFL was the most important labor group in the country, and Gompers, the guiding spirit, stayed its president, except for one year, until his death in 1924. Membership expanded from 140,000 in 1886, past 250,000 in 1892, to over 1 million by 1901. The AFL then included almost one-third of the country's skilled workers. By 1914, it had over 2 million members. The great majority of workers—skilled and unskilled—remained unorganized, but Gompers and the AFL had become a significant force in national life.

Few unions allowed women to join. The Knights of Labor had a Department of Woman's Work headed by Leonora M. Barry, a shrewd, enthusiastic organizer who established a dozen women's locals and investigated the condition of women's labor. The Knights welcomed housewives because they were "producers." The AFL either ignored or opposed women workers. Only two of its national affiliates—the Cigar Makers' Union and the Typographical Union—accepted women as members; others prohibited them outright, and Gompers himself often complained that women workers undercut the pay scales for men. Working conditions improved after 1900, but even then unions were largely a man's world. In 1910, when there were 6.3 million women at work, only 125,000 of them were in unions.

The AFL did not expressly forbid black workers from joining, but member unions used high initiation fees, technical examinations, and other means to discourage black membership. The AFL's informal exclusion practices were, all in all, a sorry record, but Gompers defended his policy toward blacks, women, and the unskilled by pointing to the dangers that unions faced. Only by restricting membership, he argued, could the union succeed.

Labor Unrest

Workers used various means to adjust to the factory age. To the dismay of managers and "efficiency" experts, they often dictated the pace and quality of their work, and set the tone of the workplace. Newly arrived immigrants got jobs for friends and relatives, taught them how to deal with factory conditions, and humanized the workplace.

Women delegates at a national meeting of the Knights of Labor in 1886. Women belonged to separate associations affiliated with local all-male unions.

Workers also formed their own institutions to deal with their jobs. Overcoming differences of race or ethnic origin, they often banded together to help each other out. They joined social or fraternal organizations, and their unions did more than argue for higher wages. Unions offered companionship, news of job openings, and much needed insurance plans for sickness, accident, or death. Workers went to the union hall to play cards or pool, sing union songs, and hear older workers tell of past labor struggles. Unions provided food for sick members, and there were dances, picnics, and parades. "The night I joined the Cattle Butchers' Union," a young Lithuanian said, "I was led into the room by a negro member. With me were Bohemians, Germans and Poles. . . . We swore to be loyal to our union above everything else except the country, the city and the State—to be faithful to each other—to protect the women workers—to do our best to understand the history of the labor movement, and to do all we could to help it on."

Many employers believed in an "iron law of wages" in which supply and demand, not the welfare of their workers, dictated wages. "If I wanted boiler iron," a steelmaker said, "I would go out on the market and buy where I could get it the cheapest, and if I wanted to employ men I would do the same thing." Wanting a docile labor force, employers fired union members, hired scabs to replace strikers, and used a new weapon, the court injunction, to quell strikes.

The injunction, which forbade workers to interfere with their employers' business, was used to break the great Pullman strike of 1894 (see Chapter 20), and the Supreme Court upheld use of the injunction in *In re Debs* (1895). Court decisions also affected the legal protection offered to workers. In *Holden* v. *Hardy* (1898), the Court upheld a law limiting working hours for miners because their work was dangerous and long hours might increase injuries. In *Lochner* v. *New York* (1905), however, it struck down a law limiting bakery workers to a sixty-hour week and ten-hour day. Because baking was safer than mining, the Court saw no need to interfere with the right of bakers to sell their labor freely.

As employers' attitudes hardened, strikes and violence broke out. The United States had the greatest number of violent confrontations between capital and labor in the industrial world. Between 1880 and 1900, there were more than 23,000 strikes involving 6.6 million workers. The railroad strike of 1877 (see "The Great Railroad Strike of 1877" on pp. 562–563) paralyzed railroads from West Virginia to California, resulted in the deaths of over a hundred workers, and required federal troops to suppress it. Another outburst of labor unrest occurred during the mid-1880s; in 1886, the peak year, 610,000 workers were off the job because of strikes and lockouts.

The worst incident took place at Haymarket Square in Chicago, where workers had been campaigning for an eight-hour workday. In early May 1886, police, intervening in a strike at the McCormick Harvester works, shot and killed two workers. The next evening, May 4, labor leaders called a protest meeting at Haymarket Square near downtown Chicago. The meeting was peaceful, even a bit dull; about three thousand people were there. Police ordered them to disperse; someone threw a dynamite bomb which instantly killed one policeman and fatally wounded six others. Police fired into the crowd and killed four people.

No one ever discovered who threw the bomb, but many Americans—not just business leaders—demanded action against labor "radicalism." Cities strengthened their police forces and armories. In Chicago, donors helped to establish nearby Fort Sheridan and the Great Lakes Naval Training Station to curb social turmoil. Uncertain who threw the bomb, Chicago police rounded up

eight anarchists who were convicted of murder. Although there was no evidence of their guilt, four were hanged, one committed suicide, and three remained in jail until pardoned by the governor in 1893. Linking labor and anarchism in the public mind, the Haymarket Riot weakened the national labor movement.

Violence again broke out in the unsettled conditions of the 1890s. In 1892, federal troops crushed a strike of silver miners in the Coeur d'Alene district of Idaho. That same year, Carnegie and Henry Clay Frick, his partner and manager, lowered wages nearly 20 percent at the Homestead steel plant. The Amalgamated Iron and Steel Workers, an AFL affiliate, struck, and Frick responded by locking the workers out of the plant. The workers surrounded it, and Frick, furious, hired a small private army of Pinkerton detectives to drive them off. But alert workers spotted the detectives, pinned them down with gunfire, and forced them to surrender. Three detectives and ten workers died in the battle.

A few days later, the Pennsylvania governor ordered the state militia to impose peace at Homestead. On July 23, an anarchist named Alexander Berkman, who was not one of the strikers, walked into Frick's office and shot him. He fired twice, then stabbed him several times. Incredibly, Frick survived, watched the police take Berkman away, called in a doctor to bandage his wounds, and stayed in the office until closing time. "I do not think I shall die," he told reporters. "But if I do or not, the company will pursue the same policy and it will win." In late July, the Homestead works reopened under military guard, and in November the strikers gave up.

Events like those at Homestead troubled many Americans who wondered whether industrialization, for all its benefits, might carry a heavy price in social upheaval, class tensions, and even outright warfare. Most workers did not share in the immense profits of the industrial age, and as the nineteenth century came to a close, there were some who rebelled against the inequity.

In the half century after the Civil War, the United States became an industrial nation—the leading one, in fact, in the world. On one hand, industrialization meant "progress," growth, world power, and in some sense, fulfillment of the American promise of abundance. National wealth grew from $16 billion in 1860 to $88 bil-

In the rioting that followed the bomb explosion in Haymarket Square in Chicago, seven police-men and four workers died and more than seventy policemen were wounded, many of them by fellow police. August Spies, one of the anarchists convicted of murder and sent to the gallows, said at his trial, "Let the world know that in A.D. 1886, in the state of Illinois, eight men were sentenced to death because they believed in a better future; because they had not lost their faith in the ultimate victory of liberty and justice!" (Actually seven of the agitators were sentenced to death, the eighth to imprisonment.)

lion in 1900; wealth per capita more than dou-bled. For the bulk of the population, the standard of living—a particularly American concept—rose.

But industrialization also meant rapid change, social instability, exploitation of labor, and grow-ing disparity in income between rich and poor. Industry flourished, but control rested in fewer and fewer hands. Maturing quickly, the young system became a new corporate capitalism: giant businesses, interlocking in ownership, managed by a new professional class, and selling an expanding variety of goods in an increasingly controlled market. As goods spread through the society, so did a sharpened, aggressive material-ism. Workers felt the strains of the shift to a new social order.

In 1902, a well-to-do New Yorker named Bessie Van Vorst decided to see what it was like to work for a living in a factory. Disguising her-self in coarse woolen clothes, a shabby felt hat, a cheap piece of fur, and an old shawl and gloves, she went to Pittsburgh and got a job in a canning factory. She worked ten hours a day, six days a week, including four hours on Saturday after-noons when she and the other women, on their hands and knees, scrubbed the tables, stands, and entire factory floor. For that she earned $4.20 a week, $3 of which went for food alone. "My hands are stiff," she said, "my thumbs almost blistered. . . . Cases are emptied and refilled; bot-tles are labeled, stamped and rolled away . . . and still there are more cases, more jars, more bottles. Oh! the monotony of it!" The noise around her was deafening; her head grew dazed and weary.

Van Vorst was lucky—when she tired of the life, she could go back to her home in New York. The working men and women around her were not so fortunate. They stayed on the factory

The Great Railroad Strike of 1877

On May 24, 1877, in the midst of a nationwide depression, the Pennsylvania Railroad announced a 10 percent cut in pay for its employees. At the time, engineers made about $3.25 a day for twelve hours of work, conductors $2.75, firemen $1.90, and brakemen $1.75. Other railroads also cut pay; the Baltimore & Ohio announced cuts totaling 20 percent. For firemen and brakemen on the B & O, that meant a wage of $.90 a day.

The wage cuts hurt. As a worker on the B & O said, "We eat our hard bread and tainted meat two days on the sooty cars up the road, and when we come home, find our children gnawing bones and our wives complaining that they cannot even buy hominy and molasses for food."

When pay cuts on the B & O took effect on July 16, anger erupted. In Martinsburg, West Virginia, one crew walked off the job leaving their cattle train standing on the tracks; the stoppage spread to other crews. Trains backed up for 2 miles east and west of town, and at the request of B & O officials, the governor of West Virginia called out the state militia.

The next day, the militia stood guard as another crew took over the cattle train. Strikers boarded the train, and one of them fired a pistol at the guards. His fire was returned, and he fell, mortally wounded. The militiamen, many of them sympathetic to the strike, turned and left the yards. Alarmed, West Virginia's governor called for federal troops to protect railroad property. President Rutherford B. Hayes hesitated, but on July 18 he issued the orders. For the first time since the 1830s, the army was ordered out in peacetime to quell a strike.

As the strike spread along the B & O, jeering crowds threw stones at passing freights. At Cumberland, Maryland, west of Martinsburg, only one freight in sixteen got through. On July 20, the governor of Maryland, too, ordered out the state militia. As one regiment emerged from the Garden Street Armory in Baltimore, the city's factories let out for the day. Homeward-bound workers pelted the bewildered soldiers with stones. Blocks away, several thousand people penned up another regiment. Shooting started, and when it ended, eleven civilians were dead and forty were wounded. At the request of Maryland's governor, President Hayes that night sent army units to Baltimore. Portions of two

Violence and fires associated with the strike destroyed railyards across the country. By the end of the strike, $10 million of railroad property had been reduced to rubble.

states were now under federal protection.

The strike spread westward through New York, Pennsylvania, and Ohio. In each one of those states the militia was called out. Workers on the giant Pennsylvania system stayed on the job until Robert Pitcairn, the aggressive superintendent of the Pittsburgh division, ordered double-headers—trains with two locomotives—on all eastbound freights. Double-headers pulled more freight and required fewer crewmen, but they were difficult to handle.

The morning the order took effect, Augustus Harris, a veteran flagman, refused to take out the 8:40 double-header. Workers and sympathizers blocked the 9:40 trains; incoming crews joined the shutdown. At noon, men from the steel mills mingled in the crowd.

During the night, Pennsylvania state officials ordered in two trainloads of militia from Philadelphia to clear the key Twenty-eighth Street railroad crossing. Several thousand people massed at the crossing and on the hillsides above. There were revolver shots, and the militia opened fire. Within minutes, twenty people lay dead, including a woman and three small children. Fifteen soldiers were hurt.

The strike spread. On Monday, July 23, the New York Central, a vital link between New York City and Chicago, shut down. Cleveland, Buffalo, and other cities were cut off from fuel and supplies. The next day, a general strike paralyzed Saint Louis, and strikes hit major railroads to the West. That night, all freight traffic in and out of Chicago, a vital railroad hub, came to a halt.

Chicago factories closed; angry crowds paraded through the streets. Bankers and lawyers armed themselves with Springfield rifles from nearby government arsenals. On Wednesday evening, July 25, violence broke out when excited policemen fired into a crowd. Citizens' militias and working people battled across the city. Shooting continued through the next day; eighteen people died.

Determined to stop the violence, President Hayes sent six companies of soldiers to Chicago and ordered the army to open the Pennsylvania line between Philadelphia and Pittsburgh. On Saturday, July 28, the break came. Nine days after the original order, the first double-header left Pittsburgh with thirty-four cars of cattle and two cars of troops.

Within a matter of days the anger was spent and the Great Strike was over. It lasted about two weeks, touched eleven states, and affected two-thirds of the country's railroad track. According to one estimate, it involved over 80,000 railroad workers and 500,000 workers in other occupations. More than one hundred people died.

Some employers responded to the strike by tightening hiring procedures, cracking down on labor unions, and strengthening police forces. Others, eager to avert another conflict, took measures to alleviate grievances. By 1880, most of the railroads had raised pay scales to earlier levels.

Many people in America and abroad studied the significance of the strike. Did it mean, as some suggested, that war

An angry mob of civilians and strikers drags soldiers from the train at Hornellsville, New York, on July 23, the day the New York Central was forced to shut down.

between capital and labor had begun? Did industrialization inevitably involve class dislocation, class tensions, and violence? Were federal troops required to maintain peace in the new industrial society?

Answers differed. In response, there was heightened demand for government intervention to regulate railroads and thereby lessen the hardships brought on by rapid industrial growth.

Like most events, however, the strike's greatest impact was on ordinary individuals whose opinions went unrecorded. In moments of individual decision, they stranded trains in Martinsburg, closed factories in Chicago, and shut down entire railroad networks.

CHRONOLOGY

1859 First oil well drilled near Titusville, Pennsylvania

1866 William Sylvis establishes National Labor Union

1869 Transcontinental railroad completed at Promontory, Utah • Knights of Labor organize

1876 Alexander Graham Bell invents the telephone • Centennial Exposition held in Philadelphia

1877 Railroads cut workers' wages, leading to bloody and violent strike

1879 Thomas A. Edison invents the incandescent lamp

1882 Rockefeller's Standard Oil Company becomes nation's first trust • Edison opens first electric generating station in New York

1883 Railroads introduce standard time zones

1886 Samuel Gompers founds American Federation of Labor (AFL) • Labor protest erupts in violence in Haymarket Riot in Chicago • Railroads adopt standard gauge

1892 Workers strike at Homestead steel plant in Pennsylvania

1893 Economic depression begins

1901 J. P. Morgan announces formation of U.S. Steel Corporation, nation's first billion-dollar company

floor, and by dint of their labor, created the new industrial society.

Recommended Reading

Samuel P. Hays, *The Response to Industrialism: 1885–1914* (1957), is an influential interpretation of the period. A detailed survey is Edward C. Kirkland, *Industry Comes of Age: Business, Labor, and Public Policy, 1860–1897* (1967). Douglass C. North, *Growth and Welfare in the American Past: A New Economic History* (1966), is stimulating. Other valu-

able overviews include Stuart Bruchey's brief *Growth of the Modern Economy* (1975), W. Elliot Brownlee's more detailed *Dynamics of Ascent: A History of the American Economy* (1974), and Robert Higgs, *The Transformation of the American Economy, 1865–1914* (1971). David Montgomery, *The Fall of the House of Labor: The Workplace, the State, and American Labor Activism, 1865–1925* (1987), is an outstanding recent study of labor in the period.

For stimulating interpretations of the period, see Robert H. Wiebe, *The Search for Order, 1877–1920* (1968), and John A. Garraty, *The New Commonwealth, 1877–1890* (1968). Thomas C. Cochran and William Miller, *The Age of Enterprise* (1942), Alfred D. Chandler, *The Visible Hand: The Managerial Revolution in American Business* (1978), Oliver Zunz, *Making America Corporate, 1870–1920* (1990), and JoAnne Yates, *Control Through Communication: The Rise of System in American Management* (1989), are perceptive. The railroad empire is treated in G. R. Taylor and I. D. Neu, *The American Railroad Network, 1861–1890* (1956); John R. Stilgoe, *Metropolitan Corridor: Railroads and the American Scene* (1983); John Hoyt Williams, *A Great & Shining Road: The Epic Story of the Transcontinental Railroad* (1988); and John F. Stover, *American Railroads* (1961). On the steel industry, see Peter Temin, *Iron and Steel in Nineteenth-Century America* (1964), and Joseph F. Wall, *Andrew Carnegie* (1970).

For the techniques of selling, see Daniel J. Boorstin, *The Americans: The Democratic Experience* (1973). Two superb books by Sam B. Warner, Jr., *Streetcar Suburbs: The Process of Growth in Boston, 1870–1900* (1962) and *The Urban Wilderness: A History of the American City* (1973), examine technology and city development. The wage earner is examined in Herbert G. Gutman, *Work, Culture, and Society in Industrializing America* (1976); Walter Licht, *Working for the Railroad* (1983); James H. Ducker, *Men of the Steel Rails* (1983); John T. Cumbler, *Working Class Community in Industrial America* (1979); Tamara K. Hareven, *Family Time and Industrial Time: The Relationship Between the Family and Work in a New England Industrial Community* (1982); James R. Barrett, *Work and Community in the Jungle: Chicago's Packinghouse Workers, 1894–1922* (1987); Richard Jules Oestreicher, *Solidarity and Fragmentation: Working People and Class Consciousness in Detroit, 1875–1900* (1986); and Gerald David Jaynes, *Branches Without Roots: Genesis of the Black Working Class in the American South, 1862–1882* (1986). Two books by Stephen Thernstrom: *Poverty and Progress: Social Mobility in the Nineteenth-Century City* (1964) and *The Other Bostonians: Poverty and Progress in the American*

Metropolis, 1880–1970 (1973), and Howard M. Gitelman, *Workingmen of Waltham: Mobility in American Urban Industrial Development 1850–1890* (1974), examine mobility. Philip S. Foner, *Women and the American Labor Movement*, 2 vols. (1979); Lois W. Banner, *Women in Modern America: A Brief History* (1974); Susan E. Kennedy, *If All We Did Was to Weep at Home* (1979); Barbara Wertheimer, *We Were There: The Story of Working Women in America* (1977); Alice Kessler-Harris, *Out to Work: A History of Wage-Earning Women in the United States* (1982); and Milton Cantor and Bruce Laurie, eds., *Class, Sex, and the Woman Worker* (1977) are excellent on the subject of women in the workplace.

Additional Bibliography

Alfred D. Chandler, *The Railroads: The Nation's First Big Business* (1965), stresses the railroads' importance; Robert Fogel, *Railroads in American Economic Growth* (1964), questions it. See also James A. Ward, *Railroads and the Character of America, 1820–1887* (1986). Julius Grodinsky, *Jay Gould* (1957); Maury Klein, *Union Pacific* (1987); the same author's *The Life and Legend of Jay Gould* (1986); and Albro Martin, *James J. Hill and the Opening of the Northwest* (1976) are superb.

For steel, see Carnegie's *Autobiography of Andrew Carnegie* (1920); Harold C. Livesay, *Andrew Carnegie and the Rise of Big Business* (1975); John Ingham, *The Iron Barons: A Social Analysis of an American Urban Elite, 1874–1965* (1978); and Ingham, *Making Iron and Steel: Independent Mills in Pittsburgh, 1820–1920* (1991). For the oil industry, see Edward N. Akin, *Flagler* (1988); Carl Solberg, *Oil Power* (1976); and Allan Nevins, *Study in Power: John D. Rockefeller*, 2 vols. (1953). Anthony F. C. Wallace, *St. Clair* (1987), and Edward J. Davies II, *The Anthracite Aristocracy* (1985), are useful on coal. Edwin Gabler, *The American Telegrapher: A Social History, 1860–1900* (1988), is perceptive on that industry. For the era's most prominent financier, see Vincent P. Carosso, *The Morgans* (1987).

On technological developments, Lewis Mumford, *Technics and Civilization* (1934); Wolfgang Schivelbusch, *Disenchanted Night* (1988); Harold L. Platt, *The Electric City: Energy in the Growth of the Chicago Area, 1880–1930* (1991); Carolyn Marvin, *When Old Technologies Were New* (1988); Charles Singer et al., eds., *History of Technology*, vol. 5, *The Late Nineteenth Century* (1958); and W. P. Strassmann, *Risk and Technological Innovation* (1959) are the places to begin. Useful studies include Andre Millard, *Edison and the Business of Innovation* (1990); John Brooks, *Telephone: The First Hundred Years* (1976); Robert W. Garnet, *The Telephone Enterprise* (1985); and Robert V. Bruce, *Alexander Graham Bell and the Conquest of Solitude* (1973).

Frank Presbrey, *The History and Development of Advertising* (1929); and James D. Norris, *Advertising and the Transformation of American Society, 1865–1920* (1990), are the best general accounts; others include J. P. Wood, *The Story of Advertising* (1958); John K. Winkler, *Five and Ten: The Fabulous Life of F. W. Woolworth* (1940); and Boris Emmet and John E. Jeuck, *Catalogues and Counters: A History of Sears, Roebuck and Company* (1950). Also, David M. Potter, *People of Plenty: Economic Abundance and the American Character* (1954).

On labor, see David Brody, *Steelworkers in America: The Nonunion Era* (1960); Shelton Stromquist, *A Generation of Boomers: The Pattern of Railroad Labor Conflict in Nineteenth-Century America* (1987); S. J. Kleinberg, *The Shadow of the Mills: Working-Class Families in Pittsburgh, 1870–1907* (1989); Eric Arnesen, *Waterfront Workers of New Orleans: Race, Class and Politics, 1863–1923* (1991); Cathy L. McHugh, *Mill Family: The Labor System in the Southern Cotton Textile Industry, 1880–1915* (1988); Cindy Sondik Aron, *Ladies and Gentlemen of the Civil Service: Middle-Class Workers in Victorian America* (1987); Joanne J. Meyerowitz, *Women Adrift: Independent Wage Earners in Chicago, 1880–1930* (1988); Susan Levine, *Labor's True Women: Carpet Weavers, Industrialization, and Labor Reform in the Gilded Age* (1984); Mary H. Blewett, *Men, Women, and Work: Class, Gender, and Protest in the New England Shoe Industry, 1780–1910* (1988); William H. Harris, *The Harder We Run: Black Workers Since the Civil War* (1982); Leon Fink, *Workingmen's Discovery: The Knights of Labor and American Politics* (1983); Harold C. Livesay, *Samuel Gompers and Organized Labor in America* (1978); and S. B. Kaufman, *Samuel Gompers and the Origins of the American Federation of Labor* (1973).

John Laslett, *Labor and the Left: A Study of Socialist and Radical Influences in the American Labor Movement, 1881–1924* (1970), is illuminating. Alexander Keyssar, *Out of Work* (1986), examines the issue of unemployment. Paul Avrich, *The Haymarket Tragedy* (1984), is a detailed account of that event. See also Bruce C. Nelson, *Beyond the Martyrs: A Social History of Chicago's Anarchists* (1988); and Eric L. Hirsch, *Urban Revolt: Ethnic Politics in the Nineteenth-Century Chicago Labor Movement* (1990). Terence V. Powderly, *Thirty Years of Labor* (1889), and Samuel Gompers, *Seventy Years of Life and Labor*, 2 vols. (1925), give the flavor of their thought.

Toward an Urban Society, 1877–1900

One day around 1900, Harriet Vittum, a settlement house worker in Chicago, went to the aid of a young Polish girl who lived in a nearby slum. The girl, fifteen, had discovered she was pregnant and had taken poison. An ambulance was on the way, and Vittum, told of the poisoning, rushed over to do what she could.

Quickly she raced up the three flights of stairs to the floor where the girl and her family lived. Pushing open the door, she found the father, several male boarders, and two or three small boys asleep on the kitchen floor. In the next room the mother was on the floor among several women boarders and one or two small children. Glancing out the window, Vittum saw the wall of another building so close she could reach out and touch it.

There was a third room; in it lay the fifteen-year-old girl, along with two more small children who were asleep. Looking at the scene, Vittum thought about the girl's life in the crowded tenement. Should she try to save her, Vittum asked herself. Should she even try to bring the girl back "to the misery and hopelessness of the life she was living in that awful place"?

The young girl died, and in later years, Vittum often told her story; it was easy to see why. The girl's life in the slum, the children on the floor, the need to take in boarders to make ends meet, the way mothers and fathers collapsed at the end of working days that began long before sunup—all reflected the experiences of millions of people living in the nation's cities.

People poured into cities in the last part of the nineteenth century, lured by glitter and excitement, by friends and relatives who were already there, and above all, by the greater opportunities for jobs and higher wages. Between 1860 and 1910 the rural population of the United States almost doubled; the number of people living in cities increased sevenfold.

Little of the increase came from natural growth, since urban families had high rates of infant mortality, a declining fertility rate, and a high death rate from injury and disease. Many of the newcomers came from rural America, and many more came from Europe, Latin America, and Asia. In one of the most significant migrations in American history, thousands of African

Americans began in the 1880s to move from the rural South to northern cities. By 1900, there were large black communities in New York, Washington, D.C., Baltimore, Chicago, and other cities. Yet to come was the even greater black migration during World War I.

Two major forces reshaped American society between 1870 and 1920. One was *industrialization* (see Chapter 18); the other was *urbanization,* the headlong rush of people from their rural roots into the modern urban environment. By 1920, the city had become the center of American economic, social, and cultural life.

THE LURE OF THE CITY

William Allen White, later a famous journalist, reflected the country's fascination with the city. He left the small Kansas town of his boyhood in 1891 to go to what he called the "gilded metropolis" of Kansas City. White was twenty-three years old, and the experience affected him for the rest of his life. He rode the cable cars and used the brand-new telephone—"always with the consciousness that I was tampering with a miracle." He purchased a secondhand dress suit, listened to the music of a sixty-piece orchestra, attended plays, and heard James Whitcomb Riley recite poetry. "Life was certainly one round of joy in Kansas City," White said.

Between 1870 and 1900, the city—like the factory—became a symbol of a new America. Drawn from farms, small towns, and foreign lands, newcomers swelled the population of older cities and created new ones almost overnight. At the beginning of the Civil War, only one-sixth of the American people lived in cities of eight thousand people or more. By 1900, one-third did; by 1920, one-half. "We live in the age of great cities," wrote the Reverend Samuel Lane Loomis in 1887. "Each successive year finds a stronger and more irresistible current sweeping in towards the centers of life."

The current brought growth of an explosive sort. Thousands of years of history had produced only a handful of cities with more than a half million in population. In 1900, the United States had six such cities, including three—New York, Chicago, and Philadelphia—with a population over one million.

Skyscrapers changed the look of many cities, including Chicago. This panoramic view, showing Dearborn, Van Buren, and Jackson streets, is from an 1897 lithograph.

Skyscrapers and Suburbs

Like so many things in these years, the city was transformed by a revolution in technology. Beginning in the 1880s, the age of steel and glass produced the skyscraper; the streetcar produced the suburbs and new residential patterns.

On the eve of the change, American cities were a crowded jumble of small buildings. Church steeples stood out on the skyline, clearly visible above the roofs of factories and office buildings. Buildings were usually made of masonry, and since the massive walls had to support their own weight, they could be no taller than a dozen or so stories. Steel frames and girders ended that limitation and allowed buildings to soar higher and higher. "Curtain walls," which concealed the steel framework, were no longer load bearing; they were pierced by many windows that let in fresh air and light. Completed in 1885, the Home Insurance Building in Chicago was the country's first metal-frame structure.

To a group of talented Chicago architects, the new trends served as a springboard for innovative forms. The leaders of the movement were John Root and Louis H. Sullivan, both of whom were attracted by the chance to rebuild Chicago after the great fire of 1871. Noting that the fire had fed on fancy exterior ornamentation, Root developed a plain stripped-down style, bold in mass and form—the keynotes of modern architecture.

He had another important insight, too. In an age of business, Root thought, the office tower, more than a church or a government building, symbolized the society, and he designed office buildings that carried out, as he said, "the ideas of modern business life: simplicity, stability, breadth, dignity."

Sullivan had studied at the Massachusetts Institute of Technology and in Paris before settling in Chicago. In 1886, at the age of thirty, he began work on the Chicago Auditorium, one of the last great masonry buildings. "Then came the flash of imagination which saw the single thing," he later said. "The trick was turned; and there swiftly came into being something new under the sun." Sullivan's skyscrapers, that "flash of imagination," changed the urban skyline.

In the Wainwright Building in St. Louis (1890), the Schiller Building (1892) and the Carson, Pirie, and Scott department store (1899) in Chicago, and the Prudential Building in Buffalo (1895), Sullivan developed the new forms. Architects must discard "books, rules, precedents," he announced; responding to the new, they should design for a building's function. "Form follows function," Sullivan believed, and he passed the idea on to a talented disciple, Frank Lloyd Wright. The modern city should stretch to the sky. A skyscraper "must be every inch a proud and soaring thing, rising in sheer exaltation . . . from bottom to top."

Electric elevators, first used in 1871, carried passengers upward in the new skyscrapers. During the same years streetcars, another innovation, carried the people outward to expanded boundaries that transformed urban life.

Cities were no longer largely "walking cities," confined to a radius of 2 or 3 miles, the distance an individual might walk. Streetcar systems extended the radius and changed the urban map. Cable lines, electric surface lines, and elevated rapid transit brought shoppers and workers into central business districts and sped them home again. Offering the modest five-cent fare with a free transfer, these mass transit systems fostered commuting; widely separated business and residential districts sprang up. The middle class moved farther and farther out to the leafy greenness of the suburbs.

As the middle class moved out of the cities, the immigrants and working class poured in. They took over the older brownstones, row houses, and workers' cottages, turning them, under the sheer weight of numbers, into the slums of the central city. In the cities of the past, classes and occupations had been thrown together; without streetcars and subways there was no other choice. The streetcar city, sprawling and specialized, became a more fragmented and stratified society with middle-class residential rings surrounding a business and working-class core.

Tenements and Privies

In the shadow of the skyscrapers, grimy rows of tenements filled the central city. Exploring them in words and photographs, Jacob Riis described *How the Other Half Lives* (1890).

Be a little careful, please! The hall is dark and you might stumble. . . . Here where the hall turns and dives into utter darkness is . . . a flight of stairs. You can feel your way, if you cannot see it. Close? Yes! What would you have? All the fresh air that enters these stairs comes from the hall-door that is forever slamming. . . . Here is a door. Listen! That short, hacking cough, that tiny, helpless wail—what do they mean? . . . The child is dying of measles. With half a chance it might have lived; but it had none. That dark bedroom killed it.

Tenement houses on small city lots crowded people into cramped apartments. In the late 1870s, architect James E. Ware won a competition for tenement design with the "dumbbell tenement." Rising seven or eight stories in height, the dumbbell tenement packed about 30 four-room apartments on a lot only 25 by 100 feet. Between four and sixteen families lived on a floor; two toilets in the hall of each floor served their needs. Narrowed at the middle, the tenement resembled a giant dumbbell in shape. The indented middle created an air shaft between adjoining buildings that provided a little light and ventilation. In case of fire, it also carried flames from one story to the next, making these buildings notorious firetraps. In 1890, nearly half the dwellings in New York City were tenements.

That year more than 1.4 million people lived on Manhattan Island, one of whose wards had a population density of 334,000 people per square mile. Many people lived in alleys and basements so dark they could not be photographed until flashlight photography was invented in 1887. Exploring the city, William Dean Howells, the prominent author, inhaled "the stenches of the neglected street . . . [and] the yet fouler and dreadfuller poverty smell which breathes from the open doorways."

Howells smelled more than poverty. In the 1870s and 1880s, cities stank. One problem was horse manure, hundreds of tons of it a day in every city. Another was the privy, "a single one of which," said a leading authority on public health, "may render life in a whole neighborhood almost unendurable in the summer."

Baltimore smelled "like a billion polecats," recalled H. L. Mencken, who grew up there. Said one New York City resident, "The stench is something terrible." Another wrote that "the stink is enough to knock you down." In 1880, the Chicago *Times* said that a "solid stink" pervaded the city. "No other word expresses it so well as stink. A stench means something finite. Stink reaches the infinite and becomes sublime in the magnitude of odiousness." In 1892, one neighborhood of Chicago, covering one-third of a square mile, had only three bathtubs.

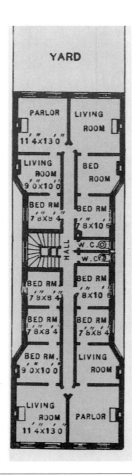

This 1879 dumbbell floor plan was meant to provide four apartments to a floor. However, a whole family might live in each room. Crowded, unsanitary conditions contributed to the spread of tuberculosis, the chief cause of death in the United States until 1909.

Cities dumped their wastes into the nearest body of water, then drew drinking water from the same site. Many built modern purified waterworks but could not keep pace with spiraling growth. In 1900, fewer than one in ten city dwellers drank filtered water. Factories, the pride of the era, polluted the urban air. At night, Pittsburgh looked and sounded like "Hell with the lid off," according to contemporary observers. Smoke poured from seventy-three glass factories, forty-one iron and steel mills, and twenty-nine oil refineries. The choking air helped prevent lung diseases and malaria—or so the city's advertising claimed.

Crime was another growing problem. The nation's homicide rate nearly tripled in the 1880s, much of the increase coming in the cities. Slum youths formed street gangs with names like the Hayes Valley gang in San Francisco or the Baxter Street Dudes, the Daybreak Boys, and the Alley Gang in New York. After remaining constant for many decades, the suicide rate rose steadily between 1870 and 1900, according to a recent study of Philadelphia. Alcoholism also rose, especially among men, though recent studies have shown that for working-class men, the urban saloon was as much a gathering spot as it was a place to drink. Nonetheless, a 1905 survey of Chicago counted as many saloons as grocery stores, meat markets, and dry goods stores combined.

Strangers in a New Land

While some of the new city dwellers came from farms and small towns, many more came from abroad. Most came from Europe, where unemployment, food shortages, and increasing threats of war sent millions fleeing across the Atlantic to make a fresh start. Often they knew someone already in the United States, a friend or relative who had written them about prospects for jobs and freer lives in a new land. Italians first came in large numbers to escape an 1887 cholera epidemic in southern Italy; tens of thousands of Jews sought refuge from the anti-Semitic massacres that swept Russia and Czarist-ruled Poland after 1880.

All told, the immigration figures were staggering. Between 1877 and 1890, more than 6.3 million people entered the United States. In one year alone, 1882, almost 789,000 people came. By 1890, about 15 percent of the population, 9 million people, were foreign born.

Most newcomers were job seekers. Nearly two-thirds were males, and the majority were between the ages of fifteen and forty. Most were unskilled laborers. Most settled on the eastern seaboard. In 1901, the Industrial Relocation Office was established to relieve overcrowding in the eastern cities; opening Galveston, Texas, as a port of entry, it attracted many Russian Jews to Texas and the Southwest. But most immigrants preferred the shorter, more familiar journey to New York, and they tended to crowd into north-

Impoverished immigrant families often lived in tiny, windowless rooms in crowded tenement districts liǐke New York City's lower East Side.

ern and eastern cities, settling in areas where others of their nationality or religion had settled.

They were often dazzled by what they saw. They stared at electric lights, indoor plumbing, soda fountains, streetcars, plush train seats for all classes, ice cream, lemons, and bananas. Relatives whisked them off to buy new "American" clothes and showed them the teeming markets, department stores, and Woolworth's new five and dime stores. "It seemed quite advanced compared with our home in Khelm," said a Polish girl. "There was a sense of safety and hope that we had never felt in Poland."

Cities had increasingly large foreign-born populations. In 1900, four-fifths of Chicago's population was foreign born or of foreign-born parentage, two-thirds of Boston's, and one-half of Philadelphia's. New York City, where most immigrants arrived and many stayed, had more Italians than lived in Naples, more Germans than lived in Hamburg, and twice as many Irish as lived in Dublin. Four out of five New York City residents in 1890 were of foreign birth or foreign parentage.

Beginning in the 1880s, the sources of immigration shifted dramatically away from northern and western Europe, the chief source of immigra-tion for over two centuries. More and more immigrants came from southern and eastern Europe: Italy, Greece, Austro-Hungary, Poland, and Russia. Between 1880 and 1910, approximately 8.4 million people came from these lands. The "new" immigrants tended to be Catholics or Jews rather than Protestants. Like their predecessors, most were unskilled rather than skilled, and they often spoke "strange" languages. Most were poor and uneducated; sticking together in close-knit communities, they clung to their native customs, languages, and religions.

More than any previous group, the so-called new immigrants troubled the mainstream society. Could they be assimilated? Did they share "American" values? Such questions preoccupied groups like the American Protective Association, a midwestern anti-Catholic organization that expanded in the 1890s and worked to limit or end immigration. Sneering epithets became part of the national vocabulary: "wop" and "dago" for Italians, "bohunk" for Bohemians, Hungarians, and other Slavs, "grease-ball" for Greeks, and "kike" for Jews. "You don't call . . . an Italian a white man?" a congressman asked a railroad construction boss in 1890. "No, sir," the boss replied. "An Italian is a Dago."

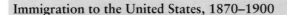

Immigration to the United States, 1870–1900

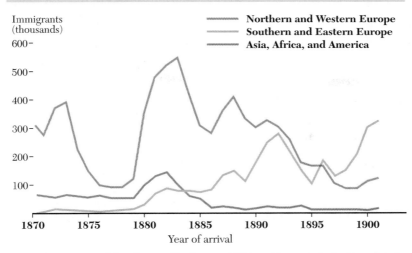

Immigrants (thousands)

— Northern and Western Europe
— Southern and Eastern Europe
— Asia, Africa, and America

Year of arrival

Note: For purposes of classification, *Northern and Western Europe* includes Great Britain, Ireland, Scandinavia, the Netherlands, Belgium, Luxembourg, Switzerland, France, and Germany. *Southern and Eastern Europe* includes Poland, Austria-Hungary, Russia, and the Baltic States, Romania, Bulgaria, European Turkey, Italy, Spain, Portugal, and Greece. *Asia, Africa, and America* includes Asian Turkey, China, Japan, India, Canada, the Caribbean, Latin America, and all of Africa.

Source: U.S. Bureau of the Census. Historical Statistics of the United States, Colonial Times to 1970, *Bicentennial Edition, Washington, D.C., 1975.*

Anti-Catholicism and anti-Semitism flared up again, as they had in the 1850s (recall Chapter 14). Edward A. Ross, a prominent sociologist, publicly decried "the lower class of Jews of Eastern Europe [who] reach here [as] moral cripples, their souls warped and dwarfed." In 1889, the head of the Fresh Air Fund, a program that sent New York City children on vacations to the suburbs, noted that "no one asked for Italian children." The Immigration Restriction League, founded in 1894, demanded a literacy test for immigrants from southern and eastern Europe. Congress passed such a law in 1896, but President Cleveland vetoed it.

Immigrants and the City

Industrial capitalism—the world of factories and foremen and grimy machines—tested the immigrants and placed an enormous strain on their families. Many immigrants came from peasant societies where life proceeded according to outdoor routine and age-old tradition. In their new city homes, they found both new freedoms and new confinements, a different language, and a novel set of customs and expectations. Historians have only recently begun to discover the remarkable ways in which they learned to adjust.

Like native-born families, most immigrant families were nuclear in structure—they consisted of two parents and their children. Though variations occurred from group to group, men and women occupied roles similar to those in native families; men were wage earners, women, housekeepers and mothers. Margaret Byington, who studied steelworkers' homes in Homestead in the early 1900s, learned that the father played a relatively small role in child rearing or managing the family's finances. "His part of the problem is to earn and hers to spend." In Chicago, social reformer Jane Addams discovered that immigrant women made it "a standard of domestic virtue that a man must not touch his pay envelope, but bring it home unopened to his wife."

Although patterns varied among ethnic groups, and between economic classes within ethnic groups, immigrants tended to marry within the group more than did the native born. In one New

In a Puck *cartoon entitled "Looking Backward," the shadows of their immigrant origins loom over the rich and powerful who wanted to deny the "new" immigrants from central and southern Europe admission to America. The caption on the cartoon reads, "They would close to the newcomer the bridge that carried them and their fathers over."*

York community, only 2 percent of French Canadian and 7 percent of Irish working men married outside their ethnic group in 1880, compared to almost 40 percent of native-born working men. Immigrants also tended to marry at a later age than natives, and they tended to have more children, a fact that worried nativists opposed to immigration.

Immigrants shaped the city as much as it shaped them. Most of them tried to retain their traditional culture for themselves and their children while at the same time adapting to life in their new country. To do this, they spoke their native language, practiced their religious faith, read their own newspapers, and established special parochial or other schools. They observed traditional holidays and formed a myriad of social organizations to maintain ties between members of the group.

Immigrant associations—there were many of them in every city—offered fellowship in a strange land. They helped newcomers find jobs and homes; they provided important services such as unemployment and health insurance. In a Massachusetts textile town, the Irish Benevolent

Society said, "We visit our sick, and bury our dead." Some groups were no larger than a neighborhood; others spread nationwide. In 1914, the Deutsch-Amerikanischer Nationalbund, the largest of the associations, had more than two million members in dozens of cities and towns. Many women belonged to and participated in the work of the immigrant associations; in addition, there were groups exclusively for women such as the Polish Women's Alliance, the Jednota Ceskyck Dam (Society of Czech Women), and the National Council of Jewish Women.

The Polish National Alliance (PNA), a typical immigrant association, was founded in 1880. Like other organizations, it helped new immigrants on their arrival, offered insurance plans, established libraries and museums, sponsored youth programs, fielded baseball teams, and organized trips back to Poland. Each year the PNA published a sought-after calendar filled with Polish holidays, information, and proverbs. Extolling Poles' contributions to their new country, it erected monuments to distinguished Americans of Polish descent.

Every major city had dozens of foreign lan-

The fiftieth anniversary issue of the Illinois Staats Zeitung, *the Chicago-area German-language newspaper with the largest circulation. There were more than twenty German-language newspapers distributed in Chicago in the 1890s.*

guage newspapers, with circulations large and small. The first newspaper published in the Lithuanian language appeared in the United States, not in Lithuania. Eagerly read, the papers not only carried news of events in the homeland, but also reported on local ethnic leaders, told readers how to vote and become citizens, and gave practical tips on adjusting to life in the United States. The Swedes, Poles, Czechs, and Germans established ethnic theaters that performed national plays and music. The most famous of these, the Yiddish (Jewish) Theater, started in the 1880s in New York City and lasted more than fifty years.

The church and the school were the most important institutions in every immigrant community. East European Jews established synagogues and religious schools wherever they settled; they taught the Hebrew language and raised their children in a heritage they did not want to leave behind. Among such groups as the Irish and the Poles, the Roman Catholic church provided spiritual and educational guidance. In the parish schools, Polish priests and nuns taught Polish American children about Polish as well as American culture in the Polish language.

Church, school, and fraternal societies shaped the way in which immigrants adjusted to life in America. By preserving language, religion, and heritage, they also shaped the country itself.

The House That Tweed Built

Closely connected with explosive urban growth was the emergence of the powerful city political machine. As cities grew, lines of responsibility in city governments became hopelessly confused, increasing the opportunity for corruption and greed. Burgeoning populations required streets, buildings, and public services; immigrants needed even more services. In this situation, political party machines played an important role.

The machines traded services for votes. Loosely knit, they were headed by a strong, influential leader—the "boss"—who tied together a network of ward and precinct captains, each of whom looked after his local constituents. In New York, "Honest" John Kelly, Richard Croker, and Charles F. Murphy led Tammany Hall, the famous Democratic party organization that dominated city politics from the 1850s to the 1930s. Other bosses included "Hinky Dink" Kenna and "Bathhouse John" Coughlin in Chicago, James McManes in Philadelphia, and Christopher A. Buckley—the notorious "Blind Boss," who used an exceptional memory for voices to make up for failing eyesight—in San Francisco.

William M. Tweed, head of the famed Tweed Ring in New York, provided the model for them all. Nearly 6 feet tall, weighing almost 300 pounds, Tweed rose through the ranks of Tammany Hall. He served in turn as city alderman, member of Congress, and New York State assemblyman. A man of culture and warmth, he moved easily between the rough back alleys of New York and the parlors and clubs of the city's elite. Behind the scenes he headed a ring that plundered New York for tens of millions of dollars.

The New York County Courthouse—"The House That Tweed Built"—was his masterpiece.

Nestled in City Hall Park in downtown Manhattan, the three-story structure was designed to cost $250,000, but the bills ran a bit higher. Furniture, carpets, and window shades alone came to more than $5.5 million. Three tables and forty chairs cost the city $180,000. Tweed's own quarry supplied the marble; the plumber got almost $1.5 million for fixtures. Andrew Garvey, the "Prince of Plasterers," charged $500,000 for plaster work, and then $1 million to repair the same work. His total bill came to $2,870,464.06. (The *New York Times* suggested that the six cents be donated to charity.) In the end the building cost over $13 million—and in 1872, when Tweed fell, it was still not finished.

The role of the political bosses can be overemphasized. Power structures in the turn-of-the-century city were complex, involving a host of people and institutions. Banks, realtors, insurance companies, architects, and engineers, among others, played roles in governing the city. Viewed in retrospect, many city governments were remarkably successful. With populations that in some cases doubled every decade, city governments provided water and sewer lines, built parks and playgrounds, and paved streets. When it was over, Boston had the world's largest public library; New York City had the Brooklyn Bridge and Central Park, two of the finest architectural achievements of any era. By the 1890s, New York also had 660 miles of water lines, 464 miles of sewers, and 1,800 miles of paved streets, far more than comparable cities in Europe.

Bosses, moreover, differed from city to city. Buckley stayed in power in San Francisco by keeping city tax rates low. "Honest" John Kelly earned his nickname serving as a watchdog over the New York City treasury. Tweed was one of the early backers of the Brooklyn Bridge. Some bosses were plainly corrupt; others believed in *honest graft*, a term Tammany's George Washington Plunkitt coined to describe "legitimate" profits made from advance knowledge of city projects.

Why did voters keep the bosses in power? The answers are complex, but involve skillful political organization and the fact that immigrants and others made up the bosses' constituency. Most immigrants had little experience with democratic government and proved easy prey for well-oiled machines. For the most part, however, the bosses stayed in power because they paid attention to the needs of the least privileged city voters. They offered valued services in an era when neither government nor business lent a hand.

If an immigrant, tired and bewildered after the long crossing, came looking for a job, bosses like Tweed, Plunkitt, or Buckley found him one in city offices or local businesses. If a family's breadwinner died or was injured, the bosses donated food and clothing and saw to it that the family made it through the crisis. If the winter was particularly cold, they provided free coal to heat tenement apartments. They ran picnics for slum children on hot summer days and contributed to hospitals, orphanages, and dozens of worthy neighborhood causes.

Most bosses became wealthy; they were not Robin Hoods who took from the rich to give to the poor. They took for themselves as well. Reformers occasionally ousted them. Tweed fell from power in 1872, "Blind Boss" Buckley in 1891, Croker in 1894. But the reformers rarely stayed in power long. Drawn mainly from the middle and upper classes, they had little understanding of the needs of the poor. Before long, they returned to private concerns, and the bosses, who had known that they would all along, cheerily took power again.

"What tells in holdin' your grip on your district," the engaging Plunkitt once said, "is to go right down among the poor families and help them in the different ways they need help. . . . It's philanthropy, but it's politics, too—mighty good politics. . . . The poor are the most grateful people in the world."

LIFE IN AMERICA, 1877

The rise of cities and industry between 1877 and the 1890s affected all aspects of American life. Mores changed; family ties loosened. Factories turned out consumer goods, and the newly invented cash register rang up record sales. Public and private educational systems burgeoned; illiteracy declined; life expectancy increased. While many people worked harder and harder just to survive, others found they had a greater amount of leisure time. The roles of women and children changed in a number of ways, and the family took on functions it had not had before. Thanks to advancing technology, news flashed quickly across the oceans, and for the first time in history, people read of the day's events in distant lands when they opened their daily newspapers.

"We are in a period," President Rutherford B. Hayes said in 1878, "when old questions are settled, and the new ones are not yet brought forward." Old questions—questions of racial, social and economic justice, and of federal-state relations—were not settled, but people wanted new directions. Political issues lost the sharp focus of the Civil War and Reconstruction. For men and women of middle age in 1877, the issues of the Union and slavery had been the overriding public concerns throughout their adult lives. Now, with the end of Reconstruction, it seemed time for new concerns.

In 1877, the country had 47 million people. In 1900, it had grown to nearly 76 million. Nine-tenths of the population were white; just under one-tenth was black. There were 66,000 Indians, 108,000 Chinese, and 148 Japanese. The bulk of the white population, most of whom were Protestant, came from the so-called Anglo-Saxon countries of northern Europe. WASPs—white Anglo-Saxon Protestants—were the dominant members of American society.

Though the rush to the cities was about to begin, most people of 1877 still lived on farms or in small towns. Their lives revolved around the farm, the church, and the general store. In 1880, nearly 75 percent of the population lived in communities of fewer than 2,500 people. In 1900, in the midst of city growth, 60 percent still did. The average family in 1880 had three children, dramatically fewer than at the beginning of the century, and life expectancy was about forty-three years. By 1900, it had risen to forty-seven years, the result of improved health care. For blacks and other minorities, who often lived in unsanitary rural areas, life expectancy was substantially lower: thirty-three years in 1900.

In small towns, houses were usually made of wooden shingles or clapboard, set back from unpaved streets. Life was quiet. Many homes had a front porch for summertime sitting. In the backyard there were numerous outbuildings, including one—at the end of a well-worn path—with a distinctive half moon carved in the door. There was a vegetable garden and often a chicken coop or

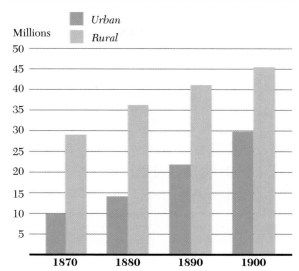

Urban and Rural Population, 1870–1900 (in millions)

Source: *U.S. Bureau of the Census. Historical Statistics of the United States, Colonial Times to 1970,* Bicentennial Edition, *Washington, D.C., 1975.*

cowshed; families—even in the cities—needed backyard produce to supplement their diets.

Meals tended to be heavy and so did people. Even breakfast had several courses and could include steak, eggs, fish, potatoes, toast, and coffee. Food prices were low. Families ate fresh homegrown produce in the summer, and "put up" their fruits and vegetables for the long winters. Toward the end of the century, eating habits changed. New packaged breakfast cereals became popular; fresh fruit and vegetables came in on fast trains from Florida and California, and commercially canned food processing became safer and cheaper. The newfangled icebox, cooled by blocks of ice, kept food fresher and added new treats such as ice cream.

Medical science was in the midst of a major revolution. Louis Pasteur's recent discovery that germs cause infection and disease created the new science of microbiology and led the way to the development of vaccines and other preventive measures. But tuberculosis, typhoid, diphtheria, and pneumonia—all now curable—were still the leading causes of death. Infant mortality declined between 1877 and 1900, but the decline was

1890 Retail Prices: Food

BACON 1 lb.	15.5¢
BUTTER 1 lb.	25.5¢
EGGS 1 dozen	20.8¢
FLOUR 5 lbs.	14.5¢
MILK ½ gal. delivered	13.6¢
PORK CHOPS 1 lb.	10.7¢
POTATOES 10 lbs.	16¢
ROUND STEAK 1 lb.	12.3¢
SUGAR 5 lbs.	34.5¢

Source: U.S. Bureau of the Census, Historical Statistics of the United States, Colonial Times to 1970, *Bicentennial Edition, Washington, D.C., 1975.*

gradual; a great drop did not come until after 1920.

There were few hospitals and no hospital insurance. Most patients stayed at home, although medical practice, especially surgery, expanded rapidly. Once brutal and dangerous, surgery in these years became relatively safe and painless. Anesthetics—ether and chloroform—eliminated pain, and antiseptic practices helped prevent postoperative infections. Antiseptic practices at childbirth also cut down on puerperal fever, an infection that for centuries had killed many women and newborn infants. The new science of psychology began to explore the mind, hitherto uncharted. William James, a leading American psychologist and philosopher, laid the foundations of modern behavioral psychology, which stressed the importance of the environment on human development.

Manners and Mores

The code of Victorian morality, its name derived from the British queen who reigned throughout the period, set the tone for the era. The code prescribed strict standards of dress, manners, and sexual behavior. It was both obeyed and disobeyed, and it reflected the tensions of a generation that was undergoing a change in moral standards.

In 1877, children were to be seen and not heard. They spoke when spoken to, listened rather than chattered—or at least that was the rule. Older boys and girls were often chaperoned, although they could always find moments alone. They played post office and spin the bottle; they puffed cigarettes behind the barn. William Allen White, later a famous journalist, recalled the high jinks of his boyhood. He and his friends smeared their naked bodies with mud and leaped out in full view of passengers on passing trains. Counterbalancing such youthful exuberance was strong pride in virtue and self-control. "Thank heaven I am absolutely pure," Theodore Roosevelt, the future president, wrote in 1880 after proposing to Alice Lee. "I can tell Alice everything I have ever done."

Gentlemen of the middle class dressed in heavy black suits, derby hats, and white shirts with paper collars. Women wore tight corsets, long dark dresses, and black shoes reaching well above the ankles. As with so many things, styles changed dramatically toward the end of the century, spurred in part by new sporting fads such as golf, tennis, and bicycling, which required looser clothing. By the 1890s, a middle-class woman wore a tailored suit or a dark skirt and a blouse, called a "shirtwaist," modeled after men's shirts. Her skirts still draped about the ankles, but more and more she removed or loosened the corset, the dread device that squeezed skin and internal organs into fashionable 18-inch waistlines.

Religious and patriotic values were strong. One of the centers of community life, the church often set the tenor for family and social relationships. In the 1880s, eight out of ten church members were Protestants; most of the rest were Roman Catholics. Evangelists like Dwight L. Moody, a former Chicago shoe salesman, and Ira B. Sankey, an organist and singer, conducted mass revival meetings across the country. Enormously successful, Moody preached to millions and sparked a spiritual awakening on American college campuses.

With slavery abolished, reformers turned their attention to new moral and political issues. One group, known as the Mugwumps, worked to end corruption in politics. Drawn mostly from the educated and upper class, they included individuals like Thomas Nast, the famous political cartoonist, George William Curtis, editor of

Harper's Weekly, and E. L. Godkin, editor of the influential *Nation*. Other zealous reformers campaigned for prohibition of the sale of intoxicating liquors, hoping to end the social evils that stemmed from drunkenness. In 1874, women who advocated total abstinence from alcoholic beverages formed the Women's Christian Temperance Union (WCTU). Their leader, Frances E. Willard, served as president of the group from 1879 until her death in 1898. By then, the WCTU had 10,000 branches and 500,000 members.

In New York City, Anthony Comstock formed the Society for the Suppression of Vice, which supervised public morality. At his request, Congress passed the Comstock Law (1873) prohibiting the mailing or transporting of "obscene, lewd or lascivious" articles. The law was not successful; within a few years Comstock reported finding 64,094 "articles for immoral use," 700 pounds of "lead moulds for making obscene matter," 202,679 obscene photographs, and 26 "obscene pictures, framed on walls of saloons."

Leisure and Entertainment

In the 1870s, people tended to rise early. On getting up, they washed from the pitcher and bowl in the bedroom, first breaking the layer of ice if it was winter. After dressing and eating, they went off to work and school. Without large refrigerators, housewives marketed almost daily. In the evening, families gathered in the "second parlor" or living room, where the children did their lessons, played games, sang around the piano, and listened to that day's verse from the Bible.

Popular games included cards, dominoes, backgammon, chess, and checkers. Many homes had a packet of "author cards" that required knowledge of books, authors, and noted quotations. The latest fad was the stereopticon or "magic lantern," which brought three-dimensional life to art, history, and nature. Like "author cards" and other games, it was instructional as well as entertaining.

The newest outdoor game was croquet, so popular that candles were mounted on the wickets to allow play at night. Croquet was the first outdoor game designed for play by both sexes, and it frequently served as a setting for courtship. Early manuals advised girls how to assume attractive poses while hitting the ball. A popular

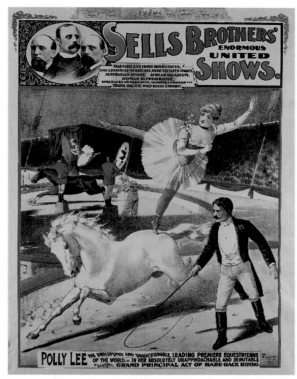

The Sells Brothers promised a world of entertainment to the patrons of their circus, which featured—according to this poster—an Australian aviary, an African aquarium, a Roman hippodrome, and an exhibit of trans-Pacific wild beasts. The principal act of the three-ring circus, however, promised to be the spectacular bareback riding of equestrienne Polly Lee.

song of the period told of a pair seated side by side as the

mallets and balls unheeded lay . . .
and I thought to myself, is that Croquet?

Sentimental ballads such as "Silver Threads Among the Gold" (1873) remained the most popular musical form, but the insistent syncopated rhythms of ragtime were being heard, reflecting the influence of the new urban culture. By the time the strains of Scott Joplin's "Maple Leaf Rag" (1899) popularized ragtime, critics complained that "a wave of vulgar, filthy and suggestive music has inundated the land." Classical music flourished. The New England Conservatory (1867), the Cincinnati College of Music (1878), and the Metropolitan Opera (1883) were new sources of civic pride; New York, Boston, and Chicago launched first-rate symphony orchestras between 1878 and 1891.

In the hamlets and small towns of America, traveling circuses were enormously popular. Hamlin Garland, an author who grew up in small Iowa villages, recalled how the circus came "trailing clouds of glorified dust and filling our minds with the color of romance. . . . It brought to our ears the latest band pieces and taught us the popular songs. It furnished us with jokes. It relieved our dullness. It gave us something to talk about." Larger circuses, run by entrepreneurs like P. T. Barnum and James A. Bailey, played the cities, but every town attracted its own smaller version.

Fairs, horse races, balloon ascensions, bicycle tournaments, and football and baseball contests attracted avid fans. The years between 1870 and 1900 saw the rise of organized spectator sports, a trend reflecting both the rise of the city and the new uses of leisure. Baseball's first professional team, the Cincinnati Red Stockings, appeared in 1869, and baseball soon became the preeminent national sport. Fans sang songs about it ("Take Me Out to the Ballgame"), wrote poems about it ("Casey at the Bat"), and made up riddles about it ("What has eighteen feet and catches flies?"). Modern rules were adopted. Umpires were designated to call balls and strikes; catchers wore masks and chest protectors and moved closer to the plate instead of staying back to catch the ball on the bounce. Fielders had to catch the ball on the fly rather than on one bounce in their caps. By 1890, professional baseball teams were drawing crowds of sixty thousand daily. In 1901, the American League was organized, and two years later the Boston Red Sox beat the Pittsburgh Pirates in the first modern World Series.

In 1869, Princeton and Rutgers played the first intercollegiate football game. Soon, other schools picked up the sport, and by the early 1890s, crowds of fifty thousand or more attended the most popular contests. Basketball, invented in 1891, gained a large following. Boxing, a popular topic of conversation in saloons and schoolyards, was outlawed in most states. For a time, championship prizefights were held in secret, with news of the result spread rapidly by word of mouth. Matches were long and bloody, fought with bare knuckles until the invention in the 1880s of the 5-ounce boxing glove. John L. Sullivan, the Boston Strong Boy and the era's most popular champion, won the heavyweight title in 1889 in a brutal seventy-five-round victory over the stubborn Jake Kilrain.

As gas and electric lights brightened the night, and streetcars crisscrossed city streets, leisure habits changed. Delighted with the new technology, people took advantage of an increasing variety of things to do. They stayed home less often. New York City's first electric sign—"Manhattan Beach Swept by Ocean Breezes"—appeared in 1881, and people went out at night, filling the streets on their way to the theater, vaudeville shows, dance halls, or just out for an evening stroll.

Family Life

Under the impact of industrialization and urbanization, family relationships were changing. On the farm, parents and children worked more or less together, and the family was a producing unit. In factories and offices, family members rarely worked together. In working-class families, mothers, fathers, and children separated at dawn and returned, ready for sleep, at dark. Morris Rosenfeld, a clothing presser lamenting that he was unable to spend more time with his son, wrote a poem entitled "My Boy."

> *I have a little boy at home,*
> *A pretty little son;*
> *I think sometimes the world is mine*
> *In him, my only one. . . .*
>
> *'Ere dawn my labor drives me forth;*
> *Tis night when I am free;*
> *A stranger am I to my child;*
> *And stranger my child to me.*

Working-class families of the late nineteenth century, like the family of the young Polish girl that Harriet Vittum saw, often lived in complex household units—taking in relatives and boarders to pay the rent. As many as one-third of all households contained people who were not members of the immediate family. Although driven apart by the daily routine, family ties among the working class tended to remain strong, cemented by the need to join forces in order to survive in the industrial economy.

The middle-class wife and children, however, became increasingly isolated from the world of work. Turning inward, the middle-class family became more self-contained. Older children spent

As early as 1866, Currier & Ives described baseball as the "American National Game." Although we can recognize some similarities between the game portrayed here and the modern game of baseball, there are also some notable differences. For example, the players depicted in the lithograph do not wear any protective gear; the batter wears no batting helmet, the catcher has no face mask or chest protector, and none of the players appears to wear baseball gloves.

more time in adolescence, and periods of formal schooling were lengthier. Families took in fewer apprentices and boarders. By the end of the century, most middle-class offspring continued to live with their parents into their late teens and twenties, a larger proportion than today.

Fewer middle-class wives participated directly in their husbands' work. As a result, they and their children occupied what contemporaries called a "separate sphere of domesticity," set apart from the masculine sphere of income-producing work. The family became a "walled garden," a place to retreat from the crass materialism of the outside world. Middle-class fathers began to move their families out of the city to the suburbs, commuting to work on the new streetcars, and leaving wives and children at home and school.

The middle-class family had once functioned in part to transmit a craft or skill, arrange marriages, and offer care for dependent kin. Now, as these functions declined, the family took on new emotional and ideological responsibilities. In a society that worried about the weakening hold of

other institutions, it became more and more important as a means of social control. It also placed new burdens on wives.

"In the old days," said a woman in 1907, "a married woman was supposed to be a frump and a bore and a physical wreck. Now you are supposed to keep up intellectually, to look young and well and be fresh and bright and entertaining." Magazines like the *Ladies' Home Journal*, which started in 1889, glorified motherhood and the home, but its articles and ads featured women as homebound, child-oriented consumers. While society's leaders spoke fondly of the value of homemaking, the status of housewives declined under the factory system, which emphasized money rewards and devalued household labor.

Underlying all these changes was one of the modern world's most important trends, a major decline in fertility rates that lasted from 1800 to 1939. Though blacks, immigrants, and rural dwellers continued to have more children than white native city dwellers, the trend affected all classes and races; among white women, the birthrate fell from 7 in 1800 to just over 4 in

W. Louis Sonntag, Jr., The Bowery at Night, *1895. Steam, steel, and electricity transformed cities. In this watercolor of New York City's Bowery in 1895, electric streetcars travel up and down the street while the elevated railroad rumbles overhead. Bright incandescent lamps light up the night.*

1880 to about 3 in 1900. People everywhere tended to marry later and have fewer children.

Since contraceptive devices were not yet widely used, the decline reflected abstinence and a conscious decision to postpone or limit families. In some cases, women decided to devote greater attention to a smaller number of children, in other cases to pursue their own careers. There was a marked increase in the number of young unmarried women working for wages or attending school; an increase in the number of women delaying marriage or not marrying at all; and a gradual decline in rates of illegitimacy and premarital pregnancy.

In large part, the decline in fertility stemmed from people's responses to the social and economic forces around them, the rise of cities and industry. In a host of individual decisions, they decided to have fewer children, and the result reshaped some of the fundamental attitudes and institutions of American society.

Changing Views: A Growing Assertiveness Among Women

In and out of the family, there was growing recognition of the self-sufficient working woman, employed in factory, telephone exchange, and business office, who was entering the work force in increasing numbers. In 1880, there were 2.6 million women gainfully employed; in 1890, 4 million. In 1882, the Census Bureau took the first census of working women; most were single and worked out of necessity rather than choice.

This "new woman" was seen by many as a corruption of the ideal vision of the American woman, in which man worshipped "a diviner self than his own," innocent, helpless, and good. Women were to be better than the world around them. They were brought up, said Ida Tarbell, a leading political reformer, "as if wrongdoing were impossible to them."

Views changed, albeit slowly. One important change occurred in the legal codes pertaining to

Female operators, called "Hello Girls," were hired to work telephone switchboards after it was discovered that male operators tended to argue too much with subscribers.

women, particularly in the common law doctrine of *femme couverte.* Under that doctrine, wives were chattel of their husbands; they could not legally control their own earnings, property, or children unless they had drawn up a specific contract before marriage. By 1890, many states had substantially revised the doctrine to allow wives control of their earnings and inherited property. In cases of divorce, the new laws also recognized women's rights to custody or joint custody of their children. Although divorce was still far from being socially acceptable, divorce rates more than doubled during the last third of the century. By 1905, one in twelve marriages was ending in divorce.

In the 1870s and 1880s, a growing number of women were asserting their own humanness. They fought for the vote, lobbied for equal pay, and sought self-fulfillment. The new interest in psychology and medicine strengthened their causes. Charlotte Perkins Gilman, author of *Women and Economics* (1898), joined other women in questioning the ideal of womanly "innocence," which, she argued, actually meant ignorance. In medical and popular literature, menstruation, sexual intercourse, and childbirth were becoming viewed as natural functions instead of taboo topics.

Edward Bliss Foote's *Plain Home Talk of Love, Marriage, and Parentage,* a best-seller that went through many editions between the 1880s and 1900s, challenged Victorian notions that sexual intercourse was unhealthy and intended solely to produce children. In *Plain Facts for Old and Young* (1881), Dr. John H. Kellogg urged parents to recognize the early awakening of sexual feelings in their children. Still, such matters were avoided in many American homes. Rheta Childe Dorr, a journalist, remembered that when a girl reached the age of fourteen, new rules were introduced, "and when you asked for an explanation you met only embarrassed silence."

Women espoused causes with new fervor. Susan B. Anthony, a veteran of many reform campaigns, tried to vote in the 1872 presidential election and was fined $100, which she refused to pay. In 1890, she helped form the National American Woman Suffrage Association to work for the enfranchisement of women (see Chapter 22). On New York's lower East Side, the Ladies Anti-Beef Trust Association, which formed to protest increases in the price of meat, established a boycott of butcher shops. When their demands were ignored, the women invaded the shops, poured kerosene on the meat, and set fire to it. "We don't riot," Rebecca Ablowitz told the judge. "But if all we did was to weep at home, nobody would notice it; so we have to do something to help ourselves."

Educating the Masses

Continuing a trend that stretched back one hundred years, childhood was becoming an even more distinct time of life. There was still only a vague concept of adolescence—the special nature of the teenage years—but the role of children was changing. Less and less were children perceived as "little adults," valued for the additional financial gain they might bring into the family. Now children were to grow and learn and be nurtured rather than rushed into adulthood.

As a result, schooling became more important and American educators came closer than ever before to universal education. By 1900, thirty-one states and territories (out of fifty-one) had enact-

The Shaping of Jim Crow
Plessy v. Ferguson

In a nation of laws, the interpretation of law can profoundly change people's lives. *Plessy* v. *Ferguson* (1896), one of the most important cases to reach the Supreme Court, changed the lives of millions of black and white Americans. Interpreting law in a way that lasted for more than a half century, it permitted the segregation of blacks in public facilities throughout the land.

Given the significance of the case, we know surprisingly little about Homer A. Plessy, the man behind it. He was young—we know that—and apparently he worked as a carpenter in Louisiana. According to the court records, he was "seven-eighths Caucasian," which perhaps was the reason he was chosen to test the constitutionality of a Louisiana law requiring railroad companies to segregate whites and blacks on trains in the state. It seemed a good law to test. Louisiana's own constitution forbade such discrimination; so did the federal Civil Rights Act of 1875, which guaranteed blacks "full and equal enjoyment" of public conveyances.

Whatever the details of his life, Plessy lived in a post-Reconstruction South in which racism was widespread but segregation was not. Where segregation did exist, it usually was not enacted into law. During the 1870s and 1880s, blacks and whites often ate together and

worked together. "I can ride in first-class cars on the railroads and in the streets. . .," a delighted black visitor wrote home from South Carolina in 1885. "I can stop in and drink a glass of soda and be more politely waited upon than in some parts of New England."

That situation changed near the end of the century. The

courts often reflect trends in the society, and whites in both North and South in the 1890s had little enthusiasm for civil rights. In addition, economic depression heightened racial tensions, and the spread of colonial imperialism in Africa and Asia led to talk about "inferior" people, both at home and abroad. Beginning in the 1870s, the

The Louisiana segregation law tested by Homer Plessy in 1892 was representative of a growing number of such laws passed in the 1880s and 1890s. Segregation legislation was neither new nor confined to the South. This 1856 engraving documents the expulsion of an African American from a railway car in Philadelphia.

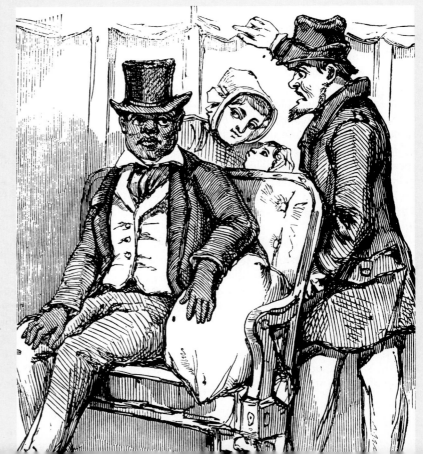

Supreme Court handed down a series of decisions that overturned much Reconstruction legislation, limited federal protection for blacks, and encouraged racial segregation.

In the *Slaughterhouse Cases* of 1873, the Supreme Court narrowed the scope of the Fourteenth Amendment protecting blacks; a decade later, in the *Civil Rights Cases* (1883), it said that Congress could not punish private individuals for acts of racial discrimination. Emboldened by such decisions, southern states passed many segregation laws, including laws requiring railroad companies to separate white and black riders. In 1890, Louisiana passed "An Act to promote the comfort of passengers" that made railroads in the state provide "equal but separate" cars.

Blacks in Louisiana protested; railroad officials, not liking the cost of the extra cars, were sympathetic. And so on June 7, 1892, to test the law, Homer A. Plessy boarded an East Louisiana Railway train in New Orleans for the 30-mile trip to Covington. He took a seat in a car reserved for whites, refused to move when a conductor asked him to, and was arrested by a

detective who was standing by for the occasion. John H. Ferguson, a local judge, ruled against Plessy's argument that the law violated his rights, and Plessy appealed to the Supreme Court.

Four years later, in a 7 to 1 decision, the Court decided against Plessy. Upholding the doctrine of "separate but equal," it held that the Louisiana law did not violate Plessy's rights. Plessy could still travel on the railroad, and there was no evidence that "the enforced separation of the two races stamps the colored race with a badge of inferiority." Justice John Marshall Harlan, the sole dissenter, scoffed at the reasoning. The Louisiana law, he said, was clearly prejudicial, designed to keep blacks from railroad cars occupied by whites. If upheld, what stood in the way of laws calling for segregation of all kinds? Laws might make blacks and whites (or for that matter, Protestants and Catholics) walk on opposite sides of the street or paint their houses different colors.

After *Plessy,* Jim Crow laws spread swiftly through the South. More and more public conveyances, schools, and restaurants were segregated. Signs say-

ing "Whites Only" or "Colored" appeared on entrances and exits, rest rooms and water fountains, waiting rooms, and even elevators. In 1905, Georgia passed the first law requiring separate public parks. In 1909, Mobile, Alabama, enacted a curfew requiring blacks to be off the streets by 10 P.M. In 1915, South Carolina forbade blacks and whites to work in the same rooms in textile factories. The Oklahoma legislature required separate telephone booths; New Orleans segregated white and black prostitutes. Atlanta had separate Bibles for black witnesses in the city courts.

Plessy v. *Ferguson* set a pattern of court-supported southern segregation that lasted sixty years. Generations of blacks and whites, children and adults alike, were deeply affected—sometimes traumatized—by it. The practice became a major focus of grievance in the growing movement for civil rights during the 1930s and 1940s. At last, in the 1954 case of *Brown* v. *Board of Education of Topeka* (see Chapter 29), the Supreme Court overturned *Plessy.* Ruling that segregated schools are inherently unequal, the Court's stand toppled segregation of many kinds.

Plessy v. Ferguson served to reinforce policies of racial segregation and eventually resulted in the institution of "separate but equal" facilities, which, like the ones shown below, were often not equal at all.

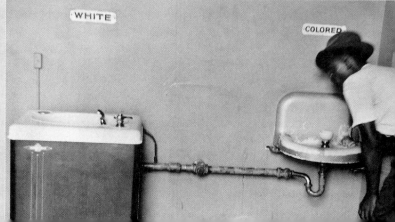

ed laws making school attendance compulsory, though most only required attendance until the age of fourteen. In 1870, there were only 160 public high schools; in 1900, there were 6,000. In the same years, public school budgets rose from $63 million to $253 million; illiteracy declined from 20 percent to just over 10 percent of the population. Still, even as late as 1900, the average adult had only five years of schooling.

Educators saw the school as the primary means to train people for life and work in an industrializing society. Hence teachers focused on basic skills—reading and mathematics—and on values—obedience and attentiveness to the clock. Most schools had a highly structured curriculum, built around discipline and routine. In 1892, Joseph Rice, a pediatrician, toured twelve hundred classrooms in thirty-six cities. In a typical classroom, he reported, the atmosphere was "damp and chilly," the teacher strict. "The unkindly spirit of the teacher is strikingly apparent; the pupils being completely subjugated to her will, are silent and motionless." One teacher asked her pupils, "How can you learn anything with your knees and toes out of order?"

Many children dropped out of school early, and not just to earn money. Helen Todd, a factory inspector in Chicago, found a group of young girls working in a hot stuffy attic. When she asked why they were not in school, Tillie Isakowsky, who was fourteen, said, "School! School is de fiercest t'ing youse kin come up against. Factories ain't no cinch, but schools is worst." A few blocks away, Todd stumbled on a thirteen-year-old boy hiding in a basement. He cried when she said he would have to go to school, blurting that "they hits ye if yer don't learn, and they hits ye if ye whisper, and they hits ye if ye have string in yer pocket, and they hits ye if yer seat squeaks, and they hits ye if ye don't stan' up in time, and they hits ye if yer late, and they hits ye if ye forget the page." Curious, Todd asked 500 children whether they would go to school or work in a factory if their families did not need the money—412 preferred the factory.

School began early; boys attended all day, but girls often stayed home after lunch, since it was thought they needed less in the way of learning. On the teacher's command, students stood and recited from *Webster's Spellers* and *McGuffey's Readers,* the period's most popular textbooks.

The work of William Holmes McGuffey, a professor of languages at Miami University in Ohio, *McGuffey's Readers* had been in use since 1836 (see Chapter 11); 100 million copies were sold in the last half of the nineteenth century. Nearly every child read them; they taught not only reading but also ethics, values, and religion. In the *Readers,* boys grew up to be heroes, girls to be mothers, and hard work always meant success:

> *Shall birds, and bees, and ants, be wise,*
> *   While I my moments waste?*
> *O let me with the morning rise,*
> *   And to my duty haste.*

The South lagged far behind in education. The average family size there was about twice as large as in the North, and a greater proportion of the population lived in isolated rural areas. State and local authorities mandated fewer weeks in the average school year, and many southern states refused to adopt compulsory education laws. Most important, Southerners insisted on maintaining separate school systems to segregate the races. Supported by the U.S. Supreme Court decision of 1896 in *Plessy* v. *Ferguson* (see "The Shaping of Jim Crow," pp. 584–585) segregated schooling added a devastating financial burden to education in the South.

North Carolina and Alabama mandated segregated schools in 1876, South Carolina and Louisiana in 1877, Mississippi in 1878, and Virginia in 1882. A series of Supreme Court decisions in the 1880s and 1890s upheld the concept of segregation. In the *Civil Rights Cases* (1883), the Court ruled that the Fourteenth Amendment barred state governments from discriminating on account of race but did not prevent private individuals or organizations from doing so. *Plessy* v. *Ferguson* (1896) established the doctrine of "separate but equal" and upheld a Louisiana law requiring different railroad cars for whites and blacks. The Court applied the doctrine directly to schools in *Cumming* v. *County Board of Education* (1899), which approved the creation of separate schools for whites, even if there were no comparable schools for blacks.

Southern school laws often implied that the schools would be "separate but equal," but they rarely were. Black schools were usually dilapidated, the teachers in them were paid considerably less than white teachers. In 1890, only 35 percent of black children attended school in the South; 55 percent of white children did. That year nearly two-thirds of the country's black population was illiterate.

Educational techniques changed after the 1870s. Educators paid more attention to early elementary education, a trend that placed young children in school and helped the growing number of mothers who worked outside the home. The kindergarten movement, started in St. Louis in 1873, spread across the country. In kindergartens, four-to six-year-olds learned by playing, not by keeping their knees and toes in order. For older children, social reformers advocated "practical" courses in manual training and homemaking. "We are impatient with the schools which lay all stress on reading and writing," Jane Addams said, for "they fail to give the child any clew to the life about him."

For the first time, education became a field of university study. European theorists like Johann Friedrich Herbart, a German educator, argued that learning occurred best in an atmosphere of freedom and confidence between teachers and pupils. Teacher training became increasingly professional. Only ten normal schools, or teacher-training institutions, existed in the United States before the Civil War. By 1900, there were 345, and one in every five elementary teachers had graduated from a professional school.

Higher Education

Nearly 150 new colleges and universities opened in the twenty years between 1880 and 1900. The Morrill Land Grant Act of 1862 gave large grants of land to the states for the establishment of colleges to teach "agriculture and the mechanic arts." The act fostered 69 "land-grant" institutions, including the great state universities of Wisconsin, California, Minnesota, and Illinois.

Private philanthropy, born of the large fortunes of the industrial age, also spurred growth in higher education. Leland Stanford gave $24 million to endow Stanford University on his California ranch, and John D. Rockefeller, founder of the Standard Oil Company, gave $34 million to found the University of Chicago. Other industrialists established Cornell (1865), Vanderbilt (1873), and Tulane (1884).

As colleges expanded, their function changed, and their curriculum broadened. No longer did they exist primarily to train young men for the ministry. They moved away from the classical curriculum of rhetoric, mathematics, Latin, and Greek toward "reality and practicality," as President David Starr Jordan of Stanford University said. The Massachusetts Institute of Technology (MIT), founded in 1861, focused on science and engineering.

Influenced by the new German universities, which emphasized specialized research, Johns Hopkins University in Baltimore opened the nation's first separate graduate school in 1876. Under President Daniel Coit Gilman, Johns Hopkins stressed the seminar and laboratory as teaching tools, bringing together student and teacher in close association. By 1900, more than nine thousand Americans had studied in Germany, and some of them returned home to become presidents of institutions such as Harvard, Yale, Columbia, the University of Chicago, and Johns Hopkins.

One of them, Charles W. Eliot, who became president of Harvard in 1869 at the age of thirty-five, moved to end, as an admirer said, the "old fogyism" that marked the institution. Revising the curriculum, Eliot set up the elective system in which students chose their own courses rather than following a rigidly prescribed curriculum. Lectures and discussions replaced rote recitation, and courses in the natural and social sciences, fine arts, and modern languages multiplied. In the 1890s, Eliot's Harvard moved to the forefront of educational innovation.

Women still had to fight for educational opportunities. Some formed study clubs, an important movement that spread rapidly between 1870 and 1900. Groups like the Decatur (Illinois) Art Class, the Boston History Class, and the Barnesville (Georgia) Shakespeare Club aimed "to enlarge the mental horizon as well as the knowledge of our members." Club members read Virgil and Chaucer, studied history and architecture, and discussed women's rights. As the Monday Club of Mount Vernon, Ohio, put it,

In ancient days when Monday came
We used our clothes to rub,
And set them boiling on the stove,
And stir them with a club.

But, Oh, our Monday Club today
Is quite a different stick;
For we've abandoned household toils
And learned a better trick.

. . . .

And with it, just as Moses did,
We drive the waves apart,
And enter on the promised land
Of learning and of art.

Clubs sprang up almost everywhere there were women: in Caribou, Maine; Tyler, Texas; and Leadville, Colorado—as well as San Francisco, New York, and Boston. Although they were usually small, study clubs sparked a greater interest among women and their daughters in education and contributed to a rapid rise in the number of women entering college in the early 1900s.

Before the Civil War, only three private colleges admitted women to study with men. After the war, educational opportunities increased for women. A number of women's colleges opened, including Vassar (1865), Wellesley (1875), Smith (1875), Bryn Mawr (1885), Barnard (1889), and Radcliffe (1893). The land-grant colleges of the Midwest, open to women from the outset, spurred a nationwide trend toward coeducation, although some physicians, like Harvard Medical School's Dr. Edward H. Clarke in his popular *Sex in Education* (1873), continued to argue that the strain of learning made women sterile. By 1900, women made up about 40 percent of college students, and four out of five colleges admitted them.

Fewer opportunities existed for blacks and other minorities. Mrs. Jane Stanford encouraged the Chinese who had worked on her husband's Central Pacific Railroad to apply to Stanford University, but her policy was unusual. Most colleges did not accept minorities, and only a few applied. W. E. B. Du Bois, the brilliant African American sociologist and civil rights leader, attended Harvard in the late 1880s but found the society of Harvard Yard closed against him. Disdained and disdainful, he "asked no fellowship of my fellow students." Chosen as one of the commencement speakers, Du Bois picked as his topic, "Jefferson Davis," treating it, said an onlooker, with "an almost contemptuous fairness."

Black students turned to black colleges such as the Hampton Normal and Industrial Institute in Virginia and the Tuskegee Institute in Alabama.

These colleges were often supported by whites who favored manual training for blacks. Booker T. Washington, an ex-slave, put into practice his educational ideas at Tuskegee, which opened in 1881. Washington began Tuskegee with limited funds, 4 run-down buildings, and only 30 students; by 1900 it was a model industrial and agricultural school. Spread over 46 buildings, it offered instruction in 30 trades to 1,400 students.

Washington stressed patience, manual training, and hard work. "The wisest among my race understand," he said in a widely acclaimed speech at the Atlanta Exposition in 1895, "that the agitation of questions of social equality is the extremest folly." Blacks should focus on economic gains; they should go to school, learn skills, and work their way up the ladder. "No race," he said at Atlanta, "can prosper till it learns that there is as much dignity in tilling a field as in writing a poem. It is at the bottom of life we must begin, and not at the top." Southern whites should help out because they would then have "the most patient, faithful, law-abiding, and unresentful people that the world has seen."

Outlined most forcefully in Washington's speech in Atlanta, the philosophy became known as the Atlanta Compromise, and many whites and some blacks welcomed it. Acknowledging white domination, it called for slow progress through self-improvement, not through lawsuits or agitation. Rather than fighting for equal rights, blacks should acquire property, and show they were worthy of their rights. But Washington did believe in black equality. Often secretive in his methods, he worked behind the scenes to organize black voters and lobby against harmful laws. In his own way, he bespoke a racial pride that contributed to the rise of black nationalism in the twentieth century.

Du Bois wanted a more aggressive strategy. Born in Massachusetts in 1868, the son of poor parents, he studied at Fisk University in Tennessee and the University of Berlin before he went to Harvard. Unable to find a teaching job in a white college, he took a low-paying research position at the University of Pennsylvania. He had no office but did not need one. Du Bois used the new discipline of sociology, which emphasized factual observation in the field, to study the condition of blacks.

Notebook in hand, he set out to examine crime in Philadelphia's black seventh ward. He inter-

viewed five thousand people, mapped and classified neighborhoods, and produced *The Philadelphia Negro* (1898), a book of nearly one thousand pages. The first study of the effect of urban life on blacks, it cited a wealth of statistics, all suggesting that crime in the ward stemmed not from inborn degeneracy but from the environment in which blacks lived. Change the environment, and people would change, too; education was a good way to go about it.

In *The Souls of Black Folk* (1903), Du Bois openly attacked Booker T. Washington and the philosophy of the Atlanta Compromise. He urged African Americans to aspire to professional careers, to fight for the restoration of their civil rights, and wherever possible, to get a college education. Calling for integrated schools with equal opportunity for all, Du Bois urged blacks to educate their "talented tenth," a highly trained intellectual elite, to lead them.

Du Bois was not alone in promoting careers in the professions. Throughout higher education there was increased emphasis on professional training, particularly in medicine, dentistry, and law. Enrollments swelled, even as standards of admission tightened. The number of medical schools in the country rose from 75 in 1870 to 160 in 1900, and the number of medical students—including more and more women—almost tripled. Schools of nursing grew from only 15 in 1880 to 432 in 1900. Doctors, lawyers, and others became part of a growing middle class that

shaped the concerns of the Progressive Era (see Chapter 22).

Although fewer than 5 percent of the college-age population attended college during the 1877–1890 period, the new trends had great impact. A generation of men and women encountered new ideas that changed their views of themselves and society. Courses never before offered, like Philosophy II at Harvard, "The Ethics of Social Reform," which students called "drainage, drunkenness, and divorce," heightened interest in social problems and the need for reform. Some graduating students burned with a desire to cure society's ills. "My life began . . . at Johns Hopkins University," Frederic C. Howe, an influential reformer, recalled. "I came alive, I felt a sense of responsibility to the world, I wanted to change things."

THE STIRRINGS OF REFORM

When Henry George, one of the era's leading reformers, asked a friend what could be done about the problem of political corruption in American cities, his friend replied: "Nothing! You and I can do nothing at all. . . . We can only wait for evolution. Perhaps in four or five thousand years evolution may have carried men beyond this state of things."

This stress on the slow pace of change reflected the doctrine of social Darwinism, based on the evolutionary theories of Charles Darwin and the

Booker T. Washington, who served as the first president of Tuskegee Institute, advocated work efficiency and practical skills as keys to advancement for African Americans. Students at Tuskegee studied academic subjects and received training in trades and professions.

writings of English social philosopher Herbert Spencer. In several influential books, Spencer applied Darwinian principles of natural selection to society, combining biology and sociology in a theory of "social selection" that explained human progress. Like animals, society evolved, slowly, by adapting to the environment. The "survival of the fittest"—a term Spencer, not Darwin, invented—preserved the strong and weeded out the weak. "If they are sufficiently complete to live, they *do* live, and it is well they should live. If they are not sufficiently complete to live, they die, and it is best they should die."

Social Darwinism had a number of influential followers in the United States, including William Graham Sumner, a professor of political and social science at Yale University. One of the country's best known academic figures, Sumner was forceful and eloquent. In writings such as *What Social Classes Owe to Each Other* (1883) and "The Absurd Effort to Make the World Over" (1894), he argued that government action on behalf of the poor or weak interfered in evolution and sapped the species. Reform tampered with the laws of nature. "It is the greatest folly of which a man can be capable to sit down with a slate and pencil to plan out a new social world," Sumner said.

The influence of social Darwinism on American thinking has been exaggerated, but in the powerful hands of Sumner and others it did influence some journalists, ministers, and policymakers. Between 1877 and the 1890s, however, it came under increasing attack. In fields like religion, economics, politics, literature, and law, thoughtful people raised questions about established conditions and suggested the need for reform.

Progress and Poverty

Read and reread, passed from hand to hand, Henry George's nationwide best-seller, *Progress and Poverty* (1879), led the way to a more critical appraisal of American society in the 1880s and beyond. The book jolted traditional thought. "It was responsible," one historian has said, "for starting along new lines of thinking an amazing number of the men and women" who became leaders of reform.

Born in 1839, the child of a poor Philadelphia family, George had little formal schooling. As a boy he went to sea, then worked as a prospector, printer, and journalist. Self-educated as an economist, he moved to San Francisco in the late 1850s and began to study "the fierce struggle of our civilized life." Disturbed by the depression of the 1870s and labor upheavals like the great railroad strikes of 1877, George saw modern society—rich, complex, with material goods hitherto unknown—as sadly flawed.

"The present century," he wrote, "has been marked by a prodigious increase in wealth-producing power. . . . It was natural to expect, and it was expected, that . . . real poverty [would become] a thing of the past." Instead, he argued,

it becomes no easier for the masses of our people to make a living. On the contrary, it is becoming harder. The wealthy class is becoming more wealthy; but the poorer class is becoming more dependent. The gulf between the employed and the employer is growing wider; social contrasts are becoming sharper; as liveried carriages appear, so do barefooted children.

George proposed a simple solution. Land, he thought, formed the basis of wealth, and a few people could grow wealthy just because the price of their land rose. Since the rise in price did not result from any effort on their part, it represented an "unearned increment," which, George argued, should be taxed for the good of society. A "single tax" on the increment, replacing all other taxes, would help equalize wealth and raise revenue to aid the poor. "Single-tax" clubs sprang up around the country, but George's solution, simplistic and unappealing, had much less impact than his analysis of the problem itself. He raised questions a generation of readers set out to answer.

New Currents in Social Thought

George's emphasis on deprivation in the environment excited a young country lawyer in Ashtabula, Ohio, Clarence Darrow. Unlike the social Darwinists, Darrow was sure that criminals were made and not born. They grew out of "the unjust condition of human life." In the mid-1880s, he left for Chicago and a forty-year career working to convince people that poverty lay at the root of crime. "There is no such thing as crime as the word is generally understood...," he told a group of startled prisoners in the Cook County jail. "If every man, woman and child in the world had a chance to make a decent, fair, honest living there would be no jails and no lawyers and no courts."

As Darrow rejected the implications of social Darwinism, in similar fashion did Richard T. Ely and a group of young economists poke holes in traditional economic thought. Fresh from graduate study in Germany, Ely in 1884 attacked classical economics for its dogmatism, simple faith in laissez-faire, and reliance on self-interest as a guide for human conduct. The "younger" economics, he said, must no longer be "a tool in the hands of the greedy and the avaricious for keeping down and oppressing the laboring classes. It

does not acknowledge laissez-faire as an excuse for doing nothing while people starve."

Accepting a post at Johns Hopkins University, Ely assigned graduate students to study labor conditions in Baltimore and other cities; one of them, John R. Commons, went on to publish a massive four-volume study, *History of Labour in the United States*. In 1885, Ely led a small band of rebels in founding the American Economic Association, which linked economics to social problems and urged government intervention in economic affairs. Social critic Thorstein Veblen saw economic laws as a mask for human greed. In *The Theory of the Leisure Class* (1899), Veblen analyzed the "predatory wealth" and "conspicuous consumption" of the business class.

Edward Bellamy dreamed of a cooperative society where poverty, greed, and crime no longer existed. A lawyer from western Massachusetts, Bellamy published *Looking Backward, 2000–1887*, in 1887 and became a national reform figure virtually overnight. The novel's protagonist, Julian West, falls asleep in 1887 and awakes in the year 2000. Wide-eyed, he finds himself in a socialist utopia; the government owns the means of production, and citizens share the material rewards. Cooperation, rather than competition, is the watchword.

The world of *Looking Backward* had limits; it was regimented, paternalistic, and filled with the gadgets and material concerns of Bellamy's own day. But it had a dramatic effect on many readers. The book sold at the rate of ten thousand copies a week, and its followers formed Nationalist Clubs to work for its objectives. By 1890, there were such clubs in twenty-seven states, all calling for the nationalization of public utilities and a wider distribution of wealth.

Walter Rauschenbusch, a young Baptist minister, read widely from the writings of Bellamy and George, along with the works of other social reformers. When he took his first church post in Hell's Kitchen, a blighted area of New York City, he soon discovered the weight of the slum environment. "One could hear," he said, "human virtue cracking and crushing all around." In the 1890s, Rauschenbusch became a professor at the Rochester Theological Seminary, and he began to expound on the responsibility of organized religion to advance social justice.

Some Protestant sects stressed individual salva-

Determined to outdo in size and splendor the mansions of his older brothers Cornelius and William, George Washington Vanderbilt acquired 125,000 acres of land in the Blue Ridge Mountains of North Carolina and commissioned architect Richard Morris Hunt to design and build a residence there. The result was Biltmore, the largest private home ever built in America. Designed in the style of a French château, Biltmore included among its 250 rooms a Baroque-style library housing some 20,000 volumes, and a 75 foot-high banquet hall furnished with medieval tapestries and hunting trophies. The grounds were designed by landscape architect Frederick Law Olmsted, who supervised the design of New York City's Central Park.

tion and a better life in the next world, not in this one. Poverty was evidence of sinfulness; the poor had only themselves to blame. "God has intended the great to be great and the little to be little," said Henry Ward Beecher, the country's best known pastor. Wealth and destitution, suburbs and slums—all formed part of God's plan.

Challenging those traditional doctrines, a number of churches in the 1880s began establishing missions in the city slums. William Dwight Porter Bliss, an Episcopal clergyman, founded the Church of the Carpenter in a working-class district of Boston. Lewis M. Pease worked in the grim Five Points area of New York; Alexander Irvine, a Jewish missionary, lived in a flophouse in the Bowery. Irvine walked his skid row neighborhood every afternoon to lend a hand to those in need. Living among the poor and homeless, the

urban missionaries grew impatient with religious doctrines that endorsed the status quo.

Many of the new trends were reflected in an emerging religious philosophy known as the "Social Gospel." As the name suggests, the Social Gospel focused on society as well as individuals, on improving living conditions as well as saving souls. Sermons in Social Gospel churches called on church members to fulfill their social obligations, and adults met before and after the regular service to discuss social and economic problems. Children were excused from sermons, organized into age groups, and encouraged to make the church a center for social as well as religious activity. Soon churches included dining halls, gymnasiums, and even theaters.

The most active Social Gospel leader was Washington Gladden, a Congregational minister and prolific writer. Linking Christianity to the social and economic environment, Gladden spent a lifetime working for "social salvation." He saw Christianity as a fellowship of love and the church as a social agency. In *Applied Christianity* (1886) and other writings, he denounced competition, urged an "industrial partnership" between employers and employees, and called for efforts to help the poor.

The Settlement Houses

A growing number of social reformers living in the urban slums shared Gladden's concern. Like Tweed and Plunkitt, they appreciated the dependency of the poor; unlike them, they wanted to eradicate the conditions that underlay it. To do so, they formed settlement houses in the slums and went to live in them to experience the problems they were trying to solve.

Youthful, idealistic, and mostly middle class, these social workers took as their model Toynbee Hall, founded in 1884 in the slums of East London to provide community services. Stanton Coit, a moody and poetic graduate of Amherst College, was the first American to borrow the settlement house idea; in 1886, he opened the Neighborhood Guild on the lower East Side of New York. The idea spread swiftly. By 1900, there were over 100 settlements in the country; five years later, there were over 200, and by 1910, more than 400.

The settlements included Jane Addams's famous Hull House in Chicago (1889); Robert A.

Woods's South End House in Boston (1892); and Lillian Wald's Henry Street Settlement in New York (1893). These reformers wanted to bridge the socioeconomic gap between rich and poor and to bring education, culture, and hope to the slums. They sought to create in the heart of the city the values and sense of community of small-town America. Of settlement workers, Wald said in *The House on Henry Street* (1915), "We were to live in a neighborhood . . . identify ourselves with it socially, and, in brief, contribute to it our citizenship."

Many of the settlement workers were women, some of them college graduates, who found that society had little use for their talents and energy. Jane Addams, a graduate of Rockford College in Illinois, opened Hull House on South Halsted Street in the heart of the Chicago slums. Twenty-nine years old, endowed with a forceful and winning personality, she intended "to share the lives of the poor" and humanize the industrial city. "American ideals," she said, "crumbled under the overpowering poverty of the overcrowded city."

Occupying an old run-down house, Hull House stressed education, offering classes in elementary English and Shakespeare, lectures on ethics and the history of art, and courses in cooking, sewing, and manual skills. A pragmatist, Addams believed in investigating a problem, then doing something to solve it. Noting the lack of medical care in the area, she established an infant welfare clinic and free medical dispensary. Because the tenements lacked bathtubs, she installed showers in the basement of the house and built a bathhouse for the neighbors. Because there was no local library, she opened a reading room. Gradually Hull House expanded to occupy a dozen buildings sprawling over more than a city block.

Like settlement workers in other cities, Addams and her colleagues studied the immigrants in nearby tenements. Laboriously they identified the background of every family in a one-third square mile area around Hull House. Finding people of eighteen different nationalities, they taught them American history and the English language, yet also encouraged them—through folk festivals and art—to preserve their own heritage.

In Boston, Robert Woods of South End House focused on the problem of school dropouts. He offered manual training, formed clubs to get young people off the streets, and established a cheap restaurant where the hungry could eat. Lillian Wald, the daughter of a middle-class family and herself a graduate nurse, concentrated on

Jane Addams founded Chicago's Hull House in 1889. The settlement house provided recreational and day-care facilities; offered extension classes in academic, vocational, and artistic subjects; and, above all, sought to bring hope to poverty-stricken slum dwellers.

providing health care for the poor. In 1898, the first Catholic-run settlement house opened in New York, and in 1900, Bronson House opened in Los Angeles to work in the Mexican American community.

Florence Kelley, an energetic graduate of Cornell University, taught night school one winter in Chicago. Watching children break under the burden of poverty, she devoted her life to the problem of child labor. Convinced of the need for political activism, she worked with Addams and others to push through the Illinois Factory Act of 1893, which mandated an eight-hour day for women in factories and for children under the age of fourteen.

The settlement house movement had its limits. Hull House, one of the best, attracted 2,000 visitors a week, still just a fraction of the 70,000 people who lived within six blocks. Immigrants sometimes resented these middle-class "strangers" who told them how to live. Dressed always in a brown suit and dark stockings, Harriet Vittum, the head resident of Chicago's Northwestern University Settlement (who told the story of the suicide victim at the beginning of this chapter), was known in the neighborhood as "the police lady in brown." She once stopped a dance because it was too wild, and then watched in disgust as the boys responded by "making vulgar sounds with their lips." Though her attempts to help were sincere, in private, Vittum called the people she was trying to help "ignorant foreigners, who live in an atmosphere of low morals . . . surrounded by anarchy and crime."

Although Addams tried to offer a few programs for blacks, most white reformers did not, and after 1900 a number of black reformers opened their own settlements. Like the whites, they offered employment information, medical care, and recreational facilities, along with concerts, lectures, and other educational events. White and black, the settlement workers made important contributions to urban life.

A Crisis in Social Welfare

The depression of 1893 (see Chapter 20) jarred the young settlement workers, many of whom had just begun their work. Addams and the Hull House workers helped form the Chicago Bureau of Charities to coordinate emergency relief.

Kelley, recently appointed the chief factory inspector of Illinois, worked even harder to end child labor, and in 1899, she moved to New York City to head the National Consumers League, which marshaled the buying power of women to encourage employers to provide better working conditions.

In cities and towns across the country traditional methods of helping the needy foundered in the crisis. Churches, Charity Organization Societies, and Community Chests did what they could, but their resources were limited, and they functioned on traditional lines. Many of them still tried to change rather than aid individual families, and people were often reluctant to call on them for help.

Gradually, a new class of professional social workers arose to fill the need. Unlike the church and charity volunteers, these social workers wanted not only to feed the poor but to study their condition and alleviate it. Revealingly they called themselves "case workers" and daily collected data on the income, housing, jobs, health, and habits of the poor. Prowling tenement districts, they gathered information about the number of rooms, number of occupants, ventilation, and sanitation, putting together a fund of useful data.

Studies of the poor popped up everywhere. Walter Wyckoff, a graduate of Princeton University, embarked in 1891 on what he called "an experiment in reality." For eighteen months he worked as an unskilled laborer in jobs from Connecticut to California. "I am vastly ignorant of the labor problems and am trying to learn by experience," he said as he set out. After working as a ditchdigger, farmhand, and logger, Wyckoff summarized his findings in *The Workers* (1897), a book immediately hailed as a major contribution to sociology.

So many others followed Wyckoff's example that sometimes it seemed the observers outnumbered those being observed. W. E. B. Du Bois did his pioneering study of urban blacks (see p. 589); Lillian Pettengill took a job as a domestic servant to see "the ups and downs of this particular dog-life from the dog's end of the chain." Others became street beggars, miners, lumberjacks, and factory laborers. Bessie and Marie Van Vorst's *The Woman Who Toils: Being the Experiences of Two Gentlewomen as Factory Girls* (1903) studied female workers, as did Helen Campbell's

Women Wage-Earners: Their Past, Their Present and Their Future (1893), which suggested that the conditions of factory employment prepared women mainly "for the hospital, the workhouse, and the prison."

William T. Stead, a prominent British editor, visited the Chicago World's Fair in 1893 and stayed to examine the city. He roamed the flophouses and tenements and dropped in at Hull House to drink hot chocolate and talk over conditions with Jane Addams. Later he wrote an influential book *If Christ Came to Chicago* (1894), and in a series of mass meetings during 1893, he called for a civic revival. In response, Chicagoans formed the Civic Federation, a group of forty leaders who aimed to make Chicago "the best governed, the healthiest city in this country." Setting up task forces for philanthropy, moral improvement, and legislation, the new group helped spawn the National Civic Federation (1900), a nationwide organization devoted to reform of urban life.

"The United States was born in the country and moved to the city," historian Richard Hofstadter said. Much of that movement occurred during the nineteenth century when the United States was the most rapidly urbanizing nation in the Western world. American cities bustled with energy; they absorbed millions of migrants who came from Europe and other distant and not-so-distant parts of the world. That migration, and the urban growth that accompanied it, reshaped American politics and culture.

By 1920, the census showed that, for the first time, most Americans lived in cities. By then, too, almost half the population was descended from people who arrived after the American Revolution. As European, African, and Asian cultures met in the American city, a culturally pluralistic society emerged. Dozens of nationalities produced a culture whose members considered themselves Polish Americans, African Americans, and Irish Americans. The melting pot sometimes softened distinctions between the various groups, but it only partially blended them into a unified society.

"Ah, Vera," said a character in Israel Zangwill's popular play, *The Melting Pot* (1908), "what is the glory of Rome and Jerusalem where all nations and races come to worship and look

CHRONOLOGY

1862 Morrill Land Grant gives land to states for establishment of colleges

1869 Rutgers and Princeton play in nation's first intercollegiate football game • Cincinnati Red Stockings, baseball's first professional team, organized

1873 Comstock Law bans obscene articles from U.S. mail • Nation's first kindergarten opens in Saint Louis, Missouri

1874 Women's Christian Temperance Union formed to crusade against evils of liquor

1876 Johns Hopkins University opens first separate graduate school

1879 Henry George analyzes problems of urbanizing America in *Progress and Poverty* • Salvation Army arrives in United States

1880 Polish National Alliance formed to help Polish immigrants adjust to life in America

1881 Booker T. Washington opens Tuskegee Institute in Alabama • Dr. John H. Kellogg advises parents to teach their children about sex in *Plain Facts for Old and Young*

1883 Metropolitan Opera opens in New York

1885 Home Insurance Building, country's first metal-frame structure, erected in Chicago • American Economic Association formed to advocate government intervention in economic affairs

1887 Edward Bellamy promotes idea of socialist utopia in *Looking Backward, 2000–1887*

1889 Jane Addams opens Hull House in Chicago

1890 National Woman Suffrage Association and the American Woman Suffrage Association, both formed in 1869, merge to consolidate the woman suffrage movement

1894 Immigration Restriction League formed to limit immigration from southern and eastern Europe

1896 Supreme Court decision in *Plessy* v. *Ferguson* establishes constitutionality of "separate but equal" facilities • John Dewey's Laboratory School for testing and practice of new educational theory opens at University of Chicago

back, compared with the glory of America, where all races and nations come to labour and look forward!" Critics scorned the play as "romantic claptrap," and indeed it was. But the metaphor of the melting pot clearly depicted a new national image. In the decades after the 1870s a jumble of ethnic and racial groups struggled for a place in society.

That society, it is clear, experienced a crisis between 1870 and 1900. Together, the growth of cities and the rise of industrial capitalism brought jarring change, the exploitation of labor, ethnic and racial tensions, poverty, and for a few, wealth beyond the imagination. At Homestead, Pullman, and a host of other places, there was open warfare between capital and labor. As reformers struggled to mediate the situation, they turned more and more to state and federal government to look after human welfare, a tendency the Supreme Court stoutly resisted. In the midst of the crisis, the depression of the 1890s struck, adding to the turmoil and straining American institutions. Tracing the changes wrought by waves of urbanization and industrialization, Henry George described the country as "the House of Have and the House of Want," almost in paraphrase of Lincoln's earlier metaphor of the "house divided." The question was, could this house, unlike that one, stand?

Recommended Reading

On urban America, see Sam Bass Warner, Jr.: *Streetcar Suburbs* (1962), and *The Urban Wilderness* (1972). Arthur M. Schlesinger, *The Rise of the City, 1878–1898* (1933), is a pioneering study; Constance M. Green, *The Rise of Urban America* (1965); Morris J. Vogel, *The Invention of the Modern Hospital: Boston, 1870–1930* (1980); William R. Taylor, *In Pursuit of Gotham: Culture and Commerce in New York* (1992); Eric H. Monkkonen, *America Becomes Urban: The Development of U.S. Cities & Towns, 1780–1980* (1988); David Schuyler, *The New Urban Landscape: The Redefinition of City Form in Nineteenth-Century America* (1986); and Howard P. Chudacoff, *The Evolution of American Urban Society*, rev. ed. (1981) are also valuable. See also two recent books by Jon C. Teaford, *The Unheralded Triumph: City Government in America, 1870–1900* (1984), and *City and Suburb: The Political Fragmentation of Metropolitan America, 1850–1970* (1979).

Kenneth T. Jackson, *Crabgrass Frontier: The Suburbanization of the United States* (1985); John R. Stilgoe, *Borderland: Origins of the American Suburb, 1820–1939* (1988); and Ann Durkin Keating, *Building*

Chicago: Suburban Developers & the Creation of a Divided Metropolis (1988), are recent treatments of the growth of the suburbs. Russel B. Nye, *The Unembarrassed Muse* (1970); and Lawrence W. Levine, *High Brow/Low Brow: The Emergence of Cultural Hierarchy in America* (1988) cover popular culture; Neil Harris, *Humbug: The Art of P. T. Barnum* (1973), is superb on both Barnum and the era. Howard P. Chudacoff, *How Old Are You?: Age Consciousness in American Culture* (1989) is fascinating on that subject. For family life, see Carl N. Degler, *At Odds: Women and the Family in America from the Revolution to the Present* (1980); Joseph Kett, *Rites of Passage: Adolescence in America* (1977); Elaine Tyler May, *Great Expectations: Marriage and Divorce in Post-Victorian America* (1980); Steven Mintz, *A Prison of Expectations: The Family in Victorian Culture* (1983); Norma Basch, *In the Eyes of the Law: Women, Marriage, and Property in Nineteenth-Century New York* (1982); and Tamara K. Hareven and Maris Vinovskis, eds., *Family and Population in Nineteenth-Century America* (1978). Karen Lystra, *Searching the Heart: Women, Men, and Romantic Love in Nineteenth-Century America* (1989), is valuable. For education, see L. A. Cremin, *The Transformation of the School* (1961); Lawrence Veysey, *The Emergence of the American University* (1965); and David B. Tyack, *The One Best System* (1974).

Oscar Handlin, *The Uprooted,* 2d ed. (1973), and John Higham, *Strangers in the Land* (1955), are classic studies. Robert H. Bremner, *From the Depths: The Discovery of Poverty in the United States* (1956); Judith Ann Trolander, *Professionalism and Social Change: From the Settlement House Movement to Neighborhood Centers, 1886 to the Present* (1987); Allen F. Davis, *Spearheads for Reform: The Social Settlements and the Progressive Movement, 1890–1914* (1967); and *American Heroine: The Life and Legend of Jane Addams* (1973), examine urban reform.

Treatments of intellectual currents include Richard Hofstadter, *Social Darwinism in American Thought,* rev. ed. (1955); Jon H. Roberts, *Darwinism and the Divine in America* (1988); Robert C. Bannister, *Sociology and Scientism* (1987); Bannister, *Social Darwinism: Science and Myth in Anglo-American Social Thought* (1979); Sidney Fine, *Laissez Faire and the General Welfare State* (1956); John L. Thomas, *Alternative America: Henry George, Edward Bellamy, Henry Demarest Lloyd and the Adversary Tradition* (1983); and Eric F. Goldman, *Rendezvous with Destiny* (1952).

Additional Bibliography

Robert H. Walker, *Life in the Age of Enterprise, 1865–1900* (1967), examines everyday life. On leisure and entertainment, see Gunther Barth, *City People*

(1980); Lary May, *Screening Out the Past: The Birth of Mass Culture and the Motion Picture Industry* (1980); Robert W. Snyder, *The Voice of the City: Vaudeville and Popular Culture in New York* (1989); and Ronald L. Davis, *A History of Music in American Life*, vol. 2 (1980). David J. Pivar, *Purity Crusade: Sexual Morality and Social Control, 1868–1900* (1973); Susan Estabrook Kennedy, *If All We Did Was to Weep at Home: A History of White Working Class Women in America* (1979); Barbara Mayer Wertheimer, *We Were There: The Story of Working Women in America* (1977); and Lois W. Banner, *Women in Modern America: A Brief History* (1974), are helpful on the topic of women in urban society.

Robert V. Bruce, *The Launching of Modern American Science, 1846–1876* (1987); Wolfgang Schivelbusch, *Disenchanted Night* (1988); and Cecelia Tichi, *Shifting Gears: Technology, Literature, Culture in Modernist America* (1987), are helpful on science and technology. For one of the era's leading architects, see Robert Twombly, *Louis Sullivan* (1986); Joseph Siry, *Carson-Pirie-Scott* (1988); and David S. Andrew, *Louis Sullivan and the Polemics of Modern Architecture* (1985). James Gilbert, *Perfect Cities: Chicago's Utopias of 1893* (1991); and Ross Miller, *American Apocalypse: The Great Fire and the Myth of Chicago* (1990) are helpful.

On education, see Sidney Hook, *John Dewey* (1939); Frederick Rudolph, *The American College and University* (1962); Donald Spivey, *Schooling for the New Slavery: Black Industrial Education, 1868–1915* (1978); Lawrence A. Cremin, *American Education: The Metropolitan Experience, 1876–1950* (1988); Robert L. McCaul, *The Black Struggle for Public Schooling in Nineteenth-Century Illinois* (1987); James D. Anderson, *The Education of Blacks in the South, 1860–1935* (1988); Gerald David Jaynes, *Branches Without Roots: Genesis of the Black Working Class in the American South, 1862–1882* (1986); Ronald Butchart, *Northern Schools, Southern Blacks, and Reconstruction, Freedmen's Education, 1862–1875* (1980); and two books by Louis R. Harlan, *Booker T. Washington: The Making of a Black Leader, 1856–1901* (1972), and *Booker T. Washington: The Wizard of Tuskegee, 1901–1915* (1953). Charles A. Lofgren, *The Plessy Case* (1987), is a detailed study of that important decision. See also Edward L. Ayers, *The Promise of the New South: Life After Reconstruction* (1992).

For immigration and urban growth, consult Barbara Solomon, *Ancestors and Immigrants* (1956); Josef J. Barton, *Peasants and Strangers* (1975); Victor R. Green, *American Immigrant Leaders, 1800–1910* (1987); Gwendolyn Mink, *Old Labor and New Immigrants in American Political Development* (1986); Leonard Dinnerstein, Roger L. Nichols, and David M. Reimers, *Natives and Strangers* (1979); Oliver Zunz, *The Changing Face of Inequality* (1982); Moses Rischin, *The Promised City: New York's Jews* (1962); David Ward, *Cities and Immigrants* (1971); Thomas L. Philpott, *The Slum and the Ghetto* (1978); Terrence J. McDonald, *The Parameters of Urban Fiscal Policy: Socioeconomic Change and Political Culture in San Francisco, 1860–1906* (1986); James Michael Russell, *Atlanta, 1847–1890: City Building in the Old South and the New* (1988); Patricia Mooney Melvin, *The Organic City: Urban Definition & Community Organization, 1880–1920* (1987); Carl V. Harris, *Political Power in Birmingham, 1871–1921* (1977); Stuart Galishoff, *Newark: The Nation's Unhealthiest City, 1832–1895* (1988); William A. Bullough, *The Blind Boss and His City* (1979); and Leo Hershkowitz, *Tweed's New York: Another Look* (1977).

See also Dorothy Rose Blumberg, *Florence Kelley* (1971); Kathy Peiss, *Cheap Amusements: Working Women and Leisure in Turn-of-the-Century New York* (1986); Lisa M. Fine, *The Souls of the Skyscraper: Female Clerical Workers in Chicago, 1870–1930* (1990); Glenna Mathews, *"Just a Housewife": The Rise and Fall of Domesticity in America* (1987); Lori D. Ginzberg, *Women and the Work of Benevolence: Morality, Politics, and Class in the Nineteenth-Century United States* (1990); Gloria Moldow, *Women Doctors in Gilded-Age Washington: Race, Gender, and Professionalization* (1987); Martha Banta, *Imaging American Women: Idea and Ideals in Cultural History* (1987); Martha Vicinus, *Independent Women: Work and Community for Single Women 1850–1920* (1985); Theodora Penny Martin, *The Sound of Our Own Voices: Women's Study Clubs, 1860–1910* (1987); Leslie Woodcock Tentler, *Wage-Earning Women: Industrial Work and Family Life in the United States, 1900–1930* (1979); Ruth Bordin, *Woman and Temperance: The Quest for Power and Liberty, 1873–1900* (1981); Mary A. Hill, *Charlotte Perkins Gilman: The Making of a Radical Feminist, 1860–1896* (1980); Mary Jo Deegan, *Jane Addams and the Men of the Chicago School, 1892–1918* (1988); Mina Carson, *Settlement Folk: Social Thought in the American Settlement Movement, 1885–1930* (1990); Reeve Rivka Schpak Lissak, *Pluralism & Progressives: Hull House and the New Immigrants, 1890–1919* (1989); Ruth Hutchinson Crocker, *Social Work and Social Order: The Settlement Movement in Two Industrial Cities, 1889–1930* (1992); John M. O'Donnell, *The Origins of Behaviorism: American Psychology, 1870–1920* (1985); Roy M. Lubove, *The Progressives and the Slums* (1962); Martin J. Schiesl, *The Politics of Efficiency: Municipal Administration and Reform in America* (1977); George Cotkin, *Reluctant Modernism: American Thought and Culture, 1880–1900* (1992); and R. C. White, Jr., and C. H. Hopkins, *The Social Gospel* (1976).

Political Realignments in the 1890s

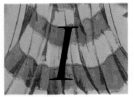

In June 1894, Susan Orcutt, a young farm woman from western Kansas, sat down to write the governor of her state a letter. She was desperate. The nation was in the midst of a devastating economic depression, and like thousands of other people, she had no money and nothing to eat. "I take my Pen In hand to let you know that we are Starving to death," she wrote. Hail had ruined the Orcutts' crops, and none of the household could find work. "My Husband went away to find work and came home last night and told me that we would have to Starve. [H]e has bin in ten countys and did not Get no work. . . . I havent had nothing to Eat today and It is three oclock[.]"

As bad as conditions were on the farms, they were no better in the cities. "There are thousands of homeless and starving men in the streets," reported a journalist in Chicago in the winter of 1893. "I have seen more misery in this last week than I ever saw in my life before." Charity societies and churches tried to help, but they could not handle the huge numbers of people who were in need. The records of the Massachusetts state medical examiner told a grim story:

K.R., 29   Suicide by drowning
Boston   October 2, 1896
Out of work and despondent for a long while. Body found floating in the Charles [River].

F.S., 29   Suicide by arsenic
Boston   January 1, 1896
Much depressed for several weeks. Loss of employment. At 7:50 a.m. Jan. 1, she called her father and told him she had taken poison and wished to die.

L.M., 38   Hanging suicide
E. Boston   October 15, 1895
Had been out of work for several weeks and was very despondent. Wife went to market at about 11 a.m. and upon returning at about 12 p.m. found him hanging from bedroom door. . . . Slipped noose about his neck and [fell] forward upon it.

R.N., 23   Suicide by bullet
            wound of brain
Boston   June 22, 1896

Out of work. Mentally depressed. About 3 p.m. June 21 shot himself in right temple. . . . Left a letter explaining that he killed himself to save others the trouble of caring for him.

Lasting until 1897, the depression was the decisive event of the decade. At its height, three million people were unemployed—fully 20 percent of the work force. The human costs were enormous, even among the well-to-do. "They were for me years of simple Hell," shattering "my whole scheme of life," said Charles Francis Adams, the descendant of two American presidents. "I was sixty-three years old and a tired man when at last the effects of the 1893 convulsion wore themselves out."

Like the depression of the 1930s that gave rise to the New Deal, the depression of the 1890s had profound and lasting effects. Bringing to a head many of the tensions that had been building in the society, it increased rural hostility toward the cities, brought about a bitter fight over the currency, and changed people's thinking about government, unemployment, and reform. There were outbreaks of warfare between capital and labor; farmers demanded a fairer share of economic and social benefits; the "new" immigrants came under fresh attack. The depression of the 1890s changed the course of American history, as did another event of that decade: the war with Spain in 1898 (see Chapter 21).

Under the cruel impact of the depression, ideas changed in many areas, including in politics. A realignment of the American political system, which had been developing since the end of Reconstruction, finally reached its fruition in the 1890s, establishing new patterns that gave rise to the Progressive Era and lasted well into the twentieth century.

POLITICS OF STALEMATE

Politics was a major fascination of the late nineteenth century, its mass entertainment and favorite sport. Political campaigns were events that involved the whole community, even though in most states men were the only ones who could vote. During the weeks leading up to an election, there were rallies, parades, picnics, and torchlight processions. Millions of Americans read party

A delegation of women's rights advocates addressed the judiciary committee of the House of Representatives to present their arguments in favor of woman suffrage. Reading the argument is Victoria Claflin Woodhull, one of the more radical activists in the women's movement.

newspapers, listened to three-hour speeches by party leaders, and in elections turned out in enormous numbers to vote. In the six presidential elections from 1876 to 1896, an average of almost 79 percent of the electorate voted, a higher percentage than voted before or after.

White males made up the bulk of the electorate; until after the turn of the century, women could vote in national elections only in Wyoming, Utah, Idaho, and Colorado. The National Woman Suffrage Association early sued for the vote, but in 1875 the Supreme Court *(Minor* v. *Happersett)* upheld the power of the states to deny this right to women. On several occasions, Congress refused to pass a constitutional amendment for woman's suffrage, and between 1870 and 1910, nearly a dozen states defeated referenda to grant women the vote.

Black men were another group kept from the polls. In 1877, Georgia adopted the poll tax to make voters pay an annual tax for the right to vote. The technique, aimed at impoverished blacks, was quickly copied across the South. In 1882, South Carolina adopted the "eight box" law, soon copied elsewhere, that required ballots for separate offices to be placed in separate boxes, a difficult task for illiterate voters.

In 1890, Mississippi required voters to be able to read and interpret the federal Constitution to the satisfaction of registration officials, all of them white. Such literacy tests, which the Supreme Court upheld in the case of *Williams* v. *Mississippi* (1898), excluded poor white voters as

well as blacks. In 1898, Louisiana got around that problem by adopting the famous "grandfather clause," which used a literacy test to disqualify black voters but permitted men who had failed the test to vote anyway if their fathers and grandfathers had voted before 1867—a time, of course, when no blacks could vote. The number of black voters decreased dramatically. In 1896, there were 130,334 registered black voters in Louisiana; in 1904, there were 1,342.

The Party Deadlock

The 1870s and 1880s were still dominated by the Civil War generation, the unusual group of people who rose to power in the turbulent 1850s. In both the North and South, they had ruled longer than most generations, with a consiousness that the war experience had set them apart. Five of the six presidents elected between 1865 and 1900 had served in the war, as had many civic, business, and religious leaders. In 1890, there were well over one million veterans of the Union Army still alive, and Confederate veterans numbered in the hundreds of thousands.

Party loyalties—rooted in Civil War traditions, ethnic and religious differences, and perhaps class distinctions—were remarkably strong. Voters clung to their old parties, shifts were infrequent, and there were relatively few "independent" voters. Although linked to the defeated Confederacy, the Democrats revived quickly after the war. In 1874, they gained control of the House of

Representatives, which they maintained for all but four of the succeeding twenty years. The Democrats rested on a less sectional base than the Republicans. Identification with civil rights and military rule cut Republican strength in the South, but the Democratic party's principles of states' rights, decentralization, and limited government won supporters everywhere.

While Democrats wanted to keep government local and small, the Republicans pursued policies for the nation as a whole, in which government was an instrument to promote moral progress and material wealth. The Republicans passed the Homestead Act (1862), granted subsidies to the transcontinental railroads, and pushed other measures to encourage economic growth. They enacted legislation and constitutional amendments to protect civil rights. They advocated a high protective tariff as a tool of economic policy, to keep out foreign products while "infant industries" grew.

In national elections, sixteen states, mostly in New England and the North, consistently voted Republican; fourteen states, mostly in the South, consistently voted Democratic. Elections, therefore, depended on a handful of "doubtful" states, which could swing elections either way. These states—New York, New Jersey, Connecticut, Ohio, Indiana, and Illinois—received special attention at election time. Politicians lavished money and time on them; presidential candidates usually came from them. From 1868 to 1912, eight of the nine Republican presidential candidates and six of the seven Democratic candidates came from the "doubtful" states, especially New York and Ohio.

The two parties were evenly matched, and elections were closely fought. In three of the five presidential elections from 1876 to 1892, the victor won by less than 1 percent of the vote; in 1876 and 1888, the losing candidates actually had more popular votes than the winners but lost in the electoral college. Knowing that small mistakes could lose elections, politicians became extremely cautious. Only twice during these years did one party control both the presidency and the two houses of Congress—the Republicans in 1888 and the Democrats in 1892.

Historians once believed that political leaders accomplished little between 1877 and 1900, but those who saw few achievements were looking in the wrong location. With the impeachment of Andrew Johnson, the authority of the presidency dwindled in relation to congressional strength. For the first time in many years, attention shifted away from Washington itself. North and South, people who were weary of the centralization brought on by war and Reconstruction looked first to state and local governments to deal with the problems of an urban-industrial society.

Experiments in the States

Across the country, state bureaus and commissions were established to regulate the new industrial society. Many of the early commissions were formed to oversee the railroads, at the time the nation's largest businesses. People who shipped goods over the railroads, especially farmers and merchants, wanted to end the policies of rate discrimination and other harmful practices. In 1869, Massachusetts established the first commission to regulate the railroads; by 1900, twenty-eight states had taken such action.

Most of the early commissions were advisory in nature; they collected statistics and published reports on rates and practices—serving, one commissioner said, "as a sort of lens" to focus public attention. Impatient with the results, legislatures in the Midwest and on the Pacific Coast established commissions with greater power to fix rates, outlaw rebates, and investigate rate discrimination. These commissions, experimental in nature, served as models for later policy at the federal level.

Illinois had one of the most thoroughgoing provisions. Responding to local merchants who were upset with existing railroad rate policies, the Illinois state constitution of 1870 declared railroads to be public highways and authorized the legislature to pass laws establishing maximum rates and preventing rate discrimination. In the important case of *Munn* v. *Illinois* (1877), the Supreme Court upheld the Illinois legislation, declaring that private property "affected with the public interest . . . must submit to being controlled by the public for the common good."

But the Court soon weakened that judgement. In the *Wabash* case of 1886 (*Wabash, St. Louis, & Pacific Railway Co.* v. *Illinois*), it narrowed the *Munn* rule and held that states could not regulate commerce extending beyond their borders. Only Congress could. The *Wabash* decision turned people's attention back to the federal government. It spurred Congress to pass the Interstate Commerce Act (1887), which created the Interstate Commerce Commission to investigate and oversee railroad activities. The act outlawed rebates and pooling agreements, and the ICC became the prototype of the federal commissions that today regulate many parts of the economy.

Reestablishing Presidential Power

Johnson's impeachment, the scandals of the Grant administrations, and the controversy surrounding the 1876 election (see Chapter 16) weakened the presidency. During the last two decades of the nineteenth century, presidents fought to reassert their authority, and by 1900, under William McKinley, they had succeeded to a remarkable degree. The late 1890s, in fact, marked the birth of the modern powerful presidency.

Rutherford B. Hayes entered the White House with his title clouded by the disputed election of 1876. Opponents called him "His Fraudulency" and "Rutherfraud B. Hayes," but soon he began to reassert the authority of the presidency. Hayes worked for reform in the civil service, placed well-known reformers in high offices, and, ordering the last troops out of South Carolina and Louisiana, ended military Reconstruction. He hoped to revive the Republican party in the South by persuading business-oriented ex-Whigs to join a national party that would support their economic interests more effectively than the Democrats did. In this attempt, however, he failed. Committed to the gold standard—the only basis, Hayes thought, of a sound currency—in 1878 he vetoed the Bland-Allison Silver Purchase bill, which called for the partial coinage of silver, but Congress passed it over his veto.

James A. Garfield, a Union Army hero and longtime member of Congress, succeeded Hayes. Winning by a handful of votes in 1880, he took office energetically, determined to unite the Republican party (which had been split by personality differences and disagreement over policy toward the tariff and the South), lower the tariff to cut taxes, and assert American economic and strategic interests in Latin America. Ambitious and eloquent, Garfield had looked forward to the presidency, yet within a few weeks he said to friends, "My God! What is there in this place that a man should ever want to get into it?"

Office seekers, hordes of them, evoked Garfield's anguish. Each one wanted a government job, and each one thought nothing of cornering the president on every occasion. The problem of government jobs also provoked a bitter fight with the powerful senator from New York, Roscoe Conkling, who resented some of Garfield's choices. On the verge of victory over Conkling, Garfield planned to leave Washington on July 2, 1881, for a vacation in New England. Walking toward his train, he was shot in the back by Charles J. Guiteau, a deranged lawyer and disappointed office seeker. Suffering through the summer, Garfield died on September 19, 1881, and Vice President Chester A. Arthur—an ally of Senator Conkling—became president.

Arthur was a better president than many had expected. Deftly he established his independence of Conkling. Conservative in outlook, he reversed Garfield's foreign policy initiatives in Latin America, but he approved the construction of the modern American navy. Arthur worked to lower the tariff, and in 1883, with his backing, Congress passed the Pendleton Act to reform the civil service. In part a reaction against Garfield's assassination, the act created a bipartisan Civil Service Commission to administer competitive examinations and appoint officeholders on the basis of merit. Initially, the act affected only about 14,000 of some 100,000 government

The Election of 1880

Candidate	Party	Popular Vote	Electoral Vote
Garfield	Republican	4,446,158	214
Hancock	Democrat	4,444,260	155
Weaver	Greenback	305,997	0

offices, but it laid the basis for the later expansion of the civil service.

In the election of 1884, Grover Cleveland, the Democratic governor of New York, narrowly defeated Republican nominee James G. Blaine, largely because of the continuing divisions in the Republican party. The first Democratic president since 1861, Cleveland was slow and ponderous, known for his honesty, stubbornness, and hard work. His term in the White House from 1885 to 1889 reflected the Democratic party's desire to curtail federal activities. Cleveland vetoed more than two-thirds of the bills presented to him, more than all his predecessors combined.

Forthright and sincere, he brought a new respectability to a Democratic party still tainted by its link with secession. Working long into the night, he reviewed veterans' pensions and civil service appointments. He continued Arthur's naval construction program and forced railroad, lumber, and cattle companies to surrender millions of acres of fraudulently occupied public domain. Late in 1887, he devoted his annual message to an attack on the tariff, "the vicious, inequitable, and illogical source of unnecessary taxation," and committed himself and the Democratic party to lowering the tariff.

The Republicans accused him of undermining American industries, and in 1888, they nominated for the presidency Benjamin Harrison, a defender of the tariff. Cleveland garnered ninety thousand more popular votes than Harrison but won the electoral votes of only two northern states and the South. Harrison won the rest of the North, most of the "doubtful" states, and the election.

The Election of 1884

Candidate	Party	Popular Vote	Electoral Vote
Cleveland	Democrat	4,874,621	219
Blaine	Republican	4,848,936	182
Butler	Greenback	175,096	0
St. John	Prohibition	147,482	0

REPUBLICANS IN POWER: THE BILLION-DOLLAR CONGRESS

Despite Harrison's narrow margin, the election of 1888 was the most sweeping victory for either party in almost twenty years; it gave the Republicans the presidency and both houses of Congress. The Republicans, it seemed, had broken the party stalemate and become the majority party in the country.

Democratic leaders hoped not, and eager to embarrass the Republicans and block Republican-sponsored laws, the Democrats in Congress used minority tactics, especially the "disappearing quorum" rule, which let members of the House of Representatives join in debate but then refuse to answer the roll call to determine if a quorum was present.

For two months, the Democrats used the rule to bring Congress to a halt. The Republicans grew angry and impatient. On January 29, 1890, they fell two votes short of a quorum, and Speaker of the House Thomas B. Reed, a crusty veteran of Maine politics, made congressional history. "The Chair," he said, "directs the Clerk to record the following names of members present and refusing to vote." Democrats shouted "Czar! Czar!" a title that stuck to Reed for the rest of his life. Tumult continued for days, but in mid-February 1890, the Republicans adopted the

Reed rules and proceeded to enact the party's program.

Tariffs, Trusts, and Silver

As if a dam had burst, law after law poured out of the Republican Congress during 1890. The Republicans passed the McKinley Tariff Act, which raised tariff duties about 4 percent, higher than ever before; it also included a novel reciprocity provision that allowed the president to lower duties if other countries did the same. In addition, the act used duties to promote new industries, like tinplate for packaging the new "canned" foods appearing on grocery store shelves. A Dependent Pensions Act granted pensions to Union Army veterans, their widows, and children. The pensions were modest—$6 to $12 a month—but the number of pensioners doubled by 1893, when nearly one million individuals received about $160 million in pensions.

With little debate, the Republicans and Democrats joined in passing the Sherman Antitrust Act, the first federal attempt to regulate big business. As the initial attempt to deal with the problem of trusts and industrial growth, the act shaped all later antitrust policy. It declared illegal "every contract, combination in the form of trust or otherwise, or conspiracy, in restraint of trade or commerce." Penalties for violation were stiff, including fines and imprisonment and the dissolution of guilty trusts. Experimental in nature, the act's terms were often vague and left precise interpretation to later experience and the courts.

One of the most important laws Congress passed, the Sherman Antitrust Act made the United States virtually the only industrial nation to regulate business combinations. It tried to harness big business without harming it. Many members of Congress did not expect the new law to have much effect on businesses, and for a decade, in fact, it did not. The Justice Department rarely filed suit under it, and in the *United States* v. *E. C. Knight Co.* (1895), the first judicial interpretation of the law, the Supreme Court severely crippled it. Though the E. C. Knight Co. controlled 98 percent of all sugar refining in the country, the Court drew a sharp distinction between commerce and manufacturing, holding that the company, as a manufacturer, was not subject to the law. But judicial interpretations changed after the turn of the century, and the Sherman Antitrust Act gained fresh power.

Another measure, the Sherman Silver Purchase Act, tried to end the troublesome problem presented by silver. As one of the two most commonly used precious metals, silver had once played a large role in currencies around the world, but by the mid-1800s, it had slipped into disuse. With the discovery of the great bonanza mines in Nevada (see Chapter 17), American silver production quadrupled between 1870 and 1890, glutting the world market, lowering the price of silver, and persuading many European nations to demonetize silver in favor of the scarcer metal, gold. The United States kept a limited form of silver coinage with congressional passage of the Bland-Allison Act in 1878.

Support for silver coinage was especially strong in the South and West, where people thought it might inflate the currency, raise wages and crop prices, and challenge the hated power of

According to the cartoon, a bimetallic system based on both silver and gold would lead to a wobbly economy.

the gold-oriented Northeast. Eager to avert the free coinage of silver, which would require the coinage of all silver presented at the U.S. mints, President Harrison and other Republican leaders pressed for a compromise that took shape in the Sherman Silver Purchase Act of 1890.

The act directed the Treasury to purchase 4.5 million ounces of silver a month and to issue legal tender in the form of Treasury notes in payment for it. The act was a compromise; it satisfied both sides. Opponents of silver were pleased that it did not include free coinage. Silverites, on the other hand, were delighted that the monthly purchases would buy up most of the country's silver production. The Treasury notes, moreover, could be cashed for either gold or silver at the bank, a gesture toward a true bimetallic system based on silver and gold.

As a final measure, Republicans in the House courageously passed a federal elections bill to protect the voting rights of blacks in the South. Although restrained in language and intent, it set off a storm of denunciation among the Democrats, who called it a "force bill" that would station army troops in the South. Because of the outcry, the bill failed in the Senate; it was the last major effort until the 1950s to enforce the Fifteenth Amendment to the Constitution.

The 1890 Elections

The Republican Congress of 1890 was one of the most important Congresses in American history. It passed a record number of significant laws that helped shape later policy, and asserted the authority of the federal government to a degree the country would not then accept. Sensing the public reaction, the Democrats labeled it the "Billion-Dollar Congress" for spending that much in appropriations and grants.

"This is a billion-dollar country," Speaker Reed replied, but the voters disagreed. The 1890 elections crushed the Republicans, who lost an extraordinary seventy-eight seats in the House. The elections also crushed Republicans in the Midwest where, again enlarging government authority, they had passed state laws prohibiting the sale of alcoholic beverages, requiring the closing of businesses on Sunday, and mandating the use of English in the public and parochial schools. Roman Catholics, German Lutherans,

and other groups resented such laws, which they saw as a direct attack on their religion and personal freedoms, and they angrily deserted the Republicans.

Political veterans went down to defeat, and new leaders vaulted into sudden prominence. Nebraska elected a Democratic governor for the first time in its history. The state of Iowa, once so staunchly Republican that a local leader had predicted that "Iowa will go Democratic when Hell goes Methodist," went Democratic in 1890.

THE RISE OF THE POPULIST MOVEMENT

The elections of 1890 drew attention to a fast-growing movement among farmers that soon came to be known far and wide as Populism. The movement had begun rather quietly, in places distant from normal centers of attention, and for a time it went almost unnoticed in the press. But during the summer of 1890, wagonloads of farm families in the South and West converged on campgrounds and picnic areas to socialize and discuss common problems. They came by the thousands, weary of drought, mortgages, and low crop prices. At the campgrounds, they picnicked, talked, and listened to recruiters from an organization called the National Farmers' Alliance and Industrial Union, which promised unified action to solve agricultural problems.

Farmers were joining the Alliance at the rate of 1,000 a week; the Kansas Alliance alone claimed 130,000 members in 1890. The summer of 1890 became "that wonderful picnicking, speech-making Alliance summer," a time of fellowship and spirit long remembered by farmers.

The Farm Problem

Farm discontent was a worldwide phenomenon between 1870 and 1900. With the new means of transportation and communication, farmers everywhere were caught up in a complex international market they neither controlled nor entirely understood.

American farmers complained bitterly about declining prices for their products, rising railroad rates for shipping them, and burdensome mortgages. Some of their grievances were valid. Farm

Selected Commodity Prices

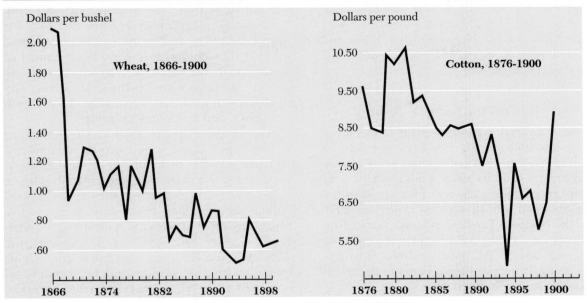

Source: U.S. Bureau of the Census. Historical Statistics of the United States, Colonial Times to 1970, Bicentennial Edition, Washington, D.C., 1975.

profits were certainly low; agriculture in general tends to produce low profits because of the ease of entry into the industry. The prices of farm commodities fell between 1865 and 1890—corn sold at sixty-three cents a bushel in 1881 and twenty-eight cents in 1890—but they did not fall as low as did other commodity prices. Despite the fact that farmers received less for their crops, their purchasing power actually increased.

Neither was the farmers' second grievance—rising railroad rates—entirely justified. Railroad rates actually fell during these years, benefiting shippers of all products. Farm mortgages, the farmers' third grievance, were common because many farmers mortgaged their property to expand their holdings or buy new farm machinery. While certainly burdensome, most mortgages did not bring hardship. They were often short, with a term of four years or less, after which farmers could renegotiate at new rates, and the new machinery the farmers bought enabled them to triple their output and increase their income.

The terms of the farm problem varied from area to area and year to year. New England farmers suffered from overworked land; farmers in western Kansas and Nebraska went broke in a severe drought that followed a period of unusual rainfall. Many southern farmers were trapped in the crop lien system that kept them in debt. They called it the "anaconda" system because of the way it coiled slowly and tightly around them.

A study of farms in the Midwest between 1860 and 1900 suggests that farm income rose substantially in the 1860s, fell during the devastating depression of the 1870s, rose in the 1880s, and remained roughly constant in the 1890s. There were also large variations in farm profits from county to county, again indicating the absence of clear nationwide patterns. Farmers who had good land close to railroad transportation did well; others did not.

Some farmers did have valid grievances, though many understandably tended to exaggerate them. More important, many farmers were *sure* their condition had declined, and this perception—as bitterly real as any actual fact—sparked a growing anger. Equally upsetting, everyone in the 1870s and 1880s seemed excited about factories, not farms. Farmers had become "hayseeds," a word that first appeared in 1889, and they watched their offspring leave for city lights and new careers. Books like *The Spider and* the Fly: or, Tricks, Traps, and Pitfalls of City Life by One Who Knows (1873) warned against such a move, but still the children went. A literature of disillusionment emerged, most notably Hamlin Garland's *Son of the Middle Border* (1890) and *Main-Travelled Roads* (1891), which described the drabness of farm life.

The Fast-Growing Farmers' Alliance

Originally a social organization for farmers, the Grange lost many of its members as it turned more and more toward politics in the late 1870s (see Chapter 17). In its place, a multitude of farm societies sprang into existence. By the end of the 1880s, they had formed into two major organizations: the National Farmers' Alliance, located on the Plains west of the Mississippi and known as the Northwestern Alliance, and the Farmers' Alliance and Industrial Union, based in the South and known as the Southern Alliance.

The Southern Alliance began in Texas in 1875 but did not assume major proportions until Dr. Charles W. Macune, an energetic and farsighted person, took over the leadership in 1886. Rapidly expanding, the Alliance absorbed other agricultural societies. Its agents spread across the South where farmers were fed up with crop liens, depleted lands, and sharecropping. They "seem like unto ripe fruit," an Alliance organizer said, "you can garner them by a gentle shake of the bush." In 1890, the Southern Alliance claimed more than a million members. It welcomed to membership the farmers' "natural friends"— country doctors, schoolteachers, preachers, and mechanics. It excluded lawyers, bankers, cotton merchants, and warehouse operators.

An effective organization, the Southern Alliance published a newspaper, distributed Alliance material to hundreds of local newspapers, and in five years sent lecturers to forty-three states and territories where they spoke to two million farm families. It was "the most massive organizing drive by any citizen institution of nineteenth-century America." Like the Grange, the Alliance also established cooperative grain elevators, marketing associations, and retail stores—all designed to bring farmers together to make greater profits. Most of the projects were short-lived, but for a time, between 1886 and 1892, cooperative enterprises blossomed in the South.

Loosely affiliated with the Southern Alliance, a separate Colored Farmers' National Alliance and Cooperative Union enlisted black farmers in the South. Claiming over a million members, it probably had closer to 250,000, but even that figure was sizable in an era when "uppity" blacks faced not merely defeat, but death. In 1891, black cotton pickers struck for higher wages near Memphis, Tennessee. Led by Ben Patterson, a thirty-year-old picker, they walked off several plantations, but a posse hunted them down and, following violence on both sides, lynched fifteen strikers, including Patterson. The abortive strike ended the Colored Farmers' Alliance.

On the Plains, the Northwestern Alliance, a smaller organization, was formed in 1880. Its objectives were similar to those of the Southern Alliance, but it disagreed with the Southerners' emphasis on secrecy, centralized control, and separate organizations for blacks. In 1889, the Southern Alliance changed its name to the National Farmers' Alliance and Industrial Union and persuaded the three strongest state alliances on the plains—those in North Dakota, South Dakota, and Kansas—to join. Thereafter, the renamed organization dominated the Alliance movement.

The Grange, personified as a farmer, rouses the sleeping citizenry to the dangers of trusts in this 1880 engraving.

The Alliance mainly sponsored social and economic programs, but it turned early to politics. In the West, its leaders rejected both the Republicans and Democrats and organized their own party; in June 1890, Kansas Alliance members formed the first major People's party. The Southern Alliance resisted the idea of a new party for fear it might divide the white vote, thus undercutting white supremacy. The Southerners instead followed leaders such as Benjamin F. Tillman of South Carolina who wanted to capture control of the dominant Democratic party.

Thomas E. Watson and Leonidas L. Polk, two politically minded Southerners, reflected the high quality of Alliance leadership. Georgia-born, Watson was a talented orator and organizer; he urged Georgia farmers, black and white, to unite against their oppressors. The president of the National Farmers' Alliance, Polk believed in scientific farming and cooperative action. Jeremiah Simpson of Kansas, probably the most able of the western leaders, was reflective and well read. A follower of reformer Henry George, he pushed for major social and economic change. Also from Kansas, Mary E. Lease—Mary Ellen to her friends, "Mary Yellin" to her opponents—helped head a movement remarkably open to female leadership. A captivating speaker, she made 160 speeches during the summer of 1890, calling on farmers to rise against Wall Street and the industrial East.

Meeting in Ocala, Florida, in 1890, the Alliance adopted the Ocala Demands, the platform it pushed for as long as it existed. First and foremost, the demands called for the creation of a "sub-treasury system," which would allow farmers to store their crops in government warehouses. In return, they could claim Treasury notes for up to 80 percent of the local market value of the crop, a loan to be repaid when the crops were sold. Farmers could thus hold their crops for the best price. The Ocala Demands also urged the free coinage of silver, an end to protective tariffs and national banks, a federal income tax, the direct election of senators by voters instead of state legislatures, and tighter regulation of railroad companies.

The Alliance strategy worked well in the elections of 1890. In Kansas, the Alliance-related People's party, organized just a few months before, elected four congressmen and a U.S. sena-

Populist Mary E. Lease advised farmers to "raise less corn and more hell." She also said ". . . if one man has not enough to eat three times a day and another man has $25 million, that last man has something that belongs to the first."

tor. Across the South, the Alliance won victories based on "the Alliance Yardstick," a demand that Democratic party candidates pledge support for Alliance measures. Alliance leaders claimed thirty-eight Alliance supporters elected to Congress, with at least a dozen more pledged to Alliance principles.

The People's Party

After the 1890 elections, Northern Alliance leaders urged the formation of a national third party to promote reform, although the Southerners remained reluctant, still hopeful of capturing control of the Democratic party. Plans for a new party were discussed at Alliance conventions in 1891 and the following year. In July 1892, a convention in Omaha, Nebraska, formed the new People's party. Southern Alliance leaders joined in, convinced now that there was no reason to cooperate with the Democrats who exploited Alliance popularity but failed to adopt its reforms.

In the South, some Populists had worked to unite black and white farmers. "They are in the ditch just like we are," a white Texas Populist said. Blacks and whites served on Populist election committees; they spoke from the same platforms, and they ran on the same tickets. Populist sheriffs called blacks for jury duty, an unheard-of practice in the close-of-the-century South. In 1892, a black Populist was threatened with lynching; he took refuge with Tom Watson, and two thousand white farmers, some of whom rode all night to get there, guarded Watson's house until the threat passed.

Many of the delegates at the Omaha convention had planned to nominate Leonidas L. Polk for president, but he died suddenly in June, and the convention turned instead to James B. Weaver of Iowa, a former congressman, Union Army general, and third-party candidate for president in 1880 (on the Greenback-Labor party ticket). As its platform, the People's party adopted many of the Ocala Demands.

Weaver waged an active campaign but with mixed results. He won 1,029,000 votes, the first third-party presidential candidate ever to attract more than a million. He carried Kansas, Idaho, Nevada, and Colorado, along with portions of North Dakota and Oregon, for a total of twenty-two electoral votes. The Populists elected governors in Kansas and North Dakota, ten congressmen, five senators, and about fifteen hundred members of state legislatures.

Despite the Populists' victories, the election brought disappointment. Southern Democrats used intimidation, fraud, and manipulation to hold down Populist votes. Weaver was held to less than a quarter of the vote in every southern state except Alabama. In most of the country, he lost heavily in urban areas with the exception of some mining towns in the Far West. He also failed to win over most farmers. In no midwestern state except Kansas and North Dakota did he win as much as 5 percent of the vote.

In the election of 1892, many voters switched parties, but they tended to realign with the Democrats rather than the Populists, whose platform on silver and other issues had relatively little appeal among city dwellers or factory workers. Although the Populists did run candidates in the next three presidential elections, they had reached their peak in 1892. That year, Farmers' Alliance

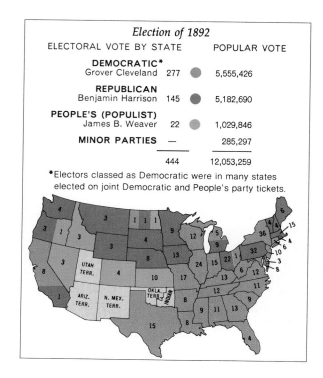

Election of 1892

ELECTORAL VOTE BY STATE		POPULAR VOTE
DEMOCRATIC* Grover Cleveland	277	5,555,426
REPUBLICAN Benjamin Harrison	145	5,182,690
PEOPLE'S (POPULIST) James B. Weaver	22	1,029,846
MINOR PARTIES	—	285,297
	444	12,053,259

*Electors classed as Democratic were in many states elected on joint Democratic and People's party tickets.

membership dropped for the second year in a row, and the organization, which was once the breeding ground of the People's party, was broken.

While it lived, the Alliance was one of the most powerful protest movements in American history. Catalyzing the feelings of hundreds of thousands of farmers, it attempted to solve specific economic problems, while at the same time advancing a larger vision of harmony and community, in which people who cared about each other were rewarded for what they produced.

THE CRISIS OF THE DEPRESSION

It was economic crisis, however, not harmony and community, that dominated the last decade of the century. Responding to the heady forces of industrialization, the American economy had expanded too rapidly in the 1870s and 1880s. Railroads had overbuilt, gambling on future growth. Companies had grown beyond their markets; farms and businesses had borrowed heavily for expansion.

The mood changed early in 1893. In mid-February, panic suddenly hit the New York stock market. In one day, investors dumped one million shares of a leading company, the Philadelphia and Reading Railroad, and it went bankrupt. Business investment dropped sharply in the railroad and construction industries, touching off the worst economic downturn to that point in the country's history.

Frightened, people hurriedly sold stocks and other assets to buy gold. The overwhelming demand depleted the gold reserve of the U.S. Treasury. Eroding almost daily, in March 1893, the Treasury's reserve slumped toward the $100 million mark, an amount that stood for the government's commitment to maintain the gold standard. On April 22, for the first time since the 1870s, it fell below $100 million.

The news shattered business confidence—the stock market broke. On Wednesday, May 3, railroad and industrial stocks plummeted, and the next day several major firms went bankrupt. When the market opened on Friday, crowds filled its galleries, anticipating a panic. Within minutes, leading stocks plunged to record lows, and there was pandemonium on the floor and in the streets outside. May 5, 1893, Wall Street's worst day until the Great Crash of 1929, became "Industrial Black Friday," "a day of terrible strain long remembered on the market."

Afterward, banks cut back on loans. Unable to get capital, businesses failed at an average rate of two dozen a day during the month of May. "The papers are full of failures—banks are breaking all over the country, and there is a tremendous contraction of credits and hoarding of money going on everywhere," an observer noted. On July 26, the Erie Railroad, one of the leading names in railroading history, failed.

August 1893 was the worst month. Across the country, factories and mines shut down. In Orange, New Jersey, Thomas A. Edison, the symbol of the country's ingenuity, laid off 240 employees at the Edison Phonograph Works. On August 15, the Northern Pacific Railroad went bankrupt; the Union Pacific and the Santa Fe soon followed. Some economists estimated unemployment at 2 million people or nearly 15 percent of the labor force. During 1893, 15,000 business firms and more than 600 banks closed.

The year 1894 was even worse. The gross national product dropped again, and by mid-year the number of unemployed stood at three million. One out of every five workers was unemployed.

"Famine is in our midst," said the head of one city's relief committee. In the summer, a heat wave and drought struck the farm belt west of the Mississippi River, creating conditions unmatched until the devastating Dust Bowl of the 1930s. Corn withered in the fields. In the South, the price of cotton fell below five cents a pound, far under the break-even point.

People became restless and angry. As one newspaper said in 1896: "On every corner stands a man whose fortune in these dull times has made him an ugly critic of everything and everybody." There was even talk of revolution and bloodshed. "Everyone scolds," Henry Adams, the historian, wrote a British friend. "Everyone also knows what ought to be done. Everyone reviles everyone who does not agree with him, and everyone differs, or agrees only in contempt for everyone else. As far as I can see, everyone is right."

Coxey's Army and the Pullman Strike

Some of the unemployed wandered across the country—singly, in small groups, and in small armies. In February 1894, police ejected 600 unemployed men who stormed the State House in Boston demanding relief. During 1894, there were some 1,400 strikes involving more than a half million workers.

On Easter Sunday 1894, an unusual "army" of perhaps three hundred people left Massillon, Ohio. At its head rode "General" Jacob S. Coxey, a mild-looking middle-aged businessman who wanted to put the nation's jobless to work building roads. Coxey wanted Congress to pass the Coxey Good Roads bill, which would authorize the printing of $500 million in paper money to finance road construction. His march to Washington—"a petition in boots," he called it— drew nationwide attention. Forty-three newspaper correspondents accompanied him, reporting every detail of the march.

Other armies sprang up around the country, and all headed for Washington to persuade the government to provide jobs on irrigation, road construction, or other projects. In the West, they commandeered freight trains and headed east. Coxey himself reached Washington on May 1, 1894, after a difficult, tiring march. Police were everywhere, lining the streets and blocking the approaches to the Capitol. Coxey made it to the

The Panic of 1893 touched off a frenzy of activity on the floor of the New York Stock Exchange as investors attempted to unload their stock. Prices on the Exchange fell to a new low on June 27. By the end of 1893, the gold reserve had dipped to $80 million.

foot of the Capitol steps, but before he could do anything, the police were on him. He and a companion were clubbed, then arrested for trespassing. A week later, Coxey was sentenced to twenty days in jail.

The armies melted away, but discontent did not. The great Pullman strike—one of the largest strikes in the country's history—began just a few days after Coxey's arrest when the employees of the Pullman Palace Car Company, living in a company town just outside of Chicago (a town in which everything was owned and meted out by the company), struck to protest wage cuts, continuing high rents, and layoffs. On June 26, 1894, the American Railway Union (ARU) under Eugene V. Debs joined the strike by refusing to handle trains that carried Pullman sleeping cars.

Within hours, the strike paralyzed the western half of the nation. Grain and livestock could not reach markets. Factories shut down for lack of coal. The strike extended into twenty-seven states and territories, tying up the economy and renewing talk of class warfare. In Washington, President Grover Cleveland, who had been reelected to the presidency in 1892, decided to break the strike on the grounds that it obstructed delivery of the mail.

On July 2, he secured a court injunction against the ARU, and he ordered troops to Chicago. When they arrived on the morning of Independence Day, the city was peaceful. Before

long, however, violence broke out, and mobs, composed mostly of nonstrikers, overturned freight cars, looted, and burned. Restoring order, the army occupied railroad yards in Illinois, California, and other points. By late July, the strike was over; Debs was jailed for violating the injunction. Many people applauded Cleveland's action, "nominally for the expedition of the mails," a newspaper said, but "really for the preservation of society."

The Pullman strike had far-reaching consequences for the development of the labor movement. Working people resented Cleveland's actions in the strike, particularly as it became apparent that he sided with the railroads. Upholding Debs's sentence in *In re Debs* (1895), the Supreme Court endorsed the use of the injunction in labor disputes, thus giving business and government an effective antilabor weapon that hindered union growth in the 1890s. The strike's failure catapulted Debs into prominence. During his time in jail, he turned to socialism, and after his release he worked to build the Socialist party of America, which experienced some success after 1900.

The Miners of the Midwest

The plight of coal miners in the Midwest illustrated the personal and social impact of the depression. Even in the best of times, mining was a dirty

Washington police escort Jacob Coxey from the steps of the U.S. Capitol and through the ranks of his 500-man army and thousands of spectators. Fifty years later Coxey finished the speech that had been interrupted with his arrest.

and dangerous business. One miner in twelve died underground; one in three suffered injury. Mines routinely closed for as long as six months a year, and wages fell with the depression. An Illinois miner earned 97 cents per ton in 1889 and only 80 cents in 1896. A bituminous coal miner made $282 a year.

Midwestern mining was often a family occupation, passed down from father to son. It demanded delicate judgments about when to blast, where to follow a seam, and how to avoid rockfalls. Until 1890, English and Irish immigrants dominated the business. They migrated from mine to mine, but nearly always lived in flimsy shacks owned by the company. Time and again the miners struck for higher wages—between 1887 and 1894 there were 116 major coal strikes in Illinois, 111 in Ohio.

After 1890, immigration from southern and eastern Europe, hitherto a trickle, became a flood. Italians, Lithuanians, Poles, Slovaks, Magyars, Russians, Bohemians, and Croatians came to the mines to find work. In three years, nearly one thousand Italians settled in Coal City, Illinois; they comprised more than one-third of the population. In other mining towns, Italian and Polish miners soon comprised almost half the population.

As the depression deepened, tensions grew between miners and their employers and between "old" miners and the "new." Many "new" miners spoke no English, and often they were "birds of passage," transients who had come to the United States to make money to take back home. Lacking the skills handed down by the "old" miners, they were often blamed for accidents, and they worked longer hours for less pay. At many a tavern after work, "old" miners grumbled about the different-looking newcomers and considered ways to get rid of them.

In April 1894, a wave of wage reductions sparked an explosion of labor unrest in the mines. The United Mine Workers, a struggling union formed just four years earlier, called for a strike of bituminous coal miners, and on April 21, virtually all midwestern and Pennsylvania miners—some 170,000 in all—quit working. The flow of crucial coal slackened; cities faced blackouts; factories closed.

The violence that soon broke out followed a significant pattern. Over the years, the English and Irish miners had built up a set of unspoken

The American Railway Union (ARU) and the United Mine Workers of America (UMWA) stood at the forefront of the labor union movement of the late nineteenth century. The UMWA scored a victory in 1897 when miners in Illinois (pictured here) and three other states struck. With assistance from the American Federation of Labor and other groups, the miners were able to stay out for two and a half months until a settlement finally brought them an average 22.5 percent wage increase.

understandings with their employers. The "new" miners had not, and they were more prone to violent action to win a strike. The depression hit them especially hard, frustrating their plans to earn money and return home. In many areas, anger and frustration turned the 1894 strikes into outright war.

For nearly two weeks in June 1894 fighting rocked the Illinois, Ohio, and Indiana coalfields. Mobs ignited mine shafts, dynamited coal trains, and defied state militias. While miners of all backgrounds participated in the violence, it often divided "old" miners and "new." In Spring Valley, Illinois, exiled Italian anarchists took over the strike leadership and incited rioting despite the opposition of the "old" miners. Elsewhere, a mine fired by arsonists burned because the "new" miners prevented the "old" ones from extinguishing the blaze.

Shocked by the violence, public opinion shifted against the strikers. The strike ended in a matter of weeks, but its effects lingered. English and Irish miners moved out into other jobs or up into supervisory positions. Jokes and songs poked cruel fun at the "new" immigrants, and the Pennsylvania and Illinois legislatures adopted laws to keep them out of the mines. Thousands of "old" miners voted Populist in 1894—the Populist platform called for restrictions on immigration—in one of the Populists' few successes

that year. The United Mine Workers, dominated by the older miners, began in 1896 to urge Congress to stop the "demoralizing effects" of immigration.

Occurring at the same time, the Pullman strike pulled attention away from the crisis in the coalfields, yet the miners' strike involved three times as many workers and provided a revealing glimpse of the tensions within American society. The miners of the Midwest were the first large group of skilled workers seriously affected by the flood of immigrants from southern and eastern Europe. Buffeted by depression, they reflected the social and economic discord that permeated every industry.

A Beleaguered President

Building on the Democratic party's sweeping triumph in the midterm elections of 1890, Grover Cleveland decisively defeated the Populist candidate James B. Weaver and incumbent president Benjamin Harrison in 1892. He won by nearly 400,000 votes, a large margin by the standards of the era, and the Democrats increased their strength in the cities and among working-class voters. For the first time since the 1850s, they controlled the White House and both branches of Congress.

The Democrats, it now seemed, had broken the party stalemate, but unfortunately for Cleveland, the panic of 1893 struck almost as he took office. He was sure that he knew its cause. The Sherman Silver Purchase Act of 1890, he believed, had damaged business confidence, drained the Treasury's gold reserve, and caused the panic. The solution to the depression was equally simple: repeal the act.

In June 1893, Cleveland summoned Congress into special session. India had just closed its mints to silver, and Mexico was now the only country in the world with free silver coinage. The silverites were on the defensive, although they pleaded for a compromise. Rejecting the pleas, Cleveland pushed the repeal bill through Congress, and on November 1, 1893, he signed it into law. Always sure of himself, he had staked everything on a single measure—a winning strategy if he succeeded, a devastating one if he did not.

Repeal of the Sherman Silver Purchase Act was probably a necessary action. It responded to the realities of international finance, reduced the flight of gold out of the country, and over the long run, boosted business confidence. Unfortunately, it contracted the currency at a time when inflation might have helped. It did not bring economic revival. The stock market remained listless, businesses continued to close, unemployment spread, and farm prices dropped. "We are hourly expecting the arrival of the benevolent man who is to pay ten cents a pound for cotton," a Virginia newspaper said.

The repeal battle of 1893, discrediting the conservative Cleveland Democrats who had dominated the party since the 1860s, reshaped the politics of the country. It confined the Democratic party largely to the South, helped the Republicans become the majority party in 1894, and strengthened the position of the silver Democrats in their bid for the presidency in 1896. It also focused national attention on the silver issue and thus intensified the silver sentiment Cleveland had intended to dampen. In the end, repeal did not even solve the Treasury's gold problem. By January 1894, the reserve had fallen to $65 million. A year later, it fell to $44.5 million.

In January 1894, Cleveland desperately resorted to a sale of $50 million in gold bonds to replenish the gold reserve; the following November, he again sold bonds; and in February 1895, arousing outrage among many, he agreed to a third bond sale that allowed financier J. Pierpont Morgan and other bankers to reap large profits. A fourth bond sale in January 1896 also failed to stop the drain on the reserve, although it further sharpened the silverites' hatred of President Cleveland.

Still another blow to the morale of the Democrats came in 1894 when they tried to fulfill their long-standing promise to reduce the tariff. Despite all their efforts, the Wilson-Gorman Tariff Act, passed by Congress in August 1894, contained only modest reductions in duties. It reduced the tariff on coal, iron ore, wool, and sugar, ended the McKinley Tariff Act's popular reciprocity agreements with other countries, and moved some duties higher than ever before. It also imposed a small income tax, a provision the Supreme Court overturned in 1895 (*Pollock* v. *Farmer's Loan and Trust Co.*). Very few Democrats, including Cleveland, were pleased with the measure, and the president let it become law without his signature.

Depression Politics

The Democrats were buried in the elections of 1894, which were some of the most important elections in American history. Suffering the greatest defeat in congressional history, they lost 113 House seats, while the Republicans gained 117. In twenty-four states, not a single Democrat was elected to Congress. Only one Democrat (Boston's John F. Fitzgerald, the grandfather of President John F. Kennedy) came from all of New England. The Democrats even lost some of the "Solid South," and in the Midwest, a crucial battleground of the 1890s, the party was virtually destroyed.

Wooing labor and the unemployed, the Populists made striking inroads in parts of the South and West, yet their progress was far from enough. In a year in which thousands of voters switched parties, the People's party elected only four senators and four congressmen. Southern Democrats again used fraud and violence to keep the Populists' totals down. In the Midwest, the Populists won double the number of votes they had received in 1892, yet still attracted less than 7 percent of the vote. Across the country, the discontented tended to vote for the Republicans, not the Populists, a discouraging sign for the Populist party.

For millions of people, Grover Cleveland became a scapegoat for the country's economic ills. Fearing attack, he placed new police barracks on the White House grounds. The Democratic party split, and southern and western Democrats deserted him in droves. At Democratic conventions, Cleveland's name evoked jeers. "He is an old bag of beef," Democratic Congressman "Pitchfork" Ben Tillman told a South Carolina audience, "and I am going to go to Washington with a pitchfork and prod him in his old fat ribs."

The elections of 1894 marked the end of the party deadlock that had existed since the 1870s. The Democrats lost, the Populists gained somewhat, and the Republicans became the majority party in the country. In the midst of the depression, the Republican doctrines of activism and national authority, which voters had repudiated in the elections of 1890, became more attractive. This was a development of great significance, because as Americans became more accepting of the use of government power to regulate the economy and safeguard individual welfare, the way lay open to the reforms of the Progressive Era, the New Deal, and beyond.

CHANGING ATTITUDES

The depression, brutal and far reaching, did more than shift political alignments. Across the country, it undermined traditional views and caused people to rethink older ideas about government, the economy, and society. As men and women concluded that established ideas had failed to deal with the depression, they looked for new ones. There was, the president of the University of Wisconsin said, "a general, all-pervasive, restless discontent with the results of current political and economic thought."

In prosperous times, Americans had thought of unemployment as the result of personal failure, affecting primarily the lazy and immoral. "Let us remember," a leading Protestant minister once said, "that there is not a poor person in the United States who was not made poor by his own shortcomings." In the midst of depression, such views were harder to maintain, since everyone knew people who were both worthy *and* unemployed. Next door, a respected neighbor might be laid off; down the block, an entire factory might be shut down.

People debated issues they had long taken for granted. New and reinvigorated local institutions—discussion clubs, women's clubs, reform societies, university extension centers, church groups, farmers' societies—gave people a place to discuss alternatives to the existing order. Pressures for reform increased, and demand grew for government intervention to help the poor and unemployed.

Everybody Works But Father

Women and children had been entering the labor force for years, and the depression accelerated the trend. As husbands and fathers lost their jobs, more and more women and children went to work. Even as late as 1901, well after the depression had ended, a study of working-class families showed that more than half the principal bread-winners were out of work. So many women and children worked that in 1905 there was a popular song, "Everybody Works But Father."

During the 1890s, the number of working women rose from 4 million to 5.3 million. Trying to make ends meet, they took in boarders and found jobs as laundresses, cleaners, or domestics. Where possible, they worked in offices and factories. Far more black urban women than white worked to supplement their husbands' meager earnings. In New York City in 1900, nearly 60 percent of all black women worked compared to 27 percent of the foreign born and 24 percent of native-born white women. Men still dominated business offices, but during the 1890s, more and more employers noted the relative cheapness of female labor. Women telegraph and telephone operators nearly tripled in number during the decade. Women worked as clerks in the new five-and-tens and department stores, and as nurses; in 1900, half a million were teachers. They increasingly entered office work as stenographers and typists, occupations in which they earned between $6.00 and $15.00 a week, compared to factory wages of $1.50 to $8.00 a week.

The depression also caused an increasing number of children to work. During the 1890s, the

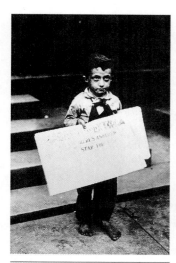

Tiny children peddling newspapers and female domestics serving the rich—their meager earnings were desperately needed.

number of children employed in southern textile mills jumped more than 160 percent, and boys and girls under sixteen years of age made up nearly one-third of the labor force of the mills. Youngsters of eight and nine years worked twelve hours a day for pitiful wages. In most cases, however, children worked not in factories but in farming and city street trades like peddling and shoeshining. In 1900, the South had more than half the child laborers in the nation.

Concerned about child labor, middle-class women in 1896 formed the League for the Protection of the Family, which called for compulsory education to get children out of factories and into classrooms. The Mothers Congress of 1896 gave rise to the National Congress of Parents and Teachers, the spawning ground of thousands of local PTAs. The National Council of Women and the General Federation of Women's Clubs took up similar issues. By the end of the 1890s, the Federation had 150,000 members who worked for various civic reforms in the fields of child welfare, education, and sanitation.

Changing Themes in Literature

The depression also gave point to a growing movement in literature toward realism and naturalism. In the years after the Civil War, literature often reflected the mood of romanticism—sentimental and unrealistic. Walt Whitman called it "ornamental confectionary" and "copious dribble," but it remained popular through the end of the century.

The novels of Horatio Alger, which provided simple lessons about how to get ahead in business and life, continued to attract large numbers of readers. A failed New York minister, Alger published some 130 novels—with titles like *Sink or Swim, Work and Win,* and *Struggling Upward*—which sold over twenty million copies. They told of poor youngsters who made their way to the top through hard work, thrift, honesty, and luck. Louisa May Alcott's *Little Women* (1868–1869) related the daily lives of four girls in a New England family; Anna Sewell's *Black Beauty* (1877) charmed readers with the story of an abused horse that found a happy home; and Lew Wallace's *Ben Hur* (1880), one of the era's best-selling books, offered a sweeping epic of life in the Roman empire.

After the 1870s, however, a number of talented authors began to reject romanticism and escapism, turning instead to realism. Determined to portray life as it was, they studied local dialects, wrote regional stories, and emphasized the "true" relationships between people. In doing so, they reflected broader trends in the society, such as industrialism, evolutionary theory, which emphasized the effect of the environment on humans, and the new philosophy of pragmatism, which stressed the relativity of values. (See Chapter 22 for a more detailed discussion of pragmatism.)

Regionalist authors like Joel Chandler Harris and George Washington Cable depicted life in the South; Hamlin Garland described the grimness of life on the Great Plains; and Sarah Orne Jewett wrote about everyday life in rural New England. Another regionalist, Bret Harte, achieved fame with stories that portrayed the local color of the California mining camps, particularly in his popular tale "The Outcasts of Poker Flat."

Harte was joined by a more talented writer, Mark Twain, who became the country's most outstanding realist author. Growing up along the Mississippi River in Hannibal County, Missouri, the young Samuel Langhorne Clemens observed life around him with a humorous and skeptical eye. Adopting a pen name from the river term "mark twain" (two fathoms), he wrote a number of important works that drew on his own experiences. *Life on the Mississippi* (1883) described his career as a steamboat pilot. *The Adventures of Tom Sawyer* (1876) and *The Adventures of Huckleberry Finn* (1884) gained international prominence. In these books, Twain used dialect and common speech instead of literary language, touching off a major change in American prose style.

William Dean Howells—after Twain, the country's most famous author—came more slowly to the realist approach. At first, he wrote about the happier sides of life, but then he grew worried about the impact of industrialization. *A Traveler from Altruria* (1894), a utopian novel, described an industrial society that consumed lives. The poem "Society" (1895), written in the midst of the depression, compared society to a splendid ball in which men and women danced on flowers covering the bodies of the poor:

> *And now and then from out the dreadful floor*
> *An arm or brow was lifted from the rest,*
> *As if to strike in madness, or implore*
> *For mercy; and anon some suffering breast*
> *Heaved from the mass and sank; and as before*
> *The revellers above them thronged and prest.*

Other writers, the "Nationalists," became impatient even with realism. Pushing Darwinian theory to its limits, they wrote of a world in which a cruel and merciless environment determined human fate. Often focusing on economic hardship, naturalist writers studied the poor, the lower classes, and the criminal mind; they brought to their writing the social workers' passion for direct and honest experience.

Stephen Crane spent a night in a seven-cent lodging house on the Bowery and in "An Experiment in Misery" captured the smells and sounds of the poor. Crane depicted the carnage of war in *The Red Badge of Courage* (1895) and the impact of poverty in *Maggie: A Girl of the Streets* (1893). His poetry suggested the unimportance of the individual in an uncaring world:

> *A man said to the universe*
> *"Sir, I exist!"*
> *"However," replied the universe,*
> *"The fact has not created in me*
> *A sense of obligation."*

Frank Norris assailed the power of big business in two dramatic novels, *The Octopus* (1901) and *The Pit* (1903), both the story of individual futility in the face of the heartless corporations. Norris's *McTeague* (1899) studied the disintegration of character under economic pressure. Jack London, another naturalist author, traced the power of nature over civilized society in novels like *The Sea Wolf* (1904) and *The Call of the Wild* (1903), his classic tale of a sled dog that preferred the difficult life of the wilderness to the world of human beings.

Theodore Dreiser, the foremost naturalist writer, grimly portrayed a dark world in which

In one of the popular literary works of the time, Mark Twain created an idyllic setting for the adventures of the irrepressible Tom Sawyer, shown here (left) convincing a gullible friend of the joys of whitewashing a fence. A powerful drawing entitled From the Depths (above) illustrated another popular work, J. Ames Mitchell's The Silent War (1906), which dealt with the class struggle.

human beings were tossed about by forces beyond their understanding or control. "My own ambition," Dreiser said, "is to represent my world, to conform to the large, truthful lines of life." In his great novel, *Sister Carrie* (1901), he followed a young farm girl who took a job in a Chicago shoe factory. He described the exhausting nature of factory work: "Her hands began to ache at the wrists and then in the fingers, and towards the last she seemed one mass of dull, complaining muscle, fixed in an eternal position, and performing a single mechanical movement."

Like other naturalists, Dreiser focused on environment and character. He thought writers should tell the truth about human affairs, not fabricate romance, and *Sister Carrie*, he said, was "not intended as a piece of literary craftsmanship, but was a picture of conditions."

THE PRESIDENTIAL ELECTION OF 1896

The election of 1896 was known as "the battle of the standards" because it focused primarily on

*T*he Wonderful Wizard of Oz

The Wicked Witch of the West.

A restless dreamer, Frank Baum tried his hand at several careers before he gained fame and fortune as a writer of children's literature. From 1888 to 1891, he ran a store and newspaper in South Dakota, where he experienced the desolation and grayness that accompanied agrarian discontent. An avid supporter of William Jennings Bryan in the "battle of the standards," Baum wrote an enduring allegory of the silver movement, *The Wonderful Wizard of Oz.* Published in April 1900, it was an immediate success.

The book opens with a grim description of Kansas:

When Dorothy stood in the doorway and looked around, she could see nothing but the great gray prairie on every side. Not a tree nor a house broke the broad sweep of flat country that reached the edge of the sky in all directions. The sun had baked the plowed land into a gray mass, with little cracks running through it. Even the grass was not green, for the sun had burned the tops of the long blades until they were the same gray color to be seen everywhere. Once the house had been painted, but the sun blistered the paint and the rains washed it away, and now the house
was as dull and gray as everything else.

Kansas had not always seemed that way. After 1854, when the Kansas-Nebraska Act opened to settlement its 50 million acres of grassland, people poured into the state to stake their claims. Many came from the hilly timbered country to the east, and breaking onto the prairie, they saw "a new world, reaching to the far horizon without break of trees or chimney stack; just sky and grass and grass and sky. . . . The hush was so loud. . . . The heavens seemed nearer than ever before and awe and beauty and majesty over all."

In later years railroads crisscrossed the state, and advertisements touted the fertile soil. Land was plentiful, rainfall somehow seemed to increase each year, crop prices held at levels high enough to pay, new farming implements yielded larger crops, and property values increased.

Yet life on the prairie was never an easy matter. Flat, lonely, and windswept, the land affected people in ways that were hard to describe to the folks back East. When Aunt Em, Dorothy's aunt, came to Kansas to live, she was young and pretty, but the sun and wind soon changed her. "They had taken the sparkle from her eyes and left
them a sober gray; they had taken the red from her cheeks and lips, and they were gray also." Like Aunt Em, Uncle Henry never laughed. "He worked hard from morning till night and did not know what joy was."

After 1887, a series of droughts struck Kansas, and as many as three out of four farms were mortgaged in some Kansas counties. Thousands of settlers like Aunt Em and Uncle Henry gave up and retraced their steps East; others trusted in the Farmers' Alliance and pinned their hopes on the free coinage of silver. While gold as a standard of currency symbolized the idle rich of the industrial Northeast, silver stood for the common folk. Added to the currency in the

Dorothy (wearing silver, not ruby, slippers in the original version) and her friends prepare to "follow the yellow brick road."

brick road, thus achieving a proper relationship between the precious metals, silver and gold. Like many of her countrymen, she does not at first recognize the power of the silver slippers, but a kiss from the Good Witch of the North (Northern voters) protects her on the road. Dorothy meets the Scarecrow (the farmer) who has been told he has no brain but actually possesses great common sense (no "hick" or "hayseed," he); the Tin Woodman (the industrial worker) who fears he has become heartless but discovers the spirit of love and cooperation; and the Cowardly Lion (reformers, particularly William Jennings Bryan) who turns out not to be very cowardly at all.

When the four companions reach the Emerald City, they meet the "Great and Terrible" Wizard who tells them that, to gain his help, they must destroy the Wicked Witch of the West (mortgage companies, heartless nature, and other things opposing progress there). Courageously, they set forth. Dorothy dissolves the witch with a bucket of water (what else for drought-ridden farmers?), but when they return to the Emerald City, they find that the great and powerful Wizard (the money power) is only a charlatan, a manipulator, whose power rests on myth and illusion. "'I thought Oz was a great Head,' said Dorothy. . . . 'And I thought Oz was a terrible Beast,' said the Tin Woodman. 'And I thought Oz was a Ball of Fire,' exclaimed the Lion. 'No; you are all wrong,' said the little man meekly. 'I have been making believe.'"

Dorothy unmasks the wizard, and with the help of Glinda, the Good Witch of the South (support

for silver was strong in the South), uses the silver slippers to return home to Kansas. Sadly, the shoes are lost in flight. Back in Oz, the Scarecrow rules the Emerald City (the triumph of the farmers), and the Tin Woodman reigns in the West (industrialism moves West). "Oz" was a familiar abbreviation to those involved in the 16 to 1 (ounces) fight over the ratio of silver to gold.

Baum wanted to write American fairy tales to "bear the stamp of our times and depict the progressive fairies of today." The land of Oz reflected his belief in the American values of freedom and independence, love of family, self-reliance, individualism, and sympathy for the underdog. *Oz*, he said in the original introduction, "aspires to being a modernized fairy tale, in which the wonderment and joy are retained and the heartaches and nightmares are left out."

The *Oz* stories have remained popular, and they still rest on many children's bookshelves. A 1939 film starring Judy Garland as Dorothy, with Ray Bolger as the Scarecrow, Jack Haley as the Tin Woodman, Bert Lahr as the Cowardly Lion, and Frank Morgan as the Wizard was spectacularly successful. Released in the midst of another depression, the film included songs designed to escape hardship, as Dorothy once had, "Somewhere over the Rainbow."

form of silver dollars, it meant more money, higher crop prices, and a return of prosperity.

Or so the supporters of silver coinage believed. In *The Wonderful Wizard of Oz*, Dorothy (every person) is carried by a cyclone (a victory of the silver forces at the polls) from drought-stricken Kansas to a marvelous land of riches and witches. Unlike dry, gray Kansas, Oz is beautiful, with rippling brooks, stately trees, colorful flowers, and bright-feathered birds. On arrival, Dorothy disposes of one witch, the Wicked Witch of the East (the eastern money power and those favoring gold), and frees the Munchkins (the common people) from servitude. To return to Kansas, she must first go to the Emerald City (the national capital, greenback-colored).

Dorothy wears magical silver slippers and follows the yellow

the gold and silver standards of money. As an election it was exciting and decisive. New voting patterns replaced old, a new majority party confirmed its control of the country, and national policy shifted to suit new realities.

The Mystique of Silver

Sentiment for free silver coinage grew swiftly after 1894, dominating the South and West, appearing even in the farming regions of New York and New England. Prosilver literature flooded the country (see "The Wonderful Wizard of Oz," pp. 620–621). Pamphlets issued by the millions argued silver's virtues.

People wanted quick solutions to the economic crisis. During 1896, unemployment shot up; farm income and prices fell to the lowest point in the decade. "I can remember back as far as 1858," an Iowa hardware dealer said in February 1896, "and I have never seen such hard times as these are." The silverites offered a solution, simple but compelling: the free and independent coinage of silver at the ratio of 16 ounces of silver to every 1 ounce of gold. Free coinage meant that the U.S. mints would coin all the silver offered to them. Independent coinage meant that the country would coin silver regardless of the policies of other nations, nearly all of which were on the gold standard.

It is difficult now to understand the kind of faith the silverites placed in silver as a cure for the depression. But faith it was, and of a sort that some observers compared to religious fervor. Underlying it all was a belief in a quantity theory of money: the silverites believed the amount of money in circulation determined the level of activity in the economy. If money was short, that meant there was a limit on economic activity and ultimately a depression. If the government coined silver as well as gold, that meant more money in circulation, more business for everyone, and thus prosperity. Farm prices would rise; laborers would go back to work. As one silverite said, "It means the reopening of closed factories, the relighting of fires in darkened furnaces; it means hope instead of despair; comfort in place of suffering; life instead of death."

By 1896, silver was also a symbol. It had moral and patriotic dimensions—by going to a silver standard, the United States could assert its independence in the world—and it stood for a wide range of popular grievances. For many, it reflected rural values rather than urban ones, suggested a shift of power away from the Northeast, and spoke for the downtrodden instead of the well-to-do. Silver represented the common people, as the vast literature of the movement showed.

William H. Harvey's *Coin's Financial School* (1894), the most popular of all silver pamphlets, had the eloquent Coin, a wise but unknown youth, tutoring famous people on the currency. Bankers, lawyers, and scholars came to argue for gold, but left shaken, leaning toward silver. *Coin's Financial School* sold five thousand copies a day at its peak in 1895, with tens of thousands of copies distributed free by silver organizations. It "is being sold on every railroad train by the newsboys and at every cigar store. . . ," a Mississippi congressman said. "It is being read by almost everybody."

Silver was more than just a political or economic issue. It was a social movement, one of the largest in American history, but its life span turned out to be brief. As a mass phenomenon, it flourished between 1894 and 1896, then succumbed to electoral defeat, the return of prosperity, and the onset of fresh concerns. But in its time, the silver movement bespoke a national mood and won millions of followers.

The Republicans and Gold

Scenting victory over the discredited Democrats, numerous Republicans fought for the party's presidential nomination, including "Czar" Thomas B. Reed of the Billion-Dollar Congress. Reed picked up early support but suffered from his reputation for biting wit. William McKinley of Ohio, his chief rival, soon passed him in the race for the nomination.

Able, calm, and affable, McKinley had served in the Union Army during the Civil War. In 1876, he won a seat in Congress where he became the chief sponsor of the tariff act named for him. In the months before the 1896 national convention, Marcus A. Hanna, his campaign manager and trusted friend, built a powerful national organization that featured McKinley as "the Advance Agent of Prosperity," an alluring slogan in a country beset with depression. When the convention met in June, McKinley had the nomination in hand, and he backed a platform that favored the gold standard against the free coinage of silver.

Republicans favoring silver proposed a pro-silver platform, but the convention overwhelmingly defeated it. Twenty-three silverite Republicans, far fewer than prosilver forces had hoped, marched out of the convention hall. The remaining delegates waved handkerchiefs and flags and shouted "Good-bye" and "Put them out." Hanna stood on a chair screaming "Go! Go! Go!" William Jennings Bryan, who was there as a special correspondent for a Nebraska newspaper, climbed on a desk to get a better view.

The Democrats and Silver

Silver, meanwhile, had virtually captured large segments of the Democratic party in the South and West. Despite President Cleveland's opposition, more than twenty Democratic state platforms came out for free silver in 1894. Power in the party shifted to the South, where it remained for decades. The party's base narrowed; its outlook increasingly reflected southern views on silver, race, and other issues. In effect, the Democrats became a sectional—no longer a national—party.

The anti-Cleveland Democrats had their issue, but they lacked a leader. Out in Nebraska, Bryan saw the opportunity to take on that role. He was barely thirty-six years old and had relatively little political experience. But he had spent months wooing support, and he was a captivating public speaker—tall, slender, and handsome, with a resounding voice that, in an era without microphones, projected easily into every corner of an auditorium. Practicing at home before a mirror, he rehearsed his speeches again and again, as his wife, Mary, a bright, sharp, and politically astute woman, listened for errors.

From the outset of the 1896 Democratic convention, the silver Democrats were in charge, and they put together a platform that stunned the Cleveland wing of the party. It demanded the free coinage of silver, attacked Cleveland's actions in the Pullman strike, and censured his gold bond sales. On July 9, as delegates debated the platform, Bryan's moment came. Striding to the

The religious symbolism in Bryan's "Cross of Gold" speech is satirized in this cartoon, but his stirring rhetoric captivated his audience and won him the Democratic presidential nomination for the election of 1896.

stage, he stood for an instant, a hand raised for silence, waiting for the applause to die down. He would not contend with the previous speakers, he began, for "this is not a contest between persons. The humblest citizen in all the land, when clad in the armor of a righteous cause, is stronger than all the hosts of error. I come to speak to you in defense of a cause as holy as the cause of liberty—the cause of humanity."

The delegates were captivated. Like a trained choir, they rose, cheered each point, and sat back to listen for more. Easterners, Bryan said, liked to praise businessmen but forgot that plain people—laborers, miners, and farmers—were businessmen, too. Shouts rang through the hall and delegates pounded on chairs. Savoring each cheer, Bryan defended silver. Then came the famous closing: "Having behind us the producing masses of this nation and the world . . . we will answer their demand for a gold standard by saying to them: 'You shall not press down upon the brow of labor this crown of thorns, you shall not crucify mankind upon a cross of gold.'"

Bryan moved his fingers down his temples, suggesting blood trickling from his wounds. He ended with his arms outstretched as on a cross. Letting the silence hang, he dropped his arms, stepped back, then started to his seat. Suddenly, there was pandemonium. Delegates shouted and cheered. When the tumult subsided, they adopted the anti-Cleveland platform, and the next day, Bryan won the presidential nomination.

Campaign and Election

The Democratic convention presented the Populists with a dilemma. The People's party had staked everything on the assumption that neither major party would endorse silver. Now it faced a painful choice: nominate an independent ticket and risk splitting the silverite forces or nominate Bryan and give up its separate identity as a party.

The choice was unpleasant, and it shattered the People's party. Meeting late in July, the party's national convention nominated Bryan, but rather than accept the Democratic candidate for vice president, it named Tom Watson instead. The Populists' endorsement probably hurt Bryan as much as it helped. It won him relatively few votes, since many Populists would have voted for him anyway, and it identified him as a Populist, which he was not, allowing the Republicans to accuse him of heading a ragtag army of malcontents. The squabble over Watson seemed to prove that the Democratic-Populist alliance could never stay together long enough to govern.

In August 1896, Bryan set off on a campaign that became an American legend. Much of the conservative Democratic eastern press had deserted him, and he took his campaign directly to the voters, the first presidential candidate in history to do so in a systematic way. By his own count, Bryan traveled 18,009 miles, visited 27 states, and spoke 600 times to a total of some 3 million people. He built skillfully on a new "merchandising" style of campaign in which he worked to educate and persuade voters.

Bryan summoned voters to an older America: a land where farms were as important as factories, where the virtues of rural and religious life outweighed the doubtful lure of the city, where common people still ruled, and opportunity existed for all. He drew on the Jeffersonian tradition of

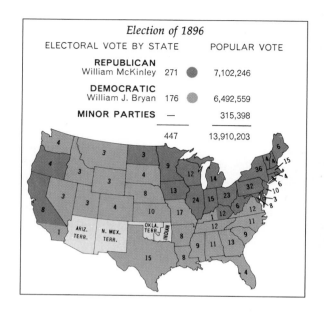

rural virtue, distrust of central authority, and abiding faith in the powers of human reason.

Urged to take the stump against Bryan, McKinley replied, "I might just as well put up a trapeze on my front lawn and compete with some professional athlete as go out speaking against Bryan." The Republican candidate let voters come to him. Railroads brought them by the thousands into McKinley's hometown of Canton, Ohio, and he spoke to them from his front porch. Through use of the press, he reached fully as many people as Bryan's more strenuous effort. Appealing to labor, immigrants, well-to-do farmers, businessmen, and the middle class, McKinley defended economic nationalism and the advancing urban-industrial society.

On election day, voter turnout was extraordinarily high, a measure of the intense interest. By nightfall, the outcome was clear: McKinley won 50 percent of the vote to Bryan's 46 percent. He won the Northeast and Midwest and carried four border states. In the cities, McKinley crushed Bryan.

The election struck down the Populists, whose totals sagged nearly everywhere. Many Populist proposals were later adopted under different leadership. The graduated income tax, crop loans to farmers, the secret ballot, and direct election of U.S. senators all were early Populist ideas. But the People's party never could win over a majority of the voters, and failing that, it vanished after 1896.

The Election of 1900

Candidate	Party	Popular Vote	Electoral Vote
McKinley	Republican	7,218,039	292
Bryan	Democrat	6,358,345	155
Woolley	Prohibition	209,004	0
Debs	Socialist	86,935	0

THE McKINLEY ADMINISTRATION

The election of 1896 cemented the voter realignment of 1894 and initiated a generation of Republican rule. For more than three decades after 1896, with only a brief Democratic resurgence under Woodrow Wilson, the Republicans remained the country's majority party.

McKinley took office in 1897 under favorable circumstances. To everyone's relief, the economy had begun to revive. The stock market rose, factories once again churned out goods, and farmers prospered. Farm prices climbed sharply during 1897 on bumper crops of wheat, cotton, and corn. Discoveries of gold in Australia and Alaska—together with the development of a new cyanide process for extracting gold from ore—enlarged the world's gold supply, decreased its price, and inflated the currency as the silverites had hoped. For the first time since 1890, the 1897 Treasury statements showed a comfortable gold reserve.

McKinley and the Republicans basked in the glow. They became the party of progress and prosperity, an image that helped them win victories until another depression hit in the 1930s. McKinley's popularity soared. Open and accessible in contrast to Cleveland's isolation, he rode the Washington streetcars, walked the streets, and enjoyed looking in department store windows. Cleveland's special police barracks vanished from the White House lawn. McKinley became the first president to ride in an automobile, reaching the speed of 18 miles an hour.

An activist president, he set the policies of the administration. Conscious of the limits of power, he maintained close ties with Congress and worked hard to educate the public on national choices and priorities. McKinley struck new relations with the press and traveled far more than previous presidents. In some ways, he began the modern presidency.

Shortly after taking office, he summoned Congress into special session to revise the tariff. In July 1897, the Dingley Tariff passed the House and Senate. It raised average tariff duties to a record level, and as the final burst of nineteenth-century protectionism, it caused trouble for the Republican party. By the end of the 1890s, consumers, critics, and the Republicans themselves were wondering if the tariff had outlived its usefulness in the maturing American economy.

From the 1860s to the 1890s, the Republicans had built their party on a pledge to *promote* economic growth through the use of state and national power. By 1900, with the industrial system firmly in place, the focus had shifted. The need to *regulate,* to control the effects of industrialism, became a central public concern of the new century. McKinley prodded the Republicans to meet that shift, but he died before his plans matured.

McKinley toyed with the idea of lowering the tariff, but one obstacle always stood in the way: the government needed revenue, and tariff duties were one of the few taxes the public would support. The Spanish-American War of 1898 (see Chapter 21) persuaded people to accept greater federal power and, with it, new forms of taxation. In 1899, McKinley spoke of lowering tariff barriers in a world that technology had made smaller. "God and man have linked the nations together. . . ," he said in his last speech at Buffalo, New York, in 1901. "Isolation is no longer possible or desirable."

In 1898 and 1899, the McKinley administration focused on the war with Spain, the peace treaty that followed, and the dawning realization that the war had thrust the United States into a position of world power. In March 1900, Congress passed the Gold Standard Act, which declared gold the standard of currency and ended the silver controversy that had dominated the 1890s.

The presidential campaign of 1900 was a replay of the McKinley-Bryan fight of 1896. McKinley's running mate was Theodore

Gold triumphs over silver in this Puck *cartoon referring to the Gold Standard Act of 1900.*

Roosevelt, hero of the Spanish-American War (see Chapter 21) and former governor of New York, who was nominated for vice president to capitalize on his popularity and, his enemies hoped, to sidetrack his political career into oblivion. Bryan stressed the issues of imperialism and the trusts; McKinley stressed his record at home and abroad. The result in 1900 was a landslide.

On September 6, 1901, a few months after his second inauguration, McKinley stood in a receiving line at the Pan-American Exposition in Buffalo. Leon Czolgosz, a twenty-eight-year-old unemployed laborer and anarchist, moved through the line, and reaching the president, shot him. Surgeons probed the wound but could find nothing. A recent discovery called the X-ray was on display at the exposition, but it was not used. On September 14, McKinley died, and Vice President Theodore Roosevelt became president. A new century had begun.

As the funeral train carried McKinley's body back to Ohio, Mark Hanna, McKinley's old friend and ally, sat slumped in his parlor car. "I told William McKinley it was a mistake to nominate that wild man at Philadelphia," he mourned. "I asked him if he realized what would happen if he should die. Now look, that damned cowboy is president of the United States!"

Hanna's world had changed, and so had the nation's—not so much because "that damned cowboy" was suddenly president, but because events of the 1890s had had powerful effects. In the course of that decade, political patterns shifted, the presidency acquired fresh power, and massive unrest prompted social change. The war with Spain brought a new empire and worldwide responsibilities. Economic hardship posed questions of the most difficult sort about industrialization, urbanization, and the quality of American life. Worried, people embraced new ideas and causes. Reform movements begun in the 1890s flowered in the Progressive period after 1900.

Technology continued to alter the way Americans lived. In 1896, Henry Ford produced a two-cylinder, four-horsepower car, the first of the famous line that bore his name. In 1899, the first automobile salesroom opened in New York, and some innovative thinkers were already imagining a network of service stations to keep the new cars running. At Kitty Hawk, North Carolina, Wilbur and Orville Wright, two bicycle manufacturers, neared the birth of powered flight.

The realignments that reached their peak in the 1890s seem distant, yet they are not. Important decisions in those years shaped nearly everything that came after them. In character and influence, the 1890s are as much a part of the twentieth century as of the nineteenth.

Recommended Reading

The most thorough account of the 1890s is in Harold U. Faulkner, *Politics, Reform and Expansion, 1890–1900* (1959), but see also Robert H. Wiebe, *The Search for Order, 1877–1920* (1967), and Samuel P. Hays, *The Response to Industrialism, 1855–1914* (1957). David P. Thelen, *The New Citizenship: Origins of Progressivism in Wisconsin, 1885–1900* (1972), stresses the impact of the depression on ideas and attitudes.

The best study of the 1890s depression is Charles Hoffman, *The Depression of the Nineties: An Economic History* (1970). Alexander Keyssar, *Out of Work: The First Century of Unemployment in Massachusetts* (1986) is also valuable. H. Wayne Morgan, *From Hayes to McKinley: National Party Politics, 1877–1896* (1969), and Richard J. Jensen, *The Winning of the Midwest: Social and Political Conflict, 1888–1896* (1971), are good on politics. See also

William R. Brock, *Investigation and Responsibility: Public Responsibility in the United States, 1865–1900* (1984). C. Vann Woodward examines the South in *Origins of the New South, 1877–1913* (1951).

Larzer Ziff, *The American 1890s* (1966); Henry Steele Commager, *The American Mind* (1950); and Justin Kaplan, *Mr. Clemens and Mark Twain* (1966), examine literary currents. On Populism, see John D. Hicks, *The Populist Revolt* (1931), and Lawrence Goodwyn, *Democratic Promise: The Populist Moment in America* (1976). C. Vann Woodward, *Tom Watson: Agrarian Rebel* (1938), is a superb biography. John L. Shover, *First Majority—Last Minority: The Transforming of Rural Life in America* (1976), examines conditions on the farms.

Additional Bibliography

On politics, see Morton Keller, *Affairs of State: Public Life in Late Nineteenth Century America* (1977); Paul John Kleppner, *The Cross of Culture: A Social Analysis of Midwestern Politics, 1850–1900* (1970), and *Continuity and Change in Electoral Politics, 1893–1928* (1987); Michael E. McGerr, *The Decline of Popular Politics: The American North, 1865–1928* (1986); Richard L. McCormick, *The Party Period and Public Policy: American Politics from the Age of Jackson to the Progressive Era* (1986); Samuel McSeveney, *The Politics of Depression* (1972); Paula Baker, *The Moral Frameworks of Public Life: Gender, Politics, and the State in Rural New York, 1870–1930* (1991); Carl V. Harris, *Political Power in Birmingham, 1871–1921* (1977); John Tomsich, *A Genteel Endeavor: American Culture and Politics in the Gilded Age* (1971); Bess Beatty, *A Revolution Gone Backward: The Black Response to National Politics, 1876–1896* (1987); Lewis Nicholas Wynne, *The Continuity of Cotton: Planter Politics in Georgia, 1865–1892* (1986); Robert D. Marcus, *Grand Old Party: Political Structure in the Gilded Age, 1880–1896* (1971); Ballard C. Campbell, *Representative Democracy: Public Policy and Midwestern Legislatures in the Late Nineteenth Century* (1980); Eric Anderson, *Race and Politics in North Carolina, 1872–1901: The Black Second* (1981); and R. Hal Williams, *Years of Decision: American Politics in the 1890s* (1978).

Biographies of the era's personalities include Allan Nevins, *Grover Cleveland* (1932); Paola E. Coletta, *William Jennings Bryan*, 3 vols. (1964–1969); Robert W. Cherny, *A Righteous Cause: The Life of William Jennings Bryan* (1985); LeRoy Ashby, *William Jennings Bryan* (1987); Kenneth Davison, *The Presidency of Rutherford B. Hayes* (1972); Ari Hoogenboom, *The Presidency of Rutherford B. Hayes,*

(1988); Justus D. Doenecke, *The Presidencies of James A. Garfield and Chester A. Arthur* (1981); Richard E. Welch, *The Presidencies of Grover Cleveland* (1988); Homer E. Socolofsky and Allan B. Spetter, *The Presidency of Benjamin Harrison* (1987); and Lewis L. Gould, *The Presidency of William McKinley* (1981). See also Peter H. Argersinger, *Populism and Politics: William Alfred Peffer and the People's Party* (1974); and Martin Ridge, *Ignatius Donnelly* (1962).

On Populism, see Steven Hahn, *The Roots of Southern Populism* (1983); Robert C. McMath, Jr., *Populist Vanguard: A History of the Southern Farmers' Alliance* (1975), and *American Populism: A Social History, 1877–1898* (1993); Bruce Palmer, *"Man Over Money": The Southern Populist Critique of American Capitalism* (1980); Barton C. Shaw, *The Wool-Hat Boys: Georgia's Populist Party* (1984); Norman Pollack, *The Just Polity: Populism, Law, and Human Welfare* (1987), and *The Humane Economy: Populism, Capitalism, and Democracy* (1990); Scott G. McNall, *The Road to Rebellion: Class Formation and Kansas Populism, 1865–1900* (1988); Lala Carr Steelman, *The North Carolina Farmers' Alliance* (1985); Worth Robert Miller, *Oklahoma Populism* (1987); Theodore R. Mitchell, *Political Education in the Southern Farmers' Alliance, 1887–1900* (1987); James E. Wright, *The Politics of Populism: Dissent in Colorado* (1974); O. Gene Clanton, *Kansas Populism: Ideas and Men* (1969), and *Populism: The Humane Preference in America, 1890–1900* (1991); Peter H. Argersinger, ed.,

Populism, Its Rise and Fall: William A. Peffer (1992); Robert W. Larson, *New Mexico Populism* (1974); Larson, *Populism in the Mountain West* (1986); and Stanley B. Parsons, *The Populist Context: Rural Versus Urban Power on a Great Plains Frontier* (1973).

Social and labor unrest is covered in Almont Lindsey, *The Pullman Strike: The Story of a Unique Experiment and of a Great Labor Upheaval* (1942); Stanley Buder, *Pullman: An Experiment in Industrial Order and Community Planning, 1880–1930* (1967); Ray Ginger, *The Bending Cross: A Biography of Eugene Victor Debs* (1969); Nick Salvatore, *Eugene V. Debs: Citizen and Socialist* (1982); Donald L. McMurry, *Coxey's Army: A Study of the Industrial Army Movement of 1894* (1929); Carlos A. Schwantes, *Coxey's Army: An American Odyssey* (1985); Shelton Stromquist, *A Generation of Boomers: The Pattern of Railroad Labor Conflict in Nineteenth-Century America* (1987); and Dorothy Schweider, *Black Diamonds: Life and Work in Iowa's Coal Mining Communities, 1895–1925* (1983). Walter T. K. Nugent, *Money and American Society* (1968), and Allen Weinstein, *Prelude to Populism: Origins of the Silver Issue, 1867–1878* (1970), explain the silver-gold controversy.

Stanley L. Jones, *The Presidential Election of 1896* (1964); Paul W. Glad, *McKinley, Bryan, and the People* (1964); and Robert F. Durden, *The Climax of Populism: The Election of 1896* (1965), examine that election.

Toward Empire

Many Americans regretted the start of the war with Spain that began in April 1898, but many others welcomed it. War was different then, shorter and more personal than the all-encompassing, lengthy, and mechanistic wars of the twentieth century. Many highly respected people believed that nations must fight every now and then to prove their power and test the national spirit.

Theodore Roosevelt, thirty-nine years old in 1898, was one of them. Nations needed to fight in order to survive, he thought. For months Roosevelt argued strenuously for war with Spain for three reasons: first, on grounds of freeing Cuba and expelling Spain from the hemisphere; second, because of "the benefit done to our people by giving them something to think of which isn't material gain"; and third, because the army and navy needed the practice.

In April 1898, Roosevelt was serving in the important post of assistant secretary of the navy. When war broke out, he quickly resigned to join the army, rejecting the advice of the secretary of the navy who warned he would only "ride a horse and brush mosquitoes from his neck in the Florida sands." The secretary was wrong—dead wrong—and later had the grace to admit it. "Roosevelt was right," he said. "His going into the Army led straight to the Presidency."

In 1898, officers supplied their own uniforms, and Roosevelt, the son of well-to-do parents, wanted his to be stylish. He wired Brooks Brothers, the expensive New York clothier, for a "regular Lieutenant-Colonel's uniform without yellow on the collar and with leggings," to be ready in a week. Joining a friend, he chose to enlist his own regiment, and after a few telephone calls to friends, and telegrams to the governors of Arizona, New Mexico, and Oklahoma asking for "good shots and good riders," he had more than enough men. The First United States Volunteer Cavalry, an intriguing mixture of Ivy League athletes and western frontiersmen, was born.

Known as the Rough Riders, it included men from the Harvard, Yale, and Princeton clubs of New York City, the Somerset Club of Boston, and New York's exclusive Knickerbocker Club. Former college athletes—football players, tennis players, and track stars—enlisted. Woodbury Kane, a wealthy yachtsman, signed up and promptly volunteered for kitchen duty.

Other volunteers came from the West—natural soldiers, Roosevelt called them, "tall and sinewy, with resolute, weather-beaten faces, and eyes that looked a man straight in the face without flinching." Among the cowboys, hunters, and prospectors, there was Bucky O'Neill, a legendary Arizona sheriff and Indian fighter, a half-dozen other sheriffs and Texas Rangers, a large number of Indians, a famous broncobuster, and an ex-marshal of Dodge City, Kansas.

Eager for war, the men trained hard, played harder, and rarely passed up a chance for an intellectual discussion—if Roosevelt's memoir of the war is to be believed. Once, he overheard Bucky O'Neill and a Princeton graduate "discussing Aryan word-roots together, and then sliding off into a review of the novels of Balzac, and a discussion as to how far Balzac could be said to be the founder of the modern realistic school of fiction." Roosevelt himself spent his spare time reading *Superiorité des Anglo-Saxons,* a French work that strove to prove the superiority of English-speaking peoples. In such a camp discipline was lax, and enlisted men got on easily with the officers.

The troops howled with joy when orders came to join the invasion army for Cuba. They won their first victories in Florida, fighting off other regiments to capture a train to take them to the wharf and then seizing the only available troopship to Cuba. The Rough Riders set sail on June 14, 1898, and Lieutenant Colonel Roosevelt, who had performed a war dance for the troops the night before, caught their mood: "We knew not whither we were bound, nor what we were to do; but we believed that the nearing future held for us many chances of death and hardship, of honor and renown. If we failed, we would share the fate of all who fail; but we were sure that we would win, that we should score the first great triumph in a mighty world-movement."

AMERICA LOOKS OUTWARD

The overseas expansion of the 1890s differed in several important respects from earlier expansionist moves of the United States. From its beginning, the American republic had been

Colonel Theodore Roosevelt poses in his custom-designed uniform. With surgeon Leonard Wood, Roosevelt organized the First U.S. Volunteer Cavalry—the Rough Riders—for service in the Spanish-American War.

expanding. After the first landings in Jamestown and Plymouth, settlers pushed westward: into the trans-Appalachian region, the Louisiana Territory, Florida, Texas, California, Arizona, and New Mexico. Most of these lands were contiguous with existing territories of the United States, and most were intended for settlement, usually agricultural.

The expansion of the 1890s was different. It sought to gain island possessions, the bulk of them already thickly populated. The new territories were held less for settlement than as naval bases, trading outposts, or commercial centers on major trade routes. More often than not, they were viewed as colonies, not as states-in-the-making.

Historian Samuel F. Bemis described the overseas expansion of the 1890s as "the great aberration," a time when the country adopted expansionist policies that did not fit with prior ex-

perience. Other historians, pointing to expansionist tendencies in thought and foreign policy that surfaced during the last half of the nineteenth century, have found a developing pattern that led naturally to the overseas adventures of the 1890s. In the view of Walter LaFeber, "the United States did not set out on an expansionist path in the late 1890s in a sudden, spur-of-the-moment fashion. The overseas empire that Americans controlled in 1900 was not a break in their history, but a natural culmination."

Catching the Spirit of Empire

Most people in most times in history tend to look inward, and Americans in these years following the Civil War were no exception. Among other things, they focused on Reconstruction, the movement westward, and simply making a living. They took seriously the well-remembered advice of George Washington's Farewell Address to "steer clear" of foreign entanglements. Throughout the nineteenth century, Americans enjoyed "free security" without fully appreciating it. Sheltered by two oceans and the British navy, they could enunciate bold policies like the Monroe Doctrine, which instructed European nations to stay out of the affairs of the Western Hemisphere, while remaining virtually impregnable to foreign attack.

In those circumstances, some people urged abolition of the foreign service, considering it an unnecessary expenditure, a dangerous profession that might lead to entanglement in the struggles of the world's great powers. A New York newspaper called it a "relic of medieval, monarchical trumpery," and if not that, it certainly became at times a dumping ground of the spoils system. Presidents named leaders who, though successful in their own fields, had no training in languages or diplomatic relations.

In the 1870s and after, however, Americans began to take an increasing interest in events abroad. There was a growing sense of internationalism, which stemmed in part from the telegraphs, telephones, and undersea cables that kept people better informed about political and economic developments in distant lands. Many Americans continued to be interested in expansion of the country's borders; relatively few were

In the late 1800s, America and Russia began to make expansionist moves in the Pacific. The cartoon, entitled "The Two Young Giants," is from the 1870s.

interested in imperialism. Expansion meant the kind of growth that had brought California and Oregon into the American system. Imperialism meant the imposition of control over other peoples through annexation, military conquest, or economic domination.

Several developments in these years combined to shift attention outward across the seas. The end of the frontier, announced officially in the census report of 1890, sparked fears about diminishing opportunities at home. Further growth, it seemed to some, must take place abroad, as John A. Kasson, an able and experienced diplomat, said in the *North American Review:* "We are rapidly utilizing the whole of our continental territory. We must turn our eyes abroad, or they will soon look inward upon discontent."

Factories and farms multiplied, producing more goods than the domestic market could consume. Both farmers and industrialists looked for new overseas markets, and the growing volume

of exports—including more and more manufactured goods—changed the nature of American trade relations with the world. American exports of merchandise amounted to $393 million in 1870, $858 million in 1890, and $1.4 billion in 1900. In 1898, the United States exported more than it imported, beginning a trend that lasted through the 1960s.

Political leaders such as James G. Blaine began to argue for the vital importance of foreign markets to continued economic growth. Blaine, secretary of state under Garfield and again under Harrison, aggressively sought wider markets in Latin America, Asia, and Africa, using tariff reciprocity agreements and other measures. To some extent, he and others were also caught up in a worldwide scramble for empire. In the last third of the century, Great Britain, France, and Germany divided up Africa and looked covetously at Asia. The idea of imperialistic expansion was in the air, and the great powers measured their greatness by the colonies they acquired. Inevitably, some Americans—certain business interests and foreign policy strategists, for example—caught the spirit and wanted to enter the international hunt for territory.

Intellectual currents that supported expansion drew on Charles Darwin's theories of evolution. Adherents pointed, for example, to *The Origin of Species,* which mentioned in its subtitle *The Preservation of Favoured Races in the Struggle for Life.* Applied to human and social development, biological concepts seemed to call for the triumph of the fit and the elimination of the unfit. "In this world," said Theodore Roosevelt, who thought of himself as one of the fit, "the nation that has trained itself to a career of unwarlike and isolated ease is bound, in the end, to go down before other nations which have not lost the manly and adventurous qualities."

Haeckel's Biogenetic Law, then a popular theory, suggested that the development of the individual repeated the development of the race. Primitive peoples thus were in the arrested stages of childhood or adolescence; they needed supervision and protective treatment. In a similar vein, John Fiske, a popular writer and lecturer, argued for Anglo-Saxon racial superiority, a result of the process of natural selection. The English and Americans, Fiske said, would occupy every land on the globe that was not already "civilized," bringing the advances of commerce and democratic institutions.

Such views were widespread among the lettered and unlettered alike. In Cuba, one of the Rough Riders ushered a visiting Russian prince around the trenches, informing him with ill-considered enthusiasm: "You see, Prince, the great result of this war is that it has united the two branches of Anglo-Saxon people; and now that they are together they can whip the world, Prince! they can whip the world!" Eminent scholars like John W. Burgess, a professor of political science at Columbia University, argued in similar though more dignified fashion that people of English origin were destined to impose their political institutions on the world.

The career of Josiah Strong, a Congregational minister and fervent expansionist, suggested the strength of the developing ideas. A champion of overseas missionary work, Strong traveled extensively through the West for the Home Missionary Society, and in 1885, drawing on his experiences, he published a book entitled *Our Country: Its Possible Future and Its Present Crisis*. An immediate best-seller, the book called on foreign missions to civilize the world under the Anglo-Saxon races. Strong became a national celebrity.

Our Country argued for expanding American trade and dominion. Trade was important, it said, because the desire for material things was one of the hallmarks of civilized people. So was the Christian religion, and by exporting both trade and religion, Americans could civilize and Christianize inferior races around the world. As Anglo-Saxons, they were members of a God-favored race destined to lead the world. Anglo-Saxons already owned one-third of the earth, Strong said, and in a famous passage he concluded that they would take more. In "the final competition of races," they would win out and "move down upon Mexico, down upon Central and South America, out upon the islands of the sea, over upon Africa and beyond."

Taken together, these developments in social, political, and economic thought prepared Americans for a larger role in the world. The change was gradual, and there was never a day when people awoke with a sudden realization of their interests overseas. But change there was, and by the 1890s, Americans were ready to reach out into the world in a more determined and

Entitled "The World Is My Market, My Customers Are All Mankind," this 1877 cartoon reflects America's interest in foreign markets. With its emphasis on agricultural produce and light industry, the cartoon understates America's role in foreign commerce.

deliberate fashion than ever before. For almost the first time, they felt the need for a foreign "policy."

Foreign Policy Approaches, 1867–1900

Rarely consistent, American foreign policy in the last half of the nineteenth century took different approaches to different areas of the world. In relation to Europe, seat of the dominant world powers, policymakers promoted trade and tried to avoid diplomatic entanglements. In North and South America, they based policy on the Monroe Doctrine, a recurrent dream of annexing Canada or Mexico, a hope for extensive trade, and Pan-American unity against the nations of the Old World. In the Pacific, they coveted Hawaii and other outposts on the sea-lanes to China.

Secretary of State William Henry Seward, who served from 1861 to 1869, aggressively pushed an expansive foreign policy. "Give me . . . fifty, forty, thirty more years of life," he told a Boston audience in 1867, "and I will give you possession of the American continent and control of the world." Seward, it turned out, had only five more years of life, but he developed a vision of an American empire stretching south into Latin America and west to the shores of Asia. This vision included Canada and Mexico; islands in the Caribbean as strategic bases to protect a canal across the isthmus; and Hawaii and other islands as stepping-stones to Asia, which Seward and many others considered a virtually bottomless outlet for farm and manufactured goods.

Seward tried unsuccessfully to negotiate a commercial treaty with Hawaii in 1867, and the same year he annexed the Midway Islands, a small atoll group 1,200 miles northwest of Hawaii. In 1867, he concluded a treaty with Russia for the purchase of Alaska (which was promptly labeled "Seward's Folly") partly to sandwich western Canada between American territory and lead to its annexation. As the American empire spread, Seward thought, Mexico City would become its capital.

Secretary of State Hamilton Fish, an urbane New Yorker, followed Seward in 1869, serving under President Ulysses S. Grant. An avid expansionist, Grant wanted to extend American influence in the Caribbean and Pacific, though Fish, more conservative, often restrained him. They moved first to repair relations with Great Britain. The first business was settlement of the *Alabama* claims—demands that Britain pay the United States for damages to Union ships caused by Confederate vessels which, like the *Alabama,* had been built and outfitted in British shipyards (see Chapter 15). Negotiating patiently, Fish signed the Treaty of Washington in 1871, providing for arbitration of the *Alabama* issue and other nettlesome controversies. The treaty, one of the landmarks in the peaceful settlement of international disputes, marked a significant step in cementing Anglo-American relations.

Grant and Fish looked most eagerly to Latin America. In 1870, Grant became the first president to proclaim the nontransfer principle— "hereafter no territory on this continent shall be regarded as subject to transfer to a European power." Fish also promoted the independence of Cuba, restive under Spanish rule, while holding off the annexation desired by the more eager Grant. Influenced by speculators, Grant tried to annex Santo Domingo in 1869 but was thwarted by powerful Republicans in the Senate who disliked foreign involvement and feared a subsequent attempt to annex Haiti.

James G. Blaine served briefly as Garfield's secretary of state and laid extensive plans to establish closer commercial relations with Latin America. His successor, Frederick T. Frelinghuysen, changed Blaine's approach but not his strategy. Like Blaine, Frelinghuysen wanted to find Caribbean markets for American goods; he negotiated separate reciprocity treaties with Mexico, Cuba and Puerto Rico, the British West Indies, Santo Domingo, and Colombia. Using these treaties, Frelinghuysen hoped not only to obtain markets for American goods but to bind these countries to American interests.

When Blaine returned to the State Department in 1889 under President Benjamin Harrison, he moved again to expand markets in Latin America. Drawing on earlier ideas, he envisaged a hemispheric system of peaceful intercourse, arbitration of disputes, and expanded trade. He also wanted to annex Hawaii. "I think there are only three places that are of value and not already taken, that are not continental," he wrote in a letter to President Harrison in 1891. "One is Hawaii and the others are Cuba and Puerto Rico." The last two might take a generation to acquire, but "Hawaii may come up for decision at any unexpected hour and I hope we shall be prepared to decide it in the affirmative."

Harrison and Blaine toyed with naval acquisitions in the Caribbean and elsewhere, but in general they focused on Pan-Americanism and tariff reciprocity. Blaine presided over the first Inter-American Conference in Washington on October 2, 1889. Delegates from nineteen American nations were present. They negotiated several agreements to promote trade and created the International Bureau of the American Republics, later renamed the Pan-American Union, for the exchange of general information including political, scientific, and cultural knowledge. The conference, a major step in hemispheric relations, led to later meetings promoting trade and other agreements.

Reciprocity, Harrison and Blaine hoped, would divert Latin American trade from Europe to the United States. Working hard to sell the idea in Congress, Blaine lobbied for a reciprocity provision in the McKinley Tariff Act of 1890 (see

Chapter 20), and once that was enacted, he negotiated important reciprocity treaties with most Latin American nations. The treaties suffered from the depression of the 1890s; nevertheless, they resulted in greater American exports of flour, grain, meat, iron, and machinery. Exports to Cuba jumped by one-third between 1891 and 1893, then dropped precipitously when the 1894 Wilson-Gorman Tariff Act ended reciprocity.

Grover Cleveland, Harrison's successor, also pursued an aggressive policy toward Latin America. In 1895, he brought the United States precariously close to war with Great Britain over a boundary dispute between Venezuela and British Guiana. Cleveland sympathized with Venezuela, and he and Secretary of State Richard Olney urged Britain to arbitrate the dispute. When Britain failed to act, Olney drafted a stiff diplomatic note affirming the Monroe Doctrine and denying European nations the right to meddle in Western Hemisphere affairs.

Four months passed before Lord Salisbury, the British foreign secretary, replied. Rejecting Olney's arguments, he sent two letters, the first bluntly repudiating the Monroe Doctrine as international law. The second letter, carefully reasoned and sometimes sarcastic, rejected Olney's arguments for the Venezuelan boundary. Enraged, Cleveland defended the Monroe Doctrine, and he asked Congress for authority to appoint a commission to decide the boundary and enforce its decision. "I am fully alive to the responsibility incurred and keenly realize all the consequences that may follow," he told Congress, plainly implying war.

Preoccupied with larger diplomatic problems in Africa and Europe, Britain changed its position. In November 1896, the two countries signed a treaty of arbitration, under which Great Britain and Venezuela divided the disputed territory. Though Cleveland's approach was clumsy—throughout the crisis, for example, he rarely consulted Venezuela—the Venezuelan incident demonstrated a growing determination to exert American power in the Western Hemisphere. Cleveland and Olney had persuaded Great Britain to recognize the United States' dominance, and they had increased American influence in Latin America. The Monroe Doctrine assumed new importance. In averting war, an era of Anglo-American friendship was begun.

The Lure of Hawaii and Samoa

The islands of Hawaii offered a tempting way station to Asian markets. In the early 1800s, they were already called the "Crossroads of the Pacific," and trading ships of many nations stopped there. In 1820, the first American missionaries arrived to convert the islanders to Christianity. Like missionaries elsewhere, they advertised Hawaii's economic and other benefits and attracted new settlers. Their children later came to dominate Hawaiian political and economic life and played an important role in annexation.

After the Civil War, the United States tightened its connections with the islands. The reciprocity treaty of 1875 allowed Hawaiian sugar to enter the United States free of duty and bound the Hawaiian monarchy to make no territorial or economic concessions to other powers. The treaty increased Hawaiian economic dependence on the United States; its political clauses effectively made Hawaii an American protectorate. In 1887, a new treaty reaffirmed these arrangements and granted the United States exclusive use of Pearl Harbor, a magnificent harbor that had early caught the eye of naval strategists.

Following the 1875 treaty, white Hawaiians became more and more influential in the islands' political life. The McKinley Tariff Act of 1890 ended the special status given Hawaiian sugar and at the same time awarded American producers a bounty of two cents a pound. Hawaiian sugar production dropped dramatically, unemployment rose, and property values fell. The following year, the weak King Kalakaua died, bringing to power a strong-willed nationalist, Queen Liliuokalani. Resentful of white minority rule, she decreed a new constitution that gave greater power to native Hawaiians.

Unhappy, the American residents revolted in early 1893 and called on the United States for help. John L. Stevens, the American minister in Honolulu, sent 150 marines ashore from the cruiser *Boston,* and within three days the bloodless revolution was over. Queen Liliuokalani surrendered "to the superior force of the United States," and the victorious rebels set up a provisional government. Stevens urged annexation, telling Washington that the "Hawaiian pear is now fully ripe, and this is the golden hour for the United States to pluck it." On February 14, 1893,

The first step toward American annexation of Hawaii came in 1893 when Queen Liliuokalani was removed from the throne. Hawaii finally became a part of the United States on August 12, 1898.

Harrison's Secretary of State John W. Foster and delegates of the new government signed a treaty annexing Hawaii to the United States.

But only two weeks remained in Harrison's term, and the Senate refused to ratify the agreement. Five days after taking office, Cleveland withdrew the treaty; he then sent a representative to investigate the cause of the rebellion. The investigation revealed that the Americans' role in it had been improper, and Cleveland decided to restore the queen to her throne. He made the demand, but the provisional government in Hawaii politely refused and instead established

the Republic of Hawaii, which the embarrassed Cleveland, unable to do otherwise, recognized.

The debate over Hawaiian annexation, continuing through the 1890s, foreshadowed the later debate over the treaty to end the Spanish-American War. People in favor of annexation pointed to Hawaii's strategic location, argued that Japan or other powers might seize the islands if the United States did not, and suggested that Americans had a responsibility to civilize and Christianize the native Hawaiians. Opponents warned that annexation might lead to a colonial army and colonial problems, the inclusion of a "mongrel" population in the United States, and rule over an area not destined for statehood.

Annexation came swiftly in July 1898 in the midst of excitement over victories in the Spanish-American War. The year before, President William McKinley had sent a treaty of annexation to the Senate, but opposition quickly arose, and the treaty stalled. Japan protested against it, pointing out that Japanese made up a quarter of the Hawaiian population. Japan dispatched a cruiser to Honolulu; the Navy Department sent the battleship *Oregon* and ordered naval forces to take Hawaii if the Japanese made threatening moves.

In 1898, annexationists redoubled arguments about Hawaii's commercial and military importance. McKinley and congressional leaders switched strategies to seek a joint resolution, rather than a treaty, for annexation. A joint resolution required only a majority of both houses, while a treaty needed a two-thirds vote in the Senate. Bolstered by the new strategy, the annexation measure moved quickly through Congress, and McKinley signed it on July 7, 1898. His signature, giving the United States a naval and commercial base in the mid-Pacific, realized a goal held by policymakers since the 1860s.

While annexation of Hawaii represented a step toward China, the Samoan Islands, 3,000 miles to the south, offered a strategic location astride the sea-lanes of the South Pacific. Americans showed early interest in Samoa, and in 1872, a naval officer negotiated a treaty granting the United States the use of Pago Pago, a splendid harbor on one of its islands. The Senate rejected the treaty, but six years later approved a similar agreement providing for a naval station there. The agreement bound the United States to use its

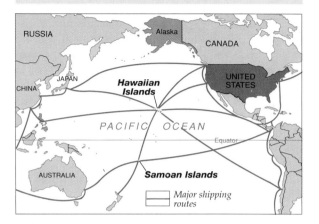

good offices to adjust any disputes between the Samoan chiefs and foreign governments. Great Britain and Germany also secured treaty rights in Samoa, and thereafter the three nations jockeyed for position.

The situation grew tense in 1889 when warships from all three countries gathered in a Samoan harbor. But a sudden typhoon destroyed the fleets, and tensions eased. A month later, delegates from Britain, Germany, and the United States met in Berlin to negotiate the problem. Britain and Germany wanted to divide up the islands; Secretary of State Blaine held out for some degree of authority by the indigenous population, with American control over Pago Pago.

The agreement, an uneasy one, ended in 1899 when the United States and Germany divided Samoa and compensated Britain with lands elsewhere in the Pacific. Germany claimed the two larger islands in the chain; the United States kept the harbor at Pago Pago.

The New Navy

Large navies were vital in the scramble for colonies, and in the 1870s the United States had almost no naval power. One of the most powerful fleets in the world during the Civil War, the American navy had fallen into rapid decline. By 1880, there were fewer than 2,000 vessels, only 48 of which could fire a gun. Ships rotted, and many officers left the service. "It was easy then,"

said George Dewey, later a hero of the war with Spain, "for an officer to drift along in his grade, losing interest and remaining in the navy only because he was too old to change his occupation."

Conditions changed during the 1880s. A group of rising young officers, steeped in a new naval philosophy, argued for an expanded navy equipped with fast, aggressive fleets capable of fighting battles across the seas. This group had its greatest influence in a special Naval Advisory Board, formed by the secretary of the navy in 1881. Big-navy proponents pointed to the growing fleets of Great Britain, France, and Germany, arguing that the United States needed greater fleet strength to protect its economic and other interests in the Caribbean and Pacific.

In 1883, Congress authorized construction of four steel ships, marking the beginning of the new navy. Experts also worked to improve naval management and the quality of fleet personnel, and between 1885 and 1889, Congress budgeted

This 1881 cartoon depicted "our top heavy navy," a decrepit vessel sinking with idle officers.

funds for thirty additional ships. The initial building program focused on lightly armored fast cruisers for raiding enemy merchant ships and protecting American shores, but after 1890, the program shifted to the construction of a seagoing offensive battleship navy capable of challenging the strongest fleets of Europe.

Alfred Thayer Mahan and Benjamin F. Tracy were two of the main forces behind the new navy. Austere and scholarly, Mahan was the era's most influential naval strategist. After graduating from the Naval Academy in 1859, he devoted a lifetime to studying the influence of sea power in history; for over two decades he headed the Newport Naval War College, where officers imbided the latest in strategic thinking. A clear, logical writer, Mahan summarized his beliefs in several major books, including *The Influence of Sea Power Upon History, 1660–1783* (1890) and *The Interest of America in Sea Power* (1897).

Mahan's reasoning was simple and, to that generation, persuasive. Industrialism, he argued, produced vast surpluses of agricultural and manufactured goods, for which markets must be found. Markets involved distant ports; reaching them required a large merchant marine and a powerful navy to protect it. Navies, in turn, needed coaling stations and repair yards. Coaling stations meant colonies, and colonies became strategic bases, the foundation of a nation's wealth and power. The bases might serve as markets themselves, but they were more important as stepping-stones to other objectives, such as the markets of Latin America and Asia.

Mahan called attention to the worldwide race for power, a race, he warned, the United States could not afford to lose. "All around us now is strife; 'the struggle of life,' 'the race of life' are phrases so familiar that we do not feel their significance till we stop to think about them. Everywhere nation is arrayed against nation; our own no less than others." To compete in the struggle, Mahan argued, the United States must expand. It needed strategic bases, a powerful, oceangoing navy, a canal across the isthmus to link the East Coast with the Pacific, and Hawaii as a way station on the route to Asia.

Mahan influenced a generation of policymakers in the United States and Europe; one of them, Benjamin F. Tracy, became Harrison's secretary of the navy in 1889. Between then and 1893,

Tracy organized the Bureau of Construction and Repair to design and build new ships, established the Naval Reserve in 1891, and ordered construction of the first American submarine in 1893. He also started the first heavy rapid-fire guns, smokeless powder, torpedoes, and heavy armor. Above all, Tracy joined with big-navy advocates in Congress to push for a far-ranging battleship fleet capable of attacking distant enemies. He wanted two fleets of battleships, eight in the Pacific and twelve in the Atlantic. He got four first-class battleships.

In 1889, when Tracy entered office, the United States ranked twelfth among world navies; in 1893, when he left, it ranked seventh and was climbing rapidly. "The sea," he predicted in 1891, "will be the future seat of empires. And we shall rule it as certainly as the sun doth rise." By the end of the decade, the navy had seventeen steel battleships, six armored cruisers, and many smaller craft. It ranked third in the world.

WAR WITH SPAIN

The war with Spain in 1898 built a mood of national confidence, altered older, more insular patterns of thought, and reshaped the way Americans saw themselves and the world. While its outcome pleased some people, it troubled others, and they raised questions about war itself, colonies, and subject peoples. The war left a lingering strain of isolationism and antiwar feeling that affected later policy. It also left an American empire, small by European standards, but quite new to the American experience by virtue of its overseas location. When the war ended, American possessions stretched into the Caribbean and deep into the Pacific. American influence went further still, and the United States was recognized as a "world power."

The Spanish-American War established the United States as a dominant force for the twentieth century. It brought America colonies and millions of colonial subjects; it brought the responsibilities of governing an empire and protecting it. For better or worse, it involved the country in other nations' arguments and affairs. The war strengthened the office of the presidency, swept the nation together in a tide of emotion, and confirmed the long-standing belief in the superiority of the New World over the Old. When it was over, Americans looked outward as never before, touched, they were sure, with a special destiny.

They seemed a chosen people, as Mr. Dooley, a character created by humorist Finley Peter Dunne, pointed out to his friend Hennessy over the Archey Road bar. "We're a gr-reat people" said Hennessy, in his rolling Irish brogue. "We ar-re that," replied Mr. Dooley. "We ar-re that. An th' best iv it is we know we ar-re."

A War for Principle

By the 1890s, Cuba and the nearby island of Puerto Rico comprised nearly all that remained of Spain's once vast empire in the New World. Several times, Cuban insurgents had rebelled against Spanish rule, including a decade-long rebellion from 1868 to 1878 (the Ten Years' War) that failed to settle the conflict. The depression of 1893 damaged the Cuban economy, and the Wilson-Gorman Tariff of 1894 prostrated it. Duties on sugar, Cuba's lifeblood, were raised 40 percent. With the island's sugar market in ruins, discontent with Spanish rule heightened, and in late February 1895, revolt again broke out.

Recognizing the importance of the nearby United States, Cuban insurgents established a junta in New York City to raise money, buy weapons, and wage a propaganda war to sway American public opinion. Conditions in Cuba were grim. The insurgents pursued a hit-and-run scorched-earth policy to force the Spanish to leave. Spain committed more than 200,000 soldiers; the Spanish commander, who had won with similar tactics in 1878, tried to pin the insurgents in the eastern part of the island where they could be cornered and destroyed.

When this strategy failed, Spain in January 1896 sent a new commander, General Valeriano Weyler y Nicolau. Relentless and brutal, Weyler gave the rebels ten days to lay down their arms. He then put into effect a "reconcentration" policy designed to move the native population into camps and destroy the rebellion's popular base. Herded into fortified areas, Cubans died by the thousands, victims of unsanitary conditions, overcrowding, and disease.

There was a wave of sympathy for the insurgents stimulated by the newspapers (see "Reporting the Spanish-American War," pp. 640–641). But "yellow" journalism did not cause the war. The conflict stemmed from larger disputes in policies and perceptions between Spain and the United States. Grover Cleveland, under whose administration the rebellion began, preferred Spanish rule to the kind of turmoil that might invite foreign intervention. Opposed to the annexation of Cuba, he issued a proclamation of neutrality and tried to restrain public opinion. In 1896, Congress passed a resolution favoring recognition of Cuban belligerency, but Cleveland ignored it. Instead, he offered to mediate the struggle, an offer Spain declined.

Taking office in March 1897, President McKinley also urged neutrality but leaned slightly toward the insurgents. He immediately sent a trusted aide on a fact-finding mission to Cuba; the aide reported in mid-1897 that Weyler's policy had wrapped Cuba "in the stillness of death and the silence of desolation." The report in hand, McKinley offered to mediate the struggle, but concerned over the suffering, he protested against Spain's "uncivilized and inhuman" conduct. The United States, he made clear, did not contest Spain's right to fight the rebellion but insisted it be done within humane limits.

Late in 1897, a change in government in Madrid brought a temporary lull in the crisis. The new government recalled Weyler and agreed to offer the Cubans some form of autonomy. It also declared an amnesty for political prisoners and released Americans in Cuban jails. The new initiatives pleased McKinley, though he again warned Spain that it must find a humane end to the rebellion. Then, in January 1898, Spanish army officers led riots in Havana against the new autonomy policy, shaking the president's confidence in Madrid's control over conditions in Cuba.

McKinley ordered the battleship *Maine* to Havana to demonstrate strength and protect American citizens if necessary. On February 9, 1898, the *New York Journal,* a leader of the "yellow press," published a letter stolen from Enrique Dupuy de Lôme, the Spanish ambassador in Washington. The letter was a private letter to a friend, and in it de Lôme called McKinley "weak," "a would-be politician," and "a bidder for the admiration of the crowd." Many Americans were angered by the insult; McKinley

Reporting the Spanish-American War

The force of the newspaper is the greatest force in civilization.

Under republican government, newspapers form and express public opinion.

They suggest and control legislation.

They declare wars.

They punish criminals, especially the powerful.

They reward with approving publicity the good deeds of citizens everywhere.

The newspapers control the nation because

THEY REPRESENT THE PEOPLE.

So proclaimed William Randolph Hearst, owner of the *New York Journal* in the paper's September 25, 1898, issue. Proud of the power of the press, Hearst and a handful of other publishers built newspaper empires that not only reported events but also influenced their outcomes.

Several of these empires took shape during the 1890s. The American population was growing rapidly, and so there were more people to read newspapers. In addition, more and more Americans were literate. Publishers did not hesitate to take advantage of the growing urban market. Technological improvements helped the spread of information: new machines made newspapers faster to print; larger type, a new half-tone engraving process for clearer pictures, and color cartoon supple-

ments made them more appealing.

In 1865, there were about 500 daily newspapers in the country with a total circulation of about 2 million. By 1900, there were over 2,000 dailies with a circulation of over 15 million. Papers sold for only one or two cents a copy. At that price, publishers could not make money on the paper itself, so they recouped their losses with advertising. Advertisers wanted readers, and to attract more and more of them, publishers used new methods. They lured buyers with banner headlines and front-page photographs. Stories stressed sex and scandals, and more cartoons and comic strips appeared.

The personalities of the "yellow journalists" attracted almost as much attention as the stories they reported. When the Journal *sent reporter Richard Harding Davis and illustrator Frederic Remington to cover the Spanish-American War, it gave the duo front-page coverage.*

One of the first publishing magnates, Joseph Pulitzer, bought the *New York World* in 1883 and within a year increased its sales from 15,000 a day to 100,000. Pulitzer had little competition until 1895 when William Randolph Hearst, an aggressive publisher from San Francisco, bought the *New York Journal.* Hearst was thirty-two. The son of a multimillionaire, he had been expelled from Harvard, had traveled widely and discovered a love for power and attention. Although he was shy and relatively inexperienced, money from his father and a desire to enter the world of newspaper publishing helped launch his career.

Fiercely competitive for "scoops" and circulation, Hearst and Pulitzer experimented with several new features: headlines that ran across the front page, profuse illustrations, a large Sunday paper with a comic section printed in color, and special sports' and women's sections. A cartoon character, "The Yellow Kid," appeared daily in both the *Journal* and the *World,* and they became known as "yellow journals." Stressing the sensational, yellow journals aimed to make news as well as report it. Hearst told his reporters: "Don't wait for things to turn up. Turn them up!"

The new journalism reached a peak in the crisis in Cuba between 1895 and 1898. When the shortlived rebellion of 1895 broke out, correspondents

flocked to Cuba to cover it. Pulitzer sent the novelist Stephen Crane and printed reports from a young Englishman named Winston Churchill. Hearst sent the star *Journal* reporter Richard Harding Davis and the famous western artist Frederic Remington to sketch scenes of Spanish cruelty. Both Hearst and Pulitzer sided with the rebels. Denouncing Spanish policy, they attacked General Valeriano Weyler—"Butcher," the *Journal* nicknamed him—and other Spanish generals.

Hearst was particularly proud of the story of Evangelina Cisneros, the seventeen-year-old niece of the rebellion's president. In August 1897, Evangelina was sentenced to twenty years in prison for aiding the rebels. Sensing the story's potential, Hearst started a letter-writing campaign to the queen of Spain to win her release. Soon he decided on a more direct method. He sent reporter Karl Decker to Havana to rescue Evangelina. Renting the house next door to the prison, Decker broke into the prison, freed Evangelina, and disguising her as a boy, smuggled her out of Havana. On October 10, 1897, the *Journal* broke the news with the headline: "An American Newspaper Accomplishes at a Single Stroke What the Best Efforts of Diplomacy Failed Utterly to Bring About in Many Months."

Once war erupted between the United States and Spain, Hearst and his rivals stepped up their efforts. They employed hundreds of correspondents and hired a fleet of swift boats to carry stories to Florida for transmission back to New York. The correspondents both reported and fought in the war. At one point, Hearst considered sinking a ship in the Suez Canal to keep the Spanish fleet from reaching the Philippines, and from aboard a chartered steamer, he personally watched the destruction of Cervera's fleet off Santiago. Waving a revolver, he waded ashore to capture a handful of Spanish sailors who survived the battle. The efforts paid off in news-paper sales. When Hearst bought the *Journal,* it was selling 77,000 copies a day. At the war's height, its sales had increased to over 1.5 million daily.

After the war, Hearst cartoonists like Homer Davenport turned their skillful attention to the trusts and other issues. Showing the lack of restraint that characterized "yellow journalism," the *Journal,* a Democratic newspaper, again and again criticized President McKinley, even suggesting that assassination might be in order. In September 1901, McKinley was shot, and when reports circulated that the assassin had a copy of the *Journal* in his pocket, the public turned on Hearst. The *Journal's* circulation dropped sharply. The new journalism continued into the twentieth century—Hearst himself went on to establish a famous publishing empire—but yellow journalism itself was never the same again.

MAINE EXPLOSION CAUSED BY BOMB OR TORPEDO?

Capt. Sigsbee and Consul-General Lee Are in Doubt—The World Has Sent a Special Tug, With Submarine Divers, to Havana to Find Out—Lee Asks for an Immediate Court of Inquiry—260 Men Dead.

IN A SUPPRESSED DESPATCH TO THE STATE DEPARTMENT THE CAPTAIN SAYS THE ACCIDENT WAS MADE POSSIBLE BY AN ENEMY.

Dr. E. C. Pendleton, Just Arrived from Havana, Says He Overheard Talk There of a Plot to Blow Up the Ship—Capt. Zalinski, the Dynamite Expert, and Other Experts Report to The World that the Wreck Was Not Accidental—Washington Officials Ready for Vigorous Action if Spanish Responsibility Can Be Shown—Divers to Be Sent Down to Make Careful Examinations.

Headlines like these in the New York World *left little doubt among readers that Spain had sunk the* Maine.

himself was more worried about other sections of the letter that revealed Spanish insincerity in the negotiations. De Lôme immediately resigned and went home, but the damage was done.

A few days later, at 9:40 in the evening of February 15, an explosion tore through the hull of the *Maine,* riding at anchor in Havana harbor. The ship, a trim symbol of the new steel navy, sank quickly; 266 lives were lost. McKinley cautioned patience and promised an immediate investigation. Crowds gathered quietly on Capitol Hill and outside the White House, mourning the lost men. Soon there was a new slogan, "Remember the *Maine* and to Hell with Spain!"

The most recent study of the *Maine* incident blames the sinking on an accidental internal explosion, caused perhaps by spontaneous combustion in poorly ventilated coal bunkers. In 1898, Americans blamed it on Spain. Spaniards were hanged in effigy in many communities. Roosevelt, William Jennings Bryan, and others urged war, but McKinley delayed, hopeful that Spain might yet agree to an armistice and perhaps Cuban independence. "I have been through one war; I have seen the dead piled up; and I do not

want to see another," he told a White House visitor.

In early March 1898, wanting to be ready for war if it came, McKinley asked Congress for $50 million in emergency defense appropriations, a request Congress promptly approved. The unanimous vote stunned Spain; allowing the president a latitude that was highly unusual for the era, it appropriated the money "for the National defense and for each and every purpose connected therewith to be expended at the discretion of the President." In late March, the report of the investigating board blamed the sinking of the *Maine* on an external (and thus presumably Spanish) explosion. Pressures for war increased.

On March 27, McKinley cabled Spain his final terms. He asked Spain to declare an armistice, end the reconcentration policy, and—implicitly— move toward Cuban independence. When the Spanish answer came, it conceded some things, but not, in McKinley's judgment, the important ones. Spain offered a suspension of hostilities (but not an armistice) and left the Spanish commander in Cuba to set the length and terms of the suspension. It also revoked the reconcentration policy. But the Spanish response made no mention of a true armistice, McKinley's offer to mediate, or Cuba's independence.

Reluctantly McKinley prepared his war message. It was long and temperate—at seven thousand words even deliberately boring; it suggested the possibility of further negotiations. Congress heard it on April 11, 1898. On April 19, Congress passed a joint resolution declaring Cuba independent and authorizing the president to use the army and navy to expel the Spanish from it. An amendment by Colorado senator Henry M. Teller pledged that the United States had no intention of annexing the island.

On April 21, Spain severed diplomatic relations. The following day, McKinley proclaimed a blockade of Cuba and called for 125,000 volunteers. On Monday, April 25, Congress passed a declaration of war. Late that afternoon, McKinley signed it.

Some historians have suggested that in leading the country toward war, McKinley was weak and indecisive, a victim of war hysteria in the Congress and country; others have called him a wily manipulator for war and imperial gains. In truth he was neither. Throughout the Spanish crisis, McKinley pursued a moderate middle course that sought to end the suffering in Cuba, promote Cuba's independence, and allow Spain time to adjust to the loss of the remnant of empire. He also wanted peace, as did Spain, but in the end, the conflicting national interests of the two countries brought them to war.

"A Splendid Little War"

Ten weeks after the declaration of war the fighting was over. For Americans, they were ten glorious, dizzying weeks, with victories to fill every headline and slogans to suit every taste. No war can be a happy occasion for those who fight it, but the Spanish-American War came closer than most. Declared in April, it ended in August. Relatively few Americans died, and the quick victory seemed to verify burgeoning American power, though Sherwood Anderson, the author, suggested that fighting a weakened Spain was "like robbing an old gypsy woman in a vacant lot at night after a fair." John Hay, soon to be McKinley's secretary of state, called it "a splendid little war."

At the outset, the United States was militarily unprepared. Unlike the navy, the army had not been rebuilt or modernized in structure, and it had shrunk drastically since the day thirty-three years before when Grant's great Civil War army marched sixty abreast, 200,000 strong, down Washington's Pennsylvania Avenue. In 1898, the regular army consisted of only 28,000 officers and men, most of them more experienced in quelling Indian uprisings than fighting large-scale battles. The Indian wars did produce effective small-scale forces, well trained and tightly disciplined, but the army was unquestionably too small for war against Spain.

When McKinley called for 125,000 volunteers, as many as 1 million young Americans responded. Ohio alone had 100,000 volunteers. Keeping the regular army units intact, War Department officials enlisted the volunteers in National Guard units that were then integrated into the national army. Men clamored to join. William Jennings Bryan, a pacifist by temperament, took command of a regiment of Nebraska volunteers; Roosevelt chafed to get to the front; and young Cordell Hull, who became secretary of state in the 1930s, was "wildly eager to leave at once." The secre-

tary of war feared "there is going to be more trouble to satisfy those who are not going than to find those who are willing to go."

In an army inundated with men, problems of equipment and supply quickly appeared. The regulars had the new .30 caliber Krag-Jorgensen rifles, but National Guard units carried Civil War Springfield rifles that used old black powder cartridges. The cartridges gave off a puff of smoke when fired, neatly marking the troops' position. Spanish troops were better equipped; they had modern Mausers with smokeless powder, which they used to devastating effect. Food was also a problem, as was sickness. The War Department fell behind in supplies and received many complaints about the canned beef it offered the men. Tropical disease felled many soldiers. Scores took ill after landing in Cuba and the Philippines, and it was not uncommon for half a regiment to be unable to answer the bugle call.

Americans then believed that "a foreign war should be fought by the hometown military unit acting as an extension of their community." Soldiers identified with their hometowns, dressed in the local fashion, and thought of themselves as members of a town unit in a national army. The poet Carl Sandburg, twenty years old in 1898, rushed to join the army and called his unit a "living part" of his hometown of Galesburg, Illinois. And the citizens of Galesburg, for their part, took a special interest in Sandburg's unit, in a fashion repeated in countless towns across the country.

Not surprisingly, then, National Guard units mirrored the social patterns of their communities. Since everyone knew each other, there was an easygoing familiarity, tempered by the deference that went with hometown wealth, occupation, education, and length of residence. Enlisted men resented officers who grabbed too much authority, and they expected officers and men to call each other by their first names. Sandburg knew most of the privates in his unit, had worked for his corporal, and had gone to school with the first lieutenant. "Officers and men of the Guard mingle on a plane of beautiful equality," said a visitor to one volunteer camp. "Privates invade the tents of their officers at will, and yell at them half the length of the street."

Each community thought of the hometown unit as its own unit, an extension of itself. In later wars, the government censored news and dominated press relations; there was little censorship in the war with Spain, and the freshest news arrived in the latest letter home. Small-town newspapers printed news of the men; townswomen knit special red or white bellybands of stitched flannel, thought to ward off tropical fevers; towns sent food, clothing, and occasionally even local doctors to the front. At the close of the war, the Clyde (Ohio) Ladies Society collected funds to provide each member of the town's company a medal struck on behalf of the town.

"Smoked Yankees"

When the invasion force sailed for Cuba, nearly one-fourth of it was African American. In 1898, the regular army included four regiments of African American soldiers, the Twenty-fourth and Twenty-fifth Infantry and the Ninth and Tenth Cavalry. Black regiments had served with distinction in campaigns against the Indians in the West. Most African American troops in fact

were posted in the West; no eastern community would accept them. A troop of the Ninth Cavalry was stationed in Virginia in 1891, but whites protested and the troop was ordered back to the West.

When the war broke out, the War Department called for five black volunteer regiments. The army needed men, and military authorities were sure that black men had a natural immunity to the climate and diseases of the tropics. But most state governors refused to accept black volunteers. Only Alabama, Ohio, and Massachusetts mustered in black units in response to McKinley's first call for volunteers. Company L of the Sixth Massachusetts Regiment took part in the invasion of Puerto Rico in July 1898, the only one of the black volunteer units to see action in the Caribbean. African American leaders, among them P. B. S. Pinchback, former acting governor of Louisiana, and George White of North Carolina, the lone African American member of Congress, protested the discrimination. The McKinley administration intervened, and in the

Charge of the 24th and 25th Colored Infantry and Rescue of the Rough Riders at San Juan Hill, July 2, 1898, *colored lithograph by Kurz and Allison, 1899 (left). The 24th and 25th Colored Infantry regiments served with exceptional gallantry in the Spanish-American War. Charles Young (below), an 1889 graduate of West Point, was the only African American officer in the army during the Spanish-American War except for a few chaplains.*

end, the volunteer army included over ten thousand black troops.

Orders quickly went out to the four black regular army regiments in the West to move to camps in the South to prepare for the invasion of Cuba. Crowds and cheers followed the troop trains across the Plains, but as they crossed into Kentucky and Tennessee, the cheering stopped. Welcoming crowds were kept away from the trains, and the troops were hustled onward. Station restaurants refused to serve them; all waiting rooms were segregated. "It mattered not if we were soldiers of the United States, and going to fight for the honor of our country," Sergeant Frank W. Pullen of the Twenty-fourth Infantry wrote; "we were 'niggers' as they called us and treated us with contempt."

Many soldiers were not prepared to put up with the treatment. Those stationed near Chickamauga Park, Tennessee, shot "at some whites who insulted them" and forcibly desegregated the railroad cars on the line into Chattanooga. Troops training near Macon, Georgia, refused to ride in the segregated "trailers" attached to the trolleys, and fights broke out. Discovering a Macon park with a sign saying "Dogs and niggers not allowed," they invaded it and removed the sign. They also chopped down a tree in the park that had been used for lynchings.

More than four thousand black troops training near Tampa and Lakeland, Florida, found segregated saloons, cafes, and drugstores. "Here the Negro is not allowed to purchase over the same counter in some stores as the white man purchases over. . . ," Chaplain George W. Prioleau charged. "Why sir, the Negro of this country is a freeman and yet a slave. Talk about fighting and freeing poor Cuba and of Spain's brutality; of Cuba's murdered thousands, and starving reconcentradoes. Is America any better than Spain?"

Near Lakeland, units of the Tenth Cavalry pistol-whipped a drugstore owner who refused to serve a black soldier at the soda fountain. Just before the army's departure for Cuba, the tensions in Tampa erupted in a night of rioting. Drunken white soldiers from an Ohio regiment shot at a black child, black soldiers retaliated, and when the night ended, three white and twenty-seven black soldiers were wounded.

When the invasion force sailed a few days later, segregation continued on some of the troop ships. Blacks were assigned to the lowest decks, or whites and blacks were placed on different sides of the ship. But the confusion of war often ended the problem, if only temporarily. Blacks took command as white officers died, and Spanish troops soon came to fear the "smoked Yankees," as they called them. Black soldiers played a major role in the Cuban campaign and probably staved off defeat for the Rough Riders at San Juan Hill. In Cuba, they won twenty-six Certificates of Merit and five Congressional Medals of Honor.

The Course of the War

Mahan's Naval War College had begun studying strategy for a war with Spain in 1895. By 1898, it had a detailed plan for operations in the Caribbean and Pacific. Naval strategy was simple: destroy the Spanish fleet, damage Spain's merchant marine, and harry the colonies on the coast of Spain. Planners were excited; two steam-powered armored fleets had yet to meet in battle anywhere in the world. The army's task was more difficult. It must defend the United States, invade Cuba and probably Puerto Rico, and undertake possible action in far-flung places like the Philippines or Spain.

Even before war was declared, the secretary of war arranged joint planning between the army and navy. Military intelligence was plentiful, and planners knew the numbers and locations of the Spanish troops. Earlier they had rejected a proposal to send an officer in disguise to map Cuban harbors; such things, they said, were simply not done in peacetime. Still, the War Department's new Military Information Division, a sign of the increasing professionalization of the army, had detailed diagrams of Spanish fortifications in Havana and other points. On the afternoon of April 20, 1898, McKinley summoned the strategists to the White House, and to the dismay of those who wanted a more aggressive policy, they decided on the limited strategy of blockading Cuba, sending arms to the insurgents, and annoying the Spanish with small thrusts by the army.

Victories soon changed the strategy. In case of war, long-standing naval plans had called for a holding action against the Spanish base in the Philippines. On May 1, 1898, with the war barely a week old, Commodore George Dewey, commander of the Asiatic Squadron located at Hong Kong, crushed the Spanish fleet in Manila Bay.

Spanish-American War: Pacific Theater
Commodore Dewey, promoted to admiral immediately after the naval victory at Manila Bay, was the first hero of the war.

American force under Admiral William T. Sampson bottled Cervera up.

In early June, a small force of Marines seized Guantanamo Bay, the great harbor on the south of the island. They established depots for the navy to refuel and pinned down Spanish troops in the area. On June 14, an invasion force of about seventeen thousand men set sail from Tampa. Seven days later, they landed at Daiquiri on Cuba's southeastern coast. All was confusion, but the Spanish offered no resistance. Helped by Cuban insurgents, the Americans immediately pushed west toward Santiago, which they hoped to surround and capture. At first, the advance through the lush tropical countryside was peaceful.

The first battle broke out at Las Guasimas, a crossroads on the Santiago road. After a sharp fight, the Spanish fell back. On July 1, the Rough Riders, troops from the four black regiments, and the other regulars reached the strong fortifications at El Caney and San Juan Hill. Black soldiers of the Twenty-fifth Infantry charged the El Caney blockhouses, surprising the Spanish defenders with Comanche yells. For the better part of a day, the defenders fought stubbornly and held back the army's elite corps. In the confusion of battle, Roosevelt rallied an assortment of infantry and cavalry to take Kettle Hill, adjacent to San Juan Hill.

They charged directly into the Spanish guns, Roosevelt at their head, mounted on a horse, a blue polka-dot handkerchief floating from the brim of his sombrero. "I waved my hat and we went up the hill with a rush," he recalled in his autobiography. Actually it was not quite so easy. Losses were heavy; eighty-nine Rough Riders were killed or wounded in the attack. Dense foliage concealed the enemy; smokeless powder gave no clue to their position. At nightfall, the surviving Spanish defenders withdrew, and the Americans prepared for the counterattack. "We have won so far at a heavy cost," Roosevelt wrote home, "but the Spaniards fight very hard and charging these entrenchments against modern rifles is terrible. We are within measurable distance of a terrible military disaster."

American troops now occupied the ridges over-looking Santiago. They were weakened by sickness, a fact unknown to the Spanish who decided the city was lost. The Spanish command in Havana ordered Cervera to run for the open

Suddenly, Manila and the Philippines lay within American grasp. At home, Dewey portraits, songs, and poems blossomed everywhere, and his calm order to the flagship's captain—"You may fire when ready, Gridley"—hung on every tongue. Dewey had two modern cruisers, a gunboat, and a Civil War paddle steamer. He sank eight Spanish warships. Dewey had no troops to attack the Spanish army in Manila, but the War Department, stunned by the speed and size of the victory, quickly raised an expeditionary force. On August 13, 1898, the troops accepted the surrender of Manila, and with it, the Philippines.

McKinley and his aides were worried about Admiral Pascual Cervera's main Spanish fleet, thought to be headed across the Atlantic for an attack on Florida. On May 13, the navy found Cervera's ships near Martinique in the Caribbean but then lost them again. A few days later, Cervera slipped secretly into the harbor of Santiago de Cuba, a city on the island's southern coast. But a spy in the Havana telegraph office alerted the Americans, and on May 28, a superior

Spanish-American War: Caribbean Theater

President McKinley set up a "war room" in the White House, following the action on giant war maps with red and white marking pins.

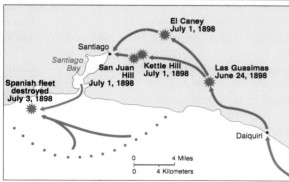

sea, although he knew the attempt to escape was hopeless. On the morning of July 3, Cervera's squadron steamed down the bay and out through the harbor's narrow channel, but the waiting American fleet closed in, and in a few hours every Spanish vessel was destroyed. Two weeks later, Santiago surrendered.

Soon thereafter, army troops, meeting little resistance, occupied Puerto Rico. Cervera had commanded Spain's only battle fleet, and when it sank, Spain was helpless against attacks on the colonies or even its own shores. The war was over. Lasting 113 days, it took relatively few lives, most of them the result of accident, yellow fever, malaria, and typhoid in Cuba. Of the 5,500 Americans who died in the war, only 379 were killed in battle. The navy lost one man in the battle at Santiago Bay, and only one to heatstroke in the stunning victory in Manila Bay.

DEBATE OVER EMPIRE

Late in the afternoon of August 12, 1898, representatives of Spain and the United States met in McKinley's White House office to sign the preliminary instrument of peace. Secretary of State William R. Day beckoned a presidential aide over to a large globe, remarking, "Let's see what we get by this."

What the United States got was an expansion of its territory and an even larger expansion of its responsibilities. According to the preliminary agreement, Spain granted independence to Cuba, ceded Puerto Rico and the Pacific island of Guam to the United States, and allowed Americans to occupy Manila until the two countries reached final agreement on the Philippines. To McKinley, the Philippines were the problem. Puerto Rico was close to the mainland, and it appealed even to many of the opponents of expansion. Guam was small and unknown; it escaped attention. The Philippines, on the other hand, were huge, sprawling, and thousands of miles from America.

McKinley weighed a number of alternatives for the Philippines, but he liked none of them. He felt he could not give the islands back to Spain; public opinion would not allow it. He might turn them over to another nation, but then they would fall, as he later said, "a golden apple of discord, among the rival powers." Germany, Japan, Great Britain, and Russia had all expressed interest in acquiring them. Germany even sent a large fleet to Manila and laid plans to take the Philippines if the United States let them go.

Rejecting those alternatives, McKinley considered independence for the islands but was soon talked out of it. People who had been there, reflecting the era's racism, told him the Filipinos were not ready for independence. He thought of establishing an American protectorate but discarded the idea, convinced it would bring American responsibilities without full American control. Sifting the alternatives, McKinley decided there was only one practical policy: annex the Philippines, with an eye to future independence after a period of tutelage.

At first hesitant, American opinion was swinging to the same conclusion. Religious and missionary organizations appealed to McKinley to hold on to the Philippines in order to "Christianize" them. Some merchants and industrialists saw them as the key to the China market and the wealth of Asia. Many Americans simply regarded them as the legitimate fruits of war. In October 1898, representatives of the United States and Spain met in Paris to discuss a peace treaty. Spain agreed to recognize Cuba's independence, assume the Cuban debt, and cede Puerto Rico and Guam to the United States.

Acting on instructions from McKinley, the American representatives demanded the cession of the Philippines. "Grave as are the responsibilities and unforeseen as are the difficulties which are before us, the President can see but one plain path of duty—the acceptance of the archipelago," the instructions said. In return, the United States offered a payment of $20 million. Spain resisted but had little choice, and on December 10, 1898, the American and Spanish representatives signed the Treaty of Paris.

Submitted to the Senate for ratification, the treaty set off a storm of debate throughout the country. Industrialist Andrew Carnegie, reformer Jane Addams, labor leader Samuel Gompers, prominent Republicans like Thomas B. Reed and John Sherman, Mark Twain, William Dean Howells, and a host of others argued forcefully against annexing the Philippines. Annexation of the Philippines, the anti-imperialists protested over and over again, violated the very principles of independence and self-determination on which the country was founded.

Some labor leaders feared the importation of cheap labor from new Pacific colonies. Gompers warned about the "half-breeds and semi-barbaric people" who might undercut wages and the union movement. Other anti-imperialists argued against assimilation of different races, "Spanish-Americans," as one said, "with all the mixture of Indian and negro blood, and Malays and other unspeakable Asiatics, by the tens of millions!" Such racial views were also common among those favoring expansion, and the anti-imperialists usually focused on different arguments. If the United States established a tyranny abroad, they were sure, there would soon be tyranny at home. "This nation," declared William Jennings Bryan, "cannot endure half republic and half colony—half free and half vassal."

Charles Francis Adams, Jr., warned that the possession of colonies meant big armies, government, and debts ("an income tax looms up in the largest possible proportions," he said). Bryan scoffed at the argument that colonies were good for trade, pointing out that "It is not necessary to own people to trade with them." E. L. Godkin, the editor of *The Nation,* George F. Hoar, a leading Republican senator, and many others thought there was no way to reconcile the country's republican ideals with the practice of keeping

A Puck *cartoon entitled "School Begins" satirizes Uncle Sam's course in civilization, in which he tells his students that they will soon be glad for all they will learn.*

people under heel abroad. As one of them put it, "Dewey took Manila with the loss of one man—and all our institutions."

William James, the psychologist, said America was about to "puke up its heritage." Unless the Philippines were freed, Americans would rob Filipinos of "the one sacred thing in the world, the spontaneous budding of a national life." To Booker T. Washington, the country had more important things to think about at home, including its treatment of Indians and blacks. Carnegie was so upset he offered to buy Filipino independence with a personal check for $20 million. He was sure that keeping the Philippines would divert attention from industrial development to foreign adventure, would glorify physical force, and would lead to a war against the Filipinos themselves, in which American soldiers who had signed up "to fight the oppressor" would end up "shooting down the oppressed."

In November 1898, opponents of expansion formed the Anti-Imperialist League to fight against the peace treaty. Local leagues sprang up in Boston, New York, Philadelphia, and many other cities; the parent league claimed thirty thousand members and over half a million "contributors." Membership centered in New England; the cause was less popular in the West and South. It enlisted more Democrats than Republicans, though never a majority of either. The anti-imperialists were weakened by the fact that they lacked a coherent program. Some favored keeping naval bases in the conquered areas. Some wanted Hawaii and Puerto Rico but not the Philippines. Others wanted nothing at all to do with any colonies. Most simply wished that Dewey had sailed away after beating the Spanish at Manila Bay.

The treaty debate in the Senate lasted a month. Pressing hard for ratification, McKinley earlier toured the South to rally support and consulted closely with senators. Though opposed to taking the Philippines, Bryan supported ratification in order to end the war; his support influenced some Democratic votes. Still, on the final weekend before the vote, the treaty was two votes short. That Saturday night, news reached Washington that fighting had broken out between American troops and Filipino insurgents who demanded immediate independence. The news increased pressure to ratify the treaty, which the Senate did on February 6, 1899, with two votes to spare. An amendment promising independence as soon as the Filipinos established a stable government lost by one vote. The United States had a colonial empire.

Guerrilla Warfare in the Philippines

Historians rarely write of the Philippine-American War, but it was an important event in American history. The war with Spain was over a few months after it began; war with the Filipinos lasted more than three years. Four times as many American soldiers fought in the Philippines as in Cuba. For the first time, Americans fought men of a different color in an Asian guerrilla war. The Philippine-American War of 1898–1902 took a heavy toll: 4,300 American lives and untold thousands of Filipino lives (estimates range from 50,000 to 200,000).

Emilio Aguinaldo, the Filipino leader, was twenty-nine years old in 1898. An early organizer of the anti-Spanish resistance, he had gone into exile in Hong Kong, from where he welcomed the outbreak of the Spanish-American War. Certain the United States would grant independence, he worked for an American victory. Filipino insurgents helped guide Dewey into Manila Bay, and Dewey himself sent a ship to Hong Kong to bring back Aguinaldo to lead a native uprising against the Spanish. On June 12, 1898, the insurgents proclaimed their independence.

Cooperating with the Americans, they drove the Spanish out of many areas of the islands. In the liberated regions, Aguinaldo established local governments with appointed provincial governors. He waited impatiently for American recognition, but McKinley and others had concluded that the Filipinos were not ready. Soon, warfare broke out between the Filipinos and Americans over the question of Filipino independence.

By late 1899 the American army had defeated and dispersed the organized Filipino army, but claims of victory proved premature. Aguinaldo and his advisers shifted to guerrilla tactics, striking suddenly and then melting into the jungle or friendly native villages. In many areas, the Americans ruled the day, the guerrillas the night. There were terrible atrocities on both sides. The Americans found themselves using brutal, Weyler-like tactics. After any attack on an

Emilio Aguinaldo (seated, in vest) and his advisors in the Philippines, 1896. Aguinaldo's forces helped the Americans drive Spain out of the Philippines, expecting that the United States would recognize Filipino independence. When the United States failed to do so, Aguinaldo led his forces in warfare against the Americans.

American patrol, the Americans burned all the houses in the nearest district. They tortured people and executed prisoners. They established protected "zones" and herded Filipinos into them. Seizing or destroying all food outside the zones, they starved many guerrillas into submission.

Bryan tried to turn the election of 1900 into a debate over imperialism, but the attempt failed. For one thing, he himself refused to give up the silver issue, which cost him some support among anti-imperialists in the Northeast who were for gold. McKinley, moreover, was able to take advantage of the surging economy, and he could defend expansion as an accomplished fact. "It is no longer a question of expansion with us," he told one audience. "If there is any question at all it is a question of contraction; and who is going to contract?" Riding a wave of patriotism and prosperity, McKinley won the election handily— by an even larger margin than he had in 1896 (see Chapter 20).

In 1900, McKinley sent a special Philippine Commission under William Howard Taft, a prominent Ohio judge. Directed to establish a civil government, the commission organized municipal administrations and, in stages, created a government for the Philippines. In March 1901, five American soldiers tricked their way into Aguinaldo's camp deep in the mountains and took him prisoner. Back in Manila, he signed a proclamation urging his people to end the fighting. Some guerrillas held out for another year but to no avail. On July 4, 1901, authority was transferred from the army to Taft, who was named civilian governor of the islands, and his civilian commission. McKinley reaffirmed his purpose to grant the Filipinos self-government as soon as they were ready for it.

Given broad powers, the Taft Commission introduced many changes. New schools provided education and vocational training for Filipinos of all social classes. The Americans built roads and bridges, reformed the judiciary, restructured the tax system, and introduced sanitation and vaccination programs. They established local governments built on Filipino traditions and hierarchies. Taft encouraged Filipino participation in government. During the following decades, other measures broadened Filipino rights; independence finally came on July 4, 1946, nearly fifty years after Aguinaldo proclaimed it.

Governing the Empire

Ruling the colonies raised new and perplexing questions. How could—and how should—the distant dependencies be governed? Did their inhabitants have the rights of American citizens? Some people contended that acquisition did not automatically incorporate the new possessions into the United States and endow them with constitutional privileges. Others argued that "the Constitution followed the flag," meaning that acquisition made the possessions part of the nation and thus entitled them to all constitutional guarantees. A third group suggested that only "fundamental" constitutional guarantees—citizenship, the right to vote, and the right to trial by jury—not "formal" privileges—the right to use American currency, the right to be taxed, and the right to run for the presidency—were applicable to the new empire.

In a series of cases between 1901 and 1904 (*De Lima* v. *Bidwell, Dooley* v. *U.S.,* and *Downes* v. *Bidwell),* the Supreme Court asserted the principle that the Constitution did not automatically and immediately apply to the people of an annexed territory and did not confer upon them all the privileges of U.S. citizenship. Instead, Congress could specifically extend such constitutional provisions as it saw fit. "Ye-es," the Secretary of War said of the Court's ambiguous rulings, "as near as I can make out the Constitution follows the flag—but doesn't quite catch up with it."

Four dependencies—Hawaii, Alaska, Guam, and Puerto Rico—were organized quickly. In 1900, Congress granted territorial status to Hawaii, gave American citizenship to all citizens of the Hawaiian republic, authorized an elective legislature, and provided for a governor appointed from Washington. A similar measure made Alaska a territory in 1912. Guam and American Samoa were simply placed under the control of naval officers.

Unlike the Filipinos, Puerto Ricans readily accepted the war's outcome, and McKinley early withdrew troops from the island. The Foraker Act of 1900 established civil government in Puerto Rico. It organized the island as a territory, made its residents citizens of Puerto Rico (U.S. citizenship was extended to them in 1917), and empowered the president to appoint a governor general and a council to serve as the upper house of the legislature. A lower house of delegates was to be elected.

Cuba proved a trickier matter. McKinley asserted the authority of the United States over conquered territory and promised to govern the island until the Cubans had established a firm and stable government of their own. "I want you to go down there to get the people ready for a republican form of government," he instructed General Leonard Wood, commander of the army in Cuba until 1902. "I leave the details of procedure to you. Give them a good school system, try to straighten out their ports, and put them on their feet as best you can. We want to do all we can for them and to get out of the island as soon as we safely can."

Wood moved quickly to implement the instructions. Early in 1900, he completed a census of the Cuban population, conducted municipal elections, and arranged the election of delegates to a constitutional convention. The convention adopted a constitution modeled on the U.S. Constitution and, at Wood's prodding, included provisions for future relations with the United States. Known as the Platt Amendment to the new Cuban Constitution, the provisions stipulated that Cuba should make no treaties with other powers that might impair its independence, acquire no debts it could not pay, and lease naval bases like Guantanamo Bay to the United States. Most important, the amendment empowered the United States to intervene in Cuba to maintain orderly government.

Between 1898 and 1902, the American military government worked hard for the economic and political revival of the island, though it often demonstrated a paternalistic attitude toward the Cubans themselves. It repaired the damage of the civil war, built roads and schools, and established order in rural areas. A public health campaign headed by Dr. Walter Reed, an army surgeon, wiped out yellow fever. Most troops withdrew at the end of 1899, but a small American occupation force remained until May 1902. When it sailed for home, the Cubans at last had a form of independence, but they were still under the clear domination of their neighbor to the north.

The Open Door

Poised in the Philippines, the United States had become an Asian power on the doorstep of China. Weakened by years of warfare, China in 1898 and 1899 was unable to resist foreign influence. Japan, England, France, Germany, and Russia eyed it covetously, dividing parts of the

American Empire, 1900

With the Treaty of Paris, the United States gained an expanded colonial empire stretching from the Caribbean to the far Pacific. It embraced Puerto Rico, Alaska, Hawaii, part of Samoa, Guam, the Philippines, and a chain of Pacific islands. The dates on the map refer to the date of U.S. acquisition.

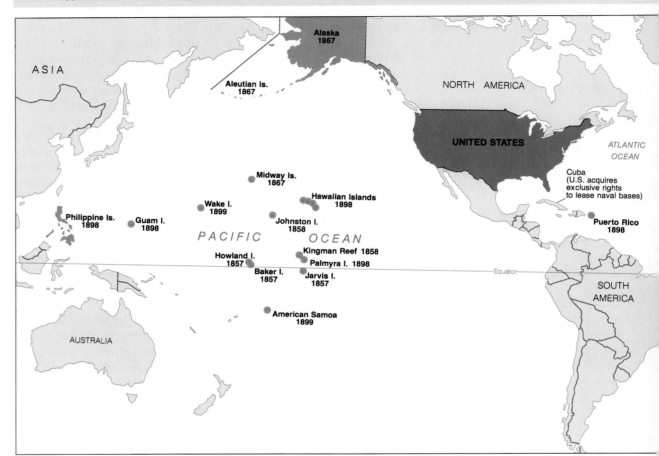

country into "spheres of influence." They forced China to grant "concessions" that allowed them exclusive rights to develop particular areas and threatened American hopes for extensive trade with the country.

McKinley first outlined a new China policy in September 1898 when he said that Americans sought more trade, "but we seek no advantages in the Orient which are not common to all. Asking only the open door for ourselves, we are ready to accord the open door to others." In September 1899, Secretary of State John Hay addressed identical diplomatic notes to England, Germany, and Russia, and later to France, Japan, and Italy, asking them to join the United States in establishing the "Open Door." The policy urged three agreements: nations possessing a sphere of influence would respect the rights and privileges of other nations in that sphere; the Chinese government would continue to collect tariff duties in all spheres; and nations would not discriminate against other nations in levying port dues and railroad rates within their respective spheres of influence.

Under the Open Door policy, the United States would retain many commercial advantages it might lose if China was partitioned into spheres of influence. McKinley and Hay also attempted to preserve for the Chinese some semblance of national authority. Great Britain most nearly accepted the principle of the Open Door. Russia declined to approve it, and the other powers, sending evasive replies, stated they would only agree if all the other nations did. Hay turned the

situation to American advantage by boldly announcing in March 1900 that all the powers had accepted the Open Door policy.

The policy's first test came just three months later with the outbreak of the Boxer Rebellion in Peking (now Beijing). In June 1900, a secret, intensely nationalistic Chinese society called the Boxers tried to oust all foreigners from their country. Overrunning Peking, they drove foreigners into their legations and penned them up for nearly two months. In the end, the United States joined Britain, Germany, and other powers in sending troops to lift the siege.

Fearing that the rebellion gave some nations, especially Germany and Russia, an excuse to expand their spheres of influence, Hay took quick action to emphasize American policy. In July, he sent off another round of Open Door notes affirming U.S. commitment to equal commercial opportunity and respect for China's independence. While the first Open Door notes had implied recognition of China's continued independence, the second notes explicitly stated the need to preserve it. Together, the two notes comprised the Open Door policy, which became a central element in American policy in the Far East.

To some degree, the policy tried to help China, but it also led to further American meddling in the affairs of another country. Moreover, by committing itself to a policy that Americans were not prepared to defend militarily, the McKinley administration left the opportunity for later controversy with Japan and other expansion-minded powers in the Pacific.

The war with Spain over, Roosevelt and the Rough Riders sailed for home in mid-August 1898. They sauntered through the streets of New York, the heroes of the city. A few weeks later, Roosevelt bade them farewell. They presented him with a reproduction of Frederick Remington's famed bronze, *The Bronco-Buster*, and close to tears, he told them, "I am proud of this regiment beyond measure." Roosevelt later wrote an account of the war in which he played so central a role that Mr. Dooley suggested "If I was him, I'd call th' book 'Alone in Cubia.'" By then Roosevelt was already governor of New York and on his way to the White House.

Other soldiers were also glad to be home, although they were sometimes resentful of the reception they found. "The war is over now," said Winslow Hobson, a black trooper from the

CHRONOLOGY

1867 United States purchases Alaska from Russia • Midway Islands are annexed

1871 Treaty of Washington between United States and Great Britain sets precedent for peaceful settlement of international disputes

1875 Reciprocity treaty with Hawaii binds Hawaii economically and politically to United States

1878 United States acquires naval base in Samoa

1883 Congress approves funds for construction of first modern steel ships; beginning of modern navy

1887 New treaty with Hawaii gives United States exclusive use of Pearl Harbor

1889 First Inter-American Conference meets in Washington, D.C.

1893 American settlers in Hawaii overthrow Queen Liliuokalani; provisional government established

1895 Cuban insurgents rebel against Spanish rule

1898 Battleship *Maine* explodes in Havana harbor (February) • Congress declares war against Spain (April) • Commodore Dewey defeats Spanish fleet at Manila Bay (May) • United States annexes Hawaii (July) • Americans defeat Spanish at El Caney, San Juan Hill (actually Kettle Hill), and Santiago (July) • Spain sues for peace (August) • Treaty of Paris ends Spanish-American War (December)

1899 Congress ratifies Treaty of Paris • United States sends Open Door notes to Britain, Germany, France, Russia, Japan, and Italy • Philippine-American War erupts

1900 Foraker Act establishes civil government in Puerto Rico

1901 Platt Amendment authorizes American intervention in Cuba

1902 Philippine-American War ends with American victory

Ninth Ohio, "and Roosevelt . . . and others (white of course) have all there is to be gotten out of it." Bravery in Cuba and the Philippines won some recognition for black soldiers, but the war itself set back the cause of civil rights. It spurred talk about "inferior" races, at home and abroad, and united whites in the North and South. "The Negro might as well know it now as later," a black editor said, "the closer the North and South get together by this war, the harder he will have to fight to maintain a footing." A fresh outburst of segregation and lynching occurred during the decade after the war.

McKinley and the Republican party soared to new heights of popularity. Firmly established, the Republican majority dominated politics until 1932. Scandals arose about the canned beef and the conduct of the War Department, but there was none of the sharp sense of deception and betrayal that was to mark the years after World War I. In a little more than a century, the United States had grown from thirteen states stretched along a thin Atlantic coastline into a world power that reached from the Caribbean to the Pacific. As Seward and others had hoped, the nation now dominated its own hemisphere, dealt with European powers on more equal terms, and was a major power in Asia.

Recommended Reading

The best general account of the development of American foreign policy during the last part of the nineteenth century is Walter LaFeber, *The New Empire: An Interpretation of American Expansion, 1860–1898* (1963). Robert L. Beisner, *From the Old Diplomacy to the New, 1865–1900* (1975), and Charles S. Campbell, Jr., *Transformation of American Foreign Relations, 1865–1900* (1976), give useful overviews that suggest important changes that took place in the 1890s. J. A. S. Grenville and George Berkeley Young present a series of significant essays in *Politics, Strategy and American Diplomacy: Studies in Foreign Policy, 1873–1917* (1966). William Appleman Williams, *The Tragedy of American Diplomacy* (1959), examines the economic motives for expansion. See also Paul Wolman, *Most Favored Nation: The Republican Revisionists and U.S. Tariff Policy, 1897–1912* (1992).

Ernest R. May analyzes the causes of the Spanish-American war in *Imperial Democracy: The Emergence of America as a Great Power* (1961); for a briefer treatment, see H. Wayne Morgan, *America's Road to Empire: The War with Spain and Overseas Expansion*

(1965). Lewis L. Gould persuasively reassesses McKinley's diplomacy and wartime leadership in *The Presidency of William McKinley* (1980).

Graham A. Cosmas presents a detailed account of military organization and strategy in *An Army for Empire: The United States Army in the Spanish-American War* (1971); Willard B. Gatewood, Jr., *"Smoked Yankees" and the Struggle for Empire: Letters from Negro Soldiers, 1898–1902* (1971), offers a fascinating glimpse of the thoughts of some black soldiers in the war. Gerald F. Linderman relates the war to the home front in *The Mirror of War: American Society and the Spanish-American War* (1974).

Additional Bibliography

On American foreign policy during this period, see David M. Pletcher, *The Awkward Years: American Foreign Relations Under Garfield and Arthur* (1962); David F. Healy, *U.S. Expansionism: The Imperialist Urge in the 1890's* (1970); Milton Plesur, *America's Outward Thrust: Approaches to Foreign Affairs, 1865–1890* (1971); Richard W. Leopold, *The Growth of American Foreign Policy* (1962); Michael H. Hunt, *Ideology and U.S. Foreign Policy* (1987); John Dobson, *America's Ascent: The United States Becomes a Great Power, 1880–1914* (1978); Adrian Cook, *The Alabama Claims* (1975); Michael J. Devine, *John W. Foster: Politics and Diplomacy in the Imperial Era, 1873–1917* (1981); and Tom E. Terrill, *The Tariff, Politics, and American Foreign Policy, 1874–1901* (1973).

For policies toward specific areas, see R. P. Gilson, *Samoa 1830 to 1900: The Politics of a Multi-Cultural Community* (1970); Charles S. Campbell, Jr., *Anglo-American Understanding, 1898–1903* (1957); Paul S. Holbo, *Tarnished Expansion: The Alaska Scandal, The Press, and Congress, 1867–1871* (1983); Thomas D. Schoonover, *The United States and Central America, 1860–1911* (1991); Joseph Smith, *Unequal Giants: Diplomatic Relations Between the United States and Brazil, 1889–1930* (1991); Thomas J. McCormick, *China Market: America's Quest for Informal Empire, 1893–1901* (1967); Michael H. Hunt, *The Making of a Special Relationship: The United States and China to 1914* (1983); David L. Anderson, *Imperialism and Idealism: American Diplomats in China, 1861–1898* (1985); Marilyn B. Young, *Rhetoric of Empire: American China Policy, 1895–1901* (1968); Merze Tate, *The United States and the Hawaiian Kingdom: A Political History* (1965); and William A. Russ, Jr., *The Hawaiian Republic, 1894–98 and Its Struggle to Win Annexation* (1961).

Books on naval and military developments during these years include Walter R. Herrick, *The American Naval Revolution* (1966); William R. Braisted, *The United States Navy in the Pacific, 1897–1909* (1958); Peter Karsten, *The Naval Aristocracy* (1972); Benjamin J. Cooling, *Gray Steel and Blue Water Navy* (1979); and Kenneth J. Hagan, *American Gunboat Diplomacy and the Old Navy, 1877–1889* (1973).

For the background of the war with Spain, see David F. Trask, *The War with Spain in 1898* (1981); Julius W. Pratt, *Expansionists of 1898: The Acquisition of Hawaii and the Spanish Islands* (1936); Walter Millis, *The Martial Spirit: A Study of Our War with Spain* (1931); Philip S. Foner, *The Spanish-Cuban-American War and the Birth of American Imperialism, 1895–1902*, 2 vols. (1972); J. E. Wisan, *The Cuban Crisis as Reflected in the New York Press, 1895–1898* (1934); John L. Offner, *An Unwanted War: The Diplomacy of the United States and Spain over Cuba, 1895–1898* (1992); and Hyman G. Rickover, *How the Battleship* Maine *Was Destroyed* (1976).

Biographies of the period's leading personalities include H. Wayne Morgan, *William McKinley and His America* (1963); Margaret Leech, *In the Days of McKinley* (1959); Robert Seager, II, *Alfred Thayer Mahan* (1977); and Ronald Spector, *Admiral of the New Empire: The Life and Career of George Dewey* (1974). See also Theodore Roosevelt, *The Rough Riders* (1899); John D. Long, *The New American Navy*, 2 vols. (1903); and H. Wayne Morgan, ed., *Making Peace with Spain: The Diary of Whitelaw Reid, September–December 1898* (1965).

The course of the war itself can be followed in Frank Freidel, *The Splendid Little War* (1958); Orestes Femara, *The Last Spanish War* (1937); Frederick Funston, *Memories of Two Wars: Cuba and Philippine Experiences* (1914); Charles H. Brown, *The Correspondents' War: Journalists in the Spanish-American War* (1967); David A. Gerber, *Black Ohio and the Color Line, 1860–1915* (1976); and Herschel V. Cashin et al., *Under Fire with the Tenth U.S. Cavalry* (1899). Willard B. Gatewood, Jr., *Black Americans and the White Man's Burden, 1898–1903* (1975), is a thorough and thought-provoking study.

For the debate over expansion and the treaty with Spain, consult Richard E. Welch, Jr., *George Frisbie Hoar and the Half-Breed Republicans* (1971); E. Berkeley Tompkins, *Anti-Imperialism in the United States: The Great Debate, 1890–1920* (1970); Daniel B. Schirmer, *Republic or Empire: American Resistance to the Philippine War* (1972); Thomas J. Osborne, *"Empire Can Wait"; American Opposition to Hawaiian Annexation, 1893–1898* (1981); and Göran Rystad, *Ambiguous Imperialism: American Foreign Policy and Domestic Politics at the Turn of the Century* (1975).

Policy toward Cuba and the Philippines is covered

in Richard E. Welch, Jr., *Response to Imperialism: The United States and the Philippine-American War, 1899–1902* (1979); H. W. Brands, *Bound to Empire: The United States and the Philippines* (1992); David F. Healy, *The United States in Cuba, 1898–1902* (1963), and *Drive to Hegemony: The United States in the Caribbean, 1898–1917* (1988); James H. Hitchman, *Leonard Wood and Cuban Independence, 1898–1902* (1971); John Morgan Gates, *Schoolbooks and Krags: The United States Army in the Philippines, 1898–1902* (1973); Glenn A. May, *Social Engineering in the Philippines* (1980); Stuart Creighton Miller, *"Benevolent Assimilation": The American Conquest of the Philippines, 1899–1903* (1982); Brian McAllister Linn, *The U.S. Army and Counterinsurgency in the Philippine War, 1899–1902* (1989); and Peter W. Stanley, *A Nation in the Making: The Philippines and the United States, 1899–1921* (1974).

The Progressive Era

*I*n 1902, Samuel S. McClure, the shrewd owner of *McClure's Magazine,* sensed something astir in the country that his reporters were not covering. Like *Life, Munsey's,* the *Ladies' Home Journal,* and *Cosmopolitan, McClure's* was reaching more and more people—over one-quarter of a million readers a month. Americans were snapping up the new popular magazines filled with eye-catching illustrations and up-to-date fiction. Advances in photoengraving during the 1890s dramatically reduced the cost of illustrations; at the same time, income from advertisements rose sharply. By the turn of the century, some magazines earned as much as $60,000 an issue from advertising alone, and publishers could price them as low as 10 cents a copy.

McClure was always chasing new ideas and readers, and in 1902, certain that something was happening in the public mood, he told one of his editors, thirty-six-year-old Lincoln Steffens, a former Wall Street reporter, to find out what it was. "Get out of here, travel, go—somewhere. . . ," he said to Steffens. "Buy a railroad ticket, get on a train, and there, where it lands you, there you will learn to edit a magazine."

McClure's, it turned out, had an unpaid bill from the Lackawanna Railroad, and Steffens traveled west. In Saint Louis, he came across a young district attorney named Joseph W. Folk who had found a trail of corruption linking politics and some of the city's respected business leaders. Eager for help, Folk did not mind naming names to the visiting editor from New York. "It is good business men that are corrupting our bad politicians. . . ," he stressed again and again. "It is the leading citizens that are battening on our city." Steffens's story, "Tweed Days in St. Louis," appeared in the October 1902 issue of *McClure's.*

The November *McClure's* carried the first installment of Ida Tarbell's scathing "History of the Standard Oil Company," and in January 1903, Steffens was back with "The Shame of Minneapolis," another tale of corrupt partnership between business and politics. McClure had what he wanted, and in the January issue he printed an editorial, "Concerning Three Articles in This Number of *McClure's,* and a Coincidence That May Set Us Thinking." Steffens on Minneapolis, Tarbell on Standard Oil, and an article on abuses in labor unions—all, McClure said, on different topics but actually on the same theme: corruption in American life. "Capitalists, workingmen, politicians, citizens—all breaking the law, or letting it be broken."

Readers were enthralled, and articles and books by other muckrakers—Theodore Roosevelt coined the unflattering term in 1906 to describe the practice of exposing the corruption of public and prominent figures—spread swiftly. *Collier's* had articles on questionable stock market practices, patent medicines, and the beef trust. Novelist Upton Sinclair tackled the meat packers in *The Jungle* (1906). In 1904, Steffens collected his *McClure's* articles in *The Shame of the Cities,* with an introduction expressing confidence that reform was possible, "that our shamelessness is superficial, that beneath it lies a pride which, being real, may save us yet."

Muckraking flourished from 1903 to 1909, and while it did, good writers and bad investigated almost every corner of American life: government, labor unions, big business, Wall Street, health care, the food industry, child labor, women's rights, prostitution, ghetto living, and life insurance. "Time was," Mr. Dooley, the fictional character of humorist Finley Peter Dunne, said to Mr. Hennessy, when magazines

was very ca'ming to the mind. Angabel an' Alfonso dashin' f'r a marriage license. Prom'nent lady authoresses makin' pomes at the moon. . . . Th' idee ye got fr'm these here publications was that life was wan glad sweet song. . . .

But now whin I pick me fav-rite magazine off th' flure, what do I find? Ivrything has gone wrong. . . . All th' pomes by th' lady authoresses that used to begin: "Oh, moon, how fair!" now begin: "Oh, Ogden Armour, how awful!" . . . Graft ivrywhere. "Graft in th' Insurance Companies," "Graft in Congress," "Graft be an Old Grafter," "Graft in Its Relations to th' Higher Life". . . .

An' so it goes, Hinnissy . . . till I don't thrust anny man anny more. . . . I used to be nervous about burglars, but now I'm afraid iv a night call fr'm th' prisidint iv th' First National Bank.

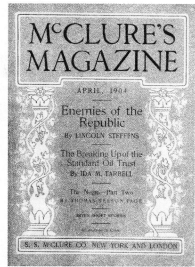

During the Progressive Era, McClure's Magazine *was at the front of the journalistic crusade for reform, which took the form of muckraking articles by such writers as Ida Tarbell (right). Her exposé of the Standard Oil Company ran side by side with Lincoln Steffens's article on the alliances between business and corrupt political machines in several cities.*

The muckrakers were a journalistic voice of a larger movement in American society. Called *progressivism,* it lasted from the mid-1890s through World War I. Like muckraking itself, progressivism reflected worry about the state of society, the effects of industrialization and urbanization, social disorder, political corruption, and a host of other issues. With concerns so large, progressivism often had a sense of crisis and urgency although it was rooted in a spirit of hopefulness and confidence in human progress. For varying reasons, thousands of people became concerned about their society, and separately and together, they set out to cure some of the ills they saw around them. Known later as the "progressives," their efforts changed the nation and gave the era its name.

As McClure had hoped, Steffens *had* found something astir in the country, something so important and pervasive that it altered the course of American history in the twentieth century. This chapter examines in detail the economic, social, and intellectual conditions that gave rise to progressivism. Chapter 23 examines progressivism itself, in the cities, states, and nation.

THE CHANGING FACE OF INDUSTRIALISM

"Life in the States," an English visitor said in 1900, "is one perpetual whirl of telephones, telegrams, phonographs, electric bells, motors, lifts, and automatic instruments." If not quite as automated as the visitor described, conditions in America were better than just a few years before. Farms and factories were once again prosperous; in 1901, for the first time in years, the economy reached full capacity. Farm prices rose almost 50 percent between 1900 and 1910. Unemployment dropped. "In the United States of today," a Boston newspaper said in 1904, "everyone is middle class. The resort to force, the wild talk of the nineties are over. Everyone is busily, happily getting ahead."

Everyone, of course, was not middle class, nor was everyone getting ahead. "Wild talk" persisted. Many of the problems that had angered people in the 1890s continued into the new century, and millions of Americans still suffered from poverty and disease. Racism sat even more heavily on African Americans in both South and North, and there was increasing hostility against immigrants from southern and eastern Europe, Mexico, and Asia. Yet to some degree the Boston newspaper was right: economic conditions *were* better for many people, and as a result, prosperity became one of the keys to understanding the era and the nature of progressive reform.

The start of the new century was another key as well, for it influenced people to take a fresh look at themselves and their times. Excited about beginning the twentieth century, people believed technology and enterprise would shape a better life. Savoring the word *new,* they talked of the new poetry, new cinema, new history, new democracy, new woman, new art, new immigration, new morality, and new city. Magazines picked up the word; there were the *New Republic* and the *New Statesman*. Presidents Theodore Roosevelt and Woodrow Wilson called their political programs the New Nationalism and the New Freedom.

The word *mass* also cropped up frequently. Victors in the recent war with Spain, many Americans took pride in teeming cities, burgeoning corporations, and other marks of the mass society. They enjoyed the fruits of mass production, read mass circulation newspapers and magazines, and took mass transit from the growing spiral of suburbs into the central cities.

Behind mass production lay significant changes in the nation's industrial system. Businesses grew at a rapid rate. They were large in the three decades after the Civil War, but in the years between 1895 and 1915, they became mammoth, employing thousands of workers and equipped with assembly lines to turn out huge numbers of the company's product. Inevitably, changes in management attitudes, business organization, and worker roles influenced the entire society. Inevitably, too, the growth of giant businesses gave rise to a widespread fear of "trusts" and a desire among many progressive reformers to break them up or regulate them.

The Innovative Model T

In the movement toward large-scale business and mass production, the automobile industry was one of those that led the way. In 1895, there were only four cars on the nation's roads; in 1917, there were nearly five million, and the automobile had already helped work a small revolution in industrial methods and social mores.

Mass production of automobiles began in the first years of the century. Using an assembly-line system that foreshadowed later techniques, Ransom E. Olds turned out five thousand Olds runabouts in 1904. But Olds's days of leadership were numbered. In 1903, Henry Ford and a small group of associates formed the Ford Motor Company, the firm that transformed the business.

Ford was forty years old. He had tried farming and hated it; during the 1890s, he worked as an engineer for Detroit's Edison Company but spent his spare time designing internal combustion engines and automobiles. At first, like many others in the industry, he concentrated on building luxury and racing cars. Racing his own cars, Ford became the "speed demon" of Detroit; in 1904, he set the world's land speed record—over 90 miles per hour—in the 999, a large red racer that shot flames from the motor.

In 1903, Ford sold the first Ford car. The price was high, and in 1905, Ford raised prices still higher. Sales plummeted. In 1907, he lowered the price; sales and revenues rose. Ford learned an important lesson of the modern economy: a smaller unit profit on a large number of sales meant enormous revenues. Early in 1908, he introduced the Model T, a four-cylinder, 20-horsepower "Tin Lizzie," costing $850, and available only in black. Eleven thousand were sold the first year.

"I am going to democratize the automobile," Ford proclaimed. "When I'm through everybody will be able to afford one, and about everyone will have one." The key was mass production, and after many experiments, Ford copied the techniques of meat packers who moved animal carcasses along overhead trolleys from station to station. Adapting the process to automobile assembly, Ford in 1913 set up moving assembly lines in his plant in Highland Park, Michigan, that dramatically reduced the time and cost of producing cars. Emphasizing continuous movement, he strove for a nonstop flow from raw material to finished product. In 1914, he sold 248,000 Model T's.

That year, Ford workers assembled a car in ninety-three minutes, one-tenth the time it had taken just eight months before. By 1925, the Ford plant turned out 9,109 Model T's, a new car for every ten seconds of the working day.

While Ford was putting more and more cars on the road, the 1916 Federal Aid Roads Act, a little-noticed measure, set the framework for road building in the twentieth century. Removing control from county governments, it required every state desiring federal funds to establish a highway department to plan routes, oversee construction, and maintain roads. In states that had such departments, the federal government paid half the cost of building the roads. Providing for a planned highway system, the act produced a

Workers assembling small parts on the Ford assembly line.

ties and steel. Rockefeller's Standard Oil owned about 85 percent of the oil business. Large companies like Standard Oil and American Tobacco had weathered the depression of the 1890s, and after 1898, financiers and industrialists followed their example and formed the Amalgamated Copper Company, Consolidated Tobacco, U.S. Rubber, and a host of others.

By 1909, just 1 percent of the industrial firms were producing nearly half of all manufactured goods. Giant businesses reached abroad for raw materials and new markets. United Fruit, an empire of plantations and steamships in the Caribbean, exploited opportunities created by victory in the war with Spain. U.S. Steel worked with overseas companies to fix the price of steel rails, an unattainable dream just a few years before. For decades, competition had sent rail prices up and down; now they stayed at $28 a ton, and through the famous "Gary dinners" in which Elbert H. Gary of U.S. Steel brought steel executives from "competing" firms together to set prices over dinner, market conditions were fixed for wide areas of the industry.

Though the trend has been overstated, finance capitalists like J. P. Morgan tended to replace the

national network of two-lane all-weather intercity roads.

The Burgeoning Trusts

As businesses like Ford's grew, capital and organization became increasingly important, and the result was the formation of a growing number of trusts. Standard Oil started the trend in 1882 (see Chapter 18), but the greatest momentum came two decades later. Between 1898 and 1903, a series of mergers and consolidations swept the economy. Many smaller firms disappeared, swallowed up in giant corporations. By 1904, large-scale combinations of one form or another controlled nearly two-fifths of the capital in manufacturing in the country.

The result was not monopoly, but oligopoly—control of a commodity or service by a small number of large powerful companies. Six great financial groups dominated the railroad industry; a handful of holding companies controlled utili-

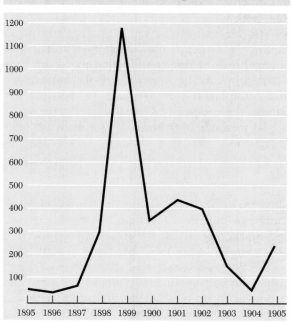

Business Consolidations (Mergers), 1895–1905

industrial capitalists of an earlier era. Able to finance the mergers and reorganizations, investment bankers played a greater and greater role in the economy. A multibillion-dollar financial house, J. P. Morgan and Company operated a network of control that ran from New York to every industrial and financial center in the nation. Like other investment firms, it held directorships in many corporations, creating "interlocking directorates" that allowed it to control many businesses. In 1913, two banking groups—Morgan's and Rockefeller's—held 341 directorships in 112 corporations with an aggregate capital of more than $22 billion.

Massive business growth set off a decade-long debate over what government should do about the trusts. Some critics who believed the giant companies were responsible for stifling individual opportunity and raising prices wanted to break them up into small competitive units. Others argued that large-scale business was a mark of the times; it produced more goods and better lives.

The debate over the trusts was one of the issues that shaped the Progressive Era, but it was never a simple contest between high-minded reformers and greedy business titans. Some progressives favored big business; others wanted it broken up. Business leaders themselves were divided in their viewpoints, and some welcomed reform-led assaults on giant competitors. As a rule, both progressives and business leaders drew on similar visions of the country: complex, expansive, hopeful, managerially minded, and oriented toward results and efficiency. They both believed in private property and the importance of economic progress. In fact, in working for reform, the progressives often drew on the managerial methods of a business world they sought to regulate.

Managing the Machines

Mass production changed the direction of American industry. Size, system, organization, and marketing became increasingly important. Management focused on speed and product, not on workers. Assembly-line technology changed tasks and, to some extent, values. The goal was no longer to make a unique product that would be better than the one before. "The way to make

As early as 1886, cartoonist Thomas Nast attacked trusts. Here the people's welfare is sinking as the Statue of Liberty is defaced.

automobiles," Ford said as early as 1903, "is to make one automobile like another automobile, to make them all alike, to make them come through the factory just alike."

In a development that rivaled assembly lines in importance, businesses established industrial research laboratories where scientists and engineers developed new products. General Electric founded the first one in 1900, housed in a barn. It soon attracted experts who designed improvements in light bulbs, invented the cathode-ray tube, worked on early radio, and even tinkered with atomic theory. Du Pont opened its labs in 1911, Eastman Kodak in 1912, and Standard Oil in 1919. As the source of new ideas and technology, the labs altered life in the twentieth century.

Through all this, business became large scale, mechanized, and managed. While many shops still employed fewer than a dozen workers, the proportion of such shops shrank. By 1920, close to one-half of all industrial workers worked in factories employing more than 250 people. More than one-third worked in factories that were part of multiplant companies.

Industries that processed materials—iron and steel, paper, cement, and chemicals—were increasingly continuous and automatic. In the glass industry, machines ended the domination of highly skilled and well-paid craft workers. In 1908, Irving W. Colburn invented a machine to manufacture plate glass; the Libbey-Owens-Ford Company bought the patent; and Ford soon had a glassmaking machine from which emerged every day for two years a $3^1/_2$-mile ribbon of automobile window glass, eventually reaching a length of almost 2,000 miles.

Workers tending such ribbons could not fall behind. Foremen still managed the laborers on the factory floor, but more and more, the rules came down from a central office where trained professional managers supervised production flow. Systematic record keeping, cost accounting, and inventory and production controls became widespread. Workers lost control of the work pace. "If you need to turn out a little more," a manager at Swift and Company said, "you speed up the conveyor a little and the men speed up to keep pace." It worked. For that and other reasons, in the automobile industry, output per man-hour multiplied an extraordinary four times between 1909 and 1919.

Folkways of the workplace—workers passing job-related knowledge to each other, performing their tasks with little supervision, setting their own pace, and in effect running the shop—began to give way to "scientific" labor management. More than anyone else, Frederick Winslow Taylor, an inventive mechanical engineer, strove to extract maximum efficiency from each worker. (See "Frederick Winslow Taylor and the Rise of Scientific Management," pp. 664–665.)

Taylor proposed two major reforms. First, management must take responsibility for job-related knowledge and classify it into "rules, laws, and formulae." Second, management should control the workplace "through *enforced* standardization of methods, *enforced* adoption of the best implements and working conditions, and *enforced* cooperation." Although few factories wholly adopted Taylor's principles, he had great influence, and the doctrines of scientific management spread through American industry.

Workers caught up in the changing industrial system experienced the benefits of efficiency and productivity; in some industries, they earned more. But they suffered important losses as well. Performing repetitive tasks, they seemed part of the machinery, to the pace and needs of which they moved. Bored, they might easily lose pride of workmanship, though many workers, it is clear, did not. Efficiency engineers experimented with tools and methods, a process many workers found unsettling. Yet the goal was to establish routine—to work out, as someone said of a garment worker, "one single precise motion each second, 3,600 in one hour, and all exactly the same." Praising that worker, the manager said, "She is a sure machine."

Jobs became not only monotonous but dangerous. As machines and assembly lines sped up, boredom or miscalculation could bring disaster. Meat cutters sliced fingers and hands. Illinois steel mills, a magazine said, were "Making Steel and Killing Men"; one mill had forty-six deaths in 1906 alone. Injuries were part of many jobs. "The machines go like mad all day," a garment worker said, "because the faster you work the more money you get. Sometimes in my haste I get my finger caught and the needle goes right through it . . . I bind the finger up with a piece of cotton and go on working."

In March 1911, a fire at the Triangle Shirtwaist Company in New York focused nationwide attention on unsafe working conditions. When the fire started, five hundred men and women, mostly Italians and Jews from eastern Europe, were just finishing their workday. Firefighters arrived within minutes, but they were already too late. Terrified seamstresses raced to the exits to try to escape the flames, but most exit doors were closed, locked by the company to prevent theft and shut out union organizers. Many died in the stampede down the narrow stairways or the single fire escape. Still others, trapped on the building's top stories far above the reach of the fire department's ladders, jumped to their deaths on the street below. One hundred forty-six people died.

Frederick Winslow Taylor and the Rise of Scientific Management

Between 1880 and 1920, American businesses underwent revolutionary changes. For one thing, they grew larger and larger, employing thousands of people and turning out products sold around the world. Some grew so large they owned the mines or farms that produced the raw materials, the railroads and steamships that transported them, the factories that turned raw materials into a finished product, and the retailing system that marketed it. As businesses grew in size, they also grew more bureaucratic, with layers of people between the owners and the shop floor. In the years after 1880 a new "science" of management sprang up to help managers organize and control the giant new businesses of the industrial age.

Frederick Winslow Taylor, an ingenious inventor and engineer, was the leader in this effort. Born in Philadelphia in 1856, Taylor was headed for Harvard when his parents, afraid that studying was hurting his eyesight, urged him to drop out of school and get a job. He went to work for Midvale Steel in Philadelphia, first as a clerk and machinist, and then as subforeman in the machine shop, his first managerial post. Taylor was aggressive and ambitious, and he soon began to step up the pace in the shop. The men refused. As late as the 1880s, workers in factories like Midvale tended to

Frederick Winslow Taylor.

make the rules themselves, regardless of orders from the top. They established their own quotas, worked at their own pace, and resisted attempts to hurry them up.

Impatient, Taylor tinkered with ways to improve the machinery and, before long, the factory system itself. "My head," he said, "was full of wonderful and great projects to simplify the processes, to design new machines, to revolutionize the methods of the whole establishment." Among other products, he invented high-speed tool steel for cutting hard metals, an innovation crucial to modern industry. At the same time he developed a broad plan of scientific management for every industry, certain, he said, that "the best management is a true science, resting upon clearly defined laws, rules, and principles."

Setting out to uncover those

laws, he studied each job in a factory, trying to reduce it to the simplest components. How did the worker's arms move? Were there wasted motions? Did he or she have the right tools? The right instructions? By 1889, when he left Midvale, Taylor had settled on four principles of scientific management: (1) centralized planning of the factory and its output; (2) systematic analysis of each job; (3) detailed instruction and supervision of each worker; and (4) an incentive wage scale that would get workers to follow the instructions. Managers, he said, not workers, should determine what happens on the shop floor. "In the past the man has been first; in the future the system must be first."

To prove the point Taylor told the story of "Schmidt," an ordinary laborer at the Bethlehem Steel plant. When war with Spain broke out in 1898, Bethlehem had 80,000 tons of pig iron stacked in piles in a field. With the sudden demand for arms the price soared, and Bethlehem asked Taylor to load it quickly for the market. Running a railroad track into the field, he studied what to do. Each bar of pig iron weighed 92 pounds; to load it, a worker had to pick it up, carry it up a ramp into a boxcar, stack it, and return for another bar. A worker usually loaded $12^{1}/_{2}$ long tons of pig iron a day. But someone working efficiently, Taylor thought, should load almost four times that much—$47^{1}/_{2}$ long tons (106,400 pounds)—a day.

That was no small difference, and when Taylor offered his men higher wages to do the job, they refused, thinking it was all just an excuse to get everyone in the factory to work harder. Starting again, Taylor chose one worker, Henry Noll, whom he made famous in his writings as "Schmidt." He had watched Noll carefully and liked the way he worked hard all day and trotted a mile home at night. Taking Noll aside, Taylor offered him a chance to earn $1.85 a day, instead of the usual $1.15. To earn the higher wage, he just had to work exactly as he was told. Noll leaped at the chance, and after a bit, others joined him. The pig iron was soon loaded and on its way.

From his experiments with Schmidt, Taylor derived a "law of heavy laboring" that told workers when to work and when to rest. Studying the shoveling of iron ore, he came up with a "science of shoveling." He designed fifteen kinds of shovels for different conditions and prescribed the exact motions for using each one. Companies adopting his ideas were often able to lay off workers and cut costs—one company cut its shoveling crew from 600 men to 140 for the same work—but Taylor argued that those who remained earned more and were happier.

In the last years of his life Taylor spent most of his time writing, consulting, and lecturing. His book, *The Principles of Scientific Management* (1911), was read widely by managers; workers passed copies of it around so everyone could fight Taylorism whenever it appeared. At his death in 1915 Taylor ranked with Henry Ford as an American industrial hero. Business leaders, of course, liked his efforts to increase productivity, but Taylor was also popular because he had much in common with the generation of progressivism. Like the progressives, he believed in experts, efficiency, systematic planning, and the application of science to human life. Theodore Roosevelt praised him; Milwaukee, Pittsburgh, Seattle, and Philadelphia used his ideas to streamline city government. Taylor and the progressives wanted to bring order to the industrial society. "There have been times in recent years," a leading progressive said of him,

Two of Taylor's principles of scientific management were systematic analysis of each job and detailed instruction of each worker. Here workers at Bethlehem Steel study the Taylor-designed charts that describe each of the tasks they are to perform.

"when it seemed as though our civilization were being throttled by things, by property, by the very weight of industrial mechanism, and it is no small matter when a man arises who can show us new ways of commanding our environment."

Since Taylor's time, researchers have found that workers care about job security, working conditions, and fringe benefits, not just higher wages, as Taylor had believed. Today, more emphasis is placed on the quality of the work, not just the time on the job, and some managers have even begun encouraging the kind of decision making on the shop floor that Taylor fought so hard to get rid of at Midvale. The Japanese, recognized today as the foremost management specialists, combine Taylor's ideas about centralized planning with Midvale's way of involving workers in some decisions. Yet when people go to their jobs in industrial nations around the world, the conditions they find are still shaped by Frederick Winslow Taylor's principles of scientific management, developed more than three-quarters of a century ago.

For companies that adopted the "art and science of shoveling" that he prescribed, Taylor predicted yearly savings of $75,000 to $80,000. Although fewer workers would be required, those who remained employed would see their daily wages rise from $1.15 to $1.88.

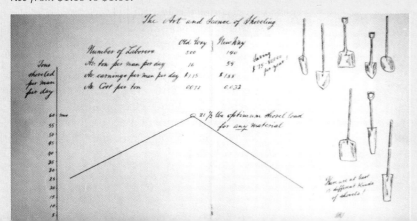

Fire nets were of no avail to the Triangle workers who jumped from the upper stories to escape the flames. Speaking to a mass meeting after the fire, labor organizer Rose Schneiderman inveighed against a system that treated human beings as expendable commodities.

A few days later, eighty thousand people marched silently in the rain in a funeral procession up Fifth Avenue. A quarter of a million peo-

ple watched. At a mass meeting held to protest factory working conditions, Rose Schneiderman, a twenty-nine-year-old dynamic organizer for the Women's Trade Union League, told New York City's civic and religious leaders that they had not done enough, they had not cared. "We have tried you good people of the public and we have found you wanting. . . . Every week I must learn of the untimely death of one of my sister workers. Every year thousands of us are maimed. The life of men and women is so cheap and property is so sacred."

The outcry impelled New York's governor to appoint a State Factory Investigating Commission that recommended laws to shorten the workweek and improve safety in factories and stores.

SOCIETY'S MASSES

Spreading consumer goods through society, mass production not only improved people's lives, but sometimes cost lives, too. Tending the machines, as Rose Schneiderman pointed out, took hard, painful labor, often under dangerous conditions. As businesses expanded, they required more and more people, and the labor force increased tremendously to keep up with the demand for workers in the factories, mines, and forest. Women, African Americans, Asian Americans, and Mexican Americans played larger and larger roles. Immigration soared. Between 1901 and 1910, nearly 8.8 million immigrants entered the United States; between 1911 and 1920, another 5.7 million came.

For many of these people, life was harsh, spent in crowded slums and long hours on the job. Fortunately, the massive unemployment of the 1890s was over, and in many skilled trades, like cigar making, there was plenty of work to go around. Though the economic recovery helped nearly everyone, the less skilled continued to be the less fortunate. Migrant workers, lumberjacks, ore shovelers, and others struggled to find decent-paying jobs.

Under such circumstances, many people fought to make a living, and many, too, fought to improve their lot. Their efforts, along with the efforts of the reform-minded people who came to their aid, became another important hallmark of the Progressive Era.

Better Times on the Farm

While people continued to flee the farms—by 1920, fewer than one-third of all Americans lived on farms; fewer than one-half lived in rural areas—farmers themselves prospered, the beneficiaries of greater production and expanding urban markets. Rural Free Delivery, begun in 1893, helped diminish the farmers' sense of isolation, and changed farm life. The delivery of mail to the farm door opened that door to a wider world; it exposed farmers to urban thinking, national advertising, and political events. In 1911, over one billion newspapers and magazines were delivered over RFD routes.

Parcel post (1913) permitted the sending of packages through the U.S. mail. Mail-order houses flourished; rural merchants suffered. Packages went both ways—President Woodrow Wilson's first parcel-post delivery had 8 pounds of New Jersey apples—and within a year, 300 million packages were being mailed annually. While telephones and electricity did not reach most rural areas for decades, better roads, mail-order catalogs, and other innovations knit farmers into the larger society. Early in the new century, Mary E. Lease—who in her Populist days had urged Kansas farmers to raise less corn and more Hell—moved to Brooklyn.

Farmers still had problems. Land prices rose with crop prices, and farm tenancy increased, especially in the South. Tenancy grew from one-quarter of all farms in 1880 to more than one-third in 1910. In South Carolina, Georgia, Alabama, and Mississippi, nearly two-thirds of the farms were run by tenant farmers. Many southern tenant farmers were African Americans, and they suffered from farm-bred diseases. In one of the reforms of the Progressive Era, in 1909, the Rockefeller Sanitary Commission, acting on recent scientific discoveries, began a sanitation campaign that eventually wiped out the hookworm disease, and in 1912, the U.S. Public Health Service began work on rural malaria.

In the arid West, irrigation transformed the land as the federal government and private landholders joined to import water from mountain watersheds. The dry lands bloomed, and so did a rural class structure that sharply separated owners from workers. Under the Newlands Act of 1902, the secretary of the interior formed the U.S. Reclamation Service, which gathered a staff of

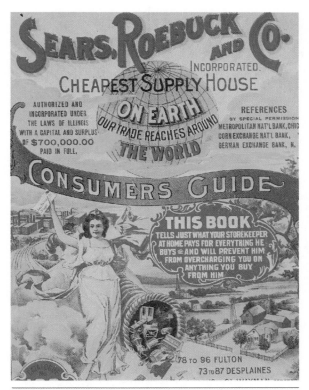

With Rural Free Delivery, people in even the most remote areas had access to the goods in the catalogs of the large mail-order houses, such as Sears, Roebuck and Co. Sears advertised itself as the "cheapest supply house on earth" with a reach that extended around the world.

thousands of engineers and technicians, "the largest bureaucracy ever assembled in irrigation history."

Dams and canals channeled water into places like California's Imperial Valley, and as the water streamed in, cotton, cantaloupes, oranges, tomatoes, lettuce, and a host of other crops streamed out to national markets. By 1920, Idaho, Montana, Utah, Wyoming, Colorado, and Oregon had extensive irrigation systems, all drawing on scarce water supplies; California, the foremost importer of water, had 4.2 million acres under irrigation, many of them picked by migrant workers from Mexico, China, and Japan. The work was backbreaking—and poorly paid. A worker from India called picking asparagus a "ghastly" job, paid at the rate of ten cents a box:

They gave us miles and miles of asparagus rows. As soon as I had knelt down with my knife and cut out one head and

Irrigation and Conservation in the West to 1917

To make the arid lands of the Western states productive, the state and federal governments regulated the water supply through irrigation projects and the creation of water reservoirs. The federal government also created land reserves.

Irrigation projects

Reservoirs and lakes used as reservoirs

Federal land reserves

put it in the box, there would be another one sprouting before me. Then I would have to stoop again, and it was continuous picking and stooping that made it a terrible form of exercise. It is walk and bend, bend and walk, from half past four [in the morning] or thereabouts, until seven in the evening.

Women at Work

Women worked in larger and larger numbers. In 1900, more than five million worked—one-fifth of all adult women—and among those aged fourteen to twenty-four, the employment rate was almost one-third. Of those employed, single women outnumbered married women by seven to one, yet more than one-third of married women worked. Most women held service jobs. Only a small number held higher paying jobs as professionals or managers.

In the 1890s, women made up over one-quarter of medical school graduates. Using a variety of techniques, men gradually squeezed them out, and by the 1920s, only about 5 percent of the graduates were women. Few women taught in colleges and universities, and those who did were expected to resign if they married. In 1906, Harriet Brooks, a promising physicist at Barnard College in New York, became engaged and refused to resign; the dean told her icily that Barnard expected a married woman to "dignify her home-making into a profession, and not assume that she can carry on two full professions at a time."

More women than men graduated from high school, and with professions like medicine and science largely closed to them, they often turned to the new "business schools" that offered training in stenography, typing, and bookkeeping. In 1920, over one-quarter of all employed women held clerical jobs. Many others taught school.

In 1907 and 1908, investigators studied 22,000 women workers in Pittsburgh; 60 percent of them earned less than $7 a week, a minimum for "decent living." Fewer than 1 percent held skilled jobs; most tended machines, wrapped and labeled, or did handwork that required no particular skill. In New York, many women toiled six days a week as garment workers from eight in the morning to six in the evening, with an extra hour off on Saturdays. They earned $7 to $12 a week, nothing at all during slack season. They had to buy their own needles and thread and pay for electricity and chairs to sit on.

Critics charged that women's employment endangered the home, threatened their reproductive functions, and even, as one man said, stripped them of "that modest demeanor that lends a charm to their kind." Adding to these fears, the birthrate continued to drop between 1900 and 1920, and the divorce rate soared, in part because working-class men took advantage of the newer moral freedom and deserted their families in growing numbers. By 1916, there was one divorce for every nine marriages as compared to one for twenty-one in 1880.

PICKING SLATE

Breaker boys, who picked out pieces of slate from the coal as it rushed past, often became bent-backed after years of working fourteen hours a day in the coal mines. Accidents—and death—were common.

David Graham Phillips, a novelist troubled by the woman's problem, depicted a husband's oppression of his wife in *The Hungry Heart,* published in 1909. "He kissed her, patted her cheek, went back to his work." When the wife grew restless, the husband knew why: "A few more years'll wash away the smatter she got at college, and this restlessness of hers will yield to nature, and she'll be content and happy in her womanhood. . . . As grandfather often said, it's a dreadful mistake, educating women beyond their sphere." Such views, mild as they were, got Phillips assassinated by a lunatic who claimed the novelist was "trying to destroy the whole ideal of womanhood."

Many children worked. In 1900, about three million children—nearly 20 percent of those between the ages of five and fifteen—held full- or almost full-time jobs. Twenty-five thousand boys under sixteen worked in mining; twenty thousand children under twelve, mainly girls, worked in southern cotton mills. Gradually the use of child labor shrank, as public indignation grew.

Determined to do something about the situation, the Women's Trade Union League (p. 672) lobbied the federal Bureau of Labor to investigate the conditions under which women and children worked. Begun in 1907, the investigation took four years and resulted in nineteen volumes of data, some of it shocking, all of it factual. In 1911, spurred by the data, the Children's Bureau was formed within the U.S. Bureau of Labor, with Grace Abbott, a social worker, at its head. It immediately began its own investigations, showing among other things the need for greater protection of maternal and infant health. In 1921, Congress passed the Sheppard-Towner Maternity and Infancy Protection Act, which helped fund maternity and pediatric clinics. Providing a precedent for the Social Security Act of 1935, it demonstrated the increasing effectiveness of women reformers in the Progressive Era.

Numerous middle-class women became involved in the fight for reform, while many others, reflecting the ongoing changes in the family (see Chapter 19), took increasing pride in homemaking and motherhood. Mother's Day, the national holiday, was formally established in 1913. With families preferring smaller numbers of children, birth control became a more acceptable practice. Margaret Sanger, a nurse and outspoken social reformer, led a campaign to give physicians broad discretion in prescribing contraceptives. When Sanger became involved in the birth control movement, the federal Comstock Law banned the interstate transport of contraceptive devices and information (see "Margaret Sanger and the Birth Control Movement," pp. 700–701).

The Niagara Movement and the NAACP

Black women had always worked, and in far larger numbers than their white counterparts. The reason was usually economic; an African American man or woman alone could rarely earn enough to support a family. Unlike many white women, black women tended to remain in the labor force after marriage or the start of a family. They also had less opportunity for job advancement, and in 1920, between one-third and one-half of all African American women who were working were restricted to personal and domestic service jobs.

For the first time since their arrival in North America, the percentage of African American women who worked would decline with the migration north during World War I (see Chapter 24), but at the turn of the century eight of every ten African Americans still lived in rural areas, mainly in the South. Most were poor sharecroppers. "Jim Crow" laws segregated many schools, railroad cars, hotels, and hospitals. Poll taxes and other devices disfranchised blacks and many poor whites. Violence was common; from 1900 to 1914, white mobs murdered over a thousand black people.

Two murders occurred near Vicksburg, Mississippi, in 1904, and they revealed a great deal about the kind of violence African Americans faced. Looking for the killer of a white planter, a mob captured a black man and woman, their guilt or innocence unknown. They were tied to trees, and their fingers and ears were cut off as souvenirs. "The most excruciating form of punishment consisted in the use of a large corkscrew in the hands of some of the mob. This instrument was bored into the flesh of the man and the woman, in the arms, legs and body, and then pulled out, the spirals tearing out big pieces of raw, quivering flesh every time it was withdrawn." Finally, both people were thrown on a fire and burned to death, "a relief," a witness said, "to the maimed and suffering victims."

Many African Americans labored in the cotton farms, railroad camps, sawmills, and mines of the South under conditions of peonage. Peons traded their lives and labor for food and shelter. Often illiterate, they were forced to sign contracts allowing planters "to use such force as he or his agents may deem necessary to require me to remain on his farm and perform good and satisfactory services." Armed guards patrolled the camps and whipped those trying to escape. "In the woods," a peon said, "they can do anything they please, and no one can see them but God."

Few blacks belonged to labor unions, and blacks almost always earned less than whites in the same job. In Atlanta, white electricians earned $5.00 a day, blacks $3.50. Black songs like "I've Got a White Man Workin' for Me" (1901) voiced more hope than reality. The illiteracy rate among African Americans dropped from 45 percent in 1900 to 30 percent in 1910, but nowhere were they given equal school facilities, teachers' salaries, or educational materials. In 1910, scarcely eight thousand African American youths were attending high schools in all the states of the Southeast. South Carolina spent $13.98 annually for the education of each white child, $1.13 for each black child.

African American leaders grew increasingly impatient with this kind of treatment, and in 1905 a group of them, led by sociologist W. E. B. Du Bois, met near Niagara Falls, New York (they met on the Canadian side of the Falls, since no hotel on the American side would take them). There they pledged action in the matters of voting, equal access to economic opportunity, integration, and equality before the law. Rejecting Booker T. Washington's gradualist approach, the Niagara movement claimed for African Americans "every single right that belongs to a freeborn American, political, civil and social; and until we get these rights we will never cease to protest."

The Niagara movement focused on equal rights and the education of African American youth, of whom it said, "They have a right to know, to think, to aspire." Keeping alive a program of militant action, it spawned later civil rights movements. Du Bois was its inspiration. In *The Souls of Black Folk* (1903) and other works, he called eloquently for justice and equality. "By every civilized and peaceful method," he said, "we must strive for the right which the world accords to man."

Peace was sometimes hard to come by. Race riots broke out in Atlanta, Georgia, in 1906 and Springfield, Illinois, in 1908, the latter the home of Abraham Lincoln. Unlike the riots of the 1960s, white mobs invaded black neighborhoods, burning, looting, and killing. They lynched two blacks—one eighty-four years old—in Springfield.

William E. Walling, a wealthy southerner and settlement house worker; Mary Ovington, a white anthropology student; and Oswald Garrison Villard, grandson of the famous abolitionist William Lloyd Garrison, were outraged. Along with other reformers, white and black (among them, Jane Addams and John Dewey), they issued a call for the conference that organized the National Association for the Advancement of Colored People, which swiftly became the most important civil rights organization in the country. Created in 1910, within four years the NAACP grew to 50 branches and more than 6,000 members. Walling headed it, and Du Bois, the only African American among the top officers, directed publicity and edited *The Crisis,* the voice of the organization.

Joined by the National Urban League, which was created in 1911, the NAACP pressured employers, labor unions, and the government on behalf of African Americans. It had some victories. In *Guinn* v. *United States* (1915), the Supreme Court overturned a "grandfather clause" that kept African Americans from voting in Oklahoma, and in *Buchanan* v. *Worley* (1917), it struck down a law in Louisville, Kentucky, requiring residential segregation. In 1918, in the midst of World War I, the NAACP and the National Urban League persuaded the federal government to form a special Bureau of Negro Economics within the Labor Department to look after the interests of African American wage earners.

Despite these gains, African Americans continued to experience disenfranchisement, poor job opportunities, and segregation. As Booker T.

Washington said in 1913, "I have never seen the colored people so discouraged and so bitter as they are at the present time."

"I Hear the Whistle": Immigrants in the Labor Force

While women and African Americans worked in growing numbers, much of the huge increase in the labor force in these years came from outside the country, particularly from Europe and Mexico. Between 1901 and 1920, the extraordinarily high total of 14.5 million immigrants entered the country, more than in any previous twenty-year period. Continuing the recent trend (see Chapter 19), many came from southern and eastern Europe. Still called the "new" immigrants, they met hostility from "older" immigrants of northern European stock who questioned their values, religion (often Catholic or Jewish), traditions, and appearance.

Labor agents—called *padroni* among the Italians, Greeks, and Syrians—recruited immigrant workers, found them jobs, and deducted a fee from their wages. Headquartered in Salt Lake City, Leonidas G. Skliris, the "Czar of the Greeks," provided workers for the Utah Copper Company and the Western Pacific Railroad. In Chicago at the turn of the century, padroni employed more than one-fifth of all Italians; in New York City, they controlled two-thirds of the entire labor force.

Immigrant patterns often departed from traditional stereotypes. Immigrants, for example, moved both to and from their homelands. Fifty percent or more of some groups returned home, although the numbers varied among groups. Jews and Czechs often brought their families to resettle in America; Serbs and Poles tended to come singly, intent on earning enough money to make a fresh start at home. Many Italian men virtually commuted, "birds of passage" who returned home every slack season. However, the outbreak of World War I interrupted the practice and trapped hundreds of thousands of Italians and others who had planned to return to Europe.

Older residents lumped the newcomers together, ignoring geographic, religious, and other differences. Preserving important regional distinctions, Italians tended to settle as Calabreses, Venetians, Abruzzis, and Sicilians. Native Americans viewed them all simply as Italians. Henry Ford and other employers tried to erase the differences through English classes and deliberate "Americanization" programs. The Ford Motor Company ran a school where immigrant employees were first taught to say, "I am a good American." At the graduation ceremony, the pupils acted out a gigantic pantomime in which, clad in their old-country dress, they filed into a large "melting pot." When they emerged, they were wearing identical American-made clothes, and each was waving a little American flag.

In similar fashion, the International Harvester Corporation taught Polish laborers to speak English, but it had other lessons in view as well. According to "Lesson One," drilled into the Polish "pupils":

I hear the whistle. I must hurry.
I hear the five minute whistle.
It is time to go into the shop.
I take my check from the gate board and hang
   it on the department board.
I change my clothes and get ready to work.
The starting whistle blows.
I eat my lunch.
It is forbidden to eat until then.
The whistle blows at five minutes of starting
   time.
I get ready to go to work.
I work until the whistle blows to quit.
I leave my place nice and clean.
I put all my clothes in the locker.
I must go home.

Labor groups soon learned to counter these techniques. The Women's Trade Union League (WTUL) urged workers to ignore business-sponsored English lessons because they did not "tell the girl worker the things she really wants to know. They do not suggest that $5 a week is not a living wage. They tell her to be respectful to her employer." Designing its own educational program, the WTUL in 1912 published "New World Lessons for Old World Peoples," which provided quite a different kind of English lesson:

Immigration to the United States, 1900–1920 (by area of origin)

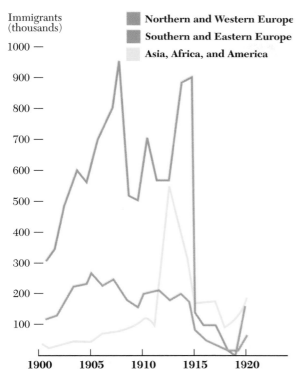

Immigrants (thousands)

Northern and Western Europe
Southern and Eastern Europe
Asia, Africa, and America

Note: For purposes of classification, *Northern and Western Europe* includes Great Britain, Ireland, Scandinavia, the Netherlands, Belgium, Luxembourg, Switzerland, France, and Germany. *Southern and Eastern Europe* includes Poland, Austria-Hungary, Russia and the Baltic States, Romania, Bulgaria, European Turkey, Italy, Spain, Portugal, and Greece. *Asia, Africa, and America* includes Asian Turkey, China, Japan, India, Canada, the Caribbean, Latin America, and all of Africa.
Source: U.S. Bureau of the Census, Historical Statistics of the United States, Colonial Times to 1970, *Bicentennial Edition, Washington, D.C., 1975.*

A Union girl takes me into the Union.
The Union girls are glad to see me.
They call me sister.
I will work hard for our Union.
I will come to all the Union meetings.

In another significant development at the beginning of the twentieth century, Mexicans for the first time immigrated in large numbers, especially after a revolution in Mexico in 1910 forced many to flee across the northern border into

Mexican Immigration to the United States, 1900–1920

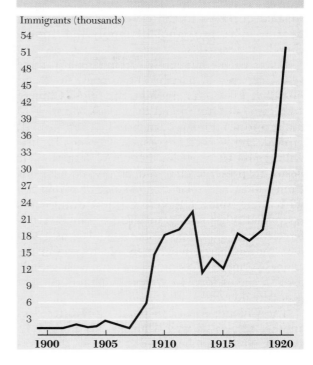

Immigrants (thousands)

Texas, New Mexico, Arizona, and California. Their exact numbers were unknown. American officials did not count border crossings until 1907, and even then, many migrants avoided the official immigration stations. Almost all came from the Mexican lower class, eager to escape peonage and violence in their native land. Labor agents—called *coyotes*—usually in the employ of large corporations or working for ranchers recruited Mexican workers.

Between 1900 and 1910, the Mexican population of Texas and New Mexico nearly doubled; in Arizona, it more than doubled; in California, it quadrupled. In all four states, it doubled again between 1910 and 1920. After the turn of the century, almost 10 percent of the total population of Mexico moved to the American Southwest.

In time, these Mexican Americans and their children transformed the Southwest. They built most of the early highways in Texas, New Mexico, and Arizona; dug the irrigation ditches that watered crops throughout the area; laid railroad track; and picked the cotton and vegetables that clothed and fed millions of Americans. Many lived in shacks and shanties along the railroad tracks, isolated in a separate Spanish-speaking world. Like other immigrant groups, they also formed enclaves in the cities, *barrios,* which became cultural islands of family life, foods, church, and festivals.

Fewer people immigrated from China in these years, deterred in part by anti-Chinese laws and hostility. Like other immigrants, most Chinese who came did not intend to remain. Wanting to make money and return home, they mined, farmed, and worked as common laborers. In their willingness to work hard for low wages, their desire to preserve clan and family associations from China, and their maintenance of strong ties with their home villages, Chinese Americans resembled other immigrant groups, but they differed in two important respects. As late as 1920, men outnumbered women by ten to one in the Chinese American population; and with a male median age of forty-two, their communities were generally dominated by the elderly.

The Chinese American population differed in another respect as well. Unlike other immigrant groups, whose numbers tended to grow, the number of Chinese Americans shrank in these years— from about 125,000 in the early 1880s to just over 60,000 in 1920. After 1910, the U.S. government set up a special immigration facility at Angel Island in San Francisco Bay, but unlike European immigrants who landed at Ellis Island in New York and quickly moved on, Chinese immigrants were kept for weeks and months, examined and reexamined, before being allowed to cross the narrow band of water to San Francisco. Angel Island remained open until 1940, and a poem carved into the wall of Building 317 showed the feelings of some of those who waited:

> *There are tens of thousands of poems composed on these walls,*
> *They are all cries of complaint and sadness.*
> *The day I am rid of this prison and attain success,*
> *I must remember that this prison once existed.*
> *In my daily needs I must be frugal.*
> *Needless extravagance leads youth to ruin.*

> *All my compatriots please be mindful.*
> *Once you have some small gains, return home early.*

> *By one from Xiangshan.*

Many Japanese also arrived at Angel Island, and though at first fewer in numbers than the Chinese, they developed communities along the Pacific Coast, where they settled mainly on farms. The number of Japanese Americans grew. In 1907, the heaviest year of immigration from Japan, nearly 31,000 Japanese entered the United States; and by 1920 there were 111,000 Japanese in the country, nearly three-quarters of them in California.

As the newcomers arrived from Asia, Europe, and Mexico, nativist sentiment, which had criticized earlier waves of immigrants, intensified. Old-stock Americans sneered at their dress and language. Racial theories emphasized the superiority of northern Europeans (see Chapter 21) and the new "science" of eugenics suggested controls over the population growth of "inferior" peoples. Hostility toward Catholics and Jews was common but touched other groups as well.

In 1902, Congress enacted a law prohibiting immigration from China. Statutes requiring literacy tests designed to curtail immigration from southern and eastern Europe were vetoed by William Howard Taft in 1913, and Woodrow Wilson in 1915 and 1917. In 1917, such a measure passed despite Wilson's veto. Other measures tried to limit immigration from Mexico and Japan.

CONFLICT IN THE WORKPLACE

Assembly lines, speedups, long hours, and low pay produced a dramatic increase in American industrial output (and profits) after 1900; they also gave rise to numerous strikes and other kinds of labor unrest. Sometimes strikes took place through the action of unions; sometimes workers just decided they had had enough and walked off the job. Whatever the cause, strikes were frequent. In one industry, in one city—the meatpacking industry in Chicago—there were 251 strikes in 1903 alone.

Strikes and absenteeism increased after 1910; labor productivity dropped 10 percent between

Immigrants from Asia arrive at the quarantine station at Angel Island, near San Francisco. Quota systems and exclusionary laws severely limited Asian immigration, while other laws placed restrictions on the immigrants, curtailing their right to own or even rent agricultural land. Some Asian immigrants, after months of detention at Angel Island, were refused permission to enter the United States and forced to return to their homelands.

1915 and 1918, the first such decline in memory. In many industries, labor turnover became a serious problem; workers changed jobs in droves. Union membership grew. In 1900, only about 1 million workers—less than 4 percent of the work force—belonged to unions. By 1920, 5 million workers belonged, increasing the unionized portion of the work force to about 13 percent.

As tensions grew between capital and labor, some people in the middle class became fearful that, unless something was done to improve the workers' situation, there might be violence or even revolution. This fear motivated some of the labor-oriented reforms of the Progressive Era. While some reform supporters genuinely wanted to improve labor's lot, others embraced reform because they were afraid of something else.

Organizing Labor

Samuel Gompers's American Federation of Labor increased from 250,000 members in 1897 to 1.7 million in 1904. By far the largest union organization, it remained devoted to the interests of skilled craftspeople. While it aimed partly at better wages and working conditions, it also sought to limit entry into the crafts and protect worker prerogatives. Within limits, the AFL found acceptance among giant business corporations eager for conservative policies and labor stability.

There were 8 million female workers in 1910, but only 125,000 belonged to unions. Gompers

continued to resist organizing them, saying they were too emotional and, as union organizers, "had a way of making serious mistakes." Margaret Dreier Robins, an organizer of proven skill, scoffed at that. "[T]hese men died twenty years ago and are just walking around dead!" she said.

Labor Union Membership, 1897–1920

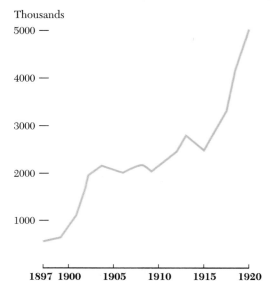

Source: U.S. Bureau of the Census. Statistical Abstract of the United States: 1982–83 *(103rd edition), Washington, D.C., 1982.*

Robins helped found the Women's Trade Union League in 1903. The WTUL led the effort to organize women into trade unions, lobby for legislation protecting female workers, and educate the public on the problems and needs of working women. It took in all working women who would join, regardless of skill (though not, at first, African American women), and it won crucial financial support from well-to-do women like Anne Morgan, daughter of the feared financier J. P. Morgan. Robins's close friend, Jane Addams (see Chapter 19), belonged, as did Mary McDowell, "The Angel of the Stockyards," who worked with slaughterhouse workers in Chicago; Julia Lathrop, who tried to improve the lot of wage-earning children; and Dr. Alice Hamilton, a pioneer in American research on the causes of industrial disease.

The WTUL never had many members—a few thousand at most—but its influence extended far beyond its membership. In 1909, it supported the "Uprising of the 20,000," a strike of shirtwaist workers in New York City. When female employees of the Triangle Shirtwaist Company tried to form a union, the company fired them, and they walked out; 20,000 men and women in 500 other shops followed. Strike meetings were conducted in three languages—English, Yiddish, and Italian—and before being forced to go back to work, the strikers won a shorter workweek and a few other gains. Sadly, the Triangle women lost out on another important demand—for unlocked shop doors and safe fire escapes. Their loss proved lethal in the famous Triangle Shirtwaist Company fire of 1911.

The WTUL also backed a strike in 1910 against Hart, Schaffner and Marx, Chicago's largest manufacturer of men's clothing. One day, Annie Shapiro, the eighteen-year-old daughter of Russian immigrants, was told her wages were being cut from $7 a week to $6.20. That was a large cut, and along with sixteen other young women, Shapiro refused to accept it and walked out. "We had to be recognized as people," she said later. Soon other women walked out, and the revolt spread. Managers quickly promised to restore the cuts, but as one woman said, "just then there was big noise outside and we all rushed to the windows and there we saw the police beating the strikers on our account, and when we saw that we went out."

In a matter of days, some forty thousand garment workers were on strike, about half of them women. Manufacturers hurried to negotiate, and the result was the important Hart, Schaffner agreement, which created an arbitration committee composed of management and labor to handle grievances and settle disputes. The first successful experiment in collective bargaining, the Hart, Schaffner agreement became the model for the kind of agreements that govern industrial relations today.

Another union, the Industrial Workers of the World (IWW), attracted by far the greatest attention (and fears) in these years. Unlike the WTUL, it welcomed everyone regardless of gender or race. Unlike the AFL, it tried to organize the unskilled and foreign-born laborers who worked in the mass production industries. Founded in Chicago in 1905, it aimed to unite the American working class into a mammoth union to promote labor's interests. Its motto—"an injury to one is an injury to all"—stressed labor solidarity as had the earlier Knights of Labor. But unlike the Knights, the IWW, or Wobblies as they were often known, urged social revolution.

"It is our purpose to overthrow the capitalist system by forcible means if necessary," William D. (Big Bill) Haywood, one of its founders, said; and he went on in his speeches to say he knew of nothing a worker could do that "will bring as much anguish to the boss as a little sabotage in the right place." Joe Hill, the IWW's legendary folk poet, reminded labor of its potential strength:

If the workers took a notion
  They could stop all speeding trains;
Every ship upon the ocean
  They can tie with mighty chains.

Every wheel in the creation
  Every mine and every mill;
Fleets and armies of the nation,
  Will at their command stand still.

IWW leaders included "Mother" Jones, a famous veteran of battles in the Illinois coalfields; Elizabeth Gurley Flynn, a fiery young radical who joined as a teenager; and Big Bill Haywood him-

Elizabeth Gurley Flynn, labor's "Joan of Arc," addresses textile workers on strike at Paterson, New Jersey.

self, the strapping one-eyed founder of the Western Federation of Miners.

The IWW led a number of major strikes. The Lawrence, Massachusetts (1912), and Paterson, New Jersey (1912), strikes attracted national attention: in Lawrence when the strikers sent their children, ill-clad and hungry, out of the city to stay with sympathetic families; in Paterson when they rented New York's Madison Square Garden for a massive labor pageant. IWW leaders welcomed the revolutionary tumult sweeping Russia and other countries. In the United States, they thought, a series of local strikes would bring about capitalist repression, then a general strike, and eventually a workers' commonwealth.

The IWW fell short of these objectives, but during its lifetime—from 1905 to the mid-1920s—it made major gains among immigrant workers in the Northeast, migrant farm labor on the Plains, and loggers and miners in the South and Far West. In factories like Ford's, it recruited workers resentful of the speedups on the assembly lines. Although IWW membership probably amounted to no more than 100,000 at any one time, workers came and left so often that its total membership may have reached as high as 1 million.

Working with Workers

Concerned about labor unrest, some business leaders used violence and police action to keep workers in line, but others turned to the new fields of applied psychology and personnel management. A school of industrial psychology emerged. As had Taylor, industrial psychologists studied workers' routines and further, they showed that output was also affected by job satisfaction. While most businesses pushed ahead with efficiency campaigns, a few did establish industrial-relations departments, hire public relations firms to improve their corporate image, and link productivity to job safety and happiness.

Ivy L. Lee, a pioneer in the field of corporate public relations, advised clients like the Pennsylvania Railroad and Standard Oil on how to improve relations with labor and the public. Calling himself a "physician to corporate bodies," Lee urged complete openness on the company's part. To please employees, companies printed newsletters and organized softball teams; they awarded prizes and celebrated retirements. Ford created a "Sociology Department" staffed by 150 experts who showed workers how to budget their incomes and care for their health. They even taught them how to shop for meat.

On January 5, 1914, Ford took another significant step. He announced the Five-Dollar Day, "the greatest revolution," he said, "in the matter of rewards for workers ever known to the industrial world." With a stroke, he doubled the wage rate for common labor, reduced the working day from nine hours to eight, and established a personnel department to place workers in appropriate jobs. The next day, ten thousand applicants stood outside the gates.

As a result, Ford had the pick of the labor force. Turnover declined; absenteeism, previously as much as one-tenth of all Ford workers every day, fell to .3 percent. Output increased; the IWW at Ford collapsed. The plan increased wages, but allowed the company greater control over a more stable labor force. Workers had to meet a behavior code in order to qualify for the Five-Dollar Day. At first scornful of the "utopian" plan, business leaders across the country soon copied it, and on January 2, 1919, Ford announced the Six-Dollar Day.

The playground at Amoskeag, provided for the children of the company's workers. The Amoskeag Textile Club, part of the employer-sponsored employee welfare program, had reading rooms, card tables, billiard and pool tables, a golf course, and a baseball field for the use of the workers. All was demolished when the mill closed in 1935. Many firms between 1910 and 1917 established employee programs similar to those introduced at Amoskeag.

Amoskeag

In size, system, and worker relations, the record of the Amoskeag Company textile mills was revealing. Located beside the Merrimack River in Manchester, New Hampshire, the mills—an enormous complex of factories, warehouses, canals, and machinery—had been built in the 1830s. By the turn of the century, they were producing nearly 50 miles of cloth an hour, more cloth each day than any other mills in the entire world.

The face of the mills, an almost solid wall of red brick, stretched nearly a mile in length. Archways and bridges pierced the facade. Amoskeag resembled a walled medieval city within which workers found "a total institution, a closed and almost self-contained world." At first the mills employed young women for labor, but by 1900, more and more immigrant males staffed the machines. French Canadians, Irish, Poles, and Greeks—seventeen thousand in all—worked there, and their experiences revealed a great deal about factory work and life at the turn of the century.

The company hired and fired at will, and it demanded relentless output from the spindles and spinning frames. Yet it also viewed employees as its "children" and looked for total loyalty in return, an expectation often realized. Workers identified with Amoskeag and, decades later, still called themselves Amoskeag men and women. "We were all like a family," one said.

Most Amoskeag workers preferred the industrial world of the mills to the farms they had left behind. They did not feel displaced; they knew the pains of industrial life; and they adapted in ways that fit their own needs and traditions. Families played a large role. They neither disintegrated nor lost their relationships. French Canadians and others often came in family units. One or two family members left the farm for the mills, maintained close ties with those back home, and then sent for others creating a form of "chain migration."

Once in Manchester, families often worked in the same workrooms. Looking after each other, they asked foremen for transfers and promotions for relatives; they taught their children technical skills and how to get along with bosses and fellow workers. Although low paid, Amoskeag employees took pride in their work, and for many of them, a well-turned-out product provided dignity and self-esteem.

The company long showed a paternal interest in employee welfare, and in 1910 it inaugurated a deliberate welfare and efficiency program. The program aimed to increase productivity, accustom immigrants to industrial work, instill company loyalty, and curb labor unrest. Playgrounds and visiting nurses, home-buying plans, a cooking school, and dental service were part of the plan. The Amoskeag Textile Club held employee dinners and picnics, organized shooting clubs and a baseball team, sponsored Christmas parties for the children, and put out the *Amoskeag Bulletin,* a monthly magazine of employee news.

From 1885 to 1919, no strike touched the mills. Thereafter, however, labor unrest increased. Overproduction and foreign competition took their toll, and Amoskeag closed in 1935.

LIFE IN AMERICA, 1920

For many Americans, the quality of life improved significantly between 1900 and 1920. Jobs were relatively plentiful, and in a development of great importance, more and more people were entering the professions as doctors, lawyers, teachers, and engineers (see Chapter 23). With comfortable incomes, a growing middle class could take advantage of new lifestyles, inventions, and forms of entertainment. Mass production could not have worked without mass consumption, and Americans in these years increasingly became a nation of consumers.

In 1900, business firms spent about $95 million on advertising; twenty years later they spent over $500 million. Ads and billboards touted cigarettes, cars, perfumes, and cosmetics. Advertising agencies boomed. Using new sampling techniques, they developed modern concepts of market testing and research. Sampling customer preferences affected business indirectly as well, making it more responsive to public opinion on social and political issues.

Mass production swept the clothing industry and dressed more Americans better than any people ever before. Using lessons learned in making uniforms during the Civil War, manufacturers for the first time developed standard clothing and shoe sizes that fit most bodies. Clothing prices dropped; the availability of inexpensive "off-the-rack" clothes lessened distinctions between rich and poor. By 1900, nine of every ten men and boys wore the new "ready-to-wear" clothes.

In 1900, people employed in manufacturing earned on average $418 a year. Two decades later, they earned $1,342 a year, though inflation took much of the increase. While the middle class expanded, the rich also grew richer. In 1920, the new income tax showed the first accurate tabulation of income, and it confirmed what many had suspected all along. Five percent of the population received almost one-fourth of all income.

An Urban Nation

In 1920, the median age of the population was only twenty-five. (It is now thirty.) Immigration accounted for part of the population's youthfulness, since most immigrants were young. Thanks to medical advances and better living conditions, death rates dropped in the early years of the century; the average life span increased. Between 1900 and 1920, life expectancy rose from forty-nine to fifty-six years for white women and from forty-seven to fifty-four years for white men. It rose from thirty-three to forty-five years for blacks and other racial minorities.

Despite the increase in life expectancy, infant mortality remained high; nearly 10 percent of white babies and 20 percent of minority babies died in the first year of life. In comparison to today, fewer babies on average survived to adolescence, and fewer people survived beyond middle age. In 1900, the death rate among people between forty-five and sixty-five was more than twice the modern rate. As a result, there were relatively fewer older people—in 1900, only 4 percent of the population was older than sixty-five compared to nearly 12 percent today. Fewer children than today knew their grandparents. Still, improvements in health care helped people live longer, and as a result, the incidence of cancer and heart disease increased.

Cities grew, and by any earlier standards, they grew on a colossal scale. Downtowns became a central hive of skyscrapers, department stores, warehouses, and hotels. Strips of factories radiated from the center. As street railways spread, cities took on a systematic pattern of socioeconomic segregation, usually in rings. The innermost ring filled with immigrants, circled by a belt of working-class housing. The remaining rings marked areas of rising affluence outward toward wealthy suburbs, which themselves formed around shopping strips and grid patterns of streets that restricted social interaction.

The giants were New York, Chicago, and Philadelphia, industrial cities that turned out every kind of product from textiles to structural steel. Smaller cities like Rochester, New York, or Cleveland, Ohio, specialized in manufacturing a

Life Expectancy, 1900–1920

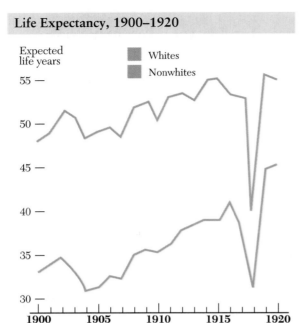

Ethnic Neighborhoods in Chicago, 1920

The ethnic groups shown here predominated in certain districts of the city, partly by choice, but also partly because of restrictive zoning practices.

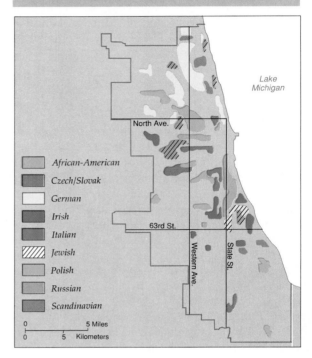

specific line of goods or processing regional products for the national market. Railroads instead of highways tied things together; in 1916, the rail network, the largest in the world, reached its peak—254,000 miles of track that carried over three-fourths of all intercity freight tonnage.

Step by step, cities adopted their twentieth-century forms. Between 1909 and 1915, Los Angeles, a city of 300,000 people, passed a series of ordinances that gave rise to modern urban zoning. For the first time, the ordinances divided a city into three districts of specified use: a residential area, an industrial area, and an area open to residence and a limited list of industries. Other cities followed. Combining several features, the New York Zoning Law of 1916 became the model for the nation; within a decade, 591 cities copied it.

Zoning ordered city development, keeping skyscrapers out of factory districts, factories out of the suburbs. It also had powerful social repercussions. In the South, zoning became a tool to extend racial segregation; in northern cities, it acted against ethnic minorities. Jews in New York, Italians in Boston, Poles in Detroit, African Americans in Chicago—zoning laws held them all at arm's length. Like other migrants, African Americans often preferred to settle together, but

zoning also helped put them there. By 1920, ten districts in Chicago were more than three-quarters black. In Los Angeles, Cleveland, Detroit, and Washington, D.C., most blacks lived in only two or three wards.

THE USES OF LEISURE

Thanks to changing work rules and mechanization, many Americans benefited from more leisure time. The average workweek for manufacturing laborers fell from sixty hours in 1890 to fifty-one in 1920. By the early 1900s, white-collar workers might spend only eight to ten hours a day at work and a half day on weekends. Greater leisure time gave more people more opportunity for play and enjoyment of the arts.

People flocked to places of entertainment. Baseball entrenched itself as the national pastime. Automobiles and streetcars carried growing numbers of fans to ballparks; attendance at major league games doubled between 1903 and 1920.

Football also drew fans, although critics attacked the sport's violence and the use of "tramp athletes," nonstudents whom colleges paid to play. In 1905, the worst year, 18 players were killed and 150 seriously injured.

Alarmed, President Theodore Roosevelt—who had once said, "I am the father of three boys [and] if I thought any one of them would weigh a possible broken bone against the glory of being chosen to play on Harvard's football team I would disinherit him"—called a White House conference to clean up college sports. The conference founded the Intercollegiate Athletic Association, which in 1910 became the National Collegiate Athletic Association (NCAA).

Movie theaters opened everywhere. By 1910, there were 10,000 of them, drawing a weekly audience of 10 million people. Admission was usually five cents, and movies stressing laughter and pathos appealed to a mass market. In 1915, D.W. Griffith, a talented and creative director, produced the first movie spectacular: *The Birth of a Nation.* Griffith adopted new film techniques, including close-ups, fade-outs, artistic camera angles, and dramatic battle scenes. (For further discussion of the film see "Changing Views of Reconstruction," pp. 490–491.)

Phonographs brought ready-made entertainment into the home. By 1901, phonograph and record companies included the Victor Talking Machine Company, the Edison Speaking Machine Company, and Columbia Records. Ornate mahogany Victrolas became standard fixtures in middle-class parlors. Early records were usually of vaudeville skits; orchestral recordings began in 1906. In 1919, 2.25 million phonographs were produced; two years later more than 100 million records were sold.

As record sales grew, families sang less and listened more. Music became a business. In 1909, Congress enacted a copyright law that provided a two-cent royalty on each piece of music on phonograph records or piano rolls. The royalty, small as it was, offered welcome income to composers and publishers, and in 1914, composer Victor Herbert and others formed the American Society of Composers, Authors and Publishers (ASCAP) to protect musical rights and royalties.

The faster rhythms of syncopated ragtime became the rage, especially after 1911 when Irving Berlin, a Russian immigrant, wrote

THE SHOW WE VISITED LAST NIGHT, "DREAMLAND" MONTROSE, COLO.

The "movies" quickly became one of the most popular forms of mass entertainment, and by the 1920s nearly 100 million Americans were going to the movies each week. Movie theaters sprang up across America, in large towns and small, offering patrons a short and inexpensive escape from daily life. The marquee on this theater in Montrose, Colorado, sums up what the movies were for many— "Dreamland."

"Alexander's Ragtime Band." Ragtime set off a nationwide dance craze. Secretaries danced on their lunch hour, the first nightclubs opened, and restaurants and hotels introduced dance floors. Waltzes and polkas gave way to a host of new dances, many with animal names: the fox-trot, bunny hop, turkey trot, snake, and kangaroo dip. Partners were not permitted to dance too close; bouncers tapped them on the shoulder if they got closer than 9 inches. The aging John D. Rockefeller hired a private instructor to teach him the tango, although Yale University banned that dance at its 1914 junior prom.

Vaudeville, increasingly popular after 1900, reached maturity around 1915. Drawing on the immigrant experience, it voiced the variety of city life and included skits, songs, comics, acrobats, and magicians. Dances and jokes showed an earthiness new to mass audiences. By 1914, stage runways extended into the crowd; performers had bared their legs and were beginning to show glimpses of the midriff. Fanny Brice, Ann Pennington, the "shimmy" queen, and Eva Tanguay—who sang "It's All Been Done Before But Not the Way I Do It"—starred in Florenz Ziegfeld's *Follies,* the peak of vaudeville.

In songs like "St. Louis Blues" (1914), W.C. Handy took the black southern folk music of the blues to northern cities. Gertrude "Ma" Rainey, the daughter of minstrels, sang in black vaudeville for nearly thirty-five years. Performing in Chattanooga, Tennessee, about 1910, she came across a twelve-year-old orphan, Bessie Smith, who became the "Empress of the Blues." Smith's voice was huge and sweeping. Recording for the "Race" division of Columbia Records, she made over eighty records that together sold nearly ten million copies.

Another musical innovation came north from New Orleans. Charles (Buddy) Bolden, a cornetist, Ferdinand "Jelly Roll" Morton, a pianist, and a youngster named Louis Armstrong played an improvisational music that had no formal name. Reaching Chicago, it became "jas," then "jass,"and finally, "jazz." Jazz jumped, and jazz musicians relied on feeling and mood. A restaurant owner once asked Jelly Roll Morton to play a waltz. "*Waltz?*" Morton exclaimed. "Man, these people want to *dance!* And you talking about waltz. This is the *Roll* you're talking to."

Popular fiction reflected changing interests. Kate Douglas Wiggins's *Rebecca of Sunnybrook Farm* (1903) and Lucy M. Montgomery's *Anne of Green Gables* (1908) showed the continuing popularity of rural themes. Westerns also sold well, but readers turned more and more to detective thrillers with hard-bitten city detectives and science fiction featuring the latest dream in technology. The Tom Swift series, begun in 1910, looked ahead to spaceships, ray guns, and gravity nullifiers.

Edward L. Stratemeyer, the mind behind Tom Swift, brought the techniques of mass production to book writing. In 1906, he formed the Stratemeyer Literary Syndicate that employed a stable of writers to turn out hundreds of Tom Swift, Rover Boys, and Bobbsey Twins stories for young readers. Burt Standish, another prolific author, took the pen name of Gilbert Patten and created the character of Frank Merriwell, wholesome college athlete. As Patten said, "I took the three qualities I most wanted him to represent— frank and merry in nature, well in body and mind—and made the name Frank Merriwell." The Merriwell books sold twenty-five million copies.

Experimentation in the Arts

"There is a state of unrest all over the world in art as in all other things," the director of New York's Metropolitan Museum said in 1908. "It is the same in literature, as in music, in painting, and in sculpture."

Isadora Duncan and Ruth St. Denis transformed the dance. Departing from traditional ballet steps, both women stressed improvisation, emotion, and the human form. "Listen to the music with your soul. . . ," Duncan told her students. "Unless your dancing springs from an inner emotion and expresses an idea, it will be meaningless." Draped in flowing robes, she revealed more of her legs than some thought tasteful, while she proclaimed the "noblest art is the nude." After a triumphant performance with the New York Symphony in 1908, her ideas and techniques swept the country. Duncan died tragically in 1927, her neck broken when her long red scarf caught in the wheel of a racing car.

The lofts and apartments of New York's Greenwich Village attracted artists, writers, and poets interested in experimentation and change. To these artists, the city was the focus of national life and the sign of a new culture. Robert Henri and the realist painters—known to their critics as the Ashcan School—relished the city's excitement. They wanted, a friend said, "to paint truth and to paint it with strength and fearlessness and individuality."

To the realists, a painting carried into the future the look of life as it happened. With the

same feel for the environment that many progressive reformers would show (see Chapter 23), their paintings depicted street scenes, colorful crowds, and slum children swimming in the river. In paintings like the *Cliff Dwellers,* George W. Bellows captured the color and excitement of the tenements; John Sloan, one of Henri's most talented students, painted the vitality of ordinary people and familiar scenes.

In 1913, a show at the New York Armory presented sixteen hundred modernist paintings, prints, and sculptures. The work of Picasso, Cézanne, Matisse, Brancusi, Van Gogh, and Gauguin dazed and dazzled American observers. Critics attacked the show as worthless and depraved; a Chicago official wanted it banned from the city because the "idea that people can gaze at this sort of thing without [it] hurting them is all bosh."

The postimpressionists changed the direction of twentieth-century art and influenced adventuresome American painters. John Marin, Max Weber, Georgia O'Keeffe, Arthur Dove, and other modernists experimented in ways foreign to Henri's realists. Defiantly avant garde, they shook off convention and experimented with new forms. Using bold colors and abstract patterns, they worked to capture the energy of urban life. "I see great forces at work, great movements," Marin said, "the large buildings and the small buildings, the warring of the great and the small. . . . I can hear the sound of their strife, and there is a great music being played."

There was an extraordinary outburst of poetry. In 1912, Harriet Monroe started the magazine *Poetry* in Chicago, the hotbed of the new poetry; Ezra Pound and Vachel Lindsay, both daring experimenters with ideas and verse, published in

Marcel Duchamp, Nude Descending a Staircase No. 2 *(1912), the most notorious exhibit at the 1913 Armory Show. The show, which was the first full-scale presentation in the United States of European abstract, Cubist, and impressionist works, had revolutionary effects on the direction of American art.*

group of poets, many of them living and writing in London, who rejected traditional meter and rhyme as artificial constraints. Eliot, Pound, and Amy Lowell, among others, believed the poet's task was to capture fleeting images in verse.

Others experimenting with new techniques in poetry included Robert Frost (*North of Boston,* 1915), Edgar Lee Masters (*Spoon River Anthology,* 1915), and Carl Sandburg (*Chicago Poems,* 1916). Sandburg's poem "Chicago" celebrated the vitality of the city:

> *Come and show me another city with lifted head singing so proud to be alive and coarse and strong and cunning.*
> . . . .
> *Fierce as a dog with tongue lapping for action, cunning as a savage pitted against the wilderness,*
> > *Bareheaded,*
> > *Shoveling,*
> > *Wrecking,*
> > *Planning,*
> > *Building, breaking, rebuilding,*
> . . . .
> *Bragging and laughing that under his wrist is the pulse, and under his ribs the heart of the people,*
> > *Laughing!*
> *Laughing the stormy, husky, brawling laughter of Youth, half-naked, sweating, proud to be Hog Butcher, Tool Maker, Stacker of Wheat, Player with Railroads and Freight Handler to the Nation.*

Manners and morals change slowly, and many Americans overlooked the importance of the first two decades of the twentieth century. Yet sweeping change was underway; anyone who doubted it could visit a gallery, see a film, listen to music, or read one of the new literary magazines. Garrets and galleries were filled with a breathtaking sense of change. "There was life in all these new things," Marsden Hartley, a modernist painter, recalled. "There was excitement, there was healthy revolt, investigation, discovery, and an utterly new world out of it all."

The ferment of progressivism in city, state, and nation reshaped the country. In a burst of reform,

the first issue. T. S. Eliot published the classic "Love Song of J. Alfred Prufrock" in *Poetry* in 1915. Attacked bitterly by conservative critics, the poem established Eliot's leadership among a

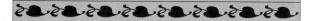

CHRONOLOGY

1898 Mergers and consolidations begin to sweep the business world, leading to fear of trusts

1903 Ford Motor Company formed • W. E. B. Du Bois calls for justice and equality for African Americans in *The Souls of Black Folk* • Women's Trade Union League (WTUL) formed to organize women workers

1905 Industrial Workers of the World (IWW) established • African American leaders inaugurate Niagara movement, advocating integration and equal opportunity for African Americans

1909 Shirtwaist workers in New York City strike in the "Uprising of the 20,000" • Campaign by Rockefeller Sanitary Commission wipes out hookworm disease

1910 NAACP founded • Strike at Hart, Schaffner and Marx leads to pioneering collective bargaining agreement • National Collegiate Athletic Association formed

1911 Fire at the Triangle Shirtwaist Company kills 146 people • Irving Berlin popularizes rhythm of ragtime with "Alexander's Ragtime Band" • Frederick Winslow Taylor publishes *The Principles of Scientific Management*

1912 Harriet Monroe begins publishing magazine *Poetry* • IWW leads strikes in Massachusetts and New Jersey

1913 Ford introduces the moving assembly line in Highland Park, Michigan, plant • Mother's Day becomes national holiday

1915 D. W. Griffith produces the first movie spectacular, *The Birth of a Nation* • T. S. Eliot publishes "The Love Song of J. Alfred Prufrock"

1916 Margaret Sanger forms New York Birth Control League • Federal Aid Roads Act creates national road network • New York Zoning Law sets the pattern for zoning laws across the nation

1917 Congress passes law requiring literacy test for all immigrants

1921 Congress passes the Sheppard-Towner Act to help protect maternal and infant health

people built playgrounds, restructured taxes, regulated business, won the vote for women, shortened working hours, altered political systems, opened kindergartens, and improved factory safety. They tried to fulfill the national promise of dignity and liberty.

Marsden Hartley, it turned out, had voiced a mood that went well beyond painters and poets. Across society, people in many walks of life were experiencing a similar sense of excitement and discovery. Racism, repression, and labor conflict were present, to be sure, but there was also talk of hope, progress, and change. In politics, science, journalism, education, and a host of other fields, people believed for a time that they could make a difference, and in trying to do so, they became part of the progressive generation.

Recommended Reading

There are several important analyses of the progressive era, including Robert H. Wiebe, *The Search for Order, 1877–1920* (1967); Richard Hofstadter, *The Age of Reform* (1955); Samuel P. Hays, *The Response to Industrialism* (1957); and Gabriel Kolko, *The Triumph of Conservatism* (1963). C. Vann Woodward, *Origins of the New South 1877–1913* (1951), is a superb account of developments in the South, along with William A. Link, *The Paradox of Southern Progressivism, 1880–1930* (1992). Lewis L. Gould, ed., *The Progressive Era* (1974), covers the period from varying perspectives; William L. O'Neill, *The Progressive Years* (1975), is a useful overview.

James T. Kloppenberg, *Uncertain Victory: Social Democracy and Progressivism in European and American Thought, 1870–1920* (1986), examines progressivism at home and abroad. C. Vann Woodward, *The Strange Career of Jim Crow* (1955), traces the civil rights setbacks of the Progressive years. Sam Bass Warner, Jr., *Streetcar Suburbs* (1962) and *The Urban Wilderness* (1972), are excellent on the subject of urban development, including zoning and industrial growth.

Work, workers, and the industrial society are perceptively treated in Herbert G. Gutman, *Work, Culture and Society in Industrializing America* (1977); David Montgomery, *Workers' Control in America: Studies in the History of Work, Technology, and Labor Struggles* (1979) and *The Fall of the House of Labor: The Workplace, the State, and American Labor Activism, 1865–1925* (1987); and David Brody, *Workers in Industrial America: Essays on the Twentieth Century Struggle* (1980). Stephen Thernstrom, *The Other Bostonians* (1973), is the best study of social and economic mobility.

Additional Bibliography

Studies of the muckrakers include David M. Chalmers, *The Social and Political Ideas of the Muckrakers* (1964); Justin Kaplan, *Lincoln Steffens* (1974); and Harold S. Wilson, *McClure's Magazine and the Muckrakers* (1970). Lincoln Steffens, *The Shame of the Cities* (1904) and *Autobiography of Lincoln Steffens* (1931), and Upton Sinclair, *The Jungle* (1906), give contemporary flavor.

Studies of youth, age, and family life include Joseph Kett, *Rites of Passage: Adolescence in America* (1977); Howard P. Chudacoff, *How Old Are You?: Age Consciousness in American Culture* (1989); W. Andrew Achenbaum, *Old Age in the New Land* (1978); William O'Neill, *Divorce in the Progressive Era* (1967); Carl N. Degler, *At Odds: Women and the Family in America* (1980); Michael Gordon, ed., *The American Family in Social-Historical Perspective* (1973); Tamara K. Hareven, ed., *Anonymous Americans* (1971) and *Transitions: The Family and Life Course in Historical Perspective* (1978). For birth control, see Linda Gordon, *Woman's Body, Woman's Right: A Social History of Birth Control in America* (1976); David M. Kennedy, *Birth Control in America: The Career of Margaret Sanger* (1970); and Ellen Chesler, *Woman of Valor: Margaret Sanger and the Birth Control Movement in America* (1993).

See also Eleanor Flexner, *Century of Struggle: The Women's Rights Movement in the United States* (1959); William L. O'Neill, *Everyone Was Brave: The Rise and Fall of Feminism in America* (1969); Ellen Fitzpatrick, *Endless Crusade: Women, Social Scientists, and Progressive Reform* (1990); Adele Heller and Lois Rudnick, eds., *1915, The Cultural Moment: The New Politics, the New Woman, the New Psychology, the New Art, & the New Theatre in America* (1991); John L. Rury, *Education and Women's Work: Female Schooling and the Division of Labor in Urban America, 1870–1930* (1991); Carole Nichols, *Votes and More for Women* (1983); Leslie Woodcock Tentler, *Wage-Earning Women: Industrial Work and Family Life in the United States, 1900–1930* (1979); Joyce Antler, *Lucy Sprague Mitchell* (1987); Noralee Frankel and Nancy S. Dye, eds., *Gender, Class, Race & Reform in the Progressive Era* (1991); Lynn D. Gordon, *Gender in Higher Education in the Progressive Era* (1990); Virginia Scharff, *Taking the Wheel: Women and the Coming of the Motor Age* (1991); Jacqueline Ann Rouse, *Lugenia Burns Hope: Black Southern Reformer* (1989); Louise Lamphere, *From Working Daughters to Working Mothers* (1987); Mary P. Ryan, *Women in Public: Between Banners and Ballots, 1825–1880* (1990); Sheila M. Rothman, *Woman's Proper Place* (1978); and Ellen Condliffe Lagemann, *A Generation of Women: Education in the Lives of the Progressive Reformers* (1979).

On labor and laborers, see Patricia A. Cooper, *Once a Cigarmaker: Men, Women, and Work Culture in American Cigar Factories, 1900–1919* (1987); Dorothy Schweider, *Black Diamonds: Life and Work in Iowa's Coal Mining Communities, 1895–1925* (1983); John Bodnar, *Workers' World* (1982); Alan Derickson, *Workers' Health, Workers' Democracy: The Western Miners' Struggle, 1891–1925* (1988); Howard M. Gitelman, *Legacy of the Ludlow Massacre* (1988); Martin Green, *New York, 1913: The Armory Show and the Paterson Strike Pageant* (1988); David M. Emmons, *The Butte Irish: Class and Ethnicity in an American Mining Town, 1875–1925* (1989); Marilyn D. Rhinehart, *A Way of Work and a Way of Life* (1992); Cathy L. McHugh, *Mill Family: The Labor System in the Southern Cotton Textile Industry, 1880–1915* (1988); Martha Vicinus, *Independent Women: Work and Community for Single Women, 1850–1920* (1985); and Richard Jules Oestreicher, *Solidarity and Fragmentation: Working People and Class Consciousness in Detroit, 1875–1900* (1986).

Roger Burlingame, *Henry Ford* (1954), and Allan Nevins and Frank E. Hill, *Ford,* 3 vols. (1954–1963), cover Ford's career; Alfred D. Chandler, *Strategy and Structure: Chapters in the History of American Industrial Enterprise* (1962); Bruce E. Seely, *Building the American Highway System: Engineers as Policy Makers* (1987); James J. Flink, *The Automobile Age* (1988); Peter L. Jakab, *Visions of a Flying Machine: The Wright Brothers and the Process of Invention* (1990); Martin J. Sklar, *The Corporate Reconstruction of American Capitalism, 1890–1916* (1988); Samuel Haber, *Efficiency and Uplift: Scientific Management in the Progressive Era* (1964); Daniel Nelson, *Frederick W. Taylor and the Rise of Scientific Management* (1980); and Frederick A. White, *American Industrial Research Laboratories* (1961), provide useful overviews. See also Tamara K. Hareven and Randolph Langenbach, *Amoskeag: Life and Work in an American Factory-City* (1978); and Judith Sealander, *Grand Plans: Business Progressivism and Social Change in Ohio's Miami Valley, 1890–1919* (1988).

The labor movement is covered in Harold Livesay, *Samuel Gompers and Organized Labor in America* (1978); Melvyn Dubofsky, *We Shall Be All: A History of the Industrial Workers of the World* (1969) and *"Big Bill" Haywood* (1987); Anne Huber Tripp, *The I.W.W. and the Paterson Silk Strike of 1913* (1987); Steve Golin, *The Fragile Bridge: Paterson Silk Strike of 1913* (1988); David J. Goldberg, *A Tale of Three Cities: Labor Organization and Protest in Paterson, Passaic, and Lawrence, 1916–1921* (1989); Clarence E.

Wunderlin, Jr., *Visions of a New Industrial Order: Social Science and Labor Theory in America's Progressive Era* (1992); Salvatore Salerno, *Red November, Black November: Culture and Community in the Industrial Workers of the World* (1989); Dee Garrison, *Mary Heaton Vorse: The Life of an American Insurgent* (1989); Elizabeth Anne Payne, *Reform, Labor, and Feminism: Margaret Dreier Robins and the Women's Trade Union League* (1988); Leslie Woodcock Tentler, *Wage-Earning Women: Industrial Work and Family Life in the United States, 1900–1930* (1979); Susan Estabrook Kennedy, *If All We Did Was to Weep at Home: A History of White Working Class Women in America* (1979); and Barbara Mayer Wertheimer, *We Were There: The Story of Working Women in America* (1977).

Leonard Dinnerstein, Roger L. Nichols, and David M. Reimers, *Natives and Strangers: Ethnic Groups and the Building of America* (1979), offer a useful overview of Mexican Americans and the "new" immigrants. See also Oscar Handlin, *The Uprooted* (1951); John Higham, *Strangers in the Land: Patterns of American Nativism* (1955); Josef J. Barton, *Peasants and Strangers* (1975); Mario T. Garcia, *Desert Immigrants: The Mexicans of El Paso, 1880–1920* (1981); William Pencak, Selma Berrol, and Randall M. Miller, eds., *Immigration to New York* (1991); Donald B. Cole, *Immigrant City: Lawrence, Massachusetts, 1845–1921* (1963); A. T. Lane, *Solidarity or Survival? American Labor and European Immigrants, 1830–1924* (1987); and John E. Bodnar, *Immigration and Industrialization* (1977). Thomas Kessner, *The Golden Door: Italian and Jewish Immigrant Mobility in New York City, 1880–1915* (1977), is excellent.

On Du Bois, see Elliot M. Rudwick, *W. E. B. Du Bois* (1968). Other useful books include George M. Frederickson, *The Black Image in the White Mind* (1971); Charles F. Kellogg, *NAACP: A History of the National Association for the Advancement of Colored People, 1909–1920* (1967); Roberta Senechal, *The Sociogenesis of a Race Riot: Springfield, Illinois, in 1908* (1990); Louis R. Harlan, *Separate and Unequal: Public School Campaigns and Racism in the Southern Seaboard States, 1900–1915* (1968); William H. Harris, *The Harder We Run: Black Workers Since the Civil War* (1982); Allen H. Spear, *Black Chicago* (1967); and Idus A. Newby, *Jim Crow's Defense: Anti-Negro Thought in America, 1900–1930* (1965). Leslie Fishbein, *Rebels in Bohemia: The Radicals of the Masses, 1911–1917* (1982); and Dewey W. Grantham, Jr., *Hoke Smith and the Politics of the New South* (1958) are valuable studies.

For the ways in which Americans entertained themselves, see Gunther Barth, *City People* (1980); Allison Danzig, *History of American Football* (1956); Russel B. Nye, *The Unembarrassed Muse: The Popular Arts in America* (1970); Nicholas E. Tawa, *The Way to Tin Pan Alley: American Popular Song, 1866–1910* (1990); John E. DiMeglio, *Vaudeville U.S.A.* (1973); Ronald L. Davis, *A History of Music in American Life, Volume II: The Gilded Years, 1865–1920* (1980); and Robert Sklar, *Movie-Made America: A Social History of the American Movies* (1975).

From Roosevelt to Wilson in the Age of Progressivism

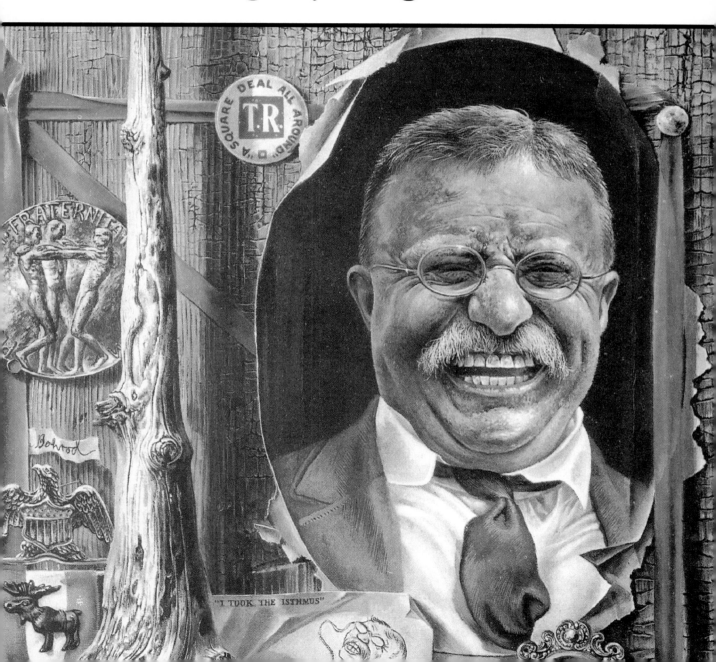

On a sunny spring morning in 1909, Theodore Roosevelt, wearing the greatcoat of a colonel of the Rough Riders, left New York for a safari in Africa. An ex-president at the age of fifty, he had turned over the White House to his chosen successor, William Howard Taft, and was now off for "the joy of wandering through lonely lands, the joy of hunting the mighty and terrible lords" of Africa, "where death broods in the dark and silent depths."

Some of Roosevelt's enemies hoped he would not return. "I trust some lion will do its duty," Wall Street magnate J. P. Morgan said. Always prepared, Roosevelt took nine extra pairs of eyeglasses, and just in case, several expert hunters accompanied him. When the nearsighted Roosevelt took aim, three others aimed at the same moment. "Mr. Roosevelt had a fairly good idea of the general direction," the safari leader said, "but we couldn't take chances with the life of a former president." Though he had built a reputation as an ardent conservationist, Roosevelt shot nine lions, five elephants, thirteen rhinoceroses, seven hippopotamuses, and assorted other game—acquiring nearly three hundred trophies in all.

It was all good fun, and afterward Roosevelt set off on a tour of Europe. He attended the funeral of the king of England with the crowned heads of Europe, dined with the king and queen of Italy—an experience he likened to "a Jewish wedding on the East Side of New York"—and happily spent five hours reviewing troops of the German empire. Less happily, he followed events back home where, in the judgment of many friends, Taft was not working out as president. Gifford Pinchot, Roosevelt's close companion in the conservation movement, came to Italy to complain personally about Taft, and at almost every stop there were letters waiting for him from other disappointed Republicans.

For his part, Taft was puzzled by it all. Honest and warmhearted, he had intended to continue Roosevelt's policies, even writing Roosevelt that he would "see to it that your judgment in selecting me as your successor and bringing about that succession shall be vindicated. . . ." But events turned out differently. The conservative and pro-gressive wings of the Republican party split, and Taft often sided with the conservatives. Among progressive Republicans, Taft's troubles stirred talk of a Roosevelt "Back from Elba" movement, akin to Napoleon's return from exile.

Thousands gathered to greet Roosevelt on his return from Europe. He sailed into New York harbor on June 18, 1910, to the sound of naval guns and loud cheers. In characteristic fashion, he had helped make the arrangements: "If there is to be a great crowd, do arrange it so that the whole crowd has a chance to see me and that there is as little disappointment as possible." Greeting Pinchot, one of Taft's leading opponents, with a hearty "Hello, Gifford," Roosevelt slipped away to his home in Oyster Bay, New York, where other friends awaited him.

He carried with him a touching letter from Taft, received just before he left Europe. "I have had a hard time—I do not know that I have had harder luck than other Presidents, but I do know that thus far I have succeeded far less than have others. I have been conscientiously trying to carry out your policies but my method of doing so has not worked smoothly." Taft invited Teddy to spend a night or two at the White House, but Roosevelt declined, saying that ex-presidents should not visit Washington. Relations between the two friends cooled. "It is hard, very hard," Taft said in 1911, "to see a devoted friendship going to pieces like a rope of sand."

A year later, there was no longer thought of friendship, only a desperate fight between Taft and Roosevelt for the Republican presidential nomination. Taft won the nomination, but angry and ambitious, Roosevelt bolted and helped form a new party, the Progressive (or "Bull Moose") party, to unseat Taft and capture the White House. With Taft, Roosevelt, Woodrow Wilson (the Democratic party's candidate), and Socialist party candidate Eugene V. Debs all in the race, the election of 1912 became one of the most exciting in American history.

It was also one of the most important. People were worried about the social and economic effects of urban-industrial growth (see Chapter 22). The election of 1912 provided a forum for those worries, and to a degree unusual in American politics, it pitted deeply opposed candidates against one another and outlined differing views of the nation's future. In the spirited battle between Roosevelt and Wilson, it also brought to the forefront some of the currents of progressive reform.

THE SPIRIT OF PROGRESSIVISM

In one way or another, progressivism touched all aspects of society. Politically, it fostered a reform movement that sought cures for the problems of city, state, and nation. Intellectually, it drew on the expertise of the new social sciences and reflected a shift from older absolutes of class and religion to newer schools of thought that emphasized physiological explanations for behavior, the role of the environment in human development, and the relative nature of truth. Culturally, it inspired fresh modes of expression in dance, film, painting, literature, and architecture. Touching individuals in different ways, progressivism became a set of attitudes as well as a definable movement.

Though broad and diverse, progressivism as a whole had a half-dozen characteristics that gave it definition. First, the progressives acted out of concern about the effects of industrialization and the conditions of industrial life. While their viewpoints varied, they did not, as a rule, set out to harm big business, but instead sought to humanize and regulate it.

In pursuing these objectives, the progressives displayed a second characteristic, a fundamental optimism about human nature, the possibilities of progress, and the capacity of people to recognize problems and take action to solve them. Progressives believed they could "investigate, educate, and legislate"—learn about a problem, inform people about it, and with the help of an informed public, find and enforce a solution.

Third, more than many earlier reformers, the progressives were willing to intervene in people's lives, confident it was their right to do so. They knew best, some of them thought, and as a result, there was an element of coercion in a number of their ideas. Fourth, while progressives preferred if possible to use voluntary means to achieve reform, they tended to turn more and more to the authority of the state and government at all levels, to put into effect the reforms they wanted.

As a fifth characteristic, many progressives drew on a combination of evangelical Protestantism, which gave them the desire (and, they thought, the duty) to purge the world of sins such as prostitution and drunkenness; and the natural and social sciences, the theories of which made them confident that they could understand and control the environment in which people lived. Progressives tended to view the environment as a key to reform, thinking (in the way some economists, sociologists, and other social scientists were suggesting) that if they could change the environment, they could change the individual.

Finally, progressivism was distinctive because it touched virtually the whole nation. Not everyone, of course, was a progressive, and there were many who opposed or ignored the ideas of the movement. But in one way or another, a remarkable number of people were caught up in it, giving progressivism a national reach and a mass base.

That was one of the features, in fact, that set it off from populism, which had grown mostly in the rural South and West. Progressivism drew support across society. "The thing that constantly amazed me," said William Allen White, a leading progressive journalist, "was how many people were with us." Progressivism appealed to the expanding middle class, prosperous farmers, and skilled laborers; it also attracted significant support in the business community.

The progressives believed in progress and disliked waste. No single issue or concern united them all. Some progressives wanted to clean up city governments, others to clean up city streets. Some wanted to purify politics or control corporate abuses, others to eradicate poverty or prostitution. Some demanded social justice in the form of women's rights, child labor laws, temperance, and factory safety. They were Democrats, Republicans, Socialists, and independents.

Progressives believed in a better world and in the ability of people to achieve it. They paid to people, as a friend said of social reformer Florence Kelley, "the high compliment of believing that, once they knew the truth, they would act upon it." Progress depended on knowledge. The progressives stressed individual morality and collective action, the scientific method, and the value of expert opinion. Like contemporary business leaders, they valued system, planning, management, and predictability. They wanted not only reform but efficiency. In the introduction to *The Shame of the Cities,* Steffens said the cure for American ills lay in "good conduct in the individual, simple honesty, courage, and efficiency."

Historians once viewed progressivism as the triumph of one group in society over another. In this view, farmers took on the hated and powerful railroads; upstart reformers challenged the city bosses; business interests fought for favorable legislation; youthful professionals carved out their place in society. Now, historians stress the way progressivism brought people together rather than drove them apart. Disparate groups united in an effort to improve the well-being of many groups in society.

The Rise of the Professions

Progressivism fed on an organizational impulse that encouraged people to join forces, share information, and solve problems. Between 1890 and 1920, a host of national societies and associations took shape—nearly four hundred of them in just three decades. Groups such as the National Child Labor Committee, which lobbied for legislation to regulate the employment and working conditions of children, were formed to attack specific issues. Other groups reflected one of the most significant developments in American society at the turn of the century—the rise of the professions.

Growing rapidly in these years, the professions—law, medicine, religion, business, teaching, and social work—were the source of much of the leadership of the progressive movement. The professions attracted young educated men and women, who in turn were part of a larger trend: a dramatic increase in the number of individuals working in administrative and professional jobs. In businesses, these people were managers, architects, technicians, and accountants. In city governments, they were experts in everything from education to sanitation. They organized and ran the urban-industrial society.

Together these professionals formed part of a new middle class, whose members did not derive their status from birth or inherited wealth, as had many members of the older middle class. Instead, they moved ahead through education and personal accomplishment. They had worked to become doctors, lawyers, ministers, and teachers. Proud of their skills, they were ambitious and self-confident, and they thought of themselves as experts who could use their knowledge for the benefit of society.

As a way of asserting their status, they formed professional societies to look after their interests and govern entry into their professions. Just a few years before, for example, a doctor had become a doctor simply by stocking up on patent medicines and hanging out a sign. The advances in medical and scientific knowledge near the turn of the century (see Chapter 19) made the practice of medicine more respectable. Doctors began to insist they were part of a medical *profession,* with educational requirements and minimum standards for practice. In 1901, they reorganized the American Medical Association (AMA) and made it into a modern, national professional society. The AMA had 8,400 members that year. A decade later, it had over 70,000, and by 1920, nearly two-thirds of all doctors belonged.

Other groups and professions showed the same pattern. Lawyers formed bar associations, created examining boards, and lobbied for regulations restricting entry into the profession. Teachers organized the National Education Association (1905) and pressed for teacher certification and compulsory education laws. Social workers formed the National Federation of Settlements (1911); business leaders created the National Association of Manufacturers (1895) and the U.S. Chamber of Commerce (1912); and farmers joined the National Farm Bureau Federation to spread information about farming and to try to improve their lot.

Working both as individuals and groups, members of the professions had a major impact on the era, as the career of one of them, Dr. Alice Hamilton, illustrated. Hamilton early decided to devote her life to helping the less fortunate. Choosing medicine, she went to the University of Michigan Medical School, one of a shrinking number of medical schools that admitted women, and then settled in Chicago where she met Jane Addams and took a room in Hull House. Soon thereafter, she traced a local typhoid epidemic to flies carrying germs from open privies. The study won national acclaim, but Hamilton had already turned her attention to the work-related illnesses she found everywhere around Hull House.

Combining field study with meticulous laboratory techniques, she pioneered research into the causes of lead poisoning and other industrial disease. In 1908, the governor of Illinois appointed her to a Commission on Occupational Diseases; two years later, she headed a statewide survey of industrial poisons. Thanks to her work, in 1911, Illinois passed the first state law providing compensation for industrial disease caused by poisonous fumes and dust. By the end of the 1930s, all major industrial states had such laws.

One of the new professionals, Hamilton had used her education and skill to broaden knowledge of her subject, change industrial practices, and improve the lives of countless workers. "For me," she said later in a comment characteristic of the progressives, "the satisfaction is that things are better now, and I had some part in it."

The Social-Justice Movement

As Alice Hamilton's career exemplified, progressivism began in the cities during the 1890s. It first took form around settlement workers and others interested in freeing individuals from the crushing impact of cities and factories.

Ministers, intellectuals, social workers, and lawyers joined in a social-justice movement that focused national attention on the need for tene-

ment house laws, more stringent child labor legislation, and better working conditions for women. They brought pressure on municipal agencies for more and better parks, playgrounds, day nurseries, schools, and community services. Blending private and public action, settlement leaders turned increasingly to government aid. "Private beneficence," Jane Addams said, "is totally inadequate to deal with the vast numbers of the city's disinherited."

Social-justice reformers were more interested in social cures than individual charity. Unlike earlier reformers, they saw problems as endless and interrelated; individuals became part of a city's larger patterns. With that insight, social-service casework shifted from a focus on an individual's well-being to a scientific analysis of neighborhoods, occupations, and classes.

In the spring of 1900, the Charity Organization Society of New York held a tenement house exhibition that graphically presented the new kind of sociological data. Put together by Lawrence Veiller, a young social worker, the exhibition included over one thousand photographs, detailed maps of slum districts, statistical tables and charts, and graphic cardboard depictions of tenement blocks. Never before had so much information been pulled together in one place. Veiller correlated data on poverty and dis-

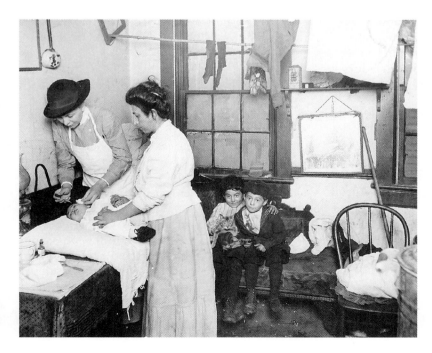

An Infant Welfare Society nurse treats the baby of an immigrant family in Chicago. A host of medical discoveries and improvements in the quality of medical education fostered an interest in public health work among the social justice reformers.

ease with housing conditions, and he pointed out that new slums were springing up in more areas of the city. Stirred by the public outcry, Governor Theodore Roosevelt appointed the New York State Tenement House Commission to do something about the problem.

With Veiller's success as a model, study after study analyzed the condition of the poor. Books and pamphlets like *The Standard of Living Among Working Men's Families in New York City* (1909) contained pages of data on family budgets, women's wages and working conditions, child labor, and other matters. Between 1910 and 1913, the U.S. Commissioner of Labor issued a massive nineteen-volume report on *Conditions of Women and Children Wage-Earners in the United States.*

Banding together to work for change, social-justice reformers formed the National Conference of Charities and Corrections, which in 1915 became the National Conference of Social Work. Controlled by social workers, the conference reflected the growing professionalization of reform. Through it, social workers discovered each other's efforts, shared methodology, and tried to establish themselves as a separate field within the social sciences. Once content with informal training sessions in a settlement house living room, they now founded complete professional schools at Chicago, Harvard, and other universities. After 1909, they had their own professional magazine, the *Survey,* and instead of piecemeal reforms they aimed at a comprehensive program of minimum wages, maximum hours, workers' compensation, and widows' pensions.

The Purity Crusade

Working in city neighborhoods, social-justice reformers were often struck by the degree to which alcohol affected the lives of the people they were trying to help. Workers drank away their wages; some men spent more time at the saloon than at home. Drunkenness caused violence, and it angered employers who did not want intoxicated workers on the job. In countless ways, alcohol wasted human resources, the reformers believed, and along with business leaders, ministers, and others, they launched a crusade to remove the evils of drink from American life.

At the head of the crusade was the Women's Christian Temperance Union (WCTU), which had continued to grow since it was founded in the 1870s. By 1911, the WCTU had nearly a quarter of a million members, the largest organization of women in American history to that time. In 1893, it was joined by the Anti-Saloon League, and together the groups pressed to abolish alcohol and the places where it was consumed. By 1916, they had succeeded in nineteen states, but as drinking continued elsewhere, they pushed for a nationwide law. In the midst of the moral fervor of World War I, they succeeded, and the Eighteenth Amendment to the Constitution, prohibiting the manufacture, sale, and transportation of intoxicating liquors, took effect in January 1920.

The amendment encountered troubles later in the 1920s as the social atmosphere changed, but at the time it passed, progressives thought prohibition was a major step toward eliminating social instability and moral wrong. In a similar fashion, some progressive reformers also worked to get rid of prostitution, convinced that poverty and ignorance drove women to the trade. By 1915, nearly every state had banned brothels, and in 1910, Congress passed the Mann Act, which prohibited the interstate transportation of women for immoral purposes. Like the campaign against liquor, the campaign against prostitution reflected the era's desire to purify and elevate, often through the instrument of government action.

Woman Suffrage, Woman's Rights

Women played a very large role in the social-justice movement. Feminists were particularly active, especially in the political sphere, between 1890 and 1914—feminists were more active then, in fact, than at any time until the 1960s. Some working-class women pushed for higher wages and better working conditions. College-educated women—five thousand a year graduated after 1900—took up careers in the professions, from which some of them supported reform. From 1890 to 1910, the work of a number of national women's organizations, including the National Council of Jewish Women, National Congress of Mothers, and the Women's Trade Union League, furthered the aims of the progressive movement.

Woman suffrage was a key element in the social-justice movement. Without the right to vote, women working actively for reform had little real power to influence elected officials to support their endeavors.

The National Association of Colored Women was founded in 1895, fifteen years before the better known male-oriented National Association for the Advancement of Colored People (NAACP). Aimed at social welfare, the women's organization was the first African-American social-service agency in the country. At the local level, African American women's clubs established kindergartens, day nurseries, playgrounds, and retirement homes.

From 200,000 members in 1900, the General Federation of Women's Clubs grew to over 1 million by 1912. The clubs met, as they had before, for coffee and literary conversation, but they also began to look closely at conditions around them. In 1904, Mrs. Sarah P. Decker, the federation's new president, told the national convention, "Ladies, you have chosen me your leader. Well, I have an important piece of news to give you. Dante is dead. He has been dead for several cen-

turies, and I think it is time that we dropped the study of his *Inferno* and turned our attention to our own."

Forming an Industrial Section and a Committee on Legislation for Women and Children, the federation supported reforms to safeguard child and women workers, improve schools, ensure pure food, and beautify the community. Reluctant at first, the federation finally lent support in 1914 to woman suffrage, a cause that dated back to the first woman's rights convention in Seneca Falls, New York, in 1848. Divided over tactics since the Civil War, the suffrage movement suffered from disunity, male opposition, indecision over whether to seek action at the state or at the national level, resistance from the Catholic church, and opposition from liquor interests, who linked the cause to prohibition.

Women in the social-justice movement needed

to influence elected officials—most of them men, whom they could not reach through the vote. Because politics was an avenue for reform, growing numbers of women activists became involved in the suffrage movement. After years of disagreement, the two major suffrage organizations, the National Woman Suffrage Association and the American Woman Suffrage Association, merged in 1890 to form the National American Woman Suffrage Association. The merger opened a new phase of the suffrage movement, characterized by unity and a tightly controlled national organization.

In 1900, Carrie Chapman Catt, a superb organizer, became president of the National American Woman Suffrage Association, which by 1920 had nearly two million members. Catt and Anna Howard Shaw, who became the association's head in 1904, believed in organization and peaceful lobbying to win the vote. Alice Paul and Lucy Burns, founders of the Congressional Union, were more militant; they interrupted public meetings, focused on Congress rather than the states, and in 1917 picketed the White House.

Significantly, Catt, Paul, and others made a major change in the argument for woman suffrage. When the campaign began in the nineteenth century, suffragists had claimed the vote as a natural right, owed to women as much as men. Now, they stressed a pragmatic argument: since women were more sensitive to moral issues than men, they would use their votes to help create a better society. They would support temperance, clean government, laws to protect workers, and other reforms. This argument attracted many progressives who believed woman's suffrage would purify politics. In 1918, the House passed a constitutional amendment stating simply that the right to vote shall not be denied "on account of sex." The Senate and enough states followed, and, after three generations of suffragist efforts, the Nineteenth Amendment took effect in 1920.

The social-justice movement had the most success in passing state laws limiting the working hours of women. By 1913, thirty-nine states set maximum working hours for women or banned the employment of women at night. Illinois had a ten-hour law; California and Washington had eight-hour laws. Wisconsin, Oregon, and Kansas allowed expert commissions to set different hours depending on the degree of strain in various occupations. As early as 1900, thanks to groups such

Woman Suffrage Before 1920

State-by-state gains in woman suffrage were limited to the Far West and were agonizingly slow in the early years of the twentieth century.

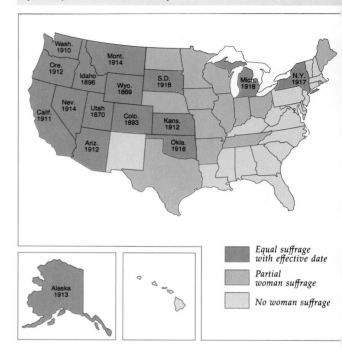

as the National Child Labor Committee, twenty-eight states had laws regulating child labor. But the courts often ruled against such laws, and families—needing extra income—sometimes ignored them. Parents sent children off to jobs with orders to lie about their ages.

In 1916, President Woodrow Wilson backed a law to limit child labor, the Keating-Owen Act, but in *Hammer* v. *Dagenhart* (1918) the Supreme Court overturned it as an improper regulation of local labor conditions. In 1919, Congress tried again in the Second Child Labor Act, and in *Bailey* v. *Drexel Furniture Company* (1922) was again struck down. Not until the 1930s did Congress succeed in passing a court-supported national child labor law.

A Ferment of Ideas

A dramatic shift in ideas became one of the most important forces behind progressive reform. Building on the developments of the 1890s (see Chapter 19), writers in law, economics, history, sociology, psychology, and a host of other fields advanced ideas that together challenged the status quo and called for change.

Most of the ideas focused on the role of the environment in shaping human behavior. Progressive reformers accepted society's growing complexity, called for factual treatment of piecemeal problems, allowed room for new theories, and above all, rejected age-encrusted divine or natural "laws" in favor of thoughts and actions that worked.

A new doctrine, called pragmatism, emerged in this ferment of ideas. It came from William James, a brilliant Harvard psychologist who became the key figure in American thought from the 1890s to World War I. A warm, tolerant person, James was impatient with theories that made truth an abstract and stagnant thing. Truth, he believed, should work for the individual, and it worked best not in abstraction, but in action. "True ideas are those we can assimilate, validate, corroborate, and verify. False ideas are those we cannot."

People, James thought, were not only shaped by their environment; they shaped it. In *Pragmatism* (1907), a book so popular it went through many editions, he praised "tough-minded" individuals who could live effectively in a world with no easy answers. The tough-minded accepted change; they knew how to pick manageable problems, gather facts, discard ideas that did not work, and act on those that did. Ideas that worked became truth. "What is the 'cash value' of a thought, idea, or belief?" James asked. Does it work? Does it make a difference to the individual who experiences it? "The ultimate test for us of what a truth means," said James, "is the conduct it dictates."

The most influential educator of the Progressive Era, John Dewey, applied pragmatism to educational reform. A friend and disciple of William James, he argued that thought evolves in relation to the environment and that education is directly related to experience. In 1896, he and his wife founded a separate School of Pedagogy at the University of Chicago, with a laboratory in which educational theory based on the newer philosophical and psychological studies could be tested and practiced.

Dewey introduced an educational revolution that stressed children's needs and capabilities. He described his beliefs and methods in a number of books, notably *School and Society* (1899) and *Democracy and Education* (1916). New ideas in education, he said, are "as much a product of the changed social situation, and as much an effort to meet the needs of the society that is forming, as are changes in modes of industry and commerce." He opposed memorization, rote learning, and dogmatic, authoritarian teaching methods; he emphasized personal growth, free inquiry, and creativity.

Providing an overarching framework within which others could fit, William James and Dewey had a great effect on other thinkers. Edward A. Ross, a reform sociologist, in *Sin and Society* (1907) called for "pure environmentalism" and a new standard of morality. Economist Richard T. Ely (see Chapter 19) rejected the conservative "laws" of classical economics and developed theories that placed economics in a changing environment. In *The Theory of the Leisure Class* (1899) and *The Instinct of Workmanship* (1914) Thorstein Veblen argued that everything was flux, the only law was the lack of laws, and modern business was an anarchic struggle for profit. Reform, to Veblen, was not only permissible, it was essential to provide order and efficiency in an industrial and entrepreneurial system characterized by disorder.

Rejecting the older view of the law as universal and unchanging, lawyers and legal theorists instead viewed it as a reflection of the environment—an instrument for social change. Law reflected the environment that shaped it. A movement grew among judges for "sociological jurisprudence" that related the law to social reform (see the Special Trial feature on *Muller* v. *Oregon,* pp. 721–725).

In Denver, Colorado, after Judge Ben Lindsey sentenced a boy to reform school for stealing coal, the boy's mother rushed forward and, grief-stricken, beat her head against the wall. Lindsey investigated the case and found the father was a smelting worker dying of lead poisoning; the family needed coal for heat. From such experiences, Lindsey concluded that children were not born with a genetic tendency to crime; they were made good or bad by the environment in which they grew. Lindsey "sentenced" youthful offenders to education and good care. He worked for playgrounds, slum clearance, public baths, and technical schools. Known as the "Kids' Judge," he attracted visitors from as far away as Japan, who wanted to study and copy his methods.

Students in the University of Chicago Laboratory School, established by John Dewey as a testing ground for his theories on education. Dewey's views on education emphasized growth and development and were directly opposed to the prevailing view, which focused on memorization and drill.

Socialism, a reformist political philosophy, grew dramatically before the First World War. Socialist political parties, composed of followers of Karl Marx, first appeared in New York, Chicago, Milwaukee, and other cities after the Civil War. They urged workers to join a worldwide revolution to overthrow capitalism. Such public appeals, however, drew little support. Leaders of a new Socialist Labor party, founded in 1877, tried in secret to gain control of important labor unions. That strategy also failed.

Daniel De Leon, a brilliant tactician, took over leadership of the Socialist Labor party during the 1890s, but he too lacked mass support. Arguing for a more moderate form of socialism, Eugene V. Debs, president of the American Railway Union, in 1896 formed a rival organization, the Social Democratic party. Gentle and reflective, not at all the popular image of the wild-eyed radical, Debs was thrust into prominence by the Pullman strike (see Chapter 20). In 1901, persuading opponents of De Leon to join him, he formed the important Socialist party of America. Neither Debs nor the party ever developed a cohesive platform, nor was Debs an effective organizer. But he was eloquent, passionate, and visionary. An excellent speaker, he captivated audiences, attacking the injustices of capitalism and urging a workers' republic.

The Socialist party of America enlisted some intellectuals, factory workers, disillusioned Populists, tenant farmers, miners, and lumberjacks. By 1911, there were Socialist mayors in thirty-two cities, including Berkeley, California; Butte, Montana; and Flint, Michigan. Although its doctrines were aimed at an urban proletariat, ·the Socialist party drew support in rural Texas, Missouri, Arkansas, Idaho, and Washington. In Oklahoma, it attracted as much as one-third of the vote. Most Socialists who won promised progressive reform rather than threatening to overthrow capitalists.

Although torn by factions, the Socialist party doubled in membership between 1904 and 1908, then tripled in the four years after that. Running for president, Debs garnered 100,000 votes in 1900; 400,000 in 1904; and 900,000 in 1912, the party's peak year.

REFORM IN THE CITIES AND STATES

Desiring reform, the progressives realized government could be a crucial agent in accomplishing their goals. They wanted to curb the influence of "special interests" and, through such measures of political reform as the direct primary and the direct election of senators, make government follow the public will. Once it did, they welcomed government action at whatever level was appropriate.

As a result of this thinking, the use of federal power increased, as did the power and prestige of the presidency. Progressives not only lobbied for government-sponsored reform, but also worked actively in their home neighborhoods, cities, and states; much of the significant change occurred in local settings, outside the national limelight. Most important, the progressives believed in the ability of experts to solve problems. At every level— local, state, and federal—thousands of commissions and agencies took form. Staffed by trained experts, they oversaw a multitude of matters ranging from railroad rates to public health.

Interest Groups and the Decline of Popular Politics

Placing government in the hands of experts was one way to get it out of the hands of politicians and political parties. The direct primary was another way. These initiatives and others like them were part of a fundamental change in the way Americans viewed their political system.

As one sign of the change, fewer and fewer people were going to the polls. Voter turnout dropped dramatically after 1900 when the intense partisanship of the decades after the Civil War gave way to media-oriented political campaigns based largely on the personalities of the candidates. From 1876 to 1900, the average turnout in presidential elections was 77 percent. From 1900 to 1916, it was 65 percent, and in the 1920s, it dropped to 52 percent, close to the average today. Turnout was lowest among young people, immigrants, the poor and, ironically, the newly enfranchised women.

It was particularly low in the South where conservative whites used restrictive election laws to keep blacks and others from the polls. Turnout in the South fell sharply, from an average of 64 percent in the presidential elections of the 1880s to just 20 percent in 1920 and 1924. Although the decline in the North was less sharp, the reasons for it were more complex. By the 1920s, as many as one-quarter of all eligible northern voters never cast a ballot.

There were numerous causes for the falloff, but among the most important was the fact that people had found another way to achieve some of the objectives they had once assigned to political parties. They had found the "interest group," a means of action that assumed importance in this era and became a major feature of politics ever after. Professional societies, trade associations, labor organizations, farm lobbies, and scores of other interest groups worked outside the party system to pressure government for things their members wanted. Social workers, women's clubs, reform groups, and others learned to apply pressure in similar ways, and the result was much significant legislation of the Progressive Era.

Reform in the Cities

During the early years of the twentieth century, urban reform movements, many of them born in the depression of the 1890s, spread across the nation. In 1894, the National Municipal League was organized, and it became the forum for debate over civic reform, changes in the tax laws, and municipal ownership of public utilities. Within a few years, nearly every city had a variety of clubs and organizations directed at improving the quality of city life.

"For two generations," Frederic C. Howe said in 1905, "we have wrought out the most admirable laws and then left the government to run itself. This has been our greatest fault." In the 1880s, reformers like Howe would call an evening conference, pass resolutions, and then go home; after 1900, they formed associations, adopted long-range policies, and hired a staff to achieve them. In the mid-1890s, only Chicago had an urban reform league with a full-time paid executive; within a decade, there were such leagues in every major city.

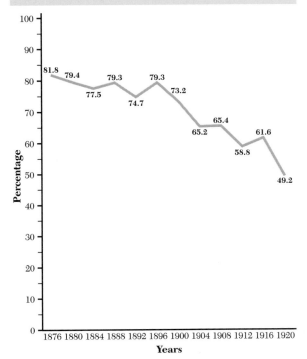

Voter Participation in Presidential Elections, 1876–1920

Margaret Sanger and the Birth Control Movement

Margaret Higgins Sanger, founder of the American Birth Control League (1921), which later became the Planned Parenthood Federation of America.

At the start of the twentieth century, birth control was an issue fraught with social and religious controversy. Devout Christians—Protestants and Catholics—opposed it as a violation of God's law; the overseers of society's moral behavior feared it might foster promiscuity. Theodore Roosevelt said it meant "race death: a sin for which there is no atonement." The Comstock Act of 1873 banned from the U.S. mails all information on birth control, and by 1914 twenty-two states had enacted laws that hindered the dissemination of such information. That year Margaret Sanger formally launched her campaign for birth control.

Born in 1883, Sanger grew up in Corning, New York. Her father, an Irish-born stonecutter, encouraged his children to think for themselves. "Leave the world better because you, my child,

have dwelt in it," he told Margaret. One of eleven children, Margaret from an early age linked poverty to large families. "Our childhood," she said, "was one of longing for things that were always denied."

Longing for excitement and romance, Sanger settled in New York City, married, and had three children. Restless, and finding her marriage confining, she discovered Greenwich Village, a favorite haunt of the period's intense young radicals. There Sanger met Socialist leader Eugene V. Debs; young reporter and revolutionary John Reed, later to be honored by the Bolsheviks and buried in the Kremlin; William D. "Big Bill" Haywood of the radical Industrial Workers of the World (IWW); and feminist and socialist agitator Emma Goldman.

The Village was filled with people determined to improve the world. Stimulated by the exciting talk, Sanger joined the Socialist party and worked to organize women for socialism in New York City. In 1912, she marched in the IWW picket lines in the great strike at the textile mills in Paterson, New Jersey. Pursuing a nursing career, Sanger worked on the lower East Side of New York where of people were crowded into tenement houses. Struck by the ignorance of tenement women about their own bodies, she wrote in 1912 a

series of newspaper articles about venereal disease and personal hygiene, entitled "What Every Girl Should Know"; the Post Office Department banned it from the mails.

That same year Sanger watched at the bedside of Sadie Sachs, a poor working woman dying from a self-induced abortion. Warned that she might not survive another pregnancy, Sachs had asked for contraceptive advice, but the doctor had suggested only that she make her husband sleep on the roof. After Sachs died, Sanger spent hours walking the streets and thinking about birth and children and poverty. She resolved that night, she later said, "to seek out the root of the evil, to do something to change the destiny of mothers whose miseries were as vast as the sky."

The answer was birth control—a term she and several friends coined in 1914. Sanger spent a year absorbing medical opinion and learning about contraceptives, and then began publishing the journal *Woman Rebel* that urged "women to look the whole world in the face with a go-to-hell look in the eyes; to have an ideal; to speak and act in defiance of convention." Aimed at the working class, the journal touched on birth control, but its chief focus was on social revolution, particularly on raising the social consciousness of working women.

It ran for only seven issues before it was banned by the post office. Sanger, indicted under the Comstock Act, fled to Europe.

There, after reflection, she decided that birth control was a medical matter, not a social or revolutionary one. It belonged in the hands of physicians and their patients, with physicians free to prescribe contraception and other measures when appropriate. Women should "decide for themselves whether they shall become mothers, under what conditions, and when." Working through the National Birth Control League and other groups, Sanger broadened the movement's base beyond the socialists and feminists who had originally backed it. Settlement house workers had been cool to birth control at first, but soon they too lent support.

Sanger returned to the United States, and the government, preoccupied with other issues, dropped the indictment against her. In October 1916, again defying the law, she opened the nation's first birth control clinic in the teeming Brownsville section of Brooklyn, New York. Police soon raided the clinic, and Sanger was sentenced to thirty days in jail. The New York State Court of Appeals upheld the sentence, but in a victory for Sanger, it ruled that physicians should have greater discretion in prescribing birth control.

Late in 1916 Sanger formed the New York Birth Control League to push for laws to give physicians even broader discretion. The league's argument that birth control would be an effective means of promoting the social welfare was a persuasive idea that convinced a wide variety of groups. Some reformers thought that smaller families would raise the standard of living of the poor. Other people thought birth control might limit the number of "undesirables" in the population. Eugenicists who wanted to improve the human species through genetic control saw it as a way to reduce the proportion of the unwanted and unfit in the society. Gradually Sanger herself reflected such arguments. "More children from the fit, less from the unfit—that is the chief issue," she said in 1919.

In 1921 Sanger organized the nationwide American Birth Control League; it held clinics and conferences to educate the public. Although the Catholic church remained opposed, the movement spread among Protestants, Jews, and those who did not attend church. In 1940, Eleanor Roosevelt, the popular First Lady, came out in support of family planning, and by the 1940s every state with the exception of Massachusetts and Connecticut had legalized the distribution of birth control information.

When Margaret Sanger died in 1966, the birth control pill had the approval of the Federal Drug Administration, and its use was widespread. The cause she had championed—once thought so shocking and radical—was won in American society.

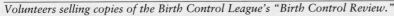

Volunteers selling copies of the Birth Control League's "Birth Control Review."

In city after city reformers reordered municipal government. Tightening controls on corporate activities, they broadened the scope of utility regulation and restricted city franchises. They updated tax assessments, often skewed in favor of corporations, and tried to clean up the electoral machinery. Devoted to efficiency, they developed a trained civil service to oversee planning and operations. The generation of the 1880s also had believed in civil service, but the goal then was mostly negative: to get spoilsmen out and "good" people in. Now the goal was efficiency and, above all, results.

In constructing their model governments, urban reformers often turned to recent advances in business management and organization. They stressed continuity and expertise, a system in which professional experts staffed a government overseen by elective officials. At the top, the elected leader surveyed the breadth of city, state, or national affairs and defined directions. Below, a corps of experts—trained in the various disciplines of the new society—funneled the definition into specific scientifically based policies.

Reformers thus created a growing number of regulatory commissions and municipal departments. They hired engineers to oversee utility and water systems, physicians and nurses to improve municipal health, and city planners to oversee park and highway development. They created specialized "academies" to train police and firefighters. Imitated by the state and federal governments, the proliferation of experts and commissions widened the gap between voters and decision makers but dramatically improved the efficiency of government.

As cities exploded in size, they freed themselves from the tight controls of state legislatures and began to experiment with their own governments. Struggling to recover from a devastating hurricane in 1900, Galveston, Texas, pioneered the commission form of government: a form of municipal government in which commissions of appointed experts, rather than elected officials, ran the city. Wanting nonpartisan expertise, Staunton, Virginia, was the first city to hire a city manager. Other cities followed, and by 1910 over one hundred cities were using either the commission or manager type of government.

In the race for reform, a number of city mayors won national reputations—among them Seth Low in New York City and Hazen S. Pingree in Detroit—working to modernize taxes, clean up politics, lower utility rates, and control the awarding of valuable city franchises. In Toledo, Ohio, Mayor Samuel M. ("Golden Rule") Jones, a wealthy manufacturer, took billy clubs away from the police, established free kindergartens, playgrounds, and night schools, and improved wages for city workers.

In Cleveland, Ohio, Tom L. Johnson demonstrated an innovative approach to city government. A millionaire who had made his fortune manipulating city franchises, Johnson one day read Henry George's *Progress and Poverty* (see Chapter 19) and turned to reform. Elected mayor of Cleveland, he served from 1901 to 1909 and collected a group of aggressive and talented young advisers. Frederic C. Howe, Newton D. Baker, and Edward Bemis—all of whom later won national reputations—shaped Johnson's ideas on taxes, prison reform, utility regulation, and other issues facing the city.

Johnson combined shrewdness and showmanship. Believing in an informed citizenry, he held outdoor meetings in huge tents. He used colorful charts to give Cleveland residents a course in utilities and taxation. He cut down on corruption, cut off special privilege, updated taxes, and gave Cleveland a reputation as the country's best governed city.

Finding it difficult to regulate powerful city utilities and keep their costs down, Johnson and mayors in other cities turned more and more to public ownership of gas, electricity, water, and transportation. Called "gas and water socialism," the idea spread swiftly. In 1896, fewer than half of American cities owned their own waterworks; by 1915, almost two-thirds did.

Action in the States

Reformers soon discovered, however, that many problems lay beyond a city's boundaries, and they turned for action to the state governments. From the 1890s to 1920, reformers worked to stiffen state laws regulating the labor of women and children, to create and strengthen commissions to regulate railroads and utilities, to impose corporate and inheritance taxes, to improve mental and penal institutions, and to allocate more funds for state universities, which were viewed as the training ground for the experts and educated citizenry needed for the new society.

Maryland passed the first workers' compensation law in 1902; soon most industrial states had such legislation. After 1900, many states adopted factory inspection laws, and by 1916, almost two-thirds of the states mandated insurance for the victims of factory accidents. By 1914, twenty-five states had enacted employers' liability laws.

New York was one of the states that led the way in adopting significant reforms. Around 1905, a series of dramatic investigations in the state revealed a systematic and corrupt alliance between politicians and business leaders in the gas, electricity, and insurance industries—all of which directly touched the general public. An angry public responded immediately, supporting greater state regulation and management by independent expert commissions. In 1905 and 1906, the state established regulatory boards to oversee utilities and insurance; it also outlawed corporate contributions to political campaigns and restricted business lobbying in the state legislature.

To regulate business, virtually every state created regulatory commissions empowered to examine corporate books and hold public hearings. Building on earlier experience, state commissions after 1900 were given new power to initiate actions, rather than await complaints, and in some cases to set maximum prices and rates. Dictating company practices, they pioneered regulatory methods later adopted in federal legislation of 1906 and 1910. Some business leaders supported the federal laws in order to get rid of "the intolerable supervision" of dozens of separate state commissions.

Historians have long praised the regulation movement, but the commissions did not always act wisely or even in the public interest. Elective commissions often produced commissioners who had little knowledge of corporate affairs. In addition, to win election, some promised specific rates or reforms, obligations that might bias the commission's investigative functions. Appointive commissions sometimes fared better, but they too had to oversee extraordinarily complex businesses like the railroads. Shaping everything from wages to train schedules, the regulatory commissions affected railroad profits and growth negatively, and in the end, damaged the railroad industry.

To the progressives, commissions offered a way to end the corrupt alliance between business and politics. There was another way, too, and that was to "democratize" government by reducing the power of politicians and increasing the influence of the electorate. To do that, progressives backed three measures to make officeholders responsive to popular will: the initiative, which allowed voters to propose new laws; the referendum, which allowed them to accept or reject a law at the ballot box; and the recall, which gave them a way to remove an elected official from office.

Oregon adopted the initiative and referendum in 1902; by 1912, twelve states had them. That year Congress added the Seventeenth Amendment to the Constitution to provide for the direct election of U.S. senators. By 1916, all but three states had direct primaries, which allowed the people, rather than nominating conventions, to choose candidates for office.

As attention shifted from the cities to the states, reform governors throughout the country earned greater visibility. Joseph Folk, Steffens's hero in Saint Louis, became the governor of Missouri in 1904. Hiram Johnson won fame in California for his shrewd and forceful campaign against the Southern Pacific Railroad. In the East, the cause of reform was upheld by Charles Evans Hughes in New York and Woodrow Wilson, the former president of Princeton University, in New Jersey.

Robert M. La Follette became the most famous reform governor. A graduate of the University of Wisconsin, La Follette served three terms in Congress during the late 1880s. A staunch Republican, he supported the tariff and other Republican doctrines but the Democratic landslide of 1890 turned him out of office. Moving to state politics, he became interested in reform, spurred in part, as so many were, by the depression of the 1890s. In 1901, he became governor of Wisconsin. Then forty-five years old, La Follette was talented, aggressive, and a superb stump speaker.

In the following six years, he put together the "Wisconsin Idea," one of the most important reform programs in the history of state government. He established an industrial commission, the first in the country, to regulate factory safety and sanitation. He improved education, workers' compensation, public utility controls, and

The most famous of the reform leaders in the states was Wisconsin's Robert M. "Fighting Bob" La Follette, pictured here campaigning in Cumberland, Wisconsin, in 1897.

resource conservation. He lowered railroad rates and raised railroad taxes. Under La Follette's prodding, Wisconsin became the first state to adopt a direct primary for all political nominations. It also became the first to adopt a state income tax.

Like other progressives, La Follette drew on expert advice and relied on academic figures like Richard Ely and Edward Ross at the University of Wisconsin. La Follette supporters established the first Legislative Reference Bureau in the university's library; the bureau stocked the governor and his allies with facts and figures to support the measures they wanted. Theodore Roosevelt called La Follette's Wisconsin "the laboratory of democracy," and the "Wisconsin Idea" soon spread to many other states, including New York, California, Michigan, Iowa, and Texas.

After 1905, the progressives looked more and more to Washington. For one thing, Teddy Roosevelt was there, with his zest for publicity and alluring grin. But progressives also had a growing sense that many concerns—corporations and conservation, factory safety and child labor—crossed state lines. Federal action seemed desirable; specific reforms fit into a larger plan perhaps best seen from the nation's center. Within a few years, La Follette and Hiram Johnson became senators, and while reform went

on back home, the focus of progressivism shifted to Washington.

THE REPUBLICAN ROOSEVELT

In September 1901, President William McKinley died of gunshot wounds (see Chapter 20); Vice President Theodore Roosevelt succeeded him in the White House. McKinley and Roosevelt had moved in similar directions, and the new president initially vowed to carry on McKinley's policies. He continued some, developed others of his own, and in the end brought to them all the particular exuberance of his own personality.

At age forty-two, Roosevelt was then the youngest president in American history. In contrast to the dignified McKinley, he was open, aggressive, and high-spirited. At his desk by 8:30 every morning, he worked through the day, usually with visitors for breakfast, lunch, and dinner. Politicians, labor leaders, industrialists, poets, artists, and writers paraded through the White House.

In personal conversation Roosevelt was persuasive and charming. He read widely and he held opinions on every issue—literature, art, marriage, divorce, conservation, business, football, and even spelling. An advocate of simplified spelling, he once instructed government printers to use "thru" for "through" and "dropt" for "dropped." Public opposition forced him to withdraw the order, and shortly afterward, as he was watching a naval review in Long Island Sound, a launch marked "Pres Bot" steamed by. Roosevelt laughed with delight.

If McKinley cut down on presidential isolation, Roosevelt virtually ended it. The presidency, he thought, was "the bully pulpit," a forum of ideas and leadership for the nation. The president was "a steward of the people bound actively and affirmatively to do all he could for the people." Self-confident, Roosevelt enlisted talented associates, including Elihu Root, secretary of war and later secretary of state; William Howard Taft, secretary of war; Gifford Pinchot, the nation's chief forester and leading conservationist; and Oliver Wendell Holmes, Jr., whom he named to the Supreme Court.

In 1901, Roosevelt invited Booker T. Washington, the prominent African American educator, to dinner at the White House. Many Southerners protested—"a crime equal to treason," a newspaper said—and they protested again when Roosevelt appointed several African Americans to important federal offices in South Carolina and Mississippi. At first Roosevelt considered building a biracial "black-and-tan" southern Republican party, thinking it would foster racial progress and his own renomination in 1904. He denounced lynching and ordered the Justice Department to act against peonage.

But Roosevelt soon retreated. In some areas of the South, he supported "lily-white" Republican organizations, and his policies often reflected his own belief in African American inferiority. He said nothing when a race riot broke out in Atlanta in 1906, although twelve persons died. He joined others in blaming African American soldiers stationed near Brownsville, Texas, after a night of violence there in August 1906. Acting quickly and on little evidence, he discharged "without honor" three companies of African American troops. Six of the soldiers who were discharged held the Congressional Medal of Honor.

Busting the Trusts

"There is a widespread conviction in the minds of the American people that the great corporations known as trusts are in certain of their features and tendencies hurtful to the general welfare," Roosevelt reported to Congress in 1901. Like most people, however, the president wavered on the trusts. Large-scale production and industrial growth, he believed, were natural and beneficial; they needed only to be controlled. Still he distrusted the trusts' impact on local enterprise and individual opportunity. Distinguishing between "good" and "bad" trusts, he pledged to protect the former while controlling the latter.

At first, Roosevelt hoped the combination of investigative journalism and public opinion would be enough to uncover and correct business evils, and in public he both praised and attacked the trusts. Mr. Dooley poked fun at his wavering: "'Th' trusts,' says he, 'are heejous monsthers built up be th' enlightened intherprise iv th' men that have done so much to advance progress in our beloved country,' he says. 'On wan hand I wud

stamp thim undher fut; on th' other hand not so fast.'"

In 1903, Roosevelt asked Congress to create a Department of Commerce and Labor, with a Bureau of Corporations empowered to investigate corporations engaged in interstate commerce. Congress balked; Roosevelt called in reporters, and in an off-the-record interview, charged that John D. Rockefeller had organized the opposition to the measure. The press spread the word, and in the outcry that followed, the proposal passed easily in a matter of weeks. Roosevelt was delighted. With the new Bureau of Corporations publicizing its findings, he thought, the glare of publicity would eliminate most corporate abuses.

Roosevelt also undertook direct legal action. On February 18, 1902, he instructed the Justice Department to bring suit against the Northern Securities Company for violation of the Sherman Antitrust Act. It was a shrewd move. A mammoth holding company, Northern Securities controlled the massive rail networks of the Northern Pacific, Great Northern, and Chicago, Burlington & Quincy railroads. Some of the most prominent names in business were behind the giant company—J. P. Morgan and Company; the Rockefeller interests; Kuhn, Loeb and Company; and railroad operators James J. Hill and Edward H. Harriman.

Shocked by Roosevelt's action, Morgan charged that the president had not acted like a "gentleman," and Hill talked glumly of having "to fight for our lives against the political adventurers who have never done anything but pose and draw a salary." Morgan rushed to Washington to complain and to ask whether there were plans to "attack my other interests," notably U.S. Steel. "No," Roosevelt replied, "unless we find out they have done something that we regard as wrong."

In 1904, the Supreme Court, in a five to four decision, upheld the suit against Northern Securities and ordered the company dissolved. Roosevelt was jubilant, and he followed up the victory with several other antitrust suits. In 1902, he had moved against the beef trust, an action applauded by western farmers and urban consumers alike. After a lull, he initiated suits in 1906 and 1907 against the American Tobacco Company, the Du Pont Corporation, the New Haven Railroad, and Standard Oil.

A 1904 Puck *cartoon depicts TR as "Jack the Giant-Killer," battling the Wall Street titans. Actually, Roosevelt dissolved relatively few trusts.*

But Roosevelt's policies were not always clear, nor his actions always consistent. He invited Morgan to the White House to confer with him and allowed the president of National City Bank to preview a draft of the president's third annual message to Congress. Roosevelt also asked for (and received) business support in his bid for reelection in 1904. Large donations came in from industrial leaders, and Morgan himself later testified that he gave $150,000 to Roosevelt's campaign. In 1907, acting in part to avert a threatened financial panic, the president permitted Morgan's U.S. Steel to absorb the Tennessee Coal and Iron Company, an important competitor.

Roosevelt, in truth, was not a "trust-buster," although he was frequently called that. William Howard Taft, his successor in the White House, initiated forty-three antitrust indictments in four years—nearly twice as many as the twenty-five Roosevelt initiated in the seven years of his presidency. Instead, Roosevelt used antitrust threats to keep businesses within bounds. Regulation, he believed, was a better way to control large-scale enterprise.

"Square Deal" in the Coalfields

A few months after announcing the Northern Securities suit, Roosevelt intervened in a major labor dispute involving the anthracite coal miners of northeastern Pennsylvania. Led by John Mitchell, a moderate labor leader, the United Mine Workers demanded wage increases, an eight-hour workday, and company recognition of the union. The coal companies refused, and in May 1902, 140,000 miners walked off the job. The mines closed.

As the months passed and the strike continued, coal prices rose. With winter coming on, schools, hospitals, and factories ran short of coal. Public opinion turned against the companies. Morgan and other industrial leaders privately urged them to settle, but George F. Baer, head of one of the largest companies, refused: "The rights and interests of the laboring man," Baer said, "will be protected and cared for—not by the labor agitators, but by the Christian men to whom God in his infinite wisdom has given the control of the property interests of this country."

Roosevelt was furious. Complaining of the companies' arrogance, he invited both sides in the dispute to an October 1902 conference at the White House. There, Mitchell took a moderate tone and offered to submit the issues to arbitration, but the companies again refused to budge. Roosevelt ordered the army to prepare to seize the mines and then leaked word of his intent to Wall Street leaders.

Alarmed, Morgan and others again urged settlement of the dispute, and at last the companies retreated. They agreed to accept the recommendations of an independent commission the president would appoint. In late October, the strikers returned to work, and in March 1903, the commission awarded them a 10 percent wage increase and a cut in working hours. It recommended, however, against union recognition. The coal companies, in turn, were encouraged to raise prices to offset the wage increase.

More and more, Roosevelt saw the federal government as an honest and impartial "broker" between powerful elements in society. Rather than leaning toward labor, he pursued a middle way to curb corporate and labor abuses, abolish privilege, and enlarge individual opportunity. Conservative by temperament, he sometimes backed reforms in part to head off more radical measures.

During the 1904 campaign, Roosevelt called his actions in the coal miners' strike a "square deal" for both labor and capital, a term that stuck to his administration. His actions stood in powerful contrast to Grover Cleveland's in the 1894 Pullman strike (see Chapter 20). Roosevelt was not the first president to take a stand for labor, but he was the first to bring opposing sides in a labor dispute to the White House to settle it. He was the first to threaten to seize a major industry, and he was the first to appoint an arbitration commission whose decision both sides agreed to accept.

Another Term

In the election of 1904, the popular Roosevelt soundly drubbed his Democratic opponent, Alton B. Parker of New York, and the Socialist party candidate, Eugene V. Debs of Indiana. Roosevelt attracted a large campaign chest and won votes everywhere. In a landslide victory, he received 57 percent of the vote to Parker's 38 percent, and on election night, he savored the public's confidence. Overjoyed, he pledged that "under no circumstances will I be a candidate for or accept another nomination," a statement he later regretted.

Following his election, Roosevelt in late 1904 laid out a reform program that included railroad regulation, employers' liability for federal employees, greater federal control over corporations, and laws regulating child labor, factory inspection, and slum clearance in the District of Columbia. He turned first to railroad regulation. In 1903, he had worked with Congress to pass the Elkins Act to prohibit railroad rebates and increase the powers of the Interstate Commerce Commission (ICC). The Elkins Act, a moderate law, was framed with the consent of railroad leaders. In 1904 and 1905, the president wanted much more, and he urged Congress to empower the ICC to set reasonable and nondiscriminatory rates and prevent inequitable practices.

The Election of 1904			
Candidate	*Party*	*Popular Vote*	*Electoral Vote*
T. Roosevelt	Republican	7,626,593	336
Parker	Democrat	5,082,898	140
Debs	Socialist	402,489	0
Swallow	Prohibition	258,596	0

Widespread demand for railroad regulation strengthened Roosevelt's hand. In the Midwest and Far West, the issue was a popular one, and reform governors La Follette in Wisconsin and Albert B. Cummins in Iowa urged federal action. Roosevelt maneuvered cannily. As the legislative battle opened, he released figures showing that Standard Oil had reaped $750,000 a year from railroad rebates. He also skillfully traded congressional support for a strong railroad measure in return for his promise to postpone a reduction of the tariff, a stratagem that came back to plague President Taft.

Triumph came with passage of the Hepburn Act of 1906. A significant achievement, the act strengthened the rate-making power of the Interstate Commerce Commission. It increased membership on the ICC from five to seven, empowered it to fix reasonable maximum railroad rates, and broadened its jurisdiction to include oil pipeline, express, and sleeping car companies. ICC orders were binding, pending any court appeals, thus placing the burden of proof of injustice on the companies. Delighted, Roosevelt viewed the Hepburn Act as a major step in his plan for continuous expert federal control over industry.

Soon he was dealing with two other important bills, these aimed at regulating the food and drug industries. Muckraking articles had touched frequently on filthy conditions in meat-packing houses, but Upton Sinclair's *The Jungle* (1906) set off a storm of indignation. Ironically, Sinclair had set out to write a novel about the packing-house workers, the "wage slaves of the Beef Trust," hoping to do for wage slavery what Harriet Beecher Stowe had done for chattel slavery. But readers largely ignored his story of the workers and seized instead on the graphic descriptions of the things that went into their meat:

> There would be meat stored in great piles in rooms; and the water from leaky roofs would drip over it, and thousands of rats would race about on it. It was too dark in these storage places to see well, but a man could run his hand over these piles of meat and sweep off handfuls of the dried dung of rats. These rats were nuisances, and the packers would put poisoned bread out for them; they would die, and then rats, bread, and meat would go into the hoppers together.

Sinclair was disappointed at the reaction. "I aimed at the public's heart," he later said, "and by accident I hit it in the stomach." He had, indeed. After reading *The Jungle*, Roosevelt ordered an investigation. The result, he said, was "hideous," and he threatened to publish the entire "sickening report" if Congress did not act. Meat sales plummeted in the United States and Europe. Demand for reform grew. Alarmed, the meat packers themselves supported a reform law, which they hoped would be just strong enough to still the clamor. The Meat Inspection Act of 1906, stronger than the packers wanted, set rules for sanitary meat packing and government inspection of meat products.

A second measure, the Pure Food and Drug Act, passed more easily. Samuel Hopkins Adams, a muckraker, exposed the dangers of patent medicines in several sensational articles in *Collier's*. Patent medicines, Adams pointed out, contained mostly alcohol, drugs, and "undiluted fraud." Dr. Harvey W. Wiley, the chief chemist in the Department of Agriculture, led a "poison squad" of young assistants who experimented with the medicines. With evidence in hand, Wiley pushed for regulation; Roosevelt and the recently reorganized American Medical Association joined the fight, and the act passed on June 30, 1906. Requiring manufacturers to list certain ingredients on the label, it represented a pioneering effort to ban the manufacture and sale of adulterated, misbranded, or unsanitary food or drugs.

An expert on birds, Roosevelt loved nature

The Pure Food and Drug Act, passed in 1906, did not ban the sale of patent medicines, nor did it curb the exaggerated claims of some of the manufacturers. Reid's Cough and Kidney Remedy, for example, promised relief within 20 minutes from colds, coughs, bronchitis, hoarseness, whooping cough, asthma, and kidney disease. The makers of the drug complied with the Pure Food and Drug Act by noting on the bottle's label that the remedy contained 30 percent grain alcohol.

and the wilderness, and some of his most enduring accomplishments came in the field of conservation. Working closely with Gifford Pinchot, chief of the Forest Service, he established the first comprehensive national conservation policy. He undertook a major reclamation program, created the federal Reclamation Service, and strengthened the forest preserve program in the Department of Agriculture. Broadening the concept of conservation, he placed power sites, coal lands, and oil reserves as well as national forest in the public domain.

When Roosevelt took office in 1901, there were 45 million acres in government preserves. In 1908, there were almost 195 million. That year, he called a National Conservation Congress attended by forty-four governors and hundreds of experts. Roosevelt formed the National Commission on the Conservation of Natural Resources to look after waters, forests, lands, and minerals. With Pinchot as head, it drew up an inventory of the nation's natural resources.

As 1908 approached, Roosevelt became increasingly strident in his demand for sweeping reforms. He attacked "malefactors of great wealth," urged greater federal regulatory powers, criticized the conservatism of the federal courts, and called for laws protecting factory workers. Many business leaders blamed him for a severe financial panic in the autumn of 1907, and conservatives in Congress stiffened their opposition. Divisions between Republican conservatives and progressives grew.

Immensely popular, Roosevelt prepared in 1908 to turn over the White House to William Howard Taft, his close friend and colleague. "The Roosevelt policies will not go out with the Roosevelt administration," a party leader said. "If Taft weakens, he will annihilate himself." As expected, Taft soundly defeated the Democratic standard-bearer William Jennings Bryan, who

was making his third try for the presidency. The Republicans retained control of Congress. Taft prepared to move into the White House, ready and willing to carry on the Roosevelt legacy.

THE ORDEAL OF WILLIAM HOWARD TAFT

The Republican national convention that nominated Taft had not satisfied either Roosevelt or Taft. True, Taft won the presidential nomination as planned, but conservative Republicans beat back the attempts of progressive Republicans to influence the convention. They named a conservative, James S. Sherman, for vice president, and built a platform that reflected conservative views on labor, the courts, and other issues. Taft want-

The Election of 1908			
Candidate	Party	Popular Vote	Electoral Vote
Taft	Republican	7,676,258	321
Bryan	Democrat	6,406,801	162
Debs	Socialist	420,380	0
Chafin	Prohibition	252,821	0

ed a pledge to lower the tariff but got only a promise of revision, which might lower—or raise—it. La Follette, Cummins, Jonathan P. Dolliver of Iowa, Albert J. Beveridge of Indiana, and other progressive Republicans were openly disappointed.

Taking office in 1909, Taft felt "just a bit like a fish out of water." The son of a distinguished Ohio family and a graduate of Yale Law School, he became an Ohio judge, solicitor general of the United States, and a judge of the federal circuit court. In 1900, McKinley asked him to head the Philippine Commission, charged with the difficult and challenging task of forming a civil government in the Philippines. Later Taft was named the first governor general of the Philippines. In 1904, Roosevelt appointed him secretary of war. In all these positions, Taft made his mark as a skillful administrator. He worked quietly behind the scenes, avoided controversy, and shared none of Roosevelt's zest for politics. A good-natured man, Taft had personal charm and infectious humor. He fled from fights rather than seeking them out and disliked political maneuvering, preferring instead quiet solitude. "I don't like politics," he said. "I don't like the limelight."

Weighing close to 300 pounds, Taft enjoyed conversation, golf and bridge, good food, and plenty of rest. Compared to the hard-working Roosevelt and Wilson, he was lazy. He was also honest, kindly, and amiable, and in his own way he knew how to get things done. Reflective, he preferred the life of a judge, but his wife, Helen H. Taft, who enjoyed politics, prodded him toward the White House. When a Supreme Court appointment opened in 1906, Taft reluctantly turned it down. "Ma wants him to wait and be president," his youngest son said.

Taft's years as president were not happy. Mrs. Taft's health soon collapsed, and as it turned out, Taft presided over a Republican party torn with tensions that Roosevelt had either brushed aside or concealed. The tariff, business regulation, and other issues split conservatives and progressives and Taft often wavered or sided with the conservatives. Taft revered the past and distrusted change; although an ardent supporter of Roosevelt, he never had Roosevelt's faith in the ability of government to impose reform and alter individual behavior. He named five corporation attorneys to his cabinet, leaned more to business than to labor, and spoke of a desire to "clean out the unions."

At that time and later, Taft's reputation suffered by comparison to the flair of Roosevelt and the moral majesty of Woodrow Wilson. He deserved better. Taft was an honest and sincere president, who—sometimes firm, sometimes befuddled—faced a series of important and troublesome problems during his term of office.

Party Insurgency

Taft started his term with an attempt to curb the powerful Republican Speaker of the House, Joseph "Uncle Joe" Cannon of Illinois. Using the powers of his position, Cannon had been setting House procedures, appointing committees, and virtually dictating legislation. Straightforward and crusty, he often opposed reform. In March 1909, thirty Republican congressmen joined Taft's effort to curb Cannon's power, and the president sensed success. But Cannon retaliated and, threatening to block all tariff bills, forced a compromise. Taft stopped the anti-Cannon campaign in return for Cannon's pledge to help with tariff cuts.

Republicans were divided over the tariff, and there was a growing party insurgency against high rates. The House quickly passed a bill providing for lower rates, but in the Senate, protectionists raised them. Senate leader Nelson W. Aldrich of Rhode Island introduced a revised bill that added over eight hundred amendments to the rates approved in the House. It placed no duties on curling stones, false teeth, canary-bird seed, and hog bristles, which brought a chuckle from Mr. Dooley. "Th' new Tariff Bill," he said, "put these familyar commodyties within th' reach iv all."

Angry, La Follette and other Republicans attacked the bill as the child of special interests. In speeches on the Senate floor they called themselves "progressives," invoked Roosevelt's name, and urged Taft to defeat the high-tariff proposal. Caught between protectionists and progressives, Taft wavered, then tried to compromise. In the end, he backed Aldrich. The Payne-Aldrich Act, passed in November 1909, called for higher rates than the original House bill, though it lowered them from the Dingley Tariff of 1897 (see

Chapter 20). An unpopular law, Payne-Aldrich helped discredit Taft and revealed the tensions in the Republican party.

Republican progressives and conservatives drifted apart. Thin-skinned, Taft resented the persistent pinpricks of the progressives who criticized him for virtually everything he did. He tried to find middle ground but leaned more and more toward the conservatives. During a nationwide speaking tour in the autumn of 1909, he praised Aldrich, scolded the low-tariff insurgents, and called the Payne-Aldrich Act "the best bill that the Republican party ever passed." Traveling through the Midwest, he pointedly ignored La Follette, Cummins, and other progressive Republicans.

By early 1910, progressive Republicans in Congress no longer looked to Taft for leadership. As before, they challenged Cannon's power, and Taft wavered. In an outcome embarrassing to the president, the progressives won, managing to curtail Cannon's authority to dictate committee assignments and schedule debate. In progressive circles there was growing talk of a Roosevelt return to the White House.

The Ballinger-Pinchot Affair

The conservation issue dealt another blow to relations between Roosevelt and President Taft. In 1909, Richard A. Ballinger, Taft's secretary of the interior, offered for sale a million acres of public land that Pinchot, who had stayed on as Taft's chief forester, had withdrawn from sale. Pinchot, fearing that Ballinger would hurt conservation programs, protested and, seizing on a report that Ballinger had helped sell valuable Alaskan coal lands to a syndicate that included J. P. Morgan, asked Taft to intervene. After investigating, Taft supported Ballinger on every count, although he asked Pinchot to remain in office.

Pinchot refused to drop the matter. Behind the scenes, he provided material for two anti-Ballinger magazine articles, and he wrote a critical public letter that Senator Dolliver of Iowa read to the Senate. Taft had had enough. He fired the insubordinate Pinchot which, though appropriate, again lost support for Taft. Although a conservationist himself, the president had fired one of the nation's leading conservationists.

Newspapers followed the controversy for months, and muckrakers assailed the administration's "surrender" to Morgan and other "despoilers of the national heritage."

The Ballinger-Pinchot controversy obscured Taft's important contributions to conservation. He won from Congress the power to remove lands from sale, and he used it to conserve more land than Roosevelt did. Still, the controversy tarred Taft, and it upset his old friend Roosevelt. Pinchot hurried to Italy where Roosevelt was on tour; he talked again with Roosevelt within days of the ex-president's arrival home in June 1910.

Taft's Final Years

Interested in railroad regulation, Taft backed a bill in 1910 to empower the ICC to fix maximum railroad rates. Progressive Republicans favored that plan but attacked Taft's suggestion of a special Commerce Court to hear appeals from ICC decisions because most judges were traditionally conservative in outlook and usually rejected attempts to regulate railroad rates. They also thought the railroads had been consulted too closely in drawing up the bill. Democratic and Republican progressives tried to amend the bill to strengthen it; Taft made support of it a test of party loyalty.

The Mann-Elkins Act of 1910 gave something to everyone. It gave the ICC power to set rates, stiffened long- and short-haul regulations, and placed telephone and telegraph companies under ICC jurisdiction. These provisions delighted progressives. The act also created a Commerce Court, pleasing conservatives. In a trade-off, conservative Republican Senate leaders pledged their support for a statehood bill for Arizona and New Mexico, which were both predicted to be Democratic. In return, enough Democratic senators promised to vote for the Commerce Court provision to pass the bill. While pleased with the act, Taft and the Republican party lost further ground. In votes on key provisions of the Mann-Elkins Act, Taft raised the issue of party regularity, and progressive Republicans defied him.

Withholding patronage, Taft attempted to defeat the progressive Republicans in the 1910 elections. He helped form antiprogressive organizations, and he campaigned against progressive

Drawn by C. R. Weed.

"WELL!—MY HUSBAND WILL HAVE TO PAY AN INCOME TAX!"

According to this cartoon, payment of the new income tax was evidence of privileged status.

Republican candidates for the Senate. In California, he opposed Hiram Johnson, the progressive Republican champion; in Wisconsin, the home of La Follette, he sent Vice President James S. Sherman to take control of the state convention. Progressive Republicans retaliated by organizing a nationwide network of anti-Taft Progressive Republican Clubs.

The 1910 election results were a major setback for Taft and the Republicans—especially conservative Republicans. A key issue in the election, the high cost of living, gave an edge to the progressive wings in both major parties, lending support to their attack on the tariff and the trusts. In party primaries, progressive Republicans overwhelmed most Taft candidates, and in the general election, they tended to fare better than the conservatives, which increased progressive influence in the Republican party.

For Republicans of all persuasions, however, it was a difficult election. The Democrats swept the urban-industrial states from New York to Illinois. New York, New Jersey, Indiana, and even Taft's

Ohio elected Democratic governors. For the first time since 1894, Republicans lost control of both the House and the Senate. In all, they lost fifty-eight seats in the House and ten in the Senate. Disappointed, Taft called it "not only a landslide, but a tidal wave and holocaust all rolled into one general cataclysm."

Despite the defeat, Taft pushed through several important measures before his term ended. With the help of the new Democratic House, he backed laws to regulate safety in mines and on railroads, create a Children's Bureau in the federal government, establish employers' liability for all work done on government contracts, and mandate an eight-hour workday for government workers.

In 1909, Congress initiated a constitutional amendment authorizing an income tax which, along with woman suffrage, was one of the most significant legislative measures of the twentieth century. The Sixteenth Amendment took effect early in 1913. A few months later, an important progressive goal was realized when the direct election of senators was ratified as the Seventeenth Amendment to the Constitution.

An ardent supporter of competition, Taft relentlessly pressed a campaign against trusts. The Sherman Antitrust Act, he said in 1911, "is a good law that ought to be enforced, and I propose to enforce it." That year, the Supreme Court in cases against Standard Oil and American Tobacco established the "rule of reason," which allowed the Court to determine whether a business presented "reasonable" restraint on trade. Taft thought the decisions gave the Court too much discretion, and he pushed ahead with the antitrust effort.

In October 1911, he sued U.S. Steel for its acquisition of the Tennessee Coal and Iron Company in 1907. Roosevelt had approved the acquisition (see p. 706), and the suit seemed designed to impugn his action. Enraged, he attacked Taft, and Taft, for once, fought back. He accused Roosevelt of undermining the conservative tradition in the country and began working to undercut the influence of the progressive Republicans. Increasingly now, Roosevelt listened to anti-Taft Republicans who urged him to run for president in 1912. In the following months, he sounded Republican sentiment for a presidential bid. In February 1912, he announced, "My hat is in the ring."

Differing Philosophies in the Election of 1912

Delighted Democrats looked on as Taft and Roosevelt fought for the Republican nomination. As the incumbent president, Taft controlled the party machinery, and when the Republican convention met in June 1912, he took the nomination. In early July, the Democrats met in Baltimore and, confident of victory for the first time in two decades, struggled through forty-six ballots before finally nominating Woodrow Wilson, the reform-minded governor of New Jersey.

A month later some of the anti-Taft and progressive Republicans—now calling themselves the Progressive party—whooped it up in Chicago. Roosevelt was there to give a stirring "Confession of Faith" and listen to the delegates sing:

> *Thou wilt not cower in the dust,*
>   *Roosevelt, O Roosevelt!*
> *Thy gleaming sword shall never rust,*
>   *Roosevelt, O Roosevelt!*

Naming Roosevelt for president, the Progressive—soon known as the "Bull Moose"—party convention set the stage for the first important three-cornered presidential contest since 1860.

Saddened, Taft was out of the running before the campaign even began. "I think I might as well give up so far as being a candidate is concerned," he said in July. "There are so many people in the country who don't like me." Taft stayed at home and made no speeches before the election. Roosevelt campaigned strenuously, even completing one speech after being shot in the chest by an anti-third-term fanatic. "I have a message to deliver," he said, "and will deliver it as long as there is life in my body."

Roosevelt's message involved a program he called the New Nationalism. An important phase in the shaping of twentieth-century American political thought, it demanded a national approach to the country's affairs and a strong president to deal with them. The New Nationalism called for efficiency in government and society. It exalted the executive and the expert, urged social-justice reforms to protect workers, women, and children, and accepted "good" trusts. The New Nationalism encouraged large concentrations of labor and capital, serving the nation's interests under a forceful federal executive.

For the first time in the history of a major political party, the Progressive campaign enlisted women in its organization. Jane Addams, the well-known settlement worker, seconded Roosevelt's nomination at Chicago, and she and other women played a leading role in his campaign. Some labor leaders, who saw potential for union growth, and some business leaders, who saw relief from destructive competition and labor strife, supported the new party.

Wilson, in contrast, set forth a program called the New Freedom that emphasized business competition and small government. A states' rights Democrat, he wanted to rein in federal authority, using it only to sweep away special privilege, release individual energies, and restore competition. Drawing on the thinking of Louis D. Brandeis, the brilliant shaper of reform-minded law, he echoed the Progressive party's social-justice objectives, while continuing to attack Roosevelt's planned state. For Wilson, the vital issue was not a planned economy but a free one. "The history of liberty is the history of the limitation of governmental power...," he said in October 1912. "If America is not to have free

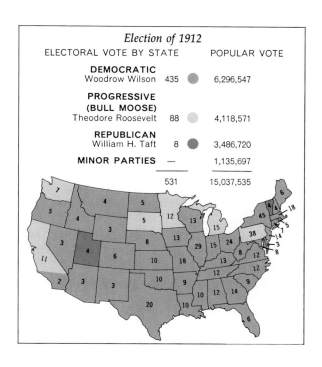

Election of 1912

ELECTORAL VOTE BY STATE		POPULAR VOTE
DEMOCRATIC Woodrow Wilson	435	6,296,547
PROGRESSIVE (BULL MOOSE) Theodore Roosevelt	88	4,118,571
REPUBLICAN William H. Taft	8	3,486,720
MINOR PARTIES	—	1,135,697
	531	15,037,535

enterprise, then she can have freedom of no sort whatever."

In the New Nationalism and New Freedom, the election of 1912 offered competing philosophies of government. Both Roosevelt and Wilson saw the central problem of the American nation as economic growth and its effect on individuals and society. Both focused on the government's relation to business; both believed in bureaucratic reform; and both wanted to use government to protect the ordinary citizen. But Roosevelt welcomed federal power, national planning, and business growth; Wilson distrusted them all.

On Election Day, Wilson won 6.3 million votes to 4.1 million for Roosevelt (who had recovered quickly from his wound) and 900,000 for Eugene V. Debs, the Socialist party candidate. Taft, the incumbent president, finished third with 3.5 million votes; he carried only Vermont and Utah for 8 electoral votes. The Democrats also won outright control of both houses.

WOODROW WILSON'S NEW FREEDOM

If under Roosevelt social reform took on the excitement of a circus, "under Wilson it acquired the dedication of a sunrise service." Born in Virginia in 1856, and raised in the South, Wilson was the son of a Presbyterian minister. As a young man, he wanted a career in public service, and he trained himself carefully in history and oratory. At age sixteen he became intrigued by the English parliamentary system, a fascination that shaped his scholarly career and perhaps his diplomacy in the First World War (see Chapter 24). A moralist, he reached judgments easily. Once reached, almost nothing shook them. Opponents called him stubborn and smug. "He gives me the creeps," a Maryland ward boss said. "The time I met him, he said something to me, and I didn't know whether God or him was talking."

After graduating from Princeton University and the University of Virginia Law School, Wilson found that practicing law bored him. Shifting to history, from 1890 to 1902 he served as professor of jurisprudence and political economy at Princeton. In 1902, he became president of the university. Eight years later, he was governor of New Jersey, where he led a campaign to reform election procedures, abolish corrupt practices, and strengthen railroad regulation.

Wilson's rise was rapid, and he knew relatively little about national issues and personalities. But he learned fast, and in some ways the lack of experience served him well. He had few political debts to repay, and he brought fresh perspectives to older issues. Ideas intrigued Wilson; details bored him. Although he was outgoing at times, he could also be cold and aloof, and aides soon learned that he preferred loyalty and flattery to candid criticism.

Prone to self-righteousness, Wilson often turned differences of opinion into bitter personal quarrels. Like Roosevelt, he believed in strong presidential leadership. A scholar of the party system, he cooperated closely with Democrats in Congress, and his legislative record placed him among the most effective presidents in terms of passing bills that he supported. Forbidding in individual conversation, Wilson could move crowds with graceful oratory. Unlike Taft, and to a greater degree than Roosevelt, he could inspire.

His inaugural address was eloquent. "The Nation," he said, "has been deeply stirred, stirred by a solemn passion, stirred by the knowledge of wrong, of ideals lost, of government too often debauched and made an instrument of evil. The feelings with which we face this new age of right and opportunity sweep across our heartstrings like some air out of God's own presence."

The New Freedom in Action

On the day of his inauguration, Wilson called Congress into special session to lower the tariff. When the session opened on April 8, 1913, Wilson himself was there, the first president since John Adams in 1801 to appear personally before Congress. In forceful language, he urged Congress to reduce tariff rates.

As the bill moved through Congress, Wilson showed exceptional skill. He worked closely with congressional leaders, and when lobbyists threatened the bill in the Senate, he appealed for popular support. The result was a triumph for Wilson and the Democratic party. The Underwood Tariff Act passed in 1913. The first tariff cut in nineteen years, it lowered rates about 15 percent and removed duties from sugar, wool, and several other consumer goods.

To make up for lost revenue, the act also levied a modest graduated income tax, authorized under the just ratified Sixteenth Amendment. Marking a significant shift in the American tax structure, it imposed a 1 percent tax on individuals and corporations earning more than $4,000 annually and an additional 1 percent tax on incomes over $20,000. Above all, the act reflected a new unity within the Democratic party which, unlike its experience under Grover Cleveland, had worked together to pass a difficult tariff law.

Wilson himself emerged as an able leader. "At a single stage," a foreign editor said, "[he went] from the man of promise to the man of achievement." Encouraged by his success, Wilson decided to keep Congress in session through the hot Washington summer. Now he focused on banking reform, and the result in December 1913 was the Federal Reserve Act, the most important domestic law of his administration.

Meant to provide the United States with a sound yet flexible currency, the act established the country's first efficient banking system since Andrew Jackson killed the Second Bank of the United States in 1832 (see Chapter 10). It created twelve regional banks, each to serve the banks of its district. The regional banks answered to a Federal Reserve Board, appointed by the president, which governed the nationwide system.

A compromise law, the act blended public and private control of the banking system. Private bankers owned the federal reserve banks but answered to the presidentially appointed Federal Reserve Board. The reserve banks were authorized to issue currency and through the discount rate—the interest rate at which they loaned money to member banks—could raise or lower the amount of money in circulation. Monetary affairs no longer depended solely on the price of gold. Within a year, nearly half the nation's banking resources were in the Federal Reserve System.

The Clayton Antitrust Act (1914) completed Wilson's initial legislative program. Like previous antitrust measures, it reflected confusion over how to discipline a growing economy without putting a brake on output. In part it was a response to the revelations of the Pujo Committee of the House, publicized by Brandeis in a disquieting series of articles, "Other People's Money."

In its investigation of Wall Street, the committee discovered a pyramid of money and power capped by the Morgan-Rockefeller empire that, through "interlocking directorates," controlled companies worth $22 billion, over one-tenth of the national wealth.

The Clayton Act outlawed such directorates and prohibited unfair trade practices. It forbade pricing policies that created monopoly, and it made corporate officers personally responsible for antitrust violations. Delighting Samuel Gompers and the labor movement, the act declared that unions were not conspiracies in restraint of trade, outlawed the use of injunctions in labor disputes unless necessary to protect property, and approved lawful strikes and picketing. To Gompers's dismay, the courts continued to rule against union activity.

A related law established a powerful Federal Trade Commission to oversee business methods. Composed of five members, the commission could demand special and annual reports, investigate complaints, and order corporate compliance, subject to court review. At first, Wilson opposed the commission concept, which was an approach more suitable to Roosevelt's New Nationalism, but he changed his mind and, along with Brandeis, called it the cornerstone of his antitrust plan. To reassure business leaders, he appointed a number of conservatives to the new commission and to the Federal Reserve Board.

In November 1914, Wilson proudly announced the completion of his New Freedom program. Tariff, banking, and antitrust laws promised a brighter future, he said, and it was now "a time of healing because a time of just dealing." Many progressives were aghast. To think society's ills were so easily cured, the *New Republic* said, "casts suspicion either upon his own sincerity or upon his grasp of the realities of modern social and industrial life."

Retreat and Advance

Distracted by the start of war in Europe, Wilson gave less attention to domestic issues for over a year. When he returned to concern with reform, he adopted more and more of Roosevelt's New Nationalism and blended it with the New Freedom to set it off from his earlier policies.

One of Wilson's problems was the Congress. To his dismay, the Republicans gained substantially in the 1914 elections. Reducing the Democratic majority in the House, they swept key industrial and farm states. At the same time, a recession struck the economy, which had been hurt by the outbreak of the European war in August 1914. Some business leaders blamed the tariff and other New Freedom laws. On the defensive, Wilson soothed business sentiment and invited bankers and industrialists to the White House. He allowed companies fearful of antitrust actions to seek advice from the Justice Department.

Preoccupied with such problems, Wilson blocked significant action in Congress through most of 1915. He refused to support a bill providing minimum wages for women workers, sidetracked a child labor bill on the ground that it was unconstitutional, and opposed a bill to establish long-term credits for farmers. He also refused to endorse woman suffrage, arguing that the right to vote was a state, not a federal matter.

Wilson's record on race disappointed African Americans and many progressives. He had appealed to African American voters during the 1912 election, and a number of African American leaders campaigned for him. Soon after the inauguration, Oswald Garrison Villard, a leader of the NAACP, proposed a National Race Commission to study the problem of race relations. Initially sympathetic, Wilson rejected the idea because he feared he might lose southern Democratic votes in Congress. A Virginian himself, he appointed many Southerners to high office, and for the first time since the Civil War, southern views on race dominated the nation's capital.

At one of Wilson's first cabinet meetings, the postmaster general proposed the segregation of all African Americans in the federal service. No one dissented, including Wilson. Several government bureaus promptly began to segregate workers in offices, shops, rest rooms, and restaurants. Employees who objected were fired. African American leaders protested, and they were joined by progressive leaders and clergymen. Surprised at the protest, Wilson backed quietly away from the policy, although he continued to insist that segregation benefited African Americans.

As the year 1916 began, Wilson made a dramatic switch in focus and again pushed for substantial reforms. The result was a virtual river of reform laws, which was significant because it began the second, more national-minded phase of the New Freedom. With scarcely a glance over his shoulder, Wilson embraced important portions of Roosevelt's New Nationalism campaign.

In part, he was motivated by the approaching presidential election. A minority president, Wilson owed his victory in 1912 to the split in the Republican party, now almost healed. Roosevelt was moving back into Republican ranks, and there were issues connected with the war in Europe that he might use against Wilson (see Chapter 24). Moreover, many progressives were voicing disappointment with Wilson's limited reforms and his failure to support more advanced reform legislation such as farm credits, child labor, and woman's suffrage.

Moving quickly to patch up the problem, Wilson named Brandeis to the Supreme Court in January 1916. Popular among progressives, Brandeis was also the first person of Jewish faith to serve on the Court. When conservatives in the Senate tried to defeat the nomination, Wilson stood firm and won, earning further praise from progressives, Jews, and others. In May, he reversed his stand on farm loans and accepted a rural credits bill to establish farm-loan banks backed by federal funds. The Federal Farm Loan Act of 1916 created a Federal Farm Loan Board to give farmers credit similar to the Federal Reserve's benefits for trade and industry.

Wilson was already popular within the labor movement. Going beyond Roosevelt's policies, which had sought a balance between business and labor, he defended union recognition and collective bargaining. In 1913, he appointed William B. Wilson, a respected leader of the United Mine Workers, as the first head of the Labor Department, and he strengthened the department's Division of Conciliation. In 1914, in Ludlow, Colorado, state militia and mine guards fired machine guns into a tent colony of coal strikers, killing twenty-six men, women, and children. Outraged, Wilson stepped in and used federal troops to end the violence while negotiations to end the strike went on.

In August 1916, a threatened railroad strike again revealed Wilson's sympathies with labor. Like Roosevelt, he invited the two sides to the

Miners in Ludlow, Colorado, went on strike in September 1913 for better working conditions and union recognition. Expecting eviction from company housing, they built a tent colony near the company town. The company, Colorado Fuel and Iron Company, hired guards to break the strike. On April 20, 1914, the guards sprayed the tents with gunfire, then soaked the tents with kerosene and set the colony afire.

White House where he urged the railroad companies to grant an eight-hour day and labor leaders to abandon the demand for overtime pay. Labor leaders accepted the proposal; railroad leaders did not. "I pray God to forgive you, I never can," Wilson said as he left the room. Soon he signed the Adamson Act (1916) that imposed the eight-hour day on interstate railways and established a federal commission to study the railroad problem. Ending the threat of a strike, the act marked a milestone in the expansion of the federal government's authority to regulate industry.

With Wilson leading the way, the flow of reform legislation continued until the election. The Federal Workmen's Compensation Act established workers' compensation for government employees. The Keating-Owen Act, the first federal child labor law, prohibited the shipment in interstate commerce of products manufactured by children under the age of fourteen. It too expanded the authority of the federal government, though it was soon struck down by the Supreme Court. The Warehouse Act, similar to the subtreasury proposal the Populists urged in the 1890s (see Chapter 20), authorized licensed warehouses to issue negotiable receipts for farm products deposited with them.

In September, Wilson signed the Tariff Commission Act creating an expert commission to recommend tariff rates. The same month, the Revenue Act of 1916 boosted income taxes and furthered tax reform. Four thousand members of the National American Woman Suffrage Association cheered when Wilson finally came out in support of woman suffrage. Two weeks later he endorsed the eight-hour day for all the nation's workers.

The 1916 presidential election was close, but Wilson won it on the issues of peace and progressivism (see Chapter 24). By the end of 1916, he and the Democratic party had enacted most of the important parts of Roosevelt's Progressive party platform of 1912. To do it, Wilson abandoned portions of the New Freedom and accepted much of the New Nationalism, including greater federal power and commissions governing trade and tariffs. In mixing the two programs, he blended some of the competing doctrines of the Progressive Era, established the primacy of the federal government, and foreshadowed the pragmatic outlook of Franklin D. Roosevelt's New Deal.

The election of 1916 showed how deeply progressivism had reached into American society. Candidates were vying for the reform-minded vote; the party of Grover Cleveland had become the party of Woodrow Wilson and, soon thereafter, of Franklin D. Roosevelt. "We have in four years," Wilson said that fall, "come very near to carrying out the platform of the Progressive party as well as our own; for we are also progressives."

In retrospect, however, 1916 also marked the beginning of progressivism's sad decline into the 1920s. At most, the years of progressive reform lasted from the 1890s to 1921, and in large measure they were compressed into a single decade between 1906 and American entry into World War I. Many problems the progressives addressed, they did not solve; and some important ones, like race, they did not even tackle. Yet their regulatory commissions, direct primaries, city improvements, and child labor laws marked an era of important and measured reform.

The institution of the presidency expanded. From the White House radiated executive departments that guided a host of activities. Independent commissions, operating within flexible laws, supplemented executive authority.

These developments owed a great deal to both Roosevelt (TR) and Wilson. To manage a complex society, TR developed a simple formula: expert advice; growth-minded policies; a balancing of business, labor, and other interests; the use of publicity to gather support; and stern but often permissive oversight of the economy. TR strengthened the executive office, and he called on the newer group of professional, educated, public-minded citizens to help him. "I believe in a strong executive," he said; "I believe in power."

At first, Wilson had different ideas, wanting to dismantle much of Roosevelt's governing apparatus. But driven by outside forces and changes in his own thinking, Wilson soon moved in directions similar to those Roosevelt had championed. Starting out to disperse power, he eventually consolidated it. Against his earlier policies, Wilson created a Federal Trade Commission to oversee business, a Tariff Commission to regulate overseas trade, and a powerful Federal Reserve Board to control money and banking.

Through such movements, government at all levels accepted responsibility for the welfare of various elements in the social order. A reform-minded and bureaucratic society took shape, in which men and women, labor and capital, political parties and social classes competed for shares in the expansive framework of twentieth-century life. But there were limits to reform. As both TR and Wilson found, the new government agencies, understaffed and underfinanced, depended on the responsiveness of those they sought to regulate.

Soon there was a far darker cloud on the horizon. The spirit of progressivism rested on a belief in human potential, peace, and progress. After Napoleon's defeat in 1815, a century of peace began in western Europe, and as the decades

CHRONOLOGY

1894 National Municipal League formed to work for reform in cities

1900 Galveston, Texas, is first city to try commission form of government

1901 Theodore Roosevelt becomes president • Robert M. La Follette elected reform governor of Wisconsin • Doctors reorganize the American Medical Association • Socialist party of America organized

1902 Roosevelt sues the Northern Securities Company for violation of Antitrust Act • Coal miners in northeastern Pennsylvania strike • Maryland is first state to pass workers' compensation law • Oregon adopts the initiative and referendum

1904 Roosevelt elected president

1906 Hepburn Act strengthens ICC • Upton Sinclair attacks meat-packing industry in *The Jungle* • Congress passes Meat Inspection Act and Pure Food and Drug Act

1908 Taft elected president • Supreme Court upholds Oregon law limiting working hours for women in *Muller* v. *Oregon*

1909 Payne-Aldrich Tariff Act divides Republican party

1910 Mann-Elkins Act passed to regulate railroads • Taft fires Gifford Pinchot, head of U.S. Forest Service • Democrats sweep midterm elections

1912 Progressive party formed; nominates Roosevelt for president • Woodrow Wilson elected president

1913 Underwood Tariff Act lowers rates • Federal Reserve Act reforms U.S. banking system • Sixteenth Amendment authorizes Congress to collect taxes on incomes

1914 Clayton Act strengthens antitrust legislation

1916 Wilson wins reelection

1918 Supreme Court strikes down federal law limiting child labor in *Hammer* v. *Dagenhart*

1920 Nineteenth Amendment gives women the right to vote

passed, war seemed a dying institution. "It looks as though this were going to be the age of treaties rather than the age of wars," an American said in 1912, "the century of reason rather than the century of force." It was not to be. Two years later, the most devastating of wars broke out in Europe, and in 1917, Americans were fighting on the battlefields of France.

Recommended Reading

George Mowry, *The Era of Theodore Roosevelt* (1958) and Arthur S. Link, *Woodrow Wilson and the Progressive Era* (1954), trace the social and economic conditions of the period. See also Henry F. Pringle's biography, *Theodore Roosevelt* (1931), John M. Blum's perceptive and brief *The Republican Roosevelt* (1954), and William H. Harbaugh's thoughtful *The Life and Times of Theodore Roosevelt,* rev. ed. (1975). Donald E. Anderson, *William Howard Taft* (1973), and Paolo E. Coletta, *The Presidency of William Howard Taft* (1973), study Taft. The definitive biography of Wilson is Arthur S. Link, *Wilson,* 5 vols. (1947–1965).

Samuel P. Hays offers an influential interpretation of progressivism in *Conservation and the Gospel of Efficiency* (1959). Albro Martin, *Enterprise Denied: Origins of the Decline of American Railroads, 1897–1917* (1971), argues persuasively that reformers damaged as well as regulated. Samuel Haber, *The Quest for Authority and Honor in the American Professions, 1750–1900* (1991) examines the changing nature of the professions. Intellectual currents are traced in Charles Forcey, *The Crossroads of Liberalism* (1961); social-justice reforms in Harold U. Faulkner, *The Quest for Social Justice, 1898–1914* (1931); and the important tax issue in Clifton K. Yearley, *The Money Machines* (1970).

Additional Bibliography

On specific issues, see O. E. Anderson, *The Health of a Nation: Harvey W. Wiley and the Fight for Pure Food* (1958); James Harvey Young, *Pure Food: Securing the Federal Food and Drugs Act of 1906* (1989); James G. Burrow, *Organized Medicine in the Progressive Era* (1977); Morris J. Vogel, *The Invention of the Modern Hospital: Boston, 1870–1930* (1980); Craig West, *Banking Reform and the Federal Reserve, 1863–1923* (1977); Eugene Nelson White, *The Regulation and Reform of the American Banking System, 1900–1929* (1983); James Livingston, *Origins of the Federal Reserve System* (1986); Stanley P. Caine, *The Myth of a Progressive Reform: Railroad Regulation in Wisconsin, 1903–1910* (1970); William J. Reese,

Power and the Promise of School Reform: Grass-Roots Movements During the Progressive Era (1986); Aileen Kraditor, *The Ideas of the Woman Suffrage Movement, 1890–1920* (1981); Christine A. Lunardini, *From Equal Suffrage to Equal Rights: Alice Paul and the National Woman's Party, 1910–1928* (1986); Susan Lehrer, *Origins of Protective Labor Legislation for Women, 1905–1925* (1987); David W. Southern, *The Malignant Heritage: Yankee Progressives and the Negro Question, 1901–1914* (1968); James H. Timberlake, *Prohibition and the Progressive Crusade* (1963); and Walter I. Trattner, *Crusade for the Children* (1970).

See also Paul Russell Cutright, *Theodore Roosevelt: The Making of a Conservationist* (1985); Linda G. Ford, *Iron-Jawed Angels: The Suffrage Militancy of the National Women's Party, 1912–1920* (1991); Ruth Rosen, *The Lost Sisterhood: Prostitution in America, 1900–1918* (1982), and *Women and Temperance* (1980); David J. Pivar, *Purity Crusade* (1973); and Norman H. Clark, *Deliver Us from Evil: An Interpretation of American Prohibition* (1976).

On politics, see George E. Mowry, *Theodore Roosevelt and the Progressive Movement* (1946); Richard L. McCormick, *The Party Period and Public Policy: American Politics from the Age of Jackson to the Progressive Era* (1986); Michael E. McGerr, *The Decline of Popular Politics* (1986); Kenneth W. Hechler, *Insurgency: Personalities and Politics of the Taft Era* (1940); David Sarasohn, *The Party of Reform: Democrats in the Progressive Era* (1989); Norman M. Wilensky, *Conservatives in the Progressive Era: The Taft Republicans of 1912* (1965); David H. Burton, *The Learned Presidency: Theodore Roosevelt, William Howard Taft, Woodrow Wilson* (1988); Francis L. Broderick, *Progressivism at Risk: Electing a President in 1912* (1989); George Juergens, *News from the White House: The Presidential-Press Relationship in the Progressive Era* (1981); and L. J. Holt, *Congressional Insurgents and the Party System, 1909–1916* (1967).

Helpful biographies include Edmund Morris, *The Rise of Theodore Roosevelt* (1979); William Manners, *TR and Will* (1969); G. Wallace Chessman, *Theodore Roosevelt and the Politics of Power* (1969); John M. Blum, *Woodrow Wilson and the Politics of Morality* (1962); John M. Mulder, *Woodrow Wilson: The Years of Preparation* (1978); Kendrick A. Clements, *Woodrow Wilson* (1987); Niels Aage Thorsen, *The Political Thought of Woodrow Wilson, 1875–1910* (1988); Henry F. Pringle, *Life and Times of William Howard Taft,* 2 vols. (1939); Robert F. Wesser, *Charles Evans Hughes* (1967); David P. Thelen, *Robert M. La Follette and the Insurgent Spirit* (1976); Fred Greenbaum, *Robert Marion La Follette* (1975); Philippa Strum, *Louis D. Brandeis* (1984); and

Alpheus Thomas Mason, *Brandeis: A Free Man's Life* (1946).

On urban reform, see John D. Buenker, *Urban Liberalism and Progressive Reform* (1973); Roy M. Lubove, *The Progressive and the Slums* (1962); William H. Wilson, *The City Beautiful Movement* (1989); Kevin J. Christiano, *Religious Diversity and Social Change: American Cities, 1890–1906* (1987); and Martin J. Schiesl, *The Politics of Efficiency* (1977). Also, Robert M. Crunden, *Ministers of Reform: The Progressives' Achievements in American Civilization, 1889–1920* (1982); Peter J. Coleman, *Progressivism and the World of Reform* (1987); James T. Patterson, *America's Struggle Against Poverty, 1900–1980* (1981); and Stephen Skowronek, *Building a New American State: The Expansion of National Administrative Capacities, 1877–1920* (1982). Bradley R. Rice, *Progressive Cities* (1977), is helpful.

Books on specific cities include Melvin Holli, *Reform in Detroit: Hazen S. Pingree and Urban Politics* (1969); Carl V. Harris, *Political Power in Birmingham, 1871–1921* (1977); James B. Crooks, *Politics and Progress: The Rise of Urban Progressivism in Baltimore, 1895–1911* (1968); Zane L. Miller, *Boss Cox's Cincinnati* (1968); and Jack Tager, *The Intellectual as Urban Reformer: Brand Whitlock and the Progressive Movement* (1968).

Statewide movements are covered in George E. Mowry's influential study, *The California Progressives* (1951); Spencer C. Olin, Jr., *California's Prodigal Sons: Hiram Johnson and the Progressives, 1911–1917* (1968); David P. Thelen, *The New Citizenship: Origins of Progressivism in Wisconsin, 1885–1900* (1972); Herbert Margulies, *The Decline of the Progressive Movement in Wisconsin, 1890–1920* (1968); Ransom E. Noble, Jr., *New Jersey Progressivism Before Wilson* (1946); John F. Reynolds, *Testing Democracy: Electoral Behavior and Progressive Reform in New Jersey, 1880–1920* (1988); James Wright, *The Progressive Yankees: Republican Reformers in New Hampshire, 1906–1916* (1987); Richard L. McCormick, *From Realignment to Reform: Political Change in New York State, 1893–1910* (1981); Sheldon Hackney, *Populism to Progressivism in Alabama* (1969); Richard M. Abrams, *Conservatism in a Progressive Era: Massachusetts Politics, 1900–1912* (1964); and H. L. Warner, *Progressivism in Ohio, 1897–1917* (1964).

For intellectual currents, see Bruce Kuklick, *The Rise of American Philosophy* (1977); John M. O'Donnell, *The Origins of Behaviorism: American Psychology, 1870–1920* (1985); George Cotkin, *William James: Public Philosopher* (1990); Daniel W. Bjork, *William James: The Center of His Vision* (1988); Robert B. Westbrook, *John Dewey and American Democracy* (1991); Joseph Brent, *Charles Sanders Peirce: A Life* (1993); Aileen S. Kraditor, *The Radical Persuasion, 1890–1917* (1981); Edward Abrahams, *The Lyrical Left: Randolph Bourne, Alfred Stieglitz, and the Origins of Cultural Radicalism in America* (1986); L. Glen Seretan, *Daniel De Leon: The Odyssey of an American Marxist* (1979); Elliott Shore, *Talkin' Socialism* (1988); John Thompson, *Closing the Frontier: Radical Response in Oklahoma, 1889–1923* (1986); Gary Marks, *Unions in Politics* (1989); and Nick Salvatore, *Eugene V. Debs: Citizen and Socialist* (1982).

Contemporary accounts include Herbert Croly, *The Promise of American Life* (1909); Walter Lippmann, *Drift and Mastery* (1914); William Allen White, *The Old Order Changeth* (1910) and *The Autobiography of William Allen White* (1946); and Charles Seymour, ed., *The Intimate Papers of Colonel House*, 4 vols. (1926–1928).

LAW & SOCIETY III

Muller v. Oregon

Expanding the Definition of Acceptable Evidence

On September 4, 1905, which happened to be Labor Day, the manager of the Grand Laundry in Portland, Oregon, the city's finest hand laundry, ordered the women who worked there to stay past the normal time, in violation of a 1903 Oregon law that barred women in factories and laundries from working more than ten hours a day. Emma Gotcher, one of the women, complained, and Curt Muller, the laundry's owner, was arrested, found guilty, and fined $10. When the Oregon Supreme Court upheld the law, Muller, with backing from business groups interested in overturning it, appealed to the U.S. Supreme Court.

Alarmed, several women in Oregon flashed word of the appeal to Florence Kelley, head of the National Consumers' League, an organization in New York City dedicated to bettering the lot of women and children. Kelley immediately saw the danger. If the Supreme Court struck down the Oregon law, similar laws in nineteen other states would be in jeopardy, along with other reform legislation as well.

Kelley needed a topflight attorney to defend the law, so she and Josephine Goldmark, the League's research director, went first to Joseph H. Choate, one of the country's most famous lawyers. But Choate was puzzled why the two women were even there. What did he, busy as he was, have to do with some Oregon law regulating the number of hours a woman could work?

"A law *prohibiting* more than ten hours a day in laundry work," he boomed. "Big, strong, laundry women. Why shouldn't they work longer?"

Getting out of Choate's office as fast as she could, Kelley turned to Goldmark: "That's over, thank God. Tomorrow we'll go to Boston."

In Boston was Louis D. Brandeis, Goldmark's brother-in-law and an attorney renowned for his work for reform. Brandeis had not always been very interested in reform. Once a prosperous corporate lawyer, he, like so many others, had changed his outlook during the depression of the 1890s. Human misfortune sharpened his social conscience, and soon Brandeis became known as the "people's attorney," a fighter against corporate abuses and political corruption.

To Brandeis, the law was a living, evolving thing, not just law books and legal precedents, but part of the present—changing, growing, responsive to current needs. He liked a poem of James Russell Lowell's:

New times demand new issues and new men,
*   The world advances, and in time out-*
*   grows the laws*
That in our fathers' time were best;
*   And, doubtless, after us some purer*
*   scheme*
Will be shaped out by wiser men than we,—
*   Made wiser by the steady growth of*
*   truth.*

Evolving, the law should reflect not abstract philosophy but actual facts, carefully gathered and "scientifically" interpreted. In this, Brandeis mirrored the outlook of his progressive generation: define the problem, collect the facts bearing on it, and devise a solution.

At first glance, however, the facts in the *Muller* case posed some major difficulties. For one thing, Brandeis had barely a month to get ready before the case came before the Court.

Even more troublesome, the Court in the case of *Lochner* v. *New York* (1905) had just struck down a New York state law setting maximum hours for bakery workers, calling it a wrongful

721

Laundry owner Curt Muller, standing in the laundry doorway with his arms folded, challenged an Oregon law limiting the length of the working day for women.

attempt "to regulate the hours of labor between the master and his employees." In trying to justify the law, the Court held, the state of New York had not shown enough of a link between the law and the health of the bakers. The *Lochner* decision heartened conservatives who were tired of progressive reforms; *Muller,* they thought, with all its similarities to the New York case, must surely be decided in the same way.

But there was an opening in *Lochner,* and both Kelley and Brandeis saw it at once. They had to do for *Muller* what the state of New York had failed to do for the bakers. They had to link the Oregon law squarely to the safety and welfare of the women it covered.

The way to do that, they thought, was to offer the Court detailed evidence showing the effects of long hours of labor on women. Enlisting ten women from various reform groups in New York City, Kelley and Goldmark haunted the city's libraries. "In these days of abundant tools of research," Goldmark recalled decades later, "the paucity of our means seems almost laughable." Using pencils and loose-leaf notebooks, the researchers combed reports from American and European factory inspectors, medical commissions, labor unions, economists, and social workers. A young medical student gathered statistics

on the hygiene of occupations. As the evidence piled up, it was taken to Boston, where Brandeis organized it in the legal brief he would present to the Court.

That brief, the "Brandeis brief," was soon famous worldwide. In a dramatic departure from prior custom, it included only two pages of traditional legal precedents. Fifteen pages were devoted to showing that other states and countries believed long hours of labor affected women's health. The brief closed with nearly a hundred pages on "The World's Experience upon which the Legislation Limiting the Hours of Labor for Women is Based."

"Long hours of labor are dangerous for women primarily because of their special physical organization," the brief argued, citing as proof eleven authorities, including a British parliamentary committee, reports of the Nebraska and Massachusetts bureaus of labor statistics, and medical handbooks. "The evil effect of overwork before as well as after marriage upon childbirth is marked and disastrous." Nine authorities supported that conclusion, and six more said that "Accidents to working women occur most frequently at the close of the day, or after a long period of uninterrupted work."

According to twenty-three sources, "When the

Lawyer Louis D. Brandeis used sociological data to defend the Oregon law limiting women's working hours when he argued the case before the Supreme Court. This portrait photograph of Brandeis was taken just after he was appointed to the Supreme Court by President Woodrow Wilson in 1916.

the Oregon law infringed on a woman's right to hire out her labor. The law, he suggested, did not protect women but instead discriminated against them. "[W]e may regret that all women may not be sheltered in happy homes, free from the exacting demands upon them in pursuit of a living, but their right to pursue any honorable vocation . . . is just as sacred . . . as the same right enjoyed by men."

Brandeis, as usual, was eloquent and imposing in rebuttal. Building from the evidence in his brief, he argued it was "common knowledge" that women differed from men, a line of reasoning that makes interesting reading today:

> *In structure and function women are differentiated from men. Besides these anatomical and physiological differences, physicians are agreed that women are fundamentally weaker than men in all that makes for endurance: in muscular strength, in nervous energy, in the powers of persistent attention and application. Overwork, therefore, which strains endurance to the utmost, is more disastrous to the health of women than of men, and entails upon them more lasting injury.*

Women, more than men, Brandeis argued, felt the strain of modern industry, and when the health of a nation's women was injured, it imperiled the future of the nation and "the race."

In its decision a few weeks later, the Court agreed unanimously with Brandeis, even taking the unusual step of mentioning him by name. It was "obvious," the Court said in upholding the Oregon law, that "woman's physical structure and the performance of maternal functions place her at a disadvantage in the struggle for subsistence."

> *This is especially true when the burdens of motherhood are upon her . . . and as healthy mothers are essential to vigorous offspring, the physical well-being of woman becomes an object of public interest and care in order to preserve the strength and vigor of the race.*
>
> *Still again, history discloses the fact that woman has always been dependent upon man. He established his control at*

health of women has been injured by long hours, . . . the deterioration is handed down to succeeding generations. . . . The overwork of future mothers thus directly attacks the welfare of the nation." Long hours also kept women from their housework, the brief argued, and with little time for leisure or home life, they sought relief in alcohol "and other excesses." "I have noticed that the hard, slavish overwork is driving those girls into the saloons. . . ," a male mill worker was quoted as saying.

Brandeis's "authorities" would not satisfy standards today, but they were the best he had, and he cited over ninety of them on the link between the number of hours worked and a person's physical and moral well-being. It all seemed very "scientific," though Brandeis wanted to title his brief "What Any Fool Knows."

On January 15, 1908, five days after the brief was finished and rushed to Washington, the Supreme Court heard the arguments in the case. Muller's attorney took a traditional tack, arguing from legal precedent—including *Lochner*—that

the outset by superior physical strength, and this control in various forms, with diminishing intensity, has continued to the present. . . . Doubtless there are individual exceptions, and there are many respects in which she has an advantage over him; but looking at it from the view point of the effort to maintain an independent position in life, she is not upon an equality.

Set off by such matters from men, the Court concluded, "[woman] is properly placed in a class by herself, and legislation designed for her protection may be sustained, even when like legislation is not necessary for men and could not be sustained."

The decision in hand, Brandeis, Kelley, and other reformers celebrated. Kelley, who had done so much to shape the case, called it "epoch-making," and Goldmark spoke of the "incalculable benefit it bestows on working women." "There have been," a leading journal said, "military victories acclaimed with the ringing of bells and with bonfires that have had no more significance for the future of the land than this sober decision. It is, in brief, that American women can be protected by law against commercial greed. . . . Although nominally a Constitutional question, it is really a vast social question that the Court has answered."

Muller soon became a landmark in the history of American law and the Supreme Court, one of the most famous and influential cases ever argued. The "Brandeis brief," based on sociological and other data rather than on legal precedent, influenced lawyers, courts, and legislatures across the country. "Far and wide this little volume spread its message of humanity and hope," Goldmark wrote. "Gone was the deadening weight of legal precedent. A movement to extend and strengthen women's hour legislation spread over the country."

Goldmark in a sense was right, but there were those who raised questions about just what *Muller* in fact had accomplished. That famous "Brandeis brief," after all, had classified women as different, dependent, and subordinate, a judgment with which the Supreme Court had clearly agreed. Reformers like Kelley and Goldmark tended to accept parts of this, believing, as

Goldmark once said, that "women *as women* should have certain safeguards secured by law, that women need special legislation."

But other people did not accept it, including a number who were devoted to improving women's rights. Had not Brandeis, they asked, invited a Supreme Court composed entirely of men to agree that women were the "weaker" sex, dependent on men like themselves for protection and safekeeping? Had *Lochner* and *Muller* been decided in different ways simply because one involved men and the other women? Why did Brandeis's arguments and the Court's decision touch so little on the welfare of women themselves and instead focus on women as mothers and homemakers? Wasn't there a tendency in that to view women as property rather than as people on a par with men? Were women, or any group in society for that matter, benefited or harmed from securing special consideration under the law?

Questions of this sort about *Muller* have mounted through the years. While some people have continued to praise the decision as a breakthrough for women and reform, others have called it "crudely patronizing" and "romantic paternalism," arguing that measures like the Oregon law made women "the virtual victims of a form of protection that in practice perpetuated their dependency." Critics have also noted that legislatures and employers, in some cases using *Muller* itself, have "protected" women right out of their jobs.

Ruth Bader Ginsburg, just the second woman to sit on the Supreme Court, has recently noted that "From a contemporary perspective, *Muller* v. *Oregon* has been described as a 'roadblock to full equality for women.'"

In the decade after *Muller,* Brandeis, Kelley, and their allies won other important court decisions using similar methods. Their briefs, filled with the kind of so-called scientific data Brandeis had used, grew longer and longer, in some cases reaching a thousand pages or more. Florence Kelley continued to fight for special protection for women, rejecting the arguments of "topsy-turvy" feminists, as she called them, until her death in 1932 at the age of seventy-two. In 1916, Brandeis himself was appointed to the Supreme Court, and sociological jurisprudence of the kind he pioneered continued to play a large role in legal thinking. Among other instances, it strongly influenced the Supreme Court's 1954 ruling in *Brown* v. *Board of Education* to end segregation in the nation's public schools.

Back in Portland, Oregon, meanwhile, the story of *Muller* v. *Oregon* had taken another twist. The Supreme Court having ruled against him, Curt Muller fired the women who worked in the laundry and hired men instead.

The Nation at War

LET'S KEEP THE GLOW IN OLD GLORY AND THE FREE IN FREEDOM TOO

On the morning of May 1, 1915, the German government took out the following important advertisement in the *New York World* as a warning to Americans and other voyagers setting sail for England:

NOTICE—

Travellers intending to embark on the Atlantic voyage are reminded that a state of war exists between Germany and her allies and Great Britain and her allies; that the zone of war includes the waters adjacent to the British Isles; that, in accordance with formal notice given by the Imperial German Government, vessels flying the flag of Great Britain, or of any of her allies, are liable to destruction in those waters and that travellers sailing in the war zone on ships of Great Britain or her allies do so at their own risk.

At 12:30 that afternoon, the British steamship *Lusitania* set sail from New York to Liverpool. Secretly, it carried a load of ammunition as well as passengers.

The steamer was two hours late in leaving, but it held several speed records and could easily make up the time. The passenger list of 1,257 was the largest since the outbreak of war in Europe. Alfred G. Vanderbilt, the millionaire sportsman, was aboard; so were Charles Frohman, a famous New York theatrical producer, and Elbert Hubbard, a popular writer who jested that a submarine attack might help sell his new book. While some passengers chose the *Lusitania* for speed, others liked the modern staterooms, more comfortable than the older ships of the competing American Line.

Six days later, the *Lusitania,* back on schedule, reached the coast of Ireland. German U-boats were known to patrol these dangerous waters. When the war began in 1914, Great Britain imposed a naval blockade of Germany. In return, Germany in February 1915 declared the area around the British Isles a war zone; all enemy vessels, armed or unarmed, were at risk. Germany

had only a handful of U-boats, but the submarines were a new and frightening weapon. On behalf of the United States, President Woodrow Wilson protested the German action, and on February 10 he warned Germany of its "strict accountability" for any American losses resulting from U-boat attacks.

Off Ireland, the passengers lounged on the deck of the *Lusitania.* As if it were peacetime, the ship sailed straight ahead, with no zigzag maneuvers to throw off pursuit. But the submarine U-20 was there, and the commander, seeing a large ship, fired a single torpedo. Seconds after it hit, a boiler exploded and blew a hole in the *Lusitania*'s side. The ship listed immediately, hindering the launching of lifeboats, and in eighteen minutes it sank. Nearly 1,200 people died, including 128 Americans. As the ship's bow lifted and went under, the U-20 commander for the first time read the name: *Lusitania.*

The sinking, the worst since the *Titanic* went down with 1,500 people in 1912, horrified Americans. Theodore Roosevelt called it "an act of piracy" and demanded war. On the French front, the Germans had just introduced poison gas, another alarming new weapon, and there were reports of German atrocities in Belgium. Still, most Americans wanted to stay out of war; like Wilson, they hoped negotiations could solve the problem. "There is such a thing," Wilson said a few days after the sinking, "as a man being too proud to fight. There is such a thing as a nation being so right that it does not need to convince others by force."

In a series of diplomatic notes, Wilson demanded a change in German policy. The first *Lusitania* note (May 13, 1915) called on Germany to abandon unrestricted submarine warfare, disavow the sinking, and compensate for lost American lives. Germany sent an evasive reply, and Wilson drafted a second *Lusitania* note (June 9) insisting on specific pledges. Fearful the demand would lead to war, Secretary of State William Jennings Bryan resigned rather than sign the note. Wilson sent it anyway and followed with a third note (July 21)—almost an ultimatum—warning Germany that the United States would view similar sinkings as "deliberately unfriendly."

Unbeknownst to Wilson, Germany had already ordered U-boat commanders not to sink passen-

With the sinking of the Lusitania, the American people learned first-hand of the horrors of total war. President Wilson's decision to protest the incident through diplomacy kept the United States out of the war—but only temporarily.

ger liners without warning. In August 1915, a U-boat mistakenly torpedoed the British liner *Arabic,* killing two Americans. Wilson protested, and Germany, eager to keep the United States out of the war, backed down. The *Arabic* pledge (September 1) promised that U-boats would stop and warn liners, unless they tried to resist or escape. Germany also apologized for American deaths on the *Arabic,* and for the rest of 1915, U-boats hunted freighters, not passenger liners.

Although Wilson's diplomacy had achieved his immediate goal, the *Lusitania* and *Arabic* crises contained the elements that led to war. Trade and travel tied the world together, and Americans no longer hid behind safe ocean barriers. New weapons, such as the submarine, strained old rules of international law. But while Americans sifted the conflicting claims of Great Britain and Germany, they hoped for peace. A generation of progressives, inspired with confidence in human progress, did not easily accept war.

Wilson also hated war, but he found himself caught up in a worldwide crisis that demanded the best in American will and diplomacy. In the end, diplomacy failed, and in April 1917, the United States entered a war that changed the nation's history.

A NEW WORLD POWER

As they had in the late nineteenth century, Americans after 1900 continued to pay relatively little attention to foreign affairs. Newspapers and magazines ran stories every day about events abroad, but people paid closer attention to what was going on at home. As Walter Lippmann, one of this century's most outstanding political commentators, once said, "I cannot remember taking any interest whatever in foreign affairs until after the outbreak of the First World War."

For Americans at the time, foreign policy was something to be left to the president in office, an attitude the presidents themselves favored. Foreign affairs became an arena in which they could exert a free hand largely unchallenged by Congress or the courts, and Roosevelt, Taft, and Wilson all took advantage of the opportunity to do so.

The foreign policy they pursued from 1901 to 1920 was aggressive and nationalistic. During these years, the United States intervened in Europe, the Far East, and Latin America. It dominated the Caribbean.

In 1898, the United States left the peace table possessing the Philippines, Puerto Rico, and

Guam. Holding distant possessions required a colonial policy; it also required a change in foreign policy, reflecting an outward approach. From the Caribbean to the Pacific, policymakers paid attention to issues and countries they had earlier ignored. Like other nations in these years, the United States built a large navy, protected its colonial empire, and became increasingly involved in international affairs.

The nation also became more and more involved in economic ventures abroad. Turning out goods from textiles to steel, mass production industries sold products overseas, and financiers invested in Asia, Africa, Latin America, and Europe. During the years between the Spanish-American War and World War I, investments abroad rose from $445 million to $2.5 billion. While investments and trade never wholly dictated American foreign policy, they fostered greater involvement in foreign lands.

"I Took the Canal Zone"

Convinced the United States should take a more active international role, Theodore Roosevelt spent his presidency preparing the nation for world power. Along with Secretary of War Elihu Root, he modernized the army, using lessons learned from the war with Spain. Roosevelt and Root established the Army War College, imposed stiff tests for the promotion of officers, and in 1903 created a general staff to oversee military planning and mobilization. Determined to end dependence on the British fleet, Roosevelt doubled the strength of the navy during his term in office.

Stretching his authority to the limits, Roosevelt took steps to consolidate the country's new position in the Caribbean and Central America. European powers, which had long resisted American initiatives there, now accepted American supremacy. Preoccupied with problems in Europe and Africa, Great Britain agreed to U.S. plans for an isthmian canal in Central America and withdrew much of its military force from the area.

Roosevelt wanted a canal to link the Atlantic and Pacific oceans across the isthmus connecting North and South America. When the war with Spain started in 1898, it took the battleship *Oregon* seventy-one days to sail from San Francisco around Cape Horn to its battle station in the Atlantic; years later, naval experts still shuddered at the thought. Secretary of State John Hay negotiated with Britain the Hay-Pauncefote Treaty of 1901 that permitted the United States to construct and control an isthmian canal, providing it would be free and open to ships of all nations.

Delighted, Roosevelt began selecting the route. One route, 50 miles long, wandered through the rough, swampy terrain of the Panama region of Colombia. A French company had recently tried and failed to dig a canal there. Northwest of Panama, another route ran through mountainous Nicaragua. Although 200 miles in length, it followed natural waterways, a factor that would make construction easier.

An Isthmian Canal Commission investigated both routes in 1899 and recommended the shorter route through Panama. Roosevelt backed the idea, and he authorized Hay to negotiate an agreement with the Colombian chargé d'affaires, Tomas Herrán. The Hay-Herrán Convention (1903) gave the United States a ninety-nine-year lease, with option for renewal, on a canal zone 6 miles in width. In exchange, the United States agreed to pay Colombia a onetime fee of $10 million and an annual rental of $250,000.

To Roosevelt's dismay, the Colombian Senate rejected the treaty, in part because it infringed on Colombian sovereignty. The Colombians also wanted more money. Calling them "jack rabbits" and "contemptible little creatures," Roosevelt considered seizing Panama, then hinted he would welcome a Panamanian revolt from Colombia. In November 1903, the Panamanians took the hint, and Roosevelt moved quickly to support them. Sending the cruiser *Nashville* to prevent Colombian troops from putting down the revolt, he promptly recognized the new Republic of Panama.

Two weeks later, the Hay–Bunau-Varilla Treaty with Panama granted the United States control of a canal zone 10 miles wide across the Isthmus of Panama. In return, the United States guaranteed the independence of Panama and agreed to pay the same fees offered Colombia. Using giant steam shovels and thousands of laborers from Jamaica, engineers cut their way across the isthmus. On August 15, 1914, the first

The Panama Canal Zone

Construction of the canal began in 1904, and despite landslides, steamy weather, and yellow fever, work was completed in 1914.

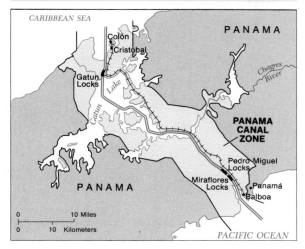

ocean steamer sailed through the completed canal, which had cost $375 million to build.

Roosevelt's actions angered many Latin Americans. Trying to soothe feelings, Wilson agreed in 1914 to pay Colombia $25 million in cash, give it preferential treatment in using the canal, and express "sincere regret" over American actions. Roosevelt was furious, and his friends in the Senate blocked the agreement. Colombian-American relations remained strained until 1921, when the two countries signed a treaty that included Wilson's first two provisions but omitted the apology.

For his part, Roosevelt took great pride in the canal, calling it "by far the most important action in foreign affairs." Defending his methods, he said in 1911, "If I had followed traditional conservative methods, I would have submitted a dignified state paper of 200 pages to Congress and the debate on it would have been going on yet; but I took the Canal Zone and let Congress debate; and while the debate goes on the Canal does also."

The Roosevelt Corollary

With interests in Puerto Rico, Cuba, and the canal, the United States developed a Caribbean policy to ensure its dominance in the region. It established protectorates over some countries and subsidized others to keep them dependent. When necessary, the United States purchased islands to keep them out of the hands of other powers, as in the case of the Danish West Indies (now the Virgin Islands), bought in 1917 to prevent the Germans from acquiring them.

From 1903 to 1920, the United States intervened often in Latin America to protect the canal, promote regional stability, and exclude foreign influence. One problem worrying American policymakers was the scale of Latin American debts to European powers. Many countries in the Western Hemisphere owed money to European governments and banks, and often these nations were poor, prone to revolution, and unable to pay. The situation invited European intervention. In 1902, Venezuela defaulted on debts; England, Germany, and Italy sent Venezuela an ultimatum and blockaded its ports. American pressure forced a settlement of the issue, but the general problem remained.

Roosevelt was concerned about it, and in 1904, when the Dominican Republican defaulted on its debts, he was ready with a major announcement. Known as the Roosevelt Corollary of the Monroe Doctrine, the policy warned Latin American nations to keep their affairs in order or face American intervention.

Applying the new policy immediately, Roosevelt in 1905 took charge of the Dominican Republic's revenue system. American officials collected customs and saw to the payment of debt. Within two years, Roosevelt also established protectorates in Cuba and Panama. In 1912, the U.S. Senate added the Lodge Corollary, which warned foreign corporations not to purchase harbors and other sites of military significance in Latin America. Continued by Taft, Wilson, and other presidents, the Roosevelt Corollary guided American policy in Latin America until the 1930s, when Franklin D. Roosevelt's Good Neighbor policy replaced it.

Ventures in the Far East

The Open Door policy toward China (see Chapter 21) and possession of the Philippine Islands shaped American actions in the Far East. Congress refused to arm the Philippines, and the islands were vulnerable to the growing power of Japan. Roosevelt wanted to balance Russian and Japanese power, and he was not unhappy at first when war broke out between them in 1904. As Japan won victory after victory, however, Roosevelt grew worried. Acting on a request from Japan, he offered to mediate the conflict, and both Russia and Japan accepted: Russia because it was losing, and Japan because it was financially drained.

In August 1905, Roosevelt convened a peace conference at Portsmouth, New Hampshire. The conference ended the war, but Japan emerged as the dominant force in the Far East. Adjusting policy, Roosevelt sent Secretary of War Taft to Tokyo to negotiate the Taft-Katsura Agreement (1905), which recognized Japan's dominance over Korea in return for its promise not to invade the Philippines. Giving Japan a free hand in Korea violated the Open Door policy, but Roosevelt argued that he had little choice.

Relations between Japan and the United States were again strained in 1906 when the San Francisco school board ordered the segregation of Japanese, Chinese, and Korean children into a separate Oriental school. A year later, the California legislature considered a bill limiting the immigration of Japanese laborers into the state. As resentment mounted in Japan, Roosevelt intervened to persuade the school board to rescind its order, while at the same time he got from Japan the "Gentlemen's Agreement" (1907) promising to stop the flow of Japanese agricultural laborers into the United States.

In case Japan viewed his policy as a sign of weakness, Roosevelt sent sixteen battleships of the new American fleet around the world, including a stop in Tokyo in October 1908. Critics at home predicted dire consequences, and European naval experts felt certain Japan would attack the fleet. Instead, the Japanese welcomed it, even posting ads to sell the sailors Mitsukoshi washing powder to "rid yourselves of the seven blemishes on the way home." For the moment, Japanese-American relations improved, and in 1908 the two nations, in an exchange of diplomatic notes,

A cartoon from *Judge* entitled "The World's Constable." The Roosevelt Corollary claimed the right of the United States to exercise "an international police power."

reached the comprehensive Root-Takahira Agreement in which they promised to maintain the status quo in the Pacific, uphold the Open Door, and support Chinese independence.

In later years, tensions again grew in the Far East. Anger mounted in Japan in 1913 when the California legislature prohibited Japanese residents from owning property in the state. At the start of the First World War, Japan seized some German colonies, and in 1915 it issued the Twenty-One Demands insisting on authority over China. Coveting an Asian empire, Japan eyed American possessions in the Pacific.

Taft and Dollar Diplomacy

In foreign as well as domestic affairs, President Taft tried to continue Roosevelt's policies. For secretary of state he chose Philander C. Knox, Roosevelt's attorney general, and together they pursued a policy of "dollar diplomacy" to promote American financial and business interests abroad. The policy had profit-seeking motives, but it also aimed to substitute economic ties for military alliances with the idea of increasing American influence and bringing lasting peace.

Intent, like Roosevelt, on supremacy in the Caribbean, Taft worked to replace European loans with American ones, thereby reducing the danger of outside meddling. In 1909, he asked American bankers to assume the Honduran debt in order to fend off English bondholders. A year later, he persuaded them to take over the assets of the National Bank of Haiti, and in 1911 he helped Nicaragua secure a large loan in return for American control of Nicaragua's National Bank. When Nicaraguans revolted against the agreement, Taft sent marines to put them down. A marine detachment remained in the country intermittently until the 1930s.

In the Far East, Knox worked closely with Willard Straight, an agent of American bankers, who argued that dollar diplomacy was the financial arm of the Open Door. Straight had close ties to Edward H. Harriman, the railroad magnate, who wanted to build railroads in Manchuria. Roosevelt had tacitly promised Japan he would keep American investors out of the area, and Knox's plan reversed the policy. Trying to organize an international syndicate to loan China money to purchase the Manchurian railroads, Knox approached England, Japan, and Russia. In January 1910, all three turned him down.

The outcome was a blow to American policy and prestige in Asia. Russia and Japan found reasons to cooperate with each other, and staked out spheres of influence in violation of the Open Door. Japan resented Taft's initiatives in Manchuria, and China's distrust of the United States deepened. Instead of cultivating friendship, as Roosevelt had envisioned, Taft had started an intense rivalry with Japan for commercial advantage in China.

FOREIGN POLICY UNDER WILSON

When he took office in 1913, Woodrow Wilson knew little about foreign policy. As a Princeton professor, he had studied Congress and the presidency, but his books made only passing reference to foreign issues, and during the 1912 campaign he mentioned foreign policy only when it affected domestic concerns. "It would be the irony of fate if my administration had to deal chiefly with foreign affairs," he said to a friend before becoming president. And so it was. During his two terms, Wilson faced crisis after crisis in foreign affairs, including the outbreak of World War I.

A supremely self-confident man, Wilson conducted his own diplomacy. He composed important diplomatic notes on his own typewriter, sent personal emissaries abroad, and carried on major negotiations without the knowledge of his secretaries of state. Failing to find the right persons for key diplomatic posts, he filled these positions with party regulars like James W. Gerard, his ambassador to Germany, for whom he had contempt. On Gerard's dispatches, Wilson penciled notes: "Ordinarily our Ambassador ought to be backed up as [a matter] of course, but—this ass? It is hard to take it seriously." Or, the next day: "Who can fathom this? I wish they would hand this idiot his passports!"

The idealistic Wilson believed in a principled, ethical world in which militarism, colonialism, and war were brought under control. He stressed moral purposes over material interests and said during one crisis, "The force of America is the force of moral principle." Rejecting the policy of dollar diplomacy, Wilson initially chose a course of moral diplomacy, designed to bring right to the world, preserve peace, and extend to other peoples the blessings of democracy.

Conducting Moral Diplomacy

William Jennings Bryan, whom Wilson appointed as secretary of state, was also an amateur in foreign relations. Trusting in the common people, Bryan was skeptical of experts in the State Department. To key posts abroad he appointed "deserving Democrats," believing they could do the job as well as career diplomats. Bryan was a fervent pacifist, and like Wilson, he believed in the American duty to "help" less-favored nations.

In 1913 and 1914, he embarked on an idealistic campaign to negotiate treaties of arbitration throughout the world. Known as "cooling-off" treaties, they provided for submitting all international disputes to permanent commissions of investigation. Neither party could declare war or increase armaments until the investigation ended, usually within one year. The idea drew on the era's confidence in commissions and the sense that human reason, given time for emotions to fade, could settle problems without war. Bryan negotiated cooling-off treaties with thirty nations, including Great Britain, France, and Italy. Germany refused to sign one. Based on a generous idea, the treaties were naive, and they did not work.

Wilson and Bryan promised a dramatic new approach in Latin America, concerned not with the "pursuit of material interest" but with "human rights" and "national integrity." Signaling the change, in 1913 they negotiated the treaty with Colombia apologizing for Roosevelt's Panamanian policy. Yet in the end, Wilson, distracted by other problems and impatient with the results of his idealistic approach, continued the Roosevelt-Taft policies. He defended the Monroe Doctrine, gave unspoken support to the Roosevelt Corollary, and intervened in Latin America more than had either Roosevelt or Taft.

In 1914, Wilson negotiated a treaty with Nicaragua to grant the United States exclusive rights to build a canal and lease sites for naval bases. This treaty made Nicaragua an American satellite. In 1915, he sent marines into Haiti to quell a revolution; they stayed until 1934. In 1916, he occupied the Dominican Republic, establishing a protectorate that lasted until 1924. By 1917, American troops "protected" Nicaragua, Haiti, the Dominican Republic, and Cuba—four nations that were U.S. dependencies in all but name.

Troubles Across the Border

Wilson's moral diplomacy encountered one of its greatest challenges across the border in Mexico. Porfirio Diaz, president of Mexico for thirty-seven years, was overthrown in 1911. Diaz had encouraged foreign investments in Mexican mines, railroads, oil, and land; by 1913, Americans had invested over $1 billion. But most Mexicans remained poor and uneducated, and Diaz's overthrow led to a decade of violence that tested Wilson's policies and brought the United States close to war with Mexico.

A liberal reformer, Francisco I. Madero, followed Diaz as president in 1911. But Madero could not keep order in the troubled country, and opponents of his reforms undermined him. With support from wealthy landowners, the army, and the Catholic church, General Victoriano Huerta ousted Madero in 1913, threw him in jail, and arranged his murder. Most European nations immediately recognized Huerta, but Wilson, calling him a "butcher," refused to do so. Instead, he announced a new policy toward revolutionary regimes in Latin America. To win American recognition, they must not only exercise power but reflect "a just government based upon law, not upon arbitrary or irregular force."

On that basis, Wilson withheld recognition from Huerta and maneuvered to oust him. Early in 1914, he stationed naval units off Mexico's ports to cut off arms shipments to the Huerta regime. The action produced trouble. On April 9, 1914, several American sailors, who went ashore in Tampico to purchase supplies, were arrested. They were promptly released, but the American admiral demanded an apology and a twenty-one-gun salute to the American flag. Huerta agreed—if the Americans also saluted the Mexican flag.

Wilson asked Congress for authority to use military force if needed; then, just as Congress acted, he learned that a German ship was landing arms at Veracruz on Mexico's eastern coast. With Wilson's approval, American warships shelled the harbor, and marines went ashore. Against heavy resistance, they took the city. Outraged, Mexicans of all factions denounced the invasion, and for a time the two countries hovered on the edge of war.

Retreating hastily, Wilson explained that he desired only to help Mexico. Argentina, Brazil, and Chile came to his aid with an offer to mediate the dispute, and tensions eased. In July 1914, weakened by an armed rebellion, Huerta resigned. Wilson recognized the new government, headed by Venustiano Carranza, an associate of Madero. Early in 1916, Francisco ("Pancho") Villa, one of Carranza's generals, revolted. Hoping to goad the United States into an action that would help him seize power, he raided border towns, injuring American civilians. In January, he removed seventeen Americans from a train in Mexico and murdered them. Two months later he invaded Columbus, New Mexico, killing sixteen Americans and burning the town.

Stationing militia along the border, Wilson ordered General John J. Pershing on a punitive expedition to seize Villa in Mexico. Pershing led six thousand troops deep into Mexican territory. At first, Carranza agreed to the drive, but as the Americans pushed farther and farther into his country, he changed his mind. As the wily Villa

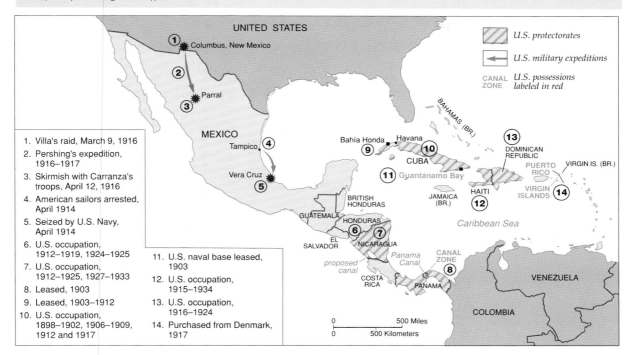

Activities of the United States in the Caribbean, 1898 to the 1930s

During the first three decades of the twentieth century, the United States policed the Caribbean, claiming the right to take action when it judged Latin American countries were doing a bad job of running their affairs.

UNITED STATES

① Columbus, New Mexico

②

③ Parral

MEXICO
Tampico ④

Vera Cruz ⑤

Bahía Honda ⑨   Havana
CUBA ⑩
⑪ Guantánamo Bay

BAHAMAS (BR.)

⑬ DOMINICAN REPUBLIC

PUERTO RICO
VIRGIN IS. (BR.)
VIRGIN ISLANDS ⑭

JAMAICA (BR.)   HAITI ⑫

Caribbean Sea

BRITISH HONDURAS
GUATEMALA
HONDURAS
⑥   ⑦
EL SALVADOR   NICARAGUA

proposed canal
Panama Canal
COSTA RICA
PANAMA ⑧
CANAL ZONE

VENEZUELA

COLOMBIA

U.S. protectorates
→ *U.S. military expeditions*
CANAL ZONE *U.S. possessions labeled in red*

1. Villa's raid, March 9, 1916
2. Pershing's expedition, 1916–1917
3. Skirmish with Carranza's troops, April 12, 1916
4. American sailors arrested, April 1914
5. Seized by U.S. Navy, April 1914
6. U.S. occupation, 1912–1919, 1924–1925
7. U.S. occupation, 1912–1925, 1927–1933
8. Leased, 1903
9. Leased, 1903–1912
10. U.S. occupation, 1898–1902, 1906–1909, 1912 and 1917
11. U.S. naval base leased, 1903
12. U.S. occupation, 1915–1934
13. U.S. occupation, 1916–1924
14. Purchased from Denmark, 1917

0   500 Miles
0   500 Kilometers

eluded Pershing, Carranza protested bitterly, and Wilson, worried about events in Europe, ordered Pershing home.

Wilson's policy had laudable goals; he wanted to help the Mexicans achieve political and agrarian reform. But his motives and methods were condescending. Wilson tried to impose gradual progressive reform on a society sharply divided along class and other lines. With little forethought, he interfered in the affairs of another country, and in doing so he revealed the themes—moralism, combined with pragmatic self-interest and a desire for peace—that also shaped his policies in Europe.

TOWARD WAR

In May 1914, Colonel Edward M. House, Wilson's close friend and adviser, sailed to Europe on a fact-finding mission. Tensions there were rising. "The situation is extraordinary," he reported to Wilson. "It is jingoism [extreme nationalism] run stark mad. . . . There is too much hatred, too many jealousies."

Large armies dominated the European continent. A web of alliances entangled nations, maximizing the risk that a local conflict could produce a wider war. In Germany, the ambitious Kaiser Wilhelm II coveted a world empire to match those of Britain and France. Germany had military treaties with Turkey and Austria-Hungary, a sprawling central European country of many nationalities. Linked in another alliance, England, France, and Russia agreed to aid each other in case of attack.

On June 28, 1914, a Bosnian assassin linked to Serbia murdered Archduke Franz Ferdinand, heir to the Austro-Hungarian throne. Within weeks Germany, Turkey, and Austria-Hungary (the Central Powers) were at war with England, France, and Russia (the Allied Powers). Americans were shocked at the events. "I had a feeling that the end of things had come. . . ," one of Wilson's cabinet members said. "I stopped in my tracks, dazed and horror-stricken." Wilson

European Alliances and Battlefronts, 1914–1917

Allied forces suffered early defeats on the Eastern Front (Tannenberg) and in the Dardanelles (Gallipoli). In 1917, the Allies were routed on the southern flank (Caporetto); the Western Front then became the critical theater of the war.

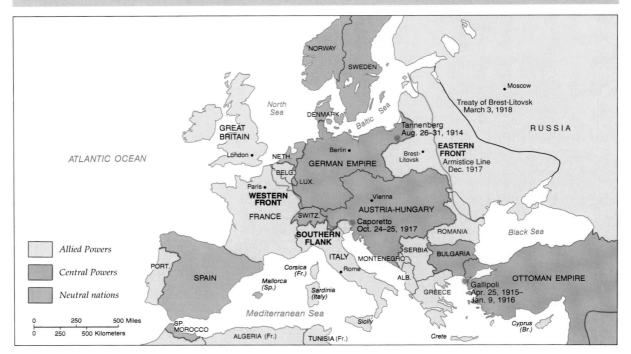

immediately proclaimed neutrality and asked Americans to remain "impartial in thought as well as in action."

The war, he said, was one "with which we have nothing to do, whose causes cannot touch us." In private, Wilson was stunned. A man who loved peace, he had long admired the British parliamentary system, and he respected the leaders of the British Liberal party, who supported social programs akin to his own. "Everything I love most in the world," he said, "is at stake."

The Neutrality Policy

In general, Americans accepted neutrality. They saw no need to enter the conflict, especially after the Allies in September 1914 halted the first German drive toward Paris. America resisted involvement in other countries' problems and had a tradition of freedom from foreign entanglements.

For the nation's large number of progressives, there were additional reasons to resist. War, they thought, violated the very spirit of progressive reform. Why demand safer factories in which people could work and then kill them by the millions in war? To many progressives, moreover, England represented international finance, an institution they detested. Germany, on the other hand, had pioneered some of their favorite social reforms.

Furthermore, progressives and others tended to put the blame for war on the greed of "munition manufacturers, stockbrokers, and bond dealers" eager for wartime profits. "Do you want to know the cause of the war?" Henry Ford, who was no progressive, asked. "It is capitalism, greed, the dirty hunger for dollars." Above all, progressives were sure that war would end reform. It consumed money and attention; it inflamed emotions.

As a result, Jane Addams, Florence Kelley, Frederic C. Howe, Lillian Wald, and other pro-

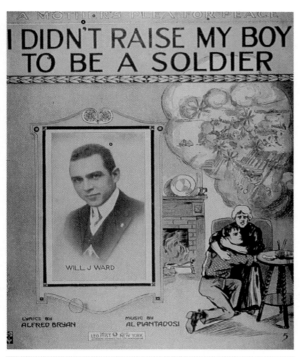

Opposition to U.S. participation in World War I was expressed in many ways. This sheet music cover for "I Didn't Raise My Boy to Be a Soldier" captured the sentiments of many parents.

gressives fought to keep the United States out of war. In late 1915, they formed the American Union Against Militarism, to throw, they said, "a monkey wrench into the machinery" of war. Throughout 1915 and 1916, *La Follette's Magazine,* the voice of the progressive leader, railed against the Morgans, Rockefellers, Du Ponts, and "the thirty-eight corporations most benefited by war orders." In 1915, Addams and Wald helped organize the League to Limit Armament, and shortly thereafter, Addams and Carrie Chapman Catt formed the Woman's Peace Party to organize women against the war.

The war's outbreak also tugged at the emotions of millions of immigrant Americans. Those who came from the British Isles tended to support the Allies; those from Ireland tended to support Germany, hoping Britain's wartime troubles might free their homeland from British domination. The large population of German Americans often sympathized with the Central Powers. But many people thought that, in a nation of immigrants, a policy of neutrality would be wise from a domestic point of view as well as from the viewpoint of foreign policy.

At the deepest level, a majority in the country, bound by common language and institutions, sympathized with the Allies and blamed Germany for the war. Like Wilson, many Americans admired English literature, customs, and law; they remembered Lafayette and the times when France had helped the United States in its early years. Germany, on the other hand, seemed arrogant and militaristic. When the war began, it invaded Belgium to strike at France and violated a treaty which the German chancellor called "just a scrap of paper." Many Americans resented the violation, and they liked it even less when German troops executed Belgian civilians who resisted.

Both sides sought to sway American opinion, and fierce propaganda campaigns flourished. The German Literary Defense Committee distributed over a million pamphlets during the first year of the war. German propaganda tended to stress strength and will; Allied propaganda called on historical ties and took advantage of German atrocities, both real and alleged. In the end, the propaganda probably made little difference. Ties of heritage and the course of the war, not propaganda, decided the American position. At the outset, no matter which side they cheered for, Americans of all persuasions preferred simply to remain at peace.

Freedom of the Seas

The demands of trade tested American neutrality and confronted Wilson with difficult choices. Under international law, neutral countries were permitted to trade in nonmilitary goods with all belligerent countries. But Great Britain controlled the seas, and it intended to cut off shipments of war materials to the Central Powers.

As soon as war broke out, Britain blockaded German ports and limited the goods Americans could sell to Germany. American ships had to carry cargoes to neutral ports from which, after examination, they could be carried to Germany. As time passed, Britain stepped up the economic sanctions by forbidding the shipment to Germany of all foodstuffs and most raw materials, seizing and censoring mail, and "blacklisting" American firms that dealt directly with the Central Powers. British ships often stopped American ships and confiscated cargoes.

Again and again Wilson protested against such infringements on neutral rights. Sometimes Britain complied, sometimes not, and Wilson often grew angry. But needing American support and supplies, Britain pursued a careful strategy to disrupt German-American trade without disrupting Anglo-American relations. After forbidding cotton shipments to Germany in 1915, it agreed to buy enough cotton to make up for the losses. When necessary, it also promised to reimburse American businesses after the war's end.

Other than the German U-boats, there were no constraints on trade with the Allies, and a flood of Allied war orders fueled the American economy. England and France bought huge amounts of arms, grain, cotton, and clothing. To finance the purchases, the Allies turned to American bankers for loans. By 1917, loans to Allied governments exceeded $2 billion; loans to Germany came to only $27 million.

In a development that influenced Wilson's policy, the war produced the greatest economic boom in the nation's history. Loans and trade drew the United States ever closer to the Allied cause. And even though Wilson often protested English maritime policy, the protests involved American goods and money whereas Germany's submarine policy threatened American lives.

The U-Boat Threat

A relatively new weapon, the *Unterseeboot,* or submarine, strained the guidelines of international law. Traditional law required a submarine to surface, warn the target to stop, send a boarding party to check papers and cargo, then allow time for passengers and crew to board lifeboats before sinking the vessel. Flimsy and slow, submarines could ill afford to surface while the prey radioed for help. If they did surface, they might be rammed or blown up by deck guns.

When Germany announced the submarine campaign in February 1915, Wilson protested sharply, calling the sinking of merchant ships without checking cargo "a wanton act." The Germans promised not to sink American ships— an agreement that lasted until 1917—and thereafter the issue became the right of Americans to sail on the ships of belligerent nations. In March, an American citizen aboard the British liner *Falaba* perished when the ship was torpedoed off the Irish coast. Bryan urged Wilson to forbid Americans to travel in the war zones, but the

A new and terrifying weapon of the war was the German U-boat, which attacked silently and without warning.

president, determined to stand by the principles of international law, refused.

Wilson reacted more harshly in May and August of 1915 when U-boats sank the *Lusitania* and *Arabic*. He demanded that the Germans protect passenger vessels and pay for American losses. At odds with Wilson's understanding of neutrality, Bryan resigned as secretary of state and was replaced by Robert Lansing, a lawyer and counselor in the State Department. Lansing brought a very different spirit to the job. He favored the Allies and believed that democracy was threatened in a world dominated by Germany. He urged strong stands against German violations of American neutrality.

In February 1916, Germany declared unrestricted submarine warfare against all *armed* ships. Lansing protested and told Germany it would be held strictly accountable for American losses. A month later, a U-boat torpedoed the unarmed French channel steamer *Sussex,* without warning, injuring several Americans. Arguing that the sinking violated the *Arabic* pledge, Lansing urged Wilson to break relations with Germany. Wilson rejected the advice, but on April 18 sent an ultimatum to Germany, stating that unless the Germans immediately called off attacks on cargo and passenger ships, the United States would sever relations.

The kaiser, convinced he did not yet have enough submarines to risk war, yielded. In the *Sussex* pledge of May 4, 1916, he agreed to Wilson's demands and promised to shoot on sight only ships of the enemy's navy. But he attached the condition that the United States compel the Allies to end their blockade and comply with international law. Wilson accepted the pledge but turned down the condition.

The *Sussex* pledge marked the beginning of a short period of friendly relations between Germany and the United States. The agreement applied not only to passenger liners, but to *all* merchant ships, belligerent or not. There was one problem: Wilson had taken such a strong position that if Germany renewed submarine warfare on merchant shipping, war was likely. Most Americans, however, viewed the agreement as a diplomatic stroke for peace by Wilson, and the issues of peace and preparedness dominated the presidential election of 1916.

Roosevelt's campaign for preparedness became a personal attack on Wilson, whom TR called a coward and a weakling.

"He Kept Us Out of War"

The "preparedness" issue pitted antiwar groups against those who wanted to prepare for war. The American Rights Committee, the National Security League, and other groups urged stepped-up military measures in case of war. In the summer of 1915, they persuaded the War Department to hold a training camp in Plattsburg, New York, in which regular army officers trained 1,200 civilian volunteers in modern warfare. The following summer, 16,000 volunteers participated in such training camps.

Bellicose as always, Teddy Roosevelt led the preparedness campaign. He called Wilson "yellow" for not pressing Germany harder and scoffed at the popular song, "I Didn't Raise My Boy to Be a Soldier," which he compared to singing "I Didn't Raise My Girl to Be a Mother." Defending the military's state of readiness, Wilson refused to be stampeded just because "some amongst us are nervous and excited." In fact, when government revenue dropped in 1915, he cut military appropriations.

Wilson's position was attacked from both sides as preparedness advocates charged cowardice, while pacifists denounced any attempt at military readiness. The difficulty of his situation, plus the growing U-boat crisis, soon changed Wilson's mind. In mid-1915, he asked the War Department to increase military planning, and he quietly notified congressional leaders of a switch in policy. Later that year, Wilson approved large increases in the army and navy, a move that upset many peace-minded progressives. In January 1916, he toured the country to promote preparedness, and in June, with an American flag draped over his shoulder, he marched in a giant preparedness parade in Washington.

For their standard-bearer in the presidential election of 1916, the Republicans nominated Charles Evans Hughes, a moderate justice of the Supreme Court. Hughes seemed to have all the qualifications for victory. A former reform governor of New York, he could lure back the Roosevelt progressives while at the same time appealing to the Republican conservatives. To woo the Roosevelt wing, Hughes called for a tougher line against Germany, thus allowing the Democrats to label him the "war" candidate. Even so, Roosevelt and others considered Hughes a "bearded iceberg," a dull campaigner who wavered on important issues.

The Democrats renominated Wilson in a convention marked by spontaneous demonstrations for peace. Determined to outdo Republican patriotism, Wilson himself had ordered the convention's theme to be "Americanism." The delegates were to sing "America" and "The Star-Spangled Banner," and to cheer any mention of America and the flag. They did it all dutifully but then broke into spontaneous applause at the mention of Wilson's careful diplomatic moves. As the keynote speaker reviewed them, the delegates shouted, "What did we do? What did we do?" The speaker shouted back, "We didn't go to war! We didn't go to war!"

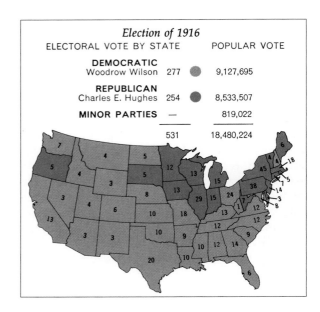

Picking up the theme, perhaps with reservation, Wilson said in October, "I am not expecting this country to get into war." The campaign slogan, "He kept us out of war" was repeated again and again, and just before the election, the Democrats took full-page ads in leading newspapers:

You Are Working—Not Fighting!
Alive and Happy—Not Cannon Fodder!
Wilson and Peace with Honor?
or
Hughes with Roosevelt and War?

On election night, Hughes had swept most of the East, and Wilson retired at 10 P.M., thinking he had lost. During the night, the results came in from California, New Mexico, and North Dakota; all supported Wilson—California by a mere 3,773 votes. Wilson won with 9.1 million votes against 8.5 million for Hughes. Holding the Democratic South, he carried key states in the Midwest and West and took large portions of the labor and progressive vote. Women—who were then allowed to vote in presidential elections in twelve states—also voted heavily for Wilson.

The Final Months of Peace

Just before Election Day, Great Britain further limited neutral trade, and there were reports from

Germany of a renewal of unrestricted submarine warfare. Fresh from his victory, Wilson redoubled his efforts for peace. Aware that time was running out, he hoped to start negotiations to end the bloodshed and create a peaceful postwar world.

In December 1916, he sent messages to both sides asking them to state their war aims. Should they do so, he pledged the "whole force" of the United States to end the war. The Allies refused, although they promised privately to negotiate if the German terms were reasonable. The Germans replied evasively and in January 1917 revealed their real objectives. Close to forcing Russia out of the war, Germany sensed victory and wanted territory in eastern Europe, Africa, Belgium, and France.

On January 22, in an eloquent speech before the Senate, Wilson called for a "peace without victory." Outlining his own ambitious aims, he urged respect for all nations, freedom of the seas, arms limitations, and a league of nations to keep the peace. "Only a peace between equals can last, only a peace the very principle of which is equality and a common participation in a common benefit." The speech made a great impression on many Europeans, but it was too late. The Germans had decided a few weeks before to unleash the submarines and gamble on a quick end to the war. Even as Wilson spoke, U-boats were in the Atlantic west of Ireland, preparing to attack.

On January 31, the German ambassador in Washington informed Lansing that beginning February 1, U-boats would sink on sight all ships—passenger or merchant, neutral or belligerent, armed or unarmed—in the waters around England and France. Staking everything on a last effort, the Germans calculated that if they could sink 600,000 tons of shipping a month, they could defeat England in six months. As he had pledged in 1916, Wilson broke off relations with Germany, although he still hoped for peace.

On February 25, the British government privately gave Wilson a telegram intercepted from Arthur Zimmermann, the German foreign minister, to the German ambassador in Mexico. A day later, Wilson asked Congress for authority to arm merchant ships to deter U-boats attacks. When La Follette and a handful of others threatened to filibuster, Wilson divulged the contents of the Zimmermann telegram.

It proposed an alliance with Mexico in case of war with the United States, offering financial support and recovery of Mexico's "lost territory" in New Mexico, Texas, and Arizona.

Spurred by a wave of public indignation toward the Germans, the House passed Wilson's measure, but La Follette and others still blocked action in the Senate. On March 9, 1917, Wilson ordered merchant ships armed on his own authority. Three days later, he announced the arming, and on March 13, the navy instructed all vessels to fire on submarines. Between March 12 and March 21, U-boats sank five American ships, and Wilson decided to wait no longer.

He called Congress into special session and at 8:30 in the evening on April 2, 1917, asked for a declaration of war. "It is a fearful thing to lead this great peaceful people into war, into the most terrible and disastrous of all wars, civilization itself seeming to be in the balance. But the right is more precious than peace, and we shall fight for the things which we have always carried nearest our hearts,—for democracy, . . . for the rights and liberties of small nations, for a universal dominion of right by such a concert of free peoples as shall bring peace and safety to all nations and make the world itself at last free."

Congressmen broke into applause and crowded the aisles to congratulate Wilson. "My message today was a message of death for our young men," he said afterward. "How strange it seems to applaud that."

Pacifists in Congress continued to hold out, and for four days they managed to postpone action. Finally, on April 6, the declaration of war passed, with fifty members of the House and six Senators voting against it. Even now, the country was divided over entry into the war.

OVER THERE

With a burst of patriotism, the United States entered a war its new allies were in danger of losing. That same month, the Germans sank 881,000 tons of Allied shipping, the highest amount for any one month during the war. There were mutinies in the French army; a costly British drive in Flanders stalled. In November, the Bolsheviks seized power in Russia, and led by V.I. Lenin, they soon signed a separate peace treaty with Germany (see the map on p. 736), freeing

$\mathcal{M}$easuring the Mind

From 1870 to 1920, scientists and physicians explored new ideas about the mind. In Europe, the Viennese psychiatrist Sigmund Freud studied the unconscious, which, he thought, shaped human behavior. Russia's Ivan Pavlov tested the conditioned reflex in mental activity (Pavlov's dogs), and in the United States William James, the psychologist and philosopher, examined emotions and linked psychology to everyday problems.

As one way of understanding *the mind,* psychologists studied the mental processes of a great many minds, a task to which the relatively new science of statistics lent a hand. Testing large samples of subjects, they developed the concept of the "normal" and "average," helpful boundaries used to determine an individual's place in the population. In 1890, the psychologist James McKeen Cattell tested one hundred freshmen at the University of Pennsylvania for vision and hearing, sensitivity to pain, reaction time, and memory. He called these examinations by a new name—"mental tests"—and the idea spread. In 1895, the American Psychological Association (APA) set up a special committee to promote the nationwide collection of mental statistics.

Work was underway on both sides of the ocean, and in 1905 Alfred Binet and Theodore Simon, two French psychologists, devised a metric intelligence scale. Seizing on the idea that until maturity, intelligence increases with age, they tested children of various ages to find an average level of performance for each age. Once they had determined the average, they could compare any child's test performance with it and thus distinguish between the child's "mental age" and chronological age. In 1912, William Stein, a German psychologist, introduced the "Intelligence Quotient," found by dividing a person's mental age by the chronological age. In 1916, Lewis M. Terman of Stanford University improved Binet's test, and the term *IQ* became part of the American vocabulary.

Employers and educators, however, remained skeptical of measuring intelligence. Thus, when the United States entered World War I, psychologists at once saw the opportunity to overcome the doubts and prove their theories. Huge numbers of men needed to be recruited, classified, and assigned to units quickly. Why not use the new mental tests? APA leaders formed twelve committees, including one on the Psychological Examination of Recruits, to explore the military uses of psychology.

Preferring to issue promotions on the basis of seniority, the army resisted the "mental meddlers," but the APA persuaded the War Department to use the tests. In

Administered to soldiers in groups, the IQ test was used in World War I to classify recruits and determine which of them were "officer material." The results of the tests not only raised questions about the mental abilities and backgrounds of the men, but also about the possible biases in the tests themselves.

early 1918, psychological examiners were posted at all training camps to administer the Alpha Test to literates and the Beta Test (with instructions given in pantomime) to illiterates and those who did not understand English: At the start of each Alpha Test, the examiners put the men at ease by explaining that the army was "not looking for crazy people. The aim is to help find out what we are best fitted to do." On the Beta Test, which was made up largely of pictures, the examiners were reminded that Beta men "sometimes sulk and refuse to work."

On the basis of the tests, the examiners classified recruits as "superior," "average," or "inferior." From the "superior" category, they selected men for officer training, a helpful winnowing process in an army that expanded quickly from 9,000 officers to 200,000. They then distributed the remaining "superior," "average," and "inferior" men among each military unit. In all, the examiners tested 1.7 million men—by far the largest testing program in human history to that time. To some degree the tests served their purpose, but they also seemed to raise questions about the education and mental ability of many American men.

For one thing, there was the extent of illiteracy—nearly one-quarter of the draft-age men in 1918 could neither read nor write. (One-third, incidentally, were physically unfit for service.) There was also the limited schooling of the recruits, most of whom had left school between the fifth and seventh grades. More alarming, according to the test results, 47 percent of the white draftees and 89 percent of the black draftees had a "mental age" of twelve years

or under, which classified them as "feebleminded." Did that mean half or more of the American population was feebleminded?

The tests also turned up racial and national distinctions—or so some of the examiners concluded. Men of "native" backgrounds and "old" immigrant stock (from northern Europe and the British Isles) tended to score well and fall in the "superior" category; "new" immigrants (from central and southern Europe) tended to score less well and rank as "inferior." Among Russian, Polish, and Italian draftees, more than half were classified as "inferior." Such results came as no surprise to those who had long doubted the intelligence of the "new" immigrants, nor did the fact that 80 percent of the African Americans taking the Alpha Test scored in the inferior range.

Some observers, however, wondered what the tests really measured. The APA examiners claimed they measured "native intelligence," but questions about Edgar Allan Poe's poem "The Raven" or the paintings of Rosa Bonheur, a French artist of the mid-nineteenth century, required answers that native intelligence alone could not supply. When blacks and whites scored comparably on the early Beta Test, the examiners decided that something must be wrong with the test, so they changed the questions until the

scores showed the expected racial differences. Most of those taking the Beta Test had never taken a written test before; many had probably never held a pencil.

Still skeptical, the army discontinued the tests the moment the war ended, but what the army rejected, the nation adopted. Businesses, government, and above all, educational institutions found greater and greater uses for intelligence testing. In 1926, the College Entrance Examination Board (CEEB) administered the first Scholastic Aptitude Test (SAT), designed to test "intelligence" and predict performance in college. In 1935, it established scoring ranges from 200 to 800, with the average score set at 500. During World War II SAT tests were widely used. In 1947, the CEEB became part of a new Educational Testing Service that spurred an educational revolution by making intelligence instead of social or economic standing the main criterion of college admissions.

Before long, intelligence testing—the measuring of minds—touched every aspect of American life. Shaping lives and careers, it pushed some people forward and held others back, in the military, industry, the civil service, and higher education. "Intelligence tests . . . " an expert said in 1971, "have more and more become society's instrument for the selection of human resources."

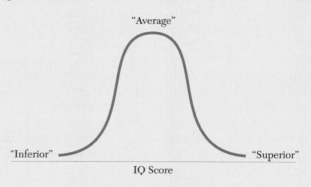

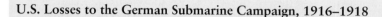

U.S. Losses to the German Submarine Campaign, 1916–1918

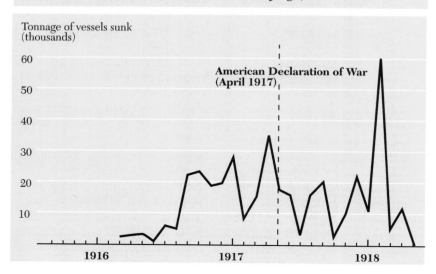

Tonnage of vessels sunk (thousands)

American Declaration of War (April 1917)

1916   1917   1918

German troops to fight in the West. German and Austrian forces routed the Italian army on the southern flank, and the Allies braced for a spring 1918 offensive.

Mobilization

The United States was not prepared for war. Some Americans hoped the declaration of war itself might daunt the Germans; there were those who thought that naval escorts of Allied shipping would be enough. Others hoped money and arms supplied to the Allies would be sufficient to produce victory without sending troops. "Good Lord!" an influential senator exclaimed just after war was declared. "You're not going to send soldiers over there, are you?"

Bypassing older generals, Wilson named "Black Jack" Pershing, leader of the Mexican campaign, to head the American Expeditionary Force (AEF). Pershing inherited an army unready for war. In April 1917, it had 200,000 officers and men, equipped with 300,000 old rifles, 1,500 machine guns, 55 out-of-date airplanes, and 2 field radio sets. Its most recent battle experience had been chasing Pancho Villa around northern Mexico. It had not caught him.

The armed forces had just two war plans: War Plan Orange, for a defensive war against Japan in the Pacific, and War Plan Black, to counter a pos-

sible German attack in the Caribbean. Wilson had ordered military commanders not to plan because it violated neutrality. "When the Acting Chief of Staff went to look at the secret files where the plans to meet the situation that confronted us should have been found," Pershing later said, "the pigeonhole was empty."

Although some in Congress preferred a voluntary army of the kind that had fought in the Spanish-American War, Wilson turned to conscription, which he felt was both efficient and democratic. In May 1917, Congress passed the Selective Service Act, providing for the registration of all men between the ages of twenty-one and thirty (later changed to eighteen and forty-five). Early in June, 9.5 million men registered for the draft. The act ultimately registered 24.2 million men, about 2.8 million of whom were inducted into the army. Defending the draft, Wilson said it was not really a draft at all, but a "selection from a nation which has volunteered in mass."

The draft included black men as well as white and four African American regiments were among the first sent into action. Despite their contributions, however, no black soldiers were allowed to march in the victory celebrations that eventually took place in Paris. Nor were they included in a French mural of the different races in the war, even though black servicemen from English and French colonies were represented.

The failure of poorly planned missions cast a pall of gloom over British and French troops. British artist John Nash painted an eyewitness record in Over the Top. *Nash—one of twelve survivors out of a company of eighty—recalled, "It was bitterly cold and we were easy targets against the snow and in daylight."*

War in the Trenches

World War I may have been the most terrible war of all time, more terrible even than World War II and its vast devastation. After the early offensives, the European armies dug themselves into trenches only hundreds of yards apart in places. Artillery, poison gas, hand grenades, and a new weapon—rapid-fire machine guns—kept them pinned down.

Even in moments of respite, the mud, rats, cold, fear, and disease took a heavy toll. Deafening bombardments shook the earth, and there was a high incidence of shell shock. From time to time, troops went "over the top" of the trenches in an effort to break through the enemy's lines, but the costs were enormous. The German offensive at Verdun in 1916 killed 600,000 men; the British lost 20,000 on the first day of an offensive on the Somme.

The first American soldiers reached France in June 1917. By March of the following year, 300,000 Americans were there, and by war's end, 2 million men had crossed the Atlantic. No troop ships were sunk, a credit to the British and American navies. In the summer of 1917, Admiral William S. Sims, a brilliant American strategist, pushed through a convoy plan that used Allied destroyers to escort merchant vessels across the ocean. At first resisted by English captains who liked to sail alone, the plan soon cut shipping losses in half.

As expected, on March 21, 1918, the Germans launched a massive assault in western Europe. Troops from the Russian front added to the force, and by May they had driven Allied forces

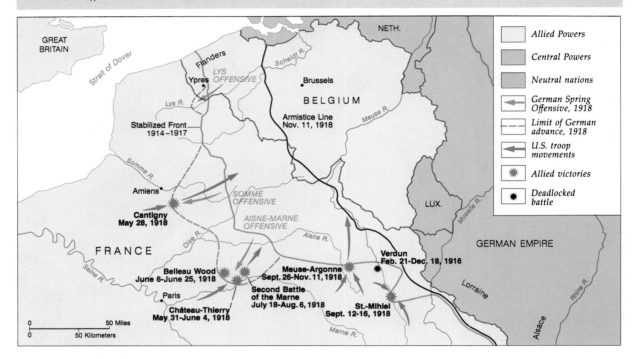

The Western Front: U.S. Participation, 1918

The turning point of the war came in July, when the German advance was halted at the Marne. The "Yanks," now a fighting force, were thrown into the breach. They played a dramatic role in stemming the tide and mounting the counteroffensives that ended the war.

back to the Marne River, just 50 miles from Paris. There, the Americans saw their first action. The American forces blocked the Germans at the town of Château-Thierry, and four weeks later forced them out of Belleau Wood, a crucial stronghold. On July 15, the Germans threw everything into a last drive for Paris, but they were halted at the Marne, and in three days of battle they were finished. "On the 18th," the German chancellor said, "even the most optimistic among us knew that all was lost. The history of the world was played out in three days."

With the German drive stalled, the Allies counterattacked along the entire front. On September 12, 1918, half a million Americans and a smaller contingent of French drove the Germans from the St. Mihiel salient, 12 miles south of Verdun. Two weeks later, 896,000 American soldiers attacked between the Meuse River and the Argonne Forest. Focusing their efforts on a main railroad supply line for the German army in the West, American troops broke through in early

November, cut the line, and drove the Germans back along the whole front.

The German high command knew that the war was lost. On October 6, 1918, Germany appealed to Wilson for an armistice, and by the end of the month, Turkey, Bulgaria, and Austria-Hungary were out of the war. At 4 A.M. on November 11, Germany signed the armistice. The AEF lost 48,909 dead and 230,000 wounded; losses to disease brought the total of dead to over 112,000.

The American contribution, although small in comparison to the enormous costs to European nations, was vital. Fresh, enthusiastic American troops raised Allied morale; they helped turn the tide at a crucial point in the war.

OVER HERE

Victory at the front depended on economic and emotional mobilization at home. Consolidating federal authority, Wilson moved quickly in 1917

German prisoners and American wounded returning from the front lines of the Meuse-Argonne. More Americans died in that campaign than in the rest of the war. The painting is by Harvey Dunn, one of eight official artists with the American Expeditionary Force.

and 1918 to organize war production and distribution. An idealist who knew how to sway public opinion, he also recognized the need to enlist American emotions. To him, the war for people's minds, the "conquest of their convictions," was as vital as events on the battlefield.

The Conquest of Convictions

A week after war was declared, Wilson formed the Committee on Public Information (CPI) and asked George Creel, an outspoken progressive journalist, to head it. Creel hired progressives like Ida Tarbell and Ray Stannard Baker, and recruited thousands of people in the arts, advertising, and film industries to publicize the war. He worked out a system of voluntary censorship with the press, plastered walls with colorful posters, and issued more than 75 million pamphlets.

Creel also enlisted 75,000 "four-minute men" to give quick speeches at public gatherings and places of entertainment on "Why We Are Fighting" and "The Meaning of America." At first, they were instructed to stress facts and stay away from emotions, particularly hatred, but by the beginning of 1918, the instructions shifted; the Germans were to be depicted as bloodthirsty Huns bent on world conquest. Exploiting a new medium, the CPI promoted films like *The Prussian Cur* and *The Kaiser, the Beast of Berlin.* Creel secretly subsidized several prowar groups

and formed the CPI's Division of Industrial Relations to rally labor to the war.

Helped along by the propaganda campaign, anti-German sentiment spread rapidly. Many schools stopped offering instruction in the German language—California's state education board called it a language "of autocracy, brutality, and hatred." Sauerkraut became "liberty cabbage"; saloon keepers removed pretzels from the bar. Orchestral works by Bach, Beethoven, and Brahms vanished from some symphonic programs, and the New York Philharmonic agreed not to perform the music of living German composers. Government agents harassed Karl Muck, the German conductor of the Boston Symphony, imprisoned him for over a year, and then after the war ended, deported him. German Americans and antiwar figures were badgered, beaten, and in some cases killed.

Vigilantism, sparked often by superpatriotism of a ruthless sort, flourished. Frequently it focused on radical antiwar figures like Frank Little, an IWW official in Butte, Montana, who was taken from his boardinghouse in August 1917, tied to the rear of an automobile, and dragged through the streets until his kneecaps were scraped off. Little was then hanged from a railroad trestle. In April 1918, a Missouri mob seized Robert Prager, a young man whose sole crime was being born in Germany. They bound him with an American flag, paraded him through town, and then lynched him. A jury acquitted the mob's members—who wore red, white, and blue ribbons to court—as one juror shouted, "Well, I guess nobody can say we aren't loyal now."

Rather than curbing the repression, Wilson encouraged it. "Woe be to the man or group of men that seeks to stand in our way," he told peace advocates soon after the war began. At his request, Congress passed the Espionage Act of 1917, which imposed sentences of up to twenty years in prison for persons found guilty of aiding the enemy, obstructing recruitment of soldiers, or encouraging disloyalty. It allowed the postmaster general to remove from the mails materials that incited treason or insurrection. The Trading-with-the-Enemy Act of 1917 authorized the government to censor the foreign language press.

In 1918, Congress passed the Sedition Act, imposing harsh penalties on anyone using "disloyal, profane, scurrilous, or abusive language" about the government, flag, or armed forces uniforms. In all, over fifteen hundred persons were arrested under the new laws. People indicted or imprisoned included a Californian who laughed at rookies drilling at an army camp, a woman who greeted a Red Cross solicitor in a "hostile" way, and an editor who printed this sentence: "We must make the world safe for democracy even if we have to 'bean' the Goddess of Liberty to do it."

The sedition laws clearly went beyond any clear or present danger. There were, to be sure, German spies in the country, Germans who wanted to encourage strikes in American arms factories. Moreover, the U.S. government and other national leaders were painfully aware of how divided Americans had been about entering the war. They set out to promote unity—by force, if necessary—in order to convince Germany that the nation was united behind the war.

But none of these matters warranted a nationwide program of repression. Conservatives took advantage of wartime feelings to try to stamp out American socialists, who in fact were vulnerable because, unlike their European counterparts, they continued to oppose the war even after their country had entered it. Using the sedition laws, conservatives harried the Socialist party and another favorite target, the Industrial Workers of the World (see Chapter 22). In 1921, ill and facing imprisonment, Big Bill Haywood, one of the

Eugene V. Debs, serving time in an Atlanta penitentiary for speaking out against the war, is shown here after receiving word of his nomination for the presidency. Debs campaigned in 1920 from behind bars.

IWW's best known members, fled to the Soviet Union where he died a few years later.

Wilson's postmaster general banned from the mails more than a dozen socialist publications, including the *Appeal to Reason* that went to over half a million people weekly. In 1918, Eugene V. Debs, the Socialist party leader, delivered a speech denouncing capitalism and the war. He was convicted for violation of the Espionage Act and spent the war in a penitentiary in Atlanta. Nominated as the Socialist party candidate in the presidential election of 1920, Debs—prisoner 9653—won nearly a million votes, but the Socialist movement never fully recovered from the repression of the war.

In fostering hostility towards anything that smacked of dissent, the war also gave rise to the great "Red Scare" that began in 1919 (see

Chapter 25). Pleased at first with the Russian revolution, Americans in general turned quickly against it, especially after Lenin and the Bolsheviks seized control late in 1917. The Americans feared Lenin's anticapitalist program, and they denounced his decision in early 1918 to make peace with Germany because it freed German troops to fight in France.

Once again, Wilson himself played a prominent role in the development of anti-Bolshevik sentiment. In the summer of 1918, he sent fifteen thousand American troops into the Soviet Union, where they joined other Allied soldiers. Ostensibly, the troops were there to protect Allied supplies from the Germans and to rescue a large number of Czechs who wanted to return home to fight Germany. But the underlying reason for their presence was that Wilson and others hoped to bring down the fledgling Bolshevik government, fearful it would spread revolution around the world.

Besides sending troops, Wilson joined in an economic blockade of Russia, sent weapons to anti-Bolshevik insurgents, and refused to recognize Lenin's government. He also blocked Russian participation in the peace conference that ended the war. American troops remained in Russia until April 1920, and on the whole, American willingness to interfere soured Russian American relations for decades to come.

The United States Food Administration urged immigrants and newcomers to America to make sacrifices in the cause of freedom.

A Bureaucratic War

Quick, effective action was needed to win the war. To meet the need, Wilson and Congress set up an array of new federal agencies, nearly five thousand in all. Staffed largely by businessmen, the agencies drew on funds and powers of a hitherto unknown scope. At night, the secretary of the treasury sat in bed, a yellow pad on his knees, adding up the money needed to finance the war. "The noughts attached to the many millions were so boisterous and prolific," he later said, "that, at times, they would run clear over the edge of the paper."

By the time the war was over, the "noughts" had boisterously added up to $32 billion in direct war expense—in an era when the entire federal budget rarely exceeded $1 billion. To raise the money, the administration sold about $23 billion in "Liberty Bonds" and, using the new Sixteenth

Amendment (see Chapter 23), boosted taxes on corporations and personal incomes. The taxes brought in another $10 billion to help pay for the war.

At first Wilson tried to organize the wartime economy along decentralized lines, almost in the fashion of his early New Freedom thinking. But that proved unworkable, and he moved instead to a series of highly centralized planning boards, each with broad authority over a specific area of the economy. There were boards to control virtually every aspect of transportation, agriculture, and manufacturing. Though only a few of them were as effective as Wilson had hoped, they did coordinate the war effort to some degree.

The War Industries Board, one of the most powerful of the new agencies, oversaw the production of all American factories. Headed by millionaire Bernard M. Baruch, a Wall Street broker and speculator, it determined priorities, allocated raw materials, and fixed prices. It told manufacturers what they could and could not make. The WIB set the output of steel and regulated the number of stops on elevators. Working closely with business, Baruch for a time acted as the dictator of the American economy.

Herbert Hoover, the hero of a campaign to feed starving Belgians, headed a new Food Administration, and he set out with customary energy to supply food to the armies overseas. Appealing to the "spirit of self-sacrifice," Hoover convinced people to save food by observing "meatless" and "wheatless" days. He fixed prices to boost production, bought and distributed wheat, and encouraged people to plant "victory gardens" behind homes, churches, and schools. He sent half a million persons door to door to get housewives to sign cards pledging their cooperation. One householder—Wilson—set an example by grazing sheep on the White House lawn.

At another new agency, the Fuel Administration, Harry A. Garfield, the president of Williams College, introduced daylight saving time, rationed coal and oil, and imposed gasless days when motorists could not drive. To save coal, he shut down nonessential factories one day a week, and in January 1918, he closed all factories east of the Mississippi for four days to divert coal to munitions ships stranded in New York harbor. A fourth agency, the Railroad Administration, dictated rail traffic over nearly 400,000 miles of track—standardizing rates, limiting passenger travel, and speeding arms shipments. The War Shipping Board coordinated shipping, the Emergency Fleet Corporation supervised shipbuilding, and the War Trade Board oversaw foreign trade.

As never before, the government intervened in American life. When strikes threatened the telephone and telegraph companies, the government simply seized and ran them. Businessmen, paid a nominal dollar a year, flocked to Washington to run the new agencies, and the partnership between government and business grew closer. As government expanded, business expanded as well, responding to wartime contracts. Industries like steel, aluminum, and cigarettes boomed, and corporate profits increased threefold between 1914 and 1919.

Labor in the War

The war also brought organized labor into the partnership with government, although the results were more limited than in the business-government alliance. Samuel Gompers, president of the AFL, served on Wilson's Council of National Defense, an advisory group formed to unify business, labor, and government. Gompers hoped to trade labor peace for labor advances, and he formed a War Committee on Labor to enlist workers' support for the war. With the blessing of the Wilson administration, membership in the AFL and other unions grew from about 2.7 million in 1916 to more than 4 million in 1919.

Hoping to encourage production and avoid strikes, Wilson adopted many of the objectives of the social-justice reformers. He supported an eight-hour day in war-related industries and improved wages and working conditions. In May 1918, he named Felix Frankfurter, a brilliant young law professor, to head a new War Labor Board. The agency standardized wages and hours, and at Wilson's direction, it protected the right of labor to organize and bargain collectively. Although it did not forbid strikes, it used various tactics to discourage them. It enforced decisions in well-publicized cases; when the Smith and Wesson arms factory in Massachusetts and

Housewives did not leave home for the factory en masse in 1917 as they later did during World War II, but many women already employed outside the home found new, well-paying opportunities in jobs previously held by men.

the Western Union telegraph company disobeyed the WLB's union rules, the agency took them over.

The WLB also ordered that women be paid equal wages for equal work in war industries. In 1914, the flow of European immigrants suddenly stopped because of the war, and in 1917, the draft began to take large numbers of American men. The result was a labor shortage, filled by women, African Americans, and Mexican Americans. One million women worked in war industries. Some of them took jobs previously held by men, but for the most part, they moved from one set of "women's jobs" into another. From the beginning of the war to the end, the number of women in the work force held steady at about eight million, and unlike the experience in World War II, large numbers of housewives did not leave the home for machine shops and arms plants.

Still, there were some new opportunities and in some cases higher pay. In food, airplane, and electrical plants, women made up one-fifth or more of the work force. As their wages increased, so did their expectations; some became more militant, and conflict grew between them and male co-workers. To set standards for female employment, a Women's Bureau was established in the Department of Labor, but the government's influence varied. In the federally run railroad industry, women often made wages equal to those of men; in the federally run telephone industry, they did not.

Looking for more people to fill wartime jobs, corporations found another major source among southern blacks. Beginning in 1916, northern labor agents traveled across the South, promising jobs, high wages, and free transportation. Soon the word spread, and the movement northward became a flood. Between 1916 and 1918, over 450,000 African Americans left the Old South for the booming industrial cities of Saint Louis, Chicago, Detroit, and Cleveland. In the decade before 1920, Detroit's black population grew by over 600 percent, Cleveland's by over 300 percent, and Chicago's by 150 percent.

Most of the newcomers were young, unmarried, and skilled or semiskilled. The men found jobs in factories, railroad yards, steel mills, packing houses, and coal mines; black women worked in textile factories, department stores, and restaurants. In their new homes, African Americans found greater racial freedom but also different living conditions. If the South was often hostile, the North could be impersonal and lonely. Accustomed to the pace of the farm—ruled by the seasons and the sun—those blacks who were able to enter the industrial sector now worked for hourly wages in mass production industries, where time clocks and foremen dictated the daily routine.

Racial tensions increased, resulting in part from growing competition for housing and jobs. In mid-1917, a race war in East Saint Louis, Illinois, killed nine whites and about forty blacks. In July 1919, the month President Wilson returned from the peace conference in Paris, a race riot in Washington, D.C., killed six people. Riots in Chicago that month killed thirty-eight—fifteen whites and twenty-three blacks—and there were later outbreaks in New York City and Omaha. Lynch mobs killed forty-eight blacks in 1917, sixty-three in 1918, and seventy-eight in 1919. Ten of the victims in 1919 were war veterans, several still in uniform.

Blacks were more and more inclined to fight back. Two hundred thousand blacks served in France—42,000 as combat troops. Returning home, they expected better treatment. "I'm glad I went," a black veteran said. "I done my part and I'm going to fight right here till Uncle Sam does his." Roscoe Jameson, Claude McKay, and other black poets wrote biting poetry, some of it—like Fenton Johnson's "The New Day"—drawn from the war experience:

For we have been with thee in No Man's Land,
Through lake of fire and down to Hell itself;
And now we ask of thee our liberty,
Our freedom in the land of Stars and Stripes.

"Lift Ev'ry Voice and Sing," composed in 1900, became known as the "Negro National Anthem." Parents bought black dolls for their children, and W. E. B. Du Bois spoke of a "New Negro," proud and more militant: "We return. We return from fighting. We return fighting."

Eager for cheap labor, farmers and ranchers in the Southwest persuaded the federal government to relax immigration restrictions, and

The 369th infantry regiment returning from the war on the Stockholm *in February 1919. They were awarded the Croix de Guerre for bravery in the Meuse-Argonne.*

between 1917 and 1920 over 100,000 Mexicans migrated into Texas, Arizona, New Mexico, and California. The Mexican American population grew from 385,000 in 1910 to 740,000 in 1920. Tens of thousands of Mexican Americans moved to Chicago, Saint Louis, Omaha, and other northern cities to take wartime jobs. Often scorned and insecure, they created urban *barrios,* similar to the Chinatowns and Little Italys around them.

Like most wars, World War I affected patterns at home as much as abroad. Business profits grew, factories expanded, and industries turned out huge amounts of war goods. Government authority swelled, and people came to expect different things of their government. Labor made some gains, as did women and blacks. Society assimilated some of the shifts, but social and economic tensions grew, and when the war ended, they spilled over in the strikes and violence of the Red Scare that followed.

The United States emerged from the war the strongest economic power in the world. In 1914, it was a debtor nation, and American citizens owed foreign investors about $3 billion. Five years later, the United States had become a creditor nation. Foreign governments owed over $10 billion, and foreign citizens owed American investors nearly $3 billion. The war marked a shift in economic power rarely equaled in history.

THE TREATY OF VERSAILLES

Long before the fighting ended, Wilson began to formulate plans for the peace. Like many others, he was disconcerted when the new Bolshevik government in Russia began revealing the terms of secret agreements among Britain, France, and Czarist Russia to divide up Germany's colonies. To try to place the war on a higher plane, he appeared before Congress on January 8, 1918, and outlined terms for a far-reaching, nonpunitive settlement. Wilson's Fourteen Points were generous and farsighted, but they failed to satisfy wartime emotions that sought vindication.

England and France distrusted Wilsonian idealism as the basis for peace. They wanted Germany disarmed and crippled; they wanted its colonies; and they were skeptical of the principle of self-determination. As the end of the war neared, the Allies, who had in fact made secret commitments with one another, balked at making the Fourteen Points the basis of peace. When Wilson threatened to negotiate a separate treaty with Germany, however, they accepted.

Wilson had won an important victory, but difficulties lay ahead. As Georges Clemenceau, the seventy-eight-year-old French premier, said, "God gave us the Ten Commandments, and we broke them. Wilson gives us the Fourteen Points. We shall see."

A Peace at Paris

Unfortunately, Wilson made a grave error just before the peace conference began. He appealed to voters to elect a Democratic Congress in the November 1918 elections, saying that any other result would be "interpreted on the other side of the water as a repudiation of my leadership." Many Republicans were furious, especially those who had supported the Fourteen Points; Wilson's problems worsened when the Democrats went on to lose both the House and Senate.

Wilson's opponents immediately announced that voters had rejected his policies, as he had suggested they could. In fact, the Democratic

Woodrow Wilson's Fourteen Points, 1918: Success and Failure in Implementation	
1. Open covenants of peace openly arrived at	Not fulfilled
2. Absolute freedom of navigation upon the seas in peace and war	Not fulfilled
3. Removal of all economic barriers to the equality of trade among nations	Not fulfilled
4. Reduction of armaments to the level needed only for domestic safety	Not fulfilled
5. Impartial adjustments of colonial claims	Not fulfilled
6. Evacuation of all Russian territory; Russia to be welcomed into the society of free nations	Not fulfilled
7. Evacuation and restoration of Belgium	**Fulfilled**
8. Evacuation and restoration of all French lands; return of Alsace-Lorraine to France	**Fulfilled**
9. Readjustment of Italy's frontiers along lines of Italian nationality	Compromised
10. Self-determination for the former subjects of the Austro-Hungarian Empire	Compromised
11. Evacuation of Rumania, Serbia, and Montenegro; free access to the sea for Serbia	Compromised
12. Self-determination for the former subjects of the Ottoman Empire; secure sovereignty for Turkish portion	Compromised
13. Establishment of an independent Poland, with free and secure access to the sea	**Fulfilled**
14. Establishment of a League of Nations affording mutual guarantees of independence and territorial integrity	Not fulfilled

Sources: Data from G. M. Gathorne-Hardy, *The Fourteen Points and the Treaty of Versailles* (Oxford Pamphlets on World Affairs, no. 6, 1939), pp. 8–34; Thomas G. Paterson et al., *American Foreign Policy, A History Since 1900*, 2d ed., Vol. 2, pp. 282–93.

losses stemmed largely from domestic problems, such as the price of wheat and cotton. But they hurt Wilson, who had alienated some important Republican party leaders. Soon, he would be negotiating with European leaders buoyed by rousing victories at their own polls.

Two weeks after the elections, Wilson announced he would attend the peace conference. This was a dramatic break from tradition, and his personal involvement drew attacks from Republicans. They renewed criticism when he named the rest of the delegation: Secretary of State Lansing, Colonel House, General Tasker H. Bliss, a military expert, and Henry White, a career diplomat. Wilson named no member of the Senate, and the only Republican in the group was White.

In selecting the delegation, Wilson passed over Henry Cabot Lodge, the powerful Republican senator from Massachusetts who opposed the Fourteen Points and would soon head the Senate Foreign Relations Committee. He also decided not to appoint Elihu Root or ex-President Taft,

both of them enthusiastic internationalists. Never good at accepting criticism or delegating authority, Wilson wanted a delegation he could control—an advantage at the peace table but not in any battle over the treaty at home.

Upon his arrival, Wilson received a tumultuous welcome in England, France, and Italy. Never before had such crowds acclaimed a democratic political figure. In Paris, two million people lined the Champs-Elysées, threw flowers at him, and shouted "Wilson *le Juste* [the just]" as his carriage drove by. Overwhelmed, Wilson was sure that the people of Europe shared his goals and would force their leaders to accept *his* peace. He was wrong. Like their leaders, many people on the Allied side hated Germany and wanted victory unmistakably reflected in the peace.

Opening in January 1919, the Peace Conference at Paris continued until May. Although twenty-seven nations were represented, the "Big Four" dominated it: Wilson; Clemenceau of France, tired and stubborn, determined to end the German threat forever; David

Sir William Orpen, The Signing of Peace in the Hall of Mirrors, Versailles, 28th of May 1919. *Although the United States played a major role in drafting the treaty, the Senate never ratified the document. Instead, the United States made a separate peace with Germany in 1921.*

Europe After the Treaty of Versailles, 1919
The treaty changed the map of Europe, creating a number of new and reconstituted nations. (Note the boundary changes from the prewar map on p. 736.)

Lloyd George, the crafty British prime minister who had pledged to squeeze Germany "until the pips squeak"; and the Italian prime minister, Vittorio Orlando. A clever negotiator, Wilson traded various "small" concessions for his major goals—national self-determination, a reduction in tensions, and a League of Nations to enforce the peace.

Wilson had to surrender some important principles. Departing from the Fourteen Points by violating the principle of self-determination, the treaty created two new independent nations—Poland and Czechoslovakia—with large German-speaking populations. It divided up the German colonies in Asia and Africa. Instead of a peace without victory, it made Germany accept responsibility for the war and demanded enormous reparations—which eventually totaled $33 billion. It made no mention of disarmament, free trade, or freedom of the seas. Instead of an open covenant openly arrived at, the treaty was drafted behind closed doors.

But Wilson deflected some of the most extreme Allied demands, and he won his coveted Point 14, a League of Nations, designed "to achieve international peace and security." The League included a general Assembly; a smaller Council composed of the United States, Great Britain, France, Italy, Japan, and four nations to be elected by the Assembly; and a court of international justice. League members pledged to submit to arbitration every dispute threatening peace and to enjoin military and economic sanctions against nations resorting to war. Article X, for Wilson the heart of the League, obliged members to look out for one another's independence and territorial integrity.

The draft treaty in hand, Wilson returned home in February 1919 to discuss it with Congress and the people. Most Americans, the polls showed, favored the League; thirty-three governors endorsed it. But over dinner with the Senate and House Foreign Relations Committees, Wilson learned of the strength of congressional opposition to it. On March 3, Senator Lodge produced a "round robin" signed by thirty-seven senators declaring they would not vote for the treaty without amendment. Should the numbers hold, Lodge had enough votes to defeat it.

Returning to Paris, Wilson attacked his critics, while he worked privately for changes to improve the chances of Senate approval. In return for major concessions, the Allies amended the League draft treaty, agreeing that domestic affairs remained outside League jurisdiction (exempting the Monroe Doctrine) and allowing nations to withdraw after two years' notice. On June 28, 1919, they signed the treaty in the Hall of Mirrors at Versailles, and Wilson started home for his most difficult fight.

Rejection in the Senate

There were ninety-six senators in 1919, forty-nine of them Republicans. Fourteen Republicans, led by William E. Borah of Idaho, were the "irreconcilables" who opposed the League on any grounds. "If the Savior of man," Borah said, "would revisit the earth and declare for a League of Nations, I would be opposed to it." Frank B. Kellogg of Minnesota led a group of twelve "mild reservationists" who accepted the treaty but wanted to insert several reservations that would not greatly weaken it. Finally, there were the Lodge-led "strong reservationists," twenty-three of them in all, who wanted major changes that the Allies would have to approve.

With only four Democratic senators opposed to the treaty, the Democrats and Republicans willing to compromise had enough votes to ratify it, once a few reservations were inserted. Bidding for time to allow public opposition to grow, Lodge scheduled lengthy hearings and spent two weeks reading the 268-page treaty aloud. Democratic leaders urged Wilson to appeal to the Republican "mild reservationists," but he refused: "Anyone who opposes me in that I'll crush!"

Fed up with Lodge's tactics, Wilson set out in early September to take the case directly to the people. Crossing the Midwest, his speeches aroused little emotion, but on the Pacific Coast he won ovations, which heartened him. On his way back to Washington, he stopped in Pueblo,

Colorado, where he delivered one of the most eloquent speeches of his career. People wept as he talked of Americans who died in battle and the hope that they would never fight again in foreign lands. That night Wilson felt ill. He returned to Washington, and on October 2, Mrs. Wilson found him lying unconscious on the floor of the White House, the victim of a stroke that paralyzed his left side.

After the stroke, Wilson could not work more than an hour or two at a time. No one was allowed to see him except family members, his secretary, and his physician. For over seven months, he did not meet with the cabinet. Secretary of State Lansing convened cabinet meetings, but when Wilson learned of them, he ordered Lansing to stop and then cruelly forced him to resign. Focusing his remaining energy on the fight over the treaty, Wilson lost touch with other issues, and critics charged that his wife, Edith Bolling Wilson, ran the government.

On November 6, 1919, while Wilson convalesced, Lodge finally reported the treaty out of committee, along with "Fourteen Reservations," one for each of Wilson's points. The most important reservation stipulated that implementation of Article X, Wilson's key article, required the action of Congress before any American intervention abroad.

The next day, the president's floor leader in the Senate told him that the Democrats could not pass the treaty without reservations. "Is it possible?" Wilson asked sadly. "It might be wise to compromise," the senator said. "Let Lodge compromise!" Wilson replied. When Mrs. Wilson urged her husband to accept the Lodge reservations, he said, "Better a thousand times to go down fighting than to dip your colors to dishonorable compromise."

On November 19, the treaty—with the Lodge reservations—failed, 39 to 55. Following Wilson's instructions, the Democrats voted against it. A motion to approve without the reservations lost 38 to 53, with only one Republican voting in favor. The defeat brought pleas for compromise, but neither Wilson nor Lodge would back down. When the treaty with reservations again came up for vote on March 19, 1920, Wilson ordered the Democrats to hold firm against it. Although twenty-one of them defied him, enough obeyed his orders to defeat it, 49 to

The Election of 1920

Candidate	Party	Popular Vote	Electoral Vote
Harding	Republican	16,133,314	404
Cox	Democrat	9,140,884	127
Debs	Socialist	913,664	0

35, seven votes short of the necessary two-thirds majority.

To Wilson, walking now with the help of a cane, one chance remained: the presidential election of 1920. For a time, he thought of running for a third term himself, but his party shunted him aside. The Democrats nominated Governor James M. Cox of Ohio, along with the young and popular Franklin D. Roosevelt, assistant secretary of the navy, for vice president. Wilson called for "a great and solemn referendum" on the treaty. The Democratic platform endorsed the treaty but agreed to accept reservations that clarified the American role in the League.

On the Republican side, Senator Warren G. Harding of Ohio, who had nominated Taft in 1912, won the presidential nomination. Harding waffled on the treaty, but it made little difference. Voters wanted a change. Harding won in a landslide, taking 61 percent of the vote and beating Cox by seven million votes. Without a peace treaty, the United States remained technically at war, and it was not until July 1921, almost three years after the last shot was fired, that Congress passed a joint resolution ending the war.

After 1919, there was disillusionment. World War I was feared before it started, popular while it lasted, and hated when it ended. To a whole generation that followed, it appeared futile, killing without cause, sacrificing without benefit. Books, plays, and movies—Hemingway's *A Farewell to Arms,* John Dos Passos's *Three Soldiers* (1921), Laurence Stallings and Maxwell Anderson's *What Price Glory?* (1924), among others—showed it as waste, horror, and death.

The war and its aftermath damaged the humanitarian, progressive spirit of the early years

CHRONOLOGY

1901 Hay-Pauncefote Treaty with Great Britain empowers United States to build Isthmian canal

1904 Theodore Roosevelt introduces corollary to Monroe Doctrine

1904–1905 Russo-Japanese War

1905 Taft-Katsura Agreement recognizes Japanese power in Korea

1908 Root-Takahira Agreement vows to maintain status quo in the Pacific • Roosevelt sends the fleet around the world

1911 Revolution begins in Mexico

1913–1914 Bryan negotiates "cooling-off" treaties to end war

1914 World War I begins • U.S. Marines take Veracruz • Panama Canal completed

1915 Japan issues Twenty-One Demands to China (January) • Germany declares water around British Isles a war zone (February) • *Lusitania* torpedoed (May) • Bryan resigns; Robert Lansing becomes secretary of state (June) • *Arabic* pledge restricts submarine warfare (September)

1916 Germany issues *Sussex* pledge (March) • General John J. Pershing leads unsuccessful punitive expedition into Mexico to seize Pancho Villa (April) • Wilson wins reelection

1917 Wilson calls for "peace without victory" (January) • Germany resumes unrestricted U-boat warfare (February) • United States enters World War I (April) • Congress passes Selective Service Act (May) • First American troops reach France (June) • War Industries Board established (July)

1918 Wilson outlines Fourteen Points for peace (January) • Germany asks for peace (October) • Armistice ends the war (November)

1919 Peace negotiations begin in Paris (January) • Treaty of Versailles defeated in Senate

1920 Warren G. Harding elected president

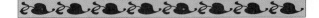

of the century. It killed "something precious and perhaps irretrievable in the hearts of thinking men and women." Progressivism survived well into the 1920s and the New Deal, but it no longer had the old conviction and broad popular support. Bruising fights over the war and the League drained people's energy and enthusiasm.

Confined to bed, Woodrow Wilson died in Washington in 1924, three years after Harding, the new president, promised "not heroics but healing; not nostrums but normalcy; not revolution but restoration." Nonetheless, the "war to end all wars" and the spirit of Woodrow Wilson left an indelible imprint on the country.

Recommended Reading

American foreign policy between 1901 and 1921 has been the subject of considerable study. Richard W. Leopold, *The Growth of American Foreign Policy* (1962), is balanced and informed. Howard K. Beale, *Theodore Roosevelt and the Rise of America to World Power* (1956), traces foreign policy during the early years; Robert E. Osgood, *Ideals and Self-Interest in America's Foreign Relations* (1953), and William Appleman Williams, *Roots of the Modern American Empire* (1969), explore the forces underlying American foreign policy.

David McCullough gives a lively account of the building of the Panama Canal in *The Path Between the Seas* (1977). For American policy toward Latin America, see Dana G. Munro's detailed account, *Intervention and Dollar Diplomacy in the Caribbean, 1900–1920* (1964). Arthur S. Link examines Wilson's foreign policy in his exceptional five-volume biography, *Wilson* (1947–1965), and in *Woodrow Wilson: Revolution, War, and Peace* (1979). N. Gordon Levin, Jr., *Woodrow Wilson and World Politics: America's Response to War and Revolution* (1968), places Wilson in the larger context of world events.

Ernest R. May studies American policy before the war in *The World War and American Isolation, 1914–1917* (1959). Bradford Perkins, *The Great Rapprochement: England and the United States, 1895–1914* (1968), examines the growing friendship between the two countries. Studies of events at home during the war include David M. Kennedy, *Over Here* (1980); Robert D. Cuff, *The War Industries Board* (1973); and Maurine W. Greenwald, *Women, War, and Work* (1980).

Woodrow Wilson and the Lost Peace (1944) and *Woodrow Wilson and the Great Betrayal* (1945) by Thomas A. Bailey are dated but thorough on Wilson's

efforts at Versailles. Arthur Walworth, *America's Moment, 1918: American Diplomacy at the End of World War I* (1977), also examines Wilson's attempt to create a peaceful world order.

Additional Bibliography

For background to American policy in these years, see Richard D. Challener, *Admirals, Generals, and American Foreign Policy, 1898–1914* (1973); Michael Pearlman, *To Make Democracy Safe for America: Patricians and Preparedness in the Progressive Era* (1984); Lloyd C. Gardner, *Safe for Democracy: The Anglo-American Response to Revolution, 1913–1923* (1984); William C. Widenor, *Henry Cabot Lodge and the Search for an American Foreign Policy* (1980); and Paul P. Abrahams, *The Foreign Expansion of American Finance and Its Relationship to the Foreign Economic Policies of the United States, 1907–1921* (1976). David H. Burton, *Theodore Roosevelt, Confident Imperialist* (1968); Frederick Marks III, *Velvet on Iron: The Diplomacy of Theodore Roosevelt* (1979); and C. E. Neu, *An Uncertain Friendship: Theodore Roosevelt and Japan, 1906–1909* (1967), trace Roosevelt's policies.

On Taft and Wilson, see Ralph E. Minger, *William Howard Taft and United States Foreign Policy* (1975); Walter V. Scholes and Marie V. Scholes, *The Foreign Policies of the Taft Administration* (1970); Frederick S. Calhoun, *Power and Principle: Armed Intervention in Wilsonian Foreign Policy* (1986); Kendrick A. Clements, *William Jennings Bryan: Missionary Isolationist* (1983) and *Woodrow Wilson: World Statesman* (1987); Robert W. Cherny, *A Righteous Cause: The Life of William Jennings Bryan* (1985); Robert H. Ferrell, *Woodrow Wilson and World War I* (1985); Michael Pearlman, *To Make Democracy Safe for America: Patricians and Preparedness in the Progressive Era* (1984); Thomas J. Knock, *To End All Wars: Woodrow Wilson and the Quest for a New World Order* (1992); and John Morton Blum, *Woodrow Wilson and the Politics of Morality* (1956). For relations with Latin America, see Dexter R. Perkins, *The United States and the Caribbean*, rev. ed. (1966); Richard L. Lael, *Arrogant Diplomacy: U.S. Policy Toward Colombia, 1903–1922* (1987); David Healy, *Drive to Hegemony: The United States in the Caribbean, 1898–1917* (1988); Richard H. Collin, *Theodore Roosevelt's Caribbean: The Panama Canal, the Monroe Doctrine, and the Latin American Context* (1990); and two books by Lester D. Langley: *Struggle for the American Mediterranean* (1975) and *The United States and the Caribbean, 1900–1970* (1980).

On Mexico, see Peter Calvert, *The Mexican Revolution, 1910–1914* (1968); Lloyd Gardner, *Wilson and Revolutions, 1913–1921* (1976); and

Robert E. Quirk, *An Affair of Honor: Woodrow Wilson and the Occupation of Veracruz* (1962). Several books deal with policies in the Far East, including Charles Vevier, *United States and China, 1906–1913* (1955); Charles S. Campbell, *Special Business Interests and the Open Door Policy* (1951); Warren I. Cohen, *America's Response to China,* 2d ed. (1980); Raymond A. Esthus, *Theodore Roosevelt and Japan* (1966); and Jerry Israel, *Progressivism and the Open Door: America and China, 1905–1921* (1971).

Historians have long debated the reasons for America's entry into the war; see, for example, Charles Seymour, *American Diplomacy During the World War* (1934) and *American Neutrality, 1914–1917* (1935); Patrick Devlin, *Too Proud to Fight: Woodrow Wilson's Neutrality* (1974); David M. Smith, *Robert Lansing and American Neutrality* (1958); Ross Gregory, *The Origins of American Intervention in the First World War* (1971); John W. Coogan, *The End of Neutrality: The United States, Britain, and Maritime Rights, 1899–1915* (1981); and Jeffrey J. Safford, *Wilsonian Maritime Diplomacy* (1978).

The war at home is followed in Ronald Schaffer, *America in the Great War: The Rise of the Welfare State* (1991); Valerie Jean Conner, *The National War Labor Board: Stability, Social Justice, and the Voluntary State in World War I* (1983); Neil A. Wynn, *From Progressivism to Prosperity: World War I and American Society* (1986); John Whiteclay Chambers II, *To Raise an Army: The Draft Comes to Modern America* (1987); Paul L. Murphy, *World War I and the Origin of Civil Liberties in the United States* (1979); John G. Clifford, *The Citizen Soldiers* (1972); William Preston, Jr., *Aliens and Dissenters: Federal Suppression of Radicals, 1903–1933* (1963); H. C. Peterson and Gilbert C. Fite, *Opponents of War, 1917–1918* (1957); Carol S. Gruber, *Mars and Minerva: World War I and the Uses of Higher Learning in America* (1975); and Stephen Vaughn, *Holding Fast the Inner Lines:*

Democracy, Nationalism, and the Committee on Public Information (1980); James R. Grossman, *Land of Hope: Chicago, Black Southerners, and the Great Migration* (1989); and Carole Marks, *Farewell—We're Good and Gone: The Great Black Migration* (1989), trace the movement of African Americans to the North. John A. Thompson, *Reformers and War: American Progressive Publicists and the First World War* (1987), examines the war's effects on reform journalists.

On military intervention, see Harvey DeWeerd, *President Wilson Fights His War* (1968); E. M. Coftman, *The War to End All Wars* (1968); Frank E. Vandiver, *Black Jack: The Life and Times of John J. Pershing,* 2 vols. (1977); Russell F. Weigley, *The American Way of War* (1973); Laurence Stallings, *The Doughboys* (1963); and Arthur E. Barbeau and Henri Florette, *The Unknown Soldiers: Black American Troops in World War I* (1974).

The Treaty of Versailles and the struggle for ratification are covered in Arno J. Mayer, *Politics and Diplomacy of Peacemaking* (1967); Charles L. Mee, Jr., *The End of Order, Versailles, 1919* (1980); Lloyd E. Ambrosius, *Woodrow Wilson and the American Diplomatic Tradition: The Treaty Fight in Perspective* (1987); Herbert F. Margulies, *The Mild Reservationists and the League of Nations Controversy in the Senate* (1989); Arthur Walworth, *Wilson and His Peacemakers: American Diplomacy at the Paris Peace Conference, 1919* (1986); Warren F. Kuehl, *Seeking World Order* (1969); L. W. Martin, *Peace Without Victory* (1958); and Ralph A. Stone, *The Irreconcilables* (1970).

Wesley M. Bagby, *The Road to Normalcy* (1962); Seward W. Livermore, *Politics Is Adjourned: Woodrow Wilson and the War Congress, 1916–1918* (1966); and David Burner, *The Politics of Provincialism: The Democratic Party in Transition, 1918–1932* (1967), are excellent studies of domestic politics of the era.

Transition to Modern America

The moving assembly line that Henry Ford perfected in 1913 for manufacture of the Model T marked only the first step toward full mass production and the beginning of America's worldwide industrial supremacy. A year later, Ford began buying large plots of land along the Rouge River southeast of Detroit, Michigan. He already had a vision of a vast industrial tract where machines, moving through a sequence of carefully arranged manufacturing operations, would transform raw materials into finished cars, trucks, and tractors. The key would be control over the flow of goods at each step along the way—from lake steamers and railroad cars bringing in the coal and iron ore, to overhead conveyor belts and huge turning tables carrying the moving parts past the stationary workers on the assembly line. "Everything must move," Ford commanded, and by the mid-1920s at River Rouge, as the plant became known, it did.

Ford began fulfilling his industrial dream in 1919 when he built a blast furnace and foundry to make engine blocks for both the Model T and his tractors. By 1924, more than forty thousand workers were turning out nearly all the metal parts used in making Ford vehicles. One tractor factory was so efficient that it took just over twenty-eight hours to convert raw ore into a new farm implement.

Visitors from all over the world came to marvel at River Rouge. Some were disturbed by the jumble of machines (by 1926, there were 43,000 in operation) and the apparent congestion on the plant floor, but industrial experts recognized that the arrangement led to incredible productivity because "the work moves and the men stand still." A trained engineer summed it up best when he wrote that a visitor to the plant "sees each unit as a carefully designed gear which meshes with other gears and operates in synchronism with them, the whole forming one huge, perfectly-timed, smoothly-operating industrial machine of almost unbelieveable efficiency."

In May 1927, after producing over fifteen million Model Ts, Ford closed the assembly line at Highland Park. For the next six months, his engineers worked on designing a more compact and efficient assembly line at River Rouge for the Model A, which went into production in November. By then, River Rouge had more than justified Ford's vision. "Ford had brought together everything at a single site and on a scale no one else had ever attempted," concluded historian Geoffrey Perrett. "The Rouge plant became to a generation of engineers far more than a factory. It was a monument."

Mass production, born in Highland Park in 1913 and perfected at River Rouge in the 1920s, became the hallmark of American industry. Other carmakers copied Ford's methods and soon his emphasis on the flow of parts moving past stationary workers became the standard in nearly every American factory. The moving assembly line—with its emphasis on uniformity, speed, precision, and coordination—took away the last vestiges of craftsmanship and turned workers into near robots. It led to amazing efficiency that produced both high profits for manufacturers and low prices for buyers. By the mid-1920s, the cost of the Model T had dropped from $950 down to only $290.

Most important, mass production led to a consumer goods revolution. American factories turned out a flood of automobiles and electric appliances that made life easier and more pleasant for the vast majority of the American people. The result was the creation of a new America, one in which individualism was sacrificed to conformity as part of the price to be paid for a new era of abundance.

The 1920s, often seen as a time of escape and frivolity before the onset of the Depression, actually marked a beginning, a time when the American people learned to adapt to life in the city, when they decided (wisely or not) to center their existence on the automobile, and when they rejected their rural past while still longing for the old values it had created. It is in the 1920s that we can find the roots of modern America—the America we know today.

THE SECOND INDUSTRIAL REVOLUTION

The first Industrial Revolution in the late nineteenth century had catapulted the United States into the forefront among the world's richest and most highly developed nations. With the advent of the new consumer goods industries, the American people by the 1920s enjoyed the highest standard of living of any nation on earth. After a brief postwar depression, 1922 saw the beginning of a great boom that peaked in 1927 and lasted until 1929. In this brief period, American industrial output nearly doubled, and the gross national product rose by 40 percent. Most of this explosive growth took place in industries producing consumer goods—automobiles, appliances, furniture, and clothing. Equally important, the national per capita income increased by 30 percent to $681 in 1929. American workers became the highest paid in history and thus were able to buy the flood of new goods they were turning out on the assembly lines.

The key to the new affluence lay in technology. The moving assembly line pioneered by Ford became a standard feature in nearly all American plants. Electric motors replaced steam engines as the basic source of energy in factories; by 1929, 70 percent of all industrial power came from electricity. Efficiency experts broke down the industrial process into minute parts using time and motion studies and then showed managers and workers how to maximize the output of their labor. Production per man-hour increased an amazing 75 percent over the decade; in 1929, a work force no larger than that of 1919 was producing almost twice as many goods.

The Automobile Industry

The nature of the consumer goods revolution can best be seen in the automobile industry, which became the nation's largest in the 1920s. Rapid growth was its hallmark. In 1920, there were 10 million cars in the nation; by the end of the decade, 26 million were on the road. Production jumped from less than 2 million units a year to over 5 million by 1929.

The automobile boom, at its peak from 1922 to 1927, depended on the apparently insatiable appetite of the American people for cars. But as the decade continued, the market became saturated as more and more of those who could afford the new luxury had become car owners. Marketing became as crucial as production. Automobile makers began to rely heavily on advertising and annual model changes, seeking to make customers dissatisfied with their old vehicles and eager to order new ones. Despite these

On the assembly line at Ford's River Rouge plant, workers performed repetitive tasks on the car chassis that rushed by at a rate of six feet per minute.

efforts, sales slumped in 1927 when Ford stopped making the Model T, picked up again the next year with the new Model A, but began to slide again in 1929. The new industry revealed a basic weakness in the consumer goods economy; once people had bought an item with a long life, they would be out of the market for a few years.

In the affluent 1920s, few noticed the emerging economic instability. Instead, contemporary observers focused on the stimulating effect the automobile had on the rest of the economy. The mass production of cars required huge quantities of steel; entire new rolling mills had to be built to supply sheet steel for car bodies. Rubber factories boomed with the demand for tires, and paint and glass suppliers had more business than ever before. The auto changed the pattern of city life, leading to a suburban explosion. Real estate developers, no longer dependent on streetcars and railway lines, could now build houses in ever wider concentric circles around the central cities.

The automobile had a profound effect on all aspects of American life in the 1920s. Filling sta-

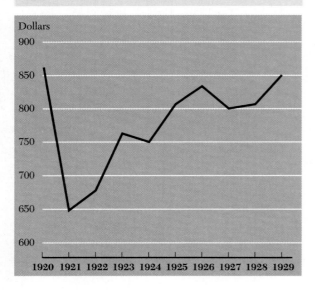

Gross National Product (Per Capita), 1920–1929

cess of KDKA in Pittsburgh stimulated the growth of more than eight hundred independent radio stations, and by 1929, NBC had formed the first successful radio network. Five nights a week, "Amos 'n Andy," a comic serial featuring two "blackface" vaudevillians, held the attention of millions of Americans. The film industry thrived in Hollywood, reaching its maturity in the mid-1920s when in every large city there were huge theaters seating as many as four thousand people. With the advent of the "talkies" by 1929, average weekly movie attendance climbed to nearly 100 million.

Other industries prospered as well. Production of light metals such as aluminum and magnesium grew into a major business. Chemical engineering came of age with the invention of synthetics, ranging from rayon for clothing to cellophane for packaging. Americans found a whole new spectrum of products to buy—cigarette lighters, wristwatches, heat-resistant glass cooking dishes, and rayon stockings to name just a few.

The corporation continued to be the dominant economic unit in the 1920s. Growing corporations now had hundreds of thousands of stockholders; and one individual or family rarely held more than 5 percent of the stock. The enormous profits generated by these corporations enabled their managers to finance growth and expansion internally, thus freeing companies from their earlier dependence on investment bankers like J. P. Morgan. Voicing a belief in social responsibility and enlightened capitalism, the new professional class operated independently, free from outside restraint. In the final analysis, the corporate managers were accountable only to other managers.

Another wave of mergers accompanied the growth of corporations during the 1920s. From 1920 to 1928, some eight thousand mergers took place as more and more small firms proved unable to compete effectively with the new giants. By the end of the decade, the two hundred largest nonfinancial corporations owned almost half of the country's corporate wealth. The oligopoly in the automobile industry set an example for other areas. The greatest abuses took place in public utilities where promoters like Samuel Insull built vast paper empires by gaining control of operating power companies and then draining them of their assets.

tions appeared on the main streets, replacing the smithies and stables of the past. In Kansas City, Jess D. Nichols built the first shopping center, Country Club Plaza, and thus set an example quickly followed by other suburban developers.

Even in smaller communities, the car ruled. In Munice, Indiana, site of a famous sociological survey in the 1920s, one elder replied when asked what was taking place, "I can tell you what's happening in just four letters: A-U-T-O!" A nation that had always revered symbols of movement, from the Mayflower to the covered wagon, now had a new icon to worship.

Patterns of Economic Growth

Automobiles were the most conspicuous of the consumer products that flourished in the 1920s but certainly not the only ones. The electrical industry grew almost as quickly. Central power stations, where massive steam generators converted coal into electricity, brought current into the homes of city and town dwellers. Two-thirds of all American families enjoyed electricity by the end of the decade, and they spent vast sums on washing machines, vacuum cleaners, refrigerators, and ranges. The new appliances eased the burdens of the housewife and ushered in an age of leisure.

Radio broadcasting and motion picture production also boomed in the 1920s. The early suc-

The most distinctive feature of the new consumer-oriented economy was the emphasis on

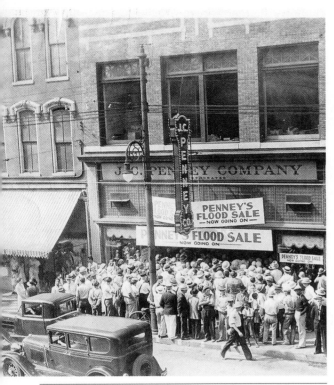

J. C. Penney's, one of the popular chain stores of the 1920s, attracted a flood of customers to its flood sale.

marketing. Advertising earnings rose from $1.3 billion in 1915 to $3.4 billion in 1926. Skillful practitioners like Edward Bernays and Bruce Barton sought to control public taste and consumer spending by identifying the good life with the possession of the latest product of American industry, whether it be a car, a refrigerator, or a brand of cigarettes. Chain stores advanced rapidly at the expense of small retail shops. A&P dominated the retail food industry, growing from 400 stores in 1912 to 15,500 by 1932. Woolworth's "five and tens" spread almost as rapidly, while such drugstore chains as Rexall and Liggetts— both owned by one huge holding company— opened outlets in nearly every town and city in the land.

Uniformity and standardization, the characteristics of mass production, now prevailed. The farmer in Kansas bought the same kind of car, the same groceries, and the same pills as the factory worker in Pennsylvania. Sectional differences in dress, food, and furniture began to disappear. Even the regional accents that distinguished Americans in different parts of the country were threatened with extinction by the advent of radio and films which promoted a stantard national dialect devoid of any local flavor.

Economic Weaknesses

The New Era, as businessmen labeled the decade, was not as prosperous as it first appeared. The revolution in consumer goods disguised the decline of many traditional industries in the 1920s. Railroads, overcapitalized and poorly managed, suffered from internal woes and from competition with the growing trucking industry. The coal industry was also troubled, with petroleum and natural gas beginning to replace coal as a fuel. The use of cotton textiles declined with the development of rayon and other synthetic fibers. The New England mills moved south in search of cheap labor, leaving behind thousands of unemployed workers and virtual ghost towns in the nation's oldest industrial center.

Hardest hit of all was agriculture. American farmers had expanded production to meet the demands of World War I, when they fed their own nation and most of Europe as well. A sharp cutback of exports in 1919 caused a rapid decline in prices. By 1921, farm exports had fallen by more than $2 billion. Throughout the 1920s, the farmers' share of the national income dropped until by 1929, the per capita farm income was only $273, compared to the national average of $681.

Workers were better off than farmers in the 1920s, but they did not share fully in the decade's affluence. The industrial labor force remained remarkably steady for a period of economic growth; technical innovations meant the same number of workers could produce far more than before. Most new jobs appeared in the lower-paying service industry. During the decade, factory wage rates rose only a modest 11 percent; by 1929, nearly half of all American families had an income of less than $1,500. At the same time, however, conditions of life improved. Prices remained stable, even dropping somewhat in the early 1920s, so that workers enjoyed a gain in real wages.

Organized labor proved unable to advance the interests of workers in the 1920s. Conservative leadership in the AFL neglected the task of organizing the vast number of unskilled laborers in the mass production industries. Aggressive management weakened the appeal of unions by portraying them as radical organizations after a series of strikes in 1919. Many businessmen used the injunction and "yellow-dog" contracts—which forbade employees to join unions—to establish open shops and deny workers the benefits of collective bargaining. Other employers wooed their workers away from unions using techniques of welfare capitalism, spending money to improve plant conditions and winning employee loyalty with pensions, paid vacations, and company cafeterias. The net result was a decline in union membership from a postwar high of five million to less than three million by 1929.

Black workers remained on the bottom, both economically and socially. Nearly half a million African Americans had migrated northward from the rural South during World War I. Some found jobs in northern industries, but many more worked in menial service areas, collecting garbage, washing dishes, and sweeping floors. Yet even these jobs offered them a better life than they found on the depressed southern farms, where millions of African Americans still lived in poverty, and so the migration continued. The black ghettos in northern cities grew rapidly in the 1920s; Chicago's African American population doubled during the decade, while New York's rose from 152,467 to 327,706, with most African Americans living in Harlem.

Middle- and upper-class Americans were the groups who thrived in the 1920s. The rewards of this second Industrial Revolution went to the managers—the engineers, bankers, and executives—who directed the new industrial economy. Corporate profits nearly doubled in ten years, and income from dividends rose 65 percent, nearly six times the rate of workers' wages. Bank accounts, reflecting the accumulated savings of the upper-middle and wealthy classes, rose from $41.1 billion to $57.9 billion. These were the people who bought the fine new houses in the suburbs and who could afford more than one car. Their conspicuous consumption helped fuel the prosperity of the 1920s, but their disposable income eventually became greater than their material wants. The result was speculation, as those with idle money began to invest heavily in the stock market to reap gains from the industrial growth.

The economic trends of the decade had both positive and negative implications for the future. On the one hand, there was the solid growth of new consumer-based industries. Automobiles and appliances were not passing fancies; their production and use became a part of the modern American way of life, creating a high standard of living that roused the envy of the rest of the world. The future pattern of American culture—cars and suburbs, shopping centers and skyscrapers—was determined by the end of the 1920s.

But at the same time, there were ominous signs of danger. The unequal distribution of wealth, the saturation of the market for consumer goods, and the growing speculation all created economic instability. The boom of the 1920s would end in a great crash; yet the achievements of the decade would survive even that dire experience to shape the future of American life.

THE NEW URBAN CULTURE

The city replaced the countryside as the focal point of American life in the 1920s. The 1920 census revealed that for the first time, slightly more than half of the population lived in cities (defined broadly to include all places of more than 2,500 people). During the decade, the metropolitan areas grew rapidly as both whites and blacks from rural areas came seeking jobs in the new consumer industries. Between 1920 and 1930, cities with populations of 250,000 or more had added some 8 million people to their ranks. New York alone grew by nearly 25 percent, while Detroit more than doubled its population during the decade.

The skyscraper soon became the most visible feature of the city. Faced with inflated land prices, builders turned upward—developing a distinctively American architectural style in the process. New York led the way with the ornate Woolworth Building in 1913. The sleek 102-story Empire State Building, completed in 1930, was for years the tallest building in the world. Other cities erected their own jagged skylines. By 1929, there were 377 buildings over 20 stories tall across the nation. Most significantly, the sky-

Its 102 stories rising 1,250 feet into the sky (222 feet were added in 1950), the Empire State Building had space for 25,000 tenants.

scraper came to symbolize the new mass culture. "The New York skyscrapers are the most striking manifestation of the triumph of numbers," wrote one French observer. "One cannot understand or like them without first having tasted and enjoyed the thrill of counting or adding up enormous totals and of living in a gigantic, compact and brilliant world."

In the metropolis, life was different. The old community ties of home, church, and school were absent, but there were important gains to replace them—new ideas, new creativity, new perspectives. Some city dwellers became lost and lonely without the old institutions; others thrived in the urban environment.

Women and the Family

The urban culture of the 1920s witnessed important changes in the American family. This vital institution began to break down under the impact of economic and social change. A new freedom for women and children seemed to be emerging in its wake.

Women had already begun to leave the home in the early twentieth century as the second Industrial Revolution opened up new jobs for them. World War I sped up the process, but in the 1920s there was no great permanent gain in the number of working women. Although two million more women were employed in 1930 than in 1920, this represented an increase of only 1 percent. Most women workers, moreover, had low-paying jobs, ranging from stenographers to maids. The number of women doctors actually decreased, and even though women earned nearly one-third of all graduate degrees, only 4 percent of the full professors were female. For the most part, the professions were reserved for men, with women relegated to such stereotypical fields as teaching and nursing.

To be sure, women had won the right to vote in 1920, but the Nineteenth Amendment proved to have less impact than its proponents had hoped. Once achieved, it robbed women of a unifying cause, and the exercise of the franchise itself did little to change the prevailing sex roles in society. Men remained the principal breadwinners in the family; women cooked, cleaned, and reared the children. "The creation and fulfillment of a successful home," a *Ladies Home Journal* writer advised women, "is a bit of craftsmanship that compares favorably with building a beautiful cathedral."

The feminist movement, however, still showed signs of vitality in the 1920s. Social feminists pushed for humanitarian reform, and were successful in gaining enactment of the Sheppard-Towner Act of 1921, which provided for federal aid to establish state programs for maternal and infant health care. Although the failure to enact the child labor amendment in 1925 marked the beginning of a decline in humanitarian reform, for the rest of the decade women's groups continued to work for good-government measures, for the inclusion of women on juries, and for consumer legislation.

One of the hard-won rights that women finally realized in 1920 was the right to vote, celebrated here in a cover from Leslie's Illustrated Weekly Newspaper.

One group of activists, led by Alice Paul's National Women's Party (NWP), lobbied for full equality for women under the law. In 1923, the NWP succeeded in having an Equal Rights Amendment introduced in Congress. The amendment stated "Men and women shall have equal rights throughout the United States and every place subject to its jurisdiction." Most other women's organizations, notably the League of Women Voters, opposed the amendment because it threatened gender-specific legislation like the Sheppard-Towner Act that women had fought so hard to enact. The drive for the ERA in the 1920s failed.

Growing assertiveness had a profound impact on feminism in the 1920s. Instead of crusading for social progress, young women concentrated on individual self-expression by rebelling against Victorian restraints. In the larger cities, some quickly adopted what critic H. L. Mencken called the flapper image, portrayed most strikingly by artist John Held, Jr. Cutting their hair short, raising their skirts above the knee, and binding their breasts, "flappers" set out to compete on equal terms with men on the golf course and in the speakeasy. Young women delighted in shocking their elders—they rouged their cheeks and danced the Charleston. For the first time, women smoked cigarettes and drank alcohol in public. The flappers assaulted the traditional double standard in sex, demanding that equality with men should include sexual fulfillment before and during marriage. New and more liberal laws led to a sharp rise in the divorce rate; by 1928, there were 166 divorces for every 1,000 marriages, compared to only 81 in 1900.

The sense of woman's emancipation was heightened by a continuing drop in the birthrate and the abundance of consumer goods. With fewer children to care for and with washing machines and vacuum cleaners to ease their household labor, it seemed that women of the 1920s would have more leisure time. Yet appearances were deceptive. Advertisers eagerly sought out women as buyers of labor-saving consumer products, but wives exercised purchasing power only as delegated by their husbands. In addition, many women were not in the position to put the new devices to use—one-fourth of the homes in Cleveland lacked running water in the 1920s, and three-quarters of the nation's families did not have washing machines. The typical childless woman spent between 43 and 50 hours a week on household duties; for mothers, the average work week was 56 hours, far longer than that of their husbands. And despite the talk of the "new woman," the flappers fell victim to the sex-role conditioning of their parents. Boys continued to play with guns and grew up to head their families; girls played with dolls and looked forward to careers as wives and mothers. "In the 1920s, as in the 1790s," concluded historian June Sochen, "marriage was the only approved state for women."

The family, however, did change. It became smaller as new techniques of birth control enabled couples to limit their offspring. More and more married women took jobs outside the home, bringing in an income and gaining a measure of independence (although their rate of pay was always lower than that for men). Young people, who had once joined the labor force when they entered their teens, now discovered adolescence as a stage of life. A high school education was no longer uncommon, and college attendance increased.

Prolonged adolescence led to new strains on the family in the form of youthful revolt. Freed of the traditional burden of earning a living at an early age, youths in the 1920s went on a great spree. Heavy drinking, casual sexual encounters, and a constant search for excitement became the hallmarks of the upper-class youth immortalized by F. Scott Fitzgerald. "I have been kissed by dozens of men," one of his characters commented. "I suppose I'll kiss dozens more." The theme of rebellion against parental authority, which runs through all aspects of the 1920s, was at the heart of the youth movement.

The Roaring Twenties

Frivolity and excitement ran high in the cities as both crime waves and highly publicized sports events flourished. Prohibition ushered in such distinctive features of the decade as speakeasies, bootleggers, and bathtub gin. Crime rose sharply as middle- and upper-class Americans willingly broke the law to gain access to alcoholic beverages. City streets became the scene of violent shoot-outs between rival bootleggers; by 1929, Chicago had witnessed over five hundred gangland murders. Underworld czars like Al Capone controlled illicit empires; Capone's produced revenue of $60 million a year.

Sports became a national mania in the 1920s as people found more leisure time. Golf boomed, with some two million men and women playing on nearly five thousand courses across the country. Spectator sports attracted even more attention. Boxing drew huge crowds to see fighters like Jack Dempsey and Gene Tunney. Baseball attendance soared. More than twenty million fans attended games in 1927, the year Babe Ruth became a national idol by hitting sixty home runs. On college campuses, football became more popular than ever. Universities vied with each other in building massive stadiums, seating upward of seventy thousand people.

In what Frederick Lewis Allen called "the ballyhoo years," the popular yearning for excitement led people to seek vicarious thrills in all kinds of ways—applauding Charles Lindbergh's solo flight across the Atlantic, cheering Gertrude Ederle's swim across the English Channel, and flocking to such bizarre events as six-day bicycle races, dance marathons, and flagpole sittings. It was a time of

Movie stars became the heroes of the roaring twenties, although Paramount Pictures described Thomas Meighan, one of the actors under contract to the moviemaker, as not "so much a motion picture star" but rather as "the sort of a friend [you] would like to have come visiting [your] home."

pure pleasure seeking, when people sought to escape from the increasingly drab world of the assembly line by worshiping heroic individuals.

Sex became another popular topic in the 1920s as Victorian standards began to crumble. Sophisticated city dwellers seemed to be intent on exploring a new freedom in sexual expression. Plays and novels focused on adultery, and the new urban tabloids—led by the *New York Daily News*—delighted in telling their readers about love nests and kept women. The popular songs of the decade, like "Hot Lips" and "Burning Kisses," were less romantic and more explicit than those of years before. Hollywood exploited the obsession with sex by producing movies with such provocative titles as *Up in Mable's Room, A Shocking Night,* and *Women and Lovers*. Theda Bara and Clara Bow, the "vamp" and the "it" girl, set the model for feminine seductiveness while Rudolph Valentino became the heartthrob of millions of American women. Young people embraced the new permissiveness joyfully, with the automobile giving couples an easy way to escape parental supervision.

There is considerable debate, however, over the extent of the sexual revolution in the 1920s. Later studies by Dr. Alfred C. Kinsey showed that premarital intercourse was twice as common among women born after 1900 than for those born before the turn of the century. But a contemporary survey of over two thousand middle-class women by Katherine B. Davis found that only 7 percent of those who were married had had sexual relations before marriage and that only 14 percent of the single women had engaged in intercourse. Actual changes in sexual behavior are beyond the historian's reach, hidden in the privacy of the bedroom, but the old Victorian prudishness was a clear casualty of the 1920s. Sex was no longer a taboo subject, at least in urban areas; men and women now could discuss it openly and many of them did.

The Literary Flowering

The greatest cultural advance of the 1920s was visible in the outpouring of literature. The city gave rise to a new class of intellectuals—writers who commented on the new industrial society. Many had been uprooted by World War I. They were bewildered by the rapidly changing social patterns of the 1920s and appalled by the materialism of American culture. Some fled to Europe to live as expatriates, congregating in Paris cafés to bemoan the loss of American innocence and purity. Others stayed at home, observing and condemning the excesses of a business civilization. All shared a sense of disillusionment and wrote pessimistically of the flawed promise of American life. Yet, ironically, their body of writing revealed a profound creativity that suggested America was coming of age intellectually.

The exiles included the poets Ezra Pound and T. S. Eliot and the novelist Ernest Hemingway. Pound discarded rhyme and meter in a search for clear, cold images that conveyed reality. Like many of the writers of the 1920s, he reacted against World War I, expressing a deep regret for the tragic waste of a whole generation in defense of a "botched civilization."

Eliot, who was born in Missouri but became a

T. S. Eliot, whose long poem The Waste Land *owed much to Ezra Pound's critical eye, set the standard by which modern American poetry was judged in the mid-twentieth century. The painting is by English artist Wyndham Lewis.*

British citizen, displayed even more profound despair. In *The Waste Land*, which appeared in 1922, he evoked images of fragmentation and sterility that had a powerful impact on the other disillusioned writers of the decade. He reached the depths in *The Hollow Men* (1925), a biting description of the emptiness of modern man.

Ernest Hemingway sought redemption from the modern plight in the romantic individualism of his heroes. Preoccupied with violence, he wrote of men alienated from society who found a sense of identity in their own courage and quest for personal honor. His own experiences, ranging from driving an ambulance in the war to stalking lions in Africa, made him a legendary figure; his greatest impact on other writers, however, came from his sparse, direct, and clean prose style.

The writers who stayed home were equally disdainful of contemporary American life. F. Scott

Fitzgerald chronicled American youth in *This Side of Paradise* (1920) and *The Great Gatsby* (1925), writing in bittersweet prose about "the beautiful and the damned." Amid the glitter of life among the wealthy on Long Island's North Shore came the haunting realization of emptiness and lack of human concern.

Sinclair Lewis became the most popular of the critical novelists. *Main Street,* published in 1920, satirized the values of small-town America as dull, complacent, and narrow-minded; *Babbitt,* which appeared two years later, poked fun at the commercialism of the 1920s, portraying George Babbitt as the stereotype of the lazy, smug, middle-class businessman who hailed the decade as a New Era.

Most savage of all was H. L. Mencken, the Baltimore newspaperman and literary critic who founded *American Mercury* magazine in 1923. Declaring war on "homo boobiens," Mencken mocked everything he found distasteful in America from the Rotary Club to the Ku Klux Klan. "From Boy Scouts, and from Home Cooking, from Odd Fellows' funerals, from Socialists, from Christians—Good Lord, deliver us," he pleaded. It was not difficult to discover what Mencken disliked (including Jews, as his recently published diary makes clear); the hard part was finding out what he affirmed, other than wit and a clever turn of phrase. A born cynic, he served as a zealous guardian of public rationality in an era of excessive boosterism.

The cultural explosion of the 1920s was surprisingly broad. It included novelists like Sherwood Anderson and John Dos Passos, who described the way the new machine age undermined such traditional American values as craftsmanship and a sense of community, and playwrights such as Eugene O'Neill, Maxwell Anderson, and Elmer Rice, who added greatly to the stature of American theater. Women writers were particularly effective in dealing with regional themes. Edith Wharton continued to write penetratingly about eastern aristocrats in books like *The House of Mirth* (1905) and *The Age of Innocence* (1921); Willa Cather and Ellen Glasgow focused on the plight of women in the Midwest and the South, respectively, in their short stories and novels. These writers portrayed their heroines in the traditional roles of wives and mothers; playwright Zona Gale on the other hand (who won the Pulitzer Prize for drama in 1920 for *Miss Lulu Bett*) used her title character to depict the dilemmas facing an unmarried woman in American society.

Art and music lagged behind literature but still made significant advances. Edward Hopper and Charles Burchfield captured the ugliness of city life and the loneliness of its inhabitants in their realistic paintings. Aaron Copland and George

Archibald Motley, The Jazz Singers. *Motley, one of the artists of the Harlem Renaissance, combined the traditions of his native New Orleans with the energy and rhythms of 1920s Harlem.*

Gershwin added a new vitality to American music. But African Americans migrating northward brought the most significant contribution: the spread of jazz—first to Saint Louis, Kansas City, and Chicago, and finally to New York. The form of jazz known as the blues, so expressive of the suffering of African Americans, became an authentic national folk music, and performers such as Louis Armstrong enjoyed popularity around the world.

The cultural growth of the 1920s was the work of blacks as well as whites. W. E. B. Du Bois, the editor of the newspaper *Crisis*, became the intellectual voice of the black community developing in New York City's Harlem. In 1917, James Weldon Johnson, who had been a professor of literature at Fisk University, published *Fifty Years and Other Poems* in which the title poem commented on the half century of suffering that had followed the Emancipation Proclamation. As other African American writers gathered around them, Du Bois and Johnson became the leaders of the Harlem Renaissance. The NAACP moved its headquarters to Harlem, and in 1923, the Urban League began publishing *Opportunity*, a magazine devoted to scholarly studies of racial issues. (See "Marcus Garvey: Racial Redemption and Black Nationalism," pp. 778–779.)

African American literature blossomed rapidly. In 1922, critics hailed the appearance of Claude McKay's book of verses, *White Shadows*. In stark images, McKay expressed both his resentment against racial injustice and his pride in blackness. Countee Cullen and Langston Hughes won critical acclaim for the beauty of their poems and the eloquence in their portrayals of the black tragedy.

Art and music also flourished during Harlem's golden age. Plays and concerts at the 135th Street YMCA; floor shows at Happy Rhone's nightclub (attended by many white celebrities); rent parties where jazz musicians played to raise money to help writers, artists, and neighbors pay their bills—all were part of the ferment that made Harlem "the Negro Capital of the World" in the 1920s. "Almost everything seemed possible above 125th Street in the early twenties for these Americans who were determined to thrive separately to better proclaim the ideals of integration," comments historian David Lewis. "You could be black and proud, politically assertive and economically independent, creative and disciplined—or so it seemed."

Although its most famous writers were identified with New York's Harlem, the new African American cultural awareness spread to other cities in the form of poetry circles and theater groups. The number of African American college graduates rose from 391 in 1920 to 1,903 by 1929. Although blacks were still an oppressed minority in the America of the 1920s, they had

W. E. B. Du Bois (left), editor of The Crisis, *was one of the intellectual and political leaders of the Harlem Renaissance, which fostered the rise of such literary figures as Zora Neale Hurston (center) and Langston Hughes (right). Hurston wrote four novels and two books of black folklore that "helped to remind the Renaissance . . . of the richness in racial heritage." Hughes wrote sensitively and eloquently of the world of common black people.*

taken major strides toward achieving cultural and intellectual fulfillment.

In retrospect, there is a striking paradox about the literary flowering of the 1920s. Nearly all the writers, black as well as white, cried out against the conformity and materialism of the contemporary scene. They were critical of mass production and reliance on the machine; they wrote wistfully of the disappearance of the artisan and of a more relaxed way of life. Few took any interest in politics or in social reform. They retreated instead into individualism, seeking an escape into their art from the prevailing business civilization. Whether they went abroad or stayed home, the writers of the 1920s turned inward to avoid being swept up in the consumer goods revolution. Yet despite their withdrawal, and perhaps because of it, they produced an astonishingly rich and varied body of work. American writing had a greater intensity and depth than in the past; American writers, despite their alienation, had placed their country in the forefront of world literature.

THE RURAL COUNTERATTACK

The shift of population from the countryside to the city led to heightened social tensions in the 1920s. Intent on preserving traditional social values, rural Americans saw in the city all that was evil in contemporary life. Saloons, whorehouses, little Italys and little Polands, communist cells, free love, and atheism—all were identified with the city. Accordingly, the countryside struck back at the newly dominant urban areas, aiming to restore the primacy of the Anglo-Saxon and predominantly Protestant culture they revered. This counterattack won considerable support in the cities from those so recently uprooted from their rural backgrounds.

Other factors contributed to the intensity of the counterattack. The war had unleashed a nationalistic spirit that craved unity and conformity. In a nation where one-third of the people were foreign born, the attack on immigrants and the call for 100 percent Americanism took on a frightening zeal. When the war was over, groups like the American Legion tried to root out "un-American" behavior and insisted on cultural as well as political conformity. The prewar progressive reform spirit added to the social tension. Stripped of much of its former idealism, progressivism focused on such social problems as drinking and illiteracy to justify repressive measures like Prohibition and immigration restriction. The result was tragic. Amid the emergence of a new urban culture, the movements aimed at preserving the values of an earlier America succeeded only in complicating life in an already difficult period of cultural transition.

The "Red Scare"

The first and most intense outbreak of national alarm came in 1919. The heightened nationalism of World War I, aimed at achieving unity at the expense of ethnic diversity, found a new target in bolshevism. The Russian Revolution and the triumph of Marxism frightened many Americans. A growing turn to communism among American radicals (especially the foreign born) accelerated these fears. Although the numbers involved were tiny—at most there were sixty thousand communists in the United States in 1919—they were highly visible. Located in the cities, their influence appeared to be magnified with the outbreak of widespread labor unrest.

A general strike in Seattle, a police strike in Boston, and a violent strike in the iron and steel industry thoroughly alarmed the American people in the spring and summer of 1919. A series of bombings led to panic. First the mayor of strike-bound Seattle received a small brown package containing a homemade bomb; then an alert New York postal employee detected sixteen bombs addressed to a variety of famous citizens (including John D. Rockefeller); and finally, on June 2, a bomb shattered the front of Attorney General A. Mitchell Palmer's home. Although the man who delivered it was blown to pieces, authorities quickly identified him as an Italian anarchist from Philadelphia.

In the ensuing public outcry, Attorney General Palmer led the attack on the alien threat. A Quaker and progressive, Palmer abandoned his earlier liberalism to launch a massive roundup of foreign-born radicals. In a series of raids that began on November 7, federal agents seized suspected anarchists and communists and held them for deportation with no regard for due process of law. In December, 249 aliens—including such well-known radical leaders as Emma Goldman and Alexander Berkman—were sent to Russia aboard the *Buford,* dubbed the "Soviet Ark" by the press. Nearly all were innocent of the charges against them. A month later, Palmer rounded up nearly four thousand suspected communists in a single evening. Federal agents broke into homes, meeting halls, and union offices without search warrants. Many native-born Americans were caught in the dragnet and spent several days in jail before being released; aliens rounded up were deported without hearings or trials.

For a time, it seemed that this Red Scare reflected the prevailing views of the American people. Instead of condemning their government's action, citizens voiced their approval and even urged more drastic steps. One patriot said his solution to the alien problem was simple:

The explosion in Wall Street on September 16, 1920, left 33 dead and nearly 200 wounded. Attorney General Palmer saw the blast as the work of a Communist conspiracy, but relatively few Americans subscribed to his view.

Ben Shahn's The Passion of Sacco and Vanzetti *(1931–1932) depicts the members of the committee who investigated the trial and confirmed its fairness.*

"S.O.S.—ship or shoot." General Leonard Wood, the former army chief of staff, favored placing Bolsheviks on "ships of stone with sails of lead," while evangelist Billy Sunday preferred to take "these ornery, wild-eyed Socialists" and "stand them up before a firing squad and save space on our ships." Inflamed by public statements like these, a group of legionnaires in Centralia, Washington, dragged a radical from the town jail, castrated him, and hanged him from a railway bridge. The coroner's report blandly stated that the victim "jumped off with a rope around his neck and then shot himself full of holes."

The very extremism of the Red Scare led to its rapid demise. In early 1920, courageous govern-

ment officials from the Department of Labor insisted on due process and full hearings before anyone else was deported. Prominent public leaders began to speak out against the acts of terror. Charles Evans Hughes, the defeated GOP candidate in 1916, offered to defend six Socialists expelled from the New York legislature; Ohio Senator Warren G. Harding, the embodiment of middle-class values, expressed his opinion that "too much has been said about bolshevism in America." Finally, Palmer himself, with evident presidential ambition, went too far. In April 1920, he warned of a vast revolution to occur on May 1; the entire New York City police force, some eleven thousand strong, was placed on duty to prepare for imminent disaster. When no bombings or violence took place on May Day, the public began to react against Palmer's hysteria. Despite a violent explosion on Wall Street in September that killed thirty-three people, the Red Scare died out by the end of 1920. Palmer passed into obscurity, the tiny Communist party became torn with factionalism, and the American people tried hard to forget their loss of balance.

Yet the Red Scare exerted a continuing influence on American society in the 1920s. The foreign born lived in the uneasy realization that they were viewed with hostility and suspicion. Two Italian aliens in Massachusetts, Nicola Sacco and Bartolomeo Vanzetti, were arrested in May 1920 for a payroll robbery and murder. They faced a prosecutor and jury who condemned them more for their ideas than for any evidence of criminal conduct and a judge who referred to them as "those anarchist bastards." Despite a worldwide effort that became the chief liberal cause of the 1920s, the courts rejected all appeals. Sacco and Vanzetti, a shoemaker and a fish peddler, died in the electric chair on August 23, 1927. Their fate symbolized the bigotry and intolerance that lasted through the 1920s and made this decade one of the least attractive in American history.

Prohibition

In December 1917, Congress adopted the Eighteenth Amendment, prohibiting the manufacture and sale of alcoholic beverages. A little over a year later, Nebraska was the necessary thirty-sixth state to ratify, and Prohibition became the law of the land.

As implemented under the Volstead Act, beginning January 16, 1920, it was illegal for anyone to make, sell, or transport any drink that contained more than one-half of 1 percent alcohol by volume. Prohibition was the result of both a rural effort of the Anti-Saloon League, backed by Methodist and Baptist clergymen, and the urban Progressive concern over the social disease of drunkenness, especially among industrial workers. The moral issue had already led to the enactment of Prohibition laws in twenty-six states by 1920; the real tragedy would occur in the effort to extend this "noble experiment" to the growing cities, where it was deeply resented by ethnic groups like the Germans and the Irish and was almost totally disregarded by the well-to-do and the sophisticated.

Prohibition did in fact lead to a decline in drinking. Americans consumed much less alcohol in the 1920s than in the prewar years. Rural areas became totally dry, and in the cities, the consumption of alcoholic beverages dropped sharply among the lower classes, who could not afford the high prices for bootleg liquor. Among the middle class and the wealthy, however, drinking became fashionable. Bootleggers supplied whiskey, which quickly replaced lighter spirits such as wine and beer. The alcohol was either smuggled from abroad (a $40 million per year business by 1924) or illicitly manufactured in America. Such exotic products as Jackass Brandy, Soda Pop Moon, and Yack Yack Bourbon were common—and all could be fatal. Despite the risk of illness or death from extraordinarily high alcohol content or poorly controlled distillation, Americans consumed some 150 million quarts of liquor a year in the 1920s. Bootleggers took in nearly $2 billion annually, about 2 percent of the gross national product.

Urban resistance to Prohibition finally led to its repeal in 1933. But in the intervening years, it damaged American society by breeding a profound disrespect for the law. The flamboyant excesses of bootleggers were only the more obvious evils spawned by Prohibition. In city after city, police openly tolerated the traffic in liquor, and judges and prosecutors agreed to let bootleggers pay merely token fines, creating almost a system of licenses. Prohibition satisfied the countryside's desire for vindication, yet rural and urban America alike suffered from this overzealous attempt to legislate morals.

The Ku Klux Klan

The most ominous expression of protest against the new urban culture was the rebirth of the Ku Klux Klan. On Thanksgiving night in 1915, on Stone Mountain in Georgia, Colonel William J. Simmons and thirty-four followers founded the modern Klan. Only "native born, white, gentile Americans" were permitted to join "the Invisible Empire, Knights of the Ku Klux Klan." Membership grew slowly during World War I, but after 1920, fueled by postwar fears and shrewd promotional techniques, the Klan mushroomed. In villages, towns, and small cities across the nation, Anglo-Saxon Protestant men flocked into the newly formed chapters, seeking to relieve their anxiety over a changing society by embracing the Klan's unusual rituals and by demonstrating their hatred against blacks, aliens, Jews, and Catholics.

The Klan of the 1920s, unlike the night riders of the post–Civil War era, was not just antiblack; the threat to American culture, as Klansmen perceived it, came from aliens—Italians and Russians, Jews and Catholics. They attributed much of the tension and conflict in society to the prewar flood of immigrants, foreigners who spoke different languages, worshiped in strange churches, and lived in distant, threatening cities. The Klansmen struck back by coming together and enforcing their own values. They punished blacks who did not know their place, women who practiced the new morality, and aliens who refused to conform. Beating, flogging, burning with acid—even murder—were condoned. They also tried more peaceful methods of coercion, formulating codes of behavior and seeking communitywide support.

The Klan entered politics, at first hesitantly, then with growing confidence. The KKK gained control of the legislatures in Texas, Oklahoma, Oregon, and Indiana; in 1924, it blocked a resolution of censure at the Democratic National Convention. With an estimated five million members by the mid-1920s, the Klan seemed to be fully established.

Its appeal lay in the sanctuary it offered to insecure and anxious people. Protestant to the core, the members found in the local Klavern a reassurance missing in their churches. The poor and ignorant became enchanted with the titles, ranging from Imperial Wizard to Grand Dragon, and gloried in the ritual that centered around the

letter "K." Thus each Klan had its own Klalendar, held its weekly Klonklave in the local Klavern, and followed the rules set forth in the Kloran. Members found a sense of identity in the group activities, whether they were peaceful picnics, ominous parades in white robes, or fiery cross burnings at night.

Although it was a male organization, the Klan did not neglect the family. There was a Women's Order, a Junior Order for boys, and a Tri-K Klub for girls. Members had to be born in America, but foreign-born Protestants were allowed to join a special Krusaders affiliate. Only blacks, Catholics, Jews, and prostitutes were beyond redemption to these lonely and anxious men who came together to chant:

United we stick
Divided we're stuck.
The better we stick
The better we Klux!

The Klan fell even more quickly than it rose. Its more violent activities—which included kidnapping, lynching, setting fire to synagogues and Catholic churches, and in one case, murdering a priest—began to offend the nation's conscience. Misuse of funds and sexual scandals among Klan leaders, notably in Indiana, repelled many of the rank and file; effective counterattacks by traditional politicians ousted the KKK from control in Texas and Oklahoma. Membership declined sharply after 1925; by the end of the decade, the Klan had virtually disappeared. But its spirit lived on, testimony to the recurring demons of nativism and hatred that have surfaced periodically throughout the American experience.

Immigration Restriction

The nativism that permeated the Klan found its most successful outlet in the immigration legislation of the 1920s. The sharp increase in immigration in the late nineteenth century had led to a broad-based movement. Spearheaded by organized labor and by New England aristocrats like Henry Cabot Lodge, the movement acted to restrict the flow of people from Europe. In 1917, over Wilson's veto, Congress enacted a literacy test that reduced the number of immigrants allowed into the country. The war caused a much more drastic decline—from an average of 1 million a year between 1900 and 1914 to only 110,000 in 1918.

After the armistice, however, rumors began to spread of an impending flood of people seeking to escape war-ravaged Europe. Kenneth Roberts, a popular historical novelist, warned that all Europe was on the move, with only the limits of available steamship space likely to stem the flow. Worried congressmen spoke of a "barbarian horde" and a "foreign tide" that would inundate the United States with "dangerous and deadly enemies of the country." Even though the actual number of immigrants, 810,000 in 1920 (less than the prewar yearly average), did not match these projections, Congress responded in 1921 by passing an emergency immigration act. The new quota system restricted immigration from Europe to 3 percent of the number of nationals from each country living in the United States in 1910.

The 1921 act failed to satisfy the nativists. The quotas still permitted more than 500,000 Europeans to come to the United States in 1923, nearly half of them from southern and eastern Europe. The declining percentage of Nordic immigrants alarmed writers like Madison Grant, who warned the American people the Anglo-Saxon stock that had founded the nation was about to be overwhelmed by lesser breeds with inferior genes. "These immigrants adopt the language of the native American, they wear his clothes and are beginning to take his women, but they seldom adopt his religion or understand his ideals," Grant wrote.

Psychologists, relying on primitive IQ tests used by the army in World War I, confirmed this judgment (see "Measuring the Mind," pp. 742–743). One senator claimed that all the nation's ills were due to an "intermingled and mongrelized people" as he demanded that racial purity replace the older reliance on the melting pot. In 1924, Congress adopted the National Origins Quota Act, which limited immigration from Europe to 150,000 a year; allocated most of the available slots to immigrants from Great Britain, Ireland, Germany, and Scandinavia; and banned all Asian immigrants. The measure passed Congress with overwhelming rural support.

The new restrictive legislation marked the most enduring achievement of the rural counter-attack. Unlike the Red Scare, Prohibition, and the Klan, the quota system would survive until the 1960s, enforcing a racist bias that excluded Asians and limited the immigration of Italians, Greeks, and Poles to a few thousand a year while permitting a steady stream of Irish, English, and Scandinavian immigrants. The large corporations, no longer dependent on armies of unskilled immigrant workers, did not object to the 1924 law; the machine had replaced the immigrant on the assembly line. Yet even here the victory was not complete. A growing tide of Mexican laborers, exempt from the quota act, flowed northward across the Rio Grande to fill the continuing need for unskilled workers on the farms and in the service trades. The Mexican immigrants, as many as 100,000 a year, marked the strengthening of an element in the national ethnic mosaic that would grow in size and influence until it became a major force in modern American society.

The Fundamentalist Controversy

The most famous of all attacks on the new urban culture was the Scopes trial held in Dayton, Tennessee. There in 1925, William Jennings Bryan, who had unsuccessfully run for president several times in previous decades, engaged in a crusade against the theory of evolution, appearing as a chief witness against John Scopes. Scopes, a high school biology teacher, had initiated the case by deliberately violating a new Tennessee law that forbade the teaching of Darwin's theory.

In the trial, Bryan testified under oath that he believed Jonah had been swallowed by a big fish and declared, "It is better to trust in the Rock of Ages than in the age of rocks." Chicago defense attorney Clarence Darrow succeeded in making Bryan look ridiculous. The court found Scopes guilty but let him off with a token fine; Bryan, exhausted by his efforts, died a few days later. H. L. Mencken, who covered the trial in person, rejoiced in the belief that fundamentalism was dead.

In reality, however, traditional rural religious beliefs were stronger than ever. As middle- and upper-class Americans drifted into a genteel Christianity that stressed good works and respectability, the Baptist and Methodist churches continued to hold on to the old faith. In addi-

Crowds of spectators throng the courtroom during the Scopes trial as defense attorney Clarence Darrow rests on the table during the proceedings. Scopes is seated to Darrow's right with his arms interlocked, staring straight ahead.

tion, aggressive fundamentalist sects such as the Churches of Christ, the Pentecostals, and Jehovah's Witnesses grew rapidly. While church membership increased from 41.9 million in 1916 to 54.5 million in 1926, the number of churches actually declined during the decade. More and more rural dwellers drove their cars into town instead of going to the local crossroads chapel.

Many of those who came to the city in the 1920s brought their religious beliefs with them and found new outlets for their traditional ideas. Thus evangelist Aimee Semple McPherson enjoyed amazing success in Los Angeles with her "Four-Square Gospel," building the Angelus Temple to seat over 5,000 worshipers. And in Fort Worth, the Reverend J. Frank Norris erected a 6,000-seat sanctuary for the First Baptist Church, bathing it in spotlights so it could be seen for 30 miles across the north Texas prairie.

Far from dying out, as divinity professor Thomas G. Oden noted, biblical fundamentalism retained "remarkable grass-roots strength among the organization men and the industrialized mass society of the 20th century." The rural counterattack, while challenged by the city, did enable some older American values to survive in the midst of the new mass production culture.

POLITICS OF THE 1920S

The tensions between the city and the countryside also shaped the course of politics in the 1920s. On the surface, it was a Republican decade. The GOP ("Grand Old Party") controlled the White House from 1921 to 1933 and had majorities in both houses of Congress from 1918 to 1930. The Republicans used their return to power after World War I to halt further reform legislation and to establish a friendly relationship between government and business. Important shifts were taking place, however, in the American electorate. The Democrats, although divided into competing urban and rural wings, were laying the groundwork for the future by winning over millions of new voters, especially among the ethnic groups in the cities. The rising tide of urban voters indicated a fundamental shift away from the Republicans toward a new Democratic majority.

Harding, Coolidge, and Hoover

The Republicans regained the White House in 1920 with the election of Warren G. Harding of Ohio. A dark-horse contender, Harding won the GOP nomination when the convention deadlocked and he became the compromise choice.

Marcus Garvey
Racial Redemption and Black Nationalism

Marcus Garvey.

World War I brought blacks to northern cities in unprecedented numbers. In the postwar economic slump, the scramble for jobs aggravated existing racial tensions, and violence erupted in cities across the country. Urban slums, job discrimination, disenfranchisement, segregation—black disillusionment with white America gave powerful resonance to the message of racial redemption preached by Marcus Garvey, a Jamaican black nationalist.

Garvey's upbringing under the color-based caste system of the British-ruled West Indies convinced him that only black racial solidarity could overturn the traditions that pitted blacks against each other, locked out of the privileges of white society. Studying in London in 1912, he espoused black nationalism and dreamed of an independent black Africa; from Booker T. Washington he adopted the doctrine of economic self-help. He molded these ideas into a vision of the black race redeemed through his new organization, the United Negro Improvement Association (UNIA). Its purpose was racial unity; its program included the strengthening of self-identity and racial pride, education, international commerce, industry, and the reconstruction of an independent black Africa.

In 1916, Garvey toured the United States. American blacks responded so strongly to his message of racial redemption and black nationalism that he decided to move UNIA headquarters to Harlem. With a new weekly, the *Negro World,* Garvey advanced his crusade for pride in black heritage and separatism. The paper extolled the beauty of black skin color and African features; his editorials echoed B. T. Washington's message of economic self-reliance, but with a new militant tone. "Up, you mighty race," he exhorted, "you can accomplish what you will."

In 1919, Garvey put his principles into practice, opening a consulting firm to assist black entrepreneurs and launching a steamship company. With the Black Star Line, Garvey hoped to demonstrate black competence in business, to enhance black pride, and to strengthen the bonds among blacks worldwide. The idea caught the popular imagination, though American black leadership was skeptical. A company brochure offered every black investor the promise of easy dividends and an opportunity to climb the ladder of success for only $5 per share. In November 1919, the BSL launched its first of three ships and stock sales soared.

Spirits were high at the first international convention of UNIA in 1920. Several thousand delegates from all 48 states and more than 20 foreign countries came to New York. After leading the opening-day parade, which stretched for several miles through the streets of Harlem, Garvey delivered the keynote address before a crowd of 25,000 at Madison Square Garden. His message was black nationalism and separatism:

> *We are the descendents of a suffering people. We are the descendents of a people determined to suffer no longer. We shall now organize the 400,000,000 Negroes of the world into a vast organization to plant the banner of freedom on the great continent of Africa. . . . If Europe is for Europeans, then Africa shall be for the black peoples of the world. We say it; we mean it.*

Garvey's ill-fated plans for African redemption began with his Liberian Rehabilitation Project. The black African republic welcomed his offer of financial and technical assistance through the

Marcus Garvey's advocacy of black nationalism and independent black entrepreneurship were, in part, discredited by his trial and conviction for mail fraud.

UNIA, and in late 1920 Garvey began to raise money for a reconstruction loan. In subsequent months, however, he diverted much of the proceeds to keep the ailing BSL afloat. With large capital outlays, poor management, and high operating costs, Garvey's dream of a maritime empire verged on financial collapse.

The "establishment" black press accused Garvey of adventurism, opportunism, and diversion from the real paths of progress. His views on the Ku Klux Klan made him even more controversial. While deploring Klan terror and violence, Garvey voiced appreciation of Klan candor on race relations:

> I regard the Klan, the Anglo-Saxon Clubs, and White American societies as better friends of the race than all other groups of hypocritical whites put together. I like honesty and fair play. You may call me a Klansman if you will, but potentially every white man is a Klansman, as far as the Negro in competition with whites socially, economically, and politically is concerned, and there is no use lying about it.

So stark a statement of racial separatism and suspicion of whites appalled other black leaders and Garvey found himself under attack from all sides. W. E. B. Du Bois called Garvey "the most dangerous enemy of the Negro race," but he was uncertain if Garvey were "a lunatic or a traitor."

Garvey's battle with black leaders was but one of his challenges. In May 1923, he and three of his associates went on trial for mail fraud in the sale of BSL stock. Defending himself, Garvey used the courtroom as much to preach his philosophy as to plead his case. Although the government documented the BSL's record of mismanagement and overspending, the legal issue was Garvey's intent; had he and his associates sold BSL stock knowing the company was insolvent? E. D. Cronon, Garvey's most meticulous biographer, finds the evidence equivocal. Garvey's business acumen was questionable and his bookkeeping atrocious, but neither he nor his executives drew large salaries from the BSL or lived lavishly at company expense. The BSL, concludes Cronon, may have been "ill-advised and even foolish," but not willfully fraudulent. The jury, unmoved by Garvey's eloquence, found him guilty while acquitting his codefendants; the judge, a white member of the NAACP, sentenced Garvey to the maximum five-year term.

A federal appeals court upheld Garvey's conviction and on February 8, 1925, he began serving his term in the federal penitentiary at Atlanta. Ironically, once he was behind bars, Garvey gained the support of many of his erstwhile detractors who protested the severity of white justice. Under mounting pressure, President Coolidge commuted Garvey's sentence late in 1927. Immediate deportation followed, as required by U.S. immigration law.

Garvey tried in vain to revitalize the UNIA in Jamaica, but with the onset of the Great Depression, American blacks concentrated more on survival than on racial redemption. Garvey slipped into obscurity and died in 1940 at the age of fifty-two.

His movement inspired blacks disgusted by the hypocrisy of American democracy and frustrated by the failure of gradualism to improve their lot. He gave them an alternative to the litigation and legislation approach of the more conservative black establishment. Although his projects offered no lasting solutions to the problems of race relations, his stress on pride of heritage and ties to Africa influenced many black Americans in succeeding generations.

Handsome and dignified, Harding reflected both the virtues and blemishes of small-town America. Originally a newspaper publisher in Marion, he had made many friends and few enemies throughout his career as a legislator, lieutenant governor, and finally, after 1914, a U.S. senator. Conventional in outlook, Harding was a genial man who lacked the capacity to govern and who, as president, broadly delegated power.

He made some good cabinet choices, notably Charles Evans Hughes as secretary of state and Herbert C. Hoover as secretary of commerce, but two corrupt officials—Attorney General Harry Daugherty and Secretary of the Interior Albert Fall—sabotaged his administration. Daugherty became involved in a series of questionable deals that led ultimately to his forced resignation; Fall was the chief figure in the Teapot Dome scandal. Two oil promoters gave Fall nearly $400,000 in loans and bribes; in return, he helped them secure leases on naval oil reserves in Elk Hills, California, and Teapot Dome, Wyoming. The scandal came to light after Harding's death from a heart attack in 1923. Fall eventually served a year in jail, and the reputation of the Harding administration never recovered.

Vice President Calvin Coolidge assumed the presidency upon Harding's death, and his honesty and integrity quickly reassured the nation. Coolidge, born in Vermont of old Yankee stock, had first gained national attention in 1919 as governor of Massachusetts when he had dealt firmly with a Boston police strike by declaring, "There is no right to strike against the public safety by anybody, anywhere, any time." A reserved, reticent man, Coolidge became famous for his epigrams, which contemporaries mistook for wisdom. "The business of America is business," he proclaimed. "The man who builds a factory builds a temple; the man who works there worships there." Consistent with this philosophy, he believed his duty was simply to preside benignly, not govern the nation. "Four fifths of all our troubles in this life would disappear," he said, "if we would just sit down and be still." Calvin Coolidge, one observer noted, "aspired to become the least President the country ever had; he attained his desire." Satisfied with the prosperity of the mid-1920s, the people responded favorably. Coolidge was elected to a full term by a wide margin in 1924.

When Coolidge announced in 1927 that he did not "choose to run," Herbert Hoover became the Republican choice to succeed him. By far the ablest GOP leader of the decade, Hoover epitomized the American myth of the self-made man. Orphaned as a boy, he had worked his way through Stanford University and had gained both wealth and fame as a mining engineer. During World War I, he had displayed admirable administrative skills in directing Wilson's food program at home and relief activities abroad. Sober, intelligent, and immensely hard working, Hoover embodied the nation's faith in individualism and free enterprise.

As secretary of commerce under Harding and Coolidge, he had sought cooperation between government and business. He used his office to assist American manufacturers and exporters in expanding their overseas trade, and he strongly supported a trade association movement to encourage cooperation rather than cutthroat competition among smaller American companies. He did not view business and government as antagonists. Instead, he saw them as partners, working together to achieve efficiency and affluence for all Americans. His optimistic view of the future led him to declare in his speech accepting the Republican presidential nomination in 1928 that "we in America today are nearer to the final triumph over poverty than ever before in the history of any land."

Republican Policies

During the 1920 campaign, Warren Harding urged a return to "not heroism, but healing, not nostrums, but normalcy." Misreading his speechwriter's "normality," he coined a new word that became the theme for the Republican administrations of the 1920s. Aware that the public was tired of zealous reform-minded presidents like Teddy Roosevelt and Woodrow Wilson, Harding and his successors sought a return to traditional Republican policies. In some areas they were successful, but in others the Republican leaders were forced to adjust to the new realities of a mass production society. The result was a mixture of traditional and innovative measures that was neither wholly reactionary nor entirely progressive.

The most obvious attempt to go back to the Republicanism of William McKinley came in tariff and tax policy. Fearful of a flood of postwar European imports, Congress passed an emergency tariff act in 1921 and followed it a year later with the protectionist Fordney-McCumber Tariff Act. The net effect was to raise the basic rates substantially over the moderate Underwood Tariff schedules of the Wilson period.

Secretary of the Treasury Andrew Mellon, a wealthy Pittsburgh banker and industrialist, worked hard to achieve a similar return to normalcy in taxation. Condemning the high wartime tax rates on businesses and wealthy individuals, Mellon pressed for repealing an excess profits tax on corporations and slashing personal rates on the very rich. Using the new budget system adopted by Congress in 1921, he reduced government spending from its World War I peak of $18 billion to just over $3 billion by 1925, thereby creating a slight surplus. Congress responded in 1926 by cutting the highest income tax bracket to a modest 20 percent.

The revenue acts of the 1920s greatly reduced the burden of taxation; by the end of the decade, the government was collecting one-third less than it had in 1921, and the number of people paying income taxes dropped from over 6.5 million to 4 million. Yet the greatest relief went to the wealthy. The public was shocked to learn in the 1930s that J.P. Morgan and his nineteen partners had paid no income tax at all during the depths of the Depression.

The growing crisis in American farming during the decade forced the Republican administrations to seek new solutions. The end of the European war led to a sharp decline in farm prices and a return to the problem of overproduction. Southern and western lawmakers formed a farm bloc in Congress to press for special legislation for American agriculture. The farm bloc supported the higher tariffs, which included protection for constituents' crops, and helped secure passage of legislation to create federal supervision over stockyards, packinghouses, and grain trading.

This special-interest legislation failed to get at the root of overproduction, however. Farmers then supported more controversial measures designed to raise domestic crop prices by having the government sell the surplus overseas at low world prices. Coolidge vetoed the legislation on grounds that it involved unwarranted government interference in the economy.

Yet the government's role in the economy

Attorney General Daugherty struggles to keep the scandals of the Harding administration hidden in the closet.

increased rather than lessened in the 1920s. Republicans widened the scope of federal activity and nearly doubled the ranks of government employees. Herbert Hoover led the way in the Commerce Department, establishing new bureaus to help make American industry more efficient in housing, transportation, and mining. Under his leadership, the government encouraged corporations to develop welfare programs that undercut trade unions, and he tried to minimize labor disturbances by devising new federal machinery to mediate disputes. Instead of going back to the laissez-faire tradition of the nineteenth century, the Republican administrations of the 1920s were pioneering a close relationship between government and private business.

The Divided Democrats

While the Republicans ruled in the 1920s, the Democrats seemed bent on self-destruction. The

Wilson coalition fell apart in 1920 as pent-up dissatisfaction stemming from the war enabled Harding to win by a landslide. The pace of the second Industrial Revolution and the growing urbanization split the party in two. One faction was centered in the rural South and West. Traditional Democrats who had supported Wilson stood for Prohibition, fundamentalism, the Klan, and other facets of the rural counterattack against the city. In contrast, a new breed of Democrat was emerging in the metropolitan areas of the North and Midwest. Immigrants and their descendants began to become active in the Democratic party. Catholic or Jewish in religion and strongly opposed to Prohibition, they had little in common with their rural counterparts.

The split within the party surfaced dramatically at the national convention in New York in 1924. Held in Madison Square Garden, a hall built in the 1890s and too small and cramped for the more than one thousand delegates, the convention soon degenerated into what one observer described as a "snarling, cursing, tenuous, suicidal, homicidal roughhouse." City slickers mocked the "rubes and hicks" from the "sticks"; populist orators struck back by denouncing the city as "wanting in national ideals, devoid of conscience . . . rooted in corruption, directed by greed and dominated by selfishness." An urban resolution to condemn the Ku Klux Klan led to a spirited response from the rural faction and its defeat by a single vote. Then for nine days, in the midst of a stifling heat wave, the delegates divided between Alfred E. Smith, the governor of New York, and William G. McAdoo of California, Wilson's secretary of the treasury. When it became clear that neither the city nor the rural candidate could win a majority, both men withdrew; on the 103rd ballot, the weary Democrats finally chose John W. Davis, a former West Virginia congressman and New York corporation lawyer, as their compromise nominee.

The Election of 1924

Candidate	Party	Popular Vote	Electoral Vote
Coolidge	Republican	15,717,553	382
Davis	Democrat	8,386,169	136
La Follette	Progressive	4,814,050	13

In the ensuing election, the conservative Davis had difficulty in distinguishing his views from those of Republican president Calvin Coolidge. For the discontented, Senator Robert La Follette of Wisconsin offered an alternative by running on an independent Progressive party ticket. Coolidge won easily, receiving 15 million votes to 8 million for Davis and nearly 5 million for La Follette. Davis had made the poorest showing of any Democratic candidate in the twentieth century.

Yet the Democrats were in far better shape than this setback indicated. Beginning in 1922, the party had made heavy inroads into the GOP majority in Congress. The Democrats took seventy-eight seats away from Republicans in that election, many of them in the cities of the East and Midwest. In New York alone, they gained thirteen new congressmen, all but one in districts with heavy immigrant populations. Even in 1924, the Republican vote in large cities declined as many urban voters chose La Follette in the absence of an attractive Democratic candidate. By 1926, the Democrats were within one vote of controlling the Senate and had picked up nine more seats in the House in metropolitan areas. The large cities were swinging clearly into the Democratic column; all the party needed was a charismatic leader who could fuse the older rural elements with the new urban voters.

The Election of 1928

The selection of Al Smith as the Democratic candidate in 1928 indicated the growing power of the city. Born on the lower East Side of Manhattan of mixed Irish-German ancestry, Smith was the prototype of the urban Democrat. He was Catholic; he was associated with a big-city machine; he was a "wet" who wanted to end Prohibition. Starting out in the Fulton Fish Market as a boy, he had joined Tammany Hall and gradually climbed the political ladder, rising from subpoena server to state legislator to governor, a post he held with distinction for nearly a decade. Rejected by rural Democrats in 1924, he still had to prove he could unite the South and West behind his leadership. His lack of education, poor grammar, and distinctive New York accent all hurt him, as did his eastern provincialism. When reporters asked him about his appeal

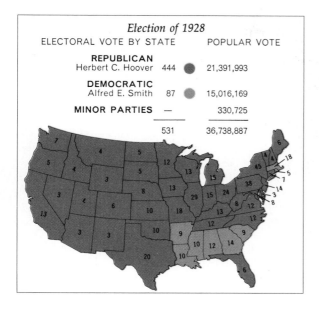

Election of 1928

ELECTORAL VOTE BY STATE   POPULAR VOTE

REPUBLICAN
Herbert C. Hoover   444   21,391,993

DEMOCRATIC
Alfred E. Smith   87   15,016,169

MINOR PARTIES   —   330,725

531   36,738,887

CHRONOLOGY

1919   U.S. agents arrest 1,700 in Red Scare raids • Congress passes Volstead Act over Wilson's veto (October)

1920   Budget Bureau set up to oversee federal spending • Nineteenth Amendment passed, granting women the right to vote • Transcontinental airmail service inaugurated (September) • WWJ-Detroit broadcasts first commercial radio program (November)

1921   Congress enacts quotas for European immigrants

1923   Newspapers expose KKK graft, torture, murder • Henry Luce begins publishing *Time* magazine (March)

1924   Senate probes Teapot Dome scandal • Veterans' World War I bonus bill passed

1925   John Scopes convicted of teaching theory of evolution in violation of Tennessee law (July)

1926   First Martha Graham modern dance recital (April)

1927   Charles Lindbergh completes first nonstop transatlantic flight from New York to Paris (May) • Coolidge vetoes farm price-control bill • Sacco and Vanzetti executed (August) • The movie *The Jazz Singer* features singing-talking soundtrack

in the states west of the Mississippi, he replied, "What states *are* west of the Mississippi?"

The choice facing the American voter in 1928 seemed unusually clear cut. Herbert Hoover was a Protestant, a dry, and an old-stock American who stood for efficiency and individualism; Smith was a Catholic, a wet, and a descendant of immigrants who was closely associated with big-city politics. Just as Smith appealed to new voters in the cities, so Hoover won the support of many old-line Democrats who feared the city, Tammany Hall, and the pope.

Yet beneath the surface, as Allan J. Lichtman points out, there were "striking similarities between Smith and Hoover." Both were self-made men who embodied the American belief in freedom of opportunity and upward mobility. Neither advocated any significant degree of economic change nor any redistribution of national wealth or power. Though religion proved to be the most important issue in the minds of the voters, hurting Smith far more than Prohibition or his identification with the city, the Democratic candidate's failure to spotlight the growing cracks in prosperity or to offer alternative economic policies ensured his defeat.

The 1928 election was a dubious victory for the Republicans. Hoover won easily, defeating Smith by more than six million votes and carrying such traditionally Democratic states as Oklahoma, Texas, and Florida. But Smith suc-

ceeded for the first time in winning a majority of votes for the Democrats in the nation's twelve largest cities. A new Democratic electorate was emerging, consisting of Catholics and Jews, Irish and Italians, Poles and Greeks. Now the task was to unite the traditional Democrats of the South and West with the urban voters of the Northeast and Midwest.

The growing influence of the city on politics of the 1920s reflected the sweeping changes taking place throughout the decade in American social and economic development. Al Smith, despite his defeat in 1928, symbolized the emergence of the city as the center of twentieth-century American life. An older nation founded on rural values had given way to a new urban society in which the production and use of consumer goods led to a very different lifestyle. Just as nineteenth-century American culture had revolved around the farm and the railroad, modern America focused on the automobile and the city. Yet despite the genuine economic progress achieved in the 1920s, the decade ended in a severe depression that lasted all through the 1930s. Only after World War II would the American people finally enjoy an abundance and prosperity rooted in the urban transformation that began in the 1920s.

Recommended Reading

William Leuchtenburg provides the best overview of the 1920s in *The Perils of Prosperity, 1914–1932* (1958). He stresses the theme of rural-urban conflict and claims the achievements of the decade were more significant than its failures. The essays in John Braeman, Robert H. Bremner, and David Brody, eds., *Change and Continuity in Twentieth Century America: The 1920s* (1968), illuminate important aspects of the period.

A fully detailed account of economic developments in the decade is George Soule, *Prosperity Decade* (1947). Two classic studies, Frederick Lewis Allen, *Only Yesterday* (1931), and Helen Lynd and Robert Lynd, *Middletown* (1929), offer valuable insights into social and cultural trends. The most recent overview of the decade is Geoffrey Perrett, *America in the Twenties* (1982).

The spirit of rural discontent with the new urban society is captured best in Lawrence Levine, *Defender of the Faith* (1965), an account of the last ten years of William Jennings Bryan's life. For changing political alignments of the 1920s, see David Burner, *The Politics of Provincialism* (1968).

Additional Bibliography

General surveys of the 1920s include Ellis W. Hawley, *The Great War and the Search for a Modern Order* (1979), and Donald McCoy, *Coming of Age* (1973). Books on economic themes are John B. Rae, *The American Automobile* (1965); James J. Flink, *The Car Culture* (1975) and *The Automobile Age* (1988); Allen Nevins and Frank E. Hill, *Ford: Expansion and Challenge, 1915–1933* (1957); James Prothro, *The Dollar Decade* (1954); Otis A. Pease, *The Responsibilities of American Advertising* (1959); Roland Marchand, *Advertising the American Dream,* *1920–1940* (1985); Martha L. Olney, *Buy Now, Pay Later: Advertising, Credit and Consumer Durables in the 1920s* (1991); and Alfred D. Chandler, Jr., *Strategy and Structure* (1962). The best books on labor are Irving Bernstein, *The Lean Years* (1960), and Robert H. Zieger, *Republicans and Labor, 1919–1929* (1969). James Shideler discusses the postwar agricultural depression in *Farm Crisis* (1957).

Social history is covered in Preston Slosson, *The Great Crusade and After* (1930); Paul Carter, *Another Part of the Twenties* (1976); Stanley Coben, *Rebellion Against Victorianism: The Impetus for Cultural Change in 1920s America* (1991); Elizabeth Stevenson, *Babbitts and Bohemians* (1967); and Paula S. Fass, *The Damned and the Beautiful* (1977).

The role of women in the 1920s is examined in William Chafe, *The American Woman* (1972); J. Stanley Lemons, *The Woman Citizen* (1973); Susan D. Becker, *The Origins of the Equal Rights Amendment* (1981); Dorothy M. Brown, *Setting a Course* (1987); Nancy Cott, *The Grounding of American Feminism* (1987); and Winifred D. Wandersee, *Women's Work and Family Values, 1920–1940* (1981). For blacks in the 1920s, see Nathan Huggins, *Harlem Renaissance* (1971); Gilbert Osofsky, *Harlem* (1966); and David Levering Lewis, *When Harlem Was in Vogue* (1981), a lively account of black culture. The career of Marcus Garvey is traced in E. David Cronon, *Black Moses* (1955), and Judith Stein, *The World of Marcus Garvey* (1986). Ricardo Romo explores one aspect of Mexican American experience in *East Los Angeles: History of a Barrio* (1983).

Frederick Hoffman, *The Twenties* (1955), and Alfred Kazin, *On Native Grounds* (1942), survey the literary trends during the decade. Other studies of this subject are Roderick Nash, *The Nervous Generation* (1969); Robert Crunden, *From Self to Society* (1972); Malcolm Cowley, *Exile's Return* (1934); and Edmund Wilson, *Shores of Light* (1952). Biographies of major literary figures of the period include William Manchester, *Disturber of the Peace* (1951) on H. L. Mencken; Arthur Mizener, *The Far Side of Paradise* (1951) on F. Scott Fitzgerald; Mark Shorer, *Sinclair Lewis* (1961); and Carlos Baker, *Hemingway* (1956).

Studies of political fundamentalism include Robert K. Murray, *Red Scare* (1955); William Young and David E. Kaiser, *Postmortem: New Evidence in the Case of Sacco and Vanzetti* (1985); and Stanley Coben, *A. Mitchell Palmer* (1963), on the postwar panic over radicalism; Andrew Sinclair, *Prohibition* (1962), and Herbert Asbury, *The Great Illusion* (1950), on the noble experiment; David Chalmers, *Hooded Americans* (1965); Arnold S. Rice, *The Ku Klux Klan in American Politics* (1962); Leonard Moore, *Citizen Klansmen: The Ku Klux Klan in Indiana, 1921–1928* (1991); and

Franklin D. Roosevelt and the New Deal

*T*he prosperity of the 1920s came to an abrupt halt in October 1929. The stock market, which had boomed during the decade, suddenly faltered. Investors who had borrowed heavily to take part in the speculative mania that had swept Wall Street suddenly were forced to sell their securities to cover their loans. The wave of selling triggered an avalanche. On October 24, later known as Black Thursday, nearly thirteen million shares were traded as highfliers like RCA and Westinghouse lost nearly half their value. In the afternoon, a group of New York bankers, led by the House of Morgan, pooled their resources and began to buy stocks to stem the decline. The stock market rallied for the next two days, but on Tuesday, October 29, the downslide resumed. Frightened sellers dumped over 16 million shares and the industrial average fell by forty-three points. The panic ended in November, with stocks at 1927 levels. For the next four years, there was a steady drift downward, until by 1932, prices were 80 percent below their 1929 highs.

The Great Depression which followed the crash of 1929 was the most devastating economic blow ever suffered by the nation. It lasted for more than ten years, dominating every aspect of American life during the 1930s. Unemployment rose to 12 million by 1932, and though it dipped midway through the decade, it still stood at 10 million by 1939. Children grew up thinking that economic deprivation was the norm rather than the exception in America. Year after year, people kept looking for a return to prosperity, but the outlook remained dismal. Intractable and all encompassing, the Depression loosened its grip on the nation only after the outbreak of World War II. And even then, it left enduring psychological scars—never again would the Americans who lived through it be quite so optimistic about their economic future.

The Depression led to a profound shift in American political loyalties. The Republicans, dominant since the 1890s, gave way to a new Democratic majority. The millions of immigrants who had come to the United States before World War I became more active politically, as did their children who were beginning to reach voting age. The result was the election of Franklin D. Roosevelt to the presidency and the development of the New Deal, a broad program of relief, recovery, and reform that greatly increased the role of government in American life.

THE GREAT DEPRESSION

The economic collapse altered American attitudes. In the 1920s, optimism had prevailed as people looked forward to an ever-increasing flow of consumer goods and a better way of life. But after 1929, despair set in. Factories closed, machines fell silent, and millions upon millions of people walked the streets, looking for jobs that did not exist.

The Great Bull Market

The consumer goods revolution contained the seeds of its own collapse. The steady expansion of the automobile and appliance industries led gradually to a saturation of the market. Each year after 1924, the rate of increase in the sale of cars and refrigerators and ranges slowed, a natural consequence as more and more people already owned these durable goods. Production began to falter, and in 1927, the nation underwent a mild recession. The sale of durable goods declined, and construction of houses and buildings fell slightly. If corporate leaders had heeded these warning signs, they might have responded by raising wages or lowering prices, both effective ways to stimulate purchasing power and sustain the consumer goods revolution. Or if government officials had recognized the danger signals and forced a halt in installment buying and slowed bank loans, the nation might have experienced a sharp but brief depression.

Neither government nor business leaders were so farsighted. The Federal Reserve Board lowered the discount rate, charging banks less for loans in an attempt to stimulate the economy. Much of this additional credit, however, went not into solid investment in factories and machinery but instead into the stock market, touching off a new wave of speculation that obscured the growing economic slowdown and ensured a far greater crash to come.

Individuals with excess cash began to invest heavily in the stock market, betting the already impressive rise in security prices would bring them even greater windfall profits. The market

Unemployment, 1929–1942

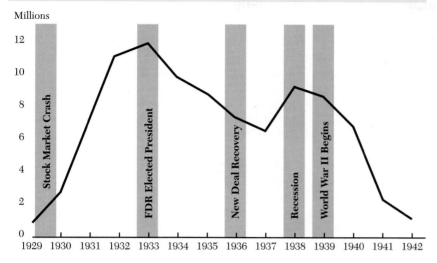

had advanced in spurts during the decade; the value of all stocks listed on the New York Stock Exchange rose from $27 billion in 1925 to $67 billion in early 1929. The strongest surge began in the spring of 1928, when investors ignored the declining production figures in the belief they could make a killing in the market. People took their savings and bet on speculative stocks. Corporations used their large cash reserves to supply money to brokers who in turn loaned it to investors on margin; in 1929, for example, the Standard Oil Company of New Jersey loaned out $69 million a day in this fashion.

Investors could now play the market on credit, buying stock listed at $100 a share with $10 down and $90 on margin, the broker's loan for the balance. If the stock advanced to $150, the investor could sell and reap a gain of 500 percent on the $10 investment. And in the bull market climate of the 1920s, everyone was sure the market would go up.

By 1929, it seemed the whole nation was engaged in speculation. In city after city, brokers opened branch offices, each complete with a stock ticker and a huge board covered with the latest Wall Street quotations. People crowded into the customers' rooms in the offices, filling the seats and greeting the latest advances of their favorite stocks with shouts of approval. So great was the public's interest in the stock market that newspapers carried the stock averages on their front pages.

In reality, though, more people were spectators than speculators; fewer than 3 million Americans owned stocks in 1929, and only about 500,000 were active buyers and sellers. But the bull market became a national obsession, assuring everyone the economy was healthy and preventing any serious analysis of its underlying flaws. When the market soared to over $80 billion in total value by midsummer, the *Wall Street Journal* discounted any possibility of a decline, proclaiming, "The outlook for the fall months seems brighter than at any time."

The great crash in October 1929 put a sudden and tragic end to the speculative mania. The false confidence that had kept the economy from collapsing in 1927 evaporated overnight. Suddenly, corporations and financial institutions were no longer willing to provide capital for stock market purchases. More important, investors and bankers cut off consumer credit as well, drying up buying power and leading to a sharp decline in the sales of consumer goods. Factories began to cut back production, laying off some workers and reducing hours for others. The layoffs and cutbacks lowered purchasing power even further, so fewer people bought cars and appliances. More factory layoffs resulted, and some plants closed entirely, leading to the availability of even less money for the purchase of consumer goods.

This downward economic spiral continued for four years. By 1932, unemployment had swelled to 25 percent of the work force. Steel production was down to 12 percent of capacity, and the vast assembly lines in Detroit produced only a trickle of cars each day. The gross national product fell to 67 percent of the 1929 level. The bright promise of mass production had ended in a nightmare.

The basic explanation for the Great Depression lies in the fact that U.S. factories produced more goods than the American people could consume. The problem was not that the market for such products was fully saturated. In 1929, there were still millions of Americans who did not own cars or radios or refrigerators, but many of them could not afford the new products. There were other contributing causes—unstable economic conditions in Europe, the agricultural decline since 1919, corporate mismanagement, and excessive speculation—but it all came down to the fact that people did not have enough money to buy the consumer products coming off the assembly lines. Installment sales helped bridge the gap, but by 1929 the burden of debt was just too great.

The new economic system had failed to distribute wealth more broadly. Too much money had gone into profits, dividends, and industrial expansion, and not enough had gone into the hands of the workers, who were also consumers. Factory productivity had increased 43 percent during the decade, but the wages of industrial workers had only gone up 11 percent (see Chapter 25). If the billions that went into stock market speculation had been used instead to increase wages—which would then have increased consumer purchasing power—production and consumption could have been brought into balance. Yet it is too much to expect that the prophets of the new era could have foreseen this flaw and corrected it. They were pioneering a new industrial system, and only out of the bitter experience of the Depression would they discover the full dynamics of the consumer goods economy.

Effect of the Depression

It is difficult to measure the human cost of the Great Depression. The material hardships were bad enough. Men and women lived in lean-tos made of scrap wood and metal, and families went without meat and fresh vegetables for months, existing on a diet of soup and beans. The psycho-

logical burden was even greater: Americans suffered through year after year of grinding poverty with no letup in sight. The unemployed stood in line for hours waiting for relief checks, veterans sold apples or pencils on street corners, their manhood—once prized so highly by the nation—now in question. People left the city for the countryside but found no salvation on the farm. Crops rotted in the fields because prices were too low to make harvesting worthwhile; sheriffs fended off angry crowds as banks foreclosed long overdue mortgages on once prosperous farms.

Few escaped the suffering. African Americans who had left the poverty of the rural South for factory jobs in the North were among the first to be laid off. Mexican Americans, who had flowed in to replace European immigrants, met with competition from angry citizens, now willing to do stoop labor in the fields and work as track layers on the railroads. Immigration officials used technicalities to halt the flow across the Rio Grande and even to reverse it; nearly a half million Mexicans were deported in the 1930s, including families with children born in the United States.

The poor—black, brown, and white—survived because they knew better than most Americans how to exist in poverty. They stayed in bed in cold weather, both to keep warm and to avoid unnecessary burning up of calories; they patched their shoes with pieces of rubber from discarded tires, heated only the kitchens of their homes, and ate scraps of food that others would reject.

The middle class, which had always lived with high expectations, was hit hard. Professionals and white-collar workers refused to ask for charity even while their families went without food; one New York dentist and his wife turned on the gas and left a note saying, "We want to get out of the way before we are forced to accept relief money." People who fell behind in their mortgage payments lost their homes and then faced eviction when they could not pay the rent. Health care declined. Middle-class people stopped going to doctors and dentists regularly, unable to make the required cash payment in advance for services rendered.

Even the well-to-do were affected, giving up many of their former luxuries and weighed down with guilt as they watched former friends and business associates join the ranks of the impoverished. "My father lost everything in the

Unemployment devastated thousands, who turned to sell-ing apples or advertising their labor. The suddenly home-less gathered in hobo camps, like the New York City "Hooverville" at left, while others crowded together on The Park Bench, as shown in this detail of the painting by Reginald Marsh (above).

Depression" became an all-too-familiar refrain among young people who dropped out of college.

Many Americans sought escape in movement. Men, boys, and some women, rode the rails in search of jobs, hopping freights to move south in the winter or west in the summer. On the Missouri Pacific alone, the number of vagrants increased from just over 13,000 in 1929 to nearly 200,000 in 1931. One town in the Southwest hired special policemen to keep vagrants from leaving the boxcars. Those who became tramps had to keep on the move, but they did find a sense of community in the hobo jungles that sprang up along the major railroad routes. Here a man could find a place to eat and sleep, and peo-ple with whom to share his misery. Louis Banks, a black veteran, told interviewer Studs Terkel what these informal camps were like:

> Black and white, it didn't make any dif-ference who you were, 'cause everybody was poor. All friendly, sleep in a jungle. We used to take a big pot and cook food, cabbage, meat and beans all together. We all set together, we made a tent. Twenty-five or thirty would be out on the side of the rail, white and colored: They didn't

have no mothers or sisters, they didn't have no home, they were dirty, they had overalls on, they didn't have no food, they didn't have anything.

FIGHTING THE DEPRESSION

The Great Depression presented an enormous challenge for American political leadership. The inability of the Republicans to overcome the eco-nomic catastrophe provided the Democrats with the chance to regain power. Although they failed to achieve full recovery before the outbreak of World War II, the Democrats did succeed in alle-viating some of the suffering and establishing political dominance.

Hoover and Voluntarism

Herbert Hoover was the Depression's most prominent victim. When the economic downturn began in late 1929, he tried to rally the nation with bold forecasts of better days ahead. His repeated assertion that prosperity was just around the corner bred cynicism and mistrust. Expressing complete faith in the American eco-nomic system, Hoover blamed the depression on foreign causes, especially unstable European banks. The president rejected proposals for bold governmental action and relied instead on voluntary cooperation within business to halt the slide. He called the leaders of industry to the White House and secured their agreement to maintain prices and wages at high levels. Yet within a few months, employers were reducing wages and cutting prices in a desperate effort to survive.

Hoover also believed in voluntary efforts to relieve the human suffering brought about by the Depression. He called on private charities and local governments to help feed and clothe those in need. But when these sources were exhausted, he rejected all requests for direct federal relief, asserting that such handouts would undermine the character of proud American citizens.

As the Depression deepened, Hoover reluctantly began to move beyond voluntarism to undertake more sweeping governmental measures. A new Federal Farm Board loaned money to aid cooperatives and bought up surplus crops in the open market in a vain effort to raise farm prices. At Hoover's request, Congress cut taxes in an attempt to restore public confidence and adopted a few federal public-works projects, such as Boulder (Hoover) Dam, to provide jobs for idle men.

To help imperiled banks and insurance companies, Hoover proposed the Reconstruction Finance Corporation, which Congress established in early 1932. The RFC loaned government money to financial institutions to save them from bankruptcy. Hoover's critics, however, pointed out that while he favored aid to business, he still opposed measures such as direct relief and massive public works that would help the millions of unemployed.

By 1932, Hoover's efforts to overcome the Depression had clearly failed. The Democrats had gained control of the House of Representatives in the 1930 elections and were pressing the president to take bolder action, but Hoover stubbornly resisted. His public image suffered its sharpest blow in the summer of 1932 when he ordered General Douglas MacArthur to clear out the "bonus army." This ragged group of some 22,000 World War I veterans had come to Washington in the summer of 1932 to lobby for Congress to pay a bonus for military service due them in 1945 immediately. After the Senate rejected the bonus bill, some of the veterans stayed in Washington, living in ramshackle huts in Anacostia Flats along the Potomac. Mounted troops drove the bonus army out of the capital, blinding the veterans with tear gas and burning their shacks.

Meanwhile, the nation's banking structure approached collapse. Bank failures rose steadily in 1931 and 1932 as customers responded to rumors of bankruptcy by rushing in to withdraw their deposits, thereby causing a bank's failure. The banking crisis completed the nation's disenchantment with Hoover; the people were ready for a new leader in the White House.

The Emergence of Roosevelt

The man who stepped forward to meet this national need was Franklin D. Roosevelt. Born into the old Dutch colonial aristocracy of New York, FDR was a distant cousin of the Republican Teddy. He grew up with all the advantages of wealth—private tutors, his own sailboat and pony, frequent trips to Europe, and education at Groton and Harvard. His strong-willed mother smoothed all the obstacles in the path of her only

The Dust Bowl
In the Plains states, farms already burdened with the economic hardship of the Depression were plagued by drought and dust storms. Farm families were forced to leave their homes to find work farther west.

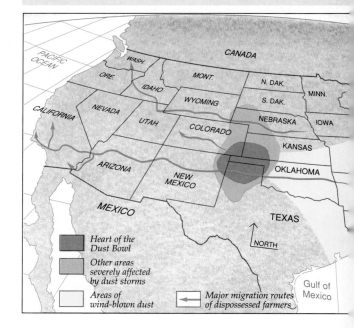

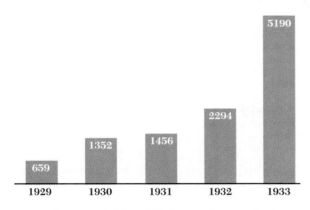

Source: Data compiled from C. D. Bremer, American Bank Failures (New York: Columbia University Press, 1935), p. 42.

child and gave him a priceless sense of inner security. After graduation from Harvard, he briefly attended law school but left to plunge into politics. He served in the New York legislature and then went to Washington as assistant secretary of the navy under Wilson, a post he filled capably during World War I. He met with defeat in 1920 as the Democratic vice presidential candidate and had begun a banking career when an attack of polio crippled him in the summer of 1921. Refusing to give in, he fought back bravely, and though he never again walked unaided, he reentered politics in the mid-1920s and was elected governor of New York in 1928.

Roosevelt's dominant trait was his ability to persuade and convince other people. He possessed a marvelous voice, deep and rich, a winning smile, and a bouyant confidence he could easily transmit to others. Some felt he was too vain and superficial as a young man, but his bout with polio gave him both an understanding of human suffering and a broad political appeal as a man who had faced heavy odds and overcome them. He understood the give-and-take of politics, knew how to use flattery to win over doubters, and was especially effective in exploiting the media, whether in bantering with newspaper reporters or reaching out to the American people on the radio. Although his mind was quick and agile, he had little patience with philosophical nuances; he dealt with the appearance of issues, not their deeper substance, and he dis-

played a flexibility toward political principles that often dismayed even his warmest admirers.

Roosevelt took advantage of the opportunity offered by the Depression. With the Republicans discredited, he cultivated the two wings of the divided Democrats, appealing to both the traditionalists from the South and West and the new urban elements in the North. After winning the party's nomination in 1932, he broke with tradition by flying to Chicago and accepting in person, telling the cheering delegates, "I pledge you—I pledge myself to a new deal for the American people."

In the fall, he defeated Herbert Hoover in a near landslide for the Democrats. Roosevelt tallied 472 electoral votes as he swept the South and West and carried nearly all the large industrial states as well. Farmers and workers, Protestants and Catholics, immigrants and native born rallied behind the new leader who promised to restore prosperity. Roosevelt not only met the challenge of the Depression but also solidified the shift to the Democratic party and created an enduring coalition that would dominate American politics for a half century.

The Hundred Days

When Franklin Roosevelt took the oath of office on March 4, 1933, the nation's economy was on the brink of collapse. Unemployment stood at nearly thirteen million, one-fourth of the labor

Presidential Voting in Chicago by Ethnic Groups, 1924–1932 (percentage democratic)			
	1924	*1928*	*1932*
Czechoslovakians	40	73	83
Poles	35	71	80
Lithuanians	48	77	84
Yugoslavs	20	54	67
Italians	31	63	64
Germans	14	58	69
Jews	19	60	77

Source: John M. Allswang, *A House for All Peoples: Ethnic Politics in Chicago, 1890–1936* (Lexington: University of Kentucky Press, 1971).

force; banks were closed in thirty-eight states. On inauguration morning, the governors of New York and Illinois closed the banks in the nation's two largest cities, thus bringing the country's financial transactions to a halt. Speaking from the steps of the Capitol, FDR declared boldly, "First of all, let me assert my firm belief that the only thing we have to fear is fear itself—nameless, unreasoning, unjustified terror." Then he announced he would call Congress into special session and request "broad executive power to wage a war against the emergency, as great as the power that would be given to me if we were in fact invaded by a foreign foe."

Within the next ten days, Roosevelt won his first great New Deal victory by saving the nation's banks. On March 5, he issued a decree closing the banks and called Congress back into session. His aides drafted new banking legislation and presented it to Congress on March 9; a few hours later, both houses passed it, and FDR signed the new legislation that evening. The measure provided for government supervision and aid to the banks. Strong ones would be reopened with federal support, weak ones closed, and those in difficulty bolstered by government loans.

On March 12, FDR addressed the nation by radio in the first of his fireside chats. In conversational tones, he told the public what he had done. Some banks would begin to reopen the next day, with the government standing behind them. Other banks, once they became solvent, would open later, and the American people could safely put their money back into these institutions. The

next day, March 13, the nation's largest and strongest banks opened their doors; at the end of the day, customers had deposited more cash than they withdrew. The crisis was over; gradually other banks opened, and the runs and failures ceased.

"Capitalism was saved in eight days," boasted one of Roosevelt's advisers. Most surprising was the conservative nature of FDR's action. Instead of nationalizing the banks, he had simply thrown the government's resources behind them and preserved private ownership. Though some other New Deal measures would be more radical, Roosevelt set a tone in the banking crisis. He was out to reform and restore the American economic system, not change it drastically. He drew on the Progressive tradition and his experience with World War I mobilization to fashion a moderate program of governmental action.

For the next three months, until it adjourned in June, Congress responded to a series of presidential initiatives. During these "Hundred Days," Roosevelt sent fifteen major requests to Congress and received back fifteen pieces of legislation. A few created permanent agencies that have become a part of American life: the Tennessee Valley Authority (TVA) proved to be the most successful and enduring of all Roosevelt's New Deal measures. This innovative effort at regional planning resulted in the building of a series of dams in seven states along the Tennessee River to control floods, ease navigation, and produce electricity. This last feature created cheap and abundant power that helped transform the poverty-stricken upper South into a relatively prosperous industrial area.

Other New Deal agencies were temporary in nature, designed to meet the specific economic problems of the Depression. None were completely successful; the Depression would continue for another six years, immune even to Roosevelt's magic. But psychologically the nation turned the corner in the spring of 1933. Under FDR, the government seemed to be responding to the economic crisis, enabling people for the first time since 1929 to look to the future with hope.

Roosevelt and Recovery

Two major New Deal programs launched during the Hundred Days were aimed at industrial and agricultural recovery. The first was the National

With his fireside chats, FDR became the first president to use radio to reach and reassure the American people.

Recovery Administration (NRA), FDR's attempt to achieve economic advance through planning and cooperation between government, business, and labor. In the midst of the Depression, businessmen were intent on stabilizing production and raising prices for their goods. Spokesmen for labor were equally determined to spread work through maximum hours and to put a floor under workers' income with minimum wages.

The NRA hoped to achieve both goals by permitting companies in each major industry to cooperate in writing codes of fair competition that would set realistic limits on production, allocate percentages to individual producers, and set firm guidelines for prices. Section 7a of the enabling act mandated protection for labor in all the codes by establishing maximum hours, minimum wages, and the guarantee of collective bargaining by unions. No company could be compelled to join, but the New Deal sought complete participation by appealing to patriotism. Each firm that took part could display a blue eagle and stamp this symbol on its products. With energetic Hugh Johnson in charge, the NRA quickly enrolled the nation's leading companies and unions. By the summer of 1933, more than five hundred industries had adopted codes that covered 2.5 million workers.

The NRA quickly bogged down in a huge bureaucratic morass. The codes proved to be too detailed to enforce easily. Written by the largest companies, these rules favored big business at the expense of smaller competitors. Labor quickly

became disenchanted with Section 7a. The minimum wages were often near starvation level, while business got around the requirement for collective bargaining by creating company unions that did not represent the real needs of workers. After a brief upsurge in the spring of 1933, industrial production began to sag as disillusionment

Although the NRA quickly bogged down in a bureaucratic morass, the NRA blue eagle became a widely respected symbol of a business' patriotism.

with the NRA grew. By 1934, more and more businessmen were complaining about the new agency, calling it the "National Run Around." When the Supreme Court finally invalidated the NRA in 1935 on constitutional grounds, few mourned its demise. The idea of trying to overcome the Depression by relying on voluntary cooperation between competing businessmen and labor leaders had collapsed in the face of individual self-interest and greed.

The New Deal's attempt at farm recovery fared a little better. Henry A. Wallace, FDR's secretary of agriculture, came up with an answer to the farmers' old dilemma of overproduction. The government would act as a clearinghouse for producers of major crops, arranging for them to set production limits for wheat, cotton, corn, and other leading crops. Under the Agricultural Adjustment Act (AAA) passed by Congress in May 1933, the government would allocate acreage among individual farmers, encouraging them to take land out of production by paying them subsidies (raised by a tax on food processors). Unfortunately, Wallace preferred not to wait until the 1934 planting season to implement this program, and so farmers were paid in 1933 to plow under crops they had already planted and to kill livestock they were raising. Faced with the problem of hunger in the midst of plenty, the New Deal seemed to respond by destroying the plenty.

The AAA program worked better in 1934 and 1935 as land removed from production led to smaller harvests and rising farm prices. Farm income rose for the first time since World War I, increasing from $2 billion in 1933 to $5 billion by 1935. Severe weather, especially Dust Bowl conditions in the Great Plains, contributed to the crop-limitation program, but most of the gain in farm income came from subsidy payments themselves rather than from higher market prices.

On the whole, large farmers benefited most from the program. Possessing the capital to buy machinery and fertilizer, they were able to farm more efficiently than before on fewer acres of land. Small farmers, tenants, and sharecroppers did not fare as well, receiving very little of the government payments and often being driven off the land as owners took the acreage previously cultivated by tenants and sharecroppers out of production. Some three million people left the

land in the 1930s, crowding into the cities where they swelled the relief rolls. In the long run, the New Deal reforms improved the efficiency of American agriculture, but at a real human cost.

The Supreme Court eventually found the AAA unconstitutional in 1936, but Congress reenacted it in modified form that year and again in 1938. The system of allotments, now financed directly by the government, became a standard feature of the farm economy. Other New Deal efforts to assist the rural poor, notably the Farm Security Administration (FSA), sought to loan tenants and sharecroppers money to acquire land of their own, but the sums appropriated by Congress were too modest. The FSA was able to extend loans to fewer than 2 percent of the nation's tenant farmers. "Obviously," the FSA director informed Roosevelt, "this . . . program can be regarded as only an experimental approach to the farm tenancy problem." The result of the New Deal for American farming was to hasten its transformation into a business in which only the efficient and well capitalized would thrive.

Roosevelt and Relief

The New Deal was far more successful in meeting the most immediate problem of the 1930s—relief for the millions of unemployed and destitute citizens. Roosevelt never shared Hoover's distaste for direct federal support; on May 12, 1933, in response to FDR's March request, Congress authorized the RFC to distribute $500 million to the states to help individuals and families in need.

Roosevelt brought in Harry Hopkins to direct the relief program. A former social worker who seemed to live on black coffee and cigarettes, Hopkins set up a desk in the hallway of the RFC building and proceeded to spend over $5 million in less than two hours. By the end of 1933, Hopkins had cut through red tape to distribute money to nearly one-sixth of the American people. The relief payments were modest in size, but they enabled millions to avoid starvation and stay out of humiliating breadlines.

Another, more imaginative early effort was the Civilian Conservation Corps (CCC), which was Roosevelt's own idea. The CCC enrolled youth from city families on relief and sent them to the nation's parks and recreational areas to build trails and improve public facilities. Ultimately,

Two Missouri families, carrying with them all their possessions, pause on their way to the California peafields. More than 3 million people migrated from the Plains states during the 1930s, driven off the land by devastating dust storms that destroyed their crops, their farms, and their way of life.

more than two million young people served in the CCC, contributing both to their families' incomes and to the nation's welfare.

Hopkins realized the need to do more than just keep people alive, and he soon became an advocate of work relief. Hopkins argued that the government should put the jobless to work, not just to encourage self-respect, but also to enable them to earn enough to purchase consumer goods and thus stimulate the entire economy. A Public Works Administration (PWA) headed by Secretary of the Interior Harold Ickes had been authorized in 1933, but Ickes, intent on the quality of the projects rather than human needs, failed to put many people to work. In the fall of 1933, Roosevelt created the Civil Works Administration (CWA) and charged Hopkins with getting people off the unemployment lines and relief rolls and back to work. Hopkins had over four million men and women at work by January 1934, building roads, schools, playgrounds, and athletic fields. Many of the workers were unskilled, and some of the projects were shoddy, but the CWA at least enabled people to work and earn enough money to survive the winter. Roosevelt, appalled at the huge expenditures involved, shut down the CWA in 1934 and forced Hopkins to return to

federal relief payments as the only source of aid to the jobless.

The final commitment to the idea of work relief came in 1935 when Roosevelt established the Works Progress Administration (WPA) to spend nearly $5 billion authorized by Congress for emergency relief. The WPA, under Hopkins, put the unemployed on the federal payroll so they could earn enough to meet their basic needs and help stimulate the stagnant economy. Conservatives complained the WPA amounted to nothing more than hiring the jobless to do make-work tasks with no real value. But Hopkins cared less about what was accomplished than about helping those who had been unemployed for years to get off the dole and gain self-respect by working again.

In addition to funding the usual construction and conservation projects, the WPA tried to preserve the skills of American artists, actors, and writers. The Federal Theatre Project produced plays, circuses, and puppet shows that enabled entertainers to practice their crafts and to perform before people who often had never seen a professional production before. Similar projects for writers and artists led to a series of valuable state guidebooks and to murals that adorned

Federal work relief programs helped millions maintain their self-respect. Workers in the CCC (top, left) received $30 a month for planting trees and digging drainage ditches. As indicated on the painting of the map, the PWA hired workers to build schools, irrigation ditches, sewage treatment plants, and bridges across the country. Artists and writers found work with the WPA (top, right).

public buildings across the land. A separate National Youth Administration (NYA) found part-time jobs for young people still in school and developed projects—ranging from automobile repairing in New York City to erecting tuberculosis isolation units in Arizona—for 2.5 million young adults.

The WPA helped ease the burden for the unemployed, but it failed to overcome the Depression. Rather than spending too much, as his critics charged, Roosevelt's greatest failure was not spending enough. The WPA never employed at any one time more than 3 million of the 10 million jobless. The wages, although larger than relief payments, were still pitifully low, averaging only $52 a month. Thus the WPA failed to prime the American economy by increasing consumer purchasing power. Factories remained closed and machinery idle because the American people still did not have the money, either from relief or the WPA, to buy cars, radios, appliances, and the other consumer goods that had been the basis for the prosperity of the 1920s. By responding to basic human needs, Roosevelt had made the Depression bearable. The New Deal's failure, however, to go beyond relief to achieve prosperity led to a growing frustration and the appearance of more radical alternatives that challenged the conservative nature of the New Deal and forced FDR to shift to the left.

ROOSEVELT AND REFORM

In 1935, the focus of the New Deal shifted from relief and recovery to reform. During his first two years in office, FDR had concentrated on fighting the Depression by shoring up the sagging American economy. Only a few new agencies, notably TVA, sought to make permanent changes in national life. Roosevelt was developing a "broker-state" concept of government, responding to pressures from organized elements such as corporations, labor unions, and farm groups while ignoring the needs and wants of the dispossessed who had no clear political voice. The early New Deal tried to assist bankers and industrialists, large farmers, and members of the labor unions, but it did little to help unskilled workers and sharecroppers.

The continuing depression and high unemployment began to build pressure for more sweeping changes. Roosevelt faced the choice of either providing more radical programs, ones designed to end historical inequities in American life, or deferring to others who put forth solutions to the nation's ills. Bolstered by an impressive Democratic victory in the 1934 congressional elections, Roosevelt responded by embracing a reform program that marked the climax of the New Deal.

Angry Voices

The signs of discontent were visible everywhere by 1935. In the upper Midwest, progressives and agrarian radicals, led by Minnesota governor Floyd Olson, were calling for government action to raise farm and labor income. "I am a radical in the sense that I want a definite change in the system," Olson declared. "I am not satisfied with patching." Upton Sinclair, the muckraking novelist, nearly won the governorship of California in 1934 running on the slogan "End Poverty in California," while in the East a violent strike in the textile industry shut down plants in twenty states. The most serious challenge to Roosevelt's leadership, however, came from three demagogues who captured national attention in the mid-1930s.

The first was Father Charles Coughlin, a Roman Catholic priest from Detroit, who had originally supported FDR. Speaking to a rapt nationwide radio audience in his rich, melodious voice, Coughlin appealed to the discontented with a strange mixture of crank monetary schemes and anti-Semitism. He broke with the New Deal in late 1934, denouncing it as the "Pagan Deal," and founded his own National Union for Social Justice. Increasingly vitriolic, he called for monetary inflation and the nationalization of the banking system in his weekly radio sermons to an audience of more than thirty million.

A more benign but equally threatening figure appeared in California. Dr. Francis Townsend, a sixty-seven-year-old physician, came forward in 1934 with a scheme to assist the elderly, who were suffering greatly during the Depression. The Townsend Plan proposed giving everyone over the age of sixty a monthly pension of $200 with the proviso that it must be spent within thirty days. Although designed less as an old-age pension plan than as a way to stimulate the economy, the proposal understandably had its greatest appeal among the elderly. They embraced it as a holy cause, joining Townsend Clubs across the country. Despite the criticism from economists that the plan would transfer over half the national income to less than 10 percent of the population, more than ten million people signed petitions endorsing the Townsend Plan, and few politicians dared oppose it.

The third new voice of protest was that of Huey Long, the flamboyant senator from Louisiana. Like Coughlin, an original supporter of the New Deal, Long turned against FDR and by 1935 had become a major political threat to the president. A shrewd, ruthless, yet witty man, Long had a remarkable ability to mock those in power. The Kingfish (a nickname he borrowed from "Amos 'n Andy") announced a nationwide "Share the Wealth" movement in 1934. He spoke grandly of taking from the rich to make "Every Man a King," guaranteeing each American a home worth $5,000 and an annual income of $2,500. To finance the plan, Long advocated seizing all fortunes of more than $5 million and levying a tax of 100 percent on incomes over $1 million. By 1935, Long claimed to have founded 27,000 Share the Wealth Clubs and had a mailing list of over 7 million people, including workers, farmers, college professors, and even bank presidents. Threatening to run as a third-party candidate in 1936, Long generated fear among Democratic leaders that he might attract 3 or 4 million votes, possibly enough to swing the election to the Republicans. Although an assassin killed Huey Long in Louisiana in late 1935, his popularity showed the need for the New Deal to do more to help those still in distress.

Social Security

When the new Congress met in January 1935, Roosevelt was ready to support a series of reform measures designed to take the edge off national dissent. The recent elections had increased Democratic congressional strength significantly, with the Republicans losing thirteen seats in the House and retaining less than one-third of the Senate. Many of the Democrats were to the left of Roosevelt, favoring increased spending and more sweeping federal programs. "Boys—this is our hour," exulted Harry Hopkins. "We've got to get everything we want . . . now or never." Congress

Despite the administration's boosterism, many felt that Social Security could not fulfill its promises.

quickly appropriated $4.8 billion for the WPA and was prepared to enact virtually any proposal that Roosevelt offered.

The most significant reform enacted in 1935 was the Social Security Act. The Townsend movement had reminded Americans that the United States, alone among modern industrial nations, had never developed a welfare system to aid the aged, the disabled, and the unemployed. A cabinet committee began studying the problem in 1934, and President Roosevelt sent its recommendations to Congress the following January.

The proposed legislation had three major parts. First, it provided for old-age pensions financed equally by a tax on employers and workers, without government contributions. In addition, it gave states federal matching funds to provide modest pensions for the destitute elderly. Second, it set up a system of unemployment compensation on a federal-state basis, with employers paying a payroll tax and with each state setting benefit levels and administering the program locally. Finally, it provided for direct federal grants to the states, on a matching basis, for welfare payments to the blind, handicapped, needy elderly, and dependent children.

Although there was criticism from conservatives who mourned the passing of traditional American reliance on self-help and individualism, the chief objections came from those who argued the administration's measure did not go far enough. Democratic leaders, however, defeated efforts to incorporate Townsend's proposal for $200-a-month pensions and increases in unemployment benefits. Congress then passed the Social Security Act by overwhelming margins.

Critics began to point out its shortcomings as they have ever since. The old-age pensions were paltry. Designed to begin in 1942, they ranged from $10 to $85 a month. Not everyone was covered; those who most needed protection in their old age, such as farmers and domestic servants, were not included. The regressive feature of the act was even worse. All participants, regardless of income or economic status, paid in at the same rate, with no supplement from the general revenue. The trust fund also took out of circulation money that was desperately needed to stimulate the economy in the 1930s.

Other portions of the act were equally open to question. The cumbersome unemployment system offered no aid to those currently out of work, only to people who would lose their jobs in the future, and the benefits (depending on the state) ranged from barely adequate to substandard. The outright grants to the handicapped and dependent children were minute in terms of the need; in New York City, for example, a blind person received only $5 a week in 1937.

The conservative nature of the legislation reflected Roosevelt's own fiscal orthodoxy, but even more it was a product of his political realism. Despite the severity of the Depression, he realized that establishing a system of federal welfare went against deeply rooted American convictions. He insisted on a tax on participants to give those involved in the pension plan a vested interest in Social Security. He wanted them to feel they had earned their pensions and that in the future no one would dare take them away. "With those taxes in there," he explained privately, "no damned politician can ever scrap my social security program." Above all, FDR had succeeded in establishing the principle of governmental responsibility for the aged, the handicapped, and the unemployed. Whatever the defects of the legislation, Social Security stood as a landmark of the New Deal, creating a system to provide for the welfare of individuals in a complex industrial society.

Labor Legislation

The other major reform achievement in 1935 was passage of the National Labor Relations Act. Senator Robert Wagner of New York introduced legislation in 1934 to outlaw company unions and other unfair labor practices in order to ensure collective bargaining for unions. FDR, who had little knowledge of labor-management relations and apparently little interest in them, opposed the bill. In 1935, however, Wagner began to gather broad support for his measure, which passed the Senate in May with only twelve opposing votes, and the president, seeing passage as likely, gave it his approval. The bill moved quickly through the House, and Roosevelt signed it into law in July.

The Wagner Act, as it became known, created a National Labor Relations Board to preside over labor-management relations and enable unions to engage in collective bargaining with federal support. The act outlawed a variety of union-busting tactics and in its key provision decreed that whenever the majority of a company's workers voted for a union to represent them, management would be compelled to negotiate with the union on all matters of wages, hours, and working conditions. With this unprecedented government sanction, labor unions could now proceed to recruit the large number of unorganized workers throughout the country. The Wagner Act, the most far reaching of all New Deal measures, led to the revitalization of the American labor movement and a permanent change in labor-management relations.

Three years later, Congress passed a second law that had a lasting impact on American workers—the Fair Labor Standards Act. A long-sought goal of the New Deal, this measure aimed to establish both minimum wages and maximum hours of work per week. Since labor unions usually were able to negotiate adequate levels of pay and work for their members, the act was aimed at unorganized workers and met with only grudging support from unions. Southern conservatives opposed it strongly, both on ideological grounds (it meant still greater government involvement in private enterprise) and because it threatened the low southern wages that had attracted northern industry since Reconstruction.

Roosevelt finally succeeded in winning passage of the Fair Labor Standards Act in 1938, but only at the cost of exempting many key industries from its coverage. The act provided for a minimum wage of forty cents an hour by 1940 and a standard workweek of forty hours, with time and a half for overtime. Despite its loopholes, the legislation did lead to pay raises for the twelve million workers earning less than forty cents an hour. More important, like Social Security it set up a system—however inadequate—that Congress could build on in the future to reach more generous and humane levels.

Other New Deal reform measures met with a mixed reception in Congress. Proposals to break up the huge public utility holding companies created by promoters in the 1920s and to levy a "soak-the-rich" tax on the wealthy stirred up bitter debate, and these bills were passed only in greatly weakened form. Roosevelt was more successful in passing a banking act that made important reforms in the Federal Reserve System. He also gained congressional approval of the Rural Electrification Administration (REA), which helped bring electricity to the 90 percent of American farms that still did not have it in the 1930s.

All in all, Roosevelt's record in reform was similar to that in relief and recovery—modest success but no sweeping victory. A cautious and pragmatic leader, FDR moved far enough to the left to overcome the challenges of Coughlin, Townsend, and Long without venturing too far from the mainstream. His reforms improved the quality of life in America significantly, but he made no effort to correct all the nation's social and economic wrongs.

IMPACT OF THE NEW DEAL

The New Deal had a broad influence on the quality of life in the United States in the 1930s. Government programs reached into areas hitherto untouched. Many of them brought about long overdue improvements, but others failed to make any significant dent in historic inequities. The most important advances came with the dramatic growth of labor unions; the conditions for working women and minorities in nonunionized industries showed no comparable advance.

Rise of Organized Labor

Trade unions were weak at the onset of the Depression, with a membership of fewer than three million workers. Most were in the American Federation of Labor (AFL), composed of craft unions that served the needs of skilled workers. The nation's basic industries like steel and automobiles were unorganized; the great mass of unskilled workers thus fared poorly in terms of wages and working conditions. Section 7a of the NRA had led to some growth in AFL ranks, but the Federation's conservative leaders, eager to cooperate with business, failed to take full advantage of the opportunity to organize the mass production industries.

John L. Lewis, head of the United Mine Workers, took the lead in forming the Committee on Industrial Organization (CIO) in 1935. The son of a Welsh coal miner, Lewis was a dynamic and ruthless man. He had led the mine workers since 1919 and was determined to spread the benefits of unions throughout industry. Lewis first battled with the leadership of the AFL, and then—after being expelled—he renamed his group the Congress of Industrial Organizations and announced in 1936 he would use the Wagner Act to extend collective bargaining to the nation's auto and steel industries.

Within five years, Lewis had scored a remarkable series of victories. Some came easily. The big steel companies, led by U.S. Steel, surrendered without a fight in 1937; management realized that with federal support the unions were in a strong position. There was greater resistance in the automobile industry. When General Motors, the first target, resisted, the newly created United Automobile Workers (UAW) developed an effective strike technique. In late December 1936, GM workers in Flint, Michigan, simply sat down in the factory, refusing to leave until the company recognized their union, and threatening to destroy the valuable tools and machines if they were removed forcibly. When the Michigan gov-

In some cases, striking union members met with brute force. Philip Evergood's 1937 painting,
The American Tragedy, *recounts the violence of the Republic Steel strike.*

ernor refused to call out the National Guard to break the strike, General Motors conceded defeat in the sit-down strike and signed a contract with the UAW. Chrysler quickly followed suit, but Henry Ford refused to give in and fought the UAW, hiring strikebreakers and beating up organizers. In 1941, however, Ford finally recognized the UAW. Smaller steel companies, led by Republic Steel, engaged in even more violent resistance; in one incident in 1937, police shot ten strikers. The companies eventually reached a settlement with the steelworkers' union in 1941.

By the end of the 1930s, the CIO had some five million members, slightly more than the AFL. The successes were remarkable—in addition to the automaking and steel unions, organizers for the CIO and the AFL had been successful in the textile, rubber, electrical, and metal industries. For the first time, unskilled as well as skilled were

unionized. Women and African Americans benefited from the creation of the CIO, not because the union followed enlightened policies, but simply because they made up a substantial proportion of the unskilled work force that the CIO organized.

Yet despite these impressive gains, only 28 percent of all Americans (excluding farm workers) belonged to unions by 1940. Millions in the restaurant, retail, and service trades remained unorganized, working long hours for very low wages. Employer resistance and traditional hostility to unions blocked further progress, as did the aloof attitude of President Roosevelt, who commented to labor and management, "A plague on both your houses" during the steel strike. The Wagner Act had helped open the way, but labor leaders like Lewis, Philip Murray of the Steel Workers Organizing Committee, and Walter

Reuther of the United Automobile Workers deserved most of the credit for union achievements.

The New Deal Record on Help to Minorities

The Roosevelt administration's attempts to aid the downtrodden were least effective with African Americans and other racial minorities. The Depression had hit blacks with special force. Sharecroppers and tenant farmers had seen the price of cotton drop from eighteen to six cents a pound, far below the level to sustain a family on the land. In the cities, the saying "First Fired, Last Hired" proved all too true; by 1933, over 50 percent of urban blacks were unemployed. Hard times sharpened racial prejudice. "No Jobs for Niggers Until Every White Man Has a Job" became a rallying cry for whites in Atlanta.

The New Deal helped African Americans survive the Depression, but it never tried to confront squarely the racial injustice built into the federal relief programs. Although the programs served blacks as well as whites, in the South the weekly payments blacks received were much smaller. In the early days, NRA codes permitted lower wage scales for blacks, while the AAA led to the eviction of thousands of Negro tenants and sharecroppers. African American leaders referred to the NRA as standing for "Negro Robbed Again" and dismissed the AAA as "a continuation of the same old raw deal." Nor did later reform measures help very much. Neither the minimum wage nor Social Security covered those working as farmers or domestic servants, categories that comprised 65 percent of all African American workers. Thus an NAACP official commented that Social Security "looks like a sieve with the holes just large enough for the majority of Negroes to fall through."

Despite this bleak record, African Americans rallied behind Roosevelt's leadership, abandoning their historic ties to the Republican party. In 1936, over 75 percent of those African Americans who voted supported FDR. In part, this switch came in response to Roosevelt's appointment of a number of prominent African Americans to high-ranking government positions, such as William H. Hastie in the Interior Department and Mary McLeod Bethune (founder and president of Bethune-Cookman College) in the National

With the statue of Abraham Lincoln as a backdrop, African American contralto Marian Anderson sang on the steps of the Lincoln Memorial in a concert given April 9, 1939.

Youth Administration. Eleanor Roosevelt spoke out eloquently throughout the decade against racial discrimination, most notably in 1939 when the Daughters of the American Revolution refused to let African American contralto Marian Anderson sing in Constitution Hall. The First Lady and Interior Secretary Harold Ickes arranged for the singer to perform at the Lincoln Memorial, where 75,000 people gathered to hear her on Easter Sunday.

Perhaps the most influential factor in the African Americans' political switch was the color-blind policy of Harry Hopkins. He had more than one million blacks working for the WPA by 1939, many of them in teaching and artistic positions as well as in construction jobs. Overall, the New Deal provided assistance to 40 percent of the nation's blacks during the Depression. Uneven as his record was, Roosevelt had still done more to aid this oppressed minority than any previous president since Lincoln. One African American newspaper commented that while "relief and WPA are not ideal, they are better than the Hoover bread lines and they'll have to do until the real thing comes along."

The New Deal did far less for Mexican Americans. Engaged primarily in agricultural labor, these people found their wages in California fields dropping from thirty-five to fourteen cents an hour by 1933. The pool of unemployed migrant labor expanded rapidly with Dust Bowl conditions in the Great Plains and the subsequent flight of "Okies" and "Arkies" to the cotton fields of Arizona and the truck farms of California. The Roosevelt administration cut off any further influx from Mexico by barring entry of any immigrant "likely to become a public charge"; local authorities rounded up and shipped migrants back to Mexico to reduce the welfare rolls.

The New Deal relief program did aid many thousands of Mexican Americans in the Southwest in the 1930s, although migrant workers had difficulty meeting state requirements. The WPA hired Mexican Americans for a variety of construction and cultural programs, but after 1937 such employment was denied to aliens. Overall, the pattern was one of great economic hardship and relatively little federal assistance for Mexican Americans.

The Native American, after decades of neglect, fared slightly better under the New Deal. Roosevelt appointed John Collier, a social worker who championed Indian rights, to serve as commissioner of Indian affairs. In 1934, Congress passed the Indian Reorganization Act, a reform measure designed to stress tribal unity and auton-

omy instead of attempting (as previous policy had done) to transform Indians into self-sufficient farmers by granting them small plots of land (see Chapter 17). Collier employed more Native Americans in the Indian Bureau, supported educational programs on the reservations, and encouraged tribes to produce native handiwork such as blankets and jewelry. Despite modest gains however, the nation's one-third of a million Indians remained the most impoverished citizens in America.

Women at Work

The decade witnessed no significant gain in the status of American women. In the midst of the Depression, there was little concern expressed for protecting or extending their rights. The popular idea that women worked for "pin money" while men were the breadwinners for their families led employers to discriminate in favor of men when cutting the work force. Working women "are holding jobs that rightfully belong to the God-intended providers of the household," declared a Chicago civic group. More than three-fourths of the nation's school boards refused to hire wives, and more than half of them fired women teachers who married. Federal regulations prohibited more than one member of a family from working in the civil service, and almost always it was the wife who had to defer to her husband. A Gallup poll revealed that 82 percent of the people disap-

Roosevelt appointed John Collier as commissioner of Indian affairs to bring the New Deal to Native Americans. Under the Indian Reorganization Act of 1934, over 7 million acres of land were restored to Native American control. Still, many Indians continued to distrust the government and its New Deal programs. Collier is shown here with a group of Flathead Indian chiefs standing behind Secretary of the Interior Harold L. Ickes on October 28, 1935, as Ickes signs the first constitution providing for Indian self-rule. Previously the Bureau of Indian Affairs had directed the government of the Indians.

proved of working wives, with 75 percent of the women polled agreeing.

Many of the working women in the 1930s were either single or the sole supporters of an entire family. Yet their wages remained lower than those for men, and their unemployment rate ran higher than 20 percent throughout the decade. Women over forty found it particularly hard to find or retain jobs during the Depression. The New Deal offered little encouragement. NRA codes sanctioned lower wages for women, permitting laundries, for example, to pay them as little as fourteen cents an hour. The minimum wage did help those women employed in industry, but too many worked as maids and waitresses—jobs not covered by the law—to have much overall effect. Despite these hardships, the number of married women and women between the ages of twenty-five and forty in the labor force increased during the 1930s. Relatively few women worked in heavy industry, where unemployment was greatest; most were employed in the clerical and service sectors, areas of traditional female employment, in which jobs were more plentiful.

The one area of advance in the 1930s came in government. Eleanor Roosevelt set an example that encouraged millions of American women. Instead of presiding sedately over the White House, she traveled continually around the country, always eager to uncover wrongs and bring them to the president's attention (see "Eleanor Roosevelt and the Quest for Social Justice," pp. 808–809). Frances Perkins, the secretary of labor, became the first woman cabinet member, and FDR appointed women as ambassadors and federal judges for the first time.

Women also were elected to office in larger numbers in the 1930s. Hattie W. Caraway of Arkansas succeeded her husband in the Senate, winning a full term in 1934. That same year voters elected six women to the House of Representatives. Public service, however, was one of the few professions open to women. The nation's leading medical and law schools discouraged women from applying, and the percentage of female faculty members in colleges and universities continued to decline in the 1930s. In sum, a decade that was grim for most Americans was especially hard on American women.

END OF THE NEW DEAL

The New Deal reached its high point in 1936, when Roosevelt was overwhelmingly reelected and the Democratic party strengthened its hold on Congress. This political triumph was deceptive. In the next two years, Roosevelt met with a series of defeats in Congress. Yet despite these setbacks, he remained a popular political leader

Government employment was one of the few areas in which working women made advances in the 1930s. Secretary of Labor Frances Perkins, shown here inspecting the Golden Gate Bridge, was the first woman cabinet member, one of a number of women appointed by FDR to posts previously held only by men.

who had restored American self-confidence as he strove to meet the challenges of the Depression.

The Election of 1936

Franklin Roosevelt enjoyed his finest political hour in 1936. A man who loved the give-and-take of politics, FDR faced challenges from both the left and the right as he sought reelection. Father Coughlin and Gerald L. K. Smith, who inherited Huey Long's following after the senator's assassination in 1935, organized a Union party, with North Dakota Progressive Congressman William Lemke heading the ticket. At the other extreme, a group of wealthy industrialists formed the Liberty League to fight what they saw as the New Deal's assault on property rights. The Liberty League attracted prominent Democrats, including Al Smith, but in 1936 it endorsed the Republican presidential candidate, Governor Alfred M. Landon of Kansas. A moderate, colorless figure, Landon disappointed his backers by refusing to campaign for repeal of the popular New Deal reforms.

Roosevelt ignored Lemke and the Union party, focusing attention instead on the assault from the right. Democratic spokesmen condemned the Liberty League as a "millionaire's union" and reminded the American people of how much Roosevelt had done for them in fighting unemployment and providing relief. In his speeches, FDR condemned the "economic royalists" who were "unanimous in their hatred for me." "I welcome their hatred," he declared, and promised that in his second term these forces would meet "their master."

This frank appeal to class sympathies proved enormously successful. Roosevelt won easily, receiving five million more votes than he had gotten in 1932 and outscoring Landon in the electoral college by 523 to 8. The Democrats did almost as well in Congress, piling up margins of 331 to 89 in the House and 76 to 16 in the Senate (with 4 not aligned with either major party).

Equally important, the election marked the stunning success of a new political coalition that would dominate American politics for the next three decades. FDR, building on the inroads into the Republican majority that Al Smith had begun in 1928, carried urban areas by impressive margins, winning 3.6 million more votes than his opponents in the nation's twelve largest cities. He held on to the traditional Democratic votes in the South and West and added to them by appealing strongly to the diverse religious and ethnic groups in the northern cities—Catholics and Jews, Italians and Poles, Irish and Slavs. The strong support of labor, together with three-quarters of the black vote, indicated that the nation's new alignment followed economic as well as cultural lines. The poor and the oppressed, who in the Depression years included many middle-class Americans, became attached to the Democratic party, leaving the GOP in a minority position, limited to the well-to-do and rural and small-town Americans of native stock.

The Supreme Court Fight

FDR proved to be far more adept at winning electoral victories than in achieving his goals in Congress. In 1937, he attempted to use his recent success to overcome the one obstacle remaining in his path—the Supreme Court. During his first term, the Court had ruled several New Deal programs unconstitutional, most notably the NRA and the AAA. Only three of the nine justices were sympathetic to the need for emergency measures in the midst of the Depression. Two others were unpredictable, sometimes approving New Deal

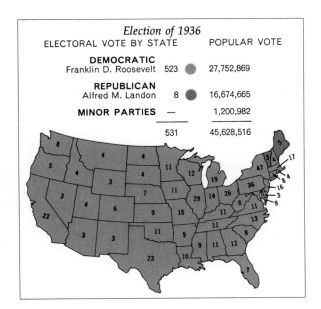

Election of 1936

ELECTORAL VOTE BY STATE		POPULAR VOTE
DEMOCRATIC Franklin D. Roosevelt	523	27,752,869
REPUBLICAN Alfred M. Landon	8	16,674,665
MINOR PARTIES	—	1,200,982
	531	45,628,516

Eleanor Roosevelt and the Quest for Social Justice

Eleanor Roosevelt entered public life as a reformer long before she became the First Lady. Although she loved and admired her uncle Theodore, her side of the Roosevelt family was more active in New York society than politics. In a family environment where the social graces were highly prized, Eleanor grew up shy and insecure. She turned to voluntary social work for fulfillment, where her relationships were based on common interests and ideals rather than social standing. Before her marriage to Franklin Roosevelt in 1905, she had been active in the New York settlement house movement and the Consumers' League. Like many reformers of her day, she found her sense of social justice upset by the existence of poverty and inequality. Avoiding politics, which she then considered a

"sinister affair," she limited her activities to nonpartisan reform and relief organizations.

After her marriage, she curtailed her social work, placing her responsibilities as a wife and mother first, as she believed a woman should. Though always a supportive partner, Mrs. Roosevelt did not develop a taste for politics despite her husband's tenure in the New York State Senate and later as assistant secretary of the navy during World War I. But when FDR was stricken with polio in 1921, she was determined that he return to political life as soon as possible; such a goal, she thought, was the best antidote to his pain and depression. While she worked tirelessly to speed his physical recovery, she also struck out on her own to keep the Roosevelt name alive in New York politics.

In the newly formed League of Women Voters, the Women's City Club, the Non-Partisan Legislative Committee, and the New York State Democratic party, Eleanor Roosevelt brought her reformer's impulse to politics. In these organizations she formed the nucleus of an "old-girls' network" that she would employ extensively during the New Deal years. Her newly acquired political and organizational skills as well as her knowledge and speeches served her husband well in his gubernatorial and presidential campaigns.

In a speech delivered in 1928, Mrs. Roosevelt commented on the need to "bring government closer to the people" and to "develop the human side of government." Focusing on those whose needs were greatest, Eleanor Roosevelt was an advo-

A modest, self-effacing woman with tremendous popular appeal, Eleanor Roosevelt played the traditional role of first lady, graciously hosting such gatherings as the one shown here. She also took on less traditional roles, fighting actively for social justice.

cate for the dispossessed. She advanced their interests within the administration, working hardest for women and African Americans, whose voices were least often heard.

FDR appealed to the "forgotten man"; his wife concerned herself with the "forgotten woman." She worked with Harry Hopkins to achieve equity for women on relief and to create more jobs for women under the auspices of the CWA and the WPA. With Frances Perkins, she arranged to establish camps for unemployed girls patterned after the CCC while she continued to work with the Women's Trade Union League to guarantee women equal pay for equal work on federal projects. In her syndicated newspaper column "My Day," she often dealt with the problems faced by women during the Depression. She even held press conferences to which only women reporters were invited to ensure employment for at least a handful of female journalists.

The First Lady's office became, in effect, a clearinghouse for federally sponsored programs for women, and her endorsement often meant the difference between success or failure. She took advantage of her position to expedite the programs she thought most important.

She worked equally hard for African Americans, but with little more to show for her efforts. "We can have no group beaten down, underprivileged," said the First Lady in a radio address in 1934, "without reaction on the rest." In one sentence, she captured the essence of her appeal for justice and equality for blacks. Social justice was not merely desirable for blacks; it was necessary to ensure the vitality of American democracy. She

spoke eloquently in favor of equal opportunity for blacks and sought their inclusion in New Deal programs. She worked with Hopkins to include more blacks in federal projects and lobbied within the administration for the appointment of black men and women to administer the programs designed specifically for them. Publicly, she endeavored to set an example by addressing black audiences throughout the country, presiding over a more egalitarian White House, and resigning her membership in the DAR over the Marian Anderson incident (see p. 804).

In her struggle against racial discrimination, Mrs. Roosevelt sometimes found her desires to be in conflict with her husband's attempts to keep the coalition of Democratic voters intact. His fear of alienating southern supporters caused him to temporize on the antilynching bill and abolition of the poll tax, both of which he considered desirable but not "must" legislation. Mrs. Roosevelt's support of these measures, however, put the Roosevelt name behind them. In her efforts to secure passage of the legislation, she arranged for meetings between FDR and Walter White of the NAACP. She briefed White to prepare him for FDR's objections in his conference with the president. When she asked FDR if he minded her public support of the antilynching bill, he replied, "Certainly not. . . . I can always say, 'Well, that is my wife; I can't do anything about her.'" Thus it appears that the president and Mrs. Roosevelt were of one mind, but she was able to support a cause that he felt it impolitic to advocate himself.

This distinction between the First Lady's activities as a representative of the Roosevelt admin-

Eleanor Roosevelt visited many sites in her efforts to bring the New Deal to the forgotten and the dispossessed. She is shown here visiting an African American nursery school run by the WPA in Des Moines, Iowa.

istration and her actions as a private citizen was often a difficult one to establish. It is even harder to assess accurately her impact on the policies of the New Deal. Eleanor Roosevelt was revered by millions of Americans who saw in her the very essence of American ideals. Her support of women and blacks was instrumental in swaying their support to the Roosevelt coalition. Still, the telling fact remains that the plight of the two groups to which she devoted the lion's share of her attention during the Depression—women and blacks—was only slightly relieved. This is not to minimize her achievements. As the self-appointed conscience of the Roosevelt administration, she exposed the areas where the New Deal had not been realized. Her accessibility to the public and her willingness to serve its interests gave encouragement to those who had lost all hope. Her courage and vitality in the pursuit of human rights and equality made her the embodiment of reform and social justice in the New Deal.

Year Created	Act or Agency	Provisions
1933	Agricultural Adjustment Administration (AAA)	Attempted to regulate agricultural production through farm subsidies; reworked after the Supreme Court ruled its key regulatory provisions unconstitutional in 1936; coordinated agricultural production during World War II, after which it was disbanded.
	Banking Act of 1933 (Glass-Steagall Act)	Prohibited commercial banks from selling stock or financing corporations; created FDIC.
	Civilian Conservation Corps (CCC)	Young men between the ages of 18 and 25 volunteered to be placed in camps to work on regional environmental projects mainly west of the Mississippi; they received $30 a month of which $25 was sent home; disbanded during World War II.
	Civil Works Administration (CWA)	Emergency work relief program put over four million people to work during the extremely cold winter of 1933–1934, after which it was disbanded.
	Federal Deposit Insurance Corporation (FDIC)	A federal guarantee of savings bank deposits initially of up to $2,500, raised to $5,000 in 1934, and frequently thereafter; continues today with a limit of $100,000.
	Federal Emergency Relief Administration (FERA)	Combined cash relief to needy families with work relief, superseded in early 1935 by the extensive work relief projects of the WPA and unemployment insurance established by Social Security.
	National Recovery Administration (NRA)	Attempted to combat the Depression through national economic planning by establishing and administering a system of industrial codes to control production, prices, labor relations, and trade practices among leading business interests; ruled unconstitutional by the Supreme Court in 1935.
	Public Works Administration (PWA)	Financed construction of over 34,000 federal and nonfederal construction projects at a cost of over $6 billion; initiated the first federal public housing program, made the federal government the nation's leading producer of power, and advanced conservation of the nation's natural resources; discontinued in 1939 due to its effectiveness at reducing unemployment and promoting private investment.
	Tennessee Valley Authority (TVA)	An attempt at regional planning, including provisions for environment and recreational design, architectural, educational, and health projects, as well as its controversial public power projects; continues today to meet the Tennessee Valley's energy and flood control needs.

Year Created	Act or Agency	Provisions
1934	Federal Communications Commission (FCC)	Regulatory agency with wide discretionary powers established to oversee wired and wireless communication; reflected growing importance of radio in everyday lives of Americans during the Depression; continues to regulate television as well as radio.
	Federal Housing Administration (FHA)	Expanded private home ownership among moderate income families through federal guarantees of private mortgages, the reduction of down payments from 30 to 10 percent, and the extension of repayment from 20 to 30 years; continues to function today.
	Securities and Exchange Commission (SEC)	Continues today to regulate trading practices in stocks and bonds according to federal laws.
1935	National Labor Relations Board (NLRB); established by Wagner Act	Greatly enhanced power of American labor by overseeing collective bargaining; continues to arbitrate labor-management disputes today.
	National Youth Administration (NYA)	Established by the WPA to reduce competition for jobs by supporting education and training of youth; paid grants to over two million high school and college students in return for work performed in their schools; also trained another 2.6 million out-of-school youths as skilled labor to prepare them for later employment in the private sector; disbanded during World War II.
	Rural Electrification Administration (REA)	Transformed American rural life by making electricity available at low rates to American farm families in areas private power companies refused to service; closed cultural gap between rural and urban everyday life by making modern amenities, such as radio, available in rural areas.
	Social Security Act	Guaranteed retirement payments for enrolled workers beginning at age 65, set up federal-state system of unemployment insurance and care for dependent mothers and children, the handicapped, and public health; continues today.
	Works Progress Administration (WPA)	Massive work relief program funded projects ranging from construction to acting; disbanded by FDR during World War II.
1937	Farm Security Administration (FSA)	Granted loans to small farmers and tenants for rehabilitation and purchase of small-sized farms; Congress slashed its appropriations during World War II when many poor farmers entered the armed forces or migrated to urban areas.
1938	Fair Labor Standards Act	Established a minimum wage of forty cents an hour and a maximum work week of forty hours for businesses engaged in interstate commerce.

measures and sometimes opposing them. Four justices were bent on using the Constitution to block Roosevelt's proposals. All were elderly men, and one, Willis Van Devanter, had planned to retire in 1932 but remained on the Court because he believed Roosevelt to be "unfitted and unsafe for the Presidency."

When Congress convened in 1937, the president offered a startling proposal to overcome the Court's threat to the New Deal. Instead of seeking a constitutional amendment either to limit the Court's power or to clarify the constitutional issues, FDR chose an oblique attack. Declaring the Court was falling behind schedule because of the age of its members, he asked Congress to appoint a new justice for each member of the Court over the age of seventy, up to a maximum of six.

Although this "court-packing" scheme, as critics quickly dubbed it, was perfectly legal, it outraged not only conservatives but liberals as well, who realized it could set a dangerous precedent for the future. Republicans wisely kept silent, letting prominent Democrats such as Senator Burton Wheeler of Montana lead the fight against Roosevelt's plan. Despite all-out pressure from the White House, resistance in the Senate blocked early action on the proposal.

The Court defended itself well. Chief Justice Charles Evans Hughes testified tellingly to the Senate Judiciary Committee, pointing out that in fact the Court was up to date and not behind schedule as Roosevelt charged. The Court then surprised observers with a series of rulings approving such controversial New Deal measures as the Wagner Act and Social Security. In the midst of the struggle, Justice Van Devanter resigned, enabling FDR to make his first appointment to the Court since taking office in 1933. Feeling he had proved his point, the president allowed his court-packing plan to die in the Senate.

During the next few years, four more vacancies occurred, and Roosevelt was able to appoint such distinguished jurists as Hugo Black, William O. Douglas, and Felix Frankfurter to the Supreme Court. Yet the price was high. The court fight had badly weakened the president's relations with Congress, opening up deep rifts with members of his own party. Many senators and representatives who had voted reluctantly for Roosevelt's mea-

sures during the depths of the Depression now felt free to oppose any further New Deal reforms.

The New Deal in Decline

The legislative record during Roosevelt's second term was meager. Aside from the minimum wage and a minimum-hour law passed in 1938, Congress did not extend the New Deal into any new areas. Attempts to institute national health insurance met with stubborn resistance, as did efforts by civil rights advocates to pass antilynching legislation. Disturbed by this growing congressional resistance, Roosevelt set out in the spring of 1938 to defeat a number of conservative Democratic congressmen and senators, primarily in the South. His targets gleefully charged the president with interference in local politics; only one of the men he sought to defeat lost in the primaries. The failure of this attempted purge further undermined Roosevelt's strained relations with Congress.

The worst blow came in the economic sector. The slow but steady improvement in the economy suddenly gave way to a sharp recession in the late summer of 1937. In the next ten months, industrial production fell by one-third, and nearly four million workers lost their jobs. Critics of the New Deal quickly labeled the downturn "the Roosevelt recession," and businessmen claimed it reflected a lack of confidence in FDR's leadership.

Actually, Roosevelt was at fault. In an effort to reduce expanding budget deficits, he had cut back sharply on WPA and other government programs after the election. Federal contributions to the consumer purchasing power fell from $4.1 billion in 1936 to less than $1 billion in 1937. For several months, Roosevelt refused to heed calls from economists to renew heavy government spending. Finally, in April 1938, Roosevelt asked Congress for a $3.75 billion relief appropriation, and the economy began to revive. But FDR's premature attempt to balance the budget had meant two more years of hard times and had marred his reputation as the energetic foe of the Depression.

The political result of the attempted purge and the recession was a strong Republican upsurge in the elections of 1938. The GOP won an impressive 81 seats in the House and 8 more in the Senate, as well as 13 governorships. The party many thought dead suddenly had new life. The Democrats still held a sizable majority in Congress, but their margin in the House was particularly deceptive. There were 262 Democratic representatives to 169 Republicans, but 93 southern Democrats held the balance of power. More and more often after 1938, anti-New Deal Southerners voted with Republican conservatives to block social and economic reform measures. Thus not only was the New Deal over by the end of 1938, but a new bipartisan conservative coalition that would prevail for a quarter century had formed in Congress.

Evaluation of the New Deal

The New Deal lasted a brief five years, and most of its measures came in two legislative bursts in the spring of 1933 and the summer of 1935. Yet its impact on American life was enduring. Nearly every aspect of economic, social, and political development in the decades that followed bore the imprint of Roosevelt's leadership.

The least impressive achievement of the New Deal came in the economic realm. Whatever credit Roosevelt is given for relieving human suffering in the depths of the Depression must be balanced against his failure to achieve recovery in the 1930s. The moderate nature of his programs, especially the unwieldy NRA, led to slow and halting industrial recovery. Although much of the advances that were made came as a result of government spending, FDR never embraced the concept of planned deficits, striving instead for a balanced budget. As a result, the nation had barely reached the 1929 level of production a decade later, and there were still nearly ten million men and women unemployed.

Equally important, Roosevelt refused to make any sweeping changes in the American economic system. Aside from the TVA, there were no broad experiments in regional planning and no attempt to alter free enterprise beyond imposing some limited forms of governmental regulation. The New Deal did nothing to alter the basic distrubution of wealth and power in the nation. The outcome was the preservation of the traditional capitalist system with a thin overlay of federal control.

More significant change occurred in American society. With the adoption of Social Security, the government acknowledged for the first time its responsibility to provide for the welfare of those

Courtesy, D. R. Fitzpatrick. St. Louis Post-Dispatch, June 28, 1935

FDR's battle with the Supreme Court provoked both sympathy and contempt among political cartoonists of the day. In the cartoon on the right, the NRA blue eagle lies dead, nailed to the wall by the Supreme Court. The cartoon on the left, entitled "That's the kind of sailor he is," satirizes FDR's court-packing scheme.

unable to care for themselves in an industrial society. The Wagner Act helped stimulate the growth of labor unions to balance corporate power, and the minimum wage law provided a much needed floor for many workers.

Yet the New Deal tended to help only the more vocal and organized groups, such as union members and commercial farmers. Those without effective voices or political clout—African Americans, Mexican Americans, women, sharecroppers, restaurant and laundry workers—received little help from the New Deal. For all the appealing rhetoric about the "forgotten man," Roosevelt did little more than Hoover in responding to the long-term needs of the dispossessed.

The most lasting impact of the Roosevelt leadership came in politics. Taking advantage of the emerging power of ethnic voters and capitalizing on the frustration growing out of the Depression, FDR proved to be a genius at forging a new coalition. He overcame the friction between rural and urban Democrats that had prolonged Republican supremacy in the 1920s and attracted new groups to the Democratic party, principally African Americans and organized labor. His political success led to a major realignment that lasted long after he left the scene.

His political achievement also reveals the true nature of Roosevelt's success. He was a brilliant politician who recognized the essence of leadership in a democracy—appealing directly to the people and giving them a sense of purpose. He succeeded in infusing them with the same indomitable courage and jaunty optimism that had marked his own battle with polio. Thus despite his limitations as a reformer, Roosevelt proved to be the leader the American people needed in the 1930s—a president who provided the psychological lift that helped them endure and survive the Great Depression.

Recommended Reading

The best overall account of political developments in the 1930s is William Leuchtenburg, *Franklin D. Roosevelt and the New Deal* (1963). Leuchtenburg offers a balanced treatment but concludes by defending Roosevelt's record. For a more critical view, see James MacGregor Burns, *Roosevelt: The Lion and the Fox* (1956), which portrays FDR as an overly cautious political leader; and Robert A. McElvaine, *The Great Depression: America, 1929–1941* (1984), which laments the New Deal's failure to make more sweeping changes in American life. An exhaustive study of the New Deal through 1936 is Arthur M. Schlesinger, Jr., *The Age of Roosevelt*, 3 vols. (1957–1960), written from a sympathetic point of view. The best critique of Roosevelt's policies is the brief but perceptive book by Paul Conkin, *The New Deal* (1967).

Additional Bibliography

General accounts of the 1930s include Broadus Mitchell, *Depression Decade* (1947), on economic developments; Dixon Wecter, *The Age of the Great Depression* (1948), on social themes; John Braeman, Robert H. Bremner, and David Brody, eds., *The New Deal*, 2 vols. (1975), a collection of essays on both national and state trends; Joseph P. Lash, *Dealers and Dreamers* (1988), a sympathetic view of key New Deal figures; Jordan A. Schwarz, *The New Dealers* (1993), a more critical account; and Harvard Sitkoff, ed., *Fifty Years Later—The New Deal Evaluated* (1985), a scholarly reappraisal.

CHRONOLOGY

1932 Franklin D. Roosevelt elected president

1933 Emergency Banking Relief Act passed in one day (March) • Twenty-first Amendment repeals Prohibition (December)

1934 Securities and Exchange Commission authorized (June)

1935 Works Progress Administration (WPA) hires unemployed (April) • Wagner Act grants workers collective bargaining (July) • Congress passes Social Security Act (August)

1936 FDR wins second term as president

1937 Auto Workers' sit-down strike forces General Motors contract (February) • FDR loses court-packing battle (July) • Roosevelt recession begins (August)

1938 Congress sets minimum wage at forty cents an hour (June)

Books on the Great Depression include John Kenneth Galbraith, *The Great Crash* (1955); Robert Sobel, *The Great Bull Market* (1968); Michael A. Bernstein, *The Great Depression* (1987); and Studs Terkel, *Hard Times* (1970). Harris Warren, *Herbert Hoover and the Great Depression* (1959); Jordan Schwartz, *Interregnum of Despair* (1970); and Albert Romasco, *The Poverty of Abundance* (1965), all deal with Hoover's failure to stem the Depression.

Frank Freidel, *Franklin D. Roosevelt*, 4 vols. (1952–1976) is the most comprehensive biography of FDR, but the last volume only covers through mid-1933. Friedel covers FDR's entire life in broad outline in *Franklin D. Roosevelt: A Rendezvous with Destiny* (1990). Other biographical accounts of value are Rexford G. Tugwell, *The Democratic Roosevelt* (1957); Kenneth Davis, *FDR: The New Deal Years, 1933–1937* (1986); Sean J. Savage, *Roosevelt: The Party Leader, 1932–1945* (1991); and Alfred B. Rollins, *Roosevelt and Howe* (1962). The rich memoir literature for the New Deal includes Frances Perkins, *The Roosevelt I Knew* (1946); Raymond Moley, *The First New Deal* (1966); and Samuel I. Rosenman, *Working with Roosevelt* (1952). For biographies of Eleanor Roosevelt, see Joseph Lash, *Eleanor and Franklin* (1971); Lois Scharf, *Eleanor Roosevelt* (1987); Tamara K. Hareven, *Eleanor Roosevelt* (1968); Blanche Cook, *Eleanor Roosevelt, 1884–1933* (1992). Susan Ware traces the role of women in the New Deal in *Beyond Suffrage* (1981). J. Joseph Huthmacher has written a fine biography of a major New Deal figure, *Senator Robert Wagner and the Rise of Urban Liberalism* (1968).

Recent biographies of important New Deal leaders include John Kennedy Ohl, *Hugh S. Johnson and the New Deal* (1986); Roy Talbert, Jr., *FDR's Utopian: Arthur Morgan of the TVA* (1987); Graham White and John Maze, *Harold Ickes and the New Deal* (1985); and George McJimsky, *Harry Hopkins* (1987).

The transition from Hoover and the beginning of the New Deal is traced in Elliot Rosen, *Hoover, Roosevelt, and the Brain Trust* (1977). Gary Dean Best is very critical of FDR's efforts to overcome the Depression in *Pride, Prejudice and Politics: Roosevelt Versus Recovery, 1933–1938* (1990). The best of many books dealing with farm problems in the 1930s are Richard Kirkendall, *Social Scientists and Farm Politics in the Age of Roosevelt* (1966); Paul Conkin, *Tomorrow a New World* (1959); Van Perkins, *Crisis in Agriculture* (1969); Sidney Baldwin, *Poverty and Politics* (1968); Theodore Saloutos, *The American Farmer and the New Deal* (1982); Janet Poppendieck, *Breadlines Knee-Deep in Wheat* (1986); and two books on the impact of drought on Great Plains farmers, Donald Worster, *Dust Bowl* (1979), and James N.

Gregory, *American Exodus* (1989), on the Okie migration to California. Searle F. Charles traces Harry Hopkins's role in the New Deal in *Minister of Relief* (1963); William McDonald describes the WPA's cultural activities in detail in *Federal Relief Administration and the Arts* (1969). For labor developments, see Sidney Fine, *Sit Down: The General Motors Strike of 1936–37* (1969); John Barnard, *Walter Reuther and the Rise of the Auto Workers* (1983); Robert H. Zieger, *John L. Lewis* (1988); and Steven Fraser, *Labor Will Rule: Sidney Hillman and the Rise of American Labor* (1991). Irving Bernstein surveys the impact of the Depression on workers in two books, *The Turbulent Years* (1970) and *A Caring Society* (1985).

Among the many books surveying the various New Deal programs, the most useful are John Salmond, *The Civilian Conservation Corps, 1933–1942* (1967); William R. Brock, *Welfare, Democracy, and the New Deal* (1988); William R. Childs, *Trucking and the Public Interest* (1985); Albert Romasco, *The Politics of Recovery* (1983); Thomas K. McCraw, *TVA and the Power Fight, 1933–1939* (1971); Jane D. Mathews, *The Federal Theatre, 1935–1939* (1967); and Richard A. Reiman, *The New Deal and American Youth* (1992). Two other important books on the New Deal are Otis L. Graham, Jr., *An Encore for Reform* (1967), and Ellis Hawley, *The New Deal and the Problem of Monopoly, 1933–1939* (1965).

Studies by critics of the New Deal include George Wolfskill, *Revolt of the Conservatives* (1962); T. Harry Williams, *Huey Long* (1969); William Ivy Hair, *The Kingfish and His Realm* (1991); Abraham Holtzman, *The Townsend Movement* (1963); Charles Tull, *Father Coughlin and the New Deal* (1965); Sheldon Marcus, *Father Coughlin* (1973); Glen Jeansonne, *Gerald L. K. Smith: Minister of Hate* (1988); and Alan Brinkley, *Voice of Protest: Huey Long, Father Coughlin, and the Great Depression* (1982). For intellectual radicalism in the 1930s, see Daniel Aaron, *Writers on the Left* (1960); Terry A. Cooney, *The Rise of the New York Intellectuals* (1986); and Richard Pells, *Radical Visions and American Dreams* (1973).

Raymond Wolters offers a critical view of Roosevelt's policies toward blacks in *Negroes and the Great Depression* (1970); Harvard Sitkoff is more positive in *A New Deal for Blacks* (1978). For the plight of African Americans in New York, see Cheryl Lynn Greenberg, *"Or Does It Explode": Black Harlem in the Great Depression* (1991). Nancy Weiss traces the shift of blacks to the Democratic party in *Farewell to the Party of Lincoln* (1984). Abraham Hoffman deals with the repatriation issue in *Unwanted Mexican-Americans in the Great Depression* (1974). For the impact of the Depression on women, see William H.

Chafe, *The American Woman* (1972); Susan Ware, *Holding Their Own* (1982); and Lois Sharf, *To Work and to Wed* (1980).

Leonard Baker describes Roosevelt's attempt to pack the Supreme Court in *Back to Back* (1967). The best account of the waning of the reform impulse in Congress is James T. Patterson, *Congressional Conservatism and the New Deal* (1967).

America and the World, 1921–1945

On August 27, 1928, U.S. Secretary of State Frank B. Kellogg, French Foreign Minister Aristide Briand, and representatives of twelve other nations met in Paris to sign a treaty outlawing war. Several hundred spectators crowded into the ornate clock room of the Quai d'Orsay to watch the historic ceremony. Six huge kleig lights illuminated the scene so photographers could record the moment for a world eager for peace. Briand opened the ceremony with a speech in which he declared, "Peace is proclaimed," and then Kellogg signed the document with a foot-long gold pen given to him by the citizens of Le Havre as a token of Franco-American friendship. In the United States, a senator called the Kellogg-Briand Treaty "the most telling action ever taken in human history to abolish war."

In reality, the Pact of Paris was the result of a determined American effort to avoid involvement in the European alliance system. In June 1927, Briand had sent a message to the American people inviting the United States to join with France in signing a treaty to outlaw war between the two nations. The invitation struck a sympathetic response, especially among pacifists who had advocated the outlawing of war throughout the 1920s, but the State Department feared correctly that Briand's true intention was to establish a close tie between France and the United States. The French had already created a network of alliances with the smaller countries of eastern Europe; an antiwar treaty with the United States would at least ensure American sympathy, if not involvement, in case of another European war. Kellogg delayed several months and then outmaneuvered Briand by proposing the pledge against war not be confined just to France and the United States, but instead be extended to all nations. An unhappy Briand, who had wanted a bilateral treaty with the United States, had no choice but to agree, and so the diplomatic charade finally culminated in the elaborate signing ceremony in Paris.

Eventually the signers of the Kellogg-Briand Treaty included nearly every nation in the world, but the effect was negligible. All promised to renounce war as an instrument of national policy, except of course, as the British made clear in a reservation, in matters of self-defense. Enforce-

ment of the treaty relied solely on the moral force of world opinion. The Pact of Paris was, as one senator shrewdly commented, only "an international kiss."

Unfortunately, the Kellogg-Briand Pact was symbolic of American foreign policy in the years after World War I. Instead of asserting the role of leadership its resources and power commanded, the United States kept aloof from other nations. America went its own way, extending trade and economic dominance but refusing to take the lead in maintaining world order. This retreat from responsibility seemed unimportant in the 1920s when exhaustion from World War I ensured relative peace and tranquillity. But in the 1930s, when threats to world order arose in Europe and Asia, the American people retreated even deeper, searching for an isolationist policy that would spare them the agony of another great war.

There was no place to hide in the modern world. The Nazi onslaught in Europe and the Japanese expansion in Asia finally led to American entry into World War II in late 1941, at a time when the chances for an Allied victory seemed most remote. With incredible swiftness, the nation mobilized its military and industrial strength. American armies were soon fighting on three continents, the U.S. Navy controlled the world's oceans, and the nation's factories were sending a vast stream of war supplies to more than twenty Allied countries.

When victory came in 1945, the United States was by far the most powerful nation in the world. But instead of the enduring peace that might have permitted a return to a less active foreign policy, the onset of the Cold War with the Soviet Union brought on a new era of tension and conflict. This time the United States could not retreat from responsibility. World War II was a coming of age for American foreign policy.

RETREAT, REVERSAL, AND RIVALRY

"The day of the armistice America stood on the hilltops of glory, proud in her strength, invincible in her ideals, acclaimed and loved by a world free of an ancient fear at last," wrote journalist George Creel in 1920. "Today we writhe in a pit of our own digging; despising ourselves and despised by the betrayed peoples of earth." The

"Married Again" is the caption of this 1928 cartoon depicting the hopeful promise of the Kellogg-Briand Treaty. The wicked world is once again pledging fidelity to peace "forever and ever."

bitter disillusionment Creel described ran through every aspect of American foreign policy in the 1920s. In contrast to diplomatic actions under Wilsonian idealism, American diplomats in the 1920s made loans, negotiated treaties and agreements, and pledged the nation's good faith, but were careful not to make any binding commitments on behalf of world order. The result was neither isolation nor involvement but rather a cautious middle course that managed to alienate friends and encourage foes.

Retreat in Europe

The United States emerged from World War I as the richest nation on earth, displacing England from its prewar position of economic primacy. The Allied governments owed the United States a staggering $10 billion in war debts, money they had borrowed during and right after the conflict. Each year of the 1920s saw the nation increase its economic lead as the balance of trade tipped heavily in America's favor. The war-ravaged countries of Europe borrowed enormous amounts from American bankers to rebuild their economies; Germany alone absorbed over $3 billion in American investments during the decade.

By 1929, American exports totaled more than $7 billion a year, three times the prewar level, and American overseas investment had risen to $17.2 billion.

The European nations could no longer compete on equal terms. The high American tariff, first imposed in 1922 and then raised again in 1930, frustrated attempts by England, France, and a defeated Germany to earn the dollars necessary to meet their American financial obligations. The Allied partners in World War I asked Washington to cancel the $10 billion in war debts, particularly after they were forced to scale down their demands for German reparations payments. American leaders from Wilson to Hoover indignantly refused this request, claiming the ungrateful Allies were trying to repudiate their sacred obligations.

Only a continuing flow of private American capital to Germany allowed the payment of reparations to the Allies and the partial repayment of the Allies war debts in the 1920s. The financial crash of 1929 halted the flow of American dollars across the Atlantic and led to subsequent default on the debt payments, with accompanying bitterness on both sides of the ocean.

Political relations fared little better. The United States never joined the League of Nations, nor did it take part in the attempts by England and France to negotiate European security treaties. American observers attended League sessions and occasionally took part in economic and cultural missions in Geneva. But the Republican administrations of the 1920s refused to compromise American freedom of action by embracing collective security, the principle on which the League was founded. And FDR, always realistic, made no effort to renew Wilson's futile quest. Thus the United States remained aloof from the European balance of power and refused to stand behind the increasingly shaky Versailles settlement.

The U.S. government ignored the Soviet Union throughout the 1920s. American businesses, however, exported large quantities of heavy machinery to Russia as part of her rapid industrialization. When that trade began to slump after 1930, business leaders hoped to revive it by calling on Washington to extend diplomatic recognition to the Bolshevik regime which had come to power in the Russian Revolution of 1917. In 1933, Franklin Roosevelt finally ended the long estrangement by signing an agreement opening up diplomatic relations between the two countries. The Soviets soon went back on promises to stop all subversive activity in the United States and to settle prerevolutionary debts, but even if they rarely understood one another, at least the two nations had opened a channel of communication.

Cooperation in Latin America

U.S. policy in the Western Hemisphere was both more active and more enlightened than in Europe. The State Department sought new ways in the 1920s to pursue traditional goals of political dominance and economic advantage in Latin America. The outcome of World War I lessened any fears of European threats to the area and thus enabled the United States to dismantle the interventions in the Caribbean carried out by Roosevelt, Taft, and Wilson (see Chapter 24). At the same time, both Republican and Democratic administrations worked hard to extend American trade and investment in the nations to the south.

Under Harding, Coolidge, and Hoover, American marines were withdrawn from Haiti and the Dominican Republic, and in 1924 the last detachment left Nicaragua, ending a twelve-year occupation. Renewed unrest there the next year, however, led to a second intervention in Nicaragua, which did not end until the early 1930s.

Showing a new sensitivity, the State Department released the Clark Memorandum in 1930, a policy statement repudiating the controversial Roosevelt Corollary to the Monroe Doctrine. Under the Monroe Doctrine, the United States had no right to intervene in neighboring states, declared Under Secretary of State J. Reuben Clark, although he asserted a traditional claim to protect American lives and property under international law.

When FDR took office in 1933, relations with Latin America were far better than they had been under Wilson, but American trade in the hemisphere had fallen drastically as the Depression worsened. Roosevelt moved quickly to solidify the improved relations and gain economic benefits. With his usual flair for the dramatic, he proclaimed a policy of the "good neighbor" and then proceeded to win goodwill by renouncing the imperialism of the past.

In 1933, Secretary of State Cordell Hull signed a conditional pledge of nonintervention at a Pan-American conference in Montevideo, Uruguay. A year later, the United States renounced its right to intervene in Cuban affairs under the Platt Amendment and loosened its grip on Panama. By 1936, American troops were no longer occupying any Latin American nation. FDR personally cemented the new policy by traveling to Buenos Aires to sign an agreement that forbade intervention "directly or indirectly, and for whatever reason" in the internal affairs of a Central or South American state.

The United States had not changed its basic goal of political and economic dominance in the hemisphere; rather, the new policy of benevolence reflected Roosevelt's belief that cooperation and friendship were more effective tactics than threats and armed intervention. Mexico tried his patience in 1938 by nationalizing its oil resources; with admirable restraint, the president finally negotiated a settlement in 1941 on terms favorable to Mexico. Yet this economic loss was more than offset by the new trade opportunities opened up by the Good Neighbor policy. American commerce with Latin America increased fourfold in the 1930s, and investment rose substantially from its Depression low. Most important, FDR succeeded in forging a new policy of regional collective security. As the ominous events leading to World War II unfolded in Europe and Asia, the nations of the Western Hemisphere looked to the United States for protection against external danger.

Rivalry in Asia

In the years following World War I, the United States and Japan were on a collision course in the Pacific. The Japanese, lacking the raw materials to sustain their developing industrial economy, were determined to expand onto the Asian mainland. They had taken Korea by 1905, and during World War I had extended their control over the mines, harbors, and railroads of Manchuria, the industrial region of northeast China. The American Open Door policy remained the primary obstacle to complete Japanese dominion over China. The United States thus faced the clear-cut choice of either abandoning China or forcefully opposing Japan's expansion. American efforts to avoid making this painful decision postponed the eventual showdown but not the growing rivalry.

The first attempt at a solution came in 1921 when the United States convened the Washington Conference, which included delegates from the United States, Japan, Great Britain, and six other nations. The major objective was a political settlement of the tense Asian situation, but the most pressing issue was a dangerous naval race between Japan and the United States. Both nations were engaged in extensive shipbuilding programs begun during the war. Great Britain was forced to compete in order to preserve its traditional control of the sea; even so, projected construction indicated that both the United States and Japan would overtake the British navy by the end of the decade. Japan, spending nearly one-third of its total budget on naval construction, was eager for an agreement; in the United States, growing congressional concern over appropriations suggested the need for slowing the naval buildup.

In his welcoming address at the Washington Conference, Secretary of State Charles Evans Hughes outlined a specific plan for naval disarmament, calling for the scrapping of sixty-six battleships—thirty American, nineteen British, and seventeen Japanese. Three months later, delegates signed a Five Power Treaty embodying the main elements of Hughes's proposal: limitation of capital ships (battleships and aircraft carriers) in a ratio of 5–5–3 for the United States, Britain, and Japan, respectively, and 1.67–1.67 for France and Italy. England reluctantly accepted equality with the United States, while Japan agreed to the lower ratio only in return for an American pledge not to fortify Pacific bases such as the Philippines and Guam. The treaty cooled off the naval race even though it did not include cruisers, destroyers, or submarines.

The Washington Conference produced two other major agreements: the Nine Power Treaty and the Four Power Treaty. The first simply pledged all of the countries involved to uphold the Open Door policy, while the other compact replaced the old Anglo-Japanese alliance with a new Pacific security pact signed by the United States, Great Britain, Japan, and France. Neither document contained any enforcement provision beyond a promise to consult in case of a violation. In essence, the Washington treaties formed a parchment peace, a pious set of pledges that attempted to freeze the status quo in the Pacific.

This compromise lasted less than a decade. In September 1931, Japanese forces overran Manchuria, violating the Nine Power Treaty and the Kellogg-Briand Pact in a brutal act of aggression. The United States, paralyzed by the Depression, responded feebly. Secretary of State Henry L. Stimson sent an observer to Geneva to assure cooperation with the League of Nations, which was content to investigate the "incident." In January 1932, Stimson fell back on moral force, issuing notes vowing the United States would not recognize the legality of the Japanese seizure of Manchuria. Despite ultimate concurrence by the League on nonrecognition, the Japanese ignored the American moral sanction and incorporated the former Chinese province, now renamed Manchukuo, into their rapidly expanding empire.

Aside from the good neighbor approach in the Western Hemisphere, American foreign policy faithfully reflected the prevailing disillusionment with world power that gripped the country after World War I. The United States avoided taking any constructive steps toward preserving world order, preferring instead the empty symbolism of the Washington treaties and the Kellogg-Briand Pact.

ISOLATIONISM

The retreat from an active world policy in the 1920s turned into a headlong flight back to isolationism in the 1930s. Two factors were responsible. First, the Depression made foreign policy seem remote and unimportant to most Americans. As unemployment increased and the economic crisis intensified after 1929, many people grew apathetic about events abroad. Second, the danger of war abroad, when it did finally penetrate the American consciousness, served only to strengthen the desire to escape involvement.

Three powerful and discontented nations were on the march in the 1930s—Germany, Italy, and Japan. In Germany, Adolf Hitler came to power in 1933 as the head of a National Socialist, or Nazi, movement. A shrewd and charismatic leader, Hitler capitalized on both domestic discontent and bitterness over World War I. Blaming the Jews for all of Germany's ills and asserting the supremacy of the "Aryan" race of blond, blue-eyed Germans, he quickly imposed a totalitarian dictatorship in which the Nazi party ruled and the führer was supreme. At first, his foreign policy seemed harmless, but as he consolidated his power, the ultimate threat to world peace became clearer. Hitler took Germany out of the League of Nations, reoccupied the Rhineland, and formally denounced the Treaty of Versailles. His boasts of uniting all Germans into a Greater Third Reich that would last a thousand years filled his European opponents with terror, blocking any effective challenge to his regime.

In Italy, another dictator, Benito Mussolini, had come to power in 1922. Emboldened by Hitler's success, he embarked on an aggressive foreign policy in 1935. His invasion of the independent African nation of Ethiopia led its emperor, Haile Selassie, to call on the League of Nations for support. With England and France far more concerned about Hitler, the League's

Millions of Germans idolized Adolf Hitler, portrayed in this captured German painting as a white knight. After the painting came into American hands, a GI slashed Hitler's face to indicate his displeasure with the mystique of the Führer.

halfhearted measures utterly failed to halt Mussolini's conquest. "Fifty-two nations had combined to resist aggression," commented historian A. J. P. Taylor; "all they accomplished was that Haile Selassie lost all his country instead of only half." Collective security had failed its most important test.

Japan formed the third element in the threat to world peace. Militarists began to dominate the government in Tokyo by the mid-1930s, using tactics of fear and even assassination against their liberal opponents. By 1936, Japan had left the League of Nations and had repudiated the Washington treaties. A year later, its armies began an invasion of China that marked the beginning of the Pacific phase of World War II.

The resurgence of militarism in Germany, Italy, and Japan undermined the Versailles settlement and threatened to destroy the existing balance of power. England and France in Europe proved as powerless as China in Asia to stop the tide of aggression. In 1937, the three totalitarian nations signed an anti-Comintern pact completing a Berlin-Rome-Tokyo axis. Their alliance ostensibly was aimed at the Soviet Union, but in fact it threatened the entire world. Only a determined American response could unite the other nations against this Axis threat. Unfortunately, the United States deliberately abstained from assuming this role of leadership until it was nearly too late.

The Lure of Pacifism and Neutrality

The growing danger of war abroad led to a rising American desire for peace and noninvolvement. Memories of World War I contributed heavily. The novel *All Quiet on the Western Front,* as well as the movie based on it, reminded people of the brutality of war. Historians began to treat the Great War as a mistake, criticizing Wilson for failing to preserve American neutrality and claiming the clever British had duped the United States into entering the war. Walter Millis advanced this thesis in a popular book, *America's Road to War, 1914–1917,* published in 1935. It was hailed as a vivid description of the process by which "a peace-loving democracy, muddled but excited, misinformed and whipped to a frenzy, embarked upon its greatest foreign war."

American youth made clear their determina-

The pacifism that swept college campuses in the 1930s touched students at the University of Chicago. The university undergraduates shown here hold placards bearing antiwar slogans as they wait to join a parade as part of a nationwide demonstration against war.

tion not to repeat the mistakes of their elders. Pacifism swept across college campuses. A Brown University poll indicated 72 percent of the students opposed military service in wartime. At Princeton, undergraduates formed the Veterans of Future Wars, a parody on veterans' groups, to demand a bonus of $1,000 apiece before they marched off to a foreign war! In April 1934, students and professors alike walked out of class to attend massive antiwar rallies, which became an annual rite of spring in the 1930s. Amid demonstrators carrying signs reading "Abolish the R.O.T.C." and "Build Schools—Not Battleships," pacifist orators urged students to sign a pledge not to support their country "in any war it might conduct."

The pacifist movement found a scapegoat in the munitions industry. The publication of several books exposing the unsavory business tactics of large arms dealers such as Krupp in Germany and Vickers in Britain led to a demand to curb these "merchants of death." Senator Gerald Nye of North Dakota headed a special Senate committee that spent two years investigating American munitions dealers. The committee revealed the

enormous profits such firms as Du Pont reaped from World War I, but Nye went further, charging that bankers and munitions makers were responsible for American intervention in 1917. No proof was forthcoming, but the public—prepared to believe the worst of businessmen during the Depression—accepted the "merchants-of-death" thesis.

The Nye Committee's revelations culminated in neutrality legislation. In 1935, Senator Nye and another Senate colleague introduced measures to ban arms sales and loans to belligerents and to prevent Americans from traveling on belligerent ships. By outlawing the activities that led to World War I, they hoped the United States could avoid involvement in the new conflict. This "never-again" philosophy proved irresistible. In August 1935, Congress passed the first of three neutrality acts. The 1935 law banned the sale of arms to nations at war and warned American citizens not to sail on belligerent ships. In 1936, a second act added a ban on loans, and in 1937, a third neutrality act made these prohibitions permanent and required, on a two-year trial basis, that all trade other than munitions be conducted on a cash-and-carry basis.

President Roosevelt played a passive role in the adoption of the neutrality legislation. At first opposed to the arms embargo, he finally approved it for six months in 1935 in a compromise designed to save important New Deal legislation in Congress. Yet he also appeared to share the isolationist assumption that a European war would have no impact on vital national interests. He termed the first neutrality act "entirely satisfactory" when he signed it. Others in the administration criticized the mandatory nature of the new law, pointing out that it prevented the United States from distinguishing between aggressors and their victims. Privately, Roosevelt expressed some of the same reservations, but publicly he bowed to the prevailing isolationism. He signed the subsequent neutrality acts without protest, and during the 1936 election, he delivered an impassioned denunciation of war. "I hate war," he told an audience in Chautauqua, New York. "I have passed unnumbered hours, I shall pass unnumbered hours, thinking and planning how war may be kept from this nation."

Yet FDR did take a few steps to try to limit the nation's retreat into isolationism. His failure to invoke the neutrality act after the Japanese invasion of China in 1937 enabled the hard-pressed Chinese to continue buying arms from the United States. In January 1938, he used his influence to block a proposal by Indiana Congressman Louis Ludlow to require a nationwide referendum before Congress could declare war. FDR's strongest public statement came earlier, in Chicago in October 1937, when he denounced "the epidemic of world lawlessness" and called for an international effort to "quarantine" this disease. When reporters asked him if his call for "positive efforts to preserve peace" signaled a repeal of the neutrality acts, however, Roosevelt quickly reaffirmed this isolationist legislation. Whatever his private yearning for cooperation against aggressors, the president had no intention of challenging the prevailing public mood of the 1930s.

War in Europe

The neutrality legislation played directly into the hands of Adolf Hitler. Bent on the conquest of Europe, he could now proceed without worrying about American interference. In March 1938, he seized Austria in a bloodless coup. Six months later, he was demanding the Sudetenland, a province of Czechoslovakia with a large German population. When the British and French leaders agreed to meet with Hitler at Munich, FDR voiced his approval. Roosevelt carefully kept the United States aloof from the subsequent surrender of the Sudetenland. At the same time, he gave his tacit approval of the Munich agreement by telling the British prime minister that he shared his "hope and belief that there exists today the greatest opportunity in years for the establishment of a new order based on justice and on law."

Six months after the meeting at Munich, Hitler violated his promises by seizing nearly all of Czechoslovakia. In the United States, Roosevelt permitted the State Department to press for neutrality revision. The administration proposal to repeal the arms embargo and place *all* trade with belligerents, including munitions, on a cash-and-carry basis soon met stubborn resistance from isolationists. They argued that cash-and-carry would favor England and France, who controlled the sea. The House rejected the measure by a narrow margin, and the Senate's Foreign Relations Committee voted 12 to 11 to postpone any action on neutrality revision.

In July 1939, Roosevelt finally abandoned his aloof position and held a meeting with Senate leaders to plead for reconsideration. Warnings of the imminence of war in Europe by both the president and the secretary of state failed to impress the isolationists. Senator William Borah, who had led the fight against the League of Nations in 1919, responded that he felt the chances for war in Europe were remote. After canvassing the senators present, Vice President John Nance Garner bluntly told FDR that the neutrality revision was dead. "You haven't got the votes," Garner commented, "and that's all there is to it."

On September 1, 1939, Hitler began World War II by invading Poland. England and France responded two days later by declaring war, although there was no way they could prevent the German conquest of Poland. Russia had played a key role, refusing Western overtures for a common front against Germany and finally signing a nonaggression treaty with Hitler in late August. The Nazi-Soviet Pact enabled Germany to avoid a two-front war; the Russians were rewarded with a generous slice of eastern Poland.

President Roosevelt reacted to the outbreak of war by proclaiming American neutrality, but the successful aggression by Nazi Germany brought into question the isolationist assumption that American well-being did not depend on the European balance of power. Strategic as well as ideological considerations began to undermine the earlier belief that the United States could safely pursue a policy of neutrality and noninvolvement. The long retreat from responsibility was about to end as Americans came to realize their own democracy and security were at stake in the European war.

THE ROAD TO WAR

For two years, the United States tried to remain at peace while war raged in Europe and Asia. In contrast to Wilson's attempt to be impartial during most of World War I, however, the American people displayed an overwhelming sympathy for the Allies and total distaste for Germany and Japan. Roosevelt made no secret of his preference for an Allied victory, but a fear of isolationist

Hitler sent his armies into Poland with tremendous force and firepower, devastating the country. When Jews, such as these residents of the Warsaw Ghetto, fell into the hands of the Nazi occupiers, they were deported to slave labor camps that soon became the sites of mass extermination.

criticism compelled him to move slowly, and often deviously, in adopting a policy of aid for England and France.

From Neutrality to Undeclared War

Two weeks after the outbreak of war in Europe, Roosevelt called Congress into special session to revise the neutrality legislation. He wanted to repeal the arms embargo in order to supply weapons to England and France, but he refused to state this aim openly. Instead he asked Congress to replace the arms embargo with cash-and-carry regulations. Belligerents would be able to purchase war supplies in the United States, but they would have to pay cash and transport the goods in their own ships. Public opinion strongly supported the president, and Congress passed the revised neutrality policy by heavy margins in early November 1939.

A series of dramatic German victories had a profound impact on American opinion. Quiet during the winter of 1939–1940, the Germans struck with lightning speed and devastating effect in the spring. In April, they seized Denmark and Norway, and on May 10, 1940, they unleashed the *blitzkrieg* (lightning war) on the western front. Using tanks, armored columns, and dive bombers in close coordination, the German army

cut deep into the Allied lines, dividing the British and French forces. Within three weeks, the British were driven off the continent. In another three weeks, France fell to Hitler's victorious armies.

Americans were stunned. Hitler had taken only six weeks to achieve what Germany had failed to do in four years of fighting in World War I. Suddenly they realized they did have a stake in the outcome; if England fell, Hitler might well gain control of the British navy. The Atlantic would no longer be a barrier; instead, it would be a highway for German penetration of the New World.

Roosevelt responded by invoking a policy of all-out aid to the Allies, short of war. In a speech at Charlottesville, Virginia, in June (just after Italy entered the war by invading France), he denounced Germany and Italy as representing "the gods of force and hate" and vowed "the whole of our sympathies lies with those nations that are giving their life blood in combat against these forces." It was too late to help France, but in early September, FDR announced the transfer of fifty old destroyers to England in exchange for rights to build air and naval bases on eight British possessions in the Western Hemisphere. Giving warships to a belligerent nation was clearly a breach of neutrality, but Roosevelt stressed the importance of guarding the Atlantic approaches, calling the destroyers-for-bases deal "the most important action in the reinforcement of our national defense that has been taken since the Louisiana Purchase."

Isolationists cried out against this departure from neutrality. A bold headline in the St. Louis *Post-Dispatch* read, "Dictator Roosevelt Commits Act of War." A group of Roosevelt's opponents in the Midwest formed the America First Committee to protest the drift toward war. Such diverse individuals as aviator-hero Charles Lindbergh, conservative Senator Robert A. Taft of Ohio, socialist leader Norman Thomas, and liberal educator Robert M. Hutchins condemned FDR for involving the United States in a foreign conflict. Voicing belief in a "Fortress America," they denied that Hitler threatened American security and claimed the nation had the strength to defend itself regardless of what happened in Europe.

To support the administration's policies, opponents of the isolationists organized the Committee to Defend America by Aiding the Allies. Eastern Anglophiles, moderate New Dealers, and liberal Republicans made up the bulk of the membership, with Kansas newspaper editor William Allen White serving as chairman. The White Committee, as it became known, advocated unlimited assistance to England short of war, although some of its members privately favored entry into the conflict. Above all, the interventionists challenged the isolationist premise that events in Europe did not affect American security. "The future of western civilization is being decided upon the battlefield of Europe," White declared.

In the ensuing debate, the American people gradually came to agree with the interventionists. The battle of Britain helped. "Every time Hitler bombed London, we got a couple of votes," noted one interventionist. Frightened by the events in Europe, Congress approved large sums for preparedness, increasing the defense budget from $2 billion to $10 billion during 1940. Roosevelt courageously asked for a peacetime draft, the first in American history, to build up the army; in September, Congress agreed.

The sense of crisis affected domestic politics. Roosevelt ran for an unprecedented third term in 1940 because of the European war; the Republicans nominated Wendell Willkie, a former Democratic businessman who shared FDR's

The Election of 1940			
Candidate	Party	*Popular Vote*	*Electoral Vote*
Roosevelt	Democrat	27,263,448	449
Willkie	Republican	22,336,260	82

commitment to aid for England. Both candidates made appeals to peace sentiment during the campaign, but Roosevelt's decisive victory made it clear that the nation supported his increasing departure from neutrality.

After the election, FDR took his boldest step. Responding to British Prime Minister Winston Churchill's warning that England was running out of money, the president asked Congress to approve a new program to lend and lease goods and weapons to countries fighting against aggressors. Roosevelt's call for America to become "the great arsenal of democracy" seemed straightforward enough, but he acted somewhat deviously by naming the program lend-lease and by comparing it to loaning a neighbor a garden hose to put out a fire.

Isolationists angrily denounced lend-lease as both unnecessary and untruthful. "Lending war equipment is a good deal like lending chewing gum," commented Senator Taft. "You don't want it back." In March 1941, however, Congress voted by substantial margins to authorize the president to "sell, transfer title to, exchange, lease, lend, or otherwise dispose of" war supplies to "any country the President deems vital to the defense of the United States." The accompanying $7 billion appropriation ended the "cash" part of cash-and-carry and ensured Britain full access to American war supplies.

The "carry" problem still remained. German submarines were sinking over 500,000 tons of shipping a month. England desperately needed the help of the American navy in escorting convoys across the U-boat-infested waters of the North Atlantic. Roosevelt, fearful of isolationist reaction, responded with naval patrols in the western half of the ocean. Hitler placed his submarine commanders under strict restraints to avoid drawing America into the European war.

Nevertheless, incidents were bound to occur. In September 1941, after a U-boat narrowly missed torpedoing an American destroyer tracking it, Roosevelt denounced the German submarines as the "rattlesnakes of the Atlantic" and issued orders for the navy to convey British ships halfway across the ocean.

Undeclared naval war quickly followed. On October 17, 1941, a German submarine damaged the U.S. destroyer *Kearney;* ten days later, another U-boat sank the *Reuben James,* killing more than one hundred American sailors. FDR issued orders for the destroyers to shoot U-boats on sight. He also asked Congress to repeal the "carry" section of the neutrality laws and permit American ships to deliver supplies to England. In mid-November, Congress approved these moves by slim margins. Now American merchant ships as well as destroyers would become targets for German attacks. By December, it seemed only a matter of weeks—or months at most—until repeated sinkings would lead to a formal declaration of war against Germany.

In leading the nation to the brink of war in Europe, Roosevelt opened himself to criticism from both sides in the domestic debate. Interventionists felt he had been too cautious in dealing with the danger to the nation from Nazi Germany. Isolationists were equally critical of the president, claiming he had misled the American people by professing peace while plotting for war. Roosevelt was certainly less than candid, relying on executive discretion to engage in highly provocative acts in the North Atlantic. He agreed with the interventionists that in the long run American security would be threatened by a German victory in Europe. But he also was aware that a poll taken in September 1941 showed nearly 80 percent of the American people wanted to stay out of World War II. Realizing that leading a divided nation into war would be disastrous, FDR played for time, inching the country toward war while waiting for the Axis nations to make the ultimate move. Japan finally obliged at Pearl Harbor.

Showdown in the Pacific

Japan had taken advantage of the war in Europe to expand further in Asia. Although successful after 1937 in conquering the populous coastal areas of China, the Japanese had been unable to defeat Chiang Kai-shek, whose forces retreated into the vast interior of the country. The German defeat of France and the Netherlands in 1940, however, left their colonial possessions in the East Indies and Indochina vulnerable and defenseless. Japan now set out to incorporate these territories—rich in oil, tin, and rubber—into a Greater East Asia Co-Prosperity Sphere.

The Roosevelt administration countered with economic pressure. Japan was heavily dependent on the United States for shipments of petroleum and scrap metal. In July 1940, President

Roosevelt signed an order setting up a licensing and quota system for the export of these crucial materials to Japan and banned the sale of aviation gasoline altogether. With Britain fighting for survival and France and the Netherlands occupied by Germany, the United States was now employing economic sanctions to defend Southeast Asia against Japanese expansion.

Tokyo appeared to be unimpressed. In early September, Japanese troops occupied strategic bases in the northern part of French Indochina. Later in the month, Japan signed the Tripartite Pact with Germany and Italy, a defensive treaty that confronted the United States with a possible two-ocean war. The new Axis alignment confirmed American suspicions that Japan was part of a worldwide totalitarian threat. Roosevelt and his advisers, however, saw Germany as the primary danger; thus they pursued a policy of all-out aid to England while hoping that economic measures alone would deter Japan.

The embargo on aviation gasoline, extended to include scrap iron and steel in late September 1940, was a burden Japan could bear, but a possible ban on all oil shipments was a different matter. Japan lacked petroleum reserves of its own and was entirely dependent on imports from the United States and the Dutch East Indies. In an attempt to ease the economic pressure through negotiation, Japan sent a new envoy to Washington in the spring of 1941. But these talks quickly broke down. Tokyo wanted nothing less than a free hand in China and an end to American sanctions, while the United States insisted on an eventual Japanese evacuation of all China.

In July 1941, Japan invaded southern Indochina, beginning the chain of events that led to war. Washington knew of this aggression before it occurred. Naval intelligence experts had broken the Japanese diplomatic code and were intercepting and reading all messages between Tokyo and the Japanese embassy in Washington. President Roosevelt responded on July 25, 1941, with an order freezing all Japanese assets in the United States. This step, initially intended only as a temporary warning to Japan, soon became a permanent embargo due to positive public reaction and State Department zeal. Trade with Japan, including the vital oil shipments, came to a complete halt. When the Dutch government-in-exile took similar action, Japan faced a dilemma: in order to have oil shipments resumed, Tokyo would have to end its aggression; the alternative would be to seize the needed petroleum supplies in the Dutch East Indies, an action that would mean war.

After one final diplomatic effort failed, General Hideki Tojo, an army militant, became the new premier of Japan. To mask its war preparations, Tokyo sent yet another envoy to Washington with new peace proposals. Code breaking enabled American diplomats to learn that the Japanese terms were unacceptable even before they were formally presented. Army and navy leaders urged President Roosevelt to seek at least a temporary settlement with Japan to give them time to prepare American defenses in the Pacific. Secretary of State Cordell Hull, however, refused to allow any concession; on November 26, he sent a stiff ten-point reply to Tokyo that included a demand for Japanese withdrawal from China.

The Japanese response came two weeks later. On the evening of December 6, 1941, the first thirteen parts of the reply to Hull's note arrived in Washington, with the fourteenth part to follow the next morning. Naval intelligence actually decoded the message faster than the Japanese embassy clerks. A messenger delivered the text to President Roosevelt late that night; after glancing at it, he commented, "This means war." The next day, December 7, the fourteenth part arrived, revealing that Japan totally rejected the American position.

Officials in Washington immediately sent warning messages to American bases in the Pacific, but they failed to arrive in time. At 7:55 in the morning, just before 1 P.M. in Washington, squadrons of Japanese carrier-based planes caught the American fleet at Pearl Harbor totally by surprise. In little more than an hour, they crippled the American Pacific fleet and its major base, sinking eight battleships and killing more than 2,400 American sailors.

In Washington, the Japanese envoys had requested a meeting with Secretary Hull at 1 P.M. Just before the meeting, news arrived of the attack on Pearl Harbor. An irate Cordell Hull read the note the Japanese handed him and then, unable to restrain himself any longer, burst out, "In all my fifty years of public service, I have

American ships were destroyed in the surprise attack on Pearl Harbor, December 7, 1941. Caught completely off guard, U.S. forces still managed to shoot down twenty-nine enemy planes.

never seen a document that was more crowded with infamous falsehoods and distortions—on a scale so huge that I never imagined until today that any government was capable of uttering them."

Speaking before Congress the next day, President Roosevelt termed December 7, "a date which will live in infamy" and asked for a declaration of war on Japan. With only one dissenting vote, both branches did so. On December 11, Germany and Italy declared war against the United States; the nation was now fully involved in World War II.

The whole country united behind Roosevelt's leadership to seek revenge for Pearl Harbor and to defeat the Axis threat to American security. After the war, however, critics charged that FDR had entered the conflict by a back door, claiming the president had deliberately exposed the Pacific fleet to attack. Subsequent investigations uncovered negligence in both Hawaii and Washington but no evidence to support the conspiracy charge. Commanders in Hawaii, like most military experts, believed the Japanese would not launch an attack on a base 4,000 miles away from Japan. FDR, like too many Americans, had badly

underestimated the daring and skill of the Japanese; he and the nation alike paid a heavy price for this cultural and racial prejudice. But there was no plot. Roosevelt could not have known that Hitler, so restrained in the Atlantic, would reverse his policy and foolishly declare war against the United States after Pearl Harbor. Perhaps the most frightening aspect of the whole episode is that it took the shock of the Japanese sneak attack to make the American people aware of the extent of the Axis threat to their well-being and lead them to end the long American retreat from responsibility.

TURNING THE TIDE AGAINST THE AXIS

In the first few months after the United States entered the war, the outlook for victory was bleak. In Europe, Hitler's armies controlled virtually the entire continent, from Norway in the north to Greece in the south. Despite the nonaggression pact, German armies had penetrated deep into Russia after an initial invasion in June 1941. Although they had failed to capture either

Moscow or Leningrad, the Nazi forces had conquered the Ukraine and by the spring of 1942 were threatening to sweep across the Volga and seize the vital oil fields in the Caucasus. In North Africa, General Erwin Rommel's Afrika Korps had pushed the British back into Egypt and threatened the Suez Canal (see the map on p. 832).

The situation was no better in Asia. The Pearl Harbor attack had enabled the Japanese to move unopposed across Southeast Asia. Within three months they had conquered Malaya and the Dutch East Indies, with its valuable oil fields, and were pressing the British back both in Burma and New Guinea. American forces under General Douglas MacArthur had tried vainly to block the Japanese conquest of the Philippines. MacArthur finally escaped by torpedo boat to Australia; the American garrison at Corregidor surrendered after a long siege, the survivors then enduring the cruel death march across the Bataan peninsula. With the American navy still recovering from the devastation at Pearl Harbor, Japan controlled the western half of the Pacific (see the map on p. 833).

Over the next two years, the United States and its allies would finally halt the German and Japanese offensives in Europe and Asia. But then they faced the difficult process of driving back the enemy, freeing the vast conquered areas, and finally defeating the Axis powers on their home territory. It would be a difficult and costly struggle that would require great sacrifice and heavy losses; World War II would test American will and resourcefulness to the hilt.

Wartime Partnerships

The greatest single advantage that the United States and its partners possessed was their willingness to form a genuine coalition to bring about the defeat of the Axis powers. Although there were many strains within the wartime alliance, it did permit a high degree of coordination. In striking contrast was the behavior of Germany and Japan, each fighting a separate war without any attempt at cooperation.

The United States and Britain achieved a complete wartime partnership. Prewar military talks led to the formation of a Combined Chiefs of Staff, headquartered in Washington, which directed Anglo-American military operations. The close cooperation between President Roosevelt and Prime Minister Churchill ensured a common strategy. The leaders decided at the outset that a Germany victory posed the greater danger and thus gave priority to the European theater in the conduct of the war. In a series of meetings in December 1941, Roosevelt and Churchill signed a Declaration of the United Nations, eventually subscribed to by twenty-six countries, that pledged them to fight together until the Axis powers were defeated.

Relations with the other members of the United Nations coalition in World War II were not quite so harmonious. The decision to defeat Germany first displeased the Chinese, who had been at war with Japan since 1937. Roosevelt tried to appease Chiang Kai-shek with a trickle of supplies, flown in at great risk by American airmen over the Himalayas from India. France posed a more delicate problem. FDR virtually ignored the Free French government in exile under General Charles de Gaulle. Roosevelt preferred to deal with the Vichy regime, despite its collaboration with Germany, because it still controlled the French fleet and retained France's overseas territories.

The greatest strain of all within the wartime coalition was with the Soviet Union. Although Roosevelt had ended the long period of nonrecognition in 1933, close ties had failed to develop. The Russian refusal to pay prerevolutionary debts, together with continued Soviet support of domestic communist activity in the United States in the 1930s, intensified American distaste for Stalin's regime. The great Russian purge trials and the temporary Nazi-Soviet alliance from 1939 to 1941, along with deep-seated cultural and ideological differences, made wartime cooperation difficult.

Ever the pragmatist, Roosevelt tried hard to break down the old hostility and establish a more cordial relationship with Russia during the war. Even before Pearl Harbor, he extended lend-lease aid to Russia, and after American entry into the war, this economic assistance grew rapidly, limited only by the difficulty in delivering the supplies. Eager to keep Russia in the war, the president promised a visiting Russian diplomat in May 1942 that the United States would create a second front in Europe by the end of that year, a pledge he could not fulfill. In January 1943, Roosevelt joined with Churchill at the

Casablanca conference to declare a policy of unconditional surrender, vowing the Allies would fight until the Axis nations were completely defeated.

Despite these promises, the Soviet Union bore the brunt of battle against Hitler in the early years of the war, fighting alone against more than two hundred German divisions. The United States and England, grateful for the respite to build up their forces, could do little more than offer promises of future help and send lend-lease supplies. The result was a rift that never fully healed—one that did not prevent the defeat of Germany but did ensure future tensions and uncertainties between the Soviet Union and the Western nations.

Halting the German Blitz

From the outset, the United States favored an invasion across the English Channel. Army planners, led by Chief of Staff George C. Marshall and his protégé, Dwight D. Eisenhower, were convinced such a frontal assault would be the quickest way to win the war. Roosevelt concurred, in part because it fulfilled his second-front commitment to the Soviets.

The initial plan, drawn up by Eisenhower, called for a full-scale invasion of Europe in the spring of 1943, with provision for a temporary beachhead in France in the fall of 1942 if necessary to keep Russia in the war. Marshall surprised everyone by placing Eisenhower, until then a relatively junior general, in charge of implementing the plan.

But the British, remembering the heavy casualties of trench warfare in World War I, preferred a perimeter approach, with air and naval attacks around the edge of the continent until Germany was properly softened up for the final invasion. Their strategists assented to the basic plan but strongly urged that a preliminary invasion of North Africa be launched in the fall of 1942. Roosevelt, too, wanted American troops engaged in combat against Germany before the end of 1942 to offset growing pressure at home to concentrate on the Pacific; hence, after he overruled objections from his military advisers, American and British troops landed on the Atlantic and Mediterranean coasts of Morocco and Algeria in November 1942.

The British launched an attack against

Rommel at El Alamein in Egypt and soon forced the Afrika Korps to retreat across Libya to Tunisia. Eisenhower, delayed by poor roads and bad weather, was slow in bringing up his forces, and in their first encounter with Rommel at the Kasserine Pass in the desert south of Tunis, inexperienced American troops suffered a humiliating defeat. General George Patton quickly rallied the demoralized soldiers, and by May 1943, Germany had been driven from Africa, leaving behind nearly 300,000 troops.

During these same months, the Red Army had broken the back of German military power in the battle of Stalingrad. Turned back at the critical bend in the Volga, Hitler had poured in division after division in what was ultimately a losing cause; never again would Germany be able to take the offensive in Europe.

At Churchill's insistence, FDR agreed to follow up the North African victory with the invasion first of Sicily and then Italy in the summer of 1943. Italy dropped out of the war when Mussolini fled to Germany, but the Italian campaign proved to be a strategic dead end. Germany sent in enough divisions to establish a strong defensive line in the mountains south of Rome; American and British troops were forced to fight their way slowly up the peninsula, suffering heavy casualties.

More important, these Mediterranean operations delayed the second front, postponing it eventually to the spring of 1944. Meanwhile, the Soviets began to push the Germans out of Russia and looked forward to the liberation of Poland, Hungary, and Romania, where they could establish "friendly" communist regimes. Having borne the brunt of the fighting against Nazi Germany, Russia was ready to claim its reward—the postwar domination of eastern Europe.

Checking Japan in the Pacific

Both the decision to defeat Germany first and the vast expanses of the Pacific dictated the nature of the war against Japan. The United States conducted amphibious island-hopping campaigns rather than attempting to reconquer the Dutch East Indies, Southeast Asia, and China. There would be two separate American operations. One, led by Douglas MacArthur based in Australia, would move from New Guinea back to the Philippines, while the other, commanded by

World War II in Europe and North Africa

The tide of battle shifted in this theater during the winter of 1942–1943. The massive German assault on the eastern front was turned back by the Russians at Stalingrad, and the Allied forces recaptured North Africa.

Admiral Chester Nimitz from Hawaii, was directed at key Japanese islands in the Central Pacific. The original plan called for the two offensives to come together for the final invasion of the Japanese home islands.

Success in the Pacific depended above all else on control of the sea. The devastation at Pearl Harbor gave Japan the initial edge, but fortunately the United States had not lost any of its four aircraft carriers. In the battle of the Coral Sea in May 1942, American naval forces blocked a Japanese thrust to outflank Australia. The turning point came one month later at Midway. A powerful Japanese task force threatened to seize

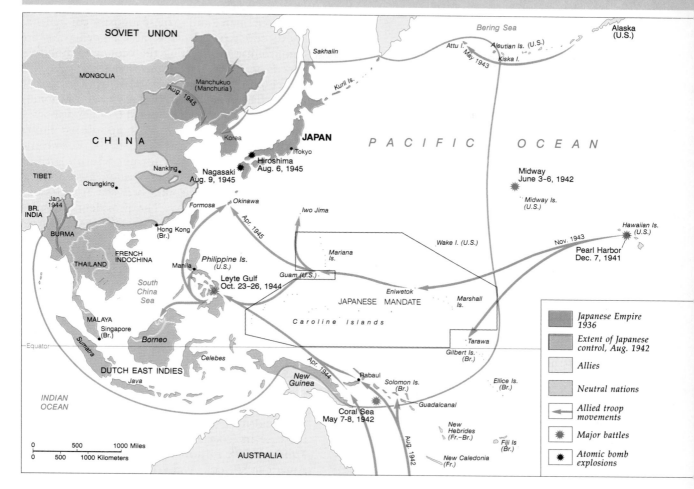

World War II in the Pacific

The tide of battle turned in the Pacific the same year as in Europe. The balance of sea power shifted back to the United States from Japan after the naval victories of 1942.

	Japanese Empire 1936
	Extent of Japanese control, Aug. 1942
	Allies
	Neutral nations
←	Allied troop movements
✷	Major battles
✸	Atomic bomb explosions

this remote American outpost over a thousand miles west of Pearl Harbor; Japan's real objective was the destruction of what remained of the American Pacific fleet. Superior American air power enabled Nimitz's forces to engage the enemy at long range. Japanese fighters shot down thirty-five of forty-one attacking torpedo bombers, but a second wave of dive bombers scored hits on three Japanese carriers. The battle of Midway ended with the loss of four Japanese aircraft carriers compared to just one American. It was the first defeat the modern Japanese navy had ever suffered, and it left the United States in control of the Central Pacific.

Encouraged by this victory, American forces launched their first Pacific offensive in the Solomon Islands, east of New Guinea, in August 1942. Both sides suffered heavy losses, but six months later the last Japanese were driven from the key island of Guadalcanal. At the same time, MacArthur began the long, slow, and bloody job of driving the Japanese back along the north coast of New Guinea.

By early 1943, the defensive phase of the war with Japan was over. The enemy surge had been halted in both the Central and the Southwest Pacific, and the United States was preparing to penetrate the Gilbert, Marshall, and Caroline islands and recapture the Philippines. Just as Russia had broken German power in Europe, so the United States, fighting alone except for Australia and New Zealand, had halted the

Japanese. And, like the Soviet plans for eastern Europe, America expected to reap the rewards of victory by dominating the Pacific in the future.

THE HOME FRONT

World War II had a greater impact than the Depression on the future of American life. While American soldiers and sailors fought abroad, the nation underwent sweeping social and economic changes at home.

American industry made the nation's single most important contribution to victory. Even though over fifteen million Americans served in the armed forces, it was the nearly sixty million who worked on farms and factories who achieved the miracle of production that ensured the defeat of Germany and Japan. The manufacturing plants that had run at half capacity through the 1930s now hummed with activity. In Detroit, automobile assembly lines were converted to produce tanks and airplanes; Henry Ford built the giant Willow Run factory, covering 67 acres, where 42,000 workers turned out a B-24 bomber every hour. Henry J. Kaiser, a California industrialist who constructed huge West Coast shipyards to meet the demand for cargo vessels and landing craft, operated on an equally large scale. His Richmond, California, plant lowered the time to build a merchant ship from 105 to 14 days. In part, America won the battle of the Atlantic by building ships faster than German U-boats could sink them.

This vast industrial expansion, however, created many problems. In 1942, President Roosevelt appointed Donald Nelson, a Sears, Roebuck executive, to head a War Production Board (WPB). A jovial, easygoing man, Nelson soon was outmaneuvered by the army and the navy, which preferred to negotiate directly with large corporations. The WPB allowed business rapid depreciation, and thus huge tax credits, for new plants and awarded lucrative cost-plus contracts for urgently needed goods. Shortages of such critical materials as steel, aluminum, and copper led to an allocation system based on military priorities. Rubber, cut off by the Japanese conquest of Southeast Asia, was particularly scarce; the administration finally began gasoline rationing in 1943 to curb pleasure driving and prolong tire life. The government itself built fifty-one synthetic rubber plants, which by 1944 were producing nearly 1 million tons for the tires of American airplanes and military vehicles. All in all, the nation's factories turned out twice as many goods as did German and Japanese industry combined.

Roosevelt revealed the same tendency toward compromise in directing the economic mobilization as he did in shaping the New Deal. When the Office of Price Administration—which tried to curb inflation by controlling prices and rationing scarce goods like sugar, canned food, and shoes—clashed with the WPB, FDR appointed James Byrnes to head an Office of Economic Stabilization. Byrnes, a former South Carolina senator and Supreme Court justice, used political judgment to settle disputes between agencies and keep all groups happy. The president was also forced to compromise with Congress, which pared down the administration's requests for large tax increases. Half the cost of the war was financed by borrowing; the other half came from revenues. A $7 billion revenue increase in 1942 included so many first-time taxpayers that in the following year the Treasury Department instituted a new practice—withholding income taxes from workers' wages.

The result of this wartime economic explosion was a growing affluence. Despite the federal incentives to business, heavy excess-profit taxes and a 94 percent tax rate for the very rich kept the wealthy from benefiting unduly. The huge increase in federal spending, from $9 billion in 1940 to $98 billion in 1944, spread through American society. A government agreement with labor unions in 1943 held wage rates to a 15 percent increase, but the long hours of overtime resulted in doubling and sometimes tripling the weekly paychecks of factory workers. Farmers shared in the new prosperity as their incomes quadrupled between 1940 and 1945. For the first time in the twentieth century, the lowest fifth of wage earners increased their share of the national income in relation to the more affluent; their income rose by 68 percent between 1941 and 1945, compared to a 20 percent increase for the well-to-do. Most important, this rising income ensured postwar prosperity. Workers and farmers saved their money, channeling much of it into government war bonds, waiting for the day when they could buy the cars and home appliances they had done without during the long years of depression and war.

American war production was twice that of all the Axis countries. Here, Boeing aircraft workers celebrate the completion of their five-thousandth bomber.

A Nation on the Move

The war led to a vast migration of the American population. Young men left their homes for training camps and then for service overseas. Defense workers and their families, some nine million people in all, moved to work in the new booming shipyards, munitions factories, and aircraft plants. Norfolk, Virginia; San Diego, California; Mobile, Alabama, and other centers of defense production grew by more than 50 percent in just a year or two. Rural areas lost population while coastal regions, especially along the Pacific and the Gulf of Mexico, drew millions of people. The location of army camps in the South and West created boom conditions in the future Sunbelt, as did the concentration of aircraft factories and shipyards in this region. California had the greatest gains, adding nearly two million to its population in less than five years.

This movement of people caused severe social problems. Housing was in short supply. Migrating workers crowded into house trailers and boardinghouses, bringing unexpected windfalls to landlords. In one boomtown, a reporter described an old Victorian house that had five bedrooms on the second floor. "Three of them," he wrote, "held two cots apiece, the two others held three cots." But the owner revealed that "the third floor is where we pick up the velvet. . . . We rent to workers in different shifts . . . three shifts a day . . . seven bucks a week apiece."

Family life suffered under these crowded living conditions. An increase in the number of marriages, as young people searched for something to hang on to in the midst of wartime turmoil, was offset by a rising divorce rate. The baby boom that would peak in the 1950s began during the war and brought its own set of problems. Only a few publicly funded day-care centers were available, and working mothers worried about their "latch-key children." Schools in the boom areas were unable to cope with the influx of new students; a teacher shortage, intensified by the lure of higher wages in war industries, compounded the educational crisis.

Despite these problems, women found the war a time of economic opportunity. The demand for workers led to a dramatic rise in female employment, from 14 million working women in 1940 to 19 million by 1945. Most of the new women workers were married and many were middle aged, thus broadening the composition of the female work force, which in the past had been

"*Inside the Vicious Heart*"

The liberation of the Nazi death camps near the end of World War II was not a priority objective; nor was it a planned operation. Convinced that military victory was the surest way to end Nazi oppression, Allied strategists organized their campaigns without specific reference to the camps; they staged no daring commando raids to rescue the survivors of Nazi genocide. It was by chance that Allied forces first stumbled upon the camps, and the GIs who threw open the gates to that living hell were totally unprepared for what they found.

Not until November 1944, did the U.S. Army discover its first camp, Natzwiller-Struthof, abandoned by the Germans months before. Viewing Natzwiller from a distance, Milton Bracker of the *New York Times* noted its deceptive similarity to an American Civilian Conservation Corps camp: "The sturdy green barracks buildings looked exactly like those that housed forestry trainees in the U.S. during the early New Deal."

As he toured the grounds, however, he faced a starker reality and slowly came to think the unthinkable. In the crematorium, he reported, "I cranked the elevator tray a few times and slid the furnace tray a few times, and even at that moment, I did not believe what I was doing was real."

"There were no prisoners," he wrote, "no screams, no burly guards, no taint of death in the air as on a battlefield." Bracker had to stretch his imagination to its limits to comprehend the camp's silent testimony to Nazi barbarism. U.S. military personnel who toured Natzwiller shared this sense of the surreal. In their report to headquarters, they carefully qualified every observation. They described "what appeared to be a disinfection unit," a room "allegedly used as a lethal gas chamber," "a cellar room with a special type elevator," and "an incinerator room with equipment obviously intended for the burning of human bodies." They saw before them the evidence of German atrocities, but the truth was so horrible, they could not quite bring themselves to draw the obvious conclusions.

Inside the Vicious Heart, Robert Abzug's study of the liberation of the concentration camps, refers to this phenomenon as "double vision." Faced with a revelation so terrible, witnesses could not fully comprehend the evidence of mass murder without meaning or logic. But as the Allied armies advanced into Germany, the shocking evidence mounted. On April 4, 1945, the Fourth Armored Division of the Third Army unexpectedly discovered Ohrdruf, a relatively small concentration camp. Ohrdruf's liberation had a tremendous impact on American forces. It was the first camp discovered intact, with its grisly array of the dead and dying. Inside the compound, corpses were piled in heaps in the barracks. An infantryman recalled, "I guess the most vivid recollection of the whole camp is the pyre that was located on the edge of the camp. It was a big pit, where they stacked bodies—

Photos of the death camps, such as these, made the almost unimaginable atrocities of the Führer's regime real to Americans at home.

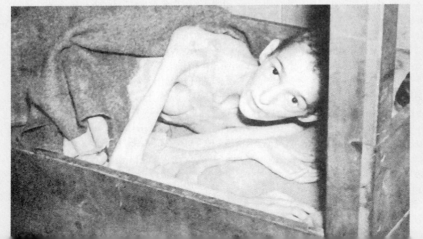

stacked bodies and wood and burned them."

On April 12, generals Eisenhower, Bradley, and Patton toured Ohrdruf. The generals, professional soldiers familiar with the devastation of battle, had never seen its like. Years later, Bradley recalled, "The smell of death overwhelmed us even before we passed through the stockade. More than 3,200 naked, emaciated bodies had been flung into shallow graves. Others lay in the street where they had fallen."

Eisenhower ordered every available armed forces unit in the area to visit Ohrdruf. "We are told that the American soldier does not know what he is fighting for," said Eisenhower. "Now at least he will know what he is fighting against." He urged government officials and journalists to visit the camps and tell the world. In an official message Eisenhower summed it up:

We are constantly finding German camps in which they have placed political prisoners where unspeakable conditions exist. From my own personal observation, I can state unequivocally that all written statements up to now do not paint the full horrors.

On April 11, the Timberwolf Division of the Third Army uncovered Nordhausen. They found 3,000 dead and only 700 survivors. The scene sickened battle-hardened veterans.

The odors, well there is no way to describe the odors. . . . Many of the boys I am talking about now—these were tough soldiers, there were combat men who had been all the way through

Victims at the Bergen-Belsen concentration camp were buried in a mass grave. The camp was liberated by the Allies April 14, 1945, less than a month before Germany's surrender.

the invasion—were ill and vomiting, throwing up, just at the sight of this. . . .

For some, the liberation of Nordhausen changed the meaning of the war.

I must also say that my fellow GIs, most thought that any stories they had read in the paper . . . were either not true or at least exaggerated. And it did not sink in, what this was all about, until we got into Nordhausen.

If the experience at Nordhausen gave many GIs a new sense of mission in battle, it also forced them to distance themselves from the realities of the camps. Only by closing off their emotions could they go about the grim task of sorting out the living from the dead and tending to the survivors. Margaret Bourke-Whitw, whose *Life* magazine photographs brought the horrors of the death camps to millions on the home front, recalled working "with a veil over my mind."

People often ask me how it is possible to photograph

such atrocities. In photographing the murder camps, the protective veil was so tightly drawn that I hardly knew what I had taken until I saw prints of my own photographs.

By the end of 1945, most of the liberators had come home and returned to civilian life. Once home, their experiences produced no common moral responses. No particular pattern emerged in their occupational, political, and religious behavior, beyond a fear of the rise of postwar totalitarianism shared by most Americans. Few spoke publicly about their role in the liberation of the camps; most found that after a short period of grim fascination, their friends and families preferred to forget. Some had nightmares, but most were not tormented by memories. For the liberators the ordeal was over. For the survivors of the hell of the camps, liberation was but the first step in the tortuous process of rebuilding broken bodies and shattered lives.

837

During and immediately after the war, ration stamps were issued for scarce food items, shoes, tires, and gasoline.

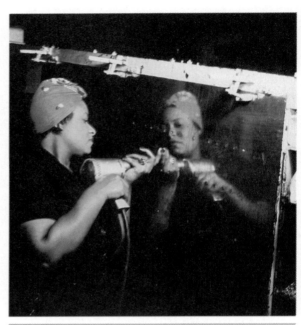

As men left for military service in World War II and U.S. industry expanded to keep up with defense needs, millions of women joined the paid labor force. By 1944, the peak year for female wartime employment, women comprised 36 percent of the American work force. Women took jobs that before the war had been done by men, such as riveting, welding, and operating heavy equipment. "Rosie the Riveter," a popular song of the era, celebrated women's new role in the labor force.

composed primarily of young single women. Women entered industries once viewed as exclusively male; by the end of the war, they worked alongside men tending blast furnaces in steel mills and welding hulls in shipyards. Few challenged the traditional view of sex roles, yet the wartime experience helped temporarily undermine the concept that woman's only proper place was in the home. Women enjoyed the hefty weekly paychecks, which rose by 50 percent from 1941 to 1943, and they took pride in their contributions to the war effort. "To hell with the life I have had," commented a former fashion designer. "This war is too damn serious, and it is too damn important to win it."

African Americans shared in the wartime migration, but their social and economic gains were limited by racial prejudice. Nearly one mil-

lion served in the armed forces, but relatively few saw combat. The army placed black soldiers in segregated units, usually led by white officers, and used them for service and construction tasks. The navy was even worse, relegating them to menial jobs until late in the war. African Americans were denied the chance to become petty officers, Secretary of the Navy Frank Knox explained, because experience had shown that "men of the colored race . . . cannot maintain discipline among men of the white race."

African American civilians fared a little better. In 1941, black labor leader A. Philip Randolph threatened a massive march on Washington to force President Roosevelt to end racial discrimination in defense industries and government employment and to integrate the armed forces. FDR compromised, persuading Randolph to call off the march and drop his integration demand in return for an executive order creating a Fair Employment Practices Committee (FEPC) to ban

The migration of African Americans from the South to northern cities was recorded in a series of sixty tempera panels by African American artist Jacob Lawrence. The paintings are done in sharp primary colors and a forceful but simple design. They form a continuous narrative of visual history and African American experience.

Detroit. The next day, a full-scale riot broke out in which twenty-three blacks and nine whites died. The fighting raged for twenty-four hours until National Guard troops were brought in to restore order. Later that summer, only personal intervention by New York mayor Fiorello LaGuardia quelled a Harlem riot that took the lives of six blacks.

These outbursts of racial violence fueled the resentments that would grow into the postwar civil rights movement. For most African Americans, despite economic gains, World War II was a reminder of the inequality of American life. "Just carve on my tombstone," remarked one black soldier in the Pacific, "here lies a black man killed fighting a yellow man for the protection of a white man."

One-third of a million Mexican Americans served in the armed forces and shared some of the same experiences as African Americans. Although

racial discrimination in war industries. As a result, African American employment by the federal government rose from 60,000 in 1941 to 200,000 by the end of the war. The FEPC proved less successful in the private sector. Weak in funding and staff, the FEPC was able to act on only one-third of the eight thousand complaints it received. The nationwide shortage of labor was more influential than the FEPC in accounting for the rise in black employment during wartime. African Americans moved from the rural South to northern and western cities, finding jobs in the automobile, aircraft, and shipbuilding industries.

This movement of an estimated 700,000 people helped transform black/white relations from a regional issue into a national concern that could no longer be ignored. The limited housing and recreational facilities for both black and white war workers created tensions that led to urban race riots. On a hot Sunday evening in June 1943, blacks and whites began exchanging insults and then blows near Belle Isle recreation park in

African American Migration from the South, 1940–1950

Movement was from the Southeast to the Mid-Atlantic and New England states and from the south central states to the Midwest and Far West.

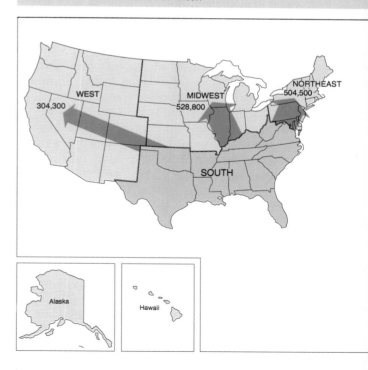

A bewildered Nisei toddler, tagged like a piece of luggage and guarded by a GI, waits to be taken to a detention camp.

they were not as completely segregated, many served in the Eighty-eighth Division, made up largely of Mexican American officers and troops, which earned the nickname "Blue Devils" in the Italian campaign. At home, Spanish-speaking people left the rural areas of Texas, New Mexico, and California for jobs in the cities, especially in aircraft plants and petroleum refineries. Despite low wages and union resistance, they improved their economic position substantially. But they still faced discrimination based both on skin color and language, most notably in the Los Angeles "zoot-suit" riots in 1943 when white sailors attacked Mexican American youths dressed in their distinctive long jackets and flared pants tightly pegged at the ankles. The racial prejudice heightened feelings of ethnic identity and led returning Mexican American veterans to form organizations such as the American G.I. Forum to press for equal rights in the future.

A tragic counterpoint to the voluntary movement of American workers in search of jobs was the forced relocation of 120,000 Japanese Americans from the West Coast. Responding to racial fears in California after Pearl Harbor, President Roosevelt approved an army order in February 1942 to move all Japanese Americans

on the West Coast to concentration camps in the interior. More than two-thirds of those detained were *Nisei*, native-born Americans whose only crime was their Japanese ancestry. Forced to sell their farms and businesses at distress prices, the Japanese Americans lost not only their liberty but also most of their worldly goods. Herded into ten hastily built detention centers in seven western and southern states, they lived as prisoners in tar-papered barracks behind barbed wire, guarded by armed troops.

Appeals to the Supreme Court proved fruitless; in 1944, six justices upheld relocation on grounds of national security in wartime. Beginning in 1943, individual Nisei could win release by pledging their loyalty and finding a job away from the West Coast. Some 35,000 left the camps during the next two years, including over 13,000 who joined the armed forces. The all-Nisei 442nd Combat Team served gallantly in the European theater, losing over five hundred men in battle and winning more than one thousand citations for bravery. One World War II veteran remembers that when his unit was in trouble, the commander would issue a familiar appeal, "Call in the Japs."

For other Nisei, the experience was bitter. More than five thousand renounced their American citizenship and chose to live in Japan at the war's end. The government did not close down the last detention center until March 1946. Japanese Americans never experienced the torture and mass death of the German concentration camps, but their treatment was a disgrace to a nation fighting for freedom and democracy. Finally in 1988, Congress voted an indemnity of $1.2 billion for the estimated sixty thousand surviving Japanese Americans detained during World War II. Susumi Emori, who had been moved with his wife and four children from his farm in Stockton, California to a camp in Arkansas, felt vindicated. "It was terrible," he said, with tears in his eyes, "but it was a time of war. Anything can happen. I didn't blame the United States for that."

Win-the-War Politics

Franklin Roosevelt used World War II to strengthen his leadership and maintain Democratic political dominance. As war brought about prosperity and removed the economic discontent that had sustained the New Deal, FDR announced "Dr. New Deal" had given way to "Dr. Win-the-War." Congress, already controlled by a conservative coalition of southern Democrats and northern Republicans, had almost slipped into GOP hands in 1942. With a very low voter turnout, due in part to the large numbers of men in service and uprooted workers who failed to meet residency requirements for voting, the Republicans won forty-four new seats in the House and nine in the Senate and elected governors in New York and California as well.

In 1944, Roosevelt responded to the Democratic slippage by dropping Henry Wallace, his liberal and visionary vice president, for Harry Truman, a moderate and down-to-earth Missouri senator who was acceptable to all factions of the Democratic party. Equally important, FDR received increased political support from organized labor, which had grown in membership during the war from ten to fifteen million. The newly organized Political Action Committee (PAC) of the CIO, headed by Sidney Hillman, conducted massive door-to-door drives to register millions of workers and their families.

The Republicans nominated Thomas E. Dewey, who had been elected governor of New York after gaining fame as a prosecutor of organized crime. Dewey, moderate in his views, played down opposition to the New Deal and instead tried to make Roosevelt's age and health the primary issues, along with the charge that the Democrats were soft on communism.

Despite his abrasive campaign style, Dewey did not advocate a return to isolationism. The Republican party was trying hard to shake the obstructionist image it had gained during the League of Nations fight in 1919; it went on record in 1943 as favoring American postwar cooperation for world peace. Indeed, Dewey pioneered a bipartisan approach to foreign policy. He accepted wartime planning for the future United Nations and kept the issue of an international organization out of the campaign.

Reacting to the issues of his age and health, especially after a long bout with influenza in the spring, FDR disregarded the advice of his doctors and took a five-hour rain-soaked drive through the streets of New York City in an open car just before the election. His vitality impressed the vot-

The Election of 1944			
Candidate	Party	Popular Vote	Electoral Vote
Roosevelt	Democrat	25,611,936	432
Dewey	Republican	22,013,372	99

ers, and in November 1944 he swept back into office for a fourth term, although the margin of 3.6 million votes was his smallest yet. The campaign, however, had taken its toll. The president, suffering from high blood pressure and congestive heart failure, had only a few months left to lead the nation.

VICTORY

World War II ended with surprising swiftness. By 1943, the Axis tide had been turned in Europe and Asia, and it did not take long for Russia, the United States, and England to mount the offensives that drove Germany and Japan back across the vast areas they had conquered and set the stage for their final defeat.

The long-awaited second front finally came on June 6, 1944. For two years, the United States and England concentrated on building up an invasion force of nearly three million troops and a vast armada of ships and landing craft to carry them across the English Channel. In hopes of catching Hitler by surprise, Eisenhower chose the Normandy peninsula, where the absence of good harbors had led to lighter German fortifications. Allied aircraft bombed the roads, bridges, and rail lines of northern France for six weeks preceding the assault in order to block the movement of German reinforcements once the invasion began.

D-Day was originally set for June 5, but bad weather forced a delay. Relying on a forecasted break in the storm, Eisenhower gambled on going ahead on June 6. During the night, three divisions parachuted down behind the German defenses; at dawn, the British and American troops fought their way ashore at five points along a 60-mile

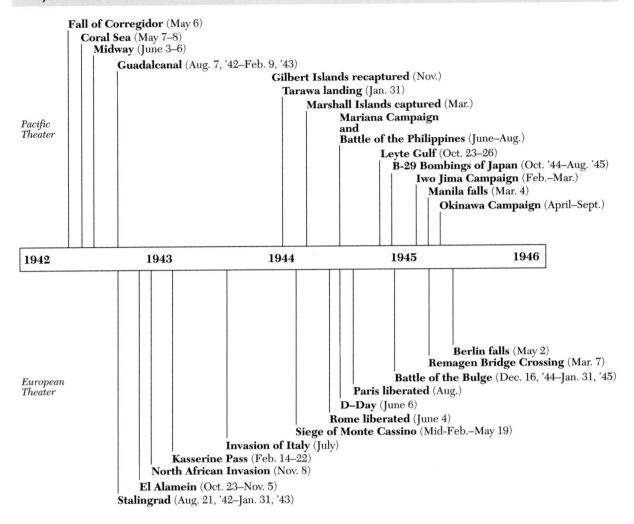

Pacific Theater

Fall of Corregidor (May 6)
Coral Sea (May 7–8)
Midway (June 3–6)
Guadalcanal (Aug. 7, '42–Feb. 9, '43)
Gilbert Islands recaptured (Nov.)
Tarawa landing (Jan. 31)
Marshall Islands captured (Mar.)
Mariana Campaign and Battle of the Philippines (June–Aug.)
Leyte Gulf (Oct. 23–26)
B-29 Bombings of Japan (Oct. '44–Aug. '45)
Iwo Jima Campaign (Feb.–Mar.)
Manila falls (Mar. 4)
Okinawa Campaign (April–Sept.)

1942   1943   1944   1945   1946

European Theater

Berlin falls (May 2)
Remagen Bridge Crossing (Mar. 7)
Battle of the Bulge (Dec. 16, '44–Jan. 31, '45)
Paris liberated (Aug.)
D–Day (June 6)
Rome liberated (June 4)
Siege of Monte Cassino (Mid-Feb.–May 19)
Invasion of Italy (July)
Kasserine Pass (Feb. 14–22)
North African Invasion (Nov. 8)
El Alamein (Oct. 23–Nov. 5)
Stalingrad (Aug. 21, '42–Jan. 31, '43)

stretch of beach, encountering stiff German resistance at several points. By the end of the day, however, Eisenhower had won his beachhead; a week later, more than one-third of a million men were slowly pushing back the German forces through the hedgerows of Normandy. The breakthrough came on July 25 when General Omar Bradley decimated the enemy with a massive artillery and aerial bombardment at Saint-Lô, opening a gap for General George Patton's Third Army. American tanks raced across the French countryside, trapping thousands of Germans and liberating Paris by August 25. Allied troops reached the Rhine River by September, but a shortage of supplies, especially gasoline, forced a three-month halt.

Hitler took advantage of this breathing spell to deliver a daring counterattack. In mid-December, the remaining German armored divisions burst through a weak point in the Allied lines in the Ardennes Forest, planning a breakout to the coast that would have cut off nearly one-third of Eisenhower's forces. A combination of tactical surprise and bad weather, which prevented Allied air support, led to a huge bulge in the American lines. But an airborne division dug in at the key crossroads of Bastogne, in Belgium, and held off a much larger German force. Allied reinforcements and clearing weather then combined to end the attack. By committing nearly all his reserves to the Battle of the Bulge, Hitler had delayed Eisenhower's advance into Germany, but he also had fatally weakened German resistance in the West.

The end came quickly. A massive Russian offensive began in mid-January and swept across the Oder River toward Berlin. General Bradley's troops, finding a bridge left virtually intact by the retreating Germans, crossed the Rhine on March 7. Eisenhower overruled the British, who favored one concentrated drive on Berlin. Instead the Allied forces advanced on a broad front, capturing the industrial Ruhr basin and meeting the Russians at the Elbe by the last week in April. With the Red Army already in the suburbs of Berlin, Adolf Hitler committed suicide on April 30. A week later, on May 7, 1945, Eisenhower accepted the unconditional surrender of all German forces. Just eleven months and a day after the landings in Normandy, the Allied forces had brought the war in Europe to a successful conclusion.

The nation's grief at FDR's death is mirrored in the face of this serviceman as the President's funeral cortege passes.

War Aims and Wartime Diplomacy

The American contribution to Hitler's defeat was relatively minor compared to the damage inflicted by the Soviet Union. At the height of the German invasion of Russia, more than 300 Soviet divisions had been locked in battle with 250 German ones, a striking contrast to the 58 divisions the United States and Britain used in the Normandy invasion. As his armies overran Poland and the Balkan countries, Joseph Stalin was determined to retain control over this region, which had been the historic pathway for Western invasion into Russia. Delay in opening the second front and an innate distrust of the West convinced the Soviets that they should maximize their territorial gains by imposing communist regimes on eastern Europe.

American postwar goals were quite different. Now believing the failure to join the League of Nations in 1919 had led to the coming of World War II, the American people and their leaders vowed to put their faith in a new attempt at collective security. At Moscow in 1943, Secretary of State Cordell Hull had won Russian agreement to participate in a future world organization at the war's end. The first wartime Big Three conference brought together Roosevelt, Churchill, and Stalin at Teheran, Iran, in late 1943. Stalin reaffirmed this commitment and also indicated to President Roosevelt that Russia would enter the war against Japan once Germany was defeated.

By the time the Big Three met again at Yalta, in February 1945, the military situation favored the Russians. While British and American forces were still recovering from the Battle of the Bulge, the Red Army was advancing to within 50 miles of Berlin. Stalin drove a series of hard bargains. He refused to give up his plans for communist domination of Poland and the Balkans, although he did agree to Roosevelt's request for a Declaration of Liberated Europe, which called for free elections without providing for any method of enforcement or supervision. More important for the United States, Stalin promised to enter the Pacific war three months after Germany surrendered. In return, Roosevelt offered extensive concessions in Asia, including Russian control over Manchuria. While neither a sellout nor a betrayal, as some critics have charged, Yalta was a significant diplomatic victory for the Soviets—one that reflected Russia's major contribution to a victory in Europe.

For the president, the long journey to Yalta proved to be too much. His health continued to fail after his return to Washington. In early April, FDR left the capital for Warm Springs, Georgia, where he had always been able to relax. He was sitting for his portrait at midday on April 12, 1945, when he suddenly complained of a "terrific headache," then slumped forward and died.

The nation mourned a man who had gallantly met the challenge of depression and global war. Unfortunately, FDR had taken no steps to prepare his successor for the difficult problems that lay ahead. The defeat of Nazi Germany dissolved the one strong bond between the United States and the Soviet Union. With very different histories, cultures, and ideologies, the two nations were bound to drift apart. It was now up to the inexperienced Harry Truman to manage the growing rivalry that was destined to develop into the future Cold War.

Triumph and Tragedy in the Pacific

The total defeat of Germany in May 1945 turned all eyes toward Japan. Although the combined chiefs of staff had originally estimated it would take eighteen months after Germany's surrender to conquer Japan, American forces moved with surprising speed. Admiral Nimitz swept through the Gilbert, Caroline, and Marshall islands in 1944, securing bases for further advances and building airfields for American B-29s to begin a deadly bombardment of the Japanese home islands. General MacArthur cleared New Guinea of the last Japanese defender in early 1944 and began planning his long-heralded return to the Philippines. American troops landed on the island of Leyte on October 20, 1944, and Manila fell by the end of the year. The Japanese navy, in a Pacific version of the Battle of the Bulge, launched a daring three-pronged attack on the American invasion fleet in Leyte Gulf. The U.S. Navy rallied to blunt all three Japanese thrusts, sinking four carriers and ending any further Japanese naval threat.

The defeat of Japan was now only a matter of time. The United States had three possible ways to proceed. The military favored a full-scale invasion, beginning on the southernmost island of Kyushu in November 1945 and culminating with an assault on Honshu (the main island of Japan)

and a climatic battle for Tokyo in 1946; casualties were expected to run into the hundreds of thousands. Diplomats suggested a negotiated peace, urging the United States to modify the unconditional surrender formula to permit Japan to retain the institution of the emperor. At Potsdam, Churchill and Truman did issue a call for surrender, warning Japan it faced utter destruction, but they made no mention of the emperor.

The third possibility involved the highly secret Manhattan Project. Since 1939, the United States had spent $2 billion to develop an atomic bomb based on the fission of radioactive uranium and plutonium. Scientists, many of them refugees from Europe, worked at the University of Chicago; Oak Ridge, Tennessee; Hanford, Washington; and a remote laboratory in Los Alamos, New Mexico, to perfect this deadly new weapon. In the New Mexico desert on July 16, 1945, they successfully tested the first atomic bomb, creating a fireball brighter than several suns and a telltale mushroom cloud that rose some 40,000 feet above an enormous crater in the desert floor.

Informed of this achievement upon his arrival at Potsdam, President Truman authorized the army air force to use the atomic bomb against Japan. Truman had been unaware of the existence of the Manhattan Project before he became president on April 12. Now he simply followed the recommendation of a committee headed by Secretary of War Henry L. Stimson to drop the bomb on a Japanese city. The committee discussed but rejected the possibility of inviting the Japanese to observe a demonstration shot at a remote Pacific site and even ruled out the idea of giving advance notice of the bomb's destructive power. Neither Truman nor Stimson had any qualms about the decision to drop the bomb without warning. They viewed it as a legitimate wartime measure, one designed to save the lives of hundreds of thousands of Americans—and Japanese—that would be lost in a full-scale invasion.

Weather conditions on the morning of August 6 dictated the choice of Hiroshima as the bomb's target. The explosion incinerated 4 square miles of the city, instantly killing more than sixty thousand. Two days later, Russia entered the war against Japan, and the next day, August 9, the

These traumatized victims of the first A-bomb blast on August 6, 1945, over Hiroshima are seeking first aid a few hours after the explosion.

United States dropped a second bomb on Nagasaki. There were no more atomic bombs available, but no more were needed. The emperor personally broke a deadlock in the Japanese cabinet and persuaded his ministers to surrender unconditionally on August 14, 1945. Three weeks later, Japan signed a formal capitulation agreement on the decks of the battleship *Missouri* in Tokyo Bay to bring World War II to its official close.

Many years later, scholars charged that Truman had more in mind than defeating Japan when he decided to use the atomic bomb. Citing air force and naval officers who claimed Japan could be defeated by a blockade or by conventional air attacks, these revisionists suggested the real reason for dropping the bomb was to impress the Soviet Union with the fact that the United States had exclusive possession of the ultimate weapon. The available evidence indicates that while Truman and his associates were aware of the possible effect on the Soviet Union, their primary motive was to end World War II as quickly and effortlessly as possible. The saving of American lives, along with a desire for revenge

for Pearl Harbor, were uppermost in the decision to bomb Hiroshima and Nagasaki. Yet in using the atomic bomb to defeat Japan, the United States virtually guaranteed a postwar arms race with the Soviet Union.

The second great war of the twentieth century has had a lasting impact on American life. For the first time, the nation's military potential had been reached. In 1945, the United States was unquestionably the strongest country on the earth, with 11 million men and women in uniform, a vast array of shipyards, aircraft plants, and munitions factories in full production, and a monopoly over the atomic bomb. For better or worse, the nation was now launched on a global career. In the future, the United States would be involved in all parts of the world, from western Europe to remote jungles in Asia, from the nearby Caribbean to the distant Persian Gulf. And despite its enormous strength in 1945, the nation's new world role would encompass failure and frustration as well as power and dominion.

The legacy of war was equally strong at home. Four years of fighting brought about industrial recovery and unparalleled prosperity. The old pattern of unregulated free enterprise was as much a victim of the war as of the New Deal; big government and huge deficits had now become the norm as economic control passed from New York and Wall Street to Washington and Pennsylvania Avenue. The war led to far-reaching changes in American society that would only become apparent decades later. Such distinctive patterns of recent American life as the baby boom and the growth of the Sunbelt can be traced back to wartime origins. The Second World War was a watershed in twentieth-century America, ushering in a new age of global concerns and domestic upheaval.

Recommended Reading

The best general account of American attitudes toward the world in the 1920s can be found in Warren I. Cohen, *Empire Without Tears* (1987). Robert Dallek provides a thorough account of FDR's diplomacy in *Franklin D. Roosevelt and American Foreign Policy, 1932–1945* (1979). For a more critical view, see Robert A. Divine, *Roosevelt and World War II* (1969).

Two good books on the continuing controversy over Pearl Harbor are Roberta Wohlstetter, *Pearl Harbor: Warning and Decision* (1962), and Gordon W. Prange, *At Dawn We Slept* (1981). Both authors deny the charge that Roosevelt deliberately exposed the naval base to attack.

In his brief overview of wartime diplomacy, *American Diplomacy During the Second World War*, 2d ed. (1985), Gaddis Smith stresses the tensions within the victorious coalition. The two best accounts of the home front are Richard Polenberg, *War and Society* (1972), and John W. Blum, *V Was for Victory* (1976).

Additional Bibliography

On American foreign policy in the period between the wars, see Selig Adler, *The Isolationist Impulse* (1957); Arnold A. Offner, *The Origins of the Second World War* (1975); Robert H. Ferrell, *Peace in Their Time* (1952); Charles Chatfield, *For Peace and Justice* (1971); Charles DeBenedetti, *Origins of the Modern American Peace Movement, 1915–1929* (1978); Michael J. Hogan, *Informal Entente* (1977); Melvin P. Leffler, *The Elusive Quest* (1978); Akira Iriye, *After Imperialism* (1965); Roger Dingman, *Power in the Pacific* (1976); Thomas H. Buckley, *The United States and the Washington Conference, 1921–1922* (1970); and Robert F. Smith, *The United States and Revolutionary Nationalism in Mexico, 1916–1932* (1972).

For foreign policy during the Hoover years, see Robert H. Ferrell, *American Diplomacy in the Great Depression* (1957); Alexander DeConde, *Herbert Hoover's Latin American Policy* (1951); and Armin Rappaport, *Henry L. Stimson and Japan* (1963). Diplomatic developments in the 1930s under FDR are covered in Dorothy Borg, *The United States and the Far Eastern Crisis of 1933–1938* (1964); Stephen E. Pelz, *Race to Pearl Harbor* (1974); Bryce Wood, *The Making of the Good Neighbor Policy* (1961); Irwin F. Gellman, *Good Neighbor Diplomacy* (1979); Dick Steward, *Trade and Hemisphere* (1979); Manfred Jonas, *Isolationism in America, 1935–1941* (1966); Robert A. Divine, *The Illusion of Neutrality* (1962); and Wayne S. Cole, *Senator Gerald Nye and American Foreign Relations* (1963).

Examinations of Roosevelt's policies during World War II include Robert Sherwood, *Roosevelt and Hopkins* (1948); James M. Burns, *Roosevelt: Soldier of Freedom* (1970); Wayne S. Cole, *Roosevelt and the Isolationists* (1983); and Warren Kimball, *The Juggler* (1991). For details of the American entry into the war, see William L. Langer and S. Everett Gleason, *The Challenge to Isolation* (1950) and *The Undeclared War* (1953); Robert A. Divine, *The Reluctant Belligerent*, 2d ed. (1979); Bruce Russett, *No Clear and Present Danger* (1972); Wayne S. Cole, *America First* (1953); Warren F. Kimball, *The Most Unsordid Act: Lend-Lease, 1939–1941* (1969); David Reynolds, *The Creation of the Anglo-American Alliance, 1937–1941* (1982); Saul Friedlander, *Prelude to Downfall: Hitler* and the United States (1967); Waldo Heinrichs, *Threshold of War* (1988); Patrick J. Hearden, *Roosevelt Confronts Hitler* (1987); Herbert Feis, *The Road to Pearl Harbor* (1950); Paul W. Schroeder, *The Axis Alliance and Japanese-American Relations: 1941* (1958); Jonathan Utley, *Going to War with Japan, 1937–1941* (1985); Akira Iriye, *The Origins of the Second World War in Asia and the Pacific* (1987); Dorothy Borg and Shumpei Okamoto, eds., *Pearl Harbor as History* (1973); and Harry Elmer Barnes, ed., *Perpetual War for Perpetual Peace* (1953).

Military and strategic aspects of World War II are covered in A. Russell Buchanan, *The United States and World War II*, 2 vols. (1964); Chester Wilmot, *The Struggle for Europe* (1952); Eric Larrabee, *Commander in Chief: Franklin Delano Roosevelt, His Lieutenants, Their War* (1987); John Dower, *War Without Mercy: Race and Power in the Pacific War* (1986); Michael Sherry, *The Rise of American Air Power* (1987); David Eisenhower, *Eisenhower: At War, 1943–1945* (1986); Kent Roberts Greenfield, *American Strategy in World War II* (1963); and Mark A. Stoler, *The Politics of the Second Front, 1941–1943* (1977). For wartime diplomacy, see Herbert Feis, *Churchill, Roosevelt and Stalin* (1957); William H. McNeill, *America, Britain, and Russia, 1941–1946* (1953); Michael Schaller, *The U.S. Crusade in China, 1936–1945* (1979); Akira Iriye, *Power and Culture* (1981); Julian G. Hurstfield, *America and the French Nation, 1939–1945* (1986); Russell Buhite, *Decision at Yalta* (1986); Diane Clemens, *Yalta* (1970); Ralph B. Levering, *American Opinion and the Russian Alliance, 1939–1945* (1976); and Warren F. Kimball, ed., *Churchill and Roosevelt: The Complete Correspondence*, 3 vols. (1984).

On the atomic bomb, see Richard G. Hewlett and Oscar E. Anderson, *The New World, 1939–1946* (1962); Richard Rhodes, *The Making of the Atomic Bomb* (1987); Gar Alperovitz, *Atomic Diplomacy* (1965); Martin Sherwin, *A World Destroyed* (1975); Herbert Feis, *The Atomic Bomb and the End of World War II* (1966); and Robert J. C. Butow, *Japan's Decision to Surrender* (1954). Social developments during World War II are examined in Roger Daniels, *Concentration Camps, USA* (1971); Peter Irons, *Justice at War* (1984); Karen Anderson, *Wartime Women* (1981); Susan Hartmann, *The Home Front and Beyond* (1982); D'Ann Campbell, *Women at War with America* (1985); Ruth Milkman, *Gender at Work* (1987); Sherna Berger Gluck, *Rosie the Riveter Revisited* (1987); Neil A. Wynn, *The Afro-Americans and the Second World War* (1976); Mauricio Mazon, *The Zoot-Suit Riots* (1984); and Clete Daniel, *Chicano Workers and the Politics of Fairness* (1991). Harold G. Vatter surveys wartime economic trends in *The U.S. Economy in World War II* (1986). Holly Cowan Shulman, *The Voice of America* (1990), describes the role of American wartime radio propaganda; for the motion picture industry's contribution, see Clayton R. Koppes and Gregory D. Black, *Hollywood Goes to War* (1987).

The American relationship to the Holocaust can be traced in David Wyman, *The Abandonment of the Jews* (1985); Monty M. Penkower, *The Jews Were Expendable* (1983); and Robert Abzug, *Inside the Vicious Heart* (1985). For a realistic assessment of the brutality of World War II see Paul Fussell, *Wartime* (1989).

Truman and the Cold War

"I am getting ready to go see Stalin and Churchill," President Truman wrote to his mother in July 1945, "and it is a chore." On board the cruiser *Augusta,* the new president continued to complain about the upcoming Potsdam conference in his diary. "How I hate this trip!" he confided. "But I have to make it win, lose or draw and we must win. I am giving nothing away except to save starving people and even then I hope we can only help them to help themselves."

Halfway around the world, Joseph Stalin left Moscow a day late because of a slight heart attack. The Russian leader hated to fly, so he traveled by rail. Moreover, he ordered the heavily guarded train to detour around Poland for fear of an ambush, further delaying his arrival. When he made his entrance into Potsdam, a suburb of Berlin miraculously spared the total destruction that his forces had created in the German capital, he was ready to claim the spoils of war.

These two men, one the veteran revolutionary who had been in power for two decades, the other an untested leader in office for barely three months, symbolized the enormous differences that now separated the wartime allies. Stalin was above all a realist. Brutal in securing total control at home, he was more flexible in his foreign policy, bent on exploiting Russia's victory in World War II rather than aiming at world domination. Cunning and caution were the hallmarks of his diplomatic style. Small in stature, ungainly in build, he radiated a catlike quality as he waited behind his unassuming facade, ready to dazzle an opponent with his "brilliant, terrifying tactical mastery." Truman, in contrast, personified traditional Wilsonian idealism. Lacking Roosevelt's guile, the new president placed his faith in international cooperation. Like many Americans, he believed implicitly in his country's innate goodness. Self-assured to the point of cockiness, he came to Potsdam clothed in the armor of self-righteousness.

Truman and Stalin met for the first time on July 17, 1945. "I told Stalin that I am no diplomat," the president recorded in his diary, "but usually said yes and no to questions after hearing all the argument." The Russian dictator's reaction to Truman remains a mystery, but Truman felt the first encounter went well. "I can deal with Stalin," he wrote. "He is honest—but smart as hell."

Together with Winston Churchill and his replacement, Clement Attlee, whose Labour party had just triumphed in British elections, Truman and Stalin clashed for the next ten days over such difficult issues as reparations, the Polish border, and the fate of eastern Europe. Truman presented the ideas and proposals formulated by his advisers; he saw his task as essentially procedural, and when he presided, he moved the agenda along in brisk fashion. After he had "banged through" three items one day, he commented, "I am not going to stay around this terrible place all summer, just to listen to speeches. I'll go home to the Senate for that." In an indirect, roundabout way, he informed Stalin of the existence of the atomic bomb, tested successfully in the New Mexico desert just before the conference began. Truman offered no details, and the impassive Stalin asked for none, commenting only that he hoped the United States would make "good use of it against the Japanese."

Reparations proved to be the crucial issue at Potsdam. The Russians wanted to rebuild their war-ravaged economy with German industry; the United States feared it would be saddled with the entire cost of caring for the defeated Germans. A compromise was finally reached. Each side would take reparations primarily from its own occupation zone, a solution that foreshadowed the future division of Germany. "Because they could not agree on how to govern Europe," wrote historian Daniel Yergin, "Truman and Stalin began to divide it." The other issues were referred to the newly created Council of Foreign Ministers, which would meet in the fall in London.

The conference thus ended on an apparent note of harmony; beneath the surface, however, the bitter antagonism of the Cold War was festering. America and Russia, each distrustful of the other, were preparing for a long and bitter confrontation. A dozen years later, Truman reminisced to an old associate about Potsdam. "What a show that was!" Describing himself as "an innocent idealist" surrounded by wolves, he claimed that all the agreements reached there were "broken as soon as the unconscionable Russian Dictator returned to Moscow!" He added ruefully, "And I liked the little son of a bitch."

Attlee, Truman, and Stalin in the palace garden at the end of the Potsdam conference in August 1945. The conference revealed the growing divergence among the wartime allies that soon led to the onset of the Cold War.

THE COLD WAR BEGINS

The conflict between the United States and the Soviet Union began gradually. For two years, the nations tried to adjust their differences over the division of Europe, postwar economic aid, and the atomic bomb through discussion and negotiation. The Council of Foreign Ministers provided the forum. Beginning in London during the fall of 1945 and meeting with their Russian counterparts in Paris, New York, and Moscow, American diplomats searched for a way to live in peace with a suspicious Soviet Union.

The Division of Europe

The fundamental disagreement was over who would control postwar Europe. In the east, the Red Army had swept over Poland and the Balkans, laying the basis for Soviet domination there. American and British forces had liberated western Europe from Scandinavia to Italy. The Russians, mindful of past invasions from the west across the plains of Poland, were intent on imposing Communist governments loyal to Moscow in the Soviet sphere. The United States, on the other hand, upheld the principle of national self-determination, insisting the people in each country

should freely choose their postwar rulers. The Soviets saw this demand for free elections as subversive, since they knew that popularly chosen regimes would be unfriendly to Russia. Suspecting American duplicity, Stalin brought down an "Iron Curtain" (Churchill's phrase) from the Baltic to the Adriatic as he created a series of satellite governments.

Germany was the key. The temporary zones of occupation gradually hardened into permanent lines of division. Ignoring the Potsdam Conference agreement that the country be treated as an economic unit, the United States and Great Britain were by 1946 refusing to permit the Russians to take reparations from the industrial western zones. The initial harsh occupation policy gave way to more humane treatment of the German people and a slow but steady economic recovery. The United States and England merged their zones and championed the idea of the unification of all Germany. Russia, fearing a resurgence of German military power, responded by intensifying the communization of its zone, which included the jointly occupied city of Berlin. By 1947, England, France, and the United States were laying plans to transfer their authority to an independent West Germany.

Europe After World War II

The heavy black line splitting Germany shows in graphic form the division of Europe between the Western and Soviet spheres of influence. The two power blocs faced each other across an "iron curtain."

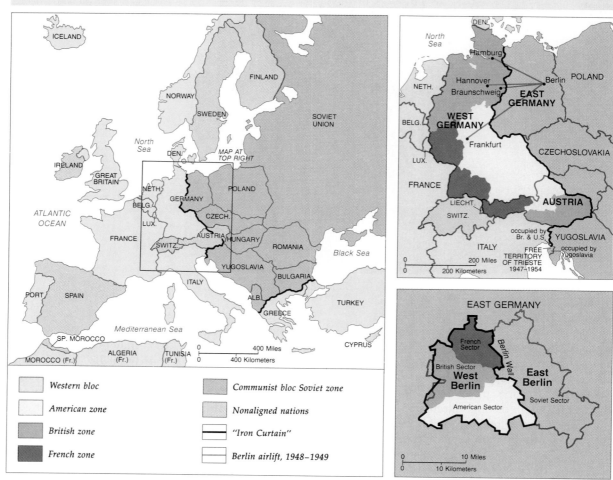

The Soviet Union consolidated its grip on eastern Europe in 1946 and 1947. One by one, communist regimes replaced coalition governments in Poland, Hungary, Rumania, and Bulgaria. Moving cautiously to avoid provoking the West, Stalin used communism as a means to dominate half of Europe, both to protect the security of the Soviet state and to advance its international power. The climax came in March 1948 when a coup in Czechoslovakia overthrew a democratic government and gave the Soviets a strategic foothold in central Europe.

The division of Europe was an inevitable after-effect of World War II. Both sides were intent on imposing their values in the areas liberated by their troops. The Russians were no more likely to withdraw from eastern Europe than the United States and Britain were from Germany, France, and Italy. A frank recognition of competing spheres of influence might have avoided further escalation of tension. But the Western nations, remembering Hitler's aggression in the 1930s, began to see Stalin as an equally dangerous threat to their well-being. Instead of accepting him as a cautious leader bent on protecting Russian security, they perceived him as an aggressive dictator leading a communist drive for world domination.

Withholding Economic Aid

The Second World War had inflicted enormous damage on Russia. The brutal fighting had taken between 15 and 20 million Russian lives, destroyed over 30,000 factories, and torn up 40,000 miles of railroad track. The industrialization that Stalin had achieved at such great sacrifice in the 1930s had been badly set back; even agricultural production had fallen by half during the war. Outside aid and assistance were vital for the reconstruction of the Soviet Union.

American leaders knew of Russia's plight and hoped to use it to good advantage. Wartime ambassador Averell Harriman wrote in 1944 that economic aid was "one of the most effective weapons at our disposal" in dealing with Russia. President Truman was convinced that economically "we held all the cards and the Russians had to come to us."

There were two possible forms of postwar assistance: loans and lend-lease. In January 1945, the Soviets requested a $6 billion loan to finance postwar reconstruction. Despite initial American encouragement, President Roosevelt deferred action on this request; as relations with Russia cooled, the chances for action dimmed. "Our experience," commented Harriman in April 1945, had "incontrovertibly proved it was not possible to bank goodwill in Moscow." By the war's end, the loan request, though never formally turned down, was dead.

Lend-lease proved no more successful. In the spring of 1945, Congress instructed the administration not to use lend-lease for postwar reconstruction. President Truman went further, however, by signing an order on May 11, 1945, terminating all shipments to Russia, including those already at sea. The State Department saw the action as applying "leverage against the Soviet Union"; Stalin termed it "brutal." Heeding Russian protests, Truman resumed lend-lease shipments, but only until the war was over in August. After that, all lend-lease ended.

Deprived of American assistance, the Russians were forced to rebuild their economy through reparations. American and British resistance prevented them from taking reparations in western Germany, but the Soviets systematically removed factories and plants from other areas they controlled, including their zone of Germany, eastern Europe, and Manchuria. Slowly the Russian economy recovered from the war, but the bitterness over the American refusal to extend aid convinced Stalin of Western hostility and thus deepened the growing antagonism between the Soviet Union and the United States.

The Atomic Dilemma

Overshadowing all else was the atomic bomb. Used by the United States with deadly success at Hiroshima and Nagasaki, the new weapon raised problems that would have been difficult for even friendly nations to resolve. Given the uneasy state of Soviet-American relations, the effect was disastrous.

The wartime policy followed by Roosevelt and Churchill ensured a postwar nuclear arms race. Instead of informing their major ally of the developing atomic bomb, they kept it a closely guarded secret. Stalin learned of the Manhattan Project through espionage and responded by starting a Soviet atomic program in 1943. By the time Truman informed Stalin of the weapon's existence at Potsdam, the Russians were well on the way to making their own bomb.

After the war, the United States developed a disarmament plan that would turn control of fissionable material, then the processing plants, and ultimately the American stockpile of bombs over to an international agency. When President Truman appointed financier Bernard Baruch to present this proposal to the United Nations, Baruch insisted on changing it in several important ways, adding sanctions against violators and exempting the international agency from the UN veto. Ignoring scientists who pleaded for a more cooperative position, Baruch followed instead the advice of Army Chief of Staff Dwight D. Eisenhower, who cited the rapid demobilization of American armed forces (from nearly 12 million in 1945 to less than 2 million in 1947) to argue that "we cannot at this time limit our capability to produce or use this weapon." In effect, the Baruch Plan, with its multiple stages and emphasis on inspection, would preserve the American atomic monopoly for the indefinite future.

The Soviets responded predictably. Diplomat Andrei Gromyko presented a simple plan calling for a total ban on the production and use of the new weapon as well as the destruction of all existing bombs. The Russian proposal was founded on the same perception of national self-interest as the Baruch Plan. Though Russia had also demobilized rapidly, it still had nearly three million men under arms in 1947 and wished to use its conventional strength to the utmost by outlawing the atomic bomb.

No agreement was possible. Neither the United States nor the Soviet Union could abandon its position without surrendering a vital national interest. Wanting to preserve its monopoly, America stressed inspection and control; hoping to neutralize the U. S. advantage, Russia advocated immediate disarmament. The nuclear dilemma, inherent in the Soviet-American rivalry, blocked any national settlement. Instead, the two superpowers agreed to disagree. Trusting neither each other nor any form of international cooperation, each concentrated on taking maximum advantage of its wartime gains. Thus the Russians exploited the territory they had conquered in Europe while the United States retained its economic and strategic advantages over the Soviet Union. The result was the Cold War.

CONTAINMENT

A major departure in American foreign policy occurred in January 1947, when General George C. Marshall, the wartime army chief of staff, became secretary of state. Calm, mature, and orderly of mind, Marshall had the capability—honed in World War II—to think in broad strategic terms. An extraordinarily good judge of ability, he relied on gifted subordinates to handle the day-to-day implementation of his policies. In the months after taking office, he came to rely on two men in particular: Dean Acheson and George Kennan.

Acheson, an experienced Washington lawyer and bureaucrat, was appointed undersecretary of state and given free rein by Marshall to conduct American diplomacy. In appearance, he seemed more British than American, with his impeccable Ivy League clothes and bushy mustache. A man of keen intelligence, he had a carefully cultivated reputation for arrogance and a low tolerance for mediocrity. As an ardent anglophile, he wanted to see the United States take over a faltering Britain's role as the supreme arbiter of world affairs. Recalling the lesson of Munich, he opposed appeasement and advocated a policy of negotiating only from strength.

Marshall's other mainstay was George Kennan, who headed the newly created Policy Planning Staff. A career foreign service officer, Kennan had become a Soviet expert, mastering Russian history and culture as well as speaking the language fluently. He served in Moscow after U.S. recognition in 1933 and again during World War II, developing there a profound distrust for the Soviet regime. In a crucial telegram in 1946, he warned that the Kremlin believed "that there can be no compromise with rival power" and advocated a policy of containment, arguing that only strong and sustained resistance could halt the outward flow of Russian power. As self-assured as Acheson, Kennan believed neither Congress nor public opinion should interfere with the conduct of foreign policy by the experts.

In the spring of 1947, a sense of crisis impelled Marshall, Acheson, and Kennan to set out on a new course in American diplomacy. Dubbed "containment," after an article by Kennan in *Foreign Affairs,* the new policy both consolidated the evolving postwar anticommunism and established guidelines that would shape America's role in the world for more than two decades. What Kennan proposed was "a long-term, patient but firm, and vigilant containment of Russian expansive tendencies." Such a policy of halting Soviet aggression would not lead to any immediate victory, Kennan warned. In the long run, however, he felt that the United States could force the Soviet Union to adopt more reasonable policies and live in peace with the United States.

The Truman Doctrine

The initial step toward containment came in response to an urgent British request. Since March 1946, England had been supporting the Greek government in a bitter civil war against communist guerillas. On February 21, 1947, the British informed the United States that they could no longer afford to aid Greece or Turkey, the latter under heavy pressure from the Soviets for access to the Mediterranean. Believing the Russians responsible for the strife in Greece (in fact, they were not), Marshall, Acheson, and Kennan quickly decided the United States would have to assume Britain's role in the eastern Mediterranean.

Worried about congressional support, especially since the Republicans had gained control of Congress in 1946, Marshall called a meeting with the legislative leadership in late February. He outlined the problem, then Acheson took over to describe "a highly possible Soviet breakthrough" that might open three continents to Soviet penetration." Comparing the situation in Greece to one rotten apple spoiling an entire barrel, Acheson warned "the corruption of Greece would infect Iran and all to the east. It would also carry infection to Africa through Asia Minor and Egypt, and to Europe through Italy and France." Claiming the Soviets were "playing one of the greatest gambles in history," Acheson concluded "we and we alone were in a position to break up the play."

The bipartisan group of congressional leaders was deeply impressed. Finally, Republican Senator Arthur M. Vandenberg spoke up, saying he would support the president, but adding that to ensure public backing, Truman would have to "scare hell" out of the American people.

The president followed the senator's advice. On March 12, 1947, he asked Congress for $400 million for military and economic assistance to Greece and Turkey. In stating what would become known as the Truman Doctrine, he made clear that more was involved than just these two countries—the stakes in fact were far higher. "It must be the policy of the United States," Truman told the Congress, "to support free peoples who are resisting attempted subjugation by armed minorities or by outside pressure." After a brief debate, both the House and the Senate approved the program by margins of better than three to one.

The Truman Doctrine marked an informal declaration of cold war against the Soviet Union. Truman used the crisis in Greece to secure congressional approval and build a national consensus for the policy of containment. In less than two years, the civil war in Greece ended, but the American commitment to oppose communist expansion, whether by internal subversion or external aggression, placed the United States on a collision course with the Soviet Union around the globe.

The Marshall Plan

Despite American interest in controlling Soviet expansion into Greece, western Europe was far more vital to U.S. interests than was the eastern Mediterranean. Yet by 1947 many Americans felt that western Europe was open to Soviet penetration. The problem was economic in nature. Despite $9 billion in piecemeal American loans, England, France, Italy, and the other European countries had great difficulty in recovering from World War II. Food was scarce, with millions existing on less than fifteen hundred calories a day; industrial machinery was broken down and obsolete; and workers were demoralized by years of depression and war. The cruel winter of 1947, the worst in fifty years, compounded the problem. Resentment and discontent led to growing communist voting strength, especially in Italy and France. If the United States could not reverse the process, it seemed as though all Europe might drift into the communist orbit.

Critics expressed doubts about the Truman Doctrine, as in this cartoon, but the national mood was shifting toward approval of the containment policy.

In the weeks following proclamation of the Truman Doctrine, American officials dealt with this problem. Secretary of State Marshall, returning from a frustrating Council of Foreign Ministers meeting in Moscow, warned that "the patient is sinking while the doctors deliberate." Acheson believed it was time to extend American "economic power" in Europe both "to call an effective halt to the Soviet Union's expansionism" and "to create a basis for political stability and economic well-being." The experts drew up a plan for the massive infusion of American capital to finance the economic recovery of Europe. Speaking at a Harvard commencement on June 5, 1947, Marshall presented the broad outline. He offered extensive economic aid to all the nations of Europe if they could reach agreement on ways to achieve "the revival of a working economy in the world so as to permit the emergence of political and social conditions in which free institutions can exist."

The fate of the Marshall Plan depended on the reaction of the Soviet Union and the U.S. Congress. Marshall had taken, in the words of one American diplomat, "a hell of a gamble" by including Russia in his offer of aid. At a meeting of the European nations in Paris in July 1947, the Soviet foreign minister ended the suspense by abruptly withdrawing. Neither the Soviet Union nor its satellites would take part, apparently because Moscow saw the Marshall Plan as an American attempt to weaken Soviet control over eastern Europe. The other European countries then made a formal request for $17 billion in assistance over the next four years.

Congress responded cautiously to this proposal, appointing a special joint committee to investigate. The administration lobbied vigorously, pointing out the Marshall Plan would help the United States by stimulating trade with Europe as well as checking Soviet expansion. It was the latter argument, however, that proved decisive. When the Czech coup touched off a war scare in March 1948, Congress quickly approved the Marshall Plan by heavy majorities. Over the next four years, the huge American investment paid rich dividends, generating a broad industrial revival in western Europe that became self-sustaining by the 1950s. The threat of communist domination faded, and a prosperous Europe proved to be a bonanza for American farmers, miners, and manufacturers.

The Western Military Alliance

The third and final phase of containment came in 1949 with the establishment of the North Atlantic Treaty Organization (NATO). NATO grew out of European fears of Russian military aggression. Recalling Hitler's tactics in the 1930s, the people of western Europe wanted assurance that the United States would protect them from attack as they began to achieve economic recovery. American diplomats were sympathetic. "People could not go ahead and make investments for the future," commented Averell Harriman, "without some sense of security."

England, France, and the Low Countries (Belgium, the Netherlands, and Luxembourg) began the process in March 1948 when they signed the Brussels Treaty, providing for collective self-defense. In January 1949, President Truman called for a broader defense pact including the United States; ten European nations, from Norway in the north to Italy in the south, joined the United States and Canada in signing the North Atlantic Treaty in Washington on April 4, 1949. This historic departure from the traditional policy of isolation—the United States had not signed such a treaty since the French alliance in the eighteenth century—caused extensive debate, but the Senate ratified it in July by a vote of 82 to 13.

There were two main features of NATO. First, the United States committed itself to the defense of Europe in the key clause, which stated that "an armed attack against one or more shall be considered an attack against them all." In effect, the United States was extending its atomic shield over Europe. The second feature was designed to reassure worried Europeans that the United States would honor this commitment. In late 1950, President Truman appointed General Dwight D. Eisenhower to the post of NATO supreme commander and authorized the stationing of four American divisions in Europe to serve as the nucleus of the NATO army. The threat of American troop involvement in any Russian assault would deter the Soviet Union from making such an attack.

The Western military alliance escalated the developing Cold War. Whatever its advantage in building a sense of security among worried Europeans, it represented an overreaction to the Soviet danger. Americans and Europeans alike

A Greek Orthodox priest blesses a truck-load of much-needed American flour brought to Athens under the Marshall Plan. The plan was an economic, social, and political success, creating an enormous reservoir of European goodwill toward the United States.

were attempting to apply the lesson of Munich to the Cold War. But Stalin was not Hitler, and the Soviets were not the Nazis. There was no evidence of any Russian plan to invade western Europe, and in the face of the American atomic bomb, none was likely. NATO only intensified Russian fears of the West and thus increased the level of international tension.

The Berlin Blockade

The main Russian response to containment came in 1948 at the West's most vulnerable point. American, British, French, and Soviet troops each occupied a sector of Berlin, but the city was located over 100 miles within the Russian zone of Germany (see the map of postwar Europe on p. 852). Stalin decided to test his opponents' resolve by cutting off all rail and highway traffic to Berlin on June 20, 1948.

The timing was very awkward for Harry Truman. He had his hands full resisting efforts to force him off the Democratic ticket, and he faced a difficult reelection effort against a strong Republican candidate, Governor Thomas E. Dewey of New York. Immersed in election-year politics, Truman was caught unprepared by the Berlin blockade. The alternatives were not very appealing. The United States could withdraw its forces and lose not just a city, but the confidence of all Europe; it could try to send in reinforcements and fight for Berlin; or it could sit tight and attempt to find a diplomatic solution. Truman made the basic decision in characteristic fashion, telling the military that there would be no thought of pulling out. "We were going to stay, period," an aide reported Truman as saying.

In the next few weeks, the president and his advisers developed ways to implement this decision. Rejecting proposals for provoking a showdown by sending an armored column down the main highway, the administration adopted a two-phase policy. The first part was a massive airlift of food, fuel, and supplies for both the 10,000 troops and the 2 million civilians in Berlin. A fleet of fifty-two C-54s and eighty C-47s began making two daily round-trip flights to Berlin, carrying 2,500 tons every twenty-four hours. Then, to guard against Soviet interruption of the airlift, Truman transferred sixty American B-29s, planes capable of delivering atomic bombs, to bases in England. The president was bluffing; the B-29s were not equipped with atomic bombs, but at the time, the threat was effective.

For a few weeks, the world teetered on the edge of war. Stalin did not attempt to disrupt the flights to Berlin, but he rejected all American diplomatic initiatives. Although at any time the Russians could have halted it by jamming radar or shooting down the defenseless cargo planes, the airlift gradually increased to more than 4,000 tons a day. Governor Dewey patriotically supported the president's policy, thus removing foreign policy from the presidential campaign. Yet

Changing Views of the Cold War
The Debate Among Historians

The outbreak of the Cold War between the United States and the Soviet Union was the subject of intense and bitter controversy among American historians. One group blamed the conflict solely on the Soviet Union, claiming the Russians were bent on world domination; opponents argued the United States had provoked the Cold War through attempts to establish a Pax Americana after World War II.

The scholarly debate followed the course of the Cold War itself. When the diplomatic contest between the United States and Russia was at its height in the 1950s, American historians maintained the Cold War was clearly the result of Soviet aggression. This orthodox view was that American actions stemmed from an attempt to absorb the lessons of the 1930s, when the Western democracies

had failed to halt the aggression of Germany and Japan until it was almost too late. Citing Munich and the folly of appeasement, historians asserted that Stalin and the Soviet Union were pursuing the same kind of expansionist policies in Europe that Hitler and Nazi Germany had been guilty of in the 1930s. Some saw the Russians as aiming at dominance in Europe; others believed the Soviets desired world domination. The most influential of these writers, former State Department official Herbert Feis, found the origin of the Cold War in the failure of Franklin D. Roosevelt to prepare the American people for the postwar expansion of the Soviet Union.

According to this orthodox view, the Russians nearly achieved their aggressive plan. Weak American diplomacy enabled Stalin to establish an Iron Curtain over eastern Europe, and by 1947 there was a growing danger of communist penetration into such western European countries as Italy and France. Then in the spring of 1947, American policy suddenly met the challenge. According to Joseph Jones in *The Fifteen Weeks,* the president and the secretary of state reversed American policy at the last minute with the Truman Doctrine and the

Marshall Plan. These two measures, along with NATO in 1949, formed the essence of containment, the American determination to preserve a favorable balance of power in Europe to check the Russian drive for world control.

This highly nationalistic view of how the Cold War began prevailed through the early 1960s. It justified heavy American military expenditures by portraying the United States as the protector of the free world. The belated and defensive American response to Soviet aggression also fit neatly into a familiar pattern. Three times in the twentieth century—in 1917, in 1941, and again in 1947—the United States had reluctantly acted to preserve a decent and civilized world.

In the next decade, however, two developments undermined this complacent explanation. First, the escalation of the Vietnam War in 1965 led to a new mood of doubt and dissent over American foreign policy. As the wisdom of U.S. intervention in Vietnam came into question, historians began to probe the roots of the Cold War to find out why Americans had ended up fighting an unpopular war in Southeast Asia. Second, the State Department archives and the private papers of American diplomats were opened for historical research in the 1960s, providing scholars with a behind-the-scenes view of policy making that often contradicted the accepted version.

The early revisionists, notably Denna F. Fleming and Gar Alperovitz, tended to blame the Cold War on the transfer of power from Roosevelt to Truman and particularly on the decision to drop the atomic bomb. According to this view, Roosevelt tried hard to cooperate with the Soviets, relying on his personal ties with Stalin to ensure postwar cooperation. FDR understood the historic Russian concern over security, which led to an insistence on friendly regimes in eastern Europe. Truman, however, lacking Roosevelt's experience in foreign policy, immediately antagonized the Russians by challenging their control over Poland and the Balkans. According to Alperovitz, Truman even tried to use the atomic bomb to force a Russian retreat in eastern Europe, and his decision to use this dread weapon was based as much on a desire to overwhelm the Soviets as to defeat Japan. Later revisionists gave greater weight to economic factors in accusing the United States of starting the Cold War. Writers such as Gabriel Kolko argued it was an American need to dominate world markets that lay behind the refusal to accept Soviet control of eastern Europe. A capitalist system that needed to expand overseas to overcome its own inherent weaknesses prevented the United States from reaching a territorial settlement with Russia that could have led to a peaceful world. Thus a powerful and

Khrushchev and Eisenhower face each other in the British cartoon entitled "Handshake."

expansionist United States, not an insecure Soviet Union, was responsible for the Cold War.

In the 1970s, as détente mellowed Soviet-American relations, a more balanced view of the origins of the diplomatic conflict emerged. Writers like John Lewis Gaddis and Daniel Yergin, who became known as postrevisionists, began to treat the Cold War as a historical event that transcended simple accusations of national guilt. Rather than challenging the revisionists completely, they tried to incorporate their views into a broader explanation that stressed the inevitability of the Cold War.

The postrevisionists based their explanation on the confusion and misunderstanding prevalent at the end of the World War II. The United States, misled by the experience with Hitler in the 1930s, mistook Stalin's attempt to bolster Russian security in eastern Europe for a design for world conquest. When Truman responded with contain-

ment, which was essentially an effort to preserve the balance of power in postwar Europe, the Russians thought America and its allies were bent on encircling and eventually destroying the Soviet Union. A vicious cycle then began, with each nation perceiving every step taken by the other as a threat to its existence. Neither the United States nor the Soviet Union alone was guilty of beginning the Cold War; both must share responsibility for this tragedy.

The postrevisionist explanation is very close to an early explanation for the Cold War advanced by historian William H. McNeill. Writing in 1950, McNeill pointed out that throughout history, victorious coalitions had split apart as soon as the common enemy was overcome. The defeat of the Axis had created a vacuum of power in which the United States and the Soviet Union were bound to clash to determine who would control the future of Europe.

Yet even this view does not explain why the competition between the two nations became so intense. Other wartime alliances dissolved without creating such a fierce rivalry. Here is where the atomic bomb played a key role. The existence of a new weapon of vast destructive power added an unknown element to the international arena, one beyond all previous experience. The very survival of the two antagonists became a genuine matter of concern in the nuclear age. Thus Hiroshima not only ended the Second World War; it also created the unstable diplomatic climate that gave rise to the Cold War.

The Berlin airlift of 1948–1949 broke the Soviet blockade. Called "Operation Vittles," it provided food and fuel for West Berliners. Here children wait for the candy that American pilots dropped in tiny handkerchief parachutes.

for Truman, the tension was fierce. In early September, he asked his advisers to brief him "on bases, bombs, Moscow, Leningrad, etc." "I have a terrible feeling afterward that we are very close to war," he confided in his diary. "I hope not."

Slowly the tension eased. The Russians did not shoot down any planes, and the daily airlift climbed to nearly 7,000 tons. Truman, a decided underdog, won a surprising second term in November over a complacent Dewey (see p. 866), in part because the Berlin crisis had rallied the nation behind his leadership. In early 1949, the Soviets gave in, ending the blockade in return for another meeting of the Council of Foreign Ministers on Germany—a conclave that proved as unproductive as all the earlier ones.

The Berlin crisis marked the end of the initial phase of the Cold War. The airlift had given the United States a striking political victory, showing the world the triumph of American ingenuity over Russian stubbornness. Yet it could not disguise the fact that the Cold War had cut Europe in two. Behind the Iron Curtain, the Russians had consolidated control over the areas won by their troops in the war, while the United States had used the Marshall Plan to revitalize western

Europe. But a divided continent was a far cry from the wartime hopes for a peaceful world. And the rivalry that began in Europe would soon spread into a worldwide contest between the superpowers.

THE COLD WAR EXPANDS

The rivalry between the United States and the Soviet Union grew in the late 1940s and early 1950s. Both sides ended the postwar demobilization and began to rebuild their military forces with new methods and new weapons. Equally significant, the diplomatic competition spread from Europe to Asia as each of the superpowers sought to enhance its influence in the Orient. By the time Truman left office in early 1953, the Cold War had taken on global proportions.

The Military Dimension

After World War II, American leaders were intent on reforming the nation's military system in light of their wartime experience. Two goals were uppermost. First, nearly everyone agreed in the aftermath of Pearl Harbor that the U.S. armed services should be unified into an integrated military system. The developing Cold War reinforced this decision. Without unification, declared George Marshall in 1945, "there can be little hope that we will be able to maintain through the years a military posture that will secure for us a lasting peace." Equally important, planners realized, was the need for new institutions to coordinate military and diplomatic strategy so the nation could cope effectively with threats to its security.

In 1947, Congress responded by passing the National Security Act. It established a Department of Defense, headed by a civilian secretary of cabinet rank presiding over three separate services—the army, the navy, and the new air force. In addition, the act created the Central Intelligence Agency (CIA) to coordinate the intelligence-gathering activities of various government agencies. Finally, the act provided for a National Security Council (NSC)—composed of the service secretaries, the secretary of defense, and the secretary of state—to advise the president on all matters regarding the nation's security.

Despite the appearance of equality among the services, the air force quickly emerged as the dominant power in the atomic age, based on its capability both to deter an enemy from attacking and to wage war if deterrence failed. President Truman, intent on cutting back defense expenditures, favored the air force in his 1949 military budget, allotting this branch over one-half the total sum. After the Czech coup and the resulting war scare, Congress granted an additional $3 billion to the military. The appropriation included funds for a new B-36 to replace the B-29 as the nation's primary strategic bomber.

American military planners received even greater support in the fall of 1949 when the Soviet Union exploded its first atomic bomb. President Truman appointed a high-level committee to explore mounting an all-out effort to build a hydrogen bomb to maintain American nuclear supremacy.

Some scientists had technical objections to the H-bomb, which was still far from being perfected, while others opposed the new weapon on moral grounds, claiming its enormous destructive power (intended to be one thousand times greater than the atomic bomb) made it unthinkable. George Kennan suggested a new effort at international arms control with the Soviets, but Dean Acheson—who succeeded Marshall as secretary of state in early 1949—felt it was imperative that the United States develop the hydrogen bomb before the Soviet Union. When Acheson presented the committee's favorable report to the president in January 1950, Truman took only seven minutes to decide to go ahead with the awesome new weapon.

At the same time, Acheson ordered the Policy Planning Staff (now headed by Paul Nitze after Kennan resigned in protest) to draw up a new statement of national defense policy. NSC-68, as the document eventually became known, was based on the premise that the Soviet Union sought "to impose its absolute authority over the rest of the world" and thus "mortally challenged" the United States. Rejecting such options as appeasement or a return to isolation, Nitze advocated a massive expansion of American military power so the United States could halt and overcome the Soviet threat. Contending the nation could afford to spend "upward of 50 percent of its gross national product" for security, NSC-68 proposed increasing defense spending from $13 to $45 billion annually. Approved in principle by the National Security Council in April 1950, NSC-68 stood as a symbol of the Truman administration's determination to win the Cold War regardless of cost.

The Cold War in Asia

The Soviet-American conflict developed more slowly in Asia. At Yalta, the two superpowers had agreed to a Far Eastern balance of power, with the Russians dominating Northeast Asia and the Americans in control of the Pacific, including both Japan and its former island empire.

The United States moved quickly to consolidate its sphere of influence. General Douglas MacArthur, in charge of Japanese occupation, denied the Soviet Union any role in the reconstruction of Japan. Instead, he supervised the transition of the Japanese government into a constitutional democracy, shaped along Western lines, in which communists were barred from all government posts. The Japanese willingly renounced war in their new constitution, relying instead on American forces to protect their security. American policy was equally nationalistic in the Pacific. A trusteeship arrangement with the United Nations merely disguised the fact that the United States held full control over the Marshall, Mariana, and Caroline islands. American scientists conducted atomic bomb tests at Bikini atoll in 1946, and by 1949, MacArthur was declaring that the entire Pacific "had become an Anglo-Saxon lake and our line of defense runs through the chain of islands fringing the coast of Asia."

As defined at Yalta, China lay between the Soviet and American spheres. When World War II ended, the country was torn between Chiang Kai-shek's Nationalists in the South and Mao Tse-tung's Communists in the North. Chiang had many advantages, including American political and economic backing and official Soviet recognition. But corruption was widespread among the Nationalist leaders, and a raging inflation that soon reached 100 percent a year devastated the Chinese middle classes and thus eroded Chiang's base of power. Mao used tight discipline and patriotic appeals to strengthen his hold on the peasantry and extend his influence. When the Soviets abruptly vacated Manchuria in 1946, after stripping it of virtually all the industrial machinery Japan had installed, Mao inherited control of this rich northern province. Ignoring American advice, Chiang rushed north to occupy Manchurian cities, overextending his supply lines and exposing his forces to Communist counterattack.

American policy sought to prevent a Chinese civil war. Before he became secretary of state, George Marshall undertook the difficult task of forming a coalition government between Chiang and Mao. For a few months in early 1946, Marshall appeared to have succeeded, but Chiang's attempts to gain control of Manchuria doomed the agreement. In reality, there was no basis for compromise. Chiang insisted he "was going to liquidate Communists," while Mao was trying to play the United States against Russia in his bid for power. By 1947, as China plunged into full-scale civil war, the Truman administration had given up any meaningful effort to influence the outcome. Political mediation had failed, military intervention was out of the question so soon after World War II, and a policy of contin-

ued American economic aid served only to appease domestic supporters of Chiang Kai-shek; 80 percent of the military supplies ended up in Communist hands.

The Chinese conflict climaxed at the end of the decade. Mao's forces drove the Nationalists out of Manchuria in late 1948 and advanced across the Yangtze by mid-1949. Acheson released a lengthy White Paper justifying American policy in China on the grounds that the civil war there "was beyond the control of the government of the United States." An American military adviser concurred, telling Congress that the Nationalist defeat was due to "the world's worst leadership" and "a complete loss of will to fight." Republican senators, however, disagreed, blaming American diplomats for sabotaging the Nationalists and terming the White Paper "a 1054-page whitewash of a wishful, do-nothing policy." While the domestic debate raged over responsibility for the loss of China, Chiang's forces fled the mainland for sanctuary on Formosa Taiwan in December 1949. Two months later, Mao and Stalin signed a

During World War II, Mao Tse-tung (center), leader of the Communist forces in China, fought the Japanese, sometimes alongside American GIs. Later, Mao triumphed over the Nationalists and created a Marxist China.

Sino-Soviet treaty of mutual assistance that clearly placed China in the Russian orbit.

The American response to the Communist triumph in China was twofold. First, the State Department refused to recognize the legitimacy of the new regime in Peking, maintaining instead formal diplomatic relations with the Nationalists on Formosa. Citing the Sino-Soviet alliance, Assistant Secretary of State Dean Rusk called the Peking regime "a colonial Russian government" and declared, "It is not the Government of China. It does not pass the first test. It is not Chinese." Then, to compensate for the loss of China, the United States focused on Japan as its main ally in Asia. The State Department encouraged the buildup of Japanese industry, and the Pentagon expanded American bases on the Japanese home islands and Okinawa. A Japanese-American security pact led to the end of American occupation by 1952. The Cold War had now split Asia in two.

The Korean War

The showdown between the United States and the Soviet Union in Asia came in Korea. Traditionally the cockpit of international rivalry in Northeast Asia, Korea had been divided at the thirty-eighth parallel in 1945. The Russians occupied the industrial North, installing a communist government under the leadership of Kim Il-Sung. In the agrarian South, Syngman Rhee, a conservative nationalist, emerged as the American-sponsored ruler. Neither regime heeded a UN call for elections to unify the country. The two superpowers pulled out most of their occupation forces by 1949. The Russians, however, helped train a well-equipped army in the North, while the United States—fearful Rhee would seek unification through armed conquest—gave much more limited military assistance to South Korea.

On June 25, 1950, the North Korean army suddenly crossed the 38th parallel in great strength. The Soviet role in this act of aggression is shrouded in mystery. Presumably Stalin ordered the attack in an attempt to expand the Soviet sphere in Asia and to counter the American buildup of Japan. Yet there is also evidence to suggest Kim Il-Sung acted on his own, confident the Russians would have no choice but to back his move.

There was nothing ambiguous about the American response. President Truman saw the invasion as a clear-cut case of Soviet aggression reminiscent of the 1930s. "Communism was acting in Korea just as Hitler, Mussolini, and the Japanese had acted ten, fifteen, and twenty years earlier," he commented in his memoirs. Following the advice of Acheson, the president convened the UN Security Council and, taking advantage of a temporary Soviet boycott, secured a resolution condemning North Korea as an aggressor and calling on the member nations to engage in a collective security action. Within a few days, American troops from Japan were in combat in South Korea. The conflict, which would last for more than three years, was technically a police action fought under UN auspices; in reality, the United States was at war with a Soviet satellite in Asia.

In the beginning, the fighting went badly as the North Koreans continued to drive down the peninsula. But by August, American forces had halted the communist advance near Pusan. In September, General MacArthur changed the whole complexion of the war by carrying out a brilliant amphibious assault at Inchon, on the waist of Korea, cutting off and destroying most of the North Korean army in the South. Encouraged by this victory, Truman began to shift from his original goal of restoring the 38th parallel, to a new one: the unification of Korea by military force.

The administration ignored warnings from Peking against an American invasion of North Korea; "I should think it would be sheer madness for the Chinese to intervene," commented Dean Acheson. MacArthur was even more confident. "We are no longer fearful of their intervention," he told Truman at a Wake Island conference in mid-October. Noting that the Chinese had no air force, the general prophesied that if they crossed the Yalu River into Korea, "there would be the greatest slaughter."

Rarely has an American president received worse advice than Truman did from Acheson and MacArthur. The UN forces crossed the 38th parallel in October, advanced confidently to the Yalu in November, and then were completely routed by a massive Chinese counterattack that drove them out of all North Korea by December. MacArthur finally stabilized the fighting near the 38th parallel, but when Truman decided to give up his attempt to unify Korea, the general

The Korean War, 1950–1953

After a year of rapid movement up and down the Korean peninsula, the fighting stalled just north of the 38th parallel. The resulting truce line has divided North and South Korea ever since the July 1953 armistice.

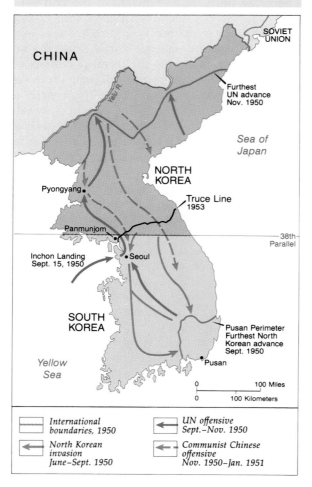

CHINA

SOVIET UNION

Yalu R.

Furthest UN advance Nov. 1950

Sea of Japan

NORTH KOREA

Pyongyang

Truce Line 1953

Panmunjom

38th Parallel

Inchon Landing Sept. 15, 1950

Seoul

SOUTH KOREA

Yellow Sea

Pusan Perimeter Furthest North Korean advance Sept. 1950

Pusan

| | 0 | 100 Miles |
| | 0 | 100 Kilometers |

International boundaries, 1950		UN offensive Sept.–Nov. 1950
North Korean invasion June–Sept. 1950		Communist Chinese offensive Nov. 1950–Jan. 1951

Soviet attack. General Omar Bradley, Truman's chief military adviser, succinctly pointed out that a "showdown" with communism in Asia would be "the wrong war, at the wrong place, at the wrong time, and with the wrong enemy."

Congress and the American people came to accept MacArthur's recall. The Korean War settled into a stalemate near the 38th parallel as truce talks with the communists bogged down for the rest of Truman's term in office. The president could take heart from the fact that he had achieved his primary goal, defense of South Korea and the principle of collective security. Yet by taking the gamble to unify Korea by force, he had confused the American people and humiliated the United States in the eyes of the world.

In the last analysis, the most significant result of the Korean conflict was the massive American rearmament it brought about. The war led to the implementation of NSC-68—the army expanded to 3.5 million troops, the defense budget increased to $50 billion a year by 1952, and the United States acquired distant military bases from Saudi Arabia to Morocco. America was now committed to waging a global contest against the Soviet Union with arms as well as words.

After being relieved of his command by President Truman, General Douglas MacArthur was hailed as a hero on his return to the United States in 1951. Here, he waves to an enthusiastic crowd in San Francisco.

protested to Congress, calling for a renewed offensive and proclaiming, "There is no substitute for victory."

Truman courageously relieved the popular hero of the Pacific of his command on April 11, 1951. At first, MacArthur seemed likely to force the president to back down. Huge crowds came forward to welcome him home and hear him call for victory over the communists in Asia. At a special congressional hearing, the administration struck back effectively by warning that MacArthur's strategy would expose all Europe to

THE COLD WAR AT HOME

The Cold War cast a long shadow over American life in the late 1940s and early 1950s. Harry Truman tried to carry on the New Deal reform tradition he had inherited from FDR, but the American people were more concerned about events abroad. The Republican party used growing dissatisfaction with both postwar economic adjustment and fears of communist penetration of the United States to revive its sagging fortunes and regain control of the White House in 1952 for the first time in twenty years.

Truman's Troubles

Matching his foreign policy successes with equal achievements at home was not easy for Harry S. Truman. As a loyal supporter of Franklin D. Roosevelt's New Deal programs during his Senate career, Truman had earned a reputation for being a hard-working, reliable, and intensely partisan legislator. But he was relatively unknown to the general public and his background as a Missouri county official associated with Kansas City machine politics did little to inspire confidence in his ability to lead the nation. Surprisingly well read—especially in history and biography—

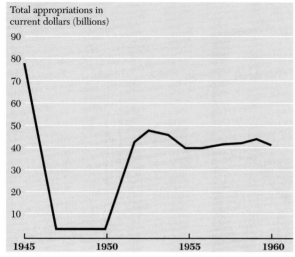

National Defense Outlays, 1945–1960

Total appropriations in current dollars (billions)

Source: *Compiled from U.S. Bureau of the Census,* Historical Statistics of the United States, Colonial Times to 1970, *Bicentennial Edition, Washington, D.C., 1975.*

Truman possessed sound judgment, the ability to reach decisions quickly, and a fierce and uncompromising sense of right and wrong.

Two weaknesses marred his performance in the White House. One was a fondness for old friends, which resulted in the appointment of many Missouri and Senate cronies to high office. Men like Attorney General Tom Clark, Secretary of the Treasury Charles Snyder, and White House military aide Harry Vaughn brought little credit to the Truman administration, while the loss of such effective public servants as Secretary of the Interior Harold Ickes and Labor Secretary Frances Perkins hurt it. The president's other serious limitation was his lack of political vision. Failing to pursue a coherent legislative program of his own, he tried to perpetuate FDR's New Deal, and as a result, engaged in a running battle with Congress.

The postwar mood was not conducive to an extension of New Deal reforms. Americans were weary of shortages and sacrifices; they wanted the chance to buy the consumer goods denied them under wartime conditions. But in the rush to convert industry from producing planes and tanks to cars and appliances, problems soon emerged. Prices and wages rose quickly as Congress voted to end wartime controls. With prices going up 25 percent in two years, workers demanded higher wages to offset the loss of overtime pay. A wave of labor unrest swept over the country in the spring of 1946, culminating in two critical strikes: a walkout by coal miners that threatened to close down much of American industry and a paralyzing strike by railroad workers.

President Truman was caught in the middle. Sensitive to union demands, he permitted businessmen to negotiate large pay increases for their workers and then pass on the cost to consumers in the form of higher prices. He criticized Congress for weakening wartime price controls, but he failed to offer anything else to curb inflation. Housewives blamed him for the rising price of food, while organized labor condemned Truman as the country's "No. 1 Strikebreaker" when he asked Congress for power to draft striking railway workers into the army.

In the face of this rising discontent, Truman's efforts to extend the New Deal met with little success. Congress ignored his September 1945 call for a series of measures to ensure economic security and enacted only the Employment Act of 1946. While this measure created the Council of Economic Advisers to assist the president and asserted the principle that the government was responsible for the state of the economy, it failed to include Truman's original goal of mandatory federal planning to achieve full employment.

The Republicans took advantage of growing public dissatisfaction with postwar economic woes to attack the Democrats. "To err is Truman," the GOP proclaimed, and then adopted a very effective two-word slogan for the 1946 congressional elections, "Had enough?" The American people, weary of inflation and labor unrest, responded by electing Republican majorities in both the House and Senate for the first time since 1930.

Truman Vindicated

The president's relations with Congress became even stormier after the GOP victory in the 1946 election. Truman successfully vetoed two GOP measures to give large tax cuts to the wealthy, but Congress overrode his veto of the Taft-Hartley Act in 1947. Designed to correct the imbalance in labor-management relations created by the Wagner Act, the Taft-Hartley Act outlawed specific unfair labor union activities—including the closed shop and secondary boycotts—and it permitted the president to invoke an

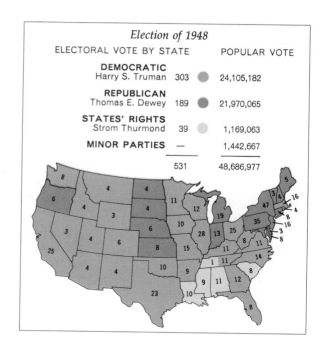

Election of 1948

ELECTORAL VOTE BY STATE		POPULAR VOTE
DEMOCRATIC Harry S. Truman	303	24,105,182
REPUBLICAN Thomas E. Dewey	189	21,970,065
STATES' RIGHTS Strom Thurmond	39	1,169,063
MINOR PARTIES	—	1,442,667
	531	48,686,977

eighty-day cooling-off period to delay strikes that might endanger national health or safety. Despite Truman's claim that it was a "slave-labor" bill, unions were able to survive its provisions.

President Truman's political fortunes reached their lowest ebb in early 1948. Former vice president Henry A. Wallace, claiming to represent the New Deal, announced his third-party (Progressive) candidacy in the presidential contest that year. Worried Democratic party leaders

A jubilant Harry Truman, on the morning after his 1948 election win, displays the headline blazoned on the front page of the Chicago Tribune—*a newspaper that believed the pollsters.*

sought to persuade Truman to step aside and allow General Dwight D. Eisenhower to become the Democratic candidate. When Eisenhower turned down bids from both parties, the Democrats reluctantly nominated Truman. His prospects for victory in the fall, however, looked very dim—especially after disgruntled Southerners bolted the Democratic party in protest over a progressive civil rights platform. The Dixiecrats, as they became known, nominated Strom Thurmond, the governor of South Carolina, on a States' Rights party ticket.

The defection of the Dixiecrats in the South and Wallace's liberal followers in the North led political experts to predict an almost certain Republican victory. Governor Thomas E. Dewey of New York, the GOP candidate, was so certain of winning that he waged a cautious and bland campaign designed to give him a free hand once he was in the White House. With nothing to lose, Truman barnstormed around the country denouncing the "do-nothing" Republican Eightieth Congress. The president's "give-'em hell" tactics reminded voters of how much they owed the Democrats for helping them survive the Depression. To the amazement of the pollsters, Truman won a narrow but decisive victory in November. The old Roosevelt coalition—farmers, organized labor, urban ethnic groups, and blacks—had held together, enabling Truman to remain in the White House and the Democrats to regain control of Congress.

There was one more reason for Truman's win in 1948. During this election, held at the height of the Berlin crisis, the GOP failed to challenge Truman's conduct of the Cold War. Locked in a tense rivalry with the Soviet Union, the American people saw no reason to reject a president who had countered aggression overseas with the Truman Doctrine and the Marshall Plan. The Republicans, committed to support the bipartisan policy of containment, had allowed the Democrats to preempt the foreign policy issue. Until they found a way to challenge Truman's Cold War policies, GOP leaders had little chance to regain the White House.

The Loyalty Issue

Despite Truman's surprising victory in 1948, there was one area on which the Democrats were vulnerable. The fear of communism abroad that

The conviction of Alger Hiss convinced many Americans that internal subversion threatened the nation's survival.

Three days before Julius and Ethel Rosenberg were executed for treason, their two young sons, ten and six years old, marched to the White House to plead executive clemency for their parents.

had led to the bipartisan containment policy could be used against them at home by politicians who were more willing to exploit the public's deep-seated anxiety.

Fear of radicalism had been a recurrent feature of American life since the early days of the republic. Federalists had tried to suppress dissent with the Alien and Sedition Acts in the 1790s; the Know-Nothings had campaigned against foreigners and Catholics in the 1850s, and the Red Scare after World War I had been directed against both aliens and radicals. The Cold War heightened the traditional belief that subversion from abroad endangered the republic. Bold rhetoric from members of the Truman administration, portraying the men in the Kremlin as inspired revolutionaries bent on world conquest, frightened the American people. They viewed the Soviet Union as a successor to Nazi Germany—a totalitarian police state that threatened the basic liberties of a free people.

A series of revelations of communist espionage activities reinforced these fears. Canadian officials uncovered a Soviet spy ring in 1946, and the House Un-American Activities Committee held hearings indicating that communist agents had flourished in the Agriculture and Treasury departments in the 1930s.

The most famous disclosure came in August 1948, however, when Whittaker Chambers, a repentant communist, accused Alger Hiss of having been a Soviet spy in the 1930s. When Hiss, who had been a prominent State Department official, denied the charges, Chambers led investigators to a hollowed-out pumpkin on his Maryland farm. Inside the pumpkin were microfilms of confidential government documents. Chambers claimed that Hiss had passed these State Department materials to him in the late 1930s. Although the statute of limitations prevented a charge of treason against Hiss, he was convicted of perjury in January 1950 and sentenced to a five-year prison term.

Although Truman tried to dismiss the loyalty issue as a "red herring," he felt compelled to take protective measures, thus lending substance to the charges of subversion. In March 1947, he had initiated a loyalty program, ordering security checks of government employees in order to root out communists. Originally intended to remove subversives for whom "reasonable grounds exist for belief that the person involved is disloyal," within four years the Loyalty Review Board was dismissing workers as security risks if there was "reasonable doubt" of their loyalty. Thousands of government workers lost their jobs, charged with guilt by association with radicals or with membership in left-wing organizations. Often those who were charged had no chance to face their accusers.

In 1948, the Justice Department further heightened fears of subversion. It charged eleven officials of the Communist party with advocating the violent overthrow of the government. After a long trial, the jury found them guilty, and the party officials received prison sentences and heavy fines; in 1951, the Supreme Court upheld these convictions as constitutional.

Such repressive measures failed, however, to reassure the nation. Events abroad intensified the sense of danger. The Communist triumph in China in the fall of 1949 came as a shock; soon there were charges that "fellow travelers" in the State Department were responsible for "the loss of China." In September 1949, when the Truman administration announced that the Russians had detonated their first atomic bomb, the ending of America's nuclear monopoly was blamed on Soviet espionage. In early 1950, Klaus Fuchs—a British scientist who had worked on the wartime Manhattan Project—admitted giving the Russians vital information about the A-bomb.

A few months later, the government charged American communists Ethel and Julius Rosenberg with conspiracy to transmit atomic secrets to the Soviet Union. In 1951, a jury found the Rosenbergs guilty of treason, and Judge Irving Kaufman sentenced them to die for what he termed their "loathsome offense." Despite their insistent claims of innocence and worldwide appeals on their behalf, the Rosenbergs were electrocuted on June 19, 1953. Thus by the early 1950s, nearly all the ingredients were at hand for a new outburst of hysteria—fear of Russia, evidence of espionage, and a belief in a vast unseen conspiracy. The only element missing was a leader to release this new outburst of intolerance.

McCarthyism in Action

On February 12, 1950, Senator Joseph R. McCarthy of Wisconsin delivered a routine

Lincoln's Birthday speech in Wheeling, West Virginia. This little known Republican suddenly attracted national attention when he declared, "I have here in my hand a list of 205—a list of names that were made known to the secretary of state as being members of the communist party and who nevertheless are still working and shaping policy in the State Department." The charge that there were communists in the State Department—repeated on different occasions with the number changed to fifty-seven, then eighty-one —was never substantiated. But McCarthy's Wheeling speech triggered a four-and-a-half-year crusade to hunt down alleged communists in government. The stridency and sensationalism of the senator's accusations soon won the name "McCarthyism."

McCarthy's basic technique was the multiple untruth. He leveled a bevy of charges of treasonable activities in government. While officials were refuting his initial accusations, he brought forth a steady stream of new ones, so the corrections never caught up with the latest blast. He failed to unearth a single confirmed communist in government, but he kept the Truman administration in turmoil. Drawing on an army of informers, primarily disgruntled federal workers with grievances against their colleagues and superiors, he charged government agencies with harboring and protecting communist agents, and he accused the State Department of deliberately losing the Cold War. His briefcase bulged with documents, but he did very little actual research, relying instead on reports (often outdated) from earlier congressional investigations. He exploited the press with great skill, combining current accusations with promises of future disclosures to guarantee headlines.

The secret of McCarthy's power was the fear he engendered among his Senate colleagues. In 1950, Maryland Senator Millard Tydings, who headed a committee critical of McCarthy's activities, failed to win reelection when McCarthy opposed him; after that, other senators ran scared. McCarthy delighted in making sweeping, startling charges of communist sympathies against prominent public figures. A favorite target was patrician Secretary of State Dean Acheson, whom McCarthy ridiculed as the "Red Dean," with his "cane, spats and tea-sipping little finger"; he even went after General George Marshall, claiming the wartime army chief of staff was an agent of the communist conspiracy. Nor were follow Republicans immune. One GOP senator was described as "a living miracle in that he is without question the only man who has lived so long with neither brains nor guts."

These attacks on the wealthy, famous, and privileged won McCarthy a devoted national following, though at the height of his influence in early 1954 he gained the approval of only 50 percent of the respondents in a Gallup poll. McCarthy drew a disproportionate backing from working-class Catholics and ethnic groups, especially the Irish, Poles, and Italians, who normally voted Democratic. He offered a simple solution

The Election of 1952			
Candidate	Party	Popular Vote	Electoral Vote
Eisenhower	Republican	33,936,137	442
Stevenson	Democrat	27,314,649	89

Eisenhower's landslide victories in the presidential elections of 1952 and 1956 seemed to prove his slogan that Americans did, indeed, "like Ike."

to the complicated Cold War: defeat the enemy at home rather than continue to engage in costly foreign aid programs and entangling alliances abroad. Above all, McCarthy appealed to conservative Republicans in the Midwest who shared his right-wing views and felt cheated by Truman's upset victory in 1948. Even GOP leaders who viewed McCarthy's tactics with distaste, such as Robert A. Taft of Ohio, quietly encouraged him to attack the vulnerable Democrats.

The Republicans in Power

In 1952, the GOP capitalized on a growing sense of national frustration to capture the presidency. The stalemate in Korea and the second Red Scare created a desire for political change; revelations of scandals by several individuals close to Truman intensified the feeling that someone

needed to clean up "the mess in Washington." In Dwight D. Eisenhower, the Republican party found the perfect candidate to explore what one senator called K_1C_2—Korea, communism, and corruption.

Immensely popular because of his amiable manner, winning smile, and heroic stature, Eisenhower alone appeared to have the ability to unite a divided nation. In the 1952 campaign, Ike displayed hidden gifts as a politician in running against Adlai Stevenson, the eloquent Illinois governor whose appeal was limited to die-hard Democrats and liberal intellectuals. Eisenhower allowed his young running mate, Senator Richard M. Nixon of California, to hammer away at the Democrats on the communist and corruption issues, but he himself delivered the most telling blow of all on the Korean War. Speaking in Detroit in late October, just after the fighting had intensified again in Korea, Ike promised if elected he would go personally to the battlefield in an attempt "to bring the Korean War to an early and honorable end."

"That does it—Ike is in," several reporters exclaimed after they heard this pledge. The hero of World War II had clinched his election by committing himself to end an unpopular war. Ten days later, he won the presidency handily, carrying thirty-nine states, including four in the formerly solid Democratic South. The Republican party, however, did not fare as well in Congress; it gained just a slight edge in the House and controlled the Senate by only one seat.

Once elected, Eisenhower moved quickly to fulfill his campaign pledge. He spent three days in early December touring the battlefront in Korea, quickly ruling out the new offensive the military favored. "Small attacks on small hills," he later wrote, "would not end the war." Instead he

McCarthy's relentless barrage of accusations went on for four years, but when he began to attack the upper echelon of the U.S. Army, McCarthy (left) was finally brought down. Millions of Americans tuned in to watch the televised hearings as army counsel Joseph Welch (right) destroyed the credibility of McCarthy's panel of informers.

turned to diplomacy, relying on subtle hints to China on the possible use of nuclear weapons to break the stalemated peace talks. These tactics, together with the death of Joseph Stalin in early March, finally led to the signing of an armistice on July 27, 1953, which ended the fighting but left Korea divided—as it had been before the war—near the 38th parallel.

The new president was less effective in dealing with the problem raised by Senator Joseph McCarthy's continuing witchhunt. Instead of toning down his anticommunist crusade after the Republican victory in 1952, McCarthy used his new position as chairman of the Senate Committee on Government Operations as a base for ferreting out communists on the federal payroll. He made a series of charges against the foreign affairs agencies and demanded that certain books be purged from American information libraries overseas. Eisenhower's advisers urged the president to use his own great prestige to stop McCarthy. But Ike refused such a confrontation, saying, "I will not get into a pissing contest with a skunk." Eisenhower preferred to play for time, hoping the American people would eventually come to their senses.

The Wisconsin senator finally overreached himself. In early 1954, he uncovered an army dentist suspected of disloyalty and proceeded to attack the upper echelons of the U.S. Army, telling one much decorated general that he was "not fit to wear the uniform." The controversy culminated in the televised Army-McCarthy hearings. For six weeks, the senator revealed his crude, bullying behavior to the American people. Viewers were repelled by his frequent outbursts that began with the insistent cry, "Point of order, Mr. Chairman, point of order," and by his attempt to slur the reputation of a young lawyer associated with army counsel Joseph Welch. This last maneuver led Welch to condemn McCarthy for his "reckless cruelty" and ask rhetorically, as millions watched on television, "Have you no sense of decency, sir?"

Courageous Republicans, led by Senators George Aiken of Vermont and Margaret Chase Smith of Maine, joined with Democrats to bring about the Senate's censure of McCarthy in December 1954, by a vote of 67 to 22. Once rebuked, McCarthy fell quickly from prominence. He died three years later virtually unnoticed and unmourned.

Yet his influence was profound. Not only did he paralyze national life with what a Senate subcommittee described as "the most nefarious campaign of half-truth and untruth in the history of the Republic," but he also helped impose a political and cultural conformity that froze dissent for the rest of the 1950s. Long after McCarthy's passing, the nation tolerated loyalty oaths for teachers, the banning of left-wing books in public libraries, and the blacklisting of entertainers in radio, television and films. Freedom of expression was inhibited, and the opportunity to try out new

CHRONOLOGY

1945 Truman meets Stalin at Potsdam conference (July) • World War II ends with Japanese surrender (August)

1946 Winston Churchill gives "Iron Curtain" speech

1947 Truman Doctrine announced to Congress (March) • George Marshall outlines Marshall Plan (June) • Truman orders loyalty program for government employees (March)

1948 Soviets begin blockade of Berlin (June) • Truman scores upset victory in presidential election

1949 NATO treaty signed in Washington (April) • Soviet Union tests its first atomic bomb (August)

1950 Truman authorizes building of hydrogen bomb (January) • Senator Joseph McCarthy claims communists in government (February) • North Korea invades South Korea (June)

1951 Truman recalls MacArthur from Korea

1952 Dwight D. Eisenhower elected president

1953 Julius and Ethel Rosenberg executed for atomic-secrets spying (June) • Korean War truce signed at Panmunjom (July)

ideas and approaches was lost as the United States settled into a sterile Cold War consensus.

While Dwight Eisenhower could claim his policy of giving McCarthy enough rope to hang himself had worked, it is possible a bolder and more forthright presidential attack on the senator might have spared the nation some of the excesses of the second Red Scare.

By the early 1950s, the Cold War had become an enduring reality of American life. The initial disagreements between the United States and the Soviet Union had settled down into a deadly rivalry with no end in sight. Thus World War II had led to neither the era of peace and tranquility that so many had looked forward to nor to the period of American world dominance that some thought possible. Although the United States emerged from the war more powerful than at any time in the nation's history, it faced a seemingly endless struggle against a determined and dangerous foe. And as the second Red Scare had so vividly demonstrated, it was a contest that was bound to affect every aspect of American life in the postwar era.

Recommended Reading

The Cold War spawned a vast array of books, some enduring in nature and many that are already outdated. The best general guide to American diplomacy since World War II is Walter LaFeber, *America, Russia and the Cold War, 1945–1992,* 7th ed. (1993). LaFeber, who writes from a moderately revisionist perspective, is more concerned with explaining the course of American foreign policy than in criticizing it. On the much debated question of the origins of the Cold War, the best balanced account is Daniel Yergin, *Shattered Peace* (1977), a book that characterizes American policy as flawed by misunderstanding rather than by illwill.

The classic account of containment is still the lucid recollection of its chief architect, George Kennan, *Memoirs, 1925–1950* (1967). John L. Gaddis uses Kennan's ideas as a point of departure for his account of the changing nature of American Cold War policy in *Strategies of Containment* (1982). Melvyn P. Leffler offers a full account of the development of containment in *A Preponderance of Power* (1992). For developments in the Far East, consult the perceptive book by Akira Iriye, *The Cold War in Asia* (1974).

The best book on the Truman period is Alonzo L. Hamby, *Beyond the New Deal* (1973), which focuses on Truman's attempts to preserve and extend the liberal reform tradition. Richard M. Fried offers a perceptive overview of the postwar anticommunist crusade in *Nightmare in Red: The McCarthy Era in Perspective* (1990).

Additional Bibliography

Surveys of American foreign policy since 1945 include Stephen Ambrose, *Rise to Globalism,* 7th ed. (1993); John Spanier, *American Foreign Policy Since World War II,* 12th ed. (1991); Ralph Levering, *The Cold War, 1945–1972* (1982); James A. Nathan and James K. Oliver, *United States Foreign Policy and World Order,* 2d ed. (1981); and Thomas S. McCormick, *America's Half Century* (1990). For perceptive essays on the Cold War, see John Lewis Gaddis, *The Long Peace* (1987), and Thomas G. Paterson, *Meeting the*

Communist Threat (1988). Adam B. Ulam provides a perceptive summary of Soviet-American relations for this period in *The Rivals* (1971). For a good critique, see John C. Donovan, *The Cold Warriors* (1974).

Gar Alperovitz began the revisionist controversy over the origins of the Cold War in *Atomic Diplomacy* (1965), which focuses on Truman's use of the atomic bomb as a veiled diplomatic weapon. Other revisionist accounts include Lloyd Gardner, *Architects of Illusion* (1970); Joyce Kolko and Gabriel Kolko, *The Limits of Power* (1972); Thomas G. Paterson, *Soviet-American Confrontation* (1973); and Lawrence Wittner, *American Intervention in Greece, 1943* (1982). For a brief moderate revisionist view, see Thomas G. Paterson, *On Every Front* (1979). Robert Tucker offers a shrewd assessment of revisionism in *The Radical Left and American Foreign Policy* (1971). Postrevisionist studies include John L. Gaddis, *The United States and the Origins of the Cold War* (1972); Vojtech Mastny, *Russia's Road to the Cold War* (1979); Robert L. Messer, *The End of an Alliance* (1982); James L. Gormly, *The Collapse of the Grand Alliance, 1945–1948* (1987); and Randall B. Woods and Howard Jones, *Dawning of the Cold War* (1991). For a lively account of the Potsdam Conference, see Charles L. Mee, *Meeting at Potsdam* (1975).

The foreign policy of the Truman administration is covered in Harry S. Truman, *Memoirs*, 2 vols. (1955, 1956); Dean Acheson, *Present at the Creation* (1969); and two works by Robert J. Donovan: *Conflict and Crisis* (1977) and *Tumultuous Years* (1982). Biographical studies of major Cold War figures include Forrest Pogue, *George C. Marshall: Statesman, 1945–1949* (1987); Mark Stoller, *George C. Marshall: Soldier-Statesman* (1989); Gaddis Smith, *Dean Acheson* (1972); David S. McClellan, *Dean Acheson* (1976); Walter Hixson, *George F. Kennan* (1990); Anders Stephanson, *Kennan and the Art of Foreign Policy* (1989); David Mayers, *George Kennan and the Dilemmas of American Foreign Policy* (1988); Wilson Miscamble, *George F. Kennan and the Making of American Foreign Policy, 1947–1950* (1992); Kai Bird, *The Chairman: John J. McCloy* (1992); Thomas A. Schwartz, *America's Germany: John J. McCloy and the Federal Republic of Germany* (1991); Rudy Abramson, *Spanning the Century: The Life and Times of W. Averell Harriman* (1992); Townsend Hoopes and Douglas Brinkley, *Driven Patriot: The Life and Times of James Forrestal* (1992); David Callahan, *Dangerous Capabilities: Paul Nitze and the Cold War* (1989); Jean Edward Smith, *Lucius D. Clay* (1990); H. W. Brands, *Inside the Cold War* (1991), on Loy Henderson; and Walter Issacson and Evan Thomas, *The Wise Men* (1986), a group biography of the foreign policy elite.

For military policy, see Walter Millis, ed., *The Forrestal Diaries* (1951); Richard F. Haynes, *The Awesome Power* (1973); Lawrence S. Kaplan, *NATO and the United States* (1988); Warner R. Schilling et al., *Strategy, Politics and Defense Budgets* (1962); Thomas H. Etzold and John L. Gaddis, eds., *Containment* (1976); and Chester J. Pach, Jr., *Arming the Free World* (1991). Studies of special interest include Gregg Herken, *The Winning Weapon* (1980), on atomic diplomacy under Truman; Michael Hogan, *The Marshall Plan* (1987), a standard account; Howard Jones, *"A New Kind of War"* (1989), on the Truman Doctrine; Avi Shlaim, *The United States and the Berlin Blockade, 1948* (1983); Randall Woods, *A Changing of the Guard: Anglo-American Relations, 1941–1946* (1990); Sallie Pisani, *The CIA and the Marshall Plan* (1991); and two books on France, John W. Young, *France, the Cold War and the Western Alliance, 1944–1949* (1990), and Irwin M. Wall, *The United States and the Making of Postwar France, 1944–1954* (1991).

For the Cold War in the Far East, consult Mark S. Gallicchio, *The Cold War Begins in Asia* (1988); Michael Schaller, *The American Occupation of Japan* (1985); Howard B. Schonberger, *Aftermath of War* (1989); Dorothy Borg and Waldo Heinrichs, eds., *The Uncertain Years: Chinese-American Relations, 1947–1950* (1980); Russell D. Buhite, *Soviet-American Relations in Asia, 1945–1954* (1982); William W. Streck, *The Road to Confrontation* (1981); Nancy B. Tucker, *Patterns in the Dust* (1983); Robert M. Blum, *Drawing the Line* (1982); and June M. Grasso, *Harry Truman's Two-China Policy, 1948–1950* (1987). Books on the Korean War include David Rees, *Korea: The Limited War and American Politics* (1968); Charles W. Dobbs, *The Unwanted Symbol* (1981); Bruce Cumings, *The Origins of the Korean War*, 2 vols. (1981 and 1991); John W. Spanier, *The Truman-MacArthur Controversy and the Korean War* (1959); two books by Rosemary Foot, *The Wrong War* (1985) and *A Substitute for Victory* (1990); Roy E. Appleman, *Disaster in Korea: The Chinese Confront MacArthur* (1989); and Burton Kaufman, *The Korean War* (1986).

Biographies of Truman include Merle Miller, *Plain Speaking* (1973); Margaret Truman, *Harry S. Truman* (1973); Richard L. Miller, *Truman: The Rise to Power* (1986); Robert H. Ferrell, *Harry S. Truman and the Modern American Presidency* (1982); Roy Jenkins, *Truman* (1986); William E. Pemberton, *Harry S. Truman: Fair Dealer and Cold Warrior* (1989); and David McCullogh, *Truman* (1992). Studies of specific policies include Barton J. Bernstein, ed., *Politics and Policies of the Truman Administration* (1970); R. Alton Lee, *Truman and Taft-Hartley* (1966); Susan M. Hartmann, *Truman and the 80th Congress* (1971); Donald R. McCoy, *The Presidency of Harry S. Truman* (1984); and Monte M. Poen, *Harry S. Truman and the Medical Lobby* (1979).

Three studies of the 1948 election are Irwin Ross, *The Loneliest Campaign* (1968); Norman D. Markowitz, *The Rise and Fall of the People's Century: Henry A. Wallace and American Liberalism, 1941* (1973); and Allen Yarnell, *Democrats and Progressives* (1973). Clark Clifford, one of Truman's key advisers, explains his role in *Counsel to the President* (1991). For Republican leaders, see two perceptive biographies, James T. Patterson, *Mr. Republican* (1968), on Senator Robert A. Taft, and Richard N. Smith, *Thomas E. Dewey and His Times* (1982).

The relationship of the Truman administration to the communist issue is covered in Earl Latham, *The Communist Conspiracy in Washington* (1966); Allan D. Harper, *The Politics of Loyalty* (1970); Athan G. Theoharis, *Seeds of Repression* (1971); and Richard Freeland, *The Truman Doctrine and the Origins of McCarthyism* (1972). Other works on the second Red Scare are Stanley Kutler, *The American Inquisition* (1982); Ronald Radosh and Joyce Milton, *The Rosenberg File* (1983); Victor Navasky, *Naming Names* (1980); Allen Weinstein, *Perjury: The Hiss-Chambers Case* (1978); and William L. O'Neil, *A Better World* (1982), which examines its impact on American intellectuals. Among the many books on McCarthyism, the best are Thomas C. Reeves, *The Life and Times of Joe McCarthy* (1982); Richard H. Rovere, *Senator Joe McCarthy* (1959); Michael P. Rogin, *The Intellectuals and McCarthy* (1967); Robert Griffith, *The Politics of Fear* (1970); Richard M. Fried, *Men Against McCarthy* (1976); William Ewald, *Who Killed Joe McCarthy?* (1984); Ellen W. Schrecker, *No Ivory Tower: McCarthyism in the Universities* (1986); and David Oshinsky, *A Conspiracy So Immense: The World of Joe McCarthy* (1983).

CHAPTER

29

Affluence and Anxiety

From the Fair Deal to the Great Society

On May 7, 1947, William Levitt announced plans to build 2,000 rental houses in a former potato field on Long Island, 30 miles from midtown Manhattan. Using mass production techniques he had learned while erecting navy housing during the war, Levitt quickly built 4,000 homes and rented them to young veterans eager to leave crowded city apartments or their parents' homes to begin raising families. A change in government financing regulations led him to begin offering his houses for sale in 1948 for a small amount down and a low monthly payment. Young couples, many of them the original renters, quickly bought the first 4,000; by the time Levittown—as he called the new community—was completed in 1951, it contained over 17,000 homes. So many babies were born in Levittown that it soon became known as "Fertility Valley" and "The Rabbit Hutch."

Levitt eventually built two more Levittowns, one in Pennsylvania and one in New Jersey; each contained the same curving streets, neighborhood parks and playgrounds, and community swimming pools as did the first development. Some observers denounced Levittown, seeing it as a symbol of conformity and materialism, but William Levitt had tapped the postwar desire of young Americans to move to the suburbs and raise their children outside the central city.

The secret of Levittown's appeal was the basic house, a 720-square-foot Cape Cod design built on a concrete slab. It had a kitchen, two bedrooms and bath, a living room complete with a fireplace and 16-foot picture window, and an expansion attic with room for two more bedrooms. Levitt built only one interior, but there were four different facades to break the monotony. The original house sold for $6,990 in 1948; even the improved model, a ranch-style house, sold for less than $10,000 in 1951.

Levitt's houses were ideal for young people just starting out in life. They were cheap, comfortable, and efficient, and each home came with a refrigerator, cooking range, and washing machine. Despite the conformity of the houses, the three Levittowns were surprisingly diverse communities; residents had a wide variety of religious, ethnic, and occupational backgrounds. African Americans, however, were rigidly exclud-ed. In time, as the more successful families moved on to larger homes in more expensive neighborhoods, the Levittowns became enclaves for lower-middle-class families.

Levittown symbolized the most significant social trend of the postwar era in the United States—the flight to the suburbs. The residential areas surrounding cities like New York and Chicago nearly doubled in the 1950s. While central cities remained relatively stagnant during the decade, suburbs grew by 46 percent; by 1960, some sixty million people, one-third of the nation, lived in suburban rings around the cities. This massive shift in population from the central city was accompanied by a baby boom that started during World War II. Young married couples began to have three, four, or even five children (compared with only one or two children in American families during the 1930s). These larger families led to a 19 percent growth in the nation's population between 1950 and 1960, the greatest increase in growth rate since 1910.

The economy boomed as residential construction soared. By 1960, one-fourth of all existing homes were less than ten years old and factories were turning out large quantities of appliances and television sets for the new households. A multitude of new consumer products—ranging from frozen foods to filter cigarettes, from high-fidelity phonographs to cars equipped with automatic transmissions and tubeless tires—appeared in stores and showrooms. In the suburbs, the supermarket replaced the corner grocer, carrying a vast array of items that enabled homemakers to provide their families with a more varied diet.

A new affluence replaced the poverty and hunger of the Great Depression for most Americans, but many could not forget the haunting memories of the 1930s. The obsession with material goods took on an almost desperate quality, as if a profusion of houses, cars, and home appliances could guarantee the nightmare of depression would never return. Critics were quick to disparage the quality of life in suburban society. They condemned the conformity, charging the newly affluent with forsaking traditional American individualism to live in identical houses, drive look-alike cars, and accumulate the same material possessions. Folksinger Malvina Reynolds caught the essence of postwar suburbia in her 1963 song:

Little boxes on the hillside,
Little boxes made of ticky tacky
Little boxes on the hillside,
Little boxes all the same.
There's a green one and a pink one
And a blue one and a yellow one
And they're all made out of ticky tacky
And they all look just the same. *

Events abroad added to the feeling of anxiety in the postwar years. Nuclear war became a frighteningly real possibility. The rivalry with the Soviet Union had led to the second Red Scare, with charges of treason and disloyalty being leveled at loyal Americans. Many Americans joined with Senator Joseph McCarthy in searching for the communist enemy at home rather than abroad. Loyalty oaths and book burning revealed how insecure Americans had become in the era of the Cold War. Thus beneath the bland surface of suburban affluence, a dark current of distrust and insecurity marred the picture of a nation fulfilling its economic destiny.

THE POSTWAR BOOM

For fifteen years following World War II, the nation witnessed a period of unparalleled economic growth. A pent-up demand for consumer goods fueled a steady industrial expansion. And heavy government spending during the Cold War added an extra stimulus to the economy, offsetting brief recessions in 1949 and 1953 and moderating a steeper one in 1957–1958. By the end of the 1950s, the American people had achieved an affluence that finally erased the lingering memories of the Great Depression.

Postwar Prosperity

The economy began its upward surge as the result of two long-term factors. First, American consumers—after being held in check by depression and then by wartime scarcities—finally had a chance to indulge their suppressed appetites for material goods. At the war's end, personal sav-

ings in the United States stood at more than $37 billion, providing a powerful stimulus to consumption. Initially, American factories could not turn out enough automobiles and appliances to satisfy the horde of buyers. By 1950, however, production lines had finally caught up with the demand. In that year, Americans bought more than six million cars, and the gross national product (GNP) reached $318 billion (50 percent higher than in 1940).

The Cold War provided the additional stimulus the economy needed when postwar expansion slowed. The Marshall Plan and other foreign aid programs financed a heavy export trade. Then the outbreak of the Korean War helped overcome a brief recession and ensured continued prosperity as the government spent massive amounts on guns, planes, and munitions. In 1952, the nation spent $44 billion, two-thirds of the federal budget, on national defense. Although Eisenhower managed to bring about some modest reductions, defense spending continued at a level of $40 billion throughout the decade.

The nation achieved a level of affluence in the 1950s that made the persisting fear of another Great Depression seem irrational. The baby boom and the spectacular growth of suburbia served as great stimulants to the consumer goods industries. Manufacturers turned out an ever-increasing number of refrigerators, washing machines, and dishwashers to equip the kitchens of Levittown and its many imitators across the country. The automobile industry thrived with suburban expansion as two-car families became more and more common. In 1955, in an era when oil was abundant and gasoline sold for less than thirty cents a gallon, Detroit sold a record eight million cars. The electronics industry boomed. Consumers were eager to acquire the latest marvel of home entertainment—the television set.

In addition, commercial enterprises snapped up office machines and the first generation of computers; industry installed electronic sensors and processors as it underwent extensive automation, and the military displayed an insatiable appetite for electronic devices for its planes and ships. As a result, American industry averaged more than $10 billion a year in capital investment, and the number of persons employed rose above the long-sought goal of sixty million nationwide.

Birth rate, 1940–1970

Births per thousand
women aged 15–44

[Line graph showing birth rate from 1940 to 1970. Values begin near 80 in 1940, rise to about 95 in 1943, dip to about 86 in 1945, climb sharply to about 112 in 1948, dip to about 107, rise steadily to a peak of about 123 in 1957, then decline through the 1960s to about 67 in 1970. Y-axis marked 60, 70, 80, 90, 100, 110, 120. X-axis marked 1940, 1945, 1950, 1955, 1960, 1965, 1970.]

Source: Compiled from U.S. Bureau of the Census, Historical Statistics of the United States, Colonial Times to 1970, Bicentennial Edition, Washington, D.C., 1975.

The well-stocked refrigerator suggests the abundance available in the booming postwar era. Manufacturers rushed to satisfy consumers' pent-up demands for household appliances, which had been unaffordable before the war and unattainable during it, and advertisers sought to attract buyers with glowing words and attractive images of "the good life."

Yet the economic abundance of the 1950s was not without its problems. While some sections of the nation (notably the emerging Sunbelt areas of the South and West) benefited enormously from the growth of the aircraft and electronics industries, older manufacturing regions, such as New England, did not fare as well. The steel industry increased its capacity during the decade, but it began to fall behind the rate of national growth. Agriculture continued to experience bumper crops and low prices, so rural regions, like the vast areas of the Plains states, failed to share in the general affluence. Unemployment persisted despite the boom, rising to over 7 percent in a sharp recession that hit the country in the fall of 1957 and lasted through the summer of 1958. The rate of economic growth slowed in the second half of the decade, causing concern about the continuing vitality of the American economy.

None of these flaws, however, could disguise the fact that the nation was prospering to an extent no one dreamed possible in the 1930s. The GNP grew to $440 billion by 1960, more than double the 1940 level. More important, workers now labored fewer than forty hours a week; they rarely worked on Saturdays, and nearly all enjoyed a two-week paid vacation each year. By the mid-1950s, the average American family had twice as much real income to spend as its counterpart had possessed in the boom years of the 1920s. From 1945 to 1960, per capita disposable income rose by $500—to $1,845—for every man, woman, and child in the country. The American people, in one generation, had moved from poverty and depression to the highest standard of living the world had ever known.

Life in the Suburbs

Sociologists had difficulty describing the nature of suburban society in the 1950s. Some saw it as classless, while others noted the absence of both the very rich and the very poor and consequently labeled it "middle class." Rather than forming a homogeneous social group, though, the suburbs contained a surprising variety of people, whether classified as "upper lower," "lower middle," and "upper middle" or simply as blue collar, white collar, and professional. Doctors and lawyers often lived in the same developments as shoe salesmen and master plumbers. The traditional distinctions of ancestry, education, and size of residence no longer differentiated people as easily as they had in the past.

Yet suburbs could vary widely, from working-class communities clustered near factories built in the countryside to old, elitist areas like Scarsdale, New York, and Shaker Heights, Ohio. Most were almost exclusively white and Christian, but suburbs like Great Neck on Long Island and Richmond Heights outside Miami enabled Jews and blacks to take part in the flight from the inner city.

Life in all these suburban communities depended on the automobile. Highways and expressways allowed fathers to commute to jobs in the cities, often an hour or more away. Children might ride buses to and from school, but mothers had to drive them to piano lessons and Little League ball games. Two cars became a necessity for almost every suburban family, thus helping spur the boom in automobile production. In 1948, only 59 percent of American families owned a car; just a few years later, nearly every family above the poverty line had at least one vehicle, and many had several.

In the new drive-in culture, people shopped at the stores that first grew up in "miracle miles"

A suburban Sunday in the 1950s. The family car, laden with shiny chrome and elongated tailfins, became an essential part of suburban life.

along the highways and later at the shopping centers that began to dot the countryside by the mid-1950s. There were only eight shopping centers in the entire country in 1946; hundreds appeared over the next fifteen years, including Poplar Plaza

Massive housing developments made single-family dwellings available—and affordable—to millions of Americans, drawing them away from the cities to the new suburbs. Inside the identical-looking homes, a dream kitchen, equipped with stove, cooking range, and refrigerator, awaited the homemaker.

in Memphis, with one large department store, thirty retail shops, and parking for over 500 cars. In 1956, the first enclosed air-conditioned mall, the Southdale Shopping Center, opened outside Minneapolis.

Despite the increased mobility provided by the car, the home became the focus for activities and aspirations. The postwar shortage of housing that often forced young couples to live with their parents or in-laws created an intense demand for new homes in the suburbs. When questioned, prospective buyers expressed a desire for "more space," for "comfort and roominess," and for "privacy and freedom of action" in their new residences. Men and women who moved to the suburbs prized the new kitchens with their built-in dishwashers, electric ovens, and gleaming counters; the extra bedrooms that ensured privacy from and for the children; the large garages that could be converted into recreation rooms; and the small neat lawns that gave them an area for outdoor activities as well as a new way to compete with their neighbors. "Togetherness" became the code word of the 1950s. Families did things together, whether gathering around the TV sets that dominated living rooms, attending community activities, or taking vacations in the huge station wagons of the era.

But there were some less attractive consequences of the new suburban lifestyle. The extended family, where several generations had lived in close proximity, was a casualty of the boom in small detached homes. As Kenneth Jackson has noted, suburban life "ordained that most children would grow up in intimate contact only with their parents and siblings." Grandparents, aunts and uncles, cousins, and more distant relatives would become remote figures, seen only on special occasions.

The nuclear family, typical of the suburb, did nothing to encourage the development of feminism. The end of the war saw many women who had entered the work force return to the home, where the role of wife and mother continued to be viewed as the ideal for women in the 1950s. Trends toward getting married earlier and having larger families reinforced the pattern of women devoting all their efforts to housework and child raising rather than acquiring professional skills and pursuing careers outside the home. Adlai Stevenson, extolling "the humble role of house-

Married Women in the Labor Force, 1950–1960	
Year	Percentage (as percentage of all married women)
1950	24.8
1951	26.7
1952	26.8
1953	27.7
1954	28.1
1955	29.4
1956	30.2
1957	30.8
1958	31.4
1959	32.3
1960	31.7

Source: Compiled from U.S. Bureau of the Census, *Historical Statistics of the United States, Colonial Times to 1970, Bicentennial Edition*, Washington, D.C., 1975.

wife," told Smith College graduates that there was much they could do "in the living room with a baby in your lap or in the kitchen with a can opener in your hand." Dr. Benjamin Spock's 1946 best-seller, *Baby and Child Care*, became a fixture in millions of homes, while the traditional women's magazines like *McCall's* and *Good Housekeeping* thrived by featuring articles on natural childbirth and inspirational pieces such as "Homemaking Is My Vocation."

Nonetheless, the number of working wives doubled between 1940 and 1960. By the end of the 1950s, 40 percent of American women, and nearly one-third of all wives, had jobs outside the home. The heavy expenses involved in rearing and educating children led wives and mothers to seek ways to augment the family income, inadvertently preparing the way for a new demand for equality in the 1960s.

THE GOOD LIFE?

Consumerism became the dominant social theme of the 1950s. Yet even with an abundance of creature comforts and added hours of leisure time, the quality of life left many Americans anxious and dissatisfied.

Areas of Greatest Growth

Organized religion flourished in the climate of the 1950s. Ministers, priests, and rabbis all commented on the rise in church and synagogue attendance in the new communities. Will Herberg claimed that religious affiliation had become the primary identifying feature of modern American life, dividing the nation into three separate segments—Protestant, Catholic, and Jewish.

Some observers condemned the bland, secular nature of suburban churches, which seemed to be an integral part of the consumer society. "On weekdays one shops for food," wrote one critic, "on Saturdays one shops for recreation, and on Sundays one shops for the Holy Ghost." But the popularity of religious writer Norman Vincent Peale, with his positive gospel that urged people to "start thinking faith, enthusiasm and joy," suggested that the new churches filled a genuine if shallow human need. At the same time, the emergence of neo-orthodoxy in Protestant seminaries (notably through the ideas of Reinhold Niebuhr) and the rapid spread of radical forms of fundamentalism (such as the Assemblies of God) indicated that millions of Americans still were searching for a more personal religious faith.

Schools provided an immediate problem for the growing new suburban communities. The unprecedented increase in the number of school-age children, from twenty to thirty million in the first eight grades, overwhelmed the resources of many local districts, leading to demands for federal aid. Congress granted limited help for areas affected by defense plants and military bases, but Eisenhower's reluctance to unbalance the budget—along with traditional adherence to state control over public education—blocked further federal assistance prior to 1957 when the government reacted to *Sputnik* (see p. 883).

Equally important, a controversy arose over the nature of education in the 1950s. Critics of "progressive" education called for sweeping educational reforms and a new stress on traditional academic subjects. Suburban communities often had bitter fights; affluent parents demanded kindergarten enrichment programs and grade school foreign language instruction while working class people resisted such costly innovations.

Television cameras zoom in on Jason Robards, Jr., and Maria Schell in a scene from For Whom the Bell Tolls, *broadcast by Playhouse 90 in 1959. At a cost of $300,000, the adaptation of the Ernest Hemingway novel was Playhouse 90's most ambitious project.*

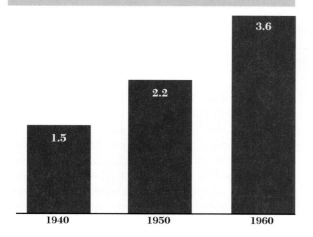

College Student Enrollment, 1940–1960 (in millions)

- 1940: 1.5
- 1950: 2.2
- 1960: 3.6

Novelist Jack Kerouac and his fellow "beat" poets bemoaned the moral bankruptcy of popular culture. Their conversational writing styles and intensely personal subject matter influenced other poets.

The one thing all seemed to agree on was the desirability of a college education. The number of young people attending colleges increased from 1.5 million in 1940 to 3.6 million in 1960, leading to rapid expansion of university enrollment.

The largest advances were made in the exciting new medium of television. From a shaky start just after the war, TV boomed in the 1950s, pushing radio aside and undermining many of the nation's magazines. By 1957, three networks controlled the airwaves, reaching 40 million sets over nearly 500 stations. Advertisers soon took charge of the new medium, using techniques first pioneered in radio—including pretaped commercials, quiz shows, and soap operas.

At first, the insatiable demand for programs encouraged a burst of creativity. Playwrights such as Reginald Rose, Rod Serling, and Paddy Chayefsky wrote a series of notable dramas for *Playhouse 90, Studio One,* and the *Goodyear Television Playhouse.* Broadcast live from cramped studios, these productions thrived on tight dramatic structures, movable scenery, and frequent closeups of the actors.

Advertisers, however, quickly became disillusioned with the live anthology programs, which usually dealt with controversial subjects or focused on ordinary people and events. In contrast, sponsors wanted shows that stressed excitement, glamor, and instant success. Aware that audiences were fascinated by contestants with unusual expertise (a shoemaker answering tough questions on operas, a grandmother stumping experts on baseball), producers began giving away huge cash prizes on *The $64,000 Question* and *Twenty-one.* In 1959, the nation was shocked when Charles Van Doren, a Columbia University professor, confessed he had been given the answers in advance to win $129,000 on *Twenty-one.* The three networks quickly dropped all the big-prize quiz programs, replacing them with comedy, action, and adventure shows such as *The Untouchables* and *Bonanza.* Despite its early promise of artistic innovation, television had become a technologically sophisticated but safe conveyor of the consumer culture.

Critics of the Consumer Society

One striking feature of the 1950s was the abundance of self-criticism. A number of widely read books explored the flaws in the new suburbia. John Keats's *The Crack in the Picture Window* described the endless rows of tract houses "vomited up" by developers as "identical boxes spreading like gangrene." Their occupants—whom he dubbed the Drones, the Amiables, and the Fecunds—lost any sense of individuality in their obsession with material goods.

Richard and Katherine Gordon were more concerned about the psychological toll of suburban life in their 1960 book *The Split Level Trap.* They labeled the new lifestyle "Disturbia" and bemoaned the "haggard" men, "tense and anxious" women, and the "gimme" kids it produced. The most sweeping indictment came in William H. Whyte's *The Organization Man* (1956), based on a study of the Chicago suburb of Park Forest. Whyte perceived a change from the old Protestant ethic, with its emphasis on hard work and personal responsibility, to a new social ethic, where everything centered on "the team" and the ultimate goal was "belongingness." The result was a stifling conformity and the loss of personal identity.

The most influential social critic of the 1950s was Harvard sociologist David Riesman. His book *The Lonely Crowd* appeared in 1950 and set the tone for intellectual commentary about suburbia for the rest of the decade. Riesman described the shift from the "inner-directed" Americans of the past who had relied on such traditional values as self-denial and frugality to the "other-directed" Americans of the consumer society who constantly adapted their behavior to conform to social pressures. The consequences—a decline in individualism and a tendency for people to become acutely sensitive to the expectations of others—produced a bland and tolerant society of consumers lacking creativity and a sense of adventure.

C. Wright Mills was a far more caustic, though less popular, commentator on American society in the 1950s. Anticipating government statistics that revealed white-collar workers (sales clerks, office workers, bank tellers) now outnumbered blue-collar workers (miners, factory workers, millhands), Mills described the new middle class in ominous terms in his books *White Collar* (1951) and *Power Elite* (1956). The corporation was the villain for Mills, depriving office workers of their own identities and imposing an impersonal discipline through manipulation and propaganda. The industrial assembly line had given way to an even more dehumanizing workplace, the modern office. "At rows of blank-looking counters sat rows of blank-looking girls with blank, white folders in their blank hands, all blankly folding blank papers."

This disenchantment with the consumer culture reached its most eloquent expression with the "beats," literary groups that rebelled against the materialistic society of the 1950s. Jack Kerouac's novel *On the Road,* published in 1957, set the tone for the new movement. The name came from the quest for beatitude, a state of inner grace sought in Zen Buddhism. Flouting the respectability of suburbia, the "beatniks"—as middle-America termed them—were easily identified by their long hair, bizarre clothing, and penchant for sexual promiscuity and drug experi-

mentation. They were conspicuous dropouts from a society they found senseless. Poet Lawrence Ferlinghetti, who held forth in the City Lights Bookshop in San Francisco (a favorite resort of the beats), summed it up this way: "I was a wind-up toy someone had dropped wound up into a world already running down."

Despite the disapproval they evoked from mainstream Americans, the beat generation had only compassion for their detractors. "We love everything," Kerouac proclaimed, "Billy Graham, the Big Ten, Rock and Roll, Zen, apple pie, Eisenhower—we dig it all." Yet as highly visible nonconformists in an era of stifling conformity, the beats demonstrated a style of social protest that would flower into the counterculture of the 1960s.

The Reaction to *Sputnik*

The profound insecurity that underlay American life throughout the 1950s burst into view in October 1957, when the Soviets sent the satellite *Sputnik* into orbit around the earth. The public's reaction to this impressive scientific feat was panic. The declining rate of economic growth; the recession of 1957–1958; the growing concern that American schools, with their frills and frivolities and their emphasis on social adjustment, were lagging behind their Russian counterparts—all contributed to a conviction that the nation had somehow lost its previously unquestioned primacy in the eyes of the world.

In the late 1950s, the president and Congress moved to restore national confidence. Eisenhower appointed James R. Killian, president of the Massachusetts Institute of Technology, as his special assistant for science and technology and to oversee a crash program in missile development. The House and Senate followed by creating the National Aeronautics and Space Administration (NASA) in 1958. Congress appropriated vast sums to allow the agency to compete with the Russians in the space race. Soon a new group of heroes, the astronauts, began the training that led to suborbital flights and eventually to John Glenn's five-hour flight around the globe in 1962.

Congress also sought to match the Soviet educational advances by passing the National Defense Education Act (NDEA). This legislation authorized federal financing of scientific and for-

Rise of a New Idiom in Modern Painting
Abstract Expressionism

In the 1950s, New York replaced Paris as the Western world's capital of avant-garde art. The artists at the center of this phenomenon were the abstract expressionists—notably Jackson Pollock, Mark Rothko, Robert Motherwell, Willem De Kooning, Barnett Newman, Adolph Gottlieb, and Franz Kline. These artists did not share a common style or motif of painting. Rather they shared a mutual conception of what constituted art: a portrayal of individual feelings and psychological traumas through improvised visual expressions.

The abstract expressionists abandoned representational art—the use of figures—and geometric design for a freer use of color and line. They strove to express transcendental themes by capturing a moment in their own lives rather than depicting a figure or a premeditated idea. Their work, wrote art critic Harold Rosenberg, "was not a picture but an event."

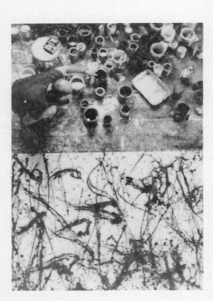

Pollock began each painting without a preconceived plan, spontaneously dripping pigment across a canvas on the floor until the composition began to suggest its own development. His Convergence (1952), a typically complex work of varied colors, is shown below.

The careers of Jackson Pollock and Mark Rothko exemplify the common and contrasting themes that characterized the abstract expressionists. Jackson Pollock was born in Cody, Wyoming, in 1912. Mark Rothko was born nine years earlier in Dvinsk, Russia, emigrated to the United States as a boy, and was reared in Portland, Oregon. By the early 1930s, both painters had settled in New York City, the crucible of avant-garde American painting during the Great Depression.

The New Deal's Federal Art Project under the Works Progress Administration (WPA) contributed to the development of a self-conscious artistic community in New York. The Project also provided Pollock and Rothko their first opportunities to paint full time. Like many artists of their generation, they adopted leftist political concerns. Their early 1930s works in social realism—a style of monumental narrative painting that emphasized social themes and collective action—reflected these beliefs.

In the late 1920s and 1930s, several important museums opened in New York. Among them, the Museum of Modern Art, opened in 1929, displayed works by such masters as Pablo Picasso. These collections gave New York artists the opportunity to study first hand the leaders of the dominant movements in twentieth-century European art. Pollock, for instance, studied Wassily Kandinsky's expressionist works while working as a custodian at the Museum of Non-Objective Art (today's Solomon R. Guggenheim Museum). Also, prominent European artists—such as André Breton, Mark Chagall, André Masson, Piet Mondrian, and Yves Tanguy, to name a few—fled to New York to escape fascist regimes. The arrival of the Europeans provided "American painters," noted critic Clement Greenberg, "the sense, wholly new in this country, of being in the center of art in their time."

The presence of these artists had a major impact on Pollock and Rothko. With the onset of World War II, they abandoned their leftist politics and what they now considered the provincialism of social realism. Inspired by cubism's radical abstraction of figures and surrealism's juxtaposition of ordinary objects and symbols in psychologically provocative ways, Pollock and Rothko each began to experiment. Both became intrigued, for instance, with the surrealists' use of automatism—a form of free association in painting—to probe the unconscious.

The Depression and World War II compelled American artists to explore ways to confront the national consciousness forged by these two momentous events. This search for a new idiom evolved into abstract expressionism. Like other artists in their circle, Pollock's and Rothko's work in the early 1940s focused on archetypal myths—present in the unconscious of the individual and basic to human experience—as a source for examining universal psychological themes. Such fundamental concepts would transcend the cultural and social differences that separated individuals in complex modern societies like the United States.

The absence of any new generation of European talent after World War II augmented the growing self-assurance of American artists. In the late 1940s, Rothko and Pollock led the transition into the new genre of abstract expressionism.

Pollock physically involved himself in the painting process by using the floor of his studio as an easel. This allowed him to traverse the canvas while he cathartically dripped paint. Although Rothko worked more conventionally, his visions were as radical as Pollock's. Rothko painted introspective floating color masses that captured the somber mood of his more conventional 1930s paintings. Their shared commitment "to work from within" rather than "go to a subject matter outside from themselves," as Pollock put it, conceptually linked their very different visions.

Avant-garde painters, like many other artists and intellectuals in the 1950s, abhorred the dominance of middle-class cultural values and social conformity that stifled individualism and led to alienation. And although the avant-garde painters avoided political interpretations of their work, there was an intellectual agreement between their aesthetic concerns—which emphasized freedom—and the emerging Cold War ethos condemning totalitarianism. According to art historian Serge Guilbaut, the abstract expressionists became the "protégé of the new liberalism," that sought to defend freedom from the "authoritarianism of the left and the right."

Whatever their social message, these artists tapped feelings that produced moving paintings but sometimes had tragic impact on

Number 10 (1950) by Mark Rothko. (Collection, The Museum of Modern Art, New York. Gift of Philip Johnson.)

their lives. After 1953, Pollock's work declined as he turned to alcohol. Following much personal anguish, he died in a possibly suicidal 1956 automobile accident. Mark Rothko battled serious bouts of depression throughout his career; he took his own life in 1970.

Pollock, Rothko, and the other abstract expressionists collectively left an enduring legacy. Their paintings stand as both a striking aesthetic commentary on culture in the Cold War and as testimony to the emergence of the United States as the center of avant-garde art and New York City as its capital.

Sputnik I *on its support stand before launching. The first news of* Sputnik *was not carried in Soviet newspapers until two days after the launch.*

eign language programs in the nation's schools and colleges. Soon American students were hard at work mastering the "new physics" and the "new math."

The belief persisted, however, that the faults lay deeper, that in the midst of affluence and abundance Americans had lost their competitive edge. Economists pointed to the higher rate of Soviet economic growth, and social critics bemoaned a supermarket culture that stressed consumption over production, comfort over hard work. Disturbed by the charge that the nation had lost its sense of purpose, President Eisenhower finally appointed a Commission on National Goals "to develop a broad outline of national objectives for the next decade and longer." Ten prominent citizens from all walks of life, led by Henry W. Wriston of Brown University, issued a report that called for increased military spending abroad, greater economic growth at home, broader educational opportunities, and more government support for both scientific research and the advancement of the arts. The consensus seemed to be that rather than a change of direction, all the United States needed was a renewed commitment to the pursuit of excellence.

FAREWELL TO REFORM

It is not surprising that the spirit of reform underlying the New Deal failed to flourish in the post-war years. Growing affluence took away the sense of grievance and the cry for change that was so strong in the 1930s. Eager to enjoy the new prosperity after years of want and sacrifice, the American people turned away from federal regulation and welfare programs.

Truman and the Fair Deal

Harry Truman tried to capitalize on his upset victory in 1948 to offer a broad program of reform to the nation on January 5, 1949. Venturing beyond earlier proposals by FDR to increase the minimum wage and broaden Social Security coverage, he called for a "Fair Deal," a reform package that comprised a new program of national medical insurance, federal aid to education, enactment of a Fair Employment Practices Commission (FEPC) to prevent economic discrimination against blacks, and an overhaul of the farm subsidy program.

The Fair Deal was never enacted. Except for raising the minimum wage to seventy-five cents an hour and broadening Social Security to cover ten million more Americans, Congress refused to pass any of Truman's health, education, or civil rights measures. The nation's doctors waged an effective campaign against the president's health insurance plan, and southern senators blocked any action on FEPC. Aid to education, repeal of Taft-Hartley, and the new farm program all failed to win congressional approval. In part, Truman was to blame for trying to secure too much too soon; if he had selected one or two measures and given them priority, he might have been more successful. More important, however, was the fact that despite the Democratic victory in 1948, Congress remained under the control of a bipartisan conservative coalition of northern Republicans and southern Democrats, the same alignment that had halted Roosevelt's reforms after 1938.

Although his legislative failure became certain in 1950 when war once again subordinated domestic issues to foreign policy, President Truman deserves credit for maintaining and consolidating the New Deal. His spirited leadership prevented any Republican effort to repeal the gains of the 1930s. Moreover, even though he failed to get any new measures enacted, he broadened the reform agenda and laid the groundwork for future advances in health care, aid to education, and civil rights.

Eisenhower's Modern Republicanism

The American people found that moderation was the keynote of the Eisenhower presidency. His major goal from the outset was to restore calm and tranquility to a badly divided nation. Unlike FDR and Truman, Eisenhower had no commitment to social change or economic reform. Ike was a fiscal conservative who was intent on balancing the budget. Yet unlike some Republicans of the extreme right wing, he had no plans to dismantle the social programs of the New Deal. He sought instead to keep military spending in check, to encourage as much private initiative as possible, and to reduce federal activities to the bare minimum. Defining his position as "Modern Republicanism," he claimed that he was "conservative when it comes to money and liberal when it comes to human beings."

On domestic issues, Eisenhower preferred to delegate authority and to play a passive role. He concentrated his own efforts on the Cold War abroad. The men he chose to run the nation reflected his preference for successful corporation executives. Thus George Humphrey, an Ohio industrialist, carried out a policy of fiscal stringency as secretary of the treasury, while Charles E. Wilson (the former head of General Motors) sought to keep the Pentagon budget under control as secretary of defense. Neither man was wholly successful, and both were guilty of tactless public statements. Humphrey warned that unless Congress showed budgetary restraint "we're gonna have a depression which will curl your hair," and Wilson gained notoriety by proclaiming "what was good for our country was good for General Motors, and vice versa."

Eisenhower was equally reluctant to play an active role in dealing with Congress. A fervent believer in the separation of powers, Ike did not wish to engage in intensive lobbying. He left congressional relations to aides such as Sherman Adams, a former New Hampshire governor who served as White House chief of staff. Adams's skill at resolving problems at lower levels insulated Eisenhower from many of the nation's pressing domestic problems.

Relations with Congress were weakened further by Republican losses in the midterm election of 1954. The Democrats regained control of both houses and kept it throughout the 1950s. The president had to rely on two Texas Democrats, Senate Majority Leader Lyndon B. Johnson and House Speaker Sam Rayburn, for legislative action; at best, it was an awkward and uneasy relationship.

The result was a very modest legislative record. Eisenhower did continue the basic social measures of the New Deal. In 1954, he signed bills extending Social Security benefits to more than 7 million Americans, raising the minimum wage to $1 an hour, and adding 4 million workers to those eligible for unemployment benefits. He consolidated the administration of welfare programs by creating the Department of Health, Education and Welfare in 1953. Oveta Culp Hobby, the first woman to hold a cabinet post in a Republican administration, headed the new department. But Ike steadfastly opposed Democratic plans for compulsory health insurance—which he condemned as the "socialization of medicine"—and comprehensive federal aid to education, preferring to leave everything except school construction in the hands of local and state authorities. This lack of presidential support and the continuing grip of the conservative coalition in Congress blocked any further reform in the 1950s.

The one significant legislative achievement of the Eisenhower years came with the passage of the Highway Act of 1956. After a twelve-year delay, Congress appropriated funds for a 41,000-mile interstate highway system consisting of multilane divided expressways that would connect the nation's major cities. Justified on grounds of national defense, the 1956 act pleased a variety of highway users: the trucking industry, automobile clubs, organized labor (eager for construction jobs), farmers (needing to speed their crops to market), and state highway officials (anxious for the 90 percent funding contributed by the federal government). Eisenhower's insistence that general revenue funds not be used to provide the federal share—estimated at $25 billion—of the total cost led to the creation of a highway trust fund raised by taxes on fuel, tires, and new cars and trucks. Built over the next twenty years, the interstate highway system had a profound influence on American life. It stimulated the economy and shortened travel time dramatically, while at the same time intensifying the nation's dependence on the automobile and distorting metropolitan growth patterns into long strips paralleling the new expressways.

Overall, the Eisenhower years marked an era of political moderation. The American people, enjoying the abundance of the 1950s, seemed quite content with legislative inaction. The president was sensitive to the nation's economic health; when recessions developed in 1953 and again in 1957 after his landslide reelection victory, he quickly abandoned his goal of a balanced budget in favor of a policy advocating government spending to restore prosperity. These steps, along with modest increases in New Deal welfare programs, led to a steady growth in the federal budget from $29.5 billion in 1950 to $76.5 in 1960. Eisenhower was able to balance the budget in only three of his eight years in office, and the $12 billion deficit in 1959 was larger than any ever before recorded in peacetime. In this manner, Eisenhower was able to maintain the New Deal legacy of federal responsibility for social welfare and the state of the economy while at the same time he successfully resisted demands for

		Popular	Electoral
Candidate	Party	Vote	Vote
Eisenhower	Republican	35,585,245	457
Stevenson	Democrat	26,030,172	73

The Election of 1956

more extensive government involvement in American life.

THE STRUGGLE OVER CIVIL RIGHTS

Despite President Eisenhower's reluctance to champion the cause of reform, powerful pressures for change forced long overdue action in one area of American life—the denial of basic rights to the nation's black minority. In the midst of the Cold War, the contradiction between the denunciation of the Soviet Union for its human-rights violations and the second-class status of African Americans began to arouse the national conscience. Fighting for freedom against communist tyranny abroad, Americans had to face the reality of the continued denial of freedom to a submerged minority at home.

African Americans had benefited economically from World War II, but they were still a seriously disadvantaged group. Those who had left the South for better opportunities in northern and western cities were concentrated in blighted and segregated neighborhoods, working at low-paying jobs, suffering economic and social discrimination, and failing to share fully in the postwar prosperity.

In the South, conditions were much worse. State laws forced blacks to live almost totally segregated from white society. Not only did African Americans attend separate (and almost always inferior) schools, but they also were rigidly segregated in all public facilities. They were forced to use separate waiting rooms in train stations, separate seats on all forms of transportation, separate drinking fountains, and even separate telephone booths. "Segregation was enforced at all places of public entertainment, including libraries, audito-

The Interstate Highway System

The 1956 plan to create an interstate highway system drastically changed America's landscape and culture. Today, the system covers about 45,000 miles, only a few thousand more miles than called for in the original plan.

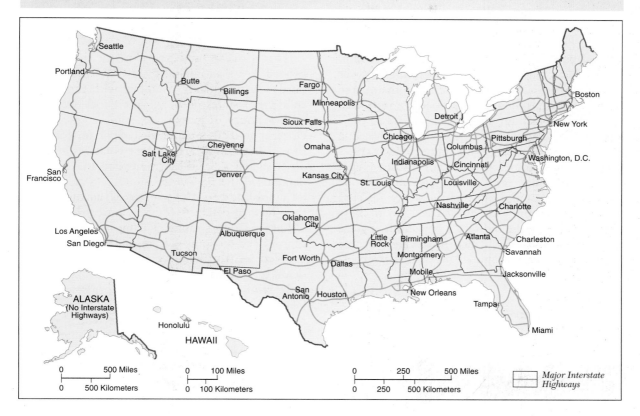

riums, and circuses," Chief Justice Earl Warren noted. "There was segregation in the hospitals, prisons, mental institutions, and nursing homes. Even ambulance service was segregated."

Civil Rights as a Political Issue

Truman was the first president to attempt to alter the historic pattern of racial discrimination in the United States. In 1946, he appointed a presidential commission on civil rights. A year later, in a sweeping report entitled "To Secure These Rights," the commission recommended the reinstatement of the wartime Fair Employment Practices Committee (FEPC), the establishment of a permanent civil rights commission, and the denial of federal aid to any state that condoned segregation in schools and public facilities. The president's ten-point legislative program in 1948 included some of these measures, notably the establishment of a permanent FEPC and a civil rights commission. But southern resistance blocked any action by Congress, and the inclusion of a strong civil rights plank in the 1948 Democratic platform led to the walkout of some southern delegations and a separate States' Rights (Dixiecrat) ticket in several states of the South that fall.

African American voters in the North responded by backing Truman overwhelmingly over Dewey in the 1948 election. The African American vote in key cities—Los Angeles, Cleveland, and Chicago—ensured the Democratic victory in California, Ohio, and Illinois. Truman responded by including civil rights legislation in his Fair Deal program in 1949. Once again, however, determined southern opposition blocked congressional action on both a permanent FEPC and an antilynching measure.

Even though President Truman had been unable to secure any significant legislation, he had succeeded in adding civil rights to the liberal agenda. From this time forward, it would be an integral part of the Democratic reform program. And Truman was able to use his executive power to assist African Americans. He strengthened the civil rights division of the Justice Department, which aided black groups in their efforts to challenge school segregation and restrictive housing covenants in the courts. Most important, in 1948 Truman issued an order calling for the desegregation of the armed forces. The navy and the air force quickly complied, but the army resisted until the personnel needs of the Korean War finally overcame the military's objections. By the end of the 1950s, the armed forces had become far more integrated than American society at large.

Desegregating the Schools

The nation's schools soon became the primary target of civil rights advocates. The NAACP concentrated first on universities, successfully waging an intensive legal battle to win admission for qualified African Americans to graduate and professional schools. Led by Thurgood Marshall, NAACP lawyers then took on the broader issue of segregation in the country's public schools. Challenging the 1896 Supreme Court decision (*Plessy* v. *Ferguson*) that upheld the constitutionality of separate but equal public facilities (see "The Shaping of Jim Crow," pp. 584–585), Marshall argued that even substantially equal but separate schools did profound psychological damage to African American children and thus violated the Fourteenth Amendment.

The Supreme Court was unanimous in its 1954 decision in the case of *Brown* v. *Board of Education of Topeka*. Chief Justice Earl Warren, recently appointed by President Eisenhower, wrote the landmark opinion which flatly declared "separate educational facilities are inherently unequal." To divide grade school children "solely because of their race," Warren argued, "generates a feeling of inferiority as to their status in the community that may affect their hearts and minds in a way unlikely ever to be undone." Despite this sweeping language, Warren realized it would be difficult to change historic patterns of segregation quickly. Accordingly, in 1955 the Court ruled that implementation should proceed "with all deliberate speed" and left the details to the lower federal courts.

The process of desegregating the schools proved to be agonizingly slow. Officials in the border states quickly complied with the Court's ruling, but states deeper in the South responded with a policy of massive resistance. Local white citizens' councils organized to fight for retention of racial separation; 101 representatives and senators signed a Southern Manifesto in 1956 that denounced the *Brown* decision as "a clear abuse of judicial power." School boards, encouraged by this show of defiance, found a variety of ways to evade the Court's ruling. The most successful was the passage of pupil placement laws. These laws enabled local officials to assign individual students to schools on the basis of scholastic aptitude, ability to adjust, and "morals, conduct, health and personal standards." These stalling tactics led to long disputes in the federal courts; by the end of the decade, less than 1 percent of the black children in the Deep South attended school with whites.

A conspicuous lack of presidential support fur-

Angry whites taunt one of the African American students trying to pass through the lines of Arkansas National Guardsmen to enroll in Little Rock's Central High School in 1957.

ther weakened the desegregation effort. Dwight Eisenhower was not a racist, but he believed people's attitudes could not be changed by "cold lawmaking"—only "by appealing to reason, by prayer, and by constantly working at it through our own efforts." Quietly and unobtrusively, he worked to achieve desegregation in federal facilities, particularly in veterans' hospitals, navy yards, and the District of Columbia school system. Yet he refrained from endorsing the *Brown* decision, which he told an aide he believed had "*set back* progress in the South *at least fifteen years.*"

Southern leaders mistook Ike's silence for tacit support of segregation. In 1957, Governor Orville Faubus of Arkansas called out the National Guard to prevent the integration of Little Rock's Central High School on grounds of a threat to public order. After 270 armed troops turned back nine young African American students, a federal judge ordered the guardsmen removed; but when the blacks entered the school, a mob of 500 jeering whites surrounded the building. Eisenhower, who had told Faubus "the

Federal Constitution will be upheld by me by every legal means at my command," sent in 1,000 paratroopers to ensure the rights of the nine students to attend Central High. The children finished the school year under armed guard. Then Little Rock authorities closed Central High School for the next two years; when it reopened, there were only three African Americans in attendance.

Despite the snail's pace of school desegregation, the *Brown* decision led to other advances. In 1957, the Eisenhower administration proposed the first general civil rights legislation since Reconstruction. Strong southern resistance and compromise by both the administration and Senate Democratic Leader Lyndon B. Johnson of Texas weakened the bill considerably. The final act, however, did create a permanent Commission for Civil Rights, one of Truman's original goals. It also provided for federal efforts aimed at "securing and protecting the right to vote." A second civil rights act in 1960 slightly strengthened the voting-rights section.

Like the desegregation effort, the attempt to ensure African American voting rights in the

Linda Brown (left). Her parents were the plaintiffs in the Brown v. *Board of Education of* Topeka *landmark Supreme Court case.* Thurgood Marshall (right), *a leading African American civil rights lawyer, was chief counsel for the Browns.*

South was still largely symbolic. Southern registrars used a variety of devices, ranging from intimidation to unfair tests, to deny African Americans suffrage. Yet the actions of Congress and the Supreme Court marked a vital turning point in national policy toward racial justice.

The Beginnings of Black Activism

The most dynamic force for change came from African Americans themselves. The shift from legal struggles in the courts to protest in the streets began with an incident in Montgomery, Alabama. On December 1, 1955, Rosa Parks—a black seamstress who had been active in the local NAACP chapter—violated a city ordinance by refusing to give up her seat to a white person on a local bus. After her arrest, African Americans gathered to protest and found a young eloquent leader in Martin Luther King, Jr. The son of a successful Atlanta preacher, King had studied theology at Boston University and only recently had taken his first church in Montgomery. He agreed to lead a massive boycott of the city's bus system, which depended heavily on African American patronage.

The Montgomery bus boycott started out with a modest goal. Instead of challenging the legality of segregated seating, King simply asked that seats be taken on a first-come, first-served basis, with African Americans being seated from the back and the whites from the front of each bus. As the protest continued, however, and as they endured both legal harassment and sporadic acts of violence, the protesters began to be more assertive. An effective system of car pools enabled them to avoid using the city buses. Soon they were insisting on a complete end to segregated seating as they sang their new song of protest:

Ain't gonna ride them buses no more
Ain't gonna ride no more
Why in the hell don't the white folk know
That I ain't gonna ride no more.

The boycott ended in victory a year later when the Supreme Court ruled the Alabama segregated seating law unconstitutional. King had won far more than this limited dent in the wall of segregation, however. He had emerged as the charismatic leader of a new civil rights movement—a man who won acclaim not only at home but around the world. He visited Third World leaders in Africa and Asia and paid homage to India's Mahatma Gandhi, who had influenced his reliance on civil disobedience. He led a triumphant Prayer Pilgrimage to Washington in 1957 on the third anniversary of the *Brown* decision, stirring the crowd of thirty thousand with his ringing demand for the right to vote. His cry, "Give us the ballot," boomed in salvos that civil rights historian Taylor Branch likened to "cannon bursts in a diplomatic salute." His remarkable voice became familiar to the entire nation. Unlike many African American preachers, he never shouted, yet he captured his audience by presenting his ideas with both passion and a compelling cadence. "Though still a boy to many of his older listeners," Branch noted, "he had the commanding air of a burning sage."

Even more important, he had a strategy and message that fitted perfectly with the plight of his followers. Drawing on sources as diverse as Gandhi and Henry David Thoreau, King came out of the bus boycott with the concept of passive

Rosa Parks's refusal to give up her seat to a white man on a Montgomery, Alabama bus led to a citywide bus boycott that brought its leader, the Rev. Martin Luther King, Jr., to prominence.

resistance. "If cursed," he had told protesters in Montgomery, "do not curse back. If struck, do not strike back, but evidence love and goodwill at all times." The essence of his strategy was to use the apparent weakness of southern blacks—their lack of power—and turn it into a conquering weapon. His message to southern whites was clear and unmistakable: "We will match your capacity to inflict suffering with our capacity to endure suffering. We will meet your physical force with soul force. We will not hate you, but we will not obey your evil laws. We will soon wear you down by pure capacity to suffer."

His ultimate goal was to unite the broken community through bonds of Christian love. He hoped to use nonviolence to appeal to middle-class white America, "to the conscience of the great decent majority who through blindness, fear, pride or irrationality have allowed their consciences to sleep." The result, King prophesied, would be to enable future historians to say of the effort, "There lived a great people—a black people—who injected new meaning and dignity into the veins of civilization."

A year after the successful bus boycott, King founded the Southern Christian Leadership Conference (SCLC) to direct the crusade against segregation. Then in February 1960 another spontaneous event sparked a further advance for passive resistance. Four African American students from North Carolina Agricultural and Technical College sat down at a dime-store lunch counter in Greensboro, North Carolina, and refused to move after being denied service. Other students, both whites and blacks, joined in similar "sit-ins" across the South, as well as "kneel-ins" at churches and "wade-ins" at swimming pools. By the end of the year, some fifty thousand young people had succeeded in desegregating public facilities in over a hundred southern cities. Several thousand of the demonstrators were arrested and put in jail, but the movement gained strength, leading to the formation of the Student Nonviolent Coordinating Committee (SNCC) in April 1960. From this time on, SCLC and SNCC, with their tactic of direct, though peaceful, confrontation, would replace the NAACP and its reliance on court action in the forefront of the civil rights movement. The change would eventually lead to dramatic success for the movement, but it also ushered in a period of heightened tension and social turmoil in the 1960s.

KENNEDY AND THE NEW FRONTIER

On Monday evening, September 26, 1960, John F. Kennedy and Richard M. Nixon faced each other in the nation's first televised debate between two presidential candidates. Kennedy, as the relatively unknown Democratic challenger, had proposed the debates; Nixon, confident of his mastery of television, had accepted even though, as Eisenhower's vice president and early

Lunch counter sit-ins proved an effective tactic in the hard-fought effort to desegregate public facilities in southern cities.

front-runner in the election, he had more to lose and less to gain.

Nixon arrived at the Chicago studio looking tired and ill at ease. The Republican candidate was still recovering from a knee injury that had slowed his campaign and left him pale and weak as he pursued a hectic catch-up schedule. The TV cameras were merciless, highlighting his heavy jowls and accentuating his pallor. In contrast, Kennedy, tanned from open-air appearances in California and rested by a day spent free from other campaign activities, looked fresh and robust.

Before a nationwide audience estimated at 77 million, the Democratic challenger took the initiative, accusing the Republicans of letting the country drift at home and abroad. "I think it's time America started moving again," Kennedy declared. Nixon agreed the problems facing the nation were serious, claiming only that he had better solutions. For more than an hour, the two candidates answered questions from a panel of journalists. Radiating confidence and self-assurance, Kennedy used a flow of statistics and details to create the image of a man deeply knowledgeable about all aspects of government. On the defensive, Nixon fought back by citing Eisenhower's record of peace and prosperity, but he appeared tense and uncomfortable in front of the cameras.

Polls taken over the next few weeks revealed a sharp swing to Kennedy. Many Democrats and independents who had thought him too young or too inexperienced were impressed by his performance. Nixon suffered more from his unattractive image than from what he said; those who heard the debate on radio thought the Republican candidate more than held his own. In the three additional debates held during the campaign, Nixon improved his performance notably by wearing makeup to soften his appearance and by taking the offensive from Kennedy on the issues. But the damage had been done. A postelection poll revealed that of 4 million voters who were influenced by the debates, 3 million voted for Kennedy.

The televised debates were only one of many factors influencing the outcome of the 1960 election. In essence, Kennedy won because he took full advantage of all his opportunities. Lightly regarded by Democratic leaders, he won the nom-

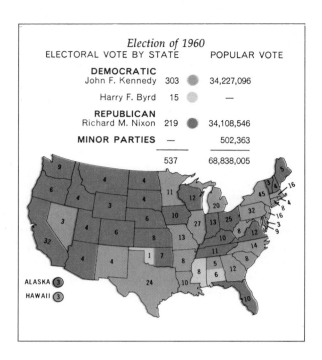

Election of 1960

	ELECTORAL VOTE BY STATE		POPULAR VOTE
DEMOCRATIC			
John F. Kennedy	303		34,227,096
Harry F. Byrd	15		—
REPUBLICAN			
Richard M. Nixon	219		34,108,546
MINOR PARTIES	—		502,363
	537		68,838,005

ination by appealing to the rank and file in the primaries, but then astutely chose Lyndon Johnson of Texas as his running mate to blunt Nixon's southern strategy.

During the fall campaign, Kennedy exploited the national mood of frustration that had followed *Sputnik*. At home, he promised to stimulate the lagging economy and carry forward long overdue reforms in education, health care, and civil rights under the banner of the "New Frontier." Abroad, he pledged a renewed commitment to the Cold War, vowing he would lead the nation to victory over the Soviet Union. He met the issue of his Catholicism head on, telling a group of Protestant ministers in Houston that as president he would always place country above religion. In the shrewdest move of all, he won over African American voters by helping to secure the release of Martin Luther King, Jr., from a Georgia jail where the civil rights leader was being held on a trumped-up charge.

The Democratic victory in 1960 was paper thin. Kennedy's edge in the popular vote was only two-tenths of 1 percent, and his wide margin in the electoral college (303 to 219) was tainted by voting irregularities in several states—notably Illinois and Texas—which went Democratic by very slender majorities. Yet even though he had

Both candidates performed well in the televised Kennedy–Nixon debates, but Nixon lost the advantage of greater name recognition, while Kennedy won supporters with his healthier appearance and more confident manner.

no mandate, Kennedy's triumph did mark a sharp political shift. In contrast to the aging Eisenhower, Kennedy symbolized youth, energy, and ambition. His mastery of the new medium of television reflected his sensitivity to the changes taking place in American life in the 1960s. He came to office promising reform at home and advance abroad. Over the next five years, he and Lyndon Johnson achieved many of their goals, only to find the nation caught up in new and even greater dilemmas.

The New Frontiersmen

The election of John F. Kennedy marked the arrival of a new generation of leadership. For the first time, people born in the twentieth century who had entered political life after World War II were in charge of national affairs. Kennedy himself had first been elected to Congress in 1946 at the age of twenty-nine and then had won a Senate seat in 1952. Although he had not sponsored any significant legislation as a senator, he championed the traditional Democratic reforms during

his presidential campaign, labeling them the New Frontier. Above all, he had criticized the Republicans for allowing sluggish economic growth and failing to deal with such pressing social problems as health care and education. His call to get the nation moving again was particularly attractive to young people, who had shunned political involvement during the Eisenhower years.

The new administration reflected Kennedy's aura of youth and energy. Major cabinet appointments went to activists—notably Connecticut governor Abraham Ribicoff as secretary of health, education, and welfare; labor lawyer Arthur J. Goldberg as secretary of labor; and Arizona congressman Stuart Udall as secretary of the interior. The most controversial choice was Robert F. Kennedy, the president's brother, as attorney general. Critics scoffed at his lack of legal experience, leading JFK to note jokingly he wanted to give Bobby "a little experience before he goes out to practice law." In fact, the president prized his brother's loyalty and shrewd political advice.

Equally important were the members of the White House staff who handled domestic affairs. Like their counterparts in foreign policy, these New Frontiersmen—Kenneth O'Donnell, Theodore Sorensen, Richard Goodwin, and Walter Heller—prided themselves on being tough-minded and pragmatic. In contrast to Eisenhower, Kennedy relied heavily on academics and intellectuals to help him infuse the nation with energy and a new sense of direction.

Kennedy's greatest asset was his own personality. A cool, attractive, and intelligent man, he possessed a sense of style that endeared him to the American public. He invited artists and musicians as well as corporate executives to White House functions; and his speeches were filled with references to Emerson and Shakespeare. He seemed to be a new Lancelot, bent on calling forth the best in national life; admirers likened his inner circle to King Arthur's court at Camelot. Reporters loved him, both for his fact-filled and candid press conferences and for his witty comments. Thus, after an embarrassing foreign policy failure, when his standing in the polls actually went up, he remarked, "It's just like Eisenhower. The worse I do, the more popular I get."

The Congressional Obstacle

Neither Kennedy's wit nor charm proved strong enough to break the logjam in Congress. Since the late 1940s, a series of reform bills ranging from health care to federal aid to education had been stalled on Capitol Hill. Despite his own triumph, however, the election of 1960 clouded the outlook for the New Frontier program. The Democrats had lost twenty seats in the House and two in the Senate; even though they retained majorities in both branches, a conservative coalition of northern Republicans and southern Democrats opposed all efforts at reform.

The situation was especially critical in the House, where 101 southern representatives held the balance of power between 160 northern Democrats and 174 Republicans. Aided by Speaker Sam Rayburn, Kennedy was able to enlarge the Rules Committee and overcome a traditional conservative roadblock, but the narrowness of the vote, 217 to 212, revealed how difficult it would be to enact reform measures. "There is no sense in raising hell and then not being suc-

cessful," JFK noted ruefully after Catholic objections to his aid to education bill—which excluded federal money for church schools—led to its defeat in the House. Discouraged, the president gave up the fight for health care in the Senate; he settled instead for a modest increase in the minimum wage and the passage of manpower training and area-redevelopment legislation.

Kennedy had no more success in enacting his program in 1962 and 1963. The conservative coalition stood firmly against education and health-care proposals. Shifting ground, the president did win approval for a trade expansion act in 1962 designed to lower tariff barriers, but no significant reform legislation was passed. Although the composition of Congress was his main obstacle, Kennedy's greater interest in foreign policy and his distaste for legislative infighting contributed to the outcome. JFK did not enjoy "blarneying with pompous congressmen and simply would not take the time to do it," one observer noted. As a result, the New Frontier languished in Congress.

Economic Advance

Kennedy gave a higher priority to the sluggish American economy. During the last years of Eisenhower's administration, the rate of economic growth had slowed to just over 2 percent annually, while unemployment rose to new heights with each recession. JFK was determined to recover quickly from the recession he had inherited and to stimulate the economy to achieve a much higher rate of long-term growth. In part, he wanted to redeem his campaign pledge to get the nation moving again; he also felt the United States had to surpass the Soviet Union in economic vitality.

Kennedy received conflicting advice from the experts. Those who claimed the problem was essentially a technological one urged manpower training and area-redevelopment programs to modernize American industry. Others called for long overdue federal spending to rebuild the nation's public facilities—from parks and playgrounds to decaying bridges and courthouses in the cities. Kennedy sided with the first group, largely because Congress was opposed to massive spending on public works.

The actual stimulation of the economy, however, came not from social programs but from greatly increased appropriations for defense and space. A $6 billion increase in the arms budget in 1961 gave the economy a great lift, and Kennedy's decision to send an astronaut to the moon eventually cost $25 billion. By 1962, over half the federal budget was devoted to space and defense; aircraft and computer companies in the South and West benefited, but unemployment remained uncomfortably high in the older industrial areas of the Northeast and Midwest.

The administration's desire to keep the inflation rate low led to a serious confrontation with the business community. Kennedy relied on informal wage and price guidelines to hold down the cost of living. But in April 1962, just after the president had persuaded the steelworkers' union to accept a new contract with no wage increases and only a few additional benefits, U.S. Steel head Roger Blough informed Kennedy that his company was raising steel prices by $6 a ton. Outraged, the president publicly called the increase "a wholly unjustifiable and irresponsible defiance of the public interest" and accused Blough of displaying "contempt for the interests of 185 million Americans." Privately, Kennedy was even blunter. He confided to aides, "My father always told me that all businessmen were sons-of-bitches, but I never believed it till now."

Roger Blough soon gave way. The president's tongue lashing, along with a cutoff in Pentagon steel orders and the threat of an antitrust suit, forced him to reconsider. When several smaller steel companies refused to raise their prices in hopes of expanding their share of the market, U.S. Steel rolled back its prices. The business community deeply resented the president's action, and when the stock market, which had been rising steadily since 1960, suddenly fell sharply in late May 1962, analysts were quick to label the decline "the Kennedy market."

Troubled by his strained relations with business and by the continued lag in economic growth, the president decided to adopt a more unorthodox approach in 1963. Walter Heller, chairman of the Council of Economic Advisers, had been arguing for a major cut in taxes since 1961 in the belief it would stimulate consumer spending and give the economy the jolt it needed. The idea of a tax cut and resulting deficits during a period of prosperity went against economic orthodoxy, but Kennedy finally gave his

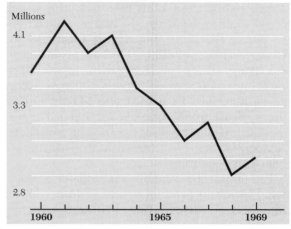

Unemployment, 1960–1969

Millions

Source: Compiled from U.S. Bureau of the Census, Historical Statistics of the United States, Colonial Times to 1970, Bicentennial Edition, Washington, D.C., 1975.

approval. In January 1963, the president proposed a tax reduction of $13.5 billion, asserting "the unrealistically heavy drag of federal income taxes on private purchasing power" was the "largest single barrier to full employment." When finally enacted by Congress in 1964, the massive tax cut led to the longest sustained economic advance in American history.

Kennedy's economic policy was far more successful than his legislative efforts. Although the rate of economic growth doubled to 4.5 percent by the end of 1963 and unemployment was reduced substantially, the cost of living rose only 1.3 percent a year. Personal income went up 13 percent in the early 1960s, but the greatest gains came in corporate profits—up 67 percent in this period. Yet critics pointed to the Kennedy administration's failure to close the glaring loopholes in the tax laws that benefited the rich and its lack of effort to help those at the bottom by forcing redistribution of national wealth. Despite the overall economic growth, the public sector continued to be neglected. "I am not sure what the advantage is," complained economist John Kenneth Galbraith, "in having a few more dollars to spend if the air is too dirty to breathe, the water too polluted to drink, the commuters are losing out in the struggle to get in and out of the cities, the streets are filthy, and the schools so bad that the young, perhaps wisely, stay away."

Moving Slowly on Civil Rights

Kennedy faced a genuine dilemma over the issue of civil rights. Despite his own lack of a strong record while in the Senate, he had portrayed himself during the 1960 campaign as a crusader for African American rights. He had promised to launch an attack on segregation in the Deep South and had endeared himself to people across the nation when he helped win Martin Luther King's release from a Georgia jail. Kennedy's fear of alienating the large bloc of southern Democrats, however, forced him to downplay civil rights legislation.

The president's solution was to defer congressional action in favor of executive leadership in this area. He directed his brother, Attorney General Robert Kennedy, to continue and expand the Eisenhower administration's efforts to achieve voting rights for southern blacks. To register previously disfranchised citizens, the Justice Department worked with the civil rights movement—notably the Student Non-Violent Coordinating Committee (SNCC)—in the Deep South. In two years, the Kennedy administration increased the number of voting rights suits fivefold. Yet the attorney general could not force the FBI to provide protection for the civil rights volunteers who risked their lives by encouraging African Americans to register. "SNCC's only contact with federal authority," noted one observer, "consisted of the FBI agents who stood by taking notes while local policemen beat up SNCC members."

Other efforts had equally mixed results. Vice President Lyndon Johnson headed a presidential Commission on Equal Employment Opportunities that worked with defense industries and other government contractors to increase jobs for African Americans. But a limited budget and a reliance on voluntary cooperation prevented any dramatic gains; African American employment improved only in direct proportion to economic growth in the early 1960s.

Kennedy did succeed in appointing a number of African Americans to high government positions: Robert Weaver became chief of the federal housing agency, and Thurgood Marshall, who pleaded the *Brown* v. *Topeka* school desegregation case before the Supreme Court, was named to the U.S. Circuit Court. On the other hand, among his judicial appointments, Kennedy included one Mississippi jurist who referred to African Americans in court as "niggers" and once compared them to "a bunch of chimpanzees."

The civil rights movement refused to accept Kennedy's indirect approach. In May 1961, the Congress of Racial Equality (CORE) sponsored a "freedom ride" in which a biracial group attempted to test a 1960 Supreme Court decision outlawing segregation in all bus and train stations used in interstate commerce. When they arrived in Birmingham, Alabama, the freedom riders were attacked by a mob of angry whites. "It's the most horrible thing I've ever seen," a Justice Department official reported. "It's terrible, terrible." The attorney general quickly dispatched several hundred federal marshals to protect the freedom riders, but the president, deeply involved in the Berlin crisis, was more upset at the distraction the protesters created. Kennedy directed one of his aides to get in touch with the leaders of CORE. "Tell them to call it off," he demanded. "Stop them."

In September, after the attorney general finally convinced the Interstate Commerce Commission to issue an order banning segregation in interstate terminals and buses, the freedom rides ended. The Kennedy administration then sought to prevent further confrontations by involving civil rights activists in its voting drive.

A pattern of belated reaction to southern racism marked the basic approach of the Kennedys. When James Meredith courageously sought admission to the all-white University of Mississippi in 1962, the president and the attorney general worked closely with Mississippi governor Ross Barnett to avoid violence. A transcript of Robert Kennedy's conversation with Governor Barnett on September 25 indicates that the attorney general's concerns were for the legal rather than the moral issues involved:

RFK:

I think the problem is that the federal courts have acted and when there is a conflict between your state and the federal courts under arrangements made some years ago—

BARNETT:

The institution is supported by the taxpayers of this state and controlled by the Trustees.

The attempts of African Americans to end discrimination and secure their civil rights met violent resistance in Birmingham, Alabama, where police used snarling dogs, fire hoses, clubs, and electric cattle prods to turn back the unarmed demonstrators.

RFK:

Governor, you are a part of the United States.

BARNETT:

. . . I am going to treat you with every courtesy, but I won't agree to let that boy get to Ole Miss. I will never agree to that. I would rather spend my whole life in a penitentiary than do that.

RFK:

I have a responsibility to enforce the laws of the United States.

BARNETT:

I appreciate that. You have a responsibility. Why don't you let the NAACP run their own affairs and quit cooperating with that crowd? . . .

Despite Barnett's later promise of cooperation, the night before Meredith enrolled at the University of Mississippi, a mob attacked the federal marshals and National Guard troops sent to protect him. The violence left 2 dead and 375 injured, including 166 marshals and 12 guardsmen, but Meredith attended the university and eventually graduated.

In 1963, Kennedy sent the deputy attorney general to face down Governor George C. Wallace, an avowed segregationist who had promised "to stand in the schoolhouse door" to prevent the integration of the University of Alabama. After a brief confrontation, Wallace yielded to federal authority, and two African American students peacefully desegregated the state university.

"I Have a Dream"

Martin Luther King, Jr., finally forced Kennedy to abandon his cautious tactics and come out openly in behalf of racial justice. In the spring of 1963, King began a massive protest in Birmingham, one of the South's most segregated cities. Public marches and demonstrations aimed at integrating public facilities and opening up jobs for African Americans quickly led to police harassment and many arrests, including that of King himself. Police Commissioner Eugene "Bull" Connor was determined to crush the civil rights movement; King was equally determined to prevail. Writing from his cell in Birmingham, he vowed an active campaign to bring the issue of racial injustice to national attention. When several Alabama clergymen asked him to open negotiations rather than provoke violence, King responded from jail, "Nonviolent direct action seeks to create such a crisis and foster such a tension that a community which has constantly refused to negotiate is forced to confront the issue."

Bull Connor played directly into King's hands. On May 3, as six thousand children marched in place of the jailed protesters, authorities broke up a demonstration with clubs, snarling police dogs, and high-pressure water hoses strong enough to take the bark off a tree. With a horrified nation watching scene after scene of this brutality on television, the Kennedy administration quickly intervened to arrange a settlement with the Birmingham civic leaders that ended the violence and granted the protesters most of their demands.

More important, Kennedy finally ended his long hesitation and sounded the call for action. "We are confronted primarily with a moral issue," he told the nation on June 11. "It is as old as the Scriptures and is as clear as the American Constitution." Eight days later, the administration sponsored civil rights legislation providing equal access to all public accommodations as well as an extension of voting rights for African Americans.

Despite pleas from the government for an end to demonstrations and protests, the movement's leaders decided to keep pressure on the administration. They scheduled a massive march on Washington for August 1963. The president and the attorney general persuaded the sponsors to tone down their rhetoric—notably one speech by a SNCC leader that termed the Kennedy legislation "too little, too late." On August 28, more than 200,000 marchers gathered for a day-long rally in front of the Lincoln Memorial where they listened to hymns, speeches, and prayers for racial justice. The climax of the event was Martin Luther King's eloquent description of his dream for America. It concluded:

> When we let freedom ring, when we let it ring from every village and every hamlet, from every state and every city, we will be able to speed up that day when all God's children, black men and white men, Jews and Gentiles, Protestants and Catholics, will be able to join hands and sing, in the words of that old Negro spiritual, "Free at last! Free at last! Thank God almighty, we are free at last!"

By the time of Kennedy's death in November 1963, his civil rights legislation was well on its way to passage in Congress. Yet even this achievement did not fully satisfy his critics. For two years, they had waited for him to deliver on his campaign promise to wipe out housing discrimination "with a stroke of the pen." When the executive order on housing was finally issued in November 1962, it proved disappointing; it ignored all past discrimination and applied only to homes and apartments financed by the federal government. For many, Kennedy had raised hopes for racial equality that he never fulfilled.

But unlike Eisenhower, he had provided presidential leadership for the civil rights movement. His emphasis on executive action gradually paid off, especially in extending voting rights. By early 1964, 40 percent of southern blacks had the franchise, compared to only 28 percent in 1960. Moreover, Kennedy's sense of caution and restraint, painful and frustrating as it was to African American activists, had proved well founded. Avoiding an early, and possibly fatal, defeat in Congress, he had waited until a national consensus emerged and then had carefully channeled it behind effective legislation. Behaving very much the way Franklin Roosevelt did in guiding

The 1963 march on Washington gave the civil rights movement a national focus.

Moments after this photograph was taken in Dallas police headquarters, accused presidential assassin Lee Harvey Oswald was fatally shot. Millions of television viewers watched in horrified disbelief as the television cameras recorded Oswald's murder.

Aboard Air Force One on the return from Dallas to Washington, D.C., Judge Sarah Hughes administers the presidential oath of office to a grim Lyndon Johnson.

the nation into World War II, Kennedy chose to be a fox rather than a lion on civil rights.

The Supreme Court and Reform

The most active impulse for social change in the early 1960s came from a surprising source: the usually staid and conservative Supreme Court. Under the leadership of Earl Warren, a pragmatic jurist more noted for his political astuteness than his legal scholarship, the Court ventured into new areas. A group of liberal judges—especially William O. Douglas, Hugo Black, and William J. Brennan, Jr.—argued for social reform, while advocates of judicial restraint (such as John Marshall Harlan and Felix Frankfurter) fought stubbornly against the new activism.

In addition to ruling against segregation, the Warren Court in the Eisenhower years had angered conservatives by protecting the constitutional rights of victims of McCarthyism. In *Yates* v. *U.S.* (1956), the judges reversed the conviction of fourteen communist leaders, claiming government prosecutors had failed to prove that the accused had actually organized a plot to overthrow the government. Mere advocacy of revolution, the Court said, did not justify conviction. In 1957, the Court issued a series of rulings that led

dissenting Justice Tom Clark to protest what he saw as giving defendants "a Roman holiday for rummaging through confidential information as well as vital national secrets."

The resignation of Felix Frankfurter in 1962 enabled President Kennedy to appoint Secretary of Labor Arthur Goldberg, a committed liberal, to the Supreme Court. With a clear majority now favoring judicial intervention, the Warren Court issued a series of landmark decisions designed to extend to state and local jurisdictions the traditional rights afforded the accused in federal courts. Thus in *Gideon* v. *Wainwright* (1963), *Escobedo* v. *Illinois* (1964), and *Miranda* v. *Arizona* (1966), the majority decreed that defendants had to be provided lawyers, had to be informed of their constitutional rights, and could not be interrogated or induced to confess to a crime without defense counsel being present. In effect, the Court extended to the poor and the ignorant those constitutional guarantees that had always been available to the rich and to the legally informed—notably hardened criminals.

The most far-reaching Warren Court decisions came in the area of legislative reapportionment—a "political thicket" that Justice Frankfurter had always refused to enter. In 1962, the Court ruled in *Baker* v. *Carr* that Tennessee had to redistribute its legislative seats to give citizens in Memphis equal representation. Subsequent decisions reinforced the ban on rural overrepresentation as the Court proclaimed that places in all legislative bodies, including the House of Representatives, be allocated on the basis of "people, not land or trees or pastures." The principle of "one man, one vote" greatly increased the political power of cities at the expense of rural areas; it also involved the Court directly in the reapportionment process, frequently forcing judges to draw up new legislative and congressional districts.

The activism of the Supreme Court stirred up a storm of criticism. The rulings that extended protection to criminals and those accused of subversive activity led some Americans to charge that the Court was encouraging crime and weakening national security. The John Birch Society, an extreme anticommunist group, demanded the impeachment of Chief Justice Warren. Decisions banning school prayers and permitting pornography incensed many conservative Americans, who saw the Court as undermining moral values. "They've put the Negroes in the schools," complained one southern congressman, "and now they've driven God out." Legal scholars worried more about the weakening of the Court's prestige as it became more directly involved in the political process. On balance, however, the Warren Court helped achieve greater social justice by protecting the rights of the underprivileged and by permitting dissent and free expression to flourish.

"LET US CONTINUE"

The New Frontier came to a sudden and violent end on November 22, 1963, when Lee Harvey Oswald assassinated John F. Kennedy as the president rode in a motorcade in downtown Dallas. The shock of losing the young president, who had become a symbol of hope and promise for a whole generation, stunned the entire world. The American people were bewildered by the rapid sequence of events: the brutal killing of their beloved president; the televised slaying of Oswald by Jack Ruby in the basement of the Dallas police station; the composure and dignity of Kennedy's widow, Jacqueline, at the ensuing state funeral; and the hurried Warren Commission report, which identified Oswald as the lone assassin. Afterward, critics would charge Oswald had been

part of a vast conspiracy, but at the time the prevailing national reaction was a numbing sense of loss.

Vice President Lyndon B. Johnson moved quickly to fill the vacuum left by Kennedy's death. Sworn in on board Air Force One as he returned to Washington, he soon met with a stream of world leaders to reassure them of American political stability. Five days after the tragedy in Dallas, Johnson spoke eloquently to a special joint session of Congress. Recalling JFK's summons in his inaugural address, "Let us begin," the new president declared, "Today in the moment of new resolve, I would say to all my fellow Americans, 'let us continue.'" Asking Congress to enact Kennedy's tax and civil rights bills as a tribute to the fallen leader, LBJ concluded, "Let us here highly resolve that John Fitzgerald Kennedy did not live or die in vain."

Johnson in Action

Lyndon Johnson suffered from the inevitable comparison with his young and stylish predecessor. LBJ was acutely aware of his own lack of polish; he sought to surround himself with Kennedy advisers and insiders, hoping their learning and sophistication would rub off on him. Johnson's assets were very real—he possessed an intimate knowledge of Congress, an incredible energy and determination to succeed, and a fierce ego. When a young marine officer tried to direct him to the proper helicopter, saying, "This one is yours," Johnson replied, "Son, they are all my helicopters."

LBJ's height and intensity gave him a powerful presence; he dominated any room he entered, and he delighted in using his physical power of persuasion. One Texas politican explained why he had given in to Johnson: "Lyndon got me by the lapels and put his face on top of mine and he talked and talked and talked. I figured it was either getting drowned or joining."

Yet LBJ found it impossible to project his intelligence and vitality to large audiences. Unlike Kennedy, he wilted before the camera, turning his televised speeches into stilted and awkward performances. Trying to belie his reputation as a riverboat gambler, he came across like a foxy grandpa, clever, calculating, and not to be trusted. He lacked Kennedy's wit and charm, and reporters delighted in describing the way he

A shrewd politician and a master of the legislative process, Johnson always knew what votes he could count on—and those he couldn't. Here, he studies the tally of a Congressional head count to gauge his support in Congress.

berated his aides or shocked the nation by baring his belly to show the scar from a recent operation.

Whatever his shortcomings in style, however, Johnson possessed far greater ability than Kennedy in dealing with Congress. He entered the White House with more than thirty years of experience in Washington as a legislative aide, congressman, and senator. His encyclopedic knowledge of the legislative process and his shrewd manipulation of individual senators had enabled him to become the most influential Senate majority leader in history. Famed for "the Johnson treatment," a legendary ability to use personal persuasion to reach his goals, Johnson in fact relied more on his close ties with the Senate's power brokers—or "whales," as he called them— than on his exploitation of the "minnows."

Above all, Johnson sought consensus. Indifferent to ideology, he had moved easily from New Deal liberalism to oil-and-gas conservatism as his career advanced. He had carefully cultivated Richard Russell of Georgia, leader of the Dixie

bloc, but he also had taken Hubert Humphrey, a Minnesota liberal, under his wing. He had performed a balancing act on civil rights, working with the Eisenhower administration on behalf of the 1957 Voting Rights Act, yet carefully weakening it to avoid alienating southern Democrats. When Kennedy dashed Johnson's own intense presidential ambitions in 1960, LBJ had gracefully agreed to be his running mate and had endured the humiliation of the vice presidency loyally and silently. Suddenly thrust into power, Johnson used his gifts wisely. Citing his favorite scriptural passage from Isaiah, "Come now, and let us reason together, saith the Lord," he concentrated on securing passage of Kennedy's tax and civil rights bills in 1964.

The tax cut came first. Aware of the power wielded by Senate Finance Committee Chairman Harry Byrd, a Virginia conservative, Johnson astutely lowered Kennedy's projected $101.5 billion budget for 1965 to $97.9 billion. Although Byrd voted against the tax cut, he let the measure out of his committee, telling Johnson, "I'll be working for you behind the scenes." In February, Congress reduced personal income taxes by more than $10 billion, touching off a sustained economic boom. Consumer spending increased by an impressive $43 billion in the next eighteen months, and new jobs opened up at the rate of one million a year.

Johnson was even more influential in passing the Kennedy civil rights measure. Staying in the background, he encouraged liberal amendments that strengthened the bill in the House. With Hubert Humphrey leading the floor fight in the Senate, Johnson refused all efforts at compromise, counting on growing public pressure to force northern Republicans to abandon their traditional alliance with southern Democrats. Everett M. Dirksen of Illinois, the GOP leader in the Senate, met repeatedly with Johnson at the White House. When LBJ refused to yield, Dirksen finally announced, "The time has come for equality of opportunity in sharing in government, in education, and in employment," and led a Republican vote to end a fifty-seven-day filibuster.

The 1964 Civil Rights Act, signed on July 2, made illegal the segregation of African Americans in public facilities, established an Equal Employment Opportunity Commission to lessen racial discrimination in employment, and protected the voting rights of African Americans. An amendment sponsored by segregationists in an effort to weaken the bill added gender to the prohibition of discrimination in Title VII of the act; in the future, women's groups would use this clause to secure government support for greater equality in employment and education.

The Election of 1964

Passage of two key Kennedy measures within six months did not satisfy Johnson. Having established the theme of continuity, he now set out to win the presidency in his own right. Eager to surpass Kennedy's narrow victory in 1960, he hoped to win by a great landslide.

Searching for a cause of his own, LBJ found one in the issue of poverty. Beginning in the late 1950s, economists had warned that the prevailing affluence only disguised a persistent and deep-seated problem of poverty. John Kenneth Galbraith had urged a policy of increased public spending to help the poor, but Kennedy ignored Galbraith's advice. In 1962, however, Michael Harrington's book *The Other America* attracted national attention. Writing with passion and eloquence, Harrington claimed that nearly one-fifth of the nation, some 35 million Americans, lived in poverty.

Three groups predominated among the poor— African Americans, the aged, and households headed by women. The problem, Harrington contended, was that the poor were invisible, living in slums or depressed areas like Appalachia and cut off from the educational facilities, medical care, and employment opportunities afforded more affluent Americans. Moreover, poverty was a vicious cycle. The children of the poor were trapped in the same culture of poverty as their parents, living without hope or knowledge of how to enter the mainstream of American life.

Johnson quickly took over proposals that Kennedy had been developing and made them his own. In his State of the Union address in January 1964, LBJ announced, "This administration, today, here and now, declares unconditional war on poverty in America." Over the next eight months, Johnson fashioned a comprehensive poverty program under the direction of R. Sargent Shriver, Kennedy's brother-in-law. The

The Election of 1964

president added $500 million to existing programs to come up with a $1 billion effort that Congress passed in August 1964.

The new Office of Economic Opportunity (OEO) set up a wide variety of programs, ranging from Head Start for preschoolers to the Job Corps for high school dropouts in need of vocational training. The emphasis was on self-help, with the government providing money and know-how so the poor could reap the benefits of neighborhood day-care centers, consumer education classes, legal aid services, and adult remedial reading programs. The level of funding was never high enough to meet the OEO's ambitious goals, and a controversial attempt to include representatives of the poor in the Community Action Program led to bitter political feuding with city and state officials. Nonetheless, the war on poverty, along with the economic growth provided by the tax cut, helped reduce the ranks of the poor by nearly ten million between 1964 and 1967.

For Johnson, the new program established his reputation as a reformer in an election year. He still faced two challenges to his authority. The first was Robert F. Kennedy, the late president's brother who continued as attorney general but who wanted to become vice president and Johnson's eventual successor in the White House. Desperate to prove his ability to succeed without Kennedy help, LBJ commented, "I don't need that little runt to win," and chose Hubert Humphrey as his running mate.

The second challenge was the Republican candidate, Senator Barry Goldwater, an outspoken conservative from Arizona. An attractive and articulate man, Goldwater openly advocated a rejection of the welfare state and a return to unregulated free enterprise. To Johnson's delight,

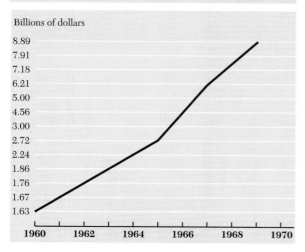

Federal Aid to Education, 1960–1970

Billions of dollars

8.89
7.91
7.18
6.21
5.00
4.56
3.00
2.72
2.24
1.86
1.76
1.67
1.63

1960   1962   1964   1966   1968   1970

Source: Compiled from U.S. Bureau of the Census, Historical Statistics of the United States, Colonial Times to 1970, *Bicentennial Edition, Washington, D.C., 1975.*

Goldwater chose to place ideology ahead of political expediency. The senator spoke out boldly against the Tennessee Valley Authority, denounced Social Security, and advocated a hawkish foreign policy. "In Your Heart, You Know He's Right," read the Republican slogan, leading the Democrats to reply, "Yes, Far Right," and in reference to a careless Goldwater comment about using nuclear weapons, Johnson backers punned, "In Your Heart, You Know He Might."

Johnson stuck carefully to the middle of the road, embracing the liberal reform program—which he now called "The Great Society"—while stressing his concern for balanced budgets and fiscal orthodoxy. The more Goldwater sagged in the polls, the harder Johnson campaigned, determined to achieve his treasured landslide. On election day, LBJ did even better than FDR had in 1936, receiving 61.1 percent of the popular vote and an overwhelming majority in the electoral college; Goldwater carried only Arizona and five states of the Deep South. Equally important, the Democrats achieved huge gains in Congress, controlling the House by a margin of 295 to 140 and the Senate by 68 to 32. Kennedy's legacy and Goldwater's candor had enabled Johnson to break the conservative grip on Congress for the first time in a quarter of a century.

The Triumph of Reform

LBJ moved quickly to secure his legislative goals. Despite solid majorities in both Houses, including seventy freshman Democrats who had ridden into office on his coattails, Johnson knew he would have to enact the Great Society as swiftly as possible. "You've got to give it all you can, that first year," he told an aide. "Doesn't matter what kind of majority you come in with. You've got just one year when they treat you right, and before they start worrying about themselves."

Johnson gave two traditional Democratic reforms—health care and education—top priority. Aware of strong opposition to a comprehensive medical program, LBJ settled for Medicare, which mandated health insurance under the Social Security program for Americans over age sixty-five, with a supplementary Medicaid program for the indigent. To symbolize the end of a long struggle, Johnson flew to Independence, Missouri, so Truman could witness the ceremonial signing of the Medicare law, which had its origins in Truman's 1949 health insurance proposal.

LBJ overcame the religious hurdle on education by supporting a child-benefit approach, allocating federal money to advance the education of students in parochial as well as public schools. The Elementary and Secondary Education Act of 1965 provided over $1 billion in federal aid, the largest share going to school districts with the highest percentage of impoverished pupils. During his administration, federal aid to education increased sharply.

Civil rights proved to be the most difficult test of Johnson's leadership. Martin Luther King, concerned that three million southern blacks were still denied the right to vote, in early 1965 chose Selma, Alabama, as the site for a test case. The white authorities in Selma, led by Sheriff James Clark, used cattle prods and bullwhips to break up the demonstrations. Over two thousand African Americans were jailed. Johnson intervened in March, after TV cameras showed Sheriff Clark's deputies brutally halting a march from Selma to Montgomery. The president ordered the Alabama National Guard to federal duty to protect the demonstrators, had the Justice

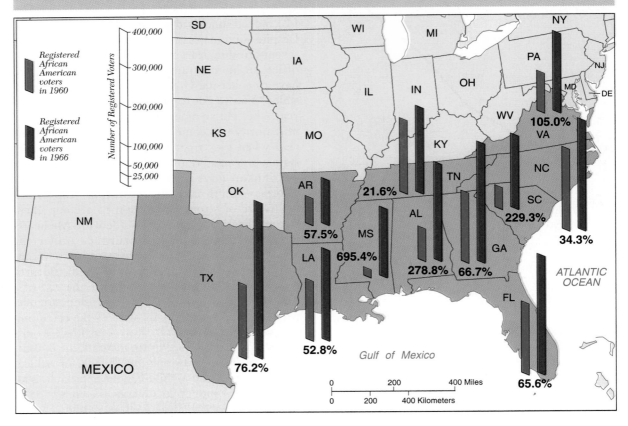

African American Voter Registration Before and After the Voting Rights Act of 1965

The Voting Rights Act of 1965 empowered federal supervision and eliminated literacy tests for voter registration. (The percentages shown on the map are the percentage increase in African American voter registration between 1960 and 1966.)

Department draw up a new voting-rights bill, and personally addressed the Congress on civil rights. "I speak tonight for the dignity of man and the destiny of democracy," he began. Calling the denial of the right to vote "deadly wrong," LBJ issued a compelling call to action. "Their cause must be our cause too. Because it is not just Negroes, but really it is all of us who must overcome the crippling legacy of bigotry and injustice."

Five months later, Congress passed the Voting Rights Act of 1965. Once again Johnson had worked with Senate Republican leader Dirksen to break a southern filibuster and assure passage of a measure. The act banned literacy tests in states and counties in which less than half the population had voted in 1964 and provided for federal registrars in these areas to assure African Americans the franchise.

The results were dramatic. In less than a year, 166,000 African Americans were added to the voting rolls in Alabama; African American registration went up 400 percent in Mississippi. By the end of the decade, the percentage of eligible African American voters who had registered had risen from 40 to 65 percent. For the first time since Reconstruction, African Americans were playing an active and effective role in southern politics.

Before the Eighty-ninth Congress ended its first session in the fall of 1965, it had passed eighty-nine bills. These included measures to create two new cabinet departments (Transportation, and Housing and Urban Affairs); acts to provide for

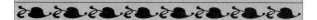

CHRONOLOGY

1946	Republicans win control of both houses of Congress in November elections
1947	Truman orders loyalty program for government employees (March) • William Levitt announces first Levittown (May)
1948	Truman orders end to segregation in armed forces (July) • Truman scores upset victory in presidential election
1949	Minimum wage raised from forty to seventy-five cents an hour
1950	Senator Joseph McCarthy claims communists in government
1952	Republican Dwight Eisenhower elected president
1953	Julius and Ethel Rosenberg executed for atomic-secrets spying (June)
1954	Supreme Court orders schools desegregated in *Brown* v. *Board of Education of Topeka* (May)
1955	Dr. Jonas Salk reports success of antipolio vaccine (April) • African Americans begin boycott of Montgomery, Alabama bus company (December)
1956	Eisenhower reelected in landslide victory
1957	Congress passes first Civil Rights Act since Reconstruction (August) • Soviets launch *Sputnik* (October)
1960	African American college students stage sit-in in Greensboro, North Carolina (February)
1961	Kennedy commits United States to landing an astronaut on the moon by 1969 (May)
1962	James Meredith is first African American to enroll at University of Mississippi (September)
1963	Kennedy assassinated; Lyndon B. Johnson sworn in as president (November)
1964	President Johnson declares war on poverty (January) • Johnson wins presidency in landslide victory (November)
1965	Martin Luther King, Jr., leads Selma-Montgomery march (March) • Medicare legislation provides aged with medical care (July)

highway safety and to ensure clean air and water; and large appropriations for higher education, public housing, and the continuing war on poverty. In nine months, Johnson had enacted the entire Democratic reform agenda, moving the nation beyond the New Deal by mandating federal concern for health, education, and the quality of life in both city and country.

The man responsible for this great leap forward, however, had failed to win the public adulation he so deeply desired. His legislative skills had made the most of the opportunities offered by the 1964 Democratic landslide, but the people did not respond to Johnson's leadership with the warmth and praise they had showered on Kennedy. Reporters continued to portray him as a crude wheeler-dealer; as a maniac who drove around Texas back roads at 90 miles an hour, one hand on the wheel and the other holding a can of beer; or as a bully who picked up his dog by the ears. No one was more aware of this lack of affection than LBJ himself. His public support, he told an aide, is "like a Western river, broad but not deep."

Johnson's realization of the fleeting nature of his popularity was all too accurate. The dilemmas of the Cold War began to divert his attention from domestic concerns and eventually, in the case of Vietnam, would overwhelm him. Yet his legislative achievements were still remarkable. In one brief outburst of reform, he had accomplished more than any president since FDR.

Difficulties abroad would dim the luster of the Johnson presidency, but they could not diminish the lasting impact of the Great Society on American life. Federal aid to education, the enactment of Medicare and Medicaid, and, above all, the civil rights acts of 1964 and 1965 changed the nation irrevocably. The aged and the poor now were guaranteed access to medical care, communities saw an infusion of federal funds to improve local education and African Americans could now begin to attend integrated schools, enjoy public facilities and gain political power by exercising the right to vote. But even at this moment of triumph for liberal reform, new currents of dissent and rebellion were brewing.

Recommended Reading

Two excellent books survey the social, cultural, and political trends in the United States during the postwar period. In *One Nation Divisible* (1980), Richard Polenberg analyzes class, ethnic, and racial changes; William Leuchtenburg offers a fine overview of American life since 1945 in *A Troubled Feast,* updated ed. (1983).

Richard Pells provides a sweeping survey of the American intellectual community's response to the Cold War in *The Liberal Mind in a Conservative Age* (1985). The broadest account of American life during the decade is David Halberstam, *The Fifties* (1993).

Charles Alexander provides a balanced view of the Eisenhower years in *Holding the Line* (1975), portraying the Republican president as an able chief executive who was well suited to the times. For the 1960s, the best general account is Jim F. Heath, *Decade of Disillusionment* (1975), which stresses the continuity in policy between the Kennedy and Johnson administrations. Richard Reeves offers a full account of the Kennedy administration in *President Kennedy* (1993); Eric Goldman offers a sympathetic view of the Johnson years in *The Tragedy of Lyndon Johnson* (1969).

Taylor Branch gives a comprehensive account of the genesis of the civil rights movement in *Parting the Waters: America in the King Years, 1954–1963* (1988). Three fine biographies—David L. Lewis's *King* (1970), Stephen B. Oates's *Let the Trumpet Sound* (1982), and David Garrow's *Bearing the Cross* (1986)—present perceptive portraits of Martin Luther King, Jr., the movement's most influential leader.

Additional Bibliography

Books on social and cultural trends in the 1950s include Bernard Rosenberg and D. M. White, eds., *Mass Culture* (1957); Douglas Miller and Marion Novak, *The Fifties: The Way We Really Were* (1977); Robert H. Bremer and Gary Reichard, eds., *Reshaping America* (1982); Stephen J. Whitfield, *The Culture of the Cold War* (1990); Elaine Tyler May, *Homeward Bound: American Familes in the Cold War Era* (1988); William O'Neill, *American High* (1986); J. Ronald Oakley, *God's Country* (1986); Paul Carter, *Another Part of the Fifties* (1983); David Potter, *People of Plenty* (1954); Herbert Gans, *The Levittowners* (1967); Scott Donaldson, *The Suburban Myth* (1969); Kenneth A. Jackson, *Crabgrass Frontier* (1986); Diane Ravitch, *The Troubled Crusade* (1983), on education; Serge Guilbaut, *How New York Stole the Idea of Modern Art* (1983); Irving Sandler, *The Triumph of American Painting* (1970); Will Herberg, *Protestant, Catholic, Jew* (1955); Mark Silk, *Spiritual Politics* (1988); Lawrence Lipton, *The Holy Barbarians* (1959); Eric Barnouw, *The Image Empire* (1970); Kent Anderson, *Television Fraud* (1978); William Boddy, *Fifties Television* (1990); and Robert J. Donovan and Ray

Scherer, *Silent Revolution* (1992), on television news. For the role of women in the postwar years, see Eugenia Kaledin, *Mothers and More* (1984), and Leila Rupp and Verta Taylor, *Survival in the Doldrums* (1987).

Paul Boyer examines the initial response of the American people to the nuclear age in *By the Bomb's Early Light* (1985); Allan M. Winkler describes the continuing impact of the bomb in *Life Under a Cloud* (1993). On *Sputnik* and the beginning of the space program, see Lloyd Swenson et al., *This New Ocean* (1966); Clayton Koppes, *JPL and the American Space Program* (1982); Walter A. MacDougall, *The Heavens and the Earth* (1985); and Robert A. Divine, *The Sputnik Challenge* (1993).

Truman's contributions to the civil rights movement are surveyed critically in Harry C. Berman, *The Politics of Civil Rights in the Truman Administration* (1970), and more sympathetically in Donald R. McCoy and Richard T. Ruetten, *Quest and Response* (1973). Other important books on civil rights are Richard Dalfiume, *Desegregation of the U.S. Armed Forces* (1969); Richard Kluger, *Simple Justice* (1975), on the *Brown* decision; Benjamin Muse, *Ten Years of Prelude* (1964); Steven Lawson, *Black Ballots* (1977), on the voting rights issue; Robert F. Burk, *The Eisenhower Administration and Civil Rights* (1985); Adam Fairclough, *To Redeem the Soul of America* (1987); Stephen J. Whitfield, *A Death in the Delta* (1988); Juan Williams, *Eyes on the Prize* (1986); and Numan V. Bartley, *The Rise of Massive Resistance* (1969), on the southern reaction.

Herbert Parmet began the scholarly reappraisal of Dwight Eisenhower in *Eisenhower and the American Crusades* (1973). Stephen E. Ambrose portrays Ike sympathetically in his two-volume biography, *Eisenhower* (1983, 1984); for a more critical view, see Piers Brendon, *Ike: His Life and Times* (1986). Other useful books on the Eisenhower years include Fred Greenstein, *The Hidden Hand Presidency* (1982); Elmo Richardson, *The Presidency of Dwight D. Eisenhower* (1979); Robert F. Burk, *Dwight D. Eisenhower* (1986); Barbara R. Clowse, *Brainpower and the Cold War* (1981); Garry Wills, *Nixon Agonistes* (1971); John Bartlow Martin, *Adlai Stevenson and the World* (1977); Gilbert Fite, *Richard B. Russell, Jr.,: Senator from Georgia* (1991); Herbert Brownell, *Advising Ike* (1993); James L. Sundquist, *Politics and Policy: The Eisenhower, Kennedy and Johnson Years* (1968); Gary W. Reichard, *The Reaffirmation of Republicanism: Eisenhower and the 83rd Congress* (1975); Mark Rose, *Interstate* (1979); and R. Alton Lee, *Eisenhower and Landrum-Griffin* (1989).

For economic developments during the 1950s, consult Edward S. Flash, *Economic Advice and*

Presidential Leadership (1965); Harold G. Vatter, The U.S. Economy in the 1950s (1962); two books by John Kenneth Galbraith: American Capitalism (1952) and The Affluent Society (1958); John W. Sloan, Eisenhower and the Management of Prosperity (1991); Ivan W. Morgan, Eisenhower vs. "the Spenders" (1990); and Raymond J. Salunier, Constructive Years (1992).

Kennedy's career before he became president is discussed in James MacGregor Burns, John Kennedy, 2d ed. (1961); Joan Blair and Clay Blair, Jr., The Search for JFK (1976); Herbert Parmet, Jack (1980); and Nigel Hamilton, Reckless Youth (1992). Favorable evaluations of the Kennedy presidency include Arthur M. Schlesinger, Jr., A Thousand Days (1965); Theodore Sorensen, Kennedy (1965); Arthur M. Schlesinger, Jr., Robert Kennedy and His Times (1978); Richard Goodwin, Remembering America (1988); Benjamin Bradlee, Conversations with Kennedy (1975); Lewis J. Paper, The Promise and the Performance (1975); and Irving Bernstein, Promises Kept (1991). For a more critical view, see Bruce Miroff, Pragmatic Illusions (1976); Henry Fairlie, The Kennedy Promise (1973); Thomas C. Reeves, A Question of Character (1991); and Garry Wills, The Kennedy Imprisonment (1981), the latter dealing with Robert and Edward Kennedy as well. For more balanced treatment, see Herbert Parmet, JFK: The Presidency of John F. Kennedy (1983); David Burner, John F. Kennedy and a New Generation (1988); and James K. Giglio, The Presidency of John F. Kennedy (1991). William Manchester, Death of a President (1967), gives the standard view of JFK's assassination; the best of the many dissenting accounts is Edward J. Epstein, Inquest (1966), while Gerald Posner offers the most convincing rebuttal to the conspiracy theorists in Case Closed (1993).

British journalist Louis Heren offers an objective and lucid survey of the Johnson presidency in No Hail, No Farewell (1970); Vaughn Bornet gives a more detailed account in The Presidency of Lyndon Johnson (1983). Joseph A. Califano offers a revealing account by an insider in The Triumph & Tragedy of Lyndon Johnson (1992). The best brief biography is Paul Conkin, Big Daddy from the Pedernales (1986). Other books on LBJ include the president's memoirs, The Vantage Point (1971); Harry McPherson, A Political Education (1972); George Reedy, Lyndon Johnson: A Memoir (1982). Robert Novak and Rowland Evans, Lyndon B. Johnson (1966); Doris Kearns, Lyndon Johnson and the American Dream (1976); Merle Miller, Lyndon (1980); Paul R. Henggeler, In His Steps: Lyndon Johnson and the Kennedy Mystique (1991); and two books that focus on his Texas background, Alfred Steinberg, Sam Johnson's Boy (1965),

and Ronnie Dugger, The Politician (1982). Robert Caro provides the most detailed and most critical account of Johnson's early career in The Path to Power (1982) and The Means of Ascent (1990); Robert Dallek gives a more balanced view of Johnson's prepresidential years in Lone Star Rising (1991). Three books edited by Robert A. Divine, Exploring the Johnson Years (1981), The Johnson Years, Volume Two (1987), and The Johnson Years, Volume Three (1994) contain essays surveying major themes of the Johnson administration.

For political developments in the first half of the 1960s, see Theodore White, The Making of the President (1961), the first in a series of election books; Sidney Kraus, The Great Debates (1962), on the Nixon-Kennedy TV debates; and two memoirs by prominent Democrats, Larry O'Brien, No Final Victories (1974), and Hubert H. Humphrey, The Education of a Public Man (1976); and a first-rate biography: Carl Solberg, Hubert Humphrey (1984).

Books on economic developments include Seymour Harris, Economics of the Kennedy Years (1964); Hobart Rowen, The Free Enterprisers (1964); and Jim F. Heath, John F. Kennedy and the Business Community (1969). Among studies of the Supreme Court are Alexander Bickel, Politics and the Warren Court (1965); Richard C. Cortner, The Apportionment Cases (1970); Anthony Lewis, Gideon's Trumpet (1965); G. Edward White, Earl Warren (1982); Melvin Urofsky, Felix Frankfurter (1991); Bruce Allen Murphy, Fortas (1988); and Laura Kalman, Abe Fortas (1990).

Victor S. Navasky's account of Robert Kennedy as attorney general, Kennedy Justice (1971), is quite critical. More sympathetic books on the same topic are Arthur Schlesinger, Jr., Robert Kennedy and His Times (1976); Carl Brauer, John F. Kennedy and the Second Reconstruction (1977); and Harris Wofford, Of Kennedys and Kings (1980). For civil rights developments in the 1960s, consult Benjamin Muse, The American Negro Revolution (1969); Mark Stern, Calculating Visions (1992); Hugh Davis Graham, The Civil Rights Era, 1960–1972 (1990); Nancy Weiss, Whitney Young, Jr., and the Struggle for Civil Rights (1989); David Garrow, Protest at Selma (1976); Michal Belknap, Federal Law and Southern Order (1987); and Doug McAdams, Freedom Summer (1988).

The Great Society, particularly in regard to welfare and the war on poverty, can be traced in Allen J. Matusow, The Unraveling of America (1984); Marshall Kaplan and Peggy Cuciti, eds., The Great Society and Its Legacy (1986); John C. Donovan, The Politics of Poverty (1973); Gilbert Steiner, The State of Welfare (1971); Sar Levitan, The Great Society's Poor

Law (1969); James T. Patterson, *America's Struggle Against Poverty* (1982); and Julie Roy Jeffrey, *Education for the Children of the Poor* (1976).

Robert H. Bremner, Gary Reichard, and Richard J. Hopkins, eds., *American Choices* (1986), contains essays on public policy issues of the 1960s. For environmental concerns, see Samuel P. Hays, *Beauty, Health and Permanence* (1987), and Lewis L. Gould, *Lady Bird Johnson and Beautification* (1987).

Vietnam and the Escalating Cold War, 1953–1968

On November 20, 1953, French planes dropped over eighteen hundred elite paratroopers into Dien Bien Phu, a remote heart-shaped valley in North Vietnam. This move was the latest effort by France to crush the rebellion of the Vietminh, a communist movement led by Ho Chi Minh, which had been fighting for the independence of Vietnam since 1946. The paratroopers quickly gained control of Dien Bien Phu with only minor casualties, built airstrips to receive supplies and reinforcements, and then prepared for the expected onslaught from the Vietminh. The French hoped to engage the elusive guerrilla forces in a pitched battle using the superior French firepower to gradually sap the strength of the Vietminh insurgency.

By March 1954, the French garrison, now composed of 13,000 troops, was in a desperate position. The Vietminh had moved 50,000 troops into the hills surrounding Dien Bien Phu and had brought in heavy Russian artillery supplied by China and American weapons captured in Korea. Vietnamese soldiers wearing woven helmets and rubber tire sandals carried the disassembled pieces of cannons and mortars through the jungle to the hilltops overlooking the French positions in the valley below. The French seemed to have ignored the classic Chinese military advice, "Never fight on a terrain which looks like a tortoise turned upside down."

When the first attack began in mid-March, the Vietminh quickly overran three French outposts at Dien Bien Phu and wiped out two entire battalions in the first few days of fighting. Surprisingly accurate antiaircraft fire made it increasingly difficult for the French planes to bring in supplies and reinforcements. What had begun as an attempt to decimate the Vietminh had turned into a showdown battle in which France's control of Indochina was thrown into jeopardy.

In desperation, the French sent a high official to Washington in late March to seek American military help in relieving their beseiged garrison. Although the United States had begun extending military and financial assistance to France in Indochina in May 1950, President Dwight D. Eisenhower in 1954 was not prepared to commit American forces to bail out the French. Instead, he and Secretary of State John Foster Dulles sought only to prevent Indochina from falling under communist control by trying to arrange for diplomatic and political support for the French effort among other Western nations. Although Admiral Arthur Radford, chairman of the Joint Chiefs of Staff, came forward with a bold plan for an American air strike to relieve the pressure at Dien Bien Phu, neither the president nor his other military advisers were ready to involve American forces in another Asian war so soon after Korea.

While political leaders searched for a negotiated settlement, the Vietminh tightened the vise on Dien Bien Phu. The French were in a hopeless tactical position. Their garrison was more than 200 miles behind the enemy's lines and was being pounded relentlessly by artillery shells. By mid-April, a devastating five-night attack had closed the last remaining airstrip, limiting supplies to those dropped by air and preventing even the evacuation of the wounded. When the French government made a last-minute appeal for Radford's air strike, President Eisenhower used characteristically indirect means to turn it down. Fearful an air attack would lead to an intervention by American ground forces, Ike insisted that both Congress and American allies in Europe approve the use of American forces in advance. Congressional leaders, recalling the recent Korean debacle, were reluctant; the British were appalled and ruled out any joint action.

The president used these objections to turn down intervention in Indochina in 1954. Much later, just before the American involvement in the Vietnam War in the 1960s, he stated his reasons more candidly. "The jungles of Indochina would have swallowed up division after division of United States troops," he explained. Equally important, he believed U.S. involvement in France's war would have compromised the American "tradition of anticolonialism. . . . The standing of the United States as the most powerful of the anticolonial powers is an asset of incalculable value to the Free World," he concluded.

On May 7, the Vietminh attackers overcame the last stronghold at Dien Bien Phu. A French officer saw a white flag on a Vietminh rifle only 50 feet away. "You're not going to shoot anymore?" asked a Vietminh soldier. "No, I am not going to shoot anymore," the Frenchman replied. And then, writes historian Bernard Fall, "all around them, as on some gruesome Judgment

Hoping to maintain colonial rule in Indochina, France dropped paratroopers into the valley of Dien Bien Phu to prepare a decisive attack against Vietnamese guerrilla forces.

Day, mud-covered soldiers, French and enemy alike, began to crawl out of their trenches and stand erect as firing ceased everywhere."

At an international conference held in Geneva a few months later, Indochina was divided at the seventeenth parallel. Ho Chi Minh gained control of North Vietnam, while the French continued to rule in the South, with provision for a general election within two years to unify the country. The election was never held, largely because Eisenhower feared it would result in an overwhelming mandate for Ho. Instead the United States gradually took over from the French, sponsoring a new government in Saigon headed by Ngo Dinh Diem, a Vietnamese nationalist from a northern Catholic family. While Eisenhower can be given credit for refusing to engage American forces on behalf of French colonialism in Indochina, his determination to resist communist expansion had committed the United States to a long and eventually futile struggle to prevent Ho Chi Minh from achieving his long-sought goal of a unified, independent Vietnam.

EISENHOWER WAGES THE COLD WAR

Dwight D. Eisenhower came into the presidency in 1952 unusually well prepared to lead the nation at the height of the Cold War. His long years of military service had exposed him to a wide variety of international issues, both in Asia and in Europe, and to an even broader array of world leaders, such as Winston Churchill and Charles de Gaulle. He was not only an experienced military strategist, but a gifted politician and diplomat as well. He was blessed with a sharp, pragmatic mind and organizational genius that enabled him to plan and carry out large enterprises, grasping the precise relationship between the parts and the whole. Above all, he had a serene confidence in his own ability. At the end of his first day in the White House, he confided in his diary: "Plenty of worries and difficult problems. But such has been my portion for a long time—the result is that this just seems like a continuation of all I've been doing since July 1941."

Eisenhower chose John Foster Dulles as his secretary of state. The myth soon developed that Ike had given Dulles free rein to conduct American diplomacy. Appearances were deceptive. Eisenhower preferred to work behind the scenes. He let Dulles make the public speeches and appearances before congressional committees, where the secretary's hard-line views placated GOP extremists. But Dulles carefully consulted with the president before every appearance, meeting frequently with Eisenhower at the White House and telephoning him several times a day. Ike respected his secretary of state's broad knowledge of foreign policy and his skill in conducting American diplomacy, but he made all the major decisions himself. "There's only one man I know who has seen *more* of the world and talked with more people and *knows* more than he does," Ike said of Dulles, "and that's me."

From the outset, Eisenhower was determined to bring the Cold War under control. Ideally, he wanted to end it, but as a realist, he would settle for a relaxation of tensions with the Soviet Union. In part, he was motivated by a deeply held budgetary concern. Defense spending had increased from $13 billion to $50 billion under Truman; Ike was convinced the nation was in danger of going bankrupt unless military spending was reduced. As president, he inaugurated a "new look" for American defense, cutting back on the army and navy and relying even more heavily than Truman had on the air force and its nuclear striking power. As a result, the defense budget dropped below $40 billion annually. In 1954, Dulles announced reliance on massive retaliation—in fact a continuance of Truman's policy of deterrence. Rather than becoming involved in limited wars such as Korea, the United States would consider the possibility of using nuclear weapons to halt any communist aggression that threatened vital U.S. interests anywhere in the world.

While he permitted Dulles to make his veiled nuclear threats, Eisenhower's fondest dream was to end the arms race. Sobered by the development of the hydrogen bomb, successfully tested by the United States in November 1952 and by the Soviet Union in August 1953, the president began a new effort at disarmament with the Russians. Yet before this initiative could take effect, Ike had to weather a series of crises around the world that tested his skill and patience to the utmost.

Containing China

The communist government in Peking posed a serious challenge for the Eisenhower administration. Senate Republicans, led by William Knowland of California, blamed the Democrats for the "loss" of China. They viewed Mao as a puppet of the Soviet Union and insisted the United States recognize the Nationalists on Formosa as the only legitimate government of China. While State Department experts realized there were underlying tensions between China and Russia, Mao's intervention in the Korean War had convinced most Americans that the Chinese communists were an integral part of a larger communist effort at world domination. Thus Truman and Acheson had abandoned any hope of trying to exploit differences between Mao and Stalin by wooing China away from the Soviet Union.

Eisenhower and Dulles chose to accentuate the potential conflict between Russia and China. By taking a strong line against China, the United States could make the Chinese realize that Russia was unable to protect their interests; at the same time, such a hawkish policy would please congressional conservatives like Knowland. Ultimately Eisenhower and Dulles hoped a policy of firmness would not only contain communist Chinese expansion in Asia, but also drive a wedge between Moscow and Peking.

A crisis in the Formosa Straits provided the first test of the new policy. In the fall of 1954, communist China threatened to seize coastal islands, notably Quemoy and Matsu, occupied by the Nationalists. Fearful that seizure of these offshore islands would be the first step toward an invasion of Formosa, Eisenhower permitted

Secretary of State John Foster Dulles reports to President Eisenhower and the nation after a European tour in 1955. Cartoonist Herblock, a sharp critic of Dulles's hard line, depicts him in a Superman suit pushing Uncle Sam to the brink of nuclear war.

Dulles to sign a security treaty with Chiang Kai-shek committing the United States to defend Formosa. When the communists began shelling the offshore islands, Eisenhower persuaded Congress to pass a resolution authorizing him to use force to defend Formosa and "closely related localities."

Despite repeated requests, however, the president refused to say whether he would use force to repel a Chinese attack on Quemoy or Matsu. Instead he and Dulles hinted at the use of nuclear weapons, carefully stating their action would depend on whether they considered an attack on the offshore islands part of a larger offensive aimed at Formosa. The Chinese leaders, unsure whether Eisenhower was bluffing, decided not to test American resolve. The shelling ended in 1955, and when the communists resumed it again in 1958, another firm but equally ambiguous American response forced them to desist. The apparent refusal of the Soviet Union to come to China's aid in these crises with the United States contributed to a growing rift between these two communist nations by the end of the 1950s. Unfortunately, the Eisenhower administration failed to take full advantage of the opportunity that it had helped to create.

Turmoil in the Middle East

The gravest crisis for Eisenhower came in the Middle East when Egyptian leader Gamal Nasser seized the Suez Canal in July 1956. England and France were ready to use force immediately; their citizens owned the canal company, and their economies were dependent on the canal for the flow of oil from the Persian Gulf. President Eisenhower, however, was staunchly opposed to intervention, preferring to seek a diplomatic solution with Nasser, who kept the canal running smoothly. For three months, Dulles did everything possible to restrain the European allies, but finally they decided to take a desperate gamble—they invaded Egypt and seized the canal, relying on the United States to prevent any Russian interference.

Eisenhower was furious when England and France launched their attack in early November. Campaigning for reelection against Adlai Stevenson on the slogan of keeping the peace, Ike had to abandon domestic politics to deal with the threat of war. "The White House crackled with barracks-room language," reported one observer; the president told an aide that the Western allies had made "a complete *mess* and *botch* of things." Unhesitatingly, he instructed Dulles to sponsor a UN resolution calling for British and French withdrawal from Egypt. Yet when the Russians supported the American proposal and went further, threatening rocket attacks on British and French cities and even offering to send "volunteers" to fight in Egypt, Eisenhower made it clear he would not tolerate Soviet interference. He put the Strategic Air Command on alert and said of the Russians, "If those fellows start something, we may have to hit 'em—and, if necessary, with everything in the bucket."

Just after noon on Election Day, November 6, 1956, British Prime Minister Anthony Eden called the president to inform him that England and France were ending their invasion. Eisenhower breathed a sigh of relief. American voters rallied behind Ike, electing him to a second term by a near landslide. As a result of the Suez crisis, the United States replaced England and France as the main Western influence in the Middle East. With Russia strongly backing Egypt and Syria, the Cold War had found yet another battleground.

Two years later, Eisenhower found it necessary to intervene in the strategic Middle Eastern country of Lebanon. Political power in this neutral nation was divided between Christian and Moslem elements. When the outgoing Christian president, Camille Chamoun, broke with tradition by seeking a second term, Moslem groups (aided by Egypt and Syria) threatened to launch a rebellion. At first, Eisenhower turned down Chamoun's request for American intervention to avert a civil war, but after an unexpected nationalist coup overthrew the pro-Western government of Iraq, Ike decided to act in order to uphold the U.S. commitment to political stability in the Middle East.

American marines from the Sixth Fleet moved swiftly ashore on July 15, 1958, securing the Beirut airport and preparing the way for a force of some fourteen thousand troops airlifted from bases in Germany. The military wanted to occupy the entire country, but Eisenhower insisted on limiting American forces to the area of Beirut. The mission of the troops, he argued, was "not primarily to fight," but simply to show the flag. Lebanese political leaders quickly agreed on a

One of the early skirmishes of the Cold War occurred in the Middle East. Here, British tanks patrol the main streets of Port Said, Egypt, while other troops stand guard. Following the Suez crisis, the United States emerged as the representative of Western interests in the Middle East.

successor to Chamoun, and American soldiers left the country before the end of October. This restrained use of force achieved Eisenhower's primary goal of quieting the explosive Middle East. It also served, as Secretary of State Dulles pointed out, "to reassure many small nations that they could call on us in a time of crisis."

Covert Actions

Amid these dangerous crises, the Eisenhower administration worked behind the scenes in the 1950s to expand the nation's global influence. In 1953, the CIA was instrumental in overthrowing a popularly elected government in Iran and placing the shah in full control of that country. American oil companies were rewarded with lucrative concessions, and Eisenhower felt he had gained a valuable ally on the Russian border. But these short-run gains created a deep-seated animosity among Iranians that would haunt the United States in the future.

Closer to home, in Latin America, Eisenhower once again relied on covert action. In 1954, the CIA masterminded the overthrow of a leftist regime in Guatemala. The immediate advantage was in denying the Soviets a possible foothold in the Western Hemisphere, but Latin Americans resented the thinly disguised interference of the United States in their internal affairs. More important, when Fidel Castro came to power in Cuba in 1959, the Eisenhower administration—after a brief effort at conciliation—adopted a hard line that helped drive Cuba into the Soviet orbit and led new attempts at covert action.

Eisenhower's record as a cold warrior was thus mixed. His successful ending of the Korean War and his peacekeeping efforts in Indochina and Formosa and in the Suez crisis are all to his credit. Yet his reliance on coups and subversion directed by the CIA in Iran and Guatemala reveal Ike's corrupting belief that the ends justified the means. And despite the 1952 campaign call for the liberation of eastern Europe, Eisenhower accepted Soviet domination of this region, refusing to act on behalf of East German protesters in 1953 or Hungarian freedom fighters in 1956.

Nevertheless, Eisenhower did display an admirable ability to stay calm and unruffled in moments of great tension, reassuring the nation and the world. And above all, he could boast, as he did in 1962, of his ability to keep the peace. "In those eight years," he reminded the nation, "we lost no inch of ground to tyranny. One war was ended and incipient wars were blocked."

Waging Peace

Eisenhower hoped to ease Cold War tensions by ending the nuclear arms race. The advent of the hydrogen bomb intensified his concern over nuclear warfare; by 1955, both the United States and the Soviet Union had added this dread new weapon to their arsenals. With new long-range ballistic missiles being perfected, it was only a matter of time before Russia and the United

States would be capable of destroying each other completely. Peace, as Winston Churchill noted, now depended on a balance of terror.

Throughout the 1950s, Eisenhower sought a way out of the nuclear dilemma. In April 1953, shortly after Stalin's death, he gave a speech in which he called on the Russians to join him in a new effort at disarmament, pointing out that "every warship launched, every rocket fired signifies, in the final sense, a theft from those who hunger and are not fed, those who are cold and are not clothed." When the Soviets ignored this appeal, the president tried again in December 1953. Addressing the UN General Assembly, he outlined an "atoms-for-peace" plan whereby the United States and the Soviet Union would donate fissionable material to a new UN agency to be used for peaceful purposes. Despite Ike's appeal "to serve the needs rather than the fears of mankind," the Russians again rebuffed him. Undaunted, Eisenhower tried once more. At the Geneva summit conference in 1955, Ike proposed to Nikita Khrushchev, just emerging as Stalin's successor after a two-year struggle for power, a way to break the disarmament deadlock. "Open skies," as reporters dubbed the plan, would overcome the traditional Russian objection to on-site inspection by having both superpowers open their territory to mutual aerial surveillance. Unfortunately, Khrushchev dismissed open skies as "a very transparent espionage device," and the Geneva Conference ended without any significant breakthrough in the Cold War.

After his reelection in 1956, the president made a new effort to initiate nuclear arms control. Concern over atmospheric fallout from nuclear testing had led presidential candidate Adlai Stevenson to propose a mutual ban on such experiments. At first, Eisenhower rejected the test-ban idea, arguing it could be effective only as part of a comprehensive disarmament agreement, but the Russians supported it. Finally, in 1958, the president changed his mind after American and Soviet scientists developed a system to detect nuclear testing in the atmosphere without on-site inspection. In October 1958, Eisenhower and Khrushchev each voluntarily suspended further weapons tests pending the outcome of a conference held at Geneva to work out a test-ban treaty. Although the Geneva Conference failed to make progress, neither the United States nor the Soviet Union resumed testing for the remainder of Ike's term in office.

The suspension of testing halted the pollution of the world's atmosphere, but it did not lead to the improvement in Soviet-American relations that Eisenhower sought. Instead, the Soviet feat in launching *Sputnik*, the first artificial satellite to orbit the earth, served to intensify the Cold War. Fearful the Russians were several years ahead of the United States in the development of intercontinental ballistic missiles (ICBMs), Democrats criticized Eisenhower for not spending enough on defense and warned that a dangerous missile gap would open up by the early 1960s—a time when the Russians might have such a commanding lead in ICBMs that they could destroy America with a first strike. Despite the president's belief that the American missile program was in good shape, he allowed a major increase in defense spending to speed up the building of American ICBMs and the new Polaris submarine-launched intermediate range missile (IRBM).

Nikita Khrushchev took full advantage of the furor over *Sputnik* to put the United States on the defensive. "We will bury you," he boasted, telling Americans, "Your grandchildren will live under communism." The most serious threat of all came in November 1958 when the Russian leader declared that within six months he would sign a separate peace treaty with East Germany, calling for an end to American, British, and French occupation rights in Berlin.

Eisenhower met the second Berlin crisis as firmly as Truman had the first. He refused to abandon the city, but also tried to avoid a military showdown. Prudent diplomacy forced Khrushchev to extend his deadline indefinitely. After a trip to the United States, culminating in a personal meeting with Eisenhower at Camp David, the Russian leader agreed to attend a summit conference in Paris in May 1960.

This much heralded meeting never took place. On May 1, two weeks before the leaders were to convene in Paris, the Soviets shot down an American U-2 plane piloted by Francis Gary Powers. The United States had been overflying Russia since 1956 in these high-altitude spy planes, gaining vital information about the Soviet missile program which showed there was little basis for the public fear the Russians had opened up a dangerous missile gap. After initially deny-

From *Straight Herblock* (Simon & Schuster, 1964)

Cartoonist Herblock's view of the Khrushchev–Eisenhower meetings.

ing any knowledge, Eisenhower took full responsibility for Powers's overflight and Khrushchev responded with a scathing personal denunciation and a refusal to meet with the American president.

Eisenhower deeply regretted the breakup of the Paris summit, telling an aide that "the stupid U-2 mess" had destroyed all his efforts for peace. Sadly he concluded that "he saw nothing worthwhile left for him to do now until the end of his presidency." Khrushchev marked time for the next nine months, waiting for the American people to choose a new president. Eisenhower did make a final effort at peace, however. Three days before leaving office, he delivered a farewell address in which he gave a somber warning about the danger of massive military spending. "In the councils of government, we must guard against the acquisition of unwarranted influence, whether sought or unsought, by the military-industrial complex," he declared. "The potential for the disastrous rise of misplaced power exists and will persist."

Rarely has an American president been more prophetic. In the next few years, the level of defense spending would skyrocket as the Cold

War escalated under his successors in the White House. The military-industrial complex reached its acme of power in the 1960s when the United States realized the full implications of Truman's doctrine of containment. Eisenhower had succeeded in keeping the peace for eight years, but he had failed to halt the momentum of the Cold War he had inherited from Harry Truman. Ike's efforts to ease tension with the Soviet Union were dashed by his own distrust of communism and by Khrushchev's belligerent rhetoric and behavior. Still, he had begun to relax tensions, a process that would survive the troubled 1960s and, after several false starts, would finally begin to erode the Cold War by the end of the 1980s.

KENNEDY INTENSIFIES THE COLD WAR

John F. Kennedy was determined to succeed where he felt Eisenhower had failed. Critical of

In his inaugural address, President Kennedy called upon the American people to "ask not what your country can do for you; ask what you can do for your country."

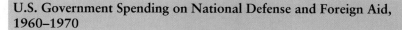

U.S. Government Spending on National Defense and Foreign Aid, 1960–1970

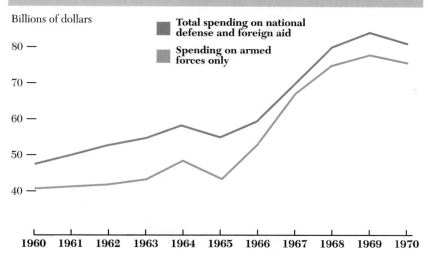

Billions of dollars

- Total spending on national defense and foreign aid
- Spending on armed forces only

Source: *Compiled from U.S. Bureau of the Census,* Historical Statistics of the United States, Colonial Times to 1970, *Bicentennial Edition, Washington, D.C., 1975.*

his predecessor for holding down defense spending and apparently allowing the Soviet Union to open up a dangerous lead in ICBMs, Kennedy sought to warn the nation of its peril and lead it to victory in the Cold War.

In his inaugural address, the young president sounded the alarm. Ignoring the domestic issues aired during the campaign, he dealt exclusively with the world. "Let every nation know, whether it wishes us well or ill, that we shall pay any price, bear any burden, meet any hardship, support any friend, oppose any foe," Kennedy declared, "to assure the survival and success of liberty. We will do all this and more."

From the day he took office, John F. Kennedy gave foreign policy top priority. In part, this decision reflected the perilous world situation, the immediate dangers ranging from the unresolved Berlin crisis, through a developing civil war in Vietnam, to the emergence of Fidel Castro as a Soviet ally in Cuba. But it also corresponded to Kennedy's personal priorities. As a congressman and senator, he had been an intense cold warrior, supporting containment after World War II, lamenting the loss of China, and accusing the Eisenhower administration of allowing the Russians to open up a dangerous missile gap.

Bored by committee work and legislative details, he had focused on foreign policy in the Senate, gaining a seat on the Foreign Relations Committee and publishing a book of speeches, *The Strategy of Peace,* in early 1960.

His appointments reflected his determination to win the Cold War. His choice of Dean Rusk, an experienced but unassertive diplomat, to head the State Department indicated that Kennedy planned to be his own secretary of state. He surrounded himself with young pragmatic advisers who prided themselves on toughness: McGeorge Bundy, dean of Harvard College, became national security adviser; Walt W. Rostow, an MIT economist, was Bundy's deputy; and Robert McNamara, the youthful president of the Ford Motor Company, took over as secretary of defense.

These New Frontiersmen, later dubbed "the best and the brightest" by journalist David Halberstam, all shared a hard-line view of the Soviet Union and the belief that American security depended on superior force and the willingness to use it. Walt Rostow summed up their view of the contest with Russia best when he wrote, "The cold war comes down to this test of whether we and the democratic world are fundamentally tougher and more purposeful in the defense of our vital interests than they are in the pursuit of their global ambitions."

Flexible Response

The first goal of the Kennedy administration was to build up the nation's armed forces. During the 1960 campaign, Kennedy had warned the Soviets were opening a missile gap. In fact, due largely to Eisenhower's foresight, the United States had a significant lead in nuclear striking power by early 1961, with a fleet of over 600 B-52 bombers, 2 Polaris submarines, and 16 Atlas ICBMs capable of delivering more than 2,000 warheads against Russian targets. Nevertheless, the new administration, intent on putting the Soviets on the defensive, authorized the construction of an awesome nuclear arsenal that included 1,000 Minuteman solid-fuel ICBMs (five times the number Eisenhower had felt necessary) and 32 Polaris submarines carrying 656 missiles. The United States thus opened a missile gap in reverse, creating the possibility of a successful American first strike.

At the same time, the Kennedy administration augmented conventional military strength. Secretary of Defense McNamara developed plans to add five combat-ready army divisions, three tactical air wings, and a ten-division strategic reserve. These vast increases led to a $6 billion jump in the defense budget in 1961 alone. The president took a personal interest in counterinsurgency. He expanded the Special Forces unit at Fort Bragg, North Carolina, and insisted, over army objections, that it adopt a distinctive green beret as a symbol of its elite status.

The purpose of this buildup was to create an alternative to Eisenhower's policy of massive retaliation. Instead of responding to communist moves with nuclear threats, the United States could now call on a wide spectrum of force—ranging from ICBMs to Green Berets. Thus, as Robert McNamara explained, the new strategy of flexible response meant the United States could "choose among several operational plans. We shall be committed only to a system that gives us the ability to use our forces in a controlled and deliberate way." The danger was that such a powerful arsenal might tempt the new administration to test its strength against the Soviet Union.

Entrance and egress between East and West Berlin was controlled by a series of checkpoints. "Checkpoint Charlie" was the gateway between the American and Soviet zones.

Crisis over Berlin

The first confrontation came in Germany. Since 1958, Soviet Premier Khrushchev had been threatening to sign a peace treaty that would put access to the isolated western zones of Berlin under the control of East Germany. The steady flight of skilled workers to the West through the Berlin escape route weakened the East German regime dangerously, and the Soviets felt they had to resolve this issue quickly.

At a summit meeting in Vienna in June 1961, Kennedy and Khrushchev focused on Berlin as the key issue. Pointing out that sixteen years had passed since the end of World War II, the Russian leader called the current situation "intolerable" and announced the Soviet Union would proceed with an East German peace treaty. Kennedy was equally adamant, defending the American presence in Berlin and refusing to give up occupation rights that he considered crucial to the defense of western Europe. In their last session, the failure to reach agreement took on an ominous tone. "I want peace," Khrushchev declared, "but, if you want war, that is your problem." "It is you, not I," the young president replied, "who wants to force a change." When the Soviet leader said he would sign a German peace treaty by December, Kennedy added, "It will be a cold winter."

The climax came sooner than either man expected. On July 25, Kennedy delivered an impassioned televised address to the American people in which he called the defense of Berlin "essential" to "the entire Free World." Announcing a series of arms increases, including $3 billion more in defense spending and a nationwide program of fallout shelters, the president took the unprecedented step of calling more than 150,000 reservists and National Guardsmen to active duty. Above all, he sought to convince Khrushchev of his determination and resolve. "I hear it said that West Berlin is militarily untenable," he commented. "And so was Bastogne. And so, in fact, was Stalingrad. Any dangerous spot is tenable if men—brave men—will make it so."

Aware of superior American nuclear striking power, Khrushchev settled for a stalemate. On August 13, the Soviets sealed off their zone of the city. They began the construction of the Berlin Wall to stop the flow of brains and talent to the West. For a brief time, Russian and American tanks maneuvered within sight of each other at Checkpoint Charlie (where the American and Soviet zones met), but by fall, the tension gradually eased. The Soviets signed a separate peace treaty that did not affect U.S. occupation rights; Berlin—like Germany and, indeed, all of Europe—remained divided between the East and the West. Neither side could claim a victory, but Kennedy felt that at least he had proved to the world America's willingness to honor its commitments.

Containing Fidel Castro

Two weeks before Kennedy's inauguration, Nikita Khrushchev gave a speech in Moscow in which he declared Soviet support for "wars of national liberation." The Russian leader's words were actually aimed more at China than the United States; the two powerful communist nations were now rivals for influence in the Third World. But the New American president, ignoring the growing Sino-Soviet split, concluded the United States and Russia were locked in a struggle for the hearts and minds of the uncommitted in Asia, Africa, and Latin America.

Calling for a new policy of nation-building, Kennedy advocated financial and technical assistance designed to help Third World nations achieve economic modernization and stable pro-Western governments. Measures ranging from the formation of the idealistic Peace Corps to the ambitious Alliance for Progress—a massive economic aid program for Latin America—were part of this effort. Unfortunately, Kennedy relied even more on counterinsurgency and the Green Berets to beat back the communist challenge in the Third World.

Kennedy's determination to check global communist expansion reached a peak of intensity in Cuba. In the 1960 campaign, pointing to the growing ties between the Soviet Union and Fidel Castro's regime, he had accused the Republicans of permitting a "communist satellite" to arise on "our very doorstep." Kennedy had even issued a statement backing "anti-Castro forces in exile," calling them "fighters for freedom" who held out hope for "overthrowing Castro."

In reality, the Eisenhower administration had been training a group of Cuban exiles in Guatemala since March 1960 as part of a CIA plan to topple the Castro regime. Many of the new president's advisers had doubts about the proposed invasion. Some saw little chance for success because the operation depended heavily

Cold War allies, Soviet Premier Nikita Khrushchev (left) and Cuban Premier Fidel Castro (right).

on a broad uprising of the Cuban people. Others—notably Senator William Fulbright of Arkansas, chairman of the Foreign Relations Committee—viewed it as an immoral act that would discredit the United States. "The Castro regime is a thorn in the flesh," Fulbright argued, "but it is not a dagger in the heart." The president, however, committed by his own campaign rhetoric and assured of success by the military, decided to go ahead.

On April 17, 1961, fourteen hundred Cuban exiles moved ashore at the Bay of Pigs on the southern coast of Cuba. Even though the United States had masterminded the entire operation, Kennedy insisted on covert action, even canceling at the last minute a planned American air strike on the beachhead. With air superiority, Castro's well-trained forces had no difficulty in quashing the invasion. They killed nearly five hundred exiles and forced the rest to surrender within forty-eight hours.

Aghast at the swiftness of the defeat, President Kennedy took personal responsibility for the failure. In his address to the American people, however, he showed no remorse for arranging the violation of a neighboring country's sovereignty, only regret at the outcome. Above all, he expressed renewed defiance, warning the Soviets that "our restraint is not inexhaustible." He went on to assert that the United States would resist "communist penetration" in the Western Hemisphere, terming it part of the "primary obligations . . . to the security of our nation." For the remainder of his presidency, Kennedy continued to harass the Castro regime, imposing an economic blockade on Cuba, supporting a continuing series of raids by exile groups operating out of Florida, and failing to stop the CIA from experimenting with bizarre plots to assassinate Fidel Castro.

At the Brink

The climax of Kennedy's crusade came in October 1962 with the Cuban missile crisis. Throughout the summer and early fall, the Soviets engaged in a massive arms buildup in Cuba, ostensibly to protect Castro from an American invasion. In the United States, Republican candidates in the 1962 congressional elections called for a firm American response; Kennedy contented himself with a stern warning

To his great embarrassment, Kennedy's handling of the Bay of Pigs invasion backfired like an exploding Cuban cigar.

against the introduction of any offensive weapons, believing their presence would directly threaten American security. Khrushchev publicly denied any such intent, but secretly he took a daring gamble, building twenty-four medium-range (1,000-mile) and eighteen intermediate-range (2,000-mile) missile sites in Cuba. Later he claimed his purpose was purely defensive, but most likely he was responding to the pressures from his own military to close the enormous strategic gap in nuclear striking power that Kennedy had opened.

On October 14, 1962, American U-2 planes finally discovered the missile sites that were nearing completion. As soon as he learned of the Russian action, Kennedy decided to seek a showdown with Khrushchev. Insisting on absolute secrecy, he convened a special group of advisers to consider the way to respond.

An initial preference for an immediate air strike gradually gave way to discussion of either a full-scale invasion or a naval blockade. The president and his advisers ruled out diplomacy, rejecting a proposal to offer the withdrawal of obsolete American Jupiter missiles from Turkey in return for a similar Russian pullout in Cuba. Kennedy finally agreed to a two-step procedure. He would proclaim a quarantine of Cuba to prevent the arrival of new missiles and threaten a nuclear confrontation to force the removal of those already there. If the Russians did not cooperate, then the United States would invade Cuba and dismantle the missiles by force.

On the evening of October 22, the president informed the nation of the existence of the Soviet missiles and his plans to remove them. He spared no words in blaming Khrushchev for "this clandestine, reckless and provocative threat to world peace," and he made it clear that any missile attack from Cuba would lead to "a full retaliatory response upon the Soviet Union."

For the next six days, the world hovered on the brink of nuclear catastrophe. Khrushchev replied defiantly, accusing Kennedy of pushing mankind "to the abyss of a world nuclear-missile war." In the Atlantic, some sixteen Soviet ships continued on course toward Cuba, while the American navy was deployed to intercept them 500 miles from the island. In Florida, nearly one-quarter of a million men were being concentrated in the largest invasion force ever assembled in the continental United States.

The first break came at midweek when the Soviet ships suddenly halted to avert a confrontation at sea. "We're eyeball to eyeball," commented Secretary of State Dean Rusk, "and I think the other fellow just blinked." Kennedy was relieved on Friday when Khrushchev sent him a long, rambling letter offering a face-saving way out—Russia would remove the missiles in return for an American promise never to invade Cuba. The president was ready to accept when a second Russian message raised the stakes by insisting the American Jupiter missiles be withdrawn from Turkey. Kennedy refused to bargain; Khrushchev had endangered world peace by putting the missiles in Cuba secretly, and he must take them out immediately. Nevertheless, while the military went ahead with plans for the invasion of Cuba, the president, heeding his brother's advice, decided to make one last appeal for peace. Ignoring the second Russian message, he sent a cable to Khrushchev accepting his original offer.

On Saturday night, October 27, Robert Kennedy—the president's brother and most trusted adviser—met with Soviet ambassador Anatoly Dobrynin to make it clear this was the last chance to avert nuclear confrontation. "We had to have a commitment by tomorrow that those bases would be removed," Robert Kennedy recalled

telling him. "He should understand that if they did not remove those bases, we would remove them." Then the president's brother calmly remarked that if Khrushchev did not back down, "there would be not only dead Americans but dead Russians as well."

In reality, John F. Kennedy was not quite so ready to risk nuclear war. Secretary of State Dean Rusk more recently revealed that the president had instructed him to propose a deal through the United Nations involving "the removal of both the Jupiters and the missiles in Cuba." "I am not," Kennedy told Rusk, "going to go to war over missiles in Turkey."

President Kennedy never had to make this final concession. At nine the next morning, Khrushchev agreed to remove the missiles in return for Kennedy's promise not to invade Cuba. The crisis was over.

On the surface, Kennedy appeared to have won a striking personal and political victory. His party successfully overcame the Republican challenge in the November elections and his own popularity reached new heights in the Gallup

BOOK-OF-THE-MONTH

At the time, Kennedy's handling of the Cuban missile crisis seemed to be the greatest triumph of his presidency. In the long run, however, the missile crisis heightened Cold War tensions and escalated the arms race between the superpowers.

poll. The American people, on the defensive since Sputnik, suddenly felt that they had proved their superiority over the Russians; they were bursting with national pride. Arthur Schlesinger, Kennedy's confidant and later his biographer, claimed the Cuban crisis showed the "whole world . . . the ripening of an American leadership unsurpassed in the responsible management of power. . . . It was this combination of toughness and restraint, of will, nerve and wisdom, so brilliantly controlled, so matchlessly calibrated, that dazzled the world."

The Cuban missile crisis had more substantial results as well. Shaken by their close call, Kennedy and Khrushchev agreed to install a "hot line" to speed direct communication between Washington and Moscow in an emergency. Long-stalled negotiations over the reduction of nuclear testing suddenly resumed, leading to the limited test ban treaty of 1963, which outlawed tests in the atmosphere while still permitting them underground. Above all, Kennedy displayed a new maturity as a result of the crisis. In a speech at American University in June 1963, he shifted from the rhetoric of confrontation to that of conciliation. Speaking of the Russians, he said, "Our most basic common link is the fact that we all inhabit this planet. We all breathe the same air. We all cherish our children's future. And we are all mortal."

Despite these hopeful words, the missile crisis also had an unfortunate consequence. Those who believed that the Russians understood only the language of force were confirmed in their penchant for a hard line. Hawks who had backed Kennedy's military buildup felt events had justified a policy of nuclear superiority. The Russian leaders drew similar conclusions. Aware the United States had a four-to-one advantage in nuclear striking power during the Cuban crisis, one Soviet official told his American counterpart, "Never will we be caught like this again." After 1962, the Soviets embarked on a crash program to build up their navy and to overtake the American lead in nuclear missiles. Within five years, they had the nucleus of a modern fleet and had surpassed the United States in ICBMs. Kennedy's fleeting moment of triumph thus ensured the escalation of the arms race. His legacy was a bittersweet one of short-term success and long-term anxiety.

JOHNSON ESCALATES THE VIETNAM WAR

Lyndon Johnson stressed continuity in foreign policy just as he had in enacting Kennedy's domestic reforms. He not only inherited the policy of containment from his fallen predecessor, but he shared the same Cold War assumptions and convictions. And feeling less confident about dealing with international issues, he tended to rely heavily on Kennedy's advisers—notably Secretary of State Rusk, Secretary of Defense McNamara, and McGeorge Bundy (the national security adviser until he was replaced in 1966 by the even more hawkish Walt Rostow).

Johnson had broad exposure to national security affairs. He had served on the Naval Affairs Committee in the House before and during World War II and as Senate majority leader he had been briefed and consulted regularly on the crises of the 1950s. A confirmed cold warrior, he took to heart the supposed lesson of Munich; he was convinced that wars came from weakness, not from strength.

He had also seen in the 1940s the devastating political impact on the Democratic party of the communist triumph in China. "I am not going to lose Vietnam," he told the American ambassador to Saigon just after taking office in 1963. "I am not going to be the President who saw Southeast Asia go the way China went."

Aware of the problem Castro had caused John Kennedy, LBJ moved firmly to contain communism in the Western Hemisphere. When a military junta overthrew a leftist regime in Brazil, Johnson offered covert aid and open encouragement. He was equally forceful in compelling Panama to restrain rioting aimed at the continued American presence in the Canal Zone.

In 1965, to block the possible emergence of a Castro-type government, LBJ sent twenty thousand American troops to the Dominican Republic. Johnson's flimsy justifications—ranging from the need to protect American tourists to a dubious list of suspected communists among the rebel leaders—served only to alienate liberal critics in the United States, particularly Senate Foreign Relations Committee Chairman J. William Fulbright, a former Johnson favorite. The intervention ended in 1966 with the election of a conservative government. Senator Fulbright, however, continued his criticism of Johnson's foreign policy by publishing *The Arrogance of Power,* a biting analysis of the fallacies of containment. Fulbright's defection symbolized a growing gap between the president and liberal intellectuals; the more LBJ struggled to uphold the Cold War policies he had inherited from Kennedy, the more he found himself under attack from Congress, the media, and the universities.

Civil War in Vietnam

It was Vietnam rather than Latin America that became Lyndon Johnson's obsession and led ultimately to his political downfall. He inherited both the problem of civil war in South Vietnam and the American commitment to Diem's regime in Saigon from Eisenhower and Kennedy.

The American decision to back Ngo Dinh Diem (see p. 913) had prevented the holding of elections throughout Vietnam in 1956, as called for in the Geneva accords. Instead, Diem sought to establish a separate government in the South with large-scale American economic and military assistance. By the time Kennedy entered the White House, however, the communist government in North Vietnam, led by the venerable Ho Chi Minh, was directing the efforts of Vietcong rebels in the South. As the guerrilla war intensified in the fall of 1961, the president sent two trusted advisers, Walt Rostow and General Maxwell Taylor, to South Vietnam. They returned favoring the dispatch of eight thousand American combat troops. "As an area for the operation of U.S. troops," reported General Taylor, "SVN [South Vietnam] is not an excessively difficult or unpleasant place to operate. . . . The risks of backing into a major Asian war by way of SVN, are present but are not impressive."

The president decided against sending in combat troops in 1961, but he authorized substantial increases in economic aid to Diem and in the size of the military mission in Saigon. The number of American advisers in Vietnam grew from fewer than one thousand in 1961 to over sixteen thousand by late 1963. The flow of supplies and the creation of "strategic hamlets," fortified villages designed to protect the peasantry from the Vietcong, slowed the communist momentum. American helicopters gave government forces mobility against the Vietcong for the first time,

but by 1963, the situation had again become critical. Diem had failed to win the support of his own people; Buddhist monks set themselves aflame in public protests against him; and even Diem's own generals plotted his overthrow.

President Kennedy was in a quandary. He realized that the fate of South Vietnam would be determined not by America but by the Vietnamese. "In the final analysis," he said in September 1963, "it is their war. They are the ones who have to win it or lose it." But at the same time, Kennedy was not prepared to accept the possible loss of all Southeast Asia. Saying it would be "a great mistake" to withdraw from South Vietnam, he told reporters, "Strongly on our mind is what happened in the case of China at the end of World War II, where China was lost. We don't want that." Although aides later claimed he planned to pull out after the 1964 election, Kennedy raised the stakes by tacitly approving a coup that led to Diem's overthrow and death on November 1, 1963. The resulting power vacuum in Saigon made further American involvement in Vietnam almost certain.

The Vietnam Dilemma

Lyndon Johnson had little choice but to continue Kennedy's policy in Vietnam. The crisis created by Diem's overthrow only three weeks before Kennedy's assassination led to a vacuum of power in Saigon that prevented the new president from conducting a thorough review and reassessment of the strategic alternatives in Southeast Asia. In 1964, seven different governments ruled South Vietnam; the government changed hands three times within one month. According to an American officer, the atmosphere in Saigon "fairly smelled of discontent," with "workers on strike, students demonstrating, [and] the local press pursuing a persistent campaign of criticism of the new government."

Resisting pressure from the Joint Chiefs of Staff for direct American military involvement, LBJ continued Kennedy's policy of economic and technical assistance. He sent in seven thousand more military advisers and an additional $50 million in aid. While he insisted it was still up to the Vietnamese themselves to win the war, he expanded American support for covert operations, including amphibious raids on the North.

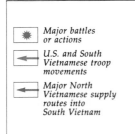

Southeast Asia and the Vietnam War

American combat forces in South Vietnam rose from 16,000 in 1963, to 500,000 in 1968, but a successful conclusion to the conflict was no closer.

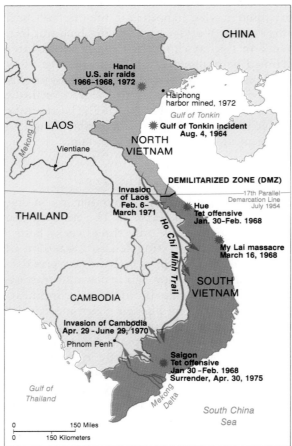

raid nearby. The *Maddox* escaped unscathed, but to show American resolve, the navy sent in another destroyer, the *C. Turner Joy*. On the evening of August 4, the two destroyers, responding to sonar and radar contacts, opened fire on North Vietnamese gunboats in the area. Johnson ordered retaliatory air strikes on North Vietnamese naval bases. Later investigation suggested that the North Vietnamese gunboats had not launched a second attack on the American ships.

The next day the president asked Congress to pass a resolution authorizing him to take "all necessary measures to repel any armed attack against the forces of the United States and to prevent further aggression." He did not in fact need this authority; he had already ordered the retaliatory air strike without it. Later, critics charged that LBJ wanted a blank check from Congress to carry out the future escalation of the Vietnam War, but such a motive is unlikely. He had already rejected immediate military intervention. In part, he wanted the Gulf of Tonkin Resolution to demonstrate to North Vietnam the American determination to defend South Vietnam at any cost. "The challenge we face in Southeast Asia today," he told Congress, "is the same challenge that we have faced with courage and that we have met with strength in Greece and Turkey, in Berlin and Korea." He also wanted to preempt the Vietnam issue from his Republican opponent, Barry Goldwater, who had been advocating a tougher policy. By taking a firm stand on the Gulf of Tonkin incident, Johnson could both impress the North Vietnamese and outmaneuver a political rival at home.

Congress responded with alacrity. The House acted unanimously, while only two senators voted against the Gulf of Tonkin Resolution. Johnson appeared to have won a spectacular victory. His standing in the Gallup poll shot up from 42 to 72 percent, and he had effectively blocked Goldwater from exploiting Vietnam as a campaign issue.

In the long run, however, this easy victory proved costly. Having used force once against North Vietnam, LBJ was more likely to do so in the future. And although he apparently had no intention of widening the conflict in August 1964, the congressional resolution was phrased broadly enough to enable him to use whatever level of force he wished—including unlimited mil-

These undercover activities led directly to the Gulf of Tonkin affair. On August 2, 1964, North Vietnamese torpedo boats attacked the *Maddox,* an American destroyer engaged in electronic intelligence gathering in the Gulf of Tonkin. The attack was prompted by the belief the American ship had been involved in a South Vietnamese

itary intervention. Above all, when he did wage war in Vietnam, he left himself open to the charge of deliberately misleading Congress. Presidential credibility proved to be Johnson's ultimate Achilles' heel; his political downfall began with the Gulf of Tonkin Resolution.

Escalation

The full-scale American involvement in Vietnam began in 1965 in a series of steps designed primarily to prevent a North Vietnamese victory. With the political situation in Saigon growing more hopeless every day, the president's advisers urged the bombing of the North as the only conceivable solution. American air attacks would serve several purposes: they would block North Vietnamese infiltration routes, make Hanoi pay a heavy price for its role, and lift the sagging morale of the South Vietnamese. But most important, as McGeorge Bundy reported after a visit to Pleiku (site of a Vietcong attack on an American base which took nine lives), "Without new U.S. action defeat appears inevitable—probably not in a matter of weeks or perhaps even months, but within the next year or so." Johnson responded in February 1965 by ordering a long-planned aerial bombardment of a set of selected North Vietnamese targets.

The air strikes, aimed at impeding the communist supply line and damaging Hanoi's economy, proved ineffective. In April, Johnson authorized the use of American combat troops in South Vietnam, but restricted them to defensive operations intended to protect American air bases. The Joint Chiefs then pressed the president for both unlimited bombing of the North and the aggressive use of American ground forces in the South. In mid-July, Secretary of Defense McNamara recommended sending 100,000 combat troops to Vietnam, more than doubling the American forces there. He felt this escalation would lead to a "favorable outcome," but also told the president that an additional 100,000 soldiers might be needed in 1966 and that American battle deaths could rise as high as 500 a month (by early 1968, they hit a peak of over 500 a week).

At the same time, other advisers, most notably Undersecretary of State George Ball, spoke out against military escalation in favor of a political settlement. Warning the United States was likely to suffer France's fate in Vietnam, "national

humiliation," Ball told the president he had "serious doubt that an army of westerners can successfully fight Orientals in an Asian jungle."

Lyndon Johnson was genuinely torn, asking his advisers at one point: "Are we starting something that in two to three years we simply can't finish?" But he finally decided he had no choice but to persevere in Vietnam. Although he insisted on paring down McNamara's troop request, LBJ settled on a steady military escalation designed to compel Hanoi to accept a diplomatic solution. In late July, the president permitted a gradual increase in the bombing of North Vietnam and allowed American ground commanders to conduct offensive operations in the South. Most ominously, he approved the immediate dispatch of 50,000 troops to Vietnam and the future commitment of 50,000 more.

These July decisions formed "an open-ended commitment to employ American military forces as the situation demanded," writes historian George Herring, and they were "the closest thing to a formal decision for war in Vietnam." Convinced that withdrawal would destroy American credibility before the world and that an invasion of the North would lead to World War III, Johnson opted for large-scale but limited military intervention. Moreover, LBJ feared the domestic consequences of either extreme. A pullout could cause a massive political backlash at home, as conservatives condemned him for betraying South Vietnam to communism. All-out war, however, would mean the end of his social programs. Once Congress focused on the conflict, he explained to biographer Doris Kearns, "that bitch of a war" would destroy "the woman I really loved—the Great Society." So he settled for a limited war, committing a half-million American troops to battle in Southeast Asia, all the while pretending it was a minor engagement and refusing to ask the American people for the support and sacrifice required for victory (see "Surviving Vietnam," pp. 930–931).

Lyndon Johnson was not solely responsible for the Vietnam War. He inherited both a policy that assumed Vietnam was a vital national interest and a deteriorating situation in Saigon that demanded a more active American role. Truman, Eisenhower, and Kennedy had taken the United States deep into the Vietnam maze; it was Johnson's fate to have to find a way out. But LBJ must bear full responsibility for the way he tried

The Strategists

Although the United States conducted thousands of air strikes over North Vietnam and committed half a million troops to the South, it failed to win the advantage. Vietcong North Vietnamese regulars and Vietcong guerrillas were better able to use the jungle terrain to advantage than their American adversaries. At right, cartoonist Bill Mauldin depicts Johnson's two options—all-out war or complete pullout—as equally precarious.

to resolve his dilemma. The failure to confront the people with the stark choices the nation faced in Vietnam, the insistence on secrecy and deceit, the refusal to acknowledge he had committed the United States to a dangerous military involvement—these were Johnson's sins in Vietnam. His lack of self-confidence in foreign policy and fear of domestic reaction led directly to his undoing.

Stalemate

For the next three years, Americans waged an intensive war in Vietnam and succeeded only in preventing a communist victory. In the air, American bombing of the North proved ineffective. The rural, undeveloped nature of the North Vietnamese economy meant there were few industrial targets; a political refusal to bomb the main port of Haiphong allowed Soviet and Chinese arms to flow freely into the country. Nor were the efforts at interdiction any more success-

ful. American planes pounded the Ho Chi Minh trail that ran down through Laos and Cambodia, but the North Vietnamese used the jungle panoply effectively to hide their shipments and massive manpower to repair damaged roads and bridges. In fact, the American air attacks, with their inadvertent civilian casualties, gave North Vietnam a powerful propaganda weapon, which it used to sway world opinion against the United States.

The war in the South went no better. Despite the steady increase in American ground forces, from 184,000 in late 1965 to more than 500,000 by early 1968, the Vietcong still controlled much of the countryside. The search-and-destroy tactics employed by the American commander, General William Westmoreland, proved ill suited. The Vietcong, aided by North Vietnamese regulars, were waging a war of insurgency, avoiding fixed positions and striking from ambush. In a vain effort to destroy the enemy, Westmoreland used

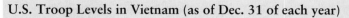

U.S. Troop Levels in Vietnam (as of Dec. 31 of each year)

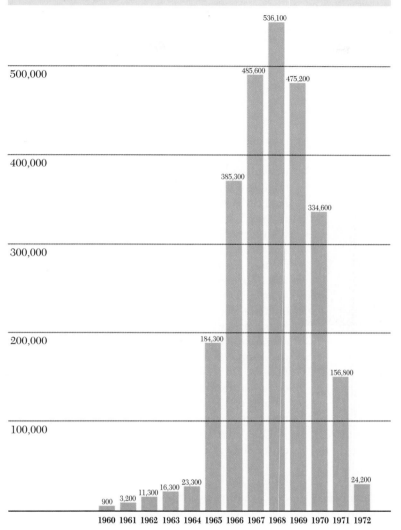

Source: U.S. Department of Defense.

superior American firepower wantonly, devastating the countryside, causing many civilian casualties, and driving the peasantry into the arms of the guerrillas. Inevitably, these tactics led to the slaughter of innocent civilians, most notably at the hamlet of My Lai. In March 1968, an American company led by Lieutenant William Calley, Jr., killed over two hundred unarmed villagers.

The main premise of Westmoreland's strategy was to wage a war of attrition that would finally reach a "crossover point" when communist losses each month would be greater than the number of new troops they could recruit. He hoped to lure

the Vietcong and the North Vietnamese regulars into pitched battles where American firepower would inflict heavy casualties. But soon it was the communists who were deciding where and when the fighting would take place, provoking American attacks in remote areas of South Vietnam that favored the defenders and made Westmoreland pay heavily in American lives for the communist losses. In late 1967, the North Vietnamese began a borders strategy designed to lure the bulk of American troops into battle in the Central Highlands and the areas bordering on Laos and Cambodia. The main attack came

Surviving Vietnam

The stark, black, angled wall that forms the Vietnam Veterans' Memorial is engraved from top to bottom along its entire length with the names of U.S. personnel killed or thought to be missing in Vietnam.

Vietnam ranks after World War II as America's second most expensive war. Between 1950 and 1975, the United States spent $123 billion on combat in Southeast Asia. More importantly, Vietnam ranks—after our Civil War and World Wars I and II—as the nation's fourth deadliest war, with 57,661 Americans killed in action.

Yet, when the last U.S. helicopter left Saigon, Americans suffered what historian George Herring terms "collective amnesia." Everyone, even those who had fought in 'Nam, seemed to want to forget Southeast Asia. It took nearly ten years for the nation to erect a national monument to honor those who died in Vietnam. The Vietnam Veterans Memorial in Washington, D.C.,

was dedicated in November 1982; on its polished black granite walls are carved the names of the dead and missing in action. And only in 1981 did collections of oral histories of some of those who served in Vietnam begin to appear: Al Santoli's well-documented *Everything We Had: An Oral History of the Vietnam War by Thirty-three American Soldiers Who Fought It* and Mark Baker's *Nam: The Vietnam War in the Words of the Men and Women Who Fought There*. Both books demonstrate that in the steaming jungles of Vietnam one thing mattered most: survival.

One Vietnam veteran expressed the general feeling of men in combat: "War is not killing. Killing is the easiest part. . . . Sweating twenty-four hours a day, seeing guys drop all around you from heatstroke, not having food, not having water, sleeping only three hours a night for weeks at a time, that's what war is. Survival."

During his term President Kennedy ordered a more than tenfold increase in the number of U.S. advisers in Vietnam. Yet, for the ten to twelve thousand predominantly career soldiers there by December of 1962, Vietnam seemed a nice little nine-to-five war. Recalls radio technician Jan Barry of the army's 18th Aviation Company, "If we wanted to go out and

chase people around and shoot at them . . . we had a war going. If we didn't . . . they left us alone." In those early days, even the Special Forces Green Berets "used to stop at four-thirty and have a happy hour and get drunk," says Barry, adding that "there was no war after four-thirty. On Saturdays, no war. On Sundays, no war. On holidays, no war. That's right, a nine-to-five war."

Within two years, however, the Joint Chiefs of Staff and President Johnson committed 50,000 American troops to combat in Vietnam, and the nice little war turned grim. By mid-1967, in fact, more than 400,000 Americans were fighting in Vietnam. As many as 300 died each week. Combat, recalls 26th Marine Division scout-sniper James Hebron, turned out "totally different" from what he had expected when he had joined the corps at age seventeen early in 1967. "There was no romance at all," says Hebron. During one combat period, Hebron's Bravo Company went without a hot meal for seven months. During that same operation, he notes, "I didn't brush my teeth for two months," explaining that "they sent toothbrushes . . . we had to use them to clean our rifles."

The Screaming Eagles of the elite 101st Airborne Division arrived in Vietnam shortly before the Tet offensive of January

930

1968. Lieutenant Robert Santos, destined to become one of the division's most decorated men, told his platoon, "two things can happen to you. You can get wounded and go home early. Or you can die." He added that the "best way to go home is whole. If you stick with me . . . and learn from the [more experienced men] you won't get wounded. You won't die." Santos and his men earned a basketful of medals for valor in combat. Lieutenant Santos explains those medals in grim terms: "My responsibility was to kill and in the process of killing to be so good at it that I indirectly saved my men's lives." So, notes Santos, "You come home with the high body count, high kill ratio," but, he concludes, "there's nothing, nothing, that's very satisfying about that."

Few who served in Vietnam survived unscathed, whether psychologically or physically. One of the 303,600 Americans wounded during the long war was 101st Airborne platoon leader James Bombard, first shot and then blown up by a mortar round during the bitter Tet fighting at Hue in February 1968. He describes his traumatic experience as

> feeling the bullet rip into your flesh, the shrapnel tear the flesh from your bones and the blood run down your leg. . . . To put your hand on your chest and to come away with your hand red with your own blood, and to feel it running out of your eyes and out of your mouth, and seeing it spurt out of your guts, realizing you were dying. . . . I was

> ripped open from the top of my head to the tip of my toes. I had forty-five holes in me.

Somehow Bombard survived Vietnam.

The fighting continued for four years after President Nixon took office. Robert Rawls served as a rifleman with the 1st Cavalry Division from early 1969 to early 1970. He recalls:

> We got fire fights after fire fights. My first taste of death. After fire fights you could smell it. They brought the [dead men] back wrapped in ponchos. . . . [T]hey just threw them up on the helicopter and [piled empty, reusable supply cases] on top of them. You could see the guys' feet hanging out. . . . I had nightmares. . . . I can still see those guys.

As the war dragged on, pacifist frustration at home paralleled the bitterness of those who had fought in Vietnam. John Muir's experience is typical. Early in the war, Muir had served as a rifleman with the 1st Marine Division during the battle of Dong Ha. Muir's single company fought continuously for four days and four nights, frequently in hand-to-hand combat, against two divisions of the North Vietnamese Army. When the marines were relieved, only ninety-one men—all wounded—were still able to fight at all. Muir's squad, however, had been wiped out: he had ended up throwing rocks at his attackers.

"It was a major battle," recalls Muir. "We did a fine job there. If it had happened in World War II, they still would be

An exhausted marine succumbs to grief after learning that one of the wounded comrades he had rescued had died. Larry Brown, the English photographer who took this picture at the marine base in Danang, South Vietnam, in 1965, was himself killed in 1971 when the helicopter carrying him to cover the South Vietnamese invasion of Laos was shot down.

telling stories about it. But it happened in Vietnam, so nobody knows about it."

Withdrawing U.S. forces from Vietnam ended only the combat. Returning veterans fought government disclaimers concerning the toxicity of the defoliant Agent Orange. VA hospitals across the nation still contain thousands of para- and quadriplegic Vietnam veterans, as well as the maimed from earlier wars. Throughout America the "walking wounded" find themselves still embroiled in the psychological aftermath of Vietnam. To this day, says former 1st Infantry Division combat medic David Ross, "If I'm walking someplace and there's grass, I find myself sometimes doing a shuffle and looking down at the ground. . . . I'm looking for a wire or a piece of vine that looks too straight, might be a [land mine] trip wire. Some of the survival habits you pick up stay residual for a long time."

931

Chronology of America's Longest War: Vietnam, 1950–1975

Date	Event	Significance
May 1950	Truman authorizes $10 million in aid to the French in Indochina fighting a war against guerrilla forces led by Ho Chi Minh	Beginning of the American involvement in Vietnam
May 1954	Fall of Dien Bien Phu	End of French dominance in Indochina
July 1954	Geneva Conference	Division of Vietnam at 17th parallel. Ho's forces gain control of North Vietnam
Oct. 1954	Eisenhower backs Diem regime in Saigon, capital of South Vietnam	U.S. replaces France as chief Western supporter of South Vietnam
Nov. 1961	Kennedy sends thousands of military "advisers" to Vietnam	The way is opened for an American combat role in Vietnam
Nov. 1963	Overthrow and assassination of Ngo Dinh Diem after Kennedy gives tacit approval to coup	Political vacuum of power created in Saigon
Aug. 1964	Congress passes Gulf of Tonkin Resolution	President Johnson is given authority to use unlimited military force in Vietnam
Feb. 1965	U.S. begins bombing of North Vietnam. It proves ineffectve	Johnson commits U.S. prestige to prevent defeat of South Vietnam
July 1965	Johnson announces decision to send 50,000 ground troops to Vietnam	U.S. involvement escalates in an effort to compel a diplomatic settlement
Jan. 1968	American ground troops reach the 500,000 mark. Vietcong launch Tet offensive	Public support for Vietnam War erodes in United States
March 1968	Johnson announces he will not run for reelection	End of American escalation in Vietnam
May 1968	Paris peace talks begin	U.S. and North Vietnam quickly deadlock on peace terms
June 1969	Nixon announces withdrawal of 25,000 American troops from Vietnam	Beginning of policy of Vietnamization
April 1970	Nixon orders invasion of Cambodia	Widening of war to include all Indochina
May 1972	Nixon authorizes mining of Haiphong harbor and intensified bombing of North Vietnam	U.S. attempts to pressure North Vietnam into agreeing to peace terms
Jan. 1973	Cease-fire agreements signed in Paris. U.S. agrees to remove its troops within 60 days	End of direct American military involvement in Vietnam
Jan. 1975	North Vietnam invades South Vietnam	U.S. unwilling to try again to rescue South Vietnam
April 1975	Fall of Saigon	Abrupt withdrawal of U.S. from South Vietnam

A flight of U.S. planes sprays chemical defoliants to remove the protective jungle covering in Vietcong areas. The chemicals used claimed many civilian victims and destroyed crops and livestock. Years after the war, the land remained devastated and evidence began to link a variety of physical and genetic disorders to exposure to the chemicals, particularly Agent Orange.

against the marines at Khe Sahn in the northern interior, drawing more than 40 percent of all American infantry and armor battalions into the two northernmost provinces of South Vietnam.

The Vietcong (VC) then used the traditional lull in the fighting at Tet, the lunar New Year, to launch a surprise attack in the heavily populated cities. Beginning on January 30, 1968, the VC struck at 36 of the 44 provincial capitals; the most daring raid came at the American embassy compound in Saigon. Although the guerrillas were unable to penetrate the embassy proper, for six hours television cameras caught the dramatic battle that ensued in the courtyard before military police finally overcame the attackers. Prompt response by American and South Vietnamese forces quickly repulsed the Tet offensive everywhere except Hue, the old imperial capital, which was only retaken after three weeks of heavy fighting had left this beautiful city, in the words of one observer, "a shattered, stinking hulk, its streets choked with rubble and rotting bodies."

Tet proved to be the turning point of the Vietnam War. Although the communists suffered a major military defeat, losing an estimated fifty thousand men, they scored an impressive political victory. For months, President Johnson had been telling the American people the war was almost over and victory in sight; suddenly it appeared to be nearly lost. CBS-TV newscaster Walter Cronkite took a quick trip to Saigon to find out what had happened. Horrified at what he saw, he

exclaimed to his guides, "What the hell is going on? I thought we were winning the war." He returned home to tell the American people, "It seems now more certain than ever that the bloody experience of Vietnam is to end in a stalemate."

President Johnson reluctantly came to the same conclusion after the Joint Chiefs of Staff requested an additional 205,000 troops to achieve victory in Vietnam following the Tet offensive. He began to listen to his new secretary of defense, Clark Clifford, who replaced Robert McNamara in January 1968. In mid-March, after receiving advice from the "wise men," a group of experienced cold warriors that included such illustrious figures as Dean Acheson and Omar Bradley, the president decided to limit the bombing of North Vietnam in an effort to open up peace negotiations with Hanoi. In a speech to the nation on Sunday evening, March 31, 1968, Johnson outlined his plans for a new effort at ending the war peacefully, and then concluded by saying, as proof of his sincerity, "I shall not seek, and I will not accept, the nomination of my party for another term as your President."

In the fourteen years since the seige of Dien Bien Phu, American policy had gone full cycle in Vietnam. Even though Eisenhower had decided against using force to rescue the French, his commitment to the Diem regime in Saigon had led eventually to American military involvement on a massive scale. Three years of inconclusive fighting and a steadily mounting loss of American lives

Johnson stunned the nation with his announcement that he would not run for reelection in 1968. Poor results in the March presidential primaries and public opinion polls indicated that support for LBJ was eroding.

had disillusioned the American people and finally cost Lyndon Johnson the presidency. And the full price the nation would have to pay for its folly in Southeast Asia was still unknown—the Vietnam experience would continue to cast a shadow over American life for years to come.

The failure in Vietnam reflected the difficulty the United States faced in pursuing containment on a global scale. The policies that had worked well in Europe in the 1940s had little relevance to a very different situation in Southeast Asia. Intent on halting the spread of communism, American leaders never grasped the political realities in Vietnam. The United States ended up backing a series of corrupt regimes in Saigon while the Vietcong won the struggle for the hearts and minds of the Vietnamese people. More than anything else, the Vietnam War revealed the need for a thorough reexamination of the basic premises of American foreign policy in the Cold War.

Recommended Reading

The best introduction to the Vietnam War is the balanced survey by George Herring, *America's Longest War*, 2d ed. (1985). Lloyd Gardner offers a persuasive analysis of the early American involvement through 1954 in *Approaching Vietnam* (1988); George McT. Kahin, *Intervention* (1986), is excellent on what led to the escalation of the 1960s.

Stephen E. Ambrose exemplifies the recent reevaluation of Dwight D. Eisenhower by historians in the second volume of his biography, *Eisenhower: The President* (1985). For an equally favorable analysis, see Robert A. Divine, *Eisenhower and the Cold War* (1981).

Roger Hilsman, *To Move a Nation* (1967), is a revealing account of Kennedy's foreign policy by an insider; the best recent study is Michael R. Beschloss, *The Crisis Years: Kennedy and Khrushchev, 1960–1963* (1991).

Additional Bibliography

H. W. Brands gives a good overview of Eisenhower's foreign policy team in *Cold Warriors* (1988). Other books on Ike's foreign policy include Emmet J. Hughes, *The Ordeal of Power* (1962), a revealing memoir; Peter Lyon, *Eisenhower: Portrait of the Hero* (1974), a critical biography; William B. Ewald, *Eisenhower the President* (1981), a sympathetic account; and Blanche W. Cook, *The Declassified Eisenhower* (1981), a critique of his diplomacy. Eisenhower's two volumes of memoirs, *Mandate for Change* (1963) and *Waging Peace* (1966), are full and revealing accounts. For Eisenhower's secretary of state, see Richard H. Immerman, ed., *John Foster Dulles and the Diplomacy of the Cold War* (1989).

The best accounts of early American involvement in Vietnam are Andrew Rotter, *The Path to Vietnam* (1988), on events before 1954; Ellen J. Hammer, *The Struggle for Indochina, 1940–1955* (1966); Melvin Gurtov, *The First Vietnamese Crisis* (1967); Bernard B. Fall, *Hell in a Very Small Place* (1966), and Melanie Billings-Yun, *Decision Against War* (1988), on Dien Bien Phu and Eisenhower's refusal to intervene; James Arnold, *The First Domino* (1992), and David Anderson, *Trapped By Success* (1991), on Eisenhower's commitment to the Diem regime. On Latin America, the best accounts are Richard Immerman, *The CIA in Guatemala* (1982); Piero Gleijeses, *Shattered Hope: The Guatamalan Revolution and the United States, 1944–1954* (1991); and Stephen Rabe, *Eisenhower and Latin America* (1988). For information on specific topics, see Chester Cooper, *The Lion's Last Roar* (1978); Donald Neff, *Warriors at Suez* (1981); Diane Kunz, *The Economic Diplomacy of the Suez Crisis* (1991); and Peter L. Hahn, *The United States, Great Britain and Egypt, 1945–1956* (1991), on the Suez crisis; David A. Mayers, *Cracking the Monolith* (1986); Gordon Chang, *Friends and Enemies: The United States, China, and the Soviet Union, 1948–1972* (1990); and Warren Cohen and Akira Iriye, eds., *The Great Powers in East Asia, 1953–1960* (1990), on Asian policy; Robert A. Divine, *Blowing on the Wind* (1978), and Richard Hewlett and Jack Holl, *Atoms for Peace and War, 1953–1961* (1989), on nuclear issues; Michael R. Beschloss, *May-Day* (1986), on the U-2 crisis; and Burton Kaufman, *Trade and Aid* (1982), on foreign economic policy.

Kennedy's foreign policy is subjected to critical scrutiny in Richard J. Walton, *Cold War and Counterrevolution* (1972), and Louise FitzSimmons, *The Kennedy Doctrine* (1972); the most recent scholarly reappraisal is Thomas Paterson, ed., *Kennedy's Quest for Victory* (1989). Books on LBJ's foreign policy include Philip Geyelin, *Lyndon B. Johnson and the World* (1966); Walt W. Rostow, *The Diffusion of Power* (1972); and Paul Y. Hammond, *LBJ and the Presidential Management of Foreign Affairs* (1992).

Concerning nuclear weapons in the 1960s, consult Michael Mandelbaum, *The Nuclear Question* (1979); Desmond Ball, *Politics and Force Levels* (1981); Harland B. Moulton, *Nuclear Superiority and Parity* (1972); and two broader studies of the arms race since 1945, McGeorge Bundy, *Danger and Survival* (1989), and Ronald Powaski, *March to Armageddon* (1987).

On Latin America, Theodore Draper, *Castro's Revolution* (1962); Richard E. Welch, *Response to Revolution* (1985); Trumbull Higgins, *The Perfect Failure* (1987); and Peter Wyden, *The Bay of Pigs* (1979), all deal with Castro's Cuba. For the Cuban Missile crisis, see Elie Abel, *The Missile Crisis* (1966); Robert F. Kennedy, *Thirteen Days* (1968); Graham Allison, *The Essence of Decision* (1971); Raymond Garthoff, *Reflections on the Cuban Missile Crisis* (1987); James G. Blight and David A. Welch, *On the Brink* (1989); Herbert Dinerstein, *The Making of the Missile Crisis* (1976); Dino Brugioni, *Eyeball to Eyeball* (1992); Robert Smith Thompson, *The Missiles of October* (1992); and James G. Blight, *The Shattered Crystal Ball* (1990). Books on Johnson's intervention in the Dominican Republic include John B. Martin, *Overtaken by Events* (1966); Jerome Slater, *Intervention and Negotiation* (1970); Abraham Lowenthal, *The Dominican Intervention* (1972); Piero Gleijeses, *The Dominican Crisis* (1976); and Bruce Palmer, *Intervention in the Caribbean* (1989).

Kennedy's handling of a key European problem is traced in Norman Gelb, *The Berlin Wall* (1986), and Honore Catudel, *Kennedy and the Berlin Wall Crisis* (1980). For other regions, see Richard D. Mahoney, *JFK: Ordeal in Africa* (1983); Thomas J. Noer, *Cold War and Black Liberation* (1985); and Timothy P. Maga, *John F. Kennedy and the New Pacific Community, 1961–1963* (1990).

Stanley Karnow offers a broad view of the Vietnam War in *Vietnam: A History* (1983). Other general accounts of the war in Vietnam include Guenther Lewy, *American in Vietnam* (1978); Gabriel Kolko, *Anatomy of a War* (1986); Chester Cooper, *The Lost Crusade* (1970); Leslie H. Gelb and Richard K. Betts, *The Irony of Vietnam* (1979); and David Halberstam, *The Best and the Brightest* (1972). For Kennedy's role, see William J. Rust, *Kennedy in Vietnam* (1985); Ellen J. Hammer, *A Death in November* (1987); and John M. Newman, *JFK and Vietnam* (1992). Neil Sheehan, ed., *The Pentagon Papers* (1971), contains important documents on the war.

Lyndon Johnson's Vietnam decisions and their consequences are traced in two books by Larry Berman, *Planning a Tragedy* (1982) and *Lyndon Johnson's War* (1989); two books on the Gulf of Tonkin incident are Joseph C. Goulden, *Truth Is the First Casualty*

(1969); and Anthony Austin, *The President's War* (1971); David Barrett, *Uncertain Warriors: Lyndon Johnson and His Vietnam Advisers* (1993); Kathleen Turner, *Lyndon Johnson's Dual War* (1985), cover LBJ and the media; Townsend Hoopes, *The Limits of Intervention* (1969); and Herbert Y. Schandler, *The Unmaking of a President* (1977), cover Johnson's change of heart in 1968.

Analyses of the military issues involved in the Vietnam War include Bruce Palmer, Jr., *The 25-Year War* (1984); Harry G. Summers, Jr., *On Strategy* (1982); Timothy Lomperis, *The War Nobody Lost— and Won* (1984); Mark Clodfelter, *The Limits of Air Power: The American Bombing of North Vietnam* (1989); James W. Gipson, *The Perfect War* (1986); Don Oberdorfer, *Tet!* (1971); James J. Wirtz, *The Tet Offensive* (1991); and Larry Cable, *Unholy Grail: The U.S. and the War in Vietnam, 1965–1968* (1992). Neil Sheehan, *A Bright Shining Lie* (1988), explores the war through the eyes of John Paul Vann.

Biographies and memoirs relating to foreign policy include Warren Cohen, *Dean Rusk* (1980); Thomas J. Schoenbaum, *Waging Peace and War: Dean Rusk* (1988); Dean Rusk, *As I Saw It* (1990); Deborah Shapley, *Promise and Power: The Life and Times of Robert McNamara* (1993); Clark Clifford, *Counsel to the President* (1991); Douglas Brinkley, *Dean Acheson, The Cold War Years, 1953–71* (1992); Douglas Kinnard, *The Certain Trumpet: Maxwell Taylor and the American Experience in Vietnam* (1991); Chester Bowles, *Promises to Keep* (1971); George Ball, *The Past Has Another Pattern* (1982); David L. DiLeo, *George Ball, Vietnam and the Rethinking of Containment* (1991); Glen T. Seaborg, *Kennedy, Khrushchev and the Test Ban* (1982) and *Stemming the Tide* (1987); and Thomas Powers, *The Man Who Kept the Secrets* (1979), which uses the career of Richard Helms to illuminate the history of the CIA.

A Crisis in Confidence, 1965–1980

"We are the people of this generation, bred in at least modest comfort, housed now in universities, looking uncomfortably to the world we inherit." So began the preamble to the Port Huron Statement, a manifesto of the newly reorganized Students for a Democratic Society (SDS), which became the call to arms for the vanguard of an entire generation. Only fifty-nine delegates attended the convention held at a union summer camp in Port Huron, Michigan, in June 1962. The two main organizers, Al Haber and Tom Hayden, hoped to transform their small student protest group into the vehicle that would rid American society of poverty, racism, and violence.

Their timing was perfect. College enrollments were climbing rapidly as a result of the post–World War II baby boom and growing affluence. Before the end of the decade, more than half the American population would be under age thirty. And many, repelled by the crass materialism of American life—with its endless suburbs and shopping centers—were ready to embrace a new lifestyle based on the belief that "man is sensitive, searching, poetic, and capable of love." They were ready to create a counterculture.

In some ways, the sixty-six-page proposal adopted at Port Huron was prosaic, repeating many conventional liberal reforms, such as expanded public housing and broader health insurance programs. But it offered a startling new approach by advocating "participatory democracy" as its main tactic for social change. In contrast to both traditional liberalism and old-fashioned socialism, the SDS sought salvation through the individual rather than the group. Personal control of one's life and destiny, not the creation of new bureaucracies, was the hallmark of the New Left.

In the next few years, the SDS grew phenomenally. Spurred on by the Vietnam War and massive campus unrest, the SDS could count more than 100,000 followers and was responsible for disruptions at nearly a thousand colleges in 1968. Yet its very emphasis on the individual and its fear of bureaucracy left it leaderless and subject to division and disunity. By 1970, a split between factions, some of which were given to violence, led to its complete demise.

The meteoric career of the SDS symbolized the turbulence of the 1960s. For a brief time, it seemed as though the nation's youth had gone berserk, indulging in a wave of experimentation with drugs, sex, and rock music. Older Americans felt all the nation's traditional values, from the Puritan work ethic to the family, were under attack.

Not all American youth joined in the cultural insurgency, however. In small towns and among blue-collar families in the cities, young people went to Friday night high school football games, cheered John Wayne as he wiped out the Vietcong in the movie, *The Green Berets,* and attended church with their parents on Sunday. The rebellion was generally limited to children of the upper middle class. But like the flappers of the 1920s, they set the tone for an entire era and left a lasting impression on American society.

YEARS OF TURMOIL

The agitation of the 1960s was at its height from 1965 to 1968, the years that marked the escalation of the Vietnam War. Disturbances on college campuses reflected growing discontent in other parts of society, from the ghettos of the cities to the lettuce fields of the Southwest. All who felt disadvantaged—students, African Americans, Hispanics, Native Americans, women, hippies—took to the streets to give vent to their feelings.

The Student Revolt

The first sign of student rebellion came in the fall of 1964 at the prestigious University of California at Berkeley. A small group of radical students resisted university efforts to deny them a place to solicit volunteers and funds for off-campus causes. Forming the Free Speech Movement, they struck back by occupying administration buildings and blocking the arrest of a nonstudent protester. For the next two months, the campus was in turmoil.

In the end, the protesters won the rights of free speech and association that they championed. Their hero was Mario Savio, a student who had eloquently summed up the cause by likening the university to a great machine and telling others,

"You've got to put your bodies upon the gears, and upon the wheels, upon the levers, upon all the apparatus, and you've got to make it stop."

The Free Speech Movement at Berkeley offered many insights into the causes of campus unrest. It was fueled in part by student suspicion of an older, Depression-born generation that viewed affluence as the answer to all problems. Unable to exert much influence on the power structure that directed the consumer society, the students turned on the university. They viewed higher education as the faithful servant of a corporate culture that trained hordes of technicians, harbored the research laboratories which perfected dreadful weapons, and regimented its students with IBM punch cards. The feeling of powerlessness that underlay the Berkeley riots was best revealed by the protester carrying the sign that read, "I am a UC student. Please don't bend, fold, spindle or mutilate me."

War, racism, and poverty were the three great evils that student radicals addressed. Many first became involved in the civil rights cause, but by 1965, white militants found a new issue—the Vietnam War. The first student teach-ins began at the University of Michigan in March 1965; soon they spread to campuses across the nation. More than twenty thousand protesters, under SDS aus-

pices, gathered in Washington in April to listen to entertainers Joan Baez and Judy Collins sing anti-war songs. "End the War in Vietnam Now, Stop the Killing," read the signs.

One of the great ironies of the Vietnam War was the system of student draft deferments, which enabled most of those enrolled in college to avoid military service. As a result, the children of the well-to-do, who were more likely to attend college, were able to escape the draft. One survey revealed that men from disadvantaged families, including a disproportionately large African American and Hispanic representation, were twice as likely to be drafted and engage in combat in Vietnam as those from more privileged backgrounds. Consequently, a sense of guilt led many college activists who were safe from Vietnam because of their student status to take the lead in denouncing an unjust war.

As the fighting in Southeast Asia intensified in 1966 and 1967, the protests grew larger and the slogans more extreme. "Hey, Hey, LBJ, How Many Kids Have You Killed Today?" chanted students as they proclaimed, "Hell, No, We Won't Go!" At the Pentagon in October 1967, over 100,000 demonstrators—mainly students, but housewives, teachers, and young professionals as well—confronted a cordon of military

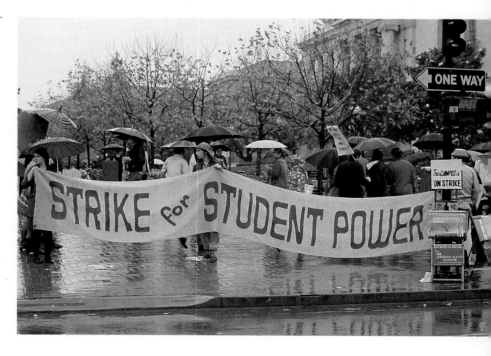

Feeling powerless but determined to gain the "Establishment's" attention, students—largely from upper middle- and middle-class backgrounds— began their crusade against poverty, racism, and war by "taking it to the streets."

policemen guarding the heart of the nation's war machine.

The climax came in the spring of 1968. Driven both by opposition to the war and concern for social justice, the SDS and African American radicals at Columbia University joined forces in April. They seized five buildings, effectively paralyzing one of the country's leading colleges. After eight days of tension, the New York City police regained control. The brutal repression quickened the pace of protest elsewhere. Students held sit-ins and marches at more than one hundred colleges, from Cheyney State in Pennsylvania to Northwestern in Illinois.

The students failed to stop the war, but they did succeed in gaining a voice in their education. University administrations allowed undergraduates to sit on faculty curriculum-planning committees and gave up their once rigid control of dormitory and social life. But the students' greatest impact lay outside politics and the campus. They spawned a cultural uprising that transformed the manners and morals of America.

The Cultural Revolution

In contrast to the elitist political revolt of the SDS, the cultural rebellion by youth in the 1960s was pervasive. Led by college students, young people challenged the prevailing adult values in clothing, hairstyles, sexual conduct, work habits, and music. Blue jeans and love beads took the place of business suits and wristwatches; long hair and unkempt beards for men, bare feet and bralessness for women became the new uniform of protest. Families gave way to communes for the "flower children" of the 1960s.

Music became the touchstone of the new departure. Folk singers like Joan Baez and Bob Dylan, popular for their songs of social protest in the mid-1960s, gave way first to rock groups such as the Beatles, whose lyrics were often suggestive of drug use, and finally to "acid rock" as symbolized by the Grateful Dead. The climactic event of the decade came at the Woodstock concert at Bethel in upstate New York when 400,000 young people indulged in a three-day festival of rock music, drug experimentation, and public sexual activity.

Former Harvard psychology professor Timothy Leary encouraged youth to join him in trying out the drug scene. Millions accepted his invitation "Tune in, turn on, drop out," literally, as they experimented with marijuana and with LSD, a new and dangerous chemical hallucinogen. The ultimate expression of insurgency was the Yippie movement, led by Jerry Rubin and Abbie Hoffman. Shrewd buffoons who mocked the consumer culture, they delighted in capitalizing on the mood of social protest to win attention. Once, when testifying before a congressional committee investigating internal subversion, Rubin dressed as a revolutionary war soldier; Hoffman appeared in the gallery of the New York Stock Exchange in 1967, raining money down on the cheering brokers below.

"Black Power"

The civil rights movement, which had spawned the mood of protest in the 1960s, fell on hard times later in the decade. The legislative triumphs of 1964 and 1965 were relatively easy victories over southern bigotry; now the movement faced the far more complex problem of achieving economic equality in the cities of the North, where more than half of the nation's African Americans lived in poverty. The civil rights movement had raised the expectations of urban African Americans for improvement; frustration mounted as they failed to experience any significant economic gain.

The first sign of trouble came in the summer of 1964, when African American teenagers in Harlem and Rochester, New York, rioted. The next summer, a massive outburst of rage and destruction swept over the Watts area of Los Angeles as the inhabitants burned buildings and looted stores. Riots in the summer of 1966 were less destructive, but in 1967 the worst ones yet took place in Newark and Detroit, where forty-three were killed and hundreds were injured. The mobs attacked the shops and stores, expressing a burning grievance against a consumer society from which they were excluded by their poverty.

The civil rights coalition fell apart, a victim of both its legislative success and economic failure. Black militants took over the leadership of the Student Nonviolent Coordinating Committee (SNCC); they disdained white help and even reversed Martin Luther King's insistence on nonviolence. SNCC's new leader, Stokely Carmichael,

The cultural revolution climaxed in August 1969 at the Woodstock music festival, billed as "Three Days of Peace and Music." Despite rainy weather, food and water shortages, and massive traffic jams, the three-day happening inspired visions of a "Woodstock nation."

told blacks they should seize power in those parts of the South where they outnumbered whites. "I am not going to beg the white man for anything I deserve," he said, "I'm going to take it." Soon his calls for "black power" became a rallying cry for more militant blacks who advocated the need for African Americans to form "our own institutions, credit unions, co-ops, political parties" and even write "our own history."

Others went further than calls for ethnic separation. H. Rap Brown, who replaced Carmichael as the leader of SNCC in 1967, told an African American crowd in Cambridge, Maryland, to "get your guns" and "burn this town down"; Huey Newton, one of the founders of the militant Black Panther party, proclaimed, "We make the statement, quoting from Chairman Mao, that Political Power comes through the Barrel of a Gun."

King suffered the most from this extremism. His denunciation of the Vietnam War cost him the support of the Johnson administration and alienated him from the more conservative civil rights groups like the NAACP and the Urban League. He finally seized on poverty as the proper enemy for attack, but before he could lead his Poor People's March on Washington in 1968, he was assassinated in Memphis in early April.

Both blacks and whites realized the nation had lost its most eloquent spokesman for racial harmony. His tragic death elevated King to the status of a martyr, but it also led to one last outbreak of urban violence. African Americans exploded in angry riots in 125 cities across the nation; the worst rioting took place in Washington, D.C., where buildings were set on fire within a few blocks of the White House. "It was as if the city were being abandoned to an invading army," wrote a British journalist. "Clouds of smoke hung over the Potomac, evoking memories of the London blitz. . . ."

Yet there was a positive side to the emotions engendered by black nationalism. Leaders began to urge African Americans to take pride in their ethnic heritage, to embrace their blackness as a positive value. African Americans began to wear Afro hairstyles and dress in dashikis, stressing their African roots. Students began to demand new black studies programs in the colleges; the word *Negro*—identified with white supremacy of the past—virtually disappeared from usage overnight, replaced by the favored "Afro-American" or "black." Singer James Brown best expressed the sense of racial identity: "Say It Loud—I'm Black and I'm Proud."

Ethnic Nationalism

Other groups quickly emulated the African American phenomenon. Native Americans decried the callous use of their identity as football mascots; in response, universities such as Stanford changed their symbols. Puerto Ricans demanded their history be included in school and college texts. Polish, Italian, and Czech groups insisted on respect for their nationalities. Congress acknowledged these demands with passage of the Ethnic Heritage Studies Act of 1972. Instead of trying to melt all groups down into a standard American type, Congress now gave what one sponsor of the measure called "official recognition to ethnicity as a positive constructive force in our society today."

Mexican Americans were in the forefront of the ethnic groups that became active in the 1970s. The primary impulse came from the efforts of César Chávez to organize the poorly paid grape pickers and lettuce workers in California into the National Farm Workers Association (NFWA). Chávez appealed to ethnic nationalism in mobilizing Mexican American field hands to strike against grape growers in the San Joaquin Valley in 1965. A national boycott of grapes by Mexican Americans and their sympathizers among the young people of the counterculture led to a series of hard-fought victories over the growers. The five-year struggle resulted in a union victory in 1970, but at an enormous cost—95 percent of the farm workers involved had lost their homes and their cars. Nevertheless, Chávez succeeded in raising the hourly wage of farm workers in California to $3.53 by 1977 (it had been $1.20 in 1965).

Chávez's efforts helped spark an outburst of ethnic consciousness among Mexican Americans that swept through the urban barrios of the Southwest. Mexican American leaders campaigned for bilingual programs and improved educational opportunities. Young activists began to call themselves Chicanos, which had previously been a derogatory term, and to take pride in their cultural heritage; in 1968, they succeeded in establishing the first Mexican American studies program at California State College at Los Angeles. Campus leaders called for reform, urging high school students to insist on improvements. Heeding such appeals, nearly ten thousand students at East Los Angeles high schools walked out of class in March 1968. These walkouts sparked similar movements in San Antonio, Texas, and Phoenix, Arizona, and led to the introduction of bilingual programs in grade

In March 1966, César Chávez, shown here speaking at the first United Farm Workers convention, led the striking grape pickers on a 250-mile march from Delano, California, to the state capital in Sacramento to dramatize the plight of migrant farm workers. With the slogan, "God Is Beside You on the Picket Line," the march took on the character of a religious pilgrimage.

schools and the hiring of more Chicano teachers at all levels.

Women's Liberation

Active as they were in the civil rights and antiwar movements, women soon learned the male leaders of these causes were little different from corporate executives—they expected women to fix the food and type the communiqués while the men made the decisions. Understandably, women soon realized they could only achieve respect and equality by mounting their own protest.

In some ways, the position of women in American society was worse in the 1960s than it had been in the 1920s. After forty years, there was a lower percentage of women enrolled in the nation's colleges and professional schools. Women were still relegated to stereotyped occupations like nursing and teaching; there were few female lawyers and even fewer women doctors. And gender roles, as portrayed on television commercials, continued to call for the husband to be the breadwinner and the wife to be the homemaker.

Betty Friedan was one of the first to seize on the sense of grievance and discrimination that developed among white middle-class women in the 1960s. The beginning of the effort to raise women's consciousness was her 1963 book, *The Feminine Mystique*. Calling the American home "a comfortable concentration camp," she attacked the prevailing view that women were completely contented with their housekeeping and child-rearing tasks, claiming housewives had no self-esteem and no sense of identity. "I'm a server of food and putter on of pants and a bedmaker," a mother of four told Friedan, "somebody who can be called on when you want something. But who am I?"

The 1964 Civil Rights Act helped women attack economic inequality head-on by making it illegal to discriminate in employment on the basis of sex. Women filed suit for equal wages, demanded that companies provide day care for their infants and preschool children, and entered politics to lobby against laws which—in the guise

of protection of a weaker sex—were unfair to women. As the women's liberation movement grew, its advocates began to attack laws banning abortion and waged a campaign to toughen the enforcement of rape laws.

The women's movement met with many of the same obstacles as other protest groups in the 1960s. The moderate leadership of the National Organization for Women (NOW), founded by Betty Friedan in 1966, soon was challenged by those with more extreme views. Ti-Grace Atkinson and Susan Brownmiller attacked revered institutions—the family and the home—and even denounced sexual intercourse with men, calling it a method of male domination. Many women were repelled by the harsh rhetoric of the extremists and expressed satisfaction with their lives. But despite these disagreements, most women supported the effort to achieve equal status with men, and in 1972, Congress responded by voting to send the Equal Rights Amendment to the state legislatures for ratification.

THE RETURN OF RICHARD NIXON

The turmoil of the 1960s reached a crescendo in 1968 as the American people responded to the two dominant events of the decade—the war in Vietnam and the cultural insurgency at home. In an election marked by a series of bizarre events, including riots and an assassination, Richard Nixon staged a remarkable comeback to win the post denied him in 1960.

The Democrats Divide

Lyndon Johnson's withdrawal from the presidential race after the Tet offensive set the tone for the 1968 election. LBJ's decision had come in response to political as well as military realities. By 1966, the antiwar movement had spread from the college campuses to Capitol Hill. Chairman J. William Fulbright gave the protests a new respectability when his Senate Foreign Relations Committee held probing hearings on the war, broadcast on television to the entire country. Johnson began to feel like a prisoner in the White House, since in his infrequent public appearances he was hounded by larger and larger groups of antiwar demonstrators, whose taunts and jeers wounded him.

Married Working Women, 1960–1969	
Year	Percentage (as percentage of all married women)
1960	31.7
1961	34.0
1962	33.7
1963	34.6
1964	35.3
1965	35.7
1966	36.5
1967	37.8
1968	39.1
1969	40.4

Source: Compiled from U.S. Bureau of the Census, *Historical Statistics of the United States, Colonial Times to 1970,* Bicentennial Edition, Washington, D.C., 1975.

The essentially leaderless protest against the war took on a new quality on January 3, 1968, when Senator Eugene McCarthy, a Democrat from Minnesota, announced he was challenging LBJ for the party's presidential nomination. Intellectual, cool, aloof, and almost arrogant, McCarthy raised the banner of idealism, telling audiences, "Whatever is morally necessary must be made politically possible." College students flocked to his campaign, shaving their beards and cutting their hair to be "clean for Gene." In the New Hampshire primary in early March, the nation's earliest political test, McCarthy shocked the political experts by coming within a few thousand votes of defeating President Johnson.

McCarthy's strong showing in New Hampshire led Robert Kennedy, who had been weighing the risks in challenging Johnson, to enter the presidential race. Elected senator from New York in 1964, Bobby Kennedy had become an effective spokesman for the disadvantaged, as well as an increasingly severe critic of the Vietnam War. Unlike McCarthy, whose appeal was largely limited to upper-middle-class whites and college students, Kennedy attracted strong support among blue-collar workers, African Americans, Chicanos, and other minorities who formed the nucleus of the continuing New Deal coalition.

Lyndon Johnson's dramatic withdrawal caused an uproar in the Democratic party. With Johnson's tacit backing and strong support from party regulars and organized labor, Vice President Hubert H. Humphrey immediately declared his candidacy. Humphrey, a classic Cold War liberal who had worked equally hard for social reform at home and American expansion abroad, was totally unacceptable to the antiwar movement. Accordingly, he decided to avoid the primaries and work for the nomination within the framework of the party.

Kennedy and McCarthy, the two antiwar candidates, were thus left to compete in the spring primaries, requiring agonizing choices among those who desired change. Kennedy won everywhere except in Oregon, but his narrow victory in California ended in tragedy when a Palestinian immigrant, Sirhan Sirhan, assassinated him in a Los Angeles hotel.

With his strongest opponent struck down, Hubert Humphrey had little difficulty at the Chicago convention. Backed by that city's political boss, Mayor Richard Daley, the vice president relied on party leaders to defeat an antiwar resolution and win the nomination on the first ballot by a margin of more than two to one. Those hoping for change had to be content with one small victory—the abolition of the unit rule among state delegations, which would make open conventions possible in the future.

Humphrey's triumph was marred by violence outside the heavily guarded convention hall. Radical groups had urged their members to come to Chicago to agitate; the turnout was relatively small but included many who were ready to provoke the authorities in their despair over the convention's outcome. Epithets and cries of "pigs" brought on a savage response from Daley's police. "The cops had one thing on their mind," commented journalist Jimmy Breslin. "Club and then gas, club and then gas, club and then gas."

The bitter fumes of tear gas hung in the streets for days afterward; the battered heads and bodies of demonstrators and innocent bystanders alike flooded the city's hospital emergency rooms.

Alarmed by antiwar demonstrators drawn to the Democratic convention, Chicago Mayor Richard Daley erected barbed wire fences in an attempt to control access to the convention hall.

What an official investigation later termed a "police riot" marred Humphrey's nomination and made a sad mockery out of his call for "the politics of joy." The Democratic party itself had become the next victim of the Vietnam War.

The Republican Resurgence

The primary beneficiary of the Democratic debacle was Richard Nixon. Written off as politically dead after his unsuccessful race for governor of California in 1962, Nixon had slowly rebuilt his place within the party by working loyally for Barry Goldwater in 1964 and for GOP congressional candidates two years later. Positioning himself squarely in the middle, he quickly became the front-runner for the Republican nomination. At the GOP convention in Miami Beach, Nixon won an easy first ballot nomination and chose Maryland governor Spiro Agnew as his running mate. Agnew, little known on the national scene, had won the support of conservatives by taking a strong stand against African American rioters.

In the fall campaign, Nixon opened up a wide lead by avoiding controversy and reaping the benefit of discontent with the Vietnam War. He played the peace issue shrewdly, appearing to advocate an end to the conflict without ever taking a definite stand. The United States should "end the war and win the peace," he declared, hinting he had a secret formula for peace but never revealing what it was. Above all, he chose the role of reconciler for a nation torn by emotion, a leader who promised to bring a divided country together again.

Humphrey, in contrast, found himself hounded by antiwar demonstrators who heckled him constantly. He walked a tightwire, desperate for the continued support of President Johnson but handicapped by LBJ's stubborn refusal to end all bombing of North Vietnam. Only when he broke with Johnson in late September by announcing that if elected he would "stop the bombing of North Vietnam as an acceptable risk for peace" did his campaign begin to gain momentum.

Unfortunately for Humphrey, a third-party candidate cut deeply into the normal Democratic majority. George Wallace had first gained national attention as the racist governor of Alabama whose motto was, "Segregation now . . . segregation tomorrow . . . segregation forever." In 1964,

he had shown surprising strength in Democratic primaries in northern states. By attacking both black leaders and their liberal white allies, Wallace appealed to the sense of powerlessness among the urban working classes. "Liberals, intellectuals and long hairs have run the country for too long," Wallace told his followers. "When I get to Washington," he promised, "I'll throw all these phonies and their briefcases into the Potomac."

Running on the ticket of the American Independent Party, Wallace was a close third in the September polls, gaining support from more than 20 percent of the electorate. But as the election neared, his following declined. Humphrey continued to gain, especially after Johnson agreed in late October to end all bombing of North Vietnam. By the first week in November, the outcome was too close for the experts to call.

Nixon won the election with the smallest share of the popular vote of any winning candidate since 1916. But he swept a broad band of states from Virginia and the Carolinas through the Midwest to the Pacific for a clear-cut victory in the electoral college. Humphrey held on to the urban Northeast; Wallace took just five states in the Deep South, but his heavy inroads into blue-collar districts in the North shattered the New Deal coalition.

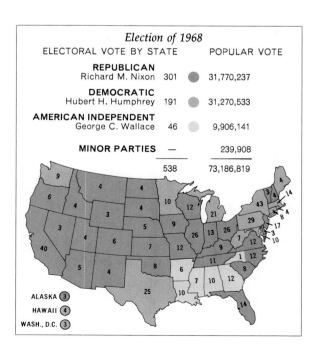

Election of 1968

ELECTORAL VOTE BY STATE		POPULAR VOTE
REPUBLICAN Richard M. Nixon	301	31,770,237
DEMOCRATIC Hubert H. Humphrey	191	31,270,533
AMERICAN INDEPENDENT George C. Wallace	46	9,906,141
MINOR PARTIES	—	239,908
	538	73,186,819

ALASKA ③
HAWAII ④
WASH., D.C. ③

The election marked a repudiation of the politics of protest and the cultural insurgency of the mid-1960s. The combined popular vote for Nixon and Wallace, 56.5 percent of the electorate, signified there was a silent majority that was fed up with violence and confrontation. A growing concern over psychedelic drugs, rock music, long hair, and sexual permissiveness had offset the usual Democratic advantage on economic issues and led to the election of a Republican president.

Nixon in Power

The man who took office as the thirty-sixth president of the United States on January 20, 1969, seemed to be a new Nixon. Gone were the fiery rhetoric and the penchant for making enemies. In their place, observers found an air of moderation and restraint. He appeared to have his emotions under firm control, but beneath the surface he remained bitter, hurt, and sensitive to criticism.

An innately shy man, Nixon hoped to enjoy the power of the presidency in splendid solitude. Described by Barry Goldwater as "the most complete loner I've ever known," Nixon assembled a powerful White House staff whose main task was to isolate him from Congress, the press, and even his own cabinet. Loyal subordinates like H. R. Haldeman and John Ehrlichman took charge of domestic issues, often making decisions without even consulting Nixon. Foreign policy was Nixon's great passion, and here he relied heavily on Henry Kissinger, his national security adviser, to formulate policy, leaving Secretary of State William Rogers to keep the State Department bureaucrats busy with minor details.

The Nixon White House soon could be likened to a fortress under siege. Distrusting everyone, from the media to members of his own party, the president sought to rule the nation without help from either Congress or his cabinet. In his quest for privacy, the president cut himself off from the nation and thus sowed the seeds of his downfall.

Reshaping the Great Society

Nixon began his first term on a hopeful note, promising the nation peace and respite from the chaos of the 1960s. Rejecting the divisions that had split Americans apart, he promised in his inaugural address to "bring us together." "We cannot learn from one another until we stop shouting at one another—until we speak quietly enough so that our words can be heard as well as our voices."

Nixon's moderation promised a return to the politics of accommodation that had characterized the Eisenhower era. Faced with a Democratic Congress, Nixon, like Ike, appeared ready to accept the main outlines of the welfare state. Instead of any massive overthrow of the Great Society, he focused on making the federal bureaucracy function more efficiently.

Nixon was successful in shifting responsibility for social problems from Washington to state and local authorities. He developed the concept of revenue sharing, by which federal funds would be dispersed to state, county, and city agencies to meet local needs. In 1972, Congress finally approved a measure to share $30.1 billion with local governments over a five-year period. An accompanying ceiling of $2.5 billion a year on federal welfare payments, however, meant that much of the revenue-sharing payments had to be allocated by cities and states to programs previously paid for by the federal government.

In the area of civil rights, Nixon made a shrewd political move. Action by Congress and the outgoing Johnson administration had ensured that massive desegregation of southern schools, delayed for over a decade by legal action, would finally begin just as Nixon took office. Nixon and his attorney general, John Mitchell, decided to shift the responsibility for this process to the courts. In the summer of 1969, the Justice Department asked a federal judge to delay the integration of thirty-three school districts in Mississippi. The Supreme Court quickly ruled against the Justice Department, declaring "the obligation of every school district is to terminate dual school systems at once." Thus, in the minds of southern white voters, it was the hated Supreme Court, not Richard Nixon, who had forced them to integrate their schools.

Nixon used similar tactics in his attempt to reshape the Supreme Court along more conservative lines. His appointment of Warren Burger, an experienced federal judge with moderate views, to replace the retiring Earl Warren as Chief

Justice, met with little objection. But liberal Democrats succeeded in blocking the nomination first of Clement Haynesworth of South Carolina and then of G. Harrold Carswell of Florida. Nixon denounced his opponents for insulting "millions of Americans who live in the South" by turning down his two southern nominees. Once again, the president had used the Supreme Court to enhance his political appeal to Southerners.

Nixon finally filled the Court position with Harry Blackmun, a respected moderate from Minnesota, who easily won confirmation. Subsequently, the president appointed Lewis Powell, a distinguished Virginia lawyer, and William Rehnquist, a rigidly conservative Justice Department attorney form Arizona, to the Supreme Court. Surprisingly, the Burger Court, despite its more conservative makeup, did not engage in any massive overturn of the Warren Court's decisions. It continued to uphold the legality of desegregation, ruling in 1971 that bussing was a necessary and proper way to achieve integrated schools.

The moderation of the Supreme Court and the legislative record of the Nixon administration indicated that the nation was not yet ready to abandon the reforms adopted in the 1960s. The pace of change slowed down in areas such as civil rights and welfare, but the commitment to social justice was still clear.

Nixonomics

The economy posed a more severe test for Richard Nixon. He inherited a growing inflation that accompanied the Vietnam War, the product of Lyndon Johnson's unsuccessful attempt to wage the war without raising taxes. The budget deficit was a staggering $25 billion in 1968 and the inflation rate had risen to 5 percent. Strongly opposed to the idea of federal controls, Nixon at first opted for a reduction in government spending while encouraging the Federal Reserve Board to raise interest rates, thereby slowing the rate of business expansion.

The result was disastrous. Inflation continued, reaching nearly 6 percent by the end of 1970, the highest rate since the Korean War. At the same time the economy underwent its first major recession since 1958. Unemployment rose to 6 percent by the end of 1970, and business failures jumped alarmingly. The collapse of the Penn Central Railroad was the most spectacular bankruptcy in the nation's history. Democrats quickly coined a new word, "Nixonomics," to describe the disaster.

Conditions seemed to worsen in 1971. Inflation continued unabated, and the nation's balance of trade became negative as imports exceeded exports by a substantial margin, leading to a weakening of the dollar abroad.

In mid-August, Nixon acted boldly to halt the economic decline. Abandoning his earlier resistance to controls, he announced a ninety-day freeze on wages and prices to be followed by federally imposed guidelines in both areas. The new secretary of the treasury, Democrat John Connally, carried out a devaluation of the dollar which, along with a 10 percent surtax on all imports, led to a greatly improved balance of trade. The sudden Nixon economic reversal quickly ended the recession with industrial production increasing by over 5 percent in the first quarter of 1972.

Building a Republican Majority

"The Great Nixon Turnaround," as historian Lloyd Gardner termed it, came too late to help the Republicans in the 1970 congressional elections. From the time he took office in 1969, the president was obsessed with the fact that he had received only 43 percent of the popular vote in 1968. The Republicans were still a minority party, and to be reelected in 1972, Nixon would need to win over southern whites and blue-collar workers who had voted for Wallace in 1968.

Attorney General John Mitchell, who had been Nixon's campaign manager in 1968, had devised a southern strategy to help achieve a Republican majority by 1972. The administration's well-publicized objection to school desegregation in the South and the attempt to put Haynesworth and Carswell on the Court were part of this design. Kevin Phillips, one of Mitchell's aides, urged the Nixon administration to direct its appeal to "middle Americans"—southern whites, Catholic ethnic groups, blue-collar workers, and, above all, the new suburbanites of the South and West, the emerging Sunbelt.

Nixon unleashed Vice President Spiro Agnew in an attempt to exploit the social issue in the 1970 election. Blaming all of society's problems—from drug abuse and sexual permissiveness to crime in the streets—on Democratic liberals and their allies in the media, Agnew delivered a series of scathing speeches. He denounced intellectuals as "an effete corps of impudent snobs," branded television commentators as "a tiny and closed fraternity of privileged men," and damned the press in general as "nattering nabobs of negativism."

The Democrats struck back by changing their tactics. Warned by Richard Scammon and Ben Wattenberg in *The Real Majority* (1970) that most voters were not young, black, or poor, Democratic candidates were careful to stress economic issues, blaming the Republicans for both inflation and recession. On the social issue, they joined in the chorus against crime, pornography, and drugs.

The outcome was a standoff. Agnew's attacks helped the GOP limit the usual off-year losses in the House to nine seats, while the Republicans gained two votes in the Senate. But the Democrats did well in state elections and proved once again that economic issues were crucial in American politics. Nixon and the Republicans still did not command a national majority.

In Search of Détente

Richard Nixon gave foreign policy top priority, and he proved surprisingly adept at it. In Kissinger, he had a White House specialist who had devoted his life to the study of diplomacy. A refugee from Nazi Germany, Kissinger had become a professor of government at Harvard, the author of several influential books, and an acknowledged authority on international affairs. Nixon and Kissinger approached foreign policy from a similar realistic perspective. Instead of viewing the Cold War as an ideological struggle for survival with communism, they saw it as a traditional great power rivalry, one to be managed and controlled rather than to be won.

Kissinger and Nixon had a grand design. Realizing that recent events, especially the Vietnam War and the rapid Soviet arms buildup of the 1960s, had eroded America's position of primacy in the world, they planned a strategic retreat. Russia had great military strength, but its economy was weak and it had a dangerous rival in China. Kissinger planned to use American trade—notably grain and high technology—to

Kissinger's search for détente began with a calculated decision to improve relations with China, a rival with whom the USSR shared a long, fortified border. In a highly publicized state visit, Nixon and Chinese leaders were photographed sharing banquets and touring the Great Wall of China.

induce Soviet cooperation, while at the same time improving U.S. relations with China.

Nixon and Kissinger shrewdly played the China card as their first step toward achieving détente—that is, a relaxation of tension—with the Soviet Union. In February 1972, accompanied by a planeload of reporters and television camera crews, Nixon made a triumphal tour of China, meeting with the communist leaders and ending more than two decades of Sino-American hostility. Nixon agreed to establish an American liaison mission in Beijing as a first step toward ultimate recognition.

The Soviets, who viewed China as a dangerous adversary along a 2,000-mile frontier in Asia, responded by agreeing to reach an arms control pact with the United States. The Strategic Arms Limitation Talks (SALT) had been underway since 1969. During a visit to Moscow in May 1972, President Nixon signed two vital docu-

ments with Soviet leader Leonid Brezhnev. The first limited the two superpowers to two hundred antiballistic missiles (ABMs) apiece; the second froze the number of offensive ballistic missiles for a five-year period. SALT I recognized the existing Soviet lead in missiles, but the American deployment of multiple warheads that could each be individually targeted (MIRV) ensured a continuing American strategic advantage.

The SALT I agreements were most important as a symbolic first step toward control of the nuclear arms race. They signified that the United States and Russia were trying to achieve a settlement of their differences by peaceful means.

Ending the Vietnam War

Vietnam remained the one foreign policy challenge that Nixon could not overcome. He had a three-part plan to end the conflict—renewed bombing, a hard line in negotiations with Hanoi, and the gradual withdrawal of American troops. The plan involved training the troops of South Vietnam to take over the American combat role. The number of American soldiers in Vietnam fell from 543,000 in early 1969 to under 30,000 by 1972; domestic opposition to the war declined sharply with the accompanying drop in casualties and reductions in the draft call.

Renewed bombing proved the most controversial part of the plan. As early as the spring of 1969, Nixon secretly ordered raids on communist supply lines in neutral Cambodia. Then in April 1970, he ordered both air and ground strikes into Cambodia, causing a massive outburst of antiwar protests at home. Students demonstrated against the invasion of Cambodia on campuses across the nation. Tragedy struck at Kent State University in Ohio in early May. After rioters had firebombed an ROTC building, the governor sent in national guard troops who were taunted and harassed by irate students. The guardsmen then opened fire, killing four students and wounding eleven more. The victims were innocent bystanders; two were young women caught in the fusillade on their way between classes. A week later, two African American student demonstrators were killed at Jackson State College in Mississippi; soon riots and protests raged on more than four hundred campuses across the country.

Nixon had little sympathy for the demonstrators, telling aides they were "bums" who were intent on "blowing up the campuses." The "silent majority" to whom he appealed seemed to agree; one poll showed that most Americans blamed the students, not the national guard, for the deaths at Kent State. An "Honor America Day" program, held in Washington, D.C., on July 4 attracted 250,000 people who heard Billy Graham and Bob Hope endorse the president's policies. Nixon's Cambodian invasion did little to shorten the Vietnam War, but the public reaction reinforced the president's resolve not to surrender.

The third tactic, negotiation with Hanoi, finally proved successful. Beginning in the summer of 1969, Kissinger held a series of secret meetings with North Vietnam's foreign minister, Le Duc Tho. In the summer and fall of 1972, the two sides were near agreement, but South Vietnamese objections blocked a settlement before the 1972

election. When the North Vietnamese tried to make last-minute changes, Nixon ordered a series of savage B-52 raids on Hanoi that finally led to the signing of a truce on January 27, 1973. In return for the release of all American prisoners of war, the United States agreed to remove its troops from South Vietnam within sixty days. The political clauses allowed the North Vietnamese to keep their troops in the South, thus virtually guaranteeing future control of all Vietnam by the communists.

The agreement was, in fact, a disguised surrender, but finally the American combat role in the Vietnam War was over. After eight years of fighting, the United States had emerged from the quagmire in Southeast Asia. Yet known only to a few insiders around the president, the nation was already deeply enmeshed in another dilemma— what Gerald R. Ford termed "the long national nightmare" of Watergate.

THE CRISIS OF DEMOCRACY

"The illegal we do immediately; the unconstitutional takes a little longer," Henry Kissinger once said jokingly of the Nixon administration. Unfortunately, he was far closer to the truth than anyone realized.

The Politics of Deceit

Richard Nixon's consuming distrust of even his own associates quickly led to a series of underhanded and illegal activities. In the spring of 1969, he ordered the bombing of Cambodia without informing Congress. When details began to leak to the press, the president ordered wiretaps on the telephones of both reporters and members of Kissinger's National Security Council staff. Only the opposition of FBI director J. Edgar Hoover, jealously guarding against rivals, blocked the scheme of a White House aide to engage in extensive electronic eavesdropping and even outright burglary in the name of national security.

When the *New York Times* and the *Washington Post* began publishing the Pentagon Papers (see "The Pentagon Papers Affair," pp. 952–953), a classified Defense Department study of the Vietnam War, Nixon decided to take dras-

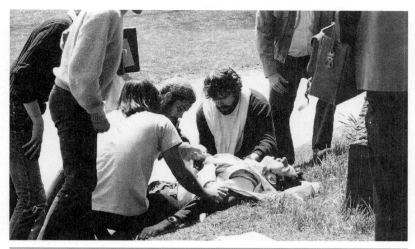

The renewed bombing of North Vietnam and invasion of Cambodia ordered by Nixon in hopes of ending the conflict precipitated student protests at many campuses. At Kent State University in Ohio, demonstrators and bystanders were shot by national guardsmen. An end to U.S. armed intervention in the war was finally negotiated by Henry Kissinger and Le Duc Tho in 1973.

tic measures to plug any further leaks of secret documents. His aides created a self-styled "plumbers" unit within the White House directed by G. Gordon Liddy, a former FBI agent, and E. Howard Hunt, a veteran of the CIA. Charged with preserving secrecy and discrediting those who kept the press informed, Hunt and Liddy set out to embarrass Daniel Ellsberg, the Defense Department official who had leaked the Pentagon Papers.

Elsewhere in the White House, aides John Dean and Charles Colson were busy preparing an enemies list, which contained the names of several hundred prominent Americans, ranging from movie stars like Jane Fonda and Paul Newman to journalists and educators such as columnist James Reston and Kingman Brewster, president of Yale University. The White House labored under a siege mentality that seemed to justify any and all measures necessary to defeat its opponents, who were thought to include the media, the intellectual community, and virtually all minority groups.

Nixon went to great lengths to guarantee his reelection in 1972. A Committee to Re-elect the President (CREEP) was formed, headed by Attorney General John Mitchell. Specialists in dirty tricks harassed Democratic contenders,

while G. Gordon Liddy, of the White House plumbers, developed an elaborate plan to spy on the opposition that included bugging the Democratic national headquarters in the Watergate complex in Washington. In the early morning hours of June 17, James McCord and four other men working under the direction of Hunt and Liddy were caught by police during a break-in at the Watergate. The continuing abuse of power had finally culminated in an illegal act that soon threatened to bring down the entire Nixon administration.

The Election of 1972

The irony of the Watergate break-in was that by the time it occurred, Nixon's election was assured. Aided by Republican dirty tricks, the Democrats self-destructed. First Edmund Muskie, the front-runner, replying in the New Hampshire primary to a letter accusing him of prejudice against French Canadians, lost his composure. Then a lone assassin, Arthur Bremer, shot and seriously wounded George Wallace. Paralyzed, Wallace was forced to drop out of the race, leaving Nixon with a complete monopoly over the political right.

$\mathcal{T}$he Pentagon Papers Affair

On June 13, 1971, the *New York Times* published an extraordinary front-page story on the history of America's war in Vietnam. The feature was based on the findings of a top-secret Defense Department study—the so-called Pentagon Papers. It was

Daniel Ellsberg after the opening session of his trial. Ellsberg was indicted for espionage, theft, and conspiracy, but the case was dismissed on the grounds of government misconduct.

the first in a series of articles detailing the way successive presidents had embroiled the United States in war in Southeast Asia.

The appearance of the *Times* special led to a dramatic showdown between the press and the government; immediately after the story broke, the Nixon administration fought hard to prevent any further release of classified material. And in the wake of the whole affair, the Nixon White House developed a siege mentality—an attitude that contributed in the long run to the Watergate break-in and cover-up.

In the summer of 1967, Secretary of Defense Robert McNamara commissioned a review of America's Vietnam policy since World War II. A team of analysts led by Leslie Gelb, a civilian Pentagon official, collected and commented on thousands of documents. Over the course of two years, scores of individuals contributed to this history, which ultimately ran to more than 7,000 pages in 47 volumes.

The man responsible for leaking this classified study was Daniel Ellsberg, a talented defense analyst who had worked on the project briefly. He became so disillusioned with the Vietnam War that he felt compelled to share the disturbing material in the Papers with the American

people. Gaining access to the manuscript at the Rand Corporation, Ellsberg photocopied thousands of pages from the Papers and offered them to several senators. When they showed little interest in the documents, Ellsberg went to the press. In March 1971, Neil Sheehan of the *New York Times* agreed to take the documents and use them to write a special series on the war.

When the story broke on June 13, the Nixon administration moved quickly to enjoin any further disclosure of the Papers. In seeking an injunction against the *Times,* the White House claimed that the Papers' release had "prejudiced the defense interests of the United States" and that continued publication would "result in irreparable injury" to the nation.

The administration's action was surprising. Traditionally, under the First Amendment there had been few, if any, instances of "prior restraint" (efforts to block publication in advance). Moreover, the contents of the Papers pertained to the policies of previous presidents, and some members of the White House staff believed they could use the Papers to embarrass the Democrats, who had, after all, led the United States into Vietnam. But President Nixon and National Security Adviser

With frustration over the "Establishment's" handling of the Vietnam War at a high, Ellsberg's leak of the Pentagon Papers reinforced the public suspicion that government actions were based on deceit.

Henry Kissinger saw in the release of the Papers a massive breach of security—a signal to foreign governments that the United States could not be trusted to keep sensitive undertakings with other nations confidential. Unknown to the public, Kissinger was then conducting three sensitive negotiations: with China, on opening up relations; with the Soviet Union, on limiting strategic arms; and with North Vietnam, on ending the war. He and Nixon saw in the release of the Pentagon Papers a threat to the very essence of their secretive approach to diplomacy.

The battle in court lasted more than two weeks. Initially, the administration claimed the top-secret classification of the Papers was reason enough to prohibit further disclosure, since the Espionage Act forbade the publication of classified material. Before the Supreme Court, however, government attorneys singled out the release of just a few portions of the study that they claimed posed a risk to national security.

The administration's case suffered from several crucial weaknesses. Part of the problem lay in the classification system. In the case of Vietnam, so much material had already been released, in many cases by government offi-

cials from the president on down, that the distinction between classified and nonclassified had long since lost any meaning. There can be no doubt that the material in the Papers embarrassed many American policymakers. But the government failed to prove to the Court that publication of stories based on the Papers or even of the documents themselves would harm the national security.

Equally important, the government's effort came too late to be effective. Ellsberg also gave the Papers to the Washington *Post,* which began publishing them on July 18. The administration responded with legal action, but the dam had burst. By the time the Court ruled, some twenty newspapers, including the Boston *Globe* and the St. Louis *Post-Dispatch,* were publishing various portions of the Papers.

On June 30, the Supreme Court voted 6 to 3 to dismiss the government's case. In the view of the majority, the government had failed to carry the heavy burden of proof necessary to overcome the presumption against "prior restraint." Yet the press's victory was limited, since each of the nine justices presented his own opinion—several of which were as critical of the newspapers as they were of the

government. The Court did not hold that the First Amendment prevented *any* injunction against publication. As one expert explained, the court battle over the Papers proved "that there *can* be prior restraint of publication while a case is being reviewed in the courts."

Although the publication of the Papers did not lead to the dire consequences its lawyers had predicted in their arguments before the Court, the White House remained resentful about the whole affair. President Nixon still believed there were too many leaks to the press and he set out to solve the problem by organizing investigative working groups, later known as "plumbers." Loyal only to the president, these men were willing to go beyond the law to ensure secrecy. The president also approved a revision of the classification system to allow his administration to operate in even greater secrecy. Most significant of all, a siege mentality now pervaded the White House. Fearful of the antiwar movement and increasingly wary of the press, the Nixon administration initiated an unprecedented series of steps that culminated in the Watergate scandal.

Senator George McGovern of South Dakota finally emerged as the Democratic nominee. He ran on a platform that advocated a negotiated settlement in Vietnam, the right to abortion, and tolerance of diverse lifestyles. The South Dakota senator hoped to unite the New Left with traditional Democratic voters, but his strong stand against the Vietnam War and in favor of income redistribution at home was perceived as "anti-establishment" by middle-class America and greatly strengthened Nixon's appeal.

Instead of focusing on his own record in office, Richard Nixon shrewdly let McGovern's apparent extremism and New Left support become the main issue in the campaign. Staying carefully aloof from partisanship, Nixon let others campaign for him, relying heavily on the recent improvement in the economy and his foreign policy triumphs with China and Russia to sway the nation's voters.

The result was a stunning victory. Nixon won a popular landslide with 60.8 percent of the vote—second only to Lyndon Johnson's record in 1964—and an even more decisive sweep of the electoral college, taking every state but Massachusetts. The very low turnout and Democratic control of both Houses of Congress suggests the election was primarily a repudiation of McGovern, rather than an endorsement of Richard Nixon. The voting patterns did suggest, however, the beginning of a major political realignment, as only blacks, Jews, and low-income voters continued to vote overwhelmingly Democratic, while the GOP made significant gains in the Sunbelt states of the South and West.

The Watergate Scandal

Only Richard Nixon knew how fragile his victory was in 1972. The president apparently had no foreknowledge of the Watergate break-in, but he was deeply implicated in the attempt to cover up the involvement of White House aides in the original burglary. On June 23, only six days after the crime, he ordered the CIA to keep the FBI off the case, on the specious grounds that it involved national security. The president even urged his aides to lie under oath, if necessary. "I don't give a [expletive deleted] what happens," Nixon said to John Mitchell. "I want you all to stonewall it, let them plead the Fifth Amendment, cover-up, or anything else. . . ."

In the short run, the cover-up, directed by White House counsel John Dean, worked. Hunt and Liddy were convicted for their roles in the Watergate break-in, but they carefully avoided implicating either CREEP or Nixon's inner circle of advisers.

The first thread unraveled when federal judge John Sirica, known for his firmness toward criminals, sentenced the burglars to long jail terms. James McCord was the first to crack, informing Sirica he had received money from the White House and had been promised a future pardon in return for his silence. By April 1973, Nixon was forced to fire John Dean, who refused to become the scapegoat for the cover-up, and to allow Haldeman and Ehrlichman, who were deeply implicated, to resign. The Senate then appointed a special committee to investigate the Watergate episode. In a week of dramatic testimony, John Dean revealed the president's personal involvement in the cover-up. Still, it was basically a matter of whose word was to be believed, that of the president or of a discredited aide, and Nixon hoped to weather the storm.

The existence of tapes of conversations in the Oval Office, recorded regularly since 1970, final-

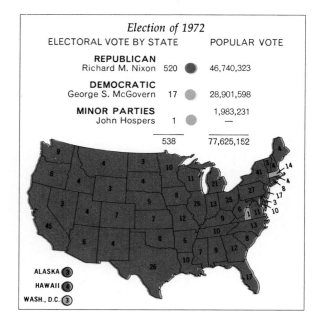

Election of 1972

ELECTORAL VOTE BY STATE		POPULAR VOTE
REPUBLICAN Richard M. Nixon	520	46,740,323
DEMOCRATIC George S. McGovern	17	28,901,598
MINOR PARTIES John Hospers	1	1,983,231 —
	538	77,625,152

ALASKA 3
HAWAII 4
WASH., D.C. 3

ly brought Nixon down. At first the president tried to invoke executive privilege to withhold the tapes. When Archibald Cox, appointed as Watergate special prosecutor, demanded the release of the tapes, Nixon responded by firing Cox. But the new Watergate prosecutor, Leon Jaworski, continued to press for the tapes. Nixon tried to release only a few of the less damaging ones, but the Supreme Court ruled unanimously in June 1974 that the tapes had to be turned over to Judge Sirica.

By that time the House Judiciary Committee, acting on evidence compiled by the staff of the Senate committee, voted three articles of impeachment, charging Nixon with obstruction of justice, abuse of power, and contempt of Congress. Faced with the release of tapes that directly implicated him in the cover-up, the president finally chose to resign on August 9, 1974.

Nixon's resignation proved to be the culmination of the Watergate scandal. The entire episode revealed both the weaknesses and strengths of the American political system. Most regrettable was the abuse of presidential authority—a reflection both of the growing power of the modern presi-

An embattled Richard Nixon waves good-bye after resigning the presidency on August 9, 1974.

dency and of the fatal flaws in Richard Nixon's character. Unlike such previous executive branch scandals as the Whiskey Ring and Teapot Dome, Watergate involved a lust for power rather than for money. Realizing he had reached the White House almost by accident, Nixon did everything possible to retain his hold on his office. He used the plumbers to maintain executive secrecy and he directed the Internal Revenue Service and the Justice Department to punish his enemies and reward his friends.

But Watergate also demonstrated the vitality of a democratic society. The press showed how investigative reporting could unlock even the most closely guarded executive secrets. Judge Sirica proved that an independent judiciary was still the best bulwark for individual freedom. And Congress rose to the occasion, both by carrying out a successful investigation of executive misconduct and by following a scrupulous and nonpartisan impeachment process that left Nixon with no chance to escape his ultimate fate.

The nation survived the shock of Watergate with its institutions intact. Attorney General John Mitchell and twenty-five presidential aides were sentenced to jail terms. Congress, in decline since Lyndon Johnson's exercise of executive dominance, was rejuvenated, with its members now intent on extending congressional authority into all areas of American life.

ENERGY AND THE ECONOMY

In the midst of Watergate, the outbreak of war in the Middle East threatened a vital national interest—the supply and price of the fuel on which the American way of life was based. In the course of the 1970s, the resulting energy crisis helped touch off an inflationary impulse that had a profound impact on the national economy.

The October War

On October 6, 1973, Egypt and Syria launched a surprise attack on Israel. The fighting caught American leaders completely off guard. After recovering from the initial shock, President Nixon and Henry Kissinger, who had become secretary of state in September, expected Israel to repel the Arab invaders and display the same military dominance it had used to win the Six Day War in 1967. In that conflict, Israel had devastated its Arab neighbors, taking possession of the Golan Heights from Syria, the Sinai peninsula from Egypt, and Jerusalem and the West Bank from Jordan. Instead of increasing Israeli security, however, these conquests had only added to Middle East tensions. They unified the Arab countries, who now called for the return of their lands, and increased Egyptian and Syrian dependence on the Soviet Union for arms and political support.

Henry Kissinger used the outbreak of the October War as an opportunity to shift American policy from its traditional pro-Israeli position to a more neutral stance—as the honest broker between Israel and its Arab neighbors. At first, Nixon and Kissinger had to approve a massive resupply in mid-October to help Israel stem the Egyptian and Syria offensives. But when the Israelis quickly routed their opponents, the United States intervened diplomatically to prevent a victory for Israel that would preclude American mediation. The fighting finally ended in late October; Israel had repulsed the Arab attack but had been stopped short of complete victory.

Kissinger's apparent diplomatic triumph, however, was offset by an unforeseen consequence of the Yom Kippur War. On October 17, the Arab members of the Organization of Petroleum Exporting Countries (OPEC) announced a 5 percent cut in oil production, with additional cuts of 5 percent each month until Israel gave up the lands it had seized in 1967. President Nixon announced a $2.2 billion aid package for Israel on October 19, and the next day Saudi Arabia cut off oil shipments to the United States and to the Netherlands, the European nation that had most strongly supported American policy in the Middle East.

The Arab oil embargo had a disastrous impact on the American economy. First, it produced a worldwide shortage of oil. Arab producers cut production by 25 percent from the September 1973 level, leading to a curtailment of 10 percent in the world supply. For the United States, which imported one-third of its daily consumption, this meant a loss of nearly 2 million barrels a day. Long lines formed at automobile service stations as motorists kept filling their tanks in fear of running out of gas.

The age of cheap and abundant oil was ending. As prices climbed and supplies dwindled, Americans found themselves waiting in long lines to fill their cars' gas tanks. Service stations reduced their operating hours and restricted the amount of gasoline drivers could buy, but many stations still ran out of fuel before they could accommodate all their customers.

A dramatic increase in oil prices proved to be a far more significant result of the embargo. After the Arab embargo began, OPEC, led by the shah of Iran, raised crude oil prices fourfold. In the United States, gasoline prices at the pumps nearly doubled in a few weeks time while the cost of home heating fuel rose even more sharply.

President Nixon responded with a series of temporary measures, including pleas to turn down thermostats in homes and offices, close service stations on weekends to curb pleasure driving, and reduce automobile speed limits to 50 miles per hour. When the Arab oil embargo ended in March, after Kissinger negotiated an Israeli pullback in the Sinai, the American public relaxed. Gasoline once again became plentiful, thermostats were raised, and people resumed their love affair with the automobile.

The energy crisis, however, did not end with the lifting of the embargo. The Arab action marked the beginning of a new era in American history. The United States, with only 6 percent of the world's population, had been using nearly 40 percent of the earth's energy supplies. In 1970, domestic oil production began to decline; the embargo served only to highlight the fact that the nation was now dependent on other countries, notably those in the Persian Gulf, for its economic well-being. A nation that based its way of life on abundance and expansion suddenly was faced with the reality of limited resources and economic stagnation.

The Oil Shocks

Cheap energy had been the underlying force behind the amazing growth of the American economy after World War II. The world price of oil had actually declined in the 1950s and 1960s as huge new fields in the Middle East and North Africa began to produce. The GNP had more than doubled between 1950 and 1973; the American people had come to base their way of life on gasoline prices that averaged about thirty-five cents a gallon. The huge gas-guzzling cars, the flight to the suburbs, the long drives to work each day, the detached houses heated by fuel oil and natural gas and cooled by central air-conditioning represented a dependence on inexpensive energy that everyone took for granted.

The first great oil shock of the 1970s came with the October War and the resulting Arab oil embargo. Few had noticed a gradual increase in OPEC prices in the early 1970s; global demand for oil, intensified by the explosive economic development of western Europe and Japan as well as the United States, had now caught up with oil production. In the ensuing shortfall, the OPEC nations quickly raised prices, first from $3 to over $5 a barrel, then to $11.65.

The effect on the American economy was devastating. Gasoline prices jumped from 35 to 65 cents a gallon; the cost of manufacturing went up proportionately, while utility rates rose sharply as a result of the higher cost of fuel oil and natural gas. Suddenly Americans faced drastic and unexpected increases in such everyday expenses as driving to work and heating their homes.

The result was a sharp decline in consumer spending and the worst recession since World War II. The GNP dropped by 6 percent in 1974 and unemployment rose to over 9 percent, the highest level since the Great Depression of the 1930s. Detroit was hit the hardest. Buyers shied away from big cars with their low gas mileage, but many were skeptical of the first generation of American-made small cars. Sales declined by 20 percent, and by the fall of 1974, Detroit's big three automakers had laid off more than 225,000 workers.

President Gerald R. Ford, who followed Richard Nixon into the White House (see p. 961), was concerned at first with inflation; he responded belatedly to the economic crisis by proposing a tax cut to stimulate consumer spending. Congress passed a $22.8 billion reduction in taxes in early 1975, which led to a gradual recovery by 1976. The resulting budget deficits, however, helped keep inflation above 5 percent and prevented a return to full economic health.

The next administration, headed by Jimmy Carter of Georgia (see p. 962), had little more success in achieving a rapid rate of economic growth. Continued federal deficits and relatively high interest rates kept the economy sluggish throughout 1977 and 1978. Then in 1979, the outbreak of the Iranian Revolution and the overthrow of the shah touched off another oil shock. Although the cutoff of Iranian oil led to a shortfall of only 3 percent of the world's oil supply, the members of the OPEC cartel took advantage of the situation to double prices over the next eighteen months. A barrel of crude oil now cost more than $30. Gasoline prices climbed to more than $1 a gallon at American service stations, leading to an even greater wave of inflation than in 1973.

The American people panicked. When lines began to form at gas stations in California and Florida in early May 1979, drivers started filling their tanks every day or two. The long lines frustrated American drivers; incidents of violence began to mount and the public took out its fury on the Carter administration. In June, the president's staff warned him of the danger in the "worsening short-term energy crisis." "Nothing else has so frustated, confused, angered the American people," Carter was told, "or so targeted their distress at you personally."

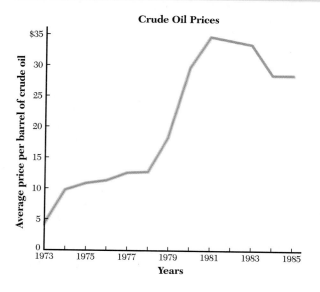

Crude Oil Prices

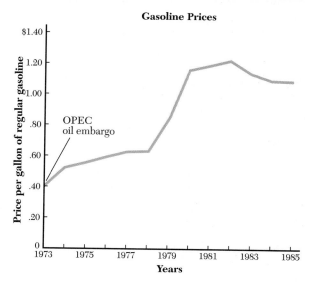

Gasoline Prices

By the fall of 1979, world supply had caught up with demand, and the oil scare ended. But the price of gasoline remained at over $1 a gallon and the inflation rate began to reach double-digit levels again. The twin oil shocks of the 1970s had left the economy battered and had undermined the average American's faith in the future.

The Search for an Energy Policy

The oil shocks of 1973 and 1979 were but two symptoms of a much deeper energy crisis. Put simply, the United States was running out of the fossil fuels on which it had relied for its economic growth in the past. Domestic oil production peaked in 1970 and declined every year thereafter; there were more ample reserves of natural gas, but both fuels were nonrenewable sources of energy that would eventually be exhausted. American political leaders had to devise a national policy to meet not only the temporary shortfalls of the 1970s but also the long-term energy problem inherent in past reliance on fossil fuels.

The success of the environmental movement in the late 1960s and early 1970s compounded the problem. Efforts to protect the environment and curtail pollution of the nation's air and water had led to significant legislative restrictions on American industry. Congress created the Environmental Protection Agency in 1970 to monitor industry and passed a Clean Air Act that encouraged public utilities to shift from using coal, which polluted the atmosphere, to clean-burning fuel oil and natural gas to generate electricity.

The energy crunch pitted the environmentalists and advocates of economic growth in direct confrontation with each other. Those who put ecology first lost out. By the end of the decade, groups such as the Sierra Club and Friends of the Earth had failed in their efforts to halt the gradual relaxation of environmental regulations that prohibited strip mining of coal and offshore drilling for oil.

The nation's leaders had a difficult time devising a coherent and workable long-term national energy policy. Gerald Ford placed a high premium on expanding production as a means of overcoming the shortage. The Republicans advocated removing price controls on oil and natural gas to give wildcatters the incentive to bring in new supplies of these fuels. Greater production of coal and expanded nuclear power plants were key parts of the Republican approach to the energy problem.

The Democrats, in contrast, stressed price controls and conservation. In Congress, Democratic leaders were intent on shielding American consumers from the full brunt of the world price increase. They wanted to continue an elaborate system of price controls instituted by Nixon in 1973, and they favored stand-by plans for gas rationing over reliance on the marketplace as a better way to allocate scarce supplies.

The nation failed to adopt either the Republican or the Democratic energy plans; instead, Congress tried to muddle through with elements of both approaches. Thus, on the production front, Ford was able to win approval for building the Alaskan pipeline, which made an additional 1.5 million barrels of oil a day available to American consumers. Carter placed a strong emphasis on reviving the lagging American coal industry. Congress continued the price controls on domestic oil for another forty months in late 1975 and mandated annual increases in automobile gasoline mileage that forced Detroit to produce more fuel-efficient cars. Since nearly 10 percent of the world's oil production was burned up every day on American highways, this one congressional act eventually resulted in substantial gasoline savings.

The overall outcome, however, was a patchwork that fell far short of a coherent national strategy for solving the energy problem. Oil

imports actually increased by 50 percent between 1973 and 1979, rising from 6 million to 9 million barrels a day, an amount nearly half of the nation's daily petroleum usage.

The Great Inflation

The gravest consequence of the oil shocks was inflation. The startling increase in price levels in the 1970s stemmed from many causes. The Vietnam War created budget deficits that grew from $63 billion for the entire decade of the 1960s to a total of $420 billion in the 1970s. A worldwide shortage of food, resulting from both rapid population increases and poor harvests around the globe in the mid-1970s, triggered a 20 percent rise in American food prices in 1973 alone. But above all else, the primary source of the great inflation of the 1970s was the sixfold increase in petroleum prices.

The impact on consumers was staggering. The price of an automobile jumped 72 percent between 1973 and 1978. During the decade, the price of a hamburger doubled, milk went from 28 to 59 cents a quart, and the cost of a loaf of bread—the proverbial staff of life—rose from 24 to 89 cents. Corresponding wage increases failed to keep pace with inflation; in 1980, the real income of the average American family fell by 5.5 percent.

Curbing inflation proved to be beyond the power of the federal government. President

Despite the environmental risk, construction of an Alaskan pipeline to tap that state's rich oil fields went forward in the mid-1970s.

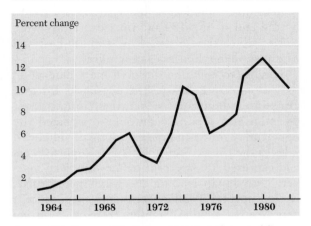

Inflation, 1962–1981

Percent change

Source: U.S. Bureau of the Census, Statistical Abstract of the United States: 1982–83 *(103rd edition), Washington, D.C., 1982.*

Ford's early efforts to roll back prices by rhetoric were a casualty of the 1974 recession. President Carter proved equally powerless. Finally, in October 1979, the Federal Reserve Board, led by Carter appointee Paul Volcker, began a sustained effort to halt inflation by mandating increased bank reserves to curtail the supply of money in circulation. The new tight money policy served only to heighten inflation in the short run by driving interest rates up to record levels. By the spring of 1980, the prime interest rate reached 20 percent.

The Shifting American Economy

Inflation and the oil shocks helped bring about significant changes in American business and industry in the 1970s. The most obvious result was the slowing of the rate of economic growth, with the GNP advancing only 3.2 percent for the decade, compared to 3.7 percent in the 1960s. More important, American industry began to lose its position of primacy in world markets. In 1959, U.S. firms had been the leaders in eleven of thirteen major industrial sectors, ranging from manufacturing to banking. By 1976, American companies led in only seven areas, and in all but one category—aerospace—U.S. corporations had declined in relation to Japanese and western European competitors.

The most serious losses came in the heavy industries where the United States had once led the world. New steel producers in western Europe, Japan, and the Third World, using more advanced technology and aided by government subsidies, were producing steel far more efficiently than their American counterparts. As a result, by the end of the 1970s, American firms were closing down their obsolete mills in the East and Midwest, idling thousands of workers.

Foreign competition did even more damage in the automobile industry. The oil shocks led to a consumer demand for small efficient cars. German and Japanese automakers seized the opportunity to expand their once small volume of sales in the United States. By 1977, imported cars had captured 18.3 percent of the American market, with Japan leading the way. In response, Detroit spent $70 billion retooling to produce a new fleet of smaller, lighter, front-wheel-drive cars; but American manufacturers barely survived

the foreign invasion. Only government-backed loans helped the Chrysler Corporation stave off bankruptcy.

In other areas, American corporations fared much better. The multinationals that had emerged in the boom years of the 1960s continued to thrive. IBM sold computers all over the globe. The growth of conglomerates—huge corporations that combined many dissimilar industrial concerns—accelerated as companies like Gulf & Western and the Transamerica Corporation diversified by buying up Hollywood studios, insurance companies, and recreational equipment manufacturers. The growth of high-technology industries proved to be the most profitable new trend of the 1970s. Computer companies and electronics firms grew at a rapid rate, especially after the development of the silicon chip, a small wafer-thin microprocessor capable of performing complex calculations almost instantly.

The result was a geographic shift of American industry from the East and Midwest to the Sunbelt. Electronics manufacturers flourished in California, Texas, and North Carolina, where they grew up around major universities. The absence of well-entrenched labor unions, the availability of skilled labor, and the warm attractive climate of the southern and western states lured many new concerns to the Sunbelt. At the same time, the decline of the steel and auto industries was leading to massive unemployment and economic stagnation in the northern industrial heartland.

The overall pattern was one of an economy in transition. The oil shocks had caused serious problems of inflation, slower economic growth, and rising unemployment rates. But American business still displayed the enterprise and the ability to develop new technologies that gave promise of renewed economic vitality.

POLITICS AFTER WATERGATE

The energy crisis and the economic dislocations of the mid-1970s could not have come at a worse time. Watergate had a paralyzing impact on the American political system. An awareness that the Cold War had led to an imperial presidency created a growing demand to weaken the power of the president and strengthen congressional authority. The result was increasing tension between the White House and Capitol Hill, preventing the strong, effective leadership needed to meet the unprecedented problems of the 1970s.

The Ford Administration

Gerald R. Ford had the distinction of being the first president who had not been elected to national office. Richard Nixon had appointed him to the vice presidency to succeed Spiro Agnew, who had been forced to resign in order to avoid prosecution for accepting bribes while he was governor of Maryland. Ford, an amiable and unpretentious Michigan congressman who had risen to the post of House minority leader, seemed ready to restore public confidence in the presidency when he replaced Nixon in August 1974.

Ford's honeymoon lasted only a month. On September 8, 1974, he shocked the nation by announcing he had granted Richard Nixon a full and unconditional pardon for all federal crimes he may have committed. Some critics charged darkly that Nixon and Ford had made a secret bargain; others pointed out how unfair it was for Nixon's aides to serve their prison terms while the chief criminal went free. Ford apparently acted in an effort to end the bitterness over Watergate, but his attempt backfired, eroding public confidence in his leadership and linking him indelibly with the scandal.

Ford soon found himself fighting an equally difficult battle in behalf of the beleaguered CIA. The Watergate scandal and the Vietnam fiasco had eroded public confidence in the government and lent credibility to a startling series of disclosures about past covert actions. The president allowed the CIA to confirm some of these charges and then he made things worse by blurting out to the press the juiciest item of all: the CIA had been involved in plots to assassinate foreign leaders.

Senate and House select committees appointed to investigate the CIA now focused on the assassination issue, eventually charging that the agency was involved in no less than eight separate attempts to kill Fidel Castro. The chairman of the Senate committee, Frank Church of Idaho, worried the revelations would damage the reputations of Democratic Presidents Kennedy and Johnson, tried to put all the blame on the CIA, likening it to "a rogue elephant on the rampage."

In late 1975, President Ford finally moved to limit the damage to the CIA. He appointed George Bush, then a respected former Republican congressman, as the agency's new director and gave him the authority both to reform the CIA and to strengthen its role in shaping national security policy. Most notably, Ford issued an executive order outlawing assassination as an instrument of American foreign policy. To prevent future abuses, Congress created permanent House and Senate intelligence committees to exercise general oversight over covert CIA operations.

Ford proved less successful in his dealings with Congress on other issues. Though he prided himself on his good relations with members of both houses, he opposed such Democratic measures as federal aid to education and control over strip mining. In a little more than a year, he vetoed thirty-nine separate bills. In fact, Ford, who as a congressman had opposed virtually every Great Society measure, proved far more conservative than Nixon in the White House.

The 1976 Campaign

Ford's lackluster record and the legacy of Watergate made the Democratic nomination a prize worth fighting for in 1976. A large field of candidates entered the contest, but a virtual unknown, former Georgia governor James Earl Carter, quickly became the front-runner. Aware of the voters' disgust with politicians of both parties, Jimmy Carter ran as an outsider, portraying himself as a Southerner who had no experience in Washington and one who could thus give the nation fresh and untainted leadership.

Appearing refreshingly candid, Carter claimed to be an honest man, ready to deal fairly with the American people. On television, the basic Carter commercial showed him at his Georgia peanut farm, dressed in blue jeans, looking directly into the camera and saying, "I'll never tell a lie."

Carter swept through the primaries and won the Democratic nomination easily, naming Senator Walter Mondale of Minnesota as his running mate. The polls gave Carter a thirty-three-point lead when the campaign began, but he quickly lost ground as he began to hedge on the

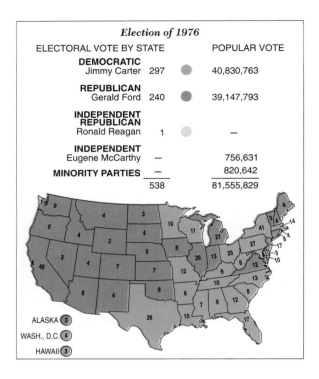

Election of 1976

ELECTORAL VOTE BY STATE		POPULAR VOTE
DEMOCRATIC Jimmy Carter	297	40,830,763
REPUBLICAN Gerald Ford	240	39,147,793
INDEPENDENT REPUBLICAN Ronald Reagan	1	—
INDEPENDENT Eugene McCarthy	—	756,631
MINORITY PARTIES	—	820,642
	538	81,555,829

ALASKA 3
WASH., D.C. 4
HAWAII 3

Disenchantment with Carter

The new president, described by an associate as "superficially self-effacing but intensely shrewd," was an ambitious and intelligent politician. He had a rare gift for sensing what people wanted and appearing to give it to them. Liberals thought he clearly stood with them; conservatives were equally convinced he was on their side. He was especially adept at utilizing symbols. He emerged from airplanes carrying his own garment bag; after his inauguration he walked up Pennsylvania Avenue hand in hand with his wife Rosalynn and daughter Amy. "Look," he seemed to be saying, "I am just an ordinary citizen who happens to be in the White House."

The substance, however, failed to match the style. He had no discernible political philosophy, no clear sense of direction. He sought the White House convinced he was brighter and better than his competitors, but once there he had no cause or mission to fulfill. He called himself a populist, but that label meant little more than an appeal to

issues. President Ford counterattacked, saying of his Democratic opponent, "he wavers, he wanders, he wiggles and he waffles." But Ford, who had developed a reputation as a bumbler from both his uninspired leadership and occasional physical stumbles on golf courses and airport ramps, reinforced his own image of ineptitude. In a televised debate, responding to a question about Iron Curtain countries, he declared, "There is no Soviet domination of eastern Europe."

Carter won an extremely narrow victory in 1976. Despite Watergate and Ford's weak record, the Democratic candidate took only 49.98 percent of the popular vote. Ford swept nearly the entire West, but Carter carried the South and key northern industrial states like New York and Ohio. Far more than most recent elections, the outcome turned on class and racial factors. "The affluent, the well-educated, the suburbanites largely went for Ford," commented one observer, "the socially and economically disadvantaged for Carter." The black vote clinched the victory for the Democrats. Carter received over 90 percent of the votes of African Americans and their ballots provided the margin of victory in Ohio, Pennsylvania, and seven southern states.

Despite his intelligence, integrity, and hard work, Jimmy Carter suffered a crisis in leadership. The electorate perceived him as ineffectual at solving problems and indecisive at setting priorities.

the common man, a somewhat ironic appeal, given Carter's personal wealth. "The idea of a millionaire populist has always amused me," commented his attorney general, fellow Georgian Griffin Bell.

The makeup of his administration reflected the conflicting tendencies that would eventually prove destructive. In the White House, he surrounded himself with close associates from Georgia, fellow outsiders like presidential adviser Hamilton Jordan and press secretary Jody Powell. Yet he picked established Democrats for key cabinet positions: Cyrus Vance, a New York lawyer, as secretary of state and Joseph Califano, a former aide to Lyndon Johnson, to head HEW. In the lower ranks, however, he selected liberal activists, followers of George McGovern, Edward M. (Ted) Kennedy, and Ralph Nader, people who were intent on regulating business and preserving the environment. The result was bound to be tension and conflict, as the White House staff and the federal bureaucracy worked at cross purposes, one group seeking change while the other attempted to protect the president.

Lacking both a clear set of priorities and a coherent political philosophy, the Carter administration had little chance to succeed. The president strove hard for a balanced budget but was forced to accept mounting deficits. Federal agencies fought to save the environment and help consumers but served only to anger industry.

In the crucial area of social services, Joseph Califano failed repeatedly in his efforts to carry out long overdue reforms. His attempts to overhaul the nation's welfare program, which had become a $30 billion annual operation serving some thirty million Americans, won little support from the White House. Carter's unwillingness to take the political risks involved in revamping the overburdened Social Security system by reducing benefits and raising the retirement age blocked Califano's efforts. And the HEW secretary finally gave up his attempt to draw up a workable national health insurance plan.

Informed by his pollsters in 1979 that he was losing the nation's confidence, Carter sought desperately to redeem himself. After a series of meetings at Camp David with a wide variety of advisers, he gave a speech in which he seemed to blame his failure on the American people, accusing them of creating "a crisis of confidence . . . that strikes at the very heart and soul and spirit of our national will." Then a week after what his critics termed the "national malaise" speech, he requested the resignation of Califano and the secretary of the treasury. But neither the attempt to pin responsibility on the American people nor the firing of cabinet members could hide the fact that Carter, despite his good intentions and hard work, had failed to provide the bold leadership the nation needed.

FROM DÉTENTE TO RENEWED COLD WAR

America's political position in the world declined sharply in the 1970s. In part, the fault was internal. The Vietnam War left the American people convinced the nation should never again intervene abroad, and Watergate discredited strong presidential leadership, shifting power over foreign policy to Congress. The new national consensus was symbolized by the War Powers Act, passed in 1973, which required the president to consult with Congress before sending American troops into action overseas. At the same time, external events and developments, notably the control over oil exercised by OPEC and the threats posed by revolutionary nationalism in the Middle East and Latin America, further weakened American foreign policy. No longer able to dominate the international scene, the United States began to play the role of spectator, and at times even of victim.

Retreat in Asia

It was Gerald Ford's fate to reap where Nixon had sown. In 1974, Congress cut in half the administration's request for $1.4 billion in military aid to South Vietnam. A year later, when a North Vietnamese offensive proved surprisingly successful, Ford was unable to get Congress to grant any additional aid. Bereft of American assistance and weakened by internal corruption, the South Vietnamese government was unable to stop the advance on Saigon in April 1975. American forces concentrated on evacuating 150,000 loyal South Vietnamese, but many more were left behind when the last helicopter left the

	Wartime Costs	Veterans' Benefits Costs	Interest Payments on War Loans	Estimated Long-Term Costs
American Revolution	100–140	28	20	170
War of 1812	87	20	14	120
Mexican War	82	26	10	120
Civil War (Union side only)*	2,300	3,289	1,200	6,800
Spanish-American War	270	2,111	60	2,400
World War I	23,700	13,856	11,100	57,600
World War II	260,000	65,231	200,000	625,200
Korean Conflict	50,000	11,391	unknown	61,400
Vietnam Conflict	140,600	13,173	unknown	153,800

*Costs of the Confederate side are estimated at $1 billion.

Source: U.S. Bureau of the Census, *Statistical Abstract of the United States: 1984,* 104th edition, Washington, D.C., 1983.

roof of the embassy in Saigon. After a quarter century of futile effort, the United States finally had to admit defeat in the nation's longest and most humiliating foreign war.

Less than a month later, Ford had a chance to remind the world of American power. The Khmer Rouge government of Cambodia seized an American freighter, the *Mayaguez,* and imprisoned its crew. When the communists ignored the initial American protest, Ford authorized an armed attack on Cambodia by two thousand marines from bases in Thailand. By the time the American forces landed on a small offshore island, Cambodia had freed the crewmen. The nation took pride in the president's resort to force, but forty Americans paid for his decision with their lives.

Accommodation in Latin America

President Carter was more successful than Ford in adjusting to the growing nationalism in the world, particularly in Central America, where the United States had imposed order for most of the twentieth century by backing reactionary regimes.

The first test came in Panama. Resentment over American ownership of the Panama Canal had led Lyndon Johnson to enter into negotiations aimed at the eventual return of the waterway to Panama. Carter completed the long diplomatic process in 1977 by signing two treaties. One restored sovereignty in the 500-square-mile canal zone to Panama, while the other provided for gradual Panamanian responsibility for operating the canal, with appropriate safeguards for its use and defense by the United States. In negotiat-

An American official punches a man trying to board a plane already overloaded with refugees during the chaotic evacuation of the city of Nha Trang in South Vietnam in the spring of 1975. Just after this plane left, Communist troops overtook the city.

ing these treaties, Carter was trying both to right an ancient wrong and create stability in a highly volatile region.

The real struggle over the treaties took place in the Senate. Conservative Republicans expressed outrage over what they termed a "giveaway" of the Panama Canal. "It's ours. We stole it fair and square," claimed California Senator S. I. Hayakawa. Intensive personal lobbying by President Carter, as well as bipartisan support from influential Republicans such as Gerald Ford and Henry Kissinger, finally led to Senate ratification with just one vote to spare, thus paving the way for the return of the canal to Panama by the year 2000.

Carter was less successful, however, in dealing with a growing problem of left-wing uprisings in Central America. In mid-1979, dictator Anastasio Somoza capitulated to the Sandinista forces in Nicaragua. Despite American attempts to moderate the Sandinista revolution, the new regime moved steadily to the left, developing close ties with Castro's Cuba. In neighboring El Salvador, a growing leftist insurgency against a repressive regime put the United States in an awkward position. Unable to find a workable alternative between the extremes of reactionary dictatorship and radical revolution in Central America, Carter tried to use American economic aid to encourage the military junta in El Salvador to carry out democratic reforms. But after the guerrillas launched a major offensive in January 1981, he authorized large-scale military assistance to the government for its war against the insurgents, setting a precedent for the future.

The Quest for Peace in the Middle East

The inconclusive results of the 1973 October War gave Henry Kissinger the opportunity to play the role of peacemaker in the troubled Middle East. Shuttling back and forth between Cairo and Jerusalem, and then to Damascus, the secretary of state finally succeeded in arranging a pullback of Israeli forces in both the Sinai and the Golan Heights. Although he failed to achieve his goal of an Arab-Israeli settlement, Kissinger had succeeded in demonstrating that the United States could play the role of neutral mediator between the

Israelis and Arabs. And equally important, he had detached Egypt from dependence on the Soviet Union, thereby weakening Russian influence in the Middle East.

In November 1977, Egyptian president Anwar Sadat stunned the world by traveling to Jerusalem in an effort to reach agreement directly with Israel. The next year, Carter invited both Sadat and Israeli prime minister Menachem Begin to negotiate under his guidance at Camp David. For thirteen days, President Carter met with Sadat and Begin, finally emerging with the ambiguous Camp David Accords. A framework for negotiations, rather than an actual peace settlement, the Camp David agreements dealt gingerly with the problem of Palestinian autonomy in the West Bank and Gaza Strip areas.

In 1979, Israel and Egypt signed a peace treaty that provided for the gradual return of the entire Sinai to Egypt but left the fate of the Palestine Arabs vague and unsettled. By excluding both the Palestine Liberation Organization (PLO) and the Soviet Union from the negotiations, the United

A highlight of Carter's presidency was his role in helping negotiate the Camp David Accords between Israeli Prime Minister Menachem Begin (right) and Egyptian President Anwar Sadat (left). The agreements set the stage for a peace treaty between Israel and Egypt.

States alienated Egypt from the other Arab nations and drove the more radical states closer to the Soviet Union.

Any sense of progress in the Middle East as a result of Camp David was quickly offset in 1979 with the outbreak of the Iranian Revolution. Under Nixon and Kissinger, the United States had come to depend heavily on the shah and his powerful army for defense of the vital Persian Gulf. Carter continued the close relationship with the shah, despite growing signs of domestic discontent with his leadership. By 1978, Iran was in chaos as the exiled Ayatollah Ruholla Khomeini led a fundamentalist Moslem revolt against the shah.

Unaware of the deep resentment most Iranians felt toward the shah—a resentment based both on dislike of sweeping modernization programs and police state rule—the Carter administration misjudged the nature of the Iranian Revolution. At first, the United States encouraged the shah to remain in Iran, but when he decided to leave the country in January 1979, Carter tried to work with a moderate regime rather than encourage an army coup. With Khomeini's return from exile, Moslem militants quickly came to power in Teheran. In October 1979, Carter permitted the exiled shah to enter the United States for medical treatment. Irate mobs in Iran denounced the United States, and on November 4, militants seized the U.S. embassy in Teheran and took fifty-eight Americans prisoner.

The prolonged hostage crisis revealed the extent to which American power had declined in the 1970s. Carter relied first on diplomacy and economic reprisals in a vain attempt to free the hostages. The United States concentrated its naval forces in the Indian Ocean as a warning to the Iranians. In his State of the Union message in January 1980, the president enunciated a new Carter Doctrine, telling the world the United States would fight to protect the vital oil supplies of the Persian Gulf. "Twin threats to the flow of oil—from regional instability and now potentially from the Soviet Union—require that we firmly defend our vital interest when threatened."

Carter was unable to back up these brave words with meaningful action. In April 1980, the president authorized a desperate rescue mission that ended in failure when several helicopters broke down in the Iranian desert. The mission

Americans were shocked by the anger Iranian mobs directed toward the U.S. embassy staff in Teheran and were frustrated by the failure to rescue the hostages.

was aborted, an accident cost the lives of eight crewmen, and Secretary of State Cyrus Vance—who had opposed the rescue attempt—resigned in protest. The hostage crisis dragged on through the summer and fall of 1980, a symbol of American weakness that proved to be a powerful political handicap to Carter in the upcoming presidential election.

The Cold War Resumes

The policy of détente was already in trouble when Carter took office in 1977. Congressional refusal to relax trade restrictions on the Soviet Union had doomed Kissinger's attempts to win political concessions from the Soviets through economic incentives. The Kremlin's repression of the growing dissident movement and its harsh policy restricting the emigration of Soviet Jews had caused many Americans to doubt the wisdom of seeking accommodation with the Soviet Union.

President Carter's emphasis on human rights appeared to the Russians to be a direct repudiation of détente. In his inaugural address, Carter reaffirmed his concern over the mistreatment of human beings anywhere in the world, declaring "our commitment to human rights must be absolute." It was easier said than done. Carter did withhold aid from authoritarian governments in Chile and Argentina, but equally repressive regimes in South Korea and the Philippines continued to receive generous American support. The Soviets, however, found even an inconsistent human rights policy to be threatening, particularly after Carter received Soviet exiles in the White House.

Secretary of State Vance concentrated on continuing the main pillar of détente, the strategic arms limitation talks (SALT). In 1974, President Ford had met with Brezhnev in Vladivostok and reached tentative agreement on the outline of SALT II. The chief provision was for a ceiling of 2,400 nuclear launchers by each side, a level that would not require either Russia or the United States to give up any existing delivery vehicles. In March 1977, Vance went to Moscow to propose a drastic reduction in this level; the Soviets, already angry over human rights, rejected the American proposal as an attempt to overcome the Russian lead in land-based ICBMs.

Zbigniew Brzezinski, Carter's national security adviser, worked from the outset to reverse the policy of détente. Commenting he was "the first Pole in three hundred years in a position to really stick it to the Russians," he favored confrontation with the Kremlin. Although Carter signed a SALT II treaty with Russia in 1979, lowering the ceiling on nuclear delivery systems to 2,250, growing opposition in the Senate played directly into Brzezinski's hands. He prevailed on the president to advocate adoption of a new MX missile to replace the existing Minuteman ICBMs, which some experts thought were now vulnerable to a Soviet first strike. This new weapons system, together with the planned Trident submarine, ensured that regardless of SALT, the nuclear arms race would be speeded up in the 1980s.

Brzezinski also was successful in persuading the president to use China to outmaneuver the Soviets. On January 1, 1979, the United States

and China exchanged ambassadors, thereby completing the reconciliation that Nixon had begun in 1971. The new relationship between Beijing and Washington presented the Soviet Union with the problem of a link between its two most powerful enemies.

The Cold War, in abeyance for nearly a decade, resumed with full fury in December 1979 when the Soviet Union invaded Afghanistan. Although this move was designed to ensure a regime friendly to the Soviet Union, it appeared to many as the beginning of a Soviet thrust toward the Indian Ocean and the Persian Gulf. Carter responded to this aggression with a series of symbolic acts: the United States banned the sale of high technology to Russia, embargoed the export of grain, resumed draft registration, and even boycotted the 1980 Moscow Olympics. These American moves did not halt the invasion of Afghanistan; instead, they put the United States and Russia back on a collision course.

The results doomed détente. Aware he could not get a two-thirds vote in the Senate, Carter withdrew the SALT II treaty. The hopeful phrases of détente gave way to belligerent rhetoric as groups like the Committee on the Present Danger called for an all-out effort against the Soviet Union. Jimmy Carter, who had come into office hoping to advance human rights and control the nuclear arms race, now found himself a victim of the renewed Cold War.

National frustration over the hostages in Iran and the Soviet invasion of Afghanistan, coupled

Soviet tanks rolled into Afghanistan in December 1979, dealing a mortal blow to East-West détente.

with anxiety over the energy crunch and rampant inflation, eroded public confidence in the Carter administration. A leader who had benefited from Vietnam and Watergate had now been betrayed by events. Despite his substantial achievements—the Camp David agreements, the Panama Canal treaties—Carter had to take the blame for developments overseas that were beyond his control. By mid-1980 the president's overall approval rating had fallen to 23 percent in the Gallup poll. The American people, disillusioned by the failures of Nixon, Ford, and Carter, yearned for new political leadership to meet the challenges facing the nation at home and abroad.

CHRONOLOGY

1966 National Organization for Women (NOW) formed

1967 Riots in Detroit kill 43, injure 2,000, leave 5,000 homeless

1968 Martin Luther King, Jr., assassinated in Memphis, Tennessee (April) • Robert F. Kennedy assassinated in Los Angeles, California (June)

1970 U.S. forces invade Cambodia (April) • Ohio National Guardsmen kill four students at Kent State University (May)

1972 President Nixon visits China (February) • U.S. and USSR sign SALT I accords in Moscow (May) • White House "plumbers" unit breaks into Democratic headquarters in Watergate complex (June) • Richard Nixon wins reelection in landslide victory over McGovern

1973 United States and North Vietnam sign truce (January) • Arab oil embargo creates energy crisis in the United States (October)

1974 Supreme Court orders Nixon to surrender White House tapes (June) • Richard M. Nixon resigns presidency (August)

1975 Last evacuation helicopter leaves roof of U.S. embassy in Saigon, South Vietnam (April)

1977 President Carter signs Panama Canal treaties restoring sovereignty to Panama

1979 Iranian militants take fifty-eight Americans hostage in U.S. embassy in Teheran (November) • Soviet invasion of Afghanistan leads to U.S. withdrawal from 1980 Moscow Olympics (December)

Recommended Reading

The most detailed account of the student protests is Todd Gitlin, *The Sixties* (1987). Gitlin, a sociologist and former SDS leader, offers a sympathetic analysis of the motives and aspirations of the youthful protesters. For other views, see James Miller, *"Democracy Is in the Streets"* (1987), which focuses on the original SDS leadership, and Irwin Unger, *The Movement* (1974), a more critical study of the New Left.

Garry Wills provides the most revealing portrait of the career and character of Richard Nixon in *Nixon Agonistes* (1970). Wills concentrates on the prepresidential years; for Nixon in office, Stephen Ambrose offers the best account in the second and third volumes of his biography, *Nixon* (1990 and 1992). See Henry Kissinger's two volumes, *The White House Years* (1979) and *Years of Upheaval* (1982), for foreign policy developments.

Stanley Kutler provides a comprehensive account of the scandal that drove Nixon from office in *The Wars of Watergate* (1990). The two volumes by journalists Bob Woodward and Carl Bernstein, *All the President's Men* (1974) and *The Final Days* (1976), are the best contemporary accounts.

In *The Prize* (1991), Daniel Yergin puts the energy crisis of the 1970s in historical perspective. The best overall account of the Carter administration is Burton I. Kaufman, *The Presidency of Jimmy Carter* (1993).

Additional Bibliography

Books on the New Left include S. Kirkpatrick Sale, *SDS* (1973); Jack Newfield, *A Prophetic Minority* (1966); Christopher Lasch, *The Agony of the American Left* (1969); Edward J. Bacciocco, *The New Left in America* (1974); Todd Gitlin, *The Whole World Is Watching* (1981); W. J. Rorabaugh, *Berkeley at War* (1989); and David Caute, *The Year of the Barricades* (1988), which places the 1968 American protests in a global context. For other aspects of the youth rebellion, see Paul Goodman, *Growing Up Absurd* (1960); Kenneth Keniston, *Young Radicals* (1968); and Lewis Feuer, *The Conflict of Generations* (1972).

The transition from the quest for integration to the assertion of black power is traced in James C. Harvey, *Black Civil Rights During the Johnson Administration* (1973); Clayborne Carson, *In Struggle* (1981); Steven

F. Lawson, *In Pursuit of Power* (1985) and *Running for Freedom* (1991); and Stokely Carmichael and C. V. Hamilton, *Black Power* (1967). For the urban riots of the 1960s, see Robert Conot, *Rivers of Blood, Years of Darkness* (1967), on Watts; John Hersey, *The Algiers Hotel Incident* (1968), and Sidney Fine, *Violence in the Model City* (1989), on Detroit; and James W. Button, *Black Violence* (1978), which shows the impact of the riots on federal policy. Bernard Schwartz traces a key Supreme Court decision on school busing in *"Swann's" Way* (1986). The growing self-consciousness of other minorities is described in Michael Novak, *The Rise of the Unmeltable Ethnics* (1973); Rodolfo Acunya, *Occupied America: A History of Chicanos*, 2d ed. (1981); and Carlos Munoz, Jr., *Youth, Identity, Power: The Chicano Generation* (1989). For the emerging feminist movement, see two books by William Chafe, *The American Woman* (1972) and *Women and Equality* (1977); Patricia G. Zelman, *Women, Work, and National Policy* (1982); Cynthia Harrison, *On Account of Sex: The Politics of Women's Issues, 1945–1968* (1988); Susan Hartmann, *From Margin to Mainstream* (1989); Sara Evans, *Personal Politics* (1979); and Alice Echols, *Daring to Be Bad: Radical Feminism in America, 1967–1975* (1989).

The best account of the 1968 election is Lewis L. Gould, *1968: The Election That Changed America* (1993); see also Theodore White, *The Making of the President, 1968* (1969), and Lewis Chester, Godfrey Hodgson, and Bruce Page, *American Melodrama* (1969). For Wallace's role, see Jody Carlson, *George C. Wallace and the Politics of Powerlessness, 1964–1976* (1981).

Fawn Brodie traces Nixon's prepresidential career critically in *Richard Nixon* (1981); Stephen Ambrose offers a more balanced view in *Nixon: The Education of a Politician, 1913–1962* (1987). The fullest account of Nixon's early career is Roger Morris, *Richard M. Nixon: The Rise of an American Politician* (1989). Other important books on Nixon include Jules Witcover, *The Resurrection of Richard Nixon* (1970); Rowland Evans and Robert Novak, *Nixon in the White House* (1971); William Safire, *Before the Fall* (1975); the president's two volumes of memoirs, *RN* (1978) and *In the Arena* (1990); Herbert Parmet, *Richard Nixon and His America* (1990); and Tom Wicker, *One of Us* (1991). For Nixon's domestic policies, see Leonard Silk, *Nixonomics* (1972); Daniel Moynihan, *Politics of a Guaranteed National Income* (1973); and two books on the Supreme Court nomination controversies by Richard Harris, *Justice* (1970) and *Decision* (1971). H. R. Haldeman offers revealing insights into the Nixon White House in *The Haldeman Diaries* (1994).

The major shifts in American politics in the late 1960s are described in Kevin Phillips, *The Emerging Republican Majority* (1969); Richard N. Scammon and Ben J. Wattenberg, *The Real Majority* (1970); S. Kirkpatrick Sale, *Power Shift* (1975); David L. Broder, *The Party's Over* (1971); Frederick G. Dutton, *The Changing Sources of Power* (1971); and John M. Blum, *Years of Discord* (1991).

Henry Brandon, *The Retreat of American Power* (1973); Tad Szulc, *The Illusion of Peace* (1978); Robert S. Litwak, *Détente and the Nixon Doctrine* (1984); and Stanley Hoffman, *Primacy of World Order* (1978), all describe Nixon's foreign policy and the search for détente. For the changing nature of relations with the Soviet Union in the 1970s, see Raymond L. Garthoff, *Détente and Confrontation* (1985), and Adam Ulam, *Dangerous Relations* (1983). The most recent account of Kissinger's contributions to American foreign policy is Walter Isaacson, *Kissinger* (1992); Robert D. Schulzinger offers a more concise view in *Henry Kissinger: Doctor of Diplomacy* (1989). Books that focus on Kissinger's role include Marvin Kalb and Bernard Kalb, *Kissinger* (1974), a sympathetic view; Roger Morris, *Uncertain Greatness* (1977), a critical analysis; Seymour Hersh, *The Price of Power* (1983), a savage indictment; and Seyom Brown, *The Crises of Power* (1979), a balanced account. For SALT, see John Newhouse, *Cold Dawn* (1973). Robert Sutter traces the new U.S. policy toward Beijing in *China Watch* (1978). William Shawcross, a British journalist, blames Kissinger for the secret bombing of Cambodia in *Sideshow* (1979).

Books on the antiwar movement and the violent protests in 1970 include Alexander Kendrick, *The Wound Within* (1974); Thomas Powers, *The War at Home* (1973); John Mueller, *War, Presidents and Public Opinion* (1973); I. F. Stone, *The Killings at Kent State* (1971); Noam Chomsky, *American Power and the New Mandarins* (1977); Melvin Small, *Johnson, Nixon and the Doves* (1988); Charles DeBenedetti and Charles Chatfield, *An American Ordeal* (1990); and Lawrence M. Baskir and William A. Strauss, *Chance and Circumstance* (1978), a study of the impact of the draft on American youth.

For the last phases of the Vietnam conflict, see Frank Snepp, *Decent Interval* (1977); Arnold R. Isaacs, *Without Honor* (1983); Nguyen Tien Hung and Jerrold Schecter, *The Palace File* (1986); and William Colby, *Lost Victory* (1989). Myra MacPherson surveys the impact of the war on an entire generation in *Long Time Passing* (1984). The different lessons drawn from the Vietnam experience are expounded in Earl C. Ravenal, *Never Again* (1978), and Norman Podhoretz, *Why We Were in Vietnam* (1982).

The election of 1972 is dealt with uncritically by Theodore White in *The Making of the President, 1972* (1973), and entertainingly by Hunter S. Thompson in *Fear and Loathing: On the Campaign Trail '72* (1973).

General accounts of Watergate include Theodore White, *Breach of Faith* (1975); Jonathan Schell, *Time of Illusion* (1976); J. Anthony Lukas, *Nightmare* (1976); and Len Colodny and Robert Gettlin, *Silent Coup* (1992). For the abuse of power that reached its culmination in the Watergate affair, see Arthur M. Schlesinger, Jr., *The Imperial Presidency* (1973); David Wise, *The American Policy State* (1976); and Athan Theoharis, *Spying on Americans* (1978). Among the many memoirs by Watergate participants, the most revealing is John Dean, *Blind Ambition* (1976).

Richard Barnet gives a thorough description of the impact of the energy crisis and foreign industrial competition on the American economy in the 1970s in *The Lean Years* (1980). Other books on this theme include Robert Stobaugh and Daniel Yergin, eds., *Energy Future* (1980); Daniel Yergin and Martin Hillenbrand, eds., *Global Insecurity* (1982); Peter R. Odell, *Oil and World Power*, 5th ed. (1979); and Franklin Tugwell, *The Energy Crisis and the American Political Economy* (1988). For other economic developments in the 1970s, see Richard Barnet and Ronald Muller, *Global Reach* (1974), on the rise of the multinationals; R. Kent Weaver, *The Politics of Indexation* (1988), on the relationship between cost-of-living increases and inflation; and Katharine Davis Fishman, *The Computer Establishment* (1981), on the early dominance of IBM.

For the Ford administration, the most useful books are Richard Reeves, *A Ford, Not a Lincoln* (1975); Clark Mollenhoff, *The Man Who Pardoned Nixon* (1976); Robert Hartmann, *Palace Politics* (1980); Edward L. and Frederick H. Schapsmeier, *Gerald R. Ford's Date with Destiny* (1989); and the president's own memoir, Gerald R. Ford, *A Time to Heal* (1979). The impact of post-Watergate reforms on the CIA can be traced in Loch Johnson, *A Season of Inquiry* (1985); James Colby, *Honorable Men* (1978); and Stansfield Turner, *Secrecy and Democracy* (1985). On the election of 1976, see Jules Witcover, *Marathon* (1977), and Elizabeth Drew, *American Journal* (1977).

The best overall accounts of the Carter administration are Charles O. Jones, *The Trusteeship Presidency* (1988), and Erwin C. Hargrove, *Jimmy Carter as President* (1988). Other books on Carter include Betty Glad, *Jimmy Carter* (1980); Haynes Johnson, *In the Absence of Power* (1980); and William Lee Miller, *Yankee from Georgia* (1978). Four memoirs offer the best insight into domestic developments during the Carter years: Joseph Califano, *On Governing America* (1981), critical of the president; Griffin Bell, *Taking Care of the Law* (1982), a defensive view by the attorney general; Jody Powell, *The Other Side of the Story* (1984), the press secretary's attack on the media; and Rosalynn Carter, *First Lady from Plains* (1984), a revealing account by the president's wife.

The conflict over foreign policy within the Carter administration can be seen clearly in the memoirs of the leading figures. Cyrus Vance defends his record as secretary of state in *Hard Choices* (1984); national security adviser Zbigniew Brzezinski is critical of Carter's handling of foreign policy in *Power and Principle* (1983); and Jimmy Carter focuses primarily on his Camp David triumph in *Keeping Faith* (1982). The best survey of the Carter administration's diplomacy is Gaddis Smith, *Morality, Reason and Power* (1985); see also Donald S. Spencer, *The Carter Implosion* (1989), a critical account, and David S. McLellan, *Cyrus Vance* (1985). For the Panama Canal treaties, see Walter LaFeber, *The Panama Canal* (1978), the broadest account; J. Michael Hogan, *The Panama Canal in American Politics* (1986); and George D. Moffett, *The Limits of Victory* (1985). Other books on foreign policy issues of the 1970s are Strobe Talbott, *Endgame* (1979), on the negotiation of SALT II; Roy Rowan, *The Four Days of the Mayaguez* (1975); William B. Quandt, *Camp David* (1986); Joshua Muravchik, *The Uncertain Crusade* (1986), highly critical of Carter's human rights policy; and Robert Pastor, *Condemned to Repetition* (1987), an insider's defense of policy toward the Nicaraguan revolution.

The best accounts of U.S. relations with the shah and the Iranian revolution are Barry Rubin, *Paved with Good Intentions* (1980); James A. Bill, *The Eagle and the Lion* (1988); and Mark Gasioroswki, *U.S. Foreign Policy and the Shah* (1991). For the hostage crisis, see Michael Ledeen and William Lewis, *Debacle* (1981), a journalistic account, and two books by members of Carter's White House staff, Hamilton Jordan, *Crisis* (1983), and Gary Sick, *All Fall Down* (1985).

The Reagan-Bush Era

The Republican National Committee sponsored a televised address by Hollywood actor Ronald Reagan on behalf of Barry Goldwater's presidential candidacy in October 1964. Reagan's speech had originally been aired on a Los Angeles station; the resulting outpouring of praise and campaign contributions led to its national rebroadcast.

In contrast to Goldwater's strident rhetoric, Reagan used relaxed, confident, and persuasive terms to put forth the case for a return to individual freedom. Instead of the usual choice between increased government activity and less governmental involvement, often couched in terms of the left and the right, Reagan presented the options of either going up or down—"up to the maximum of human freedom consistent with law and order, or down to the ant heap of totalitarianism." Then, borrowing a phrase from FDR, he told his audience: "You and I have a rendezvous with destiny. We can preserve for our children this the last best hope of man on earth or we can sentence them to take the first step into a thousand years of darkness."

Although this speech did not rescue Goldwater's unpopular candidacy, it marked the beginning of Ronald Reagan's remarkable political career. A year later, a group of wealthy friends persuaded him, largely on the basis of the success of "the speech," to run for the California governorship. Reagan proved to be an attractive candidate. His friendly, relaxed manner and his mastery of television enabled him to present his strongly conservative message without appearing to be a rigid ideologue of the right. He won handily by appealing effectively to rising middle-class suburban resentment over high taxes, expanding welfare programs, and bureaucratic regulation.

In two terms as governor, Reagan displayed natural ability as a political leader. Instead of insisting on implementing all of his conservative beliefs, he proved surprisingly flexible. Faced with a Democratic legislature, he yielded on raising taxes and increasing state spending while managing to trim the welfare rolls. Symbolic victories were his specialty; in one example he managed to confront campus radicals and fire Clark Kerr, chancellor of the University of California,

while at the same time generously funding higher education.

By the time Reagan left the governor's office in 1974, many signs pointed to a growing conservative mood across the nation. In a popular rebellion against escalating property taxes in 1978, California's voters passed Proposition 13, which called for a 57 percent cut in taxes and resulted in a gradual reduction in social services. Concern over greater acceptance of homosexuality in society and rising abortion and divorce rates impelled religious groups to engage in political activity to defend traditional family values. Jerry Falwell, a successful Virginia radio and television evangelist, founded the Moral Majority, a fundamentalist group dedicated to preserving the "American way of life." The Moral Majority held workshops and seminars to teach its followers how to become active in local politics, and it also issued "morality ratings" for congressional representatives and senators.

The population shift of the 1970s, especially the rapid growth of the Sunbelt region in the South and West (see Chapter 33), added momentum to the conservative upsurge. Those moving to the Sunbelt tended to be white, middle- and upper-class suburbanites—mainly skilled workers, young professionals, and business executives who were attracted both by economic opportunity and by a political climate stressing low taxes, less government regulation, and more reliance on the marketplace. In the West, the newcomers supported the dominant Republicans; in the South, they could choose between a growing Republican party and conservative "boll weevil" Democrats who advocated stronger national defense abroad and less government intrusion at home. The political impact of population shifts from East to West and North to South during the 1970s was reflected in the congressional gains (seventeen seats) by Sunbelt and Far West states after the 1980 census.

Conservatives also succeeded, for the first time since World War II, in making their cause intellectually respectable. Scholars and academics on the right flourished in new "think tanks"; writer William Buckley and economist Milton Friedman proved to be effective advocates of conservative causes in print and on television. Neo-conservatism, led by Norman Podhoretz's magazine

Ronald Reagan appears with the Reverend Jerry Falwell at a Moral Majority rally in Dallas, Texas, in 1980. Falwell's Moral Majority and other similar evangelical groups endorsed conservative positions on a variety of issues including abortion and school prayer. In his two presidential election campaigns, Reagan vigorously sought the support of Falwell's followers.

Commentary, became fashionable among many intellectuals who were former liberal stalwarts. They denounced liberals for being too soft on the communist threat abroad and too willing to compromise high standards at home in the face of demands for equality from African Americans, women, and the disadvantaged. Neoconservatives called for a reaffirmation of capitalism and a new emphasis on what was right about America rather than an obsessive concern with social ills.

By the end of the 1970s, Ronald Reagan was recognized as the nation's most effective spokesman for the conservative resurgence. His personal charm softened the hard edges of his right-wing call to arms, and his conviction that America could regain its traditional self-confidence by reaffirming basic ideals had a broad appeal to a nation shaken by inflation at home and humiliation abroad. In 1976, Reagan had barely lost to Gerald Ford at the Republican convention; four years later, he overcame an early upset by George Bush in Iowa to win the GOP presidential nomination handily.

In his acceptance speech at the Republican convention in Detroit, he set forth the themes that endeared him to conservatives—less government, balanced budget, family values, and peace through increased military spending. Unlike Barry Goldwater, who frightened people with his rigid ideology, Reagan offered reassurance and hope for the future. He spoke of restoring to the federal government "the capacity to do the people's work without dominating their lives." As historian Robert Dallek has pointed out, Reagan "assured his listeners that he was no radical idealist courting defeat, but a sensible, thoroughly likeable American with a surefire formula for success that would please everyone." In Ronald Reagan, the Republicans had found the perfect candidate to exploit both the American people's frustration with the domestic and foreign policy failures of the 1970s and the growing conservative mood of the nation.

THE CONSERVATIVE RESURGENCE: REAGAN IN POWER

The liberal Democratic political coalition, originally created by Franklin D. Roosevelt in the Great Depression, finally split apart by the end of the 1970s. The Watergate scandal gave the Democrats a brief reprieve, but by the end of the decade, the Republicans were using the conservative upsurge to make inroads into such normally

Democratic groups of voters as Jews, Southerners, and blue-collar workers. Yet the continuing appeal of the New Deal legacy prevented a total political realignment.

The Reagan Victory

In 1980, Jimmy Carter, the politician who had so skillfully used the Watergate trauma to win the presidency, found himself in trouble. Inflation, touched off by the second oil shock of the 1970s, reached double-digit figures—13.3 percent in 1979 and 12.4 percent in 1980. The Federal Reserve Board's effort to shrink the money supply had led to a recession, with unemployment reaching 7.8 percent by July 1980. What Ronald Reagan dubbed the "misery index," the combined rate of inflation and unemployment, hit 28 percent early in 1980 and stayed above 20 percent throughout the year.

Foreign policy proved almost as damaging to Carter. The Soviet invasion of Afghanistan eroded hopes for continued détente; the hostage crisis in Iran highlighted the nation's sense of helplessness in the face of flagrant violations of its sovereignty. In the short run, Carter used that crisis to beat back the challenge to his renomination by fellow Democrat Edward Kennedy; the president stayed in the White House during the spring primaries, reminding the voters of his devotion to duty. The Democrats rallied behind Carter, although the delegates to the party's convention displayed a notable lack of enthusiasm in renominating him.

Ronald Reagan, in the meantime, chose George Bush as his running mate. In the fall campaign, the Republican candidates hammered away at the state of the economy and the world. Reagan scored heavily among traditionally Democratic blue-collar groups by blaming Carter for inflation, which robbed workers of any gain in real wages. Reagan also accused Carter of allowing the Soviets to outstrip the United States militarily and promised a massive buildup of American forces if he was elected. Although Republican strategists feared Carter might spring an "October surprise"—a negotiated release of the American hostages at the height of the campaign—the Iranian situation actually helped Reagan by accentuating U.S. weakness in the world. Carter's position was further hurt by the

Candidate	Party	Popular Vote	Electoral Vote
Reagan	Republican	43,899,248	489
Carter	Democratic	35,481,435	49
Anderson	Independent	5,719,437	—

The Election of 1980

independent candidacy of liberal Republican John Anderson of Illinois, who appealed to voters disenchanted with Carter but not yet ready to embrace Reagan.

The president struck back by claiming Reagan was too reckless to conduct American foreign policy in the nuclear age. Charging this election would decide "whether we have peace or war," Carter tried to portray his Republican challenger as a warmonger. The attack backfired. In a televised debate arranged late in the campaign, Reagan assured the American people of his devotion to peace, leaving Carter with the onus of trying to land a low blow. At the end of the confrontation, Reagan scored impressively when he summed up the country's dire economic condition by suggesting voters ask themselves simply, "Are you better off now than you were four years ago? Is it easier for you to go and buy things in the stores than it was four years ago?"

On Election Day, the American people answered with a resounding "no." Reagan carried forty-four states and gained 51 percent of the popular vote. Carter won only six states and 41 percent of the popular vote, while John Anderson received the remaining 8 percent but failed to carry a single state. Reagan clearly benefited from the growing political power of the Sunbelt; he carried every state west of the Mississippi except Minnesota, the home state of Carter's running mate, Walter Mondale. In the South, Reagan lost only Georgia, Carter's home state. Even more impressive were Reagan's inroads into the old New Deal coalition. He received 50.5 percent of the blue-collar vote and 46 percent of the Jewish vote, the best showing by a Republican since 1928. Only one group remained loyal to Carter; African American voters gave him 85 percent of their ballots.

Republican gains in Congress were even more surprising. For the first time since 1954, the GOP gained control of the Senate, 53 to 46, and the party picked up 33 seats in the House to narrow the Democratic margin from 114 to 50. Liberals were the chief losers in Congress. Such prominent Democratic senators as George McGovern and Frank Church met with defeat, victims of a vendetta waged by the Moral Majority.

The meaning of the election was less clear than its outcome. Nearly all observers agreed the voters had rendered an adverse judgment on the Carter administration. But most experts did not assess the outcome to be a major realignment in American politics equivalent to the Democratic victory of FDR in 1932. Voters in 1980 expressed a distaste for current economic conditions, not a strongly held ideological preference. The fact that the Democrats still held a sizable majority in the House was seen as proof of their party's continuing strength. Political scientist Walter Dean Burnham termed the result "a conservative revitalization," but one that stopped short of making the GOP the dominant party.

Journalist Theodore White disagreed, viewing the outcome as a repudiation of the Democratic coalition that had dominated American politics since the days of Franklin D. Roosevelt and the New Deal. White had a strong case. In the eight presidential elections from 1952 to 1980, Republican candidates received 52.3 percent of the popular vote, compared to 47.7 percent for the Democrats; Republicans won four elections (1952, 1956, 1972, and 1980) comfortably, one (1968) narrowly, and lost two close races (1960 and 1976). Only in 1964 did the Republicans lose by a wide margin. Reagan's victory in 1980 thus marked the culmination of a Republican presidential realignment that ended a half century of Democratic dominance.

Cutting Spending and Taxes

When Ronald Reagan took office in January 1981, the ravages of inflation had cut $1,400 in purchasing power from the median family income during the 1970s. High interest rates, with the prime hovering near 20 percent, led to a decline in home building and auto sales. The government's share of the GNP had risen from 18.5 percent to over 23 percent since 1960, while the value of the dollar had dropped to just 36 cents over the same period. The new president blamed what he termed "the worst economic mess since the Great Depression" on high federal spending and excessive taxation. "Government is not the solution to our problems," Reagan announced in his inaugural address, "government is the problem."

The president embraced the concept of supply-side economics as the proper remedy for the nation's economic ills. In sharp contrast to the prevailing Keynesian theory, with its reliance on government spending to boost consumer demand, Reagan favored a reduction in both federal expenditures and revenues. Supply-side economists believed the private sector, freed of the ever-increasing burden of government spending, would shift its resources from tax shelters to productive investment, leading to an economic boom that would provide enough new income to offset the lost revenue. Although many other economists worried that the 30 percent cut in income taxes that Reagan favored would lead to staggering deficits, the president was confident his program would both stimulate the economy and reduce the role of government.

In pursuing his economic goals, Reagan relied primarily on the director of the Office of Management and Budget, David Stockman. A former Michigan congressman who had become a convert to supply-side economics, Stockman was charged with carrying out Reagan's policies of cutting government spending and sharply reducing taxes. Intelligent, combative, and shrewd, Stockman blended a missionary concern over bloated social programs with an insider's knowledge of how Congress worked. At the same time, Reagan supported the efforts of Paul Volcker, the banker Carter had appointed to head the Federal Reserve Board, to stem inflation by restricting the money supply, and even appointed him to a second four-year term in 1983.

The president and his budget director made spending the first target. Quickly deciding not to attack such popular middle-class entitlement programs as Social Security and Medicare, and sparing critical social services for the "truly deserving needy," the so-called safety net, they concentrated on slashing $41.4 billion from the budget by cutting heavily into such other social services as food stamps and by reducing public service jobs, student loans, and support for urban mass transit. Reagan used his charm and powers of persuasion to woo conservative Democrats from the West and South. Appearing before a joint session of Congress only weeks after an attempt on his life, Reagan won a commanding 253 to 176 margin of victory for his budget in the House, and an even more lopsided vote of 78 to 20 in the Senate in May. A jubilant Reagan told a Los Angeles audience that he had achieved "the greatest reduction in government spending that has ever been attempted."

The president proved equally successful in reducing taxes. Adopting a proposal originally put forth by Senator William Roth of Delaware and Congressman Jack Kemp of New York, he advocated a cut of 10 percent in personal income taxes for three consecutive years. When the Democrats countered with a two-year plan that would reduce taxes by only 15 percent, Reagan compromised with a proposal to cut taxes by 5 percent the first year but insisted on the full 10 percent reduction for the second and third years. Although some critics feared loss of revenue might result in a huge deficit, the president once again overcame Democratic resistance in Congress. In July, both houses passed the tax cut by impressive margins. In securing reductions in spending and lowering taxes, Reagan had demonstrated beyond any doubt his ability to wield presidential power effectively. As *Time* magazine commented, no president since FDR had "done so much of such magnitude so quickly to change the economic direction of the country."

Limiting the Role of Government

Reagan met with only mixed success in his other efforts to restrict governmental activity and reduce federal regulation of the economy. The concept of cutting back on the scope of federal agencies and limiting their impact on American business was a central tenet of the president's political philosophy. The goal of deregulation led to the appointment of men and women who shared his belief in relying on the marketplace rather than the bureaucracy to direct the nation's economy. To the outrage of environmentalists Secretary of the Interior James Watt opened up federal land to coal and timber production, halted the growth of national parkland, and made more than a billion acres of land available for off-

shore oil drilling. Though Watt was eventually forced to resign, the Reagan administration continued its policy of reducing governmental intervention in business long after his departure.

Transportation Secretary Drew Lewis proved to be the most effective cabinet member in the administration's first two years. He helped relieve the troubled American automobile industry of many of the regulations adopted in the 1970s to reduce air pollution and increase passenger safety. At the same time, he played a key role in the behind-the-scenes negotiations that led Japan to agree in the spring of 1981 to restrict its automobile exports to the United States for the next three years. This unilateral Japanese action enabled the Reagan administration to help Detroit's carmakers without openly violating its free market position by endorsing protectionist measures.

Lewis gained notoriety in opposing a strike by the air controllers' union (PATCO) in the summer of 1981. The president, denouncing PATCO

The Professional Air Traffic Controllers' Organization (PATCO) was one of the few unions to support Reagan in the 1980 campaign. But when PATCO struck in August 1981, Reagan unhesitatingly fired the striking air traffic controllers and refused to hire them back when the strike collapsed.

for threatening to interrupt "the protective services which are government's reason for being," fired the striking workers, decertified the union, and ordered Lewis to hire and train thousands of new air controllers at a cost of $1.3 billion. For the Reagan administration, the price was worth paying to prove no group of government employees had the right to defy the public interest.

The Reagan administration was less successful in trying to cut back on the entitlement programs that it viewed as the primary cause of the growing budget deficits. Social Security was the greatest offender. The decision to index old-age pensions to the cost of living in the 1970s had led to a 500 percent increase in benefits over the decade and threatened to bankrupt the system's trust fund by the end of the century. Reagan, overconfident from his budget victory, met a sharp rebuff when he tried to make substantial cuts in future benefits. The president finally took the issue of Social Security reform out of politics by appointing a bipartisan commission to recommend ways to protect the system's endangered trust fund. In March 1983, Congress approved a series of changes that guaranteed the solvency of Social Security by gradually raising the retirement age, delaying cost-of-living increases for six months, and taxing pensions paid to the well-to-do elderly.

The administration's record in dealing with civil rights and women's concerns proved clumsy and divisive. In federal appointments, Reagan showed far less interest than Carter in advancing minority representation. In contrast to the 12 percent African American representation in major government positions under the Democrats, the Republican figure was only 4.1 percent. Women were also slighted, falling from 12.1 percent under Carter to 8 percent under Reagan; the percentage of Hispanics dropped only slightly, from 4.1 percent to 3.8 percent.

Although feminist groups were disappointed by the administration's strong rhetorical attacks on legalized abortion (see Chapter 33), the appointment of Sandra Day O'Connor to the Supreme Court pleased them. By this one shrewd move, Reagan was able both to fulfill a campaign pledge and make a symbolic gesture to women. His appointments to the lower federal courts were a better indication of his administration's relatively low regard for women. Of the first 72 Reagan nominees to the federal judiciary, only 3 were women; just one of the 69 men was African American.

The administration's civil rights record proved especially revealing. Aware of how few African Americans had supported the GOP in 1980, Reagan made no effort to reward this group with government jobs or favors. Instead, the Justice Department actively opposed busing to achieve school integration and affirmative action measures that resulted in minority hiring quotas. The Republicans also failed to take the lead in renewing the original Voting Rights Act of 1965. After opposing key amendments designed to strengthen the historic legislation that had finally enabled African Americans to participate fully in southern politics, Reagan belatedly endorsed and signed a measure to extend the Voting Rights Act for twenty-five years.

Reaganomics

The sweeping reductions in domestic spending and income taxes that Reagan achieved in 1981 gave rise to conflicting economic expectations. Supply-side economists believed the tax relief granted investors would lead to rapid business growth, which would raise more than enough new revenue to offset the lower rates. The administration's critics, on the other hand, were sure heavy defense spending coupled with tax reductions would create massive deficits and result in economic stagnation. Neither group proved to be right.

The supply-side theory became the first economic casualty of the 1980s. The naive belief that a combination of cuts in social spending and sharply reduced taxes could unleash an economic boom that would avoid huge deficits was the victim of both Reagan's insistence on huge increases in defense spending (projected at more than $1 trillion over five years) and the Federal Reserve Board's tight money policy. It was the latter that touched off a recession that began in the fall of 1981 and grew steadily worse throughout 1982, until factory utilization fell to under 70 percent and unemployment reached a postwar high of 10.4 percent in October 1982.

Reagan responded by refusing to give up his income tax cuts. With the first major 10 percent reduction due to come in July 1982, he claimed his policies had not yet been given a chance. But he did prove flexible in other ways, slightly moderating the defense buildup, accepting fewer cuts in social programs than he proposed, and finally agreeing to a $98 billion increase in miscellaneous federal taxes. He refused, however, to cancel the final 10 percent cut in income taxes due in mid-1983. Instead he declared that all signs pointed to "a strong recovery," adding, "Our economic game plan is working."

Whether by design or good luck, the president's optimism proved justified. In the second quarter of 1983, the economy came to life, with the GNP expanding at an annual rate of 9.7 percent. The final 10 percent tax cut in July stimulated consumer spending, along with moderating inflation, which kept prices from rising so quickly. The long-depressed automobile industry, helped by Japan's voluntary quotas on car exports, began to boom, with annual sales reaching $13.6 million in 1984. The American people went on a great buying spree with consumer installment debt increasing as much in the first six months of 1983 as in all of 1982.

Best of all, inflation remained under control as the economy expanded. The recession had driven the increase in the cost of living down from 7 percent to just under 4 percent in 1982; it dropped to 3.8 percent in 1983, the lowest rate since 1972. At the same time, interest rates, which had been hovering around 16.5 percent in 1982, fell to 10.5 percent and remained below 11 percent, enabling consumers to buy goods and corporations to expand their inventories much more easily. A combination of long-term Federal Reserve policy, the impact of the recession, and a worldwide decline in energy and food prices enabled the Reagan administration to take credit for solving the problem that had proved fatal for Carter and the Democrats (see "Three Mile Island and Chernobyl," pp. 998–999).

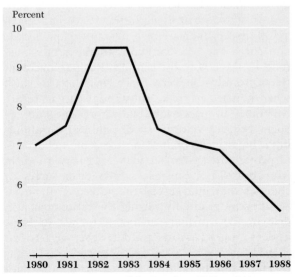

Annual Unemployment Rate, 1980–1988

Source: Economic Report of the President, 1989, p. 344.

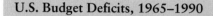

U.S. Budget Deficits, 1965–1990

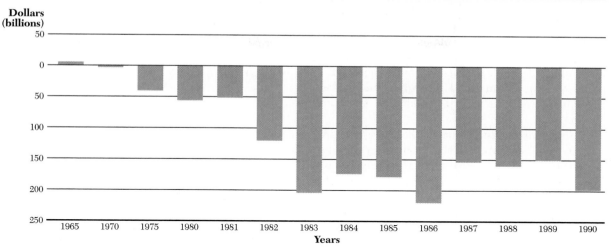

Source: Economic Report of the President.

The Growing Deficit

A new problem emerged in the mid-1980s to cloud Reagan's claims of economic recovery—the growing federal budget deficit. The 1982 recession undercut the rosy assumptions of the supply-siders. As the economy weakened and unemployment increased, tax revenues fell below projections while government spending on unemployment insurance and other social programs climbed. The deficit reached $207.8 billion in 1983, nearly triple the pre-Reagan high of $70.5 billion in 1976.

Even more frightening, some economists were predicting that at current spending and tax rates, the deficit would rise to over $300 billion a year by the end of the decade. The result, many feared, would be soaring interest rates as the government competed with the private sector for the limited amount of investment capital in the nation. In fact, a slumping world economy led to a massive infusion of foreign investment, which kept the prime rate from rising above 11 percent.

When the deficit continued to climb during the economic recovery of the mid-1980s, Congress finally came forward with what appeared to be a drastic solution. Republican senators Phil Gramm of Texas and Warren Rudman of New Hampshire joined with Democrat Ernest Hollings of South Carolina to set a series of budgetary ceilings designed to eliminate the deficit entirely by 1991 through mandatory, across-the-board spending cuts. After the Supreme Court ruled these compulsory features were unconstitutional, the revised Gramm-Rudman-Hollings Balanced Budget Act did succeed in halting the deficit spiral. As altered by Congress in 1986 and 1987, Gramm-Rudman, as it became known, stretched out the goal of ending the deficit until 1993. The president and Congress were able to lower the deficit from a peak of $221 billion in 1986 to a more manageable $155 billion by 1988. Even more important, the deficit as a percentage of the GNP fell from over 5 percent to close to 3 percent, a level common in many industrial nations.

In essence, Gramm-Rudman was a political compromise. The price Reagan had to pay for Democratic help in resolving his budgetary crisis was to stop the increase in defense spending; the Pentagon budget, which went from less than $200 billion to just under $300 billion in three years, was frozen for the rest of the decade. But at the same time, by agreeing to sizable budget deficits for the next few years, the Democrats who controlled Congress had to give up any hope of expanding existing social programs or enacting new ones, such as a comprehensive national health plan.

Concern over another alarming deficit—in the balance of overseas trade—also became an important issue in the mid-1980s. American exports had been falling steadily since the 1970s as a result of the decline in traditional manufacturing industries—iron and steel, electronics, and automobiles. The Japanese had been the biggest gainers as they dominated the American market in consumer goods such as television sets and VCRs.

A sharp rise in the value of the dollar, beginning in 1983, accentuated the problem by making American goods too expensive in foreign markets. The result was a trade deficit that grew from a modest $31 billion in 1981 to an alarming $171 billion by 1987. The only way the United States could equalize the balance of international payments was to import even more capital from abroad. Led by the Japanese, foreign investors poured large sums into the United States, buying real estate, office buildings, and even banks. As a result, in 1985, the United States, a creditor nation since World War I, suddenly became a debtor, owing the rest of the world more each year than it received from previous foreign investments. In late 1985, the Reagan administration joined with the governments of Japan and western Europe to devalue the dollar. The resulting decline in the dollar stimulated American exports and helped reduce the trade deficit to more manageable proportions by 1989, although it still remained over $100 billion a year.

In the 1980s, the American people had begun living beyond their means. Just as the government incurred large deficits rather than raising taxes to pay for the huge defense buildup, so consumers had cut back on personal saving in order to buy imported cars, television sets, and VCRs, encouraging further foreign investment. By 1988, foreigners held $400 billion in U.S. Treasury securities (almost 20 percent of the national debt), had invested another $300 billion in American industry, and owned 21 percent of the nation's banking assets. At the end of the decade, the American people were sending $60 billion a year overseas just to pay the interest on these public and private obligations. Reaganomics had succeeded in continuing America's traditional high standard of living, but at a very high price—massive borrowing that mortgaged the nation's future.

The Election of 1984

Candidate	Party	Popular Vote	Electoral Vote
Reagan	Republican	54,451,521	525
Mondale	Democratic	37,565,334	13

The Politics of Prosperity

"Are you better off now than you were four years ago?" Reagan had asked voters at the end of his 1980 debate with Jimmy Carter. By the mid-1980s, he appeared to have delivered on his implicit promise to stem inflation and revive the stagnant American economy. Yet not everyone benefited equally from Reaganomics.

The gains were impressive. The 1982 recession halted the inflationary spiral, and thanks in part to a sharp decline in oil prices, inflation remained below 4 percent for the rest of the decade. Meanwhile, the recovery that began in the final quarter of 1982 led to the creation of 16 million new jobs and a drop in the unemployment rate to just over 5 percent. The best measure of living standards, the median family income, rose slowly but steadily, going up 6.4 percent from 1980 to 1987 and 9.6 percent after the 1982 recession.

Despite these gains, the average American family was no better off by the end of the Reagan years than it had been in 1973. Measured in 1987 dollars, family income that had declined during the years of inflation had just reached the level it enjoyed before the oil shocks hit so hard. Moreover, not everyone fared equally well (see Chapter 33). Those in the top 20 percent in terms of family income benefited the most, increasing their incomes at the rate of 1.9 percent a year from 1982 to 1987, compared to only 1.4 percent a year for those in the lowest fifth. But the lower middle class did not fare as well, gaining little from the income tax changes and seeing their weekly take-home pay drop as a result of rising Social Security taxes. The rich got richer, the poor stayed poor, while middle America struggled to make ends meet.

Despite these mixed results, the Republicans were remarkably successful in persuading

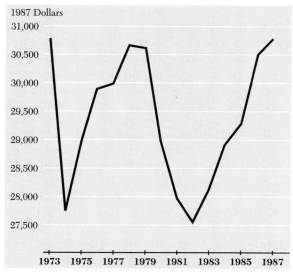

Median Family Income, 1973–1987 (in 1987 dollars)

1987 Dollars

31,000
30,500
30,000
29,500
29,000
28,500
28,000
27,500

1973 1975 1977 1979 1981 1983 1985 1987

Source: Economic Report of the President, 1989, *p. 342.*

American voters that the Reagan administration had cured the nation's economic woes. The waning of inflation, which had been the most frightening development of the 1970s, along with the

fact that wealthy Americans were far more likely to cast ballots than poorer ones, helps explain this seeming contradiction between public support of Reagan and the reality of Reaganomics.

The economic boom that began in 1983 came at just the right time for the Republican party. By early 1984, with personal income rising at an annual rate of 10.3 percent from January to June and unemployment shrinking rapidly, Democratic prospects dimmed for the 1984 election. After a long bruising primary battle, Walter Mondale, former Minnesota senator and Carter's vice president, won the Democratic nomination. In a bold break with tradition, he chose a woman as a running mate, Congresswoman Geraldine Ferraro of New York.

When the Republicans renominated Reagan and Bush, the campaign quickly came down to one issue: leadership. The GOP claimed Reagan had overcome the problems that overwhelmed Carter, notably inflation at home and disrespect abroad. Asserting he wanted to "make America great again," the president told voters if they reelected him, "You ain't seen nothin' yet."

Mondale and Ferraro, in contrast, accused Reagan of helping the rich at the expense of the poor, saddling future generations with huge

Walter Mondale and Geraldine Ferraro campaigning in 1984. Ferraro was the first woman selected by a major party as a vice-presidential candidate.

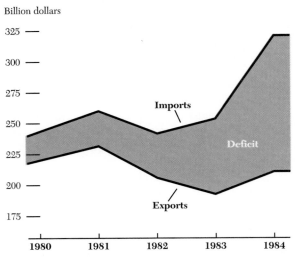

U.S. Merchandise Trade Balance, 1980–1984

Billion dollars

325 —

300 —

275 —

Imports

250 —

225 —

Deficit

200 —

Exports

175 —

1980 1981 1982 1983 1984

Source: U.S. International Trade Commission of the U.S. Department of Commerce.

deficits and risking war in the Middle East and Central America. In a surprise move, the Democratic candidate announced he intended to raise taxes to curb the deficit and then accused Reagan of harboring a "secret plan" to increase taxes himself.

These tactics failed to gain support; the outcome was a far greater Reagan victory than in 1980. With a solid base in the South and West, the president cut deeply into the normally Democratic states of the Northeast and the swing states of the Midwest to take the electoral votes of all but Minnesota and the District of Columbia. Exit surveys revealed that economic issues were uppermost in the minds of voters; in the midst of a strong economic recovery, Reagan won a majority among all voters earning more than $12,500 a year. More than two-thirds of the white males in the nation voted for Reagan, who won even a majority of the blue-collar and women's vote. Despite Ferraro's presence on the ballot, a higher percentage of women voted for Reagan in 1984 than in 1980. Of all the traditional Democratic groups, only African Americans proved loyal to the party, giving Mondale 90 percent of their votes.

The 1984 election was far more of a triumph for Reagan than for his party. In Congress, the GOP gained only fourteen seats, leaving the Democrats firmly in control of the House; in the Senate, the Republicans lost two places, narrowing their majority to 54–46. Despite minor gains at the state level, the GOP failed to achieve the party realignment it sought. Republicans were encouraged by a strong showing among the young, with Reagan taking 56 percent of the vote of the baby boomers (those aged 25 to 34) and 60 percent of the post-boomers (those aged 18 to 24). The nation seemed to be dividing politically along economic lines, with the wealthy and affluent who fared best from Reagan's economic policies supporting the president while a growing underclass of African Americans, Hispanics, and the working poor were voting solidly Democratic. Middle-class Americans who held the balance revealed their mixed feelings by backing a Republican for president and Democratic candidates for the House and Senate.

REAGAN AND THE WORLD

Ronald Reagan was even more determined to reverse the course of American policy abroad than at home. He believed that under Carter, American prestige and standing in the world had dropped to an all-time low. Intent on restoring traditional American pride and self-respect, Reagan's mission was to strengthen America's defenses and recapture world supremacy from the Soviet Union.

In reality, the new president was simply continuing the hard line that Carter had begun to take after the invasion of Afghanistan. The Democrats had begun a massive military buildup in 1979 that included plans for cruise missiles in Europe, a rapid deployment force in the Middle East, and a 5 percent increase in the defense budget.

Under Reagan, the Pentagon flourished. Secretary of Defense Caspar Weinberger, once known as a budget cutter, presented a plan that would more than double defense spending, taking it from $171 billion in 1981 to a projected $367.5 by 1986. The emphasis was on new weapons, ranging from the B-1 bomber and the controversial MX nuclear missile to the expan-

Components of Reagan's Strategic Defense Initiative (SDI) system included this tracking station, a 60-foot billboard antenna. Reagan steadfastly defended SDI against scientists who called its feasibility into question and critics who questioned its huge, open-ended cost. Even SDI defenders acknowledged that the system would cost hundred of billions of dollars to deploy.

sion of the navy from 456 to 600 ships. Despite growing opposition in Congress, by 1985 the defense budget grew to over $300 billion at the very time the administration was cutting back on domestic spending.

After some initial difficulty, Reagan proved more successful than Jimmy Carter in bringing harmony and order to the conduct of American foreign policy. His first secretary of state was Alexander Haig, a former general, NATO commander, Kissinger aide, and White House chief of staff under Nixon. Haig, outspoken and assertive, tried to establish his primacy over the policy-making process, only to alienate the entire White House staff. Finally, in mid-1982, Reagan replaced Haig as secretary of state with George Shultz, a professional economist with extensive government experience, whose low-key and relaxed style brought an air of calm reassurance to the conduct of American foreign policy. Shultz, moreover, proved more than able to hold his own in bureaucratic infighting with the White House staff, Defense Secretary Weinberger, and the administration's most outspoken hard-liner, UN Ambassador Jeane Kirkpatrick.

Despite the steady increase in defense spending and the formation of a smoothly functioning foreign policy team, Reagan soon found his diplomatic goals were more difficult to achieve than the budgetary and tax measures he had pushed through Congress so speedily. Yet in the long run

he could claim credit for a goal that had eluded his predecessors in the White House—the end of the Cold War.

Challenging the "Evil Empire"

The belief the Soviet Union was a deadly enemy that threatened the well-being and security of the United States was the central tenet of Reagan's approach to foreign policy. He saw the Russians as bent on world revolution, ready "to commit any crime, to lie, to cheat" to advance their cause. Citing what he called a "record of tyranny," Reagan denounced the Russians before the UN in 1982, claiming, "Soviet-sponsored guerrillas and terrorists are at work in Central and South America, in Africa, the Middle East, in the Caribbean and in Europe, violating human rights and unnerving the world with violence."

Given this view of Russia as "the focus of evil in the modern world," it is not surprising the new president continued the hard line that Carter had adopted after the invasion of Afghanistan. Abandoning détente, Reagan proceeded to implement a 1979 decision to place 572 Pershing II and cruise missiles in western Europe within range of Moscow and other Russian population centers to match Soviet deployment of medium-range missiles aimed at NATO countries. Despite strong protests from the Soviet Union, as well as growing uneasiness in Europe and an increasingly

Trouble Spots in the Middle East

Armed conflict and territorial attacks in this region intensified in the early and mid-1980s.

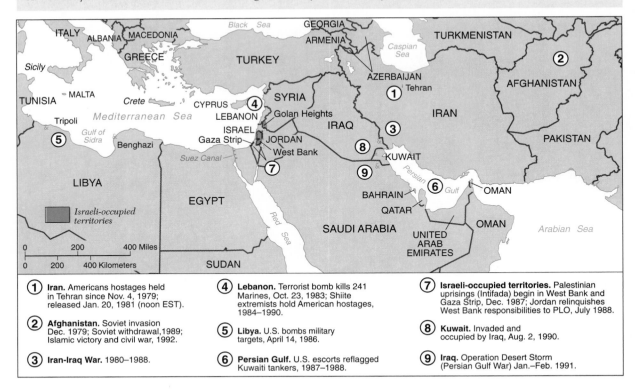

① Iran. Americans hostages held in Tehran since Nov. 4, 1979; released Jan. 20, 1981 (noon EST).

② Afghanistan. Soviet invasion Dec. 1979; Soviet withdrawal,1989; Islamic victory and civil war, 1992.

③ Iran-Iraq War. 1980–1988.

④ Lebanon. Terrorist bomb kills 241 Marines, Oct. 23, 1983; Shiite extremists hold American hostages, 1984–1990.

⑤ Libya. U.S. bombs military targets, April 14, 1986.

⑥ Persian Gulf. U.S. escorts reflagged Kuwaiti tankers, 1987–1988.

⑦ Israeli-occupied territories. Palestinian uprisings (Intifada) begin in West Bank and Gaza Strip, Dec. 1987; Jordan relinquishes West Bank responsibilities to PLO, July 1988.

⑧ Kuwait. Invaded and occupied by Iraq, Aug. 2, 1990.

⑨ Iraq. Operation Desert Storm (Persian Gulf War) Jan.–Feb. 1991.

The tragic consequence of Reagan's policy in Lebanon was the deaths of 239 marines, killed when a terrorist bomb blast destroyed their barracks. The marines, sent as part of a peace-keeping contingent, quickly became a vulnerable target in Lebanon's civil war.

vocal nuclear freeze movement at home, the United States began putting these weapons in bases in Great Britain and Germany in November 1983. The Soviets, claiming this move gave them only ten minutes of warning time in case of an American attack, responded by breaking off disarmament negotiations in Geneva.

The nuclear arms race had now reached a more dangerous level than ever before. The United States stepped up research and development of the Strategic Defense Initiative (SDI), an antimissile system based on the use of lasers and particle beams to destroy incoming missiles in outer space. SDI was quickly dubbed "star wars" by the media. Critics doubted that SDI could be perfected, but warned that even if it were, the result would be to escalate the arms race by forcing the Russians to build more offensive missiles in order to overcome the American defense system. The Reagan administration, however, defended "star wars" as a legitimate attempt to free the United States from the deadly trap of deterrence, with its reliance on the threat of

Military Power: United States vs. USSR, 1983–1984

	United States	Soviet Union
Intercontinental Ballistic Missiles (ICBMs)	1,045	1,398
Submarine-launched Ballistic Missiles (SLBMs)	568	980
Long-range Strategic Bombers	272	143
Total Delivery Vehicles (ICBMs, SLBMs, Bombers)	1,885	2,521
Nuclear Warheads (ICBMs and SLBMs)	7,297	8,342
Destructive Power (in millions of tons of TNT)	2,202	5,111
Anti-ballistic Missile Launchers (ABM)	0	32
Aircraft Carriers	14	5
Armed Forces Personnel	2,136,400	5,050,000
Related Forces		
NATO/French vs. Warsaw Pact Armed Forces	2,855,000	1,081,000
British/French SLBMs/IRBMs vs. USSR IRBMs/MRBMs	162	400

(IRBM = Intermediate-range Ballistic Missiles   MRBM = Medium-range Ballistic Missiles)

Source: *The Military Balance 1983–1984*, The International Institute for Strategic Studies, London, 1983.

nuclear retaliation to keep the peace. Meanwhile, the Soviet Union kept deploying larger and more accurate land-based ICBMs. Although both sides continued to observe the unratified SALT II agreements, the fact remained that between them the two superpowers had nearly fifty thousand warheads in their nuclear arsenals

Turmoil in the Middle East

Reagan tried to continue Carter's basic policy in the turbulent Middle East. In April 1982, the Israelis honored a Camp David pledge by making their final withdrawal from the Sinai. Reagan hoped to achieve the other Camp David objective of providing a homeland for the Palestinian Arabs on the West Bank, but Israel instead continued to extend Jewish settlements into this disputed area. The threat of the Palestine Liberation Organization (PLO), based in southern Lebanon and frequently raiding across the border into Israel, seemed to be the major obstacle to further progress.

On June 6, 1982, with tacit American encouragement, Israel's prime minister Menachem Begin began an invasion of southern Lebanon designed to secure Israel's northern border and destroy the PLO. The Reagan administration made no effort to halt this offensive, but did join with France and Italy in sending a multinational force to permit the PLO to evacuate to Tunisia. Unfortunately, the United States soon became enmeshed in the Lebanese civil war, raging since 1975. American marines, sent to Lebanon as part of the multinational force to restore order, were caught up in the renewed hostilities between Moslem and Christian militia. The Moslems perceived the marines as aiding the Christian-dominated government of Lebanon instead of acting as neutral peacekeepers, and began firing on the vulnerable American troops.

In the face of growing congressional demands for the withdrawal of the marines, Reagan declared they were there to protect Lebanon from the designs of Soviet-backed Syria. But finally, after terrorists drove a truck loaded with explosives into the American barracks, killing 239 marines, the president had no choice but to pull out. The last American unit left Beirut in late February 1984. Despite his good intentions, Reagan had experienced a humiliation similar to Carter's in Iran—one that left Lebanon in shambles and the Arab-Israeli situation worse than ever.

Confrontation in Central America

Reagan faced a difficult situation in Central America (see Chapter 31). In an area marked by great extremes of wealth, with a small landowning elite and a mass of peasants mired in dire poverty, the United States sought moderate middle-class regimes to support. Washington usually ended up backing repressive right-wing dictatorships rather than the more leftist groups who raised the radical issues of land reform and redistribution of wealth. Yet it was often oppression by U.S.-supported regimes that drove those seeking political change to embrace revolutionary tactics.

This is precisely what happened in Nicaragua, where the Sandinista coalition finally succeeded in overthrowing the repressive Somoza regime in 1979. In an effort to strengthen the many middle-class elements in the original Sandinista government and to avoid forcing Nicaragua into the Cuban and Soviet orbit, Carter extended American economic aid.

The Reagan administration quickly reversed this policy. Alexander Haig cut off all aid to Nicaragua in the spring of 1981, accusing the Sandinistas of driving out the moderates, welcoming Cuban advisers and Soviet military assistance, and serving as a supply base for leftist guerrillas in nearby El Salvador. The new policy became self-fulfilling, as Nicaragua became even more dependent on Cuba and the Soviet Union.

The United States and Nicaragua were soon on a collision course. In April 1983, declaring "the national security of all the Americas is at stake in Central America," President Reagan asked Congress for the money and authority to oust the Sandinistas. When Congress, fearful of repeating the Vietnam fiasco, refused, Reagan opted for covert action. The CIA began supplying the contras, exiles fighting against the Sandinistas from bases in Honduras and Costa Rica. The U.S.-backed rebels tried to disrupt the Nicaraguan economy, raiding villages, blowing up oil tanks, and even mining harbors. Then, in 1984, Congress passed the Boland Amendment prohibiting any U.S. agency from spending money in Central America. The withdrawal of U.S. financial backing left the contras in a precarious position.

The situation in El Salvador proved little better. There a guerrilla war had broken out in the 1970s between left-wing groups and a reactionary regime dominated by wealthy landowners. Reagan stepped up support for a government headed by middle-of-the-roader José Napoléon Duarte, ignoring charges that right-wing death squads had killed forty thousand civilians. Duarte was able to win a decisive election victory over the extreme right in 1984 and began modest reforms in an effort to undercut the appeal of the guerrillas.

The only clear-cut triumph that Reagan achieved in the hemisphere came in the Caribbean. In October 1983, a military coup led to the death of the leftist prime minister of Grenada, who was subsequently replaced by an even more radical regime. The Reagan administration, already upset by Grenada's close ties to Cuba and the construction of a large airfield on this small Caribbean island, decided to intervene to prevent the communists from acquiring a strategic military base.

Nearly two thousand U.S. marines invaded Grenada on October 25, 1983. After brief but spirited resistance from 800 Cuban workers and troops on the island, the American forces claimed a victory that cost 18 lives. The administration proudly displayed pictures of captured Soviet arms to justify the resort to force; American medical students, shown on television kissing the ground as they returned to the United States, enabled the administration to label the operation a "rescue mission."

Aside from Grenada, however, the Reagan administration had little to show for its massive military buildup. In the Middle East, its well-intentioned use of marines had ended in disaster; its determined opposition to left-wing groups in Central America had at best achieved a stalemate. Relations with the Soviet Union had fallen into one of the deepest chills of the entire Cold War with the nuclear arms race more intense than ever.

Trading Arms for Hostages

The Reagan administration's policies in the Middle East and Central America reached a tragic convergence in the Iran-contra affair. In mid-1985, Robert McFarlane, a retired marine officer

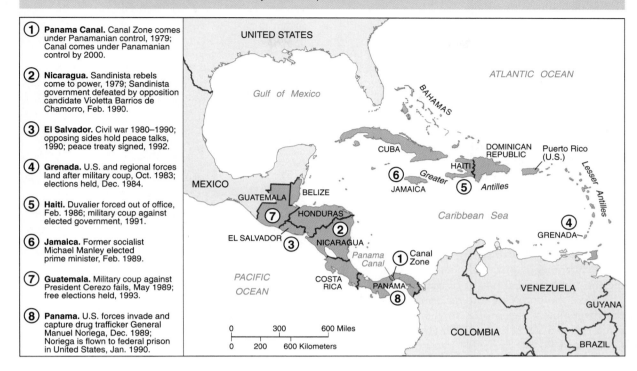

Trouble Spots in Central America and the Caribbean

U.S. involvement in Central American trouble spots intensified in the 1980s.

(1) Panama Canal. Canal Zone comes under Panamanian control, 1979; Canal comes under Panamanian control by 2000.

(2) Nicaragua. Sandinista rebels come to power, 1979; Sandinista government defeated by opposition candidate Violetta Barrios de Chamorro, Feb. 1990.

(3) El Salvador. Civil war 1980–1990; opposing sides hold peace talks, 1990; peace treaty signed, 1992.

(4) Grenada. U.S. and regional forces land after military coup, Oct. 1983; elections held, Dec. 1984.

(5) Haiti. Duvalier forced out of office, Feb. 1986; military coup against elected government, 1991.

(6) Jamaica. Former socialist Michael Manley elected prime minister, Feb. 1989.

(7) Guatemala. Military coup against President Cerezo fails, May 1989; free elections held, 1993.

(8) Panama. U.S. forces invade and capture drug trafficker General Manuel Noriega, Dec. 1989; Noriega is flown to federal prison in United States, Jan. 1990.

---

who had become national security adviser a year earlier, began a new initiative designed to restore American influence in the troubled Middle East. Concerned over the fate of six Americans held hostage in Lebanon by groups thought to be loyal to the Ayatollah Khomeini, McFarlane proposed trading American antitank missiles to Iran in return for the hostages' release. Although he realized the president was primarily concerned with the fate of the hostages, McFarlane's main goal in proposing the exchange was to establish good relations with moderate elements in Iran, anticipating the aged Khomeini's death. The Iranians, desperate for weapons in the war they had been waging against Iraq since 1980, seemed willing to comply.

McFarlane soon found himself in over his head. He relied heavily on a young marine lieutenant colonel assigned to the National Security Council (NSC), Oliver North, and North in turn sought the assistance of CIA director William Casey. A veteran of the Office of Strategic Services in World War II, Casey saw the Iran initiative as an opportunity to use the NSC to mount the kind of covert operation denied the CIA under the post-1975 congressional oversight policy. By early 1986, when John Poindexter, a naval officer with little political experience, replaced a burned-out McFarlane as national security adviser, Casey was able to persuade the president, over the strenuous objections of both Secretary of State Shultz and Secretary of Defense Weinberger, to go ahead with shipments of TOW antitank missiles and HAWK antiaircraft missiles to Iran.

The concept of trading arms for hostages was fatally flawed. Although one hostage had been released after an initial shipment of antitank missiles to Iran by way of Israel, the shipments of additional TOWs directly from the United States, as well as HAWKs, had led to the release of only two more hostages. Meanwhile, terrorist groups in Iran had seized several more Americans; by 1987, there were nine Americans being held hostage in Lebanon. As one observer commented, "As soon as Iran realized how highly we valued getting those hostages back, they apparently kept a good supply of hostages to ensure that we would do their bidding."

The arms deal with Iran was bad policy, but what came next was criminal. Ever since the Boland Amendment in late 1984 had cut off congressional funding, the Reagan administration had been searching for ways to supply the contras. Oliver North was put in charge of soliciting donations from wealthy right-wing Americans. In early 1986, North had what he later described as a "neat idea" (apparently shared by Casey as well)—he could use the enormous profits from the sale of weapons to Iran (charging as much as $10,000 for a TOW that cost the United States only $3,500) to finance the contra campaign in Nicaragua. Despite the appeal of using Khomeini's money to pay the contras and topple the Sandinistas, North's ploy was clearly not only illegal but unconstitutional, since it meant usurping the congressional power of the purse.

Unlike the policy of trading arms for hostages, the diversion of the profits to the contras was a closely held secret. Apparently only North, Casey, and Poindexter were aware of this illegal activity until November 1986, when the press finally learned of the Iranian arms sales. North then hurriedly destroyed most of the incriminating documents, but overlooked one key memo that revealed the contra diversion.

The political fallout was very heavy. The administration, having learned from the Watergate cover-up, tried to control the damage by breaking the bad news itself. Every effort was made to protect President Reagan; Attorney General Edwin Meese blamed Poindexter and North, who both were dropped from the NSC. Despite these efforts to spare the president's reputation, a CBS–New York Times poll taken in December 1986 revealed that Reagan's popularity had dropped from 67 percent to 46 percent in just a month, the steepest decline ever recorded.

The vital question of whether Ronald Reagan had approved of the contra diversion was never answered satisfactorily. Public opinion polls indicated that most Americans suspected the president was at least aware of the contra diversion. In the absence of firm evidence, however, they were willing to give Reagan the benefit of the doubt. A protracted congressional hearing in the summer of 1987 did little to clear up the confusion. Oliver

Despite Oliver North's questionable conduct, the public elevated him to near heroic status during the televised Iran–contra hearings. The bemedaled marine testified that he believed his deeds were justified as a defense of democracy.

North used his televised appearances to win public sympathy if not approval. Poindexter insisted under oath that he had never informed the president he and North had used the profits from arms sales to Iran to fund the contras in defiance of Congress. The only other man who knew what had actually happened was William Casey; his death from a brain tumor in mid-1987 left the mystery unsolved.

While Reagan escaped from the Iran-contra affair without being held fully responsible for it, his presidency was in serious trouble. In Congress, the Democrats, who gained control of the Senate as well as the House in the 1986 elections, began to override his vetoes, reject his nominees, and bring a total halt to even humanitarian aid to the contras, whose cause now became hopeless. Ronald Reagan was still in the White House, but his reliance on others to conduct the affairs of state had robbed him of his power to lead the nation.

Reagan the Peacemaker

By the end of 1987, the president had made a remarkable recovery. Stepping into the foreign affairs arena, Reagan, with strong pressure from his wife, shed his image as a hawk and set out to reverse the course of Soviet-American relations.

A momentous change in leadership in the Soviet Union proved fortunate. The illness and death of Brezhnev in 1982, followed in rapid succession by the deaths of his aged successors, Yuri Andropov and Konstantin Chernenko, led finally to the selection of Mikhail Gorbachev, a younger and more dynamic Soviet leader. Gorbachev was intent on improving relations with the United States as part of his new policy of *perestroika* (restructuring the Soviet economy) and *glasnost* (political openness). Soviet economic performance had been deteriorating steadily (Japan replaced the Soviet Union as the world's second largest producer of goods and services in the early 1980s), and the bloody war in Afghanistan, where the United States covertly supplied the Mujadeen guerrillas fighting against the Soviet invaders, had become a major liability. Gorbachev needed a breathing spell in the arms race and a reduction in Cold War tensions in order to carry out his sweeping changes at home.

The first meeting between Reagan and Gorbachev, at Geneva in 1985, went well, but did not lead to any significant agreements. A hurried summit at Reykjavik, Iceland, in October 1986, just before the Iran-contra affair had become public, nearly led to an historic breakthrough. The two men reached general agreement on the long disputed issue of Intermediate Nuclear Forces in Europe (INF). Only Soviet insistence that Reagan cancel "star wars" blocked agreement on an ambitious proposal to abolish all nuclear weapons within a decade.

The apparent failure at Reykjavik, however, did not halt the new momentum toward peace; both leaders needed a foreign policy triumph too much not to continue the dialogue. Throughout 1987, experts worked out the details of an INF agreement that promised to become the most significant achievement in disarmament since SALT I in 1972. Meeting in Washington in December 1987, Reagan and Gorbachev agreed to remove and destroy all intermediate-range missiles (approximately 3 percent of the total arsenal) and to permit on-site inspection to verify this process. Thus, not only did Reagan succeed where Carter had failed in ending the Russian deployment of sophisticated SS-20 missiles targeted at western

Reagan and Gorbachev in Red Square. During the summits between the two leaders, the American public grew to admire the Soviet premier for his policies of perestroika *(restructuring) and* glasnost *(openness).*

Europe, but he could claim his policy of building up America's defenses and talking tough to the Russians had paid off handsomely.

A fourth Reagan-Gorbachev summit in Moscow in mid-1988 did not achieve any further progress toward the goal of reducing the nuclear arsenals, but the pictures of Reagan and Gorbachev strolling amiably about Red Square in front of Lenin's tomb, saluting tourists and taking turns kissing babies, gave rise to the hope that an end to the Cold War was finally in sight.

When Reagan returned home, his popularity soared to 70 percent, higher than it had been before the Iran-contra affair. He had not only succeeded in making a major breakthrough in the nuclear arms race, but he could claim his policies had led to a moderation in Soviet behavior. During the president's last year in office, the

Soviets cooperated with the United States in pressuring Iran and Iraq to end their long war. Most impressive of all, Gorbachev moved to end the invasion of Afghanistan that had renewed the Cold War in 1979. The first Soviet units pulled out in April 1988, with the final evacuation due to be completed early the next year. By the time Reagan left office in January 1989, he had scored a series of foreign policy triumphs that offset his dismal Iran-contra fiasco and thus helped redeem his presidency.

PASSING THE TORCH

Reagan's triumphal reelection in 1984 raised Republican hopes they had achieved a major political realignment in 1980. The economic boom that had begun after the 1982 recession, along with the promise of the end of the Cold War, reinforced this trend and enabled George Bush to replace Ronald Reagan in the White House.

The Changing Palace Guard

Ronald Reagan had always been unusually dependent on aides and assistants. He saw his own role as one above the heat of bureaucratic battle—providing the nation with a set of goals and a vision of the future. As the great communicator, he would build the public consensus and let others manage the more mundane task of turning his dreams into reality.

His initial success depended heavily on the very effective White House team of James Baker, Edwin Meese, and Michael Deaver. Baker, a Texan with extensive Washington experience, became the chief of staff, managing the White House and directing legislative strategy. Shrewd and pragmatic, he outmaneuvered Californian Meese, who accepted the role of counselor to the president, advising Reagan on policy but having little to do with its implementation. Deaver, the final member of the trio, had the full confidence of Nancy Reagan and devoted himself to the goal of enhancing her husband's public image.

Ronald Reagan's laid-back style was misleading. Some thought he was little more than an actor playing the role of president, content to perform the ceremonial duties of a head of state while letting others run the country. Although it is true he preferred to be presented with solutions rather than problems, it was Reagan's personal commitment to cutting taxes, reducing domestic spending, and rebuilding America's defenses that gave shape and coherence to his administration's policies. In the Oval Office, he thrived on the interplay among Baker, Meese, and Deaver, letting them present various alternatives and then instinctively suggesting compromises. Neither brilliant nor well read, Reagan had a quick mind and a remarkable feel for the public's emotions that enabled him to perform effectively as a detached but charismatic chief executive.

An abrupt change in the White House staff in 1985 nearly proved disastrous for Reagan. Tired of the constant infighting, Baker agreed to Secretary of the Treasury Donald Regan's suggestion that the two men swap jobs. A self-made Wall Street operator, Regan possessed a confident, abrasive manner and a determination to assert his authority as White House chief of staff. When Meese became attorney general and Deaver left the government later in 1985, Regan extended his own control and thus ended the give-and-take in the Oval Office that had allowed Reagan to shape the final policy choices during his first term.

At first, Regan and Baker were able to score a major victory. Intent on lowering taxes on the wealthy still more while capitalizing on growing congressional demands for a simpler and fairer revenue system, the two men pressed for a major overhaul of the income tax. Making the necessary compromises with leaders in Congress, they shaped the 1986 Tax Reform Act, which cut the top rate from 50 to 28 percent while sharply reducing unproductive tax shelters. The new rates exempted six million people at the lower end from paying taxes while an alternative minimum tax prevented the rich from escaping their fair share. Although designed to bring in the same total revenue, the new act led to short-term increases in business taxes that kept the federal deficit from growing any larger.

The administration had only partial success in another area—appointing conservative federal judges who would simply follow the law and leave policy issues to Congress and state legislatures. Reagan was able to fill the appeals court with sympathetic judges, most of them wealthy white males. And in 1986, after a brief skirmish with the Senate, he succeeded in replacing outgoing Chief Justice Warren Burger with the Supreme Court's strongest conservative, William Rehnquist. Equally conservative appeals court judge Antonin Scalia joined the Supreme Court at the same time. But in 1987, when the president nominated Robert Bork, an outspoken opponent of judicial activism, to fill the next vacancy, Democrats drew the line. Opposition from labor and civil rights groups finally led the Senate to reject Bork's nomination by a vote of 58 to 42. It was a bittersweet victory, however, as Reagan responded by appointing the moderately conservative, but far more diplomatic, Anthony Kennedy to the Court.

The Bork defeat was especially hard on Attorney General Meese, who had been directing the administration's fight against judicial activism. But by then Meese himself had become an embarrassment to Reagan by symbolizing what came to be known as the "sleaze factor." Charges of loose financial dealings and unethical conduct in office led to the appointment of a special prosecutor. Although he found no evidence the attorney general had broken the law, the prosecutor admitted that some of Meese's dealings had the "appearance" of impropriety. The Meese affair, along with the conviction of Deaver for lying to Congress, Pentagon procurement scandals, and serious irregularities in the Department of Housing and Urban Development, left the Reagan administration with the appearance of tolerating corruption. Coupled with the far more serious Iran-contra affair, these scandals indicated that Reagan's habit of delegating authority to his subordinates had greatly weakened his presidency.

The Election of 1988

The Democrats approached the 1988 election with growing optimism. They had regained control of the Senate in 1986, Reagan no longer would be on the Republican ticket, and Iran-contra and the vast increase in the national debt since 1980 all appeared to place the GOP on the defensive. Michael Dukakis, the successful governor of Massachusetts, emerged from the grueling primary contests as the clear-cut winner. With the selection of moderate Texas senator Lloyd Bentsen as his vice presidential running mate,

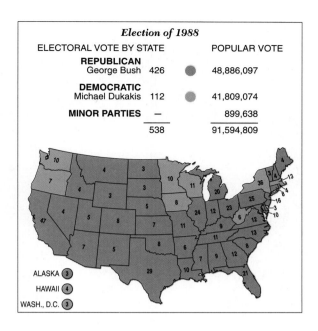

Dukakis left the convention at Atlanta confident of victory, with polls showing him ahead by 17 points.

The Republican nominee, Vice President George Bush, proved to be a much stronger candidate than anyone had expected. Despite the controversial choice of Indiana senator Dan Quayle as his running mate, Bush quickly regained the lead. The Republicans waged a ruthless attack on Dukakis, portraying him as soft on crime and defense. Across the country, viewers witnessed TV ads that accused the Massachusetts governor of furloughing dangerous criminals like Willie Horton from prison and opposing legislation requiring the Pledge of Allegiance in the schools. Above all, the GOP candidate repeatedly promised not to raise taxes, reiterating his favorite line: "Read my lips—no new taxes."

Dukakis fought back, gaining the edge over Bush in the first of two televised debates, but failing to close the narrow gap separating the two candidates in the polls. In the second debate in mid-October, Bush scored an impressive victory. In the last weeks, the vice president, with the South secure, concentrated on holding his slim leads in crucial states such as California and Ohio.

The outcome confirmed the pollsters' projections. Bush won overwhelmingly in the South, carried most of the West, and defeated Dukakis

Depositors scramble to retrieve their savings from a failing savings-and-loan (S&L) institution. During the booming economic times of the early 1980s, many S&Ls, taking advantage of relaxed regulations, used their depositors' funds to make loans on risky speculative ventures. When real estate values took a sharp downturn in 1987, the loans failed, threatening to wipe out the savings of thousands of depositors. Since the federal government, under the Federal Savings and Loan Insurance Corporation, guarantees deposits in S&Ls, the government had to make good its guarantees to individual depositors. Still, more than 500 S&Ls were forced to close, and the total cost of the S&L bailout is estimated at more than $500 billion.

in such key industrial states as Michigan and Pennsylvania. His victory reflected the continuing GOP dominance of the electoral college, as well as the natural advantage of an incumbent at a time when the economy was healthy and the world at relative peace. Yet Dukakis could take some comfort in blocking a Republican landslide that might have hurt the Democrats in Congress. Indeed, the voters seemed almost schizophrenic, choosing a Republican president but increasing the Democratic margins in both the House and Senate. Bush would be the first new president since John F. Kennedy to enter the White House while his party lost ground in Congress.

The election of 1988 indicated that, at least on the presidential level, a significant change had taken place in American politics in 1980. Bush consolidated the GOP's grip on the electoral college, winning in the Sunbelt states of the South and West. He held much of Reagan's inroads into the working-class vote, scoring 49 percent compared to Reagan's 55 percent among blue-collar voters. At the same time, racial polarization in politics continued, with Dukakis getting 88 percent of the African American vote and 69 percent

of the Hispanic ballots. The Democrats, despite their success in Congress, faced the challenge of trying to regain the support of white middle-class voters for their presidential candidates.

Defaults and Deficits

Many people expected the Bush administration to reflect the reputation of the new president—bland and cautious, lacking in vision but safely predictable. At home, he lived up to his reputation, sponsoring few initiatives in education, health care, and environmental protection while continuing the Reagan theme of limiting federal interference in the everyday lives of American citizens. He vetoed family leave legislation, refused to sponsor meaningful health-care reform, and watered down civil rights proposals in Congress. The one exception was the Americans with Disabilities Act (ADA), passed by Congress in 1991, which prohibited discrimination against the disabled in hiring, transportation, and public accommodations. Beginning in July 1992, ADA called for all public buildings, restaurants, and stores to be made accessible to those with physi-

Fed up with the corruption that accompanied the economic benefits of Chinese leader Deng Xiaoping's reforms, Chinese students demonstrated for democracy. Their nonviolent protest in Bejing's Tiananmen Square at first evoked a surprisingly passive government response. After a short time, however, military action was called for to break the students' resistance. Tanks, armored personnel carriers, and trucks cleared the square after firing randomly on the unarmed students.

cal handicaps and required that businesses with twenty-five or more workers hire new employees without regard to disability.

Most of Bush's time was taken up with two pressing domestic problems. First, the nation's savings-and-loan industry, based on U.S. government-insured deposits, was in grave trouble as a result of lax regulation and unwise, even possibly fraudulent, loan policies. After record losses of $13.4 billion in 1988, more than 250 savings and loans had been forced to close. The continuing budget deficit provided an even greater challenge. Despite Gramm-Rudman, the nation continued to spend beyond its means, with deficits still running over $150 billion a year.

The president and Congress finally reached agreement on both issues. In August 1989, Congress passed an administration bill to close or merge more than 700 ailing savings and loans at a cost of $157 billion over a ten-year period. Financial institutions would pay about two-thirds of the total, the federal government the remaining $50 billion. The proposal included a restructuring of the federal regulatory system and bond provisions to keep the thrift bailout from adding to the deficit. A new federal agency, the Resolution Trust Corporation, closed more than five hundred savings and loans, primarily in the Sunbelt states, and took over the properties on which developers had secured loans many times their

actual value and gradually sold them off at discount prices. By the time the Resolution Trust Corporation expired in 1992, the initial cost to the government was over $150 billion, and the eventual bill for the savings-and-loan cleanup, including interest, was estimated at between $500 and $700 billion.

Action on the budget proved even more difficult. Facing a Gramm-Rudman goal of $110 billion for the 1991 budget, Bush finally got Congress to accept a deficit of $105 billion in late 1989; accounting gimmicks and a surplus in the Social Security account disguised the true figure of nearly $200 billion. The following year, faced with a deficit of over $200 billion, George Bush finally agreed to break his no new taxes pledge and support a budget that included both new taxes on the wealthy along with substantial spending cuts, mainly for the military. The resulting agreement projected a savings of $500 billion over five years, half from reduced spending and half from new revenue generated by increasing the top tax rate from 28 percent to 31 percent; raising taxes on beer, wine, and cigarettes; imposing a new sales levy on luxury items like yachts, furs, jewelry, and expensive cars; and raising the gasoline tax by 5.1 cents a gallon.

Unfortunately for the president, the budget deal coincided with the beginning of a slow but painful recession that ended the Republican prosperity of the 1980s (see Chapter 33). Not only did Bush face recriminations from voters for breaking his "read my lips" pledge, but the economic decline led to greatly reduced government revenues. As a result, the deficit continued to soar, rising from $150 billion in fiscal year 1989 to just under $300 billion in 1992. Instead of reducing the deficit by $500 billion, the 1990 budget agreement had led to an increase of more than $1 trillion in the national debt during Bush's presidency.

The End of the Cold War

Abroad, the Bush administration faced an unprecedented year of change that appeared to mark the end of the post–World War II era. In country after country, communism gave way to freedom as the Cold War seemed to fade away more quickly than anyone had dared hope.

The first attempt at internal liberation proved tragically abortive. In May 1989, students in China began a month-long demonstration for freedom in Beijing's Tiananmen Square that attracted worldwide attention. Watching American television coverage of Gorbachev's visit to China in mid-May, Americans were fascinated to see the Chinese students call for democracy with a hunger strike and a handcrafted replica of the Statue of Liberty. But on the evening of June 4, the Chinese leaders sent tanks and troops to Tiananmen Square to crush the student demonstration. By the next day, full-scale repression swept over China; several hundred protesters were killed and thousands were injured. Chinese leaders imposed martial law to quell the dissent and shatter American hopes for a democratic China.

President Bush responded cautiously. While he did suspend sales of military equipment to China and stopped all government-to-government trade, he neither imposed stiffer sanctions nor engaged in harsh rhetoric. Bush wanted to preserve American influence with the Chinese government. Hence, despite official statements denouncing the crackdown, Bush permitted National Security Adviser Brent Scowcroft to undertake a secret mission to Beijing to maintain a working relationship with the Chinese leaders.

A far more promising trend toward freedom began in Europe in mid-1989. In June, Lech Walesa and his Solidarity movement came to power in free elections in Poland. Soon the winds of change were sweeping over the former Iron Curtain countries. A new regime in Hungary opened its borders to the West in September, allowing thousands of East German tourists in Hungary to flee to freedom. One by one, the repressive governments of East Germany, Czechoslovakia, Bulgaria, and Rumania fell. The most heartening scene of all took place in East Germany in early November when the new communist leaders suddenly announced the opening of the Berlin Wall. Workers quickly demolished a 12-foot-high section of this despised physical symbol of the Cold War, joyously singing a German version of "For He's a Jolly Good Fellow."

Most people realized it was Mikhail Gorbachev who was responsible for the liberation of eastern Europe. In late 1988, he signaled the spread of his reforms to the Soviet satellites by announcing the Brezhnev doctrine, which called for Soviet control of eastern Europe, was now replaced with "the Sinatra doctrine," which meant the people of this region could now do things "their way." It was Gorbachev's refusal to use armed force to keep repressive regimes in power that permitted the long-delayed liberation of the captive peoples of central and eastern Europe.

Yet by the end of 1991, both Gorbachev and the Soviet Union had become victims of the demise of communism. On August 19, 1991, eight right-wing plotters placed Gorbachev under arrest while he was vacationing in the Crimea and attempted to seize control of the government in Moscow. Boris Yeltsin, the newly elected president of the Russian Republic, however, broke up the coup by mounting a tank in Moscow and demanding Gorbachev's release. The Red Army rallied to Yeltsin's side. The coup failed and Gorbachev was released, only to resign in December 1991 after the fifteen republics dissolved the Soviet Union. Russia, by far the largest and most powerful of the former Soviet republics, took the lead in joining with ten others to form a loose alignment called the Commonwealth of Independent States (CIS). Yeltsin then disbanded the Communist party and continued the reforms begun by Gorbachev to establish democracy and a free-market system in Russia. The Bush admin-

The End of the Cold War

Free elections in Poland in June 1989 triggered the domino effect in the fall of communism in Eastern Europe and the former Soviet Union. Changes in policy have come quickly, but it is already apparent that the restructuring of social and economic institutions will take much longer.

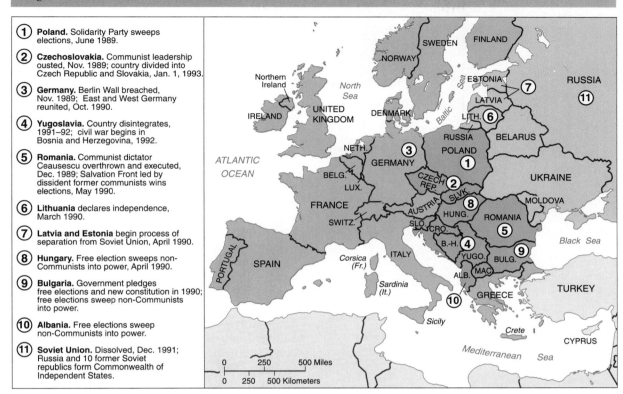

① Poland. Solidarity Party sweeps elections, June 1989.

② Czechoslovakia. Communist leadership ousted, Nov. 1989; country divided into Czech Republic and Slovakia, Jan. 1, 1993.

③ Germany. Berlin Wall breached, Nov. 1989; East and West Germany reunited, Oct. 1990.

④ Yugoslavia. Country disintegrates, 1991–92; civil war begins in Bosnia and Herzegovina, 1992.

⑤ Romania. Communist dictator Ceausescu overthrown and executed, Dec. 1989; Salvation Front led by dissident former communists wins elections, May 1990.

⑥ Lithuania declares independence, March 1990.

⑦ Latvia and Estonia begin process of separation from Soviet Union, April 1990.

⑧ Hungary. Free election sweeps non-Communists into power, April 1990.

⑨ Bulgaria. Government pledges free elections and new constitution in 1990; free elections sweep non-Communists into power.

⑩ Albania. Free elections sweep non-Communists into power.

⑪ Soviet Union. Dissolved, Dec. 1991; Russia and 10 former Soviet republics form Commonwealth of Independent States.

istration, although criticized for its cautious approach, welcomed the demise of communism and offered economic assistance to Russia and the other members of the new CIS. The most important steps came in the critical area of nuclear weapons. In 1991, Bush and Gorbachev signed START I, agreeing to reduce nuclear warheads to under 10,000 apiece; in late 1992, Bush and Yeltsin agreed on the terms of START II, which would eliminate land missiles with multiple warheads and reduce the number of nuclear weapons on each side to just over 3,000, a level not seen since the mid-1960s. Although several of the republics, notably the Ukraine, had not yet agreed even to START I, Bush could claim that by the time he left office in January 1993, the Cold War was over and the nuclear threat sharply reduced.

Waging Peace

The end of the Cold War, however, did not bring about a world free of violence. In December 1989, 27,000 American troops invaded Panama and quickly installed a new government friendly to the United States in the largest American military operation since the Vietnam War. Despite the death of twenty-three Americans and several hundred Panamanians, this action won approval from the people of both countries when it resulted in the capture of drug trafficking General Manuel Noriega. By taking such bold and decisive action in Panama, Bush was able to shake his reputation for caution. But critics noted that the president, in the best tradition of the Cold War, had waged war without consulting Congress.

Eight months later, Bush suddenly faced a much graver challenge. On August 2, 1990,

A crowd in Vilnius, the capital of Lithuania, holds lighted candles to mark Lithuanian independence. Lithuania's declaration of independence in February 1991 signaled the beginning of the break-up of the Soviet Union.

Saddam Hussein, the dictatorial ruler of Iraq, stunned the world by invading defenseless Kuwait and threatening Saudi Arabia and the oil-rich Persian Gulf region. The president responded firmly, despite an earlier balance-of-power policy of supporting Iraq against Iran. He accused Saddam of naked aggression and carefully built up a UN coalition to uphold what he termed "a new world order." Equally important, he quickly persuaded Saudi Arabia to accept a huge American troop buildup, dubbed Desert Shield. Some skeptics questioned the meaning of the "new world order," but few could quarrel with the strategic need to prevent the bulk of the world's oil reserves from falling under the control of Saddam Hussein. With the United States once again importing nearly half the oil used each day by the American people, control of the Persian Gulf was clearly a vital national interest.

Debate raged, however, on the best way to meet the Iraqi threat. Many Democrats in Congress supported Bush's efforts to place international economic sanctions on Iraq but opposed the use of force. Bush had clearly opted for a different solution by November, massing far more troops in the Persian Gulf area than were needed to defend Saudi Arabia—Operation Desert Shield was giving way to Desert Storm. After securing UN support and, heeding the criticism over the Panama invasion, winning a close vote in Congress, on January 17, 1991, Bush unleashed a devastating aerial assault on Iraq. The overwhelming American advantage in modern weaponry softened up Saddam's forces; when the ground offensive began on February 24, it took only a hundred hours to bring about the collapse of Iraq's highly overrated military forces.

Desert Storm brought mixed blessings. It was a great personal victory for George Bush, who saw his approval rating climb to an unprecedented level—nearly 90 percent, higher than even Eisenhower and Kennedy at the height of the Cold War. American military leaders felt they had finally atoned for Vietnam, a sentiment widely shared by a euphoric public. Best of all, the price of gasoline, which had climbed to a record $1.34 a gallon in October, fell back to just over $1 a gallon, enabling Americans to continue their love affair with the automobile. At the same time, however, Saddam Hussein continued to rule in Baghdad, persecuting Kurds in northern Iraq and Shi'ite Muslims in the south. Most alarming of all, the Persian Gulf War had halted a slow recovery from the lingering recession and revived growing fears for America's economic health in the post–Cold War years.

DEMOCRATIC RESURGENCE

Back in the 1940s, political historian Arthur M. Schlesinger, Sr., put forward a theory of American political cycles that proved to be remarkably accurate. Noting that periods of reform were followed by eras of conservative consolidation, Schlesinger saw a new burst of activism occurring in the 1960s that would give way to a conservative era by the 1980s. The next wave of liberal activism, he suggested, would come in the 1990s. Recent developments confirm Schlesinger's cyclical theory about the underlying rhythm of American politics.

Antiaircraft fire lights up the sky over Baghdad during the Persian Gulf war. A month of air strikes on Iraqi targets was followed by a ground offensive that lasted only 100 hours before the Iraqi troops began to surrender and President Bush declared a cease-fire.

The Election of 1992

The persistence of the recession that had begun two years earlier became the dominant political reality of 1992. As unemployment rose from 5.2 percent in 1988 to over 7 percent in mid-1992, Bush's popularity plummeted. At the same time, a decline in tax revenues due to the sluggish economy, coupled with the unexpectedly high cost of the savings-and-loan bailout, added nearly $400 billion more to the national debt, which rose to over $3 trillion. Economists warned that the interest payments on the debt, already nearly $300 billion a year, would become the largest single budget expenditure by the end of the 1990s, thereby threatening the nation's economic future.

Two men sought to capitalize on this bleak outlook. First, Arkansas governor Bill Clinton defeated a field of five other challengers for the Democratic nomination by becoming the champion of economic renewal. Forgoing traditional liberal appeals to interest groups, Clinton stressed the need for investment in the nation's future—rebuilding roads and bridges, training workers for high-tech jobs, and solving the growing national health-care crisis. One key statistic gave his message a vital appeal—in 1991, worker's wages failed to keep pace with inflation. The average family income declined by 1.9 percent, the worst economic performance since 1980.

Despite his victories in the Democratic primaries, however, Clinton faced a new rival in H. Ross Perot. An eccentric Texas billionaire, Perot singled out the deficit as the nation's gravest problem and agreed to run as an independent candidate in response to a grass-roots movement (which he financed) to place his name on the fall ballot. As a businessman, Perot made sense to millions of Americans when he charged that during the Reagan–Bush era the Washington politicians had given the country $11.4 trillion worth of programs and services while raising only $9.3 trillion in taxes. Voters got 23 percent more government than they paid for, at a hidden cost to future generations.

When Clinton succeeded in unifying the Democratic party and gaining agreement on a moderate platform promising economic change, Perot stunned his supporters by suddenly dropping out of the race in July. Clinton immediately became the front-runner, rising from 30 percent to over 50 percent in the polls, leaving Bush far

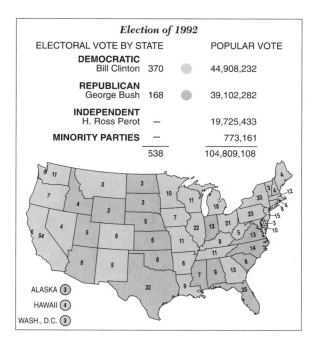

Election of 1992		
ELECTORAL VOTE BY STATE		POPULAR VOTE
DEMOCRATIC		
Bill Clinton	370	44,908,232
REPUBLICAN		
George Bush	168	39,102,282
INDEPENDENT		
H. Ross Perot	—	19,725,433
MINORITY PARTIES	—	773,161
	538	104,809,108

ALASKA ③
HAWAII ④
WASH., D.C. ③

Three Mile Island and Chernobyl
The Promise and Peril of Nuclear Power

Workers at the Three Mile Island nuclear power plant wear protective gear in an effort to guard against exposure to radiation. This photo was taken in 1989, ten years after the accident at the nuclear plant brought to light the risks and unsolved problems associated with reliance on nuclear power.

In March 1979, it appeared to the world that its worst nightmares about nuclear power might come true when a near meltdown occurred at a nuclear power plant outside of Harrisburg, Pennsylvania. An accident of even greater proportions, the explosion of a reactor in the Soviet Ukraine on April 26, 1986, stirred their fears again. Three Mile Island and Chernobyl became household words that cast doubt on the viability of nuclear power.

In the 1960s, the United States and other industrialized nations had turned to nuclear power to fulfill the need for clean, inexpensive, and renewable energy free of foreign control. By 1979, there were seventy-two power plants operating in the United States, and they generated 12.5 percent of the nation's electricity. Another ninety-two plants were under construction, and thirty more were in the planning stage. The Soviet Union had also embarked on a nuclear program. By 1984, Russia had built forty-three plants that supplied 10 percent of that country's electrical needs. Advocates insisted that nuclear power plants posed no serious danger to public health, and in both countries the industry expected to play an ever larger part in meeting the growing demand for electricity.

The accident at Three Mile Island (TMI) caught the American people by surprise and touched off a strong reaction against reliance on nuclear power. Early reports on the meltdown were sketchy. It was not clear what exactly had gone wrong, except that one unit of the TMI facility had released some radioactivity into the environment. State officials and company representatives assured the anxious public that radiation levels outside were not—repeat, not—dangerous.

Inside TMI, the water system used to cool the reactor core had broken down, and company employees, scientists, and industry experts fought to get the cooling water moving again. And even though the chain reaction inside the reactor had stopped, the radioactive materials within continued to release tremendous quantities of heat—about 6 percent of normal reactor power.

By Friday, the crisis had become intense. Radiation readings outside the plant had risen (but were not yet dangerous). Governor Richard Thornburgh advised that those most susceptible to radiation, namely pregnant women and preschool-age children living within a 5-mile radius of TMI, ought to leave. Taking no chances, more than forty thousand people streamed out of the area that afternoon and evening. The main news of the day, however, was an announcement that a hydrogen bubble had formed above the reactor core, and that as long as it was present, there existed the possibility of the ultimate catastrophe—a meltdown. The danger was real, but remote; press reports, however, were alarmist, and a cloud of fear, confusion, and uncertainty enveloped the nation.

Over the weekend, while teams of experts worked to bring the reactor under control, news reports questioned whether the hydrogen bubble was explosive. On Sunday afternoon, President Jimmy Carter paid a visit to the site in an effort to calm the public. By Monday, the bubble had shrunk dramatically, and by Tuesday, the immediate danger had passed. The crisis was contained; a meltdown did not occur, and the radiation released posed a minimal health risk.

Soviet citizens living near the Chernobyl nuclear power station were not as lucky. The Chernobyl plant housed four reactors. On April 26, 1986, while conducting a safety test in Unit IV, plant personnel violated regulations, removing all of the control rods from the reactor core. The core temperature shot up, triggering an uncontrolled nuclear reaction and steam buildup. At 1:23 A.M., the reactor exploded, destroying the concrete shield above it and causing approximately thirty fires in the immediate vicinity.

Over the course of the next ten days, Soviet officials worked to cool off the damaged core. In the meantime, the damaged reactor spewed a radioactive cloud of dust into the air—a plume that eventually spread over the Ukraine, Scandinavia, and much of central and eastern Europe.

Estimating the human cost of the Chernobyl disaster is difficult even today. The Kremlin reported that 237 persons were hospitalized for significant radiation exposure and thirty-one died in the immediate aftermath of the accident. In 1990, however, a Moscow newspaper claimed that at least 250 people had died during the accident or the subsequent rescue and cleanup operations. A more important—and controversial—question is the number of individuals who will ultimately die of cancer or various defects as a consequence of Chernobyl. According to a report by the U.S. Nuclear Regulatory Commission, the risk of cancer for those living within 20 miles of the plant is high. Dr. Robert Peter Gale, an American physician invited by the Soviets to help treat the first victims, estimates that over the next fifty years, fifty thousand lives may be lost due to cancer contracted in the wake of Chernobyl.

The two crises affected the American and Soviet nuclear power industries in strikingly similar ways. Both the American and Soviet governments stepped up their regulation of nuclear facilities rather than totally abandoning their programs. By the end of the 1980s, nuclear power plants still generated over 17 percent of America's electricity and 11 percent of the Soviet Union's.

Although nuclear power remains an important energy source in both countries, it has also lost much of its luster. In the United States, every nuclear reactor order since 1974 has either been canceled or postponed indefinitely. The Soviet Union has likewise

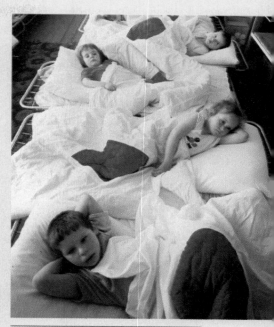

Children hospitalized for radiation sickness following the Chernobyl explosion.

scrapped some of its plans to build new stations. And in both countries, TMI and Chernobyl have left a legacy of fear that has eroded popular support for nuclear power.

Nuclear power has not, in all likelihood, been permanently discredited. Consumption of electricity in the United States has risen by one-third since the 1973 Arab oil embargo, and it promises to rise in the future. Except in certain regions where hydroelectric power, natural gas, and possibly solar energy are readily available, Americans will have to choose between coal, oil, and nuclear power. Growing environmental concern over acid rain and global warming tend to weigh against the burning of fossil fuels. In this context, the nuclear alternative may regain some of the credibility it has lost as a consequence of TMI and Chernobyl.

The candidates—Republican President George Bush, independent H. Ross Perot, and Democrat Bill Clinton—brought the issues in the 1992 presidential election to the American public in a series of three televised debates. Clinton won the election with a campaign that focused on domestic issues, including reform of the health care system and revitalization of the economy.

behind. With unemployment continuing unabated and the economy faltering even after the Federal Reserve Board dropped the interest rate to the lowest level since the 1960s, the American people turned their backs on George Bush and the Reagan revolution.

A relentless Democratic attack on the administration's lackluster economic performance overcame all the president's efforts to remind the nation of Reagan prosperity and Bush triumphs abroad. Even GOP assaults on Clinton's character, notably his evasion of the draft during the Vietnam War, failed to halt the Democratic momentum. The message that Clinton's political advisers tacked up at the Democratic candidate's headquarters in Little Rock, "THE ECONOMY, STUPID," provided the key to victory in November. Clinton wound up with 43 percent of the popular vote but with a commanding lead in the electoral college, 370 to 168 for Bush. Perot won 19 percent of the popular vote but failed to carry a single state.

For political scientists, 1992 was a clear case of a negative referendum. Voters had rejected the Reagan–Bush programs decisively. Troubled both by the frightening deficit and the sluggish economy, they had chosen Clinton's program of economic renewal over Perot's call for short-term sacrifice to achieve long-term prosperity. Clinton maintained the Democratic grip on ethnic minorities, winning 83 percent support from African Americans and 62 percent from Hispanics, gained back both the elderly and the blue-collar Reagan Democrats, and cut deeply into the crucial middle class by doing better than Bush among those earning between $30,000 and $75,000 a year.

Most important, Clinton had broken the GOP's grip on the South and West—only Texas and the interior western states had remained Republican strongholds. When the boom of the 1980s collapsed, the Sunbelt states proved to be as receptive as the rest of the nation to the call for change. Yet while there was no doubt about the rejection of Bush, there remained a question of precisely what change the electorate wanted most—responsible budgetary policies to reduce the deficit or federal spending programs to achieve jobs and economic growth.

Recommended Reading

The most detailed account of the Reagan presidency is the second volume of journalist Lou Cannon's biography, *President Reagan* (1991). Robert Schieffer and Gary Paul Gates offer a critical overview of the Reagan administration in *The Acting President* (1989), which focuses on Reagan's detached style of leadership.

The most revealing accounts by insiders are Martin Anderson, *Revolution* (1988), one of the few to give a positive view of the Reagan presidency, and George

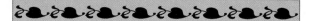

CHRONOLOGY

1980 Ronald Reagan wins presidency in landslide

1981 American hostages in Iran released after 444 days in captivity (January) • Sandra Day O'Connor becomes first woman U.S. Supreme Court justice (September)

1982 Equal Rights Amendment fails state ratification (June) • Unemployment reaches postwar record high of 10.4 percent (October)

1983 Soviets shoot down Korean airliner (September) • U.S. invades Grenada (October)

1984 Russia boycotts summer Olympics in Los Angeles (July) • Ronald Reagan reelected president (November)

1985 Mikhail Gorbachev becomes leader of the Soviet Union (March)

1986 Space shuttle *Challenger* explodes killing seven astronauts (January) • Iran-contra affair made public (November)

1987 Reagan and Gorbachev sign INF treaty at Washington summit

1988 George Bush defeats Michael Dukakis decisively in presidential election

1989 *Exxon Valdez* oil spill pollutes over 500 square miles of Alaskan waters (March) • San Francisco rocked by massive earthquake (October) • Berlin Wall crumbles (November)

1990 Bush breaks "no new taxes" campaign pledge (June) • Saddam Hussein invades Kuwait (August)

1991 Operation Desert Storm frees Kuwait and crushes Iraq (January–February) • Carl Lewis sets new world record for 100-meter dash at World Track and Field Championships (August)

1992 Hurricane Andrew devastates southern Florida (August) • Clinton defeats Bush and Perot (November)

1993 Terrorists bomb World Trade Center in New York City (February)

Shultz, *Turmoil and Triumph* (1992), the complete treatment of Reagan's foreign policy.

Additional Bibliography

Theodore White offers a stimulating account of the political changes in the 1970s that led to Reagan's election to the presidency in *America in Search of Itself* (1982). Books on the 1980 election include Elizabeth Drew, *Portrait of an Election* (1981); Jack W. Germond and Jules Witcover, *Blue Smoke and Mirrors* (1981); and Thomas Ferguson and Joel Rogers, eds., *The Hidden Election of 1980* (1981). For the conservative resurgence see Peter Steinfels, *The Neo-Conservatives* (1979); Sidney Blumenthal, *The Rise of the Counter-Establishment* (1986), a critical account; and F. Clifton White and William Gil, *Why Reagan Won: The Conservative Movement, 1964–1981* (1982), a more sympathetic view. In books with the same title, *October Surprise,* Barbara Honegger (1989) and Gary Sick (1992) argue the Republicans conspired with the Iranians to prevent the release of the hostages at the height of the campaign.

For Reagan's prepresidential years, see the first volume of Lou Cannon's biography, *Reagan* (1982), and Garry Wills, *Reagan's America* (1987), a more provocative analysis. For other interpretive accounts, see Robert Dallek, *Ronald Reagan* (1984), and Michael Paul Rogin, *Ronald Reagan: The Movie* (1987). Reagan stresses the highlights of his career in *An American Life* (1990).

Michael Schaller, *Reckoning with Reagan* (1992), and Haynes Johnson, *Sleepwalking Through History* (1991), offer critical overviews of the Reagan administration. The best account of Reagan's early success in cutting taxes and domestic spending is Lawrence Barrett, *Gambling with History* (1983); Walt Williams offers a critique of Reagan's style of governing in *Mismanaging America* (1991). C. Brandt Short traces the conservation debate in *Ronald Reagan and the Public Lands* (1989).

A full account of the 1984 election is Peter Goldman and Tony Fuller, *The Quest for the Presidency 1984* (1985), but see also Elizabeth Drew, *Campaign Journal* (1985); Jack W. Germond and Jules Witcover, *Wake Us When It's Over* (1985); and Geraldine Ferraro, *My Story* (1985). Thomas Ferguson and Joel Rogers analyze the political realignment of the 1980s in *Right Turn* (1985).

Memoirs by White House staffers, many containing revelations embarrassing to the administration, include David Stockman, *The Triumph of Politics* (1986), critical of Reaganomics; Michael Deaver, *Behind the Scenes* (1987); Larry Speakes, *Speaking Out* (1988); and Donald Regan, *For the Record* (1988), a particularly vengeful account by the former White House chief of staff. Insider accounts more supportive of the Reagan presidency include Peggy Noonan, *What I Saw at the Revolution* (1990), by the president's favorite speechwriter; Terrell Bell, *The Thirteenth Man* (1988), by Reagan's first secretary of education; and Edwin Meese, *With Reagan* (1992), the attorney general's stout defense of the administration. Nancy Reagan replied to her detractors, primarily Donald Reagan, in *My Turn* (1989).

William G. Hyland provides an overview of American diplomacy in the 1980s in *The Reagan Foreign Policy* (1987) as does Coral Bell in *The Reagan Paradox* (1990). Reagan's first secretary of state, Alexander M. Haig, Jr., gives his views in *Caveat* (1984). On Central America, see the essays edited by Kenneth M. Coleman and George C. Herring, *The Central American Crisis* (1985), and Thomas Carrothers, *In the Name of Democracy* (1990). The best accounts of the increases in defense spending in the 1980s are Daniel Wirls, *Buildup* (1992), and the memoir of Secretary of Defense Caspar Weinberger, *Fighting for Peace* (1990). Paul B. Stares traces the development of the Strategic Defense Initiative in *Space and National Security* (1987). The best studies of arms control in the 1980s are two books by Strobe Talbott, *Deadly Gambits* (1984), on the failure of Reagan's early efforts, and *The Master of the Game* (1988), on the role of Paul Nitze.

Full accounts of the Iran-contra affair are Jane Mayer and Doyle McManus, *Landslide* (1988), and Theodore Draper, *A Very Thin Line* (1991). For views of insiders, see *Perilous Statecraft* (1988) by Michael A. Ledeen, one of the original conspirators; *Men of Zeal* (1988) by William S. Cohen and George J. Mitchell, the two Maine senators who served on the congressional investigating committee; and *Under Fire* (1991) by Oliver North. Bob Woodward traces CIA director William Casey's role in the Iran-contra affair, as well as other covert activities of the 1980s, in *Veil* (1987).

Don Oberdorfer offers a factual account of the startling shift in Soviet-American relations during the late 1980s in *The Turn: From the Cold War to the New Era* (1991). For developments in the early 1990s, see Michael Beschloss and Strobe Talbott, *At the Highest Levels* (1993), which focuses on exchanges between Bush and Gorbachev. The many books of commentary on this topic include John Lewis Gaddis, *The End of the Cold War* (1992); Michael Hogan, ed., *The End of the Cold War* (1992); Richard M. Nixon, *Seize the Moment* (1992); and Ted G. Carpenter, *A Search for Enemies* (1992).

For the election of 1988, see Jack W. Germond and Jules Witcover, *Whose Broad Stripes and Bright Stars?* (1989); Sidney Blumenthal, *Pledging Allegiance* (1990); and Richard Ben Cramer, *Whatever It Takes* (1992), the most detailed account. Fitzhugh Green offers a sympathetic view in his biography, *George Bush* (1989). The best account of the first two years of the Bush administration can be found in the essays edited by Colin Campbell and Bert Rockman, *The Bush Presidency: First Appraisals* (1991).

There is a large and growing literature on the Persian Gulf War. Bob Woodward traces the decisions leading to war in *The Commanders* (1991). On military operations, full accounts are Norman Friedman, *Desert Victory* (1991); James F. Dunnigan and Austin Bay, *From Shield to Storm* (1992); Lawrence Freedman and Efraim Karsh, *The Gulf Conflict, 1990–1991* (1992); and H. Norman Schwarzkopf, *It Doesn't Take a Hero* (1993). Authors who focus more broadly on the diplomatic and strategic implications and who are more critical of American policy include Roger Hilsman, *George Bush vs. Saddam Hussein* (1992); Jean Edward Smith, *George Bush's War* (1992); and Stephen Graubard, *Mr. Bush's War* (1992).

LAW & SOCIETY IV

Bakke v. Regents of the University of California

The Question of Affirmative Action

In June 1974, an attorney for NASA engineer and Vietnam veteran Allan Bakke filed a complaint against the University of California. Bakke could not have realized he was beginning a legal battle that would last four years and end in the U.S. Supreme Court. His case would capture the attention of the nation and raise concerns about the direction of civil rights in America. In his lawsuit, Bakke claimed to be a victim of racial discrimination. His case attracted so much attention because Allan Bakke was white.

The civil rights victories of the early 1960s had benefited minorities in many ways, but economic progress was not one of them. Most minority Americans continued to live in poverty. In 1965, President Lyndon Johnson heralded the "next and the more profound stage of the battle for civil rights," as he called for efforts to improve the economic status of minorities. "We seek not just freedom but opportunity," LBJ declared. Polls showed that most Americans approved of financial aid and job training programs that assisted minorities in competing equally for educational opportunities and employment. However, Americans did not approve of programs that set quotas guaranteeing minorities a certain percentage of jobs. As the economy began to stagnate in the early 1970s and competition for work and school admissions became more fierce, many white Americans came to believe "affirmative action" programs gave opportunities to unqualified minorities at the expense of more deserving whites. The Bakke case would make this concern the subject of a national debate to be decided in the courts.

The School of Medicine at the University of California at Davis had voluntarily created a special admissions program in 1969. The university reserved sixteen of the hundred entering class seats for students accepted under an alternative admissions program known as the Task Force. A separate admissions committee composed of faculty and minority students reviewed the applications of students who claimed to have come from "educationally and economically disadvantaged backgrounds." Bakke learned about the Task Force program after the university rejected his application for the 1973 school year. He discovered that several students admitted through Task Force had lower grade point averages and Medical College Aptitude Test scores than he did. Bakke also learned no white student had ever been accepted through the alternative admissions program. When the university rejected his application for the 1974 school year, Bakke, claiming he had been denied the opportunity to compete for sixteen of the hundred seats solely because he was white, initiated his lawsuit accusing the university of racial discrimination.

Bakke v. *Regents of the University of California* was first heard in court on September 27, 1974, in the Superior Court in Yolo County, California. Judge F. Leslie Manker presided over a nearly empty courtroom; no one at the time realized Bakke's case would become nationally famous. Bakke's attorney, Reynold Colvin, contended the Task Force program was in fact a racial quota system. Bakke had been prevented from competing for one of the sixteen seats solely because of his race, a violation of the Equal Protection Clause of the Fourteenth Amendment, which guarantees that "no state shall deny to any person within its jurisdiction the equal protection under the laws." Colvin argued that if "the Constitution prohibits exclusion of blacks and other minorities on racial grounds it cannot per-

Supporters of affirmative action protested the decision of the U.S. Supreme Court in the Bakke *case. The Court ruled against the use of racial quota systems to achieve racial balance. However, the Court did uphold the principle of affirmative action by ruling that race could be one of several factors used in making hiring or admissions decisions.*

mit the exclusion of whites on racial grounds. For it must be the exclusion on racial grounds that offends the Constitution and not the particular skin color of the person excluded." Colvin asked the judge to issue an order directing the university to admit Bakke immediately.

The university not only argued against Bakke's admission, it asked the judge to declare the special admissions program to be lawful. University officials and attorneys argued that the Task Force program, far from violating the Equal Protection Clause, ensured that minorities would have an equal opportunity to attend medical school—without the Task Force program, the student body would be overwhelmingly white. The attorneys maintained that the university had a "compelling interest" in promoting diversity in the student body and the medical profession. Minority physicians would bring new viewpoints to the

medical community. They would serve as role models to minority children. They would be more likely to return to disadvantaged neighborhoods, which typically suffered from a dearth of physicians. The admission of minorities through the Task Force thus benefited not only the students but society as a whole.

The decision Judge Manker issued on November 22, 1974, pleased no one. He found that since no whites had been admitted under Task Force, it was in fact a racial quota system. No matter how beneficial its operation was to society, the program was racially discriminatory and therefore illegal:

This Court cannot conclude that there is any compelling or even legitimate public purpose to be served in granting preference to minority students in admission to the medical school when to do so denies white persons an equal opportunity for admittance. Accordingly, the Court holds in this case that the special admissions program at the Davis Medical School as the same in operation at the time of plaintiff's rejection as an applicant to the school and as the school intends to continue it is violative of the Equal Protection Clause of the Fourteenth Amendment of the United States Constitution.

Much to Bakke's dismay, however, the judge did not order the university to admit him. Judge Manker declared that Bakke had not proven he would have been admitted if the Task Force did not exist. Other students with higher scores than Bakke had been denied admission, and one of those students, not Allan Bakke, might have been accepted.

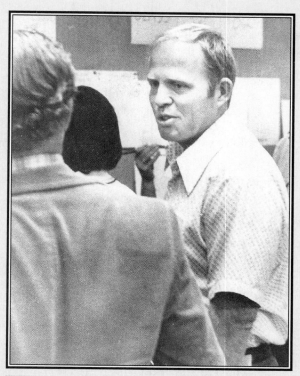

Allan Bakke finally won admission to the medical school at the University of California at Davis. Here, he chats with fellow students after his first day of class on September 26, 1978.

Justice Lewis F. Powell, Jr., wrote the deciding opinion in the Bakke case. He argued that both the Fourteenth Amendment to the U.S. Constitution and Title VI of the Civil Rights Act of 1964 allowed schools to use race as one criterion in their admissions decisions. The UC-Davis Task Force was invalid, however, because it used race as the sole factor in determining admissions.

Dissatisfied with Judge Manker's ruling, both sides appealed. The California Supreme Court accepted the case on the grounds that it was "of great and pressing state-wide importance." The case began attracting national attention. Civil rights groups, which had been confident the university would win in the trial court, now worried about the impact of an adverse decision on affirmative action programs. Nine organizations filed briefs with the court presenting their opinions on the case. The courtroom was crowded on March 18, 1976, when the justices heard oral arguments. Aware of the California Supreme Court's reputation as the most progressive court in the country, supporters of the university's program hoped for a favorable decision.

The court surprised civil rights groups with its ruling on September 16, 1976. By a 6 to 1 vote the court ruled the admissions program was illegal because it violated the equal protection clause—race could never be the determining factor in the admissions process. The university could fulfill its "compelling interest" of providing opportunities for minorities through nondiscriminatory methods such as remedial schooling programs or expanded admissions. In addition, the court ordered Bakke's admission to the medical school because the university could not prove he would have been rejected if the Task Force program had not existed:

> [S]ince Bakke successfully demonstrated that the University had unconstitutionally discriminated against him, the burden of proof shifted to the University to establish that he would not have been admitted to the 1973 or 1974 entering class without the invalid preferences. . . . Therefore, he is entitled to an order that he be admitted to the University.

The lone dissenter argued the students admitted under Task Force were fully qualified to be medical students, and that the university could use nonacademic factors, including race, in determining which qualified students to accept. He contended that the Constitution permitted racial classifications which had a positive effect, such as the compelling interests that the University claimed:

> [N]umerous decisions recognize that as a practical matter racial classifications frequently must be employed if the effects of past discrimination and exclusion are to be overcome and if integration of currently segregated institutions is to be achieved; these cases establish that the Constitution does not forbid such use of remedial racial classifications. By failing to distinguish between invidious racial classifications and remedial or "benign" racial classifications, the majority utilize the wrong constitutional standard in evaluating the validity of the Davis special admissions program.

Although the California Supreme Court found in his favor, Bakke still could not enter medical school. The university obtained a stay of the ruling from the court while debating whether to appeal to the U.S. Supreme Court, which, with four of the nine justices being Nixon appointees, now had a strongly conservative cast. Fearful of an adverse decision, concerned civil rights groups counseled the university not to appeal; they preferred to wait for a case more favorable to their position. Nonetheless, in November 1976 the university regents voted to appeal the case to the U.S. Supreme Court.

The justices of the Supreme Court vote on which cases the Court will hear. In 1974, the Court had avoided ruling on a similar case involving a law student, Marco Defunis, and the University of Washington. Five justices had voted to declare the Defunis case moot, since Defunis, unlike Bakke, had been allowed to attend school and was in his final semester when the case reached the Supreme Court. Although Justice William Brennan had wanted to rule on Defunis, he objected to hearing the Bakke case in the belief the university's weak position would lead to a decision that would jeopardize the principle of affirmative action. Despite Brennan's opposition, in February 1977 a majority of justices voted to hear the university's appeal of the California ruling in favor of Bakke.

Bakke's case now captured the attention of the nation. Demonstrators opposing Bakke held rallies and parades in California and Washington, D.C. Articles about the case appeared in newspapers and magazines. Fifty-eight individuals and organizations filed briefs containing their opinions. Eager to hear the case, people began lining up outside the Court on October 11, the evening before oral arguments were to be heard. An overflow audience watched attorneys for the two sides present their arguments on October 12, 1977, but those in attendance, along with the rest of the nation, had to wait another eight months before the Court rendered its verdict.

Court insiders later revealed that the justices "really agonized" over the Bakke case. Drafts of the decision were recalled from the printer three times for revisions. Finally, on June 28, 1978, Justice Lewis Powell, author of the majority opinion, addressed the courtroom. After acknowledging the difficulties of the Bakke case, Powell announced that six different opinions had been written, and that the court's judgment was divided. Four justices, Stevens, Burger, Rehnquist, and Stewart, upheld the judgment of the California Supreme Court. Avoiding the constitutional issues, they declared Task Force in violation of Title VI of the Civil Rights Act of 1964. Largely ignored in the earlier trials, Title VI bans racial discrimination "under any program or activity receiving Federal assistance." These four justices agreed that Bakke should be admitted to the medical school. Justices Brennan, Marshall, White, and Blackmun maintained that Title VI prohibited "only those uses of racial criteria that would violate the Fourteenth Amendment if employed by a State or its agencies; it does not bar the preferential treatment of racial minorities as a means of remedying past societal discrimination." Speaking for the four justices who upheld the university's Task Force approach under the Fourteenth Amendment, Harry Blackmun asserted, "In order to get beyond racism, we must first take account of race."

Justice Powell held the deciding vote. He agreed the Fourteenth Amendment and not Title VI should be used in judging the case. Powell argued that Task Force, which used race as the sole determining factor for admissions, violated the equal protection clause. He declared Task Force invalid. However, pointing to Harvard University's admissions procedure, Powell ruled that programs which used race as one of many factors in selecting students would not be invalid. Powell had adroitly left the door open for affirmative action programs. Finally, Powell affirmed the California Supreme Court's judgment that Bakke should be admitted to medical school.

The mixed public reaction reflected the split nature of the Court's ruling. Many viewed the decision as a blow to civil rights. A UC Davis employee complained, "there goes all the progress, everything that's happened in the past ten years," and a science major worried that "this decision seems like a step backwards to before the '60s." Jesse Jackson claimed that universities might use the ruling as an excuse to scale back their affirmative action programs. Other observers were more optimistic. Civil rights leader Vernon Jordan claimed the decision gave "a green light to go forward with acceptable affirmative-action programs," and Stanford law professor John Kaplan argued that "the Bakke people have lost. There are five votes on the Supreme Court saying that while you can't have quotas, you can manipulate admissions standards to get a desired level of minorities."

The Court's complex decision had long-reaching impact on both the life of Allan Bakke and the future of American race relationships. Bakke was a clear winner. Although he refused to comment on the verdict, part of his consistent effort to protect his privacy, he did smile broadly at the inquiring reporters. He entered the UC Davis medical school that fall and graduated in 1982. He became an anesthesiologist and began practicing at a community hospital in Minnesota. In the long run, however, Bakke's brief moment of fame, like that of so many others in the annals of the Supreme Court—Dred Scott, Homer Plessy, Ernesto Miranda—matters less than the constitutional principles to which he appealed. The American people will remember Bakke, not as the aspiring medical student who fought to become a doctor, but as a symbol of the ongoing debate over the wisdom and justice of affirmative action.

America in Flux, 1970–1993

On June 27, 1991, Thurgood Marshall, the first African American to sit on the Supreme Court, informed President Bush he was retiring due to ill health. A month later, Bush announced the nomination of Clarence Thomas, a black judge on the Court of Appeals in Washington, to take his place.

The contrast between the two justices was startling. Marshall had gained national fame for arguing the case for the *Brown* decision in 1954 that desegregated the nation's schools. A firm believer in affirmative action, he had been the Court's most liberal member. Thomas, on the other hand, was a conservative who believed in black self-help. Born in poverty in Georgia, he took to heart the admonition of the grandfather who raised him: "Anything you got you got by the sweat of your brow." After graduating from Holy Cross College and Yale Law School, Thomas eventually headed the Equal Employment Opportunity Commission (EEOC) in the Reagan years. Dismissing affirmative action as "social engineering" that creates a "narcotic of dependency," he opposed racial quotas, calling them "race-conscious legal devices that only further deepen the original problem."

Despite his color, black organizations like the NAACP opposed the confirmation of a judge who had once said that civil rights leaders did nothing but "bitch, bitch, bitch, moan and whine." At the Senate Judiciary Committee hearings on his nomination, Thomas refused to reveal his views on sensitive issues like abortion, but he did retreat from some of his earlier conservative opinions, even acknowledging that his own career had benefited from affirmative action programs.

Although the Judiciary Committee deadlocked 7 to 7 on his nomination, observers expected the full Senate to confirm his appointment by a wide margin when it voted on October 8. Just before the vote, however, sensational charges of sexual harassment finally led to three days of new hearings before the Judiciary Committee that were televised to the entire nation. Anita Hill, a black law professor at the University of Oklahoma, testified that while working for Thomas at both the Justice Department and the EEOC she had turned down his attempts to date her. She then accused Thomas of sexual harassment, recalling in vivid detail the way Thomas described to her scenes of bestiality, rape, and group sex from pornographic movies he had seen and then boasted of his own sexual prowess. Despite his unwelcome advances, Hill admitted she had followed Thomas from the Justice Department to the EEOC and had called on him on occasion in later years for advice and career assistance.

Thomas categorically denied all the charges. He accused the Judiciary Committee of conducting "a high-tech lynching of an uppity black who in any way deigns to think for himself." His lawyers brought forth four women who had worked with him in the 1980s who all testified his conduct was above reproach, with one suggesting Anita Hill had had a crush on Thomas that he discouraged.

It came down to whom you believed was telling the truth. Four witnesses recalled Anita Hill telling them about Thomas's advances; at her own request, she took and passed a lie detector test. But a public opinion poll taken at the close of the televised hearings indicated that 58 percent of the American people believed Thomas while only 24 percent believed Hill.

A bare majority of the senators apparently agreed. On October 15, the Senate confirmed Thomas by a vote of 52 to 48, the narrowest margin ever for a Supreme Court appointment. Eleven Democrats joined with the Republican minority to elevate Thomas to the nation's highest court, where he would reinforce the conservative majority already in control.

The Clarence Thomas-Anita Hill confrontation raised issues that did not end with his confirmation. The extent to which the nation should extend affirmative action to help offset past discrimination was a matter of concern and debate in regard to university admissions and employment opportunities. The question of sexual harassment, a traditional feminist grievance, took on new importance. American women in particular resented the way the all-male Judiciary Committee had treated the polite and composed Anita Hill. Instead of showing her sympathy and understanding, the Republican members, notably Senator Arlen Specter of Pennsylvania, had cross-examined her ruthlessly, suggesting she was either a disappointed suitor or mentally unstable.

Voters recalled the hearings during the 1992 campaign. Even though Specter narrowly won reelection over a female opponent, Carol Mosely

Braun used the treatment of Anita Hill to unseat Illinois senator Alan Dixon, who had voted for Thomas. Four Democratic women were elected to the Senate in 1992, and two of them won places on the Judiciary Committee, breaking the male monopoly.

Most of all, the televised hearings over the Thomas nomination were indicative of the social unrest that characterized American life in the last third of the twentieth century. The place of women in society, the continuing racial tension following the early civil rights victories, changes in family structure, the constantly shifting nature of the American population—all created a feeling of uneasiness. In addition, cumulative changes in the economic well-being of the American people, particularly the decline of manufacturing, the trend toward greater inequality in income, and the drop in defense spending with the end of the Cold War, contributed to the sense of disruption. People could rejoice in escaping the fear of nuclear annihilation, but they missed the old certainties of the Cold War era and were unsure of what the future held for them.

THE CHANGING AMERICAN POPULATION

From the *Mayflower* to the covered wagon, movement has always characterized the American people. The 1970s and 1980s witnessed two significant shifts in the American population: movement internally to the Sunbelt region of the South and West and a remarkable influx of immigrants from developing nations. These changes led to increased urbanization, greater ethnic diversity, and growing social unrest.

A People on the Move

The most striking finding in the 1980 census was that for the first time in American history more than half the people lived in the South and West; the Sunbelt had boomed. The Sunbelt, best defined as a broad band running across the country below the thirty-seventh parallel from the Carolinas to southern California, had begun to flourish with the buildup of military bases and defense plants during World War II. Rapid population growth continued with the stimulus of heavy Cold War defense spending and accelerated in the 1970s when both new high-technology firms and more established industries were attracted by lower labor costs and the favorable climate of the Sunbelt states. Florida, Texas, and California led the way, each gaining more than two million new residents in the 1970s.

In the next decade, the flow continued, but at a slower rate. The Northeast and Midwest continued to lose population to the South and West, but by the late 1980s, with the slowing of defense spending, rising real estate prices, and growing congestion, states like Texas and California no longer attracted so many new residents and even began experiencing an outflow to less populated areas like Oregon, Arizona, and New Mexico.

Migration to the Sunbelt, 1970–1981
Florida, California, and Texas gained the most people in the 1970s; New York, Ohio, and Illinois suffered the heaviest losses.

Net Population Gain from In-migration

- More than 1,000,000
- 200,000 to 1,000,000
- 0 to 200,000

Net Population Loss from Out-migration

- 0 to 100,000
- More than 100,000

Sunbelt—37th Parallel

Wash. 518,000
Ore. 388,000
Mont. 30,000
N. Dak. -19,000
Minn. -14,000
N.H. 143,000
Vt. 38,000
Maine 77,000
Idaho 129,000
S. Dak. -39,000
Wis. 8,000
Mich. -438,000
N.Y. -1,582,000
Mass. -120,000
Wyo. 108,000
Nev. 294,000
Nebr. -21,000
Iowa -98,000
Ill. -476,000
Ind. -160,000
Ohio -649,000
Pa. -328,000
R.I. -31,000
Conn. -41,000
N.J. -109,000
Calif. 2,338,000
Utah 164,000
Colo. 484,000
Kans. -23,000
Mo. 3,000
W. Va. 103,000
Del. 6,000
Md. 70,000
D.C. -161,000
Ky. 178,000
Va. 392,000
Ariz. 753,000
N. Mex. 147,000
Okla. 341,000
Ark. 224,000
Tenn. 380,000
N.C. 429,000
S.C. 286,000
Texas 2,112,000
Miss. 66,000
Ala. 168,000
Ga. 492,000
La. 233,000
Fla. 3,124,000
Alaska 38,000
Hawaii 75,000

The South, particularly Florida, continued to boom, and cities throughout the Sunbelt thrived. By 1990, Los Angeles had displaced Chicago as the nation's second largest city, and Houston had passed Philadelphia in the fourth position. Eight of the nation's cities now had more than one million residents; four were in the Sunbelt and of the rest, only New York gained in population in the 1980s.

The increasing urbanization of America had both positive and negative aspects. People living in the large metropolitan areas were both more affluent and better educated than their rural counterparts. Family income among people living in the bigger cities and their suburbs ran $9,000 a year more, while three-fourths of the urban population had graduated from high school, compared to two-thirds of other Americans. A metropolitan American was twice as likely to be a college graduate than a rural resident. Yet these advantages were offset by rising urban crime rates, longer commuting time in heavy traffic, and higher living costs. Nevertheless the big cities and their

suburbs continued to thrive, accounting for 75.2 percent of all Americans by 1990, up from 73.7 percent in 1980.

Another striking population trend was the nationwide rise in the number of the elderly. At the beginning of the century, only 4.1 percent of the population was age 65 or older; by 1990, those over 65 made up 12.6 percent of the population, with the 3 million over 85 the fastest growing group of all. Major advances in medicine increased life expectancy from 63 in the 1930s to over 75 by the 1990s. The Census Bureau projected a slower rate of increase to 2010, when the elderly will make up 13.2 percent of the population, and then a big jump as the baby boomers reach 65. By the year 2030, one out of every five Americans will be over 65.

Six of every ten older Americans were women, and they tended to have a higher rate of chronic disease and to be worse off economically. Many of the oldest old, those over 85, lived in nursing homes and accounted for one-third of all Medicaid payments. Yet only 12.4 percent of the

Growth of the Population 65 and Over

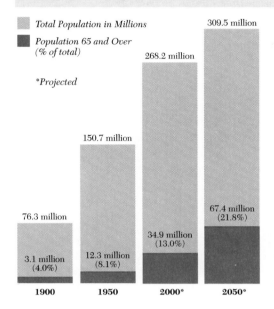

Total Population in Millions

Population 65 and Over (% of total)

*Projected

309.5 million

268.2 million

150.7 million

76.3 million

67.4 million (21.8%)

34.9 million (13.0%)

12.3 million (8.1%)

3.1 million (4.0%)

1900 1950 2000° 2050°

Life Expectancy at Birth, 1850–1985

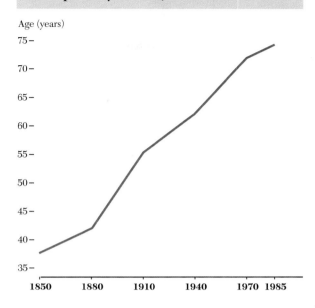

Age (years)

75 –
70 –
65 –
60 –
55 –
50 –
45 –
40 –
35 –

1850   1880   1910   1940   1970 1985

elderly lived below the poverty line; the annual cost of living increases in Social Security payments spared them the worst ravages of inflation. The average family income of those over 65 was just under $20,000 a year in 1985 and three-fourths owned their own homes. Most impressive of all was their political power: 65 percent of those over 65 voted regularly, compared to just 46 percent of the entire population. The American Association of Retired People (AARP), with more than 30 million members, proved very effective in protecting the interests of the elderly in Washington.

The Revival of Immigration

A change in immigration policy in the 1960s led to a rising flow of immigrants into the United States that reached record proportions by the early 1990s. The Immigration and Nationality Act adopted in 1965 abolished the old national origins quota system, which limited immigration from Europe and Asia to just over 150,000 a year, with no restriction on the Western Hemisphere. The new system placed limits of 170,000 visas for persons from Europe, Asia, and Africa and 120,000 for those coming from other Western Hemisphere nations. Instead of national

quotas, preferences were allocated on the basis of family relationships and job skills needed in the United States. Immediate family members— spouses, minor children, and parents of U.S. citizens—were exempted from the numerical limits, as were refugees seeking political asylum in the United States.

In the 1970s, immigration rose rapidly, reaching the level of 700,000 a year by the end of the decade. The numbers continued to increase in the 1980s, with over 7 million immigrants entering the United States. Despite some minor changes in the law in 1990, designed mainly to place numerical limits on family-sponsored preferences (226,000) and those based on employment skills (140,000), 704,000 immigrants entered the United States in 1991 and 810,635 in 1992. When the estimated 200,000 illegal immigrants, mainly from Mexico, are added, immigration runs at about 1 million a year, the level of the previous peak years from 1900 to 1910.

The new wave of immigrants came mainly from Latin American and Asia, compared to the earlier overwhelming European majority. In the 1980s, Mexico supplied the largest number of immigrants, 1.6 million, followed by the Philippines with over half a million; in contrast, all Europe supplied only 761,550 immigrants,

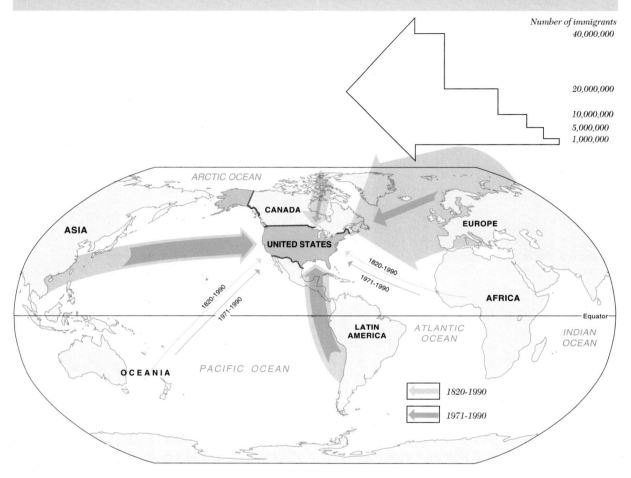

Immigration to the United States, 1820–1990

During the nineteenth century, most immigrants to the United States came from Europe. Patterns of immigration have shifted, and in the late twentieth century most immigrants come from Asia and Latin America.

Number of immigrants
40,000,000

20,000,000

10,000,000
5,000,000
1,000,000

1820-1990

1971-1990

just over 10 percent, with the largest number, 159,173, coming from the United Kingdom.

This influx from developing nations created a sharp increase in the number of foreign-born in the United States. By 1990, there were 20 million residents born abroad, 7.9 percent of the population, compared to 4.7 percent in 1970, but much lower than the 13.5 percent in 1910. The new immigrants tended to settle in urban areas in six states—California, Texas, New York, Florida, Illinois, and New Jersey. In California, the influx of immigrants from Asia and Mexico created growing pressure on public services, especially during the recession of the early 1990s. The result was growing resentment of immigrants and demands for a more restrictive policy. A

Newsweek poll in 1993 found that 60 percent of the American people felt immigration was "a bad thing for this country today." A similar New York Times/CBS survey reported that 61 percent favored a decrease in immigration, up from 49 percent in 1986.

One consequence of the increasing immigration from Latin America and Asia, along with higher birthrates among people from these areas, was a change in the racial and ethnic composition of the United States. In 1990, minority groups, primarily black, Hispanic, and Asian, made up about 25 percent of the total population. By 2050, according to Census Bureau projections, the country would be almost evenly divided between non-Hispanic whites and minorities.

Refugees from Haiti arrive in Miami. During the 1980s and 1990s many Caribbean and Central American refugees came to the United States to escape political unrest, war, and economic deprivation in their native lands.

Social harmony in the next century would depend on whether the melting pot continued to melt, blending ethnic groups into mainstream America, or whether these groups, as their numbers grew, would insist on retaining their separate identity.

Advance and Retreat for African Americans

African Americans formed the largest of the nation's ethnic groups. In 1990, there were just over 31 million blacks in the United States, 12.3 percent of the population, slightly higher than in 1970. Although there had been some reverse movement of African Americans back to the South, the great majority lived in the crowded ghettos of cities in the Northeast, Midwest, and Pacific Coast. New York had the largest concentration of blacks, 2.9 million, with California just behind at 2.1 million.

Middle-class African Americans had made some gains during the 1970s and 1980s. By 1976, one-third of all black workers held white-collar jobs—double the rate of 1960—and nearly 30 percent earned more than $12,000 a year. Education proved the key to African American advances. Black graduates of the nation's colleges and universities had relatively easy entry into higher paying jobs in banks, corporations, and government agencies. With more than one million blacks enrolled in college by 1980, the opportuni-

ties for a middle-class lifestyle were greatly increased.

Many well-educated and affluent African Americans tended to behave like whites in similar circumstances. Some joined the flight to the suburbs, leaving the central city in even larger proportions than whites. Others flocked to the Sunbelt. By the 1980s, many young African Americans, trained as doctors, lawyers, or business executives, returned to cities in the South to pursue their careers. A 1978 survey by *Ebony* magazine identified Atlanta, Dallas, and Houston among the ten most attractive cities for African Americans. Atlanta and New Orleans both had black mayors by 1980, and in 1988 Virginia elected the South's first African-American governor since Reconstruction, L. Douglas Wilder. In fact, the South had become the most thoroughly integrated of all the nation's regions.

Yet despite these gains, there were setbacks as well for African Americans. In the *Bakke* decision (see Special Trial feature, pp. 1003–1007), the Supreme Court ruled against racial quotas for blacks at the University of California at Davis medical school, although the ruling did permit universities to consider race as "simply one element" in efforts to select a diverse student body. In subsequent decisions, the Court upheld an affirmative action program designed by Kaiser Aluminum to help advance minority workers and ordered American Telephone and Telegraph to hire more African Americans and women to make up for past discrimination.

A series of Supreme Court decisions in 1989 sharply narrowed the scope of affirmative action programs. In one case involving setting aside 30 percent of all city contracts in Richmond for minority contractors, the Court ruled against such rigid racial quotas. "The 30-percent quota cannot in any realistic sense be tied to any injury suffered by anyone," wrote Justice Sandra Day O'Connor in the majority opinion. A year later, Congress passed a new civil rights bill to restore full affirmative action programs. President Bush vetoed the measure, calling it a "racial quota" bill; the Senate failed to override by one vote. Finally, in 1991, the president and Congress compromised on a new civil rights act that restored in large measure the rights of both blacks and women to sue businesses for acts of racial discrimination and sexual harassment.

Affirmative action yielded only mixed results for blacks. For those able to gain university admission, such programs proved helpful, but even blacks who graduated from college did not do as well economically as their white counterparts. The Census Bureau reported in 1991 that African American college graduates received only 77 percent as much as white graduates employed in executive and administrative positions. The median annual salary for black college graduates was $30,910, compared to $37,490 for whites. For black males with a high school degree, the gap was even larger; they earned only $60 for every $100 paid to white men with comparable educations. "It seems whether with a high school education or a bachelor's degree," commented a Census Bureau demographer, "the earnings differential is still there for black and white men."

For the many blacks without education, the situation was much worse. Even in the boom years of the 1980s, unemployment rates for African Americans remained over 10 percent, more than double that for whites, and among black teenagers, the level was a staggering 40 percent. The recession of 1990–1991 had an even greater impact. Black workers lost 59,579 jobs between July 1990 and March 1991; white, Asian, and Hispanic employment all registered small gains during the same period. The old cry, "last hired, first fired," seemed to be valid. Blue-collar African American workers were especially

hard hit, losing one-third of the 180,210 blue-collar jobs lost during the recession. Individual companies denied any racial motivation, attributing the job cuts to "corporate downsizing," but African American leaders lashed out at what they termed "black removal programs."

Rodney King became the symbol of black frustration in the United States. In April 1991, a bystander videotaped four Los Angeles policemen brutally beating King, who had been stopped for a traffic violation. The pictures of the rain of blows on King shocked the nation. Nearly a year later, when an all-white jury acquitted the four officers of charges of police brutality, rioting erupted in South Central Los Angeles that for a time threatened the entire city when the police failed to respond promptly. Looting stores at will, attacking and injuring passing motorists, and setting businesses on fire, the rioters focused the nation's attention on the plight of urban blacks. In the aftermath of the riot, which took 53 lives (compared to 34 deaths in the 1965 riot in the nearby Watts area) and did more than $1 billion in damage, government and state agencies promised new efforts to help the ghetto dwellers. Urban blacks, however, saw little hope for improvement. A poll taken in April 1992 revealed that 51 percent of African Americans felt life had "gotten worse" over the past ten years, up from 35 percent in mid-1991. For black youth in Los Angeles, surrounded by gang warfare and drive-by shootings, their only aspiration was simply to stay alive.

The Emerging Hispanics

People with Spanish surnames, labeled Hispanics by the Census Bureau, formed the nation's second largest ethnic group. Growing rapidly, there were over 23 million Hispanics in 1990, a gain of 9 million in the decade of the 1980s alone. Both a high birthrate and heavy immigration from Western Hemisphere countries helped Hispanics account for 9.3 percent of the nation's population, and demographers predicted they would replace African Americans as the nation's largest minority group by the year 2010.

The Census Bureau identified four major Hispanic categories. Mexican Americans, the largest group at 13.5 million, were concentrated in the Southwest, primarily in California and Texas. There were 2.7 million Puerto Ricans,

The acquittal of four police officers on charges of police brutality in the Rodney King case touched off the worst incidence of urban violence in the twentieth century. More than fifty people died in the rioting in Los Angeles, and property damage exceeded $1 billion.

mainly living in or near New York City. Cuban Americans, located primarily in south Florida, numbered just over 1 million. Finally, there were just over 5 million in the Census Bureau category "other Hispanics," consisting mainly of the original Hispanic population of New Mexico and recent immigrants from Central America living in California.

These Hispanic groups had several features in common. All were relatively youthful, with a median age of twenty-two and a high fertility rate. They tended to be relatively poor, with one-fourth falling below the poverty line. Those who were employed were concentrated in low-paying positions—manual laborers, domestic servants, and migrant workers. Although Hispanics had improved themselves considerably in the boom years of the 1980s, increasing their buying power 70 percent between 1982 and 1990, they still lagged behind mainstream America. The poverty rate among Hispanics was twice the national average; family median income in 1990 was $19,500, just 66 percent of the level for other Americans.

Education was a key factor in preventing economic progress for Hispanics. The American Council on Education released a report in 1991 that found Hispanics "are grossly under-represented at every rung of the educational ladder." The high school graduation rate for this group dropped to 55.9 percent by 1989, down from 62.9 percent in 1985. Only 24.5 percent of Hispanic children aged three and four were

enrolled in preschool programs, and Hispanics had the nation's highest school dropout rate at over 50 percent. In Texas, a 1989 survey showed only 45.2 percent of Hispanics graduating from high school, compared to 69.8 percent for blacks and 74.9 percent for whites. Hispanic leaders warned these figures boded ill not just for their own group, but for society as a whole. "You either educate us," claimed Edward Codina of San Antonio, "or you pay for building more jails or for more welfare."

In the 1970s, Chicanos, as Mexican American activists preferred to call themselves, became vocal in expressing their grievances. They succeeded in winning a federal mandate for bilingual education, compelling elementary schools in states like Texas and California to teach Hispanic children in Spanish as well as English. Mexican American, Puerto Rican American, and Cuban American political leaders became a force in local politics, leading the major parties to bid for their votes. The heavy gain in Hispanic population led to the creation of several Hispanic congressional seats in redistricting after the 1990 census. In 1992, over 60 percent of Hispanics cast their vote for Clinton, compared to 25 percent for Bush and 16 percent for Perot. The new president chose two Hispanics for his cabinet: former San Antonio mayor Henry Cisneros for housing and urban development and former Denver mayor Federico Pena as secretary of transportation.

The entry of several million illegal immigrants from Mexico, once derisively called "wetbacks"

U.S. Hispanic Population, 1980s

In the Western border states of California, Arizona, New Mexico, and Texas, most Hispanic immigrants come from Mexico. In the years since World War II, immigrants from Puerto Rico and Central and South America have come to the United States, settling primarily in urban areas in New York and Florida.

PERCENT
OF STATE
POPULATION

	0–5
	6–11
	12–17
	18–23
	24–29
	38

and now known as "undocumented aliens," created a substantial social problem for the nation and especially for the Southwest. Critics charged that the flagrant violation of the nation's border with Mexico had led to an "invisible subculture outside the boundaries of law and legitimate institutions." They argued that these aliens took jobs away from U.S. citizens, kept wages artificially low, and received extensive welfare and medical benefits that strained budgets in states like Texas and California.

Defenders of the undocumented aliens contended the nation gained from the abundant supply of workers who were willing to do the backbreaking jobs in fields and factories shunned by most Americans. Moreover, these illegal entrants usually paid sales and withholding taxes but rarely used government services for fear of being deported. Whichever view is correct, by the mid-1980s there was an exploited class of illegal

aliens living on the edge of poverty. The *Wall Street Journal* summed it up best by observing, "The people who benefit the most from this situation are certainly the employers, who have access to an underground market of cheap, productive labor, unencumbered by minimum wage laws, union restrictions or pension requirements."

Concern over economic competition from an estimated four million Mexican "illegals" led Congress to pass a major immigration reform bill in 1986. To discourage employers from hiring undocumented Mexican workers, the legislation imposed fines and possible prison sentences on those who knowingly employed illegal immigrants. Mexican American leaders feared these sanctions would discourage businesses from hiring anyone of Mexican descent, but they approved of an amnesty provision that enabled aliens who could prove they were living in the

U.S. Asian Population, 1980s

Immigration from Asia increased dramatically during the 1980s, with most Asian immigrants of Filipino, Chinese, or Japanese origin. Other Asian immigrants have come from Korea, Vietnam, Thailand, Laos, and Cambodia.

NUMBER OF RESIDENTS (in thousands)
- More than 500
- 100-500
- 25-100
- 5-25
- Less than 5

United States before January 1, 1982, to become legal residents.

The 1986 law failed to stem the problem of illegal immigration. Although by 1992 the government had extended legal status to nearly 4 million undocumented aliens, mainly of Mexican origin, the flow continued. Authorities noted a decline in the estimated 200,000 illegal entrants a year in the late 1980s, but by the early 1990s there was a new surge from Mexico, Central America, and China. In 1993, Lawrence H. Fuchs, acting chair of the U.S. Commission on Immigration Reform, estimated the numbers of illegals to be as high as 500,000 a year. Fuchs believed there were already between 2 and 3 million illegal aliens living in the United States, in addition to the nearly 4 million granted legal status under the 1986 act. Thus the projections for the Hispanic population, 23 percent of the total by the middle of the next century, may well prove

to be too low (see "Transnational Realities of U.S.–Mexico Relations," pp. 1020–1021).

Asian Americans on the March

Asian Americans were the fasting growing minority group in the 1980s. In 1990, there were 7.3 million Americans of Asian or Pacific Island descent. Although they represented just 3 percent of the total population, they were growing at seven times the national rate and future projections indicated that by 2050 one in ten Americans would be of Asian ancestry.

The Chinese, at 1.6 million, formed the largest single group of Asian Americans, followed closely by Filipinos at 1.4 million. Japanese, Indian, and Korean groups came next, at just under 1 million each; Vietnamese were the smallest of the six major Asian ethnic classifications at almost 600,000. Immigration was the primary reason for

Transnational Realities of U.S.– Mexico Relations

An example of the influence of Hispanic culture in the United States is this photo of a Cinco de Mayo festival in Boise, Idaho. Cinco de Mayo, the national holiday of Mexico, commemorates the Battle of Puebla in 1862 in which Mexican soldiers, outnumbered 3 to 1, fought off invading French troops.

Since the United States established diplomatic relations with Mexico in 1823, it has sought freer trade with its southern neighbor. And since that time, the question of trade with the United States has been a controversial issue in Mexico. Nationalist-minded politicians, from rightist and leftist positions, have warned against overly close political and economic relations with its more developed neighbor as a threat to national political, economic, and cultural sovereignty.

From World War II until the mid-1980s Mexico sought to protect national industry (mainly light manufacturing of consumer and intermediate goods) from international competition. Despite increasing involvement of U.S. multinational corporations in the Mexican economy, expanded Mexican commercial agricultural production dependent on U.S. markets, and growing political collaboration between the U.S. and Mexican governments since World War II, the Mexican state has been leery of free trade with the United States. But by the late-1980s, dominant Mexican as well as U.S. elites viewed a North American Free Trade Agreement (NAFTA) as the best solution to problems facing each nation's political economy.

In the 1980s, U.S. capital operating in Mexico's border area generated a form of freer bilateral trade. In places like heavily polluted Ciudad Juárez, U.S. companies built assembly plants, *maquiladoras*, where Mexican workers—often young women—completed the production of manufactured goods begun in the United States. The best of these jobs, such as in automobile factories, paid better than ones in Mexican-owned industries but still averaged less than one-seventh of comparable U.S. jobs, even though Mexican worker productivity often matched or exceeded that of U.S. workers. The companies only paid duty on value added, that is, the difference in the cost of an assembled product from that of its individual parts, when transferring finished goods to the U.S. market. Lower wages and tariffs increased profits for U.S. corporations; in addition, by producing in Mexico these companies escaped stricter U.S. environmental laws and enforcement. The profitability of this type of production accounted for the growth in Mexican *maquiladora* employment from 131,000 workers in 1981 to 505,000 in 1992, bringing intensive social changes to Mexico's border area. This growth also affected U.S. development. For example, the economies of U.S. border cities increasingly depended on Mexican consumers whose incomes were directly or indirectly tied to *maquilas,* and the region—especially the Rio Grande Valley—felt the environmental impact of modernization. Nationally, it represented the transfer of U.S. jobs to Mexico.

Historically, as one would expect, it is the transnational borderland that has produced much of the social history of U.S.-Mexico relations. In many ways NAFTA merely was a political manifestation of 150 years of social and cultural contact between the nations. Since so much of the western United States was at one time Mexico (see p. 1013), large segments of the U.S. population—whether called Chicano/a, *Tejano/a,* Mexican American, or, more generically, Hispanic or Latino/a—are descendants of Mexican citizens. In other words, much of what is politically North American is in fact socioculturally Mexican.

Since the end of Mexico's armed revolution in 1920, legal and illegal migration from all parts of Mexico to the United States has resulted in massive population movements (see pp. 1016–1019). The combined Mexican American and Mexican contributions to U.S. life and the position of the United States (as myth and reality) in the daily lives of people living south of the Rio Grande have created an unprecedented transnational cultural experience—reflected in over 250 Spanish-language radio and TV stations and 1,500 periodicals produced in the United States today. These patterns also underlie social structures that unite artificially divided city complexes such as Nuevo Laredo/Laredo, Ciudad Juárez/El Paso, and Tijuana/San Diego—part of a vast transnational border area, Mexamerica.

Postwar Los Angeles, the capital of Mexamerica, has been the cultural crucible where Mexican American youth fashioned nationally recognized subcultures—such as low-riding *Pachucos*—analogous to other ethnic and Anglo forms of U.S. urban youth culture. Like African American, Chicano musical production was repackaged beginning in the 1950s and mass marketed through radio and records to a multicultural national audience that identified (in its own ways) with Chicano expressions of alienation and marginality in postwar America while enjoying the new sound. Its production reflects the interplay of traditional Mexican music with rock and roll, rhythm and blues, and other popular genres (often emanating from similarly marginalized U.S. communities) disseminated over urban radio stations and in local dance halls. As cultural historian George Lipsitz has shown, the work of nationally popular Mexican American rock musicians from the great Ritchie Valens, born Valenzuela, in the 1950s up through Los Lobos's success in the 1980s "featured variations on melodies and harmonies common to Mexico *fiesta* music," such as in the classic *La Bamba.* And its mass-market popularity does not negate the music's "quite conscious cultural politics that seeks inclusion in the American mainstream by transforming it."

In 1992, Taco Bell (another example of the central position of Mexican representations in U.S. mass culture) opened its first restaurant south of the border, in Mexico City, where it joined the proliferation of McDonald's and other U.S. fast-food chains as Mexico relaxed restrictions on foreign retailers in the late 1980s. Mexico has no short supply of *taquerías:* convenient, inexpensive traditional eateries serving tacos. And anyone who has eaten authentic Mexican food knows how little U.S. fast-food imitations have in common with it. But that is not the appeal. Taco Bell's presence in Mexico is indicative of the popularity among middle-class Mexicans of North American fast food as a status symbol representing modernity and U.S.-style leisure.

U.S. pop culture—the dominant non-national force in Mexican mass society—is transmitted by transnational corporations (like Taco Bell and Hollywood concerns); frequently Mexican producers imitate and adapt its symbols and forms. In the United States, Mexican and Mexican American communities are influenced, appropriated, and reinvented by mainstream mass culture. In Mexamerica, Mexicans, Chicanos, Anglos, and others create complex multicultural local realities involving conflict and resistance as well as accommodation and interdependence and ultimately coexistence with national and transnational forces. It is such sociocultural processes involving everyday Mexican and North American life, more than NAFTA, that hold the key to understanding contemporary U.S.-Mexico relations.

the rapid growth of all these groups except the Japanese; in the 1980s, Asia provided 46 percent of all immigrants to the United States. As a result, Asian Americans had the highest percentage of foreign born of any ethnic group, an astonishing 64 percent.

Compared to other minorities, Asian Americans were relatively well educated and affluent. Approximately 75 percent of all Asian youth graduate from high school, compared to 51 percent of blacks and 43 percent for Hispanics. Nearly 33 percent of Asian Americans over the age of twenty-five have at least four years of college, compared to 17 percent for whites. Many Asians have entered professional fields, and as a result, the median income for Asian-American families is more than $2,000 higher than the national level.

Not all Asian Americans have fared well, however. Refugees from Southeast Asia have experienced both economic hardship and persecution. The median income for Vietnamese Americans in the mid-1980s was $8,000 below the white median; nearly half the Laotian refugees living in Minnesota were unemployed because they had great difficulty learning to read and write English. Vietnamese fishermen who settled on the Gulf Coast experienced repeated attacks on their livelihood in Texas and Louisiana; the Ku Klux Klan burned three Vietnamese fishing boats and fire-bombed one house in Seadrift, Texas. And in the Los Angeles riots in 1992, Korean stores and shops became a main target for looting and fire-bombing.

The overall experience of Asian Americans has been a positive one. They came to America seeking economic opportunity, or as many put it, "to climb the mountain of gold." "People are looking for a better life," a Chinese spokeswoman explained; "it's as simple as that, and we will continue to come here, especially if the situations over there (in Asia) stay tight, or get worse." Their progress has been remarkable. Nearly 11 percent of Harvard's entering class in 1985 was Asian. Individual Asian Americans, like conductor Seiji Ozawa of the Boston Symphony Orchestra and world renown architect I. M. Pei, have made striking contributions to American culture. Asian Americans, according to sociologist Peter I. Rose, are part of "the most upwardly mobile group in the country. They have caught up to and are even surpassing the Joneses and the Smiths, as well as the Cohens and the Levines."

Melting Pot or Multiethnic Diversity?

"Cultural diversity probably accelerated more in the 1980s than any other decade," noted demographer Carl Haub. The influx of people from all around the world, not just from Europe, had profound implications for American culture. Traditionally, the favorite American self-image was the melting pot, the title of Israel Zangwill's play written in 1908, at the height of European immigration into the nation. "America is God's crucible, the great Melting-Pot where all the races of Europe are melting and re-forming," one of his characters proclaimed. "Germans and Frenchmen, Irishmen and Englishmen, Jews and Russians—into the Crucible with you all! God is making the American!"

The melting pot image carried with it the concept of stripping newcomers of their culture and national traits and casting them into an Anglo-Saxon mold. Dubious for European immigration in view of the way each ethnic group proudly retained its separate identity, this analogy has seemed irrelevant to the Third World migration to America in recent times. Instead of reforming immigrants into an American type, immigration could better be seen as broadening the diversity that has always characterized the United States. Now, instead of the usual division between blacks and whites, America is composed of Asians as well as Europeans, Hispanics as well as African Americans.

The new awareness of ethnic diversity manifested itself in many ways. In public education, blacks led a crusade against Eurocentric curriculum and demanded a new emphasis on the influence of African culture; on college campuses, the call for multicultural courses and separate departments for African American and Hispanic studies created controversy. Citing the forecasts of a declining Anglo dominance and the rise of minority groups in the next century, ethnic leaders advocated cultural pluralism. Raul Yzaguirre, president of the national council of La Raza, argued we had never had a real melting pot where all races contributed to the mix. "What we've had is a pressure cooker, where everybody has had to come in and become anglophiles."

Yzaguirre claimed the "new demographics ask America to live up to its own conception of itself as a pluralistic society."

Many Americans found themselves perplexed and uncertain of their cultural identity by the end of the twentieth century. A Census Bureau survey, asking people to state their ancestry, revealed that fully one-fourth of Americans listed Germany first, with Ireland and England a distant second and third. Some Hispanics found the census racial classifications—black, Asian-Pacific Islander, white, or American Indian—meaningless. "I don't really consider myself Caucasian," objected Jose Arroyo of San Jose, California. "My roots go down into the Indians of Mexico." People of Arab descent felt equally confused. Maha El-Sheikh, a Californian of mixed Egyptian and Jordanian parentage, resented the fact that "on tests and things like that, I either have to put that I'm 'Caucasian' or I'm 'Asian'—which I'm not. . . . I say I am Arabic—or I leave it blank." Congressman Tom Sawyer, an Ohio Democrat, noting that one-fourth of Americans are people of color and many are recent immigrants, commented, "Traditional measurements of ethnicity and race may no longer reflect the growing diversity." Maha El-Sheikh agreed, saying a person's nationality no longer made any difference. "We are all citizens of the U.S.: that's what matters," she asserted. Asking people to categorize themselves "just brings more racism."

Horace Kallen, one of the early critics of Zangwill's melting pot analogy, offered a more appealing image of the nation's diverse heritage. He likened the United States to a symphony orchestra, in which each nationality and ethnic group contributed its "own specific *timbre* and *tonality*" to create "a multiplicity in a unity, an orchestration of mankind." As Americans wrestle with the continuing dilemma embodied in the national motto, *E Pluribus Unum,* the image of a great symphony in which all groups blend together harmoniously offers a way to balance the pride individuals find in ethnic identity with the need for national unity.

PRIVATE LIVES—PUBLIC ISSUES

The 1970s and 1980s witnessed sweeping changes in the private lives of the American peo-
ple. The traditional American family, with the husband the wage earner and the wife the homemaker, gave way to much more diverse living arrangements. The number of working women, including wives and mothers, increased sharply; the wage gap between the sexes narrowed, but women still lagged noticeably behind men in earnings. Finally, the last two decades saw the emergence of an active gay rights movement as more and more homosexuals began to disclose their sexual identities and demand an end to discrimination.

The Changing American Family

Family life underwent a number of significant shifts between 1970 and 1990. The most notable was a decline in the number of families with two parents and one or more children under eighteen. This group declined from 40 percent in 1970 to only 26 percent of all households two decades later. And unlike the earlier period, by 1990 in only 21 percent of these two-parent families was the wife solely engaged in child rearing. A few husbands stayed at home with the children, but in the great majority of these families, both parents worked outside the home.

The number of married couple households without children remained nearly constant at 30 percent, but there was a marked increase in the number of people living alone. By 1990, men living alone made up nearly 10 percent of all households and women living alone another 15 percent. With 25 percent of all families consisting of just one person, it is not surprising to find that marriages declined and those getting married did so at a later age. Thus 63 percent of women under twenty-five in 1990 were single (up from 36 percent in 1970) and 79 percent of men (up from 55 percent twenty years earlier). The birthrate, however, after a steady fall in the 1970s and early 1980s, climbed again as the baby boom generation began to mature. From a high of 3.5 in the mid-1960s, the number of births for every woman during her childbearing years dropped to 1.8 in 1974 and then stayed at that low level until the late 1980s, rising to just over 2.1 by 1990. There was a marked increase in the number of births to women over thirty, as well as a very high proportion of children born to single

A teacher at the Illinois Islamic School helps a student. With the increase in immigration from Latin American and Asia has come an increase in the religious diversity of the United States. Islam, one of the world's great monotheistic faiths (along with Judaism and Christianity), is expanding in the United States through both immigration and conversion.

mothers—27 percent of all births, compared to just 11 percent twenty years earlier.

Other changes in living patterns revealed that the divorce rate, which had doubled between the mid-1960s and the late 1970s, leveled off in the 1980s. There were three million couples of the opposite sex living together in 1990, up from half a million in 1970, but the number of same-sex households remained steady at 2 percent of the national total. The most striking, and potentially tragic, demographic figure was the doubling in the proportion of children living with one parent. By 1990, 25 percent of all children lived with only one parent—in most cases with the mother, and all too often in poverty. One-third of all impoverished familes were headed by women without partners, contributing to the fact that children made up almost 40 percent of the nation's poor.

The picture that emerges is the decline of family life in modern America. A surprisingly large number of people either never marry or postpone marriage until late in the childbearing period. The traditional family unit with the working father and the mother rearing the children at home is rapidly declining. Today most mothers work outside the home and many are the sole support for their children. Given the lower wages earned by women, the result is a high poverty rate for chil-

dren (19.6 percent in 1990). Although politicians, especially Republicans, keep referring to family values during campaigns, the fact remains that the American family underwent great stress due to social changes in the last third of the twentieth century, and children have suffered disproportionately.

Gains and Setbacks for Women

American women have experienced significant changes in their way of life and their place in society in the past twenty years. The prevailing theme is the increasing percentage of working women. There was a rapid movement of women into the labor force in the 1970s, so that by 1980 52 percent of all adult women were employed, including six million more working wives than in 1970 as two incomes became increasingly necessary to keep up with inflation. In the Reagan years, the trend continued. Fully 61 percent of the nearly 19 million new jobs created in the 1980s were filled by women. Even though many were entry-level or low-paying service positions, women succeeded in narrowing the gender pay gap from 60 percent of men's earnings in 1980 to 72 percent by 1990.

Women scored some impressive breakthroughs. They began to enter corporation boardrooms, became presidents of major universities, and were admitted to West Point and Annapolis. Women entered blue-collar, professional, and small business fields traditionally dominated by men; by 1990, women owned one in four of the country's businesses. Reagan's appointment of Sandra Day O'Connor to the Supreme Court in 1981 marked an historic first; Clinton doubled the number of women on the Court with his selection of Ruth Bader Ginsberg.

Yet at the same time women encountered a great deal of resistance. Although in 1990 one of four lawyers under 30 was a woman, for every female lawyer there were 170 women who were clerical workers, 50 sales clerks, 20 waitresses, and 15 female nurse's aides. Most women continued to work in female-dominated fields—as nurses, secretaries, teachers, and waitresses. Those who entered such male areas as management and administration soon encountered "the glass ceiling." In 1990, only 4.3 percent of corporate officers were women. Most in business worked at the middle and lower rungs of management with staff jobs in personnel and public relations, not key operational positions in sales and marketing that would lead to the boardroom; women held fewer than 3 percent of the top jobs in Fortune 500 companies.

As a result, even after the gains of the 1980s, women's wages averaged only 72 percent of male earnings. A college education helped cut the gap, but even women with degrees made only $600 a year more on the average than men with high school diplomas. Younger women did best; those between 16 and 24 earned almost 90 cents for every dollar paid to a male in the same age group. Older women, who often had no other source of support, fared poorly; those over the age of 50 earned only 64 percent as much as men their age. And the recession of 1990–1991 hit women hard, widening the gender gap as women's wages fell from 72 to 70 percent of the men's level. Feminists had once hoped to close the gender gap by the year 2000, but experts predicted women would not reach pay equity with men until 2018.

Beyond closing the gender gap in wages, the women's movement had two goals in recent years. The first was ratification of the Equal Rights Amendment (ERA). Approved by Congress in 1972, the ERA stated simply, "Equality of rights under the law shall not be denied or abridged by the United States or any state on account of sex." Within a year, twenty-two states had approved the amendment, but the efforts gradually faltered just three states short of ratification. The opposition came in part from working-class women who feared, as one union leader explained, that those employed as "maids, laundry workers, hospital cleaners, or dishwashers" would lose the protection of state laws that regulated wages and hours of work for women. Right-wing activist Phyllis Schlafly led an organized effort to defeat ERA, claiming the amendment would lead to unisex toilets, homosexual marriages, and the drafting of women. The National Organization of Women (NOW) fought back, persuading Congress to extend the time for ratification by three years and waging intense campaigns for approval in Florida and Illinois. But the deadline for ratification finally passed on June 30, 1982, with the ERA forces still three states short. NOW leader Eleanor Smeal vowed a continuing struggle: "The crusade is not over. We know that we are the wave of the future."

The women's movement focused even more of its energies in protecting a major victory it had won in *Roe* v. *Wade* in 1973. The Supreme Court, in a majority opinion written by Nixon-appointee Harry Blackmun, ruled that state laws restricting a woman's right to an abortion were unconstitutional. Asserting a basic right to privacy, the Court ruled out state action to prevent an abortion except during the third trimester. Right-to-life groups, consisting mainly of orthodox Catholics, fundamentalist Protestants, and conservatives who believed life began at conception, fought back. In 1978, with strong support from President Carter, Congress passed the Hyde amendment, which denied the use of federal funds to pay for abortions for poor women. Nevertheless, prochoice family groups organized privately funded family planning agencies and abortion clinics to give all women a chance to exercise their constitutional right of abortion.

As presidents Reagan and Bush appointed more conservative judges to the Court, however, prochoice groups began to fear the future overturn of *Roe* v. *Wade*. The Court avoided a direct challenge, contenting itself with lesser actions that upheld the rights of states to restrict abortion

The visit of Pope John Paul II to Denver, Colorado, in August 1993, drew crowds of young people as well as demonstrators on both sides of the abortion issue.

clinics, impose a 24-hour waiting period, and require the approval of one parent or a judge before a minor could have an abortion performed. Abortion became an issue in the 1988 and 1992 presidential contests, with the Republicans upholding a prolife position and the Democrats taking a prochoice stand. Clinton's election and appointment of Ruth Bader Ginsburg to the Court appeared to end the danger to *Roe* v. *Wade,* but the Democratic Congress continued

to vote in favor of the Hyde amendment. And even the exercise of the right of abortion proved difficult and sometimes dangerous in view of the often violent protests of prolife groups outside abortion clinics. For women, abortion was a hard-won right they still had to struggle to protect.

The Gay Liberation Movement

On the evening of July 29, 1969, a squad of New York policemen raided the Stonewall Inn, a Greenwich Village bar frequented by drag queens and lesbians. As the patrons were being herded into vans, a crowd of gay onlookers began to jeer and taunt the police. A riot quickly broke out. "Beer cans and bottles were heaved at the windows and a rain of coins descended on the cops," reported the *Village Voice.* "Almost by signal the crowd erupted into cobblestone and bottle heaving." The next night, more than 400 policemen battled 2,000 gay demonstrators through the streets of Greenwich Village. The two-day Stonewall riots marked the beginning of the modern gay liberation movement. Refusing to play the role of victims any longer, gays decided to affirm their sexual preference and demand an end to discrimination against homosexuals.

Within a few days, two new organizations were formed in New York, the Gay Liberation Front and the Gay Activist Alliance, with branches and offshoots quickly appearing in cities across

Voting on the Equal Rights Amendment
By the end of 1974, thirty-four states had ratified the ERA; Indiana finally approved the amendment in 1977, but the remaining fifteen states held out, leaving ratification three states short of the required three-fourths majority.

States ratifying

States not ratifying

the country. The basic theme of gay liberation was to urge all homosexuals to come out of the closet and affirm with pride their sexual identity. Instead of shame, they would find freedom and self-respect in the very act of coming out. "Come Out for Freedom! Come Out Now!" proclaimed the Gay Liberation Front's newspaper. "Come Out of the Closet Before the Door Is Nailed Shut!"

In the course of the 1970s, hundreds of thousands of gays and lesbians responded to this call. They formed more than a thousand local clubs and organizations and won a series of notable victories. In 1974, the American Psychiatric Association stopped classifying homosexuality as a mental disorder, and by the end of the decade, half the states had repealed their sodomy statutes. Gays fought hard in cities and states for laws forbidding discrimination against homosexuals in housing and employment and in 1980 they finally succeeded in getting a gay rights plank in the Democratic National Platform.

In the 1980s, the onset of the AIDS epidemic (see pp. 1028–1029) forced the gay liberation movement on the defensive. Stung by the accusation that AIDS was a "gay disease," male homosexuals faced new public condemnation at a time when they were trying desperately to care for the growing number of victims of the disease within their ranks. The gay organizations formed in the 1970s to win new rights now had to channel their energies into caring for the ill, promoting safe sex practices, and fighting for greater public funding to help conquer AIDS. In 1986, ACT UP (AIDS Coalition to Unleash Power) began a series of violent demonstrations in an effort to shock the nation into doing more about AIDS. ACT UP members disrupted public meetings, chained themselves to a New York Stock Exchange balcony, and spray painted outlines of corpses on the streets of San Francisco to call attention to those who had died of AIDS.

The movement also continued to stimulate gay consciousness in the 1980s. In 1987, an estimated 600,000 gays and lesbians took part in a march on Washington on behalf of gay rights. Every year afterward gay groups held a National Coming Out Day in October to encourage homosexuals to proclaim proudly their sexual identity. In a more controversial move, some gay leaders encouraged "outing"—releasing the names of prominent homosexuals, primarily politicians and movie stars, in an effort to make the nation aware of how many Americans were gay or lesbian. Gay leaders claimed there were more than 20 million gays and lesbians in the nation, basing this estimate on a Kinsey report which had reported that in the late 1940s that one in ten American males had engaged in homosexual behavior. A sociological survey released in the spring of 1993 contradicted these numbers, finding only 1.1 percent of American males exclusively homosexual. Whatever the actual number, it was clear by the 1990s that gays and lesbians formed a significant minority which had succeeded in forcing the nation, however grudgingly, to respect its rights.

There was one battle, however, in which victory eluded the gay liberation movement. In the 1992 election, gays and lesbians had strongly backed Democratic candidate Bill Clinton, who had promised if elected to end the ban on homosexuals in the military. In his first days in office, however, President Clinton stirred up great resistance in the Pentagon and Congress when he tried to issue an executive order forbidding such discrimination. The Joint Chiefs of Staff and many Democrats, led by Georgia senator Sam Nunn, warned that acceptance of gays and lesbians would destroy morale and seriously weaken the armed forces. Clinton finally settled for the Pentagon's compromise "don't ask, don't tell" policy that would permit homosexuals to continue serving in the military as they had in the past as long as they did not reveal their sexual preference. However disappointed gays and lesbians were in Clinton's retreat, their leaders realized the real problem was the resistance of mainstream America to full acceptance of homosexuality.

SOCIAL DILEMMAS

Two complex social issues arose in the 1980s that went against the grain of the general sense of well-being in the Reagan and Bush years. A massive viral epidemic and a new drug crisis threatened the social fabric of the United States, yet the government failed to respond promptly or effectively to either one.

The AIDS Epidemic

The outbreak of AIDS (acquired immune deficiency syndrome) in the early 1980s took most Americans by surprise. Even health experts had difficulty grasping the nature and extent of the new public health threat. Doctors first noticed a few cases of a rare form of pneumonia and an unusual type of skin cancer in male patients in New York and San Francisco in 1981. The Centers for Disease Control noted the phenomenon in a June 1981 bulletin, but it was several years before researchers finally identified it as a hitherto unknown virus that had spread from Central Africa by way of Haiti and had found its first American victims primarily among gay men.

Initially, AIDS was perceived as only a threat to gay men. With a growing sense of urgency as the death toll mounted, gay men began to practice safer sex, using condoms and confining themselves to trusted partners. It soon became apparent, however, that AIDS could not be so easily contained. It began to appear among intravenous (IV) drug users who shared the same needles and eventually among hemophiliacs and others receiving frequent blood transfusions. The possibility of a contaminated national blood supply terrified middle-class America, as did the possibility of the spread of AIDS to heterosexuals.

Scientists tried to reassure the public by explaining the virus could be spread only by the exchange of bodily fluids, primarily blood and semen, and not by casual contact. The death of movie star Rock Hudson in the summer of 1985 intensified the sense of national panic. Controversy soon developed over proposals for mandatory blood tests for suspected carriers and the segregation of AIDS victims. The integrity of hospital blood supplies caused the most realistic

A gay pride parade in Atlanta, Georgia. President Clinton was unable to deliver on his promise to remove the ban on homosexuals serving in the military.

concern; in 1985, a new test finally gave reassurance that transfusions could be performed safely.

The Reagan administration proved slow and halting in its approach to the AIDS epidemic. The lack of sympathy for gays and a need to reduce the deficit worked against any large increase in health spending; what little money was devoted to AIDS went almost entirely for research rather than for educational measures to slow its spread. The only real leadership came from Surgeon General C. Everett Koop who surprised his conservative backers in 1986 by coming out boldly with proposals for sex education, the use of condoms to ensure "safer sex," and confidential blood testing to help contain the disease.

While the administration dallied, the grim toll mounted. Because the average time between the initial infection and the first symptoms was five years and could be as long as fourteen years, efforts at prevention had little immediate impact. In November 1983, there were 2,803 known cases and 1,416 deaths; by the time Rock Hudson died in mid-1985, over 12,000 cases and more than 6,000 deaths had been reported.

Growing public concern finally led to action. In 1987, Ronald Reagan appointed a special presidential commission headed by Admiral James Watkins, a former chief of naval operations, to study the AIDS epidemic. The Watkins report in 1988 criticized the administration's AIDS efforts as "inconsistent" and recommended a new effort that included antidiscrimination legislation and explicit prevention education. Koop responded by sending out a pamphlet entitled "Understanding AIDS" to 107 million households, while in the fall, Congress voted to spend $1.3 billion to fight AIDS, with much of the money going for confidential testing and counseling and home care for victims.

Despite these new efforts, the epidemic continued to grow. In 1987, there were 50,000 cases; by mid-1989, the count had reached 100,000. The U.S. Centers for Disease Control in Atlanta reported over 200,000 cases at the end of 1991; the toll had increased to 253,448 on December 31, 1992. Although the rate of infection was slowing among homosexual males due to increased education and safer sexual practices, more than half the 142,626 victims were gay. IV drug users, whose tainted needles spread the disease, were the second largest group at 57,412, with another 15,889 consisting of gay IV drug users. The remaining 15 percent were heterosexuals, hemophiliacs, victims of tainted blood transfusions, and children of infected mothers who were born with AIDS. Despite public education campaigns aimed at the general population, experts argued the epidemic could be contained by focusing prevention on two groups—male homosexuals and IV drug users.

What was once known as the "gay disease" was likely to spread far beyond that one group in society. In the 1990s, most of the new victims were forecast to be drug users among the urban poor, many of them racial minorities, betrayed by their reliance on tainted needles. The social cost will be very heavy—as just one example, babies of drug users born with the virus are frequently abandoned in city hospitals, which are already burdened with staggering health costs at a time of declining tax revenues. Most frightening of all is the time bomb ticking away in those exposed to the virus in the 1980s, which makes the experts' forecast of as many as 500,000 cases by the mid-1990s all too believable. With no cure in sight, AIDS promises to be the most deadly disease in American history.

The War on Drugs

The 1980s witnessed the rapid spread of cocaine use in America, leading to a growing sense of social crisis by the end of the decade. Cocaine had long been viewed as a relatively harmless recreational drug used by only a few people—rock musicians, Hollywood producers, and the very wealthy. By the end of the 1970s, the snorting of the pure white powder distilled from the leaves of coca plants grown in the foothills of the Andes had spread throughout the upper middle class. Bankers, lawyers, and doctors began to use it occasionally to achieve a moment of ecstasy, striving for what has been called "the illusion of instant happiness." The costs, however, were very high—$100 for a few snorts and the danger of dying from an overdose or figuratively blowing one's mind. "Chronic cocaine use," warned one expert, "is the same as putting one's car in neutral with the brakes on and pressing the accelerator to the floor for hours—eventually, the engine will burn out." Nevertheless, the number of users reached over four million by 1982.

In the mid-1980s, cocaine suddenly was perceived as a danger to American society. The deaths of several celebrities from cocaine overdoses, notably movie star John Belushi and Maryland basketball player Len Bias, alarmed the public. More ominously, Jamaican drug gangs began to sell crack, a cheap cocaine derivative that could be smoked in a pipe to give a very intense high. Dealers sold this new form of cocaine for as little as $10 a dose, opening up a vast new market among the poor in the urban ghettos. The phenomenon of teenage pushers selling small vials of crack first appeared in Miami and Los Angeles and soon spread to inner-city districts in New York, Houston, and Detroit. By 1986, an estimated 5.8 million people were using cocaine at least once a month and over 600,000 were confirmed addicts.

Despite its relatively low cost, crack led to an explosion of urban crime. The brief but intense high lasted only a few minutes, leading users to keep smoking more, desensitizing their nervous systems and thus forcing them to use still larger amounts to achieve the by now indispensable euphoria. Needing as much as $1,000 of crack each day to sustain their habits, users began to go on literal crime sprees to gain the necessary funds. By 1987, over 70 percent of all those arrested for burglary in Manhattan tested positive for cocaine.

The Reagan administration tried several approaches to the problem posed by cocaine. In 1982, First Lady Nancy Reagan chose drug education as her special project. Using the slogan "Just Say No," she urged schools, churches, and civic groups to inform young people about the dangers of cocaine. Her program helped educate the middle class but had little impact on the crack smokers in the ghetto.

In the mid-1980s, the administration began to place greater emphasis on interdiction, using agents of the Drug Enforcement Agency (the DEA—a body created by Nixon in 1973), the Customs Bureau, and the Coast Guard to try to seal off the nation's borders. An international cartel of drug dealers, led by a group of Colombians, overcame this effort by saturating the nation with cocaine, losing only a fraction to the hard-pressed DEA. In reality, the Reagan administration was unwilling to devote the personnel and resources that truly effective interdiction would require; with one eye on the deficit, Washington was content with a few highly publicized skirmishes in what it termed the War on Drugs.

The very nature of the cocaine industry frustrated a third, and potentially most promising, countermeasure—wiping out the coca fields and processing plants in South America. The adminis-

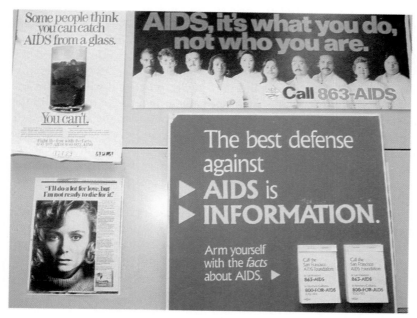

Among the problems that make the AIDS epidemic difficult to control are misinformation about how AIDS is contracted and spread, and an illusion of invulnerability among many persons, especially teenagers, at risk for the disease. Educational campaigns addressing these problems are one method used to fight the spread of this deadly disease.

Global Drug Traffic

Despite public concern over the drug problem, the United States remains one of the world's largest markets for illegal drugs.

Major opium poppy growing countries

General opium and heroin supply routes

Major coca leaf growing countries

General cocaine supply routes

tration relied on diplomatic efforts in cooperation with the governments of Colombia, Bolivia, and Peru to curb the trade in cocaine, but with little success. Colombian processors set up new labs almost as soon as old ones were destroyed; well-publicized campaigns against growing coca, such as Operation Blast Forward in Bolivia in 1986, barely made a dent in crop production. South American farmers could make five times as much money growing coca leaves as food crops; it was estimated that Bolivia received $600 million a year in hard currency from the drug trade, compared to profits of only $400 million from tin and other legal exports.

By the time Ronald Reagan left office, the problem remained as serious as ever, despite actions by Congress in 1986 and 1988 to allocate

more funds for drug education and enforcement, to legalize the death sentence for some drug-related killings, and to create a new federal drug czar. Latin America was producing nearly 400 tons of cocaine a year, five times the amount consumed in the United States; the wholesale price of a kilogram of the white powder in Miami and Los Angeles had dropped from $50,000 to less than $15,000 between 1982 and 1987. A government report in mid-1989 claimed that overall use of drugs, including heroin and marijuana, had declined 25 percent since 1985, while the number of people using cocaine at least once a week had risen from 647,000 to 862,000.

Only one thing had changed dramatically—public awareness. A Gallup poll taken in the summer of 1989 showed that for the first time in recent history, the American people regarded illegal drugs as their greatest concern. Twenty-seven percent of those polled placed drugs highest on the national agenda, a result George Gallup found "virtually unprecedented," since in the past social issues had always come in behind economic and international concerns.

Despite this new awareness, the efforts of the Bush administration proved no more successful than the Reagan program. An ambitious "Andean Strategy," funded at over $2 billion, pledged American support for antidrug programs in Columbia, Bolivia, and Peru. Yet by 1992, coca leaf production had reached a record level of 336,300 tons, nearly three times as high as in 1984. As one critic, Ted Galen Carpenter, explained, "The United States is asking Latin American governments to do the impossible: wage war on a drug trade that now represents a vital part of their economies and around which have arisen powerful political constituencies." The Clinton administration signaled a shift away from an emphasis on cutting off the supply of cocaine through interdiction to an attempt to reduce demand through a new focus on treatment of addicts. Yet it still sought to apprehend major drug traffickers and asked Congress to continue spending over $13 billion a year for a War on Drugs that gave no promise of success.

ECONOMIC CROSSCURRENTS

The strains that first hit the American economy in the lean years of the 1970s continued to erode the confidence of the American people. Despite a lessening of inflation and a seven-year boom in the 1980s, recessions in 1982 and 1990 led to heavy unemployment and prevented any real growth in family income. At the same time, structural changes in the economy and the Reagan tax policies led to important shifts in income distribution, with blue-collar workers suffering and upper income groups benefiting the most.

The Rich Grow Richer

The 1980s witnessed both advances and retreats for the American economy. A short but deep recession in 1981–1982 helped halt inflation and led to a seven-year boom. At the same time, how-

ever, a continuing decline in American manufacturing and a rising tide of imports led to a growing trade deficit and a steady decline in blue-collar jobs.

There were undeniable gains in the Reagan years. Inflation fell from double-digit levels by 1982 and averaged about 4 percent for the rest of the decade. A sharp drop in the world price of oil in late 1985 helped lower the trade deficit and brought inflation down to less than 2 percent, although cheap oil had a devastating impact on oil-producing states like Texas, Louisiana, and Oklahoma.

After the end of the 1982 recession, employment grew steadily; by 1990, there were nearly nineteen million more Americans working than in 1980. There were losers as well as winners, however. Blue-collar jobs declined as American industry, notably steel and autos, streamlined operations by closing obsolete plants, switching to automated production, and farming out manufacturing to foreign producers with far lower labor costs. Companies that specialized in labor-intensive consumer products, like Eastman Kodak and General Electric, virtually stopped all manufacturing in the United States, concentrating instead on marketing and distributing goods made to their specifications abroad. At the same time, however, the service sector expanded rapidly, especially the financial, transportation, and health-care industries. Accountants, lawyers, and technicians flourished, with women especially benefiting from the change from blue to white-collar jobs. Union membership no longer guaranteed a high-wage job; education and technical training were the keys to success in the postindustrial economy. By 1990, nearly one in three workers was an executive, technician, or professional; only one in five worked in factories. Labor unions were especially hard hit; union membership dropped from 23 percent of the work force in 1980 to 15.5 percent by 1992.

The most striking change in the decade was the growing inequality of wealth in America. In the five income categories used by the Census Bureau, the lowest 20 percent of Americans fared badly, dropping 6 percent in pretax income in the 1980s. The three middle groups gained about 5 percent, largely as a result of the increased employment of women as two wage earners became increasingly necessary for middle-class families to maintain a decent standard of living. The top fifth did far better, increasing their incomes by 20 percent over the decade. The top 1 percent, the truly rich, did best of all, doubling their aftertax income in ten years. By 1989, the top fifth made as much money as the other 80 percent combined, while the top 1 percent alone earned as much as the middle fifth of the population.

This income disparity was the product of both economic restructuring and Republican tax policy. The decline in manufacturing meant that many assembly-line workers who averaged over $20 an hour in the 1970s had lost their jobs and were working for little more than the minimum wage in the service sector. At the same time, the income tax cuts and adjustments reduced the top rate from 70 percent to 31 percent. A parallel increase in Social Security payroll taxes meant that by the end of the decade the tax burden for a middle-class family was 37.3 cents of every dollar earned, compared to 35 cents for the wealthy.

The economic inequities of the 1980s were most clearly reflected in the transfer of actual wealth—housing, property, stocks, savings, and retirement accounts. Between 1983 and 1989, family wealth increased from $13.6 trillion to $16.1 trillion; 55 percent of the gain in net assets went to the top one-half percent of the population. The poor and the lower middle class actually lost $256 billion in wealth during this boom period. As a result, wealth became even more concentrated than income in the 1980s. By the end of the decade, the top fifth of the population owned 80 percent of the nation's entire household wealth.

Recession and Stagnation

In July 1990, the American economy, which had been steadily expanding for seven years, suddenly plunged into a recession. For the next eight months, the gross domestic product (GDP) fell by 2.2 percent and unemployment shot up from 5.5 percent to a peak of 7.7 percent. Although mild by postwar standards—in 1982, the GDP fell by 3.3 percent and unemployment reached 10.8 percent—the 1990 recession proved unusually stubborn. The recovery, which began just after the

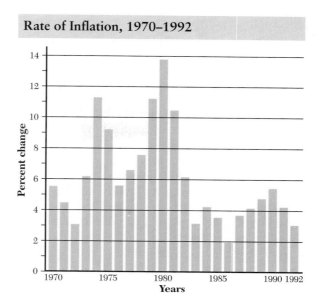

Rate of Inflation, 1970–1992

end of the Gulf War, proved slow and uneven as it stalled twice before leading to renewed growth in mid-1992. Unemployment remained flat eighteen months after the recession ended, and the GDP went up just 2.9 percent in the same period, only one-third of the average growth following other postwar recessions.

The political impact was devastating for the Bush administration. By June 1992, there were nearly ten million Americans unemployed, compared to less than seven million when Bush had taken office in 1989. In 1991, the real income of the average American declined by 1.9 percent, the worst fall since 1970, as per capita growth failed to keep pace with inflation. Unlike the 1982 recession, which had hit hardest in the industrial heartland, the 1990 downturn was felt most strongly in New England and California, the boom areas of the 1980s. And in contrast to previous recessions in which blue-collar workers had fared the worst, many white-collar employees and college graduates lost their jobs. Some could only find part-time positions as companies sought to cut their payroll costs; those who kept working experienced a 2.4 percent drop in wages. The poverty rate, which had remained steady throughout the 1980s, climbed nearly a full point to 14.2 percent.

The sluggish recovery was primarily the result of the massive restructuring of the American economy brought on by the end of the Cold War.

The fall of the Berlin Wall had resulted in annual reductions of over 5 percent in defense spending in the early 1990s; military expenditures, which had once made up over 7 percent of the nation's annual output of goods and services, dropped to 5.5 percent by 1992. Base closings and contract terminations forced the defense industry to lay off workers; General Dynamics eliminated 17,000 jobs in nineteen months. Between 1990 and 1992, defense contractors dismissed 225,000 workers, accounting for more than 15 percent of the almost 1.5 million jobs lost during the recession.

In contrast to Ronald Reagan, George Bush shared Jimmy Carter's bad luck. It was his misfortune that the long sought end of the Cold War coincided with the 1990 recession. For more than three decades, heavy military spending had kept the nation prosperous while masking a growing lack of competitiveness in the global economy. The sudden cutback in defense spending, coupled with the surging economic performance of nations like Japan and Germany unburdened by military expenditures, put the United States in a difficult position. The average American worker, whose paycheck dropped from $454 a week in 1988 to $440 by 1992, sought relief by ending the twelve years of Republican rule.

The Plight of the Middle Class

No economic issue had more political impact by 1992 than the widespread belief in the decline of the American middle class. Democratic challenger Bill Clinton based his successful bid for the presidency on the charge that Reaganomics had favored the wealthy at the expense of the average American.

The actual fate of middle-class Americans since the early 1970s reveals a more complicated pattern. The most frequently cited measure of economic well-being is median family income. Between 1947 and 1973, family income doubled, going from $17,765 to $35,474 (measured in constant dollars). But since 1973, median family income has failed to advance. Inflation caused it to drop in the late 1970s, and the recession of 1982 led to a second decline. Family income rose steadily in the boom years of the 1980s, finally reaching the 1973 level in 1987, only to fall back with the 1990 recession. In 1992, family income stood at $35,353, slightly below the 1973 figure. Middle-class Americans, used to steady postwar growth and schooled to believe things would always get better and better, suddenly realized that for 20 years their economic position had remained stagnant.

NOT AS WELL OFF AS OUR PARENTS WERE AT OUR AGE

Dana Fradon

The economic inequities of the 1980s, with the growing disparity in income between rich and poor and tax policies that favored the rich over the poor and middle class, came to a head in the recession of the early 1990s. Drawing by Dana Fradon; copyright © 1992. The New Yorker Magazine, Inc.

Percent of Persons with High, Middle, and Low Relative Incomes, 1964–1989

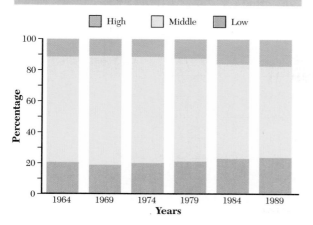

Percent Change in Gross Domestic Product, 1990–1992

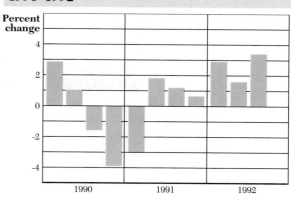

Economists offered conflicting views of the plight of the middle class. A report by the New York City Department of Consumer Affairs claimed that most Americans had to work longer just to keep even. A house in 1990 required 5.37 years of labor, compared to 3.68 in 1972; two wage earners had to work for a combined 82.2 hours a week to meet household expenses that once took only 65.4 hours. Working wives became a necessity; it took two incomes and many more hours of work in the 1980s for the average family with children to maintain a decent standard of living. As a result, the middle class declined from 71.2 percent of the population in 1969 to 63.3 percent by 1989.

A Congressional Budget Office report in 1993, however, indicated that baby boomers were better off than their parents. The older half, those between 35 and 44, fared best, but even the young boomers who entered the work force in the 1980s enjoyed higher incomes than their parents, earning an average of $30,000 a year compared to just $22,000 for the earlier generation. The rise in disposable personal income (see p. 1036) reflected the same trend. The amount that individuals had to save and spend after taxes increased from $11,013 in 1973 to $14,154 in 1990. One reason for the decline in the middle class was that almost as many advanced into the wealthier category (3.8 percent) as fell back into the low income group (4.2 percent) in the 1980s.

More important than the numbers was the growing belief of middle-class Americans that the next generation would not fare as well as their parents had. The feeling of diminished expectations was the product of many factors. The rapid expansion and affluence of the 1950s and 1960s was a happy accident unlikely to occur again. The inflation in real estate by the 1980s added greatly to the net worth of an older generation but made it very difficult for their children to enjoy the same standard of living. The resurgence

An increase in new home sales offered some hope that the nation was beginning to recover from the recession of the early 1990s.

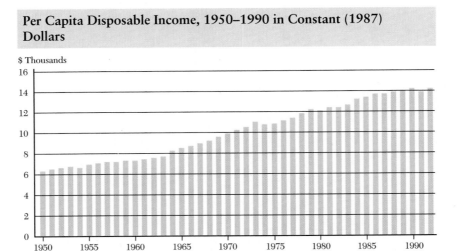

Per Capita Disposable Income, 1950–1990 in Constant (1987) Dollars

$ Thousands

Source: U.S. Department of Commerce.

of Japan and Germany and the relative decline of American industry ensured a much lower rate of national economic growth. Above all, the baby boom generation took the affluence of postwar America for granted and expected to continue to enjoy all the blessings of an abundant society.

The reality of two decades of stagnation in median family income and successive recessions that held back long-term economic growth raised serious questions for a generation that had never known the deprivations of the Great Depression and World War II. They began to wonder if they would be denied the American dream, when in reality they enjoyed a standard of living that was the envy of most of the world's population. The vast increase in immigration in the 1980s and early 1990s was proof enough that the United States was still viewed as the land of opportunity where the combination of political freedom and economic affluence made it the most desirable place to live in the world. Despite the recent setbacks, the attraction of what poet Emma Lazarus so eloquently called "the golden door" reminded all Americans of the limitless possibilities inherent in our national culture.

Recommended Reading

The best account of recent immigration into the United States from developing countries is David Reimers, *Still the Golden Door* (2d ed., 1992). Randy Shilts, *And the Band Played On* (1987), is the classic account of the initial outbreak of the AIDS epidemic in the 1980s.

Steven F. Lawson, *Running for Freedom* (1991), traces the growth of black participation in American politics since World War II, with special emphasis on the South. Susan Hartmann, *From Margin to Mainstream* (1989), highlights the role of women in society and politics since 1960.

Kevin Phillips, a Republican political commentator, has offered the most penetrating analysis of the impact of Reaganomics on economic inequality in two books: *The Politics of Rich and Poor* (1990) and *Boiling Point* (1993).

Additional Bibliography

Ronald Takaki offers a broad history of the many ethnic groups that have flourished in America in *A Different Mirror* (1993). On African Americans, especially in regard to political advances, see Steven F. Lawson, *In Pursuit of Power* (1985), and Manning Marable, *Black American Politics* (1985). The fate of affirmative action is traced in Allan P. Sindler, *Bakke, Defunis, and Minority Admissions* (1978), and J. Harvie Wilkinson, III, *From Brown to Bakke* (1979). On the women's movement, consult Jo Freeman, *The Politics of Women's Liberation* (1979); Winifred D. Wandersee, *On the Move: American Women in the 1970s* (1988); and Mary Frances Berry, *Why ERA Failed* (1988). Sarah Weddington, the lawyer for the plaintiff, describes her victory in *Roe* v. *Wade* in *A Question of Choice* (1992).

Studies on immigration include Julian Simon, *The Economic Consequences of Immigration* (1989), which

CHRONOLOGY

1965 President Johnson signs bill ending immigration quotas based on national origins

1969 Gays riot in New York's Greenwich Village after police raid on Stonewall Inn

1973 U.S. Supreme Court rules abortion constitutional in *Roe v. Wade*

1974 Henry Aaron hits 715th home run, breaking Babe Ruth's record

1976 Bicentennial celebration marks two hundred years of American independence

1977 Elvis Presley dies at Graceland, his home in Memphis

1978 Congress passes a law raising mandatory retirement age for most Americans from 65 to 70

1981 Sandra Day O'Connor becomes first woman to sit on U.S. Supreme Court

1982 Antitrust suit forces breakup of AT&T

1983 President Reagan declares Martin Luther King's birthday a national holiday

1985 United States becomes a debtor nation for first time since 1914

1987 Stock market falls 508 points on October 19 ("Black Tuesday")

1989 *Exxon Valdez* spills 11 million gallons of oil in Gulf of Alaska

1991 Magic Johnson retires from NBA after testing positive for AIDS

1992 Riots devastate South Central Los Angeles after verdict in Rodney King beating case

1993 General Motors announces largest one-year loss in American corporate history—$23.4 billion

and Mexico, see Lester Langley, *MexAmerica: Two Countries, One Future* (1988), and George Lipsitz, *Time Passages: Collective Memory and Popular American Culture* (1990).

The best overall history of sexuality in American life is John D'Emilio and Estelle B. Freedman, *Intimate Matters* (1988). Books on the gay liberation movement include John D'Emilio, *Sexual Politics, Sexual Communities* (1983); Warren J. Blumenfeld and Diane Raymond, *Looking at Gay and Lesbian Life* (1988); and Margaret Cruikshank, *The Gay and Lesbian Liberation Movement* (1992).

The Reagan administration's attempts to deal with the cocaine problem are traced in Elaine Shannon, *Desperados* (1988), and James A. Inciardi, *The War on Drugs* (1986). Stephen C. Joseph describes the difficulty in trying to contain the AIDS epidemic in *Dragon Within the Gates* (1992).

General accounts of recent economic trends include Michael J. Boskin, *Reagan and the Economy* (1987); Robert Hamrin, *America's New Economy* (1988); and Bertrand Bellon and Jorge Niosi, *The Decline of the American Economy* (1988). For the growing economic inequality and its impact on the middle class, see Denny Braun, *The Rich Get Richer* (1991), and Katherine S. Newman, *Declining Fortunes* (1993), a case study of a New Jersey suburb.

takes a positive view; Barry R. Chiswick, *Illegal Aliens* (1988), a dispassionate analysis; and Arthur Corwin, *Immigrants—and Immigrants* (1978), a critical account. The most recent survey of the nation's second largest minority group is Peter Skerry, *Mexican-Americans* (1993), which focuses on the issue of assimilation. For cultural relations between the United States

APPENDIX

The Declaration of Independence

The Articles of Confederation

*The Constitution of the United States
of America*

Amendments to the Constitution

Choosing the President

Cabinet Members

Supreme Court Justices

Admission of States into the Union

*Ten Largest Cities by Population,
1700–1990*

*A Demographic Profile of the
American People*

The Declaration of Independence

In Congress, July 4, 1776

**The Unanimous Declaration
of the Thirteen United States of America,**

When, in the course of human events, it becomes necessary for one people to dissolve the political bonds which have connected them with another, and to assume, among the powers of the earth, the separate and equal station to which the laws of nature and of nature's God entitle them, a decent respect to the opinions of mankind requires that they should declare the causes which impel them to the separation.

We hold these truths to be self-evident: That all men are created equal; that they are endowed by their Creator with certain unalienable rights; that among these are life, liberty, and the pursuit of happiness; that, to secure these rights, governments are instituted among men, deriving their just powers from the consent of the governed; that whenever any form of government becomes destructive of these ends, it is the right of the people to alter or to abolish it, and to institute new government, laying its foundation on such principles, and organizing its powers in such form, as to them shall seem most likely to effect their safety and happiness. Prudence, indeed, will dictate that governments long established should not be changed for light and transient causes; and accordingly all experience hath shown that mankind are more disposed to suffer, while evils are sufferable, than to right themselves by abolishing the forms to which they are accustomed. But when a long train of abuses and usurpations, pursuing invariably the same object, evinces a design to reduce them under absolute despotism, it is their right, it is their duty, to throw off such government, and to provide new guards for their future security. Such has been the patient sufferance of these colonies; and such is now the necessity which constrains them to alter their former systems of government. The history of the present King of Great Britain is a history of repeated injuries and usurpations, all having in direct object the establishment of an absolute tyranny over these states. To prove this, let facts be submitted to a candid world.

He has refused his assent to laws, the most wholesome and necessary for the public good.

He has forbidden his governors to pass laws of immediate and pressing importance, unless suspended in their operation till his assent should be obtained; and, when so suspended, he has utterly neglected to attend to them.

He has refused to pass other laws for the accommodation of large districts of people, unless those people would relinquish the right of representation in the legislature, a right inestimable to them, and formidable to tyrants only.

He has called together legislative bodies at places unusual, uncomfortable, and distant from the depository of their public records, for the sole purpose of fatiguing them into compliance with his measures.

He has dissolved representative houses repeatedly, for opposing, with manly firmness, his invasions on the rights of the people.

He has refused for a long time, after such dissolutions, to cause others to be elected; whereby the legislative powers, incapable of annihilation, have returned to the people at large for their exercise; the state remaining, in the mean time, exposed to all the dangers of invasions from without and convulsions within.

He has endeavored to prevent the population of these states; for that purpose obstructing the laws for naturalization of foreigners; refusing to pass others to encourage their migration hither, and raising the conditions of new appropriations of lands.

He has obstructed the administration of justice, by refusing his assent to laws for establishing judiciary powers.

He has made judges dependent on his will alone, for the tenure of their offices, and the amount and payment of their salaries.

He has erected a multitude of new offices, and sent hither swarms of officers to harass our people and eat out their substance.

He has kept among us, in times of peace, standing armies, without the consent of our legislatures.

He has affected to render the military independent of, and superior to, the civil power.

He has combined with others to subject us to a jurisdiction foreign to our constitution, and unacknowledged by our laws, giving his assent to their acts of pretended legislation:

For quartering large bodies of armed troops among us;

For protecting them, by a mock trial, from punishment for any murder which they should commit on the inhabitants of these states;

For cutting off our trade with all parts of the world;

For imposing taxes on us without our consent;

For depriving us, in many cases, of the benefits of trial by jury;

For transporting us beyond seas, to be tried for pretended offenses;

For abolishing the free system of English laws in a neighboring province, establishing therein an arbitrary government, and enlarging its boundaries, so as to render it at once an example and fit instrument for introducing the same absolute rule into these colonies;

For taking away our charters abolishing our most valuable laws, and altering fundamentally the forms of our governments;

For suspending our own legislatures, and declaring themselves invested with power to legislate for us in all cases whatsoever.

He has abdicated government here, by declaring us out of his protection and waging war against us.

He has plundered our seas, ravaged our coasts, burned our towns, and destroyed the lives of our people.

He is at this time transporting large armies of foreign mercenaries to complete the works of death, desolation, and tyranny already begun with circumstances of cruelty and perfidy scarcely paralleled in the most barbarous ages, and totally unworthy the head of a civilized nation.

He has constrained our fellow-citizens, taken captive on the high seas, to bear arms against their country, to become the executioners of their friends and brethren, or to fall themselves by their hands.

He has excited domestic insurrection among us, and has endeavored to bring on the inhabitants of our frontiers the merciless Indian savages, whose known rule of warfare is an undistinguished destruction of all ages, sexes, and conditions.

In every stage of these oppressions we have petitioned for redress in the most humble terms; our repeated petitions have been answered only by repeated injury. A prince, whose character is thus marked by every act which may define a tyrant, is unfit to be the ruler of a free people.

Nor have we been wanting in our attentions to our British brethren. We have warned them, from time to time, of attempts by their legislature to extend an unwarrantable jurisdiction over us. We have reminded them of the circumstances of our emigration and settlement here. We have appealed to their native justice and magnanimity; and we have conjured them, by the ties of our common kindred, to disavow these usurpations, which would inevitably interrupt our connections and correspondence. They, too, have been deaf to the voice of justice and of consanguinity. We must, therefore, acquiesce in the necessity which denounces our separation, and hold them, as we hold the rest of mankind, enemies in war, in peace friends.

We, therefore, the representatives of the United States of America, in General Congress assembled, appealing to the Supreme Judge of the world for the rectitude of our intentions, do, in the name and by the authority of the good people of these colonies, solemnly publish and declare, that these United Colonies are, and of right ought to be, FREE AND INDEPENDENT STATES; that they are absolved from all allegiance to the British crown, and that all political connection between them and the state of Great Britain is, and ought to be, totally dissolved; and that, as free and independent states, they have full power to levy war, conclude peace, contract alliances, establish commerce, and do all other acts and things which independent states may of right do. And for the support of this declaration, with a firm reliance on the protection of Divine Providence, we mutually pledge to each other our lives, our fortunes, and our sacred honor.

JOHN HANCOCK

BUTTON GWINNETT
LYMAN HALL
GEO. WALTON
WM. HOOPER
JOSEPH HEWES
JOHN PENN
EDWARD RUTLEDGE
THOS. HEYWARD, JUNR.
THOMAS LYNCH, JUNR.
ARTHUR MIDDLETON
SAMUEL CHASE
WM. PACA
THOS. STONE
CHARLES CARROLL
    OF CARROLLTON
GEORGE WYTHE
RICHARD HENRY LEE
TH. JEFFERSON
BENJ. HARRISON

THOS. NELSON, JR.
FRANCIS LIGHTFOOT LEE
CARTER BRAXTON
ROBT. MORRIS
BENJAMIN RUSH
BENJA. FRANKLIN
JOHN MORTON
GEO. CLYMER
JAS. SMITH
GEO. TAYLOR
JAMES WILSON
GEO. ROSS
CAESAR RODNEY
GEO. READ
THO. M'KEAN
WM. FLOYD
PHIL. LIVINGSTON
FRANS. LEWIS
LEWIS MORRIS

RICHD. STOCKTON
JNO. WITHERSPOON
FRAS. HOPKINSON
JOHN HART
ABRA. CLARK
JOSIAH BARTLETT
WM. WHIPPLE
SAML. ADAMS
JOHN ADAMS
ROBT. TREAT PAINE
ELBRIDGE GERRY
STEP. HOPKINS
WILLIAM ELLERY
ROGER SHERMAN
SAM'EL HUNTINGTON
WM. WILLIAMS
OLIVER WOLCOTT
MATTHEW THORNTON

The Articles of Confederation

Between the States of New Hampshire, Massachusetts Bay, Rhode Island and Providence Plantations, Connecticut, New York, New Jersey, Pennsylvania, Delaware, Maryland, Virginia, North Carolina, South Carolina, Georgia

Article 1.

The stile of this confederacy shall be "The United States of America."

Article 2.

Each State retains its sovereignty, freedom and independence, and every power, jurisdiction, and right, which is not by this confederation expressly delegated to the United States, in Congress assembled.

Article 3.

The said states hereby severally enter into a firm league of friendship with each other for their common defence, the security of their liberties and their mutual and general welfare; binding themselves to assist each other against all force offered to, or attacks made upon them, or any of them, on account of religion, sovereignty, trade, or any other pretence whatever.

Article 4.

The better to secure and perpetuate mutual friendship and intercourse among the people of the different states in this union, the free inhabitants of each of these states, paupers, vagabonds, and fugitives from justice excepted, shall be entitled to all privileges and immunities of free citizens in the several states; and the people of each State shall have free ingress and regress to and from any other State, and shall enjoy therein all the privileges of trade and commerce, subject to the same duties, impositions, and restrictions, as the inhabitants thereof respectively; provided, that such restrictions shall not extend so far as to prevent the removal of property, imported into any State, to any other State of which the owner is an inhabitant; provided also, that no imposition, duties, or restriction, shall be laid by any State on the property of the United States, or either of them.

If any person guilty of, or charged with treason, felony, or other high misdemeanor in any State, shall flee from justice and be found in any of the United States, he shall, upon demand of the governor or executive power of the State from which he fled, be delivered up and removed to the State having jurisdiction of his offence.

Full faith and credit shall be given in each of these states to the records, acts, and judicial proceedings of the courts and magistrats of every other State.

Article 5.

For the more convenient management of the general interests of the United States, delegates shall be annually appointed, in such manner as the legislature of each State shall direct, to meet in Congress, on the 1st Monday in November in every year, with a power reserved to each State to recall its delegates, or any of them, at any time within the year, and to send others in their stead for the remainder of the year.

No State shall be represented in Congress by less than two, nor by more than seven members; and no person shall be capable of being a delegate for more than three years in any term of six years; nor shall any person, being a delegate, be capable of holding any office under the United States, for which he, or any other for his benefit, receives any salary, fees, or emolument of any kind.

Each State shall maintain its own delegates in a meeting of the states, and while they act as members of the committee of the states.

In determining questions in the United States, in Congress assembled, each State shall have one vote.

Freedom of speech and debate in Congress shall not be impeached or questioned in any court or place out of Congress: and the members of Congress shall be protected in their persons from arrests and imprisonments, during the time of their going to and from, and attendance on Congress, *except for treason,* felony, or breach of the peace.

Article 6.

No State, without the consent of the United States, in Congress assembled, shall send any embassy to, or receive any embassy from, or enter into any conference, agreement, alliance, or treaty with any king, prince, or state; nor shall any person, holding any office of profit or trust under the United States, or any of them, accept of any present, emolument, office or title, of any kind whatever, from any king, prince, or foreign state; nor shall the United States, in Congress assembled, or any of them, grant any title of nobility.

No two or more states shall enter into any treaty, confederation, or alliance, whatever, between them, without the consent of the United States, in Congress assembled, specifying accurately the purposes for which the same is to be entered into, and how long it shall continue.

No State shall lay any imposts or duties which may interfere with any stipulations in treaties entered into by the United States, in Congress assembled, with any king, prince, or state, in pursuance of any treaties already proposed by Congress to the courts of France and Spain.

No vessels of war shall be kept up in time of peace by any State, except such number only as shall be deemed necessary by the United States, in Congress assembled, for the defence of such State or its trade; nor shall any body of forces be kept up by any State, in time of peace, except such number only as, in the judgment of the United States, in Congress assembled, shall be deemed requisite to garrison the forts necessary for the defence of such State; but every State shall always keep up a well regulated and disciplined militia, sufficiently armed and accoutred, and shall provide, and constantly have ready for use, in public stores, a due number of field pieces and tents, and a proper quantity of arms, ammunition and camp equipage.

No State shall engage in any war without the consent of the United States, in Congress assembled, unless such State be actually invaded by enemies, or shall have received certain advice of a resolution being formed by some nation of Indians to invade such State, and the danger is so imminent as not to admit of a delay till the United States, in Congress assembled, can be consulted; nor shall any State grant commissions to any ships or vessels of war, nor letters of marque or reprisal, except it be after a declaration of war by the United States, in Congress assembled, and then only against the kingdom or state, and the subjects thereof, against which war has been so declared, and under such regulations as shall be established by the United States, in Congress assembled, unless such States be infested by pirates, in which case vessels of war may be fitted out for that occasion, and kept so long as the danger shall continue, or until the United States, in Congress assembled, shall determine otherwise.

Article 7.

When land forces are raised by any State for the common defence, all officers of or under the rank of colonel, shall be appointed by the legislature of each State respectively, by whom such forces shall be raised, or in such manner as such State shall direct; and all vacancies shall be filled up by the State which first made the appointment.

Article 8.

All charges of war and all other expences, that shall be incurred for the common defence or general welfare, and allowed by the United States, in Congress assembled, shall be defrayed out of a common treasury, which shall be supplied by the several states, in proportion to the value of all land within each State, granted to or surveyed for any person, as such land and the buildings and improvements thereon shall be estimated according to such mode as the United States, in Congress assembled, shall, from time to time, direct and appoint.

The taxes for paying that proportion shall be laid and levied by the authority and direction of the legislatures of the several states, within the time agreed upon by the United States, in Congress assembled.

Article 9.

The United States, in Congress assembled, shall have the sole and exclusive right and power of determining on peace and war, except in the cases mentioned in the 6th article; of sending and receiving ambassadors; entering into treaties and alliances, provided that no treaty of commerce shall be made, whereby the legislative power of the respective states shall be restrained from imposing such imposts and duties on foreigners as their own people are subjected to, or from prohibiting the exportation or importation of any species of goods or commodities whatsoever; of establishing rules for deciding, in all cases, what captures on land or water shall be legal, and in what manner prizes, taken by land or naval forces in the service of the United States, shall be divided or appropriated; of granting letters of marque and reprisal in times of peace; appointing courts for the trial of piracies and felonies committed on the high seas, and establishing courts for receiving and determining, finally, appeals in all cases of captures; provided, that no member of Congress shall be appointed a judge of any of the said courts.

The United States, in Congress assembled, shall also be the last resort on appeal in all disputes and differences now subsisting, or that hereafter may arise between two or more states concerning boundary, jurisdiction or any other cause whatever; which authority shall always be exercised in the manner following: whenever the legislative or executive authority, or lawful agent of any State, in controversy with another, shall present a petition to Congress, stating the matter in question, and praying for a hearing, notice thereof shall be given, by order of Congress, to the legislative or executive authority of the other State in controversy, and a day assigned for the appearance of the parties by their lawful agents, who shall then be directed to appoint, by joint consent, commissioners or judges to constitute a court for hearing and determining the matter in question; but, if they cannot agree, Congress shall name three persons out of each of the United States, and from the list of such persons each party shall alternately strike out one, in the petitioners beginning, until the number shall be reduced to thirteen; and from that number not less than seven, nor more than nine names, as Congress shall direct, shall, in the presence of Congress, be drawn out by lot; and the persons whose names shall be drawn, or any five of them, shall be commissioners or judges to hear and finally determine the controversy, so always as a major part of the judges who shall hear the cause shall agree in the determination; and if either party shall neglect to attend at the day appointed, without shewing reasons which Congress shall judge sufficient, or, being present, shall refuse to strike, the Congress shall proceed to nominate three persons out of each State, and the secretary of Congress shall strike in behalf of such party absent or refusing; and the judgment and sentence of the court to be appointed, in the manner before prescribed, shall be final and conclusive; and if any of the parties shall refuse to submit to the authority of such court, or to appear or defend their claim or cause, the court shall nevertheless proceed to pronounce sentence or judgment, which shall, in like manner, be final and decisive, the judgment or sentence and other proceedings being, in either case, transmitted to Congress, and lodged among the acts of Congress for the security of the parties concerned: provided, that every commissioner, before he sits in judgment, shall take an oath, to be administered by one of the judges of the supreme or superior court of the State where the cause shall be tried, "well and truly to hear and determine the matter in question, according to the best of his judgment, without favour, affection, or hope of reward": provided, also, that no State shall be deprived of territory for the benefit of the United States.

All controversies concerning the private right of soil, claimed under different grants of two or more states, whose jurisdictions, as they may respect such lands and the states which passed such grants, are adjusted, the said grants, or either of them, being at the same time claimed to have originated antecedent to such settlement of jurisdiction, shall, on the petition of either party to the Congress of the United States, be finally determined, as near as may be, in the same manner as is before prescribed for deciding disputes respecting territorial jurisdiction between different states.

The United States, in Congress assembled, shall also have the sole and exclusive right and power of regulating the alloy and value of coin struck by their own authority, or by that of the respective states; fixing the standard of weights and measures throughout the United States; regulating the trade and managing all affairs with the Indians not members of any of the states; provided that the legislative right of any State within its own limits be not infringed or violated; establishing and regulating post offices from one State to another throughout all the United States, and exacting such postage on the papers passing through the same as may be requisite to defray the expences of the said office; appointing all officers of the land forces in the service of the United States, excepting regimental officers; appointing all the officers of the naval forces, and commissioning all officers whatever in the service of the United States; making rules for the government and regulation of the said land and naval forces, and directing their operations.

The United States, in Congress assembled, shall have authority to appoint a committee to sit in the recess of Congress, to be denominated "a Committee of the States," and to consist of one delegate from each State, and to appoint such other committees and civil officers as may be necessary for managing the general affairs of the United States, under their direction; to appoint one of their number of preside; provided that no person be allowed to serve in the office of president more than one year in any term of three years; to ascertain the necessary sums of money to be raised for the service of the United States, and to appropriate and apply the same for defraying the public expences; to borrow money or emit bills on the credit of the United States, transmitting, every half year, to the respective states, an account of the sums of money so borrowed or emitted; to build and equip a navy; to agree upon the number of land forces, and to make requisitions from each State for its quota, in proportion to the number of white inhabitants in such State; which requisitions shall be binding; and, thereupon, the legislature of each State shall appoint the regimental officers, raise the men, and cloathe, arm, and equip them in a soldier-like manner, at the expence of the United States; and the officers and men so cloathed, armed, and equipped, shall march to the place appointed and within the time agreed on by the United States, in Congress assembled; but if the United States, in Congress assembled, shall, on consideration of circumstances, judge proper that any State should not raise men, or should raise a smaller number than its quota, and that any other State should raise a greater number of men than the quota thereof, such extra number shall be raised, officered, cloathed, armed, and equipped in the same manner as the quota of such State, unless the legislature of such State shall judge that such extra number cannot be safely spared out of the same, in which case they shall raise, officer, cloathe, arm, and equip as many of such extra number as they judge can be safely spared. And the officers and men so cloathed, armed, and equipped, shall march to the place appointed and within the time agreed on by the United States, in Congress assembled.

The United States, in Congress assembled, shall never engage in a war, nor grant letters of marque and reprisal in time of peace, nor enter into any treaties or alliances, nor coin money, nor regulate the value thereof, nor ascertain the sums and expences necessary for the defence and welfare of the United States, or any of them: nor emit bills, nor borrow money on the credit of the United States, nor appropriate money, nor agree upon the number of vessels of war to be built or purchased, or the number of land or sea forces to be raised, nor appoint a commander in chief of the army or navy, unless nine states assent to the same; nor shall a question on any other point, except for adjourning from day to day, be determined, unless by the votes of a majority of the United States, in Congress assembled.

The Congress of the United States shall have power to adjourn to any time within the year, and to any place within the United States, so that no period of adjournment be for a longer duration than the space of six months, and shall publish the journal of their proceedings monthly, except such parts thereof, relating to treaties, alliances or military operations, as, in their judgment, require secrecy; and the yeas and nays of the delegates of each State on any question shall be entered on the journal, when it is desired by any delegate; and the delegates of a State, or any of them, at his, or their request, shall be furnished with a transcript of the said journal, except such parts as are above excepted, to lay before the legislatures of the several states.

Article 10.

The committee of the states, or any nine of them, shall be authorized to execute, in the recess of Congress, such of the powers of Congress as the United States, in Congress assembled, by the consent of nine states, shall, from time to time, think expedient to vest them with; provided, that no power be delegated to the said committee for the exercise of which, by the articles of confederation, the voice of nine states, in the Congress of the United States assembled, is requisite.

Article 11.

Canada acceding to this confederation, and joining in the measures of the United States, shall be admitted into and entitled to all the advantages of this union; but no other colony shall be admitted into the same, unless such admission be agreed to by nine states.

Article 12.

All bills of credit emitted, monies borrowed and debts contracted by, or under the authority of Congress before the assembling of the United States, in pursuance of the present confederation, shall be deemed and considered as a charge against the United States, for payment and satisfaction whereof the said United States and the public faith are hereby solemnly pledged.

Article 13.

Every State shall abide by the determinations of the United States, in Congress assembled, on all questions which, by this confederation, are submitted to them. And the articles of this confederation shall be inviolably observed by every State, and the union shall be perpetual; nor shall any alteration at any time hereafter be made in any of them, unless such alteration be agreed to in a Congress of the United States, and be afterwards confirmed by the legislatures of every State.

These articles shall be proposed to the legislatures of all the United States, to be considered, and if approved of by them, they are advised to authorize their delegates to ratify the same in the Congress of the United States; which being done, the same shall become conclusive.

The Constitution of the United States of America

Preamble

We the People of the United States, in Order to form a more perfect Union, establish Justice, insure domestic Tranquility, provide for the common defence, promote the general Welfare, and secure the Blessings of Liberty to ourselves and our Posterity, do ordain and establish this Constitution for the United States of America.

Article I.

Section 1   All legislative Powers herein granted shall be vested in a Congress of the United States, which shall consist of a Senate and House of Representatives.

Section 2   The House of Representatives shall be composed of Members chosen every second Year by the People of the several States, and the Electors in each State shall have the Qualifications requisite for Electors of the most numerous Branch of the State Legislature.

No Person shall be a Representative who shall not have attained to the Age of twenty five Years, and been seven Years a Citizen of the United States, and who shall not, when elected, be an inhabitant of that State in which he shall be chosen.

Representatives and direct Taxes shall be apportioned among the several States which may be included within this Union, according to their respective Numbers, *which shall be determined by adding to the whole Number of free Persons, including those bound to Service for a Term of Years, and excluding Indians not taxed, three fifths of all other Persons.* * The actual Enumeration shall be made within three Years after the first Meeting of the Congress of the United States, and within every subsequent Term of ten Years, in such Manner as they shall by Law direct. The Number of Representatives shall not exceed one for every thirty Thousand, but each State shall have at Least one Representative; *and until such enumeration shall be made, the State of New Hampshire shall be entitled to chuse three, Massachusetts eight, Rhode-Island and Providence Plantations one, Connecticut five, New York six, New Jersey four, Pennsylvania eight, Delaware one, Maryland six, Virginia ten, North Carolina five, South Carolina five, and Georgia three.*

When vacancies happen in the Representation from any State, the Executive Authority thereof shall issue Writs of Election to fill such Vacancies.

The House of Representatives shall chuse their Speaker and other Officers; and shall have the sole Power of Impeachment.

Section 3   The Senate of the United States shall be composed of two Senators from each State, *chosen by the Legislature thereof,* for six Years; and each Senator shall have one Vote.

Immediately after they shall be assembled in Consequence of the first Election, they shall be divided as equally as may be into three Classes. The Seats of the Senators of the first Class shall be vacated at the Expiration of the second Year, of the second Class at the Expiration of the fourth Year, and of the third Class at the Expiration of the sixth Year so that one third may be chosen every second Year; *and if Vacancies happen by Resignation, or otherwise, during the Recess of the Legislature of any state, the Executive thereof may make temporary Appointments until the next Meeting of the Legislature, which shall then fill such Vacancies.*

No Person shall be a Senator who shall not have attained to the Age of thirty Years, and been nine Years a Citizen of the United States, and who shall not, when elected, be an Inhabitant of that State for which he shall be chosen.

The Vice President of the United States shall be President of the Senate, but shall have no Vote, unless they be equally divided.

The Senate shall chuse their other Officers, and also a President *pro tempore,* in the Absence of the Vice President, or when he shall exercise the Office of President of the United States.

The Senate shall have the sole Power to try all Impeachments. When sitting for that Purpose, they shall be on Oath or Affirmation. When the President of the United States is tried the Chief Justice shall preside: And no Person shall be convicted without the Concurrence of two thirds of the Members present.

Judgment in Cases of Impeachment shall not extend further than to removal from Office, and disqualification to hold and enjoy any Office of honor, Trust or Profit under the United States: but the Party convicted shall nevertheless be liable and subject to Indictment, Trial, Judgment and Punishment, according to Law.

Section 4   The Times, Places and Manner of holding Elections for Senators and Representatives, shall be prescribed in each State by the Legislature thereof; but the Congress may at any time by Law make or alter such Regulations, except as to the Places of chusing Senators.

The Congress shall assemble at least once in every Year, and such Meeting *shall be on the first Monday in December, unless they shall by Law appoint a different Day.* *

---

*Passages no longer in effect are printed in italic type.

Section 5   Each House shall be the Judge of the Elections, Returns and Qualifications of its own Members, and a Majority of each shall constitute a Quorum to do Business; but a smaller Number may adjourn from day to day, and may be authorized to compel the Attendance of absent Members, in such Manner, and under such Penalties as each House may provide.

Each House may determine the Rules of its Proceedings, punish its Members for disorderly Behaviour, and, with the Concurrence of two thirds, expel a Member.

Each House shall keep a Journal of its Proceedings, and from time to time publish the same, excepting such Parts as may in their Judgment require Secrecy; and the Yeas and Nays of the Members of either House on any question shall, at the Desire of one fifth of those Present, be entered on the Journal.

Neither House, during the Session of Congress, shall, without the Consent of the other, adjourn for more than three days, nor to any other Place than that in which the two Houses shall be sitting.

Section 6   The Senators and Representatives shall receive a Compensation for their Services, to be ascertained by Law, and paid out of the Treasury of the United States. They shall in all Cases, except Treason, Felony and Breach of the Peace, be privileged from Arrest during their Attendance at the Session of their respective Houses, and in going to and returning from the same; and for any Speech or Debate in either House, they shall not be questioned in any other Place.

No Senator or Representative shall, during the Time for which he was elected, be appointed to any civil Office under the Authority of the United States, which shall have been created, or the Emoluments whereof shall have been encreased during such time, and no Person holding any Office under the United States, shall be a Member of either House during his Continuance in Office.

Section 7   All Bills for raising Revenue shall originate in the House of Representatives; but the Senate may propose or concur with Amendments as on other Bills.

Every Bill which shall have passed the House of Representatives and the Senate, shall, before it become a Law, be presented to the President of the United States; If he approve he shall sign it, but if not he shall return it, with his Objections to the House in which it shall have originated, who shall enter the Objections at large on their Journal, and proceed to reconsider it. If after such Reconsideration two thirds of that House shall agree to pass the Bill, it shall be sent, together with the Objections, to the other House, by which it shall likewise be reconsidered, and if approved by two thirds of that House, it shall become a Law. But in all such Cases the Votes of both Houses shall be determined by yeas and Nays, and the Names of the Persons voting for and against the Bill shall be entered on the Journal of each House respectively. If any Bill shall not be returned by the President within ten Days (Sundays excepted) after it shall have been presented to him, the Same shall be a Law, in like Manner as if he had signed it, unless the Congress by their Adjournment prevent its Return, in which Case it shall not be a Law.

Every Order, Resolution, or Vote to which the Concurrence of the Senate and House of Representatives may be necessary (except on a question of Adjournment) shall be presented to the President of the United States; and before the Same shall take Effect, shall be approved by him, or being disapproved by him, shall be repassed by two thirds of the Senate and House of Representatives, according to the Rules and Limitations prescribed in the Case of a Bill.

Section 8   The Congress shall have Power To lay and collect Taxes, Duties, Imposts and Excises, to pay the Debts and provide for the common Defence and general Welfare of the United States; but all Duties, Imposts and Excises shall be uniform throughout the United States;

To borrow Money on the credit of the United States;

To regulate Commerce with foreign Nations, and among the several States, and with the Indian Tribes;

To establish an uniform Rule of Naturalization, and uniform Laws on the subject of Bankruptcies throughout the United States;

To coin Money, regulate the Value thereof, and of foreign Coin, and fix the Standard of Weights and Measures;

To provide for the Punishment of counterfeiting the Securities and current Coin of the United States;

To establish Post Offices and post Roads;

To promote the Progress of Science and useful Arts, by securing for limited Times to Authors and Inventors the exclusive Right to their respective Writings and Discoveries;

To constitute Tribunals inferior to the supreme Court;

To define and punish Piracies and Felonies committed on the high Seas, and Offences against the Law of Nations;

To declare War, grant Letters of Marque and Reprisal, and make Rules concerning Captures on Land and Water;

To raise and support Armies, but no Appropriation of Money to that Use shall be for a longer Term than two Years;

To provide and maintain a Navy;

To make Rules for the Government and Regulation of the land and naval Forces;

To provide for calling forth the Militia to execute the Laws of the Union, suppress Insurrections and repel Invasions;

To provide for organizing, arming, and disciplining, the Militia, and for governing such Part of them as may be employed in the Service of the United States, reserving to the States respectively, the Appointment of the Officers, and the Authority of training the Militia according to the discipline prescribed by Congress;

To exercise exclusive Legislation in all Cases whatsoever, over such District (not exceeding ten Miles square) as may, by Cession of particular States, and the Acceptance of Congress, become the Seat of the Government of the United States, and to exercise like Authority over all Places purchased by the Consent of the Legislature of the State in which the Same shall be, for the Erection of Forts, Magazines, Arsenals, dock-Yards, and other needful Buildings;—And

To make all Laws which shall be necessary and proper for carrying into Execution the foregoing Powers, and all other Powers vested by this Constitution in the Government of the United States, or in any Department of Officer thereof.

Section 9 *The Migration or Importation of such Persons as any of the States now existing shall think proper to admit, shall not be prohibited by the Congress prior to the Year one thousand eight hundred and eight, but a Tax or duty may be imposed on such Importation, not exceeding ten dollars for each Person.*

The Privilege of the Writ of Habeas Corpus shall not be suspended, unless when in Cases of Rebellion or Invasion the public Safety may require it.

No Bill of Attainder or ex post facto Law shall be passed.

No Capitation, or other direct, Tax shall be laid, unless in Proportion to the Census or Enumeration herein before directed to be taken.

No Capitation, or other direct, Tax shall be laid, unless in Proportion to the Census or Enumeration herein before directed to be taken.

No Tax or Duty shall be laid on Articles exported from any State.

No Preference shall be given by any Regulation of Commerce or Revenue to the Ports of one State over those of another: nor shall Vessels bound to, or from, one State, be obliged to enter, clear, or pay Duties in another.

No Money shall be drawn from the Treasury, but in Consequence of Appropriations made by Law; and a regular Statement and Account of the Receipts and Expenditures of all public Money shall be published from time to time.

No Title of Nobility shall be granted by the United States: And no Person holding any Office of Profit or Trust under them, shall, without the Consent of the Congress, accept of any present, Emolument, Office, or Title, of any kind whatever, from any King, Prince, or foreign State.

Section 10 No State shall enter into any Treaty, Alliance, or Confederation; grant Letters of Marque and Reprisal; coin Money; emit Bills of Credit; make any Thing but gold and silver Coin a Tender in Payment of Debts; pass any Bill of Attainder, ex post facto Law, or Law impairing the obligation of Contracts, or grant any Title of Nobility.

No State shall, without the Consent of the Congress, lay any Imposts or Duties on Imports or Exports, except what may be absolutely necessary for executing its inspection Laws: and the net Produce of all Duties and Imposts, laid by any State on Imports or Exports, shall be for the Use of the Treasury of the United States; and all such Laws shall be subject to the Revision and Controul of the Congress.

No State shall, without the Consent of Congress, lay any Duty of Tonnage, keep Troops, or Ships of War in time of Peace, enter into any Agreement or Compact with another State, or with a foreign Power, or engage in War, unless actually invaded, or in such imminent Danger as will not admit of delay.

Article II.

Section 1 The executive Power shall be vested in a President of the United States of America. He shall hold his Office during the Term of four Years, and, together with the Vice President, chosen for the same Term, be elected, as follows:

Each State shall appoint, in such Manner as the Legislature thereof may direct, a Number of Electors, equal to the whole Number of Senators and Representatives to which the State may be entitled in the Congress: but no Senator or Representative, or Person holding an Office of Trust or Profit under the United States, shall be appointed an Elector.

The Electors shall meet in their respective States, and vote by Ballot for two Persons, of whom one at least shall not be an Inhabitant of the same State with themselves. And they shall make a List of all the Persons voted for, and of the Number of Votes for each; which List they shall sign and certify, and transmit sealed to the Seat of the Government of the United States, directed to the President of the Senate. The President of the Senate shall, in the Presence of the Senate and House of Representatives, open all the Certificates, and the Votes shall then be counted. The Person having the greatest Number of Votes shall be the President, if such Number be a Majority of the whole number of Electors appointed; and if there be more than one who have such Majority, and have an equal Number of Votes, then the House of Representative shall immediately chuse by Ballot one of them for President; and if no Person have a Majority, then from the five highest on the List the said House shall in like Manner chuse the President. But in chusing the President, the Votes shall be taken by States, the Representation from each State having one Vote; A quorum for this Purpose shall consist of a Member or Members from two thirds of the States, and a Majority of all the States shall be necessary to a Choice. In every Case, after the Choice of the President, the Person having the greatest Number of Votes of the Electors shall be the Vice President. But if there should remain two or more who have equal Votes, the Senate shall chuse from them by Ballot the Vice President.

The Congress may determine the time of chusing the Electors, and the Day on which they shall give their Votes; which Day shall be the same throughout the United States.

No person except a natural born Citizen, *or a Citizen of the United States, at the time of the Adoption of this Constitution,* shall be eligible to the Office of President; neither shall any Person be eligible to that Office who shall not have attained to the Age of thirty five Years, and been fourteen Years a Resident within the United States.

In Case of the Removal of the President from Office, or of his Death, Resignation, or Inability to discharge the Powers and Duties of the said Office, the Same shall devolve on the Vice President, and the Congress may by Law provide for the Case of Removal, Death, Resignation or Inability, both of the President and Vice President, declaring what Officer shall then act as President, and such Officer shall act accordingly, until the Disability be removed, or a President shall be elected.

The President shall, at stated Times, receive for his Services, a Compensation, which shall neither be encreased nor diminished during the Period for which he shall have been elected, and he shall not receive within that period any other Emolument from the United States, or any of them.

Before he enter on the Execution of his Office, he shall take the following Oath or Affirmation:—"I do solemnly swear (or affirm) that I will faithfully execute the Office of President of the United States, and will to the best of my Ability, preserve, protect and defend the Constitution of the United States."

Section 2   The President shall be Commander in Chief of the Army and Navy of the United States, and of the Militia of the several States, when called into the actual Service of the United States; he may require the Opinion, in writing, of the principal Officer in each of the executive Departments, upon any Subject relating to the Duties of their respective Offices, and he shall have Power to grant Reprieves and Pardons for Offences against the United States, except in Cases of Impeachment.

He shall have Power, by and with the Advice and Consent of the Senate, to make Treaties, provided two thirds of the Senators present concur; and he shall nom-

inate, and by and with the Advice and Consent of the Senate, shall appoint Ambassadors, other public Ministers and Consuls, Judges of the supreme Court, and all other Officers of the United States, whose Appointments are not herein otherwise provided for, and which shall be established by Law: but the Congress may by Law vest the Appointment of such inferior Officers, as they think proper in the President alone, in the Courts of Law, or in the Heads of Departments.

The President shall have Power to fill up all Vacancies that may happen during the Recess of the Senate, by granting Commissions which shall expire at the End of their next Session.

Section 3   He shall from time to time give to the Congress Information of the State of the Union, and recommend to their Consideration such Measures as he shall judge necessary and expedient; he may, on extraordinary Occasions, convene both Houses, or either of them, and in Case of disagreement between them, with Respect to the Time of Adjournment, he may adjourn them to such Time as he shall think proper; he shall receive Ambassadors and other public Ministers; he shall take Care that the Laws be faithfully executed, and shall Commission all the officers of the United States.

Section 4   The President, Vice President and all civil Officers of the United States, shall be removed from Office on Impeachment for, and Conviction of, Treason, Bribery or other high Crimes and Misdemeanors.

Article III.

Section 1   The judicial Power of the United States, shall be vested in one supreme Court, and in such inferior Courts as the Congress may from time to time ordain and establish. The Judges, both of the supreme and inferior Courts, shall hold their offices during good Behaviour, and shall, at stated Times, receive for their Services, a Compensation, which shall not be diminished during their Continuance in Office.

Section 2   The judicial Power shall extend to all Cases, in Law and Equity, arising under this Constitution, the Laws of the United States, and Treaties made, or which shall be made, under their Authority;—to all Cases affecting Ambassadors, other public Ministers and Consuls;—to all Cases of admiralty and maritime Jurisdiction;—to Controversies to which the United States shall be a Party;—to Controversies between two or more States;—*between a State and Citizens of another State;*—between Citizens of different States,—between Citizens of the same State claiming Lands under Grants of different States, and between a State, or the

Citizens thereof, and foreign States, Citizens or Subjects.

In all Cases affecting Ambassadors, other public Ministers and Consuls, and those in which a State shall be Party, the supreme Court shall have original Jurisdiction. In all the other Cases before mentioned, the supreme Court shall have appellate Jurisdiction, both as to Law and Fact, with such Exceptions, and under such Regulations as the Congress shall make.

The Trial of all Crimes, except in Cases of Impeachment, shall be by Jury; and such Trial shall be held in the State where the said Crimes shall have been committed, but when not committed within any State, the Trial shall be at such Place or Places as the Congress may by Law have directed.

Section 3 Treason against the United States, shall consist only in levying War against them, or in adhering to their Enemies, giving them Aid and Comfort. No person shall be convicted of Treason unless on the Testimony of two Witnesses to the same overt Act, or on Confession in open Court.

The Congress shall have Power to declare the Punishment of Treason, but no Attainder of Treason shall work Corruption of Blood, or Forfeiture except during the Life of the Person attainted.

Article IV.

Section 1 Full Faith and Credit shall be given in each State to the public Acts, Records, and judicial Proceedings of every other State. And the Congress may be general Laws prescribe the Manner in which such Acts, Records and Proceedings shall be proved, and the Effect thereof.

Section 2 The Citizens of each State shall be entitled to all Privileges and Immunities of Citizens in the several States.

A Person charged in any State with Treason, Felony, or other Crime, who shall flee from Justice, and be found in another State, shall on Demand of the executive Authority of the State from which he fled, be delivered up, to be removed to the State having Jurisdiction of the Crime.

No Person held to Service or Labour in one State, under the Laws thereof, escaping into another, shall, in Consequence of any Law or Regulation therein, be discharged from such Service or Labour, but shall be delivered up on Claim of the Party to whom such Service or Labour may be due. *

Section 3 New States may be admitted by the Congress into this Union; but no new State shall be formed or erected within the Jurisdiction of any other State; nor any State be formed by the Junction of two or more States, or Parts of States, without the Consent of the Legislatures of the States concerned as well as of the Congress.

The Congress shall have Power to dispose of and make all needful Rules and Regulations respecting the Territory or other Property belonging to the United States; and nothing in this Constitution shall be so construed as to Prejudice any Claims of the United States, or of any particular States.

Section 4 The United States shall guarantee to every State in this Union a Republican Form of Government, and shall protect each of them against Invasion; and on Application of the Legislature, or of the Executive (when the Legislature cannot be convened) against domestic violence.

Article V.

The Congress, whenever two thirds of both Houses shall deem it necessary, shall propose Amendments to this Constitution, or, on the Application of the Legislatures of two thirds of the several States, shall call a Convention for proposing Amendments, which, in either Case, shall be valid to all Intents and Purposes, as Part of this Constitution, when ratified by the Legislatures of three fourths of the several States, or by Conventions in three fourths thereof, as the one or the other Mode of Ratification may be proposed by the Congress; Provided *that no Amendment which may be made prior to the Year One thousand eight hundred and eight shall in any Manner affect the first and fourth Clauses in the Ninth Section of the first Article;* and that no State without its Consent, shall be deprived of its equal Suffrage in the Senate.

Article VI.

All Debts contracted and Engagements entered into, before the Adoption of this Constitution, shall be as valid against the United States under this Constitution, as under the Confederation.

This Constitution, and Laws of the United States which shall be made in Pursuance thereof; and all Treaties made, or which shall be made, under the Authority of the United States, shall be the supreme Law of the Land; and the Judges in every State shall be bound thereby, any Thing in the Constitution or Laws of any State to the Contrary notwithstanding.

The Senators and Representatives before mentioned, and the Members of the several State Legislatures, and all executive and Judicial Officers, both of the United States and of the several States, shall be bound by Oath or Affirmation, to support this Constitution; but no religious Test shall ever be required as a Qualification to any Office of public Trust under the United States.

Article VII.

The Ratification of the Conventions of nine States, shall be sufficient for the Establishment of this Constitution-between the States so ratifying the Same.

Done in Convention by the Unanimous Consent of the States present the Seventeenth Day of September in the Year of our Lord one thousand seven hundred and Eighty seven and of the Independence of the United States of America the Twelfth* IN WITNESS whereof We have hereunto subscribed our Names,

George Washington
President and Deputy from Virginia

New Hampshire
JOHN LANGDON
NICHOLAS GILMAN

Massachusetts
NATHANIEL GORHAM
RUFUS KING

Connecticut
WILLIAM S. JOHNSON
ROGER SHERMAN

New York
ALEXANDER HAMILTON
New Jersey
WILLIAM LIVINGSTON
DAVID BREARLEY
WILLIAM PATERSON
JONATHAN DAYTON

Pennsylvania
BENJAMIN FRANKLIN
THOMAS MIFFLIN
ROBERT MORRIS
GEORGE CLYMER
THOMAS FITZSIMONS
JARED INGERSOLL
JAMES WILSON
GOUVERNEUR MORRIS

Delaware
GEORGE READ
GUNNING BEDFORD, JR.
JOHN DICKINSON
RICHARD BASSETT
JACOB BROOM

Maryland
JAMES MCHENRY
DANIEL OF ST. THOMAS JENIFER
DANIEL CARROLL

Virginia
JOHN BLAIR
JAMES MADISON, JR.

North Carolina
WILLIAM BLOUNT
RICHARD DOBBS SPRAIGHT
HU WILLIAMSON

South Carolina
J. RUTLEDGE
CHARLES G. PINCKNEY
PIERCE BUTLER

Georgia
WILLIAM FEW
ABRAHAM BALDWIN

The Constitution was submitted on September 17, 1787, by the Constitutional Convention, was ratified by the conventions of several states at various dates up to May 29, 1790, and became effective on March 4, 1789.

Amendments to the Constitution

Amendment I

Congress shall make no law respecting an establishment of religion, or prohibiting the free exercise thereof; or abridging the freedom of speech, or of the press; or the right of the people peaceably to assemble, and to petition the Government for a redress of grievances.

Amendment II

A well regulated Militia being necessary to the security of a free State, the right of the people to keep and bear Arms, shall not be infringed.

Amendment III

No Soldier shall, in time of peace be quartered in any house, without the consent of the Owner, nor in time of war, but in a manner to be prescribed by law.

Amendment IV

The right of the people to be secure in their persons, houses, papers, and effects, against unreasonable searches and seizures, shall not be violated, and no Warrants shall issue, but upon probable cause, supported by Oath or affirmation, and particularly describing the place to be searched, and the persons or things to be seized.

Amendment V

No person shall be held to answer for a capital, or otherwise infamous crime, unless on a presentment or indictment of a Grand Jury, except in cases arising in the land or naval forces, or in the Militia, when in actual service in time of War or public danger; nor shall any person be subject for the same offense to be twice put in jeopardy of life or limb; nor shall be compelled in any criminal case to be a witness against himself, nor be deprived of life, liberty, or property, without due process of law; nor shall private property be taken for public use, without just compensation.

Amendment VI

In all criminal prosecutions, the accused shall enjoy the right to a speedy and public trial, by an impartial jury of the State and district wherein the crime shall have been committed, which district shall have been previously ascertained by law, and to be informed of the nature and cause of the accusation; to be confronted with the witnesses against him; to have compulsory process for obtaining witnesses in his favor, and to have the Assistance of Counsel for his defence.

Amendment VII

In Suits at common law, where the value in controversy shall exceed twenty dollars, the right of trial by jury shall be preserved, and no fact trial by a jury, shall be otherwise re-examined in any Court of the United States, than according to the rules of the common law.

Amendment VIII

Excessive bail shall not be required, nor excessive fines imposed, nor cruel and unusual punishments inflicted.

Amendment IX

The enumeration in the Constitution, of certain rights, shall not be construed to deny or disparage others retained by the people.

Amendment X*

The powers not delegated to the United States by the Constitution, nor prohibited by it to the States, are reserved to the States respectively, or to the people.

Amendment XI
[Adopted 1798]

The Judicial power of the United States shall not be construed to extend to any suit in law or equity, commenced or prosecuted against one of the United States by Citizens of another State, or by Citizens or Subjects of any Foreign State.

Amendment XII
[Adopted 1804]

The Electors shall meet in their respective states, and vote by ballot for President and Vice-President, one of whom, at least, shall not be an inhabitant of the same state with themselves; they shall name in their ballots the person voted for as President, and in distinct ballots the person voted for as Vice-President, and they shall make distinct lists of all persons voted for as President, and of all persons voted for as Vice-President, and of the number of votes for each, which lists they shall sign and certify, and transmit sealed to the seat of the government of the United States, directed to the President of the Senate;—The President of the Senate shall, in the presence of the Senate and House of Representatives,

---

*The first ten amendments (the Bill of Rights) were ratified and adoption certified on December 15, 1791.

open all the certificates and the votes shall then be counted;—The person having the greatest number of votes for President, shall be the President, if such number be a majority of the whole number of Electors appointed; and if no person have such majority, then from the persons having the highest numbers not exceeding three on the list of those voted for as President, the House of Representatives shall choose immediately, by ballot, the President. But in choosing the President, the votes shall be taken by states, the representation from each state having one vote; a quorum for this purpose shall consist of a member or members from two-thirds of the states, and a majority of all the states shall be necessary to a choice. And if the House of Representatives shall not choose a President whenever the right of choice shall devolve upon them, before *the fourth day of March* next following, then the Vice-President shall act as President, as in the case of the death or other constitutional disability of the President.—The person having the greatest number of votes as Vice-President, shall be the Vice-President, if such number be a majority of the whole number of Electors appointed, and if no person have a majority, then from the two highest numbers on the list, the Senate shall choose the Vice-President; a quorum for the purpose shall consist of two-thirds of the whole number of Senators, and a majority of the whole number shall be necessary to a choice. But no person constitutionally ineligible to the office of President shall be eligible to that of Vice President of the United States.

Amendment XIII [Adopted 1865]

Section 1   Neither slavery nor involuntary servitude, except as a punishment for crime whereof the party shall have been duly convicted, shall exist within the United States, or any place subject to their jurisdiction.

Section 2   Congress shall have power to enforce this article by appropriate legislation.

Amendment XIV [Adopted 1868]

Section 1   All persons born or naturalized in the United States, and subject to the jurisdiction thereof, are citizens of the United States and of the State wherein they reside. No State shall make or enforce any law which shall abridge the privileges or immunities of citizens of the United States; nor shall any State deprive any person of life, liberty, or property, without due process of law; nor deny to any person within its jurisdiction the equal protection of the laws.

Section 2   Representatives shall be apportioned among the several States according to their respective numbers, counting the whole number of persons in each State, excluding Indians not taxed. But when the right to vote at any election for the choice of electors for President and Vice-President of the United States, Representatives in Congress, the Executive and Judicial officers of a State, or the members of the Legislature thereof, is denied to any of the male inhabitants of such State, being twenty-one years of age, and citizens of the United States, or in any way abridged, except for participation in rebellion, or other crime, the basis of representation therein shall be reduced in the proportion which the number of such male citizens shall bear to the whole number of male citizens twenty-one years of age in such State.

Section 3   No person shall be a Senator or Representative in Congress, or elector of President and Vice President, or hold any office, civil or military, under the United States, or under any State, who, having previously taken an oath, as a member of Congress, or as an officer of the United States, or as a member of any State legislature, or as an executive or judicial officer of any State, to support the Constitution of the United States, shall have engaged in insurrection or rebellion against the same, or given aid or comfort to the enemies thereof. But Congress may be a vote of two-thirds of each House, remove such disability.

Section 4   The validity of the public debt of the United States, authorized by law, including debts incurred for payment of pensions and bounties for services in suppressing insurrection or rebellion, shall not be questioned. But neither the United States nor any State shall assume or pay any debt or obligation incurred in aid of insurrection or rebellion against the United States, or any claim for the loss or emancipation of any slave; but all such debts, obligations and claims shall be held illegal and void.

Section 5   The Congress shall have power to enforce, by appropriate legislation, the provisions of this article.

Amendment XV [Adopted 1870]

Section 1   The right of citizens of the United States to vote shall not be denied or abridged by the United States or by any State on account of race, color, or previous condition of servitude.

Section 2   The Congress shall have power to enforce this article by appropriate legislation.

Amendment XVI
[Adopted 1913]

The Congress shall have power to lay and collect taxes on incomes, from whatever source derived, without apportionment among the several States, and without regard to any census or enumeration.

Amendment XVII
[Adopted 1913]

The Senate of the United States shall be composed of two Senators from each State, elected by the people thereof, for six years; and each Senator shall have one vote. The electors in each State shall have the qualifications requisite for electors of the most numerous branch of the State legislatures.

When vacancies happen in the representation of any State in the Senate, the executive authority of such State shall issue writs of election to fill such vacancies: *Provided,* That the legislature of any State may empower the executive thereof to make temporary appointments until the people fill the vacancies by election as the legislature may direct.

This amendment shall not be so construed as to affect the election or term of any Senator chosen before it becomes valid as part of the Constitution.

Amendment XVIII
[Adopted 1919, repealed 1933]

Section 1 *After one year from the ratification of this article the manufacture, sale, or transportation of intoxicating liquors within, the importation thereof into, or the exportation thereof from the United States and all territory subject to the jurisdiction thereof for beverage purposes is hereby prohibited.**

Section 2 *The Congress and the several States shall have concurrent power to enforce this article by appropriate legislation.*

Section 3 *This article shall be inoperative unless it shall have been ratified as an amendment to the Constitution by the legislatures of the several States, as provided in the Constitution, within seven years from the date of the submission hereof to the States by the Congress.*

Amendment XIX
[Adopted 1920]

The right of citizens of the United States to vote shall not be denied or abridged by the United States or by any State on account of sex.

Passages no longer in effect are printed in italic type.

Congress shall have power to enforce this article by appropriate legislation.

Amendment XX
[Adopted 1933]

Section 1 The terms of the President and Vice President shall end at noon on the 20th day of January, and the terms of Senators and Representatives at noon on the 3d day of January, of the years in which such terms would have ended if this article had not been ratified and the terms of their successors shall then begin.

Section 2 The Congress shall assemble at least once in every year, and such meeting shall begin at noon on the 3d day of January, unless they shall by law appoint a different day.

Section 3 If, at the time fixed for the beginning of the term of the President, the President elect shall have died, the Vice President elect shall become President. If a President shall not have been chosen before the time fixed for the beginning of his term, or if the President elect shall have failed to qualify, then the Vice President elect shall act as President until a President shall have qualified; and the Congress may by law provide for the case wherein neither a President elect nor a Vice President elect shall have qualified, declaring who shall then act as President, or the manner in which one who is to act shall be selected, and such person shall act accordingly until a President or Vice President shall have qualified.

Section 4 The Congress may by law provide for the case of the death of any of the persons from whom the House of Representatives may choose a President whenever the right of choice shall have devolved upon them, and for the case of the death of any of the persons from whom the Senate may choose a Vice President whenever the right of choice shall have devolved upon them.

Section 5 Sections 1 and 2 shall take effect on the 15th day of October following the ratification of this article.

Section 6 This article shall be inoperative unless it shall have been ratified as an amendment to the Constitution by the legislatures of three fourths of the several States within seven years from the date of its submission.

Amendment XXI [Adopted 1933]

Section 1 The eighteenth article of amendment to the Constitution of the United States is hereby repealed.

Section 2 The transportation or importation into any State, Territory, or possession of the United States for delivery or use therein of intoxicating liquors in violation of the laws thereof, is hereby prohibited.

Section 3 This article shall be inoperative unless it shall have been ratified as an amendment to the Constitution by conventions in the several States, as provided in the Constitution, within seven years from the date of the submission hereof to the States by the Congress.

Amendment XXII [Adopted 1951]

Section 1 No person shall be elected to the office of the President more than twice, and no person who has held the office of President, or acted as President, for more than two years of a term to which some other person was elected President shall be elected to the office of the President more than once. But this Article shall not apply to any person holding the office of President when this Article was proposed by the Congress, and shall not prevent any person who may be holding the office of President, or acting as President, during the term within which this Article becomes operative from holding the office of President or acting as President during the remainder of such term.

Section 2 This article shall be inoperative unless it shall have been ratified as an amendment to the Constitution by the legislatures of three-fourths of the several States within several years from the date of its submission to the States within seven years from the date of its submission to the States by the Congress.

Amendment XXIII [Adopted 1961]

Section 1 The District constituting the seat of Government of the United States shall appoint in such manner as the Congress shall direct:

A number of electors of President and Vice President equal to the whole number of Senators and Representatives in Congress to which the District would be entitled if it were a State, but in no event more than the least populous State; they shall be in addition to those appointed by the States, but they shall be considered, for the purposes of the election of President and Vice President, to be electors appointed by a State; and they shall meet in the District and perform such duties as provided by the twelfth article of amendment.

Section 2 The Congress shall have power to enforce this article by appropriate legislation.

Amendment XXIV [Adopted 1964]

Section 1 The right of citizens of the United States to vote in any primary or other election for President or Vice President, for electors for President or Vice President, or for Senator or Representative in Congress, shall not be denied or abridged by the United States or any state by reason of failure to pay any poll tax or other tax.

Section 2 The Congress shall have the power to enforce this article by appropriate legislation.

Amendment XXV [Adopted 1967]

Section 1 In case of the removal of the President from office or his death or resignation, the Vice President shall become President.

Section 2 Whenever there is a vacancy in the office of the Vice President, the President shall nominate a Vice President who shall take the office upon confirmation by a majority vote of both houses of Congress.

Section 3 Whenever the President transmits to the President pro tempore of the Senate and the Speaker of the House of Representatives his written declaration that he is unable to discharge the powers and duties of his office, and until he transmits to them a written declaration to the contrary, such powers and duties shall be discharged by the Vice President as Acting President.

Section 4 Whenever the Vice President and a majority of either the principal officers of the executive departments or of such other body as Congress may by law provide, transmit to the President pro tempore of the Senate and the Speaker of the House of Representatives their written declaration that the President is unable to discharge the powers and duties of his office, the Vice President shall immediately assume the powers and duties of the office as Acting President.

Thereafter, when the President transmits to the President pro tempore of the Senate and the Speaker of the House of Representatives his written declaration that no inability exists, he shall resume the powers and duties of his office unless the Vice President and a majority of either the principal officers of the executive department or of such other body as Congress may by law provide, transmit within four days to the President pro tempore of the Senate and the Speaker of the House of Representatives their written declaration that the President is unable to discharge the powers and duties of his office.

Thereupon Congress shall decide the issue, assembling within 48 hours for that purpose if not in session. If the Congress, within 21 days after receipt of the latter written declaration, or, if Congress is not in session, within 21 days after Congress is required to assemble, determines by two-thirds vote of both houses that the President is unable to discharge the powers and duties of his office, the Vice President shall continue to discharge the same as Acting President; otherwise, the President shall resume the powers and duties of his office.

Amendment XXVI [Adopted 1971]

Section 1 The right of citizens of the United States, who are 18 years of age or older, to vote shall not be de

nied or abridged by the United States or any state on account of age.

Section 2 The Congress shall have the power to enforce this article by appropriate legislation.

Amendment XXVII [Adopted 1992]

No law, varying the compensation for the services of the Senators and Representatives shall take effect, until an election of Representatives shall have intervened.

Choosing the President

Presidential Election Year	Elected to Office			
	President	Party	Vice President	Party
1789	George Washington		John Adams	Parties not yet established
1792	George Washington		John Adams	Federalist
1796	John Adams	Federalist	Thomas Jefferson	Democratic-Republican
1800	Thomas Jefferson	Democratic-Republican	Aaron Burr	Democratic-Republican
1804	Thomas Jefferson	Democratic-Republican	George Clinton	Democratic-Republican
1808	James Madison	Democratic-Republican	George Clinton	Democratic-Republican
1812	James Madison	Democratic-Republican	Elbridge Gerry	Democratic-Republican
1816	James Monroe	Democratic-Republican	Daniel D. Tompkins	Democratic-Republican
1820	James Monroe	Democratic-Republican	Daniel D. Tompkins	Democratic-Republican
1824	John Quincy Adams Elected by House of Representatives because no candidate received a majority of electoral votes.	National Republican	John C. Calhoun	Democratic
1828	Andrew Jackson	Democratic	John C. Calhoun	Democratic
1832	Andrew Jackson	Democratic	Martin Van Buren	Democratic
1836	Martin Van Buren	Democratic	Richard M. Johnson First and only vice president elected by the Senate (1837), having failed to receive a majority of electoral votes.	Democratic

Major Opponents		Electoral Vote		Popular Vote
For President	*Party*			
		Washington	69	Electors selected
		J. Adams	34	by state legislatures
George Clinton	Democratic-Republican	Washington	132	Electors selected
		J. Adams	77	by state legislatures
		Clinton	50	
Thomas Pinckney	Federalist	J. Adams	71	Electors selected
Aaron Burr	Democratic-Republican	Jefferson	68	by state legislatures
		Pinckney	59	
John Adams	Federalist	Jefferson	73	Electors selected
Charles Cotesworth Pinckney	Federalist	J. Adams	65	by state legislatures
Charles Cotesworth Pinckney	Federalist	Jefferson	162	Electors selected
		Pinckney	14	by state legislatures
Charles Cotesworth Pinckney	Federalist	Madison	122	Electors selected
		Pinckney	47	by state legislatures
George Clinton	Eastern Republican			
De Witt Clinton	Democratic-Republican (antiwar faction) and Federalist	Madison	128	Electors selected
		Clinton	89	by state legislatures
Rufus King	Federalist	Monroe	183	Electors selected
		King	34	by state legislatures
		Monroe	231	Electors selected
		J. Q. Adams	1	by state legislatures
Andrew Jackson	Democratic	J. Q. Adams	84	113,122
Henry Clay	Democratic-Republican	Jackson	99	151,271
		Clay	37	47,531
William H. Crawford	Democratic-Republican	Crawford	41	40,856
John Quincy Adams	National Republican	Jackson	178	642,553
		J. Q. Adams	83	500,897
Henry Clay	National Republican	Jackson	219	701,780
		Clay	49	482,205
William Wirt	Anti-Masonic	Wirt	7	100,715
		Floyd (Ind. Dem.)	11	
		Delegates chosen by South Carolina legislature		
Daniel Webster	Whig	Van Buren	170	764,176
Hugh L. White	Whig	W. Harrison	73	550,816
William Henry Harrison	Anti-Masonic	White	26	146,107
		Webster	14	41,201
		Mangum (Ind. Dem.)	11	
		Delegates chosen by South Carolina legislature		

Presidential Election Year	Elected to Office			
	President	Party	Vice President	Party
1840	William Henry Harrison	Whig	John Tyler	Whig
1844	James K. Polk	Democratic	George M. Dallas	Democratic
1848	Zachary Taylor	Whig	Millard Fillmore	Whig
1852	Franklin Pierce	Democratic	William R. King	Democratic
1856	James Buchanan	Democratic	John C. Breckinridge	Democratic
1860	Abraham Lincoln	Republican	Hannibal Hamlin	Republican
1864	Abraham Lincoln	National Union Republican	Andrew Johnson	National Union/ Democratic
1868	Ulysses S. Grant	Republican	Schuyler Colfax	Republican
1872	Ulysses S. Grant	Republican	Henry Wilson	Republican
1876	Rutherford B. Hayes Contested result settled by special election commission in favor of Hayes	Republican	William A. Wheeler	Republican
1880	James A. Garfield	Republican	Chester A. Arthur	Republican
1884	Grover Cleveland	Democratic	Thomas A. Hendricks	Democratic
1888	Benjamin Harrison	Republican	Levi P. Morton	Republican

Major Opponents		Electoral Vote		Popular Vote
For President	Party			
Martin Van Buren	Democratic	W. Harrison	234	1,274,624
James G. Birney	Liberty	Van Buren	60	1,127,781
Henry Clay	Whig	Polk	170	1,338,624
James G. Birney	Liberty	Clay	105	1,300,097
		Birney	—	62,300
Lewis Cass	Democratic	Taylor	163	1,360,967
Martin Van Buren	Free-Soil	Cass	127	1,222,342
		Van Buren	—	291,263
Winfield Scott	Whig	Pierce	254	1,601,117
John P. Hale	Free-Soil	Scott	42	1,385,453
		Hale	—	155,825
John C. Frémont	Republican	Buchanan	174	1,832,955
Millard Fillmore	American (Know-Nothing)	Frémont	114	1,339,932
		Fillmore	8	871,731
John Bell	Constitutional Union	Lincoln	180	1,865,593
Stephen A. Douglas	Democratic	Breckinridge	72	848,356
John C. Breckinridge	Democratic	Douglas	12	1,382,713
		Bell	39	592,906
George B. McClellan	Democratic	Lincoln	212	2,218,388
		McClellan	21	1,812,807
		Eleven secessionist states did not participate		
Horatio Seymour	Democratic	Grant	286	3,598,235
		Seymour	80	2,706,829
		Texas, Mississippi, and Virginia did not participate		
Horace Greeley	Democratic and Liberal Republican	Grant	286	3,598,235
Charles O'Conor	Democratic	Greeley	80	2,834,761
James Black	Temperance	Greeley died before the electoral college met. His electoral votes were divided among the four minor candidates.		
Samuel J. Tilden	Democratic	Hayes	185	4,034,311
Peter Cooper	Greenback	Tilden	184	4,288,546
Green Clay Smith	Prohibition	Cooper	—	75,973
Winfield S. Hancock	Democratic	Garfield	214	4,446,158
James B. Weaver	Greenback	Hancock	155	4,444,260
Neal Dow	Prohibition	Weaver	—	305,997
James G. Blaine	Republican	Cleveland	219	4,874,621
John P. St. John	Prohibition	Blaine	182	4,848,936
Benjamin F. Butler	Greenback	Butler	—	175,096
		St. John	—	147,482
Grover Cleveland	Democratic	B. Harrison	233	5,447,129
Clinton B. Fisk	Prohibition	Cleveland	168	5,537,857
Alson J. Streeter	Union Labor			

Presidential Election Year	Elected to Office			
	President	Party	Vice President	Party
1892	Grover Cleveland	Democratic	Adlai E. Stevenson	Democratic
1896	William McKinley	Republican	Garret A. Hobart	Republican
1900	William McKinley	Republican	Theodore Roosevelt	Republican
1904	Theodore Roosevelt	Republican	Charles W. Fairbanks	Republican
1908	William Howard Taft	Republican	James S. Sherman	Republican
1912	Woodrow Wilson	Democratic	Thomas R. Marshall	Democratic
1916	Woodrow Wilson	Democratic	Thomas R. Marshall	Democratic
1920	Warren G. Harding	Republican	Calvin Coolidge	Republican
1924	Calvin Coolidge	Republican	Charles G. Dawes	Republican
1928	Herbert C. Hoover	Republican	Charles Curtis	Republican
1932	Franklin D. Roosevelt	Democratic	John N. Garner	Democratic
1936	Franklin D. Roosevelt	Democratic	John N. Garner	Democratic
1940	Franklin D. Roosevelt	Democratic	Henry A. Wallace	Democratic
1944	Franklin D. Roosevelt	Democrat	Harry S Truman	Democratic

Major Opponents		Electoral Vote		Popular Vote
For President	*Party*			
Benjamin Harrison	Republican	Cleveland	277	5,555,426
James B. Weaver	Populist	B. Harrison	145	5,182,600
John Bidwell	Prohibition	Weaver	22	1,029,846
William Jennings Bryan	Democratic, Populist, and National Silver	McKinley	271	7,102,246
		Bryan	176	6,492,559
Joshua Levering	Republican			
John M. Palmer	Prohibition, National Democratic			
William Jennings Bryan	Democratic and Fusion	McKinley	292	7,218,039
	Populist	Bryan	155	6,358,345
Wharton Barker	Anti-Fusion	Woolley	—	209,004
Eugene V. Debs	Populist	Debs	—	86,935
John G. Woolley	Social Democratic, Prohibition			
Alton B. Parker	Democratic	T. Roosevelt	336	7,626,593
Eugene V. Debs	Socialist	Parker	140	5,082,898
Silas C. Swallow	Prohibition	Debs	—	402,489
		Swallow	—	258,596
William Jennings Bryan	Democratic	Taft	321	7,676,258
		Bryan	162	6,406,801
Eugene V. Debs	Socialist	Debs	—	420,380
Eugene W. Chafin	Prohibition	Chafin	—	252,821
William Howard Taft	Republican	Wilson	435	6,296,547
Theodore Roosevelt	Progressive (Bull Moose)	T. Roosevelt	88	4,118,571
Eugene V. Debs	Socialist	Taft	8	3,486,720
Eugene W. Chafin	Prohibition			
Charles E. Hughes	Republican	Wilson	277	9,127,695
Allen L. Benson	Socialist	Hughes	254	8,533,507
J. Frank Hanley	Prohibition			
Charles W. Fairbanks	Republican			
James M. Cox	Democratic	Harding	404	16,133,314
Eugene V. Debs	Socialist	Cox	127	9,140,884
		Debs	—	913,664
John W. Davis	Democratic	Coolidge	382	15,717,553
Robert M. La Follette	Progressive	Davis	136	8,386,169
		La Follette	13	4,814,050
Alfred E. Smith	Democratic	Hoover	444	21,391,993
Norman Thomas	Socialist	Smith	87	15,016,169
Herbert C. Hoover	Republican	F. Roosevelt	472	22,809,638
Norman Thomas	Socialist	Hoover	59	15,758,901
Alfred M. Landon	Republican	F. Roosevelt	523	27,752,869
William Lemke	Union	Landon	8	16,674,665
Wendell L. Willkie	Republican	F. Roosevelt	449	27,263,448
		Willkie	82	22,336,260
Thomas E. Dewey	Republican	F. Roosevelt	432	25,611,936
		Dewey	99	22,013,372

Presidential Election Year	Elected to Office			
	President	Party	Vice President	Party
1948	Harry S Truman	Democratic	Alben W. Barkley	Democratic
1952	Dwight D. Eisenhower	Republican	Richard M. Nixon	Republican
1956	Dwight D. Eisenhower	Republican	Richard M. Nixon	Republican
1960	John F. Kennedy	Democratic	Lyndon B. Johnson	Democratic
1964	Lyndon B. Johnson	Democratic	Hubert H. Humphrey	Democratic
1968	Richard M. Nixon	Republican	Spiro T. Agnew	Republican
1972	Richard M. Nixon	Republican	Spiro T. Agnew	Republican
1976	Jimmy Carter	Democratic	Walter Mondale	Democratic
1980	Ronald Reagan	Republican	George Bush	Republican
1984	Ronald Reagan	Republican	George Bush	Republican
1988	George Bush	Republican	J. Danforth Quayle	Republican
1992	William Clinton	Democrat	Albert Gore, Jr.	Democrat

Major Opponents		Electoral Vote		Popular Vote
For President	*Party*			
Thomas E. Dewey	Republican	Truman	303	24,105,182
J. Strom Thurmond	States' Rights,	Dewey	189	21,970,065
	Democratic	Thurmond	39	1,169,063
Henry A. Wallace	Progressive	H. Wallace	—	1,157,326
Adlai E. Stevenson	Democratic	Eisenhower	442	33,936,137
		Stevenson	89	27,314,649
Adlai E. Stevenson	Democratic	Eisenhower	457	35,585,245
		Stevenson	73	26,030,172
Richard M. Nixon	Republican	Kennedy	303	34,227,096
		Nixon	219	34,108,546
		H. Byrd (Ind. Dem.)	15	—
Barry M. Goldwater	Republican	Johnson	486	43,126,584
		Goldwater	52	27,177,838
Hubert H. Humphrey	Democratic	Nixon	301	31,770,237
George C. Wallace	American Independent	Humphrey	191	31,270,533
		G. Wallace	46	9,906,141
George S. McGovern	Democratic	Nixon	520	46,740,323
		McGovern	17	28,901,598
		Hospers (Va.)	1	—
Gerald R. Ford	Republican	Carter	297	40,830,763
Eugene McCarthy	Independent	Ford	240	39,147,793
		E. McCarthy	—	756,631
Jimmy Carter	Democratic	Reagan	489	43,899,248
John B. Anderson	Independent	Carter	49	35,481,435
Ed Clark	Libertarian	Anderson	—	5,719,437
Walter Mondale	Democratic	Reagan	525	54,451,521
David Bergland	Libertarian	Mondale	13	37,565,334
Michael Dukakis	Democratic	Bush	426	47,946,422
		Dukakis	111	41,016,429
		Bentsen	1	—
George Bush	Republican	Clinton	357	43,728,275
H. Ross Perot	Independent	Bush	168	38,167,416
		Perot	—	19,237,245

Cabinet Members

The Washington Administration

Secretary of State	Thomas Jefferson	1789-1793
	Edmund Randolph	1794-1795
	Timothy Pickering	1795-1797
Secretary of Treasury	Alexander Hamilton	1789-1795
	Oliver Wolcott	1795-1797
Secretary of War	Henry Knox	1789-1794
	Timothy Pickering	1795-1796
	James McHenry	1796-1797
Attorney General	Edmund Randolph	1789-1793
	William Bradford	1794-1795
	Charles Lee	1795-1797
Postmaster General	Samuel Osgood	1789-1791
	Timothy Pickering	1791-1794
	Joseph Habersham	1795-1797

The John Adams Administration

Secretary of State	Timothy Pickering	1797-1800
	John Marshall	1800-1801
Secretary of Treasury	Oliver Wolcott	1797-1800
	Samuel Dexter	1800-1801
Secretary of War	James McHenry	1797-1800
	Samuel Dexter	1800-1801
Attorney General	Charles Lee	1797-1901
Postmaster General	Joseph Habersham	1797-1801
Secretary of Navy	Benjamin Stoddert	1798-1801

The Jefferson Administration

Secretary of State	James Madison	1801-1809
Secretary of Treasury	Samuel Dexter	1801
	Albert Gallatin	1801-1809
Secretary of War	Henry Dearborn	1801-1809
Attorney General	Levi Lincoln	1801-1805
	Robert Smith	1805
	John Breckinridge	1805-1806
	Caesar Rodney	1807-1809
Postmaster General	Joseph Habersham	1801
	Gideon Granger	1801-1809
Secretary of Navy	Robert Smith	1801-1809

The Madison Administration

Secretary of State	Robert Smith	1809-1811
	James Monroe	1811-1817
Secretary of Treasury	Albert Gallatin	1809-1813
	George Campbell	1814
	Alexander Dallas	1814-1816
	William Crawford	1816-1817
Secretary of War	William Eustis	1809-1812
	John Armstrong	1813-1814
	James Monroe	1814-1815
	William Crawford	1815-1817
Attorney General	Caesar Rodney	1809-1811
	William Pinkney	1811-1814
	Richard Rush	1814-1817
Postmaster General	Gideon Granger	1809-1814
	Return Meigs	1814-1817
Secretary of Navy	Paul Hamilton	1809-1813
	William Jones	1813-1814
	Benjamin Crowninshield	1814-1817

The Monroe Administration

Secretary of State	John Quincy Adams	1817-1825
Secretary of Treasury	William Crawford	1817-1825
Secretary of War	George Graham	1817
	John C. Calhoun	1817-1825
Attorney General	Richard Rush	1817
	William Wirt	1817-1825
Postmaster General	Return Meigs	1817-1823
	John McLean	1823-1825
Secretary of Navy	Benjamin Crowninshield	1817-1818
	Smith Thompson	1818-1823
	Samuel Southard	1823-1825

The John Quincy Adams Administration

Secretary of State	Henry Clay	1825-1829
Secretary of Treasury	Richard Rush	1825-1829
Secretary of War	James Barbour	1825-1828
	Peter Porter	1828-1829
Attorney General	William Wirt	1825-1829
Postmaster General	John McLean	1825-1829
Secretary of Navy	Samuel Southard	1825-1829

The Jackson Administration

Secretary of State	Martin Van Buren	1829-1831
	Edward Livingston	1831-1833

Secretary of State	Louis McLane	1833-1834
	John Forsyth	1834-1837
Secretary of Treasury	Samuel Ingham	1829-1831
	Louis McLane	1831-1833
	William Duane	1833
	Roger B. Taney	1833-1834
	Levi Woodbury	1834-1837
Secretary of War	John H. Eaton	1829-1831
	Lewis Cass	1831-1837
	Benjamin Butler	1837
Attorney General	John M. Berrien	1829-1831
	Roger B. Taney	1831-1833
	Benjamin Butler	1833-1837
Postmaster General	William Barry	1829-1835
	Amos Kendall	1835-1837
Secretary of Navy	John Branch	1829-1831
	Levi Woodbury	1831-1834
	Mahlon Dickerson	1834-1837

The Van Buren Administration

Secretary of State	John Forsyth	1837-1841
Secretary of Treasury	Levi Woodbury	1837-1841
Secretary of War	Joel Poinsett	1837-1841
Attorney General	Benjamin Butler	1837-1838
	Felix Grundy	1838-1840
	Henry D. Gilpin	1840-1841
Postmaster General	Amos Kendall	1837-1840
	John M. Niles	1840-1841
Secretary of Navy	Mahlon Dickerson	1837-1838
	James Paulding	1838-1841

The William Harrison Administration

Secretary of State	Daniel Webster	1841
Secretary of Treasury	Thomas Ewing	1841
Secretary of War	John Bell	1841
Attorney General	John J. Crittenden	1841
Postmaster General	Francis Granger	1841
Secretary of Navy	George Badger	1841

The Tyler Administration

Secretary of State	Daniel Webster	1841-1843
	Hugh S. Legaré	1843
	Abel P. Upshur	1843-1844
	John C. Calhoun	1844-1845
Secretary of Treasury	Thomas Ewing	1841
	Walter Forward	1841-1843
	John C. Spencer	1843-1844
	George Bibb	1844-1845
Secretary of War	John Bell	1841
	John C. Spencer	1841-1843
	James M. Porter	1843-1844
	William Wilkins	1844-1845
Attorney General	John J. Crittenden	1841
	Hugh S. Legaré	1841-1843
	John Nelson	1843-1845
Postmaster General	Francis Granger	1841
	Charles Wickliffe	1841
Secretary of Navy	George Badger	1841
	Abel P. Upshur	1841
	David Henshaw	1843-1844
	Thomas Gilmer	1844
	John Y. Mason	1844-1845

The Polk Administration

Secretary of State	James Buchanan	1845-1849
Secretary of Treasury	Robert J. Walker	1845-1849
Secretary of War	William L. Marcy	1845-1849
Attorney General	John Y. Mason	1845-1846
	Nathan Clifford	1846-1848
	Isaac Toucey	1848-1849
Postmaster General	Cave Johnson	1845-1849
Secretary of Navy	George Bancroft	1845-1846
	John Y. Mason	1846-1849

The Taylor Administration

Secretary of State	John M. Clayton	1849-1850
Secretary of Treasury	William Meredith	1849-1850
Secretary of War	George Crawford	1849-1850
Attorney General	Reverdy Johnson	1849-1850
Postmaster General	Jacob Collamer	1849-1850
Secretary of Navy	William Preston	1849-1850
Secretary of Interior	Thomas Ewing	1849-1850

The Fillmore Administration

Secretary of State	Daniel Webster	1850-1852
	Edward Everett	1852-1853
Secretary of Treasury	Thomas Corwin	1850-1853

Secretary of War	Charles Conrad	1850-1853
Attorney General	John J. Crittenden	1850-1853
Postmaster General	Nathan Hall	1850-1852
	Sam D. Hubbard	1852-1853
Secretary of Navy	William A. Graham	1850-1852
	John P. Kennedy	1852-1853
Secretary of Interior	Thomas McKennan	1850
	Alexander Stuart	1850-1853

The Pierce Administration

Secretary of State	William L. Marcy	1853-1857
Secretary of Treasury	James Guthrie	1853-1857
Secretary of War	Jefferson Davis	1853-1857
Attorney General	Caleb Cushing	1853-1857
Postmaster General	James Campbell	1853-1857
Secretary of Navy	James C. Dobbin	1853-1857
Secretary of Interior	Robert McClelland	1853-1857

The Buchanan Administration

Secretary of State	Lewis Cass	1857-1860
	Jeremiah S. Black	1860-1861
Secretary of Treasury	Howell Cobb	1857-1860
	Philip Thomas	1860-1861
	John A. Dix	1861
Secretary of War	John B. Floyd	1857-1861
	Joseph Holt	1861
Attorney General	Jeremiah S. Black	1857-1860
	Edwin M. Stanton	1860-1861
Postmaster General	Aaron V. Brown	1857-1859
	Joseph Holt	1859-1861
	Horatio King	1861
Secretary of Navy	Isaac Toucey	1857-1861
Secretary of Interior	Jacob Thompson	1857-1861

The Lincoln Administration

Secretary of State	William H. Seward	1861-1865
Secretary of Treasury	Salmon P. Chase	1861-1864
	William P. Fessenden	1864-1865
	Hugh McCulloch	1865
Secretary of War	Simon Cameron	1861-1862
	Edwin M. Stanton	1862-1865

Attorney General	Edward Bates	1861-1864
	James Speed	1864-1865
Postmaster General	Horatio King	1861
	Montgomery Blair	1861-1864
	William Dennison	1864-1865
Secretary of Navy	Gideon Welles	1861-1865
Secretary of Interior	Caleb B. Smith	1861-1863
	John P. Usher	1863-1865

The Andrew Johnson Administration

Secretary of State	William H. Seward	1865-1869
Secretary of Treasury	Hugh McCulloch	1865-1869
Secretary of War	Edwin M. Stanton	1865-1867
	Ulysses S. Grant	1867-1868
	Lorenzo Thomas	1868
	John M. Schofield	1868-1869
Attorney General	James Speed	1865-1866
	Henry Stanbery	1866-1868
	William M. Evarts	1868-1869
Postmaster General	William Dennison	1865-1866
	Alexander Randall	1866-1869
Secretary of Navy	Gideon Welles	1865-1869
Secretary of Interior	John P. Usher	1865
	James Harlan	1865-1866
	Orville H. Browning	1866-1869

The Grant Administration

Secretary of State	Elihu B. Washburne	1869
	Hamilton Fish	1869-1877
Secretary of Treasury	George S. Boutwell	1869-1873
	William Richardson	1873-1874
	Benjamin Bristow	1874-1876
	Lot M. Morrill	1876-1877
Secretary of War	John A. Rawlins	1869
	William T. Sherman	1869
	William W. Belknap	1869-1876
	Alphonso Taft	1876
	James D. Cameron	1876-1877
Attorney General	Ebenezer Hoar	1869-1870
	Amos T. Ackerman	1870-1871
	G. H. Williams	1871-1875
	Edwards Pierrepont	1875-1876
	Alphonso Taft	1876-1877
Postmaster General	John A. Creswell	1869-1874
	James W. Marshall	1874
	Marshall Jewell	1874-1876
	James N. Tyner	1876-1877
Secretary of Navy	Adolph E. Borie	1869
	George M. Robeson	1869-1877
Secretary of Interior	Jacob D. Cox	1869-1870
	Columbus Delano	1870-1875

| Secretary of Interior | Zachariah Chandler | 1875-1877 |

The Hayes Administration

Secretary of State	William B. Evarts	1877-1881
Secretary of Treasury	John Sherman	1877-1881
Secretary of War	George W. McCrary Alex Ramsey	1877-1879 1879-1881
Attorney General	Charles Devens	1877-1881
Postmaster General	David M. Key Horace Maynard	1877-1880 1880-1881
Secretary of Navy	Richard W. Thompson Nathan Goff, Jr.	1877-1880 1881
Secretary of Interior	Carl Shurz	1877-1881

The Garfield Administration

Secretary of State	James G. Blaine	1881
Secretary of Treasury	William Windom	1881
Secretary of War	Robert T. Lincoln	1881
Attorney General	Wayne MacVeagh	1881
Postmaster General	Thomas L. James	1881
Secretary of Navy	William H. Hunt	1881
Secretary of Interior	Samuel J. Kirkwood	1881

The Arthur Administration

Secretary of State	F. T. Frelinghuysen	1881-1885
Secretary of Treasury	Charles J. Folger Walter Q. Gresham Hugh McCulloch	1881-1884 1884 1884-1885
Secretary of War	Robert T. Lincoln	1881-1885
Attorney General	Benjamin H. Brewster	1881-1885
Postmaster General	Timothy O. Howe Walter Q. Gresham Frank Hatton	1881-1883 1883-1884 1884-1885
Secretary of Navy	William H. Hunt William E. Chandler	1881-1882 1882-1885
Secretary of Interior	Samuel J. Kirkwood Henry M. Teller	1881-1882 1882-1885

The Cleveland Administration (first)

Secretary of State	Thomas F. Bayard	1885-1889
Secretary of Treasury	Daniel Manning Charles S. Fairchild	1885-1887 1887-1889
Secretary of War	William C. Endicott	1885-1889
Attorney General	Augustus H. Garland	1885-1889
Postmaster General	William F. Vilas Don M. Dickinson	1885-1888 1888-1889
Secretary of Navy	William C. Whitney	1885-1889
Secretary of Interior	Lucius Q. C. Lamar William F. Vilas	1885-1889 1888-1889
Secretary of Agriculture	Norman J. Colman	1889

The Benjamin Harrison Administration

Secretary of State	James G. Blaine John W. Foster	1889-1892 1892-1893
Secretary of Treasury	William Windom Charles Foster	1889-1891 1891-1893
Secretary of War	Redfield Proctor Stephen B. Elkins	1889-1891 1891-1893
Attorney General	William H. H. Miller	1889-1891
Postmaster General	John Wanamaker	1889-1893
Secretary of Navy	Benjamin F. Tracy	1889-1893
Secretary of Interior	John W. Noble	1889-1893
Secretary of Agriculture	Jeremiah M. Rusk	1889-1893

The Cleveland Administration (second)

Secretary of State	Walter Q. Gresham Richard Olney	1893-1895 1895-1897
Secretary of Treasury	John G. Carlisle	1893-1897
Secretary of War	Daniel S. Lamont	1893-1897
Attorney General	Richard Olney James Harmon	1893-1895 1895-1897
Postmaster General	Wilson S. Bissell William L. Wilson	1893-1895 1895-1897
Secretary of Navy	Hilary A. Herbert	1893-1897
Secretary of Interior	Hoke Smith David R. Francis	1893-1896 1896-1897

| Secretary of Agriculture | Julius S. Morton | 1893-1897 |

The McKinley Administration

Secretary of State	John Sherman	1897-1898
	William R. Day	1898
	John Hay	1898-1901
Secretary of Treasury	Lyman J. Gage	1897-1901
Secretary of War	Russell A. Alger	1897-1899
	Elihu Root	1899-1901
Attorney General	Joseph McKenna	1897-1898
	John W. Griggs	1898-1901
	Philander C. Knox	1901
Postmaster General	James A. Gary	1897-1898
	Charles E. Smith	1898-1901
Secretary of Navy	John D. Long	1897-1901
Secretary of Interior	Cornelius N. Bliss	1897-1899
	Ethan A. Hitchcock	1899-1901
Secretary of Agriculture	James Wilson	1897-1901

The Theodore Roosevelt Administration

Secretary of State	John Hay	1901-1905
	Elihu Root	1905-1909
	Robert Bacon	1909
Secretary of Treasury	Lyman J. Gage	1901-1902
	Leslie M. Shaw	1902-1907
	George B. Cortelyou	1907-1909
Secretary of War	Elihu Root	1901-1904
	William H. Taft	1904-1908
	Luke E. Wright	1908-1909
Attorney General	Philander C. Knox	1901-1904
	William H. Moody	1904-1906
	Charles J. Bonaparte	1906-1909
Postmaster General	Charles E. Smith	1901-1902
	Henry C. Payne	1902-1904
	Robert J. Wynne	1904-1905
	George B. Cortelyou	1905-1907
	George von L. Meyer	1907-1909
Secretary of Navy	John D. Long	1901-1902
	William H. Moody	1902-1904
	Paul Morton	1904-1905
	Charles J. Bonaparte	1905-1906
	Victor H. Metcalf	1906-1908
	Truman N. Newberry	1908-1909
Secretary of Interior	Ethan A. Hitchcock	1901-1907
	James R. Garfield	1907-1909
Secretary of Agriculture	James Wilson	1901-1909
Secretary of Labor and Commerce	George B. Cortelyou	1903-1904
	Victor H. Metcalf	1904-1906
	Oscar S. Straus	1906-1909
	Charles Nagel	1909

The Taft Administration

Secretary of State	Philander C. Knox	1909-1913
Secretary of Treasury	Franklin MacVeagh	1909-1913
Secretary of War	Jacob M. Dickinson	1909-1911
	Henry L. Stimson	1911-1913
Attorney General	George W. Wickersham	1909-1913
Postmaster General	Frank H. Hitchcock	1909-1913
Secretary of Navy	George von L. Meyer	1909-1913
Secretary of Interior	Richard A. Ballinger	1909-1911
	Walter L. Fisher	1911-1913
Secretary of Agriculture	James Wilson	1909-1913
Secretary of Labor and Commerce	Charles Nagel	1909-1913

The Wilson Administration

Secretary of State	William J. Bryan	1913-1915
	Robert Lansing	1915-1920
	Bainbridge Colby	1920-1921
Secretary of Treasury	William G. McAdoo	1913-1918
	Carter Glass	1918-1920
	David F. Houston	1920-1921
Secretary of War	Lindley M. Garrison	1913-1916
	Newton D. Baker	1916-1921
Attorney General	James C. McReynolds	1913-1914
	Thomas W. Gregory	1914-1919
	A. Mitchell Palmer	1919-1921
Postmaster General	Albert S. Burleson	1913-1921
Secretary of Navy	Josephus Daniels	1913-1921
Secretary of Interior	Franklin K. Lane	1913-1920
	John B. Payne	1920-1921
Secretary of Agriculture	David F. Houston	1913-1919
	Edwin T. Meredith	1919-1921
Secretary of Commerce	William C. Redfield	1913-1919
	Joshua W. Alexander	1919-1921
Secretary of Labor	William B. Wilson	1913-1921

The Harding Administration

Secretary of State	Charles E. Hughes	1921-1923
Secretary of Treasury	Andrew Mellon	1921-1923
Secretary of War	John W. Weeks	1921-1923

Attorney General	Harry M. Daugherty	1921-1923
Postmaster General	Will H. Hays Hubert Work Harry S. New	1921-1922 1922-1923 1923
Secretary of Navy	Edwin Denby	1921-1923
Secretary of Interior	Albert B. Fall Hubert Work	1921-1923 1923
Secretary of Agriculture	Henry C. Wallace	1921-1923
Secretary of Commerce	Herbert C. Hoover	1921-1923
Secretary of Labor	James J. Davis	1921-1923

The Coolidge Administration

Secretary of State	Charles B. Hughes Frank B. Kellogg	1923-1925 1925-1929
Secretary of Treasury	Andrew Mellon	1923-1929
Secretary of War	John W. Weeks Dwight F. Davis	1923-1925 1925-1929
Attorney General	Henry M. Daugherty Harlan F. Stone John G. Sargent	1923-1924 1924-1925 1925-1929
Postmaster General	Harry S. New	1923-1929
Secretary of Navy	Edwin Denby Curtis D. Wilbur	1923-1924 1924-1929
Secretary of Interior	Hubert Work Roy O. West	1923-1928 1928-1929
Secretary of Agriculture	Henry C. Wallace Howard M. Gore William M. Jardine	1923-1924 1924-1925 1925-1929
Secretary of Commerce	Herbert C. Hoover William F. Whiting	1923-1928 1928-1929
Secretary of Labor	James J. Davis	1923-1929

The Hoover Administration

Secretary of State	Henry L. Stimson	1929-1933
Secretary of Treasury	Andrew Mellon Ogden L. Mills	1929-1932 1932-1933
Secretary of War	James W. Good Patrick J. Hurley	1929 1929-1933
Attorney General	William D. Mitchell	1929-1933
Postmaster General	Walter F. Brown	1929-1933
Secretary of Navy	Charles F. Adams	1929-1933
Secretary of Interior	Ray L. Wilbur	1929-1933
Secretary of Agriculture	Arthur M. Hyde	1929-1933
Secretary of Commerce	Robert P. Lamont Roy D. Chapin	1929-1932 1932-1933
Secretary of Labor	James J. Davis William N. Doak	1929-1930 1930-1933

The Franklin D. Roosevelt Administration

Secretary of State	Cordell Hull E. R. Stettinius, Jr.	1933-1944 1944-1945
Secretary of Treasury	William H. Woodin Henry Morgenthau, Jr.	1933-1934 1934-1945
Secretary of War	George H. Dern Henry A. Woodring Henry L. Stimson	1933-1936 1936-1940 1940-1945
Attorney General	Homer S. Cummings Frank Murphy Robert H. Jackson Francis Biddle	1933-1939 1939-1940 1940-1941 1941-1945
Postmaster General	James A. Farley Frank C. Walker	1933-1940 1940-1945
Secretary of Navy	Claude A. Swanson Charles Edison Frank Knox James V. Forrestal	1933-1940 1940 1940-1944 1944-1945
Secretary of Interior	Harold L. Ickes	1933-1945
Secretary of Agriculture	Henry A. Wallace Claude R. Wickard	1933-1940 1940-1945
Secretary of Commerce	Daniel C. Roper Harry L. Hopkins Jesse Jones Henry A. Wallace	1933-1939 1939-1940 1940-1945 1945
Secretary of Labor	Frances Perkins	1933-1945

The Truman Administration

Secretary of State	James F. Byrnes George C. Marshall Dean G. Acheson	1945-1947 1947-1949 1949-1953
Secretary of Treasury	Fred M. Vinson John W. Snyder	1945-1946 1946-1953
Secretary of War	Robert P. Patterson Kenneth C. Royall	1945-1947 1947
Attorney General	Tom C. Clark J. Howard McGrath James P. McGranery	1945-1949 1949-1952 1952-1953
Postmaster General	Frank C. Walker Robert E. Hannegan Jessee M. Donaldson	1945 1945-1947 1947-1953
Secretary of Navy	James V. Forrestal	1945-1947

Secretary of Interior	Harold L. Ickes	1945-1946
	Julius A. Krug	1946-1949
	Oscar I. Chapman	1949-1953
Secretary of Agriculture	Clinton P. Anderson	1945-1948
	Charles F. Brannan	1948-1953
Secretary of Commerce	Henry A. Wallace	1945-1946
	W. Averell Harriman	1946-1948
	Charles W. Sawyer	1948-1953
Secretary of Labor	Lewis B. Schwellenbach	1945-1948
	Maurice J. Tobin	1948-1953
Secretary of Defense	James V. Forrestal	1947-1949
	Louis A. Johnson	1949-1950
	George C. Marshall	1950-1951
	Robert A. Lovett	1951-1953

The Eisenhower Administration

Secretary of State	John Foster Dulles	1953-1959
	Christian A. Herter	1959-1961
Secretary of Treasury	George M. Humphrey	1953-1957
	Robert B. Anderson	1957-1961
Attorney General	Herbert Brownell, Jr.	1953-1958
	William P. Rogers	1958-1961
Postmaster General	Arthur E. Summerfield	1953-1961
Secretary of Interior	Douglas McKay	1953-1956
	Fred A. Seaton	1956-1961
Secretary of Agriculture	Ezra T. Benson	1953-1961
Secretary of Commerce	Sinclair Weeks	1953-1958
	Lewis L. Strauss	1958-1959
	Frederick H. Mueller	1959-1961
Secretary of Labor	Martin P. Durkin	1953
	James P. Mitchell	1953-1961
Secretary of Defense	Charles E. Wilson	1953-1957
	Neil H. McElroy	1957-1959
	Thomas S. Gates, Jr.	1959-1961
Secretary of Health, Education and Welfare	Oveta Culp Hobby	1953-1955
	Marion B. Folsom	1955-1958
	Arthur S. Flemming	1958-1961

The Kennedy Administration

Secretary of State	Dean Rusk	1961-1963
Secretary of Treasury	C. Douglas Dillon	1961-1963
Attorney General	Robert F. Kennedy	1961-1963
Postmaster General	J. Edward Day	1961-1963
	John A. Gronouski	1963
Secretary of Interior	Stewart L. Udall	
Secretary of Agriculture	Orville L. Freeman	1961-1963
Secretary of Commerce	Luther H. Hodges	1961-1963
Secretary of Labor	Arthur J. Goldberg	1961-1962
	W. Williard Wirtz	1962-1963
Secretary of Defense	Robert F. McNamara	1961-1963
Secretary of Health, Education and Welfare	Abraham A. Ribicoff	1961-1962
	Anthony J. Celebrezze	1962-1963

The Lyndon Johnson Administration

Secretary of State	Dean Rusk	1963-1969
Secretary of Treasury	C. Douglas Dillon	1963-1965
	Henry H. Fowler	1965-1969
Attorney General	Robert F. Kennedy	1963-1964
	Nicholas Katzenbach	1965-1966
	Ramsey Clark	1967-1969
Postmaster General	John A. Gronouski	1963-1965
	Lawrence F. O'Brien	1965-1968
	Marvin Watson	1968-1969
Secretary of Interior	Stewart L. Udall	1963-1969
Secretary of Agriculture	Orville L. Freeman	1963-1969
Secretary of Commerce	Luther H. Hodges	1963-1964
	John T. Connor	1964-1967
	Alexander B. Trowbridge	1967-1968
	Cyrus R. Smith	1968-1969
Secretary of Labor	W. Willard Wirtz	1963-1969
Secretary of Defense	Robert F. McNamara	1963-1968
	Clark Clifford	1968-1969
Secretary of Health, Education and Welfare	Anthony J. Celebrezze	1962-1963
	John W. Gardner	1965-1968
	Wilbur J. Cohen	1968-1969
Secretary of Housing and Urban Development	Robert C. Weaver	1966-1969
	Robert C. Wood	1969
Secretary of Transportation	Alan S. Boyd	1967-1969

The Nixon Administration

Secretary of State	William P. Rogers	1969-1973
	Henry A. Kissinger	1973-1974
Secretary of Treasury	David M. Kennedy	1969-1970
	John B. Connally	1971-1972
	George P. Shultz	1972-1974
	William E. Smon	1974
Attorney General	John N. Mitchell	1969-1972
	Richard G. Kleindienst	1972-1973

	Elliot L. Richardson	1973
	William B. Saxbe	1973-1974
Postmaster General	Winton M. Blount	1969-1971
Secretary of Interior	Walter J. Hickel	1969-1970
	Rogers Morton	1971-1974
Secretary of Agriculture	Clifford M. Hardin	1969-1971
	Earl L. Butz	1971-1974
Secretary of Commerce	Maurice H. Stans	1969-1972
	Peter G. Peterson	1972-1973
	Frederick B. Dent	1973-1974
Secretary of Labor	George P. Shultz	1969-1970
	James D. Hodgson	1970-1973
	Peter J. Brennan	1973-1974
Secretary of Defense	Melvin R. Laird	1969-1973
	Elliot L. Richardson	1973
	James R. Schlesinger	1973-1974
Secretary of Health, Education and Welfare	Robert H. Finch	1969-1970
	Elliot L. Richardson	1970-1973
	Caspar W. Weinberger	1973-1974
Secretary of Housing and Urban Development	George Romney	1969-1973
	James T. Lynn	1973-1974
Secretary of Transportation	John A. Volpe	1969-1973
	Claude S. Brinegar	1973-1974

The Ford Administration

Secretary of State	Henry A. Kissinger	1974-1977
Secretary of Treasury	William E. Simon	1974-1977
Attorney General	William B. Saxbe	1974-1975
	Edward Levi	1975-1977
Secretary of Interior	Rogers Morton	1974-1975
	Stanley K. Hathaway	1975
	Thomas Kleppe	1975-1977
Secretary of Agriculture	Earl L. Butz	1974-1976
	John A. Knebel	1976-1977
Secretary of Commerce	Frederick B. Dent	1974-1975
	Rogers Morton	1975-1976
	Elliot L. Richardson	1976-1977
Secretary of Labor	Peter J. Brennan	1974-1975
	John T. Dunlop	1975-1976
	W. J. Usery	1976-1977
Secretary of Defense	James R. Schlesinger	1974-1975
	Donald Rumsfeld	1975-1977
Secretary of Health, Education and Welfare	Caspar Weinberger	1974-1975
	Forrest D. Mathews	1975-1977

Secretary of Housing and Urban Development	James T. Lynn	1973-1974
	Carla A. Hills	1975-1977
Secretary of Transportation	Claude S. Brinegar	1974-1975
	William T. Coleman	1975-1977

The Carter Administration

Secretary of State	Cyrus R. Vance	1977-1980
	Edmund Muskie	1980-1981
Secretary of Treasury	W. Michael Blumenthal	1977-1979
	G. William Miller	1979-1981
Attorney General	Griffin Bell	1977-1979
	Benjamin R. Civiletti	1979-1981
Secretary of Interior	Cecil D. Andrus	1977-1981
Secretary of Agriculture	Robert Bergland	1977-1981
Secretary of Commerce	Juanita M. Kreps	1977-1979
	Philip M. Klutznick	1979-1981
Secretary of Labor	F. Ray Marshall	1977-1981
Secretary of Defense	Harold Brown	1977-1981
Secretary of Health, Education and Welfare	Joseph A. Califano	1977-1979
	Patricia R. Harris	1979
Secretary of Health and Human Services	Patricia R. Harris	1979-1981
Secretary of Education	Shirley M. Hufstedler	1979-1981
Secretary of Housing and Urban Development	Patricia R. Harris	1977-1979
	Moon Landrieu	1979-1981
Secretary of Transportation	Brock Adams	1977-1979
	Neil E. Goldschmidt	1979-1981
Secretary of Energy	James R. Schlesinger	1977-1979
	Charles W. Duncan	1979-1981

The Reagan Administration

Secretary of State	Alexander M. Haig	1981-1982
	George P. Shultz	1982-1989
Secretary of Treasury	Donald T. Regan	1981-1985
	James A. Baker	1985-1988
	Nicholas Brady	1988-1989
Attorney General	William French Smith	1981-1985
	Edwin Meese	1985-1988
	Richard Thornburgh	1988-1989

Secretary of Interior	James Watt	1981-1983
	William P. Clark	1983-1985
	Donald Hodel	1985-1989
Secretary of Agriculture	John R. Block	1981-1985
	Richard E. Lyng	1985-1989
Secretary of Commerce	Malcolm Baldrige	1981-1987
	C. William Verity	1987-1989
Secretary of Labor	Raymond J. Donovan	1981-1985
	William E. Brock	1985-1988
	Ann Dore McLaughlin	1988-1989
Secretary of Defense	Caspar W. Weinberger	1981-1988
	Frank C. Carlucci	1988-1989
Secretary of Health and Human Services	Richard S. Schweiker	1981-1983
	Margaret M. Heckler	1983-1985
	Otis R. Bowen	1985-1989
Secretary of Education	Terrel H. Bell	1981-1985
	William J. Bennett	1985-1988
	Lauro F. Cavazos	1988-1989
Secretary of Housing and Urban Development	Samuel R. Pierce, Jr.	1981-1989
Secretary of Transportation	Drew Lewis	1981-1983
	Elizabeth H. Dole	1983-1987
	James L. Burnely	1987-1989
Secretary of Energy	James B. Edwards	1981-1982
	Donald P. Hodel	1982-1985
	John S. Herrington	1985-1989

The Bush Administration

Secretary of State	James A. Baker	1989-1992
	Lawrence S. Eagleburger	1992-1993
Secretary of Treasury	Nicholas F. Brady	1989-1993
Attorney General	Richard Thornburgh	1989-1992
	William P. Barr	1992-1993
Secretary of Interior	Manuel Lujan	1989-1993
Secretary of Agriculture	Clayton Yeutter	1989-1991
	Edward Madigan	1991-1993
Secretary of Commerce	Robert Mosbacher	1989-1992
	Barbara H. Franklin	1992-1993
Secretary of Labor	Elizabeth H. Dole	1989-1991
	Lynn Martin	1991-1993
Secretary of Defense	Richard B. Cheney	1989-1993
Secretary of Health and Human Services	Louis W. Sullivan	1989-1993
Secretary of Housing and Urban Development	Jack F. Kemp	1989-1993
Secretary of Transportation	Samuel Skinner	1989-1992
	Andrew Card	1992-1993
Secretary of Energy	James D. Watkins	1989-1993
Secretary of Education	Lauro F. Cavazos	1989-1991
	Lamar Alexander	1991-1993
Secretary of Veterans Affairs	Edward J. Derwinski	1989-1993

The Clinton Administration

Secretary of State	Warren M. Christopher	1993-
Secretary of Treasury	Lloyd Bentsen	1993-
Attorney General	Janet Reno	1993-
Secretary of Interior	Bruce Babbitt	1993-
Secretary of Agriculture	Mike Espy	1993-1994
Secretary of Commerce	Ronald Brown	1993-
Secretary of Labor	Robert R. Reich	1993-
Secretary of Defense	Les Aspin	1993-1994
	William Perry	1994-
Secretary of Health and Human Services	Donna Shalala	1993-
Secretary of Housing and Urban Development	Henry G. Cisneros	1993-
Secretary of Transportation	Federico F. Peña	1993-
Secretary of Energy	Hazel R. O'Leary	1993-
Secretary of Education	Richard W. Riley	1993-
Secretary of Veterans Affairs	Jesse Brown	1993-

Supreme Court Justices

Name	Terms of Service[1]	Appointed by	Name	Terms of Service[1]	Appointed by
John Jay	1789–1795	Washington	Rufus W. Peckham	1896–1909	Cleveland
James Wilson	1789–1798	Washington	Joseph McKenna	1898–1925	McKinley
John Rutledge	1790–1791	Washington	Oliver W. Holmes	1902–1932	T. Roosevelt
William Cushing	1790–1810	Washington	William R. Day	1903–1922	T. Roosevelt
John Blair	1790–1796	Washington	William H. Moody	1906–1910	T. Roosevelt
James Iredell	1790–1799	Washington	Horace H. Lurton	1910–1914	Taft
Thomas Johnson	1792–1793	Washington	Charles E. Hughes	1910–1916	Taft
William Paterson	1793–1806	Washington	Willis Van Devanter	1911–1937	Taft
John Rutledge[1]	1795	Washington	Joseph R. Lamar	1911–1916	Taft
Samuel Chase	1796–1811	Washington	**Edward D. White**	1910–1921	Taft
Oliver Ellsworth	1796–1800	Washington	Mahlon Pitney	1912–1922	Taft
Bushrod Washington	1799–1829	J. Adams	James C. McReynolds	1914–1941	Wilson
Alfred Moore	1800–1804	J. Adams	Louis D. Brandeis	1916–1939	Wilson
John Marshall	1801–1835	J. Adams	John H. Clarke	1916–1922	Wilson
William Johnson	1804–1834	Jefferson	**William H. Taft**	1921–1930	Harding
William Johnson	1804–1834	Jefferson	George Sutherland	1922–1938	Harding
Brockholst Livingston	1807–1823	Jefferson	Pierce Butler	1923–1939	Harding
Thomas Todd	1807–1826	Jefferson	Edward T. Sanford	1923–1930	Harding
Gabriel Duval	1811–1835	Madison	Harlan F. Stone	1925–1941	Coolidge
Joseph Story	1812–1845	Madison	**Charles E. Hughes**	1930–1941	Hoover
Smith Thompson	1823–1843	Monroe	Owen J. Roberts	1930–1945	Hoover
Robert Trimble	1826–1828	J. Q. Adams	Benjamin N. Cardozo	1932–1938	Hoover
John McLean	1830–1861	Jackson	Hugo L. Black	1937–1971	F. Roosevelt
Henry Baldwin	1830–1844	Jackson	Stanley F. Reed	1938–1957	F. Roosevelt
James M. Wayne	1835–1867	Jackson	Felix Frankfurter	1939–1962	F. Roosevelt
Roger B. Taney	1836–1864	Jackson	William O. Douglas	1939–1975	F. Roosevelt
Philip P. Barbour	1836–1841	Jackson	Frank Murphy	1940–1949	F. Roosevelt
John Cartron	1837–1865	Van Buren	**Harlan F. Stone**	1941–1946	F. Roosevelt
John McKinley	1838–1852	Van Buren	James F. Byrnes	1941–1942	F. Roosevelt
Peter V. Daniel	1842–1860	Van Buren	Robert H. Jackson	1941–1954	F. Roosevelt
Samuel Nelson	1845–1872	Tyler	Wiley B. Rutledge	1943–1949	F. Roosevelt
Levi Woodbury	1845–1851	Polk	Harold H. Burton	1945–1958	Truman
Robert C. Grier	1846–1870	Polk	**Frederick M. Vinson**	1946–1953	Truman
Benjamin R. Curtis	1851–1857	Fillmore	Tom C. Clark	1949–1967	Truman
John A. Campbell	1853–1861	Pierce	Sherman Minton	1949–1956	Truman
Nathan Clifford	1858–1881	Buchanan	**Earl Warren**	1953–1969	Eisenhower
Noah H. Swayne	1862–1881	Lincoln	John Marshall Harlan	1955–1971	Eisenhower
Samuel F. Miller	1862–1890	Lincoln	William J. Brennan, Jr.	1956–1990	Eisenhower
David Davis	1862–1877	Lincoln	Charles E. Whittaker	1957–1962	Eisenhower
Stephen J. Field	1863–1897	Lincoln	Potter Stewart	1958–1981	Eisenhower
Salmon P. Chase	1864–1873	Lincoln	Byron R. White	1962–1993	Kennedy
William Strong	1870–1880	Grant	Arthur J. Goldberg	1962–1965	Kennedy
Joseph P. Bradley	1870–1892	Grant	Abe Fortas	1965–1969	Johnson
Ward Hunt	1873–1882	Grant	Thurgood Marshall	1967–1991	Johnson
Morrison R. Waite	1873–1882	Grant	**Warren E. Burger**	1969–1986	Nixon
John M. Harlan	1877–1911	Hayes	Harry A. Blackmun	1970–1994	Nixon
William B. Woods	1881–1887	Hayes	Lewis F. Powell, Jr.	1971–1987	Nixon
Stanley Matthews	1881–1889	Garfield	William H. Rehnquist	1971–1986	Nixon
Horace Gray	1882–1902	Arthur	John Paul Stevens	1975–	Ford
Samuel Blatchford	1882–1893	Arthur	Sandra Day O'Connor	1981–	Reagan
Lucius Q. C. Lamar	1888–1893	Cleveland	**William H. Rehnquist**	1986–	Reagan
Melville W. Fuller	1888–1910	Cleveland	Antonin Scalia	1986–	Reagan
David J. Brewer	1890–1910	B. Harrison	Anthony M. Kennedy	1988–	Reagan
Henry B. Brown	1891–1906	B. Harrison	David H. Souter	1990–	Bush
George Shiras, Jr.	1892–1903	B. Harrison	Clarence Thomas	1991–	Bush
Howell E. Jackson	1893–1895	B. Harrison	Ruth Bader Ginsburg	1992–	Clinton
Edward D. White	1894–1910	Cleveland	Stephen G. Breyer	1994–	Clinton

Chief Justices in bold type.

[1]*The date on which the justice took his judicial oath is here used as the date of the beginning of his service, for until that oath is taken he is not vested with the prerogatives of his office. Justices, however, receive their commissions ("letters patent") before taking their oath—in some instances, in the preceding year.*

[2]*Acting Chief Justice; Senate refused to confirm appointment.*

Admission of States into the Union

State	Date of Admission	State	Date of Admission
1. Delaware	December 7, 1787	26. Michigan	January 26, 1837
2. Pennsylvania	December 12, 1787	27. Florida	March 3, 1845
3. New Jersey	December 18, 1787	28. Texas	December 29, 1845
4. Georgia	January 2, 1788	29. Iowa	December 28, 1846
5. Connecticut	January 9, 1788	30. Wisconsin	May 29, 1848
6. Massachusetts	February 6, 1788	31. California	September 9, 1850
7. Maryland	April 28, 1788	32. Minnesota	May 11, 1858
8. South Carolina	May 23, 1788	33. Oregon	February 14, 1859
9. New Hampshire	June 21, 1788	34. Kansas	January 29, 1861
10. Virginia	June 25, 1788	35. West Virginia	June 20, 1863
11. New York	July 26, 1788	36. Nevada	October 31, 1864
12. North Carolina	November 21, 1789	37. Nebraska	March 1, 1867
13. Rhode Island	May 29, 1790	38. Colorado	August 1, 1876
14. Vermont	March 4, 1791	39. North Dakota	November 2, 1889
15. Kentucky	June 1, 1792	40. South Dakota	November 2, 1889
16. Tennessee	June 1, 1796	41. Montana	November 8, 1889
17. Ohio	March 1, 1803	42. Washington	November 11, 1889
18. Louisiana	April 30, 1812	43. Idaho	July 3, 1890
19. Indiana	December 11, 1816	44. Wyoming	July 10, 1890
20. Mississippi	December 10, 1817	45. Utah	January 4, 1896
21. Illinois	December 3, 1818	46. Oklahoma	November 16, 1907
22. Alabama	December 14, 1819	47. New Mexico	January 6, 1912
23. Maine	March 15, 1820	48. Arizona	February 14, 1912
24. Missouri	August 10, 1821	49. Alaska	January 3, 1959
25. Arkansas	June 15, 1836	50. Hawaii	August 21, 1959

Ten Largest Cities by Population, 1700–1990

	City	Population
1700	Boston	6,700
	New York	4,937
	Philadelphia	4,400
1790	Philadelphia	42,520
	New York	33,131
	Boston	18,038
	Charleston, S.C.	16,359
	Baltimore	13,503
	Salem, Mass.	7,921
	Newport, R.I.	6,716
	Providence, R.I.	6,380
	Marblehead, Mass.	5,661
	Portsmouth, N.H.	4,720
1830	New York	197,112
	Philadelphia	161,410
	Baltimore	80,620
	Boston	61,392
	Charleston, S.C.	30,289
	New Orleans	29,737
	Cincinnati	24,831
	Albany, N.Y.	24,209
	Brooklyn, N.Y.	20,535
	Washington, D.C.	18,826
1850	New York	515,547
	Philadelphia	340,045
	Baltimore	169,054
	Boston	136,881
	New Orleans	116,375
	Cincinnati	115,435
	Brooklyn, N.Y.	96,838
	St. Louis	77,860
	Albany, N.Y.	50,763
	Pittsburgh	46,601
1870	New York	942,292
	Philadelphia	674,022
	Brooklyn, N.Y.	419,921
	St. Louis	310,864
	Chicago	298,977
	Baltimore	267,354
	Boston	250,526
	Cincinnati	216,239
	New Orleans	191,418
	San Francisco	149,473
1910	New York	4,766,883
	Chicago	2,185,283
	Philadelphia	1,549,008

	City	Population
	St. Louis	687,029
	Boston	670,585
	Cleveland	560,663
	Baltimore	558,485
	Pittsburgh	533,905
	Detroit	465,766
	Buffalo	423,715
1930	New York	6,930,446
	Chicago	3,376,438
	Philadelphia	1,950,961
	Detroit	1,568,662
	Los Angeles	1,238,048
	Cleveland	900,429
	St. Louis	821,960
	Baltimore	804,874
	Boston	781,188
	Pittsburgh	669,817
1950	New York	7,891,957
	Chicago	3,620,962
	Philadelphia	2,071,605
	Los Angeles	1,970,358
	Detroit	1,849,568
	Baltimore	949,708
	Cleveland	914,808
	St. Louis	856,796
	Washington, D.C.	802,178
	Boston	801,444
1970	New York	7,895,563
	Chicago	3,369,357
	Los Angeles	2,811,801
	Philadelphia	1,949,996
	Detroit	1,514,063
	Houston	1,233,535
	Baltimore	905,787
	Dallas	844,401
	Washington, D.C.	756,668
	Cleveland	750,879
1990	New York	7,322,564
	Los Angeles	3,485,398
	Chicago	2,783,726
	Houston	1,630,553
	Philadelphia	1,585,577
	San Diego	1,110,549
	Detroit	1,027,974
	Dallas	1,006,877
	Phoenix	983,403
	San Antonio	935,933

A Demographic Profile of the American People

Life Expectancy, 1900–1992

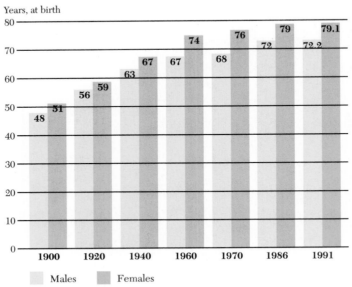

Source: U.S. Bureau of the Census, Statistical Abstract of
the United States: 1993, Washington, D.C., 1993.

Birthrate, 1820–1992

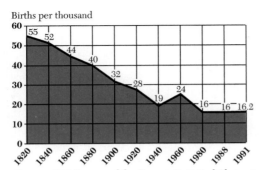

Source: U.S. Bureau of the Census, Statistical Abstract
of the United States: 1993, Washington, D.C., 1993.

Death Rate, 1900–1992

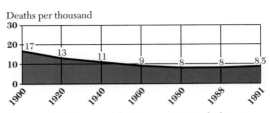

Source: U.S. Bureau of the Census, Statistical Abstract
of the United States: 1993, Washington, D.C., 1993.

Women in the Labor Force, 1890–1988

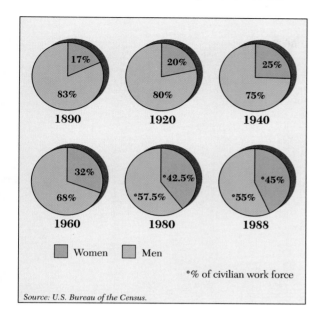

1890 — 17% / 83%
1920 — 20% / 80%
1940 — 25% / 75%
1960 — 32% / 68%
1980 — °42.5% / °57.5%
1988 — °45% / °55%

■ Women   ■ Men

°% of civilian work force

Source: U.S. Bureau of the Census.

Urban/Rural Population, 1750–1990

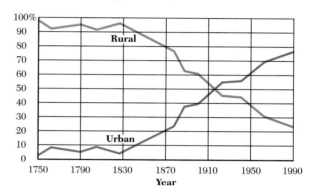

Rural

Urban

Year

Origin of Immigrants, 1820–1988

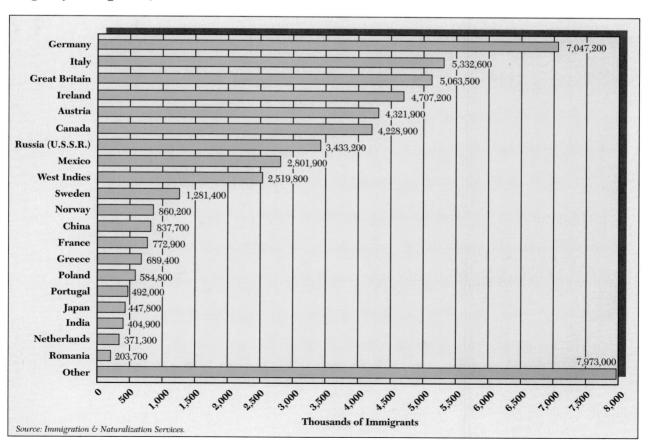

Country	Thousands of Immigrants
Germany	7,047,200
Italy	5,332,600
Great Britain	5,063,500
Ireland	4,707,200
Austria	4,321,900
Canada	4,228,900
Russia (U.S.S.R.)	3,433,200
Mexico	2,801,900
West Indies	2,519,800
Sweden	1,281,400
Norway	860,200
China	837,700
France	772,900
Greece	689,400
Poland	584,800
Portugal	492,000
Japan	447,800
India	404,900
Netherlands	371,300
Romania	203,700
Other	7,973,000

Thousands of Immigrants

Source: Immigration & Naturalization Services.

Ethnic Diversity of the United States

The classifications on this map suggest the pluralism of American society but fail to reflect completely the nation's ethnic diversity.

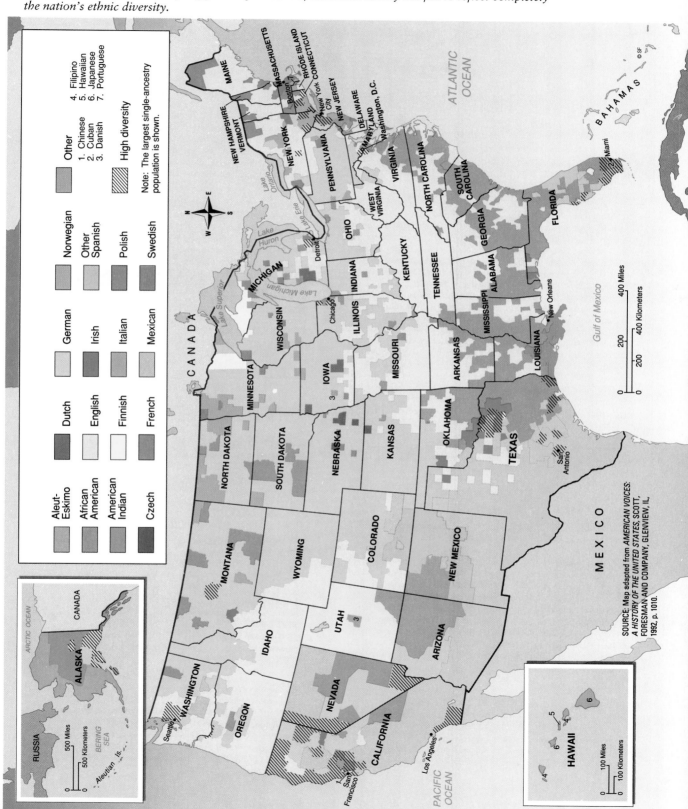

SOURCE: Map adapted from *AMERICAN VOICES: A HISTORY OF THE UNITED STATES*, SCOTT, FORESMAN AND COMPANY, GLENVIEW, IL, 1992, p. 1010.

Credits

Photos

Unless otherwise acknowledged, all photographs are the property of Scott, Foresman & Company. Positions of the photographs are indicated in abbreviated forms as follows: T top, C center, B bottom, L left, R right.

viiT New York Public Library, Astor, Lenox and Tilden Foundations/Print Collection, Miriam and Ira D. Wallach Division of Art, Prints, and Photography **viiB** The Maryland Historical Society **viiiT** Courtesy American Antiquarian Society **viiiB** Courtesy, Museum of Fine Arts, Boston **ixT** The New-York Historical Society, New York City **ixC** Lillian L. and John A. Harney Collection **ixB** Collection of Davenport West Jr. **xT** Historical Society of York County, Pennsylvania **xC** Century Association Company **xiT** St. Louis Art Museum **xiC** St. Louis Art Museum **xiB** The New-York Historical Society, New York City **xiiT** Courtesy The Museum of the Confederacy, Richmond, VA **xiiC** 1867/*Harper's Weekly* **xiiB** Thomas Gilcrease Institute of American History & Art, Tulsa **xiiiT** National Steel Company **xiiiC** The Museum of the City of New York **xiiiB** Library of Congress **xivT** George Wesley Bellows, *Warships on the Hudson,* 1909, The Hirshhorn Museum, Washington, DC, the Joseph H. Hirshhorn Bequest, 1981. Photographer: Lee Stalsworth **xivC** John Sloan, *The Coffee Line,* © 1912, The Carnegie Museum of Art, Pittsburgh, Fellows of the Museum of Art Fund, 83.29 **xvT** The National Archives **xvC** Culver Pictures **xvB** Maynard Dixon, *Okie Camp,* 1935, The Delman Collection, San Francisco **xviT** Department of Defense **xviC** Michael Rougier/*Life* Magazine/Time Warner Inc. **xviB** Cornell Capa/Magnum Photos **xviiT** Robert Ellison/Black Star **xviiC** Jullian Wasser/*Time* Magazine **xviiB** R. Bossu/Sygma **xviii** Jeffrey Markowitz/Sygma

Chapter 1

1 Print Collection, Miriam and Ira D. Wallach Division of Art, Prints, and Photography/New York Public Library, Astor, Lenox and Tilden Foundations **3T** From the Carta a Santangel Barcelona, 1493 **4T** Library of Congress **7** Ernest Haas **10L** New York Public Library, Astor, Lenox and Tilden Foundations **10R** New York Public Library, Astor, Lenox and Tilden Foundations **11T** Biblioteca Medices Laurenziana/Biblioteca Medices Laurenziana **13T** Bibliotheque Nationale, Paris **14** The Huntington Library and Art Gallery, San Marino, CA **15** Giraudon/Art Resource, New York **16** From Theodor de Bry *America* 1595/New York Public Library, Astor, Lenox and Tilden Foundations **19** Museo de America, Madrid/foto MAS **21** National Gallery of Art, Washington, DC **24** The Folger Shakespeare Library **27** Copyright the British Museum

Chapter 2

31 The Maryland Historical Society **36B** Courtesy of the Edward E. Ayer Collection. From Joan Blaeu, *Le Theatre du Monde* 1646/Courtesy of The Newberry Library, Chicago **36T** New York Public Library, Astor, Lenox and Tilden Foundations **37** Ashmolean Museum, Oxford **38** National Portrait Gallery, Smithsonian Institution **39** Smithsonian Institution **41** Enoch Pratt Free Library, Baltimore **43** Peabody Essex Museum, Salem **44** Courtesy American Antiquarian Society **46** Massachusetts Historical Society **47** Historical Pictures/Stock Montage, Inc. **52** New York Public Library, Astor, Lenox and Tilden Foundations **53** New York Public Library, Astor, Lenox and Tilden Foundations **56** New York Public Library, Astor, Lenox and Tilden Foundations

Chapter 3

63 Courtesy American Antiquarian Society **65** Courtesy of the Harvard Law School Cambridge, MA **67TL** New York Public Library, Astor, Lenox and Tilden Foundations **67TR** New York Public Library, Astor, Lenox and Tilden Foundations **71** David Hiser/Photographers/Aspen **75** National Maritime Museum, Greenwich, England **76** Duke University Library, Durham, NC **78** Courtesy American Antiquarian Society **79** Abby Aldrich Rockefeller Folk Art Center **80** New York Public Library, Astor, Lenox and Tilden Foundations **84** Photograph by Ken Burris/Shelburne Museum, Shelburne, VT **85TL** National Portrait Gallery, London **85TR** National Portrait Gallery, London **87INS** New York Public Library, Astor, Lenox and Tilden Foundations **87** Copyright the British Museum **91** North Wind Picture Archives **92** North Wind Picture Archives **93** Scott, Foresman

Chapter 4

98 Courtesy, Virginia Historical Society, Richmond **100** Special Collections Department/University of Virginia Library **102** Historical Society of Pennsylvania **103L** National Gallery of Art, Washington, DC **104** The New-York Historical Society, New York City **107** Martin Rogers **108** Courtesy of Westover **110TR** Library Company of Philadelphia **110TL** Historical Society of Philadelphia **112ALL** Library of Congress **113** Newport Historical Society **115** National Portrait Gallery, London **118** The Trustees of Sir John Soane's Museum **121** Albany Institute of History and Art **124** Copyright Yale University Art Gallery

Chapter 5

131 Courtesy, Museum of Fine Arts, Boston **133** The Colonial Williamsburg Foundation **136** Courtesy, Museum of Fine Arts, Boston **140** Bequest of Charles Allen Munn, 1924/The Metropolitan Museum of Art **143** Library of Congress **144** The New-York Historical Society, New York City **145** New York Public Library, Astor, Lenox and Tilden Foundations **148** Rare Book Division/New York Public Library, Astor, Lenox and Tilden Foundations **151** Chicago Historical Society **152TL** Library of Congress **152TR** National Portrait Gallery, London **153** Historical Society of Pennsylvania **156B** Historical Society of Pennsylvania **162** The Connecticut Historical Society

Chapter 6

165 The New-York Historical Society, New York City **168** Library Company of Philadelphia **170B** New York Public Library, Astor, Lenox and Tilden Foundations **172T** New York State Historical Association, Cooperstown **173** Friends Historical Library of Swarthmore College **175** Historical Society of Pennsylvania **180** Chicago Historical Society **181ALL** Smithsonian Institution **185** National Portrait Gallery, Smithsonian Institution **188** New York

Culver Pictures 797 Library of Congress **798TL** AP/Wide World **798B** Library of Congress **798TR** Library of Congress **800** Social Security Administration **803** Courtesy Mrs. Philip Evergood **804** Bettmann Archive **805** AP/Wide World **806** AP/Wide World **808** *Life Magazine*/Time Warner Inc.**809** The Franklin D. Roosevelt Library **813L** Historical Pictures/Stock Montage, Inc. **813R** Daniel Robert Fitzpatrick, *St. Louis Post Dispatch*

Chapter 27

817 U.S. Department of Defense **819** William A. Ireland, the *Columbus Dispatch* **822** U.S. Army Photo Center of Military History **823** AP/Wide World **825** Bettmann Archive **827** Bettmann Archive **829** Official U.S. Navy Photograph **836** Courtesy of the World Federation of Bergen-Belsen Associations **837** Courtesy of the World Federation of Bergen-Belsen Associations **838R** Library of Congress **839** The Phillips Collection, Washington, DC **840** Library of Congress **843** *Life Magazine*/Time Warner Inc. **845** AP/Wide World

Chapter 28

849 Michael Rougier/*Life* Magazine/Time Warner Inc. **851** Bettmann Archive **857** AP/Wide World **859** © 1982 by Samuel A. Tower, from *Cartoons and Lampoons*. Reprinted by permission of Julian Messner, a division of Simon & Schuster, Inc. **860** Bettmann Archive **862** Bruce Barbey/Magnum Photos **864** Wayne Miller/Magnum Photos **866** Bettmann Archive **867T** Bettmann Archive **867B** Bettmann Archive **869** Bettmann Archive **870** Ralph Morse/*Life* Magazine/Time Warner Inc. **871** AP/Wide World

Chapter 29

875 Cornell Capa/Magnum Photos **878** Frigidaire **879T** Bern Keating/Black Star **879BL** J. R. Eyerman/*Life* Magazine/Time Warner Inc. **879BR** FPG **881** CBS Photo Archives **882** Burt Glinn/Magnum Photos **884T** Rudolph Buckhardt **884C** Rudolph Buckhardt **884B** *Convergence* by Jackson Pollock/Albright-Knox Art Gallery, Buffalo **885** Mark Rothko. *Number 10* (1950). Oil on canvas, 7'6 3/8" x 57 1/8". The Museum of Modern Art, New York. Gift of Philip Johnson **886L** SOVFOTO **886R** © 1957/NYT Pictures **890** Bettmann Archive **891L** Carl Iwasaki/*Life* Magazine/Time Warner Inc. **891R** Eve Arnold/Magnum Photos **892** Bettmann Archive **893** Bruce Roberts/Photo Researchers **895** AP/Wide World **899** Charles Moore/Black Star **900** Robert W. Kelley © 1970/*Life* Magazine/Time Warner Inc. **901L** Jim Murray/Black Star **901R** Bettmann Archive **903** Photo by Okamoto/Courtesy Lyndon Baines Johnson Library, Austin, TX

Chapter 30

911 Robert Ellison/Black Star **913** AP/Wide World **914L** Bettmann Archive **914R** *Special for Today,* Simon & Schuster by Herblock in the *Washington Post* 1958 **916** AP/Wide World **918T** From *Straight Herblock,* Simon & Schuster, 1964 by Herblock in the *Washington Post* **918B** Black Star **920** Owen Franken/Stock Boston **922** Courtesy The National Library of Wales **923** Shoemaker **928L** James Pickerell/Black Star **928R** By Mauldin/Wil-Jo Associates, Inc. **930** Susan Meiselas/Magnum Photos **931** Larry Burrows/*Life* Magazine/Time Warner Inc. **933** AP/Wide World **934** Yoich R. Okamoto/Courtesy Lyndon Baines Johnson Library, Austin, TX

Chapter 31

937 Julian Wasser/*Time* Magazine **939** Wayne Miller/Magnum Photos **941** Elliott Landy/Magnum Photos **942** Bob Fitch/Black Star **944**

Bettmann Archive **947** Bettmann Archive **949** AP/Wide World **951L** Paul Fusco/Magnum Photos **951R** Bettmann Archive **952** Bettmann Archive **953** Don Wright, the *Miami News* **955** Roland Freeman/Magnum Photos **956** Tony Korody/Sygma **959** Doug Wilson/Black Star **962** SIPA-Press **964** Bettmann Archive **965** Bill Fitz-Patrick/Courtesy The White House Collection **966** Ledru/Sygma **967** SIPA/Black Star

Chapter 32

971 R. Bossu/Sygma **973** John Bryson/Sygma **976** Bettmann Archive **977** Michael Evans/Courtesy The White House Collection **981** Alan Tannenbaum/Sygma **983** Sygma **984** Stuart Franklin/Sygma **988** Fred Ward/Black Star **989** Bettmann Archive **992** Sygma **993** Black Star **996** Nikolai Ignatiev/Matrix **997** Dominique Mollard/AP/Wide World **998** Fred S. Prouser/Gamma-Liaison **999** AP/Wide World **1000** Wally McNamee/Sygma **1004** Martin Tevick/Black Star **1005T** AP/Wide World **1005B** Robert Trippett/SIPA-Press

Chapter 33

1009 Jeffrey Markowitz/Sygma **1011L** Markel/Gamma-Liaison **1011R** Markel/Gamma-Liaison **1015** Carole DeVilliers/Sygma **1017** Douglas Burrow/Gamma-Liaison **1020** David R. Frazier Photolibrary **1024** Steve Liss/*Time* Magazine **1026** Eric Lars Bakke/Black Star **1028** Rob Nelson/Black Star **1030** Liane Enkelis/Stock Boston **1035** Gerry Gropp/ Sygma

Literary

In addition, the authors and publishers acknowledge with gratitude permission to reprint, quote from, or adapt the following materials. (The numbers shown below refer to the pages of this text.)

74 (Map) Adapted from Philip D. Curtin, *Atlantic Slave Trade,* University of Wisconsin Press, 1969, pp. 88–89 **377** (Map) Adapted from Thomas Ellaison, *A Hand-Book of the Cotton Trade,* J. Woodland, Liverpool, 1838, pp. 24–25. **553** From *The Price* by Arthur Miller. Copyright © 1968, 1969 by Arthur Miller and Ingeborg M. Miller, trustee. All rights reserved/Reprinted by permission of Viking Penguin, Inc., and International Creative Management, Inc. **600** From Archives of Commonwealth, Boston. Records of the Medical Examiner, 1895. In the Executive Office of Public Safety, Medical Examiner Records. As cited in *Out of Work: The First Century of Unemployment in Massachusetts* by Alexander Keyssar, Cambridge University Press, 1986. **676** Joe Hill, "Workers of the World, Awaken!" cited in *American Folksongs of Protest* by John Greenway, University of Pennsylvania Press, 1953. **680** (Map) Adapted from *Historic City: The Settlement of Chicago,* City of Chicago, Department of Planning. **684** From "Chicago" in *Chicago Poems* by Carl Sandburg, copyright © 1916 by Holt, Rinehart and Winston, Inc.; renewed 1944 by Carl Sandburg. Reprinted by permission of Harcourt Brace Jovanovich. **708** Upton Sinclair, *The Jungle,* 1906. **751** "The New Day" by Fenton Johnson cited in *The Book of American Negro Poetry,* ed. by James Weldon Johnson. New York: Harcourt Brace and Company, 1931. **791** Studs Terkel, *Hard Times.* New York: Pantheon Books, 1970, p. 41. **900** Excerpt from "I Have a Dream" by Martin Luther King, Jr. Reprinted by arrangement with the Heirs to the Estate of Martin Luther King, Jr., c/o Joan Daves Agency as agent for the proprietor.

Index